P9-DFW-020

EVIDENCE UNDER THE RULES

ASPEN CASEBOOK SERIES

EVIDENCE UNDER THE RULES

TEXT, CASES, AND PROBLEMS

Eighth Edition

Christopher B. Mueller

Henry S. Lindsley Professor of Procedure and Advocacy
University of Colorado School of Law

Laird C. Kirkpatrick

Louis Harkey Mayo Research Professor of Law
The George Washington University Law School

Published by Wolters Kluwer in New York.

Wolters Kluwer serves customers worldwide with CCH, Aspen Publishers, and Kluwer Law International products. (www.wolterskluwerlb.com)

To contact Customer Service, e-mail customer.service@wolterskluwer.com,

call 1-800-234-1660, fax 1-800-901-9075, or mail correspondence to:

Wolters Kluwer
Attn: Order Department
PO Box 990
Frederick, MD 21705

Printed in the United States of America.

1 2 3 4 5 6 7 8 9 0

ISBN 978-1-4548-4952-0

Library of Congress Cataloging-in-Publication Data

Mueller, Christopher B., author.
Evidence under the rules: text, cases, and problems / Christopher B. Mueller, Henry S. Lindsley Professor of Procedure and Advocacy, University of Colorado School of Law; Laird C. Kirkpatrick, Louis Harkey Mayo Research Professor of Law, the George Washington University Law School.—Eighth Edition.
pages cm.—(Aspen casebook series)
Includes bibliographical references and index.
ISBN 978-1-4548-4952-0 (alk. paper)
1. Evidence (Law)—United States—Cases. I. Kirkpatrick, Laird C., author. II. Title.
KF8935.M838 2015
347.73'6—dc23
2014041082

Certified Sourcing
www.sfiprogram.org
SFI-01042

SFI label applies to the text stock

About Wolters Kluwer Law & Business

Wolters Kluwer Law & Business is a leading global provider of intelligent information and digital solutions for legal and business professionals in key specialty areas, and respected educational resources for professors and law students. Wolters Kluwer Law & Business connects legal and business professionals as well as those in the education market with timely, specialized authoritative content and information-enabled solutions to support success through productivity, accuracy and mobility.

Serving customers worldwide, Wolters Kluwer Law & Business products include those under the Aspen Publishers, CCH, Kluwer Law International, Loislaw, ftwilliam.com and MediRegs family of products.

CCH products have been a trusted resource since 1913, and are highly regarded resources for legal, securities, antitrust and trade regulation, government contracting, banking, pension, payroll, employment and labor, and healthcare reimbursement and compliance professionals.

Aspen Publishers products provide essential information to attorneys, business professionals and law students. Written by preeminent authorities, the product line offers analytical and practical information in a range of specialty practice areas from securities law and intellectual property to mergers and acquisitions and pension/benefits. Aspen's trusted legal education resources provide professors and students with high-quality, up-to-date and effective resources for successful instruction and study in all areas of the law.

Kluwer Law International products provide the global business community with reliable international legal information in English. Legal practitioners, corporate counsel and business executives around the world rely on Kluwer Law journals, looseleafs, books, and electronic products for comprehensive information in many areas of international legal practice.

Loislaw is a comprehensive online legal research product providing legal content to law firm practitioners of various specializations. Loislaw provides attorneys with the ability to quickly and efficiently find the necessary legal information they need, when and where they need it, by facilitating access to primary law as well as state-specific law, records, forms and treatises.

ftwilliam.com offers employee benefits professionals the highest quality plan documents (retirement, welfare and non-qualified) and government forms (5500/PBGC, 1099 and IRS) software at highly competitive prices.

MediRegs products provide integrated health care compliance content and software solutions for professionals in healthcare, higher education and life sciences, including professionals in accounting, law and consulting.

Wolters Kluwer Law & Business, a division of Wolters Kluwer, is headquartered in New York. Wolters Kluwer is a market-leading global information services company focused on professionals.

To Martha, Gretchen, and David
CBM

To Lind, Ryan, Morgan, and Meredith
LCK

SUMMARY OF CONTENTS

CONTENTS

PREFACE

The Federal Rules set out the law of evidence in the federal system, and these Rules have been adopted—with some variation—in 45 of the 50 states (a list of adopting states is found in footnote 2 of Chapter 1). American evidence law is unified around these Rules, and they are a natural focal point for the study of the subject. The Problems and cases in this book, and the narrative presentations too, apply and shed light on the Rules and how they work.

This edition of the book, which has now been in use for more than a quarter of a century, is substantially revised and reformatted. Some cases, particularly in the *Crawford* line of decisions interpreting confrontation rights, no longer seem so important that they should be experienced in full text, and these are presented in summary form. New Problems have been added, and the Notes are substantially revised to provide more guidance to students. The book has been redesigned to be more user-friendly, and of course it is available in an online version. We have added two new features, in the form of Picture boxes and Comment/Perspective boxes, and these are set out to differentiate them from other features of the book. The purpose of the Picture boxes is to add human interest to the materials, and the purpose of the Comment/Perspective boxes is to provide broader perspectives that should assist in understanding doctrine.

Reactions of professors and student users have strengthened our conviction that understanding evidence law requires more than cases. We consider the present work to be a *coursebook* that combines the strengths of standard materials, such as casebooks, collections of problems, and hornbooks. We set out basic ideas as narrative, and use Problems to present issues that arise every day. There are enough facts in the Problems to make evidence issues concrete and vivid. We hope these materials are self-contained—we think a conscientious student can grasp what is important about the subject from this book alone, without constantly going elsewhere to fill in gaps.

Evidence law is interesting because of its kinship with epistemology and its grounding in the real world of an adversary system: In the American courtroom, how do we go about finding the facts? Evidence law seeks to regulate a process of inquiry in a setting where lawyers, witnesses, courts, and jurors are important players. We encounter issues of policy, principle, and philosophy, often with constitutional dimensions. And because the Rules are, after all, *rules*—they are words with prescriptive meaning that is clear in core cases and less clear as we move away from the core—we grapple as well with narrow issues of application and construction. This book aims to raise both the larger and the narrower issues, to be philosophical and policy-oriented as well as practical and concrete.

These are the Problems that are new in this edition: Problem 4-B ("He Thinks I'm His Wife"), which rests on (and substitutes for) the Supreme Court's somewhat confused opinion on prior consistent statements in the *Tome* case; Problem 4-M ("Where Did She Fall?"), which explores the medical statements exception in FRE 803(4); Problem 4-N ("You Can't Offer A Police Report"), which explores uses of police reports in criminal cases under the public records exception in FRE 803(8); Problem 5-H ("The Undercover Cop Trick"), which explores use of prior acts to prove plan or scheme (replacing an earlier problem); Problem 12-F ("The Disclosure Was Inadvertent"), which explores the operation of the privilege waiver provision in FRE 502.

We offer what we call a coursebook, and claim for it a kind of completeness not found in the usual casebook, but students sometimes find it useful to resort to secondary sources (full narrative accounts) in pursuing their study of evidence law, seeking additional explanation or further coverage. We have also written a student text (often called a hornbook) that presents a straightforward account of the subject, including an analysis of each Rule and descriptions of doctrinal developments, with reference to the important decisions in point. See Christopher B. Mueller and Laird C. Kirkpatrick, Evidence (5th ed. Aspen, 2012). This book, which is available in law school libraries and bookstores, is published in both hardbound and softbound format (with different cover designs). Many other excellent studies are readily available, and we recommend these:

Paul Gianelli, Understanding Evidence (4th ed. 2013) (single-volume source)

Michael Graham, Handbook of Federal Evidence (7th ed. 2011) (8-volume set with supplementation)

Graham Lilly, Daniel Capra & Stephen Saltzburg, Principles of Evidence (6th ed. 2012) (single-volume source)

McCormick on Evidence (7th ed. 2014) (single-volume source)

Christopher Mueller & Laird Kirkpatrick, Federal Evidence (4th ed. 2013) (6-volume set with supplementation)

Roger Park, David Leonard & Steven Goldberg, Evidence Law: A Student's Guide (3d ed. 2011) (single-volume source)

Glen Weissenberger & James J. Duane, Federal Evidence (5th ed. 2006) (single-volume source)

Charles Wright & Kenneth Graham, Federal Practice and Procedure, volumes 21-26A (FRE 101 through Rejected Rule 513); 27-29 (C. Wright & V. Gold) (FRE 601-706); 30 (K. Graham) (Hearsay Policy); 31 (FRE 801-1103) (M. Graham)

Before the revision culminating in this Eighth Edition, Aspen surveyed professors who used prior editions or were familiar with them. Many were generous in providing suggestions and criticisms that we received anonymously. We looked at everything, learned from what people had to say, and made many changes as a result. To those of you who participated in this effort, we want to offer our special thanks, even though we don't know who you are. Also we thank the Honorable Gerald Rosen who has made many helpful comments over a period of years. We wish we could thank others personally as well, but we can only do so in this way because we do not know who you are. Again thank you for taking the time and giving us your thoughts.

We also want to extend special thanks to Liesa Richter, Thomas P. Hester Presidential Professor at the University of Oklahoma College of Law, who provided detailed comments on every chapter of this book. Her insightful suggestions were very useful, and we have implemented them throughout. We are deeply grateful for her extraordinary help in improving the quality and teachability of this Eighth Edition.

Finally, we want to acknowledge friends whose comments have helped us in revising this book over the years: These include David Bernstein, Chris Blair, Mark Bonner, Ron Carlson, W. Burlette Carter, Sherry Colb, David Crump, James Duane, David Faigman, Michael Green, Steven Heyman, Paul Janicke, John Junker, Edward Kimball, Ronald Lansing, Lash LaRue, Brian Leiter, Tom Lininger, Graham Lilly, Peter Lushing, Dayna Matthew, Pedro Malavet, Kevin McMunigal, David McCord, David Rudovsky, Chris Sanchirico, Fred Schauer, David Siegel, Alex Stein, George Strickler, Eleanor Swift, Peter Tague, Suja Thomas, the Honorable Richard Unis, Robert Weninger, and Mimi Wesson. All of these colleagues in evidence have commented on these pages and helped us to improve them, and the book is much the better for their suggestions.

The authors wish also to extend their appreciation to Dean Phil Weiser at Colorado, and to Interim Dean Gregory Maggs and Dean Blake Morant at George Washington, for their encouragement and support in our efforts in revising this book.

In addition, we wish especially to thank Melissa Aubin, J.D. Oregon 2004, for her extensive work on recent editions of this work.

Finally some words to families. Spouses and children, even adult children who are gone from home and making their ways in the world, are often in the thoughts of authors. Especially our spouses are expected to understand, and in many ways large and small, they support what we do. It is to our families that we dedicate this work. On Laird Kirkpatrick's side, we wish to acknowledge his wife Lind and his sons Ryan and Morgan. On Christopher Mueller's side, we wish to acknowledge his wife Martha and their children Gretchen and David. We trust that our families know how much they mean to us.

Laird C. Kirkpatrick
Washington, DC
November 2014

Christopher B. Mueller
Boulder, CO

ACKNOWLEDGMENTS

We gratefully acknowledge the following sources, which granted us permission to reprint material from the works listed below:

Books and Articles

Belli, Melvin. Demonstrative Evidence: Seeing Is Believing. Trial (July 1980). Copyright © 1980 by the American Association for Justice. Reprinted by permission.

De Lange, Nicholas. Apocrypha: Jewish Literature of the Hellenistic Age. (Viking Press 1978). Copyright © 1978 by the B'nai B'rith Commission on Adult Jewish Education. Reprinted by permission.

James, George F., Relevancy, Probability and the Law, 29 Calif. L. Rev. 689 (1941). Copyright © 1941 by the California Law Review. Reprinted by permission.

Mueller, Christopher and Laird Kirkpatrick, Federal Evidence (4th ed. 2013). Copyright © 2013 Thomson/West. Reprinted by permission.

Photographs and Illustrations

Annie Dookhan. Photograph. Copyright © Reuters / Jessica Rinaldi. Reprinted by permission.

Bhagwan Shree Rajneesh. Photograph. Copyright © JP Laffont / Sygma / Corbis. Reprinted by permission.

Export Champion. Photograph. Copyright © Carlo Martinelli. Reprinted by permission.

Exxon Valdez. Photograph. Provided courtesy of the United States Coast Guard / EPA. Reprinted by permission.

Frederick Walters. Photograph. Provided courtesy of the National Archives and Records Administration, Kansas City, MO. Courtesy of Marianne Wesson. Reprinted by permission.

Grey wolf. Photograph. Copyright © Holly Kuchera / Shutterstock. Reprinted by permission.

Jeremy Bentham (engraving by S. Freeman after painting by Worthington). Illustration. Provided courtesy of the Library of Congress. Reprinted by permission.

John Abel. Photograph. Provided courtesy of the California Department of Corrections and Rehabilitation. Reprinted by permission.

John W. Hillman (John W. Hillmon). Photograph. Provided courtesy of the National Archives and Records Administration, Kansas City, MO. Courtesy of Marianne Wesson. Reprinted by permission.

Karen Beyer. Photograph. Copyright © Karen Beyer. Reprinted by permission.

Mary Weaver. Photograph. Copyright © Deb Brammer / maryweaverstory.com. Reprinted by permission.

Mr. Baron Parke (engraving, English School, 19th century). Illustration. Private Collection © Look and Learn / Illustrated Papers Collection / Bridgeman Images. Reprinted by permission.

Sir Karl Popper. Photograph. Copyright © The Estate of Sir Karl Popper. Reprinted by permission.

Supreme Court Justice Antonin Scalia. Photograph. Copyright © Tim Sloan / AFP / Getty Images. Reprinted by permission.

Supreme Court Justice David Souter. Photograph. Copyright © Diana Walker / Time Life Pictures / Getty Images. Reprinted by permission.

Thomas Kuhn. Photograph. Copyright © Bill Pierce / The LIFE Images Collection / Getty Images. Reprinted by permission.

William A. Hinton State Laboratory Institute. Photograph. Copyright © AP Photo / Steven Senne. Reprinted by permission.

Zacarias Moussaoui. Photograph. Copyright © Getty Images / Handout. Reprinted by permission.

SPECIAL NOTICE

The problems and examples in this book are drawn, for the most part, from actual cases. But facts have been changed for predictable reasons—to add human interest, to adapt the situation to classroom use, to combine in a single example the conflicts that have arisen in several decided cases, to present particular issues or sharpen the presentation of issues, and to achieve other educational purposes. Names used in the problems and examples are inventions of the authors. None of the examples or problems should be read as referring to an actual person, and none is intended to make any comment about any person.

CBM
LCK

EVIDENCE UNDER THE RULES

CHAPTER 1

Evidence Law and the System

A WHY RULES OF EVIDENCE?

1. Why Evidence Law at All?

Many reasons are put forward in answer to the second question posed above, but five stand out. At the end of the course you will be better able to evaluate them, but keeping them in mind from the outset may help on your journey through the subject.

The first sounds strange in a republic that places great faith in the jury system, but mistrust of juries is the single overriding reason for the law of evidence. The hearsay doctrine exists largely because we believe that a lay jury (an amateur factfinder) cannot do a good job in evaluating statements made outside its presence, and the rules governing character evidence rest on the view that juries put too much weight on such proof and might use it for punitive purposes.

A second reason for the law of evidence is to serve substantive policies relating to the matter in suit. Rules that set and allocate burdens of persuasion are examples. They amount to substantive evidence law, existing in the hope and belief that they affect outcome—recovery or exoneration from liability in civil litigation and conviction or acquittal in criminal cases—in ways nearly as significant as purely substantive principles. Everyone understands that the prospect for recovery in negligence is enhanced or inhibited by adjusting substantive law to allow or preclude recovery where plaintiff is himself partly to blame. Similar results may be achieved by setting and allocating burden of persuasion: Plaintiff has a better chance if he only needs to prove his case by a "preponderance" (lowest standard known to the law), as opposed to "clear and convincing" evidence. His prospects also improve if defendant bears the burden of showing plaintiff's negligence, and diminish if plaintiff must prove due care.

A third reason is to further substantive policies *unrelated* to the matter in suit—what we may call *extrinsic* substantive policies. Typically rules in this category seek to affect behavior or quality of life outside the courtroom, and privileges are the prime example. Thus the two spousal privileges (one covering marital confidences, the other regulating the use of one spouse as witness against another) aim to protect marriage, vindicating the widespread public assumption that marital privacy is protected and removing (or limiting) the specter of pitting spouse against spouse in court.

A fourth reason for the law of evidence—and arguably this is the most important reason of all—is to ensure accurate factfinding.[1] Thus rules governing authentication of documents and things ("laying the foundation") and the Best Evidence doctrine (which requires the content of a writing to be proved by means of the writing itself) exist largely to ensure accuracy—to force litigants and courts to be careful.

The fifth reason for evidence law is pragmatic—to control the scope and duration of trials, because they must run their course with reasonable dispatch. Achieving resolution is itself valuable, even if it is not perfect. To this end, the Rules authorize the trial judge to confine and organize the dispute. Rule 403, for example, permits the judge to exclude evidence that would be otherwise admissible, simply because it would take more time than it is worth and might confuse the jury. And Rule 611 gives the judge power to control the sequence of proof and the manner of examining witnesses.

2. Why Rules Rather Than Common Law?

Accessibility is the main reason advanced by the framers of what has become the most influential body of American evidence law—the Federal Rules of Evidence. This code sets forth the bulk of the law of evidence in 63 short provisions, in language easily read and largely free from technicality and cross-referencing. The Rules can be printed in a small book easily carried to court, quickly perused and readily understandable.

Success of the Rules. It is partly the brevity and simplicity that made the Federal Rules so influential. Their quality and widespread success make them a logical focal point for a course in American evidence law, and they are central to this text.

Consider just how important the Rules have become:

They apply in federal courts across the land in both criminal and civil cases. See FRE 101 (the rules "apply to proceedings in United States courts").

[1] This concern overlaps with the first one: One way of expressing mistrust of juries is to say that we fear that they will not do a good job with some kinds of evidence and will be misled to wrong conclusions. Nobody really thinks that hearsay is worthless, and we all routinely rely on hearsay in daily life. Mistrust of juries results from a belief that jurors will not (and to some extent cannot) evaluate hearsay in the right way, which is another way of saying that we fear they will fail to perform accurate factfinding.

Generally they apply regardless whether federal or state law supplies the rule of decision. (In diversity cases where federal courts apply state substantive law, however, the Rules require federal courts to apply state evidence rules in limited areas—namely, presumptions, privileges, and competency of witnesses. See FRE 301, 501, and 601.)

Within the first 12 years after the Rules were adopted in the federal system, a majority of states adopted codes closely tracking the Federal Rules, and the number of state adoptions has reached 45.[2] Even in the six states that have not adopted the Rules, appellate opinions cite them and sometimes adopt their underlying principles.

It was not always so.

Pre-Rules evidence law. Until the Rules appeared, evidence law was mostly a creature of common law tradition. To be sure, statutes in most states addressed such matters as physician-patient privilege, business and public records, and some aspects of impeaching witnesses. Comprehensive codes were longer in coming and slower to gain acceptance.[3] Without such codes, every evidence issue—and they arise by the score in almost every trial—required resort to common law tradition, and often took lawyers and judges to caselaw and treatises to find answers.

The Rules. The Federal Rules of Evidence are the most recent and successful codification. They were proposed by a distinguished Advisory Committee comprised of practitioners, judges, and law professors appointed by the Supreme Court. The Committee was chaired by Albert Jenner (prominent Chicago trial attorney), and the principal drafting task fell to Professor Edward Cleary (then of the University of Illinois). The Committee labored more than eight years, publishing two drafts that it distributed to bench and bar, and a would-be final version, which the Court accepted and transmitted to Congress under the Enabling Act (28 USC §2072). In theory, the Rules displaced common law, but in fact common law traditions lingered as guidelines or reference points in the task of interpreting the Rules.

Under today's Enabling Act, the task of drafting and vetting Rules is assigned to a committee. Originally such committees were appointed by the Supreme Court, as was true of the Committee that prepared the Rules of Evidence. Today the committees are appointed by the Judicial Conference (chief judges of each

---

[2]As of 2015, these states have codes based on the federal model: Alabama, Alaska, Arizona, Arkansas, Colorado, Connecticut, Delaware, Florida, Georgia, Hawaii, Idaho, Illinois, Indiana, Iowa, Kentucky, Louisiana, Maine, Maryland, Michigan, Minnesota, Mississippi, Montana, Nebraska, Nevada, New Hampshire, New Jersey, New Mexico, North Carolina, North Dakota, Ohio, Oklahoma, Oregon, Pennsylvania, Rhode Island, South Carolina, South Dakota, Tennessee, Texas, Utah, Vermont, Virginia, Washington, West Virginia, Wisconsin, and Wyoming. Among the remaining five states, California and Kansas have codes that are not based on the Federal Rules. Massachusetts, Missouri, and New York do not have comprehensive evidence codes.

[3]Long ago Dean Wigmore wrote such a code, see Wigmore, Code of Evidence (1909), and the American Law Institute proposed the Model Code three decades later. See Model Code of Evidence (1942). The National Commissioners proposed a code in 1953 that was adopted in a handful of states. See Uniform Rules of Evidence (1953). In 1965, California adopted its Evidence Code, which influenced the drafters of the Federal Rules.

circuit plus a district judge from each circuit plus the chief judge of the Court of International Trade). Like similar committees, the Advisory Committee on Evidence Rules (ERC) follows a seven-step process: (1) It meets to consider and draft proposed changes; (2) with permission of the Standing Committee on Rules of Practice and Procedure (Standing Committee), the ERC publishes proposed changes for public comment; (3) the ERC considers modifications suggested in this way and, if it thinks them wise, republishes a new draft for public comment; (4) the ERC makes a final recommendation to the Standing Committee, which can approve or suggest additional modifications (usually referring the matter back to the ERC); (5) the Judicial Conference considers the recommendations, usually in September, and, if it approves them, they are transmitted to the Supreme Court; (6) the latter forwards the recommendations to Congress by May 1st of the year in which they are to take effect; (7) Congress has seven months to act (until the end of November) and, if Congress does nothing, the change takes effect on December 1st. See 28 USC §§2071-2074. Under 28 USC §2074(b), however, privilege rules take effect only if "approved by Act of Congress."

By accident of history, the Rules arrived at Congress in 1972 as the Watergate scandal was erupting. Amidst claims of executive privilege by President Nixon stirring resentment in Congress, the privilege provisions attracted attention. Acutely sensitive on the matter of legislative prerogative as against presidential power, members of Congress saw the Rules as an encroachment by the other branch—an infringement of legislative prerogative by the judiciary. Hence the Rules did not pass quietly into law (under the Enabling Act, as it existed then, Rules proposed by the Court became law after 90 days if Congress took no action). Instead Congress held hearings, changed the Rules substantially, and enacted the changed version in statutory form.

Most significant among congressional changes was the deletion of the privilege rules, and the adoption in their place of a single provision (Rule 501) leaving privilege to common law evolution. (In 2010, Congress enacted new Rule 502 on waiver of attorney-client privilege and work product protection.) Also significant, when the Rules were adopted in 1975, was congressional rejection of a proposal to admit prior inconsistent statements by testifying witnesses as "substantive" (and not merely "impeaching") evidence, by defining them as "not hearsay." Congress would not go along with this proposal, even though years earlier the Supreme Court had implied that such a provision would pass constitutional muster.

B WHAT HAPPENS AT TRIAL

In both civil and criminal cases, the trial is the culmination of preliminary work and skirmishes. The decision whether to bring a claim or prosecute charges was made long before, and evidence has been collected, witnesses located and interviewed, and negotiations aimed at settlement (plea bargaining in criminal cases) have been attempted and abandoned. The court has played a role too. Pleadings have raised factual issues—or in criminal cases charges have been denied—and pretrial motions have been resolved. In civil cases, discovery and perhaps pretrial conferences have gone forward to conclusion.

Now comes the main event—the actual trial.

1. Jury Selection

In most jurisdictions a jury panel has been assembled when the lawyers enter the courtroom on the first day of trial. Jurors may be sitting in the spectator section behind the "bar" or assembled in waiting rooms or milling in the hall. One by one the clerk summons an adequate number (usually 12 in criminal cases, sometimes less; in civil cases often 12, but as few as six) plus two alternates, who take their seats in the jury box.

The jurors usually introduce themselves one at a time, and the trial lawyers note their names. Particularly in large urban centers, the lawyers may already have information about each juror: Often jury selection forms are available to the lawyers, and private agencies rent "jury books" containing whatever information can be unearthed about members of the panel—age, marital status, occupation, prior jury service (with details about the nature and outcome of the case), and so forth.

The next step is called "voir dire," in which court and counsel try to find out whether any members of the panel should not serve. Sometimes this process brings to light that a potential juror does not meet statutory qualifications, which typically set minimum and maximum age (often 18 to 72), require that each be a citizen, and sometimes include quaint prerequisites (not being "decrepit"). But usually these standards are implemented by the clerk in issuing the summonses and do not arise during voir dire. Most people on the panel are eligible, but one or another should not serve for a reason specific to the case. If a juror is related to a party (by blood or marriage, or by business connection such as being his creditor or debtor, employer or employee), or is "prejudiced" on one or another issue or against one or another party, he should be excluded "for cause." Each party may challenge any number of people for cause, and the judge must determine any such challenge, excluding if cause is found. In addition, each party (or each side) has a fixed number of "peremptory" challenges (often three), which entitles him to exclude potential jurors for any reason at all—and the reason need not be stated.[4]

In addition to questions aimed at uncovering "cause" to exclude potential jurors, voir dire involves talking to them in general terms about the case and

---

[4]Lawyers exercising peremptory challenges must be prepared to show that they are not acting on the basis of race, see Batson v. Kentucky, 476 U.S. 79 (1986) (prosecutor); Edmonson v. Leesville Concrete Co., Inc., 500 U.S. 614 (1991) (civil litigants); Georgia v. McCollum, 505 U.S. 42 (1992) (defendant in criminal case), or gender, see J.E.B. v. Alabama *ex rel.* T.B., 511 U.S. 127 (1994) (prosecutor).

asking them whether they are ready and able to serve. In state courts, the lawyers often conduct voir dire, and they prize the right to make direct contact and use it to build rapport. In federal court and some states, the judge conducts voir dire. She may question the panel as a whole, rather than one by one, and counsel must be content with submitting questions, in hopes that she will put them to the panel.

2. Opening Statement

The opening statement gives each side its first opportunity to set before the jury the story that ensuing proof will tell. Here the lawyer presents an overview that will help the jury understand what is to come, as the actual evidence is usually fragmented and disjointed. The courtroom is a kind of theater, the trial a kind of drama, but it is not a well-made play—few witnesses on the stand perform as well as actors on stage.

Customarily the party bearing the burden of persuasion (usually plaintiff in civil litigation and prosecutor in criminal cases) has the right to make the first opening statement, and the opponent follows. (If the court permits, the opponent may delay his opening until the other party has presented her case and rested.)

In theory the opening statement is not an argument. Instead, it sums up the facts that each party contends that her proof will establish. But the opening statement *is* an argument of sorts because each lawyer tries to persuade the jury to begin to see the case in a certain way, and because lawyers know that judges are unlikely to interrupt, even when opening statements stray into argument, and that lawyers are reluctant to object at this early stage. Each lawyer points out the direction, the themes, the meaning of what is to come, so testimony and other proof can echo thoughts already in the minds of jurors, and opening remarks draw the shape of things to come. The opening statement is the first act in the theater of trial.

During opening statements, the jury learns background facts about the parties—for example, plaintiff is a laboratory technician at Carle Clinic who was driving to work when the accident occurred. Such humanizing information may not be legally relevant, but may garner sympathetic reaction, so inevitably it comes out and is likely to be mentioned early. And it is during opening statement that the jury hears that plaintiff was injured in a car accident, that he sustained serious injuries requiring treatment and convalescence, and that defendant was speeding. In a phrase that counsel will likely repeat, "the evidence will show" all these points.

3. Presentation of Proof

Presentation of proof comes next. Each party now seeks to build his case and tear down his opponent's. Ordinarily the party with the burden of persuasion goes first, followed by his adversary, and each may have additional turns. Thus plaintiff usually begins in a civil suit, followed by defendant; the prosecutor goes first in criminal cases, then the accused.

During his first appearance each party presents his "case-in-chief." He holds center stage: He doesn't have to "speak all his lines," but he can't hold much back either. He has to establish everything necessary to his case, reserving only what he may need to rebut whatever his opponent presents. When he is finished, he "rests" and yields the stage to his adversary. After both have put on their cases-in-chief, the party who opened has another chance, this time to present his "case-in-rebuttal," and then his adversary has a similar opportunity. The process may go on until each side is satisfied, or the judge decides that proof and counterproof have become repetitive. Rebuttal cases are narrower than cases-in-chief because the purpose is to give each side a chance to refute what the other side presented in its last appearance, each succeeding rebuttal being narrower than the one before.

During his case-in-chief, then, each party calls every witness on whom he depends, building his case by testimony elicited on "direct examination." He also introduces tangible evidence, such as the defective steering link that caused the accident, or the contract sued on, or medical records, or models and photographs of the accident scene. Such tangible things are often swept up under the heading "demonstrative evidence," and sometimes more particular labels apply. Thus the objects actually involved in the events in litigation (the steering link) are called "real" or "original" evidence, and almost always such things are admitted, if physical limitations of the courtroom permit. Writings are called "documentary" evidence, and they are so common that special rules apply.

During the time when a party holds center stage, he is in control. He calls the witnesses and puts the initial questions, thus determines the subjects and sequence, and lawyers prize this control. But even during his case-in-chief each party shares the stage with the opposition: After direct examination of each witness is completed, the opponent gets a turn to ask questions, this time by "cross-examination." Thus in effect the opponent interrupts the calling party's case, though in most jurisdictions the opponent can cross-examine only on subjects opened up on direct, and may not go into other relevant matters not explored on direct. (The question whether cross should be limited by the "scope of direct" is debated, as you will see soon.)

When cross-examination is finished, the calling party may engage in "redirect" examination, and then the adversary may again cross-examine (now "recross-examination"), and so on. Each succeeding round of questioning becomes narrower until the parties are satisfied or the judge decides that repetition has set in.

To sum it up, the order of proof usually goes this way (although the judge can change it for special reasons):

1. Plaintiff (or prosecutor) presents his case-in-chief, then rests;
2. Defendant presents his case-in-chief, then rests;

3. Plaintiff (or prosecutor) presents his case-in-rebuttal;
4. Defendant presents his case-in-rebuttal (sometimes called his "case-in-rejoinder");
5. Each side presents further cases-in-rebuttal (again sometimes called cases-in-rejoinder).

And the order of examination is as follows:

1. Direct examination by the calling party;
2. Cross-examination by the adverse party;
3. Redirect examination by the calling party;
4. Recross by the adverse party;
5. Further redirect and re-cross as may be necessary.

4. Trial Motions

When the evidence on both sides is in (sometimes earlier), a party confident that a reasonable person could only find in his favor may make a motion for judgment (in a criminal case, only the defense may do so). Here the court has a chance to assess the sufficiency of the proof, and to take the case from the jury if a reasonable person could resolve the dispute only one way.

In ruling on such motions, the trial judge follows well-recognized rules of thumb (they vary among jurisdictions). She assumes that the jury will believe witnesses for the party opposing the motion, which means that the judge does not determine credibility issues (or "resolves them in favor of the party opposing the motion"). In some jurisdictions the judge considers only evidence offered by the party opposing the motion, but it is usually said that she considers that evidence *and* evidence offered by the moving party that a reasonable juror could not reject. She also may take "judicial notice" of facts so well known and accepted as to be indisputable (Phoenix is hot in August). The judge only rejects evidence that runs contrary to the laws of nature or to matters that can be judicially noticed.

Typically such motions are denied. They are rarely granted for the party bearing the burden of proof in a civil case, and seldom granted in negligence cases. They are perhaps most often granted for defendants in criminal cases, and for defendants in civil contract suits. As a practical matter, they are routinely denied in jury-tried cases even where the judge is inclined to go along with the movant, if only because the outcome is better protected from reversal if the jury takes the case and comes in with a verdict for the moving party. (If the jury comes in the other way, the judge has the chance after the verdict to grant a similar motion. If she does so and is found on appeal to have erred, the verdict can be reinstated.)

5. Closing Argument

When the proof is in, the time comes for lawyers and judge to have their final say. The lawyers argue and the judge instructs. In federal court and most state systems it is done in that order (instructions are the last thing the jury hears before it "retires"). In some state systems, the judge speaks first and the lawyers have the last word, an approach much preferred by the trial bar.

The party bearing the burden of persuasion (usually plaintiff or prosecutor) has the right to make two closing arguments, one before and one after his adversary. The notion is that he needs an extra chance to persuade, since he loses if the jury finds the evidence equally balanced. In short, the party with the burden of persuasion opens first and closes first and last. His adversary goes second, in both opening and closing. (Jurisdictions may vary this pattern, allowing prosecutors only one closing argument, prior to that of the defense.)

In closing argument each side gets its chance to put its last word to the jury. The lawyer has seen how the trial has gone, and may have seen expressions of sympathy or doubt on the faces of jurors, and now he has his last chance to address such doubts, reinforce sympathetic reactions, and explain why the jury should find for his client.

Often the trial lawyer has already written a draft of his close, and he devotes final preparation to finding the best words. He concentrates on phrasing, allusions, tone, cadence. He thinks about the relationship that has grown up between him and the jury, looking for words and expressions in keeping with the positive aspects of that relationship. And he works on continuities—ideas already set out in the opening statement and supported by testimony.

The matter of closing argument is personal to each attorney and depends on the course of trial. But the attorney is not the subject of the close—the plight of the client is. A good close does not overwhelm the jury with the skill or brilliance of the lawyer, but instead leaves the jury with an inexorable feeling that the client's cause is clearly the stronger, and that any lawyer worth his salt would have shown as much.

6. Instructions

The judge instructs the jury on the law, so it understands what it must decide in order to reach a verdict for either party. Instructions explain substantive principles, and allocate and define the burdens of proof on the issues. Usually they also contain standard admonitions about the manner of conducting deliberations, the need to decide on the evidence, and so forth. The parties draft the instructions and submit their requests to the court (with copies to adverse parties) before the process of proof has been completed (in the wording of FRCP 51 and FRCrimP 30, before "the close of the evidence"), and judges often expect and get instructions before trial even begins. Any party who doesn't like a proposed instruction must object before the instruction is given.

Often the judge also instructs the jury on evidentiary matters. Such instructions may admonish the jury to exclude from consideration certain testimony or information suggested by a question during trial (often these are given when the incident occurs, and repeated at the end for good measure). These are "curative" instructions whose purpose is to save the verdict and judgment from later reversal on account of inevitable errors as the trial progresses. On some points, a curative instruction cannot work and may even be counterproductive—emphasizing the point it asks the jury to forget. Hence for the most part the question whether to give such instructions is left in the first instance to the party whose case might be damaged by the incident in question.

Often instructions advise the jury to consider certain proof only on one point and not others or against one party and not others. These are "limiting" instructions, made necessary by the fact that much important evidence has unwanted side effects, and the aim is to minimize these. Again such instructions are likely to be given during trial when such incidents occur, and the party who might be hurt by the evidence in question ordinarily decides in the first instance whether he wants an instruction at all.

Another kind of instruction seeks to convey to juries the effect of "presumptions" and certain formal inferences. Sometimes the instruction is simple. In civil cases, for example, a presumption sometimes *requires* the jury to accept a fact as proved if no counterproof has been adduced. But in criminal cases, and in civil cases where counterproof *has* been adduced, the matter of instruction is complicated. The jury is sometimes told that it may draw an inference from particular proof, although the parties may quarrel over language and may not agree that the evidence even warrants the instruction (see Chapter 10, infra).

Still other instructions tell the jury that it must decide certain points before it may consider certain evidence. In criminal cases, for example, a defendant who contends that a confession admitted against him was coerced may be entitled to have the jury consider the coercion claim before it takes the confession as proof. (The accused is constitutionally entitled to have the judge resolve his claim of coercion, but if the judge decides against him and admits the confession, the accused may be entitled to a "second bite"—that is, to make the same argument to the jury, in hopes that it will come out on his side.)

7. Deliberations

After lawyers and judge finish talking to the jury, the curtain falls. The characters leave the stage, their lines having been spoken. Judge and lawyers—producers, directors, and actors too—make their exits. Now it is the jury's turn (audience becomes actor).

The performance of the jury takes place behind closed doors. There it selects a leader and deliberates. The lines spoken in the jury room are hidden. Necessarily hidden as well are the factors that prove persuasive, and the personalities that become influential, among witnesses and lawyers, and among the jurors themselves.

This secrecy is intentional. One purpose is to encourage jurors to share their views with one another, a notion reflecting our democratic ideals and faith in the value of free expression and exchange of views—the faith that underlies the First Amendment. Another purpose is to insulate verdicts, both from public scrutiny (which would lead to relentless examination and criticism in the press) and from judicial review (which could have no purpose but to provide additional ground for reversal). Paradoxically, one reason for such precautions is the widespread belief that jury deliberations may not live up to an ideal of enlightened exchange of views and sifting of evidence, and that the jury as an institution might not survive close scrutiny of its deliberative process.

In modern practice jurors usually go home at the end of each day, although they are admonished not to discuss the case among themselves or with outsiders. If the case is notorious or controversial, the jury may be sequestered during trial and deliberations to insulate it from outside influence and pressures. Sequestration has become more challenging in the cellphone/computer age. In the Casey Anthony murder trial in Florida, for example, jurors were sequestered and required to give up their cellphones and allowed access to the internet only in a communal room under supervision by court personnel. They were allowed to make calls only on landlines, and only to family, and televised news coverage in hotel rooms was blocked.

Questions often arise during deliberations, and jurors seek clarification of testimony or instructions. Typically the leader passes a note to the bailiff to be forwarded to the judge, who summons the jury and the lawyers to the courtroom, where the jury's request can be considered. Often instructions are repeated, or parts of the trial transcript are read aloud by the reporter.

If deliberations bog down in disagreement, the leader may again communicate with the judge, and the question arises whether to declare a mistrial. Often the judge admonishes the jury to try some more, reminding it of the time already spent and the expense of a new trial and telling each juror to reconsider her position. Commonly the admonition suggests that jurors who find themselves in the minority or alone should take into account the contrary view of most of the others and consider whether that view might not be right. It suggests to those in the majority that they should reconsider the objections of others. Particularly in criminal cases, defendants object to this so-called "dynamite charge" as infringing the constitutional safeguard requiring proof beyond a reasonable doubt for conviction.

8. The Verdict

When the jury reaches its verdict, the actors in the drama assemble in court. The jury leader announces the verdict or hands a written verdict to the judge or clerk, who reads it into the record. Generally the judge asks appropriate questions to ensure that all jurors agree on the verdict as announced, closing the door to any later claim that what was announced is not what was agreed to.

Usually the jury gives a "general verdict," which in civil cases states simply who wins and (if it is the plaintiff) the amount of recovery. In criminal cases the verdict may state simply that the defendant is guilty or not guilty of the charges, but increasingly criminal verdicts also include findings on issues that relate to sentencing. Sometimes in civil cases the jury answers special interrogatories (with or without a bottom line general verdict), which ensures that the jury addresses and resolves particular issues. In criminal trials, where the death penalty is possible, the jury may retire a second time to deliberate and recommend punishment.

9. Judgment and Post-Trial Motions

After the verdict is announced, the court enters judgment. In civil cases, generally the prevailing party prepares the judgment for the court's signature, and the clerk "enters" it by notation in the docket book. Now a judgment awarding relief becomes effective in the sense that it can be "executed" against property owned by the defendant. In criminal cases where the jury returns a verdict of not guilty, a judgment of acquittal is signed by the judge and entered by the clerk forthwith, and the defendant is released from custody immediately. Where the jury returns a verdict of guilty, the judgment is signed and entered after a sentencing hearing has been held and sentence has been pronounced. In civil and criminal cases alike, entry of judgment starts the time for appeal, although the prosecutor usually has no appeal from an acquittal.

Post-trial motions present the parties with their last chance at the trial level to obtain the result they have sought. Routinely the losing parties in civil cases move for judgment as a matter of law (formerly called a JNOV or "judgment notwithstanding the verdict") and request in the alternative a new trial. In federal court and many states, such motions must be made not later than 28 days after entry of judgment, a time limit that is rigorously enforced. And routinely the defense in criminal cases moves for judgment of acquittal, which in federal court and most states is once again subject to a rigid time limit.

Other kinds of post-trial motions may be made. Some are less sweeping, like motions to correct "clerical" or "ministerial" mistakes, and or seeking permission to interview jurors (if the parties suspect some impropriety in deliberations). Others seek to begin the contest anew, like motions to reopen on account of newly discovered evidence.

10. Appellate Review

Federal courts and most state courts adhere to the final judgment rule, under which appellate review may be had only at the end of the case, when the trial court has entered a "final judgment" that dismisses claims or charges for jurisdictional or other "technical" reasons (in effect denying the relief sought) or disposes of them "on the merits" (awarding relief or perhaps not, but in any event resolving substantive issues). There are notable exceptions to the pattern: In New York, civil litigants may obtain "interlocutory" review of a wide range of orders and rulings by trial courts. And even jurisdictions following the finality principle permit interlocutory review of some rulings and orders.

The finality rule applies to appellate review of evidence points, with the result that usually a party aggrieved by a ruling on an evidence point must await final judgment before seeking review. (There are a few exceptions, taken up below in section F.)

Even when judgment has been entered, a party may obtain full review only if it "preserved" claims of error by stating its position promptly at trial (see sections C and D, infra). If these procedural steps were taken, appellate review of evidence rulings may lead to relief (reversal and often a new trial), but only if the reviewing court concludes both that the trial court erred and that the error probably affected substantial rights, hence that the error was "reversible" rather than "harmless" (see section E, infra).

MAKING THE RECORD

1. What Is the Record and How Is It Made?

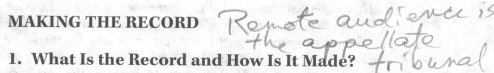

Trying a case involves a performance designed to affect both a live and a remote audience. The live audience is the judge and the jury (if any), who see and hear the goings on in the theater of trial. The remote audience is the appellate tribunal, which depends on a secondhand source—the "cold" written record. Hence lawyers are aware of the immediate impact of their performances (and those of witnesses) and are conscious of the picture their words (and those of witnesses) make when printed for remote scrutiny.

In the first instance it is the responsibility of the court reporter to prepare the record of trial. One might think that in the twenty-first century and the digital age, it would not be necessary for a human agent to hear and record a trial, and that a machine could pick up the sights and sounds and produce a readable transcript and video. That day may come, and proceedings are already recorded sometimes. And the stenograph (compact keyboard allowing the reporter to enter symbols for sound rather than spelling out words) is typically linked to a computer that produces a rough transcript simultaneously. The reporter later works from the recording or electronic transcript to produce a more literate record. (Using a recording machine has drawbacks: A reporter will speak up if he cannot hear or spell a word, and a judge protects her reporter by reminding witnesses to speak clearly and use the microphone when necessary. A machine doesn't say anything when voices become inaudible, and judges and lawyers are prone to forget that the machine is there, so transcripts produced from recordings tend to be inferior to those produced by a reporter.) For the most part, a court reporter is still found in most American trials.

The reporter is a skilled public servant and officer of the court, and his task is exactly what the title implies: He puts into permanent written form, as best he can, the words uttered at trial. He is not an editor or dramatist, and he tries not to add to or subtract from what is actually said. Hence in a real sense it is also the responsibility of court and counsel to prepare the record—to try hard to ensure that the words spoken at trial will make sense when written down—and making the record is, in the end, a cooperative venture requiring coordinated efforts by trial lawyer, judge, and reporter.

The official record of a trial actually comprises five different kinds of material:

(1) The pleadings. In civil actions these include complaint and answer, and often third-party claims, counterclaims (sometimes called cross-complaints), cross-claims, and answers to these. In criminal actions the pleadings include the indictment or complaint and the plea of the accused (usually entered orally and recorded in a verbatim transcript).

(2) Filed documents. The record includes all other papers filed in court, such as motions and accompanying briefs, documents seeking and providing discovery, jury instructions, and court orders. Many of these fade into oblivion as the action proceeds: Complaint and answer are superseded by pretrial order; many discovery requests and responses lead nowhere and are forgotten. But any one may be critical: A judgment, for example, becomes the basis for executing on a successful claim, and for enforcing the doctrines of res judicata and collateral estoppel, which block new attempts to bring the same claim or relitigate points already decided. And often jury instructions and the findings and conclusions play a central role in later appellate review.

(3) The record of proceedings. One of the most important parts of the record is the verbatim memorial of what transpires as the action is tried. It captures what is said by the parties, witnesses, and court in public session. It also captures whatever spoken words are considered important by the court or parties in private conferences, conducted sometimes in whispers at the bench, occasionally while the jury (maybe even the public) is excluded from the courtroom, and sometimes "in camera" (the office or "chambers" of the judge), at least when the court or a party requests the reporter's presence. Thus the record of proceedings puts into permanent form the testimonial evidence presented in the trial, as well as questions, objections, arguments, comments, and stipulations offered by trial lawyers during the proceedings, and orders and rulings announced orally by the judge.

It is important to note that inevitably much of the ebb and flow of the proceedings is of little or no importance later, whatever its impact on the live audience. For that reason, the reporter does *not* routinely prepare a transcript in readable printed form. Indeed, the record he produces is for the most part stored away in the original form of stenographic notes, once comprised of fanfold pages resembling an adding machine tape but now comprised of computer memory. In either case the content is the reporter's personalized arrangement of symbols. For the most part, these are readable only by their maker, being so much Greek to anybody else.

It is equally important to note that parts of this portion of the record may be critical in post-trial motions seeking a new trial or other relief, or on appellate review. Hence the reporter is ready to prepare a transcript when asked to do so—and the party who wants a transcript must pay for this service, which is not financed by taxpayers through the judicial system. In big cases, heavily supported by one or more parties, lawyers sometimes ask for daily transcripts, and the task of taking down the proceedings may be divided among reporters operating in shifts, alternately spending time in court stenographically recording what goes on, then setting down the proceedings in printed form. Through their combined efforts they produce instant transcripts for lawyers to review in preparation for the next day.

As should be obvious, this portion of the record is critical in preserving for review the various points of evidence raised during trial. Appellate opinions set out in this book depend heavily on this part of the record as a primary source, even though they may not actually quote or even mention it (sometimes they do quote and cite the record).

(4) The exhibits. The record includes all the physical exhibits offered in trial (documents or other physical objects). These are identified and lodged with the court, whether or not "admitted" for consideration by the trier of fact. Here the job of the reporter involves more care than technical skill, and doing it well is critical in preserving for review the contentions of the parties about such items of proof. Here too cooperation between reporter and lawyer is essential. In many modern courts, computers alleviate the physical clumsiness of the process, as documents can be stored in computer memory, accessed simultaneously by lawyers and court for viewing on individual screens, and "published" so a jury can see them (as printouts or images on a larger monitor).

(5) Docket entries. Finally, the record includes the court's own ledger of the proceedings—the "docket" or "docket book" kept by the court clerk, which contains dated line items entered in chronological order from the beginning to the end of the proceedings (from summons and complaint or indictment through judgment, post-trial motions, and notice of appeal). In this form the clerk simply lists each filed document and all important orders made by the judge, although the latter are generally entered in the docket book only if put in writing and filed. The docket book is a virtual table of contents, and sometimes the moment when each item is entered has great legal significance: For example, the time for appeal and for making some post-trial motions begins to run when the clerk enters the judgment in the docket book.

The record as a whole, including the five categories of material described here, is not actually assembled until and unless one or more of the parties decides to seek review. Then an early task of the appellant is to "designate" the record, part of which involves directing the reporter to prepare a transcript of important parts of the proceedings.

2. Beware the Pitfalls—What Not to Do

Trial lawyers, particularly beginners who suffer stage fright in their early performances, make a number of common mistakes that tend to muddy the record.

(1) Echoing. A nervous lawyer, particularly a novice, may fall into the habit of repeating an answer before putting the next question. This practice swells the record, distracts listeners and later the reviewing court, and conveys hesitancy and unease. While a good lawyer might repeat a point to add emphasis to an answer, there is a big difference between skilled repetition and mere echoing. No doubt echoing gives the lawyer some breathing room, but the real reason is not so much a need to think as discomfort with the surroundings. Consider this example:

Q (by Phillips): Were you present in the operating room?
A (Mr. Irwin): Yes, I was.
Q: You were. And who made the incision?
A: Dr. Young made the incision, and Dr. Hansen closed and cleaned up afterwards.
Q: Dr. Young made the incision, and Dr. Hansen closed. Very good. And were any other physicians in attendance?

(2) Overlapping. The reporter's feat in taking down the spoken word verbatim is considerable, but even skill and dedication can be overwhelmed when several voices speak at once and at cross-purposes. When lawyers or judges interrupt each other or the witness, the reporter tries to set down the words of whoever had the floor, but often the interrupted speaker stops or hesitates in surprise, and the reporter tries to pick up the ongoing words of the interrupter, which may be impossible if the original interrupting voice has itself been joined or interrupted by yet another. The result is an unreadable mishmash and a disgusted reporter. Consider the following:

A: Yes, Dr. Roth stepped in toward the end to examine the abdominal wall before—
Q (Rogers): Nothing to do with this lawsuit, and isn't even—
Q (Phillips): Interrupted by such discourtesy, which he knows, as Your Honor has again and again said you would—
A (Mr. Irwin): That again—
[Whereupon a discussion was had off the record.]

(3) Numbers, names, and big words. When a witness recites a number in her testimony, her spoken word may be susceptible to many different interpretations. What does a witness mean when she says "thirty-four O seven"? She could mean 3,407, 34.07, or even 30,407. Context may make one or another interpretation by far the more probable: "Thirty-four O seven" likely means "$3,407" (rather than either of the other two possibilities) if the witness had been asked how much it cost to rebuild the engine of the car, but the context will not always make clear the intended meaning of the answer, and the trial lawyer is well advised to clarify the record on such points.

Q (by Phillips): By "thirty-four O seven" do you mean three thousand four hundred seven dollars?
A (Rogers): Yes, that's right.

In everyday experience, names present spelling difficulties. Witnesses named "Meyer," "Myer," "Meier," "Mayer," "Meir," or "Maier" may utter the very same sound when asked their last name. What is the reporter to do? In fact, he may interrupt the proceedings and ask for a spelling then and there, but if the pace of questioning is hectic there may be no chance, and the problem may go unnoticed until the transcript appears. Sometimes the witness spells her name on her own, recognizing the problem. A thoughtful lawyer provides a list of names to the reporter in advance, so the reporter will know the spelling already.

Difficult or uncommon words, especially technical medical terms, create difficulties for the reporter. The witness who uses them should be asked first to spell them for the reporter, then explain them to the jury:

Q (by Phillips): Doctor, what did the abdominal incision reveal?
A (Dr. Young): Acute secondary peritonitis caused by bacterial invasion from the biliary system, entering through a perforation in the viscus brought on by acute cholecystitis.
Q: Doctor, would you be kind enough to assist the reporter by spelling those technical terms? Then I'll ask you to explain your answer in lay terms, as best you can, so that the jury and I can understand you.

(4) Exhibits. The problem of laying the foundation for tangible evidence is taken up in detail in Chapter 13. Suffice it to note here that in addition to laying the foundation, the trial lawyer must find an unambiguous way of referring to such evidence so his questioning is intelligible in the transcript. Instead of referring only to "that X-ray" or "the letter in your hand," the lawyer should refer to the object by its exhibit number.

Q (by Phillips): Doctor, I hand you what we have marked as plaintiff's exhibit number 35 for identification, and ask you to identify it if you can.
A (Dr. Young): Certainly. Yes, that is the X-ray which Dr. Knight prepared at my direction, showing Carl Deaver's abdominal cavity.
Q: Thank you, sir. Your Honor, if there is no objection, we now offer in evidence plaintiff's exhibit number—let's see, it'll be number 32 in evidence, I believe.
Court: Any objection?
Ms. Dreeves: No, your honor.
Court: Very well, it is admitted.

Q (by Phillips): Thank you, Your Honor. Now Dr. Young, calling your attention again to plaintiff's exhibit number 32 in evidence, can you tell us in lay terms what it shows?

(5) Pantomime, nonverbal cue, gesture, internal reference. From time to time the witnesses follow the conventions of everyday conversation, conveying information by nonverbal cues or words that refer to physical surroundings. Here the meaning is likely clear to the observer at trial, but lost to readers of the written transcript.

For example, the witness may give his answer in pantomime: Holding arm to his side with shoulder raised, elbow out and hand turned inward, he might say, "He was carrying the book this way." Here the trial lawyer conducting the questioning would be wise to state, "Let the record show that the witness is indicating that the subject carried the book at his side in one hand at about waist level." (If the lawyer on the other side disagrees, she should say so, and either the witness must convey his meaning in words or the parties must agree as to what the witness in fact indicated.)

Or the witness may answer by nonverbal cue: a nod or shake of the head, a shoulder shrug. Usually such a response evokes a reminder from trial judge or questioning lawyer: "Please give an audible response. The reporter can write down only what you say."

Sometimes the witness answers by gesture, indicating a direction or object or identifying a person by pointing. Again, usually the lawyer fills the gap: "Let the record show that the witness pointed northward" (or "up" or "at his right knee"), or "Let the record show that the witness pointed to the defendant, Leon Hall." If opposing counsel disagrees, she should so state, and silence is likely to be taken as assent.

Sometimes the witness answers by referring to objects in the courtroom, and again a clarifying remark by counsel helps, with an express or tacit stipulation by opposing counsel, or an additional answer by the witness:

A: The hammer I saw was about as big as her honor's gavel.
Q: Let the record show that the gavel has a handle about eight inches long and a head about an inch in diameter and about two inches long. That's about right, isn't it?
Ms. Dreeves: Yes, I think that's the burden of his testimony.
Q (Phillips): Thank you counsel—
A (Gordon): Yes, that's about what it was.
Q: Thank you.

(6) Going "off the record." Trial lawyers are in the habit of going "off the record" at difficult moments in depositions and occasionally during trial. The point is to avoid cluttering the transcript with bickering or long discussion that may end in agreement on a small point and a stipulation that can ultimately be briefly and simply stated.

But going off the record produces problems of its own.

For one thing, the need to do so may not appear until a discussion has begun, and one of the lawyers sings out "Off the record, don't take this down," and the discussion continues. The reporter is now in a quandary: He is professionally responsible to record all that transpires; he has no wish to be entangled in disagreement among the lawyers, in case one of them wants what is said to be recorded; if he stops taking notes, he may not know when to begin again. The better part of wisdom is to keep on recording until everyone agrees to go "off the record," then to note in his transcript, "Whereupon a discussion was held off record."

For another thing, the lawyers may forget that the reporter has stopped recording the proceedings. If an important answer or concession goes unrecorded, the lawyer who later needs it faces embarrassment. Lawyers must take care to signal the reporter that he is to begin again to record. Catching his eye or pointing to the stenograph may do it, but the careful lawyer might prefer to leave no doubt: "Alright, let's go back on the record now. We need to get this down."

(7) The sidebar conference. Frequently during trial the need arises for lawyers and court to speak on procedural or evidentiary points that might confuse the jury or convey matters that might ultimately be ruled inadmissible. See Rule 103(c). In such cases the court summons the lawyers to the bench, or one or another of them asks permission "to approach the bench." Often the judge moves her chair to the side of the bench furthest from the jury, the better to talk with the lawyers without being heard. These "sidebar" conferences are necessarily "off the record" if the court reporter cannot hear them, though he may be invited to join (and record) the huddle.

Physical limitations of the courtroom make it hard to conduct a sidebar conference that is "on the record" yet beyond hearing of nearby jurors. It can be done in modified stage whispers if the reporter hears well and moves close by, but lengthy conversations are best conducted in chambers or after the jury has been excused from the courtroom.

3. Taking Care—What to Do

As the foregoing discussion suggests by negative inference, two contributions that the trial lawyer makes in preparing a useful record of the proceedings are to insure that (1) utterances important to his cause, whether his own or those of witnesses or the judge, are spoken clearly enough to be put down by the reporter, and (2) those utterances will have meaning when they appear in printed form in the transcript. Accomplishing just these aims requires the trial lawyer to be aware of the reporter and his task, and to pitch his performance toward both the live and the remote audience.

The procedural requirements for preserving points for review by appropriate offer of proof and objection are described below, as are the formalities of introducing tangible evidence (in documentary or other form). Both require care in building the record.

D HOW EVIDENCE IS ADMITTED OR EXCLUDED

1. Getting Evidence In: Foundation and Offer

a. Testimonial Proof—Direct Examination

Almost always, the bulk of the trial (in terms of time spent) involves the presentation of live testimony by witnesses. Initially each party presents such testimony by direct examination, during which she tries to do basically three things with each witness:

First, she brings out background information—name and address and other basic facts, such as occupation and perhaps age or marital status. Several things are going on here: Opening questions help put the witness at ease, and along with the ritual of the oath impress on him that now is an occasion to behave responsibly; the jury wants to know who is talking, and needs a few moments to get used to the person and voice before focusing on the issues at hand; in a trial of public record a person giving evidence should be identified and understood, and not faceless.

Second, each party lays the foundation for the testimony to follow by asking questions that show that the witness has personal knowledge of the matters to which he will speak. These may place him at the scene of the accident or the signing of a will. In the case of an expert witness, the party brings out the special skill or training that provides a basis for his testimony on unfamiliar or technical matters.

Third, the lawyer asks "substantive questions" getting at the witness's knowledge of pertinent facts—the direction from which the car was coming, how fast it was going, which car had the light, and so forth.

Form of questioning. For the most part, direct examination must proceed by nonleading questions. See FRE 611(c). The point is that the questioning should not *unnecessarily* push the witness toward a particular response—it should not be too suggestive of the answers sought. In most cases, lawyer and witness have already gone over the substance of the expected testimony, and usually they reach an understanding of the narrative that is to unfold, so there should be no need to lead the witness.

There is no simple test for the "leading question" that is to be avoided on direct examination. Sometimes it is said that any question seeking a yes or no answer is leading, but that is plainly not so: Asking a witness whether he was at a certain place at a certain time calls for such a response, for example, but would not likely be considered leading. Consider this description of what makes a question leading:

> Sometimes it is a matter of phrasing: even in cold print, a question that begins "Isn't it a fact that" or "Did you not" suggests a response and is leading. So is one that is phrased in the alternative to highlight the desired answer in careful detail while diminishing the other choice in vagueness: "Did you understand that you were to meet him at your home at ten o'clock, or what?" But a question that frames the only likely alternatives in an evenhanded way is not leading: "Did you call him, or did he call you?" Sometimes phrasing tells little and context is more important. In a trial for battery where defendant claims he struck no blow, the defense might ask an eyewitness "Did you see the defendant beat the victim?" and it would hardly be considered leading, but the same question would be leading if put by the prosecutor. And sometimes inflection, facial expression, voice dynamics, or gestures tell the story. It is easy enough to imagine asking the question "Did he seem really angry to you?" in a leading manner that conveys clearly that either a yes or a no answer is the one sought, but also easy to imagine the same words spoken in a neutral and nonleading way.

3 C. Mueller & L. Kirkpatrick, Federal Evidence §6:65 (4th ed. 2013).

The idea is that the *witness* should do the testifying on direct examination, not the lawyer. Questions pushing too hard in one direction are bad because they may (1) invoke in the witness a false memory of events, (2) induce him to lessen efforts to relate what he actually remembers and to acquiesce instead in the examiner's suggested version, and (3) distract him from important detail by directing his attention only to selected aspects of the story. (Important departures from this pattern are taken up in Chapter 7, infra.)

b. *Testimonial Proof—Cross-Examination*

With each witness, direct examination is followed by cross-examination by the adverse party. During plaintiff's case-in-chief, defendant has a chance to cross-examine after plaintiff's direct is done, and plaintiff has a similar chance during defendant's case-in-chief. Cross-examination seeks to limit or bring out inconsistencies in the direct. So important is this process that cross-examination has been extolled as a bulwark of our liberty, and the most powerful weapon in the arsenal of the trial lawyer: Wigmore called it "the greatest engine ever invented for the discovery of truth." 5 Wigmore on Evidence §1390 (J. Chadbourn rev. 1974).

Leading questions. Cross-examination differs markedly from the direct. Here counsel is in the limelight, and the substance of what is conveyed to the jury emerges more from questions than answers—the latter serving to confirm an idea already planted by counsel in the question. Much has been written about this process, perhaps because lawyers sometimes see this function as their highest calling and greatest challenge. The following advice to practitioners gets to the heart of the matter:

> The name of the game in cross-examination is control. However, such control should perhaps more properly be categorized as subtle control. While it is certainly in your interest to control the witness, it may not be in your interest to convey the fact of control too overtly to either the witness or the jury. Sympathies are a fickle thing and can shift rather easily without much provocation or justification. Thus, you cannot make it appear, despite what you may be attempting to accomplish with respect to a particular witness, that you are taking unfair advantage of the witness, brow-beating the witness or otherwise treating the witness with less respect than you would treat any other human being. This is made all the more difficult when you know the witness is a liar or is capable of providing you with information which is extremely helpful to your case, but won't do so without a certain amount of intimidation . . . . [B]y the same token, you cannot permit the witness to take advantage of you. While there is nothing wrong with permitting it to appear as if the witness is taking advantage of you for the purpose of setting the witness up for the big fall, you cannot permit the momentum to become such that the cross-examination and its direction [are] actually being dictated by the responses of the witness as opposed to the questions you ask.

M. Dombroff on Direct and Cross-Examination 191-192 (1985).

Apart from the personality of counsel, the main instrument of control during cross-examination is the leading question. From the standpoint of the litigant, the leading question narrows the inquiry and limits the opportunity of the witness to stray from the chosen path.

From the standpoint of the system, leading the witness on cross is acceptable because the qualities in such questioning that seemed bad during direct now seem beneficial. Thus during cross-examination leading questions may (1) invoke the conscience of the witness and awaken his memory sufficiently to dislodge him from his previous version of events in favor of what he himself considers a more complete or accurate version, (2) expose limits or inaccuracies in his memory, and (3) focus his attention on important details.

Scope-of-direct rule. A critical limit on cross-examination is the principle, observed in most jurisdictions, that cross-questioning is limited to matters explored on direct. This rule aims to confine the opponent's ability to interrupt the calling party's case. It is fundamental to the philosophy of the adversary system that each party is responsible for making his own case, and each should have latitude in arranging his own presentation.

Critique of scope-of-direct rule. Scholars and some judges take issue with the scope-of-direct rule, mounting two objections: First, it is said to be hard to administer and to lead to quibbling objections. Second, it is said to be an impediment to truth, keeping the cross-examiner from exploring relevant matters within the knowledge of the witness.

(1) Administration. Difficulties in administration arise from the imprecision of the principle. Consider a suit by a contractor for final payment on a house that the owner hired the contractor to build. Plaintiff calls an architect who inspected the house and looked at the plans, and he testifies on direct that it is "substantially complete." All would agree that the owner may cross-examine the architect on things remaining undone (painting trim, completing cabinets, and so forth) because completeness is the "matter" to which the architect testified on direct.

May the owner ask about the soundness of the plan or quality of its execution—whether, for example, the foundation ought to have broader footings than the plan specifies, or whether the contractor properly graded the grounds to ensure drainage, where the contract calls for "basic grading"? If the scope-of-direct rule embraces the "transaction" described by the architect, arguably the questions are proper: After all, the architect described the contractor's performance, and the cross goes to this point. But if the rule is intended to confine the cross-examiner to the very matter opened up on direct, such questions seem improper because they do not affect "substantial completion."

May the owner ask the architect whether 11 months is a "reasonable time" to complete the house? If the rule embraces every "issue" to which the direct testimony relates, the answer would be Yes: "Substantial completion" and "timely performance" both relate to breach and damages. See Degnan, Non-Rules Evidence Law: Cross-Examination, 6 Utah L. Rev. 323, 330-331 (1959) (suggesting six interpretations of scope-of-direct limit).

(2) Impediment to truth. It has long been asserted that the scope-of-direct rule impedes the truth-finding mission by keeping the adverse party from pursuing matters relevant to the case but not raised on direct by the calling party. For reasons well put by McCormick, it is no answer that the other side may later call the witness and put such questions:

> [I]n many instances a postponement of the questions will not be the only result of a ruling excluding a cross-question as outside the scope of the direct; unless the question is vital and he is fairly confident of a favorable answer, the cross-examiner might be unwilling to run the risk of calling the adversary's witness at a later stage as his own witness. A cautious cross-examiner might well decide to abandon the inquiry.

McCormick on Evidence §23 (Kenneth S. Broun ed., 7th ed. 2014).

Defense of the scope-of-direct rule. Despite these objections, most jurisdictions observe the scope-of-direct rule. One reason has proved persuasive, and two others are often advanced in support of the result thus reached:

(1) The order of proof. The strongest single reason for the scope-of-direct rule is that it enables the parties to control the order in which they present their evidence. Trial lawyers carefully plan their presentations. While they cannot produce a well-made play, with every line spoken in just the right place, they take pains to present their case in coherent fashion, and they do not want their adversary to disrupt this process.

Does the scope-of-direct limit serve this interest? The answer seems to be yes and no. The yes part runs this way: When the calling party introduces evidence of a single act or event, limiting cross to that act or event does protect the calling party's chosen order of presentation. The no part is as follows: If Witness 1 testifies to the color of the light at the intersection and Witness 2 describes the speed of the vehicles, then disallowing cross-examination of the latter on the color of the light does not preserve the order of proof. *That* cat is already out of the bag, and the calling party would likely have questioned Witness 2 on the subject if he expected favorable answers.

(2) The special case of the accused as witness. The Fifth Amendment entitles the accused not to testify and bars the prosecutor from calling him as a witness. That constitutional protection reinforces, in this context, the tradition of limiting cross to the scope of the direct.

It is settled that when the accused does testify, he cannot raise the Fifth Amendment as a shield against reasonable cross-examination:

> [The accused] has the choice, after weighing the advantage of the privilege against self-incrimination against the advantage of putting forward his version of the facts and his reliability as a witness, not to testify at all. He cannot reasonably claim that the Fifth Amendment gives him not only this choice but, if he elects to testify, an immunity from cross-examination on the matters he has himself put in dispute. It would make of the Fifth Amendment not only a humane safeguard against judicially coerced self-disclosure but a positive invitation to mutilate the truth a party offers to tell.

Brown v. United States, 356 U.S. 148, 155-156 (1958). The question then becomes, How broad is the waiver of the Fifth Amendment right? To put it another way, Does the waiver coincide with cross-examination that would be permitted by the scope-of-direct rule, or is it broader or narrower?

Apparently waiver is limited to matters related to the direct testimony. See Brown v. United States, 356 U.S. 148, 154-155 (1958) (defendant "determines the areas of disclosure and therefore of inquiry" and thereby "the breadth of his waiver"); Fitzpatrick v. United States, 178 U.S. 304, 315-316 (1900) (after testifying to an alibi, defendant could be cross-examined on his whereabouts, but going "farther" would present "a clear case of the defendant being compelled to furnish original evidence against himself"). See also Carlson, Cross-Examination of the Accused, 52 Cornell L.Q. 705 (1967), and Scope of Cross-Examination and the Proposed Federal Rules, 32 Fed. B.J. 244 (1973). In one opinion, however, the Court squinted in the other direction. See Johnson v. United States, 318 U.S. 189, 195 (1943) (in testifying the accused waives his privilege against self-incrimination "as to *all other relevant facts*").

In the trial of kidnapped heiress Patricia Hearst for bank robbery, the reviewing court showed that even a limited waiver may be very broad. See United States v. Hearst, 563 F.2d 1331, 1341 (9th Cir. 1977) (in support of her claim that she was coerced into participating in bank robbery, defendant described her lengthy period of captivity but omitted happenings in one "lost year" in the period; on cross, the prosecutor could inquire about that "interim year" even though he might uncover other criminal acts; this line of inquiry was "more than 'reasonably related' to the subject matter" of her direct testimony), *cert. denied*, 435 U.S. 1000 (1978).

(3) The voucher principle. It was once said that the calling party "vouched" for his witnesses and was thus "bound" by their testimony. Here was a dog whose bark was worse than its bite. A party could always adduce evidence conflicting with what one of its witnesses said, and there were ways around the rule, but it rested on the half-truth that a party can choose its witnesses (proving a point may require a witness whom the party would prefer not to call) and it sometimes produced injustice. The principle meant that a party could not impeach witnesses he called, and it reinforced the notion that the calling party should not cross-examine such witnesses by leading questions. It seemed to follow that the cross-examiner should not be allowed to explore matters that had not been "opened up" on direct, for doing so would let him (1) "make his own case" by leading questions, (2) avoid "vouching" for a witness who would become "his" witness although not actually called by him, and (3) build his case by testimony of a witness for whom his opponent vouched and could not impeach.

These formalistic objections have disappeared. FRE 607 does away with the voucher rule, providing that any party may impeach, including the party that called the witness. It is clear as well that a party who cannot cross-examine a witness adequately at the outset may recall her later, without fearing that he "vouches" for her or becomes "bound" by her testimony, and he has the right to "impeach" and put "leading questions" to her. If it be argued that the freedom made possible by throwing out the voucher rule makes it *unnecessary* to permit cross-examination beyond the scope of the direct, the answer may be the one advanced by McCormick: Questioning delayed is likely to be questioning denied, for the adverse party often will not dare recall the witness later.

Striking a compromise. The framers of the Rules were unable to choose between the scope-of-direct limit or wide-open cross. They seesawed back and forth. In his testimony before Congress, the chair of the Evidence Committee and the Reporter testified that in multiple votes the matter went "one way or the other by one vote," and the outcome kept changing.[5] In all this vacillation the Committee was debating only a matter of emphasis in a flexible provision—one that would say *either* that cross-examination should be limited to "the subject matter of the direct" but that the judge may permit "inquiry into additional matters" *or* that cross-examination may delve into "any matter relevant to any issue in the case" but that the judge might "limit cross-examination with respect to matters not testified to on direct." The former was to prevail, so usually the scope-of-direct rule applies, but the judge may permit broader cross. The rule in this form largely obviates the objection that it is hard to administer, since the trial judge is not likely to be reversed for choosing either alternative

[5]Hearings on Proposed Rules of Evidence before the Special Subcommittee on Reform of Federal Criminal Laws of the House Committee on the Judiciary, 93d Cong., 1st Sess., ser. 2, at 526-527 (1973) (testimony by Albert Jenner and Edward Cleary).

and there is little "percentage" trying to make an issue out of the choice she makes in any given case.

The divisions in the Committee are reflected in conflicts in state practice. While most states adhere to the scope-of-direct rule, a substantial minority has gone the other way. By recent count, more than a dozen states have abandoned or diluted the scope-of-direct rule.[6] See Arizona Rule of Evidence 611(b) (allowing cross on "any relevant matter"); Maine Rule of Evidence 611(b) (trial judge may limit cross "in the interests of justice"); Boller v. Cofrances, 42 166 N.W.2d 129 (Wis. 1969) (adopting wide-open rule).

■ PROBLEM 1-A. How Did It Happen?

At the intersection of Folsom and Valmont, two cars collide—a yellow Fiat driven by Abby Barton, in which Carl Dreeves rode as passenger, and a blue Buick driven by Eric Felsen. In a Rules jurisdiction, Barton sues Felsen for personal injuries and property damage. During her case-in-chief, Barton calls Carl Dreeves, who testifies on direct examination that "the Buick ran a red light."

On cross-examination, Felsen's counsel asks the following questions:

Q: Now Mr. Dreeves, you and Ms. Barton are seeing each other socially, isn't that right?

Q: Isn't it true, Mr. Dreeves, that at the time of the accident Ms. Barton here had turned clear around in her seat and was looking out the back window of the car?

Q: Tell me, Mr. Dreeves, you and Ms. Barton here had just finished lunch at Sebastian's where she drank three glasses of wine just before the accident, isn't that true?

To each question Barton's counsel objects, "Improper as beyond the scope of direct, your honor." How should the judge rule in each instance, and why? What arguments do you expect from Barton and Felsen?

---

[6] In a survey updated in 2013, we found that more than half the states (28) follow the scope-of-direct rule, while a substantial minority (17) follow the wide-open rule. The other five occupy intermediate positions. Here are the 28 states that favor the scope-of-direct rule: Alaska, Arkansas, California, Colorado, Connecticut, Delaware, Florida, Hawaii, Idaho, Illinois, Indiana, Iowa, Kansas, Maryland, Minnesota, Montana, Nebraska, New Jersey, New Mexico, New York, North Dakota, Oklahoma, Oregon, Rhode Island, South Dakota, Utah, Washington, and Wyoming. Here are the 17 states that prefer the wide-open rule: Alabama, Arizona, Georgia, Kentucky, Louisiana, Maine, Massachusetts, Michigan, Mississippi, Missouri, New Hampshire, North Carolina, Ohio, South Carolina, Tennessee, Texas, and Wisconsin. The other five states fall out this way: Vermont and West Virginia allow wide open cross-examination for witnesses who are parties. Pennsylvania allows wide open cross for parties in civil cases. Nevada and Virginia leave the matter to the discretion of the judge.

c. *Real Evidence*

"Real evidence" refers to tangible things directly involved in the transactions or events in litigation—the defective steering assembly involved in the accident, the weapon used in the homicide or armed robbery, the wound or injury suffered by the claimant, the written embodiment of the terms of agreement.

Apart from writings, the law of evidence ordinarily does not *require* production of such items, and their existence and nature may be established by testimony. But the Best Evidence doctrine (Chapter 14) generally does require the introduction of writings (or an excuse for not producing them), and all such items are generally considered relevant. They are likely to be admitted unless practical considerations preclude receipt.

The proponent's task in getting them admitted is to lay a foundation. Even if the thing in question looks very much like what it is supposed to be, the law of evidence is a Doubting Thomas, taking the skeptical position that the thing may *not* be taken "at face value" and the trier of fact may *not* assume it is "what it seems to be." Instead, the proponent must prove this point, and the process is called "authenticating" the evidence. Few specific Rules govern this process, and the ones we have are found in Article IX (see Chapter 13). Usually authentication is taken care of by stipulation, or by testimony from a witness having firsthand knowledge:

Q (Ms. Phipps): Now, Lieutenant Goldbloom, I hand you a gun which has been marked for identification as People's Exhibit Number Seven, and ask whether you can tell us what it is. Don't worry, sir, I've checked to be sure that it is not loaded.

A (Mr. Goldbloom): Thank you, but I always like to check these things myself. (Witness pauses to examine the gun.) Yes, I can identify this weapon. It is a Smith & Wesson .38 caliber revolver.

Q: And have you seen this particular weapon before?

A: Yes.

Q: How can you tell?

A: Here on the handle, it has my identification mark on it, which means that I found it in the course of my duties and wrote it up in a report.

Q: And could you tell us how you happened to find it?

A: Certainly. It was during the investigation of the death of Irving Stiffle, and I found the gun on the floor of the bedroom about five feet from his body.

Q: Your honor, I now offer this gun into evidence—what number will it be, Mr. Glade?

Court Clerk: It would be People's Number Three in evidence.

Ms. Phipps: I offer this gun into evidence as People's Exhibit Number Three.

The Court: Any objection from the defense?

Mr. Darnell: Yes, your honor, I do object, on several grounds. In the first place, nothing the Lieutenant has said connects that gun to the defendant or to the alleged homicide. Moreover, his testimony fails to account for the whereabouts of that gun from the time he picked it up until now. For all we know, the Property Room has fouled up again, and that's an entirely different weapon.

The Court: Ms. Phipps, any counter?

Ms. Phipps: Yes, your honor, it should suffice that the gun was found in the same room with the victim, but in any event we will offer ballistics testimony proving that the bullet that killed the victim was fired from this gun, and testimony from Forensics that defendant's fingerprints were found on the gun. As to the objection that we have not established the chain of custody, such proof should be unnecessary when we have the Lieutenant's testimony based on his mark that this is the very weapon which he found at the scene.

The Court: I'm inclined to agree. Objection overruled. Exhibit—what number is it, now?

Court Clerk: Number Three in Evidence.

The Court: Yes, the gun is admitted as Exhibit Number Three in Evidence.

In this exchange, notice that the authenticating witness Goldbloom recognized the gun and knew from memory that it was the weapon he found at the scene. In effect, the trial court has ruled that this information suffices to authenticate the weapon, even *without* "chain-of-custody" evidence establishing that the gun he found was carefully kept in a safe place under watch (or at least lock and key). Implicit here is a judgment that the proponent need not show precautions against a switch, at least when the authenticating witness says, in effect, that no switch occurred. Note too that the trial judge did not decide whether authentication requires proof connecting the gun to the homicide (the ballistics evidence) or to the defendant (forensics evidence), taking the prosecutor at her word that she would supply such proof later. If she does not deliver, the defense may force the issue by moving to strike the evidence.

In this example, the gun was "marked for identification" before being mentioned. All physical objects that a party expects to offer are routinely marked in this preliminary way. This precaution helps keep track of them and enables the parties to refer to them, in a way that will later make sense in the transcript, even before they are admitted. If the trial judge *excludes* an object, still it is lodged with the clerk, and the record of the offer may become important later on. When the judge *admits* the object, it is renumbered as an exhibit in evidence, and the number finally assigned may differ from the one originally assigned for identification.

d. Demonstrative Evidence

As the name implies, demonstrative evidence is tangible proof that in some way makes graphic the point to be proved. It differs from real evidence in that it is created for illustrative purposes for use at trial, having played no actual role in the events or transactions leading to the suit. Diagrams, photographs, maps, and models are all within the present category. So are computer-aided reconstructions, which can depict in color and from multiple perspectives an automobile accident or a crime, such as a robbery or murder or assault. See generally Fred Galves, Where the Not-So-Wild Things Are: Computers in the Courtroom, The Federal Rules of Evidence, and the Need for Institutional Reform and More Judicial Acceptance, 13 Harv. J.L. & Tech. 161 (2000).

Such materials are usually considered relevant and are routinely admitted. Once again there are no specific rules or principles, and the proponent's task is to show that the proffered item is a fair and accurate depiction of the matter in question. The growing sophistication of computer-aided reconstructions, which can convey a sense of movement, mass, and perspective that cannot easily be captured in verbal descriptions, but also have power to distort or overwhelm, have "raised the ante" for such foundational issues. These reconstructions must usually be supported by testimony showing that the dimensions and perspectives are correct, and may require experts rather than ordinary eyewitnesses. For demonstrative evidence that is more routine and less dramatic, usually the proponent simply calls a witness who has seen the matter and who then testifies that the exhibit fairly represents it:

Q (Ms. Phipps): Lieutenant Goldbloom, may I call your attention to the drawing on the stand here, which has been marked for identification as People's Exhibit Number Eight. This drawing is intended to show the layout of the bedroom where the victim was found. Is that a fair and accurate diagram of the room as you remember it?

A (Lt. Goldbloom): Yes, the bed came out more or less from the center of the wall farthest from the door, there was a bureau along the wall to the left as you came in—that's supposed to be the bureau, isn't it?

Q: Perhaps you could label the items with this. (Counsel hands marker to Witness.)

A: OK, here's the bed. (Witness marks drawing.)

Q: You've written the word "bed." OK, Thank you. Would you also mark where the window is? (Pause. Witness marks drawing.) You've written the word "window" with an arrow. Is that where the window is located?

A: Yes.

Ms. Phipps: Your Honor, we now offer into evidence what has been marked for identification as People's Exhibit Eight.

The Court: Mr. Darnell?

Mr. Darnell: No objection, Your Honor.

The Court: Very well, then. The diagram of the room will be received as People's Exhibit—what number are we at now?

Court Clerk: This will be People's Number Four in Evidence, Your Honor.

The Court: It is admitted as People's Exhibit Number Four.

Notice in this exchange that the drawing was taken only as illustrating the testimony of the witness, Lieutenant Goldbloom. You will see that a drawing produced to make graphic the testimony of a witness has no evidential force independent of that testimony. Sometimes jurors are instructed to this effect, and sometimes the parties even argue that material of this sort should not be taken to the jury room or even displayed to them because of the risk that the jury will *treat* it as evidence, uncritically accepting the things that it represents as having been established, when in fact they have no more support than the testimony of the witness, which the material merely illustrates. Of course the same is true of computer-aided reconstructions.

e. *Writings*

Writings are one kind of physical evidence that generally *must* be introduced at trial rather than proved by testimonial description. Often writings amount to real evidence because so many transactions generating lawsuits involve documents. But often writings provide a means to prove what someone has said about a matter in dispute: Laboratory reports and medical records, for example, are routinely admitted into evidence. Again, electronic technology sometimes aids courts and litigants: Written documents can be stored and organized on computers, made available to lawyers and judges for simultaneous access on computer screens, and "published" for juries to see on larger monitors, or printed out for ease in access on a selective basis.

With writings, once again the job of the proponent is to establish authenticity, and we have some specific rules on authenticating writings (Article IX, taken up in Chapter 13). Suffice it to say that in civil suits the parties usually authenticate writings involved in the underlying transaction by means of discovery or stipulations during pretrial. Taking time at trial to authenticate such writings is a sign that there is a genuine dispute over authenticity or that trial counsel are not well prepared.

With respect to writings offered to prove what somebody has said about the matters in litigation, laying the foundation is usually a twofold task. First, the proponent establishes that the writing is what he says it is—in other words, he authenticates it. Second, he shows that it falls within a hearsay exception:

Q (Irwin): Dr. Rogers, I hand you now a book and would ask you now to look at it and tell me whether you are acquainted with this work?

A (Dr. Rogers): Oh, Appleby on Thoracic Surgery, Littleton Publishing Company, Sixth Edition 2012. Yes, this is a standard work in my field.

Q: Would you be good enough to turn to page 287 and read aloud to us the paragraph which has been marked? Mr. Steed, here is a copy of the page in question.

Mr. Steed: One minute, Your Honor, please. I have not seen this before.

The Court: Yes, of course. Dr. Rogers, please wait with your response.

Mr. Steed: I'm going to have to object, Your Honor. Obviously this book is hearsay, and since the doctor here has not said that he relied on it in formulating whatever opinion he is going to offer, the passage in question is not admissible.

Mr. Irwin: Your Honor, Dr. Rogers has testified that Appleby on Thoracic Surgery is a standard work in his field, and that should suffice to satisfy Rule 803(18), which is the exception for learned treatises.

Mr. Steed: But there's been no reliance on this book, and without reliance it cannot be offered in evidence.

Mr. Irwin: Perhaps that was the common law rule, counsel, but the Federal Rules have changed that. Exception 18 doesn't say the witness has to rely on it, so long as the book is shown to be authoritative.

The Court: Mr. Steed, I think he's right. I'm going to let it in.

In this exchange, proving that the object is what the proponent claims it to be is easy. A physician acquainted with a published work can authenticate a particular bound volume as a counterpart of that published work, and ordinarily there would be no contest on this point whatsoever. In this particular exchange, laying the foundation involves mostly a demonstration that what the book contains is competent evidence.

2. Keeping Evidence Out

a. *The Objection*

Perhaps the one practice known to everybody is that lawyers object when they want to keep evidence out. You have probably concluded that there must be a reason and that failing to object must carry a cost. Right on both points.

Broadly speaking, the aim of the rules surrounding this custom is to provide the parties a fair opportunity to make their case, but not an endless one. If a party aggrieved by evidence were allowed to await the outcome and *then* complain that it should not have been admitted, the trial process would be even more drawn out and costly. The eventual loser could hold his peace during trial, perhaps even encourage error, then avoid the result by obtaining a reversal. Requiring objections helps limit this risk. Of course this approach carries a cost, for it means that some errors (those not objected to) go uncorrected, and the fact that we take this risk is one indication that the system tolerates imperfection.

There are two other (more particular) reasons to require objections to be raised at trial. One is that the objection helps the trial court. The law of evidence is vast and sometimes complicated, and trial judges (like other mortals) do not always have the right answer close at hand. The other is to help the offering party cure on the spot any problem in his proof. If an objection is sustained, the offering party may be able to accomplish her original aim by rephrasing the question, laying a further foundation, or asking the question of another witness.

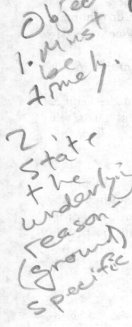

These aims imply two further points about objections:

First, the objection must be timely, meaning that it must be raised at the earliest reasonable opportunity. Thus an objection to testimony should usually be stated after the proponent has put a question but before the witness answers. If the witness "jumps the gun," perhaps with the connivance of the other lawyer, the objection can be stated after the fact, when it becomes a "motion to strike." The drawback of this "after objection" is that the jury has heard the answer, so an instruction to disregard may be ineffective, even counterproductive (emphasizing the point to be forgotten). Hence the objecting party often couples a motion to strike with a request for a mistrial, arguing that the damage cannot be undone, and therefore that the trial must begin anew before another jury. You can probably guess why this part of the motion is not likely to succeed.

Second, the objection should include a statement of the underlying reason ("ground"). In other words, the objection should be "specific," not "general." The alliterative phrase "irrelevant, incompetent, and immaterial" is a general objection, even though a detailed argument that evidence is "irrelevant" would be considered specific. (If the context leaves room for doubt, the objection should describe what the objector wants to exclude.)

The specific grounds that support an objection may be, for want of better terms, either "substantive" in nature or "formal."

Substantive objections. These rest on particular exclusionary principles in the Rules of Evidence, which are examined in detail in this course. The hope of the party raising such an objection is to keep the evidence out altogether. He may not entirely succeed, even if his objection is sustained, as the proponent may find another way to offer substantially the same proof. Examples of substantive grounds include the hearsay and Best Evidence doctrines, the attorney-client and marital confidence privileges, and the rules governing character evidence and "subsequent remedial measures" (usually framed in as limitations on the general notion of relevancy). Consider the following exchange:

Q (Mr. Parsons): Were you at the intersection of Fourth and Green in the commercial area in Champaign near campus on Wednesday afternoon, June 16th of this year?

A (Ms. Gordon): Why yes, I think I was. I can't remember the date for sure, but you're talking about the day of the accident, aren't you?

Q: Yes, that occasion. You were present then?

A: Yes.

Q: And did you see an accident between two cars at that time?

A: Well yes, I happened to be looking at the station wagon when it hit the other car.

Q: And did you have occasion to speak to Mr. Cronan shortly after that?

A: Yes, I did.

Q: And what was his reaction?

A: Well, he told me—

Mr. Dawson: I'm going to have to object, your honor. The jury has no way of knowing whether Mr. Cronan was speaking accurately or even whether he was truthful. What he said is inadmissible hearsay.

Mr. Parsons: Your Honor, Mr. Cronan's statement fits within the exception for excited utterances. That's Rule 803(2), I believe—Yes, that's it.

Mr. Dawson: He hasn't shown that that exception applies, your honor.

The Court: Well, Mr. Dawson, I'm inclined to agree. Mr. Parsons, you'd best lay the foundation first or call Mr. Cronan himself to the stand.

Pay attention to several things. One is that the objection is both specific and timely. Another is that it imparts the necessary information to the judge, and yet it conveys sympathy for the jury rather than mistrust of its judgment. Because the jury hears most objections, lawyers need to find a way to object without seeming to obstruct, to make the necessary legal point without seeming to hide information. Finally, the objection serves one of the underlying purposes, which is to alert the proponent to a problem in his proof, so he may cure it if he can, and here perhaps he can: He may be able to call Cronan ("declarant" who made the statement), hoping he will say the same thing on the stand, or to lay the foundation by satisfying the excited utterance exception so that Gordon can testify to Cronan's statement.

Formal objections. These focus on the manner of questioning, and they are standard equipment for trial lawyers. Many of them are mere tactical weapons, used to obstruct, delay, or break the cadence of the opposition. But in the right circumstances they raise proper points and are sustained. Apart from the objection to leading questions, these objections are not enshrined in the Rules, but they speak to the judge's authority to regulate the presentation of proof in the interest of getting at the truth while avoiding confusion and delay and preventing abuse of witnesses. See FRE 611, and see generally Roger C. Park, David P. Leonard & Steven H. Goldberg, Evidence Law: A Student's Guide to the Law of Evidence as Applied in American Trials, Chapter 3 (3d ed. 2011).

Here is a list of what may be the most common of these objections:

(1) "Asked and answered." Here the objecting lawyer accuses the questioner of drumming away too hard on the witness, putting the same question time and again in hopes of coercing the desired response. The questioner must be allowed to press the witness (particularly on cross) and need not take the first answer given, or else the witness would soon catch on that she can get out of the hot seat by simple denials or the time-honored evasion of "I don't know/remember." But when the questioner has gotten his response and has had a reasonable chance to expose falsehood or awaken the memory and conscience of the witness, the questioning must move on to other matters, and this objection can force the point.

(2) "Assumes facts not in evidence." If the questioner imparts information in his query, it should be supported by proof already admitted. If such support is missing, the question is objectionable as assuming too much. Thus, asking "How long did it take to drive the 20 miles from the ranch to town?" would be objectionable if nothing in the record indicated that the ranch was 20 miles from town.

(3) "Argumentative." Sometimes the questioner tries to contradict the witness or wants more to confront her with disbelief than to get a response. Questions in this vein, usually dripping with contempt, amount to "grandstanding," which may be permissible in closing argument but not while evidence is being presented. "What you mean when you say Martin wasn't speeding is that his car hadn't taken off like an airplane, isn't that it?" is a question that cannot be taken seriously and is objectionable as argument thinly disguised.

(4) "Compound." Sometimes a question apparently seeks more than one answer or suggests alternative responses, while being framed in a way that invites a yes or no response. The problem is that the witness may answer yes or no and her meaning will then be obscure. For example, "Did you telephone or see the decedent after that?" If the witness says yes, a strict construction of the question and response suggests that she telephoned *or* saw the decedent, but not both. But in the more relaxed everyday parlance the yes might mean that the witness *both* telephoned and saw the decedent, or perhaps simply that she saw the decedent (that being the last and perhaps more inclusive possibility). A careful witness might see the ambiguity and answer clearly ("I saw the decedent after that but did not speak to him on the phone"), but a timely objection will likely persuade the judge to tell the questioner to rephrase, so as to lessen the risk of ambiguity in the upcoming response.

(5) "Leading the witness." Here the suggestion is that counsel is telling the witness what to say, and the net impression is that the lawyer is doing the testifying, with the witness simply acceding to the will of counsel. We have already looked at the problems in this technique.

(6) "Misleading." Here the question misstates the evidence. If the only proof on point suggests that the ranch is 40 miles from town, a question asking "Why did it take you an hour to drive the ten miles to town?" would be objectionable as misleading. The same is true of a question that misquotes the testimony of a previous witness.

(7) "Speculation or conjecture." This objection raises the point that witnesses are expected to say what they "know," not what they "guess" or "suppose" or "expect" is true. Like objections to hearsay, this one has substantive content. It may be impossible for the questioner to offer what he wants because lay witnesses are expected to say what they know and to be factual and specific. (Experts have more leeway and often testify to what they would expect in hypothetical circumstances, where these are supported by evidence.) Asking a lay witness, for example, "what she would have done" if she knew something then that she knows now, or what someone else "was thinking when he did that," is typically objectionable on this ground. Categorical certainty is not required, since it is hard to come by. Someone who saw a robbery and "thinks" *X* did it may testify to this effect, even if she is "not absolutely certain." We expect a reasonable belief, but a "guess" is not good enough. Sometimes the problem is less substance than form, as when the questioner cannot figure out how to get what he wants in a nonleading way. A court that does not let a lawyer ask "what you would have done" with other information would probably let him ask, "What was the most important reason you did what you did?"

(8) "Calls for narrative response." A lawyer who has laid a foundation by getting the witness to say she was on the scene may want to give her free rein. "Could you tell us everything that happened then?" If the opposing lawyer thinks she is likely to say objectionable things, like repeating statements by others that could be excluded as hearsay, he might object that the question "calls for a narrative response." Judges differ on this point, and context matters—it may be preferable for a witness to be given latitude to speak in her own words. But latitude always brings some risk—and the objecting lawyer can point out particular concerns in a sidebar conference. Hence such an objection is often sustained. The questioner is told, "Ask specific questions, please."

(9) "Ambiguous, uncertain, and unintelligible." Like the alliterative general objection ("incompetent, irrelevant, and immaterial"), this protest is time-honored. It isn't pretty, but it points out the flaw in questions that cannot be understood or whose meaning depends on inflection that the record cannot capture. Sometimes the problem is that the lawyer has garbled his words and needs to start over. Sometimes the query is a close cousin to the argumentative question, where there is no serious expectation of a response. Here is an example: "In arranging the lineup, you picked seven men who weighed the same and didn't weigh the same, who were the same height but not the same height, and who looked alike but didn't look alike, didn't you?"

(10) "Nonresponsive to the question." Lawyers who ask proper questions on specific points are entitled to answers addressing those points. Suppose counsel for plaintiff asks defendant in an accident case, "Weren't you driving faster than the posted limit?" If he replies, "Maybe so, but your client darted out in front of me and I couldn't have stopped no matter how fast I was going," the questioner can ask the court to "strike the answer as nonresponsive and instruct the witness to answer the question." (The judge will do so and tell the jury to "disregard the answer.") Anyone who watches televised interviews knows questioners and respondents have agendas and work at cross-purposes—sometimes it's hard to know who's manipulating whom. In the courtroom, the judge decides such things, and ordinarily the lawyer asking questions decides what points to make and when, and the witness has to cooperate. Clients are stuck with evidence their lawyers offer, so when a witness answers a question that wasn't asked, striking the answer as nonresponsive may be important. (A fair answer to an open-ended question is *not* nonresponsive. If the lawyer says, "Tell us what happened," and the witness replies, "Your client darted out in front of me," that answer *is* responsive. The lawyer is stuck with it.)

The general objection. If overruled, a general objection does not preserve for review whatever point the objector had in mind, so it gives less than maximum protection.

Yet general objections are far from useless, and trial lawyers make them all the time. Sometimes the reason is that they do not always find the right words immediately—they sense that something is wrong but cannot say exactly what. Sometimes the reason is almost the converse—which is to say that *everybody* knows exactly what is wrong, and the point is too obvious for words. Here the trial lawyer may well resort to the alliterative "incompetent, irrelevant, and immaterial," or (better yet, to avoid evoking the stereotypical lawyer's image, never much liked by lay people) might simply say "I object, Your Honor; he can't do that" or "That's unfair" or words of similar effect.

If the problem is that the objecting attorney has for the moment lost his wits and cannot think of the specific ground, these words at least halt the proceedings while he gropes in his mind to formulate his point. If lawyers and judge already know what is wrong, the judge may sustain the objection, and a general objection sustained will survive attack on appeal if there are *any grounds* upon which it may be supported. So a general objection may be a sign of poor lawyering, but not necessarily and not always. And in the right circumstances it can aptly serve the objector's purpose.

b. The Motion in Limine

Often a party anticipates that particular evidence will be offered to which he will object. Sometimes he anticipates that an item of proof that he plans to offer will meet serious objection from the adversary. In either case, he may want to obtain a ruling in advance, and the mechanism of a "motion in limine" (literally, "at the threshold") provides the means. This procedural device is sometimes authorized by statute or rule, and it exists by common law tradition almost everywhere. (The motion to suppress evidence, which is authorized by FRCrimP 12(b) and routinely made by the defense to assert rights to exclude evidence on the basis of violations of the Fourth, Fifth, or Sixth Amendment, is the most familiar instance of this procedure in operation.)

The attraction of this device is readily explained. It provides a chance for both parties to brief an evidence issue and present more elaborate argument than is possible during trial. It allows the movant to isolate and emphasize a point and to obtain a considered ruling. It may affect trial strategy: In the common situation in which the accused seeks an order forbidding the prosecutor from questioning him on past criminal convictions, the ruling may determine whether he should testify on his own behalf. And trial judges may be more than willing to consider and rule in advance upon such matters, in hopes of making a sounder decision and avoiding delays that are awkward while trial is in process.

But motions in limine are not always satisfactory.

From the standpoint of the judge, the motion seems to seek an "advisory opinion" that she is loathe to provide. It grates on her judicial temperament to be asked to decide a point not yet actually presented, and its very isolation from the trial may persuade her that she does not yet know how the issue should be resolved. If the accused wants to foreclose questions about his own criminal convictions, ruling correctly may involve the judge in considering the nature of testimony as yet unheard. And the judge may want to know more about the entire case than she knows before trial has begun.

Motions in limine sometimes create procedural ambiguities for the parties. If the judge denies a motion to exclude evidence, must the movant object again during trial in order to protect his right to obtain later review? FRE 103(a) provides that an objection need not be renewed at trial if the judge rules definitively on a pretrial motion. If the trial goes differently from what was anticipated, however, the judge may change the ruling. See United States v. Gaertner, 705 F.2d 210, 214-216 (7th Cir. 1983) (in drug trial, court first ruled that prosecutor could not ask defendant about prior drug convictions, but after he implied in his testimony that he was a person of good character, court permitted cross-examination on prior convictions), *cert. denied*, 464 U.S. 1071 (1984). Thus, even a clear ruling in limine still leaves the lawyers with the problem of deciding when (and whether) events have gone sufficiently far astray to justify reconsideration.

3. The Offer of Proof

The counterpart to the objection is the offer of proof. Making an offer of proof is not nearly so ingrained in the popular image of lawyers as objecting, but it is equally important, and failing to make offers when necessary is a common and serious shortcoming. Here is the basic point: A lawyer faced with a ruling excluding evidence *must* make a formal offer of proof, if he wants to preserve the point for later review, which means demonstrating to the trial court what he will introduce if permitted.

Broadly speaking, offers of proof are required for the same reason as objections. The idea is to accord the offering party (the "proponent") a fair procedural opportunity to get in his proof, but not endless chances. He must be ready to present his evidence when the objection is made and must make its "substance" known to the court (see FRE 103(a)(2)). If it were otherwise, if the proponent could await the outcome and only *then* make it known that he has additional evidence and disclose the details of what he would have proved if allowed, the end result would be a costly and potentially interminable process. An offer of proof is also necessary to "preserve the record" for purposes of review. Without an offer, an appellate court normally has no way to determine whether excluded evidence might have affected the outcome.

Like the objection, the offer of proof serves a disclosive function and thus achieves two additional ends. One is to enable the objector to refine his objection if need be, or to frame it more fully. The other is to help the trial judge arrive at the right ruling, since a detailed exposition of the evidence might lead her to change her mind and admit.

If the evidence is a document or other physical exhibit, it will likely have been marked for identification before trial. At the time of the offer, the proponent hands it to the clerk ("lodge" is the usual expression), to become part of the record regardless whether it is admitted. (You saw this ritual with the gun and drawing, offered with Lieutenant Goldbloom's testimony.) For documentary evidence, technology can make the process simpler, since a document stored on computers can be accessed by judge and lawyers at the same time, and "calling it up on the screen" enables the court to consider and rule on the proffer without handing around pieces of paper. If the evidence is testimonial, usually counsel for the proponent makes his offer by describing on the record the substance of the expected testimony. If the judge doubts that the witness would testify as described, she may ask counsel to put him on the stand: In the words of FRE 103(c), the court may tell the lawyer to offer the proof in "question-and-answer form." Needless to say, in all these cases the offer of proof is made (in the words of FRE 103(d)) "to the extent practicable," in a manner that keeps inadmissible evidence from being "suggested to the jury." Hence the jury is ordinarily excused when a proffer is heard.

It should be obvious from the description of objecting that the party wishing to exclude evidence bears the initial burden of raising the objection. When the objection has been made, however, ordinarily the proponent bears the burden of showing that his evidence is admissible. In other words, in making his offer of proof he must be prepared to explain why a rule or principle supports admitting the evidence. The necessary showing may involve simply winning an argument over the meaning and applicability of the Rules, but often it involves presenting testimony or other proof of facts and conditions that bring a rule into play. The apparently successful objection voiced by Dawson in the exchange quoted above might lead to an offer of proof by Parsons:

Mr. Parsons: Your Honor, may I be heard further on this matter? I believe that I can establish that Mr. Cronan's statement fits within the excited utterance exception set out in Rule 803(2), and I would like to make an offer of proof for the record.

Mr. Dawson: Cronan's statement does not fit, and the court has quite rightly sustained my objection. If we're going to get into a legal argument on this point, may I suggest that the jury be excused while we fight it out? The jury has to leave if he's going to make an offer of proof, anyway.

The Court: Gentlemen, please approach the bench.

[Discussion is held off the record.]

The Court: Ladies and gentlemen, we have not been able to reach an understanding yet, and since the dispute concerns a technical question of law, I'd like to ask you to step out in the hall for about 20 minutes while we get to the bottom of this thing. The bailiff will show you out. You may want to go down to the snack room in the basement for a cup of coffee or other refreshment. There are some vending machines down there, and you can take a midmorning break.

[Jury leaves the courtroom.]

The Court: Alright, gentlemen, let's get this over with. Mr. Parsons, you say I should let Ms. Gordon tell us what Mr. Cronan said shortly after the accident. You claim that his statement fits within the excited utterance exception and you want to make a record of Cronan's statement, is that right?

Mr. Parsons: Exactly, Your Honor. The exception was practically designed for this very situation, and we want to preserve a record of what he said.

The Court: Alright. Mr. Dawson, you say the statement is hearsay, and I should not let Ms. Gordon testify to what Cronan said, is that right?

Mr. Dawson: Right, Your Honor. Cronan's statement is pure hearsay, and Mr. Parsons should call him as a witness if he wants the jury to hear what he has to say.

The Court: The ball's in your court, Mr. Parsons.

Q (Parsons): Thank you, Your Honor. Ms. Gordon, where were you when the accident occurred?

A (Gordon): As I said before, I was on the sidewalk about 40 feet away from where the two cars collided.

Q: And where was Mr. Cronan at the time?

A: He was about ten feet away from me.

Q: And did you two know each other?

A: No, sir. But we both got out our cellphones to call for help, and we stayed around in case we were needed. And when the police came, they took statements from both of us, and it was then that I picked up his name.

Q: I see. And shortly after the collision, but before you found out his name, did Mr. Cronan say something to you about the accident?

A: Yes.

Q: How long after the accident, would you say?

A: Well, hardly any time had passed. It's a little hard to say, since I was concerned about the condition of the people in those cars, and worried that we were going to have other collisions. But to answer your question, I would say that Mr. Cronan said what he said not more than half a minute after the impact.

Q: Thank you. And Ms. Gordon, could you tell us how he sounded? Did he speak to you in—

Mr. Dawson: Just a minute, Your Honor. He's about to put words in the mouth of the witness. Let her tell us how he sounded in her own words.

The Court: Yes, I agree. Ms. Gordon, you heard the question. Tell us how Mr. Cronan sounded.

A (Gordon): Well, he just said it. I suppose we were both a bit upset—probably more surprised than anything. You know how it is when you're walking along the street and all of a sudden out of nowhere you hear tires screech and that sound of metal crashing together and you don't know for sure whether you're out of harm's way. I'd say Mr. Cronan said the first thing that came to him, and he kind of blurted it out.

Q: You said that Mr. Cronan sounded upset. Could you elaborate on that?

A: Well, I don't know what more to say. He was startled and sounded sort of aggravated.

Q: And now tell us, please, what you heard him say.

Mr. Dawson: Your Honor, you haven't ruled yet that what Mr. Cronan said is admissible. Let me just state for the record that I continue to object that his statement is hearsay.

The Court: Yes, counsel, I haven't forgotten your objection. You may answer, Ms. Gordon. What did he say?

A (Gordon): Well, he said "I knew that guy in the station wagon wasn't going to stop. He never did slow down." Then he added something like, "Too much of a hurry to obey the rules the rest of us live by."

Mr. Parsons: Thank you, Ms. Gordon. Your Honor, I submit that Cronan's statement is within the excited utterance exception of Rule 803(2). Ms. Gordon has said that he seemed "startled," to use her word, and subdivision (2) expressly mentions statements "relating to a startling event or condition" when such statements are made while declarant was "under the stress of excitement" brought on by that event. Well, a car accident is a startling event, and Mr. Cronan was obviously excited. His statement relates to the event. It should be received.

The Court: I take your point. Mr. Dawson, your turn.

Q (Dawson): Ms. Gordon, the intersection of which you spoke was Fourth and Green, was it not?

A (Gordon): Yes.

Q: And what were the traffic conditions at the time, if you remember?

A: Well, it was about three o'clock on a Wednesday afternoon, and there were quite a few cars coming down Green from both directions, and up and down Fourth too.

Q: So would you say things were pretty quiet, or on the noisy side?

A: Well, rather noisy. It is a busy street corner, and with the buses and the students and all, it's fairly noisy.

Q: So you heard the sounds of the accident against a background of pretty substantial traffic noise?

A: Yes, I would say so.

Q: Thank you, Ms. Gordon. Your Honor, this is not a case—

The Court: Excuse me just a minute. Are you both through with the witness?

Mr. Parsons: Yes, Your Honor. For the moment.

Mr. Dawson: Yes, sir.

The Court: Ms. Gordon, you may step down. Would you be good enough to wait in the hall for a few minutes? We'll tell you shortly whether we will be needing you any further.

[Witness leaves.]

The Court: OK gentlemen, where are we?

Mr. Dawson: Your Honor, may I be heard? Ms. Gordon has told us that neither she nor Mr. Cronan were afraid for their personal safety. They were far enough away from the accident to be out of danger. She has also testified, and I don't know how she could have said otherwise, that there was considerable noise in the intersection at the time. The noise of the collision was not like a sudden thunderclap. It wasn't any more than a loud sound in the general rumble of traffic, nothing you could even call unusual. The excited utterance exception contemplates a person exclaiming something "under the stress of excitement," and these people were not under stress and were certainly not excited. No more than you or I would be under similar circumstances.

Mr. Parsons: Your Honor,—

The Court: Unless you have something new to add that you haven't already said, I'd just as soon not hear anything further.

Mr. Parsons: Let me just say that the Rule does not require the declarant to be frightened for his life. It speaks of a "a startling event" and "excitement," and we have that here. Moreover, this evidence is critical to my case.

The Court: Well, it's a close question. You've made a record of what you want to get in, Mr. Parsons, so if this case goes up on appeal you can point out exactly what you wanted to prove. I still think this is just hearsay, and I'm inclined to agree with Mr. Dawson that there wasn't enough excitement here to guarantee reliability. If you want to get in Mr. Cronan's opinion, you'll have to call him. The objection is sustained. Gentlemen, unless you have any objection, I am going to excuse Ms. Gordon. Bailiff, please ask Ms. Gordon to step back in the courtroom, and I'll tell her she is excused. Then you may bring the jury back in.

If Parsons's client loses the case and takes an appeal, he now has the fullest possible on-the-record offer of proof, done in question-and-answer form to preserve the very testimony ultimately excluded and including testimony supporting the ground on which he contends that the statement should have been admitted. If there was error, the reviewing court should be able to see it and assess its significance. Consider how much harder those tasks would be if no offer had been made—if the record had stopped short when the objection was originally sustained.

Fortunately such an elaborate offer of proof is not always necessary. In the example above, Parsons put Gordon on the stand to get her to testify to what Cronan said about the conduct of the driver of the station wagon. Testimony about what another person said raises hearsay issues, which cannot be resolved on the basis of Parsons's initial question to Ms. Gordon ("And what was his [Cronan's] reaction?"), so further inquiry is in order when the defense makes its objection. But if Parsons sought to elicit from Ms. Gordon *her own* account of what happened when the cars collided, the nature of her expected response would likely be apparent on the face of the question. Recall that Parsons placed her at the scene ("Were you at the intersection of Fourth and Green . . . ?" "Why yes, . . .") and established that she saw what happened ("And did you see an accident . . . ?" "Well yes, I happened to be looking at the station wagon . . . ."). Assume the questioning then proceeded in this way:

Q (Parsons): If you can, Ms. Gordon, please tell us about how fast the station wagon was going as it entered the intersection.

Mr. Dawson: Your Honor, please, Ms. Gordon can't give her opinion on points like that.

Mr. Parsons: Your Honor, I don't know where Mr. Dawson got that idea. Under the Rules, let's see, I think it's 701, any witness can testify to matters based on personal observation, so long as it's helpful to the jury. Certainly a person who sees a car driving along can give an estimate as to speed, and that's all I propose for Ms. Gordon to do here.

Court: No Mr. Parsons, I don't think so. She couldn't see the speedometer from outside the car and I don't think I'll allow it. Now if you want to cover any other points with her, go right ahead.

In this situation, an attorney in Parsons's position might ask permission to approach the bench and would whisper to the court, the reporter, and to opposing counsel, "Let the record show that if permitted, Ms. Gordon would testify that she saw the station wagon driving along Fourth Street at approximately 50 mph just prior to the collision." Unless court or counsel did not believe Ms. Gordon would testify this way, this representation would likely be accepted, satisfying the requirement of an offer of proof.

It is even probable that if Parsons made *no* further statement of the expected tenor of Gordon's testimony, the record would show the appellate court that Ms. Gordon was expected to testify that the vehicle was speeding and the ruling disallowing such testimony would be reviewable for error. (Most courts let an eyewitness like Ms. Gordon testify to the speed of a car, and the court probably erred in refusing to let her answer.)

4. Judicial "Mini-Hearings"

Objections and offers of proof can involve court and parties in what amounts to "mini-hearings" raising all sorts of questions. Does the hearsay doctrine permit use of *Appleby on Thoracic Surgery* to prove surgical technique? Is a gun sufficiently connected to the crime to be admitted in a murder trial, on the basis of Lieutenant Goldbloom's testimony that he found it "on the floor of the bedroom about five feet from [the victim's] body"? Was Cronan excited when he spoke, since apparently the hearsay doctrine would permit this use of his out-of-court statement about the speed of a station wagon if he was?

Obviously the judge has a role to play. But does he decide these questions himself? Or just screen them, passing them to the jury if a reasonable person could decide them either way, on the basis of the evidence or common sense and experience?

Rule 104 describes the functions of judge and jury in deciding evidence questions. Rule 104(a) says the judge determines "preliminary" questions—witness competency, privilege, and admissibility of evidence. Rule 104(b) says it is different when relevancy turns on whether some "fact" exists. Here the judge merely screens the evidence: When different answers are possible, the jury decides. That is, the jury decides whether the factual condition is satisfied, and evidence that is conditionally relevant can be admitted subject to the requirement of offering later evidence "sufficient to support a finding" by the jury that the fact exists.

Sometimes Rules 104(a) and 104(b) operate without a hitch.

Rule 104(a) applies to the first and third questions noted above because both involve the hearsay doctrine. In Rules terms, the proposed use of the treatise and the bystander's remark about speed raise questions of admissibility. Rule 104(a) also applies to questions of witness competency. The only common question of competency involves qualifying a witness as an expert, and the trial judge alone decides this point. And Rule 104(a) also allocates to the judge alone issues involving the application of privileges, such as attorney-client or spousal confidences.

There are also clear applications of Rule 104(b). It governs the question raised by the gun that Lieutenant Goldbloom found next to the body. In Rules terms, the question whether the gun is sufficiently connected to the crime raises an issue of authentication, which is treated as a matter of conditional relevancy. That is, the jury decides whether such an item is what its proponent claims. The task of the judge is to ensure that the evidence is such that a reasonable juror could conclude that the item is what it is claimed to be. Only in extreme cases does the judge take over this decision. At one extreme, the judge excludes for failure to authenticate if there is not enough foundational evidence to enable a reasonable person to find the item authentic, or where the counterproof is so cogent and compelling that a reasonable person could only find the item *not* authentic. At the opposite extreme, the judge could instruct that the item is what its proponent claims, though such an instruction is seldom given, and it might be improper against the accused in a criminal case. Rule 104(b) also applies to the question of personal knowledge of witnesses (see ACN to FRE 602).

Sometimes, however, application of Rule 104 is more difficult. While applying the hearsay doctrine is mostly a matter for the judge under Rule 104(a), a few hearsay issues are sometimes given to juries, such as the question whether a party "adopted" a statement made by another and the question whether a person who makes what is offered as a "dying declaration" actually knew he was dying. Note too the language in Rule 104(a), saying that the judge is not "bound by" the rules of evidence (apart from privileges) in deciding questions of admissibility. In other words, the judge may consider matters that the jury cannot consider when it decides the case on the merits, and this point raises issues in applying the admissions doctrine and the exception for excited utterances.

CONSEQUENCES OF EVIDENTIAL ERROR

Few trials make it from beginning to end without error on points of evidence, and claims of evidence error are commonplace in appeals. It is doubtful that perfection in administering evidence law may be had at all, let alone at a price worth paying. There are three main causes of imperfection, and for each the system has developed an adaptive technique that helps separate errors requiring correction from those that do not.

First, some evidence rules are slippery or complex. Avoiding all mistakes is too much to expect. Judges and litigating lawyers, commentators and authors of appellate opinions—all are mortals who make mistakes. This reason alone suggests that there can be no such thing as "automatic" reversal on account of evidence errors. The reviewing court awards relief only when errors seem to have made a real difference in result.

Second, some evidence rules are framed as vague standards, and close appellate scrutiny would make no more sense than trying to fix a computer with a wrench. Many of the more particular rules require someone—usually the judge—to resolve factual issues, and the remoteness of the reviewing court suggests that deference to the trial judge is very much in order. Freewheeling review of efforts by the trial judge to apply vague standards or find facts affecting application of specific rules would be demoralizing, and would discourage trial judges from taking care in the first instance.

Third, ours is an adversary system, which places the lion's share of responsibility for the conduct of trial in the litigants (acting through their lawyers). There is good reason to hold them to the choices they (their lawyers) make at trial, and to refuse relief for errors they cause or might reasonably have been expected to prevent.

In sum, our system tolerates a less-than-perfect world. The three adaptive techniques are worth a closer look.

1. Appraising Such Error on the Merits

Assume that the reviewing court means to resolve an evidence point on the merits. One of its tasks is to identify error and tell everyone how to do the right thing next time. But reversal is not automatic, so identifying error is only the beginning. The rest of the job involves distinguishing errors that matter from those that do not.

The distinction turns on two connected points. One is that the evidence error must have affected what Rule 103 calls "a substantial right," meaning essentially outcome (verdict and resultant judgment in jury cases; judgment alone in judge-tried cases). The other is that we need some standard to deal with uncertain situations because reviewing courts often cannot tell for sure that even the most egregious error actually affected the result. The usual standard directs appellate courts to reverse a judgment only for error which "probably affected" the result, although this formula tells little and does not capture the flavor of the cases.[7]

Kinds of error. Reviewing courts put evidence errors in four categories: First is "reversible" error, meaning a mistake that probably *did* affect the judgment. Generally the term also means that appellant took the necessary steps to preserve his claim of error (by raising appropriate objection or making an offer of proof).

Second is "harmless" error, meaning a mistake that probably did *not* affect the judgment. This label expresses the reviewing court's conclusion that appellant has not shown that a ruling affected the verdict.

Third is "plain" error, meaning the kind that warrants relief, in the estimation of the reviewing court, even though appellant failed to take the steps to preserve its rights (objecting or making an offer of proof). It bears emphasis that the plain error doctrine provides only a slim hope for the trial lawyer whose wits and instincts failed at an important moment, and appellate opinions routinely reject claims of plain error and emphasize that the lawyer failed to object or offer proof, thus waiving the right to argue error. Generally courts insist that error is "plain" only if it is in some sense "obvious" (the judge should have known better even if the lawyer did not) and "serious" in the sense of providing greater certainty (more even than "reversible" error imparts) that outcome was affected at trial. Sometimes courts go so far as to say that error can be viewed as plain only if the judgment below amounts to a "miscarriage of justice." See Rule 103(d).

Fourth is "constitutional" error in criminal cases, which usually means a mistake in admitting evidence for the prosecution that should have been excluded under the Constitution. Most often invoked are the search and seizure provision of the Fourth Amendment (source of the doctrine requiring exclusion of illegally seized evidence, see Mapp v. Ohio, 367 U.S. 643 (1961)), the privilege against self-incrimination in the Fifth Amendment (source of the doctrine requiring police to warn suspects in custody of their rights, see Miranda v. Arizona, 384 U.S. 436 (1966)), and the Confrontation Clause in the Sixth Amendment (source of the doctrine entitling the accused to cross-examine witnesses against him, see Davis v. Alaska, 415 U.S. 308 (1974)). Here is a place where it was once thought that the general rule required "automatic" reversal, without a showing that the error affected the results below. But the

---

[7]Most courts apply the standard quoted above, but the matter is not free of doubt. A famous scholar of the bench would reverse unless the reviewing court "believes it highly probable that the error did not affect the judgment." R. Traynor, The Riddle of Harmless Error 35 (1970). And it has been argued that in criminal cases the standard applied on review should track the standard of proof applied at trial, meaning that the prosecutor should show beyond reasonable doubt that an error did *not* affect the result. See Saltzburg, The Harm of Harmless Error, 59 Va. L. Rev. 988, 991-1007 (1973). In its most thorough consideration of the subject, the Court admonished against "technicality," emphasized the importance of considering the proceedings "in their entirety," but stated its conclusion in elusive language. Kotteakos v. United States, 328 U.S. 750, 765 (1946) (reversal proper unless court can say with "fair assurance" that error did not affect result).

Court repudiated that position in Chapman v. California, 387 U.S. 18 (1967), adopting for most such cases (though perhaps not all) a more lenient standard under which the judgment may be affirmed if the prosecution shows beyond a reasonable doubt that the error was harmless. Less often, constitutional error occurs when courts exclude evidence offered by the defense, see Chambers v. Mississippi, 410 U.S. 284 (1973).

Distinguishing "harmless" from "reversible" error. You will discover that appellate courts are likely to find that a party lost or limited her "standing" to complain of error by the way she (her lawyer) conducted herself at trial. Tremendous energy goes into explaining why one or another contention cannot be fully considered on appeal. Putting this difficulty aside for a moment, the hardest task for appellate courts (and for lawyers deciding whether to appeal) is to distinguish between harmless and reversible error.

Viewed in isolation, many errors might have affected outcome: Evidence admitted in error might have been the reason why the trier decided against the appellant on a critical issue. Evidence excluded in error might (if it had been admitted) have tipped the balance on an issue that the jury decided against the appellant. An impeaching attack (or cross-examination) undertaken by the appellant but erroneously cut short by the trial court might have undercut a critical witness for the adverse party if allowed to run its full course. And an improper attack (or cross-examination) undertaken by the adverse party might have destroyed a witness for appellant whom the trier would otherwise have believed. Convincing a court that such errors "probably" had such effect is the second task of the appellant (the first being to persuade the court that indeed there was error).

In this quest appellant usually must also convince the court that other circumstances disclosed by the record (and emphasized by the party who won below) do not turn what seems to be reversible error into harmless error. Three doctrines have evolved, each describing and responding to a circumstance that turns the poignant into the bland (reversible into harmless error):

First is the "cumulative evidence" doctrine, which supports affirmance despite errors both in admitting and in excluding. Nothing is so common as an appellate opinion stating that the trial judge did err in *admitting* evidence offered *against* the appellant, but that so much other proper evidence supported the same point that the jury would likely have found against her even if the judge had done the right thing. And you read almost as often the appellate view that the judge erred in *excluding* evidence offered *by* the appellant, but that so much other proof was admitted on the same point that the jury would not likely have changed its mind even if the judge had correctly admitted the evidence in question.

Bear in mind—and appellate opinions sometimes get this wrong—that the "cumulative evidence" doctrine does *not* justify affirmance merely because other evidence was *sufficient* to sustain the result reached below: The question is always whether evidence erroneously admitted *probably affected* outcome or whether evidence erroneously excluded *probably would have* affected outcome. If the answer is yes, the error calls for corrective action even if there is enough other evidence in the case to support the conclusion that the trier actually reached.

Second is the "curative instruction" doctrine. When a judge makes a mistake on an evidence point, he may be able to avoid reversal by an instruction to the jury. When the risk is great that evidence admitted on one point or against one party may be improperly considered by the jury as proof on a different point or against another party, a limiting instruction is possible (see FRE 105). Such instruction is usually viewed as effective, thus disposing of any contention on appeal that the evidence was used improperly. Similarly, if it becomes clear after the fact that evidence should not have come in at all, an instruction to disregard may be effective in preserving the judgment on appeal. These instructions are said to "cure" the error, making it harmless. Occasionally an instruction even cures an error in *excluding* evidence, as happens when a judge implies in his instructions that the issue has been (or should be) resolved in favor of the party who offered the evidence. Sometimes the verdict itself cures the error, as happens when the jury finds in favor of the appellant on the only issues affected by any error.

Third is the "overwhelming evidence" doctrine. If a reviewing court concludes that evidence properly admitted supports the judgment below overwhelmingly, generally it affirms, even in the face of errors admitting or excluding evidence that might otherwise be considered serious. The opinions seem to suggest that the evidence was such as to invite a directed verdict.

2. Appellate Deference: The Discretion of the Trial Judge

The doctrine of judicial discretion limits appellate review of evidential rulings. One source of discretion is found in doctrines that are framed in loose terms. It is settled, for example, that the judge may exclude even competent and relevant evidence if it seems likely to prejudice the jury against one of the parties. See FRE 403. And the judge may control the manner and sequence of questioning witnesses. See FRE 611.

Doctrines such as these may be viewed in different ways. Clearly they confer great power in the trial judge to affect the presentation of evidence. They amount to a vote of confidence in her ability to fashion sensible ad hoc solutions to the inevitable problems of trial. The generality of such doctrines concedes that specific rules do not exist and suggests that they could not be framed. Lawyers are inclined to describe the decisions invited by these doctrines in terms of balancing, by which is usually meant selecting between one course and another by considering and comparing dissimilar factors (in effect "choosing between apples and oranges").

In such cases the trial judge is likely to be upheld no matter which choice she makes. Appellate opinions refer to her "broad discretion," and often they suggest that her decision is reviewable only for "abuse," which is perhaps only another way of saying that the appellate court strongly disagrees. (If the claimed error falls into a discretionary category, sometimes reversal can be had if it can be shown that the judge failed to exercise discretion in the mistaken belief that she was bound by a particular rule.)

There is another source of judicial discretion. It is the more particular evidential doctrines whose application turns in the first instance on factfinding by the trial judge. Even in criminal trials and civil jury cases, where we think of the jury as the factfinder, the trial judge performs factfinding duties in administering the law of evidence. Recall the discussion between Parsons and Dawson over Cronan's remark about the fellow in the station wagon being in "too much of a hurry." There the trial judge was asked to apply Rule 803(2)—the "excited utterance" exception, which applies only where (1) there was an occasion which startled the declarant, (2) he spoke while excited, and (3) his statement expressed his reaction to the occasion. It is the trial judge who determines whether these requirements are satisfied, and her conclusions are reviewed under either a "clear error" or "abuse-of-discretion" standard. These terms seem in this context to coalesce, and they mean that the reviewing court defers to the conclusions of the trial judge, and reverses only if it strongly disagrees.

3. Procedural Pitfalls and Adversarial Gambits

Often reviewing courts do not reach the question whether error was harmless, or even whether it was committed. And often they do not reach the question whether a ruling should be affirmed because the matter is committed to the sound discretion of the trial judge and her decision was within reasonable parameters. Instead, courts often limit review or foreclose relief altogether because of the trial behavior of the appellant (acting through counsel). In hindsight, that behavior may fall somewhere on a continuum from gross blunder to understandable mistake, calculated risk, or carefully planned (but unsuccessful) strategy.

In general, three kinds of behavior generate such effects:

(1) Failing to object or offer proof. We have already considered the need to object and make offers of proof. When a case goes up on appeal, a serious consequence usually flows from failing to object or offer proof: Failing to object waives the right to claim error in admitting evidence, and failing to offer proof waives the right to claim error in excluding evidence. In both cases relief is denied in the absence of "plain error," and review is limited *because* appellant failed to "preserve the point" by objecting or making an offer. Plain error is seldom found in rulings admitting evidence, and almost unheard of in rulings excluding evidence (absent a record of the unoffered proof, a reviewing court can hardly tell that it would have affected the result).

More refined consequences flow from the manner of objecting or offering proof. Thus an objection on one ground suffices only to preserve that particular claim of error: If appellant unsuccessfully objected that testimony violates the hearsay doctrine, he can prevail on appeal only if the testimony did offend the hearsay doctrine (as well as outcome). He might want to argue on appeal that the testimony also offended the rule against proving conduct by character evidence, but failing to raise this ground in his objection waived his right to assert it on appeal. (He might still win on this ground, but only if the reviewing court thinks that failing to apply the character rule was plain error.)

Likewise, an unsuccessful offer of proof resting on a particular ground for admitting evidence only preserves for review arguments on that ground: If appellant invokes a hearsay exception in his offer, he can prevail only if the trial court erred in refusing to apply that exception (and the excluded evidence would likely have affected outcome). The fact that the evidence fits another exception doesn't help: Failing to advance this ground in his proffer waives his right to rely on it, and once again he can argue this new exception only if the failure to see and apply it was plain error.

And there is more:

In objecting and making offers of proof, appellant may limit or lose his right to review if part of the proof does not fit the objection or the offer. If *part* of a document is not excludable under the hearsay doctrine, an objection on that ground may be viewed as inadequate even though other parts of the document *should be excluded* for that reason. And if part of a document does *not* fit a hearsay exception, an offer of the whole document may be viewed as inadequate even though part *does* fit the exception. In short, rulings adverse to the party who later appeals may be sustained if that party was not precise enough in specifying the evidence subject to the objection or offer.

Finally, and here we see real determination of the system to sustain the trial court if possible, appellate courts often say that where the judge sustains an objection or accepts an offer of proof *on the wrong ground* (a ground later shown inapplicable or erroneous), her ruling will likely be sustained on appeal if *some other ground, though unmentioned below*, supports her action. Thus if the trial judge accepts an offer of proof that depends on a particular hearsay exception, she is likely to be sustained even though that exception does not apply, if the offering party can show that some other exception applies. In short, the system favors affirming judgments, imposing what amounts to a double standard operating in favor of the trial judge and against trial counsel.

(2) Inviting error. Trial behavior of a very different sort may affect review: Lawyers sometimes put questions that produce otherwise excludable answers. Assuming that the witness fairly replies to the question asked, the questioner is said to have "invited" any error that would otherwise arise in allowing the answer. And a party "invites" error by relying on (and in this sense endorsing) evidence offered by his opponent that he might otherwise have excluded by raising objection.

(3) Opening the door. Finally, trial behavior may "open the door" to evidence that would otherwise be excludable. In the typical instance, a party testifying on direct examination by his own counsel makes an ill-advised and overbroad assertion that he has a blemish-free past. Thus a criminal defendant sometimes testifies that he has "never been in trouble with the law before," and if this statement is false it "opens the door" to devastating evidence of prior arrests or convictions, which he might otherwise have kept out. And a party in a civil negligence suit sometimes testifies that he "has never had an accident before," which (if false) "opens the door" to damaging proof that indeed he has had other accidents. (See the material on impeaching witnesses in Chapter 8, infra.)

■ PROBLEM 1-B. He Didn't Object!

Carl Dreeves joins with Abby Barton as the second plaintiff in the suit against Eric Felsen (Problem 1-A). The defense offers testimony by police officer Hill, based on measurements of skid marks at the scene, that Barton's Fiat was traveling at a speed of about 50 mph just before entering the intersection. (The posted limit was 35 mph.) Counsel for Barton objects that "officer Hill is not qualified as an expert in accident reconstruction," and that "estimates of speed based on skid marks involve sheer speculation and are not helpful to the jury."

The court overrules the objection; the jury returns a verdict for Felsen; the court enters judgment that Barton and Dreeves take nothing, and that their claims be dismissed with prejudice. Dreeves appeals, and Felsen argues that his appeal should be dismissed because of his failure to object below. Should he prevail on this argument? Why or why not?

OBTAINING REVIEW OF EVIDENCE POINTS

1. Appeal from Judgment

Most evidence rulings are prime examples of the nonappealable interlocutory order. When such rulings are made during trial, immediate review would be impractical: The resultant interruption of trial would be an imposition on trial courts, not to mention juries and witnesses. Piecemeal review could become another weapon of delay for a party fearful of an adverse judgment. The very nature of the review would change radically if appellate courts had to evaluate evidential error without the record of a completed trial.

Hence rulings admitting or excluding evidence, rulings on examination of witnesses (whether dealing with the form or the substance of the questions), and rulings on such evidential devices as presumptions and burden of persuasion are almost always reviewed only after judgment. Generally (though not always) rulings on claims of privilege are likewise reviewed only after judgment.

2. Interlocutory Appeal

There are two important exceptions to the pattern sketched above—two instances where interlocutory appeal is commonly permitted. One arises when a person claims a privilege and refuses to answer despite an order of the trial court directing him to do so, and the other involves pretrial orders suppressing evidence in criminal cases.

Privilege rulings. Here the cases take different directions. Under one approach, the threshold question is whether the person from whom information was sought has been held in contempt. If not, no review may be had. If so, some authority would permit the reviewing court to consider the merits of the privilege ruling only if the person was held in criminal contempt, and otherwise would limit review to the matter of the authority of the trial judge to impose the contempt sanction.

Under another approach, the threshold question is whether the nondisclosing person is a party to the action. If so, he may obtain review of the privilege ruling only by suffering an adverse judgment, then raising the privilege issue on appeal from the judgment. If he is not a party, he may obtain review of the privilege issue without suffering a judgment of contempt, simply because the final judgment will not afford him a chance for review. Reinforcing the notion that parties cannot obtain immediate review of privilege rulings, the Supreme Court held in 2009 that the "collateral order" doctrine is unavailable in such situations. See Mohawk Industries, Inc. v. Carpenter, 558 U.S. 100 (2009).

Not surprisingly, many modern cases present the issue of review in the context of orders of production directed to criminal defense lawyers. As you will see, a lawyer may (indeed must) invoke the attorney-client privilege on her client's behalf, and of course *the lawyer* is not herself a party to her client's case. In this circumstance, some modern federal authority applies the doctrine of Perlman v. United States, 247 U.S. 7 (1918) (party permitted to appeal, on ground of Fourth Amendment violation, from disclosure order directed to court clerk), and permits the attorney to appeal immediately from a disclosure order overruling her claim of privilege, advanced on her client's behalf. See, e.g., In re Grand Jury Proceedings (Fine), 641 F.2d 199, 201-203 (5th Cir. 1981).

Suppression motions. In criminal cases in federal court, the applicable statute paves the way for government appeals from an order "suppressing or excluding evidence" if the U.S. Attorney certifies that the appeal has not been taken "for purpose of delay" and that the evidence is a substantial proof of a material fact (18 USC §3731). Many states have similar statutes. Most such pretrial suppression motions raise issues under the Constitution rather than the Rules, but a ruling on any defense motion to exclude evidence may generate an appeal by the prosecutor under such statutes. See, e.g., United States v. Siegel, 536 F.3d 306 (4th Cir. 2008) (government appeal from ruling in limine excluding prior crimes), *cert. denied*, 129 S. Ct. 770.

CHAPTER 2

Relevance

INTRODUCTION

"Relevance" is an everyday word describing factors that bear on the decisions we make and problems we set out to solve, and the term carries similar meaning in law. As rational beings, we know as a matter of common sense what we ought to consider in making decisions and solving problems. A picnic in the park? We think about whether we have time, whether the sun is out, what the temperature is, whether the roads are congested or the park crowded, and so forth.

Long ago, Thayer said that the very existence of a judicial system, created to resolve disputes affecting private rights of citizens and administration of regulatory and criminal laws, implies the principle that "relevant" evidence should generally be considered, and not irrelevant evidence. J. Thayer, Preliminary Treatise 264-265 (1898). This principle finds expression in FRE 402, which says that relevant evidence is generally admissible and irrelevant evidence is not.

A relational concept. By nature, relevance is relational—it carries meaning only in context. If we learn that *E* is employed as a driver by the Corporation and that this fact is "relevant," we would ask, "relevant to what?" In a suit against the Corporation for injuries caused by a truck owned by it and driven by *E,* his employment is some indication that he was acting pursuant to his duties, hence that the Corporation may be responsible under the doctrine of respondeat superior if *E* was negligent. But in a suit by *E* against *F* to collect money that *E* had leant *F* under a promissory note, *E*'s employment would not likely be relevant to any issue at hand.

The context in which relevance questions arise is defined partly by substantive law (like the doctrine of respondeat superior) and partly by the issues that the parties raise. In criminal cases the issues are raised by the information or indictment and the defendant's plea. In civil cases the pleadings raise the issues generally, though they are refined through discovery and motions and narrowed by pretrial conference and order.

No modern thinker considers it profitable to codify relevance in detail. Disputes leading to litigation are too varied, as are problems of proof. Not that the possibility of detailed rules has been ignored: John Henry Wigmore, who did much for the law of evidence, tried early in life to draft such rules, and anyone who believes the task worthwhile should begin with a look at the compendious banalities that found their way into his *Code of Evidence* (1909). Thayer hit on a more durable truth when he said "the law furnishes no test of relevancy," but relies instead on "logic and general experience." J. Thayer, Preliminary Treatise 265 (1898).

Following Thayer, FRE 401 furnishes nothing detailed enough to be called a "test," and instead sets out a general standard: Evidence is relevant if it has "any tendency" to make the existence of any consequential fact "more or less probable."

Direct and circumstantial. If the question is whether *E* is employed by the Corporation, nobody doubts the relevance of his own testimony to that effect, or testimony by *W* that she saw *E* loading boxes on a truck with the Corporation logo painted on the side. Both are relevant on the question of *E*'s employment, but here a distinction is commonly drawn: The former is usually called "direct" and the latter "circumstantial" evidence.

"Direct" describes evidence that, if accepted as genuine or believed true, necessarily establishes the point for which it is offered (if *E* is believed, the trier must conclude that he was employed by the Corporation). "Circumstantial" means evidence that, even if credited, may still fail to support (let alone establish) the point in question, simply because an alternative explanation seems as probable or more so (perhaps *E was* loading the truck, but other facts suggest he was helping a friend employed by the Corporation).

The Rules draw no distinction between direct and circumstantial evidence, and the latter is not necessarily inferior: Alternate explanations may be much less likely than the one advanced by the proponent, and direct proof may be unavailable, either because there are no witnesses or because the issue is such that direct proof cannot be had (usually "mens rea," the mental element of a crime, is proved circumstantially). Courts recognize these realities. See Michalic v. Cleveland Tankers, 364 U.S. 325, 330 (1960) (circumstantial evidence may be "more certain, satisfying and persuasive than direct evidence"). Even criminal convictions may rest on such proof, see State v. Sivo, 925 A.2d 901, 910 (R.I. 2007) (state may rely on circumstantial evidence alone, and "need not disprove all possible theories of innocence" so long as totality of proof shows guilt beyond reasonable doubt).

Still, circumstantial evidence poses special problems. In popular imagination, the term connotes weakness, and closing arguments often exploit that idea. And circumstantial evidence poses the only real challenge in administering the requirement of logical relevancy and assessing the sufficiency of proof to take a case to the jury. Moreover, circumstantial evidence raises questions of coordinating the responsibilities of judge and jury.

Rationality. There are differences between the common understanding of relevance and its meaning in the law of evidence. For one thing, experience seems time and again to affirm that even thoughtful decisions in life rest only in part on reason and logic, that decisionmaking is as much psychological as analytical, and that intuition and emotion play large roles. But evidence law, especially its notion of relevance, emphasizes reason and logic. Intuition and emotion in the trier of fact are matters to be controlled and minimized, and numerous exclusionary rules serve that end, along with a tradition of discretionary power in the trial judge to exclude evidence so as to obviate or minimize extrarational forces.

Another difference is that everyday decisions generally look forward rather than backward, while courts have the task of determining matters of historical fact—what happened, why, and how. So our legal concept of relevance describes clues that help the trier of fact understand the past, rather than decide on a future course of action. But the difference is not great, simply because the historical facts are contested by the parties and unknown to the trier.

The law of evidence serves a pragmatic profession, so it ignores the philosophical problem, which is illuminated in literature and experienced in science, whether anyone can ever really know what happened. Carl Sandburg put it this way:

> Do you solemnly swear before the everliving God that the testimony you are about to give in this cause shall be the truth, the whole truth, and nothing but the truth?
>
> No, I don't. I can tell you what I saw and what I heard and I'll swear to that by the everliving God but the more I study about it the more sure I am that nobody but the everliving God knows the whole truth and if you summoned Christ as a witness in this case what He would tell you would burn your insides with the pity and the mystery of it.

C. Sandburg, The People, Yes 193 (1936). Evidence law sets aside these doubts: It affirms implicitly that we *can* know enough, and that relevant evidence offered in court can help the trier of fact arrive at a close enough understanding to warrant entering a judgment that materially alters the positions and fortunes of the parties.

A LOGICAL RELEVANCE

1. Relevance and Materiality

Relevance readily divides into two subparts, and common law tradition distinguished them by separate terms. Evidence was "relevant" if it tended to establish the point for which it was offered, and "material" if the point bore on issues in the case.

Assume that *X* says publicly that *J* is suffering from an ailment, and tells *J* privately that he will tell *J*'s employer about it unless *J* pays *X* for his silence. If *J* brought a libel suit, and *X* raised truth as a defense, proof that *J* was being treated at a cancer clinic would be relevant in suggesting that *J* was ill. It would also be material because *J*'s illness supports *X*'s defense of truth. If *X* were prosecuted for extortion, proof that *J* was being treated at the clinic would still be relevant in tending to prove that he was ailing. It would not, however, be material, because the truth or falsity of *X*'s statements does not count in an extortion trial. Extortion means obtaining by threat something of value, and the fact that *X* was right about *J*'s situation would not matter.

All agree that evidence should be admitted only if it is both relevant and material. Since both conditions must be satisfied, insisting on two terms was a fetish, and the modern approach embraces both ideas within the single term "relevance." Under FRE 401, evidence is relevant if it tends to make more or less probable the existence of any consequential fact.

OLD CHIEF v. UNITED STATES (I)

Supreme Court of the United States
519 U.S. 172 (1997)

Justice SOUTER delivered the opinion of the Court.

[Defendant Johnny Lynn Old Chief was charged with being a convicted felon in possession of a firearm. As is usual when this charge is brought, defendant allegedly committed other crimes that are more visible and likely to attract the attention of law enforcement: Old Chief was also charged with assault with a deadly weapon and using a firearm in a crime of violence. His prior felony conviction was for assault causing serious bodily injury, so the defense offered to stipulate to the conviction in hope of keeping its title and the details from the jury. In this opinion, the Supreme Court ultimately decides that the trial court should have excluded proof of the name and details of the prior conviction as too prejudicial. (See *Old Chief (II)* in section B of this chapter, infra.) Before dealing with the prejudice issue, the Court addresses the basic question whether the name of the crimes of which Old Chief had been convicted was relevant.]

In 1993, petitioner, Old Chief, was arrested after a fracas involving at least one gunshot. The ensuing federal charges included not only assault with a dangerous weapon and using a firearm in relation to a crime of violence but violation of 18 USC §922(g)(1). This statute makes it unlawful for anyone "who has been convicted in any court, of a crime punishable by imprisonment for a term exceeding one year" to "possess in or affecting commerce, any firearm . . . ." "[A] crime punishable by imprisonment for a term exceeding one year" is defined to exclude "any Federal or State offenses pertaining to antitrust violations, unfair trade practices, restraints of trade, or other similar offenses relating to the regulation of business practices" and "any State offense classified by the laws of the State as a misdemeanor and punishable by a term of imprisonment of two years or less." 18 USC §921(a)(20).

The earlier crime charged in the indictment against Old Chief was assault causing serious bodily injury. Before trial, he moved for an order requiring the government "to refrain from mentioning—by reading the Indictment, during jury selection, in opening statement, or closing argument—and to refrain from offering into evidence or soliciting any testimony from any witness regarding the prior criminal convictions of the Defendant, except to state that the Defendant has been convicted of a crime punishable by imprisonment exceeding one (1) year." He said that revealing the name and nature of his prior assault conviction would unfairly tax the jury's capacity to hold the Government to its burden of proof beyond a reasonable doubt on current charges of assault, possession, and violence with a firearm, and he offered to "solve the problem here by stipulating, agreeing and requesting the Court to instruct the jury that he has been convicted of a crime punishable by imprisonment exceeding one (1) year." He argued that the offer to stipulate to the fact of the prior conviction rendered evidence of the name and nature of the offense inadmissible under FRE 403, the danger being that unfair prejudice from that evidence would substantially outweigh its probative value. He also proposed this jury instruction:

> The phrase "crime punishable by imprisonment for a term exceeding one year" generally means a crime which is a felony. The phrase does not include any state offense classified by the laws of that state as a misdemeanor and punishable by a term of imprisonment of two years or less and certain crimes concerning the regulation of business practices. I hereby instruct you that Defendant Johnny Lynn Old Chief has been convicted of a crime punishable by imprisonment for a term exceeding one year.

As a threshold matter, there is Old Chief's erroneous argument that the name of his prior offense as contained in the record of conviction is irrelevant to the prior-conviction element, and for that reason inadmissible under FRE 402. FRE 401 defines relevant evidence as having "any tendency to make the existence of any fact that is of consequence to the determination of the action more probable or less probable than it would be without the evidence." To be sure, the fact that Old Chief's prior conviction was for assault resulting in serious bodily injury rather than, say, for theft was not itself an ultimate fact, as if the statute had specifically required proof of injurious assault. But its demonstration was a step on one evidentiary route to the ultimate fact, since it served to place Old Chief within a particular sub-class of offenders for whom firearms possession is outlawed by §922(g)(1). A documentary record of the conviction for that named offense was thus relevant evidence in making Old Chief's §922(g)(1) status more probable than it would have been without the evidence.

Nor was its evidentiary relevance under FRE 401 affected by the availability of alternative proofs of the element to which it went, such as an admission by

Old Chief that he had been convicted of a crime "punishable by imprisonment for a term exceeding one year" within the meaning of the statute. [Court quotes ACN to FRE 401, which states: "The fact to which the evidence is directed need not be in dispute. While situations will arise which call for the exclusion of evidence offered to prove a point conceded by the opponent, the ruling should be made on the basis of such considerations as waste of time and undue prejudice (see FRE 403), rather than under any general requirement that evidence is admissible only if directed to matters in dispute."]

[If relevant evidence must sometimes be excluded because of its connection to other evidence, its exclusion must not rest on the ground] that the other evidence has rendered it "irrelevant," but on its character as unfairly prejudicial, cumulative or the like, its relevance notwithstanding.[4] . . .

[T]he Government invokes the familiar, standard rule that the prosecution is entitled to prove its case by evidence of its own choice, or, more exactly, that a criminal defendant may not stipulate or admit his way out of the full evidentiary force of the case as the government chooses to present it. The authority usually cited for this rule is Parr v. United States, 255 F.2d 86 (CA5), cert. denied, 358 U.S. 824 (1958), in which the Fifth Circuit explained that the "reason for the rule is to permit a party 'to present to the jury a picture of the events relied upon. To substitute for such a picture a naked admission might have the effect to rob the evidence of much of its fair and legitimate weight.'"

This is unquestionably true as a general matter. The "fair and legitimate weight" of conventional evidence showing individual thoughts and acts amounting to a crime reflects the fact that making a case with testimony and tangible things not only satisfies the formal definition of an offense, but tells a colorful story with descriptive richness. Unlike an abstract premise, whose force depends on going precisely to a particular step in a course of reasoning, a piece of evidence may address any number of separate elements, striking hard just because it shows so much at once; the account of a shooting that establishes capacity and causation may tell just as much about the triggerman's motive and intent. Evidence thus has force beyond any linear scheme of reasoning, and as its pieces come together a narrative gains momentum, with power not only to support conclusions but to sustain the willingness of jurors to draw the inferences, whatever they may be, necessary to reach an honest verdict. This persuasive power of the concrete and particular is often essential to the capacity of jurors to satisfy the obligations that the law places on them. Jury duty is usually unsought and sometimes resisted, and it may be as difficult for one juror suddenly to face the findings that can send another human being to prison,

[4]Viewing evidence of the name of the prior offense as relevant, there is no reason to dwell on the Government's argument that relevance is to be determined with respect to the entire item offered in evidence (here, the entire record of conviction) and not with reference to distinguishable sub-units of that object (here, the name of the offense and the sentence received). We see no impediment in general to a district court's determination, after objection, that some sections of a document are relevant within the meaning of FRE 401, and others irrelevant and inadmissible under FRE 402.

as it is for another to hold out conscientiously for acquittal. When a juror's duty does seem hard, the evidentiary account of what a defendant has thought and done can accomplish what no set of abstract statements ever could, not just to prove a fact but to establish its human significance, and so to implicate the law's moral underpinnings and a juror's obligation to sit in judgment. Thus, the prosecution may fairly seek to place its evidence before the jurors, as much to tell a story of guiltiness as to support an inference of guilt, to convince the jurors that a guilty verdict would be morally reasonable as much as to point to the discrete elements of a defendant's legal fault.

But there is something even more to the prosecution's interest in resisting efforts to replace the evidence of its choice with admissions and stipulations, for beyond the power of conventional evidence to support allegations and give life to the moral underpinnings of law's claims, there lies the need for evidence in all its particularity to satisfy the jurors' expectations about what proper proof should be. Some such demands they bring with them to the courthouse, assuming, for example, that a charge of using a firearm to commit an offense will be proven by introducing a gun in evidence. A prosecutor who fails to produce one, or some good reason for his failure, has something to be concerned about. "If [jurors'] expectations are not satisfied, triers of fact may penalize the party who disappoints them by drawing a negative inference against that party." Saltzburg, A Special Aspect of Relevance: Countering Negative Inferences Associated with the Absence of Evidence, 66 Calif. L. Rev. 1011, 1019 (1978) (footnotes omitted).[9] Expectations may also arise in jurors' minds simply from the experience of a trial itself. The use of witnesses to describe a train of events naturally related can raise the prospect of learning about every ingredient of that natural sequence the same way. If suddenly the prosecution presents some occurrence in the series differently, as by announcing a stipulation or admission, the effect may be like saying, "never mind what's behind the door," and jurors may well wonder what they are being kept from knowing. A party seemingly responsible for cloaking something has reason for apprehension, and the prosecution with its burden of proof may prudently demur at a defense request to interrupt the flow of evidence telling the story in the usual way.

In sum, the accepted rule that the prosecution is entitled to prove its case free from any defendant's option to stipulate the evidence away rests on good

[9]Cf. Green, "The Whole Truth?": How Rules of Evidence Make Lawyers Deceitful, 25 Loyola (LA) L. Rev. 699, 703 (1992) ("[E]videntiary rules . . . predicated in large measure on the law's distrust of juries [can] have the unintended, and perhaps ironic, result of encouraging the jury's distrust of lawyers. The rules do so by fostering the perception that lawyers are deliberately withholding evidence" (footnote omitted)). The fact that juries have expectations as to what evidence ought to be presented by a party, and may well hold the absence of that evidence against the party, is also recognized in the case law of the Fifth Amendment, which explicitly supposes that, despite the venerable history of the privilege against self-incrimination, jurors may not recall that someone accused of crime need not explain the evidence or avow innocence beyond making his plea. The assumption that jurors may have contrary expectations and be moved to draw adverse inferences against the party who disappoints them undergirds the rule that a defendant can demand an instruction forbidding the jury from drawing such an inference.

sense. A syllogism is not a story, and a naked proposition in a courtroom may be no match for the robust evidence that would be used to prove it. People who hear a story interrupted by gaps of abstraction may be puzzled at the missing chapters, and jurors asked to rest a momentous decision on the story's truth can feel put upon at being asked to take responsibility knowing that more could be said than they have heard. A convincing tale can be told with economy, but when economy becomes a break in the natural sequence of narrative evidence, an assurance that the missing link is really there is never more than second best.

[Court concludes, however, that the prosecutor's need for "evidentiary depth" has virtually no application "when the point at issue is a defendant's legal status, dependent on some judgment rendered wholly independently of the concrete events of later criminal behavior."]

[A dissenting opinion of Justice O'Connor, joined by Chief Justice Rehnquist and Justices Scalia and Thomas, is omitted.]

■ NOTES ON RELEVANCE, "FIT," AND OFFERS TO STIPULATE

1. *Old Chief* is right that proof of a *felony assault conviction* is relevant when the point to be proved is a *felony conviction.* The statute speaks of a conviction for "a crime punishable by imprisonment exceeding one (1) year," which means felony. It doesn't matter *what kind of felony* (except that some felonies don't count, including those for "antitrust violations, unfair trade practices, restraints of trade," and "similar offenses relating to the regulation of business practices"). Still, every conviction that *does count* will be for a particular crime, like assault. A category of what is relevant cannot require a one-to-one "fit" between the proof and the element in the case to which the proof relates.

2. Litigants regularly prove points of detail that aren't, strictly speaking, necessary. In a murder trial, for example, the prosecutor shows the circumstances (the victim was killed at home, for instance, or died of multiple stab wounds, or pled for his life, or was shot in the abdomen, and so forth). And in the negligence suit described in Problem 1-A (*How Did It Happen?*), proof that Abby Barton drove a yellow Fiat and that Eric Felsen drove a blue Buick would be relevant even if it were *not* needed as a means to connect those people to the accident. Partly the reason such proof should count as relevant is that we want witnesses to communicate in ways that are comfortable to them and to juries, and ordinary language does not easily mesh with (or reduce to) the various categories that are important in lawsuits. Partly the reason is that even "background" evidence has some relevance under FRE 401, as the ACN recognizes (evidence that is "essentially background in nature" can come in "as an aid to understanding"). See also United

States v. Daily, 842 F.2d 1380, 1388 (2d Cir. 1988) (can show "circumstances surrounding the events"). In this vein, courts let witnesses testify to their name and address, and often occupation or business, although questioning about things like hobbies may be disallowed as getting too far afield. See, e.g., United States v. Solomon, 686 F.2d 863, 873-874 (11th Cir. 1982) (barring inquiry into family history and military service). And see generally Mueller & Kirkpatrick, Evidence §§4.2 and 6.58 (5th ed. 2012).

3. *Old Chief* also makes a good choice in holding that an offer to stipulate does not make relevant evidence irrelevant. The Court rests its conclusion partly on the ACN to FRE 401. Compare Cal. Evidence Code §210 (defining relevance as "having any tendency in reason to prove or disprove *any disputed fact* that is of consequence to the determination of the action") (emphasis added). In *Old Chief*, the Court also relies on policy, stressing party autonomy in presenting evidence, jury expectations, and "descriptive richness." When you revisit this decision in *Old Chief (II)*, you will see that an offer to stipulate bears on whether evidence should be excluded under FRE 403 because of the risk of "unfair prejudice."

4. The majority in *Old Chief* also says particularized evidence is important "to sustain the willingness of jurors to draw the inferences" required for a verdict, and to convince them that a guilty verdict "would be morally reasonable." Arguably this point suggests that the *defense* should be allowed to offer particularized proof that isn't strictly relevant to the matter of guilt or innocence, but that might bear on what is "morally reasonable." See generally James Joseph Duane, "Screw Your Courage to the Sticking Place": The Roles of Evidence, Stipulations, and Jury Instructions in Criminal Verdicts, 49 Hastings L.J. 463, 469 (1998) (asking whether *Old Chief* majority would "embrace the logical implications of this position" by letting defendant "call his wife and children to testify" to the ways "their lives would be devastated" by extended incarceration, or by letting defendant show a "graphic but accurate film of living conditions" in the local prison).

5. In Shannon v. United States, 512 U.S. 573 (1994), the Court held that a defendant, who had been charged with a violent crime and offered an insanity defense, was *not* entitled to an instruction that he would be committed involuntarily if the jury accepted the defense, to keep the jury from mistakenly believing that a finding of insanity would allow him to go free. The majority in *Shannon* said the jury's function is to find the facts and decide guilt or innocence, hence that information on "the consequences of a verdict" is irrelevant. This decision has been broadly applied to deny defense requests that the jury be told about mandatory minimum sentences that follow a verdict of guilty. One commentator has argued that *Shannon* and *Old Chief* together construct a pro-prosecution bias inviting prosecutors to prove the consequences of criminal acts without letting defendants offer analogous proof about the consequences of conviction. See James Joseph Duane, supra note 4, at 474 (*Shannon* and *Old Chief* create an inconsistency that "borders on madness," since the former says juries cannot consider evidence on the moral reasonableness of a guilty verdict but the latter says juries can consider such evidence).

2. Relevance as Threshold: Standard of Probative Worth (Weight and Sufficiency Contrasted)

Rule 401 provides no particularized test of relevancy, but sets a general standard requiring a "tendency" to prove or disprove a consequential fact. So it is tempting to ask: How strong must the tendency be?

Over the years four answers have been suggested:

(1) More probably true. One might say that evidence has the required tendency only if it makes the point more probably true than not. But the relevancy standard must be applied again and again during trial because evidence is offered piece by piece. Hence defining the tendency this way seems too strict: It would exclude many items of proof that, taken together, might have high probative value.

(2) More probable than any other. One might say that evidence is relevant only if the suggested inference is more probable than any other. Some courts take this view. See Standafer v. First National Bank, 52 N.W.2d 718 (Minn. 1952) (where decedent fell down elevator shaft, error to admit evidence that heel was knocked from his shoe, offered as proof that he tripped on L-beam while working on top of elevator car; it was equally probable that heel was knocked off in fall) (harmless). But setting the standard at this level would produce a sliding scale, where evidence would be scrutinized more strictly at the beginning of trial, when little or nothing is known, than at the end, when probative worth would be more apparent in light of evidence already presented. See Trautman, Logical or Legal Relevancy—A Conflict in Theory, 5 Vand. L. Rev. 385, 390 (1952).

(3) More than minimally probative. A third approach rejects the first two, but insists that the necessary tendency requires more than minimal probative worth, hence that there is a standard of "legal relevancy" that is more strict than logic and reason alone would indicate. Wigmore took this view, saying that legal relevance demands an incremental "plus value." Sometimes courts agree. See Frank R. Jelleff, Inc. v. Braden, 233 F.2d 671, 679 (D.C. Cir. 1956). Wigmore thought the accumulation of legal precedent would lead to rules that resolve relevance problems, and that *ad hoc* resort to logic and experience is inappropriate. See 1 J. Wigmore, Evidence §28 (1943).

(4) More probable than it was before. The fourth answer holds that evidence is relevant if it makes the point to be proved more probable than it was without the evidence. Here is the most lenient standard—the one most favoring admissibility. It is the one found in FRE 401. The idea is captured in some downhome aphorisms: "A brick is not a wall," McCormick on Evidence §185 (K. Broun ed., 7th ed. 2014); "Not every witness can make a home run" (ACN to FRE 401, paraphrasing McBaine). Consider the explanation set out by Professor James, writing about evidence of intent as proof of subsequent action:

> Persons who are unwilling to agree that men's fixed designs (at least in the case of murder) are "probably" carried out—or, even conceding the fact of murder,

> that proof of *A*'s fixed design to kill *B* establishes *A*, more likely than not, as *B*'s killer—still agree that somehow this bit of evidence does have some tendency to indicate *A*'s guilt. What form of general statement can reconcile these views? Perhaps something like this: "Men having such a fixed design are more likely to kill than are men not having such a fixed design." Those who contend that even fixed designs to kill are more often abandoned or thwarted than carried out can and doubtless will still concede that enough such designs are carried to execution so that the percentage of murderers is higher among persons entertaining such a fixed design than among the general public. Obviously this proposed generalization does not lead us from *A*'s fixed design to kill *B* to the conclusion that *A* probably did kill *B*. There is nothing disturbing in this. This conclusion simply does not follow from the evidence of design. The error was in the original "direct induction." In fact, no useful conclusion about *A*'s guilt can be drawn from design or intent alone. On the basis of an acceptable generalization we are able only to place *A* in a class of persons in which the incidence of murder is greater than among the general public. We cannot now say that *A* is probably guilty, but we can say that *the apparent probability of his guilt is now greater than before the evidence of design was received.* This is logical relevancy—the only logical relevancy we can expect in dealing with practical affairs where strict demonstration is never possible. The advantage of [forcing the general premise into prominence] is that we know to what degree of proof we have attained, and do not overstate our results.

James, Relevancy, Probability and the Law, 29 Cal. L. Rev. 689, 698-699 (1941).

In effect this fourth answer holds that the question we began with has no real answer. Thayer was right: There is no test in the sense of particularized principles—only a broad standard. Trying to refine the necessary "tendency" to prove a point is like trying to bring in a test by the back door, and it won't work.

Weight and sufficiency contrasted. Put most simply, relevancy does not mean "weight" and it does not mean "sufficiency." Weight means the aggregate probative worth that the factfinder assigns to the proof in the case. Does plaintiff's proof make it more probable than not that everything plaintiff must prove is true? Does the prosecutor's evidence make it clear beyond a reasonable doubt that defendant committed the charged offense? In jury-tried cases, the question of weight is for the jury alone to decide (only in bench trials is it for the judge).

At the end, there must be *sufficient* evidence to satisfy the standard of proof that applies. What we mean is that a civil case is subject to judgment as a matter of law if the evidence as a whole, viewed by a reasonable person, can lead to only one outcome. In civil cases tried to juries, plaintiff and defendant alike can force the issue by making the appropriate motion at the end of trial under FRCP 50. A party who makes and loses such a motion can take an appeal and ask the reviewing court to award judgment as a matter of law. (In bench trials, lawyers for both sides usually argue that there is only "one way" to view the evidence, but the judge simply decides. If the party who loses thinks that no reasonable judge could decide as this one did, an appeal can test this point.) In criminal cases tried to juries, prosecutors cannot seek judgment as a matter of law on the merits of any charge, although they can sometimes strike defenses when the defendant offers nothing in support of them. Defendants, however, can seek dismissal on ground that the evidence is insufficient.

3. Establishing Relevance: The Evidential Hypothesis

Often the relevance of circumstantial evidence is obvious. Everyone can see how it bears on the case, what point it tends to prove, and why the point counts. If the question is whether defendant is the one who robbed the bank, evidence that he said he was going to do it takes no explaining.

But relevance may not be so apparent, and explanation may be needed—for the judge as well as the jury. And if the adverse party raises a relevance objection, the judge may ask the proponent to justify the proffer, even if relevance seems apparent.

Evidential hypothesis. The proponent should be prepared to put forth an "evidential hypothesis" explaining why his proof is relevant. The adverse party should be ready to refute the hypothesis, if possible, or show its limitations or offer a counterhypothesis that explains away the evidence or enlists it in aid of his own cause. (The parties will not likely agree on interpreting the evidence. Usually their differences are aired in closing argument and resolved by the trier of fact. Such differences are said to affect the "weight" of the evidence and "credibility" of witnesses, rather than "admissibility.") An evidential hypothesis contains one or more of what logicians call a "general premise"—a general proposition about the ways of the world or human nature. It also contains at least one specific premise linking the proof to the general premise. Finally, it sets out the conclusion toward which the evidence points.

The evidential hypothesis sets out the steps of reasoning and inference that logicians describe as argument by "deduction" or "induction." Both forms involve appraising known or accepted data in order to reach a new understanding of matters not directly observed. Logicians define deductive argument as one in which the stated premises *necessarily* lead to a particular conclusion. In the classic example, the major (or general) premise holds that "all humans are mortal," and the minor (or particular) premise asserts that "Socrates is human." Hence necessarily the conclusion, "Socrates is mortal." The "inductive" argument is less categorical. Logicians define it as one in which the conclusion *does not* necessarily follow from the premises, though they support the conclusion. Proving that defendant robbed a bank by evidence that he stated an intent to do so involves inductive argument: The major premises are that "People who intend to do something likely do it" and "People who state an intent likely have it." The minor premise is "Defendant stated his intent to rob the bank," and the conclusion is that "He likely did rob the bank."

Deduction. Deductive and categorical logic sometimes appears in litigation. Again consider a bank robbery trial: This time the prosecutor offers a surveillance video. This video may be well-nigh conclusive proof that a crime was committed and that the person depicted is the perpetrator, but other evidence may only circumstantially link defendant to the crime, and there may be a question whether he is the person in the video. The prosecutor might call an expert who examined the video and get his testimony that defendant is the person shown. The prosecutor might not state his argument as a deductive syllogism, but it would fit the model: The man in the video is the perpetrator; defendant is the man in the video; hence he is the perpetrator.

Induction. Not only in litigation, but in science and everyday thinking, inductive argument is more common. In a sense it is the more potent and inventive of the two forms, for it reaches further than deduction in seeking to increase understanding. One scholar put it this way:

> Valid deductive arguments are demonstrative; that is, if the premises are true, the conclusion must necessarily be true also. Because of this, the conclusion cannot embody conjectures about the empirical world that go beyond what the premises say; in this sense the conclusion of a valid deductive argument must be "contained in" its premises. However, an inductive argument . . . has a conclusion embodying empirical conjectures about the world that do go beyond what its premises say; in an inductive argument the conclusion is not wholly "contained in" the premises.

S. Barker, The Elements of Logic 223 (3d ed. 1980).

Consider again evidence that defendant said he intended to rob the bank. One major premise was, "People who intend to do something likely do it." Wigmore pointed out that this premise itself—and remember that it serves as a foundation of an inductive argument—rests on induction: How do we know people act as they intend? The answer is, by observing particular instances in which they do—in other words, by drawing an inductive inference (a generalization) to the major premise, which serves then as the basis for an inductive inference to the particular point in issue (*this* person acted on *his* intent). So Wigmore noticed that in every inductive argument it is possible to "forc[e] into prominence the implied law or generalization on which it rests more or less obscurely." But he then reached a questionable conclusion: It is "undesirable" and "useless" to do so, since forcing the premise into prominence requires the court "to take it up for examination," which can be undertaken only by resort to the very inductive inference for which the proponent argued in the first place. See 1 J. Wigmore, Evidence §12 (1943).

If you think something is fishy, you are not alone. Wigmore was confronting the riddle that plagues logicians, which is that inductive argument seems circular. In a seminal article, Professor James took Wigmore on:

> Wigmore does not deny that in every instance proof must be based upon a generalization connecting the evidentiary proposition with the proposition to be proved. Conceding this, he argues that the generalization may as well be tacitly understood as expressed, . . . "because the Court's attention is merely

> transferred from the syllogism as a whole to the validity of the inference contained in the major premise." Yet it is precisely in this transfer of attention that the value . . . lies. [Wigmore's] own examples illustrate the point. In the case of the repaired machinery we are told: "'People who make such repairs [after an accident] show a consciousness of negligence; *A* made such repairs; therefore, *A* was conscious of negligence.'" Before this . . . proof can be evaluated, ambiguity must be eliminated from the major premise. By "people" shall we understand "some people" or "all people"? If the argument is intended to read, "Some people who make such repairs show consciousness of negligence; *A* made such repairs; therefore *A* was conscious of negligence," it contains an obvious logical fallacy. If intended to read, "All people who make such repairs show consciousness of negligence; *A* made such repairs; therefore, *A* was conscious of negligence," it is logically valid. However, few could be found to accept the premise that *all* persons who repair machinery after an accident show consciousness of guilt; that is, that no single case could be found of one who, confident of his care in the past, nevertheless made repairs to guard against repetition of an unforeseeable casualty or to preserve future fools against the consequence of their future folly. Here the result of [forcing the premise into prominence] is discovery that it is invalid—at least in the terms suggested.

James, Relevancy, Probability and the Law, 29 Cal. L. Rev. 689, 696-697 (1941).

Consider evidence that defendant said he intended to rob a bank. The government advances the evidential hypothesis: People who intend to do something likely do it, and people who state their intent likely have it. Combine the evidence with the premises, and the conclusion follows—not that defendant must have robbed the bank, but that he likely did so. How likely is hard to say. James again:

> Once one attempts to deal, in a quasi-syllogistic form, not with certainties but with probabilities, additional opportunities for fallacy are presented. Suppose that it is argued: "Most *A*s are *X*, *B* is an *A*, therefore *B* is probably *X*; or nine-tenths of all *A*s are *X*, *B* is an *A*, therefore the chances are nine to one that *B* is an *X*." Neither of these arguments is logically valid except upon the assumption that *A*s may be treated as a uniform class with respect to the probability of their being *X*. This can be because there really is no way of subdividing the class, finding more *X*s in one subclass than in another, or because no subdivision can be made in terms of available data. Suppose that nine-tenths of all people in the world have dark eyes. If absolutely all one knew about *B* was that he was a person, it would be an apparent nine-to-one chance that *B* had dark eyes. But if one knew *B* to be a Swede, the percentage of dark eyes in the total population of the world would no longer be important. One would want to know about the proportion of dark-eyed Swedes, which might differ from the ratio among humans generally.

James, id. at 697.

How about the prosecutor's two premises? Do all persons having a particular intent carry it out? (Of course not, common experience cries out. Hence the conclusion is less than certain, and the argument is inductive rather than deductive.) Do most—say, seven out of ten? (Nobody knows, and we cannot be sure that the conclusion is more probable than not.) Do some—say, two out of ten? (Surely yes—often we act in accordance with earlier-formed intent—and the evidence provides some support for the conclusion.) Does it matter *what* is intended? (Just as the percentage of Swedes with dark eyes may differ—one supposes it is smaller—from the percentage of people in general with dark eyes, so the percentage of people intending to take a walk who actually do so may differ—one supposes it is higher—from the percentage of people intending to commit serious crimes who actually do so.) Does the age or circumstance of the person matter? (Surely it does: One who despairs of lawful profits and sustains himself in criminal endeavors may be more likely to carry out an intent to commit a now-familiar sort of act than, say, a hitherto law-abiding college student, who may want or need money too, but for whom the world holds promise of moderate profit from lawful pursuits.)

And what of the second premise—that persons who announce an intent likely have such intent? (Again, surely less than all who make such announcement actually harbor such intent, but at least some do. Again the nature of the announced intent may matter, and again the situation of the person in question probably matters.)

Now that you have thought about induction and evidential hypotheses, look at some real situations in which we have circumstantial proof that suggests conclusions through inductive reasoning. Develop explanations for why and how the evidence in each of these situations is relevant, paying attention in each case to the evidential hypotheses that support use of the evidence.

■ PROBLEM 2-A. Too Much Wax on the Floor?

Juliette Bryant, a 60-year-old married woman, went grocery shopping at her local Alpha Market on Tuesday, January 3. The weather was unseasonably warm and dry.

While pushing a cart down one of the aisles, Mrs. Bryant fell and sustained a distal fracture of the lower one-third of the right fibula (the small bone that goes into the ankle). Her foot and leg had to be put in a cast for six weeks, and she was hospitalized for 30 days. According to her doctor's testimony, she developed traumatic arthritis causing chronic partial disability that might be permanent.

Bryant and her husband sue Alpha Market, claiming that it failed to maintain its floor in a safe condition. At trial she shows that each Saturday night Alpha cleans the floor by scrubbing with water and detergents, followed by machine-scrubbing to remove old wax and dirt and then the application of a solution of new wax and water. The evidence indicates that the amount of water in the solution determines how much wax adheres to the floor, and that improper mixtures lead the wax to "cake" and become slick. This procedure was followed on the Saturday before the mishap, and the store was closed on the following Sunday and Monday in observance of the New Year's holiday. Mrs. Bryant was among the earliest customers on Tuesday morning.

Plaintiffs call Mr. Walters, the manager of Alpha Market, as an "adverse witness." Over Alpha's objection, plaintiffs get Walters to admit that "twice before I slipped and fell on the floor when it was overwaxed," and that he received "several other reports" of customers falling in the past year.

Should plaintiffs have been permitted to ask Walters about his prior falls? About the reports he received that others fell?

■ PROBLEM 2-B. Was He Going Too Fast?

On an open stretch of two-lane highway in Nevada, Jay Gadsby, traveling eastbound in a red Z-Car with racing stripe, collided with Roy Reinhart, headed westbound in a pickup truck with gunrack. Both Jay and Roy were killed instantly. The road was straight, the noonday sun bright overhead, and afternoon thermal winds had not yet picked up—in short, driving conditions were optimal. Physical facts yield no clues as to the cause of the accident.

In her wrongful death action against Gadsby's estate, Roy's widow offers testimony by another eastbound driver—one Hill, who was the first to come upon the accident—that 30 miles west of the point of collision the red Z-Car had overtaken him going "at least 80 miles per hour." The defense objects, arguing that Hill's testimony is "irrelevant" when offered as proof that Jay was speeding at the time of the accident, at least in the absence of further proof that Gadsby likely continued to travel at the rate observed for the 30 miles between the sighting and the point of impact.

Is the evidence relevant on the question of Gadsby's speed at the time of impact? Should the judge admit the evidence only if the proponent offers additional proof to satisfy the condition suggested by defendant?

■ PROBLEM 2-C. Boys on the Bridge

While driving under an overpass, Arthur is injured by a chunk of concrete crashing through his windshield from above. Buildright Construction Company is in the process of rebuilding the overpass, which entails removing a concrete walk and railing.

Arthur sues Buildright, and shows at trial that defendant put up a bulkhead to confine the fall of debris, and in the process broke away some concrete in order to insert steel beams for its support. No direct evidence shows what caused the piece that struck Arthur to fall from the overpass, but Buildright offers testimony by Carla that she saw four or five boys of junior high school age about four blocks from the bridge running in a direction taking them away from the scene. Arthur objects.

Should the evidence be admitted? Could Arthur ask the court to require Buildright to prove other points before letting Carla testify? Does it matter that Arthur thinks the accident happened "about 10 A.M." and that Carla thinks it might have been "just about that time" when she saw the boys?

■ PROBLEM 2-D. Flight and Guilt

As Joe and his assistant Andy are closing the mobile fish-and-chip stand they operate from a truck in a parking lot near a lighted baseball field, a man armed with a sawed-off shotgun robs them of the evening's proceeds.

The next day, Joe and Andy examine mug books at the stationhouse and independently identify Carl as the thief. Later that day, police arrest Carl at his home.

At trial, the state calls Brenda. She is Carl's girlfriend, and she answered the door at the time of the arrest. The state offers her testimony that when Carl saw the police approaching, he first ran to the back door, then hid in a closet after discovering an officer standing guard in the alley. Carl objects, arguing that proof of his behavior at the time of arrest is irrelevant. In a sidebar conference, his lawyer points out that Carl's arrest was based on an outstanding default warrant, issued two years earlier on unrelated charges.

State the evidential hypothesis supporting the proffer. State a counterhypothesis favoring exclusion. How should the judge rule, and why?

■ NOTES ON EVIDENCE OF ATTEMPTS TO AVOID CAPTURE

1. Evidence of efforts to avoid capture is generally admissible in criminal trials. We even have a Biblical aphorism: "The wicked flee when no man pursueth; but the righteous are bold as a lion." Proverbs 28:1. The Supreme Court has long thought such evidence is relevant, Allen v. United States, 164 U.S. 492, 499 (1896) (flight by the accused is competent evidence having a tendency to establish guilt), and it usually comes in. See United States v. Martinez, 681 F.2d 1248, 1257 (10th Cir. 1982) (few cases are found in which such evidence is excluded); State v. Payne, 280 S.E.2d 72, 80 n.2 (W. Va. 1981) (citing authority from all but three states approving such evidence).

2. Evidence of flight does not create a "presumption of guilt" or suffice for conviction. Hickory v. United States, 160 U.S. 408, 416 (1896). And the Court has declared that the Biblical aphorism does not state "an accepted axiom of criminal law," noting that there may be reasons for flight apart from guilt:

> Innocent men sometimes hesitate to confront a jury; not necessarily because they fear that the jury will not protect them, but because they do not wish their names to appear in connection with criminal acts, are humiliated at being obliged to incur the popular odium of an arrest and trial, or because they do not wish to be put to the annoyance or expense of defending themselves.

Alberty v. United States, 162 U.S. 499, 511 (1896). See also United States v. Stewart, 579 F.2d 356, 359 n.3 (5th Cir.) (approving instruction warning jury that flight might result from "fear of being apprehended, unwillingness to confront the police, or reluctance to confront the witness"), *cert. denied*, 439 U.S. 936 (1978). While flight bears generally on guilt, it clearly cannot be taken as proof of some specific elements in the crime. See United States v. Owens, 460 F.2d 467, 470 (5th Cir. 1972) (alleged interstate transportation of stolen money orders; defendant's flight in Louisiana could not prove that the money orders had been forged in New Jersey).

3. Such evidence can be troublesome because the very idea of flight is interpretive, amounting to a gloss or reading of human conduct. Sometimes there is no room for doubt, as happens when defendant leads arresting officers driving a clearly marked vehicle on a high-speed chase or runs when uniformed officers approach. But often the evidence is subject to doubt. It may show, for example, only that after the crime defendant could not be located in his usual haunts, see United States v. Sims, 617 F.2d 1371, 1378-1379 (9th Cir. 1980) (failure to return to "halfway house" could be viewed as flight); Commonwealth v. Toney, 433 N.E.2d 425, 431-432 (Mass. 1982) (after homicide, inability of law enforcement officers to locate defendant at her home or workplace or by contacting four sisters and one cousin amounted to evidence of flight). Or it may show only that he left the environs after the crime, see United States v. Beahm, 664 F.2d 414, 419-420 (4th Cir. 1981) (on getting note from FBI requesting interview three weeks after crime, defendant went from Virginia to Florida; not flight). Or it may show that he was arrested in another jurisdiction, with no indication when he left the area, see United States v. Howze, 668 F.2d 322, 324-325 (7th Cir. 1982) (charged with robbing bank in Illinois, defendant was arrested four months later in Minnesota; court should reconsider whether these facts indicate flight). Yet even in such cases, the inference of flight might be persuasive if other factors are present. See United States v. Martinez, 681 F.2d 1248, 1254-1259 (10th Cir. 1982) (attorney disappeared after television and newspaper reports said he was wanted in connection with letter bombs, abandoning family and law practice, allowing driver's license to lapse and failing to attend mother's funeral; seven years later he was arrested entering from Mexico with false name and passport; judge erred in excluding proof of these facts to show flight; defendant "had to know" he was wanted, and he disappeared shortly after issuance of arrest warrant).

4. Courts often suggest that relevancy depends on the reasonableness of the assumption that defendant knew he was under investigation and that this inference becomes weaker as lapsed time between the crime and alleged flight increases. See United States v. Jackson, 572 F.2d 636, 640-641 (7th Cir. 1978).

5. Important to the prosecutor is an instruction that invites the jury to consider flight as evidence of possible guilt. Kevin F. O'Malley, Jay E. Grenig & Hon. William C. Lee, Federal Jury Practice and Instruction §14.08 (6th ed. 2014); United States v. Blue Thunder, 604 F.2d 550, 556 (8th Cir.) (approving flight instruction), *cert. denied*, 444 U.S. 902 (1979). If defendant's conduct cannot support an inference of flight, it may be reversible error to invite the jury to consider flight as evidence of possible guilt. See United States v. Myers, 550 F.2d 1036, 1048-1051 (5th Cir. 1977) (conviction reversed).

6. Similar kinds of proof include evidence that the accused (1) employed false identification or aliases, (2) destroyed or concealed evidence ("spoliation"), (3) fabricated evidence or suborned perjury, (4) killed, threatened, or otherwise impeded witnesses for the prosecution, (5) sought to escape detention, (6) attempted suicide, or (7) sought to bribe public officials. See generally Mueller & Kirkpatrick, Evidence §4.4 (5th ed. 2012); Hutchins & Slesinger, Some Observations on the Law of Evidence—Consciousness of Guilt, 77 U. Pa. L. Rev. 725 (1929).

B PRAGMATIC RELEVANCE

1. Prejudice and Confusion

It is said that FRE 401 giveth, but FRE 403 taketh away. The logical relevancy standard in FRE 401 is satisfied by evidence having even slight probative worth, but FRE 403 lets the judge exclude relevant evidence on account of any "danger" described there, meaning especially "unfair prejudice," but also confusing the issues, misleading the jury, undue delay, waste of time, or needlessly presenting "cumulative evidence."

FRE 403 confers broad discretion on the trial judge. Note, however, that FRE 403 is cast in language favoring admissibility. Evidence is to be excluded only if probative value is "substantially outweighed" by any of the listed dangers and considerations. Apparently evidence is to be admitted if probative worth and (for instance) the danger of unfair prejudice are in equal balance. Does it make sense to set a low standard of relevance and then authorize exclusion in broad terms? Does the cast of FRE 403 mean that this power should be exercised sparingly?

STATE v. CHAPPLE

Arizona Supreme Court
660 P.2d 1208 (Ariz. 1983)

[Alleged first-degree murder, arising out of apparent dispute over drug money. Victim Bill Varnes was found in the bedroom of a house trailer, dead of a gunshot wound in the head. At his trial, defendant Dolan Chapple claimed to have been in another state at the time. He was convicted on the basis of testimony by Malcolm Scott and Pamela Buck, who were themselves involved in the drug transaction and who did not actually see the killing. They placed one Dee at the scene of the crime, however, and Buck testified that Dee had confessed to killing Varnes. And both Scott and Buck identified defendant as Dee by picking out his picture from a photographic display.]

FELDMAN, J.

Defendant contends that the trial court erred by admitting pictures of the charred body and skull of the victim, Bill Varnes. The four pictures were admitted in conjunction with the testimony of Detective Hanratty, the investigating officer, and Dr. Thomas Jarvis, the medical examiner. In vivid color, the photographs portray Varnes' burned body, face and skull, the entry wound of the bullet, a close-up of the charred skull with a large bone flap cut away to show the red-colored, burned dura matter on the inside rim of the skull with the pink brain matter beneath and a pencil pointing to the location of the bullet embedded in the brain. The last photograph shows the brain as the bullet is being removed. On appeal, defendant contends that these pictures were gruesome and inflammatory and therefore should not have been admitted.

We have previously stated the law on this issue as follows:

> Photographs having probative value are admissible in evidence whether they are in black and white or color. *They must, of course, be relevant* to an issue in the case and may be admitted in evidence to identify the deceased, to show the location of the mortal wounds, to show how the crime was committed and to aid the jury in understanding the testimony of the witnesses. *If the photographs have any bearing upon any issue in the case, they may be received although they may also have a tendency to prejudice the jury against the person who committed the offense.* The discretion of the trial court will not be disturbed on appeal unless it has been clearly abused.

State v. Mohr, 476 P.2d 857, 858 (Ariz. 1970) (citations omitted) (emphasis supplied).

The facts of this case and the presence of the issue of inflammatory photographs in many other cases recently argued to this court lead us to reexamine the often quoted language from *State v. Mohr*. That language should not be interpreted to mean that any photograph which is relevant may be admitted despite its tendency to prejudice the jury. If this were the rule, any photograph of the deceased in any murder case would be admissible because the fact and cause of death are always relevant in a murder prosecution. Relevancy is not the sole test of admissibility for the trial court. Where the offered exhibit is of a nature to incite passion or inflame the jury—and the photographs in the case at bench certainly fall within that category—the court must go beyond the question of relevancy and consider whether the probative value of the exhibit outweighs the danger of prejudice created by admission of the exhibit. State v. Beers, 448 P.2d 104, 108-110 (Ariz. App. 1968) . . . . We first adopted this rule in these words:

> Relevancy is thus not the sole test of the admissibility of evidence; admissibility depends, rather, on a balancing of the various effects of the admission of such evidence, considered in the light of recognized rules of law governing the administration of criminal justice.

The . . . test has since been codified in Arizona Rule 403.

Thus, the correct rule is that exhibits which may tend to inflame the jury must first be found relevant. The trial court must then consider the probative value of the exhibits and determine whether it outweighs the danger of prejudice . . . . In making this determination, the trial court must examine the purpose of the offer. In State v. Thomas, 515 P.2d 865 (Ariz. 1973), we identified the following uses for which photographs of a corpse may be admitted in a homicide prosecution: to prove the corpus delicti, to identify the victim, to show the nature and location of the fatal injury, to help determine the degree of atrociousness of the crime, to corroborate state witnesses, to illustrate or explain testimony, and to corroborate the state's theory of how and why the homicide was committed. If any of these questions is contested, either expressly or implicitly, then the trial court may find that the photographs have more than mere technical relevance; it may find that the photographs have "bearing" to prove a contested issue in the case and may, therefore, be admissible notwithstanding a tendency to create prejudice.

However, if the photographs have no tendency to prove or disprove any question which is actually contested, they have little use or purpose except to inflame and would usually not be admissible.

In this case the State had the burden of proving all the elements of first degree murder as well as responding to defendant's sole argument that he was not Dee. In meeting this burden, the State not only had to establish that the defendant was at the scene of the crime, but also that he was responsible for murder. The State argues that the photographs were relevant to these purposes for several of the reasons enumerated in *Thomas*, supra. We agree that the photographs were relevant to the issues raised by the State's burden of establishing a case for first degree murder. We also agree with the State's claim that the photographs are useful to prove that Dee (who told Buck that he had "shot that ______ in the head") had committed one of the killings.

While both of these arguments establish the relevancy of the photographs, under the facts of this case we find that they had little probative value. The fact that Varnes was killed, the medical cause of his death, and what was done with his body after death were not in controversy. The defense did not dispute, controvert or contradict the State's testimony from the two witnesses on this subject, Detective Hanratty and Dr. Jarvis, and even offered to stipulate to the cause of death. The facts illustrated in the photographs were simply not in dispute or at issue. As the prosecution accurately told the jury in final argument, the only issue to be tried was whether Malcolm Scott and Pamela Buck were correct in identifying the defendant as Dee.

While the exhibits did illustrate the testimony of Hanratty and Jarvis and thus helped the jury comprehend that testimony,[7] there was simply no conflict with regard to the point at which the bullet entered Varnes' skull, the depth of its penetration, the lobe of the brain in which it was lodged, the damage which it did, or over whether it or some other condition had caused death. Nor was there any value to the photographs on the theory that they were relevant to Buck's testimony that after the killings Dee admitted that he had shot Varnes in the head. This admission may well serve to establish that Dee was the one who killed Varnes, but defendant did not deny that Dee had killed Varnes by shooting him in the head. Defendant argued only that he was not Dee. The photographs showing the bullet hole in the skull and the bullet in the burned brain were not probative on the only issue being tried, which was whether defendant was Dee.

In summary, the narrow issue on which this case turned was identification. The matters illustrated by the photographs were cumulative of uncontradicted and undisputed testimony, as well as the subject of a stipulation offered by the defendant. We find, therefore, that the photographs in question had little probative value on the issues being tried and that their admission in evidence could have almost no value or result except to inflame the minds of the jury. Under such circumstances, there was nothing for the trial court to weigh, nothing on which its discretion could be exercised, and the admission of the photographs was error.

In reaching this conclusion, we recognize that the state cannot be compelled to try its case in a sterile setting. Exhibits which have the tendency to cause prejudice may often be admissible despite offers to stipulate or the absence of controverting or contradicting evidence. Many times the accuracy of a witness' testimony is not conceded and can be better understood when illustrated by photographs. Testimony may be difficult to comprehend without photographs, or exhibits may corroborate or illustrate controverted testimony.

---

[7]The trial judge admitted three of the photographs over objection, informing the jurors that the photographs were "distasteful, perhaps to some even shocking. The . . . sole purpose for which you are to consider their admission into evidence, is the fact that they do show where the slug which the detective described was in the skull of one of the victims." The detective and medical examiner both testified without contradiction to the area of the brain in which the bullet was found and the cumulative effect of the photographs could serve no purpose under these facts. We do not believe that the court's statement to the jury regarding the purpose of the admission can be relied upon to negate the admittedly "shocking" effect of the photographs.

In such cases, the exhibits have probative value on issues expressly or tacitly in dispute. In every case in which there is probative value to the exhibit, it is for the trial court to weigh that value against the danger of prejudice and its conclusion on this point will not be disturbed absent a clear abuse of discretion.

In this case, however, there was nothing of significance to weigh and the only possible use of the photographs would have been to inflame the minds of the jury or to impair their objectivity. Since there was so little probative value to these photographs and since their capacity to inflame is obvious, the admission was legally erroneous and an abuse of discretion . . . .

[The conviction is reversed on account of errors in admitting the photographs and excluding expert testimony offered by the defense concerning the reliability of eyewitness identification.]

OLD CHIEF v. UNITED STATES (II)

Supreme Court of the United States
519 U.S. 172 (1997)

Justice SOUTER delivered the opinion of the Court.

[Recall that Johnny Lynn Old Chief was charged with being a felon in possession of a firearm. Recall that he was also charged with assault with a dangerous weapon and use of a firearm in a violent crime. The prior conviction involved an assault causing serious bodily injury. The defense offered to stipulate to the conviction in hope of keeping details from the jury. Early in the opinion, the Court concludes that the *name* of the prior conviction is relevant, that the offer to stipulate did not make this point irrelevant, and that it is important for a variety of reasons to admit evidence rather than try cases on stipulated facts. See *Old Chief (I)* in section A of this chapter, supra. Here the Court addresses the matter of unfair prejudice under FRE 403.]

As for the analytical method to be used in FRE 403 balancing, two basic possibilities present themselves. An item of evidence might be viewed as an island, with estimates of its own probative value and unfairly prejudicial risk the sole reference points in deciding whether the danger substantially outweighs the value and whether the evidence ought to be excluded. Or the question of admissibility might be seen as inviting further comparisons to take account of the full evidentiary context of the case as the court understands it when the ruling must be made.[6] This second approach would start out like the first but be ready to go further. On objection, the court would decide whether a particular item of evidence raised a danger of unfair prejudice. If it did, the judge would go on to evaluate the degrees of probative value and unfair prejudice not only for the

[6]It is important that a reviewing court evaluate the trial court's decision from its perspective when it had to rule and not indulge in review by hindsight . . . .

item in question but for any actually available substitutes as well. If an alternative were found to have substantially the same or greater probative value but a lower danger of unfair prejudice, sound judicial discretion would discount the value of the item first offered and exclude it if its discounted probative value were substantially outweighed by unfairly prejudicial risk. As we will explain later on, the judge would have to make these calculations with an appreciation of the offering party's need for evidentiary richness and narrative integrity in presenting a case, and the mere fact that two pieces of evidence might go to the same point would not, of course, necessarily mean that only one of them might come in. It would only mean that a judge applying FRE 403 could reasonably apply some discount to the probative value of an item of evidence when faced with less risky alternative proof going to the same point. Even under this second approach, as we explain below, a defendant's FRE 403 objection offering to concede a point generally cannot prevail over the Government's choice to offer evidence showing guilt and all the circumstances surrounding the offense.[7]

The first understanding of the rule is open to a very telling objection. That reading would leave the party offering evidence with the option to structure a trial in whatever way would produce the maximum unfair prejudice consistent with relevance. He could choose the available alternative carrying the greatest threat of improper influence, despite the availability of less prejudicial but equally probative evidence. The worst he would have to fear would be a ruling sustaining a FRE 403 objection, and if that occurred, he could simply fall back to offering substitute evidence. This would be a strange rule. It would be very odd for the law of evidence to recognize the danger of unfair prejudice only to confer such a degree of autonomy on the party subject to temptation, and the Rules of Evidence are not so odd.

Rather, a reading of the companions to FRE 403, and of the commentaries that went with them to Congress, makes it clear that what counts as FRE 403 "probative value" of an item of evidence, as distinct from FRE 401 "relevance," may be calculated by comparing evidentiary alternatives. The ACN to FRE 401 explicitly say that a party's concession is pertinent to the court's discretion to exclude evidence on the point conceded . . . . As already mentioned, the Notes make it clear that such rulings should be made not on the basis of FRE 401 relevance but on "such considerations as waste of time and undue prejudice (see FRE 403) . . . ." The ACN to FRE 403 then take up the point by stating that when a court considers "whether to exclude on grounds of unfair prejudice," the "availability of other means of proof may . . . be an appropriate factor." . . . Thus the notes leave no question that when FRE 403 confers discretion by providing that evidence "may" be excluded, the discretionary judgment may be informed not only by assessing an evidentiary item's twin tendencies, but by

[7]. . . [O]ur holding is limited to cases involving proof of felon status. On appellate review of a FRE 403 decision, a defendant must establish abuse of discretion, a standard that is not satisfied by a mere showing of some alternative means of proof that the prosecution in its broad discretion chose not to rely upon.

placing the result of that assessment alongside similar assessments of evidentiary alternatives.

In dealing with the specific problem raised by §922(g)(1) and its prior-conviction element, there can be no question that evidence of the name or nature of the prior offense generally carries a risk of unfair prejudice to the defendant. That risk will vary from case to case, for the reasons already given, but will be substantial whenever the official record offered by the government would be arresting enough to lure a juror into a sequence of bad character reasoning. Where a prior conviction was for a gun crime or one similar to other charges in a pending case the risk of unfair prejudice would be especially obvious, and Old Chief sensibly worried that the prejudicial effect of his prior assault conviction, significant enough with respect to the current gun charges alone, would take on added weight from the related assault charge against him.[8]

The District Court was also presented with alternative, relevant, admissible evidence of the prior conviction by Old Chief's offer to stipulate, evidence necessarily subject to the District Court's consideration on the motion to exclude the record offered by the Government. Although Old Chief's formal offer to stipulate was, strictly, to enter a formal agreement with the Government to be given to the jury, even without the Government's acceptance his proposal amounted to an offer to admit that the prior-conviction element was satisfied, and a defendant's admission is, of course, good evidence. See FRE 801(d)(2)(A).

Old Chief's proffered admission would, in fact, have been not merely relevant but seemingly conclusive evidence of the element. The statutory language in which the prior-conviction requirement is couched shows no congressional concern with the specific name or nature of the prior offense beyond what is necessary to place it within the broad category of qualifying felonies, and Old Chief clearly meant to admit that his felony did qualify, by stipulating "that the Government has proven one of the essential elements of the offense." As a consequence, although the name of the prior offense may have been technically relevant, it addressed no detail in the definition of the prior-conviction element that would not have been covered by the stipulation or admission. Logic, then, seems to side with Old Chief.

[Here Court discusses "descriptive richness," "moral underpinnings" of the law, and jury "expectations." See *Old Chief (I)* in section A of this chapter, supra.]

[Recognition that the prosecution] needs evidentiary depth to tell a continuous story has, however, virtually no application when the point at issue is a defendant's legal status, dependent on some judgment rendered wholly independently of the

---

[8] It is true that a prior offense may be so far removed in time or nature from the current gun charge and any others brought with it that its potential to prejudice the defendant unfairly will be minimal. Some prior offenses, in fact, may even have some potential to prejudice the Government's case unfairly. Thus an extremely old conviction for a relatively minor felony that nevertheless qualifies under the statute might strike many jurors as a foolish basis for convicting an otherwise upstanding member of the community of otherwise legal gun possession. Since the Government could not, of course, compel the defendant to admit formally the existence of the prior conviction, the Government would have to bear the risk of jury nullification, a fact that might properly drive the Government's charging decision.

concrete events of later criminal behavior charged against him. As in this case, the choice of evidence for such an element is usually not between eventful narrative and abstract proposition, but between propositions of slightly varying abstraction, either a record saying that conviction for some crime occurred at a certain time or a statement admitting the same thing without naming the particular offense. The issue of substituting one statement for the other normally arises only when the record of conviction would not be admissible for any purpose beyond proving status, so that excluding it would not deprive the prosecution of evidence with multiple utility; if, indeed, there were a justification for receiving evidence of the nature of prior acts on some issue other than status (i.e., to prove "motive, opportunity, intent, preparation, plan, knowledge, identity, or absence of mistake or accident," FRE 404(b)), FRE 404(b) guarantees the opportunity to seek its admission. Nor can it be argued that the events behind the prior conviction are proper nourishment for the jurors' sense of obligation to vindicate the public interest. The issue is not whether concrete details of the prior crime should come to the jurors' attention but whether the name or general character of that crime is to be disclosed. Congress, however, has made it plain that distinctions among generic felonies do not count for this purpose; the fact of the qualifying conviction is alone what matters under the statute .... Finally, ... proof of the defendant's status goes to an element entirely outside the natural sequence of what the defendant is charged with thinking and doing to commit the current offense. Proving status without telling exactly why that status was imposed leaves no gap in the story of a defendant's subsequent criminality, and its demonstration by stipulation or admission neither displaces a chapter from a continuous sequence of conventional evidence nor comes across as an officious substitution, to confuse or offend or provoke reproach.

Given these peculiarities of the element of felony-convict status and of admissions and the like when used to prove it, there is no cognizable difference between the evidentiary significance of an admission and of the legitimately probative component of the official record the prosecution would prefer to place in evidence .... In this case, as in any other in which the prior conviction is for an offense likely to support conviction on some improper ground, the only reasonable conclusion was that the risk of unfair prejudice did substantially outweigh the discounted probative value of the record of conviction, and it was an abuse of discretion to admit the record when an admission was available.[10] ...

[10] There may be yet another means of proof besides a formal admission on the record that, with a proper objection, will obligate a district court to exclude evidence of the name of the offense. A redacted record of conviction is the one most frequently mentioned. Any alternative will, of course, require some jury instruction to explain it (just as it will require some discretion when the indictment is read). A redacted judgment in this case, for example, would presumably have revealed to the jury that Old Chief was previously convicted in federal court and sentenced to more than a year's imprisonment, but it would not have shown whether his previous conviction was for one of the business offenses that do not count, under §921(a)(2). Hence, an instruction, with the defendant's consent, would be necessary to make clear that the redacted judgment was enough to satisfy the status element remaining in the case. The Government might indeed, propose such a redacted judgment for the trial court to weigh against a defendant's offer to admit, as indeed the government might do even if the defendant's admission had been received into evidence.

The judgment is reversed, and the case is remanded to the Ninth Circuit for further proceedings consistent with this opinion.[11]

It is so ordered.

Justice O'CONNOR, with whom THE CHIEF JUSTICE, Justice SCALIA, and Justice THOMAS join, dissenting.

[The dissent argues that the relevant statute shows that Congress thought jurors would learn "the name and basic nature" of the prior offense. The statute uses the term "crime punishable by imprisonment for a term exceeding one year," and does not refer merely to "felons," and it does provide that certain "business crimes" and misdemeanors that happen to be punishable by imprisonment of two years or less do not count. Hence "crime" is not an "abstract or metaphysical" concept, and the government must prove that the defendant "committed a particular crime."

More importantly, one is not found guilty of a crime or felony, but of "a specified offense." Thus the prior case found that Old Chief "did knowingly and unlawfully assault Rory Dean Fenner, said assault resulting in serious bodily injury," and the name and nature of his crime were "inseparable from the fact of his earlier conviction."

Still more troubling is the majority's argument that the general principle favoring evidentiary depth has "virtually no application" here, for a jury is "as likely to be puzzled" by a "missing chapter" relating to a prior felony conviction as it would be by a concession of any other element in the crime.]

NOTES ON PREJUDICE, GRUESOME PHOTOGRAPHS, AND PRIOR CRIMES

1. Consider the meaning of "prejudice" in *Chapple* and *Old Chief.* It can't simply mean "harm" to the objecting party's case because *all* relevant evidence that supports one side is likely to damage the position of the other side. Rule 403 speaks of "unfair prejudice," but in common parlance "prejudice" is invariably unfair, so "unfair prejudice" seems redundant, and the idea of "fair prejudice" seems oxymoronic. Probably the purpose of the modifier "unfair" was simply to recognize that "prejudice" can also simply mean "harm," and the intent of FRE 403 is certainly not to bar evidence that harms the other side's case, but to bar evidence that does so "unfairly."

(a) In *Chapple,* unfair prejudice seems to refer to a tendency toward emotionalism—the court thinks the photographs might "incite passion or inflame the jury," and this idea of unfair prejudice is salient and common. Given our understanding that reason is affected by emotion because we are human, the

[11] In remanding, we imply no opinion on the possibility of harmless error, an issue not passed upon below.

effort of courts here is to confine the impact of emotionalism, to exclude evidence that might make the jury "see red" and react in blind anger. So the first major definition of "unfair prejudice" is evidence that enflames the passions of the jury or evokes an angry response.

(b) In *Old Chief,* unfair prejudice refers to proof that might "lure a juror into a sequence of bad character reasoning." You will see that Rule 404 bars proof of character to prove conduct, and *Old Chief* expresses the idea that "unfair prejudice" refers to evidence that the jury is likely to "misuse." The prior conviction is admissible to prove that indeed defendant is a felon, but it might be misused as proof that defendant probably did this time what he was convicted of doing before, which is to assault someone. "Jury misuse" is the second major definition of "unfair prejudice."

2. *Old Chief* holds—and *Chapple* agrees—that a stipulation does not make relevant evidence irrelevant, but a stipulation has *some effect* on the task of weighing probative worth against prejudice. A stipulation *lessens the need* to admit evidence. So while a proffered stipulation does not guarantee the exclusion of evidence, it has some effect in striking the balance between probative worth and unfair prejudice.

3. Don't be misled by *Chapple.* First, it is rare for a trial judge to be reversed for error in deciding whether relevance is outweighed by the risk of unfair prejudice. Second, *Chapple* gets it slightly wrong in saying the question is whether probative worth outweighs prejudicial impact. Rule 403 is cast in favor of *admitting* evidence, so the question is whether probative worth is "substantially outweighed" by prejudicial impact. Third, gruesome photographs are routinely admitted in homicide cases. The decision is valuable, however, because defendants convicted in homicide cases regularly appeal on this ground, which sometimes offers the best (maybe the only) chance for a reversal.

4. As in *Old Chief* and *Chapple,* defendants often offer to stipulate to the points that can be proved by evidence that has explosive impact. In bloody photograph cases, defendants may offer to stipulate to the appearance of the scene, the cause of death, position of the body, the nature and relationship of wounds—points they are unlikely to try to refute anyway—and even to stipulate to the viciousness of the attack. On one or more of these arguments, prosecutors regularly prevail. See Edwards v. United States, 767 A.2d 241 (D.C. Ct. App. 2001) (in trial for murder of 2-year-old placed in tub of hot water, admitting photographs of body despite defense offer to stipulate to the identity of the body and the cause of death; *Old Chief* did not require otherwise).

5. Often the cases hold, like *Chapple,* that the mere fact that photographs are "gruesome" does not mean they should be excluded. See State v. Smith, 684 N.E.2d 668, 687-688 (Ohio 1997) (admitting "gruesome" photographs of body, crime scene, and autopsy; details included "the depressed skull fracture caused by a hammer-like object," which conflicted with defendant's testimony about what he had done). Indeed, they are sometimes admitted *because* they demonstrate atrocity. See Cole v. State, 164 P.3d 1089 (Kan. 2007) (admitting "extremely grotesque" photos; this was "an extremely brutal crime" involving "a grown man breaking a helpless child in half" and state had to prove "willful or malicious use" of unreasonable force; nature of injuries was "hidden inside the child's body," and photos were "close up shots" of wounds showing the broken spine and separated aorta); People v. Bonilla, 160 P.3d 84 (Cal. 2007) ("as unpleasant as these photographs are, they demonstrate the real-life consequences of Bonilla's actions"); Commonwealth v. Rogers, 222 N.E.2d 766, 772 (Mass.) ("repulsive pictures of mutilated corpse, which left no gruesome detail of this macabre event to the imagination" were relevant on question whether homicide was committed with "extreme atrocity and cruelty"), *cert. denied*, 389 U.S. 991 (1967); Hopkinson v. State, 632 P.2d 79, 139 (Wyo. 1981) (photographs of victim who had been "brutally tortured before his death"; manner of death was relevant to prosecutor's theory, which was that defendant, who was himself in prison at time of slaying, arranged killing for revenge: "[I]t has never been held that *probative* evidence is inadmissible solely because of repugnancy. Murder is repugnant"), *cert. denied*, 455 U.S. 922 (1982). Color slides are sometimes allowed, magnifying the awful image of violent death. See Goffer v. State, 430 So. 2d 896, 898-899 (Ala. Crim. App. 1983) (rejecting claim that color slides of victim in hospital should have been excluded because they "produced a magnification of the wounds and a distortion of the injuries"; the slides were "just enlargements").

6. Sometimes courts exclude gruesome photographs under FRE 403 when probative worth is minimal and inflammatory impact is great. The chance for exclusion improves when the numbing impact of such pictures results from changed conditions, so they are "misleading" under FRE 403 as well as prejudicial. See People v. Coleman, 451 N.E.2d 973, 977-978 (Ill. App. 1983) (reversible error to admit "color slide of the decedent's decomposing, maggot-infested, partially autopsied body"); Terry v. State, 491 S.W.2d 161, 164 (Tex. Crim. App. 1973) (reversible error to admit pictures of month-old murder victim, showing "massive mutilation" caused by autopsy and depicting "severed parts of a human body"). And see Ritchie v. State, 632 P.2d 1244, 1245-1246 (Okla. Crim. 1981) (reversible error to display enlarged photograph of three-year-old victim taken before attack, surrounded by photographs of his body afterwards and during subsequent autopsy; jury "should not have been concerned with what the child looked like prior to the offense," and "use of a billboard to display the numerous photographs could have served no other purpose than to prejudice and arouse the passions," and "the billboard became an item of evidence notwithstanding the fact that it was never introduced").

7. Turning to *Old Chief,* the Court is right that the felon-in-possession charge did not turn on the *nature* of the prior conviction. Johnny Lynn Old Chief had been convicted of felonies that were not in the exempt category relating to "business practices," so it made no difference to *present* charges whether he was convicted of burglary, embezzlement, murder, or something else. So telling the jury the nature of the convictions served no legitimate purpose. It's also obvious that proving that Old Chief had been convicted of assault might incline the jury to conclude that he was up to no good when found in possession of a gun, and that he was a bad person who deserved to go to jail. But the Court notes also that prior acts are often relevant in a very different way: They may shed light on points like motive (defendant had committed robbery, so he needed to steal a car to get away) or intent (defendant had often sold cocaine, so this time when he possessed cocaine he probably intended to sell it). In such cases, *Old Chief* says, a defense offer to stipulate will not likely tip the balance as it did in this instance. Still, courts often exclude prior crimes in this setting when relevance seems attenuated and the risk of prejudice seems large. You will take up this issue in Chapter 5. At least one commentator thinks the typical outcomes (bloody photographs are routinely admitted; prior crimes are often excluded) are backwards. See Michael Risinger, John Henry Wigmore, Johnny Lynn Old Chief, and "Legitimate Moral Force": Keeping the World Safe for Heartstrings and Gore, 49 Hastings L.J. 403, 421 (1998) (proof of "bloody photos and weeping widows" ought to be more readily excludable than prior convictions, which at least are not "wholly irrelevant by anyone's definition," but that "the opposite is in fact the case" and *Old Chief* does not change this practical reality).

8. *Old Chief* determines an issue of federal evidence law, so its holding does not bind states. That means that states could, if they chose, continue to admit proof of the names of prior convictions in state felon-in-possession cases. Not surprisingly, however, *Old Chief* has proven influential in state courts. See Hardister v. State, 849 N.E.2d 563 (Ind. 2006) (rule of *Old Chief* applies in this state); Ferguson v. State, 210 S.W.3d 53 (Ark. 2005) (adopting *Old Chief* rule). Moreover, its reasoning has been applied in other areas. See, e.g., Diemer v. State, 225 S.W.3d 348 (Ark. 2006) (trial for killing another while incarcerated); State v. James, 81 S.W.3d 751 (Tenn. 2002) (trial for escape by convicted felon). But see Rigby v. State, 826 S.2d 694 (Miss. 2002) (in trial on felony DUI charges, prior DUI convictions were admissible despite defense offer to stipulate; in *Old Chief*, nature of prior convictions did not matter; here they do); Franklin v. State, 965 So.2d 79 (Fla. 2007) (declining to apply *Old Chief* in sentencing phase of capital trial).

Justice David Souter (served 1990-2009)

Justice David Souter served as a judge in New Hampshire, first on the trial bench (1973-1983) and then on the New Hampshire Supreme Court (1983-1990). President Bush appointed him to the federal Court of Appeals in 1990 and, on Justice Brennan's retirement a few months later, to the Supreme Court. Ten years after authoring the opinion in *Old Chief*, Justice Souter wrote the opinion in the *Twombly* case, which you likely read in Civil Procedure. *Twombly* reflects awareness that a generous relevancy standard opens the door wide in the discovery process in civil cases, and it was largely because the majority thought trial courts could not adequately control

Diana Walker / Time Life Pictures / Getty Images

discovery that the Court adopted the "plausibility standard" for complaints in civil cases. See Bell Atlantic Corp. v. Twombly, 550 U.S. 544 (2007). Justice Souter also authored the Court's main opinion dealing with the Exxon Valdez oil spill (see picture of the ship and description of the litigation in Chapter 4B5, infra). While serving on the New Hampshire Supreme Court ten years before *Old Chief,* Justice Souter had written an opinion reversing a judgment refusing involuntary civil commitment, finding error in the refusal to admit a statement in which defendant admitted killing his uncle, then trying to incinerate and hide the corpse. The jury heard about these acts, but should have heard his admissions: Their significance was not "limited to their narrative content," for evidence of "behavior in making them, and even the phrasing of his statements," could have provided "further indications" of mental condition. See In re Sanborn, 545 A.2d 726, 729 (N.H. 1988).

■ PROBLEM 2-E. The Battered Wife

Virginia died of a stab wound in her chest, and the state has charged her ex-husband Donald with murder and, in the alternative, manslaughter. Donald has pleaded innocent to the charges, claiming that the killing was accidental.

There is no doubt of the cause of death. Virginia's body was found in the trailer where she lived with Todd and Jason (children of hers from a previous marriage), dead from massive hemorrhaging caused by a chest wound. Nor is there any doubt that Donald played a role in her death: The evidence shows that he called the sheriff's office at 2:00 A.M., saying that he had just stabbed his wife and giving the address of the trailer. (Officers who went to the scene found the children asleep.)

During the state's case-in-chief, the prosecutor proves cause of death (stab wound) and introduces a knife said to be the fatal weapon, along with lab analysis connecting the blood on the knife to Virginia, forensic testimony that a knife of that size made the wound, and evidence that Donald's latent fingerprints were found on it.

During the defense case, Donald testifies that he spent the evening at the trailer watching television with Virginia while the children slept, and that the two quarreled when she said she was going to leave him and take Todd and Jason with her. He testifies that he "asked her not to go, and told her how important her children had become to him, and that he would try to get a court order to stop her from leaving." He testifies that Virginia then attacked him with a baseball bat and admits that he picked up the knife from the countertop, but says, "She just fell into the blade, and I didn't even know she was hurt, at least not right away."

During its case-in-rebuttal, the state offers testimony by a counselor at a Shelter for Battered and Abused Women that two years earlier Virginia had sought refuge there for about 30 days, during which time she divorced Donald.

Donald objects to the testimony of the counselor at the shelter, arguing that it is irrelevant and prejudicial. Should that testimony get in? How is it relevant? How is it prejudicial?

■ PROBLEM 2-F. The Exploding Gas Tank

Struck from behind by a vehicle exceeding the speed limit on the highway, the car in which Risner was riding as a passenger bursts into flames as a result of a ruptured fuel tank. Within 24 hours, Risner dies from burns sustained in the accident, and his widow thereafter sues the automaker, alleging that negligent design of the fuel tank caused Risner's death—that if the tank had been properly designed it would not have ruptured when the car was struck from behind.

At trial, defendant automaker introduces testimony by a state trooper that the impacting vehicle was going about 80 mph at the time of impact. The automaker also introduces a certified copy of a guilty plea, entered by the driver of the impacting vehicle to charges of involuntary manslaughter arising from the accident. In the end, the jury returns a verdict for defendant.

Mrs. Risner appeals, urging that the trial court should have excluded the guilty plea under FRE 403. In response, defendant automaker argues that the plea was properly received to show the speed of the impacting vehicle and establish cause of death.

Who should prevail in these arguments and why?

2. Limited Admissibility—Confining the Impact of Proof

It is a perennial headache for judges and trial lawyers that evidence tends to prove too much. Time and again, evidence that seems perfect to prove one point also tends to prove another, on which it is incompetent. Or the other point is highly prejudicial. Or evidence is admissible in support of one claim but not another, or admissible against one party but not another. Rule 403 lets the trial judge balance probative worth against risks of "unfair prejudice" or confusion of issues or "misleading the jury" and admit or exclude accordingly.

Rule 105 authorizes a very different approach: Admit the evidence, on the point for which or against the parties as to whom it is competent, but give limiting instructions to prevent misuse on other issues or as against other parties. More often than not courts admit evidence having unwanted spillover effect, and parties raising objection on this ground must content themselves with a limiting instruction. The reason is practical necessity, for little proof would be admissible if its relevance or impact in the case had to match exactly its competency. Thus a great deal of evidence is admitted for purposes of impeachment despite the fact that it cannot properly be considered as proof of any number of other points that it may seem to establish, and out-of-court statements and prior criminal acts may be proved in different contexts despite rules restricting their use.

■ PROBLEM 2-G. "My Insurance Will Cover It"

While driving on the left (inside) lane of a busy four-lane street in Miami, Lina hears a sudden metallic scraping and feels her (new shiny white) Chrysler being shoved roughly leftward. Myra, who is driving in the right (outside) lane hears the same awful noise, and feels her (bright red) Porsche being nudged sharply to the right. The two regain control of their cars. Lina drops back behind Myra, and they pull over to the curb and inspect the damage.

They exchange names and addresses, and Lina says: "Whoever screws up, her insurance pays. I'm sure my insurance will cover it. They'll pay for what happened to your Porsche."

It takes more than $6,000 to fix Myra's Porsche and almost as much to repair Lina's Chrysler. Despite their promising amicable beginning, the two women do not manage to work out their differences amicably. Myra sues, and Lina counterclaims.

At trial, Myra proposes to testify to what Lina said.

Lina objects, invoking FRE 411, which says that evidence of liability insurance cannot be offered to prove that a person "acted negligently or otherwise wrongfully." But Myra insists: "What Lina said is admissible to prove she was negligent. She admitted it, for heaven's sake."

How should the court rule, and why?

■ NOTES ON LIMITED ADMISSIBILITY

1. You will see that what a party says is usually admissible against her, under the admissions doctrine contained in Rule 801(d)(2)(A). See Chapter 4B1, infra. Myra is right that nothing prevents use of a statement by Lina to prove she was negligent. But Lina is also right that under Rule 411 the fact of insurance cannot be used to prove negligence. See Chapter 5F, infra. The challenge is to sort out the admissible from the inadmissible aspects of the proffered evidence. It would be difficult if not impossible to let Myra testify to just part of what Lina said. Hence the choice for the court is to exclude Lina's statement altogether under Rule 403 or admit it for a limited purpose under Rule 105. Of course Lina could ask for a limiting instruction that her statement could not be used to prove the fact of insurance. It seems doubtful that such an instruction would do much good. Note that FRE 105 leaves it up to the objecting party to request such an instruction or not to.

2. As a practical matter, there is no alternative to the doctrine of limited admissibility, is there? Consider these statements in defense of the doctrine:

> To say that the jury might have been confused amounts to nothing more than an unfounded speculation that the jurors disregarded clear instructions of the court in arriving at their verdict. Our theory of trial relies upon the ability of a jury to follow instructions.

Opper v. United States, 348 U.S. 84, 95 (1954) (no "confusion" resulted here).

> Unless we proceed on the basis that the jury will follow the court's instructions where those instructions are clear and the circumstances are such that the jury can reasonably be expected to follow them, the jury system makes little sense. Based on the faith that the jury will endeavor to follow the court's instructions, our system of jury trial has produced one of the most valuable and practical mechanisms in human experience for dispensing substantial justice.

Delli Paoli v. United States, 352 U.S. 232, 242-243 (1957) (but there are "practical limitations" on doctrine of limited admissibility). The Court is right, isn't it?

3. In *Opper* and *Delli Paoli*, the Court struggled with limited admissibility in a recurrent situation—the trial of several defendants in which a prosecutor offers a statement by one that mentions others. Often such a statement is admissible against the person who made it, but *not* against others. The question was whether it violates the confrontation rights of the accused if the statement is admitted against its maker with a limiting instruction to protect other defendants named in the statement. Ultimately the Court concluded that even clear limiting instructions were not good enough, noting that the prosecutor could proceed separately against the various defendants. Bruton v. United States, 391 U.S. 123 (1968) (set forth in Chapter 4B1, infra).

3. Completeness—Providing Context

Another headache for judges and trial lawyers comes from the fact that a bit of evidence that might be competent on a point is so connected with other evidence that it would be a distortion to consider the one without the other. Sometimes the difficulty is that there is not enough competent evidence to make the point fairly. But usually the problem is that the proponent chooses to present a small piece of a larger picture and thus distorts meaning.

Here again FRE 403 authorizes one approach (balance, and admit or exclude the whole accordingly). And at least in connection with "a writing or recorded statement," FRE 106 authorizes another: The adverse party may require introduction of "any other part" of the statement that "ought in fairness" to be considered at the same time as the part already offered. This "rule of completeness," as it is sometimes called, obviously could apply to statements that have not been written or recorded and to other sorts of evidence as well, and trial courts have authority enough under Rules 401 through 403 and 611 to apply the same principle to such other proof.

■ PROBLEM 2-H. "Power Rollback Caused the Crash"

While serving as a Navy flight instructor, Lieutenant Commander Erin Ranney died in a T44 training aircraft that crashed while climbing and turning hard right during "touch-and-go's" (exercises in which plane lands, then accelerates and takes off again). Her student, Ensign Dan Knowls, also died in the crash. Jim Ranney, her surviving husband and also a Navy flight instructor, sued manufacturer Rockwood Aircraft.

Jim Ranney thinks that sudden failure of engine power at a crucial moment during take-off caused the crash. Shortly afterwards, and long before suit was filed, Ranney investigated the plane and the scene and the available records, and wrote a detailed letter to Commander Martin concluding that "power rollback caused the crash."

At trial, Ranney presents his evidence of power rollback, mostly in the form of expert testimony developed for trial. During the defense case, Rockwood introduces official findings, based on Commander Martin's investigation, that pilot error caused the crash. Those findings suggest that Knowls was in the left student seat in control of the plane, that Erin Ranney did not at first see a second craft approaching from the left because Knowls blocked her view, and that when she did see the second plane she took the controls and banked right. The findings indicate that Knowls "released the stick" to let her do what she had to do, but that he had improperly trimmed the plane (the trim tabs were set wrong). Releasing the stick brought the nose up, causing a sudden loss of airspeed leading to stall and crash.

Counsel for Rockwood calls Jim Ranney as an adverse witness, and asks about comments Ranney made in his letter to Commander Martin. In one, he said the plane "violated pattern integrity as it turned crosswind" when his wife "reacted instinctively and abruptly by initiating a hard right turn" away from the nearby craft. In another, Ranney said his wife had been under "unnecessary pressure" and tried to "cancel the exercise because Knowls was tired and emotionally drained." Counsel for Ranney rose to examine:

Ranney Counsel: In the same letter you were just asked about, didn't you conclude that power rollback caused the crash?

Rockwood Counsel: Well, I'm going to have to object to that, your Honor. We went into the letter because he wrote it and we can do that, but he can't offer his own letter because it's hearsay. Of course he can go over the passages about how fatigued his wife was, and how she was out of the pattern, but he's getting into other subjects now. It's hearsay and beyond the direct.

Ranney Counsel: Your Honor, he's trying to pick and choose. If he's going to use the letter, he can't distort it. We need to correct that.

The Court: I'm going to sustain the objection. If you want to ask your client what he learned about the crash by investigating, I'll let you get into that again, just to clear up what he thinks. But don't go into other parts of the letter.

After a jury verdict and judgment for the defense, Jim Ranney appeals, arguing that the court erred under FRE 106 in restricting redirect. What result, and why?

■ NOTES ON THE COMPLETENESS DOCTRINE

1. FRE 106 invites the adverse party to "require" the proponent to offer another "writing" (or "other part" of a writing) *at the same time* as the writing (or part) being offered. But in Problem 2-H, counsel for Ranney acted to bring out additional parts of the Ranney letter during what amounted to "friendly cross-examination" *after* counsel for Rockwood had brought out part of the letter on direct. Indeed, counsel for Ranney might have deferred this effort until putting on his case-in-rebuttal. Although framed as what one commentator calls an "interruption rule," FRE 106 authorizes adverse parties to answer an incomplete presentation later, thus serving as a "rebuttal rule." See generally Dale Nance, A Theory of Verbal Completeness, 80 Iowa L. Rev. 825, 847-849 (1995).

2. You will see that what Ranney wrote in his letter could be used *against him* as his *admission*, but Ranney could not normally put the letter in evidence himself, since the admissions doctrine does not authorize one to introduce his own statements. (Probably the letter does not fit the exception for public records, although the official findings might fit this exception.) Does this fact make a difference? Some courts take the view that FRE 106 affects only the *order* or *sequence* of proof, which would mean that it does not authorize a person in Ranney's position to offer his own letter later in the trial. The better view, however, is that FRE 106 can sometimes "trump" hearsay and other objections when necessary to provide context. For a good development of this view, see

Dale Nance, Verbal Completeness and Exclusionary Rules Under the Federal Rules of Evidence, 75 Tex. L. Rev. 51 (1996).

4. "The Shortness of Life"

Trial judges can exclude even probative evidence not only because of prejudice and confusion—factors likely to distort or undermine the jury's decisionmaking process—but also for more mundane reasons. FRE 403 speaks of undue delay, of wasting time, and of needless presentation of "cumulative evidence." Here the concern is purely practical, and this aspect of judicial power amounts to what Holmes called "a concession to the shortness of life." Reeve v. Dennett, 11 N.E. 938, 943 (Mass. 1887).

Thus courts may limit the number of witnesses called to prove any particular point. See Michelson v. United States, 335 U.S. 469, 480 (1948) (judge may control number of character witnesses called by the accused); Mills v. Nahabedian, 824 A.2d 500, 503 (R.I. 2003) (in doctor's suit alleging that odors from new carpet made her patients ill, trial judge properly limited number of witnesses that plaintiff could call to five). And judges may exclude, as cumulative, evidence that is duplicative of that already presented. See United States v. Crosby, 713 F.2d 1066, 1071-1072 (5th Cir.) (judge properly excluded journal entries and poetry offered to support defense of post-traumatic stress disorder from Vietnam experience, for these were "cumulative of other testimony"), *cert. denied*, 464 U.S. 1001 (1983). Judges may also insist that a trial continue once it has begun and deny requests for time to locate new witnesses or evidence.

Consider the following explanation for these powers:

> The court's time is a public commodity that should not be squandered. Witnesses and jurors have private lives, and ought not to be asked to give more of their time than is necessary to resolve disputes. A tireless or resourceful litigant should not have unlimited freedom to wear down his opponent by repetitious proof or unnecessary waiting. In short, FRE 403 is evidence law's answer to the adage, "Enough is enough."

1 Mueller & Kirkpatrick, Federal Evidence §4:15 (4th ed. 2013).

5. The Functions of Judge and Jury

Recall that the judge decides admissibility under Rule 104(a) (Chapter 1D4, supra). Fact questions may arise in this context. In the example where Cronan said the guy in the station wagon "wasn't going to stop" because he was in "too much of a hurry," the judge was called on to decide whether the speaker was excited when he spoke, which affected the admissibility of his statement as an excited utterance. The preponderance standard applies to these preliminary matters, in civil cases and in criminal cases too, where both prosecutor and defense must satisfy this standard in laying the foundation for the evidence they offer.

When it comes to relevancy, however, the judge is only sometimes the sole decisionmaker, and often the judge and the jury have overlapping responsibilities.

Simple relevance. The judge alone decides whether a particular point, which a proffered item of evidence concededly tends to establish or refute, is consequential under FRE 401. Only a judge can decide this point, which turns on substantive and procedural rules that establish and limit the issues. See Prather v. Prather, 650 F.2d 88, 90 (5th Cir. 1981) (in suit on oral contract, error to admit statements by plaintiff describing his understanding of terms, telling jury to determine whether his belief was relevant; that was "for the court to determine," and it should have concluded that plaintiff's state of mind was not relevant). Also the judge decides whether proffered evidence actually tends to prove the point for which it is offered.

Here we speak of "simple" (as opposed to "conditional") relevance, and the judge determines the matter by thinking about the legal issues in the case and about the inductive inferences that we have sampled—for example, does conduct suggest flight, and does flight suggest guilt of the charged crime?

Conditional relevance. Rule 104(b) provides that when relevance turns on whether a fact exists, proof must be introduced that is "sufficient to support a finding" that the fact does indeed exist. Here the Rule contemplates that the judge performs only a screening function: When different answers are reasonable on the basis of the proof, the jury decides. Rule 104(b) also says the judge may decide the order in which these matters are resolved: When relevance of evidence depends on whether a fact exists, the court may admit the evidence at the outset, on condition that proof of the critical fact be introduced later, or may insist that the condition be satisfied by other proof first.

The example of the gun that Lieutenant Goldbloom found at the murder scene (Chapter 1D1c, supra) illustrates what Rule 104(b) is talking about. The relevance of the gun depends on resolution of a question of fact: Was the gun used in the crime? This question, which is viewed as an issue of "authenticity," would ordinarily be given ultimately to the jury, and the judge's role is only to ensure that the prosecutor offers evidence "sufficient to support a finding" that the gun was used in the crime. Almost always such proof is offered first, but the judge can admit the gun first and then later in trial admit the authenticating proof (evidence sufficient to show that the gun was used in the charged crime). Most issues of authenticity, such as whether a document is genuine or not, are viewed in a similar way. See generally the provisions in Article IX of the Rules (Chapter 13, infra). A similar question arises when a lay witness testifies: Whether she has sufficient personal knowledge to testify raises a question of relevancy that depends on whether a fact exists, and again the judge plays a screening role and ordinarily the jury ultimately decides whether she has knowledge. Again Rule 104(b) is applicable.

Weight and sufficiency distinguished. To revisit a point made before (section A2, supra), decisions on simple relevancy differ from weighing evidence: As a matter of timing, a judge decides whether evidence is relevant when it is offered. As a matter of function, a judge assesses relevancy in deciding whether to admit or exclude. In contrast, the factfinder (the jury if there is one) *assesses* (or "weighs") the evidence at the end of the case, performing this function for the purpose of deciding the case on the merits. But determining relevancy and weighing the evidence both involve assessing probative worth, and both involve drawing inferences (usually inductive inferences, like deciding whether conduct indicates flight and whether flight indicates consciousness of guilt). Moreover, both involve thinking about the evidence in light of reason and experience. Issues of conditional relevance are bound up in weighing the evidence, in deciding how and whether one item of proof affects another.

And let us remember as well that relevancy is not sufficiency: Issues of relevance are not scrutinized to ensure that each item of proof meets the overall standard of persuasion that applies—normally in civil cases requiring claimants to satisfy the preponderance standard and in criminal cases requiring prosecutors to prove crimes beyond a reasonable doubt. The evidence as a whole must satisfy the applicable standard for each element of a claim, defense, or charged crime, but each item need only increase the probability that some consequential point is true.

Despite this account, distinguishing conditional relevancy under FRE 104(b) from "simple" relevancy and other questions of admissibility under FRE 104(a) can be hard. Consider this problem.

■ PROBLEM 2-I. Raid on the Cedar Woods Apartment

After receiving reports about suspicious activities in the Cedar Woods apartment complex, Agent Garber raids one of the units and arrests the tenant Joseph Terry on drug charges. Garber had already come across Terry's name when speaking to Tanya Wilson, a cocaine user arrested in a disturbance in a tavern downtown. Wilson had told Garber she bought cocaine from Terry, and offered to help get Terry if the prosecutor would drop charges against Wilson herself.

In Terry's apartment, Garber found six kilograms of cocaine (street value of $148,000), and paraphernalia commonly used to prepare crack cocaine. He also found two other items. First, in a kitchen drawer was an apparent ledger written in coded language reflecting sales of "packs," "basketballs," and "quarter pounders with cheese," with dates and apparent customer names and prices. Second, on Terry's computer Garber found a retained copy of an apparent email to Terry's brother-in-law, Bryan Chambers (a lawyer) containing this statement: "I've been selling some stuff, and I think the narcs are looking for me. I might need your help. Hey don't say anything to my sister Karen, since she wouldn't understand. Tell me quick what I should do or who I should see, OK? Joe."

After the raid, Wilson phoned Garber and told him "I don't want to talk to you any more, see, because I got this call from Terry that was on my answering machine and I'm scared." Garber persuades Wilson to keep the call. He goes to her place and makes a recording of it. In the call, a male voice says: "Tanya you bitch you better watch your backside. I fixed you up when you had the shakes and then you turned snitch. If I see you within a mile of the cops you better hope your insurance is paid up. You damn whore you know who this is, and what happens to people like you." Garber traces the call to a discontinued cellphone account, but cannot link it to Terry.

At Terry's trial, three evidence issues arise:

(1) The prosecutor offers the ledger, with expert testimony interpreting the coded expressions as referring to drug transactions. In a hearing in aid of objection, Terry testifies "I never saw that before. One of my friends must have put it there on Saturday when I had a party." The defense lawyer argues thus: "Your honor, this can't come in. They haven't linked it to my client and it's not relevant unless he had something to do with it. Under FRE 104(a), you have to exclude because it's not admissible." The prosecutor replies, "Your Honor, it's up to the jury to decide this point under FRE 104(b), and there's enough so a reasonable jury could find that this is Terry's record."

(2) The prosecutor offers the retained copy of the email to Bryan Chambers, arguing that "selling stuff" is Terry's "admission that he's in the drug trade." The defense argues thus: "This email is a confidential communication to a lawyer seeking advice. The privilege question is for the court to decide under FRE 104(a)." The prosecutor replies: "Your Honor, it's not privileged. He never consulted Chambers. He was writing to a brother-in-law to vent. Anyway the jury should decide whether the privilege applies. Whether Terry was consulting Chambers to get legal advice is a fact question, and juries decide fact questions under FRE 104(b)."

(3) The prosecutor offers the recording of the threatening phonecall from Tanya Wilson's phone: "Garber was working with Wilson, but we aren't calling her to the stand. I think the jury should hear what Mr. Terry said in this message. It shows consciousness of guilt." The defense replies: "This is prejudicial because it will make the jury angry at my client, and who knows why someone was threatening Ms. Wilson? They can't prove my client was talking about this case, or even that it's him on the phone. You should rule this matter irrelevant and prejudicial under FRE 401-403, and this is your call to make as a matter of admissibility under FRE 104(a)." The prosecutor replies: "This is like the drug ledger. Whether it's linked to Mr. Terry is for the jury to decide under FRE 104(b) as a matter of conditional relevancy."

In all three arguments, the defense says the court should resolve the issues as matters of admissibility under FRE 104(a), and the prosecutor asks the court to admit the evidence in and let the jury resolve remaining issues as matters of relevance conditioned on facts as contemplated by FRE 104(b). Whose position is stronger, and why?

■ NOTES ON CONDITIONAL RELEVANCE

1. For item (1) (drug ledger), we have answers. Whether to admit the ledger raises a question of conditional relevancy under FRE 104(b)—an "authentication" question. Is it really a drug ledger? Is it sufficiently connected to Terry to be considered evidence of his involvement in the charged offense? Like the gun Lieutenant Goldbloom found near the murder victim in Chapter 1, the judge is a screening agent: He can admit the item if the circumstances (finding it in the kitchen drawer) and other proof (perhaps expert testimony interpreting the ledger as reflecting drug transactions) are *sufficient to support a jury finding* that Terry prepared or was connected with the ledger. If this foundational proof is not sufficient, the judge excludes. If the judge admits the ledger, Terry can still urge the jury to disregard it by testifying that he "never saw it before" and a friends "must have put it there." See FRE 104(e), providing that the objecting party side can "introduce before the jury evidence that is relevant to the weight or credibility of other evidence."

2. Instead of admitting the ledger, the judge might insist on more evidence that Terry prepared it—perhaps expert testimony that it was in Terry's handwriting. See FRE 901(b)(3). Under FRE 104(b), the court can insist that further proof be offered first or can admit the ledger provisionally, "subject to being connected up" later (to use the common phrase). Thus Rule 104(b) requires foundational proof, but also says the court can admit evidence "on the condition that [foundational] proof be introduced later." If the judge admits the ledger, but the expert can't say Terry wrote it, the court could "strike" the ledger or grant a mistrial. See FRE 104(a)(1)(A) (objector may move "to strike").

3. For item (2) (the email), we also know the answer. Whether the attorney-client privilege covers it turns on in part on whether it was made for purpose of obtaining legal advice. Terry says it was, but the prosecutor claims Terry was just writing to his brother-in-law as a friend. The judge resolves these matters under FRE 104(a), which states that the court must decide "any preliminary question about whether . . . a privilege exists."

4. Authentication questions, like whether Terry is connected to the ledger, go to juries because we think juries are capable of resolving them by exercising common sense, and because such questions are very closely connected to the merits of the case. Privilege questions, like whether the email fits the attorney-client privilege, go to judges because they are quintessentially questions of "law," and are loaded with policy considerations that are separate from the merits, and juries are not well equipped to answer them.

5. Item (3) (the phone threat) is hard because it seems to have one foot in each of the two camps. It looks like an authentication issue under FRE 104(b), because we are asking whether Terry is connected to it, so it resembles issues raised by the drug ledger. Did Terry make the threatening call, and does it relate to the charges against him? In this sense, we have another a question of conditional relevancy under FRE 104(b). But it also looks like an issue of admissibility under FRE 104(a), because things that Terry said can be admitted against him, or things he put another person up to saying, but not things that just anybody said. Courts have struggled with such questions. See Jakola v. Eisenberg, 781 A.2d 77 (N.J. Super. 2001) (in malpractice suit against dentist Eisenberg, plaintiff offered her new dentist's testimony describing a call from someone who identified himself as "Dr. Eisenberg" and referred to plaintiff by name and to the crown that he said he placed on her tooth; caller told new dentist, who was planning to testify for plaintiff, to "look at things differently," saying he could "make things really difficult for you" and using profane language; judge admitted evidence of the call after a preliminary hearing, and reviewing court approves; contents and substance made out a "prima facie case" that defendant was the caller, and jury could so conclude); Sweet v. Roy, 801 A.2d 694, 705 (Vt. 2002) (in suit against owners of trailer park, defendants wanted to prove threatening phonecalls from plaintiff's ex-boyfriend expressing in "aggressive and profane" terms an intent to harm defendant for "harassing and inflicting distress," but court could exclude this proof because judge can require a "foundational showing" that ex-boyfriend acted as "agent for plaintiff," and defendants offered only recordings and plaintiff's testimony that she "talked to the ex-boyfriend because he is her child's father," which did not show she knew about or authorized the threats). Because of the dangers of such evidence, the better argument is that the judge should resolve the matter under FRE 104(a).

6. Regardless whether the matter is governed by FRE 104(a) or 104(b), the judge decides issues of simple relevancy under FRE 401, and whether to exclude evidence prejudicial or misleading under FRE 403. So the judge decides whether a drug ledger (if that's what it is) tends to prove Terry's guilt, whether the email to the lawyer tends to prove guilt, and whether the threat (if it came from Terry) tends to prove guilt. If the judge decides these items are relevant, he can still exclude if prejudicial impact outweighs probative worth under FRE 403.

7. Issues of conditional relevance connect with what modern commentators call the problem of "conjunction." The fortunes of a litigant may depend on testimony by two witnesses, thus on the "conjunction" of what they say. Here the relevance of what each says might be said to be conditional on what the other says. Consider an example drawn from the ACN: *X* sues *Y* on a debt, and *X*'s case depends on proving that *Y* admitted the debt by letter. The Note describes this situation as one of conditional relevance, and the judge will likely admit testimony by *X* that he received the letter, as well as testimony by some third person *Z* that *Y* wrote or authorized it. If the proof shows a 60 percent likelihood that *X* received such a letter and a 60 percent likelihood that *Y* authorized it, should the jury find for *X*? The "product rule" describes the "conjoint" probability that two independent events occur: If there is a 50 percent likelihood of getting a head or a tail on a single coin flip, the product rule tells us that there is a 25 percent likelihood of getting a head (or a tail) twice in a row (50 percent x 50 percent). In the suit of *X* against *Y*, applying this rule suggests that the evidence favoring *X* reaches only a likelihood of 36 percent. See generally Nesson, The Evidence or the Event? On Judicial Proof and the Acceptability of Verdicts, 98 Harv. L. Rev. 1357, 1388 (1985) (here jury does "consider the conjunction of the two accounts" in deciding the issue) (probability of one times probability of the other). One commentator argued that it is simply untrue that proof of one of two interdependent points is irrelevant absent proof of the other. See Ball, The Myth of Conditional Relevancy, 14 Ga. L. Rev. 435 (1980) (arguing that unless trier determines that one of two necessary facts does not exist, evidence tending to prove one is relevant, and FRE 104(b) should be repealed).

THE RELEVANCE OF PROBABILISTIC ANALYSIS

The task of the trier of fact is to determine whether plaintiff in a civil suit has proved his case by a preponderance of the evidence, which is usually defined as establishing that the necessary facts are more probably true than not. The task in a criminal trial is to determine whether the prosecutor has proved guilt beyond a reasonable doubt, which also suggests probability but at a much higher level.

Seldom does the degree of probability suggested by evidence lend itself readily to mathematical expression or attain numeric precision. But probabilistic evidence is sometimes offered, and in certain kinds of cases (such as discrimination suits and litigation over paternity) mathematical proof has become common.

PEOPLE v. COLLINS

California Supreme Court
438 P.2d 33 (Cal. 1968)

SULLIVAN, J.

We deal here with the novel question whether evidence of mathematical probability has been properly introduced and used by the prosecution in a criminal case. While we discern no inherent incompatibility between the disciplines of law and mathematics and intend no general disapproval or disparagement of the latter as an auxiliary in the fact-finding processes of the former, we cannot uphold the technique employed in the instant case. As we explain in detail infra, the testimony as to mathematical probability infected the case with fatal error and distorted the jury's traditional role of determining guilt or innocence according to long-settled rules. Mathematics, a veritable sorcerer in our computerized society, while assisting the trier of fact in the search for truth, must not cast a spell over him. We conclude that on the record before us defendant should not have had his guilt determined by the odds and that he is entitled to a new trial. We reverse the judgment.

A jury found defendant Malcolm Ricardo Collins and his wife defendant Janet Louise Collins guilty of second degree robbery. Malcolm appeals from the judgment of conviction. Janet has not appealed.

On June 18, 1964, about 11:30 A.M. Mrs. Juanita Brooks, who had been shopping, was walking home along an alley in the San Pedro area of the City of Los Angeles. She was pulling behind her a wicker basket carryall containing groceries and had her purse on top of the packages. She was using a cane. As she stooped down to pick up an empty carton, she was suddenly pushed to the ground by a person whom she neither saw nor heard approach. She was stunned by the fall and felt some pain. She managed to look up and saw a young woman running from the scene. According to Mrs. Brooks the latter appeared to weigh about 145 pounds, was wearing "something dark," and had hair "between a dark blond and a light blond," but lighter than the color of defendant Janet Collins' hair as it appeared at trial. Immediately after the incident, Mrs. Brooks discovered that her purse, containing between $35 and $40, was missing.

About the same time as the robbery, John Bass, who lived on the street at the end of the alley, was in front of his house watering his lawn. His attention was attracted by "a lot of crying and screaming" coming from the alley. As he looked in that direction, he saw a woman run out of the alley and enter a yellow automobile parked across the street from him. He was unable to give the make of the car. The car started off immediately and pulled wide around another parked vehicle so that in the narrow street it passed within six feet of Bass. The latter then saw that it was being driven by a male Negro, wearing a mustache and beard. At the trial Bass identified defendant as the driver of the yellow automobile. However, an attempt was made to impeach his identification by his admission that at the preliminary hearing he testified to an uncertain identification at the police lineup shortly after the attack on Mrs. Brooks, when defendant was beardless.

In his testimony Bass described the woman who ran from the alley as a Caucasian, slightly over five feet tall, of ordinary build, with her hair in a dark blond ponytail, and wearing dark clothing. He further testified that her ponytail was "just like" one which Janet had in a police photograph taken on June 22, 1964.

On the day of the robbery, Janet was employed as a housemaid in San Pedro. Her employer testified that she had arrived for work at 8:50 A.M. and that defendant had picked her up in a light yellow car[2] about 11:30 A.M. On that day, according to the witness, Janet was wearing her hair in a blonde ponytail but lighter in color than it appeared at trial.[3] There was evidence from which it could be inferred that defendants had ample time to drive from Janet's place of employment and participate in the robbery. Defendants testified, however, that they went directly from her employer's house to the home of friends, where they remained for several hours.

In the morning of June 22, Los Angeles Police Officer Kinsey, who was investigating the robbery, went to defendants' home. He saw a yellow Lincoln automobile with an off-white top in front of the house. He talked with defendants. Janet, whose hair appeared to be a dark blonde, was wearing it in a ponytail. Malcolm did not have a beard. The officer explained to them that he was investigating a robbery specifying the time and place; that the victim had been knocked down and her purse snatched; and that the person responsible was a female Caucasian with blonde hair in a ponytail who had left the scene in a yellow car driven by a male Negro. He requested that defendants accompany him to the police station at San Pedro and they did so. There, in response to police inquiries as to defendants' activities at the time of the robbery, Janet stated, according to Officer Kinsey, that her husband had picked her up at her place of employment at 1 P.M. and that they had then visited at the home of friends in Los Angeles. Malcolm confirmed this. Defendants were detained for an hour or two, were photographed but not booked, and were eventually released and driven home by the police.

Late in the afternoon of the same day, Officer Kinsey, while driving home from work in his own car, saw defendants riding in their yellow Lincoln. Although the transcript fails to disclose what prompted such action Kinsey proceeded to place them under surveillance and eventually followed them home. He called for assistance and arranged to meet other police officers in the vicinity of defendants' home. Kinsey took a position in the rear of the premises. The other officers, who were in uniform and had arrived in a marked police car, approached defendants' front door. As they did so, Kinsey saw defendant Malcolm Collins run out the back door toward a rear fence and disappear behind a tree. Meanwhile the other officers emerged with Janet Collins whom they had placed under arrest. A search was made for Malcolm who was found in a closet of a neighboring home and also arrested. Defendants were again taken to the police station, were kept in custody for 48 hours, and were again released without any charges being made against them.

---

[2]Other witnesses variously described the car as yellow, as yellow with an off-white top, and yellow with an egg-shell white top. The car was also described as being medium to large in size. Defendant drove a car at or near the times in question which was a Lincoln with a yellow body and a white top.

[3]There are inferences which may be drawn from the evidence that Janet attempted to alter the appearance of her hair after June 18. Janet denies that she cut, colored or bleached her hair at any time after June 18, and a number of witnesses supported her testimony.

Officer Kinsey interrogated defendants separately on June 23 while they were in custody and testified to their statements . . . . According to the officer, Malcolm stated that he sometimes wore a beard but that he did not wear a beard on June 18 (the day of the robbery), having shaved it off on June 2, 1964.[5] He also explained two receipts for traffic fines totaling $35 paid on June 19, which receipts had been found on his person, by saying that he used funds won in a gambling game at a labor hall. Janet, on the other hand, said that the $35 used to pay the fines had come from her earnings.[6]

On July 9, 1964, defendants were again arrested and were booked for the first time. While they were in custody and awaiting the preliminary hearing, Janet requested to talk with Officer Kinsey. There followed a lengthy conversation during the first part of which Malcolm was not present. During this time Janet expressed concern about defendant and inquired as to what the outcome would be if it appeared that she committed the crime and Malcolm knew nothing about it. In general she indicated a wish that defendant be released from any charges because of his prior criminal record and that if someone must be held responsible, she alone would bear the guilt. The officer told her that no assurances could be given, that if she wanted to admit responsibility disposition of the matter would be in the hands of the court and that if she committed the crime and defendant knew nothing about it the only way she could help him would be by telling the truth. Defendant was then brought into the room and participated in the rest of the conversation. The officer asked to hear defendant's version of the matter, saying that he believed defendant was at the scene. However, neither Janet nor defendant confessed or expressly made damaging admissions although constantly urged by the investigating officer to make truthful statements. On several occasions defendant denied that he knew what had gone on in the alley. On the other hand, the whole tone of the conversation evidenced a strong consciousness of guilt on the part of both defendants who appeared to be seeking the most advantageous way out . . . . [S]ome parts of the foregoing conversation were testified to by Officer Kinsey and in addition a tape recording of the entire conversation was introduced in evidence and played to the jury.

At the seven-day trial the prosecution experienced some difficulty in establishing the identities of the perpetrators of the crime. The victim could not identify Janet and had never seen defendant. The identification by the witness Bass, who observed the girl run out of the alley and get into the automobile, was incomplete as to Janet and may have been weakened as to defendant.

---

[5]Evidence as to defendant's beard and mustache is conflicting. Defense witnesses appeared to support defendant's claims that he had shaved his beard on June 2. There was testimony that on June 19 when defendant appeared in court to pay fines on another matter he was bearded. By June 22 the beard had been removed.

[6]The source of the $35, being essentially the same amount as the $35 to $40 reported by the victim as having been in her purse when taken from her the day before the fines were paid, was a significant factor in the prosecution's case. Other evidence disclosed that defendant and Janet were married on June 2, 1964, at which time they had only $12, a portion of which was spent on a trip to Tiajuana. Since the marriage defendant had not worked, and Janet's earnings were not more than $12 a week, if that much.

There was also evidence, introduced by the defense, that Janet had worn light-colored clothing on the day in question, but both the victim and Bass testified that the girl they observed had worn dark clothing.

In an apparent attempt to bolster the identifications, the prosecutor called an instructor of mathematics at a state college. Through this witness he sought to establish that, assuming the robbery was committed by a Caucasian woman with a blond ponytail who left the scene accompanied by a Negro with a beard and mustache, there was an overwhelming probability that the crime was committed by any couple answering such distinctive characteristics. The witness testified, in substance, to the "product rule," which states that the probability of the joint occurrence of a number of *mutually independent* events is equal to the product of the individual probabilities that each of the events will occur.[8] *Without presenting any statistical evidence whatsoever in support of the probabilities for the factors selected,* the prosecutor then proceeded to have the witness *assume* probability factors for the various characteristics which he deemed to be shared by the guilty couple and all other couples answering to such distinctive characteristics.[10]

Applying the product rule to his own factors the prosecutor arrived at a probability that there was but one chance in 12 million that any couple possessed the distinctive characteristic of the defendants. Accordingly, under this theory, it was to be inferred that there could be but one chance in 12 million that defendants were innocent and that another equally distinctive couple actually committed the robbery. Expanding on what he had thus purported to suggest as a hypothesis, the prosecutor offered the completely unfounded and improper testimonial assertion that, in his opinion, the factors he had assigned were "conservative estimates" and that, in reality "the chances of anyone else

---

[8]In the example employed for illustrative purposes at the trial, the probability of rolling one die and coming up with a "2" is 1/6, that is, any one of the six faces of a die has one chance in six of landing face up on any particular roll. The probability of rolling two "2's" in succession is 1/6 × 1/6, or 1/36, that is, on only one occasion out of 36 double rolls (or the roll of two dice), will the selected number land face up on each roll or die.

[10]Although the prosecutor insisted that the factors he used were only for illustrative purposes—to demonstrate how the probability of the occurrence of mutually independent factors affected the probability that they would occur together—he nevertheless attempted to use factors which he personally related to the distinctive characteristics of defendants. In his argument to the jury he invited the jurors to apply their own factors, and asked defense counsel to suggest what the latter would deem as reasonable. The prosecutor himself proposed the individual probabilities set out in the table below. Although the transcript of the examination of the mathematics instructor and the information volunteered by the prosecutor at that time create some uncertainty as to precisely which of the characteristics the prosecutor assigned to the individual probabilities, he restated in his argument to the jury that they should be as follows:

Characteristic	*Individual probability*
A. Partly yellow automobile	1/10
B. Man with mustache	1/4
C. Girl with ponytail	1/10
D. Girl with blond hair	1/3
E. Negro man with beard	1/10
F. Interracial couple in car	1/1000

In his brief on appeal defendant agrees that the foregoing appeared on a table presented in the trial court.

besides these defendants being there, . . . having every similarity, . . . is somewhat like one in a billion."

Objections were timely made to the mathematician's testimony on the grounds that it was immaterial, that it invaded the province of the jury, and that it was based on unfounded assumptions. The objections were "temporarily overruled" and the evidence admitted subject to a motion to strike. When that motion was made at the conclusion of the direct examination, the court denied it, stating that the testimony had been received only for the "purpose of illustrating the mathematical probabilities of various matters, the possibilities for them occurring or re-occurring."

Both defendants took the stand in their own behalf. They denied any knowledge of or participation in the crime and stated that after Malcolm called for Janet at her employer's house they went directly to a friend's house in Los Angeles where they remained for some time. According to this testimony defendants were not near the scene of the robbery when it occurred. Defendant's friends testified to a visit by them "in the middle of June" although she could not recall the precise date. Janet further testified that certain inducements were held out to her during the July 9 interrogation on condition that she confess her participation.

Defendant makes two basic contentions before us: First, that the admission in evidence of the statements made by defendants while in custody on June 23 and July 9, 1964, constitutes reversible error . . . and second, that the introduction of evidence pertaining to the mathematical theory of probability and the use of the same by the prosecution during the trial was error prejudicial to defendant. We consider the latter claim first.

As we shall explain, the prosecution's introduction and use of mathematical probability statistics injected two fundamental prejudicial errors into the case: (1) The testimony itself lacked an adequate foundation both in evidence and in statistical theory; and (2) the testimony and the manner in which the prosecution used it distracted the jury from its proper and requisite function of weighing the evidence on the issue of guilt, encouraged the jurors to rely upon an engaging but logically irrelevant expert demonstration, foreclosed the possibility of an effective defense by an attorney apparently unschooled in mathematical refinements, and placed the jurors and defense counsel at a disadvantage in sifting relevant fact from inapplicable theory.

We initially consider the defects in the testimony itself. As we have indicated, the specific technique presented through the mathematician's testimony and advanced by the prosecutor to measure the probabilities in question suffered from two basic and pervasive defects—an inadequate evidentiary foundation and an inadequate proof of statistical independence. First, as to the foundation requirement, we find the record devoid of any evidence relating to any of the six individual probability factors used by the prosecutor and ascribed by him to the six characteristics as we have set them out in footnote 10, ante. To put it another way, the prosecution produced no evidence whatsoever showing, or from which it could be in any way inferred, that only one out of every ten cars which might have been at the scene of the robbery was partly yellow, that only one out of every four men who might have been there wore a mustache, that only one out of every ten girls who might have been there wore a ponytail, or that any of the other individual probability factors listed were even roughly accurate.[12]

The bare, inescapable fact is that the prosecution made no attempt to offer any such evidence. Instead, through leading questions having perfunctorily elicited from the witness the response that the latter could not assign a probability factor for the characteristics involved,[13] the prosecutor himself suggested what the various probabilities should be and these became the basis of the witness' testimony (see fn. 10, ante). It is a curious circumstance of this adventure in proof that the prosecutor not only made his own assertions of these factors in the hope that they were "conservative" but also in later argument to the jury invited the jurors to substitute their "estimates" should they wish to do so. We can hardly conceive of a more fatal gap in the prosecution's scheme of proof. A foundation for the admissibility of the witness' testimony was never even attempted to be laid, let alone established. His testimony was neither made to rest on his own testimonial knowledge nor presented by proper hypothetical questions based upon valid data in the record . . . .

But, as we have indicated, there was another glaring defect in the prosecution's technique, namely an inadequate proof of the statistical independence of the six factors. No proof was presented that the characteristics selected were mutually independent, even though the witness himself acknowledged that such condition was essential to the proper application of the "product rule" or "multiplication rule." To the extent that the traits or characteristics were not mutually independent (e.g., Negroes with beards and men with mustaches obviously represent overlapping categories[15]), the "product rule" would inevitably

---

[12]We seriously doubt that such evidence could ever be compiled since no statistician could possibly determine after the fact which cars, or which individuals, "might" have been present at the scene of the robbery; certainly there is no reason to suppose that the human and automotive populations of San Pedro, California, include all potential culprits—or, conversely, that all members of these populations are proper candidates for inclusion. Thus the sample from which the relevant probabilities would have to be derived is itself undeterminable. (See generally Yamane, Statistics, An Introductory Analysis (1964), ch. I.)

[13]The prosecutor asked the mathematics instructor:

> Now, let me see if you can be of some help to us with some independent factors, and you have some paper you may use. Your specialty does not equip you, I suppose, to give us some probability of such things as a yellow car as contrasted with any other kind of car, does it? . . . I appreciate the fact that you can't assign a probability for a car being yellow as contrasted to some other car, can you?

A. No, I couldn't.

[15]Assuming arguendo that factors *B* and *E* (see fn. 10, ante) were correctly estimated, nevertheless it is still arguable that most Negro men with beards also have mustaches (exhibit 3 herein, for instance, shows defendant with both a mustache and a beard, indeed in a hirsute continuum); if so, there is no basis for multiplying 1/4 by 1/10 to estimate the proportion of Negroes who wear beards and mustaches. Again, the prosecution's technique could never be meaningfully applied, since its accurate use would call for information as to the degree of interdependence among the six individual factors. Such information cannot be compiled, however, since the relevant samples necessarily remain unknown. (See fn. 10, ante.)

yield a wholly erroneous and exaggerated result even if all of the individual components had been determined with precision.

In the instant case, therefore, because of the aforementioned two defects—the inadequate evidentiary foundation and the inadequate proof of statistical independence—the technique employed by the prosecutor could only lead to wild conjecture without demonstrated relevancy to the issues presented. It acquired no redeeming quality from the prosecutor's statement that it was being used only "for illustrative purposes" since, as we shall point out, the prosecutor's subsequent utilization of the mathematical testimony was not confined within such limits.

We now turn to the second fundamental error caused by the probability testimony. Quite apart from our foregoing objections to the specific technique employed by the prosecution to estimate the probability in question, we think that the entire enterprise upon which the prosecution embarked, and which was directed to the objective of measuring the likelihood of a random couple possessing the characteristics allegedly distinguishing the robbers, was gravely misguided. At best, it might yield an estimate as to how infrequently bearded Negroes drive yellow cars in the company of blonde females with ponytails.

The prosecution's approach, however, could furnish the jury with absolutely no guidance on the crucial issue: *Of the admittedly few such couples, which one, if any, was guilty of committing this robbery?* Probability theory necessarily remains silent on that question, since no mathematical equation can prove beyond a reasonable doubt (1) that the guilty couple in fact possessed the characteristics described by the People's witnesses, or even (2) that only one couple possessing those distinctive characteristics could be found in the entire Los Angeles area.

As to the first inherent failing we observe that the prosecution's theory of probability rested on the assumption that the witnesses called by the People had conclusively established that the guilty couple possessed the precise characteristics relied upon by the prosecution. But no mathematical formula could ever establish beyond a reasonable doubt that the prosecution's witnesses correctly observed and accurately described the distinctive features which were employed to link defendants to the crime. Conceivably, for example, the guilty couple might have included a light-skinned Negress with bleached hair rather than a Caucasian blonde; or the driver of the car might have been wearing a false beard as a disguise; or the prosecution's witnesses might simply have been unreliable.[16]

The foregoing risks of error permeate the prosecution's circumstantial case. Traditionally, the jury weighs such risks in evaluating the credibility and probative value of trial testimony, but the likelihood of human error or of falsification obviously cannot be quantified; that likelihood must therefore be excluded from

[16]In the instant case, for instance, the victim could not state whether the girl had a ponytail, although the victim observed the girl as she ran away. The witness Bass, on the other hand, was sure that the girl whom he saw had a ponytail. The demonstration engaged in by the prosecutor also leaves no room for the possibility, although perhaps a small one, that the girl whom the victim and the witness observed was [not], in fact, the same girl.

any effort to assign a *number* to the probability of guilt or innocence. Confronted with an equation which purports to yield a numerical index of probable guilt, few juries could resist the temptation to accord disproportionate weight to that index; only an exceptional juror, and indeed only a defense attorney schooled in mathematics, could successfully keep in mind the fact that the probability computed by the prosecution can represent, at best, the likelihood that a random couple would share the characteristics testified to by the People's witnesses—*not necessarily the characteristics of the actually guilty couple.*

As to the second inherent failing in the prosecution's approach, even assuming that the first failing could be discounted, the most a mathematical computation could ever yield would be a measure of the probability that a random couple would possess the distinctive features in question. In the present case, for example, the prosecution attempted to compute the probability that a random couple would include a bearded Negro, a blonde girl with a ponytail, and a partly yellow car; the prosecution urged that this probability was no more than one in 12 million. Even accepting this conclusion as arithmetically accurate, however, one still could not conclude that the Collinses were probably the guilty couple. On the contrary, as we explain in the Appendix, the prosecution's figures actually imply a likelihood of over 40 percent that the Collinses could be "duplicated" by at least *one other couple who might equally have committed the San Pedro robbery.* Urging that the Collinses be convicted on the basis of evidence which logically establishes no more than this seems as indefensible as arguing for the conviction of *X* on the ground that a witness saw either *X* or *X*'s twin commit the crime.

Again, few defense attorneys, and certainly few jurors, could be expected to comprehend this basic flaw in the prosecution's analysis. Conceivably even the prosecutor erroneously believed that his equation established a high probability that no other bearded Negro in the Los Angeles area drove a yellow car accompanied by a ponytailed blonde. In any event, although his technique could demonstrate no such thing, he solemnly told the jury that he had supplied mathematical proof of guilt.

Sensing the novelty of that notion, the prosecutor told the jurors that the traditional idea of proof beyond a reasonable doubt represented "the most hackneyed, stereotyped, trite, misunderstood concept in criminal law." He sought to reconcile the jury to the risk that, under his "new math" approach to criminal jurisprudence, "on some rare occasion . . . an innocent person may be convicted." "Without taking that risk," the prosecution continued, "life would be intolerable . . . because . . . there would be immunity *for the Collinses, for people who chose not to be employed to go down and push old* ladies down and take their money and be immune because how could we ever be sure they are the ones who did it?"

In essence this argument of the prosecutor was calculated to persuade the jury to convict defendants whether or not they were convinced of their guilt to a moral certainty and beyond a reasonable doubt. Undoubtedly the jurors were unduly impressed by the mystique of the mathematical demonstration but were unable to assess its relevancy or value. Although we make no appraisal of the proper applications of mathematical techniques in the proof of facts, we have strong feelings that such applications, particularly in a criminal case, must be critically examined in view of the substantial unfairness to a defendant which may result from ill conceived techniques with which the trier of fact is not technically equipped to cope. We feel that the technique employed in the case before us falls into the latter category.

We conclude that the court erred in admitting over defendant's objection the evidence pertaining to the mathematical theory of probability and in denying defendant's motion to strike such evidence. The case was apparently a close one. The jury began its deliberations at 2:46 P.M. on November 24, 1964, and retired for the night at 7:46 P.M.; the parties stipulated that a juror could be excused for illness and that a verdict could be reached by the remaining 11 jurors; the jury resumed deliberations the next morning at 8:40 A.M. and returned verdicts at 11:58 A.M. after five ballots had been taken. In the light of the closeness of the case, which as we have said was a circumstantial one, there is a reasonable likelihood that the result would have been more favorable to defendant if the prosecution had not urged the jury to render a probabilistic verdict. In any event, we think that under the circumstances the "trial by mathematics" so distorted the role of the jury and so disadvantaged counsel for the defense, as to constitute in itself a miscarriage of justice. After an examination of the entire cause, including the evidence, we are of the opinion that it is reasonably probable that a result more favorable to defendant would have been reached in the absence of the above error. The judgment against defendant must therefore be reversed.

In view of the foregoing conclusion, we deem it unnecessary to consider whether the admission of defendants' extrajudicial statements constitutes error....

The judgment is reversed.

APPENDIX

[The court presents a mathematical demonstration that *if* we know that *one* couple exists in a city of about 12 million with all the characteristics noted in the case, whose scarcity is described by the numbers assumed by the prosecutor, *then* there is a 41% probability that a *second* couple also exists in the city with those characteristics. If all we know about the defendants, then, is that they were in Los Angeles and have the characteristics of the guilty couple, the calculations cannot prove guilt beyond a reasonable doubt, and "imply a very substantial likelihood" that another couple did it.]

TRAYNOR, C.J., and PETERS, TOBRINER, MOSK, and BURKE, J.J., concur.

MCCOMB, J.
I dissent. I would affirm the judgment in its entirety.

NOTES ON *COLLINS* AND THE MISUSE OF PROBABILITIES

1. The Court in *Collins* makes important technical criticisms of the prosecutor's mathematical theory and its application. The court also raises policy-based objections that apply even if the technical problems could be overcome. What are these objections?

2. For a moment, forget the policy-based objections. Assume the identical case of *Collins-2* arises, but now the prosecutor has proof of the relative frequency of the qualities of the guilty couple and shows they are independent. He makes the same statistical argument. In *Collins*, the court tells us the argument is mathematically misconceived. Why? In thinking about it, consider a parlor trick. The wizard puts three complete decks of cards in a hopper and mixes them. Blindfolded, he draws a card, which turns out to be the Queen of Hearts. He replaces it and mixes the cards, and (blindfolded) draws a second card. Lo, it too is the Queen of Hearts. His patter runs as follows:

> The 156 cards in the hopper make three complete decks, so the proportion of hearts and queens is the same that we find in a single deck. The odds of drawing a heart are one in four because a quarter of the cards in each deck are hearts. And the odds of drawing a Queen are one in 13 because each suit has 13 cards, only one of which is a Queen.
>
> Knowing we drew a heart tells us nothing about the likelihood that we drew a Queen. The reason is that even among hearts we still have only one chance in 13 of getting the Queen. And conversely, knowing we drew a Queen tells us nothing about the likelihood that we drew a heart. The reason is that even among Queens we have only one chance in four of getting a heart. In short, being a heart and being a Queen are independent qualities.
>
> So what's the probability that we will draw a Queen of Hearts? Easy: It may be calculated by the product rule, and it comes to 1/52, which is 1/4 times 1/13.
>
> Now, you just saw me draw the Queen of Hearts twice in a row. That astonishing feat was not accidental, and only the wizard can do it. There's only one chance in 52 of drawing such a card, so there's only one chance in 52 that the Queen of Hearts I picked on the second draw is a *different card* from the one I picked on the first draw. Imagine getting the same card twice. Try it if you think it's easy.

Isn't this patter similar to the argument in *Collins*? Admittedly it was a coincidence (perhaps magic) that the wizard drew a Queen of Hearts twice in a row. But the likelihood that he drew a different Queen of Hearts the second time is 2/3, isn't it? (Given three decks and replacement of the first draw, there were three Queens of Hearts in the hopper each time.) So when he said the likelihood is only 1/52 that the second card was different, he was exaggerating, if not just plain wrong.

When the wizard got 1/52 with the product rule, what does it describe? Doesn't it describe the same kind of thing that 1/12,000,000 describes in *Collins?* And just as 1/52 in the parlor trick does *not* accurately describe the likelihood that the wizard drew a different card the second time, so 1/12,000,000 in *Collins* does not accurately describe the likelihood that defendants are different from the culprits.

3. The Appendix in *Collins,* summarized at the end of the case, addresses the problem of distribution. Even if a particular outcome is likely half the time, it does not follow that this predicted frequency will occur in a particular series of events or sample. Maybe half the coin tosses produce heads, but in any series of ten tosses we might get heads four times or even ten times, or not at all. In *Collins,* if the estimates are taken as describing the frequency of the observed characteristics in the known universe, they do not necessarily describe the frequency of those characteristics in Los Angeles. In one population of 12 million couples, we might find two or three couples matching the description of the culprits; in another, we might find none. The Appendix says there is a 41% chance of finding a second "magic couple," given that we know that one such couple exists. From this fact, we can calculate the likelihood that the Collinses are the culprits—that the people that the police arrested and charged are the very people who robbed the woman in the alley. The calculation suggests about a 70% probability that the Collinses were in fact guilty, which amply justifies the court's conclusion that the numbers do *not* prove anything we could comfortably call proof "beyond a reasonable doubt" even if we were willing to quantify this concept.

4. You might think nobody would be foolish enough to make the mistake the prosecutor made in *Collins,* but such mistakes do sometimes occur. See, e.g., Wilson v. State, 803 A.2d 1034, 1047 (Md. 2002) (reversing conviction of father for murder of infant son where prosecutor argued, on basis of statistical evidence of rarity of SIDS deaths and fact that defendant's other infant son had also died of SIDS, that the chance was only "1 in 10 million that the man sitting here is innocent").

5. In two settings, the product rule has smoother sailing. One involves use of DNA evidence, where prosecutors routinely show that the genetic profile of the defendant, measured by analyzing samples of blood or other fluid or tissue, matches the genetic profile of the apparent culprit, measured by analyzing samples from the crime scene. Here prosecutors routinely offer proof of the probability that these characteristics would be found in the general population. See, e.g., State v. Belken, 633 N.W.2d 786, 790, 799-801 (Iowa 2001) (in trial for kidnapping and sexual abuse, admitting evidence that defendant's DNA matched that of sample found at scene, and there was "a random match probability of 1 in 431 billion"). As in *Collins,* such probabilities describe scarcity, and do *not* describe the probability that defendant is guilty, or even the probability that he left the sample found at the scene. The other setting in which statistical evidence is routinely accepted is paternity cases, where a "match" between the profile of the paternal gene in the child and the genes of the defendant generates a similar statistic: "Only one in ten million men chosen at random would have this genetic profile." In this setting, courts *also* admit expert testimony describing the "probability of paternity," in which essentially an expert testifies as follows: "Based on these probabilities, we can say that there is a 97 percent probability that defendant is the father." See, e.g., Child Support Enforcement Agency v. Doe, 51 P.3d 366 (Haw. 2002) (99.96 percent probability of paternity). We revisit these issues in Chapter 9D, infra.

6. On the problem of *Collins*, see McCord, A Primer for the Nonmathematically Inclined on Mathematical Evidence in Criminal Cases: *People v. Collins* and Beyond, 47 Wash. & Lee L. Rev. 741 (1990).

■ PROBLEM 2-J. The Exploding Tire

Herb Lewis installs tires and batteries for the Auto Service Center operated by Nationwide Mercantile. One day he begins to mount four snow tires on a car. He finishes three and places the fourth on the wheel rim. Inflating it, he watches the bead rise along the inner edges of the rim, waiting for the "pop" when it would jump and firmly seat itself in the lip of the rim. This time the bead strikes the lip and the tire explodes, sending Herb to the emergency room with serious injuries. Len Small, manager of the Service Center, gathered up the burst tire and sent it to be tested by Failsafe Automotive Laboratory.

Herb sues Grather Tire Company, alleging that it made the tire and it was defective. During his case-in-chief, Herb seeks to establish (1) through testimony by Len Small that Grather made the exploding tire, and (2) through testimony by Michael Treaver (who tested the tire Failsafe got from Small) that the tire was defective. Unfortunately, Small did not note the markings on the tire, and Treaver failed to record them in his report, so nobody knows who made the exploding tire.

Herb seeks to elicit from Small that Grather made 80 percent of the tires at the Service Center, and that four other manufacturers account for the remaining 20 percent in about equal proportion. Grather objects, arguing that the court should not permit "gambling odds" testimony and that "mere numbers" cannot support a verdict.

Should Small and Treaver be allowed to testify? If there is no other proof that Grather made the tire that injured Herb, should such testimony suffice to take the issue to the jury?

■ NOTES ON PROBABILISTIC PROOF IN CIVIL CASES

1. In civil litigation, the most natural way to explain preponderance of the evidence involves saying that the party bearing that burden must show that the matters in question are "more likely so than not so." See generally Kevin

F. O'Malley, Jay E. Grenig & Hon. William C. Lee, Federal Jury Practice and Instructions §104.01 (6th ed. 2014) (using that phrase). Of course "more likely so than not so" stops short of quantifying a probability. Arguably it means the evidence "preponderates" even if it *just barely* favors the party with the burden—a layperson might express the notion as a 51 percent probability (or "odds" of 51:49). If this probability satisfies the standard, should Herb Lewis get his case to the jury? The indicated answer is Yes, and yet we are not comfortable with it.

2. Recall the famous case of the two careless hunters, both of whom negligently fired guns. Sympathizing with the plaintiff because he could not show which one fired the shot that hurt him, the California court put the burden on each defendant to prove he did not cause the injury. See Summers v. Tice, 199 P.2d 1 (Cal. 1948). The idea in *Summers* found new life in theories of market-share liability and enterprise liability in cases like Sindell v. Abbott Laboratories, 607 P.2d 924 (Cal.) (market share; antimiscarriage drug DES), *cert. denied*, 449 U.S. 912 (1980), and Hall v. E.I. Du Pont De Nemours & Co., 345 F. Supp. 353 (E.D.N.Y. 1972) (enterprise; blasting caps). Under *Sindell*'s market-share liability theory, a plaintiff who sues makers of identical products may get a judgment against all, each to pay the percentage corresponding to its market share. Later the California court held that recovery is limited to the proportion of damages corresponding to the combined market share of the defendants. Brown v. Superior Court, 751 P.2d 923 (Cal. 1988). Under *Hall*'s enterprise liability theory, a plaintiff who sues all or most makers of identical dangerous products may hold each liable on a theory of joint liability, and may win a judgment against each for full damages. If these cases are sound, we come to the broader question whether we should adopt similar theories in cases like The Exploding Tire, but we are not comfortable in extending these theories to such cases.

3. Here are arguments against letting the party with the burden of persuasion prevail on the basis of "numbers alone." Doing so, it is said, would be bad because it would

(a) lead to the unjust result that each of 100 similar plaintiffs win, even though the evidence means that defendant should be liable to only 80;

(b) permit recovery on proof inherently inferior to particularized evidence, which at least tends "directly" to establish critical points;

(c) misinterpret reality, because particularized proof usually exists and failing to offer it suggests not so much that it isn't there, but that it is unfavorable to the party relying on numerical probabilities;

(d) create an undesirable counterincentive, discouraging active pursuit of particularized proof;

(e) either (1) leave nothing for the jury to decide in the exercise of reason, so that it would have to be directed to find in accordance with the numbers (thus significantly and undesirably reducing its role), or (2) render the jury's work transparent, thus subjecting particular juries and the institution of jury trial to criticism, since observers will see that juries decide cases "by" or "against" the "odds";

(f) undesirably quantify the margin for error tolerated in the system, revealing that a civil claimant may recover nothing even when the probability is as high as .49 that he should have won;

(g) lessen public respect for and acceptance of courts by showing that they "gamble" on serious matters.

To most people, items (a) and (d) seem most persuasive—letting all prevail because most should seems wrong, and in most cases plaintiffs should be able to come up with something better than just naked statistics. Consider what a plaintiff in the position of Herb Louis should be able to find. Professor Nesson has argued strongly in favor of the argument summarized as (f)—that we want jury verdicts to be accepted as the truth, and *knowing* that a verdict merely represents a particular numerical probability would undermine our respect for juries. See generally Nesson, The Evidence or the Event? On Judicial Proof and the Acceptability of Verdicts, 98 Harv. L. Rev. 1357, 1389 (1985); Tribe, Trial by Mathematics: Precision and Ritual in the Legal Process, 84 Harv. L. Rev. 489 (1970); L. Cohen, The Probable and the Provable (1977); Kaye, The Paradox of the Gatecrasher and Other Stories, 1979 Ariz. St. L.J. 101.

4. Consider again the problem of "conjunction." Lewis must prove (a) that Grather made the tire and (b) that it was defective. He can prevail only by establishing the conjunction of both elements. Assume this time that the proof is *not* "nakedly" quantified, but the evidence suggests that each element is "probably" established: Small remembers that the exploded tire was made by Grather, but his credibility is impaired on cross; Treaver gives a hedged opinion that the tire was defective. If we quantified the evidence ourselves, we might conclude there is an 80 percent likelihood that Grather made the tire that Small sent to Failsafe and a 60 percent likelihood that it was defective. A jury might do the same thing, assigning numeric values to the proof. Who should win, Lewis or Grather?

(a) If, as seems true, the two probabilities are independent, doesn't the product rule tell us the "conjoint" likelihood of the two facts crucial to Lewis is only 48 percent? One astute commentator argues that juries do not do this kind of thing, but instead they (quite rightly) determine each element separately. Trials, it is argued, generate a kind of history:

> Any narrative history recounts the occurrence of many events. If we asked what the conjunctive probability of the narrative's independent elements is and dismissed the narrative when this probability was low, then we would have no history. We would constantly face a paradox. We could accept the truth of each event comprising the narrative but could not accept the narrative itself. We could believe every element that the historian recounted, but we could not believe the history as a whole.

Nesson, The Evidence or the Event? On Judicial Proof and the Acceptability of Verdicts, 98 Harv. L. Rev. 1357, 1389 (1985). Some have criticized the Nesson view. See Allen, Rationality, Mythology, and the "Acceptability of Verdicts"

Thesis, 66 B.U. L. Rev. 541 (1986); Cohen, The Costs of Acceptability: Blue Buses, Agent Orange, and Aversion to Statistical Evidence, 66 B.U. L. Rev. 563 (1986).

(b) The problem of conjunction also affects different items of proof directed at single elements in a case (item 7 in Notes on Conditional Relevance, supra). We "conjoin" separate items of proof relating to a single element in a case (thus diminishing aggregate likelihood) but *not* the proofs of separate elements in recognition of the reality that we could seldom resolve close cases if we conjoined even the separate elements.

CHAPTER 3

Hearsay

WHAT IS HEARSAY?

1. Underlying Theory: Risks and Safeguards

A simple definition. To put it as simply as it can be put, hearsay is an out-of-court statement offered to prove the matter asserted—or as lawyers usually say, "offered to prove the truth of the matter asserted."

Assume that plaintiff Abby wants to prove the blue car ran a red light, and she calls Faraway to testify that he heard the accident happen (but did not see it) and heard Bystander (who did see it) say shortly thereafter, "the blue car ran a red light." Here Bystander's statement is being offered (through Faraway's testimony) to prove what it asserts—that the blue car ran a red light—and it is hearsay.

The result would be the same if Abby calls Faraway to lay the foundation for a letter from Bystander, in which Bystander wrote that "the blue car ran the red light." The letter too is Bystander's out-of-court statement. It too is offered to prove what it asserts, and it too is hearsay. (Nor would things change if Faraway testified to what he read in the letter from Bystander, for again Bystander's out-of-court statement is offered to prove what it asserts. As you will see, there is an additional barrier to Faraway's testimonial account of what was in the letter. The Best Evidence doctrine would require the party seeking to show what the letter says to offer the letter itself, or an excuse for not producing it. See Chapter 14.)

Assume now that Bystander is called as a witness, and that a party seeks to show that the blue car ran a red light. If Bystander is asked on the stand whether the blue car had the light in its favor, he might say "no, the blue car ran the red light." Now there would be no hearsay objection, for Bystander is saying in court what he knows and remembers.[1]

The simple one-liner suggested above gets to the heart of the matter, and everyone would agree that Faraway's testimonial account of Bystander's statement in the example is hearsay. If you look for a moment at FRE 801(a) through (c), you will see that our one-liner agrees substantially with the more elaborate formal definition adopted by the Federal Rules. But the hearsay doctrine draws a line through a vast domain of human expression, and charts a course across a boundless sea of evidential uses of human behavior, so we must take the one-liner for what it is and not expect too much. It is "right," but like the definition of justice offered by Glaucon in the early going of Plato's *Republic* ("giving every man his due") it leaves much unsaid and is capable of mischief.

Our focus now is on recognizing hearsay, not on deciding whether it is admissible. Much that is hearsay is still admissible, and much that is not hearsay is not admissible anyway. Yet it is necessary to recognize hearsay because of the general principle, central to Anglo-American evidence law, that hearsay evidence is inadmissible unless it falls within one of many exceptions. Rule 802 states that general principle and hints at the exceptions. But for the time being our *only* concern is to get straight what hearsay is.

Reasons to exclude hearsay. Why exclude hearsay? Three reasons are usually given:

First and most important is the absence of cross-examination. Out-of-court statements are not subject to this truth-testing technique, at least when uttered, and in our example Bystander was not cross-examinable when he spoke. (Never mind for the moment the question whether *deferred* cross might be just as good—in other words, whether it would do to admit his statement in evidence if Bystander takes the stand and testifies at some point during the trial, and can then be questioned about his statement.) It is true that when Faraway testifies to what Bystander said, *Faraway* can be cross-examined, which is to say that *his in-court testimonial account* of what Bystander said can be probed, and this fact is valuable in itself. But it is Bystander on whom we rely when we take his statement as evidence of what happened at the intersection.

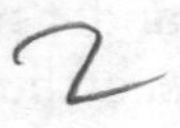

Second is the absence of demeanor evidence. The out-of-court declarant (Bystander in our example) is not under the gaze of the trier of fact, at least at the time he speaks, so the trier lacks those impressions and clues which voice, inflection, expression, and appearance convey. (Put aside for the moment the question whether *deferred* demeanor evidence might be adequate, if Bystander testifies so that his demeanor may be observed by the trier of fact when he is

[1]The hearsay objection might reappear, however, if for some reason Bystander answered the question by testifying, "I told Faraway that the blue car ran the red light." The problem is that once again Bystander's out-of-court statement is being offered as proof of what it asserts, even though *now* it is proved by Bystander's own testimony. Therefore, under our one-line definition Bystander's answer is hearsay. (The cure for the problem is to direct Bystander "to tell us what happened, and not what you told someone else," which he might not fully understand but could probably comply with.)

asked about his earlier statement.) Again it is true that Faraway's demeanor is observable by the trier and that this fact is helpful. But again we are relying on Bystander when we come to consider his statement as evidence.

Third is absence of the oath. Usually the out-of-court declarant was not under oath when he spoke (as Bystander was not, in our example), so the trier of fact has no indication that he felt any moral or legal obligation to speak the truth.[2] (Put off the question whether a *deferred* oath might suffice—whether it would be good enough to call Bystander and question him under oath at trial about his prior statement.) Of course Faraway is under oath, which helps to some extent, but still it is Bystander on whom we rely when we consider his statement.

These three reasons for the hearsay doctrine express a preference for live testimony over out-of-court statements. They also describe three safeguards in the trial process: Testifying witnesses all swear (or affirm) under penalty of perjury that they will tell the truth, their demeanor is on display for the trier of fact to observe, *and* they are subject to immediate cross-examination. Why should these safeguards matter? Remember that the hearsay issue disappears when Bystander takes the stand and testifies that "the blue car ran a red light." A testimonial account is obviously subject to the same human frailties as a substantially identical out-of-court statement. So why prefer the testimonial account?

The hearsay risks. The answer usually given is fourfold, which is to say that there are four "hearsay risks" associated with out-of-court statements that are substantially reduced (though certainly not removed entirely) by the safeguards of the trial process:

First is the risk of misperception. Maybe the car Bystander saw was not blue but silver; maybe what he thought to be a red light was glare from the sun; maybe the light changed after the blue car entered the intersection. The risk is not only a function of sensory capacity (such as acuity of vision) but of physical circumstance (such as distance and alignment of the sun) and of mental capacity and psychological condition. Even a well-situated witness with excellent vision can misinterpret or misunderstand what he sees, for lack of mental sharpness or because he is thinking of something else or is amused or expectant or angry or worried—in short, distracted or preoccupied.

Second is the risk of faulty memory. It is true that if Bystander related what he saw only moments afterwards, his statement is not likely to suffer in accuracy from failed or faulty memory. Indeed, memory problems increase with the time lapse between original observation and court appearance. But even

[2]He would have been sworn if his statement was in the form of an affidavit, executed in cooperation with a notary public. But affidavits as such do not fit a hearsay exception. To be sure, they have limited evidential use with motions for summary judgment and applications for warrants. And it is true that various kinds of certificates, which are like affidavits in being sworn out-of-court statements, have important evidential use in authenticating other documents. See FRE 902(1) through (3) and (8). But the hearsay doctrine makes affidavits generally inadmissible as proof of what they assert.

a statement that follows close on the heels of an event might be affected by something like a memory problem: If Bystander glanced at the traffic light moments before the incident, then looked elsewhere, and only *then* saw the blue car enter the intersection, his remark might reflect a conflation of memories of the earlier condition of the light and later path of the car. As to this risk, cross-examination may be useful in bringing out, eliminating, or reducing uncertainties.

Third is the risk of misstatement, often called the risk of "ambiguity" or "faulty narration." In saying the car "ran the red light," perhaps Bystander meant to say the light changed to red before the car made it across the intersection; he said "blue" but might have meant to describe the car as "silver"; maybe what he meant to say was that the blue car "did *not* run a red light." As to this risk, trial safeguards seem truly useful: Cross-examination can get at the limits and intended meaning of what Bystander has to say; the oath should bring home to him the need to speak with care; his demeanor adds dimension to the ways he affirms or qualifies his story of what happened.

Fourth is the risk of distortion (whether conscious or unconscious) and outright lying or deception, or (to put it in the customary and more gentle way) the risk of insincerity or lack of candor. Bystander may have shaded the truth in saying the blue car ran the red light, while knowing the light changed to red only after the blue car entered the intersection. Perhaps he did so because he knew and liked the other driver or felt animus toward the driver of the blue car, and the distortion may have been subconscious rather than calculated. Or he may have known full well that the driver of the blue car had the light in his favor and Bystander intended to fool the trier of fact. As to distortion, it is thought that trial safeguards do help, and we at least *hope* they do when the witness intentionally tries to deceive. There is reason to think the oath and the courtroom environment quell at least casual impulses to deceive, that the visible demeanor of the witness provides clues if she tries to mislead, and that cross-examination can bring to light subconscious distortion and sometimes succeeds in exposing lies.

2. Out-of-Court Statement Offered for Its Truth

Often the hearsay doctrine is simple in application, as illustrated by the statements of Bystander in Abby's suit. But people do not always express themselves so directly. Consider now a series of statements, all describing the same incident.

■ PROBLEM 3-A. Three See a Robbery

Higgins is charged with the armed robbery of BankSouth. As part of its case-in-chief, the state calls to the stand one Lissner, who entered BankSouth shortly after the fact and conversed with three people who apparently saw what happened. The prosecutor proposes to have Lissner describe these conversations, and specifically to testify:

1) That Plaintalk said, with reference to the robbery and to defendant, "Higgins is the one who did it";
2) That Sirchev said, again with reference to the robbery and to defendant, "That fellow Higgins went out of here carrying money bags";
3) That Oblique said, once again with reference to the robbery of BankSouth and to defendant, "they ought to put Higgins in jail for this, and throw away the key."

The defense objects that the statements by Plaintalk, Sirchev, and Oblique are inadmissible hearsay. Without worrying for the moment whether the statements are admissible, are they hearsay? Why or why not?

B A CLOSER LOOK AT THE DOCTRINE

1. What Is a Statement?

a. Assertive Conduct

The examples considered so far have obvious hearsay implications because they involve the use of language to express ideas. The very term "hearsay" describes what one person hears another say, and suggests a concern with human verbal expression. But the hearsay doctrine rests upon the four risks of misperception, faulty memory, ambiguity, and insincerity, and these risks appear not only with verbal expression but with nonverbal conduct where the actor has assertive intent.

Hence any reasonable definition of hearsay must embrace assertive conduct when offered to prove the point asserted. There has never been much doubt on this score. Rule 801(a) embraces such conduct because its definition of statement includes "nonverbal conduct" of a person, if "intended" as an assertion. A common instance of such conduct involves use of one of the standard nonverbal cues—nodding or shaking the head or shrugging the shoulders in answer to a question, pointing as a means of identifying or selecting. Evidence of such behavior, offered to prove the idea that the actor sought to convey, is hearsay. See United States v. Caro, 569 F.2d 411, 416 n.9 (5th Cir. 1978) (co-offender "pointed out" his "source" to law enforcement officers, apparently indicating a dwelling; his act was "assertive conduct" that, "like an oral declaration," was "subject to the hearsay rule"); United States v. Ross, 321 F.2d 61, 69 (2d Cir.), *cert. denied*, 375 U.S. 894 (1963) (testimony that *S* pointed to a list when asked what numbers were used by the salesmen "was not outside the hearsay rule merely because [he] used no words," for "the pointing was as much a communication as a statement . . . would have been").

Nor would it matter if the conduct were a coded signal. Evidence that one lantern had been lit in the belfry of Old North Church would be hearsay if offered in court to prove that the British had moved out from Boston toward Concord and that they were coming by land rather than sea. The evidence would tend to prove the point only if the lantern were interpreted as a signal from the minuteman immortalized in Longfellow's poem[3] and taken as proof of the very point which the appearance of one lantern in that spot was intended to communicate.

In such obvious cases the hearsay issue is easily seen and resolved. But read on.

b. Nonassertive Conduct

Perhaps surprisingly, even evidence of nonassertive human conduct implicates most of the hearsay risks—at least sometimes. How to treat such conduct in these situations has posed great challenge to the hearsay doctrine, in both theory and application. Consider now a problem that raises the question whether nonassertive conduct should ever be considered hearsay, and then read the *Wright* case, which this book presents in summary form with an edited version of a famous opinion by Baron Parke that advanced a broad view of hearsay that embraces nonassertive conduct in certain situations.

■ PROBLEM 3-B. Kenworth and Maserati

A huge Kenworth truck pulls up to an intersection regulated by traffic lights and stops in its righthand lane. An open Maserati sports car pulls up beside the truck in the left lane and stops, and Phillip behind the wheel guns his engine. The traffic light across the street is not working, and Phillip cannot see the light nearest him, above and to his right, nor can he see cross-traffic coming from his right, as the bulk of the Kenworth is in the way.

The Kenworth begins to pull forward, and Phillip in the Maserati shoots into the intersection, where he is broadsided by a blue car crossing from its right, driven by Hillary. A lawsuit follows, for personal injuries and property damage, with Phillip and Hillary each claiming the other was at fault.

---

[3]See H.W. Longfellow, The Landlord's Tale: Paul Revere's Ride, from Tales of a Wayside Inn, pt. I, st. 2 (1864-1873):

> One if by land, and two if by sea,
> And I on the opposite shore will be
> Ready to ride and spread the alarm
> Through every Middlesex village and farm.

As proof that he had the light in his favor, Phillip offers to testify that the truck pulled forward across the pedestrian lane into the intersection before he (Phillip) stepped on the accelerator. Hillary objects, her lawyer arguing that evidence of the behavior of the truckdriver at the intersection is hearsay, when offered to prove that the light had turned green for Phillip. The trial judge is astonished: "Hearsay? What in the world are you thinking of, counsel, there isn't an assertion in sight here. Overruled."

You are Hillary's lawyer. Advance her argument that evidence of the movement of the Kenworth is hearsay, when offered for the stated purpose. For the moment, do not try to apply Rule 801. Just explain to the judge exactly what logical steps are required to get from the movement of the truck to the conclusion that the light was green for Phillip, and why those steps involve the same risks that lead us to exclude an out-of-court statement ("the light's turned green"), when offered to prove what it asserts. If you can't do it, read the next case and try it again.

Baron Parke (b. 1782; d. 1868)

You are about to read Baron Parke's argument in the *Wright* case. James Parke, First Baron Wensleydale, was an English barrister who served as a judge from 1828 to 1855, including 21 years on the Court of Exchequer. Considered an insightful jurist, Baron Parke is the source of a phrase long associated with limits on the responsibility of an employer for the torts of an employee, that remains part of our law today, although we no longer say it the way Baron Parke did. In the case of Joel v. Morison, 172 Eng. Rep. 1338 (Ct. Excheq. 1834), it was Baron Parke who said a master is liable for the tort of his servant only "where the servant is acting in the course of his employment," but "if he was going on a frolic of his own, without being at all on his master's business, the master will not be liable." The enduring legacy of Baron Parke's later opinion in *Wright* is attested by the fact that the problem of applying the hearsay doctrine to a statement that doesn't seem actually to be saying what it is offered to prove still engages courts. See, e.g., see Commonwealth v. Vasquez, 2005 WL 3642768 (Mass. Superior Ct.) (analyzing *Wright* and other authorities at length and concluding that incoming calls received on a cellphone taken from defendant, in which callers sought to acquire drugs, were admissible evidence and not hearsay).

Mr Baron Parke (engraving), English School (19th century) / Private Collection / © Look and Learn / Illustrated Papers Collection / Bridgeman Images

WRIGHT v. DOE D. TATHAM

Court of Exchequer Chamber
7 Ad. & E. 313, 112 Eng. Rep. 488 (1837)

[Sandford Tatham, cousin and sole heir at law to the decedent John Marsden, brought suit to set aside his will, which was allegedly procured by fraud. By that will Marsden left valuable real property to his steward George Wright, who was named as defendant.

John Marsden, who by the standards of the time lived to the rather old age of 68, was apparently an unprepossessing fellow. By one view, advanced vigorously on behalf of Sandford Tatham, Marsden was "weak in understanding" and "ignorant of the commonest natural occurrences," hence prone "to ask childish questions on the most familiar subjects relating to his own property" and apparently "incapable of conducting business." He also displayed "imbecility in his amusements" and was "subject to irrational fears, insomuch that he sought the protection of other persons when passing by a pig or a turkey-cock." And in these unfortunate circumstances the steward George Wright "exercised an absolute control" over Marsden, treating him "with great harshness and disrespect" and even resorting to "personal violence" against him. Evidence was offered to the effect that

> Marsden was treated as a child by his own menial servants; that, in his youth, he was called, in the village where he lived, "Silly Jack," and "Silly Marsden," and was never talked to "as a man that was capable of anything, but as a child"; that a witness had seen boys shouting after him, "There goes crazy Marsden," and throwing dirt at him, and had persuaded a person passing by to see him home; and that once, when Marsden passed the evening at a gentleman's house, in company with Mr. Ellershaw . . . the elder persons of the family sat down to whist, and, Ellershaw mentioning that Marsden was unable to play, some children were sent for, and he was put to play with them at loo, at a side table, a man-servant superintending the game.

By another view (argued on behalf of the steward Wright), John Marsden "was a man of very retentive memory." While "not of strong mind or natural talent equal to the generality of men," still it was said that he had "such understanding and judgment as to be competent to conduct all the ordinary transactions of life." And in the estimate of one acquaintance, Marsden was "competent to manage his affairs with the assistance of agents and professional men, and to make such a will and codicil as these in question." 2 Russ. & M. 1, 20, 39 Eng. Rep. 295, 302 (reporting earlier proceedings in the same case).

Part of the proof adduced by George Wright was in the form of three letters written to Marsden before his death, all by persons who had themselves died before trial. One letter was personal in nature, but two others dealt with matters of business. One of the latter sort came from the Vicar of Lancaster, Oliver Marton, and it read as follows:

Dear Sir.—I beg that you will Order your Attorney to Wait on Mr. Atkinson, or Mr. Watkinson, & propose some Terms of Agreement between You and the Parish or Township or disagreeable things must unavoidably happen. I recommend that a Case should be settled by Your and their Attorneys, and laid before Council to whose Opinion both Sides should submit otherwise it will be attended with much Trouble and Expence to both Parties.—I am, Sr. with compliments to Mrs. Coockson, Your Humble Servant, &c.

OLIVER MARTON

May ye 20th 1786.
I beg the favour of an Answer to this.
John Marsden, Esq. Wennington.

When the case came to be heard in Exchequer Chamber, a majority of justices thought that the letters should not have been received. Baron Parke wrote what has come to be a famous opinion, set forth in part below.]

PARKE B. . . .

Each of the three letters, no doubt, indicates that in the opinion of the writer the testator was a rational person. He is spoken of in respectful terms in all . . . . Mr. Marton addresses him as competent to do business to the limited extent to which his letter calls upon him to act; and there is no question but that, if any of one of those writers had been living, his evidence, founded on personal observation, that the testator possessed the qualities which justified the opinion expressed or implied in his letters, would be admissible on this issue. But the point to be determined is, whether these letters are admissible as proof that he did possess these qualities?

I am of the opinion that, according to the established principles of the law of evidence, the letters are all inadmissible for such a purpose . . . .

That the three letters were each of them written . . . and sent . . . no doubt are facts . . . proved on oath; and the letters are without doubt admissible on an issue in which the fact of sending such letters . . . is relevant to the matter in dispute; as, for instance, on a feigned issue to try the question whether such letters were sent to the testator's house . . . .

But the question is, whether the contents of these letters are evidence of the fact to be proved upon this issue,—that is, the actual existence of the qualities which the testator is, in those letters, by implication, stated to possess: and those letters may be considered in this respect to be on the same footing as if they had contained a direct and positive statement that he was competent. For this purpose they are mere hearsay evidence, statements of the writers, not on oath, of the truth of the matter in question, with this addition, that they have acted upon the statements on the faith of their being true, by their sending the letters to the testator. That the so acting cannot give a sufficient sanction for the truth of the statement is perfectly plain; for it is clear that, if the same statements had been made by parol or in writing to a third person, that would have been insufficient; and this is conceded by the learned counsel for [Wright]. Yet in both cases there has been an acting on the belief of the truth, by making the statement, or writing and sending a letter to a third person; and what difference can it possibly make that this is an acting of the same nature by writing and sending the letter to the testator? It is admitted, and most properly, that you have no right to use in evidence the fact of writing and sending a letter to a third person containing a statement of competence, on the ground that it affords an inference that such an act would not have been done unless the statement was true, or believed to be true, although such an inference no doubt would be raised in the conduct of the ordinary affairs of life, if the statement were made by a man of veracity. But it cannot be raised in a judicial inquiry; and, if such an argument were admissible, it would lead to the indiscriminate admission of hearsay evidence of all manner of facts.

Further, it is clear that an acting to a much greater extent and degree upon such statements to a third person would not make the statements admissible. For example, if a wager to a large amount had been made as to the matter in issue by two third persons, the payment of that wager, however large the sum, would not be admissible to prove the truth of the matter in issue. You would not have had any right to present it to the jury as raising an inference of the truth of the fact, on the ground that otherwise the bet would not have been paid. It is, after all, nothing but the mere statement of that fact, with strong evidence of the belief of it by the party making it. Could it make any difference that the wager was between the third person and one of the parties to the suit? Certainly not. The payment by other underwriters on the same policy to the plaintiff could not be given in evidence to prove that the subject insured had been lost. Yet there is an act done, a payment strongly attesting the truth of the statement, which it implies, that there had been a loss. To illustrate this point still further, let us suppose a third person had betted a wager with Mr. Marsden that he could not solve some mathematical problem, the solution of which required a high degree of capacity; would payment of that wager to Mr. Marsden's banker be admissible evidence that he possessed that capacity? The answer is certain; it would not. It would be evidence of the fact of competence given by a third party not upon oath.

Let us suppose the parties who wrote these letters to have stated the matter therein contained, that is, their knowledge of his personal qualities and capacity for business, on oath before a magistrate, or in some judicial proceeding to which the plaintiff and defendant were not parties. No one could contend that such statement would be admissible on this issue; and yet there would have been an act done on the faith of the statement being true, and a very solemn one, which would raise in the ordinary conduct of affairs a strong belief in the truth of the statement, if the writers were faith-worthy. The acting in this case is of much less importance, and certainly is not equal to the sanction of an extra-judicial oath.

Many other instances of a similar nature, by way of illustration, were suggested by the learned counsel for [Tatham] which, on the most cursory consideration, any one would at once declare to be inadmissible in evidence. Others were supposed on the part of [Wright] which, at first sight, have the appearance of being mere facts, and therefore admissible, though on further consideration they are open to precisely the same objection. Of the first description are the supposed cases of a letter by a third person to anyone demanding a debt, which may be said to be a treatment of him as a debtor, being offered as proof that the debt was really due; a note, congratulating him on his high state of bodily vigour, being proposed as evidence of his being in good health; both of which are manifestly at first sight objectionable. To the latter class belong the supposed conduct of a family or relations of a testator, taking the same precautions in his absence as if he were a lunatic; his election, in his absence, to some high and responsible office; the conduct of a physician who permitted a will to be executed by a sick testator; the conduct of a deceased captain on a question of seaworthiness, who, after examining every part of the vessel, embarked in it with his family; all these, when deliberately considered, are, with reference to the matter in issue in each case, mere instances of hearsay evidence, mere statements, not on oath, but implied in or vouched by the actual conduct of persons by whose acts the litigant parties are not to be bound.

The conclusion at which I have arrived is, that proof of a particular fact, which is not of itself a matter in issue, but which is relevant only as implying a statement or opinion of a third person on the matter in issue, is inadmissible in all cases where such a statement or opinion not on oath would be of itself inadmissible; and therefore, in this case the letters which are offered only to prove the competence of the testator, that is the truth of the implied statements therein contained, were properly rejected, as the mere statement or opinion of the writer would certainly have been inadmissible.

■ NOTES ON NONASSERTIVE CONDUCT AS HEARSAY

1. Baron Parke says the letters "imply[] a statement or opinion" of their authors and were offered to prove "the truth of the implied statements." Obviously Parke did not mean "imply" in the usual strong sense of "intentionally suggesting." Nobody thinks the Vicar's purpose was to express or communicate that "Marsden is a man of sound mind." If his letter "implies" this point, it does so in the weak sense of the term: It "indicates," because of what it says and what it tries to do, that its author thinks one can do business with Marsden, so the author thinks Marsden is of sound mind, and so Marsden probably *is* of sound mind. That makes the Vicar's letter different from Oblique's statement in Problem 3-A ("they ought to put Higgins in jail for this"). Oblique intentionally expressed and communicated that Higgins was guilty, thus "implied" it in the strong sense. For Parke, an "implied statement" embraces everything one might infer about (and from) the thoughts of a person by reading what he writes or listening to what he says, whether he intended to convey it or not.

2. From this broad view of "imply," Parke takes a broad view of hearsay. Under his view, the behavior of the rascals in taunting "crazy Marsden" and throwing dirt at him could be hearsay too. And the same would be true of the way Ellershaw and his friends treated Marsden in arranging separate entertainment while the other adults played whist. (The *Oxford English Dictionary* describes "loo" as "a round card-game" played with three- or five-card hands, in which one "who fails to take a trick or breaks any of the laws of the game is 'looed,' i.e., required to pay a certain sum, or 'loo,' to the pool.") Apparently George Wright raised no objection to this proof. Ironically, Ellershaw wrote one of the letters Wright offered to prove that Marsden was of sound mind. Wright's lawyers argued that the Ellershaw letter was just as proper as proof that Marsden was called "Silly Marsden" and "pelted by boys." If the opposition could prove Marsden had been "treated as a child" by Ellershaw and others, Wright's lawyers argued, then Wright should be able to get in a letter from Ellershaw in which Marsden was "differently treated." They had a point, didn't they? See Maguire, The Hearsay System: Around and Through the Thicket, 14 Vand. L. Rev. 741, 749-760 (1961).

3. Baron Parke's opinion is famous for its specific holding—the letters are hearsay because they imply a statement that Marsden is sound. But Parke is even more famous for his broad account of what hearsay is, which may not be necessary to the outcome but is part of the underlying logic. He speaks of the ship captain embarking with his family after inspecting the vessel, as proof that the vessel is sound. That too implies a statement, in Parke's view. Under this view, it seems that a person accused of a crime would face a hearsay objection if he tried to prove his innocence by proving that another was observed running from the scene of the deed. And it seems that a claimant seeking workers' compensation would encounter the same objection if she tried to prove that she suffered certain injuries by introducing evidence that she was treated for such injuries.

4. Under Parke's view, Phillip's testimony that the truck started forward into the intersection would be hearsay if the purpose was to prove that the light had turned green. If the truckdriver had said to Phillip, "Hey fella, the light's green," of course that would be hearsay if offered in court to prove the point. You can see that in both cases we're using the truckdriver's behavior—whether driving forward or making a statement—to prove an act, event, or condition in the world (the light turning green). This use of human conduct involves a two-step inference, which is the same inference that is entailed when statements are offered as proof of what they assert. Here is the first step: Act or statement suggests the belief of the actor or the speaker (truckdriver's act of pulling forward or his statement that the light is green suggests what he thinks about the light). Here is the second step: The belief of the actor or speaker suggests something about acts, events, or conditions in the world (truckdriver's belief suggests that the light is indeed green). This two-step inference is the same logic described in note 1, when the letters to John Marsden are taken as proof of his soundness of mind.

5. The view of Baron Parke generated tensions that continue. The strongest argument in favor of the broad view stresses that using human conduct in support of the two-step inference brings most of the risks that the hearsay doctrine is designed to guard against. These are the risks of misperception, failed or inaccurate memory, and ambiguity. The only "missing" risk involves sincerity—if an actor (like the truckdriver) doesn't intend to assert anything, we need not worry about lying. Famously, one commentator defended Baron Parke's broad definition by stressing the hearsay risks and arguing that we can never know whether an actor intended to assert something. Citing a doctor who lets a patient be interrogated, where the doctor's conduct is offered later as proof that the patient was "physically and mentally competent to make a rational statement," Professor Finman concluded that the question whether the doctor intended an assertion cannot be answered rationally after the fact: A court is "free to decide either (a) that the actor did intend to assert the proposition his conduct is offered to prove, and thus that the offered evidence is hearsay, or (b) that the actor had no such intent, and thus that the evidence is not hearsay." Hence "such cases cannot be intelligently decided by approaching the intent issue as if it could be resolved as a question of fact," so "implied assertions should be classified as hearsay." Finman, Implied Assertions as Hearsay: Some Criticisms of the Uniform Rules of Evidence, 14 Stan. L. Rev. 682, 696-697, 707 (1962).

6. The strongest argument in favor of a narrower view, which excludes nonassertive conduct from the definition of hearsay, is that the risk of insincerity—the risk that actor might be "lying"—disappears in the case of nonassertive conduct. As Professor Judson Falknor put it, "A man doesn't lie to himself," so the risk of using nonassertive conduct in support of the two-step inference "is the same whether he is an egregious liar or a paragon of veracity," and lack of cross-examination in such cases "in relation to his veracity or lack of it, would seem to be of no substantial importance." And equally important, "conduct is evidently more dependable than an assertion," and in any event "the hearsay objection to evidence of nonassertive conduct is overlooked in practice" more often than not. Hence the definition of hearsay should exclude nonassertive conduct. See Falknor, The "Hear-Say" Rule as a "See-Do" Rule: Evidence of Conduct, 33 Rocky Mtn. L. Rev. 133, 136-137 (1961).

7. In the battle over the breadth of the hearsay doctrine, we can announce a modern winner. Most courts today reject the broad position of Baron Parke in *Wright.* So does Rule 801, as statutory prose and legislative history make clear: Under FRE 801, nonassertive conduct offered for the two-step inference—to prove the actor's belief in a fact, hence the fact itself—is not hearsay. The wording supports this conclusion because FRE 801(a)(2) defines "nonverbal conduct" of a person as hearsay *only* if "intended" as an assertion. And the ACN contrasts "nonverbal" conduct, which is "the equivalent of words, assertive in nature," against "[o]ther nonverbal conduct," saying of the latter:

> Admittedly evidence of this character is untested with respect to the perception, memory, and narration (or their equivalents) of the actor, but the Advisory Committee is of the view that these dangers are minimal in the absence of an intent to assert and do not justify the loss of the evidence on hearsay grounds. No class of evidence is free of the possibility of fabrication, but the likelihood is less with nonverbal than with assertive verbal conduct. The situations giving rise to the nonverbal conduct are such as virtually to eliminate questions of sincerity. Motivation, the nature of the conduct, and the presence or absence of reliance will bear heavily upon the weight to be given the evidence.

In short, if the trial judge thinks the driver of the Kenworth did not intend to assert that the light was green (Problem 3-B), then evidence of his pulling forward into the intersection is not hearsay under Rule 801 when offered to prove that the light changed to green. If the truckdriver had simply *said* the light turned green, his statement *would* be hearsay if offered to prove that point. And both his conduct and his statement support the two-step inference—both suggest what he thought, which in turn suggests the external fact. His conduct is nonhearsay (if nonassertive), but his statement is hearsay.

COMMENT/PERSPECTIVE: Implied Statements

Baron Parke's opinion in *Wright* is famous in the law of evidence, and is still cited by American courts. His expansive definition of hearsay reached what he called "implied statements," in which category he included what we would call nonassertive conduct when offered for the two-step inference (to prove belief, hence some act, event, or condition in the world). For years this broad definition prevailed at common law in England and throughout the United States. But Judson Falknor's argument (note 6) persuaded the framers of FRE 801 to *reject* this broad view, in favor of the narrower view that conduct is hearsay only if the actor "intended it as an assertion." Most American states follow this path too. *Wright*'s broad approach survived longer in England, being reaffirmed in *Regina v. Kearley,* 2 App. Cas. 228 (H.L. Eng. 1992), but in 2003 the United Kingdom adopted a new statutory definition of statement, see Criminal Justice Act of 2003, §115(2) ("representation of fact or opinion made by a person"), and seven years later the Court of Appeals concluded that this new definition discarded *Wright*'s broad definition, see Regina v. Chrysostomou (Mark), 2010 Crim. L. 942 (Ct. App. Crim. Div. 2010). So in federal courts and most states (and in the UK too), we are safe in saying that nodding the head "yes" can be hearsay, but not pulling forward into an intersection (unless the driver intended the act as an assertion, which is unlikely). There is one caveat: On its facts, *Wright* involved *words*—letters that sought to set up a meeting. In section D of this chapter (Borderland of Hearsay), you will see that modern courts *still* sometimes invoke *Wright*'s broad view of hearsay when words are offered to prove points that are not directly asserted but are on the mind of the speaker.

8. We should note that nonassertive conduct includes the visible psychological, physical, and emotional reaction of a person, which may of course suggest something about what happened (the two-step inference is involved once again). Consider a case in which Gwinn was charged with kidnapping and sexually assaulting a woman. On first seeing his likeness in a mugbook at the police station, the woman screamed and started crying. Her emotional reaction amounts to nonassertive conduct and was viewed as nonhearsay. People v. Gwinn, 314 N.W.2d 562, 572 (Mich. App. 1981) (crying was not a "statement" under MRE 801 because "not intended as an assertion"). Similarly the reaction of a teller, who became pale and was shaking during a robbery, is nonassertive conduct when offered to prove the robbers intimidated bank personnel, and not hearsay. See Cole v. United States, 327 F.2d 360 (9th Cir. 1964).

9. The ACN to FRE 801 also says "nonassertive verbal conduct" is excluded from the definition of hearsay. You might say "there's no such thing as nonassertive verbal conduct, because words are *always* assertive," and for the most part that's true. But it is possible that the framers had in mind involuntary verbal behavior like screaming "ouch" when struck unexpectedly, which seems reflexive more than reflective and is closer in nature to the kind of emotional reactions described above than to most verbal behavior.

CAIN v. GEORGE

United States Court of Appeals for the Fifth Circuit
411 F.2d 572 (1969)

PER CURIAM.

This is a diversity of citizenship case brought by the parents under the wrongful death statute of Texas for the death of their son who died of carbon monoxide poisoning while a guest in appellees' motel. A chair next to the heater had burned and was smoldering at the time of the arrival of the fire department. Plaintiffs alleged that the gas heater in the motel room was defective because it had been improperly installed, was improperly vented and had never been inspected or cleaned since the time of installation.

A jury verdict in the form of answers to special interrogatories found that the death of [the son] was not proximately caused by the negligence of the defendants, that the death . . . was not proximately caused by his own negligence, and that [the son's] death was due to an unavoidable accident. Thereupon, the

District Court entered a final judgment for the defendants and dismissed the action on its merits . . . .

Appellants contend that the trial court erred in allowing in evidence the testimony of the motel owners concerning the number of guests who had occupied the room where the deceased was found dead and who had made no complaints. This testimony was relevant on the issue, however, that carbon monoxide came from the smoldering chair and clothing and not from the gas heater. Such testimony merely related the knowledge of the motel owners as to whether anyone was ever harmed by the heater. It was not hearsay as it derived its value solely from the credit to be given to the witnesses themselves and it was not dependent upon the veracity or competency of other persons. This testimony of Mr. and Mrs. George was clearly the best available evidence to support their position that carbon monoxide did not come from the heater. We think it was admissible to show how the heater had acted in the past . . . .

[Judgment affirmed.]

■ NOTES ON EVIDENCE OF NONCOMPLAINT

1. The court in *Cain* says that testimony as to noncomplaint depends solely on "the credit to be given to the witnesses" who testify *and* that such evidence tended "to show how the heater had acted in the past." That can't be quite right. The credibility of the witness is crucial in deciding whether guests had stayed in the room without complaining. But whether the behavior of the guests tells us anything about the heater depends entirely on our appraisal of *their* behavior—their "credibility" in the sense of their powers of observation and the meaning of their conduct in not complaining.

2. *Cain* is entirely willing to take the out-of-court behavior of the guests in support of the two-step inference—their behavior suggests their belief that the heater was operational, which suggests that it was. Indeed, *Cain* seems to support Judson Falknor's argument (note 6 after *Wright*) that courts don't even detect hearsay issues with proof of nonassertive conduct that does not include verbal expressions. Perhaps more to the point, *Cain* is consistent with the modern approach to hearsay. The behavior of the guests would not be hearsay under FRE 801 because those who departed without complaining were probably not trying to assert anything—their conduct might *still* suggest that there was nothing amiss in the rooms, but they weren't trying to *tell* that to anybody.

3. Evidence of noncomplaint, sometimes called "negative hearsay" or "the sounds of silence" as a student note puts it (see Note, 84 Dickinson L. Rev. 605 (1980)), is usually admitted over a hearsay objection. See also Lindheimer v. United Fruit Co., 418 F.2d 606, 607-608 (2d Cir. 1969) (admitting evidence that during shipboard meeting of safety committee nobody reported an accident, "as some proof that no accident did in fact occur," where testimony indicated that "it was the duty of those present to discuss accidents occurring on the voyage"; nonreporting "is an act, not a hearsay statement"). It seems that Baron Parke would have seen such evidence as hearsay.

4. It is of course altogether a different matter if, in order to prove that no accident occurred, a witness testifies that he inquired of a person likely to know and was told that no accident had occurred. Here the person is not silent—she asserts that there was no accident. See United States v. DeLoach, 654 F.2d 763, 770-771 (D.C. Cir. 1980) (apparently hearsay), *cert. denied*, 450 U.S. 933 (1981).

c. *Indirect Hearsay*

Consider the following testimony in light of what you understand so far:

Q: Please state your name for the record.
A: My name is Emma Harris.
Q: And where were you born, please?
A: In Bangor, Maine.
Q: And your parents were Algernon Harris and Anne Harris?
A: That's right.
Q: And your mother's given name was Anne Davies, was it not?
A: Correct.
Q: Your parents immigrated from Yorkshire, England, to this country in 1984, is that correct?
A: Yes, sir.
Q: And the date of your birth?
A: November 14, 1991.

You can see at a glance that Emma Harris cannot have firsthand knowledge of any of the facts set out in her answers, and it would appear that every one of them was in substance (though not in form) a repetition of something that was common knowledge in her house and that her parents might have told her in so many words. By that quite reasonable view, they are hearsay pure and simple.

Yet common sense cries out that on the subjects to which Harris testified, such answers should be unobjectionable. There would be something wrong with a system that refused to take the word of a witness on facts like her name, parentage, and place and date of birth.

In the usual case in which such information comes out as background, such answers are routinely accepted without a second thought, even though lawyers and judges know that the hearsay doctrine is implicated. Everyone understands that matters of this sort should be provable this way—regardless of "technical" hearsay problems. It might be different if place of birth or the date that the parents arrived in this country were central points of contested fact—if, for example, such data affected citizenship rights or entitlement to benefits. Even in such cases judges would likely accept the testimony of the witness, though it might carry little weight if the other side had substantial counterproof in the nature of official records or other persuasive evidence.[4]

Here a short digression is in order. Technically, "hearsay" is not quite the right objection to the answers by Emma Harris, for she never refers to statements by others. The principle that would support an objection, if the system were administered in a wooden and unyielding way, would be that Emma lacks "personal knowledge." Rule 602 instructs that every witness must be shown to have "personal knowledge of the matter" to which she is to testify, which ordinarily means knowledge gleaned directly from the senses. Clearly Emma Harris lacks personal knowledge of the facts to which she testified. But a judge would likely give equally short shrift to a personal knowledge objection in this context. Just as the hearsay doctrine seems almost "too technical" if it could block such testimony, so too the personal knowledge requirement would seem to obstruct rather than promote justice if it could keep a witness from testifying to her own personal and familial background. (In the case of a witness who testifies to an out-of-court statement admissible under one of the hearsay exceptions, the knowledge requirement is satisfied if the witness heard the oral utterance or read the written word, although in the latter case the Best Evidence doctrine poses an additional problem. The personal knowledge requirement is considered in Chapter 6C, infra.)

In short, the system tolerates testimony of the sort illustrated here even though the witness lacks personal knowledge and is, in substance, testifying to hearsay. It is another matter altogether if a party tries to use indirect hearsay to prove contested and substantial points. Consider this appalling example of an attempt to use indirect hearsay.

UNITED STATES v. CHECK

United States Court of Appeals for the Second Circuit
582 F.2d 668 (1978)

[Sandy Check, a patrolman in the New York City Police Department, was convicted of possessing cocaine with intent to distribute, and related offenses. The key witness against him was Stephen Spinelli, a detective in the force who had been assigned to investigate allegations against Check. Spinelli operated undercover and worked through an informant named William Joseph Cali to get close to Check. Spinelli assumed the role of a prospective purchaser of narcotics in his investigation of Check.]

[4] There *are* exceptions that would likely enable the proponent of Emma's answers to vault over a hearsay objection. FRE 803(19) embraces "reputation" among family members on facts of personal or family history, like birth, marriage, and ancestry, and FRE 804(b)(4) embraces any "statement" by an unavailable declarant describing such personal matters. One or both of these exceptions would likely enable Emma to testify as she did, even if she was summarizing common knowledge in her household or telling things she gleaned from conversations with her parents.

WATERMAN, J . . . .

Spinelli testified that, as anticipated, Cali arranged for a meeting with Check which was to take place on August 8, 1974 at Dave's Corner Restaurant, located at the corner of Canal Street and Broadway in lower Manhattan. Shortly after Spinelli and Cali had entered the restaurant Check appeared outside the front window of the building and motioned to have Cali meet with him outside. This Cali did and, after a conversation with Check, Cali rejoined Spinelli who was still seated in the restaurant. Cali refused to testify at the trial. So, in view of the potential hearsay problems connected with any attempt to elicit the content of Spinelli's conversations with him, and after an objection on hearsay grounds had already been voiced, the prosecutor employed a method of questioning which he argued circumvented any hearsay problems. The prosecutor, after establishing that Check and Cali had conversed and that Cali had thereafter returned to speak to Spinelli, inquired of Spinelli (as he would ultimately inquire of him at least twelve additional times): "Without telling us what Mr. Cali said to you, what did you say to him?" In response, Spinelli told the prosecutor, and also, of course, the jury, what he had purportedly said to Cali:

> I—after we had the conversation, I instructed William Cali that by no means did I intend to front any sum of money to Sandy Check, I didn't particularly care for the fact that—initially he was supposed to come with an ounce of cocaine, and the taste which he had, which I was supposed to get prior to making the ounce buy of cocaine, was at his house, and due to the fact that it wasn't of good quality, I wasn't particularly concerned, as good faith wasn't being shown to me, especially for the fact I also told William Cali I had no intention of giving Sandy Check $300 which William Cali owed to him from a previous narcotics deal . . . .

The scene of the negotiations now shifted. After instructing Cali to continue his discussions with Check, Spinelli left the restaurant, passed Check in the street and proceeded to a nearby topless bar. Cali arrived at the bar ten minutes later and there Spinelli and Cali had another conversation. At trial, the government asked of the undercover agent: "Without telling us what Mr. Cali said to you, what did you say to him during that conversation?" In accordance with the limitations of the question, Spinelli faithfully responded:

> I told William Cali that I was willing to wait until the following day to get the ounce of cocaine, that I could understand that there was problems with Sandy Check's supplier, and that I would definitely have the money with me, and as arrangements, I would drop Cali off to meet Sandy Check and wait for him a few blocks away from the location.

The indirect dealing through Cali abruptly came to an end when Check, responding to Spinelli's gesture of disgust at the unproductive course the negotiations had followed, motioned for Spinelli to cross the street and meet with him personally . . . .

Turning to the merits, we agree with Check that for much of his testimony Spinelli was serving as a transparent conduit for the introduction of inadmissible hearsay information obviously supplied by and emanating from the informant Cali. Indeed, it would be virtually impossible to draw any other conclusion . . . .Moreover, the hearsay introduced through Spinelli was not only damaging in character but extensive in scope. Thus, the jury learned from Spinelli's "I told William Cali" responses that:

1. Check wanted Spinelli to front the money not only for the narcotics he wished to purchase from Check but also to cover $300 which William Cali owed Check from a previous narcotics deal

2. Check kept narcotics at his house

3. Check was supposed to arrive at the meeting of August 8, 1974 with an ounce of cocaine and a taste of it, but, inasmuch as the cocaine was not of good quality, Check did not bring the drugs with him . . . .

4. After seeing Spinelli in the street, after he departed Dave's Corner Restaurant, Check felt more comfortable about dealing with him and would go ahead and try to arrange for a sale of an ounce of cocaine to Spinelli

5. Check would produce the ounce of cocaine that same afternoon of August 8, 1974 . . . .

Despite its unwillingness to exclude all of Spinelli's testimony which conveyed the foregoing hearsay information, the district court did exclude or strike some of it . . . . The judge . . . expressed her misgivings about Spinelli's entire testimony by remarking that Spinelli "doesn't seem to be [testifying to just his part of the conversation]. He seems to be weaving the two together. We can't distinguish which is which." In fact some of Spinelli's "paraphrasing" was so blatant and obvious that at one point even the prosecutor felt compelled to admit that "[t]he obvious inference to be drawn [from Spinelli's testimony regarding Check's being with his runner Duky] is that he [Spinelli] knew it because Cali identified the person."

There is, furthermore, no doubt that the out-of-court statements uttered by Cali, audaciously introduced through the artifice of having Spinelli supposedly restrict his testimony to his half of his conversations with Cali, were being offered to prove the truth of the matters asserted in them. This conclusion follows inescapably from the fact that . . . the government constantly took the position at trial that the challenged portions of Spinelli's testimony avoided the proscription against the use of hearsay not because they were not being offered for the truth of the matters asserted but rather because they were Spinelli's *own* out-of-court statements and he was testifying in court and could be cross-examined. In other words, the government was apparently arguing that the out-of-court statements were admissible because they were somehow excluded from the definition of hearsay or qualified for some supposed exception to the hearsay rule . . . . A concession that *Cali's* statements would have been hearsay [as the government agreed] is an admission that the purpose for which the statements were being offered at trial (irrespective of whether they were to be regarded as Spinelli's or Cali's) was to prove the truth of the matters asserted therein. We thus conclude that, in substance, significant portions of Spinelli's testimony regarding his conversations with Cali were indeed hearsay, for that testimony was a transparent attempt to incorporate into the officer's testimony information supplied by the informant who did not testify at trial. Such a device is improper and cannot miraculously transform inadmissible hearsay into admissible evidence. The district judge . . . should have granted Check's motion to strike all of Spinelli's testimony narrating his conversations with Cali . . . .

Judgment of conviction reversed and case remanded for a new trial on all counts of the indictment.

NOTES ON INDIRECT HEARSAY

1. Judge Waterman's care in *Check* is commendable. If the government could so easily avoid the hearsay doctrine with respect to proof central to its case, the doctrine would accomplish little.

2. Reviewing courts are more relaxed in less egregious situations. See United States v. Obi, 239 F.3d 662, 668 (4th Cir. 2001) (admitting testimony by detective that he began investigating defendant because informant cooperating on another matter introduced him to underworld figure *S*, who said he was acquainted with "some dude named Obi," and rejecting claim that the statement improperly connected defendant with underworld). In *Obi*, isn't it clear that what *S* said was hearsay if offered to connect *S* with the defendant? Defendants in such cases object to being connected to underworld figures as being unfairly prejudicial, and even as an attack on character. (You will see in Chapter 5 that prosecutors cannot generally open up the subject of defendant's character.) You might wonder why courts would admit such proof, and the answer is that proof of the manner in which law enforcement personnel investigated the defendant may become important if the defendant claims that he was improperly targeted.

3. Even in situations like *Obi*, courts are sometimes very sensitive to the risks. See State v. Litzau, 650 N.W.2d 177, 182 (Minn. 2002) (reversing drug conviction, largely because police were allowed to testify that they acted against defendant on the basis of reliable tips that he was involved in crimes); Commonwealth v. Farris, 380 A.2d 486 (Pa. Super. 1977) (error to let prosecutor elicit from detective that when he arrived at robbery scene, the first thing he did was "interrogate Gary Moore," who "made a statement," as a result of which "I arrested Emanuel Farris") (testimony violated hearsay rule).

d. Machines and Animals Speak

Hearsay risks sometimes appear in cases where machines or animals seem to be the source of the factual data reported in court. Consider the following exchange:

Q: When did you check the price of Ajax stock?
A: It was 11:34 A.M.
Q: How do you happen to know that so exactly?
A: I thought it might come up, so I read the time off my smartphone—it's really a little tablet phone or tablet computer.
Q: And what was the price?
A: $47.50 for May futures.
Q: What is your source for that?
A: I called up the Wall Street Journal on my smartphone and read it off of that.

In this exchange, the witness is not stating firsthand observations: He did not check the position of the sun in the sky for the time or observe a sale of Ajax stock. One might argue that both observations are hearsay. If *a person* had told our witness the time and price, and our witness had repeated what the person had told him, then the testimony would be subject to a hearsay objection (or an objection that the witness lacks personal knowledge). Of course FRE 801(a) and (b) both refer to statements and assertive conduct by a "person," and a tablet phone or tablet computer is not a person, suggesting a strong negative inference that anything they "say" cannot be hearsay. But we cannot shrug off a hearsay objection quite so easily. Behind every human-contrived machine that provides information is, well, a human being—someone who designed the machine to do what it does, whether we're talking about clocks, speedometers, blood pressure cuffs, gas chromatographs (to measure blood alcohol content), or tablet phones or tablet computers. So we are not far off the mark in saying that *someone,* meaning some human being, engaged in the conduct that produced the machine, and designed it to generate information. To the extent that a machine reflects human input, the idea of hearsay has some application after all—information provided by any such machine is a statement by a person at one remove (or maybe many removes).

A hearsay objection to testimony about time of day would fail, if only because the human input that produces the information reflected by a clock or the time reading on a tablet phone or tablet computer is remote, and because the function of keeping and displaying time of day is so simple, so mechanical, and so familiar. Everyone understands that timekeeping machines are usually right (or close to it), even if they sometimes fail and are wrong. But a hearsay objection to testimony describing price taken from a newspaper website would be viewed as hearsay. Here, human input is more immediate, more salient, more directly connected to the substance of what the witness reports in testifying.

And what of animal statements? Suppose police discover a house burglary in progress and on entering they discover clear evidence of a theft just completed and a dog. Advised by the owners that the dog does not belong to them, the police surmise that the burglar left it while making his escape. They take the dog to the station, where he is surly to all comers. But a day later when they arrest the suspected burglar and bring him to the station the dog leaps up in obvious doggish enthusiasm—head up, ears relaxed, much licking, prancing, and tail wagging and happy squeals. If ever a dog said, "I know you/I love you," this dog has said it. In the later prosecution of the suspect, the prosecutor offers a testimonial account of the discovery of the dog, his behavior at the station, and his reaction on seeing the suspect, arguing that it all amounts to circumstantial evidence that the suspect is the culprit. Hearsay? Courts say no—an animal is not a "person," so whatever the dog said cannot be hearsay. Of course there are some risks—it is not the case that animals never make mistakes, and not even the case that they never lie. But animals cannot be sworn as witnesses or cross-examined, so from that perspective it seems pointless to treat their "statements" as hearsay.

As a practical matter, the question of "animal hearsay" arises most often in connection with proof of canine tracking and identification, and such evidence is usually held admissible. See United States v. McNiece, 558 F. Supp. 612 (E.D. N.Y. 1983) (approving videotape and testimonial description of behavior of dog who, after exposure to defendant's sock and an array of tools, exhibited an "alert" reaction on coming to boltcutters found at robbery scene, leading witness to conclude that defendant had been in contact with boltcutters). Sometimes proof of other kinds of animal behavior is admitted. See State v. Grimsley, 30 P.2d 85 (Mont. 1934) (in trial for theft of two calves, approving testimony by complaining witness that his cows seemed to be looking for their calves, which bore on proposed test to see whether cows would claim calves as their own).

But occasionally courts balk. See State v. Storm, 238 P.2d 1161, 1176 (Mont. 1951) ("Dogs and other dumb animals do not qualify as witnesses in the courts of this state. They know not the nature of an oath. They may not be sworn. They cannot be cross-examined. They testify only through professed interpreters whose translations and conclusions are always hearsay."(!)) (murder conviction reversed for error in admitting bloodhound tracking evidence).

2. When Is a Statement Not Hearsay?

Under FRE 801, a statement is hearsay when offered "to prove the truth of the matter asserted." The negative inference invited by this definition is that a statement is *not* hearsay when offered for any *other* purpose—when it is *not* "offered to prove the truth of the matter asserted." What other purposes can there be? As it turns out, there can be many. In these cases, their accuracy or truthfulness is not a critical factor. By universal custom—and there are literally thousands of cases—there are six nonhearsay categories, and here they are: (1) impeachment, (2) verbal acts (or parts of acts), (3) effect on listener or reader,

(4) verbal markers or objects, (5) circumstantial evidence of state of mind, and (6) circumstantial evidence of memory or belief. These categories are not listed anywhere in the Rules. Nonetheless they are very familiar to judges, practicing lawyers and commentators.

The verbal act category is overused and is sometimes an unthinking label for a statement offered for any nonhearsay purpose. The first four categories listed above are fairly straightforward, but the last two (circumstantial evidence of state of mind; circumstantial evidence of memory or belief) are troublesome. The next seven Problems illustrate these six nonhearsay uses in the order set out above. With this minimal guidance, and suggestions in the Notes following the Problems, you can figure out why these uses fall outside the definition of hearsay.

■ PROBLEM 3-C. "The Blue Car Ran a Red Light"

Abby sues Burton for property damages and personal injuries arising out of an intersection collision. (Abby had been driving a maroon station wagon, Burton a blue sedan.) In order to show that Burton's blue sedan ran the light, Abby's counsel calls Bystander and establishes through preliminary questions that he saw the accident.

Then the critical question: "Which car had the light in its favor?" Bystander's response: "The light was green for the station wagon. The blue car ran a red light."

On cross-examination, Burton asks Bystander about a conversation he had with insurance adjuster Charles three days after the accident. Over Abby's hearsay objection, Burton wants to ask Bystander whether he said to Charles, "The blue car had the green light in its favor." Burton replies to the objection, "Your honor, we seek only to impeach the witness, not to offer the statement for its truth."

How should the court rule on the hearsay objection, and why?

■ NOTES ON IMPEACHMENT BY PRIOR STATEMENTS

1. If Burton argued that he was using Bystander's statement to prove that the light was green, he would have "made the other side's day" because that use would make the statement hearsay. If Burton argued that Bystander's statement shows that Bystander *once thought* the light was green for Burton's car, Burton would still not be home free. Here is the reason: Even if a statement doesn't *expressly* say the speaker "thinks" that a certain fact is true, still a statement asserting the fact implies that the speaker *thinks* the fact is true. Indeed, every statement of fact says the speaker thinks what he says is so. If a statement of fact didn't also say the speaker thinks the fact is so, then we as listeners would have no reason to take the statement as proof of that fact. In short, it is a necessary condition of communication by language that factual statements express the belief of the speaker. Hence arguing that the statement is just being offered to prove what the speaker thinks, not what the reality is—doesn't get us out of the hearsay category.

2. So why is Bystander's statement not hearsay if offered to impeach? The important thing about Bystander's statement is that it differs from his trial testimony. Burton is arguing thus: "I'm proving Bystander's change of position on the color of the light." For this reason, courts universally take the view that prior inconsistent statements are not hearsay when offered to impeach. The inconsistent statement is offered to prove vacillation—the witness blows hot and cold, and it is this change in position that impeaches, not the truthfulness or correctness of the prior statement.

3. But almost always there is a rub: Usually a prior inconsistent statement that has an impeaching impact also asserts a fact that is relevant in the case. The jury might misuse the statement as proof of that very fact, and remember that jury misuse of evidence is one of the definitions of "unfair prejudice" under FRE 403. Usually, however, the objection under FRE 403 fails too, because this mechanism of impeachment is so very well accepted and considered so important in assessing credibility.

■ PROBLEM 3-D. "Any Way You Like"

The state seeks an injunction to close down the Gentleman's Massage Parlor, on ground that its owner Ratliff operates it for purposes of soliciting prostitution. The government calls undercover agent Wallis to testify that while posing as a patron there he was served by a masseuse named Debra who, in the middle of giving him a rubdown, asked whether I was "interested in a good time." Wallis testifies that he replied "that depends on when and where and how much" and that Debra replied, "the cost depends on what you want, but I'm real versatile like, and you can have it any way you like, honey."

Ratliff objects that Wallis's testimony about this verbal exchange is hearsay. Is it?

■ NOTES ON VERBAL ACTS IN CRIMINAL CASES

1. Debra and Wallis did not agree on a price, which might mean that no crime has been committed, but that does not resolve the hearsay question. Even if agreement is necessary for a crime, her statements tend to prove solicitation, which is a step toward the criminal act of prostitution. In short, this statement is a classic verbal act.

2. Note that even when offered to prove a crime (and not for the truth of the matter asserted), content counts. If Debra had said "it looks like it's going to rain today," her statement would not be a crime or a step on the way to a crime. Could Debra be guilty of solicitation even if she never intended to engage in whatever acts she describes?

3. Recall your course in Criminal Law. Can you think of other crimes that are committed by words alone? By words connected with acts? Does the definition of the crime require that the speaker intend to act in accordance with what he says?

■ PROBLEM 3-E. Whose Corn?

John Lord leased part of his farm to Frank Cartwright for payment in kind, in the amount of 40 percent of the corn Cartwright could grow. Cartwright borrowed money from First State Bank, giving the bank a security interest in the part of his crop not promised to Lord, but ultimately defaulted on the loan. The bank repossessed a double crib of corn from the farm and sold it to Dan Prager.

Lord sues Prager and the bank for conversion, claiming that the corn that the bank repossessed and sold was Lord's share of Cartwright's crop. As proof that the corn belonged to him, Lord testifies that he and Cartwright went to the field one day, and Cartwright "pointed out the corn in the double crib and said, 'Mr. Lord, this double crib of corn is your share for this year, and it belongs to you, sir.'" The bank and Prager object that Lord's description of what Cartwright said and did was hearsay.

As proof that the corn in the double crib was indeed the corn covered by its security interest, the bank offers testimony by its loan officer that "when we came out to see about selling the corn, Cartwright told us the corn in the double crib was his." Lord objects that the loan officer's description of what Cartwright said and did was hearsay.

What result on these hearsay objections, and why? Assume that if the bank got the wrong corn, Prager and the bank are liable to Lord for conversion.

■ NOTES ON VERBAL ACTS IN CIVIL CASES

1. Cartwright's statement to Lord has operative effect. In the context of their relationship, we expect Cartwright to convey part of his corn crop to

Lord. Normally a conveyance of personal property (anything other than land) requires delivery, but in the case of large objects (like a crib of corn), the law accepts symbolic delivery or merely words or gestures. Words of this sort are classic "verbal acts."

2. Now consider Cartwright's statement to the bank. It probably does not do the same thing as Cartwright's statement to Lord. The reason is that it speaks of a past act. Hence it would not be construed as conveying title.

3. Think about your courses in Torts, Property, and Contracts. Can you come up with other examples of civil transactions where words have operative effects and could qualify as nonhearsay verbal acts?

■ PROBLEM 3-F. "I'm from the Gas Company"

While working on the job at the Crane Wrecking Company, Jack Alford thought he smelled the odor of natural gas coming from a nearby pipeline running above ground. Although Alford had not yet decided to call the gas company, a man appeared on the scene shortly thereafter: "I'm Joe Forrest from Interstate Gas," he said, "Could you show me where the pipeline is, so I can check it out? We've had reports of a leak in this area."

Alford took Forrest around to the back of the building and was pointing out the pipeline when Forrest started to light up a cigarette. The burning match ignited the escaping gas, and in the explosion Alford was seriously hurt.

Alford sues Interstate Gas on a negligence theory, and Interstate raises contributory negligence as a defense, arguing that Alford should not have gone so close to what he knew or suspected to be a gas leak. At trial, Alford offers to testify to what Forrest told him just before the explosion, as proof that Forrest was an agent of Interstate Gas and that Alford's behavior was reasonable. Interstate Gas raises a hearsay objection. When offered for either or both of these purposes, is Forrest's statement hearsay?

■ NOTES ON PROVING EFFECT ON HEARER OR READER

1. Suppose a drug company defends a product liability suit by claiming the label gave proper warning against the use to which plaintiff put the pills. Is the label hearsay? Clearly not. It is offered to prove the information that defendant provided to users of the drug. Suppose the question is whether a broker knew facts about a house she was selling, and the other side seeks to prove the point by offering a document from her file. Hearsay? Clearly not, for the document proves the information that the broker had. In the gas leak problem, the words were spoken rather than written. For purposes of proving notice, that doesn't matter.

2. If the purpose were to prove that Forrest was actually an agent for Interstate Gas, the hearsay objection would reappear. Why? If plaintiff argued that what Forrest said proved agency because Interstate Gas *knew* he was going around saying such things and did nothing to stop him or alert the public, could this argument support the proffered evidence as nonhearsay proof of what the law would call "ostensible" authority? Clearly the answer is Yes, proof of such statements would be nonhearsay verbal acts if offered on this theory. But in order to prevail on the theory, the party seeking to establish the point would have to offer additional proof showing that the alleged principal knew the supposed agent was saying such things, was in a position to put a stop to it, and did nothing. Such facts sometimes appear, but are not common.

■ PROBLEM 3-G. Eagle's Rest Bar & Grill

Whitney Seaver, Greg Flawn, and Stacey Nichols are charged in United States District Court for the Southern District of Wisconsin with conspiring to distribute cocaine, and related substantive offenses. The case depends partly on showing that the three used a rundown house at 611 Elm Street in Alton, Wisconsin, as a warehouse and occasional living quarters, and that they sold the cocaine at a night spot called Eagle's Rest Bar & Grill in the nearby resort community of Pine Meadows.

As is usual in such matters, the evidence was largely circumstantial. Scattered in the array of background evidence offered by the prosecutor were the following bits and pieces: Proof that Whitney Seaver once attended the University of Illinois in Urbana-Champaign, where he (along with many fraternity brothers) was an ardent supporter of his school's football and basketball teams, known in the Big Ten as the "Fighting Illini"; proof that he was known among his friends by the nickname "Witter"; proof that Greg Flawn resided in Alton at 611 Elm Street.

The prosecutor had a hard time connecting Seaver with the drug venture, but she offered the following items of evidence on this point:

1) As proof that Seaver had been to the Eagle's Rest Bar & Grill, a book of matches found in his possession bearing the legend "Eagle's Rest Bar & Grill, Pine Meadows";
2) As proof that Seaver spent time at the house in Alton, a mug found there bearing a large orange capital "I" overprinted with the word "Illinois" and, at the bottom of the mug in block printing, the word "Witter";
3) As proof that Seaver knew Stacey Nichols, (a) testimony by a barmaid at Eagle's Rest Bar & Grill that she often saw Stacey Nichols with a

man whose name she did not know and that, when asked by police officer Isom whether Stacey had ever been there with a man, she (the barmaid) had pointed to the man that Stacey had been with, along with (b) police officer Isom's testimony that the man the barmaid pointed out was Whitney Seaver.

To each of these items of evidence, Whitney Seaver has raised a hearsay objection. Are any or all of these items hearsay? Why or why not?

NOTES ON VERBAL OBJECTS OR MARKERS

1. Sherlock Holmes could figure out where a person had been in London by looking at the mud on his boots. Can a verbal legend on a matchbook serve a similar identifying function, acting in effect as a verbal object or marker? Unlike mud, a verbal legend is a human expression: It *says* something because someone made appropriate arrangements. There's also a "declarant," even if we have trouble saying who it is. It is not the maker of the matchbooks, who is just following directions. Presumably the declarant is the person who placed the order, who wants matchbooks that bear this particular legend.

2. There is a statement, too, isn't there? Reasonably understood, such a matchbook says "there's a great bar and grill in Pine Meadows, called Eagle's Rest," and implicitly it says "you ought to come for drinks and a good meal," and "this matchbook came from there." We would normally just call it advertising. Offered to prove there is such a place in Pine Meadows, and the matchbook came from there, the legend looks like hearsay. But it would be ridiculous to use the hearsay doctrine to exclude such evidence, and Rule 902(7) simply cuts through hearsay issues and allows use of any "inscription, sign, tag or label purporting to have been affixed in the course of business and indicating origin, ownership, or control." This provision is found in Chapter 9 of the Rules (Authentication and Identification) and it makes such things "self-authenticating," so they can be taken at face value, without calling a witness to testify to source or origin. In the setting of the matchbook, Rule 902(7) says, in effect, that it can be admitted without other proof, and can be accepted by the trier of fact as being from Eagle's Rest Bar and Grill. The hearsay objection goes away.

3. Without Rule 902(7), we would have a hearsay problem if we just used the matchbook itself as proof of its own origin. If you think back to the example of mud on a boot, you'd need a witness like Sherlock Holmes to testify that the mud could only have come from a particular place. In the case of the matchbook, you'd need a witness to give similar testimony. What kind of witness could do that?

4. The beer mug presents a greater challenge. To start with, the logo or legend on the mug (orange capital "I" overtyped with the state name) are commercially affixed and might fit Rule 902(7), except for the fact that the logo or legend does not indicate "origin, ownership, or control." And the word "Witter" would be a special order customized label, and not one "affixed in the course of business." So we don't have an easy escape from a hearsay objection. Is there a statement? Clearly so: Whoever bought or owned the mug is apparently using it to say something like "My name is Witter and I'm a Fighting Illini Fan." To get around the hearsay objection, then, we need a witness who could say something like "I know Witter really well and he's a diehard Fighting Illini fan." That *might* be enough to connect the mug with Whitney Seaver. Remember, we're in Badger country, and there won't be that many Fighting Illini mugs, and "Witter" is not a common name like John, so one might simply infer that the mug belonged to Whitney Seaver on the basis of this testimony alone. Better still would be testimony by a friend of Seaver's who could say "he owns that mug." Again we're using words as verbal objects or markers rather than assertions.

5. The third example (barmaid pointing out Seaver to Isom in the bar) is harder yet. In the bar, she said "that's the guy I saw Nichols with." Then in court she testifies that the guy she pointed out is the guy she saw with Nichols, and Isom testifies that the guy she pointed out was Seaver. Neither of them is using the barmaid's statement to Isom to prove the truth of the matter asserted. Each is giving present testimony using the words spoken out of court as markers—not physical markers, like the legend on the matchbook or the logo and name on the beer mug, but oral or spoken words that have marking effect, serving as reference points for live courtroom testimony.

■ PROBLEM 3-H. Anna Sofer's Will

Anna Sofer died from injuries she suffered when run over by a bus, and her surviving husband Ira has brought a wrongful death action against the Municipal Transit Authority, operator of the bus. Under applicable law, the wrongful death claim belongs to Ira as Anna's next of kin, and he is entitled to recover for loss of companionship and expected income. Anna was a dentist with significant income.

In an attempt to show that in fact Ira would have had no reasonable expectation of future financial benefit if Anna had survived, and to suggest that the quality of companionship between the two was not what might be expected between husband and wife, the Transit Authority offers in evidence a passage from Anna's will. Anna had executed the will, with the assistance of legal counsel, only a few weeks before her death. In it she had written as follows:

> Whereas I have been a faithful and loving wife to Ira, while he has reciprocated my tender feelings with utter cruelty, disrespect, and indifference, and whereas I have foolishly spent my best years trying hard to make

> him happy and to provide a comfortable home for us while he took me for granted and wasted the resources gathered by what was supposed to be our joint endeavor upon selfish and trivial pursuits every chance he got, now therefore I limit my bequest to Ira to $1, which is more than he deserves.

Ira objects that Anna's will is hearsay, when offered for the stated purpose. Is it? Why or why not?

■ PROBLEM 3-I. "A Papier-Mâché Man"

Zinder is prosecuted for alleged sexual assault upon eight-year-old Sharon, occurring eight months before. There is clinical evidence of assault, and Sharon testifies that Zinder assaulted her. Indeed, the defense admits that Sharon was the victim of an attack of this nature, but denies that Zinder was the assailant.

To demonstrate that Zinder was the assailant, the prosecutor offers two proofs. One takes the form of an account by Officer Stalwart of the description which Sharon gave of the room to which she said she was taken by the man who assaulted her:

> She said the room contained what she called an "old fashioned iron bed" with "a curlicue design in the metal." She said that there were windows to the outside on two walls and a door to a closet which also had a window to the outside. She said that near the bed there was, to use her own words, "a green rocking chair and a little table with a lamp on it," and in the corner there was what she called "a papier-mâché man sitting on a wooden chair, and the man was painted red and green and blue and had a book on his lap, with his legs crossed, wearing a hat," and she said the man looked "really gay and funny, and kind of short, like a leprechaun."

The other proof takes the form of a testimonial account by Officer Yeoman, who made the arrest, describing the room in which Zinder resides. Yeoman's account is independent of that given by Stalwart. That is, Yeoman was not in the courtroom while Stalwart testified; he had not talked to Sharon about the room; he described what he saw with his own eyes. These proofs seem persuasive evidence that Zinder was the culprit because the descriptions given by Sharon and Yeoman are alike in all essential details, including especially the description of the papier-mâché man.

Zinder has strenuously objected to Officer Stalwart's testimony, arguing at length that "Sharon's description is hearsay, for it is offered as proof of the room in which the assault occurred, and necessarily that requires that the jury believe in the truth of her words and believe that she really thinks that the room looks as she described it."

But the court rules, "Her description is not hearsay. It is offered to prove that she knows what the room looks like. I'm going to let it in." Has the court erred? Why or why not? What additional proof might the prosecutor offer in aid of the claim that Sharon's description of the room should be viewed as nonhearsay?

■ NOTES ON CIRCUMSTANTIAL EVIDENCE OF STATE OF MIND AND OF MEMORY

1. As the introductory comment says, these categories are troublesome. We have a hearsay exception for state-of-mind statements, found in FRE 803(3), and you will study it in Chapter 4. The exception allows use of statements to prove the speaker's state of mind, including most importantly the speaker's intention, but language in FRE 803(3) blocks use of the exception to use a statement to prove a "fact remembered or believed."

2. In *Anna Sofer's Will*, Anna's statement is not offered to prove that Ira behaved badly. It would be hearsay if offered for this purpose, and the state of mind exception in FRE 803(3) could not be used (it is not available to prove a fact remembered or believed). Instead, Anna's statement is being offered to prove what she *thought* of Ira, and it is clear that she held a low opinion of him. If it tended to prove what she thought only because she was *asserting* that she thought ill of Ira (and every statement of fact tells us the speaker thinks the facts are as recited in the statement, and tells us something of what the speaker thinks), then her statement would be hearsay, but it would fit the state-of-mind exception in FRE 803(3). We can, however, look at Anna's statement in another way, and courts often do that when the words do not expressly refer to state of mind.

3. Consider the fact that she writes her statement in a will. The verbal act doctrine does not apply because the point is not to prove or give effect to the will, but to show something about the relationship of Anna and Ira. Still, making the statement in her will counts for something, as the will disinherits Ira and will become public at some point. When one of two people in an intimate relationship makes public statements critical of the other, don't we normally conclude that there are problems in the relationship? Such a conclusion does not depend on the truth of the facts asserted, but on the fact that intimate companions are acting out their grievances in public—this *behavior* tells us something about the relationship—and it isn't good—and viewing Anna's statement as verbal behavior involves a nonhearsay use.

4. In *Papier-Mâché Man*, what Sharon said is being offered to prove her memory of the room, hence to show that she was in the room. Since her statement asserts that she has seen the room and been there, it looks like hearsay. Since it is used to prove her memory of the room, it cannot be offered under the state-of-mind exception in FRE 803(3). Yet common sense calls out that her statement is *highly persuasive*, perhaps even more so than her testimony would be. The reason is that it describes a unique or highly unusual room. We can treat her statement as nonhearsay because it is hard to imagine how she could say what she said unless she had been in the room. This unique or very unusual knowledge is an argument for nonhearsay treatment. The argument wouldn't work if Sharon described an ordinary room—one with a bed and a bureau and a nightstand that had no unusual or unique qualities like those detailed in Sharon's statement: Anybody could "make up" such a description of a bedroom and the description would fit a great many bedrooms. But not anybody could make up the description that Sharon has provided.

5. Suppose Hal is tried for stealing cash from the safe of his employer, Fran. She testifies that she set the combination as 687176218, that she kept it secret, and that Hal was the only employee to whom she told the number. Hal claims Jason, another employee, committed the theft, and that he must have found the secret location where the combination was recorded. After Fran testifies, Hal calls Ike, who was sequestered and did not hear her testify or learn what she said. If allowed, Ike would testify that before the theft Jason said he "knew the combination, and wrote these numbers on a slip, which he gave to me." The digits on this slip match the combination. Hearsay, if offered to prove Jason knew the combination and might be the thief?

HEARSAY UNDER RULE 801: A REPRISE

Now let us look more closely at the definition of hearsay in Rule 801, and review the situations we have already examined in distinguishing between hearsay and nonhearsay. Most importantly, FRE 801 says that hearsay is any statement (written or oral) offered "to prove the truth of the matter asserted." And a statement includes "nonverbal conduct," but only if it is "intended . . . as an assertion."

With this definition in mind, we know that the three statements in Problem 3-A (Three See a Robbery) are hearsay under FRE 801 if offered to prove Higgins robbed the bank. And we know as well that the statements in the other problems in the section on nonhearsay uses—Problems 3-C through 3-F dealing with the red light, the massage parlor, the corn crib, and the gas company—are not hearsay. They all involve "assertive verbal conduct," so they are statements for purposes of FRE 801, but they are not hearsay because they were offered as a basis for inferring something other than "the truth of the matter asserted."

We also know that Rule 801 rejects the broad view of Baron Parke in *Wright* that hearsay embraces nonassertive conduct (captain boarding vessel with family, truck pulling forward into the intersection) when offered for the two-step inference (conduct implied belief; belief implies something about acts, events, conditions in the world).

Other choices. Before going on, it's worth noting that the framers of Rule 801 could have made other choices. Over many years, commentators had offered other suggestions that would have lessened the impact of the hearsay doctrine. One suggestion was to define hearsay as an uncross-examinable statement, when offered to prove the truth of the matter asserted, which would have had the effect of admitting any prior statements by persons who take the stand and testify. (The idea behind this approach was that being able to cross-examine the declarant is the main concern, and that "deferred" cross-examination, which takes place at trial *after* the prior statement was made, is just as good—or *almost* just as good—as "contemporaneous" cross-examination, which we have with "in court" statements by the witness.) Another suggestion was a "rule-of-preference" approach that would have defined hearsay as a statement by a person who is absent but available to the proponent, when offered to prove the truth of the matter asserted. (The idea would be to admit statements by testifying witnesses, and also statements by witnesses who cannot be called to testify, on the theory that it would be better to admit hearsay if live testimony cannot be had.) Yet another approach would have reduced the hearsay doctrine to a cautionary principle, opening the door to any hearsay that was "reliable." (The idea was to broaden the exceptions to the hearsay doctrine, replacing the "categorical" exceptions that you are about to study with "flexible" exceptions applied on an *ad hoc* basis.)

None of these reformist approaches was chosen. You will learn in Chapter 4, however, that *some* prior statements by witnesses who testify are admissible under special provisions in FRE 801(d)(1). These are defined there as "not hearsay," and they include certain "inconsistent" statements, certain "consistent" statements, and statement of "identification of a person." These statements really *are* hearsay, however, because they fit the definition in Rule 801(a)-(c). They are defined as "not hearsay" by what we might call statutory magic: Out of the "hat" of the basic definition, the drafters pull the "rabbit" of "not hearsay" for these three categories. The same statutory magic happens again in FRE 801(d)(2), which codifies the admissions doctrine. The statements described in the five clauses of that provision (A through E) are "not hearsay" only because FRE 801(d)(2) defines them in that way. This extension of the statutory magic is not so odd, however, because it connects with common law tradition, where admissions were sometimes seen as nonhearsay and sometimes as hearsay but within an exception that made them admissible.

You should note that the "not hearsay" category set up by FRE 801(d) has nothing to do with the nonhearsay uses that you just examined. The nonhearsay uses involve statements that are not offered for their truth, so they fall outside the definition of hearsay. The "not hearsay" category includes statements that *do* fit the definition of hearsay, and we just use statutory magic in labeling them "not hearsay."

D HEARSAY AND NONHEARSAY—BORDERLAND OF THE DOCTRINE

1. Statements with Performative Aspects

While FRE 801 resolves much with certainty, some situations were problematic before the Rule was adopted and are problematic still.

The hard cases involve what might be called "indirect uses" of statements. We are *not* talking about statements like those by Plaintalk, Sirchev, and Oblique in Problem 3-A (Three See a Robbery), all of which are hearsay plain and simple. In the indirect-use cases, the purpose is *not* to prove acts, events, or conditions asserted by the speaker in the ordinary meaning of his words ("Higgins is the one who did it"), *nor* to use his words this way and then draw further inferences ("Higgins went out of here carrying money bags"), *nor* to prove what the speaker *meant* to say, even though the words make the point indirectly ("they ought to put Higgins in jail for this").

In the indirect-use cases, the purpose is to use words to get at something else. In these cases, we are after something that seems to be *on the speaker's mind but is not asserted* in the statement. Recall the words of Anna Sofer in Problem 3-H ("my husband treats me with 'cruelty' and fritters away our savings 'upon selfish and trivial pursuits'") and Sharon in Problem 3-I ("there was 'a papier mâché man'"). In each case the statement suggests something else about the speaker's thoughts (Anna would not have supported her husband; Sharon must have been in that room), and it was this "something else" that the statements were offered to prove. The same is true of the Vicar's statements in the *Wright* case (business talk suggested Marsden could conduct business). These are examples of statements whose importance lies in what they suggest about what the declarant must think, without actually saying it.

Neither the language of FRE 801 nor decided cases provide clear guidance for these indirect-use cases. In fairness, we should add that there is something about the nature of hearsay and human verbal expression that makes such cases hard. We doubt that any brief statutory phrase can provide much guidance.

Let us look again at the ACN to FRE 801. After the passage about "nonverbal conduct," the Note adds:

> [V]erbal conduct which is assertive but offered as a basis for inferring something other than the matter asserted [is] also excluded from the definition of hearsay by the language of subdivision (c).

What does this comment mean? By one reading, it is perfectly bland, expressing the truism that a statement offered for a nonhearsay purpose is not hearsay. Does the comment reach further? Obviously it does not embrace what Oblique said in Problem 3-A ("they ought to put Higgins in jail for this"). Extended that far, the comment would reduce the hearsay doctrine to a foolish rule where formalism reigns supreme. Hearsay would only reach statements that say literally what they are offered to prove, and the doctrine would only occasionally achieve its purposes.

The statements by Anna Sofer and Sharon probably qualify as assertive verbal conduct offered as "a basis for inferring something other than the matter asserted." But if they escape the hearsay definition in FRE 801, is it because they are offered to prove an unspoken thought? Since all factual claims are also purposeful disclosures of the speaker's thoughts, that is not a persuasive explanation. The better explanation is that the words have performative aspects (Anna makes a public display of distaste for her husband; Sharon displays knowledge she could not have without the experience).

UNITED STATES v. SINGER

United States Court of Appeals for the Eighth Circuit
687 F.2d 1135, modified, 710 F.2d 431 (1983)

[Joseph Sazenski, Arturo Izquierdo, and others were prosecuted for drug offenses, arising out of an operation allegedly involving shipments of marijuana from Miami, Florida, to Minnetonka, Minnesota. Sazenski maintained a residence at 600 Wilshire in Minnetonka. Apparently Izquierdo used the alias of Carlos Almaden.]

HENLEY, J. . . .

The district court admitted into evidence an envelope addressed to Sazenski and "Carlos Almaden," 600 Wilshire, containing notice to terminate their tenancy. It was introduced to show that "Carlos Almaden" lived with Sazenski. We reject Sazenski's contention that this letter was hearsay.

FRE 801(c) states: "'Hearsay' is a statement, other than one made by the declarant while testifying at the trial or hearing, offered in evidence to prove the truth of the matter asserted." The Advisory Committee for the proposed Rules of Evidence noted that "[t]he effect of the definition of 'statement' is to exclude from the operation of the hearsay rule all evidence of conduct, verbal or nonverbal, not intended as an assertion . . . . [Some] nonverbal conduct . . . may be offered as evidence that the person acted as he did because of his belief in the existence of the condition sought to be proved, from which belief the existence of the condition may be inferred." This observation is consistent with the purpose of the hearsay rule—the exclusion of declarations whose veracity cannot be tested by cross-examination. There is some guarantee that an inference drawn from out-of-court behavior is trustworthy, because people base their actions on the correctness of their belief. If this letter were submitted to *assert* the implied truth of its *written contents*—that Carlos Almaden lived at 600 Wilshire—it would be hearsay and inadmissible. It is, however, admissible nonhearsay because its purpose is to imply from the landlord's *behavior*—his mailing a letter to Carlos Almaden, 600 Wilshire—that "Almaden" lived there. In addition, it is important that the letter was found in the residence at 600 Wilshire . . . .

From what has been said, it follows that the judgments of the district court should be, and they are, affirmed.

It is so ordered.

[The opinion of Arnold, Circuit Judge, concurring in part and dissenting in part, is omitted. On rehearing, the Eighth Circuit reversed the convictions, but the en banc opinion expressly "adopted and reaffirmed" much of the panel's original opinion, including the portion set out above.]

NOTES ON STATEMENTS WITH PERFORMATIVE ASPECTS

1. Forget about Sazenski, who is not important. The letter to Carlos Almaden *says* he lives (takes mail) at that address, which would support the conclusion that the address block is hearsay if offered to prove that Almaden lives (takes mail) there. The larger purpose of the owner in writing the address block on the envelope was different—he wanted the carrier to deliver the letter to the right place and wanted Almaden to get it. So we can concede that the address block is a statement, and it *says* Almaden lives at 600 Wilshire. If that were all there was to it, we have hearsay. But we can also say that the eviction notice (including the address block) is something more—an attempt to throw Almaden out, to begin a formal eviction, and that makes a difference. The owner *acted on his belief,* and took the critical legal step of giving notice, which justifies nonhearsay treatment. (If the owner had merely mailed a postcard to a friend commenting that he'd rented the place at 600 Wilshire to Almaden, the act would not be very significant, and the hearsay aspect of what he did would count more.) In evicting a tenant, mailing is crucial. It isn't just "talk," but "action" too. Thus it seems that the court in *Singer* got it right in finding the notice to be nonhearsay.

2. Suppose an FBI agent asked the owner where Carlos Almaden lived and he replied "600 Wilshire." That would be hearsay if offered to prove where Almaden lived. Suppose an undercover agent testified that he gave the owner a package for Almaden, then secretly followed him, and saw the owner deliver it to 600 Wilshire. Such testimony would *not* be subject to a hearsay objection. Which of these examples more closely resembles the actual facts of *Singer*, the first or the second?

3. When law enforcement agents bust bookmaking or drug operations, they routinely take incoming phonecalls. In the former situation, a voice at the distant end tries to place a bet. In the latter, the voice tries to line up a drug purchase. If the officer who takes the calls testifies to what the callers say, as proof that people normally on the premises take bets or sell drugs, is it hearsay? Most American courts say no. See Headley v. Tilghman, 53 F.3d 472 (2d Cir. 1995) (incoming calls could be characterized as "mixed acts and assertions" admissible because of their "performance aspects"); United States v. Long, 905 F.2d 1572, 1579-1580 (D.C. Cir.) (admitting incoming drug calls as nonhearsay proof of trafficking), *cert. denied*, 498 U.S. 948 (1990). Courts in the UK once considered such calls to be hearsay, applying the broad view of hearsay handed down by Baron Parke's opinion in *Wright*, but now they agree with American courts that such calls are not hearsay. See Regina v. Chrysostomou (Mark), 2010 WL 25150002 (Court of Appeal, Criminal Division) (2010) (cellphone text messages to defendant seeking drugs were not hearsay when offered to prove defendant was a dealer). The best explanation is that such calls have important performative aspects, like the eviction notice in *Singer*. See generally Symposium: The Reach and Reason of the Hearsay Rule: How Should (or Would) the Supreme Court Decide *Kearley*?, 16 Miss. C. L. Rev. 1 (1995) (collecting essays on an English case holding that an incoming drug call is hearsay).

■ PROBLEM 3-J. "My Husband Is in Denver"

In FBI interviews, eyewitnesses identify Greg Hensen as one of the men who robbed Girard Bank & Trust in Boston on April 10th. On April 11th, FBI agents get an arrest warrant and go to Greg's house, where they encounter his wife Barbara. "My husband is in Denver," she tells them, "because his mother just died, and he flew out to her funeral on the 9th. He's coming back day after tomorrow." On checking airline passenger and reservation lists, the FBI learn that there is no record of a Greg Hensen flying either into or out of Boston in the previous seven days, nor any reservation in his name on any incoming flights to Boston in the next three days.

On April 12, agents question another suspect, who tells them that "Greg is hiding out at his brother's in Quincy." On the basis of that tip, the agents promptly get a warrant authorizing them to search for Greg in his brother's apartment, and there they find him.

At Greg's trial in federal court for armed bank robbery, the government offers testimony by the agents describing their encounter with Barbara, quoting what she told them of her husband's whereabouts. Counsel for Greg objects: "Barbara Hensen is not on trial here, her husband is. What she said or thought is hearsay, and irrelevant besides." Is Barbara's statement relevant? Is it hearsay?

NOTES ON LYING AND HEARSAY

1. In Greg Hensen's trial, arguing for the state that the hearsay doctrine doesn't apply to Barbara Hensen's statement is duck soup, isn't it? "We're not offering it for its truth, your Honor, so it can't be hearsay." When you prevail on that point and the statement gets in, you will come in time to closing arguments. What will you say to the jury about Barbara's false statement? You would probably stress "what she was trying to do" when she talked to police, which was to mislead them, to throw them off the scent. In effect, this argument stresses the performative aspect of her statement.

2. Most courts that consider lying have said it is not hearsay, and they sometimes accept the duck soup argument. In a complicated conspiracy prosecution for casting false ballots in a federal election, for example, the Supreme Court rejected a hearsay objection to evidence that conspirators perjured themselves in local proceedings inquiring into election fraud. The perjury took the form of false statements about who came to the polls, and the Court concluded that these lies were not hearsay. They were not offered to prove "the truth of anything asserted," said the Court, but to show "they were false." Nor did the rationale of the hearsay doctrine come into play, said the Court, since defendants "had no interest in cross-examining" their lying cohorts inasmuch as the government did not contend that what they said was true. Anderson v. United States, 417 U.S. 211, 219-222 (1974) (perjured statements "helped prove the underlying motive of the conspiracy" by showing that false votes in the federal contest "were not an end in themselves," but part of an effort to control local results). Obviously perjured statements are "verbal acts" that can send the speaker to jail. Is that point critical in *Anderson*? If you were the prosecutor, wouldn't you argue very much in the way you did in the Greg Hensen case?

3. In Problem 3-J, Barbara committed a crime if she lied to the FBI about where her husband was. See 18 USC §1001 (one who "knowingly and willfully falsifies, conceals or covers up" a material fact or "makes any false, fictitious or fraudulent statements" on matters within the jurisdiction of the government is guilty of a felony). We treat such statements as crimes because they have harmful operative impact—leading police in the wrong direction, driving up costs, perhaps keeping them from the truth. Treating such statements as crimes recognizes their performative aspect, doesn't it? Even if Barbara did not commit a crime, arguably the impeding effect of deceiving FBI agents justifies treating her statement as an act.

4. When the defendant himself lies to police, it doesn't much matter whether we treat what he said as hearsay or as nonhearsay. The reason is that what a party to a suit says may always be admitted against him, at least so far as the hearsay doctrine is concerned. In the parlance of the Rules, a statement by a party, if offered against him for the truth of the matter asserted, is an "admission" and can be received in evidence. See FRE 801(d)(2)(A) (Chapter

4B, infra). But this rationale does not usually reach statements offered against a defendant but made by someone else after the crime, as in *Anderson* and Problem 3-J. Here it makes a big difference whether the statement is viewed as hearsay or nonhearsay, and often courts follow the lead of *Anderson* and admit. See, e.g., State v. Reyes, 52 P.3d 948, 958 (N.M. 2002) (admitting against one defendant false exculpatory statements, all telling the same story, separately given by himself and three co-offenders; statements by the other three were nonhearsay because offered as proof that they were false, indicating consciousness of guilt). Sometimes, however, false statements showing a guilty mind on the part of one person carry little or no weight when offered against another. See United States v. Pedroza, 750 F.2d 187, 203-204 (2d Cir. 1984) (in trial of *P* and *H* and others for kidnapping an 11-year-old boy, testimony by arresting agent that *H* falsely said she was the boy's mother was not hearsay, and showed "consciousness of guilt," but *H* lived with a third man who "masterminded the affair" and was "his principal aide," while *P* and other codefendants were only "hired hands," so on retrial it might not be proper to attribute *H*'s state of mind to "the hired hands").

■ PROBLEM 3-K. King Air YC-437-CP

Bruno and others are charged with theft of an airplane and with importation and possession of marijuana. The evidence indicates that the plane in question, a King Air bearing identification Number YC-437-CP, was stolen in Florida and flown to an airstrip on Bruno's rural Arkansas property. There federal agents attached a transponder enabling them to track the plane when Mason and Pell flew it first to Acapulco (where it was seen picking up marijuana) and then to Mississippi (where the cargo was unloaded). Arrests were made and charges brought against Bruno and three others. Pell was not charged, for he bargained a plea and testified for the government.

At his trial, Bruno contends that his involvement in the unsavory theft and drug scheme was completely innocent. He testifies that the King Air made an emergency landing at his airstrip, where he let it stay until it could be repaired, that mechanics came thereafter and fixed a ruptured oil line that forced the landing, and that the plane "was mysteriously flown away about a week later." He denies that he accepted money from his codefendants in exchange for letting the plane stay, and insists he knows nothing about the theft or use of the plane to import marijuana.

Bruno also calls Kay Dixon as a witness and offers her testimony that "Bruno told me in front of six other people that he was storing a King Air at his airstrip." He argues that the fact that he said in public that he was storing the plane supports his claim of innocence, since "a man with guilty knowledge is not likely to advertise his possession of stolen property." The prosecutor raises a hearsay objection. What result, and why?

NOTES ON THE SIGNIFICANCE OF DISCLOSURE

1. We should not say Bruno's statement avoids the hearsay category because it was a naked factual assertion ("I'm storing a King Air"), rather than a forthright revelation of knowledge ("I know about yonder King Air"). That would be like saying "The light was red" is not hearsay when offered to prove the speaker *thinks* the light was red, and what the speaker *thinks* is not *itself* hearsay if offered to prove that what he thinks is so. That would mean the end of the hearsay doctrine, wouldn't it?

2. What makes Bruno's statement relevant is not that it proves what he knows, but that he's willing *to tell others* what he knows. If you get Bruno's statement admitted, isn't that what would you tell the jury it means? Thus the statement is relevant because of *what it does*, which is to inform his listeners that Bruno knows about the airplane.

2. Using Statements to Prove Matters Assumed

UNITED STATES v. PACELLI

United States Court of Appeals for the Second Circuit
491 F.2d 1108, cert. denied, 419 U.S. 826 (1974)

[Vincent Pacelli, Jr., was charged with conspiracy to interfere with the constitutional rights of others. The charges arose out of the brutal stabbing of Patsy Parks, whose body was doused with gasoline and set afire in a desolate area of Long Island. On the day before her death, federal agents had tried to serve a subpoena on her. She had previously testified before a grand jury investigating drug dealing, where she gave evidence about a box apparently containing money that was delivered to Pacelli. The grand jury indicted Pacelli and others. In the present prosecution, the government alleged that Pacelli killed Parks to keep her from testifying.]

MANSFIELD, Circuit J. . . .

Appellant next urges that it was prejudicial error on the part of the trial court to have permitted Lipsky, over defense objections, to testify as to the conduct and statements of appellant's wife, Beverly, of his uncle, Frank Bassi, and of his friends Perez and Bracer on February 10, 1972, at the Bassis' apartment. We agree. Since the conspiracy to violate Parks' civil rights had terminated with her death, this proof was not admissible as declarations of a co-conspirator made in the course of a conspiracy or as evidence of acts designed to show illegal activity on the part of the conspirators themselves. The purpose of the evidence was to get before the jury the fact that various persons other than Lipsky, who had been closely associated with Pacelli, believed Pacelli to be guilty of having murdered Parks. Indeed the government frankly conceded this in its brief:

> The fact that Pacelli's wife summoned Lipsky to the Bassis' apartment is proof that she knew of his involvement with Pacelli in the murder. The fact that Pacelli's wife, uncle, and close friends were discussing at that meeting that the murder had been bungled by leaving the body where it could easily be found—rather than that Pacelli had been remanded for something he had not done—is strongly indicative that they knew that Pacelli caused Patsy Parks's death. . . . [T]he jury was entitled to conclude, from the close relationship to Pacelli of the persons at the February 10th meeting, that the source of their knowledge was Pacelli himself, since he was the only person besides Lipsky present at the commission of the crime.
>
> The additional fact that at this meeting Pacelli's wife told Lipsky to get instructions from Bracer, who, with Perez, then told Lipsky he should go to Florida and offered him the money to do so, was clearly evidence that they knew that Lipsky had seen Pacelli kill Parks.

Since the extra-judicial statements clearly implied knowledge and belief on the part of third person declarants not available for cross-examination as to the source of their knowledge regarding the ultimate fact in issue, i.e., whether Pacelli killed Parks, Lipsky's testimony as to them was excludable hearsay evidence.

... The admission of testimony as to the third party's declarations in the present case violated the central purpose of the hearsay rule, which is to give litigants "an opportunity to cross-examine the persons on whom the fact finder is asked to rely." Finman, Implied Assertions as Hearsay: Some Criticisms of the Uniform Rules of Evidence, 14 Stan. L. Rev. 682, 684 (1962). We cannot agree that the only source of the extra-judicial declarations and conduct could have been Pacelli himself. Cross-examination of the declarants, had they been produced as witnesses, might have established that the information came from Lipsky himself, from third persons, or from news media, especially since appellant had on the same day been jailed as a result of the discovery of Parks' body.

We consider it irrelevant . . . that the extra-judicial statements and conduct admitted in this case may not have been intended by those involved to communicate their belief that Pacelli murdered Parks. The government concedes that if Lipsky had testified that the various declarants (Beverly Jalaba, the Bassis, Perez and Bracer) had told him at the February 10th meeting that Pacelli had admitted to them his participation in the killing of Parks, the testimony would have been inadmissible hearsay. While the danger of insincerity may be reduced where implied rather than express assertions of the third parties are involved, there is the added danger of misinterpretation of the declarant's belief. Moreover, the declarant's opportunity and capacity for accurate perception or his sources of information remain of crucial importance. Here, for instance, there is no suggestion that the declarants actually observed Pacelli commit the crimes with which he was charged. Thus their extra-judicial implied assertions have even less indicia of reliability than the implied assertion involved in Krulewitch [v. United States, 336 U.S. 440 (1949)], which was held inadmissible. Pacelli was entitled to cross-examine the third party declarants in order to test the validity of the inference—which the government sought to have the jury draw—that he had told the declarants he had killed Parks....

The judgment of conviction is reversed and the case is remanded for a new trial.

MOORE, J., dissenting....

Turning now to the "hearsay" constituting, according to the majority, reversible error, of what does this hearsay, so damaging as to require reversal, consist? On February 10th at the apartment of Frank Bassi (Pacelli's uncle) were gathered, Bassi, Pacelli's wife, Beverly, Beverly's sister, Barbara, Pacelli's sister, Loretta, three friends, Al Bracer, Abby Perez and Barbara Jalaba, and a man named Bayron. By this time via the public press, Parks' murder and the burning of the body had been revealed to the public at large. Frank Bassi commented about the bungling technique used in trying to dispose of the body. Lipsky was induced to go away for a while and given $1,000 by Perez for that purpose. From this the majority conclude that these "extra-judicial statements clearly implied knowledge and belief on the part of third person declarants not available for cross-examination as to the source of their knowledge regarding the ultimate fact in issue, i.e., whether Pacelli killed Parks." However, there was no declaration that Pacelli had told them that he had killed Parks and none expressed an opinion to this effect so that any such "hearsay" problem is not before us. Thus, Lipsky's statements of the February 10th apartment conversation added so little—and this only by way of inference—to his actual eye-witness testimony as to the events on February 4th that it does not, in my opinion, fall within the category of reversible error....

■ NOTES ON USING STATEMENTS TO PROVE UNSPOKEN THOUGHTS

1. *Pacelli* is a pre-Rules decision, but applying FRE 801 would not change anything. Where is the hearsay that led to reversal? Isn't Judge Moore right in saying there was "no declaration that Pacelli had told them"? Consider these possible interpretations:

(a) Those at the meeting thought Pacelli killed Parks, and their talk about sending Lipsky into hiding expressed that belief. Hence their words are hearsay, like the words of Oblique in Problem 3-A ("They ought to put Higgins in jail for this"). By this understanding, the majority got it right.

(b) Those at the meeting didn't know what happened, but spoke and acted on rumors, perhaps traceable ultimately to statements by Lipsky or Pacelli. Hence an account of the behavior of those at the meeting conveyed "indirect hearsay," like that condemned by Judge Waterman in *Check* (section B1c, supra). By this understanding, once again the majority got it right.

(c) Those at the meeting *behaved* as though Pacelli did the deed—as though that were commonly understood. What they did was to send Lipsky into hiding to protect Pacelli. Thus their statements have a performative aspect, justifying nonhearsay treatment, in the manner of the eviction notice in *Singer* and the lies to police in Problem 3-J ("My Husband Is in Denver"). By this understanding, Judge Moore is right (no hearsay).

(d) What is persuasive about the meeting is what did *not* happen and what was *not* said. If those present thought Pacelli did not murder Parks, one would have expected protests at the conduct of agents and prosecutors in arresting and charging Pacelli. Hence what happened at the meeting resembles *Cain* (section B1b, supra), where the absence of complaint was not hearsay when offered to prove the heater worked. By this understanding, once again Judge Moore is right (no hearsay).

2. Consider a case in which Parran and Reynolds were charged with conspiracy to defraud the government by cashing unemployment checks belonging to others. Agents were tipped by a photography studio, where the clerk said two men were trying to get photo IDs but did not know what names and numbers to use(!). Watched by the agents, the two emerged from the studio, conversed briefly, and then Reynolds entered a bank, which refused to cash the check that he proffered because he had no account. Agents arrested Reynolds. When Parran approached, Reynolds told him "I didn't tell them anything about you." The government proved this statement in the trial of the two. When Parran appealed, the government argued that what Reynolds said was not offered "for the truth of the matter asserted" because Reynolds had said nothing about Parran's guilt or involvement. Consider these possible interpretations:

(a) Although his words do not say "we both know you're in this with me up to your eyeballs," that was Reynolds' message. Hence his words were hearsay like Oblique's in Problem 3-A ("They ought to put Higgins in jail for this").

(b) In his remark to Parran, Reynolds was making a gesture of solidarity, which suggests that Parran was involved because the gesture would not be needed otherwise. The gesture has a performative aspect like lying to police, as in Problem 3-J ("My Husband Is in Denver"), justifying nonhearsay treatment.

(c) Reynolds did not assert anything about Parran, merely stating a fact that is true or false (he said he had not implicated Parran; either he did or he didn't). We infer, from the fact that Reynolds said these words, that he knew Parran was involved, and the government is right—the words are not hearsay because they assume the point but do not assert it.

Which would you choose? In the case itself, the reviewing court chose the first interpretation, holding that Reynolds' statement was hearsay: "[S]tatements containing express assertions may also contain implied assertions qualifying as hearsay and susceptible to hearsay objections," and the probative value of what Reynolds said "depends on the truth of an assumed fact [that] it implies," making it inadmissible hearsay. United States v. Reynolds, 715 F.2d 99, 103 (3d Cir. 1983) (reversing).

3. In *Krulewitch* (cited in both *Pacelli* and *Reynolds*) the Supreme Court said a statement is hearsay when offered to prove something assumed by the speaker. There Kay and a woman companion were charged with transporting another woman from New York to Miami for immoral purposes. After the three were arrested, Kay's companion spoke with the woman. At Kay's trial, the latter summed up the conversation this way:

> She asked me, she says, "You didn't talk yet?" And I says, "No." And she says, "Well, don't," she says, "until we get you a lawyer." And then she says, "Be very careful what you say." And I can't put it in exact words. But she said, "It would be better for us two girls to take the blame than Kay (the defendant) because he couldn't stand it, he couldn't stand to take it."

See Krulewitch v. United States, 336 U.S. 440, 441-443 (1949) (reversing for error in admitting "hearsay declaration" attributed to his companion, since it "plainly implied [Kay] was guilty of the crime"). See also Dutton v. Evans, 400 U.S. 74 (1970) (treating as hearsay a co-offender's jailhouse comment that "we wouldn't be in this now" if it hadn't been for defendant since it "implicitly identified" defendant as murderer).

4. Suppose Nora sues Vince, claiming he is the father of Nora's infant son Christopher. Nora offers to testify that Vince's parents came to the hospital for the delivery and that Vince's brothers and sisters and other kindred "visited [the hospital] and exhibited affection" toward little Christopher after he was born. Admit in support of the claim that Vince is the father, or exclude? Is it hearsay? See Thornton v. Shows, 537 So. 2d 1363, 1366 (Miss. 1989) (exclude) (family affection for Christopher was just "a nonverbal assertion" of family's belief that defendant was the father). Did the family intend to assert that Vince was the father? If not, should family behavior be excluded anyway, because they could not know who the father was? Or does their behavior implicitly convey an admission by Vince that he was the father?

5. So difficult are cases like *Pacelli, Reynolds,* and *Krulewitch,* that courts sometimes invoke Baron Parke's approach in *Wright* in trying to solve the problem. It seems highly doubtful that these courts would really conclude that *all* human conduct, whether consisting of pure nonassertive acts (driving forward into the intersection) or statements ("let's set up a meeting") are hearsay when offered for the two-step inference described in the Notes after *Wright,* but in the setting of verbal utterances these cases apply the hearsay doctrine with maximum breadth:

(a) In the trial of Eric Stoddard for murdering a child, the question was whether to admit something that another child asked her mother. She had been with defendant at the time of the crime, and her question was whether Eric was "going to get me?" The Maryland Court of Appeals concluded that her question was hearsay when offered to prove that Eric beat the victim. The question "impliedly" said that the child saw the prior beating. Stoddard v. State, 887 A.2d 564, 581 (Md. 2005) (citing *Wright*).

(b) In the drug trial of Brett Dullard, the question was whether to admit a note found on the premises, addressed to defendant, in which the author said he "had to go inside to pee + calm my nerves," and that when he came out "there sat a black + white w/the dude out of his car facing our own direction," offered to show that the author was afraid because of drugs on the premises. The Iowa Supreme Court concluded that the note was hearsay, invoking the "implied assertion" doctrine even though it recognized that FRE 801 rejects the broad definition of hearsay. See State v. Dullard, 668 N.W.2d 585, 591-592 (Iowa 2003) (citing *Wright* and adding "we are not convinced that the absent of intent [to assert] makes the underlying belief more reliable, especially when the belief is derived from verbal conduct").

(c) In the murder trial of Sergio Ginez and Leo Reyes, the question was whether to admit against Ginez something Reyes said to arresting officers—"Well, if you don't find the gun, then you are going to let us go, right?" The gun used in the crime was never found, and the prosecutor argued what Ginez said suggests that the gun was missing because Ginez and Reyes had gotten rid of it in the few minutes that elapsed between the shooting and the arrest. Although this meaning was "implied rather than express," the court concluded that the statement was hearsay. See People v. Reyes, 70 Cal. Rptr. 903, 907 (Cal. App. 2008) (citing *Wright* as the "starting point for a discussion of the implied assertion doctrine").

6. These difficulties have persuaded some to advocate amending the definition of hearsay in FRE 801 to adopt Baron Parke's broad approach, at least with respect to verbal utterances. See M. Graham, "Stickperson Hearsay": A Simplified Approach to Understanding the Rule Against Hearsay, 1982 U. Ill. L. Rev. 887, 921; G. Wellborn, The Definition of Hearsay in the Federal Rules of Evidence, 61 Tex. L. Rev. 49, 92 n.191 (1982) (a broader definition found its way into Texas Rule 801). But problems of this sort are inevitable in a doctrine regulating the evidential use of human statements, especially since modern hearsay requires us to distinguish between *saying* and *doing*. Just as *doing something* may have an assertive quality (nodding the head, pointing), so *saying something* may have a performative quality (evicting someone). There will always be cases with one foot in each camp. See generally Mueller, Post-Modern Hearsay Reform: The Importance of Complexity, 76 Minn. L. Rev. 367, 412-423 (1992) (developing this argument); Park, "I didn't tell them anything about you": Implied Assertions as Hearsay Under the Federal Rules of Evidence, 74 Minn. L. Rev. 783 (1990) (analyzing *Reynolds* and other cases and concluding that FRE 801 should *not* be amended); Millich, Re-Examining Hearsay Under the Federal Rules: Some Method for the Madness, 39 Kan. L. Rev. 1 (1990) (proposing a test for statements offered to prove matters assumed).

3. Statements That Are Questions or Commands

In everyday usage, the term "assertion" connotes a strong claim that something is so. This term is part and parcel of the hearsay doctrine, under FRE 801 (which says a statement is an "assertion") and in common law tradition. "There is a red barn" is a quintessential assertion—a strong claim that something is so (there is a barn and it is red). But in everyday usage, other kinds of statements, like commands or imperatives ("Look at the red barn") and questions ("Is that barn red?") would not be described as assertions because they do not (at least in a formal or grammatical sense) make strong claims: The speaker is not trying to inform or persuade another about the facts to which he refers.

As is true of statements with performative aspects (the eviction notice in *Singer*) and statements offered to prove matters assumed (the conversation in *Pacelli*), commands and questions use words that tell us something about what the speaker is thinking. But when we use such a statement to prove acts, events, or conditions in the world, we are not using it to prove exactly what the declarant seems to be saying. For example, we might use the command "Look at the red barn" to prove that there is a barn or that it is red. Or we might use the question "Is that barn red?" to prove that there is a barn. (Probably such a question would have little probative force on the barn's *color*, but it is easy enough to imagine questions that *do* have probative force on the very point asked about: "How fast do you think that speed demon is going?" might very well be taken as proof that someone is driving too fast for the conditions at hand.)

Because such statements are not offered to prove exactly what the speaker is telling us, some courts have thought that they cannot be hearsay. In the *Oguns* case, for example, the court concluded that an incoming phonecall, received at an apparent drug distribution point asking about purchasing "apples" (code word for heroin) was not hearsay because the caller was simply asking questions. See United States v. Oguns, 921 F.2d 442, 448-449 (2d Cir. 1990) (an inquiry is not an assertion).

Despite *Oguns* (a few other decisions take the same view), the everyday interpretation of the term "assertion" should *not* prevail in applying the hearsay doctrine. Even questions and commands usually *express* or *communicate* something about acts, events, or conditions in the world, and the hearsay risks appear just as they do when the speaker makes a conventional strong claim about such matters. Hence the term "assertion" should be interpreted to mean essentially "express" or "communicate."

■ NOTES ON QUESTIONS OR COMMANDS AS HEARSAY

1. Recall Julius Caesar's last words in the Shakespeare play: "Et tu, Brute?" sounds a lot like a question. Still, it seems absolutely clear that these words should be viewed as hearsay if offered to prove that Brutus was among the assailants. Again, the hearsay risks are present every bit as much as they would be if Caesar had said "Brutus joined the others in stabbing me." See Craig Callen, Hearsay and Informal Reasoning, 47 Vand. L. Rev. 43, 89 (1994) (commenting that "Could it be a little more quiet in here?" may convey "the speaker's opinion that the stereo is too loud, rather than a question about applied acoustics").

2. Most modern decisions understand these points. In the *Summers* case, for example, one of the defendants said, at the time of his arrest, "How did you find us so fast?" and the court concluded that it was hearsay. See, e.g., United States v. Summers, 414 F.3d 1287 (10th Cir. 2005) (the question "contained an inculpatory assertion") (reversing bank robbery conviction).

E HEARSAY—TEST YOUR UNDERSTANDING

You have made your way through some of the hardest parts of the law of evidence. Test and refine your understanding by considering another case and taking a short quiz.

BETTS v. BETTS

Washington Court of Appeals
473 P.2d 403 (Wash. App. 1970)

[Michael Betts sued his former wife Rita in Washington and obtained a judgment awarding him custody of their daughter, five-year-old Tracey Lynn. Michael and Rita had divorced in California, and she had moved to Washington with Tracey Lynn and Tracey Lynn's brother James, the second child of the marriage.

While in Washington, Rita and the children began living with Raymond Caporale. A week later, James (then two years old) died from internal injuries and multiple bruises on the head and body. Tracey Lynn was placed in protective custody and Caporale was charged with second-degree murder in the death of James, but he was acquitted with a finding that the evidence was insufficient.

In the meantime, Michael Betts moved to Washington and remarried, and Rita married Caporale and moved to California. Tracey Lynn remained in a foster home in Washington.

On appeal, Rita urges that the trial court erred in admitting certain testimony by Tracey Lynn's foster mother.]

ARMSTRONG, C.J. . . .

The foster mother saw an item in the paper relative to the remarriage of the child's mother and with reference to it, testified as follows:

A: So I told her that her mama and Mr. Ray Caporale had got married, and she started crying. She said,—she ran and put her arms around me and her head in my lap and started crying real bad and hard and said, "He killed my brother and he'll kill my mommie too,"—and she doesn't seem to ever get that out of her mind.

Q: Does she say this often?

A: Yes, she tells all her friends—explains why she is with us, and she goes into this tale, and I don't seem to be able to get her not to tell her problems to outsiders.

Q: Did she ever make statements about this prior to the incident you have just mentioned, which apparently occurred after the trial?

A: Yes, yes, she started telling about [how] her little brother was in heaven and how he had gotten there and she always blamed him for it.

Q: By "him," who do you mean?

A: Mr. Caporale.

Q: Has anyone in your presence tried to pull this information out of this child?

A: No, because I didn't want to worry her. When she talks, we let her talk; but we don't try to change her mind, one way or the other, because we aren't there to do that—just give her a home.

The foster mother further stated, "She always mentioned, 'He's mean.' That is the word she uses—'He's mean.'"

We hold that use of this testimony does not violate the hearsay evidence rule.

The hearsay evidence rule prohibits the use of testimony in court, of a statement made by another person out of court, which is being offered to show the truth of the matter asserted therein. Such evidence derives its value, not solely from the credibility of the in-court witness himself, but also in part, from the veracity and competence of the person who made the out-of-court statement.

The statements of the child were not admitted to prove the truth of the assertions she made, but merely to indirectly and inferentially show the mental state of the child at the time of the child custody proceedings.

In finding of fact 18, the trial court stated in part: "The fact that said statements had been made would tend to create a strained relationship between said Tracey Lynn Betts and her stepfather, Raymond Don Caporale, and her mother, should she be awarded to the mother." . . .

It should be pointed out that there is a distinction between nonhearsay statements which circumstantially indicate a present state of mind *regardless of their truth,* and hearsay statements which indicate a state of mind *because of their truth.* The state of mind must be relevant in either instance. The distinction is based upon the question of whether the statement shows the mental state *regardless of the truth of the statement.* The distinction is usually disregarded in the cases because the statement will usually be admissible either under the exception to the hearsay rule or under the theory that it is not hearsay. In this case the distinction is important because if the statement is admitted as an exception to the hearsay rule, certain reliability requirements must be met.

An obvious example of an out-of-court non-hearsay statement which circumstantially indicates a state of mind regardless of the truth of the statement would be "I am Napoleon Bonaparte." This would be relevant in a sanity hearing.

The statements in question in this case are clearly nonhearsay statements which circumstantially indicate a state of mind regardless of their truth. Since they were relevant, they are admissible.

The mother further contends, however, that the out-of-court statements would not be admissible because the child was not competent to testify in court. At the time of the hearing she was 5 years old.

We need not decide whether hearsay statements introduced under an exception to the hearsay rule must be made by someone who is competent to testify as a witness. We note, however, that res gestae utterances of a child who would probably not have been competent as a witness were held admissible in [two earlier cases]. It was suggested in an article [by a Washington judge] that the better rule would be that with the exception of res gestae utterances, all hearsay statements introduced under any exception to the rule should be made by someone competent as a witness at the time the statement was made.

However, we are not considering the testimony of the 5-year-old child as an exception to the hearsay rule, but as a nonhearsay statement which circumstantially indicates the state of the child's mind regardless of the truth of the statement. Under such circumstances, the statement would be admissible even though the child may not have been competent to serve as a witness in the case....

We conclude that the rule, that out-of-court nonhearsay statements may be admitted which circumstantially indicate a state of mind regardless of the truth of the statement, is especially applicable in child custody proceedings. The mental state of the child is an important element in determining what is best for the child's welfare. The trial court should consider the truth of the child's assertion only if such statements meet the reliability test required of the "present state of mind" exception to the hearsay rule....

The judgment is affirmed.

PEARSON and PETRIE, JJ., concur.

■ NOTES ON STATEMENTS AS CIRCUMSTANTIAL EVIDENCE OF STATE OF MIND

1. What did the prosecutor seek to prove with Tracey Lynn's statements in *Betts*? Whether Tracey Lynn wanted to live with Rita and Raymond, or whether they would provide a suitable environment for her? *Betts* is far from being the only case that treats fact-laden statements as nonhearsay circumstantial evidence of state of mind. See, e.g., United States v. Parry, 649 F.2d 292, 294-295 (5th Cir. 1981) (defendant claimed he thought he was leading undercover agents to drug sources; reversible error to exclude testimony by his mother that he said the person phoning him was an agent with whom he was working; statement was nonhearsay circumstantial evidence of state of mind).

2. Should Tracey Lynn's statement be treated the same way as the statement by Anna Sofer (Problem 3-H), complaining about her husband's misbehavior? It's not as convincing, certainly, because children don't have grown-up inhibitions in talking about their elders.

3. The court says Tracey Lynn's statement indicates her state of mind without regard to its truth. In one sense, that seems correct: Although children lack adult inhibitions, the behavior of a child who charges an adult with horrible misbehavior is some indication of a relationship that is not quite right. In another sense, the truth of Tracey Lynn's statement is important: If she charges Ray Caporale with misdeeds while knowing that he didn't actually commit them, there may be trouble in their relationship, but the statement doesn't give a correct picture of that trouble. The court also says the statement "I am Napoleon" would be nonhearsay circumstantial evidence if offered to prove state of mind. That is a defensible conclusion, and it can be defended under FRE 801 as well: In the same way that we think about Tracey Lynn's statement as telling us something about her relationship with Caporale whether it's correct in describing his behavior or not, the statement "I am Napoleon" tells us something about the speaker's state of mind regardless whether he actually is (thinks he is) Napoleon.

4. The foster mother testified that Tracey Lynn "ran and put her arms around me and her head in my lap and started crying real bad" on learning that her mother Rita had married Ray. Probably a spontaneous outburst of that sort is nonhearsay (it isn't entirely voluntary and therefore arguably is not an assertion). Doesn't this behavior on Tracey Lynn's part make it easier to accept her contemporaneous statements as not hearsay?

5. If the court had decided that Tracey Lynn's statements were hearsay, two obvious hearsay exceptions might apply—the one for "excited utterances" now contained in FRE 803(2) and the one for statements describing the declarant's state of mind now contained in FRE 803(3). But the court entertains doubt as to Tracey Lynn's competency as a witness and thinks the hearsay exceptions might be unavailable. Most courts don't apply witness competency standards to out-of-court statements. See, e.g., Morgan v. Foretich, 846 F.2d 941, 948-950 (4th Cir. 1988) (admitting child's statement to doctor; competency restrictions do not apply to statements offered under hearsay exceptions).

HEARSAY QUIZ

In each example, the only question is whether the evidence offered is or is not hearsay. Assume that Rule 801(a) through (c) provides the applicable standard. You should consider the evidence to be hearsay if it fits within those definitional provisions and not hearsay if it does not. As you have seen, some statements that qualify as hearsay under those provisions are defined to be "not hearsay" by Rule 801(d). That has no bearing on these questions. In other words, answer the questions as if FRE 801(d) did not exist. Remember that the issue is hearsay versus not hearsay, not admissibility versus excludability. You will discover when you take up the exceptions that many statements that are hearsay are also admissible, so do not let your instinct that something is admissible lead you to conclude that it must not be hearsay!

1. As proof that *B* lacked testamentary capacity in April, evidence that several times in March he told friends that he was Woody Allen.

2. As proof that *C* assumed the risk of accident on account of faulty brakes in riding in *D*'s car, *D*'s testimony that "I told *C* before he got in that something was wrong with my brakes."

3. In *E*'s personal injury suit, as proof that *F* was an agent of defendant All-Cure Drugstore, *E*'s testimony that *F* said, "I'm awfully sorry, I was running an errand for my employer All-Cure Drugstore."

4. As proof that *G* stole a car, evidence that police stopped him and that his girlfriend *H* falsely stated at that time, "This car belongs to my brother."

5. As proof that *H* was frightened when *J* brandished a plastic pistol and demanded cash, evidence that *H* began sweating and shaking.

6. As proof that the time was about midnight when *K* entered the building, testimony by *L* that she saw *K* come in and mentioned it to *M* ten minutes later, coupled with *M*'s testimony that it was "just past midnight when *L* told me that she saw *K* enter."

7. As proof that *N* committed the robbery with which he is charged, testimony from bystander *O* that "I picked *N* out of the lineup as the one who did it."

8. As proof that *P* and *Q* had never met before, evidence that *Q* said to *P* on parting after a short conversation, "Very nice to meet you."

9. As proof that *R* was unusually accomplished in French, evidence that in her first year of college she was accepted into a fourth-year course.

10. As proof that defendant *S* participated in a criminal venture under duress, evidence that coparticipant *T* told him, "We will kill you if you don't help us."

11. As proof that *U* favored increasing the penalties for drunk driving, evidence that she joined an organization entitled Mothers Against Drunk Driving, coupled with proof that the principal aim of that organization is to increase such penalties.

12. As proof that defendant *V* owned a .32 caliber pistol, testimony by a police officer that when he asked *V*'s father *W* whether *V* owned such a pistol, *W* went to a drawer in the house where he and *V* lived, pulled out a .32 caliber pistol, and handed it to the officer.

13. As proof that it was raining at 10 A.M., proof that *X* said at that time, "It should stop raining in the next hour."

14. As proof that officer *Y* acted in good faith in arresting *Z*, offered by *Y* in defending against the claim brought by *Z* for violation of his rights, evidence that the prosecuting attorney told *Y*, "you have probable cause to arrest *Z*."

15. As proof that St. John's beat Georgetown in basketball, evidence that *A*, who had bet on Georgetown, paid off his debt.

16. As proof that *B* had committed a prior bank robbery, evidence that she was prosecuted for that crime and that a jury had found her guilty.

17. As proof that *C* went to New Orleans on Tuesday, evidence that on Monday he said, "Tomorrow I'm going to New Orleans."

18. As proof that his brakes were bad, evidence that *D* said, "I think I ought to reline my brakes before anybody drives the car."

19. As proof that *E* was selling pornographic literature, evidence that he received a letter from *F* enclosing a check and saying in substance "please send me that dirty book."

20. As proof that *G* knew *H*, evidence that *G* had in his cellphone directory *H*'s name and *H*'s phone number.

21. As proof of the manner in which *J* was injured in the workplace, a videotape in which *J* reenacts the events that led to her injury, offered in proof by *J*.

22. As proof that *K* did not have permission to drive the car to Sacramento, evidence that owner *L* had told *K* "not to drive it out of San Francisco."

23. As proof that tenant *L* terminated his month-to-month tenancy effective November 1, evidence that *L* sent owner *M* a letter in September that stated: "October will be my last month as tenant. I am vacating by November 1."

24. As proof that the stairs in Bloomingdeal's Department store were adequately lighted, testimony by the floor manager that in six years several customers had complained that they were a long hard climb but no one had mentioned any lighting problem.

25. As proof that *N* had been in the law library before, evidence that on entering the library she said to the attendant, "May I please have the key to the locked cage in the basement, so I can look at Starkie on Evidence?" coupled with proof that in fact that book is shelved in a locked cage at that location.

26. As proof that the hit-and-run driver drove a Porsche, testimony that the logo on the rear of the vehicle in question read "Porsche."

27. On the question whether tenant *O* had paid his rent for the month of April, testimony that in handing landlord *P* a check in the appropriate amount *O* said to *P*, "This is for the April rent."

28. On the issue set out in question 27, testimony that on the day after giving the check to *P*, *O* was heard to say, "I paid my rent for April."

29. As proof that *Q*'s boyfriend *R* was *Q*'s assailant, *Q*'s statement to a nurse in the hospital emergency room, "for god's sakes don't let my boyfriend *R* near me!"

30. As proof that the train had come from the west, testimony by eyewitness *S* that she pointed in the direction of the train when she heard it coming, coupled with testimony by a police officer present at the scene that the direction in which *T* pointed was west.

31. As proof that HiTechCorp was a bad credit risk, evidence that Din & Broodstreet gives HiTech-Corp a poor credit rating.

32. As proof that BankWest acted reasonably in refusing to refinance HiTechCorp's debt, evidence that Din & Broodstreet gives HiTechCorp a poor credit rating.

33. As proof that *U* was seriously ill, evidence that he was being kept in the intensive-care unit of the hospital.

34. As proof that *V* is an honest man, evidence that he handed the store clerk a $10 bill for a $7 purchase and, on receiving a $10 bill and three ones from the clerk in change, *V* returned the $10 bill and said, "I think you've made a mistake here."

35. As proof that *W* is a violent man, testimony that he is reputed in his community to be such.

CHAPTER 4

Hearsay Exceptions

INTRODUCTION—ORGANIZATION OF THE HEARSAY EXCEPTIONS

Now that you know what hearsay is, and you know about nonhearsay uses of out-of-court statements, we shift focus. Now we want to know whether a statement is admissible *even though it is* hearsay. First let's look at the organization of the hearsay exceptions.

Organization of exceptions. Many standard exceptions pave the way for statements offered to prove what they assert, although exclusion may be required on other grounds, like relevancy or "unfair prejudice." Many exceptions rest on notions of necessity and trustworthiness, and most of these exceptions contain criteria that implement these notions. Some exceptions, however, are outgrowths of the adversary system.

The Rules set out the exceptions in five groups.

(1) Statements by declarants who testify. The first group is in FRE 801(d)(1), which contains three exceptions. All three apply in the special situation of testifying witnesses—they apply to certain prior statements by declarants who testify. The statutory magic of FRE 801 *defines* these statements as "not hearsay" even though they fit the hearsay definition in Rule 801(a)-(c). In substance, these are hearsay exceptions.

(2) Admissions. The second group is in FRE 801(d)(2), with five exceptions—five variations on a single theme. Together they make up what we call the admissions doctrine, paving the way for statements made by opponents of the offering party. The statutory magic is at work here too: These are "not hearsay" even though they fit the definition. Again we have what amounts to hearsay exceptions.

(3) Unrestricted exceptions. The third and largest group is in FRE 803. Here we find 23 "unrestricted" exceptions—"unrestricted" in the sense that a statement fitting any of these exceptions may be used to prove what it asserts regardless whether the declarant testifies, and regardless whether he could be produced to give testimony (that is, regardless whether he is unavailable). Here we find such critical exceptions as the ones covering excited utterances, state of mind statements, and business and public records.

(4) Statements by unavailable declarants. The fourth group is in FRE 804, which contains five more exceptions. These may be invoked only if the declarant is "unavailable as a witness" under FRE 804(a). Here we find the against-interest exception, the former testimony exception, the modern forfeiture exception, the colorful exception for dying declarations, and a minor exception for statements of personal or family history.

(5) Catchall. Fifth and last is the exception found in FRE 807, known as the "catchall" exception (in contrast to "categorical" exceptions). The catchall reaches "reliable" hearsay that does not fit any categorical exception. Notably, all states now have what amount to "specialized versions" of the catchall that pave the way, under certain circumstances, to admit statements by children describing abuse. Like the catchall, these "rifle shot" exceptions do not specify criteria for gauging reliability.

Of the 37 hearsay exceptions described above, about half are used every day. The others appear only rarely. This chapter takes up the important exceptions, and notes some of the others.

EXCEPTIONS IN FRE 801(d)(1)—DECLARANT TESTIFYING

FRE 801(d)(1) defines as "not hearsay" three kinds of prior statements by testifying witnesses. Statements in the first two exceptions—certain prior inconsistencies and certain prior consistencies—would likely be admissible for limited nonhearsay purposes anyway. With respect to prior inconsistencies, recall Problem 3-C ("The Blue Car Ran a Red Light"), where such a statement was offered to impeach. The subject of impeachment by inconsistent statements is examined in Chapter 8B1, infra. With respect to consistent statements, you will see that these are sometimes admissible to support the declarant/witness, and you will take up the subject of rehabilitating witnesses in Chapter 8C. For the moment, the point is that the effect of FRE 801(d)(1)(A) and (B) is not so much to let in what would be kept out otherwise, but to permit fuller use of such statements.

The third exception—statements of identification, offered under FRE 801(d)(1)(C)—is not connected with impeachment or rehabilitation. It paves the way for some statements that might not get in otherwise. It applies primarily in criminal cases and expresses the view that identifying statements made out of court are more to be trusted than in-court identifications.

1. Prior Inconsistent Statements

The reluctance to admit prior statements by testifying witnesses expresses a strong preference for live testimony. Scholars had concluded, even before the project culminating in the Rules began, that at least some prior inconsistent statements should be admissible for all purposes (not just to impeach), and the drafters were persuaded. They tried to lift out of the definition of hearsay any prior inconsistent statement by a witness who testifies at trial and is "subject to cross-examination" about the statement. See Preliminary Draft of March 1969, Proposed Federal Rules of Evidence, Rule 8-01(c)(2)(iv), 46 F.R.D. 161, 331 (1969).

Lawyers and judges disagreed. And Congress, many of whose members are lawyers by training and inclination, refused to go along with the drafters. Lawyers and judges continue to think that admitting such statements would encourage reliance on them at trial, and that "deferred" cross-examination (questioning the witness at trial about statements made before) is inferior to contemporaneous cross-examination (asking about statements the witness now makes at trial). Rule 801(d)(1)(A) amounts to a compromise. A prior statement by a witness is "not hearsay" if three conditions are met: First, the witness must now be cross-examinable about the prior statement. Second, the statement must be "inconsistent" with his present testimony. Third, it must have been made under oath in a "trial" or "other proceeding" or "deposition."

These requirements are mostly easy to interpret. But the forgetful witness (or one who *claims* to have forgotten) brings problems in applying the first and second requirements. And where the witness denies having made a prior statement or claims it was a lie, problems arise with cross-examinability. There is even some difficulty in applying the term "other proceeding." On this point, the case you're about to read is an outlier.

STATE v. SMITH

Washington Supreme Court
651 P.2d 207 (Wash. 1982)

DIMMICK, J.

Assault victim, Rachael Conlin, wrote out a statement on a form supplied by a detective of the Pasco Police Department, which contained *Miranda* warnings, in which she named Nova Smith (defendant) as her assailant. She signed under oath with penalty of perjury before a notary. At Smith's trial a month later, she named another man as her attacker. The trial court allowed her prior inconsistent statement to be used as substantive evidence, ruling it was not hearsay under Rule of Evidence 801(d)(1)(i). The jury found Smith guilty of assault in the second degree.

Thereafter, the judge granted a new trial, reasoning that ER 801(d)(1)(i) did not authorize the statement's admissibility as it was not given in a "proceeding." The State appealed and we accepted certification from the Court of Appeals....

I

At approximately 6:30 A.M. on July 10, 1980, Rachael Conlin was cruelly and severely assaulted in a room at the Double D Motel, Pasco, Washington, which she kept for work-related activities. She was struck in the face, beaten with a wire coat hanger, a belt, and a pipe, kicked several times and pulled back into the room by her hair on her attempt to escape. She received a cracked nose, bruises, black eyes, and required several stitches on her face. At 8 A.M. a police officer was called to the hospital and Conlin stated defendant had assaulted her, she was afraid, and did not know what to do. She was advised that nothing could be done unless she was willing to testify in court. About noon the officer recontacted Conlin and asked her if she wanted to give a statement concerning the incident. She came to the police station and talked with a detective indicating she was willing to press charges and testify in court. She understood that by giving a voluntary sworn statement criminal action against defendant was likely. She thereupon wrote, in her own words, a statement describing the details of the assault and identified the defendant as her assailant. She signed each page and the detective signed as a witness on pages 2, 3, and 4 of the statement. The detective then took her before a notary and read her the affidavit portion and oath. She reread the affidavit and oath and signed the affidavit. The notary subscribed the jurat and seal to Conlin's statement.

That same day Conlin, chased by defendant, ran into her manager's apartment screaming for help. Police were called when defendant, by force, took Conlin's car keys and departed.

At trial Ms. Conlin testified to the same facts regarding her assault as her original statement indicated, except for the startling deviation that her assailant was a Mr. Gomez, and that defendant had come to her aid. She freely admitted giving the sworn, voluntary statement to the detective and telling the officer at the hospital that defendant had assaulted her. She testified that she was upset with defendant over a fight the night before and blamed him for her having to stay in the motel room overnight with Gomez rather than in her apartment where defendant also lived. She further testified that she had lived with defendant both before and after the assault, and that she had left $150 for him at the jail for cigarettes, although she denied he was her pimp.

The prosecuting attorney was surprised at trial by Conlin's change in the identification of her assailant and introduced the written statement at issue for impeachment purposes. The State then moved to have it admitted as substantive evidence also, as it was apparently the only evidence that identified defendant as the perpetrator of the assault.

As previously noted, the trial judge ruled that the statement was admissible but then reconsidered and granted a new trial declaring ER 801(d)(1)(i) did not apply.

II. . .

We are here concerned with the interpretation of the words "other proceeding" as used in [Washington Evidence Rule 801(d)(1)(i)]. Washington's rule is taken verbatim from FRE 801(d)(1)(A). Accordingly, it is proper to look at the federal rule's history and purposes in interpreting its provisions. In fact, the comment to the Washington rule ER 801 provides that the rule "conforms state law to federal practice."

The rule as adopted by the United States Supreme Court and passed by the Senate adopted the minority position allowing all prior inconsistent statements to be used as substantive evidence. The House Subcommittee disagreed with this unrestricted version and sought to limit the Rule by requiring that the statement be made under oath, subject to penalty for perjury, and given at a "trial, hearing, deposition, or before a grand jury." These requirements were to assure reliability. The House Committee on the Judiciary added that the original statement must have been subject to cross-examination and deleted the reference to grand jury proceedings. The Advisory Committee objected, asserting that an in-court cross-examination was adequate to discern the truthfulness of the prior statement. The committee finally reached a compromise resulting in the rule in question. One report in the House noted that the rule adopted covers statements before a grand jury. However, the term "other proceeding" was not discussed.

It is well accepted that "other proceeding" includes grand jury proceedings. The Ninth Circuit extended this interpretation and upon reviewing the rule's legislative history it determined that a tape-recorded statement made under oath and taken in an immigration investigation was admissible. United States v. Castro-Ayon, 537 F.2d 1055 (9th Cir.), cert. denied, 429 U.S. 983 (1976). The court determined that the Legislature intended the term "other proceeding" to be open-ended and not restricted to grand jury proceedings. The court also compared grand jury proceedings to immigration proceedings and found enough similarities between the two to admit the statements. The court specifically added: "We do not hold, as the question is not before us, that every sworn statement given during a police-station interrogation would be admissible."

We likewise decline to answer the issue broadly. We do not interpret the rule to always exclude[1] or always admit[2] such affidavits. The purposes of the

---

[1]Some federal courts would apparently exclude all affidavits made to investigating officials as substantive evidence under FRE 801(d)(1)(A). Those courts, however, have not dealt with facts identical to the ones before us. E.g., United States v. Livingston, 661 F.2d 239 (D.C. Cir. 1981) (A postal inspector asked the witness questions, took notes, typed a statement based on the witness' responses and asked her to sign it. At trial the witness gave inconsistent testimony and either did not recall making the statements to the inspector or denied them.); United States v. Ragghianti, 560 F.2d 1376 (9th Cir. 1977) (The government's witness changed her story on the stand and did not recall making the prior inconsistent statement. The circumstances surrounding the prior inconsistent statement were not set forth except that it was given to an FBI agent, the investigating officer.).

[2]At least one other state court which has adopted FRE 801(d)(1)(A) would admit an affidavit signed by a witness any time it is taken under oath before an official who is authorized to hear evidence and administer oaths. Slavens v. State, 614 S.W.2d 529 (Ark. App. 1981). Appellant relies heavily upon State v. Maestas, 584 P.2d 182 (N.M. App. 1978). The New Mexico court would seemingly always admit prior inconsistent statements such as the one made in the instant case. New Mexico, however, has adopted a different rule of evidence from Washington's which allows all prior inconsistent statements to be admitted as substantive evidence regardless of whether they were taken in a proceeding or under oath.

rule and the facts of each case must be analyzed. In determining whether evidence should be admitted, reliability is the key. In many cases, the inconsistent statement is more likely to be true than the testimony at trial as it was made nearer in time to the matter to which it relates and is less likely to be influenced by factors such as fear or forgetfulness. One commentator has addressed the question of admissibility as follows:

> Inquiry into what other statements are encompassed by the Rule should be informed by the two purposes Congress had in mind in narrowing the provision originally proposed by the Court. The first was to remove doubt as to the making of the prior statement . . . . The second purpose was to provide at least the minimal guarantees of truthfulness which an oath and the circumstance of a formalized proceeding tend to assure. Clearly, however, the prior statement need not have been subject to cross-examination at the time made, for Congress was satisfied to rely upon delayed cross-examination of the declarant at trial to expose error or falsehood in the statement.

(Footnotes omitted.) D. Louisell & C. Mueller, [Federal Evidence] §419, at 169-71 [now 4 C. Mueller & L. Kirkpatrick, Federal Evidence §8:36 (3d ed. 2007)].

Here, there was no question that the statement was made since Ms. Conlin testified to that fact. Minimal guaranties of truthfulness were met since the statement was attested to before a notary, under oath and subject to penalty for perjury. Additionally, the witness wrote the statement in her own words. The jury, seeing Rachael Conlin on the stand, under oath, and hearing her explanation of the inconsistent statement while subject to cross-examination, was in a position to determine which statement was true.

III

Another factor to be considered is the original purpose of the sworn statement. It was taken as standard procedure in one of the four legally permissible methods for determining the existence of probable cause, thus allowing charges to be filed against defendant. The four methods are [filing an information, a grand jury indictment, inquest proceedings, and filing a complaint before a magistrate].

The first method, the one used here, is usually the result of police investigations into alleged criminal activity, and the taking of statements from witnesses and the presentment of them to the prosecuting attorney. The prosecuting attorney then exercises discretion in finding probable cause and files an information. "Other proceeding" under the rule would clearly cover the other three methods of finding probable cause listed above. That is, if the witness gave a statement, necessarily under oath to a grand jury, in an inquest proceeding or to a magistrate, that statement would be admissible as substantive evidence. Since the purpose of the statements in the first method is the same as the other three methods, that is determining probable cause, it should also be covered by the rule in an appropriate case such as we have before us.

To sum up, each case depends on its facts with reliability the key. Here, the complaining witness-victim voluntarily wrote the statement herself, swore to it under oath with penalty of perjury before a notary, admitted at trial she had made the statement and gave an inconsistent statement at trial where she was subject to cross examination. ER 801(d)(1)(i) is satisfied under the totality of these circumstances.

We therefore remand to the trial court with instructions to reinstate the verdict of the jury and sentence defendant thereon.

NOTES ON PRIOR PROCEEDINGS

1. Let us start with points of certainty. The term "proceedings" in FRE 801(d)(1)(A) embraces prior trials, depositions, preliminary hearings, and grand jury proceedings. All these involve formal settings in court or under direct court supervision, and all typically produce contemporaneous verbatim records, leaving little room to doubt what was said and providing a setting in which the speaker is obliged to tell the truth ("under penalty of perjury"). See generally Mueller and Kirkpatrick, Evidence §8.24 (5th ed. 2012).

2. The decision in *Smith* pushes the envelope, and is an outlier. Interpreting "proceeding" to embrace stationhouse interviews is a stretch: Beyond the semantic difficulty, we note that usually such interviews are *not* contemporaneously recorded, and formalities that attend court proceedings are missing. *Smith* stresses that criminal charges can rest on an "information" (which can be statements taken at a stationhouse), so there is a functional similarity with grand jury proceedings that generate indictments. But this functional similarity has not convinced most courts, which refuse to apply the exception to stationhouse utterances. See, e.g., the *Livingston* case (cited in *Smith*), where questioning that produced the affidavit proceeded in the home of the witness. See also United States v. Williams, 272 F.3d 845, 869 (7th Cir. 2001) (excluding affidavit; investigative interview is not a proceeding).

3. Another outlier is *Castro-Ayon,* which applied the exception to statements given under oath at a border control station. *Castro-Ayon* took a functional approach similar to *Smith,* admitting the statements in a trial for transporting illegal aliens, after three of them (called by the government) gave testimony favorable to the defense. Each admitted making a prior statement to Agent Pearce on arrest, and the reviewing court approved their substantive use in evidence:

> [T]he immigration proceeding before Agent Pearce bears many similarities to a grand-jury proceeding: Both are investigatory, ex parte, inquisitive, sworn, basically prosecutorial, held before an officer other than the arresting officer, recorded, and held in circumstances of some legal formality. Indeed, this

> immigration proceeding provides more legal right for the witness than does a grand jury: the right to remain totally silent, the right to counsel, and the right to have the interrogator inform the witnesses of those rights.

United States v. Castro-Ayon, 537 F.2d 1055, 1056-1057 (9th Cir.), *cert. denied,* 429 U.S. 983 (1976). But see United States v. Day, 789 F.2d 1221, 1221-1223 (6th Cir. 1986) (excluding recorded statement to IRS agent under oath; refusing to follow *Castro-Ayon*).

4. *Smith* involves the "turncoat witness" who gives statements supporting criminal charges in the early going, but then waffles at trial—the very situation where FRE 801(d)(1)(A) has proved most important. Where the initial incriminating statement was made before a grand jury or in a preliminary hearing, it can be used as substantive evidence if the witness tells a different story at trial. The exception helps the accused less often because he does not participate in grand jury proceedings.

(a) Grand juries are *the* mechanism for bringing criminal charges in federal court, but states often operate (as *Smith* illustrates) on the basis of an "information" (charges based on personal interviews or police investigations). Grand juries can indict if they find probable cause that defendant committed an offense. Rule 801(d)(1)(A) reaches grand jury testimony, indicating that the key to making it admissible against defendants is the fact that they can cross-examine the witness at trial ("deferred" or after-the-fact cross). Sometimes defendants offer grand jury testimony, but not often (prosecutors call witnesses who are prepared to implicate the defendant).

(b) Preliminary hearings are common features of both state and federal courts. Again the question is whether there is "probable cause" to believe that an offense has been committed and that defendant is the culprit, but this time defendants appear through counsel and participate. When witnesses like Rachael Conlin in *Smith* change their testimony at trial and the prosecutor offers their preliminary hearing testimony as substantive evidence, defendant will have a chance to cross-examine at trial, and also had an earlier opportunity to do so. But defendants typically do not cross-examine in preliminary hearings, recognizing that there is little chance of dismissing the case at this point. So once again, as a practical matter the ability of the defense to cross-examine at trial is critical in the operation of FRE 801(d)(1)(A) when it comes to statements by turncoat witnesses. To the matter of cross-examination at trial we turn now.

■ PROBLEM 4-A. "I Got Amnesia"

Dustin Duran is tried on charges of racketeering and disrupting interstate commerce, arising out of the armed robbery of Halshire Foods on March 29, 2013.

Before a grand jury in June 2013, Peter Breen testified that he, along with Duran and a man named Zigler, "cased" Halshire Foods several times prior to the robbery. On the night in question, Breen climbed a telephone pole and broke into the store through an upstairs window. He then let Duran and Zigler in the back door. While Zigler guarded the janitor in the office, Breen and Duran wheeled in portable acetylene tanks and a blowtorch and "blew the safe." Duran, Breen, and Zigler then fled with the proceeds.

In June, 2014, the government calls Breen as its star witness at trial, but he suddenly proves unhelpful. First he claims his privilege against self-incrimination. The court immunizes him from any future use of his testimony and tells him to answer the prosecutor's questions. Then he says he can't remember what happened on March 29, 2013, because he "got under the influence of Valium in May 2013 while living at the Metropolitan Correctional Center, and that made me forget." He adds that "events in the early summer of 2013 upset me because federal agents and others threatened me so I got amnesia about what happened before then, except that I remember going in the Witness Protection Program." Finally, Breen says he cannot remember making any statement to the grand jury about the robbery.

The prosecutor argues that Breen's lack of memory is "feigned," hence that his position at trial is "inconsistent with his detailed grand jury testimony in June 2013." Invoking FRE 801(d)(1)(A), she offers a transcript of that testimony. Counsel for Duran objects:

> Your Honor, Breen's grand jury transcript is inadmissible. First, under 801(d)(1)(A), the earlier statement has to be "inconsistent" with the trial testimony, and it isn't. All Breen has said here today is that he can't remember. Second, Breen has to be "subject to cross-examination" on his prior statement, but he isn't. How can I question him on his allegations about the robbery in March of a year ago when he says he doesn't remember blowing the safe at Halshire Foods? How can I question him about what he told the grand jury last June when he can't even remember testifying? Sure, he'll sit there and let me ask questions, but that can't be all that "subject to cross-examination" means. If I can't get anything out of him, how am I supposed to test his statement?

The prosecutor replies in this vein:

> Your honor, Mr. Breen is a classic turncoat witness. In June 2013 he testified to the grand jury about the Halshire Foods robbery on March 29th, but now he's got cold feet. Selective memory loss, actually. He remembers going into the Protection Program, which was in May of 2013, and the defendant can ask him about that and going to the grand jury, and anything he wants about credibility.

The trial court admits the grand jury testimony. On cross, Breen still claims he cannot remember the robbery, but counsel for Duran gets him to admit "I've been a burglar most of my life" until deciding "to lay low while helping the government, as long as they'll keep me in the Program and pay me." Breen admits he's been in trouble with crimes while in the Program, and "got more than $40,000 from the government over the last year, you know, for helping 'em out."

Duran is convicted, and he appeals. Did the court properly admit Breen's grand jury testimony under FRE 801(d)(1)(A)? What are the best arguments on both sides?

NOTES ON SUBSTANTIVE USE OF INCONSISTENT STATEMENTS: MEMORY LOSS AND CROSS-EXAMINABILITY

1. Is Peter Breen's grand jury testimony describing the robbery inconsistent with his testimony at trial that he doesn't remember the events? Consider this approach:

> As long as people speak in nonmathematical languages, such as English . . . it will be difficult to determine precisely whether two statements are inconsistent. But we do not read the word "inconsistent" in FRE 801(d)(1)(A) to include only statements diametrically opposed or logically incompatible. Inconsistency may be "found in evasive answers, silence, or changes in positions." In addition, a purported change in memory can produce "inconsistent answers." Particularly in a case of manifest reluctance to testify, "if a witness has testified to [certain] facts before a grand jury and forgets them at trial," his grand jury testimony falls squarely within FRE 801(d)(1)(A).

United States v. Williams, 737 F.2d 594, 608 (7th Cir. 1984). *Williams* suggests that Breen's position at trial is inconsistent with his grand jury testimony.

COMMENT/PERSPECTIVE: Lack of Memory as an Inconsistency

In congressional hearings into alleged misconduct, often by administration officials or directors in federal departments or agencies, it is commonplace for the witness who is put on the spot to say, in effect, "I don't remember." Claims of lack of memory are designed not only to avoid questions on an uncomfortable topic and minimize political embarrassment, but to save the witness from charges that whatever positive statement he makes now conflicts with something he or someone else said before. Because of such obvious motivations, claims of lack of memory are treated with skepticism. In *Twelve Angry Men* (1957), a famous movie about jury deliberations in the trial of an 18-year-old Hispanic boy for allegedly murdering his father, Juror 4 (E.G. Marshall) said he didn't believe the boy's exculpatory explanation because he couldn't remember the movie he'd seen three hours after the crime, but Juror 8 (Henry Fonda) questioned Juror 4 about a movie he'd seen four days earlier, and he recalled the main feature but had trouble with the name of the second: "I'll tell you in a minute . . . The Remarkable Mrs. . . . Something. Mrs. Bainbridge. . . . It was a very inexpensive second feature, with unknown . . ." Juror 8 points out "you weren't under an emotional stress, were you?" Courts and juries are often called on to decide whether claimed lack of memory is genuine or designed to cover up something else.

2. Understandably troubled by cases in which the proponent invokes FRE 801(d)(1)(A) on the basis of a claimed lack of memory at trial, some courts insist on proof that the claim is feigned—the witness really does remember but is pretending not to. California has lots of experience in this area because its Code allows use of *all* prior inconsistent statements as substantive evidence, see California Evidence Code §1235, and California cases require proof that the claimed lack of memory at trial is feigned. See People v. Homick, 289 P.3d 791, 830 (Cal. 2013) (recognizing principle). California is not alone in this view, see State v. Amos, 658 N.W.2d 201 (Minn. 2003), and some federal decisions applying this provision express disbelief in the claimed lack of memory, see U.S. v. Cisneros-Gutierrez, 517 F.3d 751 (5th Cir. 2008) (speaking of "feigned" memory loss; witness had "selective memory" that was "more convenient than actual"). Most decisions applying FRE 801(d)(1)(A), however, seem satisfied to take at face value the claimed lack of memory, and admit prior positive statements without requiring more.

3. The central question in the Problem is whether Breen is "subject to cross-examination" about his prior statement if he cannot remember the robbery. Note that he does remember testifying before the grand jury, and that FRE 801(d)(1)(A) requires only that he be cross-examinable "about [his] prior statement," and doesn't say anything about his being cross-examinable about the events described. Note as well that the exceptions for prior consistent statements and prior statements of identification, in clauses (B) and (C) of FRE 801(d)(1), are subject to the same requirement. Consider these points:

(a) In United States v. Owens, 484 U.S. 554 (1988), the Court said the cross-examination requirement is satisfied even if the witness has forgotten the events. *Owens* involved the trial of a prison inmate for assaulting a correctional officer named Foster, who was hospitalized with serious injuries. At the trial of Owens, Foster remembered talking in the hospital with FBI Agent Mansfield where he identified Owens as his assailant, but Foster could not remember the assault, except for "feeling the blows to his head and seeing blood on the floor." Still the Court rejected the argument that Foster was not sufficiently cross-examinable: One may be subject to cross under FRE 801(d)(1)(C) even

if lack of memory about events makes him "unavailable as a witness" for purposes of FRE 804 (setting out exceptions requiring declarant's unavailability).

(b) You will discover that the Confrontation Clause deals with the use of testimonial hearsay against the accused, but allows use of hearsay if the defense has an opportunity to cross-examine (the topic is introduced in section C, and explored in section G, infra). So it is not just FRE 801(d)(1)(A) that requires declarant to be cross-examinable, but the Constitution too. The Court has made many comments indicating that the Constitution requires little or nothing more than the *Owens* construction of FRE 801(d)(1) requires.

(c) For the proposition that the cross-examination requirement means the witness must be able to give some kind of response, see United States v. DiCaro, 772 F.2d 1314, 1323 (7th Cir. 1985) (requirement should not be made "effectively meaningless," and in many if not most cases where witness suffers "total memory lapse concerning both the prior statement and its contents" he cannot be considered subject to cross). See also State v. Amos, 658 N.W.2d 201, 206 (Minn. 2003) (witness must be "testable about the statement, meaning that he must be reasonably responsive to questions on the circumstances in which he made it"). But see United States v. Keeter, 130 F.3d 297, 302 (7th Cir.) (admitting grand jury testimony by witness who feigned amnesia, which did not block defense cross), *cert. denied*, 523 U.S. 1034 (1997). Surely it would be a mistake, however, to interpret FRE 801(d)(1)(A) to mean only that the speaker must sit still long enough to answer questions, hence that one who remembers *neither* the events *nor* his statement is still "subject to cross-examination."

4. Admitting Breen's grand jury testimony against Duran raises greater concern if is the only evidence against him, or is likely to be decisive. The Senate Report on FRE 801(d)(1)(A) echoes concerns expressed by opponents of the provision. That report comments in a footnote that opposition rests on "concern that a person could be convicted solely" on a prior statement, adding that the Rule addresses admissibility, not sufficiency, and that "if this were the sole evidence, dismissal would be appropriate."

2. Prior Consistent Statements

A prior consistent statement by a testifying witness is defined as "not hearsay" under some circumstances. FRE 801(d)(1)(B) sets out three conditions: First, the witness must be cross-examinable at trial about the statement. Second, it must be consistent with his testimony. Third, it must be offered to rebut a charge of recent fabrication or improper influence or motive or to rehabilitate the witness if attacked on some other ground.

In one sense it is hard to get excited about this provision. To a large extent, a statement consistent with present testimony brings no new information and cannot be the only evidence on any point. Judgments are seldom reversed for error in admitting a prior consistency, which is largely "cumulative" of live testimony. Yet a consistent statement can be potent evidence, as you will see.

Notice two things:

First, this provision is limited because it applies only if the prior statement is otherwise admissible to refute some kind of impeachment of the witness. In effect, Rule 801(d)(1)(B) says that *if* a consistent statement is going to come in anyway (to refute such impeachment), *then* it might as well be usable for substantive purposes too—as proof of what it says. It's *not* the case that any litigant may, any time it wants, offer prior consistent statements by a testifying witness. But *if* such a statement is admissible to repair credibility, then substantive use is allowed too, and Rule 801(d)(1)(B) defines such statements as "not hearsay." The underlying belief is that deferred cross-examination is not as effective as contemporaneous cross, which is why Rule 801(d)(1)(B) is narrowly crafted. In fact this fear is most acute with *consistent* statements, for it is here—where the witness sticks to his original story—that the danger seems real that any falsehood may "harden and become unyielding to the blows of truth" struck by the cross-examiner. State v. Saporen, 285 N.W. 898, 901 (Minn. 1939).

Second, Rule 801(d)(2)(B) embraces consistent statements in any form. There is no requirement that they be uttered under oath in proceedings, so this provision can apply to any prior statement by the witness that is consistent with present testimony.

This exception raises three issues in application: First, what kind of impeaching attack paves the way to offer prior consistent statements? It turns out that only certain kinds of impeachment invite the use of consistent statements. Second, what consistent statements are admissible to rebut such attacks? It turns out that only certain statements can rebut the attack, even though Rule 801(d)(1)(B) doesn't itself impose any special requirements (no requirement of an oath or prior proceedings, for example). Third, what does "consistent" mean?

First issue: What kind of attack? Here we focus on prior statements offered to rebut what subpart (i) of Rule 801(d)(1)(B) calls "an express or implied charge" of recent fabrication or "improper influence or motive." We put off (for now) consideration of statements offered, in the words of subpart (ii), "to rehabilitate the declarant's credibility when attacked on another ground." This provision was added in 2014, having been omitted from the original Rule (probably a drafting error), and we look at the other grounds that pave the way for consistent statements when we get to the material on impeachment of witnesses. There we learn that consistent statements can also be offered to refute claimed lack of memory, to prove that a prior *inconsistent* statement was not made or that it was not inconsistent with the trial testimony (Chapter 8C2). The effect of the two subparts together is to insure that all prior consistent statements that are admissible to repair credibility can also be used as proof of what they assert.

So what is "an express or implied charge" of recent fabrication or "improper influence or motive"? Sometimes the cross-examiner suggests in so many words that the witness "just made it up" or "changed his story" because he was cajoled, paid, or frightened. Clearly FRE 801(d)(1)(B)(i) reaches these easy cases where the charge of fabrication is express. But the Rule reaches further, giving the green light where charges of influence or motive are merely "implied." Professor Graham suggests these examples where "partiality" or "fabrication" is charged by implication: "You are the mother of the defendant, aren't you?" "You would do anything you could to help your son, wouldn't you?" "Didn't you talk with plaintiff's counsel shortly before testifying here today?" "When did you first decide to change your testimony for trial?" See Graham, Prior Consistent Statements: Rule 801(d)(1)(B) of the Federal Rules of Evidence: Critique and Proposal, 30 Hastings L.J. 575, 586, 607 (1979).

Second issue: What consistent statements rebut such charges? If an attack suggests fabrication or improper influence or motive, do *all* prior statements that are consistent with the testimony of the witness tend to repel the attack? The answer is No, and here an example is necessary to make the point. Let us suppose that motorist David runs over pedestrian Paul, and that Paul sues David. Eyewitness Marian becomes involved in the pretrial skirmishing, and ultimately she testifies for motorist David:

Pretrial Events

Day 1: Marian comments, "David was driving within the speed limit."

Day 20: David talks to Marian, perhaps pressures her to support him at trial (by cajolery, threat, bribe, or appeal to sympathy), but only David and Marian know.

Day 30: Marian comments, "David was driving within the speed limit."

Trial Testimony

On direct for David, Marian testifies: "David was driving within the speed limit."

On cross by Paul, Marian concedes: "On Day 20, I talked to David, and he insisted that he was driving within the speed limit. He pressed me to support him. I decided he was right."

Paul's lawyer says: "So what you told us here today about David driving within the speed limit—the source for that was David, wasn't it?"

Given this sequence, can counsel for David (calling party) ask Marian about her statements on Days 1 and 30, which are consistent with her direct testimony that David was driving within the speed limit? The hornbook answer is that a prior consistency tends to rebut such an attack (repairing or rehabilitating the witness) *only* if uttered *before* the influence or motive came into play. On these facts, what Marian said on Day 1 would tend to refute the suggestion that her direct testimony was produced by influence or motive brought to bear on Day 20: After all, if she said the same thing on Day 1 that she says at trial, then whatever happened on Day 20 cannot account for her trial testimony.

On the other hand, Marian's utterance on Day 30 seems to *confirm* Paul's theory that the meeting with David on Day 20 is what led Marian to testify favorably for him. After all, her statement on Day 30 is consistent with her testimony, and she made the statement after talking to David, so her statement (like her testimony) reflects his influence. By tradition, courts refused to let David prove such a statement because it would not repair Marian's credibility.

Figuring out when a motive arises is often harder than the example suggests, and many courts abandoned the premotive requirement for this reason. They concluded that even postmotive statements have some probative worth, but in 1995 the Supreme Court held that Rule 801(d)(1)(B) embodies a premotive requirement when prior consistent statements are offered to refute a claim of improper influence or motive. See Tome v. United States, 513 U.S. 150 (1995).

Third Issue: What does consistent mean? Suppose the witness testifies that "the blue car ran a red light." Problem 3-C offers this example, along with an *inconsistent* statement by the same witness. This time let's assume that the witness was attacked for "improper influence or motive," and that he had said before "The blue car ran a red light, and cross-traffic was moving across the intersection." Suppose an important issue is whether indeed cross-traffic was going through the intersection, because the other side contends that it had the light and cross-traffic was *not* moving. Can the calling party offer the prior statement as evidence that indeed the cross-traffic was moving?

Suffice it to say that Rule 801(d)(1)(B) was not designed to allow the substantive use of prior statements containing critical information that is not also found in the testimony of the witness whose credibility is being repaired. The statement about cross-traffic moving in the intersection is consistent with testimony that the light was red, but it adds new information, which is not the purpose of Rule 801(d)(1)(B). That purpose was to allow substantive use of statements that merely repair credibility, not to allow such statements to prove additional facts.

Repairing and substantive use compared. Implicit in the foregoing discussion is the proposition that there is a difference between using a consistent statement to refute a claim of fabrication or motive, or to repair credibility attacked on other grounds, and the substantive use of consistent statements. It may help to remember that *inconsistent* statements may be used to impeach, which is a nonhearsay use because they show *vacillation* by the witness. Under Rule 801(d)(1)(A), *some* inconsistent statements may be used as substantive evidence (those given under oath in proceedings). Using consistent statements to repair credibility is another nonhearsay use, the theory being that they show *consistency* on the part of the witness. Under Rule 801(d)(1)(B) *any* consistent statement can be used as substantive evidence if it is also admissible to repair credibility.

In sum, what Marian said on *Day 1* can be taken as additional proof (along with her testimony) that David was driving within the speed limit. This consistent statement was made *before* David and Marian spoke, so it tends to refute any suggestion that his influence accounts for her testimony, and it fits FRE

801(d)(1)(B). Marian's statement on *Day 30,* however, came after the motive to fabricate arose, so it does not repair the attack that Paul's lawyer mounted, and can't be used that way. For the same reason, it does not fit FRE 801(d)(1)(B) and cannot be used as substantive evidence either.

■ PROBLEM 4-B. "He Thinks I'm His Wife"

Martin Trask is tried in federal court in New Mexico for the alleged abuse of his four-year-old daughter "S.T." occurring on the Navajo Indian Reservation there. S.T. had been staying with him under an agreement giving him primary custody when he and S.T.'s mother Bonnie divorced.

The summer after the divorce, S.T. went to live with her mother Bonnie in Colorado for a month. During this visit, she told Bonnie that Trask had sexually abused her. Bonnie took S.T. to be examined by a pediatrician and interviewed by a social worker. S.T. made detailed statements to both, describing the abuse and telling the social worker that Trask "gets drunk and thinks I'm his wife." Authorities were notified in New Mexico, and criminal charges were filed against Trask.

At trial, the prosecutor called S.T. to testify (she was then six and a half), but she proved reluctant to describe the alleged abuse. All the prosecutor could get from her was "yes" or "uh huh" to a leading questions, such as "Did your dad touch you in your private place?" The trial court commented on the "very difficult situation" before it.

Martin Trask's lawyer tried to conduct a gentle cross-examination, anxious to avoid the appearance of meanness to an apparent abuse victim, but he eventually asked this question: "Isn't it true that you are just making up this story about your dad because you would prefer to live with your mother in Colorado?"

In rebuttal, the government sought to refute the suggestion that S.T. had just made it all up. Invoking FRE 801(d)(1)(B), the prosecutor called Bonnie the pediatrician and the social worker to testify to the more detailed statements S.T. had made, describing the abuse. If allowed, these three witnesses would recount S.T.'s comment about Trask getting drunk and thinking S.T. was his wife, and the pediatrician and social worker would recount more specific statements (that Trask touched S.T.'s vaginal area).

In aid of an offer of proof, the prosecutor argues thus:

> Your Honor, what S.T. told her mother, the social worker, and the pediatrician are admissible as consistent statements under FRE 801(d)(1)(B), which means they can be used as substantive evidence and to repair credibility. They are consistent with her testimony here, in which she answered in the affirmative when I asked her whether Martin Trask had touched her vaginal area. They are admissible because the defense has seen fit to try to

impeach S.T. by suggesting that what she's saying is just part of an attempt to be with her mother in Colorado permanently, and that it's all made up.

In support of its hearsay objection, the defense argues thus:

Your honor, S.T.'s statements to her mother, the pediatrician, and the social worker are classic hearsay. They don't fit Rule 801(d)(1)(B)(i) for two reasons: First, what S.T. said before doesn't refute our contention that she's making up this story so she can stay with her mother in Colorado. Only statements made before the motive arose can refute claims that her testimony is motivated by that interest, and these statements were made *after* she decided she wanted to stay with her mother in Colorado. Second, the Rule requires consistency. Oh sure, you can say that multiple detailed accounts of alleged abuse are consistent with a one-word answer to the question "Were you abused?" But the devil is in the details, and the prior detailed statements are *everything* in this case. They go far beyond anything S.T. testified to. The exception was never designed to get in the only convincing evidence in the case, but for the limited purpose of repairing credibility on the points to which the witness has actually testified.

How should the court rule on these objections, and why?

NOTES ON PRIOR CONSISTENT STATEMENTS AND FRE 801(d)(1)(B)

1. The Problem tracks the facts of the *Tome* case, where the Court held that the premotive requirement is embedded in FRE 801(d)(2)(B), and it reversed a conviction of the father because the trial court did not apply a premotive requirement. See Tome v. United States, 513 U.S. 150 (1995). It is hard to figure out when S.T. was first motivated to make statements charging Trask with abuse. Perhaps the abuse supplied the motive, but the defense suggested that S.T.'s motive arose when she was in Colorado with her mother. Either way, S.T.'s statements came *after* the motive arose.

2. As the introductory material explains, consistent statements have nonhearsay significance, as they tend to prove consistency in the speaker's attitude toward whatever she's talking about. *Tome* addressed the substantive use of such statements under FRE 801(d)(1)(B)—as proof, in addition to a child's rather unsatisfactory trial testimony, that abuse occurred—it is in this context that *Tome* insists on the premotive requirement.

(a) Decisions after *Tome* split on the question whether the premotive requirement applies to the nonhearsay use of statements purely to refute a claim of improper influence of motive. Compare State v. Veis, 962 P.2d 1153, 1156 (Mont. 1998) (statement by victim identifying defendant did not satisfy

premotive requirement, so it was "not admissible as a prior consistent statement" under *Tome* and state counterpart to federal rule) and State v. Morris, 554 N.W.2d 627, 633 (Neb. 1996) (similar) with People v. Eppens, 979 P.2d 14 (Colo. 1999) (error to exclude statement by victim on ground that motive to fabricate already existed; such statements may be admitted to rehabilitate and need not satisfy premotive requirement) *and* United States v. Simonelli, 237 F.3d 19, 25-28 (1st Cir.) (when consistent statement is offered to rehabilitate, FRE 801(d)(1)(B) and its restrictions do not apply), *cert. denied*, 534 U.S. 821 (2001).

(b) If postmotive statements can't be used as substantive evidence but can still be used to repair credibility, then seemingly the mother, pediatrician, and social worker can testify, and the court would give a limiting instruction. On the facts of the Problem and *Tome*, the only difference on retrial would be just such an instruction. The ACN says the 2014 amendment (described in the introductory material) "retains the requirement of *Tome*" that a consistent statement "must have been made before the alleged fabrication or improper influence or motive arose," if it is offered to rebut such a charge. Could a limiting instruction implement *Tome* as envisioned by the ACN? Could a jury possibly understand such an instruction?

(c) All along, it seems that the intent of FRE 801(d)(1)(B) was to permit substantive use of prior consistent statements *whenever* they are admitted to repair credibility after an attack. This purpose seems all the clearer after the 2014 amendment. Hence it doesn't make much sense to apply a premotive requirement to the substantive use of prior consistent statements but not to the use of such statements to repair credibility (thus requiring a limiting instruction). Either the premotive requirement is sound, for reasons stated in the introductory material, or more trouble than it is worth because of the difficulties in pinpointing the time when the motive arose. One way or the other, the requirement should apply (or not) to both the substantive and the rehabilitating use.

3. The second defense objection seems persuasive too. S.T.'s "uh-huh" to a single leading question indicating that abuse occurred is far less informative than her prior statements. See, e.g., State v. Farrah, 735 N.W.2d 336, 344 (Minn. 2007) ("when a witness' prior statement contains assertions about events that have not been described by the witness in trial testimony, those assertions are not helpful in supporting the credibility of the witness and are not admissible"). See also Mueller and Kirkpatrick, Federal Evidence §8:38 (4th ed. 2013) ("If Abraham Lincoln testified that those who fought at Gettysburg were caught up in a great battle with the noble cause of nationhood and democracy at stake, his famous address on November 19, 1863 could be considered 'consistent' with such testimony. Consistent it might be, but the address itself would far outshine and outweigh a more general statement, and would likely have greater impact in any later appraisal of what happened at Gettysburg."). *Tome* didn't focus on this matter (addressing only the premotive issue), but this objection would have had force there too.

3. Prior Statements of Identification

At the dramatic moment of a criminal trial when an eyewitness is asked to point out, if she can, the person she saw commit the deed ("Do you see him in this courtroom?"), everybody knows the expected answer: "Yes, he is that man sitting over there." "Let the record show that the witness pointed to the defendant." No matter how the question is put, it is loaded. The risk of false identification is obvious, and there is a less obvious risk—that alert jurors will discount the courtroom identification because the setting renders it so suspect.

By comparison, pretrial identifications may be more trustworthy. In a proper lineup, for instance, the situation is less suggestive: The array does not single out the suspect, and it is possible through "blank" arrays to detect an overeager identifier or deflate any preconception that the suspect must be one of the ones before her. Often pretrial identifications are made close to the time of the offense, before pressure can be brought to bear on the witness. And where the identifier appears in court, so what she says there and what she said before can be compared, and she can be cross-examined on both, there is all the more reason for confidence.

For these reasons, FRE 801(d)(1)(C) creates what amounts to a hearsay exception for previous statements of identification, made by a witness after perceiving the subject, provided that the witness is subject at trial to cross-examination about the statement.

STATE v. MOTTA

Hawaii Supreme Court
659 P.2d 745 (Hawaii 1983)

LUM, C.J . . . .

On April 29, 1980 at about 11:30 P.M., Wendy Iwashita, a cashier on duty at Anna Miller's Coffee House in Pearlridge, was robbed at gunpoint by a man who demanded that she give him all the money she had in her cash register. Iwashita complied and the robber fled with approximately $300.00 in cash.

Iwashita gave a description of the robber to the police who arrived at the scene soon thereafter. On May 6, 1980, Iwashita met with Joe Aragon, an artist for the Honolulu Police Department, who drew a composite sketch of the robbery suspect based on Iwashita's description.

On June 3, 1980, Iwashita picked appellant's photograph from a photographic array of about twenty-five to thirty pictures. On June 9, 1980, Iwashita positively identified appellant in a preliminary hearing. At trial, Iwashita confirmed her prior identifications and pointed out the appellant as the person who robbed her.

Appellant presented an alibi defense at trial. Appellant testified that he was at a nightclub at the time of the robbery. Appellant called several other witnesses to describe his physical appearance on the date of the robbery and to corroborate his alibi.

After considering the evidence presented, the jury found appellant guilty of the offense of robbery in the first degree . . . .

Appellant also contends that the trial court erred in admitting Aragon's composite sketch based on Iwashita's description of the robbery suspect. Appellant argues that the sketch was inadmissible hearsay under HRE 802 which provides that "[h]earsay is not admissible except as provided by these rules, or by other rules prescribed by the Hawaii supreme court, or by statute." Rule 801(3) defines "hearsay" as "a statement, other than one made by the declarant while testifying at the trial or hearing, offered in evidence to prove the truth of the matter asserted."

Other courts have admitted composite sketches into evidence under various rationales. One view, expressed by the Second Circuit Court of Appeals in United States v. Moskowitz, 581 F.2d 14 (2d Cir.), cert. denied, 439 U.S. 871 (1978), is that a police sketch is not even hearsay because it does not qualify as a statement which is defined in FRE 801(a) as "(1) an oral or written assertion or (2) nonverbal conduct of a person, if it is intended by him as an assertion." Under this view, since the sketch did not constitute hearsay, it merely had to satisfy the authentication requirements of FRE 901.

Another approach taken by some state courts is to view the police sketch as hearsay, but admissible under various common-law hearsay exceptions. The Pennsylvania Superior Court in Commonwealth v. Dugan, 381 A.2d 967 (Pa. Super. 1977) took this approach and found that a sketch made by a friend of the victim was properly admitted under the res gestae exception to the hearsay rule since the sketch had been made shortly after the victim had seen the suspect. The Illinois Supreme Court in People v. Rogers, 411 N.E.2d 223 (Ill. 1980) held that the hearsay rule did not bar admission of a composite sketch used as extra-judicial identification evidence to corroborate a witness' in-court identification.

A final alternative, which is available to those courts which have adopted rules similar to the Federal Rules of Evidence, is to allow the admission of composite sketches and other pretrial identifications under the prior identification exception to the general hearsay exclusionary rule under FRE 801(d)(1)(C) . . . . The Senate Judiciary Committee which recommended the adoption of Rule 801(d)(1)(C) noted that

> Both experience and psychological studies suggest that identifications consisting of nonsuggestive lineups, photographic spreads, or similar identifications made reasonably soon after the offense, are most [sic] reliable than in-court identifications. Admitting these prior identifications therefore provides greater fairness to both the prosecution and defense in a criminal trial. Their exclusion would thus be detrimental to the fair administration of justice.

After careful review of the various alternatives, we find that the better approach is to recognize a composite sketch as hearsay but nevertheless admissible under the hearsay exception for prior identifications if it complies with HRE 802.1(3) (which is identical in substance to FRE 801(d)(1)(C)).

We recognize along with the majority of courts that a composite sketch is in fact hearsay. It has the same effect as if the victim had made a verbal description of the suspect's physical characteristics. Just because the sketch is in picture form does not change the fact that it is being offered as a statement made out of court to prove what the suspect looked like. See *United States v. Moskowitz* (Friendly, J., concurring); *Commonwealth v. Dugan* (Spaeth, J., concurring).

Although a composite sketch is hearsay, it may still be admissible as a prior identification under HRE 802.1(3) if (1) declarant testifies at trial and is subject to cross-examination concerning the subject matter of his statement and (2) the statement is one of identification of a person made after perceiving him. In the instant action, the admission of the sketch met the requirements of HRE 802.1(3): the declarant, Wendy Iwashita, testified at trial and was available for cross-examination regarding the subject matter of her description, and the sketch was an identification of the robbery suspect made after Iwashita had seen him.

Appellant contends that the composite sketch was admitted solely to corroborate Wendy Iwashita's in-court identification. Appellant consequently argues that since corroborating evidence is only admissible when offered to rebut testimony impeaching the witness and no such impeaching evidence was introduced, the sketch is inadmissible.

Appellant misapprehends the nature of the prior identification exception to the hearsay rule. Unlike the common-law extra-judicial identification exception . . . , the prior identification exception . . . allows the admission of pretrial identifications, not merely as corroborative evidence, but also as substantive proof of identity . . . . See also Gilbert v. California, 388 U.S. 263, 272, n.3 (1967) ("The recent trend . . . is to admit the prior identification under the exception that admits as substantive evidence a prior communication by a witness who is available for cross-examination at trial").

Thus . . . Rule 801(d)(1)(C) operates independently of the impeachment process and therefore the statement is admissible as substantive evidence even though it is not a prior inconsistent statement for impeachment purposes as required in FRE 801(d)(1)(A) nor a prior consistent statement for rehabilitation purposes as required in Rule 801(d)(1)(B).

The primary reason for excluding hearsay is the danger that the declarant is not available and her credibility therefore cannot be assessed by the trier of fact. That danger was not present in this case where both Joe Aragon, the police artist who made the sketch, and Wendy Iwashita, the eyewitness who provided the description, testified at trial and were subject to cross-examination by the defense. See also State v. Naeole, 617 P.2d 820, 826 (Haw. 1980) (testimony permitted with regard to photographic lineup where both the officer who conducted the lineup and the person making the identification were present at trial to testify about the prior identification and were subject to cross-examination) . . . .

Given the fact that the jury was given the opportunity to judge the credibility of both the police artist and the eyewitness at trial, we find no reason to disturb the trial court's discretion in admitting the sketch into evidence....

Affirmed.

■ NOTES ON APPLICATION OF FRE 801(d)(1)(C)

1. It was Wendy Iwashita, not sketch artist Joe Aragon, who saw the robber at Anna Miller's Coffee House, so only Iwashita can make a statement that fits FRE 801(d)(1)(C). How can Aragon's sketch be viewed as Iwashita's statement?

2. Both Iwashita and Aragon testified. The sketch could be admitted under FRE 801(d)(1)(C) on the basis of Iwashita's testimony alone. She could testify that she sat down with a sketch artist, described the culprit and recommended alterations in the sketch as it materialized, until she concluded that the sketch captured the likeness of the culprit ("that's as close to being him as I can come"). As the decision in *Motta* suggests, an identification based on a photo array ("mugshots") would satisfy the Rule as well. See United States v. Salameh, 152 F.3d 88, 125-126 (2d Cir. 1998). Like the sketch, a mugshot too can become part of the identifying witness's statement. In either case, it is probably a good idea to call as witnesses anyone who was with the identifying witness at the time, like the police officer who showed the mugshots or the artist who drew a sketch. Doing so presents a more complete picture of the identifying process.

3. If David Motta had stood in a proper lineup and Wendy Iwashita picked him out as the robber, could the officer in charge testify to her statement, or does FRE 801(d)(1)(C) require her to testify to it? See People v. Lewis, 860 N.E.2d 299, 305 (Ill. 2006) (third party can testify). But the identifier too must take the stand, for FRE 801(d)(1)(C) requires that *she* be subject to cross. See Mauet, Prior Identifications in Criminal Cases: Hearsay and Confrontation Issues, 24 Ariz. L. Rev. 29, 49 (1982) (officer may describe nature and circumstances of lineup, and identifier's words and manner, but officer's testimony cannot substitute for cross-examination of identifier going into his "ability to transfer accurately the mental images made during the commission of the crime to the place and time of the lineup").

4. FRE 801(d)(1)(C) contemplates statements by an eyewitness made after perceiving the subject. It contemplates the situation in which the declarant saw the crime (or the subject in a situation that incriminates him), then saw him again (typically in a lineup), and says, "He's the one who did it." A few decisions interpret the exception as *requiring* a second look, see State v. Shaw, 705 N.W.2d 620 (S.D. 2005), but most have concluded that no second look is required. See United States v. Lopez, 271 F.3d 472, 484-485 (3d Cir. 2001) (exception embraces statements to police, one day after the crime, indicating that declarant saw the three defendants in the area when crime was committed), *cert.*

denied, 535 U.S. 908 (2002). In other words, if a witness sees a crime, recognizes the culprit, and later says (to a friend or to police), "Tom Jones is the one who did it," the exception applies. It applies as well even if the witness only hears the voice of the culprit and says it's the defendant's voice, or hears the voice of the culprit during the offense and then hears a recording of a suspect and says "Yes, that's the voice I heard." See United States v. Ramirez, 45 F.3d 1096, 1101 (7th Cir. 1995) (entry on transcript of recorded conversation identifying voice fit exception; maker of transcript testified).

5. The Rule contemplates that the identifier (like Wendy Iwashita) will be "subject to cross-examination" about her statement. Suppose she *cannot* say "the man sitting over there is the one" (pointing to defendant), but instead says, "I don't know if he's the one, and I don't remember for sure what the guy looked like." Can an unremembering witness satisfy the cross-examination requirement? Suppose the same woman, who cannot identify defendant or remember what the culprit looked like, *does remember* going to a lineup or seeing a photo array and making an identification. Suppose she can be fully examined on this matter and on general credibility. Is that enough? See United States v. Owens, 484 U.S. 554 (1988) (cross-examination requirement satisfied despite "assertion of memory loss"). You will see that this fact probably satisfies confrontation concerns too. See Crawford v. Washington, 541 U.S. 36 (2004) (if speaker can be cross-examined at trial, Confrontation Clause places "no constraints" on use of what he said). Pretrial identifications may be more reliable than identifications at trial, but they are still subject to hearsay risks, so cross-examination at trial remains critical.

COMMENT/PERSPECTIVE: Constitutional Issues with Identifications

The Supreme Court has long recognized that getting a statement by the complaining witness identifying the culprit is a crucial stage in the investigative process. Already in 1967, the Court held that the accused is entitled to counsel in a postindictment lineup, and to notice of the lineup. See U.S. v. Wade, 388 U.S. 218 (1967). In a companion case, the Court added that denying defense rights under *Wade* requires exclusion of the lineup identification at trial. But the Court cut back on this doctrine later, holding in Kirby v. Illinois, 406 U.S. 682 (1972) that *Wade-Gilbert* does not apply to preindictment showups, nor to identifications based on photo arrays, see U.S. v. Ash, 413 U.S. 682 (1973). Other decisions recognize Due Process limits on use of pretrial identifications, and on testimony by witnesses who made such identifications, particularly those occurring in suggestive circumstances. See, e.g., Manson v. Brathwaite, 432 U.S. 98 (1977). Consider the difficulties faced by both police and defendants in cases like *Motta,* where it seems critical both to obtain from Wendy Iwashita her best recollection of the man who robbed her and to protect the rights of the eventual defendant to have a fair shot at testing statements identifying him as the culprit. There is nothing obvious on the facts of *Motta,* is there, that suggests that the police did anything wrong in putting Wendy together with sketch artist Joe Aragon?

6. Suppose Iwashita caught the eye of an officer before the culprit got away, and watched the officer arrest him. She tells the officer, "He's the one with the gun who took our money." Six months later she confronts David Motta at trial but is unsure that he's the one. She testifies that "the man I pointed out did it; I saw him do it and never let him out of my sight." The officer testifies that "defendant is the man she pointed out." FRE 801(d)(1)(C) paves the way for this testimony, but do we need a hearsay exception on these facts? Both Wendy and the officer use her statement as a "verbal marker" that gives meaning to their present testimony. You looked at this question in Problem 3-G (Eagle's Rest Bar and Grill), where the barmaid was asked whether she had seen Nichols and Seaver together. Don't such audible spoken words identify a person in the same manner that the visible written words "Fighting Illini" identify a mug in that problem? See United States v. Barbati, 284 F. Supp. 409 (E.D.N.Y. 1968) (barmaid's oral statement identifying people who passed counterfeit bills can be called nonhearsay "without doing violence to theory" by "analogizing" to identification of objects; barmaid testifies from memory that "I was given a counterfeit bill by a man, *X*, and I saw the police arrest *X*," and officer testifies, "The man we arrested was the defendant," and neither statement is hearsay).

B EXCEPTIONS IN FRE 801(d)(2)—ADMISSIONS BY PARTY OPPONENT

Before there was a hearsay doctrine, what a party said could be offered against him. Such statements continued to be admissible after the coming of the hearsay doctrine. In today's world, a driver who runs over a pedestrian and makes a comment afterwards ("I ran the red light") has made evidence against himself. The same is true if he writes it down or signs a statement.

Sometimes admissions are viewed as nonhearsay. It is true that when a statement by a party is offered against him, usually it conflicts with his position at trial (the driver may claim the light was in his favor), so it has nonhearsay significance as evidence of vacillation. If he testifies, his admission is a "prior inconsistency" that undermines his credibility. In other words, an admission often has impeaching effect and could come in even if there were no hearsay exception. But impeachment does not tell the whole story, for admissions come in as positive proof of what they assert (driver ran the red light), which unavoidably raises the hearsay issue.

Hence it is understood that the hearsay doctrine needs some special wrinkle to account for the full use of admissions. Yet a formal hearsay exception for admissions would be a curiosity, since the other exceptions are grounded in notions of necessity and trustworthiness (as you will see), and admissions do not fit this pattern. In the end, trying to classify admissions accurately in hearsay terminology seems to be a game that is not worth the candle. FRE 801(d)(2) just cuts the knot: By the same statutory magic we've seen before, it defines all admissions as "not hearsay." Once again this solution is not an entirely happy one. If admissions lie beyond the definition of hearsay (like verbal acts) there would be no need for such a provision. Maybe we should just say that admissions are statements with hearsay aspects that we treat as nonhearsay, or as hearsay exceptions.

Resolving the hearsay issue by fiat leaves the real question unanswered. Why do admissions come in as proof of what they assert? The most persuasive explanation is that the admissions doctrine expresses the philosophy of the adversary system, in which each party is responsible for making or breaking, winning or losing, his own lawsuit—by his conduct both in and out of court. And a series of somewhat related reasons points in the same direction: The hearsay doctrine is designed to protect parties against uncross-examined statements, but a party can hardly complain that he didn't have a chance to cross-examine himself; admissions are a kind of conduct, amounting to behavior by a party that provides circumstantial evidence of what they assert;[1] admissions give rise to estoppel notions and should be usable against a party for similar reasons;[2] fairness suggests that one should simply not be allowed to complain that his words are proved against him.

When a statement comes in against a party as his admission, generally it is not "binding" in the sense of foreclosing him from taking a conflicting position at trial. A party may seek to explain away or reject what he said before. Indeed, the very fact that he takes such a position often induces the adverse party to offer his admissions. Whether a party can succeed in avoiding the effect of his own prior statements is another matter: The trier may credit what he said before rather than his trial testimony, which is just a way of saying that admissions are potent evidence. (Recall from your civil procedure course that the rule is otherwise with pleadings filed in a pending civil suit, for averments in this form do constitute "judicial admissions," meaning that the party is foreclosed from offering evidence to the contrary. See FRCP 8(d), which provides in essence that what an answer does not deny is admitted.)

---

[1] Nonverbal nonassertive behavior comfortably fits this explanation. Consider cases where the accused fled the scene: Conduct suggests flight, which suggests guilty mind, which suggests guilt (see Problem 2-B). Because Rule 801 rejects *Wright v. Tatham* (Chapter 3B1b), this use of defendant's conduct is not hearsay.

[2] Estoppel usually depends on reliance by another party, while admissions may come in even if the other party did not rely on them. And estoppel ordinarily forecloses a party from taking certain positions, which goes well beyond the mere *evidential* effect given to admissions.

The modern admissions doctrine is elaborate, as a glance at the five subdivisions of FRE 801(d)(2) confirms. In a suit by or against an individual, the doctrine reaches his own statements offered against him, and it also sometimes reaches statements by others that a party makes his own by adoption. Moreover, the doctrine reaches statements by a party's authorized agents, employees, and (usually in criminal cases) fellow conspirators. In short, admissions embrace many statements associated with the party against whom they are offered.

1. Individual Admissions

In the case of individual admissions, there are almost no limits. Some sense of the reach of the doctrine is suggested by a modern trial for bank fraud, where a court admitted against a defendant an undelivered email that he had written to a radio personality, apparently conceding that he had "misappropriated" a large sum of money. See United States v. Sprick, 233 F.3d 845, 855 (5th Cir. 2000). It is true that occasional statutes restrict use of admissions, and the Constitution protects the accused against the use of some things he says in some circumstances. And important principles bar or regulate certain lines of circumstantial evidence (like proof of character and safety measures taken after an accident). These principles may incidentally require exclusion of admissions. But statements by a party are broadly admissible against him.

■ PROBLEM 4-C. Fire in the Warehouse

Martin left his truck at Carter's Automotive Repair and Refinishing in Tupelo, Mississippi, because one of the brackets securing the gastank had broken. Carter himself was in Oxford, Mississippi, at the time. The shop has separate areas for repair and maintenance, for body work, and for painting and refinishing. While the truck was being repaired, employee Dugan was working with a welding torch on a wrecked car, within five feet of the door to the paint storage room. Placing the flaming torch on the ground, he went around the side of the building to get a Coke from a vending machine. Moments later the fire alarm sounded, and Dugan returned to discover the paint shed burning out of control. The fire consumed the premises and destroyed Martin's truck.

Martin sues Carter to recover for loss of the truck. As proof that Dugan's negligence started the fire (hence that Carter is liable by respondeat superior), Martin calls an insurance adjuster named Esher. It turns out that Carter spoke to Esher after the fire in the course of advancing his insurance claim for loss of the building. If permitted, Esher will testify that Carter told him, "The fire started in the paint shed when Dugan put a flaming welding torch on the ground too close to the fumes."

Carter raises a hearsay objection, and Martin invokes the admissions doctrine and FRE 801(d)(2)(A). Should Carter's statement come in? Quite apart from what the Rule indicates, what is the sound result here?

NOTES ON INDIVIDUAL ADMISSIONS

1. Many cases reject an objection that a party whose statement is offered against him lacked knowledge, and the ACN to FRE 801 endorses this result. The dog-bite cases are typical: In a suit against a dog owner, plaintiff may prove that the latter, although she did not see the incident, said afterwards that her pet bit or attacked plaintiff. See Berkowitz v. Simone, 188 A.2d 665, 666 (R.I. 1963) (she had not seen either incident, but owner admitted that her dog bit two children); Janus v. Akstin, 20 A.2d 552 (N.H. 1941) (statement that dog "jumped on" woman and "knocked her down the steps" was admissible against pet owner even though he was not present). Still, personal knowledge would make such statements more convincing, and you will discover that most of the hearsay exceptions *apart from* admissions are crafted to insure personal knowledge. With admissions, usually the speaker has at least a kind of "circumstantial knowledge" enabling her to make an intelligent statement even if she didn't see what she describes. A dog owner likely knows something about the proclivities of the animal and would not likely say Rover bit someone if she didn't think Rover would so such a thing.

2. The cases sometimes refer to "admissions against interest," as if the doctrine reached only statements "giving up" or "conceding" some point. Requiring an "against interest" element implies that the statement of a driver that he "ran a red light" would be admissible, but not one that "he honked his horn at me" (even though, later at trial, declarant's opponent might want to establish this point). But FRE 804(b)(3) carves out a separate exception for "declarations against interest," and the admissions doctrine carries no "against interest" requirement. Even a statement designed to *advance* the interest of the declarant is admissible over his objection. See People v. Meyer, 954 P.2d 1068 (Colo. 1999) (denials of wrongdoing fit admissions doctrine; no against-interest element).

3. Consider a statement that the accident "was all my fault" or that working conditions were "safe and proper." Should the conclusory nature suffice to exclude such statements? Courts uniformly accept them, on the theory that it is better to admit probative statements than to apply, to statements made out of court, trial standards requiring more specificity. See Strickland v. Davis, 128 So. 233 (Ala. 1930) (admitting statement by defendant that he was "at fault") (admissions "need not conform to statements the witness could make on the stand"); Owens v. Atchison, T. & S.F. Ry., 393 F.2d 77, 79 (5th Cir.) (plaintiff said he considered working conditions "safe and proper" and there was nothing defendant "could have done to prevent the accident"), *cert. denied*, 393 U.S. 855 (1968).

COMMENT/PERSPECTIVE: Apologies as Admissions

Statements of apology ("I'm sorry I hurt you") fit the admissions doctrine if offered against the speaker. Hence such statements are sometimes admitted, but there is abundant evidence that claimants are often aggrieved as much because of the perceived "stonewalling" attitude of defendants as they are by the injuries suffered from accidents, or for that matter medical malpractice or product liability. Apologizing may go a long way to satisfy a claimant, making settlement more likely and even forestalling suit altogether. For this reason, statutes in some states bar the use of apologies. Compare Colorado Revised Statutes §13-25-135 (making certain statements expressing "apology, fault, sympathy, commiseration, condolence, compassion, or a general sense of benevolence" by doctors or medical providers inadmissible in malpractice cases) with California Evidence Code §1160 (making statements of apology inadmissible against the declarant in all civil cases, but providing that statements of "fault" are not covered by this principle). See Jonathan R. Cohen, Legislating Apology: The Pros and Cons, 70 U. Cin. L. Rev. 819 (2002); Jennifer K. Robbennolt, Apologies and Legal Settlement: An Empirical Examination, 102 Mich. L. Rev. 460 (2003). Are such rules a good idea?

4. What if declarant is drunk? Courts admit such statements too. See Commonwealth v. Walker, 456 N.E.2d 1154, 1156 (Mass. App. 1983) (rejecting claim that defendant "was too drunk to waive *Miranda* rights" despite officer's testimony that he was "pretty loaded") (court could find that he "had his wits sufficiently"); Sutton v. State, 228 S.E.2d 815 (Ga. 1976) (in trial of father for murdering two daughters and setting fire to home to conceal crimes; admitting his incriminating remarks, where evidence conflicted on whether he was conscious or unconscious at the time).

5. Even statements by seriously injured persons are often admissible against them. See Finnerty v. Darby, 138 A.2d 117, 126 (Pa. 1958) (admitting statement by plaintiff describing accident to officer in hospital the morning after; he "was so severely injured that his life was despaired of" and his tongue had been "sutured to his cheek to facilitate breathing" and last rites had been administered while he was unconscious; he was "mostly in an unconscious or semi-conscious state" and recovery was "most miraculous") (dissenting, Justice Musmanno notes that statement was written by his wife at his bedside); Aide v.

Taylor, 7 N.W.2d 757, 759-760 (Minn. 1943) (in suit by pedestrian struck by car, fact that plaintiff was "suffering from much pain," had taken "several hypos of morphine," and was "still semi-conscious" did not require exclusion of statement that he had run into street without looking; such facts affect "probative value and weight," but statements must be excluded where declarant is "incapacitated from making a rational admission, as where he was at the time in a coma"). In light of cases such as *Finnerty* and *Aide*, and considering the fact that the party offering a statement as an admission is often instrumental in obtaining it, the possibility of overreaching or taking advantage of the other side has sometimes persuaded legislatures to restrict the use of such statements. See, e.g., Minn. Stat. Ann. §602.01 (statement by injured person obtained within 30 days after accident is presumed fraudulent, and is inadmissible unless party obtaining it gives the injured person a copy within 30 days); Colo. Rev. Stat. §13-21-301 (barring hospitals and doctors from negotiating settlements with patients within 30 days after treatment, and excluding statements obtained by doctors or hospitals from patients within 15 days of such occurrence).

6. What if the party is asleep? Recall Iago's words from *Othello*:

> . . . I lay with Cassio lately,
> And being troubled with a raging tooth,
> I could not sleep.
> There are a kind of men so loose of soul
> That in their sleeps will mutter their affairs:
> One of this kind is Cassio.
> In sleep I heard him say 'Sweet Desdemona,
> Let us be wary, let us hide our loves';
> And then, sir, would he gripe and wring my hand,
> Cry 'O sweet creature!' then kiss me hard,
> As if he pluck'd up kisses by the roots,
> That grew upon my lips—then laid his leg
> Over my thigh—and sigh'd, and kiss'd, and then
> Cried 'Cursed fate that gave thee to the Moor!'

Shakespeare, *Othello*, Act III, Scene iii. Compare Flavell v. Flavell, 20 N.J. Eq. 211 (1869) (husband sought divorce for adultery, but wife said he too was an adulterer; he admitted that he "met a girl named Ella" while in New York and intoxicated, but the evidence fell "far short" of proving adultery even though "he called out her name in his sleep, or when partly intoxicated and half asleep") with People v. Knatz, 428 N.Y.S.3d 709 (N.Y. App. Div. 1980) (in trial for manslaughter and arson, error to admit girlfriend's testimony about statements defendant made in his sleep; fact that he slept detracted from their reliability; utterances were ambiguous and did not unequivocally relate to crime). Is sleeptalk more probative when it amorously names names than when it confesses to criminal acts? Or less so?

7. Probative worth apart, should it matter that the context is a criminal trial? There, "involuntary" confessions are barred under the Fifth Amendment, but only where a state agent plays some active role. See Colorado v. Connelly, 479 U.S. 157 (1986) (confession by defendant experiencing "command hallucinations" interfering with his "volitional abilities"—he was reacting to what he considered the "voice of God"—was voluntary for purposes of Fifth Amendment; so was his waiver of *Miranda* rights; *Miranda* protects only against "government coercion," and a "perception of coercion flowing from the 'voice of God,' . . . is a matter to which the United States Constitution does not speak"). Confessions to police by severely injured or incapacitated defendants have been excluded. See Mincey v. Arizona, 437 U.S. 385 (1978) (defendant was wounded in drug raid that resulted in death of officer; he arrived at hospital "depressed almost to the point of coma," and was questioned by detective while in intensive care, lying on his back encumbered by tubes, needles, and breathing apparatus; his confession, delivered bit by bit in written form because could not speak, was involuntary and should have been excluded); Beecher v. Alabama, 389 U.S. 35 (1967) (murder confession signed when defendant was in a "kind of slumber" from morphine, and was feverish and in intense pain, was inadmissible because involuntary).

8. What if declarant is a minor? Compare De Souza v. Barber, 263 F.2d 470 (9th Cir.) (admitting statements by alien resisting deportation, made 28 years before proceedings while he was 19 and 20 years old), *cert. denied*, 359 U.S. 989 (1959) with Fontaine v. Devonis, 336 A.2d 847, 852 (R.I. 1975) (excluding statement by three-and-one-half-year-old child that he "ran out into the street and got hit by the car") (he could hardly "elucidate upon the proper nuances to indicate his freedom from negligence").

■ PROBLEM 4-D. An Encounter Gone Bad

While on a skiing vacation in Vail, Colorado, a wealthy man named Kenneth Brixton struck up a conversation with a waitress named Sally Flynn in a bar. The two became friendly. They wound up walking the grounds close to the hotel, and eventually they went to Brixton's room. What happened in the room is in dispute, but two days later Flynn went to local police and said that Brixton had sexually assaulted her. On advice by a victim's advocate, Flynn went to a local hospital where a "rape kit" was used in collecting fluid samples and conducting an examination.

After criminal charges of felony sexual assault were filed against Brixton, Flynn went to a lawyer and filed a civil suit for damages.

In the criminal case, the lawyer for Brixton considers the possibility of entering a plea of guilty to a lesser charge of sexual contact (a misdemeanor) that would carry a lesser sentence. At a plea hearing, Brixton's lawyer knows the judge will explain the charges and range of possible sentences, and will advise Brixton that he has a right to a jury trial where the prosecutor would have to call witnesses and prove the charges against him, and that Brixton need not testify. The judge will tell Brixton that a plea of guilty waives his right to trial and leads to conviction. The judge will ask Brixton whether he committed the offense to which he is considering a plea of guilty. There Brixton will be expected to recount his version of what happened between him and Flynn in the hotel room.

Would Brixton's statements in his plea hearing be admissible against him in Flynn's civil suit? What strategies should Brixton's lawyer consider? If Brixton pleads guilty and offers his version of events showing that unlawful sexual contact occurred, would that justify summary judgment for Flynn in the civil suit? Could Brixton's conviction, based on his guilty plea, become the basis for collateral estoppel in the civil suit?

NOTES ON PRIOR GUILTY PLEAS

1. Pleading guilty to charges usually involves proceedings like those described in the Problem. Defendant is represented, and the judge explains his situation. If defendant enters a plea, usually it is admissible in a later civil damage suit. A guilty plea, and certainly the resultant conviction, can even be *binding* in later civil litigation. See Jiron v. City of Lakewood, 392 F.2d 410, 417 (10th Cir. 2004) ("a plea of guilty entered in Colorado state court can have preclusive effect in a subsequent civil proceeding").

(a) A plea of nolo contendere in the criminal proceedings can help: It's not admissible in a civil suit, but it requires defendant to submit to punishment and allow entry of a criminal judgment against him, and courts do not always allow such pleas.

(b) For defense counsel, the situation is tricky. Pleading to the criminal charges brings the risks noted above, but going forward with the civil litigation brings its own risks, including the fact that defendant would be expected to give a deposition, but would likely have to claim the privilege against self-incrimination or his answers in the deposition would be usable by the prosecutor in the criminal case. Most defense lawyers in this situation struggle mightily to resolve both the civil and the criminal matters at the same time, through settlement and plea bargain.

2. Consider a guilty plea to a traffic infraction, like speeding, failure to yield right-of-way, or making an illegal turn. Should such a plea, or any resultant conviction, be admissible in a later civil damage suit? Absent some special statute or rule, courts generally say yes. See Folino v. Young, 568 A.2d 171 (Pa. 1990) (in civil negligence suit, admitting conviction for driving at unsafe speed); Romine v. Parman, 831 F.2d 944, 946 (10th Cir. 1987) (in civil negligence suit, admitting proof that defendant paid fine for failing to yield right of way). Some statutes provide otherwise. See, e.g., Colo. Rev. Stat. §42-4-1713 (making record of conviction of traffic infraction inadmissible "in any civil action"). Considerations underlying such legislation include recognizing that people may pay tickets just because resisting isn't worth the time or effort. Hence pleading guilty, or paying fines (which serves the same function) isn't very persuasive proof of actual guilt. Even going to trial and losing might not be very persuasive, since normally so little is at stake. Excluding traffic infraction pleas and judgments has the effect of keeping relevant evidence from the trier of fact, but probably encourages the more efficient operation of traffic enforcement mechanisms. As always, such statutes bring issues of construction, and they are sometimes qualified. Thus the question arises whether barring use of a "conviction" for a traffic infraction also bar use of a guilty plea (or paying the fine)? See Jones v. Talbot, 394 P.2d 316, 319 (Idaho 1964) (statute excluding conviction also excludes guilty plea, for admitting the plea would "achieve by indirection what the statute prohibits directly"). And the Florida statute, which generally bars use of traffic infractions, makes an exception if the incident constituting the infraction kills or injures another person. See Fla. Stat. §§318.14(4) and 318.19.

3. If a state statute excludes convictions for traffic infractions, should it be honored in a federal diversity suit seeking damages? Given the purposes of such legislation, the answer is probably Yes. See Bullock v. Wayne, 623 F. Supp. 2d 1247, 1256 (D. Colo. 2009) (purpose of state statute barring use of traffic infractions was substantive; legislature "did not want these relatively small infractions to have grave consequences in civil actions where significantly more could be at stake," and statute "ameliorates docket congestion in traffic courts," as "incentive to fight a traffic ticket would grow dramatically" if they were admissible in later damage suits).

BRUTON v. UNITED STATES

United States Supreme Court
391 U.S. 123 (1968)

Mr. Justice BRENNAN delivered the opinion of the Court.

[In the trial of George Bruton and William Evans for armed postal robbery, a postal inspector testified that Evans made an oral confession saying in effect that "Bruton and I committed the robbery." Evans made this confession while being interrogated in a St. Louis jail, where he was being held on state charges. The trial court admitted the confession against Evans, but told the jury that it could not be considered "in any respect" against Bruton. At the close of trial, the judge told the jury that a confession by one defendant "may not be considered as evidence against" another who was "not present and in no way a party to" it. Each is entitled to have his case determined on "his own acts and statements," said the judge, so the jury should leave "out of consideration entirely any evidence admitted solely against" another defendant.

Bruton and Evans were convicted. The Eighth Circuit reversed the conviction of Evans because his confession should not have been admitted against him. But the reviewing court affirmed Bruton's conviction because the instructions prevented any harm. The Eighth Circuit relied on Delli Paoli v. United States, 352 U.S. 232 (1957) (limiting instructions suffice to protect one defendant when another's confession is introduced). The Supreme Court reverses.]

Delli Paoli assumed that this encroachment on the right to confrontation could be avoided by the instruction to the jury to disregard the inadmissible hearsay evidence.[3] But, as we have said, that assumption has since been effectively repudiated. True, the repudiation was not in the context of the admission of a confession inculpating a codefendant but in the context of a New York rule which submitted to the jury the question of the voluntariness of the confession itself. Jackson v. Denno, 378 U.S. 368. Nonetheless the message of *Jackson* for *Delli Paoli* was clear. We there held that a defendant is constitutionally entitled at least to have the trial judge first determine whether a confession was made voluntarily before submitting it to the jury for an assessment of its credibility. More specifically, we expressly rejected the proposition that a jury, when determining the confessor's guilt, could be relied on to ignore his confession of guilt should it find the confession involuntary. Significantly, we supported that conclusion in part by reliance upon the dissenting opinion of Mr. Justice Frankfurter for the four Justices who dissented in *Delli Paoli.*

That dissent challenged the basic premise of *Delli Paoli* that a properly instructed jury would ignore the confessor's inculpation of the nonconfessor in determining the latter's guilt. "The fact of the matter is that too often such admonition against misuse is intrinsically ineffective in that the effect of such a nonadmissible declaration cannot be wiped from the brains of the jurors. The admonition therefore becomes a futile collocation of words and fails of its purpose as a legal protection to defendants against whom such a declaration should not tell." The dissent went on to say, as quoted in the cited note in *Jackson,* "The government should not have the windfall of having the jury be influenced by evidence against a defendant which, as a matter of law, they should not consider but which they cannot put out of their minds." To the same effect, and also cited in the *Jackson* note, is the statement of Mr. Justice Jackson in his concurring opinion in Krulewitch v. United States, 336 U.S. 440, 453: "The naive assumption that prejudicial effects can be overcome by instructions to the jury . . . all practicing lawyers know to be unmitigated fiction . . . ."

In addition to *Jackson,* our action in 1966 in amending FRCrimP 14 also evidences our repudiation of *Delli Paoli*'s basic premise. Rule 14 authorizes a severance where it appears that a defendant might be prejudiced by a joint trial. The Rule was amended in 1966 to provide expressly that "[i]n ruling on a motion by a defendant for severance the court may order the attorney for the

[3] We emphasize that the hearsay statement inculpating petitioner was clearly inadmissible against him under traditional rules of evidence [citing *Krulewitch* and *Fiswick* decisions dealing with coconspirator statements], the problem arising only because the statement was . . . admissible against the declarant Evans. There is not before us, therefore, any recognized exception to the hearsay rule insofar as petitioner is concerned and we intimate no view whatever that such exceptions necessarily raise questions under the Confrontation Clause.

government to deliver to the court for inspection in camera any statements or confessions made by the defendants which the government intends to introduce in evidence at the trial." The Advisory Committee on Rules said in explanation of the amendment:

> A defendant may be prejudiced by the admission in evidence against a co-defendant of a statement or confession made by that co-defendant. This prejudice cannot be dispelled by cross-examination if the co-defendant does not take the stand. Limiting instructions to the jury may not in fact erase the prejudice....

The purpose of the amendment is to provide a procedure whereby the issue of possible prejudice can be resolved on the motion for severance....

Those who have defended reliance on the limiting instruction in this area have cited several reasons in support. Judge Learned Hand, a particularly severe critic of the proposition that juries could be counted on to disregard inadmissible hearsay, wrote the opinion for the Second Circuit which affirmed Delli Paoli's conviction. In Judge Hand's view the limiting instruction, although not really capable of preventing the jury from considering the prejudicial evidence, does as a matter of form provide a way around the exclusionary rules of evidence that is defensible because it "probably furthers, rather than impedes, the search for truth...." Nash v. United States, 54 F.2d 1006, 1007 (2d Cir. 1932). Insofar as this implies the prosecution ought not to be denied the benefit of the confession to prove the confessor's guilt, however, it overlooks alternative ways of achieving that benefit without at the same time infringing the nonconfessor's right of confrontation.[10] Where viable alternatives do exist, it is deceptive to rely on the pursuit of truth to defend a clearly harmful practice.

Another reason cited in defense of *Delli Paoli* is the justification for joint trials in general, the argument being that the benefits of joint proceedings should not have to be sacrificed by requiring separate trials in order to use the confession against the declarant. Joint trials do conserve state funds, diminish inconvenience to witnesses and public authorities, and avoid delays in bringing those accused of crime to trial. But the answer to this argument was cogently stated by Judge Lehman of the New York Court of Appeals, dissenting in People v. Fisher, 164 N.E. 336, 341 (N.Y. Ct. App.):

> We still adhere to the rule that an accused is entitled to confrontation of the witnesses against him and the right to cross-examine them.... We destroy the

---

[10] Some courts have required deletion of references to codefendants where practicable. [Court cites student notes criticizing such deletions (known as "redaction") as ineffective.] In this case Evans' confessions were offered in evidence through the oral testimony of the postal inspector. It has been said: "Where the confession is offered in evidence by means of oral testimony, redaction is patently impractical. To expect a witness to relate *X*'s confession without including any of its references to *Y* is to ignore human frailty. Again, it is unlikely that an intentional or accidental slip by the witness could be remedied by instructions to disregard." Note, 3 Col. J. of Law & Soc. Prob. 80, 88 (1967)....

> age-old rule which in the past has been regarded as a fundamental principle of our jurisprudence by a legalistic formula, required of the judge, that the jury may not consider any admissions against any party who did not join in them. We secure greater speed, economy and convenience in the administration of the law at the price of fundamental principles of constitutional liberty. That price is too high.

Finally, the reason advanced by the majority in *Delli Paoli* was to tie the result to maintenance of the jury system. "Unless we proceed on the basis that the jury will follow the court's instructions where those instructions are clear and the circumstances are such that the jury can reasonably be expected to follow them, the jury system makes little sense." We agree that there are many circumstances in which this reliance is justified. Not every admission of inadmissible hearsay or other evidence can be considered to be reversible error unavoidable through limiting instructions; instances occur in almost every trial where inadmissible evidence creeps in, usually inadvertently. "A defendant is entitled to a fair trial but not a perfect one." It is not unreasonable to conclude that in many such cases the jury can and will follow the trial judge's instructions to disregard such information. Nevertheless, as was recognized in Jackson v. Denno, supra, there are some contexts in which the risk that the jury will not, or cannot, follow instructions is so great, and the consequences of failure so vital to the defendant, that the practical and human limitations of the jury system cannot be ignored. Such a context is presented here, where the powerfully incriminating extrajudicial statements of a codefendant, who stands accused side-by-side with the defendant, are deliberately spread before the jury in a joint trial. Not only are the incriminations devastating to the defendant but their credibility is inevitably suspect, a fact recognized when accomplices do take the stand and the jury is instructed to weigh their testimony carefully given the recognized motivation to shift blame onto others. The unreliability of such evidence is intolerably compounded when the alleged accomplice, as here, does not testify and cannot be tested by cross-examination. It was against such threats to a fair trial that the Confrontation Clause was directed....

Reversed.

[Justice Black concurred, and Justice Stewart filed a separate concurring opinion. Justice Marshall took no part.]

[Justice White dissented, arguing that a defendant's confession is "probably the most damaging evidence," which explains the rule excluding them absolutely if coerced. Such confessions are *not* excluded because they are unreliable, but to serve "other ends" that juries would not understand. Statements by co-offenders are different. The holding will "severely limit" joint trials of co-offenders, and burden prosecutors unfairly.]

■ PROBLEM 4-E. His Master's Car

Napton works for Ace Building Supplies, where his duties include making deliveries in a pickup truck. While working one day, Napton negligently runs over O'Brien. Napton has long been on thin ice with Ace, and a month later he loses his job for reasons unrelated to the accident. Six months later, Napton tells O'Brien that "the brakes on that truck just failed," and "I was speeding" at the time of the accident.

O'Brien sues both Napton and Ace for personal injuries.

At trial, O'Brien offers Napton's statement as proof that the brakes were bad and that Napton was speeding, invoking the admissions doctrine. Ace objects that it is hearsay. (Assume that, as to Ace, Napton's statement is inadmissible. Napton was not employed by Ace when he spoke, so his statement does *not* fit FRE 801(d)(2)(D).) How should the court rule, and why?

■ NOTES ON *BRUTON* AND ADMISSIONS IN MULTIPARTY SITUATIONS

1. In both *Bruton* and Problem 4-E (His Master's Car), a statement by one defendant fits FRE 801(d)(2)(A) when offered against the person who spoke, but not when offered against a coparty. *Bruton* is a criminal case that addresses the common "spillover confession" problem, treating it as raising a constitutional issue under the Confrontation Clause. This issue is absent from *His Master's Car* because the Confrontation Clause does not apply in civil cases.

2. In *His Master's Car*, Ace has a legitimate objection when O'Brien offers Napton's statement, even if the Constitution is not involved. Under FRE 105, Ace can ask the court to consider the statement "I was speeding" as proof only against Napton (and not Ace), but such an instruction is unlikely to do much good. Or Ace might ask the court to exclude the statement altogether as unfairly prejudicial under FRE 403, on the ground that the jury is likely to "misuse" the statement as proof against Ace regardless what instruction the court gives (recall that "jury misuse" is one of the definitions of "unfair prejudice"). This objection seems unlikely to succeed because the statement is so clearly relevant and admissible against Napton. With respect to the other statement ("the brakes on the truck just failed") Ace has a good shot at getting it excluded altogether. While this statement is (like the one about speeding) admissible against Napton, it isn't really relevant to the claim against him (assuming that Ace, and not Napton personally, was responsible to maintain the brakes). It's relevant to the claim against Ace, but not admissible against Ace, so exclusion is a real possibility.

3. Would *Bruton* have been decided the same way if Evans' statement to the postal inspector fit an exception *other than* the admissions doctrine? In footnote 3, the Court comments that there is no exception that would make Evans' statement admissible against Bruton. The note cites the coconspirator exception, which (as you will see in section B5) does not reach statements made after a conspiracy is over (the arrest of Evans ended the conspiracy for him). It seems, then, that if Evans had been talking to someone during and in furtherance of the conspiracy (bringing the coconspirator exception into play), admitting his statement against Bruton would be alright.

4. What Evans says is admissible against him under FRE 801(d)(1)(A) as his individual admission. Why should the "spillover" effect of Evans' admission naming Bruton cause harm to Bruton that a limiting instruction can't ward off? You might be surprised to learn, given *Bruton's* insistence that a limiting instruction isn't good enough, that violations of *Bruton* can be constitutionally harmless. See Harrington v. California, 395 U.S. 250 (1969) (where defendant's own confession placed him at the scene, error in admitting co-offender's confessions also placing him there was harmless beyond reasonable doubt); Schneble v. Florida, 405 U.S. 427 (1972) (confession by co-offender placing defendant at scene violated *Bruton*; error was harmless, despite lack of evidence "independent" of defendant's confession, which was perhaps coerced).

5. Where codefendants make "interlocking" confessions that tie together in a story, can one defendant raise a *Bruton* objection if he is named (or his activities are described) in a confession by another, offered in evidence against the latter? See Cruz v. New York, 481 U.S. 186 (1987) (Yes; a codefendant's confession is "enormously damaging if it confirms, in all essential respects, the defendant's alleged confession," though it might be different "if the defendant were *standing by* his confession") (5-4 decision).

6. Assume that defendant Carol's confession describes criminal acts committed by several people but makes no reference to defendant Dan. If the confession is admitted against Carol, does Dan have a *Bruton* objection? What if the confession describes criminal acts by Carol that bear on Dan's guilt as an accomplice? See Richardson v. Marsh, 481 U.S. 200 (1987) (admitting confession by *W* describing events culminating in robbery and murder, over codefendant *M*'s *Bruton* objection; *W*'s confession only incriminated *M* "when linked with evidence introduced later" in the form of *M*'s own testimony; when "such linkage" is necessary, "it is a less valid generalization that the jury will not likely obey the instruction to disregard the evidence").

COMMENT/PERSPECTIVE: Joint Trials and the *Bruton* Problem

Prosecutors prefer trying joint offenders in a single trial, for efficiency reasons and because the criminality of one tends to "rub off" on the other. If Al and Bob are charged with crimes, and Al makes a spillover confession to police implicating himself and Bob by name, *Bruton* poses a serious problem for a joint trial. In the trials of Oklahoma City bombers Timothy McVeigh and Terry Nichols, both had made confessions implicating the other, leading Judge Matsch to sever the trials. See U.S. v. McVeigh, 169 F.R.D. 362 (D. Colo. 1996). Other than doing without Al's statement, are there other ways to proceed with a joint trial?

(1) Al might take the witness stand, and then Bob can cross-examine. *Bruton* rests on the right of confrontation, and Bob's opportunity to cross-examine satisfies this concern. You will see that the Confrontation Clause is satisfied by the chance to cross-examine at trial ("deferred" cross). Unfortunately a prosecutor cannot know in advance whether Bob will testify, so counting on this possibility is a thin reed on which to base a decision to proceed against Al and Bob jointly.

(2) Another possibility is to assemble separate juries, one to deliberate in the case against Al, the other to deliberate in the case against Bob. When Al's statement is offered, the jury for Bob's case can be excused so it doesn't hear it. But courtrooms are not set up for multiple juries, and the mechanics of proceeding this way, and of insuring that the juries don't talk to one another, are daunting.

(3) Footnote 10 of *Bruton* mentions a third possibility, which is "redaction." Al's confession could be edited to exclude any reference to Bob. But if Al said "Bob and I did it," and a redacted version says "I did it," you can imagine what objections Al would raise. A redacted statement in which Al takes sole responsibility is more damaging (and not entirely true) than the actual statement laying part of the blame on Bob. And what do we tell a witness testifying to what Al said? Should we say, "Tell the whole truth, but when it comes to Al's statement, leave out what he said about Bob?" Can we do that?

7. The technique of redaction brings other problems. In the *Gray* case, Anthony Bell and Kevin Gray were tried for the beating death of Stacey Williams, and the prosecutor offered the following redacted transcription of Bell's statement to a detective:

Q: When Stacey was beaten on Wildwood Parkway, how was he beaten?
A: Hit, kicked.
Q: Who hit and kicked Stacey?
A: I hit Stacey, he was kicked but I don't know who kicked him.
Q: Who was in the group that beat Stacey?
A: Me, ________, ________, and a few other guys.
Q: Do you have the other guys' names?
A: ________, ________, and me, I don't remember who was out there.

In each of the two places where the two blanks appear, one reference was to Kevin Gray, and the other was to a third person who had died. Gray raised a *Bruton* objection, and ultimately prevailed. See Gray v. Maryland, 523 U.S. 185 (1998) (redactions that "simply replace a name with an obvious blank space or a word such as 'deleted' or a symbol or other similarly obvious indications of alteration" leave statements that "so closely resemble *Bruton*'s unredacted statements that, in our view, the law must require the same result"). *Gray* probably doesn't mean redaction is dead as a technique for complying with *Bruton*, but it underscores the suggestion in *Bruton* that redaction doesn't work well in the case of oral confessions, and probably others in which references to co-offenders are intertwined with references to the speaker himself.

2. Adoptive Admissions

The heart of an admission by Ed need not be the words he speaks or writes: It may be a statement spoken or written by Freda. If Ed, to paraphrase the Rule, "manifests his adoption or belief in the truth" of what Freda says, then Ed becomes the "declarant" and her statement becomes his own. See FRE 801(d)(2)(B) (using these terms).

This process of attribution is not mumbo jumbo, but common sense. If, for example, Freda told Ed "I think your breaks are squeaking," and he replied "Yes, I think you're right," Ed has agreed that his breaks are squeaking. A doctrine that would admit Ed's response if it were offered against him, but exclude Freda's statement that elicited the response, would make no sense. The meaning in Freda's statement to Ed is absorbed in Ed's response to her, so we can conclude that Ed conveyed the combined message of both statements, and he adopted Freda's assertion.

Of course the human response to a statement by another does not always indicate so clearly the position of the responder. Suppose Ed replied to Freda's statement about the breaks by saying "Well, what of it?" Or suppose he said "I've got an appointment to have the car checked tomorrow, and they'll look at everything, as they always do." Do these responses indicate adoption? Finally, suppose Ed said nothing. Can silence adopt another's statement? The answer is Yes, sometimes, and we speak of "tacit" adoption.

Here is another question: Who decides whether Ed adopted Freda's statement? In a bench trial, the judge decides (there is no other factfinder), but in a jury trial the question is whether the judge still decides this point, or does it go to the jury? Under FRE 104(a), the judge decides whether evidence is "admissible," but the jury decides whether "a fact exists" whenever "the relevance of [other] evidence depends" on such a fact. Consider now a case and a Problem. The case explores adoption by silence (tacit adoption), and the Problem explores an ambivalent reply and the role of judge and jury.

UNITED STATES v. HOOSIER

United States Court of Appeals for the Sixth Circuit
542 F.2d 687 (1976)

[Herman Hoosier was convicted of the armed robbery of a federally insured bank. Four witnesses identified him as the perpetrator.]

PER CURIAM.

Another witness, Robert E. Rogers, testified that he had been with the robbery defendant before and after the bank robbery, that before the bank robbery defendant told him that he was going to rob a bank, and that three weeks after the bank robbery, he saw defendant with money and wearing what he thought were diamond rings, and that in the presence of defendant, the defendant's girlfriend said concerning defendant's affluence at that point, "That ain't nothing, you should have seen the money we had in the hotel room," and that she spoke of "sacks of money." Although both defendant and his girlfriend disputed these facts in their testimony, obviously the resolution of that fact dispute was for the jury, and we must assume the jury resolved it in favor of the government by its verdict of "guilty."

Appellant's sole appellate argument to this court, however, is that the testimony elicited from the fifth witness concerning appellant's girlfriend's statement was inadmissible hearsay, and that it was reversible error for the District Judge to fail to grant the objection to its admission.

[Court quotes FRE 801(d)(2)(B) and accompanying ACN.]

Our analysis of our present problem is made in the context of the Advisory Committee Note which is an appropriately guarded one. First, we note that the statement was made in appellant's presence, with only his girlfriend and Rogers present. Since appellant had previously trusted Rogers sufficiently to tell him his plan to rob a bank, we see little likelihood that his silence in the face of these statements was due to "advice of counsel" or fear that anything he said might "be used against him." Under the total circumstances, we believe that probable human behavior would have been for appellant promptly to deny his girlfriend's statement if it had not been true—particularly when it was said to a person to whom he had previously related a plan to rob a bank. While we agree with appellant's counsel that more is needed to justify admission of this statement than the mere presence and silence of the appellant, we observe that there was more in this record.

Finding no reversible error, the judgment of conviction is affirmed.

■ PROBLEM 4-F. "Did You Rob That Bank?"

Ivers is charged with armed bank robbery. At his trial, the prosecutor offers testimony by his friend Jessup that several days after the crime Jessup heard the following exchange between Ivers and another friend named Kerwin:

Kerwin: Are you the one who stuck up First Seacoast Bank the other day?
Ivers: Will you please leave me alone?

In deciding whether to admit Kerwin's statement and Ivers' reply, what role should the trial judge perform? Should she decide for herself whether the reply accepts the suggestion implicit in the question, treating it as a matter of admissibility under FRE 104(a). Or should she admit the evidence if she thinks a reasonable jury could reach that conclusion, passing the question to the jury as a matter of conditional relevancy under FRE 104(b).

This time assume that Jessup would testify to the following exchange:

Kerwin: You're the one who robbed First Seacoast Bank, aren't you? It just so happens that I was in the bank when the fellow came in, and it was you, wasn't it?
Ivers: Will you please leave me alone?

Is there a difference between the first and the second versions of the Kerwin-Ivers conversation that suggests a different role for the judge?

■ NOTES ON TACIT ADMISSIONS AND AMBIVALENT RESPONSES

1. *Hoosier* seems rightly decided, but the mere fact that the girlfriend spoke in the defendant's presence is not enough to support an inference of adoption—as the court said, something "more" is needed. Her statement certainly implies (like Oblique's statement in Problem 3-A that "they ought to put Higgins in jail for this") that the two of them had lots of money in the hotel room ("sacks of money"). That implicates them both in a crime, a bit like Evans' statement in *Bruton* ("Bruton and I committed the robbery"). Implicit in the court's opinion approving use of the girlfriend's statement is the proposition that "one who is implicated by another in a crime would likely deny it if he is innocent, and so failing to deny admits guilt." Courts often accept this view. The court in *Hoosier* comments that defendant had already confided in Rogers about the bank robbery plan, suggesting that this element of trust is a reason to conclude that Herman Hoosier's silence adopted the girlfriend's suggestion. Do you agree? For another case admitting against a defendant a conversation in which he participated, see United States v. Robinson, 275 F.3d 371, 383-384 (4th Cir. 2001) (in trial for carjacking trial with a fatal shooting, admitting *L*'s testimony about conversation between defendants *R* and *O* even though *L* could not say who made any given statement; he could discern separate voices and knew *R* and *O* were describing the crime; situation was such that, if one disagreed with the other, he would have said so), *cert. denied*, 535 U.S. 1006 (2002).

2. If one receives in the mail an unsolicited offer that says failure to reply will be deemed acceptance of the terms set forth, can nonreply bind the recipient? The answer is No, because one party cannot impose on another a duty to respond, and this answer is rooted at least as much in the law of contract as in the law of evidence. Of course the situation changes if two parties are in a long-standing contractual arrangement in which one provides goods or services to another and regularly submits bills that the other regularly pays. Such a course of dealing can give rise to a duty in the recipient of such bills to protest if one of them is in error. Bank depositors are familiar with the legend found in monthly statements indicating that the depositor has 30 days to point out any error—one who lets such things go for longer than that cannot later come to the bank and protest a check, and being silent for 30 days indicates agreement with the statement.

3. Assume that a party makes some use of a statement by a third person, as happens, for example, when someone covered by insurance submits a physician's statement in support of a claim. Does such use mean that one "adopts" the third-person statement for purposes of the admissions doctrine? Compare Insurance Co. v. Newton, 89 U.S. (22 Wall.) 32, 35 (1874) (beneficiary "presented to the company" findings by coroner's jury that the insured committed suicide, so findings were "admissible as representations on the part of the party for whose benefit the policies were taken") with New York Life Insurance Co. v. Taylor, 147 F.2d 297, 299 (D.C. Cir. 1944) (excluding physician's statement listing suicide as cause of death, where it had been made on a form submitted directly by carrier to physician, and beneficiary had not seen it; proofs of death are competent only where authorized by beneficiary).

4. What if the government submits an affidavit by a police officer in support of a warrant application? See United States v. Warren, 42 F.3d 647, 655 (D.C. Cir. 1994) (affidavit submitted to federal magistrate constitutes admission by government). As you will see in section B4, however, there is a real question whether statements by government agents can "bind the sovereign." On the theory that they cannot, courts sometimes refuse to apply the admissions doctrine against the government.

5. In Problem 4-F, Ivers' response ("Will you please leave me alone?") is a blunt evasion, a refusal to deal with the subject. In the first version, Kerwin asks a plain question (in substance, "Are you the one?"). In the second, Kerwin still puts a question, but embedded in it is an implied claim that Ivers is the robber (in substance, "You're the one, I was there and it was you, wasn't it?"). Whether Ivers' brushoff can possibly be construed as his admission is itself hard to decide. But one would expect more than a brushoff when confronted with a charge of criminality, and it is plausible to argue that if silence in the face of the girlfriend's statement admitted Hoosier's involvement in a bank robbery (acquisition of "bags of money"), then Ivers' brushoff has the same effect. Why didn't Ivers say "Not me," or "Why would you say that, I had nothing to do with it"?

6. In jury-tried cases, the question whether the judge or the jury should decide questions of adoption has split courts. Most conclude that it is a question for the jury. For an example of the majority trend, see U.S. v. Tocco, 135 F.2d 116, 128-129 (2d Cir. 1998) (jury decides question of adoption). For an example of the minority view, see U.S. v. Harrison, 296 F.3d 994, 1001 (10th Cir. 2002) (whether defendant adopted statement was preliminary fact question to be decided by court). On the facts of Problem 4-F, it seems that there is more danger of jury misuse in the second instance (in substance, "You're the one, I was there and it was you, wasn't it?") than the first. The reason is that the second statement actually claims that Ivers robbed the bank, so it is some evidence that he did it even if one doesn't think Ivers agreed with the suggestion. Hence there is a good reason, at least in the second instance, to give the question of adoption to the judge. See generally Mueller and Kirkpatrick, Evidence §8.29 (5th ed. 2012) (where outsider's statement "implies or openly asserts something harmful to the party against whom it is offered" and implies that the outsider "knew something," then "it is unrealistic to involve the jury" in deciding adoption).

7. Consider this description of the elements and limits of the tacit admissions doctrine:

> At a minimum, it should be made to appear that (a) the party heard the statement, (b) the matter asserted was within his knowledge, and, perhaps most importantly, (c) the occasion and nature of the statement were such that he would likely have replied if he did not mean to accept what was said. Even if these conditions be satisfied, the statement should be excluded if it appears that (d) the party did not understand the statement or its significance, (e) some physical or psychological factor explains the lack of reply, (f) the speaker was someone whom the party would likely ignore, or (g) the silence came in response to questioning or comments by a law enforcement officer (or perhaps another) during custodial interrogation after *Miranda* warnings have been (or should have been) given . . . .

C. Mueller & L. Kirkpatrick, Evidence §8.29 (5th ed. 2012). Given that admissions do not require personal knowledge, should knowledge matter for tacit admissions? The description implies that items (a)-(c) should be proved by the proponent, but that (d)-(g) must be shown by the objecting party. Does this allocation of burdens make sense?

DOYLE v. OHIO

United States Supreme Court
426 U.S. 610 (1976)

Mr. Justice POWELL delivered the opinion of the Court.

[In separate state trials in Ohio, Jefferson Doyle and Richard Wood were convicted of selling ten pounds of marijuana to William Bonnell, a well-known street person acting as a local narcotics informant.

Evidence indicated that Bonnell told law enforcement agents he had arranged a "buy" of marijuana and needed $1,750. Agents gathered $1,320 in cash and gave it to Bonnell, who left for the rendezvous under surveillance. Bonnell met Doyle and Wood in a bar and took Wood in his truck to a nearby town while Doyle drove off for the marijuana. Arriving in his own car, Doyle met the other two as agreed, and a transaction occurred in a parking lot as agents watched. Doyle and Wood discovered they had been shortchanged by $430. They circled the neighborhood looking for Bonnell. Police stopped them, and agent Kenneth Beamer arrested them, delivering *Miranda* warnings. A search of Doyle's car turned up the $1,320 in cash.

In both trials, the defense tried to show the agents did not see what happened. They saw Bonnell standing next to Doyle's car with a package, and one agent said he saw the package passed through the window to Bonnell, but the agent had not mentioned this point in the preliminary hearing, and the defense argued that he changed his story. According to the defense, Bonnell framed Doyle and Wood since the arrangement had been *for him to sell them* marijuana. Doyle had gone off to get the money, the defense argued, but had decided to buy only one or two pounds instead of ten. When Bonnell reached Doyle's car, he was already carrying the marijuana, and Doyle tried to explain his change of mind. Bonnell got mad, threw the cash into Doyle's car, and took the marijuana back to his truck. Wood and Doyle then looked for Bonnell to find out what the money was for.

Wood testified at his own trial. On cross, the prosecutor asked whether Wood had told his story to agent Beamer:

Q. [*By the prosecutor.*] Mr. Beamer did arrive on the scene?
A. [By Wood.] Yes, he did.
Q. And I assume you told him all about what happened to you? . . .
A. No.
Q. You didn't tell Mr. Beamer? . . .
A. No.
Q. You didn't tell Mr. Beamer this guy put $1,300 in your car? . . .
A. No, sir.
Q. And we can't understand any reason why anyone would put money in your car and you were chasing him around town and trying to give it back? . . .
A. I didn't understand that.
Q. You mean you didn't tell him that? . . .
A. Tell him what? . . .
Q. Mr. Wood, if that is all you had to do with this and you are innocent, when Mr. Beamer arrived on the scene why didn't you tell him? . . .
Q. But in any event you didn't bother to tell Mr. Beamer anything about this?
A. No, sir.

Reviewing courts in Ohio affirmed the conviction. Concluding that use of post-*Miranda*-warning silence violates due process, the Supreme Court reverses.]

The State pleads necessity as justification for the prosecutor's action in these cases. It argues that the discrepancy between an exculpatory story at trial and silence at time of arrest gives rise to an inference that the story was fabricated somewhere along the way, perhaps to fit within the seams of the State's case as it was developed at pretrial hearings. Noting that the prosecution usually has little else with which to counter such an exculpatory story, the State seeks only the right to cross-examine a defendant as to post-arrest silence for the limited purpose of impeachment. In support of its position the State emphasizes the importance of cross-examination in general, and relies upon those cases in which this Court has permitted use for impeachment purposes of post-arrest statements that were inadmissible as evidence of guilt because of an officer's failure to follow *Miranda*'s dictates. Thus, although the State does not suggest petitioners' silence could be used as evidence of guilt, it contends that the need to present to the jury all information relevant to the truth of petitioners' exculpatory story fully justifies the cross-examination that is at issue.

Despite the importance of cross-examination, we have concluded that the *Miranda* decision compels rejection of the State's position. The warnings mandated by that case, as a prophylactic means of safeguarding Fifth Amendment rights, require that a person taken into custody be advised immediately that he has the right to remain silent, that anything he says may be used against him, and that he has a right to retained or appointed counsel before submitting to interrogation. Silence in the wake of these warnings may be nothing more than the arrestee's exercise of these *Miranda* rights. Thus, every post-arrest silence is insolubly ambiguous because of what the State is required to advise the person arrested. Moreover, while it is true that the *Miranda* warnings contain no express assurance that silence will carry no penalty, such assurance is implicit to any person who receives the warnings. In such circumstances, it would be fundamentally unfair and a deprivation of due process to allow the arrested person's silence to be used to impeach an explanation subsequently offered at trial....

We hold that the use for impeachment purposes of petitioners' silence, at the time of arrest and after receiving *Miranda* warnings, violated the Due Process Clause of the Fourteenth Amendment.[11] The State has not claimed that such use in the circumstances of this case might have been harmless error. Accordingly, petitioners' convictions are reversed and their causes remanded to the state courts for further proceedings not inconsistent with this opinion.

So ordered.

Mr. Justice STEVENS, with whom Mr. Justice BLACKMUN and Mr. Justice REHNQUIST join, dissenting.

---

[11] It goes almost without saying that the fact of post-arrest silence could be used by the prosecution to contradict a defendant who testifies to an exculpatory version of events and claims to have told the police the same version upon arrest. In that situation the fact of earlier silence would not be used to impeach the exculpatory story, but rather to challenge the defendant's testimony as to his behavior following arrest.

[The due process rationale has "characteristics of an estoppel theory," and the key point is that the *Miranda* warning is "deceptive unless we require the State to honor an unstated promise not to use the accused's silence against him." But "there is nothing deceptive or prejudicial" in the warning, nor does it lessen the probative value of silence or make it unfair to cross-examine about silence. Here silence was "graphically inconsistent" with testimony claiming that defendants were framed. If that were so, their failure to say anything when they were arrested is "almost inexplicable." Indeed, the *Miranda* warning provides "the only plausible explanation" for their silence. If the warning really were the reason they were silent, they would have said so on cross. Instead they gave "quite a different jumble of responses." Since defendants did not rely on *Miranda* warning in failing to raise the point about being framed, the due process rationale "collapses."

Nor does use of silence violate the Fifth Amendment in *Miranda*, which says the state may not "use at trial the fact that the defendant stood mute or claimed the privilege in the face of accusations." Doyle did not remain silent, and neither he nor Wood claimed the privilege. And the *Miranda* statement is dictum that relies on Griffin v. California, 380 U.S. 609 (1965), which held that the Fifth Amendment prohibits the prosecutor from commenting on defendant's failure to testify. But Raffel v. United States, 271 U.S. 494 (1926), lets the prosecutor use defendant's silence at a prior trial and recognizes a distinction between "affirmative use" of silence and use of silence for "impeachment purposes." Under *Raffel*, a state is "free to regard the defendant's decision to take the stand as a waiver of his objection to the use of his failure to testify at an earlier proceeding or his failure to offer his version of events prior to trial."]

In my judgment portions of the prosecutor's argument to the jury overstepped permissible bounds. In each trial, he commented upon the defendant's silence not only as inconsistent with his testimony that he had been "framed," but also as inconsistent with the defendant's innocence. Comment on the lack of credibility of the defendant is plainly proper; it is not proper, however, for the prosecutor to ask the jury to draw a direct inference of guilt from silence—to argue, in effect, that silence is inconsistent with innocence. But since the two inferences—perjury and guilt—are inextricably intertwined because they have a common source, it would be unrealistic to permit comment on the former but to find reversible error in the slightest reference to the latter. In the context of the entire argument and the entire trial, I am not persuaded that the rather sophisticated distinction between permissible comment on credibility and impermissible comment on an inference of guilt justifies a reversal of these state convictions.

Accordingly, although I have some doubt concerning the propriety of the cross-examination about the preliminary hearing and consider a portion of the closing argument improper, I would affirm these convictions.

■ NOTES ON SILENCE AS ADMISSION

1. *Doyle* condemns the use of postarrest postwarning silence by the accused where he testifies to an innocent version of events. The prosecutor's argument is that silence impeaches his explanation. Suppose that defendant did not testify, but offered testimony by another witness—one close enough to hear what was said and see who passed what to whom—and this witness said Doyle tried to buy, not sell. The prosecutor might then elicit testimony by Agent Beamer that Doyle offered no such explanation after being *Mirandized,* hence that Doyle must have been the seller (and his witness is mistaken). Wouldn't a Court that condemns the use of custodial post-*Miranda* silence to impeach Doyle's testimony *also* condemn use of such silence as substantive evidence (proof of guilt) if Doyle had not testified? Even Justice Stevens was disturbed at use of defendant's silence as substantive evidence. See also James v. Illinois, 493 U.S. 307 (1990) (expanding impeachment exception to admit *Miranda*-barred statements to contradict testimony by others would "chill some defendants from presenting their best defense").

2. The court later held that *Doyle* does not apply to prearrest silence. See Jenkins v. Anderson, 447 U.S. 231 (1980). *Jenkins* emphasizes that it is the *Miranda* warning that makes it constitutionally unfair to use the silence of the accused against him. Why is it unfair? If the answer is that the warning advises the accused that what he says may be used against him, not what he doesn't say, could the problem be cured by amending the warning to say that what the accused does and what he does not say may *both* be used against him? Would that deny human dignity by subjecting defendant to the kind of cruel choice that the Fifth Amendment seeks to prevent? See Murphy v. Waterfront Commission, 378 U.S. 52, 55 (1964) (Fifth Amendment expresses "our unwillingness to subject those suspected of crime to the cruel trilemma of self-accusation, perjury or contempt"). Would a change in the warning be practical? Consider Kamisar, Police Interrogation and Confessions: Essays in Law and Policy 92 n.12 (1980): "Can a police officer be trusted to explain to a suspect how he can have 'a right to remain silent' and still have his silence used against him at trial? And even if an officer does his very best to explain, can the average person be expected to understand?"

3. If it is cruel to arrest a defendant and put him in a situation in which both what he says and what he does not say will later be usable against him, is it less cruel to arrest and hold a defendant, refrain from giving *Miranda* warnings, and then use his silence against him? See Fletcher v. Weir, 455 U.S. 603 (1982) (per curiam) (upholding use of postarrest silence where police neither question defendant nor deliver warnings). But in Griffin v. California, 380 U.S. 609 (1965), the Court said that commenting on the failure of the accused to take the stand violated the Fifth Amendment. Can these holdings be squared?

4. What if defendants testify at trial that they *did* tell arresting officers that Bonnell framed them by throwing the money at them, to make them look like sellers? Look at the Court's comment in footnote 11 about a point that "goes without saying."

5. Reconsider Hoosier and his girlfriend. Suppose both are arrested and charged with robbery, and in the squadcar she yells, "You idiot, I told you we'd never get away with it!" He doesn't reply. Should her exclamation and his apparent acquiescence be provable against him? See United States v. Harrison, 296 F.3d 994, 1001 (10th Cir. 2002) (admitting statements by child victim to FBI agent in presence of defendant, to which he replied that he was sorry and it wouldn't happen again; trial court found that defendant's response "admitted the truth"), *cert. denied*, 537 U.S. 1134 (2003).

(a) Consider the matter of *Miranda* warnings. Should it make a difference whether they were given? Whether Hoosier invoked his right to be silent or asked for a lawyer? See Illinois v. Perkins, 496 U.S. 292 (1990) (jail cell questioning by undercover agent produced incriminating answers; no warnings required because *Miranda* forbids coercion rather than "strategic deception," and coercion comes from "interaction of custody and official interrogation"); Arizona v. Mauro, 481 U.S. 520 (1987) (after being *Mirandized*, defendant declined to talk and demanded counsel; officer stayed in room and openly recorded conversation between him and his wife; his responses to her incriminated him; no *Miranda* violation because no interrogation).

(b) Whatever *Doyle* means when arresting officers pose questions, *Perkins* and *Mauro* don't leave much for Hoosier in the way of a constitutional argument on our assumed facts, do they? If arresting officers give *Miranda* warnings, could Hoosier argue that the very fact of warning precludes later construing silence in the face of nonofficial comments as an admission? Can he distinguish his case from *Mauro* by arguing that in *Mauro* defendant chose to speak, while in his own case Hoosier had no choice (his girlfriend did the talking)?

3. Admissions by Speaking Agents

Agency law defines conditions under which one person may act for another—a lawyer negotiating a contract for his client, a broker selling property by transmitting offer, counteroffer, and acceptance between buyer and seller, a corporate officer signing agreements for the company. In its own version of these principles, the admissions doctrine defines conditions in which a statement by one person is viewed as an admission by another.

When a person authorizes an agent actually to speak for him, as in arrangements between seller and broker, it seems obvious that what the one says may be offered in evidence against the other. Technically (although the point is often overlooked), what such a "speaking agent" says is not even hearsay in the common situation in which his words commit the principal and are offered to prove the commitment. The words are verbal acts, often making or accepting offers or negotiating deals or contracts. Principles of agency and notions of relevance indicate when and to what extent such words should be admissible. But sometimes words of a speaking agent are offered for a hearsay purpose, to prove that something they describe actually exists or happened.

If, for example, a seller's broker tells the buyer of Greenacre there is a tractor in the barn that is included in the price, those words are nonhearsay verbal acts if offered against the seller to show the deal includes the tractor (so the seller may have committed fraud if there was no tractor, or breached the agreement if he removed it after the deal was struck). Substantive law and principles of relevancy would lead a court to admit those words even if there were no special hearsay exception. But the same words *would be* hearsay if offered against the seller to prove there actually was a tractor in the barn, for now they are used as proof of the physical reality that they depict.

Regardless whether the broker's words be used to prove the terms of the deal or the presence of the tractor in the barn, a court would likely cite FRE 801(d)(2)(C) in concluding that they are admissible against the seller (though only in the latter instance do we actually need a special provision to admit them). Why does the hearsay doctrine make the words admissible to prove the presence of the tractor? Again, it is the philosophy of the adversary system at work. When one hires another to speak for him, it is fair to allow the words of the latter to establish facts at trial against the former.

■ PROBLEM 4-G. Couldn't He See the Boy?

Eleven-year-old Albert Garment gets out of a school bus in front of the farm where he lives with his parents. He must cross to the other side of the highway to get home, so he walks around the front of the bus. In the meantime busdriver Martin Grider checks the traffic and, unaware that Albert is crossing in front, pulls forward. As the bus enters the traffic lane it runs over and kills Albert.

The parents of Albert Garment bring a wrongful death action against Martin Grider on a negligence theory. Shortly before the statute of limitations was to run, the Garments file an amended complaint that includes a second count stating a claim in strict liability against Standard Bus Sales. The new count alleges that Standard sold the bus to the School District and that the mirrors "were so positioned that a complete view of the area within the path of the bus was not discernible by a person in the driver's seat."

But the Garments have named the wrong seller, and before trial Standard wins summary judgment on the ground that it did not sell the bus.

The case goes to trial against Martin Grider alone. Invoking FRE 801(d)(2)(C), Grider's lawyer seeks and obtains permission to read to the jury the allegations about the mirrors appearing in the now-dismissed second count. (Counsel for the Garments is also permitted to read Standard's denials of those allegations.) The jury returns a verdict for busdriver Martin Grider, and the Garments appeal, arguing that the trial court should not have permitted the superseded pleading to be read into evidence. Do they have a good argument? In defending the action of the trial judge, shouldn't Grider argue on appeal that the Garments' pleading entitled him to a directed verdict?

■ NOTES ON ADMISSIONS IN JUDICIAL PROCEEDINGS

1. Pleadings from prior lawsuits, and pleadings superseded by amendment in the pending suit, are generally admissible against the party who filed them. So are answers to interrogatories, whether filed in a prior suit or the pending action. Not so with an "admission" filed in response to requests to admit. Under FRCP 36(a), a matter admitted in this way is "conclusively established" in the pending suit, but FRCP 36(a) and (b) provide that such an admission is "for purposes of the pending action only," and is not an admission "for any other purpose and cannot be used against the party in any other proceeding." Why the difference?

2. Assume that Grider has a defense to the negligence claim if the mirrors did not let him see in front of the bus. If Albert Garment's father or mother (plaintiffs) had taken the stand and testified that they noticed that the mirrors did not permit such a view, they would not automatically lose their claim against Grider. Garment's lawyer might have a hard time "getting out from under" this statement, but Garment wouldn't likely have full or persuasive knowledge about this matter, and the lawyer might have other evidence supporting the view that the mirror did not have this effect. The point is that a statement by a party, even testimony by the party in court, is not "judicially binding," and a court or jury as factfinder in the case could still find in favor of the party who has made such a statement or testified in this vein.

3. What if the Garments offered testimony by an expert who had examined the bus, to the effect that the mirrors did not permit the necessary view of the front of the bus? Compare Fox v. Taylor Diving & Salvage Co., 694 F.2d 1349, 1354-1358 (5th Cir. 1983) ("central and explicit theme" of expert testimony presented by injured plaintiff stressed that he was "an onshore supervisory employee," and plaintiff did not question this assumption; facts justify inference of "silent adoption," and dismissal of claim dependent on seaman status) with Kirk v. Raymark Industries, Inc., 61 F.3d 147, 163-164 (3d Cir. 1995) (experts are "supposed to testify impartially," and normally do not agree to be within party's control, which precludes invoking FRE 801(d)(2)(C) as basis for admitting against a party in a later trial testimony" by expert in prior trial).

4. Admissions by Employees and Agents

A company hiring a truck driver intends that he will operate the truck, not speak for the company. In this situation notions of relevancy and substantive principles of agency would not pave the way to admit against the company what the truck driver says, and for years the common law of evidence excluded such statements. But where such an employee injures another in the course of his duties, it came to be seen as unfair that an employer legally liable for the tort might remain evidentially immune from the statements of the tortfeasor. See Martin v. Savage Truck Line, 121 F. Supp. 417, 419 (D.D.C. 1954) (railing against "legally untenable fiction" that lets truck owner hire another to drive, but not to describe accident to police; it is as if driver could make an admission usable against the company only if he were an officer or director, but "trucks are not operated that way") (excluding driver's statements denies agency that "inherently exists").

Rule 801(d)(2)(D) addresses the situation of the truck driver and similar employees, resolving the issue in favor of admissibility against the principal or employer. In the language of this provision, it paves the way to admit, against an employer or a principal, a statement by an "agent or employee" when he speaks "on a matter within the scope of that relationship while it existed."

Form of statement. Often a statement offered under the present exception is an oral utterance, described in court by someone who heard the speaker. Sometimes the statement is in writing—an ordinary document, as you will see in the *Mahlandt* case. In our electronic age, Rule 801(d)(2)(D) embraces emails and the like too. See, e.g., Zerega Ave. Realty Corp. v. Hornbeck Offshore Transportation, 571 F.3d 206, 214 (2d Cir. 2009) (email from one company employee to another was admissible under FRE 801(d)(2)(D); author was "agent of a party acting within the scope of his employment"); Sea-Land Service, Inc. v. Lozen International, L.L.C., 285 F.3d 808, 820-821 (9th Cir. 2002) ("internal company email" authored by one employee of plaintiff and forwarded to defendant by another was admissible against plaintiff company).

Agent or employee. Often there is no doubt that the speaker is an agent or employee, and the exception covers the truck driver who delivers goods (jobber delivering to a market the food that it sells) or provides services (cable company technicians going out to repair lines). But sometimes questions arise, and neither the Rule nor the ACN defines those terms, leaving the matter to courts to resolve by applying agency principles. See City of Tuscaloosa v. Harcros Chemicals, Inc., 158 F.3d 548, 551-552 (11th Cir. 1998) (exception does not define "agent," leaving the matter to be resolved by "general common law principles of agency"), *cert. denied*, 528 U.S. 812 (1999). It seems that the intent of FRE 801(d)(2)(D) was to reach two kinds of persons:

> (1) The person whose conduct produces liability for the employer or principal. Sometimes we're applying respondeat superior, where the conduct in suit

is a personal tort for which the company is liable (as happens when driver of a company truck negligently collides with another). Sometimes we're simply looking at an actor whose conduct contributes to organizational liability (as happens when a design engineer is responsible for some feature of a product that makes it dangerous).

(2) The person who is a passive observer or bystander rather than an actor, but who makes statements on matters within the scope of his duties (think of the railroad engineer who comments on the condition of the track as he passes over it). People of this description are not always authorized spokespeople. The reason to admit their statements is less compelling than the reasons to admit statements by liability-producing actors.

See generally Mueller & Kirkpatrick, Evidence §8.32 (5th ed. 2012).

One might ask whether independent contractors are agents or employees under FRE 801(d)(2)(D), and usually the answer is No. Independent contractors differ from agents or employees because the principal (who retains their services) exercises less control over what they do. See Powers v. Coccia, 861 A.2d 466, 470 (R.I. 2004) (in tenant's suit against landlord, statement by "rooter" hired to remove blockage in pipes was inadmissible; rooter was independent contractor, not agent of landlord); Murrey v. United States, 73 F.3d 1448, 1456 (7th Cir. 1996) (in suit against government alleging malpractice in government hospital, doctors retained as independent auditors were not agents or employees; their statements were not admissions by the hospital).

Even if independent contractors are not covered by FRE 801(d)(2)(D), however, sometimes actions by the one who retains their services constitutes adoption, making their statements admissible against their principal. In the *Murrey* case mentioned above, the court held that action by the Veterans Administration adopted recommendations by auditors, so their statements were admissible against the government. This principle can sidestep agency questions in other contexts. See Pekelis v. Transcontinental & Western Air, 187 F.2d 122, 128 (2d Cir.) (after crash, airline set up committee to investigate and recommend changes, which were implemented; recommendations were airline's admissions in suit by survivor), *cert. denied*, 341 U.S. 951 (1951).

Within the scope. Rule 801(d)(2)(D) applies only to statements by agents or employees that are "within the scope" of their duties. This phrase does *not* mean the exception reaches only statements made while the speaker is at work, nor does it require that the speaker have decisionmaking authority on the matters of which he speaks. See, e.g., Aliotta v. National R.R. Passenger Corp., 315 F.3d 756, 761-763 (7th Cir. 2003) (declarant served in investigative capacity and "held no decisionmaking authority," but all that is required is that "the subject matter of the admission match the subject matter of the employee's job description," and declarant's job is "to investigate accidents"); Moore v. KUKA Welding Systems & Robot Corp., 171 F.3d 1073, 1081 (6th Cir. 1999) (admitting statements by *TM* recited by *DM* "at a social occasion," since *TM* told *DM* to pass his statement along).

Still, a statement does not relate to the scope of one's duties merely because it describes working conditions. See, e.g., Williams v. Pharmacia, Inc., 137 F.3d 944, 949-950 (7th Cir. 1998) (statements by employees claiming they were being discriminated against did not fit FRE 801(d)(2)(D) when offered against company). Statements by a railroad engineer describing the condition of the track probably fit because the engineer has responsibility to attend to safety issues, and to report problems with tracks.

Some statements, even though describing matters within the scope of one's duties, may be excludable for other reasons. In the *Aliotta* case (mentioned above), the court was willing to admit against a railroad statements by a "risk manager" about the causes of an accident, but not to admit his statement theorizing that a vacuum created by a passing train pulled a bystander into its path. The reason was that the risk manager did not qualify as an expert, and such a conclusion is admissible only if it is valid science under the *Daubert* standard. (You will study the *Daubert* standard in Chapter 9, infra.)

Multiple or "layered" hearsay. As you will discover when you reach the business records exception, statements by someone who counts as an agent or employee under FRE 801(d)(2)(D) often rest on or pass along what *others* in the workplace have said. Suppose, for example, that Bob tells Arlo that Catherine as vice president for production "wants to reduce the production staff by ten people," and that all three work for the Digby Company. If, in a suit against Digby, Arlo testifies to what Bob said for the purpose of proving that Digby was reducing the production staff, this testimony involves multiple or layered hearsay. Bob's statement tends to prove what Catherine said, and her statement tends to prove Digby's intention or actions. Under FRE 805, multiple or layered hearsay is admissible if each statement fits an exception, and in this case it is entirely possible that FRE 801(d)(2)(D) would reach both what Catherine said to Bob and what Bob said to Arlo, so Arlo could testify and a hearsay objection would not succeed.

Personal knowledge. Perhaps equally important in the setting of admissions, there is no personal knowledge requirement. Recall Problem 4-C (Fire in the Warehouse), where Carter's statements were admissible against him under FRE 801(d)(2)(A) even though Carter lacked personal knowledge. When you read the *Mahlandt* case (coming next), you will see how this principle plays out in the setting of FRE 801(d)(2)(D).

Government admissions. Arguably FRE 801(d)(2)(D) reaches statements by agents and employees of the government. But the situations may not be the same, and logic runs up against the counterforce of tradition here. Traditionally statements by public employees have not been admissible against the government, on the grounds that (1) such people do not have the same sort of personal stake in the outcome of any dispute as private employees have, and (2) agents cannot bind the sovereign. See United States v. Yildiz, 355 F.3d 80, 81-82 (2d Cir. 2004) (excluding statement by informant, offered against government); United States v. Kampiles, 609 F.2d 1233, 1246 (7th Cir. 1979) (statements by

CIA agent would not be admissible against government in espionage prosecution), *cert. denied*, 446 U.S. 954 (1980).

Are there better reasons to be cautious in admitting against the government statements by its agents? Consider these points: The government must deal with citizens evenhandedly. It should not accord preferential treatment and should administer policies and benefits uniformly. This interest is threatened if statements by its agents are freely admissible. Government bureaucracy is massive, and the pertinent point is not so much the scope of an agent's employment but the authority of the agent to make policies and decisions. Do such concerns suggest that we should distinguish among statements by police officers in affidavits seeking warrants, statements by drivers of government vehicles involved in accidents, and statements by agency staffers in the IRS or EPA?

Consider context. Liability on the part of government differs from liability on the part of private entities. For example, one can sue a city under 42 USC §1983 for damages from civil rights violations, but defendant is liable only for acts by agents done pursuant to policy, law, or regulation, not on broader principles of respondeat superior. See Monell v. Department of Social Services, 436 U.S. 658 (1978). If right to recover is restricted this way, should statements by agents be admitted only if have authority to speak?

There are no easy answers. Some modern decisions question the traditional result and point toward a wider rule of admissibility. See United States v. Kattar, 840 F.2d 118, 130-131 (1st Cir. 1988) (in criminal case, government is defendant's party-opponent; it does not follow that "the entire federal government in all its capacities" fits this category, but Justice Department does; on behalf of defendant, court should have admitted sentencing memorandum and brief filed in other cases); United States v. Morgan, 481 F.2d 933, 938 (D.C. Cir. 1978) (nothing in Rules indicates intent to put government beyond reach of agent's admission doctrine).

MAHLANDT v. WILD CANID SURVIVAL & RESEARCH CENTER

United States Court of Appeals for the Eighth Circuit
588 F.2d 626 (1978)

VAN SICKLE, J.

This is a civil action for damages arising out of an alleged attack by a wolf on a child. The sole issues on appeal are as to the correctness of three rulings which excluded conclusionary statements against interest. Two of them were made by a defendant, who was also an employee of the corporate defendant; and the third was in the form of a statement appearing in the records of a board meeting of the corporate defendant.

On March 23, 1973, Daniel Mahlandt, then 3 years, 10 months, and 8 days old, was sent by his mother to a neighbor's home on an adjoining street to get his older brother, Donald. Daniel's mother watched him cross the street, and then turned into the house to get her car keys. Daniel's path took him along a walkway adjacent to the Poos' residence. Next to the walkway was a five foot chain link fence to which Sophie had been chained with a six foot chain. In other words, Sophie was free to move in a half circle having a six foot radius on the side of the fence opposite from Daniel.

Sophie was a bitch wolf, 11 months and 28 days old, who had been born at the St. Louis Zoo, and kept there until she reached 6 months of age, at which time she was given to the Wild Canid Survival and Research Center, Inc. It was the policy of the Zoo to remove wolves from the Children's Zoo after they reached the age of 5 or 6 months. Sophie was supposed to be kept at the Tyson Research Center, but Kenneth Poos, as Director of Education for the Wild Canid Survival and Research Center, Inc., had been keeping her at his home because he was taking Sophie to schools and institutions where he showed films and gave programs with respect to the nature of wolves. Sophie was known as a very gentle wolf who had proved herself to be good natured and stable during her contacts with thousands of children, while she was in the St. Louis Children's Zoo.

Sophie was chained because the evening before she had jumped the fence and attacked a beagle who was running along the fence and yapping at her.

A neighbor who was ill in bed in the second floor of his home heard a child's screams and went to his window, where he saw a boy lying on his back within the enclosure, with a wolf straddling him. The wolf's face was near Daniel's face, but the distance was so great that he could not see what the wolf was doing, and did not see any biting. Within about 15 seconds the neighbor saw Clarke Poos, about seventeen, run around the house, get the wolf off of the boy, and disappear with the child in his arms to the back of the house. Clarke took the boy in and laid him on the kitchen floor.

Clarke had been returning from his friend's home immediately west when he heard a child's cries and ran around to the enclosure. He found Daniel lying within the enclosure, about three feet from the fence, and Sophie standing back from the boy the length of her chain, and wailing. An expert in the behavior of wolves stated that when a wolf licks a child's face that it is a sign of care, and not a sign of attack; that a wolf's wail is a sign of compassion, and an effort to get attention, not a sign of attack. No witness saw or knew how Daniel was injured. Clarke and his sister ran over to get Daniel's mother. She says that Clarke told her, "a wolf got Danny and he is dying." Clarke denies that statement. The defendant, Mr. Poos, arrived home while Daniel and his mother were in the kitchen. After Daniel was taken in an ambulance, Mr. Poos talked to everyone present, including a neighbor who came in. Within an hour after he arrived home, Mr. Poos went to Washington University to inform Owen Sexton, President of Wild Canid Survival and Research Center, Inc., of the incident. Mr. Sexton was not in his office so Mr. Poos left the following note on his door:

> Owen, would [you] call me at home, 727-5080? Sophie bit a child that came in our back yard. All has been taken care of. I need to convey what happened to you.

Denial of admission of this note is one of the issues on appeal.

Later that day, Mr. Poos found Mr. Sexton at the Tyson Research Center and told him what had happened. Denial of plaintiff's offer to prove that Mr. Poos told Mr. Sexton that, "Sophie had bit a child that day," is the second issue on appeal.

A meeting of the Directors of the Wild Canid Survival and Research Center, Inc., was held on April 4, 1973. Mr. Poos was not present at that meeting. The minutes of that meeting reflect that there was a "great deal of discussion . . . about the legal aspects of the incident of Sophie biting the child." Plaintiff offered an abstract of the minutes containing that reference. Denial of the offer of that abstract is the third issue on appeal.

Daniel had lacerations of the face, left thigh, left calf, and right thigh, and abrasions and bruises of the abdomen and chest. Mr. Mahlandt was permitted to state that Daniel had indicated that he had gone under the fence. Mr. Mahlandt and Mr. Poos, about a month after the incident, examined the fence to determine what caused Daniel's lacerations. Mr. Mahlandt felt that they did not look like animal bites. The parallel scars on Daniel's thigh appeared to match the configuration of the barbs or tines on the fence. The expert as to the behavior of wolves opined that the lacerations were not wolf bites or wounds caused by wolf claws. Wolves have powerful jaws and a wolf bite will result in massive crushing or severing of a limb. He stated that if Sophie had bitten Daniel there would have been clear apposition of teeth and massive crushing of Daniel's hands and arms which were not injured. Also, if Sophie had pulled Daniel under the fence, tooth marks on the foot or leg would have been present, although Sophie possessed enough strength to pull the boy under the fence.

The jury brought in a verdict for the defense.

The trial judge's rationale for excluding the note, the statement, and the corporate minutes, was the same in each case. He reasoned that Mr. Poos did not have any personal knowledge of the facts, and accordingly, the first two admissions were based on hearsay; and the third admission contained in the minutes of the board meeting was subject to the same objection of hearsay, and [also] unreliability because of lack of personal knowledge.

The Federal Rules of Evidence became effective in July 1975 (180 days after passage of the Act). Thus, at this time, there is very little case law to rely upon for resolution of the problems of interpretation.

The relevant rule here is . . . [FRE 801]. So the statement in the note pinned on the door is not hearsay, and is admissible against Mr. Poos. It was his own statement, and as such was clearly different from the reported statement of another. Example, "I was told that . . . ." See Cedeck v. Hamiltonian Fed. Sav. & L. Assn., 551 F.2d 1136 (8th Cir. 1977). It was also a statement of which he had manifested his adoption or belief in its truth. And the same observations may be made of the statement made later in the day to Mr. Sexton that, "Sophie had bit a child . . . ."

Are these statements admissible against Wild Canid Survival and Research Center, Inc.? They were made by Mr. Poos when he was an agent or servant of the Wild Canid Survival and Research Center, Inc., and they concerned a matter within the scope of his agency, or employment, i.e., his custody of Sophie, and were made during the existence of that relationship.

Defendant argues that Rule 801(d)(2) does not provide for the admission of "in house" statements; that is, it allows only admissions made to third parties.

The notes of the Advisory Committee on the Proposed Rules, discuss the problem of "in house" admissions with reference to Rule 801(d)(2)(C) situations. This is not a (C) situation because Mr. Poos was not authorized or directed to make a statement on the matter by anyone. But the rationale developed in that comment does apply to this (D) situation. Mr. Poos had actual physical custody of Sophie. His conclusions, his opinions, were obviously accepted as a basis for action by his principal. See minutes of corporate meeting. As the Advisory Committee points out in its note on (C) situations,

> . . . communication to an outsider has not generally been thought to be an essential characteristic of an admission. Thus a party's books or records are usable against him, without regard to any intent to disclose to third persons. J. Wigmore on Evidence §1557 . . . .

After reciting a lengthy quotation which justifies the rule as necessary and suggests that such admissions are trustworthy and reliable, Weinstein states categorically [in Weinstein's Evidence §801(d)(2)(D)(01)] that although an express requirement of personal knowledge on the part of the declarant of the facts underlying his statement is not written into the rule, it should be. He feels that is mandated by Rules 805 and 403.

Rule 805 recites, in effect, that a statement containing hearsay within hearsay is admissible if each part of the statement falls within an exception to the hearsay rule. Rule 805, however, deals only with hearsay exceptions. A statement based on the personal knowledge of the declarant of facts underlying his statement is not the repetition of the statement of another, thus not hearsay. It is merely opinion testimony. Rule 805 cannot mandate the implied condition desired by Judge Weinstein.

Rule 403 provides for the exclusion of relevant evidence if its probative value is substantially outweighed by the danger of unfair prejudice, confusion of the issues, or misleading the jury, or by consideration of undue delay, waste of time, or needless presentation of cumulative evidence. Nor does Rule 403 mandate the implied condition desired by Judge Weinstein.

Thus, while both Rule 805 and Rule 403 provide additional bases for excluding otherwise acceptable evidence, neither rule mandates the introduction into Rule 801(d)(2)(D) of an implied requirement that the declarant have personal knowledge of the facts underlying his statement. So we conclude that the two statements made by Mr. Poos were admissible against Wild Canid Survival and Research Center, Inc.

As to the entry in the records of a corporate meeting, the directors as primary officers of the corporation had the authority to include their conclusions in the record of the meeting. So the evidence would fall within 801(d)(2)(C) as to Wild Canid Survival and Research Center, Inc., and be admissible. The "in house" aspect of this admission has already been discussed, Rule 801(d)(2)(D), supra.

But there was no servant, or agency, relationship which justified admitting the evidence of the board minutes as against Mr. Poos.

None of the conditions of 801(d)(2) cover the claim that minutes of a corporate board meeting can be used against a non-attending, non-participating employee of that corporation. The evidence was not admissible as against Mr. Poos.

There is left only the question of whether the trial court's rulings which excluded all three items of evidence are justified under Rule 403. He clearly found that the evidence was not reliable, pointing out that none of the statements were based on the personal knowledge of the declarant.

Again, that problem was faced by the Advisory Committee on Proposed Rules. In its discussion of 801(d)(2) exceptions to the hearsay rule, the Committee said:

> The freedom which admissions have enjoyed from technical demands of searching for an assurance of trustworthiness in some against-interest circumstances, and from the restrictive influences of the opinion rule and the rule requiring first-hand knowledge, when taken with the apparently prevalent satisfaction with the results, calls for generous treatment of this avenue to admissibility.

So here, remembering that relevant evidence is usually prejudicial to the cause of the side against which it is presented, and that the prejudice which concerns us is unreasonable prejudice; and applying the spirit of Rule 801(d)(2), we hold that Rule 403 does not warrant the exclusion of the evidence of Mr. Poos' statements as against himself or Wild Canid Survival and Research Center, Inc.

But the limited admissibility of the corporate minutes, coupled with the repetitive nature of the evidence and the low probative value of the minute record, all justify supporting the judgment of the trial court under Rule 403.

The judgment of the District Court is reversed and the matter remanded to the District Court for a new trial consistent with this opinion.

■ NOTES ON STATEMENTS BY AGENTS OR EMPLOYEES

1. Kenneth Poos told his boss Owen Sexton that Sophie bit Daniel because Clarke had said as much to Kenneth. The court finds that what Kenneth told Sexton is admissible against the Center. Certainly Kenneth's statement fits FRE

801(d)(1)(D). Using the current language of that provision, Kenneth was the Center's "agent or employee" and was speaking "on a matter within the scope of that relationship while it existed." The court comments that what Poos said was "accepted as a basis for action" by the Center, but it doesn't tell us what the Center did. Apparently it removed Sophie to a location where she probably couldn't harm anyone. If so, there is another reason to admit what Kenneth Poos said, which is that the Center adopted his statement by taking this action, and it fits FRE 801(d)(2)(B) as well as 801(d)(2)(D).

2. In *Mahlandt*, Kenneth Poos lacked personal knowledge. He relied on Clarke, even though he didn't quote Clarke or say he was relying on him. For purposes of applying the admissions doctrine, does it matter whether Kenneth quoted the person he was relying on, or instead simply restated in his own words the information he had received?

(a) Given the court's conclusion (personal knowledge is not required for this kind of admission), it seems that reliance on Clarke or anyone else should be perfectly proper. A person who knows enough to make some definite statement, while lacking personal knowledge, will usually rely on information from somewhere. Kenneth relied on his son Clarke and it is hard to see any reason for him to do otherwise.

(b) The court implies that the situation would have been different if Kenneth had written to Owen Sexton "Clarke told me Sophie bit a child." Maybe so, but consider this possibility: Regardless whether Kenneth quotes Clarke or speaks "on his own nickel," the state of his knowledge is the same. He didn't see what happened, but he heard what Clarke said, and presumably he has some idea whether Clarke can be trusted and whether Sophie might have done it. If he had quoted Clarke in his note to Sexton, the very fact that he passed along the information (adding "all has been taken care of") indicates that Kenneth too thinks Sophie bit the child, and in substance Kenneth is making Clarke's statement his own. Arguably it should not matter whether he quotes his son.

(c) In favor of the contrary view—that the note would have to be excluded if Kenneth quoted Clarke, *Mahlandt* cites the *Cedeck* case, which was a sex discrimination claim against a bank. There, plaintiff offered to testify that the branch manager told her *he* had been told she could not become a manager unless "she's flatchested and wears pants." The reviewing court concluded that this statement was excludable as "hearsay within hearsay." Surely a bank manager, if he cites another as the source of policy, would be referring to one who was in charge of such matters (call him X) or one who was in charge of being sure that policies are carried out (call him Y). If the manager is quoting X or Y, they are also bank employees speaking on matters within the scope of their duties. We may call it multiple hearsay—the manager conveys X's statement to him, or Y's statement that in turn embeds X's statement. Each layer, however, fits FRE 801(d)(2)(D) and so what the manager tells plaintiff should be admissible. For this reason, most courts disagree with *Cedeck.* See EEOC v. HBE Corp., 135 F.3d 543, 552 (8th Cir. 1998) (in enforcement suit alleging discrimination, admitting testimony that CEO did not like black employees; fact that "some of

the statements came through multiple declarants does not matter," since all were agents speaking on activities within scope of their employment).

(d) Mahlandt is different because Clarke Poos is not a higher-up (he doesn't work for the Center at all). So if Kenneth Poos had quoted Clarke in the note to Sexton, we could not invoke FRE 801(d)(2)(D) as embracing Clarke's statement. We could only admit the note if we were persuaded by the argument in (b) above, taking the view that Kenneth had adopted Clarke's view and that Kenneth himself was telling Owen Sexton that Sophie bit the child.

3. Why aren't the minutes of the meeting of the Center's directors admissible against Kenneth Poos? See, e.g., United States v. Wideyk, 71 F.3d 602, 605-606 (6th Cir. 1995) (in trial of Fund manager *W* for taking kickbacks, error to admit statements by *E* of DPS; while DPS was an agent of the Fund, it did not follow that *E* was an agent of *W*).

Endangered Wolf Center

Holly Kuchera / Shutterstock

A dog gets "one bite" without her owner being liable, but not a wolf, whose owner is strictly liable for injuries caused by a wild animal in captivity. Danny suffered serious injuries (requiring more than 200 stitches). Somehow he was scraped by barbs on the fence, either by sliding under it (plaintiff claimed Sophie dragged him under it) or by climbing over it (as the defense claimed). No witness saw Sophie bite Danny, which concerned the trial judge. He asked Poos, "Do you know—and I'm talking about eyeball knowledge or personal knowledge—do you know how he happened to get inside the fence?" "No, Your Honor, I do not," said Poos, who gave the same answer when the judge asked whether Danny was "bit, mauled, clawed, or whatever by Sophie?" Because nobody seemed to have "eyeball knowledge," the judge excluded what Poos told Owen Sexton in the note, and the jury found for the defendants. After the appeal, the case was remanded but never retried; it settled for a reportedly small sum. Sophie was not euthanized, but was sent away—reportedly to a research center in Illinois, similar to a game preserve. Danny was left with a scar on his face, and would tell people "I was bitten by a wolf." But he didn't lose his love of animals, according to his mother. In a separate suit, the carrier that insured the Poos home won a judgment that any injury caused by Sophie was excluded from coverage as related to Kenneth Poos' business. See North River Ins. Co. v. Poos, 553 S.W.2d 500 (Mo. App. 1977). Had plaintiff won a judgment, Poos might be personally liable, and the Center too. Sophie's time at the Poos residence was to be only temporary, while a wolf preserve was under construction—now it is the Endangered Wolf Center in Eureka, Missouri, 20 miles west of St. Louis. Owen Sexton, Kenneth Poos' boss at the time, is a Professor Emeritus of Biology at American University in St Louis and one of the Center's founders. For more, see Eleanor Swift, The Story of *Mahlandt v. Wild Canid Survival Center:* Encounters of Three Different Kinds, in Evidence Stories (Lempert ed., 2006).

■ PROBLEM 4-H. "I Was on an Errand for My Boss"

Driving a truck bearing the legend "Farmright Produce Corp.," Rogers collides with an automobile driven by Story. Neither is badly hurt, but the vehicles (especially the car) are damaged. Some 30 minutes after the accident, Rogers remarks to Story, "I'm sorry this happened. I was making a delivery for Farmright, and got distracted for a moment trying to read the purchase order on my clipboard."

Story sues Farmright Corp., which includes in its answer to the complaint an averment that "the driver Rogers was not acting within the scope of his employment at the time of the alleged accident." At trial, Story offers to testify to what Rogers said, invoking FRE 801(d)(2)(D). Farmright objects:

> Your Honor, that exception cannot be invoked unless plaintiff proves that Rogers was an agent of Farmright speaking of a matter within the scope of his employment. Plaintiff has not proved either point, and we are prepared to go forward with evidence that he was neither. In short, the necessary foundation for using that provision has not been laid. Moreover, Your Honor, they can't use the statement to prove the very facts which the Rule sets out as conditions of admissibility. That would be bootstrapping.

What result, and why? Check FRE 104(a).

■ NOTES ON BOOTSTRAPPING AND COINCIDENCE

1. Rogers' statement raises a bootstrapping problem because part of his statement ("I was making a delivery for Farmright") asserts a fact necessary to the application of FRE 801(d)(2)(D) (Rogers was an employee of Farmright and his duties included driving the truck). The proponent invokes this provision in offering the statement, and the question is whether proffered evidence can itself prove the fact on which its admissibility depends. Look at the last sentence of FRE 801(d), which suggests that the statement can be considered on this point, but additional evidence must be offered too. What additional evidence could the proponent be asked to come up with?

2. The statement also raises a coincidence problem because the same part of it ("I was making a delivery for Farmright") asserts a fact that is also an "ultimate fact" on which the merits depend. The judge decides admissibility under FRE 104(a), which means he must decide whether Rogers was working for Farmright and what his duties were. But the jury must resolve the same question in deciding whether Farmright is liable to Story for Rogers' alleged tort. Consider the following approach: The judge decides the question and admits or excludes the statement accordingly, but doesn't tell the jury what he thinks about Rogers' relationship to Farmright; then (if the case goes to the jury) the jury decides the same question in resolving the merits. Does that make sense?

5. Coconspirator Statements

The coconspirator exception is a venerable feature of our law. It appeared in English conspiracy trials in the eighteenth century, and in this country thereafter. The elements in the exception have not changed, and are set out in FRE 801(d)(2)(E): A coconspirator statement is admissible if (1) declarant and defendant conspired ("coventurer" requirement), and the statement was made (2) during the course of the venture ("pendency" requirement) and (3) in furtherance thereof ("furtherance" requirement).

The coconspirator exception is available in civil and criminal cases alike, and can apply even if the case does not include conspiracy charges or claims. When the exception applies, it enables one party to introduce against another statements made by persons who conspired with the latter. As a practical matter, however, proving conspiracy is an elaborate undertaking: Hence the exception seldom appears outside the context of trials on counts that include conspiracy, and most such prosecutions are in federal court.

Conspiracy prosecutions. It is worth pausing to consider why a conspiracy count is such a potent weapon in the arsenal of the federal prosecutor: It gives him an advantage in selecting venue (which can be laid where any act in the conspiracy occurred); it helps him join multiple defendants who committed different crimes at different times and places; it provides the possibility of conviction even if "substantive" counts fail (a defendant found innocent of importing drugs may yet be guilty of conspiring to do so); and it brings into play useful evidential conventions (only "slight evidence" is needed to link a defendant to a conspiracy), especially the coconspirator exception.

Applying the exception. The prosecutor must establish the predicate facts, which means that she must show that the coventurer, pendency, and furtherance requirements are satisfied.

Applying the exception has proved difficult for three reasons: First, proof of conspiracy is invariably circumstantial and diffuse. Second, the coventurer requirement introduces a problem of coincidence because conspiracy is both a predicate fact in the exception and (if defendant is charged with conspiring) an element of guilt or innocence. Third, coconspirator statements often assert or imply that declarant and defendant conspired, introducing a bootstrapping problem because the statement asserts a fact on which its admissibility depends.

Hearsay and nonhearsay uses. Almost invariably, coconspirator statements that satisfy the exception are vital evidence of the existence and operation of the conspiracy, and in proving these points they have both hearsay and nonhearsay significance.

In a case that reached the Supreme Court, for example, police had confiscated some drugs in a search of an empty house, and in another house they arrested two partners of defendant Inadi who seemed to have acquired drugs from him (they were released when no drugs were found). In later conversations, other participants in the scheme discussed these events, one suggesting that Inadi "set them up" for the arrest, but another suggesting that he was not an informant. These comments seemed indicative of a conspiracy, and suggested that Inadi may have set up the police bust, implying that he was in a conspiracy with the others. The court admitted these comments against Inadi under FRE 801(d)(2)(E). The Court rejected the argument that coconspirator statements should be admitted only where the declarant is unavailable as a witness, and spoke highly of the probative worth of such statements:

> Because [coconspirator statements] are made while the conspiracy is in progress, such statements provide evidence of the conspiracy's context that cannot be replicated, even if the declarant testifies to the same matters in court. When the Government—as here—offers the statement of one drug dealer to another in furtherance of an illegal conspiracy, the statement will often derive its significance from the circumstances in which it was made. Conspirators are likely to speak differently when talking to each other in furtherance of their illegal aims than when testifying on the witness stand. Even when the declarant takes the stand, his in-court testimony seldom will reproduce a significant portion of the evidentiary value of his statements during the course of the conspiracy.
>
> In addition, the relative positions of the parties will have changed substantially between the time of the statements and the trial. The declarant and the defendant will have changed from partners in an illegal conspiracy to suspects or defendants in a criminal trial, each with information potentially damaging to the other. The declarant himself may be facing indictment or trial, in which case he has little incentive to aid the prosecution, and yet will be equally wary of coming to the aid of his former partners in crime. In that situation, it is extremely unlikely that in-court testimony will recapture the evidentiary significance of statements made when the conspiracy was operating in full force.

United States v. Inadi, 475 U.S. 387, 395 (1986).

The conversations in *Inadi* had nonhearsay significance: The very fact that co-offenders had such conversations suggests a conspiracy in action, even without taking any assertions as proof of facts that they assert. They are nonhearsay verbal acts and could be proved even if there were no coconspirator exception. But the conversations had hearsay significance too: One speaker asserted a circumstantially relevant fact (Inadi set up the bust), tending to implicate him in the conspiracy. And arguably the other speaker implied (intended to communicate) that Inadi was one of their number (not an informant). To get the statements in for these purposes, the coconspirator exception is necessary.

Procedural issues. A statement fits this exception only if the defendant and the declarant conspired, and if the statement was made during the conspiracy, and if the statement furthered the conspiracy.

Determining these "predicate facts," as they are called, raises four procedural issues: First, who decides whether the predicate facts exist? (The choice is the judge under FRE 104(a) as a matter of admissibility or the jury under 104(b) because relevance of the coconspirator statement "depends" on whether some other fact exists.) Second, what standard of proof applies to these queries? (Possibilities include preponderance, clear and convincing, or beyond reasonable doubt.) Third, can a statement offered under the exception be counted as proof of the predicate facts, or must those facts be proved by evidence "independent" of the statement? (This issue raises the bootstrapping or circularity problem. Statements offered under the exception often tend to show that there is a conspiracy, that defendant is a member, and that he committed certain acts.) Fourth, assuming that a statement offered under the exception *can* be considered as proof of the predicate facts, is *any* independent evidence required, or can a statement offered under the exception "bootstrap" itself into admissibility without any further proof?

In its 1987 decision in the *Bourjaily* case, the Supreme Court addressed three of these issues, and noted the fourth without resolving it. The Court easily dealt with the first issue: The government and the defendant agreed "that the existence of a conspiracy and petitioner's involvement in it are preliminary questions of fact that, under Rule 104, must be resolved by the court." On the second issue (standard of proof), the Court observed that the Rules don't address this matter, and turned to case law:

> We have traditionally required that these matters be established by a preponderance of proof. Evidence is placed before the jury when it satisfies the technical requirements of the evidentiary Rules, which embody certain legal and policy determinations. The inquiry made by a court concerned with these matters is not whether the proponent of the evidence wins or loses his case on the merits, but whether the evidentiary Rules have been satisfied. Thus, the evidentiary standard is unrelated to the burden of proof on the substantive issues, be it a criminal case or a civil case. The preponderance standard ensures that before admitting evidence, the court will have found it more likely than not that the technical issues and policy concerns addressed by the Federal Rules of Evidence have been afforded due consideration . . . . We think that our previous decisions in this area resolve the matter. See, e.g., Colorado v. Connelly, 479 U.S. 157 (1986) (preliminary fact that custodial confessant waived rights must be

> proved by preponderance of the evidence); Nix v. Williams, 467 U.S. 431, 444, n.5 (1984) (inevitable discovery of illegally seized evidence must be shown to have been more likely than not); United States v. Matlock, 415 U.S. 164 (1974) (voluntariness of consent to search must be shown by preponderance of the evidence); Lego v. Twomey, 404 U.S. 477 (1972) (voluntariness of confession must be demonstrated by a preponderance of the evidence). Therefore, we hold that when the preliminary facts relevant to Rule 801(d)(2)(E) are disputed, the offering party must prove them by a preponderance of the evidence.

Bourjaily v. United States, 483 U.S. 171, 175-176 (1987).

With respect to the third issue (bootstrapping), the Court agreed that prior decisions required independent evidence of a conspiracy and did not let courts rely on the statement itself to establish a conspiracy or the participation of the defendant. In Glasser v. United States, 315 U.S. 60 (1942), for example, the Court held that "such declarations are admissible over the objection of an alleged co-conspirator, who was not present when they were made, only if there is proof *aliunde* that he is connected with the conspiracy" because otherwise "hearsay would lift itself by its own bootstraps" to admissibility. And in United States v. Nixon, 418 U.S. 683 (1974), the Court had said that statements by one defendant may be admissible on "a sufficient showing, *by independent evidence*," that the declarant and one or more defendants were conspirators. Both *Glasser* and *Nixon* were decided, however, before the Federal Rules were enacted in 1975. Hence the Court took up the question whether the Rules changed prior practice:

> . . . Rule 104, on its face, appears to allow the court to make the preliminary factual determinations relevant to Rule 801(d)(2)(E) by considering any evidence it wishes, unhindered by considerations of admissibility. That would seem to many to be the end of the matter. Congress has decided that courts may consider hearsay in making these factual determinations. Out-of-court statements made by anyone, including putative co-conspirators, are often hearsay. Even if they are, they may be considered, *Glasser* and the bootstrapping rule notwithstanding. But [defendant] nevertheless argues that the bootstrapping rule, as most Courts of Appeals have construed it, survived this apparently unequivocal change in the law unscathed and that Rule 104, as applied to the admission of coconspirator's statements, does not mean what it says. We disagree.
>
> [Defendant] claims that Congress evidenced no intent to disturb the bootstrapping rule, which was embedded in the previous approach, and we should not find that Congress altered the rule without affirmative evidence so indicating. It would be extraordinary to require legislative history to *confirm* the plain meaning of Rule 104. The Rule on its face allows the trial judge to consider any evidence whatsoever, bound only by the rules of privilege. We think that the Rule is sufficiently clear that to the extent that it is inconsistent with petitioner's interpretation of *Glasser* and *Nixon*, the Rule prevails.

Bourjaily v. United States, 483 U.S. 171, 179 (1987).

On the fourth issue (is *any* independent evidence required?), the Court punted. Implying that there was independent evidence (the judge considered the statement "and the subsequent events" in finding that the predicate facts had been established), the Court concluded that there was no error in admitting statements under the coconspirator exception. In 1997, an amendment added the language currently in FRE 801(d)(2) to the effect that a statement offered under the coconspirator exception—and any statement offered as "authorized" admissions under FRE 801(d)(2)(C) or as admissions by an agent or employee under FRE 801(d)(2)(D)—is itself to be "considered" but does not itself "establish" the predicate facts on which the operation of those exceptions depend.

■ NOTES ON PROCEDURAL ISSUES

1. *Bourjaily* says the judge alone decides under FRE 104(a) whether the coventurer, pendency, and furtherance requirements are satisfied. Here the judge resolves credibility issues. See United States v. Nichols, 695 F.2d 86, 91 (5th Cir. 1982) (in determining predicate, "judging the credibility of the witness is a matter for the trial court").

2. *Bourjaily* addresses the question *how* a court determines the predicate, but leaves open the question *when* it does so. Eight years earlier, the Fifth Circuit said the judge should hold what has come to be called a *James* hearing, preferably before admitting coconspirator statements:

> [E]vidence [of coconspirator statements] endangers the integrity of the trial because the relevancy and apparent probative value of the statements may be so highly prejudicial as to color other evidence even in the mind of a conscientious juror, despite instructions to disregard the statements or consider them conditionally. . . . Courts have on occasion allowed such statements to be heard by the jury upon the promise that the prosecutor will "connect it up" [by evidence proving the predicate facts]. . . . If . . . the judge should conclude at the end of the trial that the proper foundation has not been laid, the defendant will have been prejudiced from the jury's having heard the inadmissible evidence . . . .
>
> Both because of the "danger" to the defendant if the statement is not connected and because of the inevitable serious waste of time, energy and efficiency when a mistrial is required in order to obviate such danger, we conclude that the present procedure warrants the statement of a preferred order of proof in such a case. The district court should, whenever reasonably practicable, require the showing of a conspiracy and of the connection of the defendant with it before admitting declarations of a coconspirator. If it determines it is not reasonably practical to require the showing to be made before admitting the evidence, the court may admit the statements subject to being connected up.

United States v. James, 590 F.2d 575, 579, 581-582 (5th Cir. 1979) (en banc). A previous panel opinion in the same case went even further:

> [T]he judge cannot allow the jury to hear a coconspirator's declaration until he has determined admissibility by a preponderance of the evidence.

United States v. James, 576 F.2d 1121, 1131 (5th Cir. 1978). Other courts have said the judge can follow whatever sequence she prefers. See United States v. Smith, 320 F.3d 647, 654 (6th Cir.), *cert. denied*, 123 S. Ct. 1954 (2003). Clearly following *James* would be costly and difficult for court and witnesses and lawyers: The prosecutor would in effect try the case twice, which probably explains later decisions in *James* and other cases retreating from the position of the panel.

3. If the judge decides the conspiracy question under *Bourjaily* in determining whether to admit conconspirator statements while the jury decides the same question in determining guilt or innocence, it is possible for judge and jury to give conflicting answers. The conflict can take two forms: One arises where (a) the judge excludes the statement (finding that the evidence fails to establish a conspiracy by a preponderance) but puts the case to the jury anyway and (b) the jury convicts defendants of conspiring but acquits them of substantive charges. Here either the judge or the jury made a mistake on the conspiracy question, and the judge's view may have had decisive impact (leading to acquittal on substantive charges). The other situation arises where (a) the judge admits the statement (finding that the evidence establishes the predicate facts by a preponderance) and puts the case to the jury and (b) the jury acquits defendants of conspiring but convicts them on the substantive charges. Here perhaps judge or jury made a mistake on the conspiracy question, and the judge's opinion may have had decisive effect, this time producing conviction on the substantive charges.

4. Going in the other direction—asking the jury to determine predicate facts—leads to difficulties that are even more serious because the jury is ill-suited to resolve hearsay issues (which would require putting the statement in front of them and asking them whether the predicates are met). So *Bourjaily* makes the better choice, and one of the problems described above (jury convicts defendants of conspiring despite the exclusion of coconspirator statements), can sometimes be resolved by setting aside the conviction for insufficient evidence. Difficulties in the *Bourjaily* approach, and the alternatives, are considered in 4 Mueller & Kirkpatrick, Federal Evidence §8:62 (4th ed. 2013).

■ PROBLEM 4-I. Drugs Across the Border

Arlen and Bud decide to import cocaine from Colombia. They discuss the matter and agree that Bud will fly there with his friend Carol and acquire the stuff, while Arlen lines up customers. Bud recruits Carol to the conspiracy. Carol's friend Fiona drives them to the airport, and the three share a beer before Carol and Bud board the plane:

Fiona: So you guys are going into the import business?

Carol: Yeah, only thing I regret is Arlen. He's a real creep. Can he handle his end?

Bud: Yeah, he can talk good, and he knows how to set the price. Besides, he's fronted us the buy money for the trip, so what can you say?

Don, who works under cover for the Drug Enforcement Administration, approaches Arlen several days later:

Don: Looking for some coke. What can you do for me?
Arlen: How much you want to buy?
Don: Couple or three kilos.
Arlen: Hey man, that's a lot of bucks. You good for it?
Don: When can you produce and what's the price?
Arlen: Got some coming in on Monday. Twenty-five thou per kilo. First-rate stuff. Good price.
Don: I need to be able to count on it.
Arlen: Hey, you know Bud, don't you? He's gone south to make the buy, and he'll be back on Sunday. You can count on it. Meet you at the Alibi Club Monday at 3.
Don: OK.

At the airport on Sunday morning, other DEA agents (knowing nothing of Don's contact with Arlen) spot Carol on the basis of their drug courier profile and speak to her as she gets off the plane. Bud is on board too, but he and Carol are traveling separately, and he avoids detection. Finding nothing, the agents release but follow Carol, who finds Bud and tells him, "The feds let me go, and even apologized." On Sunday afternoon, Arlen (followed by Don's colleagues in the DEA) goes to see Bud. On Monday afternoon, Arlen keeps his engagement with Don at the Alibi, but immediately after the sale DEA agents arrest Arlen, and other agents simultaneously capture Bud and Carol at Bud's place. After receiving *Miranda* warnings, Carol implicates herself and tells the agents that "Bud made the buy in Colombia," and she "just helped carry the stuff past customs down there."

Arlen, Bud, and Carol are prosecuted together. All are charged with conspiracy to import and sell cocaine; Bud and Carol are charged with importation of cocaine; Arlen and Bud are charged with possession of cocaine; Arlen is charged with selling cocaine.

At trial, the prosecutor invokes the coconspirator exception in offering the following items of evidence: (1) testimony by Fiona describing what Bud told her in the bar (Arlen "fronted us the buy money"), over Arlen's objection; (2) testimony by Don describing what Arlen said (Bud's "gone south to make the buy"), over Bud's objection; and (3) testimony by the DEA agent describing what Carol told him ("Bud made the buy"), over Bud's objection. Do any or all of these statements fit the coconspirator exception?

■ NOTES ON THE COCONSPIRATOR EXCEPTION

1. Many cases repeat that the coconspirator exception may be invoked even if there are not conspiracy charges. Should it be available when conspiracy charges are dropped on motion to dismiss for insufficient evidence or defendant is acquitted of conspiracy? See United States v. Xheka, 704 F.2d 974, 986 (7th Cir.) (exception applies even where defendant was acquitted of conspiracy), *cert. denied*, 494 U.S. 993 (1983).

2. The exception does not reach statements made before or after a conspiracy, and the Court has been emphatic that statements made during the "concealment phase" are not ordinarily within the exception. See Krulewitch v. United States, 336 U.S. 440 (1949) (in trial for transporting women across state lines for prostitution, statement by complaining witness more than a month after her arrival in Miami did not fit the exception; conspirators "always expressly or implicitly agree to collaborate" in concealing facts to prevent detection and conviction, and "plausible arguments" could be made that most statements by one conspirator "tended to shield" another, but broadening the exception to reach such statements would "create automatically a further breach of the general rule against the admission of hearsay"). In Grunewald v. United States, 353 U.S. 391 (1957), the Court made an exception for postconspiracy statements that further "the *main* criminal objectives," suggesting that kidnappers "in hiding, waiting for ransom" commit acts of concealment "in furtherance of the objectives" of conspiracy, "just as repainting a stolen car would be in furtherance of a conspiracy to steal." See also Dutton v. Evans, 400 U.S. 74 (1970) (federal rule is not constitutionally required; state court could admit postarrest statement under its version of exception).

3. The Court has rejected constitutional challenges to the exception, and it did so again in *Bourjaily* (in passages not quoted here). You will see that current confrontation doctrine continues to allow coconspirator hearsay (section G, infra).

4. Are coconspirator statements reliable? The admissions doctrine does not rest on reliability, and commentators have suggested that the coconspirator exception should require a showing of reliability. Would this revision be wise? See generally Mueller, The Federal Coconspirator Exception: Action, Assertion, and Hearsay, 12 Hofstra L. Rev. 323 (1984); Davenport, The Confrontation Clause and the Co-Conspirator Exception in Criminal Prosecutions: A Functional Analysis, 85 Harv. L. Rev. 1378 (1978).

EXCEPTIONS IN FRE 803—UNRESTRICTED

Most hearsay exceptions apply regardless whether declarant is available as a witness. Rule 803 sets out a daunting list of 23, almost all in this category. The exceptions in Rule 803 reflect different considerations than the ones you just looked at—the ones in FRE 801(d)(1) covering some previous statements by persons who now testify and submit to cross, and the ones in FRE 801(d)(2) covering admissions that we allow in evidence on account of the philosophy of the adversary system.

The exceptions in Rule 803 are said to turn on considerations of trustworthiness and necessity—statements fitting these exceptions are considered trustworthy for one reason or another, and for various reasons they are considered necessary for rational decisionmaking. Two exceptions fall outside the pattern: Rule 803(5) paves the way for statements of past recollection recorded only if declarant testifies and lays a foundation, and Rule 803(18) reaches treatises only if an expert testifies as a witness—both turning on the fact that a live witness can shed light on the matter at hand.

Confrontation concerns. The exceptions in Rule 803 will keep us busy, but we must also keep in mind the constitutional constraints on using hearsay against criminal defendants. The Sixth Amendment says the accused has the right "to be confronted with the Witnesses against him," and this Confrontation Clause has long been understood as blocking use against the accused of some out-of-court statements, even if they fit a hearsay exception. At the heart of confrontation is the right to cross-examine, which is diminished or denied when prosecutors use such statements. The Confrontation Clause applies in both federal and state courts.

The first thing to note is that the hearsay doctrine (with its exceptions) and the Confrontation Clause operate independently. Sometimes the hearsay doctrine bars use of statements that would not offend the Confrontation Clause, and sometimes the latter bars the use of statements that could be admitted under hearsay exceptions.

Second the Confrontation Clause constrains *only* prosecutors (not the accused), and it applies *only* in criminal cases, while the hearsay doctrine and its exceptions apply to all parties in both civil and criminal trials. And the hearsay doctrine and the Confrontation Clause have different doctrinal contours. For these reasons it seems wise to go through the hearsay exceptions first, and separately to take up the Confrontation Clause afterwards. Yet hearsay exceptions don't make much sense unless you also bear in mind the basics of confrontation doctrine, so it is important to introduce the latter right now.

In Crawford v. Washington, 541 U.S. 36 (2004), the Court discarded its prior approach and concluded that the Confrontation Clause applies only to "testimonial" statements, which ordinarily cannot be used against the accused unless he has a chance to cross-examine the declarant, either at trial or before (in an earlier hearing). At issue in *Crawford* was the use, against a man charged with beating up another man, of his wife's statement to police that the victim was unarmed (defendant claimed he had something that might have been a knife). The statement fit against interest exception because the wife incriminated herself as an accessory. She never took the witness stand.

In *Crawford*, the Court decided that the wife's statement was "testimonial" because it was made to police in a criminal investigation. The Court did not offer a definition, but ventured some descriptions: Testimonial hearsay includes "material such as affidavits, custodial examinations, prior testimony that the defendant was unable to cross-examine, or similar pretrial statements that declarants would reasonably expect to be used prosecutorially," and also "extrajudicial statements" in "formalized testimonial materials, such as affidavits, depositions, prior testimony, or confessions," as well as statements "made under circumstances which would lead an objective witness reasonably to believe that the statement would be available for use at a later trial." The Court said less formal statements, especially those made in private settings ("casual statements to a neighbor"), would likely be nontestimonial and beyond the reach of the Confrontation Clause.

Prior to *Crawford*, prosecutors had invoked many exceptions, including three critical ones that you will encounter. One is the exception for excited utterances in FRE 803(2); second is the exception for against-interest statements in FRE 804(b)(3) (a state version of which applied in *Crawford*); third is the child victim hearsay exception that all states have, which usually reaches a statement by a child describing abuse if it is reliable and the child testifies or is unavailable. Sometimes these exceptions paved the way to admit statements against defendants that are now viewed as testimonial. Under *Crawford*, these statements are now *usually* excludable (unless the accused has an opportunity to cross-examine at trial or before) because *usually* they are made to police or state agents investigating crimes.

In 2006, the Court revisited *Crawford* in consolidated cases that arose in Washington and Indiana. At issue in the Washington case was a 911 call from a woman who said she had been fighting with her boyfriend. At issue in the Indiana case was a statement to a police officer by a woman at the scene of a domestic disturbance. These cases led to the opinion in Davis v. Washington, 547 U.S. 813 (2006), which held that statements made for the "primary purpose" of dealing with an ongoing emergency are admissible after all. The Court concluded that the 911 call fit the "emergency" exception because the danger was ongoing, but not the statements to officers on the scene because the emergency was past. The *Davis* emergency doctrine reduced the impact of *Crawford*.

We examine the *Crawford* doctrine more fully in section G.

1. Present Sense Impressions and Excited Utterances

The first two exceptions in Rule 803 are related and overlapping. Immediacy is the key for present sense impressions under FRE 803(1). Declarant describes what he sees as he sees it. Excitement is the key for excited utterances under FRE 803(2). Declarant is excited or "startled" by an event and makes a statement relating to it.

The exception for present sense impressions is a recent arrival. It derived from the excited utterance exception, and both were distilled from the haze of a vague common law doctrine captured in the Latin term *"res gestae"* ("things that happened"). *Res gestae* expressed the notion that the relationship between event and statement was so close that the happening impelled the words out of the declarant. Less poetically, the idea was that the connection was so close that declarant had no time to lie or forget, and she focused her attention on what she described.

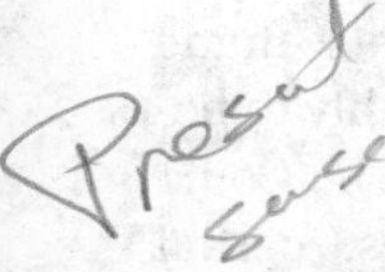

Present sense impressions under FRE 803(1). To fit this exception, a statement (1) must be made "during or immediately after" the speaker "perceived" an event or condition, and (2) must describe or explain the event or condition.

This exception paves the way for statements identifying perpetrators of crime, often moments before or moments after. Sometimes victims identify approaching assailants just before being killed, not anticipating danger. In the *Salgado* case, for example, a New Mexico court admitted a victim's statement, "Hey, Timo, what's up?" that was uttered as the victim greeted his assailant just before being shot to death. See State v. Salgado, 974 P.2d 66, 664 (N.M. 1999). And in chilling cases, victims describe something that looks ominous or scary, as in the *Bray* case, which was a murder trial in which a Kentucky court admitted the victim's statement to her sister on the phone saying that the eventual assailant was "sitting at the bottom of the hill" and had been there "quite a while" and that she feared for her life). See Bray v. Commonwealth, 177 S.W. 2d 741 (Ky. 2005).

In less vivid cases, victims or bystanders react to unfolding crimes or notice critical facts and comment about them to friends or acquaintances, or telephone friends. The exception can also apply to observations made just before an accident occurs.[3]

Usually the testifying witness has seen (and can corroborate) what is described in a present sense impression. Some states require corroboration, most notably New York. On the question whether FRE 803(1) should be interpreted as requiring corroboration, cases differ, although most reject the idea.[4] If we don't have a witness who can corroborate what the speaker says, however, it may be hard to know whether the speaker actually perceived what he describes, and we are faced once again with a bootstrapping question that arises with statements offered as admissions or as coconspirator statements (which often assert the facts on which admissibility depends). In other words, without a corroborating witness we may be forced to take the statement as proof of

---

[3] See, e.g., State v. Wright, 817 A.2d 600, 605 (R.I. 2003) (in murder trial, admitting statement by defendant's mother, talking by phone to friend about killing, describing her sudden discovery of a purse, which turned out to be the victim's); Greene v. B.F. Goodrich Avionics Systems, Inc., 409 F.3d 784 (6th Cir. 2005) (helicopter pilot's comment, just before fatal crash, "My gyro just quit") (product liability suit); Houston Oxygen Co. v. Davis, 161 S.W.2d 474 (Tex. 1942) (referring to another car, automobile passenger said "they must have been drunk" and "we would find them somewhere on the road wrecked if they kept that rate of speed up") (classic precursor to FRE 803(1)).

[4] For the New York rule, see People v. Vasquez, 670 N.E.2d 1328, 1334 (N.Y. 1996). Compare Ernst v. Commonwealth, 160 S.W.3d 744, 756 (Ky. 2005) and United States v. Ruiz, 249 F.3d 643, 646-647 (7th Cir. 2001) (both holding that exception does not require corroboration) with People v. Hendrickson, 586 N.W.2d 906, 909 (Mich. 1998) (exception does require corroboration).

the conditions of its own admissibility. Of course the court decides whether FRE 803(1) applies. Under FRE 104(a), the court isn't bound by the rules of evidence in making such decisions, and can consider the statement itself as some proof of this point, although additional proof is usually available to aid the decision. See Miller v. Crown Amusements, Inc., 821 F. Supp. 703, 706 (S.D. Ga. 1993) (911 caller "noticed" truck as it "sideswiped" car parked on road; court relies on statement and circumstances in concluding that declarant observed the incident).

In the electronic age, witnesses may "tweet" or "text" friends, or "Instagram" or use cellphones or call 911—all in order to describe crimes as they unfold or just afterwards. See, e.g., U.S. v. Boyce, 742 F.3d 792, 796 (7th Cir. 2014) (under FRE 803(1), admitting 911 call by mother of defendant's children reporting that defendant had just hit her and was "going crazy for no reason" and replying "yes" when asked whether he had a weapon, adding that he had "a gun"). Often such calls raise problems under *Crawford* because operators who receive them are connected with law enforcement, but some are admitted under the emergency doctrine. See United States v. Thomas, 453 F.3d 838 (7th Cir. 2006) (911 caller reports shooting; present sense impression fit emergency doctrine).

Excited utterances under FRE 803(2). To fit the excited utterance exception, (1) the statement must relate to the event or condition and (2) declarant must speak "under the stress of excitement that it caused." This exception commonly applies in three kinds of cases. First is the accident case. Here typically an injured party or bystander describes what happened shortly after the event, as happened in a slip-and-fall case where the injured claimant said at the time "I went flying."[5]

Second is the violent crime case. Here a victim or bystander describes what happened, as in one case where the victim sought help at the time and repeatedly said "They beat me."[6] Such statements are often "testimonial" under the *Crawford* doctrine, if given to police or law enforcement officers (unless the *Davis* emergency exception applies). These complications appear in the *Arnold* case that you will soon read, and we take up the subject in section G, infra.

Third is the child abuse case. Here child victims tell parents or adult caretakers about terrible acts.[7] One complicating factor is the involvement of social service personnel or police, making it more likely that anything the child says is

---

[5] MacDonald v. B.M.D. Golf Associates, Inc., 813 A.2d 488 (N.H. 2002) (admitting statement by injured person after accident in golf cart, "I wasn't supposed to be driving [the cart]"); Simpson v. Wal-Mart Stores, Inc., 744 A.2d 625, 628 (N.H. 1999) (admitting statement by slip-and-fall victim, "I went flying"). But see Gainer v. Wal-Mart Stores East, L.P., 933 F. Supp. 2d 920 (E.D. Mich. 2013) (excluding post-fall statement that store employee had recently mopped, made by unidentified customer, for failure to show personal knowledge and because mopping a floor is not an exciting event).

[6] Wright v. State, 368 Ark. 629 (Ark. 2007) (admitting murder victim's statement to her mother saying "me and Cory been fighting" and "he raped me" for two or three hours and "tried to kill me"); Commonwealth v. Carroll, 789 N.E.2d 1062 (Mass. 2003) ("Please help me. Help me. My eye. They beat me. They beat me").

[7] State v. Ladner, 644 S.E.2d 684 (S.C. 2007) (statement by two-and-a-half-year-old girl to caretakers indicating that her "tooch" hurt and that defendant "did it") (but adding that he "didn't do nothing").

testimonial under *Crawford* (usually the emergency doctrine does not apply because there is no immediate threat). Another complicating factor is the age of the child, which courts treat as a reason to decide that excitement lasts longer, extending the reach of the exception. Although very young children may be unable to testify effectively, courts do not let this fact block use of their statements. In the *Ladner* case cited in the footnote in this paragraph, the court said incompetency at trial does not preclude use of an excited utterance proved "through a different, competent witness." The court finessed this issue in *Betts* (Chapter 3E, supra), where Tracey Lynn said "He killed my brother and he'll kill my mommie too," and the court treated her statement as nonhearsay (so competence didn't matter).

NUTTALL v. READING CO.

United States Court of Appeals for the Third Circuit
235 F.2d 546 (1956)

[Florence Nuttall, as executrix of the estate of Clarence Nuttall, sued the railroad (Reading) under the Federal Employers' Liability Act. Clarence Nuttall worked for Reading as an engineman, and in this suit his widow claimed that Reading required him to report to work despite his objection that he was ill. The case was tried twice. In the first trial plaintiff recovered a verdict of $30,000, but the judge ordered a new trial (on the ground that an improper claim for damages on behalf of a minor child may have engendered "sympathetic emotion" in the jury).

In the second trial, the court directed a verdict against Florence Nuttall, from which she took this appeal. Here she urged error in the exclusion of evidence, including (1) two affidavits (one by Fireman John O'Hara, the other by Conductor James Snyder, both of whom worked with Nuttall on the occasion in question), (2) her own testimonial account of her husband's phone conversation with the yardmaster, and (3) testimony by the fireman about remarks Nuttall made in the trainyard on the day in question.

The affidavits were secured by the railroad after suit had been filed, but the judge excluded them as hearsay. The reviewing court here approves this ruling. Still, the affidavits tell the story that Mrs. Nuttall wanted the court to hear. They indicated that Clarence Nuttall did report to work, assuming his duties as engineman on the 7:00 A.M. Wilmington Yard shifter.

Fireman O'Hara's affidavit stated the following facts: Nuttall "did not look well," and "said he wasn't feeling too good." Nuttall was "coughing and couldn't seem to get his breath," and O'Hara relieved him after an hour while Nuttall "sort of propped himself on the Fireman's seat . . . perspiring and coughing" and having "trouble getting his breath." Nuttall "reported off until further notice" at about 1:00 P.M., declining O'Hara's offer of a lift home and driving off himself.

Conductor Snyder's affidavit confirmed O'Hara's version of events and commented that Nuttall looked "pretty ill" and "seemed choked up and his lips were blue."

Although failing on the affidavits, Florence Nuttall fared better with her claims that the judge erred in excluding testimony by herself and John O'Hara.]

Goodrich, J.

If the plaintiff in this case can prove that management forced a sick employee, of whose illness they knew or should have known, into work for which he was unfitted because of his condition, a case is made out for the jury under the Federal Employers' Liability Act. As to this general proposition we think there is no dispute....

Now we turn to the other vital piece of testimony. On the morning of January 5, 1952, Nuttall had a telephone conversation from his home with the yardmaster at Wilmington. This conversation took place in the presence of his wife and at the end there was an additional statement made to her after he had hung up the receiver. Here is [Florence Nuttal's account of] the conversation which plaintiff offered and the district judge refused...:

Q. Suppose you start again. He got on the phone and he dialed the office and he said something to George.
A. Yes. He said, "George," he said, "I am very sick, I don't think I will be able to come to work today."
Q. What was the next you heard your husband say?
A. I heard him say, "But I can't come to work today, I don't feel I can make it."
Q. What was the next thing you heard your husband say?
A. I heard him say, "but, George, why are you forcing me to come to work the way I feel?"
Q. Then did your husband say anything after that?
A. Well, he said, "I guess I will have to come out then."
Q. Was that the end of this conversation on the telephone?
A. It was.
Q. Then what did he do with the telephone?
A. He put the telephone back.
Q. Then did you help him? Then what happened? Did he go off, or go to work, or did he remain in the house, or what?
A. No, he went to work, he said to me, "I guess I will have to go."

[The court concludes that what Clarence Nuttall said to his wife was competent to prove that he was being forced to go to work. Moreover, what Nuttall said to O'Hara in the railroad yard (that he "was not feeling well, that he had requested to be off that day but was refused permission") was admissible to prove the same point.]

To hold the defendant responsible for sending a sick man into unsuitable work it must be shown that the man was not only under pressure but was under pressure to undertake the work by virtue of something the employer had done. The persecution complex is a well known psychiatric phenomenon; it would be highly unfair to hold an employer responsible for something the employee merely imagined without the employer inducing it.

Is the telephone conversation evidence of pressure by the employer? Unfortunately, both parties to the conversation are dead. Neither can minimize, enlarge, explain, or otherwise make any commentary upon the words Mrs. Nuttall heard her husband use on that morning of January 5.

We think that the conversation tends to show that Nuttall was being forced to do something by somebody. The "somebody" is identified without difficulty. He was Marquette the railroad employee in charge of operations in the yard. Knowing that Nuttall's superior was talking to him on the telephone we think that the words Nuttall used during the time and his statement immediately afterward tend to show that he was being forced to go to work. At this point we are assuming Nuttall's state of mind established and seeking probative evidence that his state of mind was induced by something his employer did. When a man talks as Nuttall did and acts as Nuttall did during and immediately following a conversation on the telephone with his boss, it has a tendency to show that the boss was requiring him to come to work against his will.

What Nuttall had to say during the telephone conversation was subject to Marquette's comment and response. In his statement to his wife following the conversation Nuttall merely reiterated what he had already said and in terms less accusatory. Mrs. Nuttall has no personal knowledge of what Marquette said and neither does anyone else for both parties to the conversation are dead. She did hear her husband characterize the statements of his boss at the very moment he heard what Marquette had to say and immediately thereafter. Such characterizations, since made substantially at the time the event they described was perceived, are free from the possibility of lapse of memory on the part of the declarant. And this contemporaneousness lessens the likelihood of conscious misrepresentation. All things considered, we think that Nuttall's statements during and immediately following the telephone conversation should be admitted into evidence to prove that he was being compelled to come to work.

[O'Hara's account of what Nuttall said in the trainyard, although admissible to prove compulsion, is not admissible to prove that Reading (acting through Marquette) was the force that created the compulsion.]

Mistakes on admissibility of evidence are almost inevitable during a hotly contested trial. Unless they seriously affect the case they are not a ground for reversal. But here the rejected evidence goes to the very heart of the plaintiff's case. It is unfortunate that this type of case must be tried three times. But that is necessary in this instance.

The judgment of the district court will be reversed and the case remanded with further proceedings not inconsistent with this opinion.

■ NOTES ON PRESENT SENSE IMPRESSIONS

1. *Nuttall* was decided almost 20 years before the Federal Rules took effect, but the case illustrates the utility of the exception for present sense impressions in FRE 803(1). Clarence Nuttall's words in his conversation with George Marquette, and immediately thereafter with his wife Florence, tend to prove that Nuttall felt pressured. Those words ("I don't think I will be able to come to work" and "I guess I will have to come out then") *could* be called nonhearsay circumstantial evidence of state of mind (like the words of Anna Sofer in Problem 3-H speaking of being a "faithful and loving wife" while Ira reciprocated with "cruelty, disrespect, and indifference"). But absent the peculiar facts of Problem 3-H (wife publicizes her ill feelings), it seems wiser to treat words like these as hearsay. One available exception is FRE 803(3) (state-of-mind statements), which we will reach shortly. Another is FRE 803(1).

2. Another thing suggested by Nuttall's words during and after the phonecall is that "somebody" was applying that pressure, namely "George" (meaning Marquette). When Nuttall's words are offered to prove this point (critical, the court says, in view of the "persecution complex"), we need something other than the state-of-mind exception, because *now* we are proving events in the world (what Marquette told Nuttal). Today we would apply FRE 803(1) in arriving at this result.

3. What Nuttall told O'Hara, on arriving at the trainyard, also tended to prove Nuttall was there under compulsion. But the court did not let the trainyard statement prove that Marquette had applied pressure. Under FRE 803(1), the result would be the same.

4. *Nuttall* resembles cases decided under FRE 803(1). See United States v. Portsmouth Paving Corp., 694 F.2d 312, 322-323 (4th Cir. 1982) (caller tells bystander what party on distant end said; immediacy requirement satisfied; statement came "no more than a few seconds" after call); United States v. Early, 657 F.2d 195, 197-198 (8th Cir. 1981) (hanging up phone, declarant said "Oh mom, what am I going to do? That sounded just like Butch"). Clearly "perceiving" (central to the exception) embraces not only what declarant sees but what he hears. See also MCA, Inc. v. Wilson, 425 F. Supp. 443, 450-451 (S.D.N.Y. 1976) (in infringement action alleging wrongful appropriation of "Boogie Woogie Bugle Boy," admitting "spontaneous reactions of cast and audience" to stage performance of allegedly infringing song during play).

5. The exception is crafted in a way that nearly insures firsthand knowledge. What if the facts leave doubt whether the speaker actually has a basis in experience for what he reports? See State v. Davis, 638 S.E.2d 57, 63 (S.C. 2006) (in trial for murder and armed robbery, error to admit statement by associate of defendant that shotgun was used to murder victim; no showing that speaker witnessed shooting) (reversing); Moe v. State, 123 P.3d 148, 151 (Wyo. 2005) (excluding statement by eyewitness that he didn't see anything wrong, offered as proof that complainant consented; no showing that speaker perceived victim consenting to sex).

6. Even comments by defendants while committing criminal acts can qualify as present sense impressions. In an Oklahoma case, for example, a defendant convicted of murder and sentenced to death won a new trial because the court refused to admit his own statement, made after shooting two people, "it was them or me," offered to show self-defense. See Williams v. State, 915 P.2d 371, 381 (Okla. Crim. App. 1996). In another case, a comment by one defendant to another was admissible against both because it fit the exception. See Welch v. State, 968 P.2d 1231, 1239 (Okla. Crim. App. 1998) ("someone's getting a spanking over a deal"), *cert. denied*, 528 U.S. 829 (1999).

7. As noted in the introduction, immediacy is critical. Suppose defendant in a criminal case made an exculpatory statement ten minutes after the fact. Can the defense offer it under the exception? See United States v. Penney, 576 F.3d 297, 312-313 (6th Cir. 2009) (No; not immediate enough), *cert. denied*, 130 S. Ct. 1536. Alighting from a train in Chicago, defendant is accosted by police searching for drugs, who ask to question her. She walks with them 100 feet to a baggage area, and one of the officers asks a redcap following with a full cart whether he has her luggage. "That's the bag she gave me," he replies, indicating a piece on the cart. Present sense impression? See United States v. Parker, 936 F.2d 950, 954 (7th Cir. 1991) (Yes; statement was contemporaneous; interval between picking up bags and speaking was "extremely short"). Moments after accident, witness arrives and hears driver say that passenger "grabbed the wheel, causing the pickup to go into the ditch and overturn." Present sense impression? See Starr v. Morsette, 236 N.W.2d 183, 186-188 (N.D. 1975) (Yes).

8. With the growth of social media and explosion of recorded data like tweets, texts, instagrams and 911 calls, which may include statements that fit the exception, some call for reform. See Jeffrey Bellin, Facebook, Twitter, and the Uncertain Future of Present Sense Impressions, 160 U. Pa. L. Rev. 331 (2012) (arguing for "percipient witness" requirement under which present sense impressions in the form of electronic statements can be presented only by a witness "present at the time the statement was made," who can "clarify, vouch for" or even "discredit" the statement). But see Leisa L. Richter, Don't Just Do Something!: E-Hearsay, The Present Sense Impression, and the Case For Caution in the Rulemaking Process, 61 Am. U. L. Rev. 1657 (2012) (existing doctrine adequately deals with e-hearsay, and percipient witness requirement would undermine utility of exception, particularly in domestic violence cases).

UNITED STATES v. ARNOLD

United States Court of Appeals for the Sixth Circuit
486 F.3d 177 (2007)

Before BOGGS, Chief Judge; MARTIN, BATCHELDER, DAUGHTREY, MOORE, COLE, CLAY, GILMAN, ROGERS, SUTTON, COOK, MCKEAGUE, and GRIFFIN, Circuit Judges.

SUTTON, Circuit Judge.

Joseph Arnold challenges his felon-in-possession-of-a-firearm conviction, contending that the evidence does not support the verdict, that the district court violated his Confrontation Clause rights by admitting testimonial hearsay and that the district court made several erroneous evidentiary rulings during the course of the trial. We affirm . . . .

II

. . . At trial, the jury learned that Tamica Gordon called 911 and told the emergency operator that Arnold had just threatened her with a gun. When officers arrived at the scene, they encountered a visibly shaken Gordon, who explained that she had just been in an argument with Arnold, her mother's boyfriend, and that he had threatened her with a gun. "Joseph Arnold," she told the officers, "pulled a gun on [me], he said he was going to kill [me]. He was arguing and [I] thought he was going to kill [me]." Gordon "stated that she . . . saw him with a gun in his hand," and "that she observed him cock the weapon." Gordon described Arnold's weapon as "a black handgun." "[B]ecause of the way she said that he cocked it"—that he "pulled back the slide"—and because of the way she described the gun, the officers concluded that the gun was a semiautomatic handgun, and that "there would be a round chambered" in it.

Soon after the officers arrived, Gordon's mother pulled up in a car with Arnold sitting in the passenger seat. "[A]s the car pulled up, [Gordon] got back excited, she started crying [and] pointing at the car saying that's him, that's the guy that pulled the gun on me, Joseph Arnold, that's him[,] . . . he's got a gun on him." When the officers approached Arnold and "asked him what was going on, . . . he basically said that they were arguing." After obtaining permission to search the car, the officers found a plastic bag containing a loaded, black, semiautomatic handgun with a round in its chamber directly under the passenger seat of the car.

[A grand jury charged Joseph Arnold with being a felon in possession of a firearm. Tamica Gordon did not testify at trial, although the government had subpoenaed her. Invoking the excited utterance exception, the trial court admitted redacted recording of the 911 call (deleting language referring to Arnold as a convicted murderer) as well as Gordon's statements at the scene.] . . .

III

Arnold . . . challenges the admissibility of three out-of-court statements—the 911 call, Gordon's initial statements to police officers upon their arrival at the crime scene and Gordon's statement to officers upon Arnold's return to the scene—under the excited-utterance exception to the hearsay rule. Under FRE 803(2), a court may admit out-of-court statements for the truth of the matter asserted when they "relat[e] to a startling event or condition made while the declarant was under the stress of excitement caused by the event or condition." To satisfy the exception, a party must show three things. "First, there must be an event startling enough to cause nervous excitement. Second, the statement must be made before there is time to contrive or misrepresent. And, third, the statement must be made while the person is under the stress of the excitement caused by the event." *Haggins v. Warden, Fort Pillow State Farm*, 715 F.2d

1050, 1057 (6th Cir. 1983). All three inquiries bear on "the ultimate question": "[W]hether the statement was the result of reflective thought or whether it was a spontaneous reaction to the exciting event." *Id.* at 1058 (internal quotation marks omitted). We apply abuse-of-discretion review to a district court's application of the rule.

The 911 Call. Gordon's statements to the 911 operator readily satisfy the first and third prongs of the test. As to the first requirement, being threatened by a convicted murderer wielding a semi-automatic handgun amounts to a startling event that would prompt at least nervous excitement in the average individual, if not outright trauma. As to the third requirement, Gordon plainly remained in this state of anxiety during the 911 call. Throughout the call, the operator had to tell her to "calm down" and "quit yelling" and often had difficulty understanding her frantic pleas for help.

The record also supports the district court's finding that the call took place soon after Arnold threatened Gordon—"slightly more than immediately" after the threat, in the district court's words—which satisfies the second factor. The district court listened to the tape of the 911 call five times, noted that Gordon said "*he's* fixing to shoot me," not that he "*was* fixing to shoot me," and ultimately concluded that there was an immediacy to her statements. Arnold does not challenge the district court's factual conclusions regarding the meaning of the tape.

Case law supports the view that Gordon made the statement "before there [was] time to contrive or misrepresent." *Haggins*, 715 F.2d at 1057. *Haggins*, for example, upheld the admission of statements by a four-year-old child made more than an hour after the incident but while the child was still suffering the trauma from it. Other cases have upheld the admission of statements that also were made after the startling event but well within the traumatic range of it. *See, e.g., United States v. Baggett*, 251 F.3d 1087, 1090 & n.1 (6th Cir. 2001) (applying the excited-utterance exception to statements made several hours after the last of several spousal beatings over a three-day period); *see also United States v. McCullough*, 150 Fed. Appx. 507, 510 (6th Cir. 2005) (applying exception to statements made "not . . . longer than two-and-a-half hours" after witnessing companion's arrest); *United States v. Green*, 125 Fed. Appx. 659, 662 (6th Cir. 2005) (applying exception to statements made three hours after the startling event); *see also United States v. Alexander*, 331 F.3d 116, 123 (D.C. Cir. 2003) (applying exception to statements made 15 to 20 minutes after the startling event); *United States v. Cruz*, 156 F.3d 22, 30 (1st Cir. 1998) (applying exception to statements made four hours after the startling event); *United States v. Tocco*, 135 F.3d 116, 128 (2d Cir. 1998) (applying exception to statements made within three hours of the startling event).

Contrary to Arnold's suggestion, our cases do not demand a precise showing of the lapse of time between the startling event and the out-of-court statement. The exception may be based solely on "[t]estimony that the declarant still appeared nervous or distraught and that there was a reasonable basis for continuing [to be] emotional[ly] upset," *Haggins*, a conclusion that eliminates an unyielding requirement of a time line showing precisely when the threatening event occurred or precisely how much time there was for contrivance. The district court made this exact finding, a finding supported by evidence that, in the words of *Haggins*, "will often suffice."

The dissent, though not Arnold, raises the concern that the uncorroborated content of an excited utterance should not be permitted by itself to establish the startling nature of an event. But this issue need not detain us because considerable nonhearsay evidence corroborated the anxiety-inducing nature of this event: (1) Gordon's act of calling 911; (2) the fear and excitement exhibited by the tenor and tone of Gordon's voice during the 911 call; (3) Gordon's distraught demeanor personally observed by Officers Brandon and Newberry upon their arrival at the scene; (4) Gordon's renewed excitement upon seeing Arnold return; and (5) the gun matching Gordon's description found underneath the passenger seat in which Arnold was sitting. This dispute, in short, is not one of the "very few cases" in which this "knotty theoretical problem" has raised its head. *See* 2 McCormick on Evidence §272 (6th ed. 2006) ("Fortunately, only a very few cases need actually confront th[e] knotty theoretical problem [of whether independent corroborating evidence of startling events is necessary] if the courts view what constitutes independent evidence broadly, as they should where the circumstances and content of the statement indicate trustworthiness.") (internal footnote omitted).

Gordon's statement to officers upon their arrival at the scene. When the officers arrived at the scene soon after learning of the 911 call, Gordon exited her car and approached the officers, "crying," "hysterical," "visibly shaken and upset," and exclaimed that Arnold had threatened her with a gun. For many of the same reasons the district court had authority to admit the 911 call, it had authority to admit this statement. It remained the case that a startling event had occurred. The time that had passed between the end of the 911 call and the officers' arrival on the scene—5 to 21 minutes, based on the officers' testimony that the dispatch contacted them "about 8:00" or "a little bit before 8:00" (meaning the dispatch could have occurred any time between the end of the 911 call at 7:45 and 8:00) and that they arrived five to six minutes later—did not give Gordon sufficient time to misrepresent what had happened. *See Alexander* ("Considering the nature of the startling occurrence—Alexander allegedly had a gun and threatened both to 'do something' to [declarant] and to 'mess [up]' her apartment—the passage of 15 to 20 minutes hardly suggests that the district court abused its discretion in admitting the 911 call."). And as shown by Gordon's frantic statements to the officers upon their arrival, she remained visibly agitated by Arnold's threat. The court did not abuse its discretion in admitting the statement.

Gordon's statement to officers when Arnold pulled up next to the police car. Soon after the officers' arrival, which is to say from 30 seconds to 5 minutes after they reached the scene, a car with Arnold in it pulled up next to the police car, at which point Gordon made the last of her statements admitted as an excited utterance. "[T]hat's him," she said, "that's the guy who pulled a gun on me, Joseph Arnold, that's him." The district court permissibly admitted this statement as part of the same emotional trauma that captured Gordon's earlier statement to the officers. On top of that, the unexpected appearance of the victim's assailant independently suffices to establish a startling event followed by an understandably excited verbal response. The district court did not abuse its discretion in admitting the statement.

The dissent's view of the excited-utterance question prompts a few responses. *First*, the dissent, though not Arnold, contends that the district court failed to place the burden of proof on the government. Yet the district court, in making this ruling, concluded that "the elements to allow the exception have been demonstrated by the government." And we, too, have placed the burden on the government.

Second, the dissent claims that, instead of saying "he's fixing to shoot me," Gordon said "he finna shoot me," thereby eliminating the "'s" between he and finna (which the dissent finds to be a slang term for "fixing to"). But Arnold has not challenged the district court's factual determination that Gordon told the 911 operator "he's fixing to shoot me," and accordingly this issue is not properly before us. Nor, at any rate, is it clearly the case, or even somewhat clearly the case, that the dissent properly interprets the tape—given the rapidity and anxiety with which Gordon spoke during the 911 call. This difficulty reinforces not only our decision to defer to the district court's interpretation of the tape but also our decision that indeed it was an excited utterance.

[All of these statements fit the emergency exception that allows use of testimonial statements under *Crawford*.]

For these reasons, we affirm.

Judge CLAY concurs and dissents.

[The opinions by Judge CLAY and Judge GRIFFIN, concurring and dissenting, are omitted.]

Judge KAREN NELSON MOORE dissents.

[The evidence is insufficient because Arnold's presence in the car and Gordon's statements are not enough. The gun found under the passenger seat had no fingerprints, and there is no basis to infer that Arnold possessed it. Nor did Gordon's critical statements on these matters qualify as excited utterances.] . . .

Lack of Time to Contrive or Misrepresent. . . . In *Haggins*, we noted that "the lapse of time between the startling event and the out-of-court statement," while "not dispositive," was still "[o]ne of the most relevant factors in determining spontaneity" and therefore admissibility.[7] Here, the majority maintains

[7] In *Haggins* we noted several factors that often will extend the window of time in which a statement may still be considered spontaneous. These factors include the declarant's age, the declarant's physical and mental condition (including shock, intervening unconsciousness, and pain), "the characteristics of the event, and the subject matter of the statements."

that the government need not establish with precision how much time passed between the two events. Even if this assumption were correct, the government (as the proponent and therefore the party bearing the burden of proof on evidentiary questions) must provide *some* indication of how closely tethered the two events were. But here, the district court placed no such requirement on the government. Instead, the district court admitted, "I don't know the time frame." Notwithstanding this uncertainty, the district court concluded *without explanation* that Gordon's phone call "appears to have been made before there was time to contrive or misrepresent." Without any explanation or any basis in the record for this conclusion, the district court's decision cannot stand.

Next, the majority places undue emphasis on its interpretation of the tape. Although I question the utility of semantically dissecting Gordon's statements, even if I take the majority's approach, the tape does not indicate that Gordon spoke to the 911 operator before sufficient time to contrive or misrepresent had passed. According to the majority, Gordon said, "he's fixing to shoot me," as opposed to "he was fixing to shoot me." After listening to the tape multiple times, I hear the words: "I guess he finna shoot me." I find this significant for two reasons. First, Gordon's inclusion of the words "I guess" (which the majority cleverly excises) renders her statement far less definitive than the majority chooses to present it. More importantly, the statement contains no auxiliary verb (e.g., "is" or "was") connected to "finna," which I understand to be a slang contraction for "fixing to," much as "gonna" serves as a contraction for "going to." *See, e.g.*, http://www.urbandictionary.com/define.php?term=finna (last visited Apr. 19, 2007) (defining "finna" as, "Abbreviation of 'fixing to.' Normally means 'going to.'").[8] The lack of an auxiliary verb renders determination of whether Gordon intended to imply the past or present tense an exercise in sheer guesswork. Accordingly, the words spoken on the tape do not establish that Gordon offered these statements before there was time to contrive or misrepresent.

[The majority's attempt to "satisfy the temporal element" by noting that Gordon seemed "nervous and distraught" fails because that simply goes to the element of excitement, "and thus impermissibly collapses the second and third prongs."]

Finally, the cases the majority relies upon are readily distinguishable. In *Haggins*, the court found the declarant's statements admissible because of her young "age and physical condition," emphasizing that "[s]he was bleeding and in critical condition." Gordon, by contrast, is an adult who suffered no physical harm. . . .

[8] Understanding Gordon's statements in the 911 tape requires an understanding of slang, which is constantly evolving. Turning to a source that operates by consensus, and thus develops along with slang usage, therefore seems unusually appropriate in this instance. UrbanDictionary.com is such a source, as it permits users to propose definitions for slang terms, and other users to vote on whether they agree with the particular definitions posited. At the time of the last visit, the definition cited above (which was posted in June 2003) had received 272 positive votes, and only 45 negative votes, making it the most popular of the twenty proposed definitions of "finna," all but one of which connote future action.

[Also Gordon's statements when officers first arrived, and her statements after Arnold arrived, were not shown to fit the exception. The government did not carry its burden of proving that the 911 call fit the emergency doctrine. By the time officers arrived, the emergency had passed, so her statements then did not fit emergency doctrine, nor her statements to officers later.]

■ NOTES ON EXCITED UTTERANCES

1. Applying FRE 803(2) requires that the speaker be under stress of excitement caused by the event and that the statement relate to the event, and it is clear that the judge must determine these points (not a jury) under FRE 104(a), as matters affecting admissibility. Everything that sheds light on the speaker's emotional state counts in determining excitement—nature of the event, speaker's relationship to it, tone of voice, demeanor, content of statement, speaker's age, whether speaker was injured. While the question is whether *this* speaker was excited (subjective standard), courts entertain reasonable assumptions because they cannot know everything one might want to know, and inevitably try to gauge the responses of a reasonable person similarly situated. See discussion in Mueller and Kirkpatrick, Evidence §8.36 (5th ed. 2012). *Arnold* considers these points and also the "act of calling 911," which in itself is some indication of excitement because one doesn't resort to this resource unless some emergency is at hand.

2. Tamica Gordon was a victim of the charged crime, which for purposes of applying the exception the judge can consider if convinced by the proof, even though defendant has not been convicted. If Ms. Gordon had been a disinterested eyewitness, the exception could still apply, but excitement is not *as* clear. See United States v. Bogan, 267 F.3d 614, 619 (7th Cir. 2001) (in trial of prisoners for assault on corrections officer, admitting exclamatory statement by eyewitness that defendants were trying to kill officer).

3. The time lapse between the event and the 911 call could not be fixed. The majority says the call came "soon after" the event, but Judge Moore argues that this point was unproved, and that the words Gordon used—either "fixing to shoot me" or "finna shoot me"—could describe something happening *now* (present progressive verb) or something that *had already* happened (past tense).

(a) Since the call was recorded, the reviewing court is as able as the trial court to appraise this point, which is unusual. Arguably the deference due to trial court findings on such points is not as clearly warranted in such a case.

(b) Assuming that the time between the event and the call was measured in minutes, does it matter whether it was four minutes or 20? Courts vary. Some have found that excitement persists for many hours after the event. See People v. Smith, 581 N.W.2d 654, 668 (Mich. 1998) (admitting statement by 16-year-old male sexual assault victim nine hours after the event; his behavior

revealed a "continuing level of stress arising from the assault that precluded any possibility of reflection"); State v. Stafford, 23 N.W.2d 832, 835 (Iowa 1946) (admitting statement by farm wife who spent the night wandering the fields, naming husband as assailant, some 14 hours after the event). Others refuse to go so far. See United States v. Marrowbone, 211 F.3d 452, 454-456 (8th Cir. 2000) (error to admit statements by 16-year-old sexual assault victim, made three hours after the event; teenagers have "acute ability to fabricate") (harmless).

4. If one drifts in and out of consciousness or lucidity for hours after being injured in an accident, should we say the stress of the event and ensuing trauma endures, so what he first says on regaining his ability to speak fits the exception? See Chestnut v. Ford Motor Co., 445 F.2d 967, 972-973 (4th Cir. 1971) (in product suit, plaintiff told his physician 20 hours after the fact that he sought to dim lights on meeting a car but closure mechanism activated instead; in applying exception, court should decide whether he had "regained his reflective powers"; apparently he spoke before, but record does not indicate whether these were rational statements or "merely the babblings of one in pain and in a state of severe shock"). Can excitement be rekindled if the declarant is suddenly reminded of a traumatic experience? The court in *Arnold* thought so. See also United States v. Tocco, 135 F.3d 116, 128 (2d Cir. 1998) (in *F*'s arson trial, admitting statement by co-offender *T*, not on trial, three hours after lighting fire; if arson itself was not exciting, *T*'s later understanding that "people could be trapped inside the burning building" would be), *cert. denied*, 423 U.S. 1096 (1998); United States v. Napier, 518 F.2d 316, 317-318 (9th Cir.) (approving exclamation by kidnap victim hospitalized for seven weeks with head injuries, on seeing newspaper picture of defendant a week after her return home, "He killed me, he killed me"), *cert. denied*, 423 U.S. 895 (1975).

5. As *Arnold* illustrates, 911 calls often fit the exception. The coming of cellphones, texting, twitter, instagrams, and other social media insures that more exciting events generate recorded accounts. For criticism of the use of such material, see Richard D. Friedman & Bridget McCormack, Dial-In Testimony, 150 U. Pa. L. Rev. 1171 (2002).

6. Noting that exciting events present to the observer "a vast number of stimuli that far transcend the span of apperception," one critic suggested long ago that the exception is "merely an artifice" for admitting unreliable evidence:

> Excitement is not a guarantee against lying, especially since the courts often hold that excitement may endure many minutes and even hours beyond the event. More important, excitement exaggerates, sometimes grossly, distortion in perception and memory especially when the observer is a witness to a nonroutine, episodic event such as occurs in automobile collision cases and crimes. The likelihood of inaccurate perception, the drawing of inferences to fill in memory gaps, and the reporting of nonfacts is high.

Stewart, Perception, Memory, and Hearsay: A Criticism of Present Law and the Proposed Federal Rules of Evidence, 1970 Utah L. Rev. 1, 8-22, 27-29. Convinced by similar arguments, one distinguished modern jurist would do away with the exceptions for present sense impressions and excited utterances. See U.S. v. Boyce, 742 F.3d 792, 796 (7th Cir. 2014) (the law should awaken from its "dogmatic slumber" and cast out the exception for present sense impressions, which is "not even common sense," nor "even good folk psychology," and asking how there can be any confidence that an "unreflective utterance" caused by excitement is reliable) (Posner, J., writing separately).

■ PROBLEM 4-J. "I Felt This Sudden Pain"

Fifty-five-year-old Eldon Sanders was employed as a pumper and well treater by Texas Oil (he was a 23-year veteran with the company). His job required him manually to load 30-gallon containers of chemicals onto a pickup truck and then drive around to wells in the field, unload the containers, and pour the contents down the wells. From time to time he also had to move pumps weighing 50 to 100 pounds, lifting them onto the truck and unloading them.

On the morning in question, Sanders had his usual coffee and doughnut at a cafe and drove the pickup into the fields at about 7:00 A.M. Two hours later he was seen en route to the "Chase Lease" to treat wells. At 10:00 A.M. he returned to town and went home, where he complained somewhat breathlessly to his wife Eleanor, "I felt this sudden pain just a few minutes ago when I had to lift one of those 30-gallon cans out on the Chase."

Eleanor drove her husband to the office of their family physician Dr. Hillier, who took an electrocardiogram. There was no indication of heart damage, though Sanders' blood pressure was elevated. Hillier administered a tranquilizer and put Sanders to bed for observation. At first he rested easy and seemed better, but in the afternoon he became uncomfortable, and at 5:00 P.M. he died of acute myocardial infarction (heart attack).

Eleanor Sanders sues Liberty Insurance Company, the workers' compensation carrier for Texas Oil, seeking benefits as surviving widow. She testifies that she was surprised to see her husband come home at that hour, and that he "never comes home at that time." She offers to testify to what he told her, and counsel invokes the excited utterance exception. Liberty objects, arguing that "there's no proof of an exciting event here, other than the statement itself, and letting the statement prove the condition on which admissibility depends would be bootstrapping." How should the court rule, and why?

NOTES ON PROVING EXCITEMENT FOR PURPOSES OF THE EXCEPTION

1. Should courts require independent evidence of an exciting event? The trend is toward *not* requiring it. *Bourjaily* sets a parallel example in the context of coconspirator statements, holding that the statement itself can be considered with other evidence in deciding whether a conspiracy exists (section B5, supra). See also People v. Barrett, 747 N.W.2d 797, 804 (Mich. 2008) (rejecting doctrine requiring independent proof); United States v. Brown, 254 F.3d 454, 459-460 (3d Cir. 2001) (independent proof not required). In the Problem, isn't there independent evidence of an exciting event? Consider that Eldon Sanders came home in the middle of the morning, went to the doctor, received medication, and died of a heart attack in the evening.

2. In *Arnold*, Judge Moore argued that there was no evidence that Arnold brandished his gun (no independent evidence of an exciting event):

> The government failed to introduce any evidence of a "startling event" outside of the hearsay statement (the 911 call) itself. The majority glosses over this fact, stating without analysis that "being threatened by a convicted murderer wielding a semi-automatic handgun amounts to a startling event that would prompt at least nervous excitement in the average individual, if not outright trauma." This may well be true, but absent some independent evidence of such an event, the district court abused its discretion by admitting the tape.
>
> [An excited utterance "cannot constitute the only evidence of a startling event," and independent evidence is necessary for two reasons:]
>
> First, relying on the putative excited utterance itself to show that a startling event occurred is endlessly circular. In such a scenario, the district court would rely on the statement itself to establish an element of the test for whether the statement is sufficiently reliable to be admitted into evidence. Such circularity is problematic in and of itself, although the problem can potentially be explained away by reference to FRE 104(a), which permits district courts to resolve preliminary questions regarding admissibility by preponderance of the evidence. *See Bourjaily v. United States*, 483 U.S. 171, 175-76 (1987) (holding that district courts may resolve preliminary questions under FRE 801(d)(2)(E) by preponderance of the evidence). Notably, the record in this case reflects no such determination under Rule 104(a).
>
> Second, and significantly, this circularity contradicts the purpose of the excited-utterance exception to the hearsay rule. As noted above, excited utterances are admissible because the startling event and corresponding state of alarm renders it "unlikely that the statement is contrived or the product of reflection." *Haggins*. And, as we have previously noted, when determining whether a statement qualifies as an excited utterance, "the ultimate question is whether the statement was the result of reflective thought or whether it was a spontaneous reaction to the exciting event." Without some corroborating evidence of such an exciting event, the district court lacks the capacity to make such a determination, or to determine even that there *was* such an event. Put differently, when the only evidence of the startling event is the proffered

statement, the proponent cannot carry its burden of establishing that the relevant circumstances "eliminate the possibility of fabrication," [*Idaho v.*] *Wright*, [497 U.S. 805, 820 (1990)], or that the statement "contain[s] inherent guarantees of truthfulness," *Haggins*. To the contrary, anyone could contrive a fact that—if real—would cause excitement, and state it in an exclamatory manner. To hold that such a statement, standing alone, is admissible for the truth of the matter asserted stands the hearsay rule on its head.

[In this case "the possibility of fabrication was alive and well." Without proof of "gun-brandishing," it is possible that Arnold and Gordon argued and Gordon "stormed away angry." Gordon knew her mother had handguns. She wanted Arnold back in jail so "her mother's relationship with him would end," and she made up a story that she relayed to the 911 operator. There was *no proof* that her statement is "more reliable than any run-of-the-mill inadmissible hearsay statement."[4]]

Reaching the same conclusion that I have, various courts have held that a hearsay statement itself cannot serve as the sole evidence of the alleged startling event that spurred the statement. [Citations to cases from Missouri, Michigan, Pennsylvania, and Texas, and opinions in Fourth and Sixth Circuits.] In its supplemental brief, the government notes that some other authorities have reached the opposite conclusion. Although some of these authorities claim that admitting such statements is the "generally prevailing rule," *see United States v. Brown*, 254 F.3d 454, 459 (3d Cir. 2001), they neither cite recent authority nor provide explanations of *why* such circular reasoning is permissible. More troubling, not one of these cases addresses the incompatibility of such bootstrapping with the foundations of the excited-utterance exception to the hearsay rule.[6] The better rule, and the one I would adopt, requires at least some corroborating evidence of the alleged startling event.

United States v. Arnold, 486 F.3d 177, 209 (6th Cir. 2007).

3. Judge Moore takes the majority in *Arnold* to task for counting both the fact that Gordon called 911 and the fact that her voice reflected "fear and excitement." But it seems that both facts suggest that something startled or excited her. She is on target in suggesting that Gordon might be making it all up

[4] Brushing this concern aside, the majority offers five items of "corroborating" evidence. As an initial matter, it is farfetched to count each of these items as an independent piece of evidence. For example, the majority attempts to parse surgically Gordon's "act of calling 911" from the "fear and excitement" in her voice, and to distinguish both of these from the statements made during the call, counting each as a separate factor indicating that the alleged startling event actually occurred. But the point remains that each item is part of the same whole, a whole that is perfectly consistent with the hypothetical contrivance recounted above. The majority's rationale thus fails to illustrate how Gordon's statements in the 911 call are more reliable than any made-up out-of-court allegation.

[6] . . . [A]uthorities generally cited in support of the government's position are of dubious value. For instance, the vast majority of such authorities predate 1943. In many of the cases cited in the McCormick treatise, independent corroborating evidence of the startling event existed. These cases are therefore distinguishable from the case at bar. Perhaps in recognition of these distinctions, the latest version of the McCormick treatise now notes that "[t]he issue [of whether an exciting event may be proved simply by relying on the statement itself] has not yet been resolved under the Federal Rules." 2 McCormick on Evidence §272 (6th ed. 2006).

in order to send Arnold back to jail, but that seems to be simply an argument that the exception doesn't assure truthfulness.

4. Reconsider Problem 4-H ("I Was on an Errand for My Boss"), but alter the facts. This time Rogers speaks immediately after the accident, obviously excited. Recall that he said he "got distracted for a moment trying to read the purchase order" while "making a delivery for Farmright." If his statement comes in under FRE 803(2), it can prove he was negligent and was employed by defendant and acting within the scope of his duties. *Now* we don't have a bootstrapping problem: We're applying an exception that doesn't require proof that the speaker was employed by the defendant and acting within the scope of his duties. See Murphy Auto Parts Co. v. Ball, 249 F.2d 508 (D.C. Cir. 1957) (driver was sorry for hitting child and was on errand for employer; exception reaches both parts of statement), *cert. denied*, 355 U.S. 932 (1958).

2. State of Mind

The state-of-mind exception, as it is usually called, also emerged from the haze of *res gestae.* It is vitally important, often invoked, and in some respects difficult. As formulated in FRE 803(3), the exception has four distinct uses: To prove (a) declarant's then-existing physical condition, (b) his then-existing mental or emotional condition, (c) his later conduct, and (d) facts about his will.

On all but the third point, what declarant said is likely the best source of information, hence less suspect than the next-best alternative. That alternative (for points a and b) would be his own backward-looking testimonial account. On the first three points (a through c), his prior statement has the virtue of immediacy. On all four points, the risk of misperception is small, and the risk of faulty memory is virtually nonexistent.

But risks of candor and ambiguity remain, and some cases hold that the exception is unavailable where circumstances suggest insincerity, a risk that may seem considerable in the case of blame-avoiding statements. See United States v. Ponticelli, 622 F.2d 985, 991-992 (9th Cir.) (defendant had time enough "to concoct an explanation"), *cert. denied*, 449 U.S. 1016 (1980); Fla. Stat. Ann. §90.803(3)(b)(2) (2010) (authorizing exclusion where circumstances indicate "lack of trustworthiness"). But see United States v. DiMaria, 727 F.2d 265, 271-272 (2d Cir. 1984) ("truth or falsity was for the jury to determine," and statement within categorical exceptions "is admissible without any preliminary finding of probative credibility by the trial judge"). Judge for yourself as you proceed whether the exception should be subject to some general power in the trial judge to exclude on account of doubts over veracity of the declarant.

a. *Then-Existing Physical Condition*

In personal injury suits, the exception is regularly invoked for statements describing aches and pains ("my shoulder hurts"). It doesn't matter whether the speaker is talking at the very time he was hurt or at the onset of the ailment, so long as his words describe how he feels now. The Supreme Court explained it this way in an early case:

> [T]he usual expressions of such feelings are original and competent evidence. Those expressions are the natural reflexes of what it might be impossible to show by other testimony. If there be such other testimony, this may be necessary to set the facts thus developed in their true light, and to give them their proper effect.

Insurance Co. v. Mosley, 75 U.S. 397, 404-405 (1869). Such statements are admissible not only when spoken to treating physicians, but also when spoken to a spouse or friend. In *Mosley*, he spoke to his son and wife. See also Mabry v. Travelers Insurance Co., 193 F.2d 497, 498 (5th Cir. 1952) (wife to husband); Casualty Insurance Co. v. Salinas, 333 S.W.2d 109, 116-118 (Tex. 1960) (worker to friends complaining of pain after injury).

b. Then-Existing Mental or Emotional Condition

When mental state of a party is in issue (it often is), the exception paves the way to use her own statements describing or reflecting it ("I just love my job"). See, e.g., L.D.G., Inc. v. Brown, 211 P.3d 1110, 1128 (Alaska 2009) (in suit against bar alleging that it let patron drink too much, leading to incident in which he shot a woman, letting her grandparent describe "her plans for the future," which entailed caring for young children; her statements could prove her state of mind and intent to spend time with them); Detroit Police Officers' Association v. Young, 608 F.2d 671, 693-694 (6th Cir. 1979) (in suit to enjoin affirmative action program, testimony describing reasons stated by former police supervisors for past discrimination was admissible in support of challenged program), *cert. denied*, 452 U.S. 938 (1981).

Sometimes the mental state of nonparties is in issue. Here too the exception applies, as in suits alleging loss of good will. See Morris Jewelers v. General Electric Credit Corp., 714 F.2d 32, 33-34 (5th Cir. 1983) (admitting "complaints and expressions of anger" in letters from customers to prove their state of mind, hence loss of good will).

Present mental state; continuity inferences. The exception reaches only statements of *present* mental state. Hence what the declarant says on Wednesday about his mental state on Monday does not fit. See Bartlett & Co., Grain v. Merchants Co., 323 F.2d 501, 509-510 (5th Cir. 1963) (statement by grain inspector months after examining load did not fit exception when offered to prove his knowledge on the earlier occasion).

Sometimes, however, it is reasonable to think that mental state persists over time, so what the declarant says on Wednesday about how he feels may shed light on his mental state both then *and* on the prior Monday and following Friday and can be admitted to prove all these points. See Rayborn v. Hayton,

208 P.2d 133 (Wash. 1949) (woman said she would part with her deed only for money; she was thereafter murdered, and husband appeared with deed in hand, claiming she delivered it to him in exchange for his promise to pay; her earlier statement was admissible to prove that she did not intend delivery); Mills v. Damson Oil Corp., 691 F.2d 715, 716-717 (5th Cir. 1982) (statement indicating that declarant knew about title to property reflected his knowledge at the time "and, by inference, prior thereto" when he dealt with grantor).

More often, however, courts refuse to draw inferences of continuity, particularly into the past. See U.S. v. Rivera-Hernandez, 497 F.3d 71, 81-82 (1st Cir. 2007) (in extortion trial, not letting defendant prove his own statement that he was providing consulting services, offered as proof of his mental state previously when he had demanded payment). And great care is warranted:

> The stream of consciousness has enough continuity so that we may expect to find the same characteristics for some distance up or down the current. But there is a point beyond which such evidence becomes irrelevant. Hudson River water at West Twenty-third St. Ferry is no proof of its quality above Fort Edward.

Chafee, The Progress of the Law—Evidence, 1919-1922, 35 Harv. L. Rev. 428, 444 (1922).

Fact-laden statements. Applying the exception to prove mental state is complicated by the fact that often relevant utterances are wholly or partially factual in nature. In what we can call "fact-laden statements," people purposefully disclose their thinking by speaking in factual terms, choosing to communicate inclinations in that oblique way. "It's too cold to be outside" is a factual statement, but it tells us that the speaker would prefer not to be outside, supporting an inference that he wasn't planning a picnic right then. Sometimes the main purpose of such statements is to communicate facts ("it's so cold that the birdbath is frozen"), but in doing so they also reveal something about inclinations, often consciously, but perhaps subconsciously or unconsciously.

Rule 803(3) contains all-important words of limitation: The exception covers a statement of "then-existing state of mind," but *not* a statement of "memory or belief to prove the fact remembered or believed" (except in wills cases). Here's a critically important point: These words do *not* mean the exception doesn't apply to the statements described in the prior paragraph ("It's too cold to be outside" and "it's so cold that the birdbath is frozen"). What these words mean is that these statements can't be used to prove the acts, events, or conditions in the world that they describe—that it's cold outside (perhaps too cold for a human to be comfortable) or that the birdbath frozen. The words of limitation leave room, however, for these fact-laden statements to prove the mental state of the speaker. Of course, if the danger is too great that a jury would misuse such words to prove something about the temperature outside, and if such misuse could make a difference in the case (because the temperature outside is an important point in itself), then an objection under Rule 403 could lead to exclusion even though the words also have a proper use (to prove the mental state of the speaker).

"You got a nonborrowing account." Consider this vivid example of fact-laden statements communicating the speaker's inclination: Oberman sues Dun & Bradstreet, alleging that it issued a false credit report causing Prudential Realty to refuse to lease a building to him. Oberman describes his telephone conversation with Rance of Prudential:

> I says, "Well, if you are buying the building you will need a lessee, so I will lease the building. . . ."
>
> He [Rance] said, "Well, you can't do that either."
>
> I said, "Why?"
>
> He said, "Well, I may as well give you the facts. I was trying to be nice to you. So I will give you the facts. I want to read a report to you I got here from Dun & Bradstreet. . . . You got a non-borrowing account at the bank. You got five thousand worth of receivables in your business. You are worth a thousand dollars. How are you going to pay one thousand four hundred thirty dollars a month for rent?"

At the end of the conversation Oberman offered to "get that corrected," but Rance replied: "Forget it. It is all over." Dun & Bradstreet objects that Rance was just "remembering a past decision" and that the state-of-mind exception does not embrace "statements of memory or belief." The reviewing court approved use of the statement:

> Rance's statements . . . do not face backward. For present purposes, it is of no moment whether the facts which gave rise to Rance's declaration were true or actually occurred, because the concern here is only with the reason for Rance's refusal to lease the Hamlin Avenue property. Thus, there are no problems of memory and perception of the declarant to be tested, and therefore, as in the usual state of mind situation, Oberman's recollection of the statement is as likely to be correct as Rance's recollection.

Oberman v. Dun & Bradstreet, 507 F.2d 349, 351-352 (7th Cir. 1974).

Rance was stating facts (describing acts, events, or conditions in the world), telling Oberman that he had a credit report from Dun & Bradstreet and reciting its content. Just as surely Rance consciously told Oberman why he couldn't lease the building, in effect saying "you're a poor credit risk." Thus Rance disclosed his (and Prudential's) reasons for their decision—his own state of mind and Prudential's institutional judgment. The reviewing court was right to apply FRE 803(3), even though on its face the statement recited facts rather than inclinations.

Recall that sometimes statements of fact are viewed as nonhearsay circumstantial evidence of state of mind. Remember the statements by Anna Sofer in Problem 3-H (Ira "reciprocated my tender feelings with utter cruelty, disrespect, and indifference") and Sharon in Problem 3-I (describing a bedroom with "a papier-mâché man"). See also Catalan v. GMAC Mort. Corp., 2011 WL

61627 (7th Cir. 2011) (loan officer's statements to plaintiff that his application for home equity loan would not be approved were "expressions of the intentions of the bank," and they either fell "outside the definition of hearsay" or they fit the state-of-mind exception).

■ PROBLEM 4-K. "He Says He'll Kill Me"

The prosecutor has evidence that defendant Otto Neff was shaking down Paul Quade, who was found dead of knife wounds in a park. Neff is a small-time tough guy, and the prosecutor thinks he was collecting "protection" money from Quade, who balked and was killed for resisting. At trial the prosecutor calls Quade's friend Roy Sarnak, who will testify (if permitted) that during the period in question Quade once told him:

> Neff is after me again. He says he'll kill me and my family if I don't pay protection. I've already paid him $5,000, and I'm trying to steer clear of him, and I need help but I just don't know what to do.

Neff raises a hearsay objection. The prosecutor invokes FRE 803(3). If the charge against Neff is extortion, what arguments and counterarguments do you expect on the admissibility of what Quade said? What if the charge against Neff is murder? If the charge were murder, would it make a difference that Neff claims self-defense?

■ NOTES ON PROVING STATE OF MIND BY FACT-LADEN STATEMENTS

1. In an extortion case, fear on the part of the victim is an element in the prosecutor's case. And his fear of defendant has *other* relevance, too, because it suggests that defendant must have done something to make the victim afraid. FRE 803(3) allows use of Quade's statement to prove his fear, but forbids use of his statement to prove Neff's behavior. The choice is to admit with a limiting instruction under FRE 105 (if requested) or exclude under FRE 403 as unfairly prejudicial. In this setting, courts usually admit the statement. See United States v. Collins, 78 F.3d 1021, 1036 (6th Cir.) (admitting statement by extortion victim indicating fear), *cert. denied*, 506 U.S. 1082 (1996).

2. If Neff were charged simply with murder, is the victim's fear still an element? The answer is No (killing can be murder regardless whether the victim was afraid). Is fear of defendant relevant? Absolutely, because it suggests that defendant did something to make him afraid, which in turn suggests that defendant had a hostile purpose or attitude toward him, which bears on the likelihood that defendant committed murder. Should the court admit Quade's statement if murder is the only charge? In this setting, most courts do *not* admit such statements. Can you see why? Fear on the victim's part is doubly relevant in extortion cases (it's an element in the charge, and it tends to prove misbehavior by the defendant), but it is only relevant in one sense in a murder case (tending to prove misbehavior by the defendant). This difference has decisive impact on balancing the risk against probative value. See Commonwealth v. Laich, 777 A.2d 1057, 1061 (Pa. 2001) (in murder trial, reversible error to admit victim's fact-laden statement indicating fear); United States v. Brown, 490 F.2d 758 (D.C. Cir. 1973) (state-of-mind exception does not generally apply to statement of fear by victim in homicide trial, especially when it describes another's conduct, unless victim's state of mind is itself an issue). And see generally C. Mueller & L. Kirkpatrick, Evidence §§8.38-8.39 (5th ed. 2012). But for another view, see Capano v. State, 781 A.2d 556, 612-615 (Del. 2001) (in kidnap-murder case, admitting statements of fear by victim as proof that she was seeking to end relationship, which tended to show motive), *cert. denied*, 536 U.S. 958 (2002).

3. In the *Shepard* case, the Supreme Court concluded that a statement by a dying wife accusing her husband of trying to kill her ("Dr. Shepard has poisoned me") did not fit the dying declaration exception, which allows proof of statements by dying persons on the cause of their coming demise. See FRE 804(b)(2) (section E3, infra). The prosecutor had another arrow for his bow, arguing that the statement should be admitted to prove Zenana Shepard's state of mind, in refutation of defendant's contention that she took her own life. But the court admitted her statement as a dying declaration, as proof that Shepard poisoned her. The Court would not go along with the state-of-mind rationale:

> The defendant had tried to show by Mrs. Shepard's declarations to her friends that she had exhibited a weariness of life and a readiness to end it, the testimony giving plausibility to the hypothesis of suicide. By proof of these declarations evincing an unhappy state of mind the defendant opened the door to the offer by the Government of declarations evincing a different state of mind, declarations consistent with the persistence of a will to live. The defendant would have no grievance if the testimony in rebuttal had been narrowed to that point. What the Government put in evidence, however, was something very different .... It will not do to say that the jury might accept the declarations for any light that they cast upon the existence of a vital urge, and reject them to the extent that they charged the death to some one else. Discrimination so subtle is a feat beyond the compass of ordinary minds. The reverberating clang of those accusatory words would drown all weaker sounds. It is for ordinary minds, and not for psychoanalysts, that the rules of evidence are framed. They have their source very often in considerations of administrative convenience, of practical expediency, and not in rules of logic. When the risk of confusion is so great as to upset the balance of advantage, the evidence goes out ....

> The testimony now questioned faced backward and not forward. This at least it did in its most obvious implications. What is even more important, it spoke to a past act, and more than that, to an act by some one not the speaker. Other tendency, if it had any, was a filament too fine to be disentangled by a jury.

Shepard v. United States, 290 U.S. 96, 103-104, 106 (1933) (Cardozo). Would *Shepard* have been different if Zenana had said, "I don't want to die from poisoned liquor"?

4. In Problem 4-K, if Neff had proof that *Quade* was making threats to kill Neff (in other words, the prosecutor had it backwards), probably such proof would be admissible. If Neff knew about such threats, it would bear on the reasonablness of his behavior in killing Quade. If Neff did not know, still the fact that Quade told others he wanted (or planned) to kill Neff would bear on the likelihood that Quade was the aggressor in the encounter that led to his death. See Allison v. United States, 160 U.S. 203, 215 (1895) (admitting communicated threats by victim against defendant); Griffin v. United States, 183 F.2d 990, 992 (D.C. Cir. 1950) (admitting victim's uncommunicated threats when self-defense is claimed and there is substantial evidence that victim attacked defendant).

COMMENT/PERSPECTIVE: Statements of Fear in the O.J. Simpson Murder Trial

In the trial of O.J. Simpson for the alleged murders of his ex-wife Nicole Brown and her friend Ronald Goldman, Judge Lance Ito excluded evidence that Brown told others she was afraid Simpson was going to kill her. To "the man or woman in the street," Judge Ito commented, such evidence has "obvious and compelling" probative worth, and it seems "only just and right" to consider the victim's own words, but courts must apply "the laws and appellate court decisions," and the California Supreme Court had given "clear guidance" in "factual situations distressingly similar" to this case. See Ruling on motion in limine, 1995 WL 21768 (Jan. 18, 1995), citing People v. Ireland, 450 P.2d 580 (Cal. 1969) (in trial of husband for murdering wife, reversible error to admit her statement to friend that she knew he was going to kill her and wished he would get it over with). Mr. Simpson was acquitted of murder, but was later found civilly liable to the Brown and Goldman families. In 2008, he was sentenced 33 years in prison for armed robbery and kidnapping, arising out of an incident in a Las Vegas hotel. Mr. Simpson had been a star running back at the University of Southern California in 1967, and then played professional football for the Buffalo Bills and San Francisco 49ers.

c. *Subsequent Conduct*

Did she embark on a journey? Her intent to go (or not to) bears on this question, and the instant exception permits use of her words to prove intent, so it is not surprising that what a person said is often admitted as proof of what she thereafter did (or did not do). If the speaker says "I'm going to drive into the city tomorrow," that is some proof that he likely drove into the city the next day, and it fits FRE 803(3) if offered for this purpose.

Two great difficulties attend this use of the exception:

One is that intent is a complicated matter. It comes to life in a tangle of understandings and beliefs about conditions in the world and the expected behavior of other people. Consequently, proof of intent often tends to prove other things as well. If Emily plans in November to take a January flight to Utah to go skiing, she likely believes or assumes there will be snow on the slopes and perhaps that discount tickets may be had and that she can stay with a friend. Proof that Emily harbored such intent, coupled with proof of even a few additional facts about her (that she is not wealthy, that she always stays in Utah with a particular friend, that she refuses to fly a certain airline), would tend not only to show that she went to Utah in January as planned but also to prove other things (that discount fares *are* available, that she has a friend with a place, that her friend is there and expects her to visit, that tickets may be had on airlines other than the one she dislikes, and so forth).

Another problem is that people often describe intent in fact-laden statements similar to those we've already looked at. Emily may speak of her plans by saying "Jan will let me stay at her house, and she's taking time off from work so we can both go skiing." Here Emily clearly intends to disclose her plans and some facts as well, including (implicitly) that she and Jan have been in touch and have agreed to get together.

The words of limitation in Rule 803(3) are once again important. The exception does not embrace "a statement of memory or belief to prove the fact remembered or believed" (except in wills cases). These words do *not* mean the exception doesn't apply to the statements described in the prior paragraph ("Jan will let me stay at her house," and so forth). Rather, these words mean that these statements can't be used to prove the acts, events, or conditions in the world that they describe—that Jan has agreed to let Emily stay with her, and so forth. The words of limitation leave room, however, for these fact-laden statements to prove the speaker's intent (she intends to visit Jan and to ski with her). Once again, if the danger is too great that a jury would misuse such words to prove that Jan is taking time off from work (and the other facts asserted), and if such misuse could make a difference in the case (because Jan's activities are important in themselves), then an objection under Rule 403 could lead to exclusion even though the words also have a proper use (to prove the mental state of the speaker).

MUTUAL LIFE INSURANCE CO. v. HILLMON

United States Supreme Court
145 U.S. 285 (1892)

[Sallie Hillmon sued Mutual Life Insurance Co. to recover $10,000 in proceeds payable under a policy on the life of her husband John Hillmon. She alleged that her husband, who was a 34-year-old cowboy and adventurer, had died in early March 1879 when accidentally shot by his companion John Brown at a campsite at Crooked Creek, Kansas, while the two were seeking out a place to start a ranch. At the same time Sallie Hillmon filed two other suits, for Hillmon had taken out two other policies on his life, each in the amount of $5,000, acquiring all of them less than four months prior to his disappearance. The three suits were consolidated for trial.

Evidence favorable to Sallie Hillmon included the deposition of Brown himself, who testified that indeed he had left Wichita with Hillmon in search of a ranch and that he did accidentally shoot Hillmon dead at Crooked Creek.

But the three insurance carriers resisted the claim, arguing that the body discovered at the campsite was not Hillmon's at all, but instead that of Adolph Walters. The defense theory was that Sallie Hillmon's suit was but the last step in a scheme by Hillmon and Brown to defraud the three carriers, and that in fact Hillmon had murdered Walters. And Brown, whose deposition supported the plaintiff, had previously signed an affidavit highly favorable to the defense position. In it Brown said that he and Hillmon had conspired to defraud the companies, that they had set out from Wichita and had thereafter met a man named "Berkley" or "Burgess" or "something like that" who joined them. Perhaps most important, Brown said that it was the latter (and not Hillmon) whose body was found at Crooked Creek, and that in fact Hillmon had fired the fatal shot.

In further support of the conspiracy theory, the defendants offered in evidence certain letters from Walters (who they claimed was the same man Brown had identified as "Berkley" or "Burgess"). In one Walters wrote to his sister in Iowa that he intended "to leave Wichita on or about March 5th, with a certain Mr. Hillmon, a sheep-trader, for Colorado or parts unknown to me." In the other, Walters wrote to his fiancée in Iowa ("Dearest Alvina," it began), indicating his intent to leave Wichita "to see a part of the country that I never expected to see when I left home, as I am going with a man by the name of Hillmon, who intends to start a sheep ranch [and has] promised me more wages than I could make at anything else."

The trial court excluded the letters, and the jury returned verdicts favorable to Sallie Hillmon against all three carriers. Defendants appealed.]

Mr. Justice GRAY . . . delivered the opinion of the Court.

This question is of the admissibility of the letters written by Walters on the first days of March, 1879, which were offered in evidence by the defendants, and excluded by the court. In order to determine the competency of these letters it is important to consider the state of the case when they were offered to be read.

The matter chiefly contested at the trial was the death of John W. Hillmon, the insured; and that depended upon the question whether the body found at Crooked Creek on the night of March 18, 1879, was his body or the body of one Walters.

Much conflicting evidence had been introduced as to the identity of the body....

The evidence that Walters was at Wichita on or before March 5th, and had not been heard from since, together with the evidence to identify as his the body found at Crooked Creek on March 18th, tended to show that he went from Wichita to Crooked Creek between those dates. Evidence that just before March 5th he had the intention of leaving Wichita with Hillmon would tend to corroborate the evidence already admitted, and to show that he went from Wichita to Crooked Creek with Hillmon. Letters from him to his family and his betrothed were the natural, if not the only attainable, evidence of his intention.

The position taken at the bar that the letters were competent evidence, ... as memoranda made in the ordinary course of business, cannot be maintained, for they were clearly not such.

But upon another ground suggested they should have been admitted. A man's state of mind or feeling can only be manifested to others by countenance, attitude, or gesture, or by sounds or words, spoken or written. The nature of the fact to be proved is the same, and evidence of its proper tokens is equally competent to prove it, whether expressed by aspect or conduct, by voice or pen. When the intention to be proved is important only as qualifying an act, its connection with that act must be shown, in order to warrant the admission of declarations of the intention. But whenever the intention is of itself a distinct and material fact in a chain of circumstances, it may be proved by contemporaneous oral or written declarations of the party. The existence of a particular intention in a certain person at a certain time being a material fact to be proved, evidence that he expressed that intention at that time is as direct evidence of the fact as his own testimony that he then had that intention would be. After his death there can hardly be any other way of proving it, and while he is still alive his own memory of his state of mind at a former time is no more likely to be clear and true than a bystander's recollection of what he then said, and is less trustworthy than letters written by him at the very time and under circumstances precluding a suspicion of misrepresentation.

The letters in question were competent not as narratives of facts communicated to the writer by others, nor yet as proof that he actually went away from Wichita, but as evidence that, shortly before the time when other evidence tended to show that he went away, he had the intention of going, and of going with Hillmon, which made it more probable both that he did go and that he went with Hillmon than if there had been no proof of such intention. In view of the mass of conflicting testimony introduced upon the question whether it was the body of Walters that was found in Hillmon's camp, this evidence might properly influence the jury in determining that question.

The rule applicable to this case has been thus stated by this court: "Wherever the bodily or mental feelings of an individual are material to be proved, the usual expressions of such feelings are original and competent evidence. Those expressions are the natural reflexes of what it might be impossible to show by other testimony. If there be such other testimony, this may be necessary to set the facts thus developed in their true light, and to give them their proper effect. As independent, explanatory, or corroborative evidence it is often indispensable to the due administration of justice. Such declarations are regarded as verbal acts, and are as competent as any other testimony, when relevant to the issue. Their truth or falsity is an inquiry for the jury." Insurance Co. v. Mosley, 8 Wall. 397, 404, 405 . . . .

Upon an indictment of one Hunter for the murder of one Armstrong at Camden, the court of errors and appeals of New Jersey unanimously held that Armstrong's oral declarations to his son at Philadelphia, on the afternoon before the night of the murder, as well as a letter written by him at the same time and place to his wife, each stating that he was going with Hunter to Camden on business, were rightly admitted in evidence. Chief Justice Beasley said:

> In the ordinary course of things, it was the usual information that a man about leaving home would communicate, for the convenience of his family, the information of his friends, or the regulation of his business. At the time it was given, such declarations could, in the nature of things, mean harm to no one. He who uttered them was bent on no expedition of mischief or wrong, and the attitude of affairs at the time entirely explodes the idea that such utterances were intended to serve any purpose but that for which they were obviously designed. If it be said that such notice of an intention of leaving home could have been given without introducing in it the name of Mr. Hunter, the obvious answer to the suggestion, I think, is that a reference to the companion who is to accompany the person leaving is as natural a part of the transaction as is any other incident or quality of it. If it is legitimate to show by a man's own declarations that he left his home to be gone a week, or for a certain destination, which seems incontestable, why may it not be proved in the same way that a designated person was to bear him company? At the time the words were uttered or written they imported no wrongdoing to any one, and the reference to the companion who was to go with him was nothing more, as matters then stood, than an indication of an additional circumstance of his going. If it was in the ordinary train of events for this man to leave word or to state where he was going, it seems to me it was equally so for him to say with whom he was going.

Hunter v. State, 40 N.J. Law, 495, 534, 536-538 (N.J. 1878).

Upon principle and authority, therefore, we are of opinion that the two letters were competent evidence of the intention of Walters at the time of writing them, which was a material fact bearing upon the question in controversy; and that for the exclusion of these letters, as well as for the undue restriction of the defendants' challenges, the verdicts must be set aside, and a new trial had . . . .

Judgment reversed, and case remanded to the circuit court, with directions to set aside the verdict and to order a new trial.

UNITED STATES v. PHEASTER

United States Court of Appeals for the Ninth Circuit
544 F.2d 353 (1976), cert. denied, 429 U.S. 1099 (1979)

[At about 9:15 P.M. on Saturday night, June 1, 1974, 16-year-old Larry Adell left his date Francine and a group of high school friends at a table in Sambo's North in Palm Springs, California, and disappeared. He had told Francine and Doug that he intended to meet "Angelo" in the parking lot to pick up some free marijuana. Larry never returned, and his family never saw him again. On the day after Larry disappeared, his father (a multimillionaire) got a phonecall making a ransom demand for $400,000 and a threat that he would never see his son alive again if he called police or the FBI. Nevertheless he did immediately contact the FBI. Three attempts to pay the ransom failed—once because delivery instructions came after the deadline had passed, once because the father wanted assurance that Larry would be released, and once because the kidnappers apparently became aware that the pickup spot was under surveillance. In the end the kidnappers cut off communications, and attempts to renew contact failed.

Angelo Inciso and another are tried on federal charges of conspiracy to kidnap and related offenses of using the mail to demand money and convey threats. At trial, Francine and Doug are permitted over defense objection to testify to Larry's description of what he planned to do. Francine testifies that when Larry picked her up that evening he told her in substance that "he was going to meet Angelo at Sambo's North at 9:30 P.M." in order to "pick up a pound of marijuana that Angelo had promised him for free." Doug testifies that Larry "made similar statements to him in the afternoon and early evening" and that on leaving the table "to go into the parking lot" Larry said "he was going to meet Angelo and he'd be right back." Francine also testifies that while with Larry on an earlier occasion she met a man named Angelo, and she identifies defendant as that man.]

RENFREW, J. [sitting by designation].

The Government's position that Larry Adell's statements can be used to prove that the meeting with Inciso did occur raises a difficult and important question concerning the scope of the so-called "*Hillmon* doctrine," a particular species of the "state of mind" exception to the general rule that hearsay evidence is inadmissible. The doctrine takes its name from the famous Supreme Court decision in Mutual Life Insurance Co. v. Hillmon, 145 U.S. 285 (1892). That the *Hillmon* doctrine should create controversy and confusion is not surprising, for it is an extraordinary doctrine. Under the state of mind exception, hearsay evidence is admissible if it bears on the state of mind of the declarant and if that state of mind is an issue in the case. For example, statements by a testator which demonstrate that he had the necessary testamentary intent are admissible to show that intent when it is in issue. The exception embodied in the *Hillmon* doctrine is fundamentally different, because it does not require that the state of mind of the declarant be an actual issue in the case. Instead, under the *Hillmon* doctrine the state of mind of the declarant is used inferentially to prove other matters which are in issue. Stated simply, the doctrine provides that when the performance of a particular act by an individual is an issue in a case, his intention (state of mind) to perform that act may be shown. From that intention, the trier of fact may draw the inference that the person carried out his intention and performed the act. Within this conceptual framework, hearsay evidence of statements by the person which tend to show his intention is deemed admissible under the state of mind exception. Inciso's objection to the doctrine concerns its application in situations in which the declarant has stated his intention to do something *with another person*, and the issue is whether he did so. There can be no doubt that the theory of the *Hillmon* doctrine is different when the declarant's statement of intention necessarily requires the action of one or more others if it is to be fulfilled.

When hearsay evidence concerns the declarant's statement of his intention to do something with another person, the *Hillmon* doctrine requires that the trier of fact infer from the state of mind of the declarant the probability of a particular act not only by the declarant but also by the other person. Several objections can be raised against a doctrine that would allow such an inference to be made. One such objection is based on the unreliability of the inference but is not, in our view, compelling.[14] A much more significant and troubling objection is based on the inconsistency of such an inference with the state of mind exception. This problem is more easily perceived when one divides what is really a compound statement into its component parts. In the instant case, the statement by Larry Adell, "I am going to meet Angelo in the parking lot to get a pound of grass," is really two statements. The first is the obvious statement of Larry's intention. The second is an implicit statement of Angelo's intention. Surely, if the meeting is to take place in a location which Angelo does not habitually frequent, one must assume that Angelo intended to meet Larry there if one is to make the inference that Angelo was in the parking lot and the meeting occurred. The important point is that the second, implicit statement has nothing to do with Larry's state of mind. For example, if Larry's friends had testified that Larry had said, "Angelo is going to be in the parking lot of Sambo's

[14] The inference from a statement of present intention that the act intended was in fact performed is nothing more than an inference. Even where no actions by other parties are necessary in order for the intended act to be performed, a myriad of contingencies could intervene to frustrate the fulfillment of the intention. The fact that the cooperation of another party is necessary if the intended act is to be performed adds another important contingency, but the difference is one of degree rather than kind. The possible unreliability of the inference to be drawn from the present intention is a matter going to the weight of the evidence which might be argued to the trier of fact, but it should not be a ground for completely excluding the admittedly relevant evidence.

North tonight with a pound of grass," no state of mind exception or any other exception to the hearsay rule would be available. Yet, this is in effect at least half of what the testimony did attribute to Larry.

Despite the theoretical awkwardness associated with the application of the *Hillmon* doctrine to facts such as those now before us, the authority in favor of such an application is impressive, beginning with the seminal *Hillmon* decision itself....

Although *Hillmon* was a civil case, the Supreme Court cited with approval a number of criminal cases in support of its decision. One of them, Hunter v. State, 11 Vroom (40 N.J.L.) 495, involved facts remarkably similar to those before us here....

The *Hillmon* doctrine has been applied by the California Supreme Court in People v. Alcalde, 24 Cal. 2d 177, 148 P.2d 627 (1944), a criminal case with facts which closely parallel those in *Hunter*. In *Alcalde* the defendant was tried and convicted of first degree murder for the brutal slaying of a woman whom he had been seeing socially. One of the issues before the California Supreme Court was the asserted error by the trial court in allowing the introduction of certain hearsay testimony concerning statements made by the victim on the day of her murder. As in the instant case, the testimony was highly incriminating, because the victim reportedly said that she was going out with Frank, the defendant, on the evening she was murdered. On appeal, a majority of the California Supreme Court affirmed the defendant's conviction, holding that *Hillmon* was "the leading case on the admissibility of declarations of intent to do an act as proof that the act thereafter was accomplished." Without purporting to "define or summarize all the limitations or restrictions upon the admissibility of" such evidence, the court did mention several prudential considerations not unlike those mentioned by Chief Justice Beasley in *Hunter*. Thus, the declarant should be dead or otherwise unavailable, and the testimony concerning his statements should be relevant and possess a high degree of trustworthiness. The court also noted that there was other evidence from which the defendant's guilt could be inferred. Applying these standards, the court found no error in the trial court's admission of the disputed hearsay testimony. "Unquestionably the deceased's statement of her intent and the logical inference to be drawn therefrom, namely, that she was with the defendant that night, were relevant to the issue of the guilt of the defendant."

In addition to the decisions in *Hillmon* and *Alcalde*, support for the Government's position can be found in the California Evidence Code and the new Federal Rules of Evidence, although in each instance resort must be made to the comments to the relevant provisions.

Section 1250 of the California Evidence Code carves out an exception to the general hearsay rule for statements of a declarant's "then existing mental or physical state." The *Hillmon* doctrine is codified in Section 1250(2) which allows the use of such hearsay evidence when it "is offered to prove or explain acts or conduct of the declarant." The comment to Section 1250(2) states that, "Thus, a statement of the declarant's intent to do certain acts is admissible to prove that he did those acts." Although neither the language of the statute nor that of the comment specifically addresses the particular issue now before us, the comment does cite the *Alcalde* decision and, therefore, indirectly rejects the limitation urged by Inciso.

Although the new Federal Rules of Evidence were not in force at the time of the trial below, we refer to them for any light that they might shed on the status of the common law at the time of the trial. The codification of the state of mind exception in Rule 803(3) does not provide a direct statement of the *Hillmon* doctrine . . . . Although Rule 803(3) is silent regarding the *Hillmon* doctrine, both the Advisory Committee on the Proposed Rules and the House Committee on the Judiciary specifically addressed the doctrine. After noting that Rule 803(3) would not allow the admission of statements of memory, the Advisory Committee stated broadly that

> The rule of *Mutual Life Ins. Co. v. Hillmon* [citation omitted] allowing evidence of intention as tending to prove the doing of the act intended, is, of course, left undisturbed.

Significantly, the Notes of the House Committee on the Judiciary regarding Rule 803(3) are far more specific and revealing:

> However, the Committee intends that the Rule be construed to limit the doctrine of *Mutual Life Insurance Co. v. Hillmon* [citation omitted] so as to render statements of intent by a declarant admissible *only to prove his future conduct, not the future conduct of another person* (emphasis added).

Although the matter is certainly not free from doubt, we read the note of the Advisory Committee as presuming that the *Hillmon* doctrine would be incorporated in full force, including necessarily the application in *Hillmon* itself. The language suggests that the Advisory Committee presumed that such a broad interpretation was the prevailing common law position. The notes of the House Committee on the Judiciary are significantly different. The language used there suggests a legislative intention to cut back on what that body also perceived to be the prevailing common law view, namely, that the *Hillmon* doctrine could be applied to facts such as those now before us.

Although we recognize the force of the objection to the application of the *Hillmon* doctrine in the instant case,[18] we cannot conclude that the district court erred in allowing the testimony concerning Larry Adell's statements to be introduced . . . .

For the reasons set out above, we affirm the convictions.

---

[18] Criticism of the *Hillmon* doctrine has come from very distinguished quarters, both judicial and academic. However, the position of the judicial critics is definitely the minority position, stated primarily in dicta and dissent. In his opinion for the Court in Shepard v. United States, 290 U.S. 96 (1933), Justice Cardozo indicated in dicta an apparent hostility to the *Hillmon* doctrine . . . . [appearing to suggest] that the *Hillmon* doctrine is limited to "suits upon insurance policies," although the cases cited by the Court in *Hillmon* refute that sug-

■ NOTES ON STATE OF MIND AS PROOF OF CONDUCT

1. *Hillmon* is on firm footing in recognizing that what someone says he intends to do can be critical in figuring out what he actually did. Courts regularly admit out-of-court statements for this purpose. Particularly vivid are cases that admit statements indicating an intent to kill someone (like Neff's statements to Quade in Problem 4-K). The state-of-mind exception is not necessary when such statements are made by defendants in murder trials (they come in as admissions), but similar statements by others are sometimes important, and the state-of-mind exception paves the way. See, e.g., State v. Yarbrough, 767 N.E.2d 216, 224-225 (Ohio 2002) (in trial of *Y* for murdering *A* on behalf of *D*, admitting *D*'s statement that "he'd have [*A*] killed or kill her himself"), *cert. denied*, 537 U.S. 1023. Also vivid are homicide cases admitting statements by a victim (later killed) describing an intent to break off a relationship with the defendant, to show that the victim acted on her intent, proving what became the motive for the crime. See, e.g., State v. Robinson, 903 P.3d 1289 (Haw. 1995) (admitting statements by murder victim, once to her friend, and once to both the friend and the defendant, that she wanted to break off her relationship with defendant).

2. In *Hillmon*, the Court says Walters's intent was "a distinct and material fact" even though it was *not* an ultimate issue (the question was whose body was at Crooked Creek). The Court describes contemporaneous expressions (letters to sister and fiancée) as "direct evidence" of intent. The Court also says

---

gestion. The decision in *Shepard* was relied upon by Justice Traynor of the California Supreme Court in his vigorous dissent from the decision reached by the majority in *People v. Alcalde*. Justice Traynor argued that the victim's declarations regarding her meeting with Frank could not be used to "induce the belief that the defendant went out with the deceased, took her to the scene of the crime and there murdered her . . . without setting aside the rule against hearsay." Any other legitimate use of the declaration, in his opinion, was so insignificant that it was outweighed by the enormous prejudice to the defendant in allowing the jury to hear it. Finally, the exhaustive analysis of a different, but related, hearsay issue by the Court of Appeals for the District of Columbia in United States v. Brown, 490 F.2d 758 (D.C. Cir. 1974), provides inferential support for the position urged by Inciso. The issue in that case was the admissibility of hearsay testimony concerning a victim's extrajudicial declarations that he was "[f]rightened that he may be killed" by the defendant. After surveying the relevant cases, the court stated a "synthesis" of the governing principles. One of the cases which was criticized by the court was the decision of the California Supreme Court in People v. Merkouris, 52 Cal. 2d 672, 344 P.2d 1 (1959), a case relied upon by the Government in the instant case. The court in *Merkouris* held that hearsay testimony showing the victim's fear of the defendant could properly be admitted to show the probable identity of the killer. The court in *Brown* expressed the following criticism of that holding, a criticism which might also apply to the application of the *Hillmon* doctrine in the instant case:

> Such an approach violates the fundamental safeguards necessary to the use of such testimony [citation omitted]. Through a circuitous series of inferences, the court reverses the effect of the statement so as to reflect on *defendant's* intent and actions rather than the state of mind of the declarant (victim). This is the very result that it is hoped the limiting instruction will prevent.

490 F.2d at 771 (emphasis in original).

For a frequently cited academic critique of the *Hillmon* doctrine, see Maguire, The *Hillmon* Case—Thirty-Three Years After, 38 Harv. L. Rev. 709 (1925).

the letters tended to show Walters "had the intention of going, and of going with Hillmon, which made it more probable both that he did go and that he went with Hillmon." Does that mean Walters' letters can prove what Hillmon did? Consider the fact that everyone agreed that Hillmon was at Crooked Creek: Plaintiff claimed the body was Hillmon's, and the carriers claimed Hillmon killed Walters there. Thus it wasn't necessary to reach the question whether letters from Walters could prove what Hillmon did.

3. *Pheaster* forced the court to confront the question that could be slid by in *Hillmon.* Could the spoken intent of one person (Larry Adell) prove what another did thereafter (Angelo Inciso)? *Pheaster* went to trial before the Rules were adopted, and the reviewing court invoked common law tradition "for any light" it might shed on the Rules. It is hard to tell whether *Pheaster* meant to *contrast* what would happen before the Rules took effect with what must happen now, or to *incorporate tradition* into the Rules in concluding that nothing has changed.

4. Before any factfinder can take letters that Walters wrote on Monday as proof of what Hillmon did on Wednesday, and *before* it can take statements by Adell at 8:00 P.M. as proof of what Angelo did at 9:30 P.M., the factfinder must draw inferences about what Walters and Adell must have done before they wrote or spoke. The trier would have to infer that the speaker had conferred with the other person and that the two had agreed to do something together (travel west, meet in the parking lot). In stating that the exception does not embrace statements of "memory or belief to prove the fact remembered or believed," FRE 803(3) is addressing those very inferences. One might try to reconcile use of statements of intent referring to other events through limiting instructions. If a brother writes to his sister saying "I'm taking Amtrak to Chicago tomorrow," perhaps we could admit his letter as proof that the brother went to Chicago the next day and took the train, but not as proof that Amtrak *actually ran* such a train. But if the real question is whether Amtrak ran the train, this approach doesn't solve anything, and if the real question is whether the brother went to Chicago, a limiting instruction wouldn't be important.

5. In *Pheaster*, there seems to have been no other evidence that Angelo went to the parking lot at Sambo's that night. Often there is independent evidence that the two people mentioned in a statement actually met, and courts have seized on this point as important. Post-*Pheaster* cases say state-of-mind statements can prove a later meeting between the speaker and another if there is additional evidence of such a meeting. Compare United States v. Nersesian, 824 F.2d 1294, 1325 (2d Cir. 1987) (to prove *M* was in a drug conspiracy, admitting statement by *A* that he planned "to see other people with my kind of brochure," coupled with evidence that *A* and *M* then met in a restaurant, where "brochure" referred to drugs; statements of "intention or future plans" are admissible against another person "when they are linked with independent evidence that corroborates the declaration") with United States v. Delvecchio, 816 F.2d 859, 862-863 (2d Cir. 1987) (error to admit statement by third person describing his intent to meet defendant and another on May 11th, absent independent evidence that defendant went to meeting). See also People v. James,

717 N.E.2d 1052, 1060 (N.Y. 1999) (statement of intent to act with others may be admitted if declarant is unavailable, statement "unambiguously contemplates some *future* action by the declarant," any past arrangement indicated by the statement was apparently made in recent past, and there is "independent evidence of reliability" and proof that "the intended future acts were at least likely to have actually taken place"). For a modern case *refusing* to admit statements by the victim indicating her intent (or expectation) to meet defendant, see Camm v. State, 908 N.E.2d 215, 226-227 (Ind. 2009) (in *D*'s trial for murdering wife *K*, error to admit friend's testimony that *K* said she expected *D* home at 7:30; exception did not allow use of *K*'s statement to prove *D*'s later actions; *K* "could not know the defendant's plans without perceiving and remembering some past fact—something the defendant (or some other person) said or did to indicate that he would arrive home at that time") (reversing).

6. Some decisions construing state rules still admit statements by one person to prove what another did with the speaker. States can adopt their own rules, and can adopt identical counterparts to FRE 803(3) *without* deferring to federal authority or history, and can assign to their own rules their own ideas about proper application. See State v. Atwood, 988 A.2d 981, 986 (Me. 2010) (in murder trial, admitting evidence that victim told others she would go to Arizona with defendant on day she disappeared; state-of-mind exception "applies to statements made by the declarant regarding the declarant's beliefs about the involvement of other people in the declarant's future plan" if they "cast light upon the future" and are "highly reliable and highly relevant"); Lisle v. State, 941 P.2d 459, 467-468 (Nev. 1997) (in trial of *J* and *K* for murdering *L*, admitting *L*'s statement, made several hours before he was killed, that he was going out with "Vatos" to get drugs and would be back in 15 minutes) ("Vatos" is what *L* called *K* and *J*), *cert. denied*, 525 U.S. 830 (1998). On the problem of using statements of intent to prove what others did, see Lynn McLain, "I'm Going to Dinner With Frank"; Admissibility of Nontestimonial Statements of Intent to Prove the Actions of Someone Other than the Speaker—And the Role of the Due Process Clause, 32 Cardozo L. Rev. 373 (2010).

7. In *Shepard*, which is quoted in the Notes following Problem 4-K ("He Says He'll Kill Me"), Justice Cardozo tried to build a dike to contain the *Hillmon* doctrine:

> There are times when a state of mind, if relevant, may be proved by contemporaneous declarations of feeling or intent. . . . [I]n suits upon insurance policies, declarations by an insured that he intends to go upon a journey with another, may be evidence of a state of mind lending probability to the conclusion that the purpose was fulfilled. *Hillmon.* The ruling in that case marks the high water line beyond which courts have been unwilling to go. It has developed a substantial body of criticism and commentary. Declarations of intention, casting light upon the future, have been sharply distinguished from declarations of memory, pointing backwards to the past. There would be an end, or nearly that, to the rule against hearsay if the distinction were ignored.

Shepard v. United States, 290 U.S. 96, 104-106 (1933). Why would there be "an end" to the hearsay doctrine ("or nearly that") if statements of memory could be admitted to prove the fact believed? After *Pheaster*, does lake spill over the dike?

Who Is Buried in Hillmon's Grave?

John Hillmon
National Archives and Records Administration, Kansas City, MO. Courtesy of Marianne Wesson

The question who is buried in Hillmon's grave presents one of the great mysteries in American evidence law. If it is John Hillmon, the insurance carriers unjustly resisted Sallie Hillmon's claim, leading to six trials and two appeals to the Supreme Court over 25 years. If it is Adolph Walters, the carriers were justified in resisting her claims, and Hillmon likely committed insurance fraud and murder. The letter Walters sent to his fiancée Alvina Kasten was persuasive evidence: When he wrote of going someplace he "never expected to see" with a man named Hillmon, perhaps the prediction included eternity. He was never seen or heard from again. But then neither was Hillmon. One scholar suggests that the insurance carrier fabricated Walter's letter and manipulated evidence. See Marianne Wesson, *"Remarkable Stratagems and Conspiracies": How Unscrupulous Lawyers and Credulous Judges Created an Exception to the Hearsay Rule*, 76 Fordham L. Rev. 1675 (2007) (tentatively concluding that the man in the grave is Hillmon). Professor Wesson unearthed the bones seeking a DNA sample to compare with one from a descendant of Hillmon, but groundwater had bleached away the DNA. A forensic anthropologist at the University of Colorado examined photos presented in the *Hillmon* trials and thinks the corpse was *not* Walters and was probably Hillmon. See Dennis Van Gerven, *A Digital Photographic Solution to the Question of Who Lies Buried in Oak Hill Cemetery* (Feb. 13, 2007), at http://www.thehillmoncase.com/results.html. See also Wesson, A Death at Crooked Creek: The Case of the Cowboy, the Cigarmaker and the Love Letter (NYU Press, 2013); Douglas McFarland, Dead Men Tell Tales: Thirty Times Three Years of the Judicial Process After *Hillmon*, 30 Vill. L. Rev. 1 (1985).

Adolph Walters
National Archives and Records Administration, Kansas City, MO. Courtesy of Marianne Wesson

V=Virginia found shot at home. Knife found close to body.

■ PROBLEM 4-L. Fright Points the Finger

Donald is tried for the murder of Virginia, who is found shot in the living room of their home. A kitchen knife is found on the floor close to her body, and the gun that fired the fatal shot is recovered. There is testimony from neighbors that their relationship had been stormy, punctuated with loud fights and occasional violence. Other evidence points toward Donald's guilt, all of it is circumstantial. The prosecutor wants to offer the following proofs to bolster his case:

(1) Several weeks before her death Virginia told her neighbor, "I'm afraid Donald is going to kill me";
(2) Days before her death Virginia told her neighbor, "I'm going to take the train to Denver to stay with mother for a while";
(3) A few months before her death Virginia left home temporarily and took refuge in a shelter for battered women.

Should these items be excluded as hearsay? Does the state-of-mind exception apply?

■ NOTES ON STATEMENTS AND BEHAVIOR BY MURDER VICTIMS INDICATING FEAR

1. Recall Problem 4-K ("He Says He'll Kill Me") and the Notes following, which make the point that the victim's fear of the defendant is an element in an extortion case, but not in a murder case. Still, such fear is relevant in a murder case. Fear suggests that defendant acted in a hostile or threatening manner, making it more likely (when she was killed) that defendant did it. Recall Problem 2-E (The Battered Wife), another "Donald and Virginia" scenario, where her flight to the woman's shelter could be taken as proof of his hostile behavior, hence as indicating that he intentionally killed her in the altercation leading to her death. Consider now Virginia's words and behavior here. We know in the answers for the first and third proofs. Start with these, and then consider the second item:

(a) The first proof ("I'm afraid Donald is going to kill me") would normally be excluded. It invites the inference forbidden by FRE 803(3)—the inference into the past that Donald threatened her or acted in a hostile manner. The answer might change if, for example, Donald claimed self-defense. Then proving that Virginia feared him would suggest that she didn't attack him in the encounter leading to her death, achieving greater relevancy. Courts would likely admit her statement in this situation.

(b) The third proof (Virginia left home and took refuge in a battered women's shelter) would be admitted. It too shows that she feared Donald; it too suggests that he did something to make her afraid (threat or hostile behavior). There is no need to worry about hearsay because the conduct is nonassertive and the two-step inference is proper (behavior suggests fear; fear suggests past actions by Donald making Virginia afraid).

(c) The second proof (Virginia told her neighbor she was going to "take the train to Denver to stay with mother") is in the middle. Unlike the first proof ("I'm afraid Donald is going to kill me"), her statement of intent points forward, and it is just such statements that FRE 803(3) normally reaches. Unlike the third proof (flight to the shelter), her statement is an assertion that brings risks that the hearsay doctrine is designed to deal with. If we could infer from her statement of intent that she left (and leaving reflected fear, not just a desire to visit mother), then it would be proper to infer from her leaving that Donald had done something wrong, and the second proof would be similar to the third (admissible). But if we can only draw that inference from the statement itself, the second proof looks more like the first and the inference is not proper (so exclude). If Virginia had not only talked to her neighbor, but actually bought a train ticket, it would be easier to admit the second proof. In short, the second proof presents the hardest issue.

2. Soon you will encounter the forfeiture exception in FRE 804(b)(6). There you will learn that a defendant who kills or frightens off a witness may lose the protection of both the hearsay doctrine and the Confrontation Clause when it comes to statements by that witness, but only if the defendant acted with the purpose of preventing the witness from testifying. If that sort of thing was going on here—if Donald was trying to keep Virginia from testifying against him in, for example, an abuse prosecution, then her statements could be admitted under the forfeiture exception. See Chapter 4E6, infra.

d. Facts About Declarant's Will

In a convoluted way, FRE 803(3) creates what might be treated as a separate exception for statements about declarant's will. (The language generally bars use of the exception to prove a "fact remembered or believed," but this restriction does not apply to statements relating to the validity or terms of "declarant's will," so the exception *can* be used to prove this particular sort of "fact remembered or believed.")

Putting this matter in the state-of-mind exception may be defended on the ground that the mental state of the testator is paramount in wills cases. Admitting what he has said on the subject makes sense because (1) he is likely to be well informed on the subject, (2) he is likely to be dead when the matter is litigated, suggesting a strong need for evidence of what he has said, and (3) his views on the subject may be as trustworthy as live testimony by interested parties disputing the disposition of the estate.

3. Statements for Medical Treatment

When a person seeks treatment from a physician, life and health may hang in the balance. There is good reason to believe that he will be careful and accurate in describing his symptoms to his doctor and telling her what he thinks caused them. Hence Rule 803(4) recognizes an exception for such statements. Note three things: First, the exception requires that the purpose of the speaker is to obtain medical diagnosis or treatment (the statement must be made "for" such purposes). Second, the statement must be "reasonably pertinent" to one of these ends. Third, the exception reaches accounts of "past" and "present" symptoms and sensations, as well as "medical history" and accounts of the "inception" or "general cause" of symptoms or sensations.

■ PROBLEM 4-M. Where Did She Fall?

On leaving Hagen Grill in Chicago after dining with friends one evening, Doris Welsh felt woozy. The next thing she knew, she awakened in a bed in nearby Emmanuel Hospital. Treating physician Paul Thorne found that Welsh was suffering from a broken hip and dislocated shoulder, apparently from a bad fall. Welsh sued Hagen Grill, alleging that a defect in the stairs leading out of the restaurant had caused her to fall. Measurements indicated that the height of risers in the stairs was $8\frac{3}{4}$ inches, almost two inches more than the standard 7 inches.

Welsh didn't remember how she got to the emergency room, but a passerby named Greg Shaw called 911 on his cellphone. After an ambulance arrived, Shaw accompanied Welsh in the ambulance to the hospital. Consider the following proffers:

(1) For plaintiff, the ambulance driver would testify that "Ms. Welsh was unconscious when he first arrived, but as she came to she complained of excruciating pain in her hip and right shoulder."

(2) Asked by plaintiff's counsel whether Welsh said anything about how it happened, Dr. Thorne would testify "She told me that she'd fallen on the stairs in the restaurant."

(3) For defendant, the hospital intake specialist would testify that "Mr. Shaw brought Ms. Welsh to the ER, and told me he saw her trip on the sidewalk in the park near the plaza east of Hagen Grill."

On proper objection, should the ambulance driver, Thorne and the intake nurse be allowed to testify as indicated? Do their statements fit FRE 803(4)?

NOTES ON THE MEDICAL STATEMENTS EXCEPTION

1. The medical statements exception in FRE 803(4) envisions statements by patients to doctors, but the exception does not actually say that the patient must be the speaker or the statement must be made to a doctor. Most courts conclude that the exception embraces at least some statements by Good Samaritans like Greg Shaw in Problem 4-M, and by parents speaking on behalf of their children in seeking medical care. See Kelly v. Haralampopoulos by Haralampopoulos, 327 P.3d 255 (Colo. 2014) (statement by patient's "then-roommate and ex-girlfriend"); Lawson v. Kreative Child Care Center, Inc., 2006 WL 245928 (Mich. App. 2006) (key to admitting statements by Good Samaritan is purpose of speaker and relationship to patient; parent's statement on behalf of child patient fits exception). But see McKinley v. Casson, 80 A.3d 618, 625 (Del. 2013) (excluding statements by bystanders describing accident; they "did not give their statements for the purpose of receiving medical treatment themselves"). Most courts also say the exception reaches statements to persons other than doctors, like the intake specialist in Problem 4-M, or to nurses or physician assistants, or others involved in patient care. See Hornaday Transp., LLC v. Fluellen, 116 So. 3d 236 (Ala. App. 2012) (exception applies to "statements made to anyone whose participation or involvement is necessary in the process of diagnosis or treatment, including hospital attendants, or even members of the family").

2. Part of what Greg Shaw told the intake specialist (Welsh tripped "on the sidewalk in the park") and part of what Welsh told the doctor ("she'd fallen down the stairs of a restaurant") are problematic. Rule FRE 803(4) reaches only statements "pertinent to" diagnosis or treatment. One might think a doctor would want to know whether the patient tripped or fell, and it is humanly difficult to describe such events without saying things like "on the sidewalk" or "on the stairs." Hence it is natural to include information referring to the place. But where the location of an accident bears directly on major questions, courts usually reject such statements. See, e.g., Rock v. Huffco Gas & Oil Co., 922 F.2d 272, 277-278 (5th Cir. 1991) (refusing to consider doctor's report that claimant twisted ankle on rusted-out step and slipped on grease in galley). Recall Problem 4-J ("I Felt This Sudden Pain"), but this time assume that Eldon Sanders went straight to Dr. Hillier's office and told *him* what happened ("I felt this sudden pain just a few minutes ago when I had to lift one of those 30-gallon cans out on the Chase"). Here too (employee suing employer), where the accident occurred is the critical fact, and courts would likely exclude this part of what Sanders said.

3. Suppose Doris Welsh had told Dr. Thorne that she'd fallen on the stairs "because the risers weren't the right height and the stairs were dangerous." The ACN comments that FRE 803(4) does not reach statements of "fault" and would not apply to a patient's statement that the car that hit him "was driven through a red light," so such a statement by Doris Welsh would certainly be excluded.

4. How about statements *by physicians?* The exception should reach statements by one physician to another about the patient, if made in diagnosing or treating the patient, inasmuch as medical care involves multiple caregivers working together, sharing information, subject to professional standards. But courts disagree on this point. Compare O'Gee v. Dobbs Houses, Inc., 570 F.2d 1084, 1088-1089 (2d Cir. 1978) (approving testimony by consulting physician reciting what patient told him that other doctors told her, where physician made it clear that he was also relying on actual reports by the doctors) with Field v. Trigg County Hosp., Inc., 386 F.3d 729 (6th Cir. 2004) (in malpractice case, error to admit defendant doctor's testimony describing phone conversations with other doctors who treated plaintiff). And courts have been reluctant to apply the exception to statements by physicians to personal injury claimants, perhaps for the reason that doing so would enable plaintiff's to get in their doctor's opinions without calling them as witnesses. See Sibbing v. Cave, 922 N.E.2d 594, 597 (Ind. 2010) (error to let plaintiff suing for injuries in car accident testify to what her doctor told her about the cause of her pain; statements by healthcare providers to patient don't share the "enhanced indicia of reliability" that come with patient statements to doctors) (harmless).

BLAKE v. STATE

Supreme Court of Wyoming
933 P.2d 474 (Wyo. 1997)

LEHMAN, Justice.

David Alfred Blake (Blake) was convicted of two counts of second degree sexual assault of his stepdaughter . . . .

Responding to a report of alleged sexual abuse of a sixteen-year-old girl, an investigator from the Department of Family Services (DFS), together with an officer from the sheriff's office, interviewed the victim at a local high school. Following the interview, the victim was transported to the hospital emergency room for medical examination. During the course of the examination, and in response to questions by Dr. Mary Bowers, the victim stated that she had been forcibly subjected to sexual intercourse by her stepfather, Blake, numerous times over the previous several years . . . .

At trial, neither the State nor Blake called the victim to the witness stand. The State relied upon Blake's typed confession, Dr. Bowers' testimony, testimony of the nurse who assisted Dr. Bowers in the examination of the victim, testimony by the DFS investigator, testimony by the officer who interviewed the victim, and testimony by the officer who interviewed and obtained a confession from Blake. Over a continuing objection by defense counsel, the district court allowed Dr. Bowers to testify concerning what the victim stated to her during the sexual assault examination, including the victim's statements identifying Blake as the sexual assault perpetrator, pursuant to WRE 803(4) [which is identical to

FRE 803(4)—Eds.]. The jury returned a verdict of guilty, convicting Blake of two counts of second degree sexual assault. Blake timely appeals . . . .

We acknowledge the general rule that statements attributing fault or identity usually are not admissible under rules identical to WRE 803(4). Goldade v. State, 674 P.2d 721, 725 (Wyo. 1983). However, we have held that in situations involving physical or sexual abuse of children, statements made by a child victim to a medical professional may be admitted.[2] Statements of identification in child abuse cases are admitted because of the special character of diagnosis and treatment in sexual abuse cases.

This court first had occasion to address this issue in *Goldade.* In that case, we upheld the admission of statements by a child victim to the treating physician under WRE 803(4). In so holding, we noted that child abuse is a unique and special problem encompassing more than physical injury. The State has expressed special concern for that problem in Wyoming's child protection statutes, and physicians and other medical personnel play a special role in detecting and dealing with the problem of child abuse.

In *Stephens* [v. State, 774 P.2d 60 (Wyo. 1989)], we emphasized that a proper foundation is essential to justify admission of identity statements under WRE 803(4). We cited with approval the two-part test set forth in United States v. Renville, 779 F.2d 430 (8th Cir. 1985), which encompasses the foundation requirement. The *Renville* test requires that, first, the declarant's motive in making the statement is consistent with the purposes of promoting treatment or diagnosis and, second, that the content of the statement is reasonably relied on by a physician in treatment or diagnosis. Because the case was remanded for a new trial, we did not decide whether the statements in *Stephens* were admissible.

More recently, this court applied the *Renville* test in *Betzle* [v. State, 847 P.2d 1010 (Wyo. 1993)] and *Owen* [v. State, 902 P.2d 60 (Wyo. 1995)]. In both those cases, we upheld the admission of hearsay testimony of an expert witness as to the identity of the perpetrator under the WRE 803(4) exception, finding the two-part test was met.

Our inquiry now turns to whether in this case the requirements of the *Renville* two-part test were fulfilled. At trial, Dr. Bowers testified as follows:

Q. What was the purpose of the examination?

A. The purpose of the examination was to provide health care because of an alleged sexual assault.

[2] [Court reports that "an overwhelming majority of jurisdictions, including at least 32 states and four federal circuits," admit statements by victims identifying the perpetrator in child physical or sexual assault cases. Many invoke the medical statements exception, but several jurisdictions admit such statements only in cases "where the perpetrator is a member of the immediate household or a relative, close family friend, or babysitter."]

Q. Did you perform any specific examination on her?
A. Yeah. I performed a comprehensive physical examination on her, including a pelvic examination . . . .
Q. Okay. Could you please just describe generally what you normally would do, what you normally do, the procedure you normally follow in a rape kit examination.
A. The kit itself has specific instructions for the health care provider; and I usually begin by explaining what the purpose of the examination is to the patient and by taking a history from that patient about what has happened to them so that I can properly use the kit, collect specimens, so that I can also provide appropriate medical care . . . .
Q. Could you describe [victim's] condition at the time?
A. [Victim] was a very—very subdued, very quiet young lady. She was—we use the term "in no acute distress." She wasn't medically unstable; but she was quite withdrawn, seemed somewhat exhausted . . . .
Q. All right. Now, during the course of your examination did you have an opportunity to ask [victim] any questions?
A. Before proceeding with the exam, I asked her a number of questions to help direct my exam and determine what might be appropriate.
Q. Okay. Generally speaking, what types of questions would you have asked?
A. I ask general questions about what kinds of assault she may have been subjected to, what kind of sexual contact may have occurred, what she remembers of what had occurred, whether or not—whether or not she was aware of body fluids present in her, whether or not she had had any symptoms of vaginal discharge, itching, abdominal pain that might represent sexually-transmitted disease, what parts of her body had been violated.
Q. What is the purpose in asking those questions?
A. To determine where to collect certain kinds of specimens, what kinds of bacteriology studies to do, what kinds of treatment might be necessary to care for her and keep her healthy, restore her to health if she's ill . . . .
Q. Do you recall what the first question was that you asked her [victim]?
A. I asked her the nature of the assault, what had transpired that brought her to the emergency room.
Q. Okay. And why did you need to know that?
A. It was important for me to understand as a physician what her emotional state was; and I explained to her that I wanted to help her, that—because this is invariably an unpleasant experience, and I wanted to find out exactly why she was there.
Q. Was it important for your purposes of diagnosis or treatment?
A. It certainly is important. Who the alleged assailant might be in a sexual assault determines frequently the extent to which testing and treatment is given.
Q. In asking that question, what did she say?
A. She told me that she had been subjected to sexual intercourse forcibly by her stepfather numerous times over the previous several years.

Q. What did you ask her next?

A. I asked her when the most recent episode had been and what had happened, under what circumstances and if there was physical trauma. . . .

Q. How did she respond?

A. She responded that approximately a week prior to that she had been forced to the floor of the bathroom in their home and had had forcible genital sexual intercourse with her stepfather.

We conclude that the State laid the proper foundation and that the elements of the *Renville* two-part test were satisfied. The victim was examined by Dr. Bowers as a result of an investigation into allegations that she had been sexually abused. Dr. Bowers testified that in a rape kit examination, she takes a history from the patient about what has happened so as to properly collect specimens and provide appropriate medical care. The doctor also described the importance of understanding a victim's emotional state in a sexual assault case. The victim's statements were consistent with the purposes for which Dr. Bowers became involved with the victim, that is, to perform tests and treat the victim as necessary. Dr. Bowers' testimony indicates that she relied on the victim's account of the circumstances surrounding the sexual assault, including the abuser's identity, to determine how to properly treat the victim.

Blake asserts that because the victim was seventeen at the time of trial, her statements lack the reliability of statements made by a younger victim. Blake attempts to distinguish *Goldade*, *Betzle* and *Owen* on the ground that the victims in those cases were much younger than the victim here. We find no merit in this argument. The age of a child and her personal characteristics go toward the weight of the hearsay statements rather than their admissibility. United States v. George, 960 F.2d 97, 100 (9th Cir. 1992). Blake had the opportunity to attack the credibility of the victim but chose not to do so. The district court did not abuse its discretion by admitting the victim's hearsay statements into evidence pursuant to WRE 803(4). . . .

[The court rejects challenge to Dr. Bowers' testimony under the pre-*Crawford* interpretation of the Confrontation Clause, finding the medical statements exception to be firmly rooted. It also finds that the state adequately proved that defendant was in a "position of authority" in the home of the victim. The court affirms the conviction.]

NOTES ON THE MEDICAL STATEMENTS EXCEPTION IN ABUSE CASES

1. Problem 4-M (Where Did She Fall?) illustrates a traditional use of the medical statements exception (patient describing pain to medical service provider), but *Blake* exemplifies a common modern use. Almost all such cases are tried in state court under state versions of the exception, but state and federal decisions mostly do the same thing in this area. In construing the Wyoming provision, *Blake* cites the federal decision in *Renville* and follows its two-part standard under which declarant's motive must be "consistent with" obtaining treatment and the content of the statement must indicate that reliance would be reasonable. It looks as though Dr. Bowers was aware of the requirements of the exception. Her testimony was tailor-made to insure that her young patient's statements would be admitted. Are you satisfied that her questions to the victim, and her answers, satisfy *Renville*? Consider this argument favoring the broad approach, advanced by Justice Castille in a Pennsylvania case:

> Child abuse . . . is one of the most devastating social ailments afflicting our society and the injuries suffered by an abused child differ dramatically from the types of injuries normally encompassed by the medical treatment exception to the hearsay rule. While most injuries are purely somatic, child abuse cases also often involve deep emotional and psychological injuries. In order to effectively treat child abuse victims, physicians must be attentive not only to the child's emotional and psychological injuries which result from this crime, but they must also take care to ensure the safety of the child when he or she is released from the physician's care, often back to the abusive situation that gave rise to the original injury. Effective treatment can only be provided for the child's physical and psychic injuries if the physician knows the identity of the abuser, especially when the abuser resides with the victim.

Justice Castille also addressed the question whether a youthful patient (five years old) is motivated to seek treatment:

> While the child's motive here may not be readily apparent, a young child is generally aware of the emotional and physical pain that she is suffering and is able to comprehend that she is receiving medical treatment to alleviate that suffering. Moreover, there is nothing in the record to suggest an ulterior motive for the child to make the statement to the nurse other than to receive medical treatment.

Commonwealth v. Smith, 681 A.2d 1288, 1293 (Pa. 1996) (dissenting opinion). See also State v. Mendez, 242 P.3d 328, 342 (N.M. 2010) (with most states, New Mexico considers statements identifying perpetrator as pertinent to diagnosis or treatment where important to separate declarant from abuser); White v. Illinois, 502 U.S. 346 (1992) (in statement to doctor, child identified assailant; court assumes exception applies).

2. From the standpoint of applying the medical statements exception, there are two serious problems in the broad view:

(a) First, recall the ACN's comment that "statements as to fault" do not ordinarily qualify. Mindful of this problem, an early case applying the exception in an abuse case stressed that the child described the abuse itself, not identifying the abuser, see United States v. Iron Shell, 633 F.2d 77, 84 (8th Cir. 1980) (identity of assailant was not in issue; statements were about "what happened

rather than who assaulted her"), but modern cases have abandoned this concern.

(b) Second, concepts like "diagnosis" and "treatment" do not normally embrace steps like removing a child from an abusive home, and doctors (main audience for statements offered under the exception) are not experts in such remedies. In Commonwealth v. Smith, 681 A.2d 1288 (Pa. 1996) (opinion generating dissent by Justice Castille quoted above), the majority concluded that a statement by five-year-old Priscilla naming her father as the one who put her in a bathtub containing scalding hot water did not satisfy the medical exception (the father claimed he was asleep on the couch when she got into the tub, and he was running cold water when the mother found the two in the bathroom). Here is the majority's view on the point:

> We fail to see how the identity of the perpetrator of the physical abuse was pertinent to the treatment of Priscilla's scalding burns. What difference would it have made to the treatment of the burns whether a total stranger inflicted the burns or a close family relative? The Commonwealth simply fails to demonstrate that the identity of the abuser is pertinent to medical treatment. [Court collects cases.] The Commonwealth argues that the statement as to identity of the perpetrator of abuse is of significance for psychological and emotional treatment of the victim as well as for the protection of the child from future abuse . . . . [W]e acknowledge that this goal is of utmost importance; however, this acknowledgement does not make the statements at issue admissible under the medical treatment exception. Protection from future abuse, as such, does not constitute medical treatment or diagnosis.
>
> The Commonwealth's argument that the statement as to identity of a perpetrator is relevant to psychological and emotional treatment of the child is, at first blush, inviting. However, "[a]s a general rule all statements made in this context [of psychological treatment], regardless of their content, are relevant to diagnosis or treatment since experts in the field view everything relating to the patient as relevant to the patient's personality." Weinstein & Berger, Evidence, ¶803(4)[01]. Thus, were we to accept the Commonwealth's argument, everything said by the patient in the context of being questioned for the purposes of psychological treatment and diagnosis would be admissible under the medical treatment exception. This would destroy the "pertinent to medical treatment" requirement. The Commonwealth's position renders the "pertinent to medical treatment" requirement meaningless as a standard for judicial analysis. "The pertinency standard is intended to impose a true limit." Christopher B. Mueller and Laird C. Kirkpatrick, 4 Federal Evidence, §442 at p.461 (2d ed. 1994).

Commonwealth v. Smith, 681 A.2d 1288, 1292-1293 (Pa. 1996). And see Mosteller, Child Sexual Abuse and Statements for the Purpose of Medical Diagnosis or Treatment, 67 N.C. L. Rev. 257 (1989) (rationale of exception cannot support its use in this context); Tuerkheimer, Convictions Through Hearsay in Child Sexual Abuse Cases: A Logic Progression Back to Square One, 72 Marq. L. Rev. 47 (1988) (statements to physicians or psychologists by child victims should not suffice to convict; courts should require nonhearsay proof of defendant's guilt by a preponderance; victim hearsay should be treated as corroborative proof).

3. The victim in *Blake* was 16 years old. What if she were six years old? Do very young children understand the importance of telling the truth to doctors or, as often happens, "forensic nurses" who are specially trained to gather information useful in diagnosis and investigating and prosecuting crime? Justice Castille thought the answer was Yes. But see VanPatten v. State, 986 N.E.2d 255 (Ind. 2013) (reversing child molestation conviction for error in admitting statements to forensic nurse examiner; no indication that two six-year-old girls understood her role or their duty to speak truthfully).

4. There is another problem with using the medical statements exception (or any other) as a means of introducing statements by children describing abuse,[3] which is the constitutional constraint brought by the *Crawford* doctrine. The statements in *Blake* were gathered in a hospital after the Department of Family Services became involved. In many places, Sexual Assault Nurse Examiners conduct such interviews. Suppose the investigator was present when the doctor examined the child. Or that police were there. Or suppose such officials were hovering in the background. Consider the fact that doctors are legally obligated to report cases of suspected abuse. With some reason, then, defendants have vigorously argued that statements by child victims are testimonial under *Crawford*, hence excludable unless the child testifies. These arguments have met with mixed success, and statements to physicians are often admitted in such cases, despite *Crawford* and regardless whether the child testifies. See section G2, infra. But see Davison v. State, 282 P.3d 1262 (Alaska 2012) (error to admit statements by 14-year-old victim to doctor who conducted special exam as part of Sexual Assault Response Team; child had received medical attention; interview was arranged by state trooper, who was there with woman's advocate; trooper took active role; doctor stressed forensic purpose; court could not conclude that purpose was medical diagnosis or treatment) (harmless).

5. The court in *Blake* called Dr. Bowers a *treating* physician, and she was cast in that light: She said her purpose was "to provide health care," and told her patient she "wanted to help." Note, however, that FRE 803(4) covers statements for "diagnosis" as well as "treatment," *expanding* the exception (at common law, it covered only statements for purposes of medical *treatment*). The idea of the expansion was to embrace statements to doctors who were to testify as experts—doctors who would diagnose the patient (usually the claimant in a civil suit) but would not be involved in treatment. Behind the expansion was the thought that *when* such a doctor testifies, anything the patient told him

[3] Child abuse trials use two other exceptions. Statements by child victims are often admitted as excited utterances under FRE 803(2), or under the catchall and rifle-shot child victim hearsay exceptions (see FRE 807 and the discussion in section F, infra). Use of the forfeiture provision has proved difficult. See FRE 804(b)(6) (section E6, infra). Special provisions let children give depositions or testify from remote locations (section G5, infra).

would come out at trial as part of the basis for the opinion. If that was going to happen, the argument ran, there is no point in limiting the statement to that use, so it might as well be usable as substantive evidence (hence FRE 803(4) expanded the exception).

(a) The wisdom of this choice is still debated. Arguments pro and con—for and against allowing use of things a patient tells an expert preparing to testify—are set out in the pre-Rules decision in the *Tramutola* case. There, the majority was *against even admitting* what the patient said, but a dissent argued in favor. Plaintiff had emerged from a lung operation with part of surgical needle in her chest, and she sued her doctor. The issue was whether her pain came from the metal fragment or spreading ribs during surgery. At her lawyer's request, she consulted Dr. Kaplan, who examined her and testified that the needle fragment caused the pain. Over defense objection, Kaplan described the history she provided, but the majority said her statements should have been excluded. Pretrial statements to a doctor in an exam aimed at qualifying him as an expert are not trustworthy in the manner of statements to a treating physician, and "the self-interest of the declarant may become a motive for distortion, exaggeration and falsehood." But the dissenting judge thought it was right to admit what she had said:

> Dr. Kaplan could not have formed an opinion as to plaintiff's mental state and psychiatric condition without being informed in at least some detail as to her prior history and complaints. His situation was not that of a treating doctor who can base an opinion on, at least, objective physical symptoms. Indeed, Dr. Kaplan said that his evaluation necessarily had to be based on his discussion with Mrs. Tramutola, and that discussion had to include her account of her past medical history.

Tramutola v. Bortone, 288 A.2d 863, 872 (N.J. Super. 1972). Contra Wise v. Monteros, 379 P.2d 116, 117-118 (Ariz. 1963) (patient statements admissible on direct examination of doctor, to "explain the basis" of her opinion, but not to prove truth of statements). Who is right? If a doctor like Bowers (or Kaplan) is to testify, should patient statements come out? For all purposes, or only for limited purposes?

(b) After the initial choice to *broaden* FRE 803(4) to reach statements to diagnosing doctors, there was a change of heart. In 2000, FRE 703 (on bases for expert testimony) was amended to bar the party calling an expert from mentioning to a jury any inadmissible "facts or data" underlying the opinion (with room to do otherwise if probative value in helping understand the opinion "substantially outweighs" prejudice). So on medical statements we've come full circle: FRE 803(4) expanded the exception because statements to testifying (diagnosing) doctors would come out, but then FRE 703 said inadmissible data could *not* come out. Yet we still have the expanded exception.

4. Past Recollection Recorded

Sometimes a witness who can't remember critical points has written down what he knew. Under some conditions, what he wrote may be admitted as a substitute for his testimony. Typically the proponent tries to refresh recollection by reminding him of the statement, quoting relevant parts or showing him the document. If the witness then *does* remember, he may testify on the basis of refreshed recollection, and his prior statement fades away (sometimes it becomes admissible as a consistent statement, to repair credibility and even as substantive evidence; or it may be usable to impeach as an inconsistent statement). Refreshing recollection is taken up in Chapter 7A.

When these avenues lead nowhere, the proponent often tries to get the statement itself into evidence. To do so, he must demonstrate that (1) the witness lacks present recollection of the matter, (2) he made or adopted the statement, (3) it accurately reflects the knowledge he once had, and (4) he did so while the matter was "fresh" in his mind. Satisfying these criteria paves the way under FRE 803(5) to admit what a testifying witness said before, on the theory that satisfying the last three criteria assures reliability, and at least some testing on cross is now possible (despite lack of memory).

OHIO v. SCOTT

Ohio Supreme Court
285 N.E.2d 344 (Ohio St. 1972)

[Randy Scott was convicted of shooting at another with intent to kill, wound, or maim, and shooting at two police officers. Victim Willard Lee was blinded by a shotgun blast in the face when he opened his front door to investigate noises outside. A guest in his house then fled by car, only to be chased by defendant in a red Ford. The guest hailed police, who pursued the Ford, and defendant allegedly fired at them.]

LEACH, J.

The principal issue involved in this case is whether the rule of evidence, referred to as "past recollection recorded," is recognized in Ohio, whether it may be employed in a criminal trial, and whether, if so employed, such rule is violative of a defendant's Sixth Amendment right of confrontation, including the opportunity of cross-examination. Although such rule of evidence has been specifically approved by the highest courts of most of our sister states, it appears that this issue has not heretofore been directly passed upon by this court.

The problem of "past recollection recorded" arises in this case from the testimony of Carol Tackett, a witness for the state. Miss Tackett had been a friend of the defendant and had held a conversation with him at the theater just prior to his arrest. She gave a handwritten, signed statement to the police concerning this conversation the day after the arrest. A portion of the statement read as follows:

> About 5 min. before the show was over Randy came in. I got up to talk to him. He had been drinking so I didn't really believe what he said. He had told me he wrecked a car and he shot a guy. I just looked [at] him and he asked me to help him. I then asked him if he was telling the truth. When he said he was I turned away from him and ran out of the theater and got in the car with my sister and we tried to find Gary [one of the policemen] to tell him.

This statement of Carol Tackett was admitted in evidence over the objection of the defendant. At the time of its admission Miss Tackett was on the witness stand. Prior to its admission she had testified, in part, as follows:

A. Well, I sat through the whole show and, well, except for the last part of it. Randy was standing in the doorway inside the show and I got up and I was talking to him in the show. That was about five, ten minutes before the show ended or something like that.
Q. All right. Now what was this conversation that you had with him at that time?
A. Well, he wanted to know if I had a car and I told him no. And he wanted—I said that Linda had a car and he wanted to know if he could go with us and I said no that he couldn't go with us.
Q. What else was said at that time?
A. Why, he was kind of upset and everything and that's when we heard the sirens outside and stuff.
Q. Did you have any other conversation with him?
A. Well he said something about somebody being shot at that time and I left the show right after that with my sister and Linda.
Q. Do you recall the police coming in the movie at that time?
A. No. I wasn't there at that time.
Q. You say you left before they came or you didn't see any police come in?
A. Yes. I left before that.
Q. Now, then, can you tell us what the words were that Randy used concerning somebody being shot?
A. I can't remember exactly what they were, just that it was something about that.
Q. Do you recall being interviewed by the police following this time?
A. Yes.
Q. Do you recall giving a statement to the police?
A. Yes.
Q. I will hand you what has been marked as state's Exhibit 17 and ask if you can identify what that is.
A. That's the statement that I made out for the policeman.
Q. Is this your handwriting on here?

A. Yes.
Q. According to this, this was made on the 24th day of November of 1969. Would that be correct?
A. Yes.
Q. And down here, this signature here, whose signature is that?
A. It's mine.
Q. Now then, at the time that you made this statement, Carol, did you make this statement according to what your knowledge was at that time?
A. To the best that I remembered.
Q. Then would you say that this was a true statement that you made at that time?
A. Yes . . . .
Q. Now Carol, at the time that you made this statement which is identified as state's Exhibit 17, was your memory better than it is now?
A. Yes.

The state argues that the statement was properly admitted under the rule of "past recollection recorded." The defendant argues that the rule of "past recollection recorded" has not been recognized in Ohio, that the statement was "hearsay" and that its admission in evidence deprived the defendant of his constitutional right of confrontation and cross-examination. We hold that the statement was properly admitted as "past recollection recorded," and that its admission did not violate defendant's constitutional rights.

While the rule of "past recollection recorded" is historically an offshoot from the practice of permitting a witness to refresh or revive his memory by examination of his own written memorandum ("present recollection refreshed"), it is fundamentally different in legal concept.

In the "present recollection refreshed" situation, the witness looks at the memorandum to refresh his memory of the events, but then proceeds to testify upon the basis of his present independent knowledge. However, in the "past recollection recorded" situation, the witness' present recollection is still absent or incomplete, but his present testimony is to the effect that his recollection was complete at the time the memorandum was written and that such recollection was accurately recorded therein.

[The court quotes four requirements for past recollection recorded proposed by McCormick, which found their way into FRE 803(5), noting that Wigmore endorsed the exception and suggested that the original record be used if available and shown to opposing counsel. And the court quotes the opinion by Justice Lockwood in Kinsey v. State, 49 Ariz. 201, 65 P.2d 1141 (1937). There Lockwood argues that recorded recollection should not be viewed as hearsay because it embodies a statement by a testifying witness, and that a witness who has made such a statement may be cross-examined on his honesty and integrity and ability to observe accurately. While he cannot be examined so well on his memory, it is "unnecessary" to do that because "he has already stated that he has *no* independent recollection of the event, which is all that could be brought out" on cross if he testified from present recollection.]

Thus, from the point of view of a procedural rule of evidence we are of the opinion that the rule of past recollection recorded is based upon sound logic and should be specifically recognized with approval in this state.

To the extent that appellant is asserting that the use of such rule in a criminal case would result in a violation of the defendant's Sixth Amendment right of confrontation, including the opportunity of cross-examination, we reject such assertion upon the basis of the holdings of the United States Supreme Court in California v. Green (1970), 399 U.S. 149, and Nelson v. O'Neil (1971), 402 U.S. 622. [The court presents a lengthy description of *Green*, which is described in section G4, infra. It then concludes that "no constitutional inhibition" prevents use of statements of past recollection recorded against criminal defendants. *O'Neil* is also described in section G4, infra.] . . .

The question remains as to whether the signed statement of Carol Tackett meets the requirements of past recollection recorded. We find that it does. The statement consisted of facts of which the witness had firsthand knowledge; the written statement was the original memorandum made near the time of the event while the witness had a clear and accurate memory of it; the witness lacked a present recollection of the words used by Randy Scott in the conversation; and the witness stated that the memorandum was accurate.

Thus, we find that the admission of the signed statement of Carol Tackett as past recollection recorded was proper, and that such did not amount to a denial of the defendant's right of confrontation or cross-examination . . . .

Judgment affirmed.

O'NEILL, C.J., and SCHNEIDER, HERBERT and STERN, JJ., concur.

CORRIGAN and BROWN, JJ., dissent.

It seems to this member of the court that a can of evidential worms is being opened and foisted into the soil of our trial procedure in Ohio with this innovative ruling adopting the precept of past recollection recorded into the criminal law of Ohio under the facts in this case. And, given time, they will emerge from that very soil in different fact situations and present problems of constitutional dimension to irk this court.

In the instant case, the written statement seems to me to be objectionable for at least four reasons:

1. the statement was not made in the presence of the defendant;
2. admitting the written paper as evidence results in it going to the deliberation room with the jury and a patent danger is that it will be given undue weight by the jury;
3. it places special emphasis on the facts recorded in the statement as against other facts testified to and contrary to the written statement; the written statement, likewise, gains an excessive value which ordinary testimony unreduced to available written form cannot have;
4. finally, under the traditional formulation of the rule, before a past recollec-

> tion recorded could be received in evidence the witness who made it must testify that he lacks present memory of the events and therefore is unable to testify concerning them.

Here, the witness, Carol Tackett, testified for the state. She was the girlfriend of the defendant. She did not say, unambiguously, that she had no present memory of the events recorded in her statement. . . .

Certainly, in that state of the proof, the witness did not expressly say that any present memory of the facts recorded was absent or that she had no independent recollection of the event. More importantly, there was no effort made by the prosecutor to refresh her recollection from her prior written statement as to the facts therein. She was not asked if the written statement revived her memory.

The admission of the statement under the facts in this criminal case was, in my view, prejudicially erroneous to the substantial rights of defendant, and I would reverse the judgment of the Court of Appeals and remand to the trial court for further proceedings.

■ NOTES ON PAST RECOLLECTION RECORDED

1. *Scott* illustrates the lack-of-memory requirement. The judge must decide whether the witness lacks memory, and whether the other requirements of the exception are met (adoption, accurate reflection of prior knowledge, freshness), which raise questions of admissibility under FRE 104(a). Had Carol Tackett forgotten? What made Judge Corrigan doubt it?

2. Consider the accuracy requirement. How can an unremembering witness testify that her prior statement accurately reflects what she once knew? Did Carol Tackett do that? Courts require some testimony outside the statement itself. See Polite v. State, 116 So. 3d 270, 275 (Fla. 2013) (essential that declarant testify to correctness of statement). Courts differ on the sufficiency of hedged testimony. Compare Hodas v. Davis, 196 N.Y.S. 801 (N.Y. App. Div. 1922) (in testifying that "he never affixed his signature 'to any paper which did not contain the true facts,'" the witness "may have stated a sufficient premise" to think his statement was accurate, but "the conclusion that he so believed was not asserted") with Walker v. Larson, 169 N.W.2d 737, 741-743 (Minn. 1969) (admitting statement signed by passenger in car involved in accident; he testified that he "would not have signed a record that was not true"; *Hodas* rule could "prevent an entirely correct and truthful statement from being presented" merely by showing "a convenient loss of memory" at trial, "which would result in impeding justice").

3. Carol Tackett satisfied the second requirement: She signed the statement (thus "made or adopted it"). Can two persons be involved in making a statement that fits the exception? Consider a bank robbery case: The perpetrators flee by car, and a bystander comes to the door of the bank (now locked) and raps on the glass. A guard goes to the door. "We're closed," he says, but the bystander replies, "The license number of that car that just drove off is WJF 6849." The guard fetches a deposit receipt, gets the bystander to repeat the number, and scribbles it down, taking the bystander's name and address. At trial, the prosecutor can link the car to the defendant and wants to use what the bystander said to link the car to the crime. Can he get the deposit slip into evidence? See United States v. Booz, 451 F.2d 719, 724-725 (3d Cir. 1971) (if the agent "can verify the accuracy of his transcription" and the observer "can testify [that] he related an accurate recollection of the number" to the agent, the evidence may come in). The ACN to FRE 803(5) seems to approve. Hence "made or adopted" embraces acts of two persons—one dictating, the other writing down—as long as both testify appropriately at trial.

4. Fresh memory is the fourth requirement in FRE 803(5), but there are no rules of thumb. One court found the requirement satisfied even where the statement was prepared three years after the event. See United States v. Senak, 527 F.2d 129, 139-142 (7th Cir.) (statement "displayed no lapses of memory" and was "specific in detail"), *cert. denied*, 424 U.S. 907 (1975). How can a court apply this factor? Consider these suggestions:

> Gaps or qualifications on the face of a statement reflecting incomplete or uncertain memory suggest it is stale; relative importance of the matters described in the life of the speaker bears on how long memory is fresh; the nature of matters recorded may be such that they would likely be fresh in the mind for a longer time, or be of such complexity or detail that time is likely to wash them away quickly; indications of care and attention in the statements may indicate freshness, particularly if the maker personally and meticulously wrote it out, or (in the case of a writing prepared by another) if he made corrections or changes, while haste and vagueness or uncritical acceptance suggest the matter is stale. Wooden rules of thumb (memory stays fresh about two weeks) are not helpful.

Mueller & Kirkpatrick, Evidence §8.43 (5th ed. 2012).

5. In *Scott,* Carol Tackett described criminal conduct to a police officer, so her statement would be testimonial under *Crawford.* Probably it would pass constitutional muster, however, because she was cross-examinable at trial. See section G4, infra.

5. Business Records

The exception for business records is a blockbuster. The eyes glaze over at the mere thought of studying such a prosaic exception, but it is critical in litigation and astonishing in breadth.

Consider the variety of material reached by the term "record" in FRE 803(6): Airline check-in and reservation data; a report by soils testing laboratory; laundromat reconciliation sheets matching washer cycles with coins in pay boxes; internal corporate memoranda, minutes of trade group meetings, diaries describing business meetings; work orders and parts requisitions; telephone toll records; credit card receipts; truck driver's notebook recording deliveries; flight training records; drilling records describing operations of oil rig.[4] Need more convincing?

As originally proposed, the business records exception extended to personal records, if routinely kept, and some pre-Rules authority applied the business records exception to such material. See Sabatino v. Curtiss National Bank, 415 F.2d 632 (5th Cir.) (depositor's account book fit exception because "routinely entered" and "routinely checked" by a person having "no motive to falsify"), *cert. denied*, 396 U.S. 1057 (1969). Congressional changes, however, made it clear that the exception does not apply to personal records (adding the term "business," with other language referring to "occupation" and "calling," to ensure that the exception reaches records of not-for-profit entities). The congressional changes also added a requirement that the record be kept as a "regular practice." See generally Mueller & Kirkpatrick, Federal Evidence §8:66 (4th ed. 2013).

The four elements of the exception are as follows:

(1) Regular business; regularly kept record. The exception embraces only records of a "regularly conducted" business, but the language is inclusive (mentioning "profession" and "occupation" and "calling," among other things). *And* the exception reaches only records that are regularly kept—made as a "regular practice."

The exception is broad enough to reach records kept by a single person who is, so to speak, "in business for himself." See Keogh v. Commissioner, 713 F.2d 496 (9th Cir. 1983) (diary kept by Las Vegas casino dealer recording gains and losses fits exception; he kept it in course of his business or occupation). It reaches too the records of illegal enterprises like drug selling. See United States v. Foster, 711 F.2d 871, 882 (9th Cir. 1983). And language in the Conference Report makes clear the intent to cover "schools, churches and hospitals." No doubt it also reaches records of labor unions, political committees and parties, and charities like the Community Chest and Red Cross.

(2) Personal knowledge of source. The source of information must be someone with personal knowledge, but that person need not be the one who made the entry, so the exception contemplates multiple hearsay—one entry based on another based on another. So the person on the loading dock, on receiving a shipment of widgets, can tell the inventory person how many widgets were received, and the latter can pass the same information to the financial people, and so forth, and entries made by each of these on

---

[4] The examples come, respectively, from United States v. Fuji, 301 F.3d 535 (7th Cir. 2002); Fortier v. Dona Anna Plaza Partners, 747 F.2d 1324 (10th Cir. 1984); State v. Evans, 932 P.2d 758 (Idaho 1997); In re Japanese Electronic Prods. Antitrust Litig., 723 F.2d 238 (3d Cir. 1983); Phoenix v. Com/Systems, 706 F.2d 1033 (9th Cir. 1983); United States v. Atchley, 699 F.2d 1055 (11th Cir. 1983); State v. Hager, 691 A.2d 1191, 1193 (Me. 1996); United States v. Cincotta, 689 F.2d 238 (1st Cir.), *cert. denied*, 459 U.S. 991 (1982); In re Aircrash in Bali, Indonesia, 684 F.2d 1301 (9th Cir. 1982); Matador Drilling Co. v. Post, 662 F.2d 1190 (5th Cir. 1981).

the basis of the information gathered by the loading dock person, can fit the exception.

(3) Contemporaneity. The exception contemplates that the information will be recorded (or at least gathered) at the time of the act or event, or when the condition was observed, but the requirement is not interpreted literally. It suffices that the record is made (or the information gathered) close to the time of the event.

(4) Foundation testimony. Every hearsay exception requires a foundation, but this one expressly contemplates either *testimony* by the "custodian" of records or other "qualified witness" *or* a *certification* by such a person, meaning an affidavit (a shortcut making it unnecessary to call a live witness). The foundation witness or certifier need not have made the record or watched its preparation, nor even have been employed when the record was made. What is required is a witness with firsthand knowledge of the system who can describe usual means of preparation. In short, the foundation witness or certifier may rely on a kind of "circumstantial" knowledge, although one who lacks this minimal knowledge cannot lay the foundation. Compare United States v. Evans, 572 F.2d 455, 490 (5th Cir.) (accountants could authenticate, regardless whether employed at the time), *cert. denied*, 439 U.S. 870 (1978) with State v. Radley, 804 A.2d 1127, 1131 (Me. 2002) (credit union manager could not authenticate reports of clearing house; she was neither employed there "nor in any way involved" in those reports).

PETROCELLI v. GALLISON

United States Court of Appeals for the First Circuit
679 F.2d 286 (1982)

[James and Beverly Petrocelli sued Dr. Davis Gallison, alleging medical malpractice in a hernia operation that Gallison performed on James on March 18, 1975. After the operation, Petrocelli suffered intense pain in his groin area. Several months later, he went to Massachusetts General Hospital and consulted Dr. Swartz. He diagnosed a recurrence of the hernia and did a second operation on September 25. This effort too failed to solve the problem, and Petrocelli underwent a third operation, suffering pain all the while.

At trial, Petrocelli described his pain after the operations. Beverly Petrocelli testified that she called Gallison after the first operation and asked whether there was anything she could do and that Gallison replied, "I could give him Darvon, but it is not going to do anything because I cut a nerve. What do you expect?" A consulting physician testified that the ilioinguinal nerve was "injured" or "traumatized" in the first operation, although he could not say that it was severed. He neither examined nor treated Petrocelli and rested his opinion on complaints, the distribution of the pain, and hospital and medical records.

The defense attacked the plaintiff's expert, pointing out that he was a thoracic surgeon rather than a neurologist, that he had not performed a hernia operation in 16 years, and that he socialized occasionally with plaintiffs' attorney. Defendant also introduced evidence that a neurologist who examined Petrocelli thought that "sensation appeared intact" in the ilioinguinal area. And Gallison himself testified that he neither severed the nerve nor told Beverly that he had.

From a jury verdict for Gallison, plaintiffs appeal, urging error in the exclusion of a sentence in Dr. Swartz's postoperative report and a surgical note by another physician.]

LEVIN H. CAMPBELL, J.

The first item of excluded evidence, noted below in italics, was contained in Dr. Swartz's report filed the day after he performed Petrocelli's second hernia operation. That report is divided into two sections, one labeled "Indications" and one labeled "Procedure." The first of these reads, in its entirety, as follows:

> INDICATIONS: This 37 year old man had a left inguinal hernia repair at an outside hospital 5 mos. prior to admission. *During the course of that surgical procedure, the left ilioinguinal nerve was severed.* A recurrence of the hernia was noted in the immediate postoperative period. He presented to this hospital for repair of the recurrence. [Emphasis added.]

There follows the section entitled "Procedure" which at great length details what Dr. Swartz himself did and observed during his repair operation. There is no mention whatever of the ilioinguinal nerve in this section.

The other excluded portion of the medical record was an entry made by a different physician at a Massachusetts General Hospital surgical clinic on October 28, 1975. In his report of Petrocelli's visit to the surgical clinic, this doctor noted, "Hernia well healed but very worried about pain from transected ilio femoral nerve . . . ." Plaintiffs assert on appeal that both of the above statements, while hearsay, should nevertheless have been admitted under the exception to the hearsay rule codified in FRE 803(6).

Rule 803(6), commonly called the business records exception, governs admissibility of "Records of regularly conducted activity." It provides that any report of "acts, events, conditions, opinions, or diagnoses, made at or near the time by, or from information transmitted by, a person with knowledge, if kept in the course of a regularly conducted business activity" should be admitted "even though the declarant is available as a witness." Plaintiffs argue that the notations describing the ilioinguinal nerve as having been "severed" at the earlier operation in a different hospital, and mentioning Petrocelli's worry about pain from "transected ilio femoral nerve," were both contained in reports kept by the hospital in the regular course, that they were made by doctors with knowledge of Petrocelli's condition, and that they should therefore have been admitted as the "opinions or diagnoses" of Petrocelli's attending physicians.

We think the district court did not abuse its discretion in excluding the parts of this hospital record which indicated that the nerve had earlier been severed.

We reach this result primarily because of the complete absence of any indication as to where this information—relating to something that had happened six months ago in another hospital—came from. To be admissible as "business records" under Rule 803(6), the referenced notations would have to represent either the opinions or diagnoses of the Massachusetts General Hospital doctors who made the notations or the diagnoses of some other "person with knowledge" (such as a medical colleague) who reported to the maker of the record as part of the usual business or professional routine of Massachusetts General Hospital. If the entries were merely relaying what Mr. Petrocelli or his wife told the reporting physicians, when providing a medical history, the matter would not be admissible solely under Rule 803(6) . . . . Rule 803(6) requires that information in a business record be "transmitted by a person with knowledge" acting "in the course of a regularly conducted business activity." The Advisory Committee Notes make clear that this encompasses only declarants—like nurses or doctors in the case of hospitals—who report to the recordkeeper as part of a regular business routine in which they are participants. Where the declarant is a hospital patient, his relating of his own history is not part of a "business" routine in which he is individually a regular participant.

Plaintiffs argued vigorously both here and below, that the notations concerning the severed nerve must be taken to reflect the medical opinions of the reporting doctors. But we think it entirely uncertain whether the reporting doctors themselves determined from ascertainable symptoms or observations, that the nerve had been "severed" or "transected" in the previous operation, or whether instead these doctors were simply recording what the patient or his wife had reported. The statements are not obviously diagnostic in quality. There is no mention of symptoms leading to a conclusion that the nerve had previously been cut. See Buckminster's Estate v. Commissioner, 147 F.2d 331 (2d Cir. 1944) (admitting medical report diagnosing party as exhibiting symptoms of cerebral hemorrhage). Nor are the statements in the nature of opinions based upon observations by the physicians. See Reed v. Order of United Commercial Travelers of America, 123 F.2d 252 (2d Cir. 1941) (statement by admitting physician in medical record that party was "still apparently well under the influence of alcohol" admitted to prove intoxication).

[The Petrocellis themselves might have been the source of the remark in the report by Dr. Swartz, and the trial court was in "no position to know" whether Dr. Swartz made an independent determination. Noting the testimony that detecting the severed nerve might be difficult during subsequent surgery because of scarring, and the absence of any mention of the point in the Procedure section of the Swartz report, the court concludes that one "bare" and "conclusory" sentence would be entitled to "no weight as reflecting the doctor's own opinion." The mention in the October 28 report is "even more cryptic" and might have rested on the report by Dr. Swartz, which may have been in the same file.]

In judging the reasonableness of exclusion under Rule 803(6), it is relevant that the excluded, elliptical reports could easily have been misconstrued by the jury as definitive opinion testimony on the most critical issue in the entire case—whether the nerve had, in fact, been severed. See FRE 403. Given the impossibility of determining from the records themselves whether these reports reflected medical judgments, and the lack of any corroborative evidence or testimony offered by the plaintiffs to assure the court that these were professional opinions, the district court could reasonably determine that the notations were simply too inscrutable to be admitted, bearing in mind that, if admitted under Rule 803(6), they would be admitted for their truth without any opportunity to cross-examine the physicians who made them. Pretrial discovery rules made it possible for plaintiffs to have deposed or otherwise sought clarification from the various physicians, including Dr. Swartz, which they apparently did not do. The trial court could thus entertain legitimate doubts as to whether the doctors who recorded these statements were actually rendering professional judgments. We emphasize that this case involves a rather narrow issue regarding the admissibility under Rule 803(6) of a business record which is so cryptic that pure guesswork and speculation is required to divine the source of the cited information. Under such circumstances the district judge acted within his discretion in determining that the hearsay statements could not be admitted as business records reflecting medical "opinions or diagnoses" under Rule 803(6).[3]

There is, to be sure, another basis for admission if we assume that Petrocelli himself or his spouse was the source of the "cut nerve" information . . . . Rule 803(4) provides for admission of patient or family statements "describing medical history, or past or present symptoms, pain, or sensations, or the inception or general character of the cause . . ." of a condition, provided the statements are "reasonably pertinent to diagnosis or treatment." Thus, if not admissible under Rule 803(6), the Petrocellis' recorded statements about the cut nerve were arguably admissible as part of patient history.[5] For the reasons which follow, however, we do not think such a theory warrants either a reversal or a new trial in this case.

First, the Petrocellis did not argue either to the court below or in their briefs on this appeal that the references in these medical records derived from statements made by Petrocelli or his wife to doctors at Massachusetts General Hospital and were, therefore, admissible as patient history. We do not ordinarily decide cases on the basis of theories never presented below nor argued to us.

One might surmise, moreover, that plaintiffs' reluctance to claim admissibility under Rule 803(4) was deliberate and strategic rather than inadvertent, making it even less appropriate for us to upset the lower court on the basis of a theory never advanced. The jury knew from the testimony of Petrocelli's wife that the Petrocellis believed the nerve had been severed by Dr. Gallison. A mere reiteration via the hospital record that Petrocelli or his wife had told Dr. Swartz

---

[3] It may also be argued, although we need not decide the issue, that the patent ambiguity as to the true source of information in this hospital record created such a "lack of trustworthiness," see FRE 803(6), as to authorize the trial judge to exclude, on that separate ground, the references to the severed nerve.

that his nerve was cut during Dr. Gallison's operation would have added little beyond corroborating what Mrs. Petrocelli had already told the jury. Yet were these statements to have been admitted under Rule 803(4), fairness would have dictated that the judge instruct the jury, if requested, that the statements were admitted for their truth solely as matters related by the patient or a member of his family, not as professional opinion. Otherwise, the jury was open to the misimpression that the notations were admitted as the medical judgments of the two Massachusetts General Hospital doctors who wrote the entries or of the hospital itself. As it would have been manifestly improper for statements admitted as patient history under Rule 803(4) to be presented to the jury as something else[6] plaintiffs' attorney understandably sought admission exclusively under Rule 803(6) . . . .

Affirmed.

■ NOTES ON MEDICAL RECORDS

1. *Petrocelli* says FRE 803(6) requires the information source to be acting in the regular course of business, which is important and correct.

2. Does the exception embrace information given by an outsider to the business, like what a doctor learns from a patient? Suppose the statement in Dr. Swartz's record ("left ilioinguinal nerve was severed") rested on something James Petrocelli said to Dr. Swartz. Could we combine FRE 803(4) (Petrocelli's statement) and 803(6) (Swartz's record)? See Merrow v. Bofferding, 581 N.W.2d 696, 702 (Mich. 1998) (in suit against landlord, admitting doctor's record saying plaintiff was hurt when his arm "went through the window"). Presumably the doctor in *Merrow* wrote down what plaintiff told him. Why doesn't this principle apply to Petrocelli's comment about the nerve?

3. Assume Dr. Swartz recorded relevant data as a "regular practice," as seems likely. Let these examples serve as a reminder that the proponent must show that *each level* of hearsay fits an exception:

---

[5] Since the medical history arguably asserted here was recorded in a hospital record, the plaintiffs would actually have had to qualify the notations under a combination of Rule 803(6) (to admit the hospital record) and Rule 803(4) (to admit the patient history). See FRE 805.

[6] It may, of course, be urged that since it is fairly certain the information in the report came from one or the other of two sources—the doctors or the Petrocellis—either of which might have qualified the statements for admission under an applicable hearsay exception, the district court should have let the information in and allowed the *jury* to decide whether the statements were, in fact, the diagnoses of the attending physicians or the statements of the Petrocellis. No such theory was posed by plaintiffs, however, and such a procedure would run counter to FRE 104(a), which gives to the *judge* the preliminary duty of determining whether—and under what theory—an item of evidence is to be admitted. More importantly, where, as here, an item in a medical record is so ambiguous as to its source as to leave a jury with no clue as to how to evaluate it (other than the fact that it appears in an official record), a trial judge would be entitled in a case like this to exclude the evidence under FRE 403 on the ground that the danger of unfair prejudice from jury confusion substantially outweighed the record's probative value . . . .

(a) James Petrocelli tells Dr. Swartz he felt no pain until five months after the operation, when he was doing weightlifting exercises, and Dr. Swartz records this information. Could Dr. Gallison offer the Swartz record against plaintiffs? See Hansen v. Abrasive Engineering & Manufacturing, Inc., 856 P.2d 625, 630-631 (Or. 1993) (in product suit against maker of sanding machine, defense introduced psychiatrist's record reflecting statements by plaintiff) (admissions and business records).

(b) Dr. Swartz phoned Dr. Gallison about Petrocelli and wrote that Gallison said the nerve was severed in the surgery. Could James and Beverly Petrocelli offer *this* Swartz record against Gallison? See O'Gee v. Dobbs Houses, Inc., 570 F.2d 1084, 1088-1089 (2d Cir. 1978) (medical statements exception reaches what one doctor tells another).

(c) Suppose Dr. Gallison forwarded to Dr. Swartz a copy of Petrocelli's patient files, and Swartz copied the information into his own record, as happens with patient referrals. Could we apply FRE 803(6) twice—once for the Gallison record, once for the Swartz record?

4. Suppose Dr. Swartz wrote in his report, "Examined patient—left ilioinguinal nerve severed or damaged, apparently in earlier surgical procedure." Would it be admissible?

5. Suppose Petrocelli consulted Dr. Swartz after suing Dr. Gallison, for purposes of getting Swartz simply to diagnose the injury. If Swartz recorded the "patient history" from what Petrocelli said, noting that "pain commenced five months after prior surgery," could Petrocelli offer this record to prove the point? What if Petrocelli consulted Swartz under a discovery order obtained by Dr. Gallison under FRCP 35 requiring Petrocelli to see Swartz? See Yates v. Bair Transport, 249 F. Supp. 681 (S.D.N.Y. 1965) (plaintiff could introduce reports by physicians who examined him on behalf of defendants, but not reports by physicians he chose who examined him in anticipation of litigation).

NORCON, INC. v. KOTOWSKI

Supreme Court of Alaska
971 P.2d 158 (Alaska 1999)

[Mary Kotowski worked on cleanup of the Exxon Valdez oil spill. Exxon retained Veco as general contractor on the project. Veco subcontracted with Purcell Security to provide security and investigate rulebreaking, and with Norcon for other services. Veco and Norcon had a policy against alcohol consumption by anyone working on the project or living in company housing.

Kotowski was sent by her union in Fairbanks to work for Norcon on a shower barge attached to a ship called the Pacific Northwest Explorer (Pacific Northwest). There she worked 12-hour days for two weeks, and was quartered on the Pacific Northwest. Her supervisor reported to Mike Posehn, a Norcon foreman. On June 28, 1989, Posehn told Kotowski to pack and move to a barge called the Foss 280. Reporting there and checking with security, she was told she had not been assigned a room but was taken to a work station. Posehn appeared. Kotowski testified that "he came up to me, he kissed me, he kind of squeezed my bottom, asked me how's it going, babe?" She testified that she was distressed but did not then complain. Later she asked Posehn if there was specific work for her. He told her to ask "one of the girls running around here . . . if they need help with anything."

At the end of the day, Kotowski returned to her quarters on the Pacific Northwest. Back on the Foss 280 the next day, she asked Posehn for instructions, adding that if she were not needed there, she had work on the Pacific Northwest. Posehn invited her to his room. She went, and Posehn poured them both whiskey. She took a sip, and he consumed his drink. He told her to calm down and go back to the Pacific Northwest for a nap, inviting her to return that evening for a party in his room and further discussion of her employment.

Back on the Pacific Northwest, Kotowski discussed events with Elmo Savell (Exxon executive). She told Savell that Posehn was harassing her and that he "had a reputation for granting employment preferences in exchange for sex." She told him he had invited her to his room that evening, and she expected alcohol to be consumed. Savell gave her a tape recorder and (at her request) a note stating she had been assigned to help gather information on alcohol/drug abuse on the Foss 280, and was to have "amnesty from prosecution and from being fired."

Back on the Foss 280, Kotowski was told she had been transferred to the "beach" (a less desirable assignment). In Posehn's room she found the party, where she recorded the conversations. As reflected in the tape, many people were there, including identifiable Norcon managers. There was sexual banter and alcohol. Posehn told her she had been assigned to the beach, but he had changed it. As the party broke up, she told him she would see him the next day. He suggested she have another drink, and they would talk about her job. Later she went to the bathroom. She returned to find everyone gone but Posehn, who was in his underwear with the lights out. She said she was leaving. He asked her to spend the night and held the door closed, but she got it open and left, leaving her coat, life vest, and hard hat.

An Exxon executive who had been at the party asked a union steward to get Kotowski to sign a statement that she had been insubordinate. Told by the steward that her job would not be terminated, Kotowski signed the statement. The steward gave the statement to the Exxon executive while he was at lunch with other managers, and saw it being passed around the table, bringing laughter. Later a senior official with Norcon told Kotowski to pack and go to Valdez, where she was questioned by people working for Norcon, Veco, and Purcell. She testified that the questioning was hostile, and she was concerned for her safety (she slept in a girlfriend's car instead of company barracks). The Exxon executive told her to "sit tight, relax, we'll figure something out."

Posehn was interviewed too. He denied drinking with Kotowski, but said that "if we had a drink that night it was after working hours."

Both Kotowski and Posehn were fired on July 10th. A never-delivered termination slip said Kotowski was terminated "for leaving work here [on the Foss 280] without permission." A second termination slip (issued and delivered) said she was terminated for "breaking camp rules" (apparently a reference to drinking). Posehn was fired for a sexual relationship with another Norcon employee. Only Kotowski was terminated for drinking.

A jury found Norcon liable for sexual harassment, and negligent and intentional infliction of emotional distress. Kotowski won $8,494 in lost earnings, $1,850 in emotional distress, and $3.8 million in punitive damages. The Alaska Supreme Court reduces the punitive award to $500,000 and deals with many issues.]

MATTHEWS, Justice . . .

Kotowski's Exhibit 7 is a three-page, handwritten memo from Bruce Ford, an investigator with Purcell Security, to Tom Varnell, his superior. Veco had contracted with Purcell to provide security for the cleanup, which included the investigation of allegations of rulebreaking on the cleanup vessels. The Ford memo summarizes the information Ford and fellow Purcell employee Mark Flechsing had gathered concerning Kotowski, Posehn, and other Norcon employees between July 2, 1989, and July 5, 1989. Kotowski offered the memo into evidence to prove the truth of the matters asserted in the following portion of the memo:

> Re: Mike Posehn. I talked with two roommates of Mike Posehn at the Foss 280 Rm. 235. The individuals were Jim Stampley and Mark Ruder and both Norcon employees. Stampley said that Posehn did have a lot of female visitors in his room and there was drinking of alcoholic beverages as a supervisor as a "springboard" for sexual activity with the females under his supervision.
>
> I also talked with Sgt. Mark Flechsing who is the head of security for Purcell at the Midway Barge. Flechsing said he had talked to Larry Coyle, one of the head supervisors for Norcon, concerning Posehn. Coyle told Flechsing that Posehn would do favors for some of his female crew in exchange for some sort of sexual activity. Coyle is now on R & R and is unavailable to be interviewed.

Norcon objected, arguing that this memo was inadmissible hearsay. Kotowski argued that the memo fell within the business records exception to the hearsay rule. See ARE 803(6) [which is identical to FRE 803(6)—EDS.]. Norcon also contested this, in part because the memo was an investigative report containing the hearsay statements of others. The superior court admitted the memo under the business records exception.

[Court quotes ARE 803(6).]

On appeal Norcon does not contest the superior court's implicit findings that Ford acquired his information as part of a regularly-conducted business activity, and that it was Purcell's regular practice to make and keep memoranda of this type. Instead, Norcon objects to the fact that the memo consisted of the "double and triple hearsay" of Coyle and Stampley, the informants who provided the information contained in the memo. According to Norcon, even if Ford acted within the regular course of business in preparing the memo, no indication exists that these informants were acting within the regular course of their business. Norcon refers this court to the commentary on Rule 803(6), which reads in part:

> Sources of information present no substantial problem with ordinary business records. All participants, including the observer or participant furnishing the information to be recorded, are acting routinely, under a duty of accuracy, with employer reliance on the result, or in short "in the regular course of business." If, however, the supplier of the information does not act in the regular course, an essential link is broken; the assurance of accuracy does not extend to the information itself, and the fact that it may be recorded with scrupulous accuracy is of no avail.

ARE 803(6) commentary. [There is a substantially identical passage in the ACN to FRE 803(6).—EDS.]

Kotowski argues that Coyle and Stampley had business reasons, as employees of Norcon, to provide accurate and truthful responses. She argues alternatively that the testimony of these informants should be regarded as nonhearsay, as admissions of a party-opponent. ARE 801(d)(2). [In a footnote, court quotes ARE 801(8)(d)(2)(A)-(E), which are substantially identical to the corresponding federal provisions, except that the latter were later amended in ways not related to this case.]

In its reply brief, Norcon does not contest the admissibility of the Ford memo based on this alternative theory. In our view, the alternative argument has merit. To use the terms of Rule 801(d)(2), both Coyle and Stampley were agents speaking at a time that they were employed by Norcon. As supervisors and safety employees, alcohol use and sexual harassment are apparently matters which their jobs required them to report, especially in response to an employer-initiated investigation. We therefore conclude that it was not error to admit the Ford memo . . . .

■ NOTES ON INTERNAL REPORTS OFFERED AS BUSINESS RECORDS

1. Private companies investigate personnel disputes. Typically there is a human resources director, often with department and staff, one of whom interviews people and makes a report. In *Norcon*, the investigation was done by an outside firm hired to monitor compliance with workplace rules (Purcell), whose staff person Tom Varnell asked Bruce Ford to prepare the report. Ford spoke to people working for Norcon and Purcell. The court invokes the business records exception as the basis for admitting the Ford report to prove what was said by Stampley, Ruder, Coyle (Norcon employees) and Flechsing (a Purcell employee). The court invokes the admissions doctrine as the basis to take those statements as proof of what they assert (that Posehn engaged in misconduct). Would either exception be enough by itself to justify the result? Consider the following:

(a) Stampley, Ruder, and Coyle are in a sense outsiders to Purcell (they work for Norcon). Does this fact mean the business records exception would not justify admitting the Ford report? In applying the exception, wouldn't it make sense to view the three companies as engaging in one business, since Norcon and Purcell combined with Veco on the cleanup? Then we view the various employees as all working for one company.

(b) One requirement of the exception is that each statement must be made in ordinary course. When Stampley spoke with Ford, and Coyle spoke with Flechsing (both providing information about drinking and behavior of Posehn), they weren't acting in regular course, were they? The court solves this problem by invoking the admissions doctrine and the business records exception.

The Exxon Valdez

US Coast Guard / EPA

The suit brought by Mary Kotowski against Exxon was important to her, and the judgment in her favor must have sent a message about workplace conduct and the responsibility of employers to deal with harassers like Posehn. But her suit was only part of the consequences of the disastrous maritime collision that led to the cleanup effort in which Kotowski was involved. The Exxon Valdez oil spill occurred on March 24, 1989, when the ship struck a reef in Prince William Sound and spilled 260,000 to 750,000 barrels of crude oil into the water (a record volume exceeded only by the 2010 Deepwater Horizon spill in the Gulf of Mexico). The captain was not on the bridge, reportedly asleep and intoxicated. The National Transportation Safety Board identified three causes—failure adequately to supervise the master and provide sufficient crew to operate the vessel safely, failure of the helmsman properly to maneuver, and failure adequately to maintain the radar collision avoidance system which would have alerted the helmsman to what was coming. The spill killed 100,000 to 250,000 seabirds, thousands of sea otters, and hundreds of seals and bald eagles, plus salmon and herring in unknown numbers. After the spill, Exxon spent some $2.1 billion in cleanup efforts, settled a civil action brought by the government and the state of Alaska for a reported $900 million, and paid another $303 million to private parties for economic damages. Other claims led to consolidated litigation in federal court in Alaska, and to a verdict on behalf of a class of some 32,000 claimants in the amount of $287 million, plus $5 billion in punitive damages. Other compensation was also paid, including $20 million to Native Alaskans and $2.6 million in settlement to claimants who opted out. The Supreme Court later reduced the punitive damage award to $507 million. See Exxon Shipping Co. v. Baker, 554 U.S. 471 (2008).

2. Suppose a different set of facts, in which Posehn is falsely accused. Suppose the Ford report exonerates Posehn, presenting statements by Stampley, Coyle, and Ruder supporting the conclusion that Posehn did nothing wrong. Could Norcon use this report as evidence in its favor? In a 1998 case, the Montana Supreme Court threw out a decision by the Board of Labor Appeals denying unemployment compensation to Mary Bean, a nurse who was dismissed from her job with the Village Health Care Center (Village). An Incident Report, prepared and offered by Village, indicated that Bean committed misconduct and had been fired for cause rather than laid off (hence not entitled to compensation). The court thought this report did not fit the business records exception because it was not prepared as part of the "routine business activity" of Village in "administering nursing services to elderly residents." Also it was made "in anticipation of litigation," meaning it was untrustworthy. See Bean v. Montana Board of Labor Appeals, 965 P.2d 256, 261-262 (Mont. 1998). Employers like Norcon and Village anticipate trouble when they investigate such employment issues. Are courts right to be suspicious when employers offer their own reports on these matters? Are they right to admit them in cases like *Norcon*, when they are offered *against* employers?

3. Employers investigate accidents in the workplace or involving their products or services: Thus airlines investigate plane crashes, railroads investigate train accidents, and makers of consumer products investigate accidents with power tools and other things. Long ago the Court decided in the *Palmer* case that a railroad accident report did not fit the statutory predecessor to FRE 803(6). In *Palmer*, a husband sued for the death of his wife in a grade crossing accident, and the railroad offered a statement by the engineer (since deceased), prepared for his signature after a question-and-answer interview with the assistant superintendent. The Court in *Palmer* would have none of it:

> An accident report may affect [a] business in the sense that it affords information on which the management may act. It is not, however, typical of entries made systematically or as a matter of routine to record events or occurrences, to reflect transactions with others, or to provide internal controls. The conduct of a business commonly entails the payment of tort claims incurred by the negligence of its employees. But the fact that a company makes a business out of recording its employees' versions of their accidents does not put those statements in the class of records made "in the regular course" of the business within the meaning of the Act . . . . If the Act is to be extended to apply not only to a "regular course" of a business but also to any "regular course" of conduct which may have some relationship to business, Congress not this Court must extend it. Such a major change which opens wide the door to avoidance of cross-examination should not be left to implication. Nor is it an answer to say that Congress has provided in the Act that the various circumstances of the making of the record should affect its weight, not its admissibility. That provision comes into play only in case the other requirements of the Act are met.

In short, it is manifest that in this case those reports are not for the systematic conduct of the enterprise as a railroad business. Unlike payrolls, accounts receivable, accounts payable, bills of lading and the like, these reports are calculated for use essentially in the court, not in the business. Their primary utility is in litigating, not in railroading. Palmer v. Hoffman, 318 U.S. 109, 113-114 (1943) (per Douglas). It should come as no surprise that the Montana Supreme Court in *Bean* (note 2, supra) relied on *Palmer*.

4. *Palmer* might have put an end to the idea that reports on workplace incidents or accidents fit the exception. But it did not. *Norcon* and *Bean* deal with workplace incidents, and sometimes courts admit accident reports (despite *Palmer*). See, e.g., Lewis v. Baker, 526 F.2d 470 (2d Cir. 1975) (admitting accident report prepared and offered by railroad in FELA suit on behalf of railroader killed in yard accident; report in *Palmer* was prepared by engineer "personally involved" in accident, who knew he was likely to be charged with wrongdoing; here report was prepared by men who were not involved and could not be target of suit; such report need not be excluded merely because it "might ultimately be of some value" in suit, nor because it "embodies an employee's version" of events or "happens to work in favor of" employer).

5. Not surprisingly, government agencies are often involved in investigating maritime, railroad, and aircraft accidents. The cooperation of private parties is expected, and statutes or regulations sometimes *require* those involved in accidents to file reports. Hence concerns arise that the prospect of litigation will affect both willingness to cooperate and the substance of information submitted. See, e.g., 49 USC §20903 (accident or incident reports filed by railroad with Secretary of Transportation may not be "used in a civil action for damages resulting from a matter mentioned in the report"); 10 USC §2254 (opinions on causation reflected in reports of military aircraft accidents prepared by secretary of department "may not be considered as evidence" in litigation). Some courts recognize a self-critical analysis privilege in related settings, offering protection for employers who take constructive steps to address workplace issues. See, e.g., Kientzy v. McDonnell Douglas Corp., 133 F.R.D. 522, 527 (E.D. Mo. 1991) (in sex discrimination suit, recognizing corporate ombudsman's privilege covering some material plaintiff sought), *rev'd on other grounds*, 990 F.2d 1051 (8th Cir. 1993).

6. Public Records

a. Introduction

The public records exception rests on the great responsibility that attends the discharge of government functions in a democracy. In effect, it is presumed that public servants go about their tasks with care, without bias or corruption, and that public scrutiny of government functions adds assurance that official records are trustworthy. The repetitive routine involved in preparing many such documents adds some assurance against misstatement, though the idea of routine is not an element in this exception.

Necessity also plays a role: Officials probably do not long remember much of what they record in the course of their duties. And public functions are so pervasive, and the importance of facts set down in public records is so great, that an exception may be necessary simply to keep litigation from interrupting public officials too often.

The range and variety of public documents are staggering, so the framers of FRE 803(8)(A) found it necessary to provide separately for various kinds of documents. They also included an escape clause where circumstances indicate "lack of trustworthiness."

Clause (i) embraces mundane documents describing "activities" of a public office. Examples include court transcripts to prove testimony given, a marshal's return to show service of process, an "antidumping proceeding notice" by the Commissioner of Customs, and a "progress sheet" prepared by the Treasury Department describing the processing and mailing of numbered government checks.[5]

Clause (ii) covers documents reporting any "matter observed" by public officials, subject to certain restrictions taken up below. Examples include reports by building inspectors indicating code violations, cargo survey reports prepared for the Agency for International Development, and a legislative preamble from a state law enacted in 1807 indicating that the Housatonic River was navigable.[6]

Clause (iii) embraces "factual findings" from official investigations, subject again to certain restrictions taken up below. Examples include findings of employment discrimination based on race and gender prepared by the Equal Economic Opportunity Commission, studies on toxic shock syndrome by the Centers for Disease Control, reports on power tool accidents prepared by the Consumer Products Safety Commission, and findings by a Coast Guard Hearing Examiner as to which of two crewmembers started a shipboard fight.[7]

Note that other narrow exceptions embrace specific records. FRE 803(9) creates an exception for records of vital statistics, like birth and death; FRE 803(14) creates an exception for records of documents affecting property interests; FRE 803(22) creates one for judgments of felony conviction; and FRE 803(23) creates one for judgments on matters of personal, family, or general history, or boundaries. In addition, FRE 803(10) creates an exception for proof of the *absence* of a public entry.

---

[5] The examples come, respectively, from United States v. Arias, 575 F.2d 253 (9th Cir.), *cert. denied*, 439 U.S. 868 (1978); United States v. Wilson, 690 F.2d 1267 (9th Cir. 1982), *cert. denied*, 464 U.S. 867 (1983); In re Japanese Electronic Prods. Antitrust Litig., 723 F.2d 238 (3d Cir. 1983); United States v. Stone, 604 F.2d 922 (5th Cir. 1979).

[6] The examples come, respectively, from United States v. Hansen, 583 F.2d 325 (7th Cir.), *cert. denied*, 439 U.S. 912 (1978); United States v. Central Gulf Lines, 747 F.2d 315 (5th Cir. 1984); Connecticut Light & Power Co. v. Federal Power Commn., 557 F.2d 349 (2d Cir. 1977).

[7] The examples come, respectively, from Chandler v. Roudebush, 425 U.S. 840 (1976); Ellis v. International Playtex, 745 F.2d 292 (4th Cir. 1984); Roth v. Black & Decker, 737 F.2d 779 (8th Cir. 1984); Lloyd v. American Export Lines, 580 F.2d 1179 (3d Cir.), *cert. denied*, 439 U.S. 969 (1978).

b. Use in Civil Cases

As you are about to see, the public records exception can play a critical role in civil litigation, where it can be used to prove not only narrow and routine points, but sometimes exceptionally important points that are central to the litigation.

BAKER v. ELCONA HOMES CORP.

United States Court of Appeals for the Sixth Circuit
588 F.2d 551 (1978), cert. denied, 441 U.S. 933 (1979)

ENGEL, J.

Early in the evening of June 7, 1973, a 1968 Plymouth Valiant automobile traveling southbound on State Route 4 and a Ford semi-tractor truck traveling westbound on U.S. Route 20 collided at the intersection of the two routes, seriously injuring one and killing the other five occupants of the Valiant. The driver of the truck did not sustain serious injury. U.S. Route 20 at that intersection was a four-lane divided highway running generally east and west; State Route 4 was a two-lane highway running generally north and south. The intersection was controlled by a traffic light.[1]

The occupants of the automobile were returning home from a high school outing when their car was struck by the truck. Joseph Slabach, the driver of the truck, was returning home after making a delivery for his employer, Elcona Homes Corporation. It is not disputed that Slabach was operating the truck in the course of his employment for Elcona Homes Corporation.

A complaint invoking the diversity jurisdiction of the district court and filed by the administrators of the estates of the four deceased passengers of the Valiant was consolidated for trial with a similar complaint brought on behalf of the seriously injured passenger, Cindy Baker. Named as defendants were Slabach and Elcona Homes Corporation.

---

[1] The traffic light at the intersection was controlled by "sensors" or trip signals. Since U.S. Route 20 was the more heavily traveled highway, the signal system was designed so that if there was no traffic approaching the intersection on State Route 4, the signal controlling U.S. Route 20 would remain a constant green until a vehicle on State Route 4 crossed the sensors. Thus the signal's "rest" position was normally green for Route 20 and red for Route 4. According to the testimony, when a vehicle approaching the intersection southbound on State Route 4 crossed its sensor, and if no vehicle had crossed the sensor on U.S. Route 20 in the last six seconds, the traffic signal for U.S. Route 20 would immediately change from a green to an amber light and would remain amber for a period of four seconds while the signal for State Route 4 would remain red. Thereafter, the signal for U.S. Route 20 would change from amber to red so that both highways received red signals for a period of one second. After the expiration of one second, the signal controlling State Route 4 would change from red to green, while the signal for U.S. Route 20 remained red. Thus when the signal system is in the "rest" position, a minimum of four seconds would elapse between the moment that a vehicle on State Route 4 crossed its sensor until the signal controlling U.S. Route 20 changed to red. However, if a vehicle had crossed the sensor on U.S. Route 20 within six seconds prior to the time that the vehicle on State Route 4 passed its sensor, then a period of time, to a maximum of six seconds, would elapse between the crossing of the sensor on State Route 4 [and] the instant that the signal for U.S. Route 20 changed to amber.

The plaintiffs' causes of action were based on the alleged negligence of the defendant Slabach. The primary factual issue in the lawsuit was which vehicle had the right-of-way at the time it entered the intersection. Since Slabach testified that he could not see the light because he was blinded by the sun, and since Cindy Baker had no recollection of the accident, there was no direct eyewitness testimony concerning this fact and the jury's resolution of the issue had to depend upon circumstantial evidence and such inferences as could be made from it. The burden of proof, of course, rested upon the plaintiffs. A jury trial resulted in a judgment in favor of the defendants; the plaintiffs appeal. We affirm.

I

The principal issue upon appeal concerns the admission into evidence of the police accident report prepared by Sgt. John N. Hendrickson, a twenty-eight year veteran of the Ohio State Highway Patrol. Hendrickson, as assistant post commander, was on duty at the Norwalk Post when the accident occurred and, upon receiving the accident report, sped directly to the scene, arriving approximately six minutes after the collision.

Sgt. Hendrickson was called as a witness by the defense, although he had been subpoenaed but not called by the plaintiffs. He testified at length about the physical circumstances at the accident scene, including the measurements taken and careful descriptions of the locations of the vehicles and physical markings, refreshing his recollection from time to time from the police accident report. He further testified to having visited the defendant Slabach at the hospital and to having taken a statement from him in which Slabach, while admitting that because of the sunlight he could not see the color of the traffic light controlling the intersection, described the location and speed of the Valiant when he first observed it emerging from behind a house located on the northeast corner of the intersection. Sgt. Hendrickson also identified a diagram of the accident scene on which were placed, on transparent overlays, the locations of the two vehicles at the point of impact and as they came to rest, calculated by the sergeant from his investigative materials and from his use of vector analysis.

While Sgt. Hendrickson was examined and cross-examined at length concerning the factual data which he incorporated in the accident report and the vector analysis he employed, he was not questioned concerning any opinion he might have as to who had the right-of-way, although he had qualified as an expert in accident reconstruction and although the plaintiffs had, in their case-in-chief, employed similarly an accident reconstruction expert who opined that the light was green for the Valiant at the time it entered the intersection.

After Sgt. Hendrickson had left the stand, however, the defense introduced the police accident report into evidence, over the hearsay objection of plaintiffs. Plaintiffs particularly objected to Sgt. Hendrickson's record of the statement of defendant Slabach[3] and to Sgt. Hendrickson's notations concerning the fault for the accident. The report included the observation that "apparently unit #2 [the Valiant] entered the intersection against a red light." Likewise, on the same page of the accident report under "contributing circumstances," Sgt. Hendrickson had checked the box provided on the form for failure of vehicle #2 [the Valiant] to yield the right-of-way and had also checked the boxes next to "driver preoccupation" for drivers of both the truck and the Valiant.

In admitting the accident report and the addenda to it, the district judge appears to have concluded that the report was admissible as a recorded recollection under FRE 803(5).[4] We conclude, however, that the report was more properly admissible as a public record under [FRE 803(8)].

. . . A police report is, in our judgment, a "public record and report" within the meaning of the first part of Rule 803(8). The direct observations and recorded data of Sgt. Hendrickson in the course of his investigation which were placed upon the report clearly are "matters observed pursuant to duty imposed by law as to which matters there was a duty to report," under FRE 803(8)(A)(i),* and are thereby not inadmissible under the hearsay rule. The principal concerns, however, are whether Slabach's statement as recorded in the police report and whether the findings of Sgt. Hendrickson as to the color of the light at the time of the accident and his markings on the boxes relative to the contributing circumstances of the accident were properly allowed to be put before the jury as substantive evidence.

We address first the question of whether the finding that the Valiant ran the red light is a "factual finding" within the meaning of Rule 803(8)(A)(iii). We conclude that it is.

In enacting the Federal Rules of Evidence, the House Judiciary Committee adopted a narrow interpretation of "factual findings." . . . The Senate, however, disagreed with this narrow interpretation . . . . While the Conference Committee finally adopted the House's version of this Rule, both the House and Senate versions employed the term "factual findings," and the differing views as to the meaning of that term were not resolved. The Advisory Committee

---

[3] [Slabach said he was going west on U.S. 20 at a speed of 50-55 m.p.h. and first saw the Valiant southbound on Route 4 "when it came out from behind the house at the corner," looking "just like a flash" and moving "about 50-60 m.p.h." Slabach couldn't tell whether he had a green light because "the sun was in my eyes," but traffic "was moving" eastbound on U.S. 20 and Slabach "saw no traffic stopped" and no cross-traffic on Route 4 apart from the Valiant.—EDS.]

[4] . . . Reliance upon Rule 803(5) is, in our opinion, insufficient here to support admissibility against the claim that it was hearsay. The parties dispute whether Sgt. Hendrickson in fact had "insufficient recollection" within the meaning of the rule and a review of the record is convincing that Sgt. Hendrickson was able to remember basically what was in the report, although he refreshed himself from time to time. There was no testimony that he needed the report to testify fully and accurately as to its contents. More important, however, is the provision of Rule 803(5) that a memorandum or record may not itself be received as an exhibit unless offered by an adverse party. Since the record was introduced by the defendants who themselves called Sgt. Hendrickson, it would not have been admissible under this subsection.

* References to FRE 803 have been changed to reflect the restyled version of the Rules.—EDS.

Notes, however, accept "evaluative reports" as being within the meaning of factual findings under Rule 803(8)(A)(iii).

Generally the courts have been liberal in determining admissibility under Rule 803(8). Thus in Melville v. American Home Assurance Company, 443 F. Supp. 1064 (E.D. Pa. 1977), the court allowed into evidence two FAA Air Worthiness directives, which impugned the mechanical safety of the model of plane which had been involved in that lawsuit. In admitting the reports, the district court took note of the conflict between the House and Senate interpretations of "factual findings," and agreed with the Senate Judiciary Committee that the Advisory Committee's methodology provided adequate guidance and safeguards for admissibility of such reports under Rule 803(8)(A)(iii).

In United States v. School District of Ferndale, Michigan, 577 F.2d 1339 (6th Cir. 1978), Judge Celebrezze reversed a determination of the district court that the findings of an HEW hearing examiner were inadmissible hearsay, untrustworthy and did not fall within the exception of Rule 803(8)(A)(iii) since they were not factual findings. There our court held that the district judge should have received under Rule 803(8) as evidence the findings of an HEW hearing examiner that a school had been established and maintained as a black school for segregatory purposes and that the district court had erred in excluding the findings as hearsay and as untrustworthy. The court stated: . . .

> We agree with the United States that the HEW findings come within the scope of Rule 803(8)(A)(iii) as they are "factual findings resulting from an investigation made pursuant to authority granted by law." The investigation vs. adjudication distinction fashioned by the district court finds no support in the rule or the cases interpreting it. The Supreme Court has construed Rule 803(8)(A)(iii) to apply in an analogous situation. Clearly, the HEW proceedings were an "investigation" into the state of affairs in the Ferndale schools within the plain meaning of that word. That the proceedings could also be labeled a "quasi-judicial hearing" is of no consequence in this regard.

Applying the rule and its background to the facts here, it is apparent that whether the light was red or green for one driver or the other at the time of the accident is distinctly a factual finding within the meaning of the rule, and certainly far more so than the HEW finding in *Ferndale*, which, we believe, is essentially an evaluative opinion resulting from evidence. It is also clear from the construction of the rule itself that factual findings admissible under Rule 803(8)(A)(iii) may be those which are made by the preparer of the report from disputed evidence, as contrasted to those facts which are "matters observed pursuant to duty imposed by law as to which matters there was a duty to report" called for under Rule 803(8)(A)(ii). The more conclusory nature of the HEW report, however, did not disturb our court in *Ferndale*, and it was concerned rather with the district judge's determination that the report lacked trustworthiness.

In determining whether the "sources of information or other circumstances" indicate lack of trustworthiness, the Advisory Committee Notes list four suggested factors for consideration: (1) the timeliness of the investigation; (2) the special skill or experience of the official; (3) whether a hearing was held on [and?] the level at which conducted, and (4) possible motivational problems. [Court quotes ACN to FRE 803(8).]

Because he did not rely on Rule 803(8), the trial judge did not make a specific finding of trustworthiness. We do not, however, consider the omission fatal . . . . The burden was upon the plaintiffs to show that the report was inadmissible because its sources of information or other circumstances indicated a lack of trustworthiness. That burden was not met here.

First, the report was timely because the police arrived at the scene of the accident minutes after it occurred. An investigation was begun immediately and although the final report was not issued for two months, a continuing effort was made to determine the facts.

Second, Sgt. Hendrickson, as a State Highway Patrolman with 28 years on the force, had investigated hundreds or even thousands of automobile accidents and his expertise and skill in accident reconstruction do not appear seriously to have been challenged. His attention to detail and his testimony concerning vector analysis make it apparent that he possessed special skill and experience in the investigation of automobile accidents.

The third factor concerns whether or not a hearing was held, and of course, no formal hearing was held in this case. The Rule, however, makes no reference to such a requirement; the factor appears only to be one of those suggested by the Advisory Committee. The evidence showed that Sgt. Hendrickson gathered all the evidence that he could from all sources. There is no indication that he neglected any one source or impermissibly preferred one over another. We do not believe that a formal hearing is a sine qua non of admissibility under Rule 803(8)(A)(iii) when other indicia of trustworthiness are present.

Finally, there is no indication that the report was made with any improper motive. Sgt. Hendrickson was completely independent of both parties and his testimony at the trial rather fully and convincingly demonstrated his impartiality.

We, therefore, conclude that the sergeant's own objective findings of fact, specifically his finding that the light was red for traffic approaching the intersection from the north, were admissible. The plaintiffs' objections go not so much to admissibility as to weight and credibility, matters which are essentially for the jury to consider. It is true, of course, that Sgt. Hendrickson was not directly questioned concerning the color of the light at the time of the accident. Nevertheless, examination and cross-examination did corroborate the accident report in most other respects and there is no showing that the plaintiffs' right of cross-examination was restricted in any way. That they did not choose to do so was no doubt a matter of proper trial strategy but cannot affect the admissibility of the report in the first place.

Likewise the trial judge carefully instructed the jury concerning the admissibility of opinion testimony and no complaint can be made that those instructions were unfair or inadequate.

The appellants also challenge the admissibility of the report insofar as it contained the statement of the driver Slabach. This would not, in our judgment, be admissible under Rule 803(8). The statement was neither an observation nor a factual finding of the police officer, although Slabach's statement, with other evidence, no doubt had a bearing upon the ultimate factual finding made by the officer. Nonetheless we need not determine to what extent, where factual findings are admissible, the underlying data considered by the investigating officer are also admissible under Rule 803(8). It appears that under Rule 801, Slabach's statement was not hearsay. [Court sets out FRE 801(d)(1)(B).]

Slabach was called for cross-examination by the plaintiffs in their case-in-chief. He was vigorously cross-examined about his recollection of the accident, particularly concerning when he had first seen the Valiant. The questioning of Slabach implied that his testimony in court differed from a statement he had made earlier, and therefore, it was proper under Rule 801 to introduce his prior statement given to the police officer as showing that, in fact, the testimony he gave at trial was consistent with prior statements and was not a recent fabrication or result of an improper influence or motive. Thus, Slabach's statement as appended to the police report was not hearsay, and thereby not inadmissible under Rule 802.

[Any error in allowing Hendrickson to testify that he issued no traffic citation to Slabach was harmless. The reviewing court rejects other claims of error and affirms the judgment below.]

■ NOTES ON PUBLIC RECORDS IN CIVIL CASES

1. Consider the different things that Hendrickson's report tends to prove:

(a) It shows that Hendrickson investigated the accident, doesn't it? This part of the report fits FRE 803(8)(A)(i) (covering "activities" of public agency).

(b) It shows what Hendrickson saw—the position of the wreckage and condition of the vehicles. This part fits FRE 803(8)(A)(ii) ("matters observed").

(c) It says the Valiant ran the red light. Does this part fit FRE 803(8)(A)(iii) ("factual findings")? Hendrickson probably relied partly on what he saw in reaching this conclusion. But probably he also relied on what truckdriver Joseph Slabach said (outsider hearsay). Consider that clause (iii) speaks of a "legally authorized investigation," and Hendrickson is *supposed* to figure out what happened, including talking to witnesses. He was a "twenty-eight-year veteran of the Ohio State Highway Patrol" and was "qualified as an expert in accident reconstruction." How does this point relate to clause (iii)? The opinion in *Baker* says the exception doesn't embrace Slabach's opinion, but that the report could prove that Slabach made the statement, which could in turn be used under FRE 801(d)(1)(B) (Slabach having testified). What is going on? Why doesn't FRE 803(8) embrace Slabach's opinion about the light?

(d) A famous New York decision held that a police accident report was inadmissible to the extent it rested on statements to officer by onlookers. See Johnson v. Lutz, 170 N.E. 517 (N.Y. 1930). The court reached that conclusion even though the statute said circumstances like "lack of personal knowledge by the entrant or maker" of the report affect "weight" rather than "admissibility." *Lutz* applied the business records exception, and today we would apply the public records exception. *Lutz* went much further than we would go today in rejecting public reports based partly on hearsay, but *Baker* insists that the public records exception does not embrace outsider statements as such.

2. Should "factual findings" in FRE 803(8)(A)(iii) exclude interpretive conclusions like Officer Hendrickson's? In its 1988 decision in a wrongful death suit against an aircraft manufacturer, the Supreme Court adopted a broad interpretation embracing "factually based conclusions or opinions." There the Court approved a report by a Navy Lieutenant Commander offered by the defense suggesting that the cause of a crash during a training mission was pilot error. See Beech Aircraft Corp. v. Rainey, 488 U.S. 153 (1988) (language of Rule yields "no clear answer," nor does legislative history; concern over applying the provision too loosely may be answered by carefully considering trustworthiness and applying other safeguards relating to relevance and prejudice; ultimate safeguard is opponent's right to offer counterproof). See also Rebelwood Apartments RP, LP v. English, 48 So. 3d 483, 493 (Miss. 2010) (conclusion in police report may be admitted in civil case if it rests on factual investigation and is trustworthy); Dortch v. Fowler, 588 F.3d 396, 402-404 (6th Cir. 2009) (admitting police accident report as trustworthy; preparer had "experience and training in accident reconstruction," and there were no problems in motivation; report rested largely on his own observations).

3. Some states with rules based on the federal model either leave out the substance of FRE 803(8)(C) (Florida, Michigan, and Ohio) or add language barring reports such as that by Officer Hendrickson. Provisions adopted by Arkansas, Idaho, Iowa, and Vermont, for example, bar or severely restrict use of "investigative reports by police and other law enforcement personnel." Even on the civil side, many states exclude police accident reports, particularly those based on eyewitness statements. See Carrigan v. Wheeler, 898 A.2d 1011 (N.H. 2006) (excluding police accident report stating motorcyclist was at fault in accident, as untrustworthy); Hewitt v. Grand Trunk Western R.R., 333 N.W.2d 264 (Mich. App. 1983) (police accident report concluding, on basis of eyewitness statements, that decedent who was struck by train had committed suicide, not within FRE 803(8)).

■ NOTES ON THE TRUSTWORTHINESS FACTOR

1. The ACN to FRE 803(8) lists the following factors affecting the assessment of trustworthiness under FRE 803(8)(C): timeliness of investigation; use of hearings; skill and motivation of investigator. See also Zenith Radio Corp. v.

Matsushita Electric Industries Co., 505 F. Supp. 1125 (D.C. Pa.), *aff'd in part*, 723 F.2d 238 (3d Cir. 1983) (suggesting additionally (1) finality of agency findings, (2) extent to which findings rest on inadmissible evidence supplied by interested parties, (3) where hearings are employed, extent to which appropriate safeguards are applied and observed, (4) extent to which there is a record on which findings are based, (5) extent to which findings express policy judgment rather than factual adjudication, (6) extent to which findings rest on findings by other bodies which may be suspect, and (7) where findings rest upon expert opinion, extent to which facts or data on which opinion is based are reasonably relied on by experts in field). See generally Note, The Trustworthiness of Government Evaluative Reports Under Federal Rules of Evidence 803(8)(C), 96 Harv. L. Rev. 492 (1982).

2. How should a court appraise trustworthiness of an official report resting on conflicting statements gathered and considered by officials? See In re Korean Air Lines Disaster, 932 F.2d 1475, 1482-1483 (D.C. Cir. 1991) (admitting investigative report by international agency on cause of Russian shoot-down of commercial plane, despite defense claim that report was not trustworthy because it rested on Russian version of intercept); Moss v. Ole South Real Estate, Inc., 933 F.2d 1300, 1306-1308 (5th Cir. 1991) (in suit claiming racial discrimination in sale of real estate, magistrate overstepped role in judging trustworthiness of investigative report by considering credibility of information sources; court should focus on manner or "methodology," not credibility of sources; report may be excluded, however, if it lacks a reasonable basis, and court would *not* say bias of sources "may never render a report unreliable").

c. Use in Criminal Cases

Prosecutors often try to use forensic lab reports as evidence—reports showing a DNA match, autopsy results, blood alcohol analyses, test results for "white powdery substances" that turn out to be proscribed drugs. Such reports are usually prepared by state or federal crime laboratories, or by private laboratories retained by prosecuting authorities, and the reports are public records. Most states have statutes regulating the use of such material, but there is no federal statute. Absent such a statute, the applicable provision dealing with hearsay issues is Rule 803(8).

Amidst doubts about the competency (sometimes the integrity) of forensic labs, the Supreme Court addressed issues in the use of such reports under the *Crawford* doctrine three times in three years—in the *Melendez-Diaz* case in 2009, in *Bullcoming* in 2011, and in *Williams* in 2012. Even before these decisions came along, however, hearsay issues surrounding the use of Rule 803(8) in connection with lab reports had surfaced, and a critical decision by the Second Circuit in the *Oates* case in 1977 (two years after the Rules were adopted) concluded that such material was inadmissible hearsay.

Forensic lab reports: The *Oates* case and hearsay issues. The decision in *Oates* construed two use restrictions in FRE 803(8)(A). Today one is in clause (ii), and it bars in criminal cases the use of public records to prove a "matter observed" by "law-enforcement personnel." The other is in clause (iii), and it bars prosecutorial use of "factual findings" from an "investigation." (The wording and numbering were changed in the 2010 restyling project, but the change is not substantive and would not affect the result or logic of *Oates*.) See U.S. v. Oates, 560 F.2d 45 (2d Cir. 1977).

Oates came to three important conclusions that prevail today. First, "law-enforcement personnel" should be given a broad construction, and it includes technicians in government crime laboratories, so their reports cannot be admitted against the accused under FRE 803(8)(A)(ii). Not every public agent who secures compliance with the law counts as "law-enforcement personnel," however. See United States v. Hansen, 583 F.2d 325 (7th Cir.) (city building inspector was not included, even though noncompliance with code may result in criminal conviction), *cert. denied*, 439 U.S. 912 (1978).

Second, crime lab reports qualify as "factual findings" that are inadmissible against the accused in a criminal case under the use restriction in FRE 803(8)(A)(iii).

Third and perhaps most importantly, these use restrictions in FRE 803(8) are *very different* from limitations in other exceptions. In substance, the use restrictions are *exclusionary rules*, so material covered by them may not generally come in under other hearsay exceptions, especially the business records exception in FRE 803(6) and the catchall in FRE 807. In one respect, however, *Oates* was overbroad. Courts have held that a forensic report may be admitted as past recollection under FRE 803(5), because the analyst is there to testify and can be cross-examined. See United States v. Marshall, 532 F.2d 1279 (9th Cir. 1976) (admitting police chemist's analysis of alleged heroin as past recollection recorded).

Oates achieved a considerable following, but most states did not find that resorting to the exception for past recollection was a satisfactory way to deal with forensic reports for two reasons. First, the past recollection recorded exception still requires production of the analyst to testify, which imposes a burden on state crime labs. Second, even if the analyst does testify, under the past recollection recorded exception the report itself is not admitted as an exhibit but only read to the jury. Thus most states passed special statutes regulating the admissibility of forensic reports that in effect modify their version of the public records hearsay exception.

These statutes were of two types. The first kind, often described a "notice and demand" statute, requires the government to notify the defendant of its intention to offer a forensic report and to call the analyst if the defendant so requests. The second kind, often described as a "subpoena" statute, allows the forensic report to be admitted without the testimony of the analyst but allows the defendant to subpoena the analyst to testify if he so chooses. In Melendez-Diaz

v. Massachusetts, 557 U.S. 405 (2009), the Supreme Court reviewed a conviction arising under the second type of statute, however, and found that it violated the defendant's right of confrontation under *Crawford.*

Forensic lab reports: *Melendez-Diaz* and confrontation issues. The *Melendez-Diaz* case was a drug prosecution involving a lab report stating that the substance seized from defendant was cocaine. Remarkably, many decisions around the country had concluded that forensic lab reports were *not* testimonial, but the Court rejected this view out of hand: The "certificates of analysis" prepared by the State Crime Laboratory fit the "core class of testimonial statements" described in *Crawford,* being solemn declarations intended to prove facts in a criminal trial.

In reaching this conclusion, the Court in *Melendez-Diaz* rejected the argument that statements by analysts are not "accusatory" (they don't directly charge anyone with wrongdoing), and rejected the argument that lab technicians are somehow special (not "ordinary" witnesses describing "historical events"). In language that proved prophetic, the Court said scientific testing is not "as neutral or as reliable" as one might think:

> Forensic evidence is not uniquely immune from the risk of manipulation. According to a recent study conducted under the auspices of the National Academy of Sciences, "[t]he majority of [laboratories producing forensic evidence] are administered by law enforcement agencies, such as police departments, where the laboratory administrator reports to the head of the agency." And "[b]ecause forensic scientists often are driven in their work by a need to answer a particular question related to the issues of a particular case, they sometimes face pressure to sacrifice appropriate methodology for the sake of expediency." A forensic analyst responding to a request from a law enforcement official may feel pressure—or have an incentive—to alter the evidence in a manner favorable to the prosecution.
>
> Confrontation is one means of assuring accurate forensic analysis. While it is true . . . that an honest analyst will not alter his testimony when forced to confront the defendant, the same cannot be said of the fraudulent analyst. Like the eyewitness who has fabricated his account to the police, the analyst who provides false results may, under oath in open court, reconsider his false testimony. And, of course, the prospect of confrontation will deter fraudulent analysis in the first place.
>
> Confrontation is designed to weed out not only the fraudulent analyst, but the incompetent one as well. Serious deficiencies have been found in the forensic evidence used in criminal trials. One commentator asserts that "[t]he legal community now concedes, with varying degrees of urgency, that our system produces erroneous convictions based on discredited forensics." One study of cases in which exonerating evidence resulted in the overturning of criminal convictions concluded that invalid forensic testimony contributed to the convictions in 60% of the cases. And the National Academy Report concluded: "The forensic science system, encompassing both research and practice, has serious

> problems that can only be addressed by a national commitment to overhaul the current structure that supports the forensic science community in this country."

Melendez-Diaz v. Massachusetts, 557 U.S. 305, 320 (2009).

Even before its decision in *Crawford*, the Court had accepted the proposition that the confrontation clause was satisfied if the declarant could be cross-examined, either at trial ("deferred cross") or in pretrial proceedings ("prior cross"). In *Melendez-Diaz*, the state sought to defend use of the lab reports by arguing that the defense "had the ability to subpoena the analysts" for cross-examination at trial. The Court replied, however, that "converting the prosecution's duty" into a defendant's privilege "shifts the consequences of adverse-witness no-shows from the State to the accused." And it is the prosecutor's burden to call its witnesses, not the defendant's. Pointedly, however, the Court approved "notice and demand" statutes under which prosecutors must notify defendants of their intent to use lab reports, and defendants can demand that *prosecutors* call lab technicians.

Four Justices dissented in *Melendez-Diaz*, arguing that lab reports differ from ordinary testimony in being scientific. A single test may involve many technicians, the dissenters argued, and forcing prosecutors to call them would "disrupt if not end" many trials depending on such evidence.

The *Bullcoming* case. The decision in *Melendez-Diaz* made it clear that the prosecutor had to call a percipient witness, but the inevitable question was whether the prosecutor had to call the very person who ran the test, which leads in turn to the question whether everyone involved in a particular test must be called. These questions surfaced in the *Bullcoming* case, which involved a DUI prosecution. There, the prosecutor offered a certified report prepared in a state lab on the basis of a gas chromatograph test for blood alcohol content. The technician who did the test was reportedly unavailable, and another testified in his stead. Invoking *Melendez-Diaz*, a majority in *Bullcoming* condemned such "surrogate testimony" as inadequate, suggesting that the defense could only expose "evasiveness, incompetence, or dishonesty" if the very person who performed the test appeared as a witness. See Bullcoming v. New Mexico, 131 S. Ct. 2705 (2011).

The same four Justices who dissented in *Melendez-Diaz* again dissented in *Bullcoming*, and this time Justice Sotomayor filed a concurring opinion, which was necessary to the majority. She sought to limit the reach of *Bullcoming* in four important ways: First, she said the case did *not* involve some "alternate purpose" or some other "primary purpose," like providing medical care. Second, she said the case was *not* one in which a "supervisor, reviewer, or someone else with a personal, albeit limited, connection to the scientific test" took the stand. Third, she said this was not a case where an expert testified to his "independent opinion" about the tests without offering the reports themselves. Fourth, this was not a case involving "only machine-generated results." In such cases, she obviously meant to say, confrontation issues might come out differently.

The *Williams* case. A year later, the Court in the *Williams* case addressed the third issue raised by Justice Sotomayor in *Bullcoming*—whether expert reliance on a forensic report that was not itself introduced in evidence violates the Confrontation Clause if the report itself would amount to testimonial hearsay. In *Williams,* an Illinois state forensic analyst testified that defendant's DNA matched the DNA on a vaginal swab taken from a rape victim. Cellmark, a private laboratory in Maryland, had produced a report setting out a DNA profile generated from the vaginal swab. The analyst's opinion that there was a match relied on the Cellmark profile, but no one from Cellmark testified and the report itself was not introduced. See Williams v. Illinois, 132 S. Ct. 2221 (2012).

A four-justice plurality (same four who dissented in *Melendez-Diaz*) wrote an opinion in *Williams* rejecting confrontation claims on the ground that the Cellmark report had not been offered, serving only as basis for the opinion of the testifying expert. The other five Justices disagreed, arguing that there is no important difference between using a report as the basis for expert opinion and offering the report as proof of what it says. These five contended that expert testimony depending on the substance of testimonial hearsay violates confrontation rights under *Melendez-Diaz* and *Bullcoming.*

As one of the five who believed that such use of a forensic report amounts to using it for its truth, however, Justice Thomas *concurred* with the plurality and voted to *reject* the confrontation claim, but on a very narrow ground. In his view, the confrontation clause reaches *only* statements bearing "indicia of solemnity," by which he meant basically sworn or certified statements, and the Cellmark report was neither (in *Melenedez-Diaz* and *Bullcoming* the reports were certified).

■ NOTES ON PROVING FORENSIC LAB REPORTS IN CRIMINAL CASES

1. It is hard to argue with a straight face that reports by state or federal laboratories are not "testimonial" for purposes of *Crawford.* Suffice it to say that that the aim of those who prepare such reports is to aid law enforcement and prosecution. Private labs (like Cellmark in the *Williams* case) are hired by state and federal prosecutors, and their reports too seem testimonial, as their purpose once again is to aid law enforcement and prosecution, and they act in effect as agents of the state or government. For purposes of the hearsay doctrine, such reports are public records, and admissibility turns on applying state statutes governing the matter or on the hearsay exception in FRE 803(8).

Troubles in Forensic Crime Laboratories

Annie Dookhan
Reuters / Jessica Rinaldi

Massachusetts Forensic Drug Laboratory
AP Photo / Steven Senne

In 2012, Governor Deval Patrick closed the Massachusetts Forensic Drug Laboratory in Jamaica Plain (MFDL), source of the report used in *Melendez-Diaz*, after chemist Annie Dookhan admitted tampering with drug samples. Ms. Dookhan reportedly signed certificates confirming that samples used in drug cases were cocaine, but later testing reached contrary results. Popular reports claimed that Dookhan engaged in "dry labbing" (guessing on basis of preliminary tests). Charged with obstructing justice and tampering with evidence, Dookhan was found guilty and sentenced to 3-5 years imprisonment. Reportedly hundreds of people were released on account of problems in the crime lab, and civil suits were filed against the state. A report on the MFDL by the Massachusetts Inspector General concluded that Dookhan was "the sole bad actor" and that "management failures" contributed to her misbehavior. The MFDL "lacked formal and uniform protocols," the report concluded, and training was "wholly inadequate." The MFDL "failed to provide potentially exculpatory evidence" and failed to use "a valid statistical approach" in estimating the weight of drugs in certain cases. The quality control system was inadequate, security was insufficient, and there were no mechanisms to document "discrepancies in chain-of-custody protocols or inconsistent testing results." In 2014, state drug testing laboratories in Colorado, Delaware, Florida, New York and elsewhere were being examined for alleged irregularities. Published reports suggest that work pressures and opportunities to profit from reselling seized drugs lie behind these difficulties.

2. In *Bullcoming*, the Court held that it wasn't enough to call a coworker to testify about a forensic report. What if the prosecutor produces the lab supervisor? An emerging consensus suggests that it suffices to call a technician who supervised, the lab where the report was prepared, or the test itself. See, e.g., State v. Gomez, 244 P.3d 1163 (Ariz. 2011) (admitting testimony by senior forensic analyst and supervisor of lab to which police submitted items from crime scene with sample of defendant's blood; supervisor testified on basis of DNA profiles and checked and described protocols followed in generating them; witness must be "familiar with" profiles and procedures).

3. Consider a case in which a driver is injured in an accident while under the influence of alcohol, and the accident also injures others. The driver and the others are hospitalized, and police get a search warrant seeking a blood sample, and obtain from the hospital a toxicology report indicating that the driver's BAC is .29 (well above the limit). Later the driver is prosecuted for assault, wanton endangerment, driving while intoxicated and related offenses. Over his objection under *Melendez-Diaz,* the prosecutor offers the toxicology report, without calling a lab technician. See Little v. Commonwealth, 422 S.W.3d 328 (Ky. 2014) (medical purpose involved; report was not testimonial). Recall Justice Sotomayor's swing vote in *Bullcoming.*

4. It is no exaggeration to say that *Williams* is a conflicted decision that did not bring clarity to the subject. Best understood, *Williams* affirms the proposition that expert testimony embracing the conclusion of a lab report is tantamount to introducing the report itself, bringing into play the obligation spelled out in *Melendez-Diaz* and *Bullcoming* to call a percipient witness—one involved in the testing that produced the report. See, e.g., Carrington v. District of Columbia, 77 A.3d 999 (D.C. 2013) (in DUI bench trial, error to admit testimony based on urine tests for blood alcohol content; witness did not "personally perform or observe" testing, but used result as basis for it; five Justices in *Williams* would not let expert present testimonial hearsay to explain opinion) (harmless); Jenkins v. United States, 75 A.3d 174 (D.C. 2013) (in murder trial, reversible error to admit FBI analyst's testimony that defendant's DNA profile matched that of unknown DNA found at crime scene).

5. At nearly the opposite extreme from the decisions in *Carrington* and *Jenkins,* which take seriously the basic approach of *Melendez-Diaz,* are decisions in other states that take full advantage of the suggestion that machine-generated results from samples prepared by others don't require much in the way of a percipient witness. See, e.g., State v. Lui, 315 P.3d 493 (Wash. 2014) (in murder trial, admitting testimony by Cellmark analyst who did not do initial testing, but examined "machine-generated data" and created DNA profile and determined that it "matches" another profile; this person, not those who participate in earlier steps, is the "witness against" the defendant).

6. Does *Melendez-Diaz* mean prosecutors must call percipient witnesses to testify to every step in the laboratory process, from the persons who gather samples to the persons who calibrate the machinery? The majority in that case said no, commenting that it was *not* saying that "anyone whose testimony may be relevant in establishing the chain of custody, authenticity of the sample, or accuracy of the testing device, must appear." *Melendez-Diaz,* 557 U.S. 305, 312 n.1 (2009). See also Speers v. State, 999 N.E.2d 850 (Ind. 2013) (need not call person who transferred blood from piece of glass to swab for testing, as he was "just one person involved in the chain of custody"); Commonwealth v. Dyarman, 73 A.3d 565, 570 (Pa. 2013) (admitting calibration and accuracy certificates for breath testing machine).

COMMENT/PERSPECTIVE: Handling Forensic Drug Reports

Consider incentives and pressures on prosecutors and defense counsel in drug cases and others in which forensic lab reports are crucial, assuming that the jurisdiction has the notice-and-demand statute that the Court approved in *Melendez-Diaz*. Prosecutors may see little gain and some risk in calling a chemist. Usually there is no question that a drug sample is a proscribed substance, and often little or no doubt about the conclusion indicated by blood alcohol analyses or DNA profiles. A chemist or technician may or may not be a good witness. Identifying the right person may be a challenge, and she may be unavailable because of other cases or things like vacation or ailment or job change, and a thorough presentation may require more than one person. There are cost issues: In New York, a trial in Syracuse requires several hours driving time for a technician from the state lab in Albany or Fort Crane, and distances in western states like Colorado could easily double that time. And technical staffs are already overworked. Defendants may be tempted to demand production of the technician or chemist just *because* it provides leverage (it usually helps to force the other side to do something it prefers not to do). But if the person appears, a defendant who is not able to mount a serious challenge risks irritating the judge for wasting time and money. Asking blind questions may bolster the expert's conclusion, and a lawyer who has no real hope of raising doubts is better off asking nothing. And how is the lawyer to know whether a report rests on shoddy procedures or whether the technician or chemist is competent or not, or corrupt or not? The defense lawyer may be able to bring out things like risks of mistake (mishandling or mislabeling samples), and limits on accuracy inherent in the procedure itself, but these are not likely to be convincing. Small wonder, then, that many modern trials go forward with lab reports and no technical witnesses, while much energy is spent litigating procedural questions.

■ PROBLEM 4-N. "You Can't Offer A Police Report"

Four days after FirstSave in Oklahoma City is robbed at 8 P.M. on Friday, June 14th, police arrest Chuck Dial and Cheryl Doran in Norman (some 20 miles from the scene of the crime). They are charged in federal court with bank robbery. Eyewitnesses place them at the scene, and their car matches the description of the vehicle apparently used by the culprits, but the proceeds of the robbery are not found, and defendants offer an alibi—they were at home in unit 5 of Stone Creek Apartments at 2640 Jefferson Street in Norman when the crime occurred, watching an episode of Big Bang Theory.

On the evening of the crime, a neighbor of Chuck and Cheryl's in Norman called police to complain about excessive noise, coming from one of the apartment units in the 2600 block of Jefferson Street. A squadcar came, and officers knocked on the doors of six residences to make inquiries, including unit 5 of Stone Creek Apartments.

(A) Assume the police report states "06/14, 8:11PM, Knocked on apt. door at 2640 Jefferson #5; occupants Chuck Dial and Cheryl Doran answered door; said they hadn't heard unusual or loud noises." In support of their alibi defense, defendants offer this report, invoking FRE 803(8). "You can't offer a police report," objects the prosecutor, invoking the relevant language. Should the court admit the report?

(B) Assume the police report states "06/14, 8:11PM, Knocked on apt. door at 2640 Jefferson #5; checked back door; looked through blinds; nobody home." To challenge the alibi defense, the prosecutor offers this this report, invoking FRE 803(8). "You can't offer a police report," objects the defense, invoking the relevant language. Should the court admit the report?

NOTES ON USE OF FRE 803(8) IN CRIMINAL CASES

1. In variant (A), when defendants offer the police report (to support their alibi), confrontation concerns play no role. We only have to worry about hearsay issues, and FRE 803(8)(A) is the relevant provision. Clause (i) doesn't apply because the point isn't to prove what police did ("activities" of police), but to prove that defendants were at home when they showed up. Arguably clause (ii) does apply, as the report reflects "a matter observed," but the use restriction says this clause doesn't reach matters observed by "law-enforcement personnel" in "a criminal case." Legislative history makes clear that the restriction in clause (ii) was designed to protect *defendants* against use of police reports, and that even in the pre-*Crawford* era the framers thought using such reports in this way would violate confrontation rights. When defendants *offer* such reports, can we ignore the literal language and let them in? See United States v. Smith, 521 F.2d 957 (D.C. Cir. 1975) (Yes); State v. Bertul, 664 P.2d 1181, 1185-1186 (Utah 1983) (admitting police booking sheet offered by defense to prove defendant was intoxicated). Arguably clause (iii) applies as well, as the report that defendants were home represents "factual findings" from an "investigation," which can be offered in any "civil case" or against the government in a criminal case.

2. In variant (B), when the prosecutor offers the report (to prove that defendants were *not* home, thus calling their alibi into question), the hearsay issue arises out of the use restrictions in clauses (ii) and (iii). Looking at clause (ii), the report again appears to reflect a "matter observed" by "law-enforcement personnel," which is inadmissible in criminal cases. Looking at clause (iii), it might be called a "finding" from an "investigation," in which case it can only be used in civil cases and against the government in criminal cases. Recall that *Oates* said these restrictions cannot be avoided by invoking other exceptions. In a series of cases, however courts constructed what is best understood as a judicially created exception allowing use of *some* police reports against defendants. The cases mostly use the phrase "routine and nonadversarial" in explaining the outcome, and the idea is that some records prepared by or for law enforcement agents are not part of an attempt to prepare charges or make evidence against any particular defendant. In the *Puente* and *Orozco* cases, for example, the prosecutor sought to prove, in trials for illegally importing drugs, that defendant drove from California to Mexico, and then back to California. When these cases came down, Treasury agents recorded the comings and goings of cars across such border checkpoints as San Ysidro in Southern California, entering data into computers connected with the Treasury Enforcement Communications System (TECS). With modern technology, such functions are carried out by automatic cameras, with no need for human input. But suppose a live government agent enters the information into official records (as actually happened in those cases). Would the information be admissible under FRE 803(8)? See United States v. Puente, 826 F.2d 1415, 1417-1418 (5th Cir. 1987); United States v. Orozco, 590 F.2d 789 (9th Cir.), *cert. denied*, 439 U.S. 1049 (1979) (both indicating Yes). See also United States v. Brown, 315 F.3d 929, 931-932 (8th Cir. 2003) (in counterfeiting trial, admitting computerized database operated by Secret Service showing that bills with certain serial numbers appeared in Detroit; such information is "routinely entered" by data entry personnel; database was not assembled "in anticipation of " defendant's trial).

3. This question naturally arises: As a matter of confrontation law, could decisions like those in *Puente, Orozco*, and *Brown* come out the same way in the age of *Crawford* and *Melendez-Diaz?* Suffice it to say that courts are applying a similar idea in confrontation cases today, suggesting that "routine and nonadversarial" records are nontestimonial. See U.S. v. Lopez, 747 F.3d 1141, 1148 (9th Cir. 2014) (verification of removal reflects "physical removal across the border," for purpose of "recording the movement of aliens," is not done in anticipation of litigation, and is routine cataloguing of unambiguous facts; nontestimonial); State v. Copeland, 306 P.3d 610 (Or. 2013) (in contempt proceeding for violating restraining order, admitting declaration by deputy sheriff that he'd served order on defendant; record does not violate confrontation rights, as primary purpose was "to serve the administrative functions of the court system").

7. Learned Treatises

Rule 803(18) permits full use of a learned treatise if (a) it is shown to be "reliable authority" and (b) either a testifying expert relies on it during direct examination or it is called to his attention on cross. The idea here, much like the idea behind expanding the medical statements exception to cover statements made to doctors who merely "diagnose" a person (and not limiting it to "treating" doctors), is that *if* an expert can rely on such material, then the jury ought to be able to do so as well.

Traditionally the rules were much more restrictive. Learned treatises were usable only as impeaching evidence. One could cross-examine an expert about a treatise but could not offer it as substantive evidence. Even this practice was restricted: Some courts only let the cross-examiner ask about treatises on which the expert relied in his testimony; some let the cross-examiner ask about the treatise of his choice if the expert relied on *any* treatise or to question him on treatises which he acknowledges as authoritative; some generously allowed the cross-examiner to ask about any treatise that could be established in some way as authoritative. Under this scheme, even if the cross-examiner could point to a passage in a treatise supporting exactly what he wanted to prove, he could use it only to argue that contrary testimony by the expert was wrong.

Four arguments supported the traditional approach. One was that technical material confuses jurors, who are likely to misread, misunderstand, and misapply it. Another was that such material may be easily wrenched out of context, so permitting substantive use would lead to unfair tactics. The third was that treatises are inferior to live testimony, meaning that live experts can shed more light on technical problems than authors. The fourth was that technical knowledge evolves so quickly that treatises are likely to convey obsolescent information. In rejecting these arguments, Rule 803(18) puts much more confidence in the capacities of juries and in the ability of courts to prevent abuses.

■ NOTES ON LEARNED TREATISES

1. Under FRE 803(18), a treatise may be "read into evidence" but not "received as an exhibit." What does the latter restriction mean?

2. To what extent is the exception useful in medical malpractice cases? Compare Smith v. Knowles, 281 N.W.2d 653, 655-656 (Minn. 1979) (in suit against treating physician for wrongful death of pregnant woman and fetus after woman apparently went into eclamptic convulsions, passages from medical treatises offered during plaintiff's cross-examination of physician were sufficient as substantive evidence "to establish the requisite standard of care" but insufficient to prove departure from this standard or causation) with Heilman v. Snyder, 520 S.W.2d 321 (Ky. 1975) (in malpractice suit against physician who failed to sterilize skin of patient before administering injections, approving treatise offered by defendant to prove that such sterilization is unnecessary).

3. Apart from medical books, what does the exception embrace? See Alexander v. Conveyors & Dumpers, 731 F.2d 1221 (5th Cir. 1984) (safety codes); Dawson v. Chrysler Corp., 630 F.2d 950 (3d Cir. 1980) (crashworthiness reports prepared by private laboratory for Department of Transportation), *cert. denied*, 450 U.S. 959 (1981).

THE MINOR EXCEPTIONS

You have looked at eight kinds of statements that are "not hearsay" under FRE 801 (really exceptions flying under another flag) and some important exceptions in Rule 803. There are 16 more exceptions in FRE 803 that are less important, though well established and necessary in particular cases. Three are worthy of special mention, and others can be summarized briefly:

(1) Ancient documents. FRE 803(16) creates an exception for statements in documents that have been around for 20 years or more. Age does not improve accuracy, but suggests three reasons to be lenient. First, forces generating the litigation are unlikely to have affected whatever was said long ago, so one major source of concern over trustworthiness is absent. Second, better evidence about events long ago may be hard to come by. Third, such events are unlikely to be pivotal in litigation. See Dallas County v. Commercial Union Assurance Co., 286 F.2d 388 (5th Cir. 1961). This hearsay exception connects with a special authentication provision in FRE 901(b)(8), which authorizes courts to accept such documents as genuine on the basis of how they look and where they came from (easing foundation requirements).

(2) Market reports, commercial lists. FRE 803(17) paves the way for a variety of data "published" and generally "relied upon by the public or by persons in particular occupations." The notion here is that widespread circulation and reliance create pressures ensuring reliability. Hence price lists published in catalogues, stock market quotations appearing in newspapers, mortality and morbidity tables used in the insurance industry, and city directories are admissible to prove the various facts they reflect. Specialty periodicals in astonishing number circulate among interested persons on subjects ranging from the marketing and servicing of rubber tires to the raising of livestock to modern commercial and banking practices, and all these are potentially within the exception. See McMillen Feeds v. Harlow, 405 S.W.2d 123 (Tex. Civ. App. 1966) (growth statistics for turkeys published in Turkey World).

It is harder to say whether the exception reaches credit ratings. These fall within the literal wording of the exception, and are widely relied on by lenders, but credit ratings are both indiscriminate and cautious in the sense of overincluding unchecked information. Compare United States v. Beecroft, 608 F.2d 753, 760-761 (9th Cir. 1979) (admitting Dun & Bradstreet report under business records exception as proof of information available to defendant) with Phillip Van Heusen, Inc. v. Korn, 460 P.2d 549 (Kan. 1969) (Dun & Bradstreet reports not admissible against third parties but admissible against person whose statements appear therein).

(3) Felony convictions. Evidence of felony convictions is admissible in carefully limited circumstances under FRE 803(22) to prove facts "essential to" the judgment. In the *Lloyd* case (section E2, infra), for example, you will see that the question was who started a shipboard fight. The court (in part of the opinion that you will not see) held that the judge erred in excluding a Japanese judgment convicting Alvarez of injuring Lloyd, a crime punishable in Japan by imprisonment for more than a year. The court found that Japanese law recognizes self-defense, while permitting the accused to be held criminally liable to the extent he used "excessive force." Lloyd v. American Export Lines, 580 F.2d 1179, 1188 (3d Cir.), *cert. denied*, 439 U.S. 969 (1978).

Notably, FRE 803(22) contains a restriction for criminal prosecutions reminiscent of the use restrictions in FRE 803(8). Thus in criminal cases the prosecutor cannot introduce prior convictions of third persons for purposes "other than impeachment." This language is responsive to a constitutional pronouncement by the Supreme Court in Kirby v. United States, 174 U.S. 47 (1899). There the accused was charged with receiving stolen property, and the Court concluded that using against him a conviction of others for theft, offered to prove that the property was indeed stolen, violated defendant's rights under the Confrontation Clause. As is true of the use restrictions in the public records exception in FRE 803(8), here too it seems that the restrictive language seeks not only to limit application of FRE 803(22) but to block resort to other exceptions for such judgments.

Several difficulties of construction lurk behind FRE 803(22). The phrase quoted above envisions the use of convictions to impeach witnesses. FRE 803(22) embraces only felonies and not misdemeanors, but FRE 609(a)(2) authorizes use of both felony and misdemeanor convictions to impeach government and defense witnesses.[14] And the restrictive language in FRE 803(22) bars use of felony convictions based on nolo pleas, which seems right in some situations but not in others, a point taken up in connection with FRE 410 (see Chapter 5D2, infra).

Perhaps the greatest difficulty in FRE 803(22) is that it is hard to imagine giving merely evidentiary (as opposed to conclusive collateral estoppel) effect to a judgment that says that so-and-so was convicted of thus-and-such. Where a party *can* obtain benefit of collateral estoppel effect from a prior judgment, he would prefer to use the judgment in this way. But evidentiary effect is what the exception contemplates, and the reviewing court in *Lloyd* concluded that the judgment should be admitted under FRE 803(22) rather than given collateral estoppel effect to bar recovery. See Motomura, Using Judgments as Evidence, 70 Minn. L. Rev. 979 (1986).

The other "minor exceptions" cover scattered territory:

[14] The limit included in FRE 803(22) seems designed to ensure that felony convictions of third parties *may* be used to impeach. The reasonable supposition is that this use of felonies implicates the hearsay doctrine (convictions are offered to prove what the witness did). But if convictions are hearsay when used this way, they must be hearsay whether the charge is a felony or a misdemeanor. Yet there is no exception for misdemeanor convictions: How do *they* overcome a hearsay objection when offered to impeach? The likely answer is that FRE 609, which addresses the subject of using convictions to impeach must be read (despite the fact that it is not in the "Hearsay" article of the Rules) as creating a hearsay exception for convictions to the extent authorized there for impeachment purposes.

Absence of record. Two provisions authorize proof of the *absence* of entries in business and public records, as evidence that some matter did not occur or exist that one would expect to see recorded in such places if it occurred or existed. See FRE 803(7) and (10). In a criminal trial, for example, the government refuted evidence that defendant loaned his car to one Dale Olson by evidence that an FBI agent checked credit records, city directories, and various public records and found no trace of such a person. United States v. Rich, 580 F.2d 929, 937-939 (9th Cir.), *cert. denied*, 439 U.S. 935 (1978).

This provision has proved important in deportation cases, where the prosecutor must prove that defendant was not given special permission to "reenter" the country after being deported, and where the prosecutor seeks to prove the defendant did not have a gun permit or was not authorized by some official to perform some role or was not employed by an official agency. Some decisions concluded that use of certificates in this setting did violate *Crawford* as interpreted in *Melendez-Diaz* (section C6c, supra). See, e.g., U.S. v. Orozco-Acosta, 607 F.3d 1156 (9th Dir. 2010). These decisions precipitated an amendment in 2013, which modified FRE 803(10) by adding language inspired by the "notice and demand" statutes that the Court had approved. Under the amendment, the absence of a public record may be proved by certificate only if the prosecutor provides written notice prior to trial and the defendant does not object in writing thereafter.

Birth, marriage, death. Several provisions authorize proof of "milestones" and assorted family matters. One paves the way to prove vital statistics (births, fetal deaths, deaths, marriage) by public records. See FRE 803(9). Another authorizes use of religious records as proof of matters of personal and family history, such as marriage, divorce, ancestry, and relationship by blood or marriage. See FRE 803(11). Yet another paves the way for "family records" as proof of matters of personal or family history (including that infamous example of legal obscurity and butt of jokes on the lore of hearsay—engravings on urns or tombstones). See FRE 803(13).

Real property. Four provisions relate to real property. The content of documents of conveyance may be proved by the records of the land office under FRE 803(14). Old land office records contain descriptions of conveyances, handwritten by public clerks, so the exception is needed if these are to prove what the originals contain. But the modern hall of records contains mechanical reproductions of the originals, and the issue is one of Best Evidence rather than hearsay. (Can the original be proved by the mechanical copy? The answer, given in Best Evidence terms by FRE 1003, is yes.) The more difficult hearsay issue is whether documents of conveyance may be used to prove the truth of matters they assert, such as source and condition of title. FRE 803(15) says yes, relying on the serious nature of such transactions as providing some assurance of trustworthiness. Yet another provision authorizes "reputation" as to "boundaries" or "customs" relating to lands in the community. FRE 803(20). The purpose is to authorize use of such hearsay to show where boundaries lie and who has what rights in the land.

Reputation evidence. Two provisions authorize evidence of personal reputation. One covers reputation of a person within his family concerning matters such as his birth, marriage, death, and relationship by blood and marriage. FRE 803(19). The other authorizes proof of reputation within the "community" as to "character." FRE 803(21). In this context hearsay issues are complicated.

You will see that evidence of the character of a person is commonly admitted to prove his out-of-court behavior (FRE 404 and 405) and in-court veracity or lack of it (FRE 608). Often the proof takes the form of testimony as to his "reputation." When reputation is offered for this purpose, clearly it is multiple hearsay. Somewhere, someone has said "*X* is a belligerent fellow" or "*X* is honest and truthful." In due course another repeats it. The word spreads, and reputation takes shape. Then comes litigation, and the question arises whether *X* started a fight or whether he should be believed as a witness. A character witness is called, and she says she knows *X*'s reputation, which indicates that he is "belligerent" or "truthful." Here the immediate aim is to prove exactly that, and the ultimate aim is to convince the trier that *X* started a fight or told the truth. Testimony by the character witness conveys hearsay—multiple hearsay, in fact—and FRE 803(21) lets it in.

Sometimes, however, reputation itself is the issue. In a libel case, for example, defendant might hope to prove that plaintiff's reputation was bad before the allegedly libelous statement was uttered. The point is not to prove what plaintiff is really like, but how he is reputed to be. "Reputation" in this sense could be viewed in either of two ways. Probably the more realistic view is that it shows "what people think": Seen this way, reputation is hearsay because it sums up a multitude of statements as proof of what various people think and say that others think. Somewhat less realistically, reputation is simply "what people say": So viewed, it amounts simply to the "noise" generated in the community, making it in effect multiple "verbal acts" and not hearsay at all. The exception created by FRE 803(21) chops through this thicket and permits receipt of "what people say" as proof of "what they (in aggregate) think" even if it is hearsay.

Complementing the provisions for "reputation" evidence is one for "judgments" as proof of "matters of personal, family or general history, or boundaries," where the finding is "essential to the judgment." FRE 803(23). This provision in effect assumes that such matters are carefully litigated and that the outcome is to be trusted as much as reputation evidence, hence that judgments may prove any point that would be provable "by evidence of reputation."

E EXCEPTIONS IN FRE 804—DECLARANT UNAVAILABLE

The five hearsay exceptions in Rule 804 envision a two-step process: First, the proponent shows that the declarant is unavailable as a witness. Second, she shows that the statement fits one of the five exceptions. (Recall that one approach to hearsay would reduce the doctrine to a rule of preference, to that showing unavailability of the declarant would pave the way to admit anything he said, but Rule 804 does not take this approach, and is in keeping with pre-Rules tradition in being more limited.) Statements fitting one of these five exceptions are thought to be good enough to be admitted (certainly better than nothing), but not so good as live testimony by the declarant. Most important are the exceptions or former testimony and declarations against interest.

Serious arguments are sometimes advanced that the unavailability requirement is either underbroad (more exceptions ought to require it) or overbroad (some that require it should not): In the *Inadi* case (quoted in section B5, supra) the Supreme Court rejected a claim that the Constitution ought to require unavailability of the declarant as a condition of resorting to the coconspirator exception. In People v. Spriggs, 389 P.2d 377 (Cal. 1964), the California Supreme Court said declarations against penal interest should be admissible regardless whether declarant is unavailable, but was overruled by the legislature. See Cal. Evidence Code §1230 (1965).

1. The Unavailability Requirement

As a glance at FRE 804(a) reveals, "unavailability as a witness" does not mean the declarant must be physically unobtainable—hiding or beyond reach of subpoena. The requirement is satisfied if his *testimony* is unobtainable. Even if someone is in court, he is unavailable under the Rule if he cannot remember, refuses to testify, or successfully claims a privilege.

The judge determines whether the declarant is unavailable, meaning that the question is one of admissibility under FRE 104(a). See United States v. Bell, 500 F.2d 1287, 1290 (2d Cir. 1974). Applying the unavailability criteria is usually straightforward, but not always. Some forms of unavailability have soft edges, as can happen if declarant is temporarily absent or ill, or if the prosecutor could have secured his presence in court but failed to take a step that would have achieved this result. Unavailability has a constitutional dimension as well.

Claim of privilege. Under FRE 804(a)(1) a declarant is unavailable if exempted from testifying by court order on ground of privilege. In criminal cases, witnesses sometimes invoke the Fifth Amendment privilege against self-incrimination, which makes them unavailable (this privilege is available in civil cases too, but less often seen there).

The Rule contemplates an actual ruling: Declarant takes the stand, claims a privilege, and the court sustains his position. Generally a party hoping to take advantage of this form of unavailability cannot simply represent that the declarant would claim a privilege if called, see United States v. Pelton, 578 F.2d 701, 709-710 (8th Cir.), *cert. denied*, 439 U.S. 964 (1978). But sometimes this hardnosed approach is relaxed. Where one defendant wants to offer a statement by another as a declaration against interest, for example, declarant's privilege against self-incrimination entitles him not even to be called as a witness. Hence he may be viewed as unavailable under FRE 804(a)(1) without being called to the stand for a ruling. United States v. Gossett, 877 F.2d 901, 907 (11th Cir.), *cert. denied*, 493 U.S. 1082 (1989).

Refusal to testify. FRE 804(a)(2) contemplates actual refusal: On the stand, declarant declines to answer and does not cooperate when ordered to do so. An effort to secure his cooperation is essential, and the Rule contemplates a threat of contempt. See United States v. MacCloskey, 682 F.2d 468, 478 n.19 (4th Cir. 1982). Where a refusal to testify rests on wrongful conduct by the other side that seeks purposefully to prevent testimony, the proponent may be able to invoke the forfeiture exception in FRE 804(b)(6) (see section E6, infra).

Lack of memory. A declarant who testifies that he does not remember "the subject matter" of his statement is unavailable under FRE 804(a)(3). In United States v. DiCaro, 772 F.2d 1314 (7th Cir. 1985), for example, one Brown participated in a robbery leading to charges against DiCaro. At DiCaro's trial, Brown testified that he couldn't remember the robbery, although he had described it to a grand jury. The robbery was the "subject matter" of what he said in his grand jury testimony, so he was unavailable at trial.

DiCaro illustrates a paradox created by FRE 801(d)(1)(A) and 804(a)(3). Brown's grand jury testimony was admissible under FRE 801(d)(1)(A), which requires declarant to be "subject to cross-examination" about his prior statement. Can it be that the same witness is at once "subject to cross-examination" under FRE 801(d)(1), yet "unavailable" under FRE 804(a)? The answer appears to be Yes. A person may remember making his statement well enough to be cross-examinable, thus satisfying FRE 801(d)(1), even though he has forgotten underlying events, thus being unavailable under FRE 804(a)(3).

Death, illness, infirmity. Under FRE 804(a)(4), determining unavailability due to death has not posed problems, but the same is not always true of "illness or infirmity." A minor ailment from which speedy recovery is expected should not satisfy the requirement, even though the declarant cannot attend trial on a given day. In this situation it should be possible to adjourn the proceedings to allow time for recovery. But a serious illness of uncertain prognosis is likely to be enough. Context is important:

> [S]ince witness availability affects the court's ability to manage its cases, the trial court's decision to refuse an adjournment and to admit prior testimony must be treated with respectful deference. In exercising discretion a trial court must consider all relevant circumstances, including: the importance of the absent witness for the case; the nature and extent of cross-examination in the earlier testimony; the nature of the illness; the expected time of recovery; the reliability of the evidence of the probable duration of the illness; any special circumstances counseling against delay.

United States v. Faison, 679 F.2d 292, 297 (3d Cir. 1982).

In some settings, mental condition makes a witness unavailable to testify even though the modern view is that insanity does not disqualify one from giving evidence. Particularly in trials for child abuse, the victim may experience apprehension, fear, or embarrassment that is so severe that she cannot cope with testifying in court. Hence statutes in almost every state recognize a form of "psychological or medical unavailability." These statutes permit use of depositions by children, who may be allowed to testify at trial from another room by use of video monitor. (Some of statutes also create what amounts to catchall exceptions for child abuse victims, which makes it even easier to put in evidence whatever they have to say.) Although abuse prosecutions are rarely brought in federal court, Congress enacted a detailed statute on the subject. See 28 USC §3509. See also the discussion of Protected Witness Testimony in section G5, infra.

Unavoidable absence. A declarant is unavailable under FRE 804(a)(5) if her presence cannot be had at trial by subpoena or "other reasonable means."

Sometimes she is beyond reach of the subpoena power. In state systems, usually the subpoena power of a court of general jurisdiction runs the length and breadth of the state. In state criminal trials, usually the forum may invoke an interstate compact to get help from another state in bringing in a needed witness. In civil litigation in the federal system, the subpoena power of the District Court reaches throughout the district, and the so-called bulge service provision extends to any point within 100 miles of the courthouse (even if outside the district). See FRCP 45(b). In isolated instances, a few statutes permit nationwide service of process. In federal criminal trials, the subpoena power runs nationwide. See FRCrimP 17(e). And in both civil and criminal cases in federal court, it is sometimes possible to subpoena a U.S. citizen traveling abroad. See 28 USC §1783.

Even a witness beyond reach of subpoena is not necessarily unavailable, for "other reasonable means" may secure her presence. Occasionally courts expect parties simply to invite her to attend, and in the case of the government in criminal cases, to offer to pay travel expenses. See Government of Virgin Islands v. Aquino, 378 F.2d 540, 549-552 (3d Cir. 1967) (in trial for rape of stewardess on Norwegian vessel, error to admit her preliminary hearing testimony; government did not show she had left country; if she had, government "would be required to reimburse her for her expenses of travel and subsistence" if necessary).

Sometimes a witness who is physically within range of the subpoena power simply cannot be found, and the question arises whether the party offering her statement under FRE 804(b) has tried hard enough to serve her. See Perricone v. Kansas City S.R.R., 630 F.2d 317, 320-321 (5th Cir. 1980) (in suit arising out of grade crossing accident, plaintiff should not have introduced testimony by witness in prior trial; plaintiff did not subpoena witness, and defendant located him at his workplace in town where accident occurred, a mile from courthouse; he had moved from another town, but dialing his old number would reach a recording giving his number; plaintiff did not make a "diligent search").

This discussion oversimplifies slightly. Rule FRE 804(a)(5) includes a qualifying phrase added by Congress when the Rules were enacted. In net effect, this phrase puts pressure on parties to obtain deposition testimony by a declarant who might be unavailable at trial. The language says that, for purposes of four of the five exceptions—the ones in FRE 804(b)(2)-(4) covering dying declarations, against-interest statements, and statements of personal or family history—a declarant is unavailable only if her attendance at trial "or [her] testimony" cannot be obtained. That means that these three exceptions can't be used, even if the declarant is now hidden in a cave in the Himalayas and cannot be reached by any means, if the proponent could have taken her deposition but failed to do so. (The fact that he could have taken her deposition means that her "testimony" is *not* unavailable, and that is what counts.) This qualifier on unavailability does not apply to the fifth exception—the one in FRE 804(b)(1) for "former testimony," because there is no point in forcing the proponent to take a deposition if what he proposes to offer is some kind of "former testimony" that is itself "as good as" a deposition.

Procurement or wrongdoing. A party who procures the absence of a declarant should not be allowed to invoke one of the exceptions that absence normally brings into play. The last sentence of FRE 804(a) so provides, though it is seldom invoked.

Should this principle keep the prosecutor from resorting to one of the exceptions in FRE 804(b) when the declarant claims her privilege against self-incrimination? The threat of prosecution can push the declarant to invoke the privilege, but if the government grants use immunity, her privilege claim would be overruled and she could be forced to testify. See Kastigar v. United States, 406 U.S. 441 (1972). Where the government threatens prosecution or refuses to immunize the witness, is it procuring her unavailability? Probably the answer is No, and the reason is that the power to grant immunity is viewed as a government tool administered by the U.S. Attorney, and not by courts. But some decisions hint that a refusal to immunize might be viewed as abuse, United States v. Morrison, 535 F.2d 223, 225-229 (3d Cir. 1976), and that courts might play a role in deciding whether immunity should be granted, United States v. Herman, 589 F.2d 1191, 1204 (3d Cir. 1978), *cert. denied*, 441 U.S. 913 (1979).

One defendant made the similar argument that "adversarial fairness" should block the government from claiming it lacked the necessary motive to cross-examine a witness who gave testimony favorable to the defendant in grand jury proceedings but claimed the Fifth Amendment at trial. If the government could be blocked from saying it lacked the motive to cross-examine at the grand jury, the defense could offer the grand jury testimony under the former testimony exception. But the Court rejected this view, and the Second Circuit held that the government lacked the necessary motive, hence the defense could not offer the grand jury testimony under FRE 804(b)(1). See United States v. Salerno, 505 U.S. 317 (1992) (rejecting "adversarial fairness" argument), *on remand*, 974 F.2d 231 (2d Cir. 1992) (government lacked similar motive to cross-examine).

Constitutional considerations; governmental dilemmas. Lurking behind the unavailability requirement in Rule 804(a) are constitutional concerns in criminal cases when it comes to offering one particular kind of hearsay against the accused. We are talking now about former testimony—testimony given in another trial, or in a deposition or preliminary hearing, which sometimes fits the former testimony exception set out in FRE 804(b)(1). We have already seen some impacts of confrontation jurisprudence on the hearsay exceptions in Rule 803 (which do not require a showing of unavailability), particularly in connection with lab reports and the *Melendez-Diaz* case (section C6c, supra). Now we look at the impacts of confrontation jurisprudence on the unavailability requirement for former testimony, which the Supreme Court has often addressed.

BARBER v. PAGE

United States Supreme Court
390 U.S. 719 (1968)

Mr. Justice MARSHALL delivered the opinion of the Court.

[Jack Barber and Charles Woods are tried for armed robbery in state court in Oklahoma. At a preliminary hearing, a lawyer named Parks represented both defendants. There Woods waived his privilege against self-incrimination, and Parks withdrew as his attorney but continued to represent Barber. In his testimony at that hearing, Woods incriminated Barber, and Parks did not cross-examine, although a lawyer for another defendant did. When Barber was tried seven months later, Woods was in federal prison in Texas, about 225 miles away. Over Barber's objection, the state introduced a transcript of the testimony given by Woods at the preliminary hearing. Barber lost in the state system, and ultimately challenged his conviction in federal court by seeking a writ of habeas corpus, where he lost both at the District Court and on appeal.]

We start with the fact that the State made absolutely no effort to obtain the presence of Woods at trial other than to ascertain that he was in a federal prison outside Oklahoma. It must be acknowledged that various courts and commentators have heretofore assumed that the mere absence of a witness from the jurisdiction was sufficient ground for dispensing with confrontation on the theory that "it is impossible to compel his attendance, because the process of the trial Court is of no force without the jurisdiction, and the party desiring his testimony is therefore helpless." 5 Wigmore, Evidence §1404 (3d ed. 1940).

Whatever may have been the accuracy of that theory at one time, it is clear that at the present time increased cooperation between the States themselves and between the States and the Federal Government has largely deprived it of any continuing validity in the criminal law.[4] For example, in the case of a prospective witness currently in federal custody, 28 U.S.C. §2241(c)(5) gives federal courts the power to issue writs of habeas corpus ad testificandum at the request of state prosecutorial authorities. In addition, it is the policy of the United States Bureau of Prisons to permit federal prisoners to testify in state court criminal proceedings pursuant to writs of habeas corpus ad testificandum issued out of state courts.

In this case the state authorities made no effort to avail themselves of either of the above alternative means of seeking to secure Woods' presence at petitioner's trial. The Court of Appeals majority appears to have reasoned that because the State would have had to request an exercise of discretion on the part of federal authorities, it was under no obligation to make any such request. Yet as Judge Aldrich, sitting by designation, pointed out in dissent below, "the possibility of a refusal is not the equivalent of asking and receiving a rebuff." In short, a witness is not "unavailable" for purposes of the foregoing exception to the confrontation requirement unless the prosecutorial authorities have made a good-faith effort to obtain his presence at trial. The State made no such effort here, and, so far as this record reveals, the sole reason why Woods was not present to testify in person was because the State did not attempt to seek his presence. The right of confrontation may not be dispensed with so lightly.

The State argues that petitioner waived his right to confront Woods at trial by not cross-examining him at the preliminary hearing. That contention is untenable. Not only was petitioner unaware that Woods would be in a federal prison at the time of his trial, but he was also unaware that, even assuming Woods' incarceration, the State would make no effort to produce Woods at trial. To suggest that failure to cross-examine in such circumstances constitutes a waiver of the right of confrontation at a subsequent trial hardly comports with this Court's definition of a waiver as "an intentional relinquishment or abandonment of a known right or privilege." Johnson v. Zerbst, 304 U.S. 458, 464 (1938); Brookhart v. Janis, 384 U.S. 1, 4 (1966).

Moreover, we would reach the same result on the facts of this case had petitioner's counsel actually cross-examined Woods at the preliminary hearing. The right to confrontation is basically a trial right. It includes both the opportunity to cross-examine and the occasion for the jury to weigh the demeanor of the witness. A preliminary hearing is ordinarily a much less searching exploration into the merits of a case than a trial, simply because its function is the

---

[4] For witnesses not in prison, the Uniform Act to Secure the Attendance of Witnesses from Without a State in Criminal Proceedings provides a means by which prosecuting authorities from one State can obtain an order from a court in the State where the witness is found directing the witness to appear in court in the first State to testify. The State seeking his appearance must pay the witness a specified sum as a travel allowance and compensation for his time. As of 1967 the Uniform Act was in force in 45 States, the District of Columbia, the Canal Zone, Puerto Rico, and the Virgin Islands. See 9 Uniform Laws Ann. 50 (1967 Supp.). For witnesses in prison, quite probably many state courts would utilize the common-law writ of habeas corpus ad testificandum at the request of prosecutorial authorities of a sister State upon a showing that adequate safeguards to keep the prisoner in custody would be maintained.

more limited one of determining whether probable cause exists to hold the accused for trial. While there may be some justification for holding that the opportunity for cross-examination of a witness at a preliminary hearing satisfies the demands of the confrontation clause where the witness is shown to be actually unavailable, this is not, as we have pointed out, such a case.

The judgment of the Court of Appeals for the Tenth Circuit is reversed and the case is remanded for further proceedings consistent with this opinion.

It is so ordered.

[The concurring opinion of Justice HARLAN is omitted.]

■ NOTES ON UNAVAILABILITY AND THE CONSTITUTION

1. *Barber* adds a constitutional dimension to the unavailability requirement. Of course Woods' testimony in the preliminary hearing would be "testimonial" under *Crawford* (a statement made before trial in the form of actual testimony in earlier proceedings in the same case can hardly help but be "testimonial"!), and language in *Crawford* confirms the constitutional unavailability requirement (*Crawford* cites *Barber* on this point). In the preliminary hearing, the lawyer Parks did not cross-examine Woods, perhaps because he knew he couldn't question a former client (Parks had represented him before) without violating the attorney-client privilege, but whether to cross-examine would have posed a dilemma for Parks even if Woods had not been his client. (Remember that the question at a preliminary hearing is whether to proceed to trial, not guilt or innocence.)

(a) If he had chosen to cross-examine Woods, Park might have torn down his testimony, or raised doubts about it, but probably he would not have gotten the case dismissed (Barber's guilt or innocence wasn't the question). Worse, he would have "tipped his hand," giving Woods and the prosecutor a chance to think of ways to counter his strategy at trial. And Park would have known that cross-examining Woods at the preliminary hearing would give the other side an argument that confrontation concerns had been satisfied. The Court in *Barber* said otherwise—saying it would have decided the case the same way even if Parks had cross-examined. More recently, however, the Court has held that prior cross-examination satisfies confrontation concerns, at least sometimes. See California v. Green, 399 U.S. 149 (1970); Ohio v. Roberts, 448 U.S. 56 (1980) (described in section G4, infra).

(b) In choosing *not* to cross-examine Woods (the choice Parks actually made), a defense lawyer would preserve his "best shot" for trial, where it would most likely count more. He would have given up the chance for "dry run," and would know that someone might later say "you had a chance to cross-examine and you didn't," so you waived confrontation rights. The Court in *Barber* had an answer to that claim—confrontation is a "trial right," so not cross-examining was not a waiver.

(c) Thus it appears that the better option for the defense is *not* to cross-examine in the preliminary hearing. Bear in mind, however, that if the witness satisfies even the constitutional standard of unavailability (perhaps dying or being truly beyond reach of the prosecutor, no matter how much effort he might expend), there is still an argument that the former testimony should be admissible, despite *Barber*'s conclusion that cross-examination is a trial right. So deciding not to cross-examine can be costly if the unexpected happens, and the witness cannot be called to testify at trial.

2. Today the prosecutor would invoke FRE 804(b)(1) (former testimony exception) in offering Woods' testimony from the preliminary hearing against Barber. You are about to see that this exception applies only if the party against whom such testimony is offered had "opportunity and similar motive" to examine the witness when he testified. We have just seen that there is a good argument that the defense does not have the requisite motive, so it is possible that this fact alone would lead to excluding Woods' testimony from trial. But the cases are in disarray on this point, and we revisit the matter later.

3. The constitutional unavailability requirement surfaced again in the *Mancusi* case a few years later. The procedural setting was complicated, but the essential holding is that a Tennessee prosecutor did not violate the confrontation rights of defendant in a murder case (Stubbs) by failing to produce at trial the victim's husband (Alex Holm). He had returned to his native Sweden (becoming a "permanent resident" there), and the Tennessee prosecutor made no effort to bring him back. The Court noted that a statute authorized federal courts to subpoena citizens living abroad, but the wording suggested that this power applied only to subpoenas to appear in federal proceedings. Hence there was no ready means to obtain Holm to testify on retrial of Stubbs in Tennessee:

> The Uniform Act to secure the attendance of witnesses from without a State, the availability of federal writs of habeas corpus ad testificandum, and the established practice of the United States Bureau of Prisons to honor state writs of habeas corpus ad testificandum, all supported the Court's conclusion in *Barber* that the State had not met its obligations to make a good-faith effort to obtain the presence of the witness merely by showing that he was beyond the boundaries of the prosecuting State. There have been, however, no corresponding developments in the area of obtaining witnesses between this country and foreign nations. Upon discovering that Holm resided in a foreign nation, the State of Tennessee, so far as this record shows, was powerless to compel his attendance at the second trial, either through its own process or through established procedures depending on the voluntary assistance of another government.

Mancusi v. Stubbs, 408 U.S. 204, 212 (1972).

4. The statute described in *Mancusi* was amended after the trial considered in that case, and now authorizes federal courts to subpoena citizens living abroad to appear "before a person or body designated by" the court. See 28 USC §1783. A federal court can also detain a material witness. See 18 USC §3144. If a federal court do these things, there is little doubt that it could now help a state prosecutor bring a person like Alex Holm back to testify. Justice Marshall was probably right in his dissenting opinion in saying that *Mancusi* is a holding of "very limited significance."

■ PROBLEM 4-O. "The Government Let Her Go"

Rick Masters is tried for importing cocaine when he and a 17-year-old Australian woman named Jane Shell are arrested as they arrive in Puerto Rico on a plane flight from Peru. Her name resulted in a "hit" during a computer check of debarking passengers, meaning that the Drug Enforcement Agency had information that she and an associate were suspected of smuggling drugs. A body search of Shell resulted in the discovery of ten packages of cocaine attached by tape inside her undergarments. Agents arrested Masters for the same reason, but a search of his person yielded no contraband.

Shell was arrested and detained in an adult prison facility, and she gave a statement that led to the indictment of Masters. Several weeks later, the U.S. Attorney sought permission to take Shell's deposition, suggesting that she might return to Australia and it would be impossible to bring her back to testify against Masters. The court permitted the deposition over defense objection, and defense counsel attended but did not question Shell. She incriminated Masters, testifying that he "hired me to carry the cocaine, which I was to turn over to him in exchange for $500 and my airline ticket to Australia when we arrived here in Puerto Rico." Shell also said she would not appear at the trial of Masters, and the U.S. Attorney returned her plane ticket and passport.

In the trial of Masters several months later, the government offers the deposition testimony of Shell, invoking the former testimony exception. The U.S. Attorney explains that "we checked with our Embassy in Australia and they found Shell, but she refuses to come back." The defense objects:

> If Shell is unavailable, your Honor, it's only because the government let her go. Indeed, they practically invited her to go by returning her ticket and passport. In the words of FRE 804(a), Shell is not unavailable because her absence is due to the procurement or wrongdoing of the government, and their purpose here was just what the Rule says—preventing the witness "from attending or testifying."

The U.S. Attorney rises to her feet and argues the other side:

> Your Honor, that provision contemplates at least negligent misbehavior and perhaps something worse, like deliberate scheming. We didn't do anything wrong. We couldn't just hold Shell in jail or deny her right to return home for two months. We knew she would likely leave, so we took her deposition with your permission. The defense was there and could cross-examine.

Should the court admit Shell's deposition? Why or why not?

NOTES ON PROCURED ABSENCE

1. Did the government do right on the facts of the Problem? Consider what else it might have done: It might have charged Shell with a crime and kept her in custody; it might have imprisoned her as a material witness; it might have taken her passport and ticket; it might have offered her money or a plane ticket to return to Puerto Rico. Should it have done any of those things? Does it matter whether she's a foreigner? Can the government behave this way toward U.S. citizens?

2. Why shouldn't the government depose an important witness? Defense counsel could attend and question Shell. Should a deposition taken under these circumstances be *less* admissible than testimony in a preliminary hearing? See Ohio v. Roberts, 448 U.S. 56 (1980) (admitting preliminary hearing testimony by witness who had left state and disappeared, where defense had called her at preliminary hearing and engaged in "functional equivalent" of cross-examination). The *Roberts* approach to confrontation was discarded in *Crawford* in 2004, but its approach to preliminary hearing testimony is consistent with current doctrine. For a case more sympathetic than the *Mancusi* case (described in notes 3 and 4 prior to the Problem) to the needs of prosecutors where witnesses are out of the country, see State v. Hacheney, 158 P.3d 1152 (Wash. 2007) (admitting depositions by state witnesses who left country while under subpoena).

3. Consider the possibility of detaining Shell as a material witness. The statute contemplates that a judge may impose conditions of release, but it forbids detention "if the testimony of such witness can adequately be secured by deposition." See 18 USC §3144. Yet in criminal cases, depositions for "use in trial" are to be taken only in "exceptional cases." FRCrimP 15(a). Do these provisions mean Shell should be deposed? If so, do they also mean she should be detained to testify at trial? If she leaves because the government does not keep her on the island (incarceration or taking her tickets or passport), do these provisions mean her deposition should be admissible? See United States v. Yida, 498 F.3d 945, 957-961 (9th Cir. 2007) (in drug trial, excluding testimony given in first trial by witness, since deported; government argued that witness and his lawyer made "oral assurances" that he would return, that he cooperated in first trial, that government was concerned about his due process rights because he was being kept in prison under material witness warrant, and government had agreed to pay expenses; government did not act reasonably; its choices "were not limited to either detaining [him] or deporting him," as government could have released him but "required him to remain" in country by confiscating passport, serving subpoena, and imposing conditions, such as "home confinement, limited travel, and/or some form of electronic detention").

2. The Former Testimony Exception

In some respects, former testimony is the closest thing to live testimony, and the exception in FRE 804(b)(1) makes only a small inroad in the general bar against hearsay. The easiest example is a case retried after a successful appeal, where a witness who testified at the first trial dies before the second. On retrial, a party wishing to make use of what the deceased witness had said may resort to the transcript, reading the original testimony as evidence: The prior statements were given under oath in a trial of the same issues, the declarant was cross-examinable, and the verbatim transcript of the earlier proceedings captures his exact words.[9]

But FRE 804(b)(1) reaches much further than the situation just described. It embraces depositions and testimony given in preliminary hearings in criminal cases, for example. And like the provision for prior inconsistent statements, the former testimony exception requires the statement to have been given in a "proceeding" but does not require a "judicial" proceeding, which opens the door to use of the former testimony exception for testimony given in administrative hearings as well.

The main limit in FRE 804(b)(1) is the cross-examination requirement. (The wording speaks of "an opportunity [on the prior occasion] and similar motive to develop" the testimony on direct, cross, or redirect. Thus "cross-examination requirement" is an inexact but useful shorthand.) The language says the exception is available in civil cases if the party against whom it is offered, or his "predecessor in interest," had a chance to cross-examine the declarant. In criminal cases, the requirement is stricter, since it will not do that a "predecessor in interest" had a chance to cross-examine before. Hence the prosecutor cannot offer former testimony against the accused if he himself did not have a previous chance to cross-examine, even if a predecessor in interest did.

As phrased in the Rule, it suffices that the party against whom the testimony is offered had "an opportunity and similar motive" to cross-examine. Often the objecting party argues that differences between the prior and the present proceedings show that on the earlier occasion there was less reason (or none) to go after the witness: The charges or issues were different in the earlier proceedings, or parties were added or dropped, or the purpose of the earlier hearing was narrower. Many such differences have no plausible effect. See United States v. Licavoli, 725 F.2d 1040, 1048-1049 (6th Cir.) (against defendants

[9] Former testimony is usually proved by a transcript, which amounts to an out-of-court assertion by the reporter that the witness said thus-and-so in the prior proceedings. Hence we have two layers of hearsay, and need an exception for each. See FRE 805. The former testimony exception paves the way to admit what the witness said as proof of what he asserts. The public records exception in FRE 803(8) paves the way to admit the transcript to prove the words uttered by the witness. See also 28 USC §753(b) (authorizing use of certified transcripts of court proceedings, as prima facie correct statements of testimony taken and proceedings that transpired). In effect we piggyback two exceptions.

in federal RICO trial, admitting testimony given in state murder trials; issues "were nearly identical," despite fact that this case required proof of criminal enterprise; defendants "failed to point to any matter that they would have raised" on cross that they did not raise before), *cert. denied*, 467 U.S. 1252 (1984).

Sometimes changes in parties or issues do matter. See United States v. Feldman, 761 F.2d 380, 385-386 (7th Cir. 1985) (deposition of codefendant *S*, taken in civil suit against corporation managed by *F* and *M*, was not admissible against them in criminal trial; they had "little personal or financial stake" in prior suit and pursued opposite strategies; the "naked opportunity" to cross-examine was not enough, absent an incentive to do so); United States v. Atkins, 618 F.2d 366, 372-373 (5th Cir. 1980) (excluding co-offender's testimony given in hearing on coconspirator statements and offered by defendant at trial; government "did not have the motivation" to examine witness on whether the "Robert" to whom he referred was the defendant, since government claimed defendant played different role in conspiracy). And sometimes other factors stifle cross-examination in the prior proceedings. See People v. Brock, 695 P.2d 209 (Cal. 1985) (in murder trial, woman dying of terminal cancer testified at preliminary hearing in hospital room; precarious condition and inability to follow and respond to questions undermined defense cross and precluded use of former testimony exception).

Note the difference between this exception and the one for prior inconsistent statements. While both require a chance for cross (and each rests heavily on this point), one requires a prior opportunity, and the other a present opportunity: The former testimony exception in FRE 804(b)(1) requires a *prior* chance to cross-examine the declarant; the exception for prior inconsistent statements in FRE 801(d)(1)(A) requires a *present* chance to cross-examine.

LLOYD v. AMERICAN EXPORT LINES, INC.

United States Court of Appeals for the Third Circuit
580 F.2d 1179, cert. denied, 439 U.S. 969 (1978)

[Frank Lloyd, an electrician on the SS Export Commerce, was involved in a shipboard altercation with Roland Alvarez, a third assistant engineer. The incident occurred in Yokohama harbor on September 7, 1974. Lloyd sued shipowner American Export Lines, alleging negligence under the Jones Act and unseaworthiness under general maritime law. American Export impleaded Alvarez as third-party defendant, and Alvarez counterclaimed against American Export, alleging negligence and unseaworthiness.

Lloyd disappeared, and the claims of Alvarez against American Export came to trial. In essence, Alvarez contended that American Export was liable because Lloyd started the fight, while American Export argued no liability because Alvarez started it. At trial, Alvarez testified that Lloyd sneaked through the open door of a resistor house on deck without warning or provocation and viciously attacked him, striking him with an unidentified object and screaming that he wanted to "kill" him. During a life-threatening struggle, Alvarez picked up a turnbuckle and struck Lloyd, ending the fight.

To prove that Alvarez was the attacker, American Export resorted to the former testimony exception. It sought (unsuccessfully) to introduce a transcript of Lloyd's testimony, taken by a Coast Guard hearing examiner during proceedings to determine whether Lloyd's merchant mariner's documents should be suspended or revoked for misconduct. At that hearing both Lloyd and Alvarez were represented by counsel, and each testified under oath. In his testimony at the Coast Guard hearing—which the jury in the present case did not hear—Lloyd described his relationship to Alvarez. Coming to the September 7 incident, he said that he entered the resistor house, saw Alvarez, asked him what he was doing, "and that's the last thing I remember" because when "I woke up" two or three days later "I was in the hospital" bleeding and "spitting up blood."

The jury returned a verdict finding American Export negligent and awarding Alvarez $95,000, but rejecting the claim that American Export had breached its warranty of seaworthiness. American Export appealed, urging error in the exclusion of Lloyd's testimony from the Coast Guard hearing, and Alvarez cross-appealed, urging error in the refusal of the trial judge to enter judgment notwithstanding the verdict for "maintenance and cure" pursuant to the unseaworthiness claim.]

ALDISERT, J. . . .

In order for the hearsay exceptions of Rule 804 to apply, it is required that the declarant be "unavailable"—in this case, that he be "absent from the hearing and the proponent of his statement [be] unable to procure his attendance . . . by process or other reasonable means." Rule 804(a)(5). In preparation for trial, as has been noted, numerous attempts were made by Export to depose Lloyd, but he repeatedly failed to appear. Finally, on the day set for trial, Export learned that Lloyd would not appear to prosecute his case. Lloyd's counsel represented to the court that extensive efforts had been made to obtain his appearance, but they had failed, due at least in part to his seafaring occupation. We are satisfied that where Export and Lloyd's own counsel were unable to obtain his appearance in an action in which he had a formidable interest as a plaintiff, his unavailability status was sufficient to satisfy the requirement of Rule 804.

We turn now to the more difficult question: did Alvarez or a "predecessor in interest" have the "opportunity and similar motive to develop the testimony by direct, cross or redirect examination" as required by Rule 804(b)(1)? In rejecting the proffered evidence, the district court took a strict view of the new rule, one that we do not share.

We note at the outset that inasmuch as Congress did not define "predecessor in interest," that interpretive task is left to the courts. We find no definitive guidance in the reports accompanying language changes made as the Rules were considered, in turn, by the Supreme Court and the houses of Congress. As originally submitted by the Supreme Court, Rule 804(b)(1) would have allowed prior testimony of an unavailable witness to be received in evidence if the party against whom it was offered, or a person with "motive and interest similar," had an opportunity to examine the witness. The House of Representatives adopted the present language, the Committee on the Judiciary offering this rationale:

> Rule 804(b)(1) as submitted by the Court allowed prior testimony of an unavailable witness to be admissible if the party against whom it is offered or a person "with motive and interest similar" to his had an opportunity to examine the witness. The Committee considered that it is generally unfair to impose upon the party against whom the hearsay evidence is being offered responsibility for the manner in which the witness was previously handled by another party. The sole exception to this, in the Committee's view, is when a party's predecessor in interest in a civil action or proceeding had an opportunity and similar motive to examine the witness. The Committee amended the Rule to reflect these policy determinations.

The Senate Committee on the Judiciary viewed the import of this change as follows:

> . . . The House amended the rule to apply only to a party's predecessor in interest. Although the committee recognizes considerable merit to the rule submitted by the Supreme Court, a position which has been advocated by many scholars and judges, we have concluded that the difference between the two versions is not great and we accept the House amendment.

We, too, fail to see a compelling difference between the two approaches.

In our analysis of this language change, we are aware of the basic thrust of subdivision (b) of Rule 804. It was originally designed by the Advisory Committee on Rules of Evidence of the Judicial Conference of the United States to strike a proper balance between the recognized risk of introducing testimony of one not physically present on a witness stand and the equally recognized risk of denying to the fact-finder important relevant evidence. Even in its slightly amended form as enacted by Congress, Rule 804 still serves the original intention of its drafters: "The rule expresses preferences: testimony given on the stand in person is preferred over hearsay, and hearsay, if of the specified quality, is preferred over complete loss of the evidence of the declarant."

Although Congress did not furnish us with a definition of "predecessor in interest," our analysis of the concept of interests satisfies us that there was a sufficient community of interest shared by the Coast Guard in its hearing and Alvarez in the subsequent civil trial to satisfy Rule 804(b)(1). Roscoe Pound has taught us that interests in law are "the claims or demands or desires which human beings, either individually or in groups or associations or relations, seek to satisfy . . . ."[8] The interest implicated here was a claim or desire or demand

---

[8] Pound, A Survey of Social Interests, 57 Harv. L. Rev. 1 (1943).

which Alvarez as an individual, and the Coast Guard as a representative of a larger group, sought to satisfy, and which has been recognized as socially valid by authoritative decision-makers in our society.

Individual interests, like those of Alvarez, are involved immediately in the individual life, in the Pound formulation, and asserted in title of that life. Public interests, like those of the Coast Guard, are involved in the life of a politically organized society, here the United States, and asserted in title of that entity. Thus, Alvarez sought to vindicate his individual interest in recovering for his injuries; the Coast Guard sought to vindicate the public interest in safe and unimpeded merchant marine service. Irrespective of whether the interests be considered from the individual or public viewpoints, however, the nucleus of operative fact[11] was the same—the conduct of Frank Lloyd and Roland Alvarez aboard the SS Export Commerce. And although the results sought in the two proceedings differed—the Coast Guard contemplated sanctions involving Lloyd's mariner's license, while Alvarez sought private substituted redress, i.e., monetary damages—the basic interest advanced by both was that of determining culpability and, if appropriate, exacting a penalty for the same condemned behavior thought to have occurred.[12] The Coast Guard investigating officer not only preferred charges against Lloyd but functioned as a prosecutor at the subsequent proceeding as well. Thus, he attempted to establish at the Coast Guard hearing what Alvarez attempted to establish at the later trial: Lloyd's intoxication, his role as the aggressor, and his prior hostility toward Alvarez. Dean Pound recognized that there can be such a community of individual and public interests as this: "It must be borne in mind that often we have here different ways of looking at the same claims or same type of claims as they are asserted in different titles."

Moreover, although our precise task is to decide whether the Coast Guard investigating officer was Alvarez' predecessor in interest, it is equally important to respect always the fundamentals that underlie the hearsay rule, and the reasons for the exceptions thereto. Any fact-finding process is ultimately a search for truth and justice, and legal precepts that govern the reception of evidence must always be interpreted in light of this. Whether it be fashioned by rules of decision in cases or controversies, or promulgated by the Supreme Court with the approval of Congress, or designed and adopted by Congress, every rule of evidence is a means to an end, not an end in itself. We strive to avoid interpretations

---

[11] Karl Llewellyn has defined an interest as "a social fact or factor of some kind, existing [in]dependent of the law," with "value independent of the law." Llewellyn, A Realistic Jurisprudence—The Next Step, 30 Colum. L. Rev. 430, 441 (1930).

[12] In this regard, McCormick takes the position that "insistence upon precise identity of issues, which might have some appropriateness if the question were one of res judicata or estoppel by judgment, are out of place with respect to former testimony where the question is not of binding anyone, but merely of the salvaging, for what it may be worth, of the testimony of a witness not now available in person . . . . It follows that neither the form of the proceeding, the theory of the case, nor the nature of the relief sought needs be the same." McCormick, Handbook of the Law of Evidence §257 at 261 (2d ed. 1972).

that are wooden or mechanical, like obsolete common law pleadings, and to favor those that facilitate the presentation of a complete picture to the fact-finder. With this approach in mind, we are satisfied that there existed, in the language of Rule 804(b)(1), sufficient "opportunity and similar motive [for the Coast Guard investigating officer] to develop [Lloyd's] testimony" at the former hearing to justify its admission against Alvarez at the later trial.[14]

While we do not endorse an extravagant interpretation of who or what constitutes a "predecessor in interest," we prefer one that is realistically generous over one that is formalistically grudging. We believe that what has been described as "the practical and expedient view" expresses the congressional intention: "if it appears that in the former suit a party having a like motive to cross-examine about the same matters as the present party would have, was accorded an adequate opportunity for such examination, the testimony may be received against the present party."[15] Under these circumstances, the previous party having like motive to develop the testimony about the same material facts is, in the final analysis, a predecessor in interest to the present party. . . .

Held

The judgment of the district court will be reversed and the cause remanded for a new trial.

Each side to bear its own costs.

STERN, J., concurring.

[Judge Stern would invoke the catchall to admit Lloyd's testimony, thus concurs in the result reached by the majority, but disagrees with the construction of "predecessor in interest" given by the majority.]

It is true that Congress nowhere defined "predecessor in interest," but it seems clear that this phrase, a term of art, was used in its narrow, substantive law sense. Although the commentators have expressed disapproval of this traditional and restrictive rule, they recognize that a "predecessor in interest" is defined in terms of a privity relationship.

---

[14] One can discern a confluence between the congressional policy determinations and our view of the interests in this case in an analysis offered by the Fourth Circuit in a case, also involving a prior Coast Guard proceeding, that predated the present rules. Tug Raven v. Trexler, 419 F.2d 536, 542-543 (4th Cir. 1969), *cert. denied sub nom.* Crown Central Petroleum Corp. v. Trexler, 398 U.S. 938 (1970).

. . . Chadwick's testimony was presented by use of a portion of the proceedings before the Coast Guard in its investigation of the catastrophe. In those proceedings Chadwick was sworn. There was a presiding officer who conducted the proceedings, ruled on the form of questions and ruled on the admissibility of evidence. The object of the inquiry was to fix responsibility for the fire—the object of these proceedings. Full cross-examination on the facts as then known by counsel for the Trexler estate, counsel for Crown and counsel for the barge and tug was permitted. The interests of those present and represented by counsel were substantially the same as those who are parties in these proceedings, but who did not appear in the Coast Guard proceedings.

[15] McCormick, supra, §256 at 619-620. The approach of the Federal Rules is to examine proffered former testimony in light of the prior opportunity and motive to develop the testimony, whether in the form of direct, redirect or cross-examination. This less restrictive approach finds support among commentators. See McCormick, supra, §255 at 617; Falknor, Former Testimony and the Uniform Rules: A Comment, 38 N.Y.U. L. Rev. 651 n.1 (1963).

> The term "privity" denotes mutual or successive relationships to the same rights of property, and privies are distributed into several classes, according to the manner of this relationship. Thus, there are privies in estate, as donor and donee, lessor and lessee, and joint tenants; privies in blood, as heir and ancestor, and co-parceners; privies in representation, as executor and testator, administrator and intestate; privies in law, where the law, without privity of blood or estate casts the land upon another, as by escheat.

Metropolitan St. Ry. v. Gumby, 99 F. 192 (2nd Cir. 1900) . . . .

The majority rejects the view that the Rule's wording signals a return to the common law approach requiring privity or a common property interest between the parties, and finds it sufficient that the Coast Guard investigator shared a community of interest with Alvarez. But community of interest seems to mean only that the investigating officer sought to establish the same facts as Alvarez attempted to prove in the instant suit. Used in this sense, community of interest means nothing more than similarity of interest or similarity of motive. But similar motive is a separate prerequisite to admissibility under 804(b)(1) and thus the majority's analysis which reads "predecessor in interest" to mean nothing more than person with "similar motive" eliminates the predecessor in interest requirement entirely.

Moreover, while I appreciate the fact that the Coast Guard investigator sought to establish Lloyd's wrongdoing and that Alvarez sought to do the same, I do not believe that this establishes the kind of "common motive" sufficient to satisfy 804(b)(1).

A prosecutor or an investigating officer represents no ordinary party. He shoulders a peculiar kind of duty, even to his very adversary, a duty which is foreign to the adversarial process among ordinary litigants. The prosecutor, it is true, must seek to vindicate the rights of the alleged victim, but his interests go far beyond that. His interest in a prosecution is not that he shall win a case, but that justice shall be done.

The interests of an attorney representing the government surely overlap with those of the private litigant, but they do not coincide. The investigating officer was under no duty to advance every arguable issue against Lloyd in the vindication of Alvarez's interests, as Alvarez's own counsel would have been. He simply did not represent Alvarez.

Thus, even if I could agree that Congress intended to relax the common law requirement of actual privity between the parties before prior testimony could be admitted, I cannot endorse a rule which would automatically render admissible against a party evidence which was elicited in a different proceeding by an unrelated person merely because both shared an interest in establishing the same facts. The majority's holding makes admissible against Alvarez the testimony of all witnesses who appeared at the Coast Guard hearing—not just Lloyd—and this without any showing of necessity by the proponent of such evidence. Indeed under the majority view, all kinds of testimony adduced at all kinds of administrative hearings—hearings before the Civil Aeronautics

Board on airplane disasters; hearings before the Federal Communications Commission on misuse of broadcast licenses; hearings before the Securities and Exchange Commission on securities fraud, just by way of example—would be admissible in subsequent civil suits, albeit that the parties were entirely different. With all due respect, I think this goes too far. The net result would be charging the party against whom the hearsay evidence is being offered with all flaws in the manner in which the witness was previously handled by another, and all flaws in another's choice of witnesses, the very result characterized by the House Judiciary Committee as "generally unfair."[2]

[Judge Stern then explains his view that the catchall can appropriately apply here.]

NOTES ON PRIOR CROSS-EXAMINATION REQUIREMENT

1. How's that again? Far from Judge Aldisert to distort congressional language by "extravagant interpretation," but the Coast Guard's investigating officer is a "predecessor in interest" to Alvarez? Could he have initiated proceedings against Lloyd to take away his seaman's license? For a discussion, see Weissenberger, The Former Testimony Exception: A Study in Rulemaking, Judicial Revisionism, and the Separation of Powers, 67 N.C. L. Rev. 295 (1989) (fairness to parties, not just accuracy in factfinding, underlay legislative judgment expressed in "predecessor in interest" clause; judicial interpretations conflict, and Court should grant review and restore meaning intended by Congress).

---

[2] Alvarez derived no benefit from the Coast Guard proceeding against Lloyd. His private action for damages in no way derives from or is enhanced by the Coast Guard hearing convened for the purpose of determining whether Lloyd's papers should be revoked or suspended. This distinguishes the instant case from In re Master Key Antitrust Litigation, 72 F.R.D. 108 (D. Conn.), aff'd without published opinion, 551 F.2d 300 (2d Cir. 1976), the only case in which 804(b)(1) has been construed. In *Master Key*, a private class action antitrust suit, defendants sought to introduce testimony given in a prior governmental antitrust action which preceded and gave rise to the private suit. The question was whether the United States could be deemed predecessor in interest of the private plaintiffs for the purpose of Rule 804(b)(1). The court held that it could, but only after weighing "special considerations."

> The unique relationship between the Government's antitrust enforcement suits and the private actions which follow has Congressional recognition and ratification, which has in turn provided special benefits to the private plaintiffs. It has, for example, tolled the applicable statute of limitations, and thus allowed them to extend the period for which they may recover .... Furthermore, the judgment in the earlier decision will be admissible in evidence (although it too is hearsay) and serves to establish their prima facie case.

72 F.R.D. at 109 (citations omitted). No such special circumstances, no quid pro quo, exist here.

S.S. Export Commerce

Carlo Martinelli

Reading *Lloyd,* you may wonder what a shipboard altercation has to do with "seaworthiness," but the concept is central to admiralty law. In the *Boudoin* case, the Supreme Court upheld a judgment against the shipowner when plaintiff was assaulted by a crew member, who had snuck into his room and stolen a bottle of brandy under plaintiff's bed, striking plaintiff with it when he woke. Justice Douglas wrote that "the warranty of seaworthiness is a species of liability without fault," although it does not mean the owner is liable for injuries from "every sailor's brawl" or "from all the fisticuffs on shipboard." Noting that everyone is "to some degree irascible" and that sailors "lead a rough life and are more apt to use their fists than office employees," the Court nevertheless upheld an award to the plaintiff. It concluded that a seaman "with a proclivity for assaulting people may, indeed, be a more deadly risk than a rope with a weak strand or a hull with a latent defect," and that the trial court was justified in thinking the assailant had "crossed the line" and "had such savage disposition as to endanger the others." See Boudoin v. Lyke Bros. S.S. Co., 348 U.S. 336, 339-340 (1955).

The Export Commerce (ship involved in Alvarez) was built in 1963 by Sun Shipbuilding and Dry Dock in Chester, Pennsylvania, and American Export Lines (AEL) operated it for 15 years. The vessel was 11,420 tons, medium sized by the standards of the time. AEL operated cruise and passenger ships too, including the S.S. Constitution, which figured in the movie *An Affair to Remember* (1957). In a scene in that movie, reprised by Tom Hanks and Meg Ryan in the 1993 film *Sleepless in Seattle,* Cary Grant waited in vain for hours on top of the Empire State Building for Deborah Kerr to arrive (see the movie to find out why), but Hanks and Ryan found a happier ending.

2. Before being too hard on Judge Aldisert, consider this case: Partners JB and JC Wright lost their building to fire and sue their casualty carrier. The latter calls Eppler and Brown, expecting that they would testify that JB Wright conspired with them to burn the building. But Eppler and Brown claim their privilege against self-incrimination. In a prior trial of JB Wright for arson, however, Eppler and Brown testified to a conspiracy, and the carrier offers a transcript of that testimony. The Oklahoma Supreme Court thought the transcript was admissible against *both* JB and JC Wright:

> Is it important that JC Wright did not have an opportunity to cross-examine in the criminal case? JB Wright had the same motive and interest in cross-examining the witnesses in the criminal case as would JC Wright in the instant case. The issues were the same in both cases .... We conclude that JB Wright's opportunity to cross-examine the witness in the criminal case on the same issue, and with the same interest and motives that JC Wright would have in the instant case, satisfies the rule of substantial identity of issues and parties and opportunity for satisfactory cross-examination.
>
> From the foregoing it is seen that the question of substantial identity of parties is important only with regard to the parties as against whom such testimony is offered; therefore the fact that the state was JB Wright's adversary in the first case rather than the insurance companies is immaterial. Such fact has no bearing upon the question of whether there has been an adequate opportunity to thoroughly sift and test such testimony by cross-examination.

Travelers Fire Insurance Co. v. Wright, 322 P.2d 417 (Okla. 1958). Didn't *Wright* reach the best result? Putting aside FRE 804(b)(1), *Lloyd* reached an equally sound result, didn't it? If *Wright* arose today under FRE 804(b)(1), could the *Lloyd* interpretation justify admitting the former testimony of Eppler and Brown against JC Wright?

3. A Blue Lines bus collides with a car, and many bus passengers are killed or injured. Bus passenger Anne brings action 1 against Blue Lines and seeks to prove that excessive speed of the bus caused the accident. But eyewitness Carl testifies for Blue Lines that the bus was traveling slowly in its own lane, and the car crossed the center line at the last minute, driving into the bus. The jury returns a verdict for Blue Lines. Thereafter bus passenger Bart sues Blue Lines, also alleging that the bus was speeding. Carl has died, and Blue Lines offers his testimony from action 1 against Bart. Does FRE 804(b)(1) permit this use of Carl's former testimony?

4. Doug sues Emville Asbestos Corporation, alleging that he contracted asbestosis while installing Emville insulation products. At trial, Dr. Gregory (physician employed by Emville) testifies to the state of medical knowledge regarding asbestos-related diseases. Then he dies. Now Eric, another insulation installer who suffers from asbestosis, sues Emville and Franklin Insulation Company, making similar allegations about products made by both companies. Can Eric offer against Emville and Franklin the testimony by Dr. Gregory in Doug's suit?

5. The idea that a person may be bound or affected by what his "predecessor in interest" has done is central to the notion of "privity." In his concurring opinion in *Lloyd*, Judge Stern quotes a standard definition of privity. That concept was also central in explaining why a person not party to a lawsuit could nevertheless be bound by it—explaining, in other words, why the person was bound by res judicata or collateral estoppel. Is it appropriate, in deciding whether testimony from a prior suit may be admitted against a party who did not participate in it, to apply the same test that determines whether the judgment in the earlier suit may have res judicata or collateral estoppel effect against that party?

3. Dying Declarations

Where a person understands that his death is imminent and speaks of his circumstance, the hearsay doctrine has long recognized an exception for his words. The exception rests on a thought passed forward from a more godfearing age that a dying person will not meet his maker with a lie on his lips, and rests also on the belief that psychological forces incline a dying person toward being truthful. There is also the point that dying declarations are likely to speak of facts in the forefront of memory.

The exception is most often invoked in homicide trials, paving way to admit the dying words of the victim identifying defendant as his assailant. See Commonwealth v. Moses, 766 N.E.2d 827, 830 (Mass. 2002) (in murder trial, admitting statement by victim to medical technician stating that "Prince" had shot him). These cases bring strong emotional appeal to listen to the last utterance of a helpless victim.

The exception as we have it in FRE 804(b)(2) applies in homicide trials and civil cases and embraces statements about "cause and circumstances" of impending death. Thus statements identifying the assailant fit the exception, as do descriptions of the accident or catastrophe that befell the declarant. See United States v. Mobley, 421 F.2d 345, 346-347 (5th Cir. 1970) (bank president shot in robbery describes events); Connor v. State, 171 A.2d 699 (Md. 1960) (run over by husband, dying wife declares, "It was no accident"), *cert. denied*, 368 U.S. 906 (1961); United Services Automobile Association v. Wharton, 237 F. Supp. 255, 257-260 (N.D.N.C. 1965) (breakthrough and colorful civil case admitting hospital statement by woman fatally injured in head-on collision, that her husband said immediately before driving into lefthand lane that they would "go to eternity together"). Probably it also embraces descriptions of prior threats and quarrels, physical pain or sensations, and matters inhaled, injected, or ingested.

■ NOTES ON DYING DECLARATIONS

1. Does the exception rest on a sound psychological premise? Consider the insight of Shakespeare, in the plea of the dying Melun:

–Melun–
What in the world should make me now deceive,
–Salisbury–
May this be possible? May this be true?
–Melun–
Have I not hideous death within my view,
Retaining but a quantity of life,
Which bleeds away, even as a form of wax
Resolveth from this figure 'gainst the fire?
What in the world should make me now deceive,
Since I must lose the use of all deceit?
Why should I then be false, since it is true

That I must die here and live hence by truth?

Shakespeare, *King John*, Act V, scene iv.

2. How should we decide whether the declarant had a settled expectancy of imminent death? See Mattox v. United States, 146 U.S. 140, 151-152 (1892) (relying on nature of wounds and advice by attending physician that declarant had no chance); State v. Buggs, 581 N.W.2d 329, 335 (Minn. 1998) (shot six times in chest and abdomen, victim was found "lying on her back on the floor in a pool of blood, 'squirming,' and struggling to breathe") (seriousness of wounds, labored breathing, and fact of death within hours were "sufficient circumstances" from which court could infer belief in impending death).

3. How imminent must the prospect of death be? Consider the trial of Charles Shepard, a doctor and army officer, for the murder of his wife Zenana. She was apparently poisoned with bichloride of mercury, her symptoms first appearing on May 20, and death following on June 15. Two days after falling ill, she asked the attending nurse to fetch a bottle of liquor from which she had drunk before collapsing, asked whether enough was left to test for poison, adding that "the smell and taste were strange" and suggesting that "Dr. Shepard has poisoned me." In a famous opinion by Justice Cardozo, the Supreme Court concluded that the exception did not apply:

> We have said that the declarant was not shown to have spoken without hope of recovery and in the shadow of impending death. Her illness began on May 20. She was found in a state of collapse, delirious, in pain, the pupils of her eyes dilated, and the retina suffused with blood. The conversation with the nurse occurred two days later. At that time her mind had cleared up, and her speech was rational and orderly. There was as yet no thought by any of her physicians that she was dangerously ill, still less that her case was hopeless. To all seeming she had greatly improved, and was moving forward to recovery. There had been no diagnosis of poison as the cause of her distress. Not till about a week afterwards was there a relapse, accompanied by an infection of the mouth, renewed congestion of the eyes, and later hemorrhage of the bowels. Death followed on June 15.
>
> Nothing in the condition of the patient on May 22 gives fair support to the conclusion that hope had then been lost. She may have thought she was going to die and have said so to her nurse, but this was consistent with hope, which could not have been put aside without more to quench it. Indeed, a fortnight later, she said to one of her physicians, though her condition was then grave, "You will get me well, won't you?" Fear or even belief that illness will end in death will not avail of itself to make a dying declaration. There must be "a settled hopeless expectation" (Willes, J. in Reg. v. Peel, 2 F. & F. 21, 22) that death is near at hand, and what is said must have been spoken in the hush of its impending presence. Despair of recovery may indeed be gathered from the circumstances if the facts support the inference. There is no unyielding ritual of words to be spoken by the dying. Despair may even be gathered though the period of survival outruns the bounds of expectation. What is decisive is the state of mind. Even so, the state of mind must be exhibited in the evidence, and not left to conjecture. The patient must have spoken with the consciousness of a swift and certain doom.

> What was said by this patient was not spoken in that mood. There was no warning to her in the circumstances that her words would be repeated and accepted as those of a dying wife, charging murder to her husband, and charging it deliberately and solemnly as a fact within her knowledge. To the focus of that responsibility her mind was never brought. She spoke as one ill, giving voice to the beliefs and perhaps the conjectures of the moment. The liquor was to be tested, to see whether her beliefs were sound. She did not speak as one dying, announcing to the survivors a definitive conviction, a legacy of knowledge on which the world might act when she had gone.

Shepard v. United States, 290 U.S. 96, 99-100 (1933). Are you persuaded? Are the words of Cardozo powerful enough to convince you of the validity of the exception? Are they just words, or do they capture a reality of the human condition?

4. Who should decide these points (that the speaker thought she was dying and that death was imminent and inevitable)? The choices are judge or jury. Common law tradition included an instruction that jury should consider statement only if it believed that declarant knew death was imminent. See Freihage v. United States, 56 F.2d 127, 134 (9th Cir. 1932) (error to withdraw question from jury). Modern cases go the other way. See Commonwealth v. Cooley, 348 A.2d 103, 108 (Pa. 1975) (question whether statement qualifies as dying declaration "is one of law" that is "not within the province of the jury") (refusing to tell jury "to assess for themselves whether the decedent believed he was about to die"). The latter seems correct under FRE 104(a), as the question whether the declarant knew he was dying affects admissibility rather than relevancy.

5. How should we deal with the question whether the declarant had personal knowledge? Compare Shepard v. United States, 290 U.S. 96, 100-102 (1933) (dying declaration admissible only if circumstances permit inference that declarant had knowledge and should be excluded if speaker expresses "suspicion or conjecture") and State v. Wilks, 213 S.W. 118 (Mo. 1919) (statement that certain people hired assailant inadmissible as dying declaration because of lack of knowledge) with Soles v. State, 119 So. 791 (Fla. 1929) (admitting statement by declarant shot in back of head identifying defendant as his assailant, without discussing personal knowledge).

4. Declarations Against Interest

a. Introduction and General Considerations

Declarations against interest are thought to be trustworthy on the ground that a person is unlikely to state facts (or make statements) harming his own interest unless they are true.

Civil cases. Traditionally the exception embraced statements against financial or proprietary interest, and was invoked in civil cases. If Sam says "I owe Tod $1,000," he concedes a debt, and the statement is against interest to that extent. It would likely be admissible to prove that he owed Tod that sum.

In a suit against Sam, Tod could offer the statement as Sam's admission—with no need for the against-interest exception. If Sam has died and Tod presses a claim against his estate, the exception may be necessary. Commonly, Dead Man's Statutes bar Tod from testifying to what Sam said (see Chapter 6), but they might not block testimony by others, or a document in which Sam acknowledges his debt.

Similarly, a statement acknowledging that the speaker received payment is likely to be against his interest. If Tod said, "Sam paid me $2,000," that statement would be against Tod's interest in suggesting that Sam now owes $2,000 less than before, and this same logic applies to an actual written receipt for payment that Tod gives Sam. In an attenuation of subtlety, it is sometimes said that if the statute of limitations permits suit, Tod's statement is against interest (it proves date of payment, and might start a new limitation period, but concedes payment), but if the statute has run, the statement is self-serving (it still concedes payment and might begin a new period, but now it revives a previously barred claim for unpaid balance).

Applying the exception is usually not so easy as this bare-bones example suggests. Even statements like Sam's and Tod's can be difficult. Consider these factors:

(1) Context. Here is a critical element. Imagine that Tod was hounding Sam to "pay back the $5,000 you owe me," and Sam said "I owe you $1,000." Sam's statement concedes a debt. But if his intent is to limit or reduce his obligation, it is not against interest, at least with respect to a claim above $1,000. Donovan v. Crisostomo, 689 F.2d 869, 876-877 (9th Cir. 1982) (statements by Philippine workers that they had not worked much were not against interest, when offered by employer in suit by Labor Secretary seeking back pay; worker who might be sent back to Philippines could feel that it was "in his interest to state he was paid properly to avoid the wrath of his employer").

(2) Conflicting interests. Every person has multiple interests, and they are often complex rather than simple, conflicting rather than consistent. Not surprisingly, a statement may further one interest and impair another. In any such case, courts applying the exception could either (a) exclude the statement because conflicting interests cancel each other, or (b) determine whether the statement was predominantly disserving or self-serving, and admit or exclude accordingly.

(3) One-way interest. A taxpayer fills out her return, stating taxable income for the year; an owner trying to sell his motel talks to a prospective buyer about gross receipts for a year. There are penalties for paying the government less than it is due and for fraudulent sales, but the immediate interest of the taxpayer is to aim low, that of the owner to aim high. Each might speak against interest—she by overstatement, he by understatement. Does the instant exception play a role here?

Some courts have thought it might. If the taxpayer dies and suit is brought for wrongful death, decedent's tax return might be offered to show that decedent made *at least* as much as it says, for she would never declare *more than* she earned. If the motel owner dies and the property is condemned, the taking agency might offer the estimate of gross receipts as proof that the commercial value of the property is *no higher*, for declarant would never say the motel earned *less than* it did. See Plisco v. United States, 306 F.2d 784, 786-789 (D.C. Cir. 1962) (in IRS jeopardy assessment suit, admitting memoranda by taxpayers to show winnings but not losses; they "had no incentive to overstate their daily profit figures" to increase their taxes, which commissioner could accept as "minima," but "did have an incentive to overstate their daily loss," which commissioner could reject), *cert. denied*, 371 U.S. 948 (1963).

(4) Circumstantially adverse facts. A statement may fit the exception without directly speaking of debts or property. Thus, a statement admitting fault in a context that might give rise to liability or loss to the declarant may satisfy the exception. In a suit by a building owner and insurance carrier against the tenant of a warehouse to recover for fire loss, for example, plaintiffs offered a statement made hours after the blaze by the tenant's employee Faulds to police officers and a fire inspector. There Faulds admitted that he and others had been drinking, and entered the warehouse at 3:00 A.M. and smoked cigarettes:

> A statement is against pecuniary and proprietary interest when it threatens the loss of employment, or reduces the chances for future employment, or entails possible civil liability . . . . Here Faulds' statement is an important link in providing a basis for concluding that Faulds and the other nighttime visitors to the warehouse were responsible for starting the fire; the possibility of civil liability against him arising from the statement is thus evident. Indeed, an effort was made to make him a defendant in this case . . . . Further, even though [the tenant] did not have a rule against smoking on the premises, Faulds' admission that he had been there after hours, for a purpose unrelated to his employment, and while there did something which may have caused the destruction of his employer's stock in trade, reflects on his responsibility and trustworthiness, and can reasonably be said to jeopardize his standing with his employer.

Gichner v. Antonio Troiano Tile & Marble Co., 410 F.2d 238 (D.C. Cir. 1969) (case remanded to determine whether Faulds was unavailable).

(5) Declarant's understanding. The exception only helps to pick out reliable statements if declarant understood his own interests and how the fact or statement could affect them. Hence courts exclude statements uttered by persons who lack the necessary information. See Filesi v. United States, 352 F.2d 339, 343-344 (4th Cir. 1965) (in suit by taxpayer to recover taxes previously assessed and paid, statement by deceased partner admitting that dancing went on in the bar was not against his interest; nothing indicated that he "realized the possible serious financial consequences" that could arise from admission that "dancing was permitted"). Granting the principle, can you believe that a tavern owner would not know about cabaret taxes?

b. *Criminal Cases—Statements Implicating the Accused*

Traditionally the exception did not reach statements against "penal" interest. In a notorious prosecution of one Donnelly for the alleged murder of an Indian named Chickasaw, the Supreme Court found that a confession by Joe Dick (who had died of consumption) that he shot Chickasaw was inadmissible. The result moved Justice Holmes to protest that "no other statement is so much against interest as a confession of murder," which should be received as "far more calculated to convince than dying declarations, which would be let in to hang a man." Donnelly v. United States, 228 U.S. 243, 278 (1913). The argument against admitting confessions like Joe Dick's is that it invites defendants to offer perjured testimony describing third-party confessions that were never made. These are hard for prosecutors to investigate (let alone disprove) because the declarant is unavailable.

The tide has turned, and FRE 804(b)(3) extends the exception to statements against penal interest. It is fair to say that nobody expected, with this extension of the exception, that it would prove so useful to prosecutors, who now use the exception to prove third-party confessions implicating the accused. This use of the exception came to the Supreme Court in the case you're about to read.

WILLIAMSON v. UNITED STATES

United States Supreme Court
512 U.S. 594 (1994)

Justice O'CONNOR delivered the opinion of the Court, except as to Part IIC. In this case we clarify the scope of the hearsay exception for statements against penal interest. FRE 804(b)(3).

I

[Stopped for weaving on the highway, Reginald Harris was arrested after a search of the trunk led to the discovery of 19 kilograms of cocaine in two suitcases. DEA Agent Donald Walton interviewed him by phone. Harris said he got the cocaine from a Cuban in Fort Lauderdale, but it belonged to Fredel Williamson and was to be delivered at a dumpster that night. Later Walton spoke personally to Harris, who said he rented the car and drove to Fort Lauderdale to meet Williamson. Harris said he got the cocaine from a Cuban, who put it in the car with a note instructing Harris how to deliver the drugs.

Agent Walton tried to arrange a controlled delivery, but Harris then said he had lied about the Cuban, the note, and the dumpster. Actually, Harris said, he was taking the cocaine to Atlanta for Williamson, who had been driving in front in another car. Williamson saw that Harris had been stopped, doubled back and drove past, seeing the ongoing search. Hence a controlled delivery was impossible. Harris said he had lied because he was afraid of Williamson. He refused to let his statement be recorded or to sign a written version. Walton promised to report his cooperation to the U.S. Attorney.

Williamson and Harris were linked by other proof: The rental agreement listed Williamson as an additional driver; the luggage bore his sister's initials; the glove compartment held an envelope addressed to him and a receipt with his girlfriend's address.

Williamson was convicted of possessing cocaine with intent to distribute, conspiracy, and traveling interstate to promote distribution. Harris refused to testify, even when offered immunity and ordered to do so. The court admitted against Fredel Williamson what Reginald Harris told Agent Walton. On appeal, Williamson claims the against-interest exception did not apply and that his rights under the Confrontation Clause were violated.]

II

A

. . . To decide whether Harris' confession is made admissible by FRE 804(b)(3), we must first determine what the Rule means by "statement," which FRE 801(a)(1) defines as an "oral or written assertion." One possible meaning, "a report or narrative," Webster's Third New International Dictionary 2229, definition 2(a) (1961), connotes an extended declaration. Under this reading, Harris' entire confession—even if it contains both self-inculpatory and non-self-inculpatory parts—would be admissible so long as in the aggregate the confession sufficiently inculpates him. Another meaning of "statement," "a single declaration or remark," definition 2(b), would make FRE 804(b)(3) cover only those declarations or remarks within the confession that are individually self-inculpatory. See also id. (defining "assertion" as a "declaration"); id. (defining "declaration" as a "statement").

Although the text of the Rule does not directly resolve the matter, the principle behind the Rule, so far as it is discernible from the text, points clearly to the narrower reading. FRE 804(b)(3) is founded on the commonsense notion that reasonable people, even reasonable people who are not especially honest, tend not to make self-inculpatory statements unless they believe them to be true. This notion simply does not extend to the broader definition of "statement." The fact that a person is making a broadly self-inculpatory confession does not make more credible the confession's non-self-inculpatory parts. One of the most effective ways to lie is to mix falsehood with truth, especially truth that seems particularly persuasive because of its self-inculpatory nature.

In this respect, it is telling that the non-self-inculpatory things Harris said in his first statement actually proved to be false, as Harris himself admitted during the second interrogation. And when part of the confession is actually self-exculpatory, the generalization on which FRE 804(b)(3) is founded becomes even less applicable. Self-exculpatory statements are exactly the ones which people are most likely to make even when they are false; and mere proximity to other, self-inculpatory, statements does not increase the plausibility of the self-exculpatory statements.

We therefore cannot agree with Justice Kennedy's suggestion that the Rule can be read as expressing a policy that collateral statements—even ones that are not in any way against the declarant's interest—are admissible. Nothing in the text of FRE 804(b)(3) or the general theory of the hearsay rules suggests that admissibility should turn on whether a statement is collateral to a self-inculpatory statement. The fact that a statement is self-inculpatory does make it more reliable, but the fact that a statement is collateral to a self-inculpatory statement says nothing at all about the collateral statement's reliability. We see no reason why collateral statements, even ones that are neutral as to interest, should be treated any differently from other hearsay statements that are generally excluded.

Congress certainly could, subject to the constraints of the Confrontation Clause, make statements admissible based on their proximity to self-inculpatory statements. But we will not lightly assume that the ambiguous language means anything so inconsistent with the Rule's underlying theory. In our view, the most faithful reading of FRE 804(b)(3) is that it does not allow admission of non-self-inculpatory statements, even if they are made within a broader narrative that is generally self-inculpatory. The district court may not just assume for purposes of FRE 804(b)(3) that a statement is self-inculpatory because it is part of a fuller confession, and this is especially true when the statement implicates someone else. "The arrest statements of a codefendant have traditionally been viewed with special suspicion. Due to his strong motivation to implicate the defendant and to exonerate himself, a codefendant's statements about what the defendant said or did are less credible than ordinary hearsay evidence." Lee v. Illinois, 476 U.S. 530, 541 (1986) (internal quotation marks omitted); see also Bruton v. United States, 391 U.S. 123, 136 (1968); Dutton v. Evans, 400 U.S. 74, 98 (1970) (Harlan, J., concurring in result).

[Quoting the CAN and the passage from McCormick that Justice Kennedy also relies on, Justice O'Connor rejects the view that "an entire narrative, including non-self-inculpatory parts (but excluding the clearly self-serving parts)," fit the exception. The CAN "is not particularly clear" and its cite to McCormick "points the other way."] Without deciding exactly how much weight to give the CAN in this particular situation, we conclude that the policy expressed in the statutory text points clearly enough in one direction that it outweighs whatever force the Notes may have. And though Justice Kennedy believes that the text can fairly be read as expressing a policy of admitting collateral statements, for the reasons given above we disagree.

B

We also do not share Justice Kennedy's fears that our reading of the Rule "eviscerates the against penal interest exception," or makes it lack "meaningful effect." There are many circumstances in which FRE 804(b)(3) does allow the admission of statements that inculpate a criminal defendant. Even the confessions of arrested accomplices may be admissible if they are truly self-inculpatory, rather than merely attempts to shift blame or curry favor.

For instance, a declarant's squarely self-inculpatory confession—"yes, I killed *X*"—will likely be admissible under FRE 804(b)(3) against accomplices of his who are being tried under a coconspirator liability theory. Likewise, by showing that the declarant knew something, a self-inculpatory statement can in some situations help the jury infer that his confederates knew it as well. And when seen with other evidence, an accomplice's self-inculpatory statement can inculpate the defendant directly: "I was robbing the bank on Friday morning," coupled with someone's testimony that the declarant and the defendant drove off together Friday morning, is evidence that the defendant also participated in the robbery.

Moreover, whether a statement is self-inculpatory or not can only be determined by viewing it in context. Even statements that are on their face neutral may actually be against the declarant's interest. "I hid the gun in Joe's apartment" may not be a confession of a crime, but if it is likely to help the police find the murder weapon, then it is certainly self-inculpatory. "Sam and I went to Joe's house" might be against the declarant's interest if a reasonable person in the declarant's shoes would realize that being linked to Joe and Sam would implicate the declarant in Joe and Sam's conspiracy. And other statements that give the police significant details about the crime may also, depending on the situation, be against the declarant's interest. The question under FRE 804(b)(3) is always whether the statement was sufficiently against the declarant's penal interest "that a reasonable person in the declarant's position would not have made the statement unless believing it to be true," and this question can only be answered in light of all the surrounding circumstances.

C

In this case, however, we cannot conclude that all that Harris said was properly admitted. Some of Harris' confession would clearly have been admissible under FRE 804(b)(3). For instance, when he said he knew there was cocaine in the suitcase, he essentially forfeited his only possible defense to a charge of cocaine possession, lack of knowledge. But other parts of his confession, especially the parts that implicated Williamson, did little to subject Harris himself to criminal liability. A reasonable person in Harris' position might even think that implicating someone else would decrease his practical exposure to criminal liability, at least so far as sentencing goes. Small fish in a big conspiracy often get shorter sentences than people who are running the whole show, especially if the small fish are willing to help the authorities catch the big ones.

Nothing in the record shows that the District Court or the Court of Appeals inquired whether each of the statements in Harris' confession was truly self-inculpatory. As we explained above, this can be a fact-intensive inquiry, which would require careful examination of all the circumstances surrounding the criminal activity involved; we therefore remand to the Court of Appeals to conduct this inquiry in the first instance....

So ordered.

Justice SCALIA, concurring....

A statement obviously can be self-inculpatory (in the sense of having so much of a tendency to subject one to criminal liability that a reasonable person would not make it without believing it to be true) without consisting of the confession "I committed *X* element of crime *Y*." Consider, for example, a declarant who stated: "On Friday morning, I went into a gunshop and (lawfully) bought a particular type of handgun and particular type of ammunition. I then drove in my 1958 blue Edsel and parked in front of the First City Bank with the keys in the ignition and the driver's door ajar. I then went inside, robbed the bank and shot the security guard." Although the declarant has not confessed to any element of a crime in the first two sentences, those statements in context are obviously against his penal interest, and I have no doubt that a trial judge could properly admit them.

Moreover, a declarant's statement is not magically transformed from a statement against penal interest into one that is inadmissible merely because the declarant names another person or implicates a possible codefendant. For example, if a lieutenant in an organized crime operation described the inner workings of an extortion and protection racket, naming some of the other actors and thereby inculpating himself on racketeering and/or conspiracy charges, I have no doubt that some of those remarks could be admitted as statements against penal interest. Of course, naming another person, if done, for example, in a context where the declarant is minimizing culpability or criminal exposure, can bear on whether the statement meets the FRE 804(b)(3) standard. The relevant inquiry, however—and one that is not furthered by clouding the waters with manufactured categories such as "collateral neutral" and "collateral self-serving"—must always be whether the particular remark at issue (and not the extended narrative) meets the standard set forth in the Rule.

Justice GINSBURG, with whom Justice BLACKMUN, Justice STEVENS, and Justice SOUTER join, concurring in part and concurring in the judgment.

[*Lee* holds that a statement implicating another is inadmissible under the Confrontation Clause, and an arrested person has "strong incentive to shift blame or downplay his own role" in hope of leniency and a shorter sentence. Hence none of the statements by Reginald Harris fit the exception, "even in part."]

Justice KENNEDY, with whom THE CHIEF JUSTICE and Justice THOMAS join, concurring in the judgment.

[Commentators debate the admissibility of collateral statements. Wigmore favored admitting the whole statement; McCormick was "more guarded," and favored admitting "collateral statements of a neutral character," but not "self-serving" ones. Jefferson favored admitting only statements proving facts that are against interest. The ACN shows that some collateral statements are admissible, including statements implicating the accused that come in as "related statements," and Congress intended to continue the principles "as they were at common law," reaching collateral statements connected with disserving statements. The Court's approach would, in the words of a commentator, "eviscerate the against penal interest exception."

Self-serving collateral statements should not be admissible, such as "one that tends to reduce the charges or mitigate the punishment for which the declarant might be liable."]

[T]here is a separate limit applicable to cases in which the declarant made his statement to authorities; this limit applies not only to collateral statements but also to the precise words against penal interest. A declarant may believe that a statement of guilt to authorities is in his interest to some extent, for example as a way to obtain more lenient treatment, or simply to clear his conscience. The ACN takes account of that potentiality and states that courts should examine the circumstances of the statement to determine whether the statement was "motivated by a desire to curry favor with the authorities." That appears consistent with McCormick's recognition that "even though a declaration may be against interest in one respect, if it appears that the declarant had some other motive whether of self-interest or otherwise, which was likely to lead him to misrepresent the facts, the declaration will be excluded." McCormick §256, p.553 . . . .

In sum, I would adhere to the following approach with respect to statements against penal interest that inculpate the accused. A court first should determine whether the declarant made a statement that contained a fact against penal interest. If so, the court should admit all statements related to the precise statement against penal interest, subject to two limits. Consistent with the ACN, the court should exclude a collateral statement that is so self-serving as to render it unreliable (if, for example, it shifts blame to someone else for a crime the defendant could have committed). In addition, in cases where the statement was made under circumstances where it is likely that the declarant had a significant motivation to obtain favorable treatment, as when the government made an explicit offer of leniency in exchange for the declarant's admission of guilt, the entire statement should be inadmissible . . . .

■ NOTES ON STATEMENTS AGAINST INTEREST THAT IMPLICATE THE ACCUSED

1. In a passage edited from the case, *Williamson* avoids taking any position on the Confrontation Clause. *Williamson* is binding on federal courts as a construction of FRE 804(b)(3), but a state court can interpret its against-interest exception in other ways. In a state that has adopted the Rules, *Williamson* is influential but not binding. Compare, e.g., State v. Keeton, 589 N.W.2d 85 (Minn.

1998) (following *Williamson*) with People v. Newton, 966 P.2d 563 (Colo. 1998) (declining to follow *Williamson*).

2. In substance, *Williamson* holds that FRE 804(b)(3) does not reach associated (or "collateral") statements. Instead, Justice O'Connor's opinion says a statement must itself be against interest. Speaking for himself and two others, Justice Kennedy disagrees. He argues that the exception does reach neutral statements that are related to against-interest statements. On this salient point of difference, both O'Connor and Kennedy stress legislative history and underlying purpose. Who has the better of the argument?

3. All nine Justices agree that statements that curry favor with police do not satisfy the against-interest exception. Almost all such statements are also testimonial under *Crawford*, which came after *Williamson*. Today, then, almost all such statements are excludable under the Confrontation Clause. In this sense *Crawford* largely eclipses *Williamson*. "Largely" is the operative word: *Williamson* remains important because of the way it interprets the against-interest exception. Many against-interest statements are made in private settings, where an alleged participant in crimes generating charges against the defendant speaks to someone else and makes statements implicating both the speaker and the defendant. *Such* statements are almost never testimonial, and their admissibility depends on whether they fit the against-interest exception (including the unavailability requirement), where *Williamson* remains influential.

4. The challenge in applying *Williamson* is to decide whether, and to what extent, a third-party statement describing behavior by the defendant fits the exception. Consider these points:

(a) Some see in *Williamson* a per se rule that third-party statements cannot fit the exception in describing behavior by the defendant. See, e.g., Smith v. State, 647 A.2d 1093 (Del. 1994) (error to admit statements by accomplice to wife that he and defendant beat victim; exception does not reach "neutral, collateral statements") (reversing). Most courts, however, do not see *Williamson* as a complete bar to such statements. See, e.g., United States v. Smalls, 605 F.3d 765, 781 (10th Cir. 2010) (*Williamson* did not say that accomplice statements implicating defendant are "presumptively unreliable regardless of the circumstances," and such statements are admissible if truly self-inculpatory).

(b) Justice O'Connor says a facially neutral statement is against interest if context makes it so. Hence "Sam and I went to Joe's house" is against interest "if a reasonable person in the declarant's shoes would realize that being linked to Joe and Sam would implicate the declarant in Joe and Sam's conspiracy." Doesn't it follow that references to what others did are not always "collateral," and a statement by one person can sometimes be used against another to prove what the latter did?

(c) The statements by Reginald Harris referring to defendant Fredel Williamson can be fairly summarized this way:

> I rented the car and went to Fort Lauderdale to meet Williamson. The cocaine in the suitcases in the trunk belonged to him, and I was transporting it to Atlanta for him. He was ahead of me in another rented car, but after I was stopped he

> turned around, came back and drove past, so he saw my car being searched. I lied about getting the drug from the Cuban because I'm afraid of Williamson.

In sum, Harris says Williamson owned the cocaine, that he was involved in transporting it, and that Harris was acting for him. These statements implicate *Harris* in a conspiracy too. Aren't they against the interest of *Harris* just as much as (if not more than) the example given by the Court as one that could come in ("Sam and I went to Joe's house")?

(d) The real question is whether a third-party statement implicating the accused had *so great a tendency* to expose the speaker to "criminal liability" that "a reasonable person" in his position would only have spoken that way if his words were true. In *Williamson*, what Harris said fails that test *not* because he mentioned Williamson, but because Harris was speaking to a DEA Agent after being caught red-handed—he was "currying favor" to minimize his own future difficulties with the criminal justice system.

(e) Putting aside such "curry favor" statements, which don't fit the exception and would also be excludable under *Crawford* as testimonial, we are left with statements by friends or colleagues of the defendant to other friends or acquaintances. In such settings, most modern decisions, including those that consider *Williamson* to be authoritative, *admit* such statements if they are even-handed in attributing blame to the speaker and the defendant, and *exclude* them if they appear to be shifting blame—attributing worse behavior to the defendant and in that sense exonerating the speaker. Compare, e.g., United States v. Smalls, 605 F.3d 765, 785 (10th Cir. 2010) (in trial for murdering informant in prison, admitting co-offender *C*'s statement to cellmate implicating defendant *S*; rather than shifting blame, *C* "opined that because all three men were involved" in murder, none could say anything; statement "plainly speaks to a conspiracy to commit murder, an act of murder, and a motive" for murder; description of murder, even though naming other participants, was against *C*'s penal interest and trustworthy) with Walter v. State, 267 S.W.3d 883 (Tex. Crim. App. 2008) (in trial for murdering employees of a steakhouse in armed robbery, error to admit statements by *M* admitting involvement but blaming defendant for actual killings; "blame-shifting statements" that do not implicate declarant and defendant "equally" are not within the exception).

c. *Criminal Cases—Statements Exonerating the Accused*

■ PROBLEM 4-P. "He Had Nothing to Do with It"

While driving an 18-wheeler north on I-55 near Bloomington, Illinois, John Garvin is stopped by State Trooper Howard for a Motor Carrier Code violation. Garvin gets out of the cab and produces his license but does not have a logbook or bill of lading. On request, he lets Howard search the cab for these items, telling them he is traveling with co-driver Will Torrens, who is resting in the bunk behind the seat.

Officer Howard asks Torrens to get out of the cab and notes a strong smell of air freshener as Torrens emerges. Howard then looks through the cab. Once inside, Howard smells a strong odor of marijuana and sees four brown suitcases, one with a sidepocket that is slightly unzipped. Howard sees duct tape through the opening and feels "bricklike objects" when he squeezes the bag. Howard radios for backup, and a trained dog is brought to the scene, leading to a search and the discovery of marijuana, which is packed in the suitcases and hidden behind the bunk in the sleeping area.

Howard reads Garvin his *Miranda* rights. Garvin tells Howard that the company assigned him to work with Torrens when Garvin's truck broke down, that the two drove from Milwaukee to Dallas to deliver a load of cheese, that on arrival in Dallas they got a hotel room, that Torrens left for several hours and on his return said the company wanted them to drive the cheese to Kansas City. Thereafter Garvin and Torrens took turns driving, and Torrens told Garvin the cheese had been delivered in Kansas City while Garvin was sleeping. Garvin said he never saw the bill of lading and knew nothing about any marijuana.

Thereafter Howard reads Torrens his *Miranda* rights and they talk outside the hearing of Garvin: Torrens tells Howard: "The marijuana belongs to me, not Garvin. He had nothing to do with it. I just wanted to get rich quick. I took a chance and lost, and now I have to do the time. I'm ready for it."

Garvin and Torrens are charged in federal court with possessing marijuana with intent to distribute. Their motion to suppress the marijuana is rejected, and Torrens pleads guilty, but Garvin does not. In Garvin's trial, Torrens refuses to testify. The government proves the truck was empty and argues that Garvin must have known that no cheese was ever carried or delivered and must have smelled the marijuana because its odor was apparent to Howard despite the air freshener. Garvin calls Howard to testify to what Torrens said about the marijuana belonging to him and Garvin having "nothing to do with it," invoking the against-interest exception. The court refuses to allow this testimony, concluding that the exception does not reach the part of the Torrens statement exonerating Garvin. Ultimately Garvin is convicted. On appeal, he argues that the court erred in excluding Torrens' statement to Howard. What result, and why?

NOTES ON STATEMENTS AGAINST INTEREST EXONERATING THE ACCUSED

1. Although Torrens is under arrest, he is not "currying favor" when he speaks to Officer Howard. To put it another way, he is not blaming someone else while implicitly offering his services to help get a conviction. Do these facts indicate that what Torrens said is trustworthy insofar as it tends to exonerate Garvin?

2. Was it against the interest of Torrens to tell Officer Howard that Garvin "had nothing to do with it"? A court following *Williamson* slavishly might exclude this part of the statement, but courts have disagreed on this point. Compare State v. White, 729 A.2d 31 (N.J. 1999) (statement exculpating defendant fits exception "if, when considered in the light of surrounding circumstances, they subject the declarant to criminal liability or if, as a related part of a self-inculpatory statement, they strengthen or bolster the incriminatory effect of the declarant's exposure to criminal liability") with United States v. Vegas, 27 F.3d 773, 782 (2d Cir. 1994) (excluding proof that *J* said he knew "who gave me the drugs and who didn't" and that *M* and defendant "didn't give me" drugs). Does it matter whether the speaker says "the contraband is mine" or says instead "the contraband doesn't belong to the other guy; it's mine"? See United States v. Hilliard, 11 F.3d 618, 619 (6th Cir. 1993) (third party acknowledged "ownership of both the drugs and the money," which satisfied against-interest requirement).

3. Sometimes applying the exception to statements exonerating the accused is easy: A third person confesses to committing the deed, making no reference to defendant, in a setting in which declarant's guilt would exonerate the accused. See Gray v. State, 796 A.2d 697, 734 (Md. 2002) (in trial of husband for murdering wife, error to exclude statement by her lover to friend, saying "I took care of her" which seemed to confess murder) (reversing).

4. Sometimes defendants offer statements by already-incarcerated people in postconviction attacks. Courts are skeptical, especially where the speaker cannot be prosecuted because charges were dropped or dismissed or the speaker is already convicted on related charges. See United States v. Albert, 773 F.2d 386, 388-389 (1st Cir. 1985) (excluding statement by convicted co-offender at plea proceeding; people speak "to help themselves, not to be sentenced to a longer term"); Witham v. Mabry, 596 F.2d 293, 296-298 (8th Cir. 1979) (excluding statement by incarcerated co-offender that defendant had nothing to do with killing) (postconviction challenge).

d. Corroboration Requirement; Other Details

For many years, the against-interest exception found in FRE 804(b)(3) required corroboration for against-interest statements offered to *exonerate* the accused, but not for against-interest statements that *implicate* the accused. Apparently the reason for this distinction was that prosecutors feared a flood of perjured confessions, and sought a way to limit defense resort to the exception. But putting a heavier burden on *defendant's* use of the exception than on the *prosecutor's* use seemed unfair. Now the exception requires corroboration whenever any party invokes the exception for a statement tending to expose the speaker to liability in a criminal case.

What does corroboration mean? Consider the following account:

> Certainly the requirement is satisfied by independent evidence that directly or circumstantially tends to prove the points for which the statement is offered. Pretty clearly the requirement can also be satisfied by independent evidence that tends directly or circumstantially to prove other important facts asserted in the statement, including, for example, proof that a declarant who admits his involvement in a crime was at the scene when it was committed.
>
> But "corroborating circumstances" is a much broader term. It reaches other kinds of circumstantial evidence that supports either the trustworthiness of the particular statement, such as indications that the statement was against interest in some very clear or to an unusual or devastating degree, or that the speaker repeated the statement on other occasions, or that the speaker could not have been motivated to falsify for the benefit of the accused. The term should also embrace other factors suggesting trustworthiness, such as spontaneity.

Mueller & Kirkpatrick, Federal Evidence §8.131 (4th ed. 2013).

5. Statements of Personal or Family History

Consider the following statements, in which a person speaks of her origins and family:

> My mother told me I was born in West Virginia.
> Donald is my son.
> Dad told me that William was my uncle and that he sent for Dad to join him in Texas.

These statements,[10] and others like them describing what we might call "family pedigree" (the Rule refers to "family history" and includes matters relating to birth, adoption, and relationship by blood or marriage) are admissible under FRE 804(b)(4) when the declarant is unavailable. The first statement would likely fit subdivision (A) of the exception because declarant speaks mostly about herself. The second and third would likely fit subdivision (B) because she speaks mostly about "another person" related to her. Note that subdivision (B) would also pave the way for statements by one who was "intimately associated" with the family of the person she describes.

Rule 804(b)(4) applies despite the fact that the declarant sometimes conveys what he heard from another and thus lacks personal knowledge (as in the first and third examples). The exception rests on the assumption that the

[10] The statements quoted above resemble those approved in Liacakos v. Kennedy, 195 F. Supp. 630, 633 (D.C. 1961); Will of T., 86 Misc. 2d 452, 382 N.Y.S.2d 916, 919 (1976); Strickland v. Humble Oil Co., 140 F.2d 83, 86 (5th Cir.), *cert. denied*, 323 U.S. 712 (1944).

speaker has adequate information, and in practice many statements are made before controversy arises (untainted by forces generating litigation).

Where a statement is offered to prove facts about people other than the speaker, courts may require independent evidence that she belongs to the family (or is an intimate of the family). See Fulkerson v. Holmes, 117 U.S. 389 (1886); United States v. Eng Suak Lun, 67 F.2d 307, 308-309 (10th Cir. 1933). But when her statement is offered to prove facts about herself (such as her marriage or children or her parents), other proof of the relationships is probably not required. See Morgan v. Susino Construction Co., 33 A.2d 607, *aff'd*, 36 A.2d 604 (N.J. 1943).

Courts sometimes exclude self-serving statements, and those motivated by greed, ill will, or other forces suggesting untruthfulness. For example, in the prosecution of Martha and Fernando Carvalho for knowing use of false alien registration receipt cards, the government tried to prove that defendants, who married after meeting in this country, were "sophisticated regarding the immigration laws." In support of this contention it offered affidavits from former spouses of each: One affiant said he married Martha "for love" several months earlier but planned "to terminate my marriage to this woman as soon as possible" and "to withdraw the application for permanent residence." The other said she married Fernando "because I felt sorry for him and out of anger because of what had happened to me" and because she "wanted to help him get his residence." The reviewing court concluded that these statements did not fit FRE 804(b)(4):

> While undoubtedly it is correct that for some purposes a statement regarding one's reasons for entering a marriage might well be a "statement concerning" one's marriage, it is also clear that evidence as to motive or purpose, highly debatable or controversial matters, is simply not within the scope of Rule 804(b)(4) . . . .
>
> The propriety of a distinction between different types of facts concerning personal or family history relating to marriage is buttressed further by a comparison of marriage to the other items on the non-exhaustive list in Rule 804(b)(4). The list includes, for example, birth, adoption, divorce, legitimacy and ancestry. It is difficult to envision how issues similar to the frame of mind at the time of entering a marital relationship could arise regarding the other items on the list. More likely, the relevant issues instead would be a date of birth, existence of an adoption, or details of one's ancestry. Since "marriage" appears in Rule 804(b)(4) in the midst of a list of items unlikely to concern complex issues of motive, we conclude that [affiants'] motives for marrying [defendants] was not a "fact" within the meaning of FRE 804(b)(4), and, accordingly, that the Rule does not provide a basis for admission of the affidavits.

United States v. Carvalho, 742 F.2d 146, 151 (4th Cir. 1984).

6. Statements Admissible Because of Forfeiture by Misconduct

Rule 804(b)(6) paves the way to admit statements against a party who wrongfully caused (or "acquiesced" in wrongdoing that caused) the speaker to be unavailable as a witness, if the party "did so intending" to achieve this result. The purpose is to deal with witness intimidation in criminal cases. One may speak of "waiver" (which suggests that the exception applies where someone "intended" to give up rights), and the exception *does contain* a component of intentionality. That component, however, goes *not* to the intent of a party to give up her right to exclude hearsay, but to her intent to *keep the speaker from testifying.* Thus "forfeiture" seems an apt term in the sense that the exception does *not* turn on proving intent to *give up a right.*

Before FRE 804(b)(6) came in 1997, some decisions had held that misconduct by a criminal defendant that kept a grand jury witness from testifying at trial was enough to cause loss of protection of both the hearsay doctrine and the Confrontation Clause. See, e.g., United States v. Thevis, 665 F.2d 616, 627-628 (6th Cir.) (admitting grand jury testimony after finding that defendant was responsible for death of witness), *cert. denied*, 456 U.S. 1008 (1982).

The *Giles* case. The Supreme Court approved the idea of a forfeiture exception in the *Giles* case, where it also held that the intent requirement is essential if the accused is to lose confrontation rights.[11] That case involved the murder prosecution of Dwayne Giles in California, arising out of the shooting death of his ex-girlfriend Brenda Avie. The altercation leading to her death occurred in the garage at the home of defendant's grandmother, and there were no eyewitnesses, but the grandmother heard the two talking, and heard Avie yell "Granny" several times followed by a series of gunshots. See Giles v. California, 554 U.S. 353 (2008).

Giles claimed self-defense, testifying at trial that Avie had been jealous and that he knew she had once shot a man and had threatened people with a knife and vandalized his home on prior occasions. On these facts, prosecutors proved statements that Avie had made to a police officer responding to a domestic violence report three weeks earlier, where she told the officer (in tears as she spoke) that Giles had accused her of having an affair and that during the ensuing argument Giles grabbed her by the shirt, lifted her off the floor, and began to choke her, later punching her in the face and head and threatening to kill her with a knife. Giles was convicted. During his ensuing appeal, the Supreme Court decided the *Crawford* case and the reviewing court in California approved use of Avie's description of their earlier altercation on the theory of forfeiture by wrongdoing.

The Supreme Court reversed. All agreed that Avie's statements to the officer were "testimonial," and the majority in *Giles* invoked 19th century cases and treatises in concluding that forfeiture requires "a showing that defendant intended to prevent a witness from testifying," not merely conduct (like murder)

---

[11] Even before *Giles*, the Court made considered comments approving the forfeiture idea. See Crawford v. Washington, 541 U.S. 36 (2004) (noting "rule of forfeiture by wrongdoing (which we accept)" and commenting that it "extinguishes confrontation claims"); Davis v. Washington, 547 U.S. 813 (2006) ("one who obtains the absence of a witness by wrongdoing forfeits the constitutional right to confrontation"). *Giles*, *Crawford*, and *Davis* deal with confrontation rights rather than rights to exclude hearsay, but they validated FRE 804(b)(6), which does deal with hearsay.

that necessarily has the effect of silencing a witness. The forfeiture doctrine seeks to remove "the otherwise powerful incentive for defendants to intimidate, bribe, and kill the witnesses against them," thus to protect the integrity of court proceedings. The intent requirement puts "boundaries" on the doctrine, and avoids an overbroad principle that would be "repugnant" to our jury system, a principle under which murder defendants "whom the judge considers guilty (after less than a full trial . . . [and] before the jury has pronounced guilt) should be deprived of fair-trial rights, lest they benefit from their judge-determined wrong." Referring to the forfeiture exception in the Rules, the Court summed it up this way:

> We have described this as a rule "which codifies the forfeiture doctrine." *Davis v. Washington*, 547 U.S. 813, 833 (2006). Every commentator we are aware of has concluded the requirement of intent "means that the exception applies only if the defendant has in mind the particular purpose of making the witness unavailable." 5 Mueller & Kirkpatrick, Federal Evidence §8:134, p. 235 (3d ed. 2007); 5 Weinstein & Berger, Weinstein's Federal Evidence §804.03[7][b], p. 804-32 (J. McLaughlin ed., 2d ed. 2008); 2 K. Broun, McCormick on Evidence 176 (6th ed. 2006).[2] The commentators come out this way because the dissent's claim that knowledge is sufficient to show intent is emphatically not the modern view. See 1 W. LaFave, Substantive Criminal Law §5.2, p. 340 (2d ed. 2003).
>
> In sum, our interpretation of the common-law forfeiture rule is supported by (1) the most natural reading of the language used at common law; (2) the absence of common-law cases admitting prior statements on a forfeiture theory when the defendant had not engaged in conduct designed to prevent a witness from testifying; (3) the common law's uniform exclusion of unconfronted inculpatory testimony by murder victims (except testimony given with awareness of impending death) in the innumerable cases in which the defendant was on trial for killing the victim, but was not shown to have done so for the purpose of preventing testimony; (4) a subsequent history in which the dissent's broad forfeiture theory has not been applied. The first two and the last are highly persuasive; the third is in our view conclusive.

Giles v. California, 554 U.S. 353, 367-368 (2008).

A concurring opinion in *Giles* agreed on the intent requirement, and echoed the majority's concern over the "near circularity" involved in admitting a victim's statement because the judge thinks the defendant committed the crime for which he is on trial. But the concurrence added that intent would ordinarily exist where a domestic abuser seeks to "isolate the victim from outside help" in a continuing relationship.

---

[2] [Court says only Oregon recognizes a broader forfeiture doctrine, not turning on intent. Seven out of 12 states recognizing forfeiture track the federal language requiring intent, including Delaware, Kentucky, North Dakota, Pennsylvania, Vermont, Tennessee, and Michigan. Two others refer to a "purpose" to make the declarant unavailable (Ohio and California), and yet two others use the word "procured," which "traditionally" means intent (Hawaii and Maryland).] [Oregon's provision now requires intent.—EDS.]

Three dissenters thought that intent to kill in a murder case necessarily includes an intent to prevent the victim from testifying, and charged the majority with converting intent into a stronger notion of "purpose."

NOTES ON THE SCOPE OF THE FORFEITURE EXCEPTION

1. *Giles* holds that a defendant forfeits confrontation rights by killing a witness (making her unavailable to testify) *only if* his conduct is "intended" or "designed" to achieve this result. Thus the Sixth Amendment forfeiture principle emerging from *Giles* and the forfeiture provision in FRE 804(b)(6) are coextensive. Before *Crawford* in 2004, this principle was a minor footnote in American law, but it has exploded since then, largely for the reasons that appear in *Giles*: Forfeiture paves the way to admit statements to police that would never be admitted otherwise, because most such statements don't fit hearsay exceptions and because they are usually "testimonial" under *Crawford.*

2. Why have a forfeiture doctrine? It is often said to rest on "equitable" principles (both *Crawford* and *Davis* say so). Is the purpose then to set right an imbalance in proof caused by defendant's wrongful conduct? Isn't equity about fairness and justice too? Can it be fair (or just) to say to defendant in a murder case, "we think you probably did it, so you can't exclude anything your victim said that is relevant, even though defendants in other situations can exclude similar evidence"? Notice that Justice Scalia's opinion for the Court (with three who join his opinion in full) and Justice Souter's concurrence (with Justice Ginsburg) comment on the circularity involved in considering a defendant guilty as charged in order to decide to admit his victim's statements, so six Justices don't accept the notion that equity means accepting such unfairness.

3. If *Giles* had come out the other way (simple "wrongdoing" causing a witness to be unavailable is enough to forfeit a confrontation objection), then everything a murder victim said would be admissible against the defendant in a trial for murder, wouldn't it (assuming relevance)? This outcome would vitiate the limits that apply to hearsay exceptions for dying declarations, excited utterances, and state-of-mind statements. It would also mean that in the trial of O.J. Simpson the court would have admitted Nicole Brown's statements reflecting fear, although they would not normally be admissible under the state-of-mind exception (the purpose was to prove past abusive conduct).

4. *Giles* differs from the paradigm case on the mind of the framers of FRE 804(b)(6): That case is one in which a defendant faces criminal charges (they're pending or he sees them coming), and realizes someone is cooperating with the prosecutor, so he kills him or takes similar wrongful steps (threats, bribes) to insure that he will not testify. The conduct that forfeits rights comes *after* the conduct generating charges, and the judicial role in deciding the forfeiture issue does not overlap with the jury's role in determining guilt or innocence. That this case is what the framers had in mind can be seen in a sentence in the ACN to FRE 804(b)(6) that was added at the last minute but left out of published versions of the Rules. The sentence says the exception "applies to actions taken *after the event* to prevent a witness from testifying" (emphasis added).

5. In describing "intent," *Giles* has in mind a strong form of the idea, close to purpose or plan. Six Justices reject a weaker form, where intent which might mean as little as "knowledge" or "foreseeable consequence." This weaker idea, supported by Justice Breyer and two others, is that *knowingly* causing the witness to be unavailable to testify is enough—a murderer *knows* that killing a witness means she won't testify. Doesn't this weak form of intent imply both too little and too much? Surely it means too *little* if it refers to the fact that *everyone* knows killing a person means he will never talk again: Should we view everyone charged with murder as interfering with the work of courts? Surely it means *too much* if the idea is that *knowing* the victim will never talk is the equivalent of thinking about testimony that will never be given: Is every murderer really thinking about testimony that will never see the light of day?

6. Trials for domestic abuse pose special challenges. Abusers may engage in ongoing conduct that frightens and isolates victims, perhaps for the purpose of discouraging efforts to seek help. The Scalia opinion comments that murder in this setting might amount to an expression of "the intent to isolate the victim and stop her" from reporting or cooperating, bringing the forfeiture doctrine into play. Justice Souter comments that the requisite intent would "normally" exist in such cases, and Justice Breyer refers to a "presumption" of intent. Sometimes the intent of abusers in cases leading to the death of the victim is clear. See, e.g., Vasquez v. People, 173 P.3d 1099, 1105 (Colo. 2007) (defendant told police he killed his wife because she "set him up" in on a prior charge, which proved intent). Consider what facts would show intent: Is it enough to show a pattern of abuse? Would it suffice if an expert testifies that the victim's behavior is consistent with patterns seen in battered women? What if the victim tells a friend she won't testify because she doesn't want the abuser jailed, or loves him?

7. Child molestation trials also pose special challenges. Perpetrators often ask their victims not to talk to others: One might agree that asking a child *in any way* to remain silent about abuse is wrongful, but if the child declines to testify it may be harder to figure out whether this conduct is the cause, or something else is going on. See People v. Stechly, 870 N.E.2d 333 (Ill. 2007) (court did not determine whether defendant intended to discourage child from testifying) (reversing); State v. Henderson, 160 P.3d 776 (Kan. 2007) (no evidence that defendant threatened mentally incompetent victim or in any way "procured her unavailability") (reversing). See also State v. Poole, 232 P.3d 519, 527 (Utah 2010) (court erred in concluding that child victim was unavailable because she refused to testify twice before, more than five months earlier; court can evaluate availability in hearing "immediately prior to trial," but must revisit the matter at time of trial to be sure unavailability persists; forfeiture requires showing that witness is unavailable as a result of defendant's wrongful acts intended for this purpose).

8. Forfeiture requires wrongful conduct. Obviously killing can be wrongful (and usually is). We can be sure other kinds of conduct are wrongful, like threatening or frightening a witness, or bribing or kidnapping her. What else? Must there be a wrongful element *apart from* being purposeful in getting a witness not to testify? What about asking someone not to testify, or persuading her not to, or reaching an "understanding"?

(a) An early decision in *Reynolds*, which the Court invoked in *Giles*, involved a bigamy trial (it is better known for disapproving of polygamy, rejecting a defense based on religious belief). There the prosecutor failed in trying to serve Amelia Schofield, whom defendant Reynolds married while being already married to Mary Tuddenham. The Deputy Marshal testified that he went to find Ms. Schofield, encountered defendant, and asked where she was: "He said she was not at home," and in response to the question where she could be found, he said "You will have to find out." The Deputy Marshal went to the house again, and encountered Ms. Tuddenham, who said Amelia "was not there" and "hadn't been there for two or three weeks." On a third visit on the day of trial, the Deputy Marshal again found that Ms. Schofield was not home. On these facts, the court admitted her testimony from defendant's first trial, and the Supreme Court approved:

> [I]f a witness is absent by his own wrongful procurement, [defendant] cannot complain if competent evidence is admitted to supply the place of that which he has kept away. The Constitution does not guarantee an accused person against the legitimate consequences of his own wrongful acts. It grants him the privilege of being confronted with the witnesses against him; but if he voluntarily keeps the witnesses away, he cannot insist on his privilege. If, therefore, when absent by his procurement, their evidence is supplied in some lawful way, he is in no condition to assert that his constitutional rights have been violated . . . .
>
> The accused was himself personally present in court when the showing was made [of the attempts to serve the witness], and had full opportunity to account for the absence of the witness, if he would, or to deny under oath that he had kept her away. Clearly, enough had been proven to cast the burden upon him of showing that he had not been instrumental in concealing or keeping the witness away. Having the means of making the necessary explanation, and having every inducement to do so if he would, the presumption is that he considered it better to rely upon the weakness of the case made against him than to attempt to develop the strength of his own. Upon the testimony as it stood, it is clear to our minds that the judgment should not be reversed because secondary evidence was admitted.

Reynolds v. U.S., 98 U.S. 145, 158-160 (1878). Do the facts in *Reynolds* really show "collusion"? Do they show wrongful behavior under FRE 804(b)(6)?

(b) Consider a 2010 Massachusetts decision in the *Szerlong* case. There an assault victim told her sister and police that defendant broke down her door, entered her home, tried to strangle her, held a knife to her throat, and tried to kill her. Later she married him, and she invoked the spousal testimonial

privilege and refused to testify. She had told a close friend she married him as "the only way that she would not have to testify" in his assault trial. The court concluded that defendant had forfeited his rights. "Even if the idea to marry originated with the victim, the defendant agreed to marry, and the spousal privilege existed only because of his agreement." Hence the judge could find that he "intended to make her unavailable," even if it was not his "sole or primary purpose." See Commonwealth v. Szerlong, 933 N.E.2d 633, 641 (Mass. 2010) (defendant had "due process" right to exclude unreliable hearsay) (statements were reliable); Commonwealth v. Edwards, 830 N.E.2d 158, 170-171 (Mass. 2005) (applying forfeiture doctrine where defendant and witness were "orchestrating" witness's departure; collusion is forfeiture if defendant "contributed to" unavailability significantly). Is marrying a witness, with no other showing of motive or purpose on part, wrongful conduct? Really?

9. What about witnesses who are unavailable not because of defendant's acts, but because of behavior by another with whom defendant was involved in conspiracy? This question arose in the *Cherry* case. There the Tenth Circuit invoked the *Pinkerton* doctrine, which defines the extent to which a conspirator is liable for substantive crimes committed by other conspirators. The Court in *Cherry* said *Pinkerton* also defines the reach of forfeiture, which occurs if (1) defendant "participated directly" in planning or procuring the declarant's unavailability, or (2) procurement "was in furtherance, within the scope, and reasonably foreseeable as a necessary or natural consequence of an ongoing conspiracy." The scope of a conspiracy "is not necessarily limited to a primary goal—such as bank robbery—but can also include secondary goals relevant to the evasion of apprehension and prosecution for that goal—such as escape, or, by analogy, obstruction of justice." And a conspirator is responsible for the acts of colleagues unless he or she "meets the burden of proving that he or she took affirmative steps to withdraw from the conspiracy before those acts were committed." See United States v. Cherry, 217 F.3d 811 (10th Cir. 2000) (relying on Pinkerton v. United States, 328 U.S. 640 (1946)), *later appeal*, 265 F.3d 1097 (10th Cir. 2001), *cert. denied*, 535 U.S. 1099 (2001).

10. In the federal system, forfeiting confrontation rights also forfeits hearsay objections, and Rule 804(b)(6) contains no trustworthiness requirement. Does it follow that unreliable statements, like statements designed to curry favor with police, are admissible? See United States v. Dhinsa, 243 F.3d 635, 654-656 (2d Cir. 2001) (courts can exclude "facially unreliable" hearsay under FRE 403 even in forfeiture cases).

11. In the states, the relationship between forfeiting confrontation rights and forfeiting hearsay objections is uncertain. The question whether a defendant has forfeited his rights under the Confrontation Clause raises an issue of constitutional law, and states must follow *Giles.* The question whether forfeiting confrontation rights also forfeits objections under state hearsay rules is a matter of state law. Most state courts that have considered these questions conclude that forfeiting confrontation rights also forfeits hearsay objections, but there is some disagreement. Compare People v. Stechly, 870 N.E.2d 333, 351

(Ill. 2007) and State v. Meeks, 88 P.2d 789, 794 (Kan. 2004) (holding that forfeiture waives hearsay as well as confrontation rights) with Vasquez v. People, 173 P.3d 1099, 1106 (Colo. 2007) ("the more prudent course is to require that the hearsay rules be satisfied separately"). Does it make sense to lift the bar against admitting testimonial statements because of misconduct, while insisting that hearsay satisfy standard exceptions?

■ PROBLEM 4-Q. "If You Want to Stay Healthy"

Lanny Keeton is charged with armed robbery of Southside Quick Serve in St. Louis, and with assault and attempted murder. The crimes occurred at 2 A.M. when two masked men entered the store carrying sawed-off shotguns. The videotape shows that the two trained their guns on Nick Owens, the night-duty clerk in the cashier's cage behind bulletproof glass. Owens turned over the cash (as he was required to do in such situations), but the amount was small (less than $100) because he had just put most of the cash from the register into the safe, which could only be opened by dialing the combination and waiting ten minutes.

One perpetrator is seen on the videotape menacing a customer with the shotgun, and the customer is forced to lie face down on the floor. The videotape shows this perpetrator firing his shotgun through the change slot that scoops below the glass in the counter, injuring Owens who is struck by pellets that ricochet up inside the cage.

Ten days later, armed with minimal information supplied by the customer and Owens describing the getaway car, police arrest Marvin Spreigel in a routine traffic stop. (A search of the Police Information Network alerted the patrolman that Spreigel and his car might have been involved in the Quick Serve robbery.) Later that same day, police also locate and arrest Lanny Keeton, and both wind up in the same station house, where they are questioned separately. Spreigel acknowledges his participation in the robbery and says Keeton fired the shotgun at Owens and threatened the customer.

The prosecutor enters a plea bargain with Spreigel, who pleads guilty to aiding and abetting and agrees to testify against Keeton. When Keeton's case comes to trial, however, Spreigel refuses to testify. In a hearing in chambers attended by Spreigel and his lawyer, from which Keeton and his lawyer were excluded, Spreigel's lawyer reads a letter that he says Spreigel received from Keeton in jail while awaiting his sentencing hearing after entering his plea. The letter says "if you and that bitch of yours want to stay healthy, you know what you should do and what you shouldn't, so I better not see you as a stoolie at my trial." Spreigel's lawyer tells the judge that Lanny Keeton made oral threats targeting both Spreigel and his girlfriend.

The judge rules that statements Spreigel gave to police and prosecutors, as well as his later guilty plea allocutions, are admissible against

Keeton under Rule 804(b)(6). Informed by the judge that the ruling rested on "conversations with Mr. Spreigel and his lawyer in chambers," the lawyer for Keeton raises a hearsay objection, and argues that "you can't find my client responsible for Spreigel's refusal to testify in an ex parte hearing on the basis of unsworn statements by a lawyer," and "besides, any finding that my client kept Spreigel off the stand must rest on proof beyond a reasonable doubt." Do these objections have merit?

■ NOTES ON PROCEDURE IN APPLYING THE FORFEITURE EXCEPTION

1. If you were the judge, how would you feel about letting Keeton participate in a hearing designed to determine whether he threatened Spreigel? Why do you suppose Marvin Spreigel wanted his lawyer to do the talking?

2. When the lawyer tells the judge that Keeton threatened his client, he is accusing Keeton of another crime. Does that suggest that the judge should require proof beyond a reasonable doubt before finding that Keeton threatened witnesses or obstructed justice? In Bourjaily v. United States, 483 U.S. 171 (1987) (described and quoted in section B5, supra), the Court held that the preponderance standard applies to decisions by the judge on the predicate facts of the coconspirator exception (one of which is that defendant and declarant conspired), and most courts hold that this standard applies in the setting of the forfeiture exception as well. Some, however, have adopted a stricter standard. See, e.g., People v. Smart, 23 N.Y.3d 213 (N.Y. 2014) ("clear and convincing evidence").

3. Does Keeton have a due process right to be present in a hearing on the question whether the forfeiture doctrine applies? See Kentucky v. Stincer, 482 U.S. 730 (1987) (in trial for sexual offenses against children, excluding defendant from hearing to determine competency of victims to testify did *not* violate due process or confrontation rights; his absence did not affect ability to cross-examine, and witnesses did not speak to merits, thus did not affect his opportunity to defend). Often what happens to a co-offender who "turns state's evidence" is that he gets killed. If the court in such a case conducts a minihearing to determine whether to admit out-of-court statements by a deceased witness under FRE 804(b)(6), this minihearing resembles a murder trial. In such cases, there is no reason to exclude the defendant from the hearing, is there?

4. How can the judge determine whether defendant intended to prevent a witness from testifying? In its decision in the *Smart* case in 2014, New York's highest court offered this analysis:

> Because witness tampering is a surreptitious activity rarely admitted by the defendant or the witness, few cases will involve direct evidence of this causal link

> between the defendant's misconduct and the witness's refusal to testify or failure to appear in court. Therefore . . . the court may infer the requisite causation from the evidence of the defendant's coercive behavior and the actions taken by the witness in direct response to or within a close temporal proximity to that misconduct . . . .

People v. Smart, 23 N.Y.3d. 213 (N.Y. 2014) (finding forfeiture on proof that defendant told witness he would "[w]ring [her] fucking neck" if she testified, and told her it would be a "good idea" for her to leave town).

THE CATCHALL EXCEPTION

1. Origin of the Catchall

Last of the exceptions in Article VIII is the so-called catchall that is now codified in FRE 807. At the heart of this provision is the idea that hearsay may be trustworthy even if it doesn't fit one of the "categorical" exceptions in Rules 801, 803, and 804, if it has "equivalent circumstantial guarantees of trustworthiness." Separate clauses impose other requirements: Hearsay offered under the catchall must go to "a material fact" and must be "more probative" than other evidence the proponent can get through reasonable effort. It must serve the "interests of justice" to admit hearsay under the catchall, and the proponent must provide "reasonable notice" (including declarant's "name and address"). If they do nothing else, these latter requirements convey the point that the catchall exception is to be, as many cases say, "sparingly invoked."

Origin: The *Dallas County* case. The classic decision behind the catchall is the *Dallas County* case. There, Dallas County sued an insurance carrier after the wooden clock tower above the courthouse in Selma, Alabama, collapsed on a Sunday morning in July. The County claimed lightning had caused the collapse, but the carrier claimed that the charred timbers came from a fire that happened while the tower was under construction many years earlier. The trial judge admitted an old newspaper clipping to prove the earlier fire. In an eloquent opinion by Judge Wisdom, the reviewing court affirmed:

> There is no procedural canon against the exercise of common sense in deciding the admissibility of hearsay evidence. In 1901 Selma, Alabama, was a small town. Taking a common sense view of this case, it is inconceivable to us that a newspaper reporter in a small town would report there was a fire in the dome of the new courthouse—if there had been no fire. He is without motive to falsify, and a false report would have subjected the newspaper and him to embarrassment in the community. The usual dangers inherent in hearsay evidence, such as lack of memory, faulty narration, intent to influence the court proceedings, and plain lack of truthfulness are not present here. To our minds, the article published in the Selma Morning-Times on the day of the fire is more reliable, more trustworthy, more competent evidence than the testimony of a witness called to the stand fifty-eight years later.

Dallas County v. Commercial Union Assur. Co., 286 F.2d 388, 391-392 (5th Cir. 1961).

The Rules. In early drafts, the framers of the Rules wanted to follow the lead of Judge Wisdom in *Dallas County*, so those drafts *began* with broad-brush provisions. Under proposed Rule 8-03, a statement by an available declarant was *not* excludable as hearsay "if its nature and the special circumstances under which it was made offer assurances of accuracy not likely to be enhanced by calling the declarant as a witness," and proposed Rule 8-04 did the same thing for a statement by an unavailable declarant if circumstances offered "strong assurances of accuracy." Both provisions then hammered home the main point by setting out lists of "examples" that track what we now call the categorical exceptions (business records, excited utterances, and so forth). These examples, however, were offered "by way of illustration only, and not by way of limitation." See the Preliminary Draft of March, 1969, 46 F.R.D. 161, 345, 377 (1969).

The legal profession was uncomfortable with this approach. Before the Rules reached Congress, the Committee changed course. It abandoned its lists of "examples" in favor of categorical exceptions that were prescriptive rather than exemplary. It moved the broad-brush provisions out of the opening lines of Rules 803 and 804, placing them at the ends of long lists, but clearly de-emphasized them. See 51 F.R.D. 315, 419-422, 439 (1971). Then Congress got into the act, introducing changes that remain in the reformulated catchall now found in FRE 807. It was Congress that stuck in the four additional requirements (beyond trustworthiness) that we see in FRE 807.

2. The Catchall and Proof of Exonerating Facts

STATE v. WEAVER

Supreme Court of Iowa
554 N.W.2d 240 (Iowa 1996)

McGIVERIN, Chief Justice.

[Mary Weaver, who had been hired to be a caretaker or babysitter for 11-month-old Melissa Mathes, was charged with murder and related crimes when Melissa died after being in Weaver's care. Her first trial resulted in a hung jury, and the prosecutor decided to bring the charges again (reprosecution after a jury is unable to reach a verdict does not violate the double jeopardy clause). Weaver then waived her right to trial by jury, and Judge Peterson presided and convicted her of first degree murder.

Mary Weaver had picked up Melissa at the Mathes home at 10:20 A.M. on Friday, January 22, 1993. At 11:14 A.M., Weaver called 911 and reported that Melissa was not breathing. The child died of respiratory arrest the next day.

An autopsy showed that Melissa had old and recent injuries, including a skull fracture, subdural hematoma, bleeding in the brain, and bilateral retinal hemorrhages, which were "consistent with shaken baby syndrome." Doctors Robinson, Folberg, and Schelper thought the skull fracture was seven to ten days old. Dr. Robinson thought the subdural hemorrhage was one to two weeks old, and that cell death and a blood clot in the brain were seven to ten days old. Melissa also suffered "acute injuries," including "diffuse subarachnoid hemorrhage, contusion (frontal cortex), bilateral retinal hemorrhage, and bilateral anterior chamber hemorrhage." These conditions "would have been nonsubtle and immediate," and occurred shortly before Melissa arrived at the hospital.

After her conviction, Mary Weaver moved for a new trial on the basis of affidavits by Robin McElroy and Mistry Lovig, who reportedly did not know each other, but said that Melissa's mother, Tessia Mathes, had said that Weaver "had not hurt Melissa" and that Melissa "had hit her head on a coffee table at the Mathes home" on the morning of January 22 before being placed in Mary Weaver's care. Judge Peterson denied the motion, concluding that the affidavits contained hearsay that fit no exception and lacked "circumstantial guarantees of trustworthiness."

The Court of Appeals affirmed the conviction, but the Iowa Supreme Court remanded the case to consider a second new trial motion based on new affidavits by three other women recounting another statement by Tessia Mathes. Chief Judge Ronald Schechtman referred the matter to Judge Alan Goode, from a nearby judicial district.[5] At the hearing on this motion, Mary Weaver adduced live testimony by all five women describing statements by Tessia Mathes. The Supreme Court, however, limits its consideration to the new affidavits by the three women, which it quotes:

> (1) Affidavit by Evelyn Braack (age 68) dated 10/20/95:
>
> Some friends of ours and my husband and I have coffee every Wednesday afternoon around 2:30 P.M. at Hardees in Marshalltown. The women sit together and the men do the same. We knew Tessia Mathes as she worked there. Shortly after the baby died (2-3 weeks) Tessia told the women present that she had been putting on the baby's snowsuit and she had thrown her head back and hit her head on a table injuring her head but she did not say how bad....
>
> (2) Affidavit by Flossie Wall (age 67) dated 10/24/95:
>
> My husband and I meet at Hardees every Wednesday for coffee with several couples. Tessia Mathes worked there. Shortly after her baby died and was

[5] Chief Judge Schechtman gave the following reasons for the special assignment: Due to the nature and circumstances of the limited remand, the nature of the motion, the fact that the original trial court was the factfinder, without a jury, and the availability of a complete transcript of the trial, the undersigned concludes that the matter warrants the assignment of a special judge, who has not been a previous trial court herein, to hear the merits of the motion for new trial. Counsel for each of the parties, as well as the defendant, have no objection to this administrative assignment. [This is the Court's footnote.—EDS.]

> buried she came back to work and came over to talk to us. She told us that one morning as she was dressing the baby to leave the house she was putting on the baby's snowsuit, [the baby] was fussing and moving around. The baby hit her head on the coffee table and was knocked unconscious. . . .
>
> (3) Affidavits by Elaine Kail (age 68) dated 10/20/95 and 10/24/95:
>
> Several friends including our husbands meet on Wednesday afternoons at about 2:30 P.M. at Hardees. A short time after the baby died, her mother Tessia told myself and Evelyn Braack, Flossie Wall, Donna Parsons, that one morning as she was dressing Melissa, the baby had hit her head on the coffee table. She did not elaborate any further. . . .
>
> This statement [is] in addition to the statement I provided on October 20, 1995. That night I thought about this further and remembered that Tessia had told us the baby had went limp after she had hit her head on the coffee table and became unconscious. My impression was that Tessia was telling us how the baby had died. It was my impression that the baby struck her head on the coffee [table] on the morning that she died.

None of the affiants "could absolutely identify the date" on which Tessia Mathes said the coffee table incident occurred, but the reviewing court does not consider this "determinative," and it notes that Judge Goode thought it was "reasonable to assume" that the affidavits referred to an incident that occurred on January 22, 1993, "some time prior to the time defendant picked up Melissa." The State and the defense agree that if she were called as a witness, Tessia Mathes would testify that Melissa "neither struck her head against a coffee table" on the fateful morning nor "ever lost consciousness for any reason while in Tessia's care," and that she (Tessia) "never described" to Braack, Wall, or Kail any "fall" against a coffee table that would have resulted in a loss of consciousness.

One question on appeal is whether Tessia Mathes's statements would be admissible in a new trial.]

After a careful consideration of the record in this matter including the findings of the district court, we believe the court did not abuse its discretion in ruling that the affidavits and testimony of Braack, Wall and Kail at the hearing on the motion were admissible hearsay evidence. Therefore, the district court properly considered that evidence in ruling on defendant's second motion for new trial.[10]

As the State contests only the trustworthiness prong of admissibility under IRE 803(24), we consider the merits of that factor only and deem the other factors waived in the State's appeal . . . .

[10] In retrial on the merits, the evidence of the witnesses Braack, Wall, and Kail must be offered in the usual way, will be subject to objection anew, and must be ruled on by the court as to admissibility. The affidavits alone of those witnesses would not be admissible at trial without agreement of both the State and the defendant.

Factors to consider in making a trustworthiness determination under rule 803(24) include: the declarant's (Tessia Mathes') propensity to tell the truth, whether the alleged statements by Tessia Mathes were made under oath, assurance of Tessia Mathes' personal knowledge, the time lapse between the alleged event and the statement by Tessia Mathes concerning the event, and the motivations of Tessia Mathes to make the alleged statements. Additional circumstances to consider include corroboration, reaffirming or recanting the statement by the declarant, credibility of the witness reporting the statement, and availability of the declarant for cross-examination.[11]

In concluding that the affidavits and testimony were trustworthy for purposes of admissibility under rule 803(24), the district court made the following findings based on the facts and trustworthiness factors to be considered:

1. The witnesses reporting the statement are very credible.
2. The declarant, Tessia Mathes, is available to testify.
3. The statement was made shortly after the incident in close proximity to events the declarant could be expected to remember.
4. The declarant had firsthand knowledge of the substance of the statement and was not relying on potentially erroneous secondary information.
5. The statement was unambiguous and explicit that the event occurred.
6. The statement was in response to an open-ended question, and was not the result of interrogation or investigation by the accused or others on her behalf.
7. The statement was made to more than one person, who agree on the substance of what was said.
8. A similar account of the episode of trauma was made on other separate occasions.
9. The statement is corroborated by objective medical evidence showing a contusion on the left occiput which has not been otherwise explained.

In addition to the above findings, several other facts convince us that the affidavits and testimony were sufficiently trustworthy to constitute admissible hearsay under IRE 803(24) under this record. The three affiants were acquaintances of Tessia Mathes, the declarant, only through her employment at Hardees. The affiants did not socialize with Tessia Mathes and only saw and spoke to her when they would go to Hardees for coffee with their friends. None of the affiants are alleged to have had a personal vendetta against Tessia Mathes and, perhaps more importantly, none of the affiants personally knew the defendant.

In opposition to the above findings, the State asserts the information provided in the affidavits is not trustworthy for several reasons, including: (1) the

[11] We do not believe the above factors are an exclusive list to be considered in any one given trustworthiness analysis.

passage of time, nearly three years from the time Tessia Mathes allegedly offered the statements to the affiants; (2) the affiants' exposure to extensive media coverage over Melissa's death and the resulting trials; and (3) the affiants' admitted collective memory efforts regarding the statements allegedly made to them by Tessia Mathes a couple of weeks after Melissa's death.

As we believe the above contentions go to the weight to be given to the evidence and not admissibility, we find the State's attempt to bar the admissibility of the affidavits to be without merit for the purposes of the hearing on the motion.

Based on the findings of the district court and additional facts herein stated which are supported by substantial evidence, we cannot conclude the court's decision to admit the evidence under IRE 803(24) was an abuse of discretion. There are facts in the record that establish the trustworthiness of the affidavits; therefore, we cannot conclude the court's ruling was clearly unreasonable or was based on clearly untenable grounds.

As the State does not contend on appeal that defendant has not satisfied the other factors required to prove admissibility under rule 803(24) at the hearing on the motion, we find those are met.

[Reaching the question whether this evidence "probably would have changed the result at trial," the court notes the State's claim that nobody believes that the retinal hemorrhages and the bilateral anterior chamber hemorrhages could have been caused by a fall against the coffee table. But the court concludes otherwise.]

One of defendant's medical experts, Dr. Blackbourne, testified at the hearing on defendant's second motion for new trial that Melissa's bilateral retinal hemorrhages could have been attributable to chronic edema that the child may have had from the alleged cookie monster chair incident on January 22, 1993. Dr. Earl Rose opined that Melissa's respiratory arrest was caused when a previously existing subdural hematoma re-bled. Based on the newly-discovered evidence, Dr. Rose believed the alleged coffee table incident caused the rebleed to occur and resulting respiratory arrest. On cross-examination, Dr. Rose agreed that the existing subdural hematoma could have either been caused by Melissa's alleged fall from the cookie monster chair on January 22, 1993 (as maintained by Tessia Mathes), or from the alleged coffee table incident on the morning of January 22, 1993 (as alleged by the three affiants).

Although the State and its medical experts vigorously challenge [these] theories concerning the cause of death, we believe the district court's conclusion that the newly-discovered evidence probably would change the result at trial was not clearly unreasonable or untenable. The State's case advocating shaken or slammed baby syndrome as the cause of death was disputed by the defendant's experts based in part on the newly-discovered evidence. There is a factual basis in the record to support the court's grant of defendant's second motion for new trial. The district court in an extensive ruling evaluated the newly-discovered evidence and assessed the credibility and weight of the new witnesses' testimony against the complete trial record and thus was in a good position to determine what evidence would and would not probably change the result at trial.

NOTES ON PROVING EXONERATING FACTS WITH THE CATCHALL

1. Three times *Weaver* speaks of admitting "affidavits and testimony" of Evelyn Braack, Flossie Wall, and Elaine Kail, but the court expects these women to testify. Using affidavits to prove Tessia made the crucial statement, which in turn indicates that Melissa hit her head on a table, would involve *double* hearsay. There is but one layer of hearsay if the women testify to what Tessia Mathes said.

2. Are you satisfied that her statement to the three women was trustworthy? The affidavits were prepared several years after Melissa died; Tessia Mathes was expected to testify; the fact being proved (Melissa hit her head) was corroborated by medical evidence; Mathes made similar statements to others (Robin McElroy and Mistry Lovig). Does these facts help explain the court's decision to invoke the catchall?

3. After this opinion, Mary Weaver was tried a third time. Tessia Mathes did testify and said nothing untoward happened to Melissa that morning. She also denied making statements describing a fall. All five of the women testified, and said Tessia Mathes told them that Melissa fell. The prior statements by Tessia Mathes would have been admissible to impeach her. Iowa has a rule similar to FRE 801(d)(1)(A) that would *not* reach her statements to the five women because they were not under oath in proceedings, so they could *only* impeach. Was the catchall exception necessary?

4. Would the statements by Tessia Mathes fit the against-interest exception? She didn't say *she* had done anything to Melissa—only that Melissa hit her head while Tessia was putting her into her snowsuit.

(a) Consider that an adult in charge is responsible to some extent for injuries suffered by infants (as the endangerment charges against Mary Weaver suggest). The possibility of an earlier skull fracture plus a head-bumping incident at home raises questions about the nature of parental care. Is there any doubt that if the state had prosecuted Tessia Mathes, her statement could come in to show she didn't take proper care of Melissa?

(b) Tessia Mathes testified, so the against-interest exception could not apply. Some courts subscribe to the "near miss" theory, under which a statement that *almost* fits a categorical exception can't be admitted under the catchall. See United States v. Vigoa, 656 F. Supp. 1149, 1504 (D.C.N.J. 1987) (catchall cannot apply to statements "covered" but excluded by other exceptions). Most courts reject this theory. See, e.g., United States v. Clarke, 2 F.3d 81, 83 (4th Cir. 1993) (rejecting near miss theory).

(c) Arguably the unavailability requirement of the against-interest exception is not so crucial that using the catchall in *Weaver* undermines policy concerns. The "near miss" theory is different from the theory adopted in the *Oates* case (section C6c, supra). There the court decided that Congress intended the use restrictions in FRE 803(8) to be exclusionary provisions, not mere qualifications on the exception.

Mary Weaver and Drama in Marshalltown

Deb Brammer / maryweaverstory.com

Mary Weaver was 41 years old in 1993 when she picked up 11-month-old Melissa Mathes on what turned out to be the last day of the child's life. Married and the mother of two small children of her own (a four-year-old daughter and three-year-old son), Weaver was tried for murder three times. The case became a focal point for what was then the new idea of "shaken baby syndrome." The first jury could not reach a verdict; in her second trial without jury, a judge found her guilty and sentenced her to life in prison; a jury in her third trial acquitted her. She spent almost four years behind bars for the alleged murder of Melissa. About 60 miles northeast of Des Moines, Marshalltown is close to the center of Iowa and had a population of about 25,000 in 1993. Reportedly Mary Weaver's husband was a cousin of Melissa's father, who owned an auto parts store. The death of Melissa and Mary Weaver's conviction in the second trial divided the town, and yard signs appeared, with Weaver supporters posing the question "Was justice done?" and those believing in her guilt answering the question "Yes, justice was done." Some continue to argue that symptoms of the sort that led to the death of Melissa are not the delayed result of earlier injuries, and that shaking a baby leads to immediate symptoms of the sort that Melissa displayed. Others argue that there was no direct proof that Mary Weaver did anything to hurt the child. The controversy inspired a book that appeared in 2013, as well as a long article in the local newspaper. See Deb Brammer, Edges of Truth: The Mary Weaver Story (2013); David Alexander, Wrongfully Convicted, Marshalltown Times Republican (Feb. 3, 2013).

5. Suppose a defendant offers a third-party statement that not only asserts facts that exculpate him (as in *Weaver*) but actually *confesses* the crime. And suppose the against-interest exception can't do the job, either because the person who confesses is available or because the person who heard him confess won't testify, but did tell others. In such cases courts only sometimes apply the catchall. Compare United States v. Hall, 165 F.3d 1095, 1110-1111 (7th Cir. 1999) (in kidnap-rape-murder trial, excluding confession by *G*, which did not fit catchall; *G* appeared psychotic, confessing to any crime about which he was questioned, lacked knowledge, and there was no corroboration) with Demby v. State, 695 A.2d 1152 (Del. 1997) (in murder trial, error to exclude videotaped statement by *L* reciting confession in which *F* said he, not defendant, shot victim; *L* and *F* invoked privilege against self-incrimination; *F*'s statement fit against-interest exception; *L*'s videotaped recitation of *F*'s statement fit catchall).

3. The Catchall and Child Abuse Prosecutions

Recall that child abuse trials have led to the use of three hearsay exceptions, including the catchall and special rifle-shot child victim hearsay exceptions (the latter resemble the catchall in resting on reliability without specific criteria).[12] And you have already seen other exceptions operating in this area. Statements by child victims are often admitted under the excited utterance exception (see FRE 803(2) and section C1, supra), the medical statements exception (see FRE 803(4) and the *Blake* case in section C3, supra), and prosecutors sometimes invoke the forfeiture provision too, but with less success (see FRE 804(b)(6), discussed in section D6, supra). In addition, special provisions allow children to give depositions or testify from remote locations, and these either modify the way of taking testimony for children or create what amount to new hearsay exceptions too. See section G, infra.

In applying the catchall to statements by abused children, courts have developed lists of factors that bear on trustworthiness, including the following: Precocious knowledge and age-appropriate language (the former gives new expression to an old idea that a statement may be trusted if it is unlikely that the speaker could say what she said without experiencing something close to what she describes; the latter means that a statement on difficult or delicate matters is more likely to be trustworthy if phrased in terms one would expect of a child); behavioral changes (often fearfulness of men, regression in toilet habits, sleep disturbances, new problems at home or school); general demeanor and affect, and particular indications of pain or emotional upset; spontaneity; the

[12] See, e.g., United States v. Dunford, 148 F.3d 385, 392-394 (4th Cir 1998) (admitting statements by daughters of defendant describing abuse; court stresses "serious nature" of statements and notes that they were repeated and consistent); State v. Rojas, 524 N.W.2d 659 (Iowa 1994) (admitting videotaped interview between ten-year-old victim and social worker under state catchall).

presence or absence of bias or other motives on the part of the speaker or the reporting witnesses; signs of tension or disagreement between the child and the person accused of abuse; the training and techniques of people who talk to the child; the number and consistency of repetitions of the basic story; the character of the child. See generally Mueller & Kirkpatrick, Evidence §8.82 (5th ed. 2012).

Since *Crawford*, much of the literature has focused on confrontation concerns in the use of child victim hearsay. See Robert Mosteller, Testing the Testimonial Concept and Exceptions to Confrontation: "A Little Child Shall Lead Them," 82 Ind. L.J. 917 (2007); Myrna Raeder, Comments on Child Abuse Litigation in a "Testimonial" World: The Intersection of Competency, Hearsay, and Confrontation, 82 Ind. L.J. 1009 (2009).

So frequent and compelling are such cases that statutory reforms across the country provide multiple means for putting before the factfinder what the young victims of abuse have to say. The simplest reform is what we call the rifle-shot child victim hearsay exception paving the way for statements by children describing abuse.[13] Let us look at the Minnesota provision, which is typical of measures adopted in all states:

> An out-of-court statement made by a child under the age of ten years . . . alleging, explaining, denying, or describing any act of sexual contact or penetration performed with or on the child or any act of physical abuse of the child . . . is admissible as substantive evidence if:
>
> (a) the court . . . finds, in a hearing conducted outside of the presence of the jury, that the time, content, and circumstances of the statement and the reliability of the person to whom the statement is made provide sufficient indicia of reliability; and
>
> (b) the child . . . either:
>
> (i) testifies at the proceedings; or
>
> (ii) is unavailable as a witness and there is corroborative evidence of the act; and
>
> (c) the proponent of the statement notifies the adverse party of the proponent's intention to offer the statement and the particulars of the statement sufficiently in advance of the proceeding at which the proponent intends to offer the statement into evidence to provide the adverse party with a fair opportunity to prepare to meet the statement.

Minnesota Stat. Ann. §595.02.

In a way, such rifle-shot exceptions are new wine in old flasks: They do not state criteria of trustworthiness in the manner of the categorical exceptions, but define a subject area (abuse) and a declarant (child victim), and direct

---

[13] Another approach involves the videotaped depositions, where a child can testify in a setting more comfortable than the witness stand, and her videotaped testimony can be offered at trial. Yet another involves special procedures for taking the testimony of the child from a remote setting, with a television monitoring system. See the discussion in section G5, infra.

courts to admit trustworthy statements. Hence the trustworthiness criteria described above, that developed in connection with the catchall exception, are now applied in cases applying the rifle-shot child abuse exceptions, and these are routinely upheld against constitutional challenge. See, e.g., Thomas v. Delaware, 725 A.2d 424 (Del. 1999) (rejecting challenge to statute similar to Minnesota's, quoted above).

In another way, these exceptions are new: The Minnesota provision acknowledges, for instance, that "the reliability of the person to whom the statement is made" counts in the calculus. And the exception requires corroboration in the event that the child does not testify. And of course there is a notice provision, reminiscent of the catchall itself.

Apart from the general problem of trustworthiness, the new child abuse exceptions bring two new issues:

One is an issue of statutory meaning, and the question is whether the existence of these special rifle-shot exceptions forecloses resort to traditional exceptions that might apply. In some cases, courts have concluded that resort to certain other exceptions, including the catchall, is inappropriate because the specific exception was meant to be the sole means to deal with such statements. See, e.g., State v. Jones, 625 So. 2d 821 (Fla. 1993) (statements to physicians are to be appraised under special exception for statements by child victims, and not under state's medical statements exception).

The other is constitutional in nature. Under the older *Roberts* regime, the Court decided that statements offered under the catchall and similar new exceptions (those that are not "firmly rooted") must satisfy a constitutional standard of trustworthiness before being used against the accused. The Court also said trustworthiness had to be assessed *without* counting corroborative evidence (looking only at "inherent" factors). See Idaho v. Wright, 497 U.S. 805 (1990). Under *Crawford*, the constitutional question is whether statements offered under such exceptions are testimonial, and this issue admits of some complications in this setting, as you are about to see.

G IMPACT OF THE CONFRONTATION CLAUSE

1. Historical Antecedents

The Sixth Amendment of the United States Constitution provides in part:

> In all criminal prosecutions, the accused shall enjoy the right . . . to be confronted with the Witnesses against him; to have compulsory process for obtaining witnesses in his favor, and to have the Assistance of Counsel for his defense.

These three clauses protect the right of the accused to defend against criminal charges. The first (Confrontation Clause) bears directly on using hearsay against the accused, but the Court took approaches in the past that were different from the approach that began in 2004 with the decision in Crawford v. Washington, 541 U.S. 36 (2004).

The Confrontation Clause does more than affect application of the hearsay doctrine. For one thing, it means that the accused is entitled to be there when witnesses testify against him, and to cross-examine. In 1988, the Court held that the Clause entitles the defendant not only to be there, and to see and hear the witnesses against him, but also *to be seen by them, to be at least in view of* them. See Coy v. Iowa, 487 U.S. 1012 (1988) (condemning use of translucent screen separating teen-aged girl from defendant in sexual assault case, designed to let defendant see her but shielding her from seeing him). But the accused may *lose* the right to be present by misbehaving, see Illinois v. Allen, 397 U.S. 337 (1970), and a court may let youthful assault victims testify from another room, their image and words conveyed into court by one-way video circuit, on the basis of a case-specific finding that this step is necessary to protect the child, see Maryland v. Craig, 497 U.S. 836 (1990), discussed in section G5, infra.

If "witness against" includes anyone who makes an out-of-court statement offered against the accused, the relevance of the Clause on use of hearsay is obvious. Even if "witness against" embraces only people who testify, letting them recite statements by others would seem to undercut the right to cross-examine, since they are not accountable for what others say. Even using prior statements by one who testifies might be seen in this light, since cross-examination envisions "striking while the iron is hot."

These possibilities raise questions: Does the Confrontation Clause entitle the accused to exclude hearsay? Always? If it blocks some hearsay but not all, how do we separate what is allowed from what is not? What if the declarant is unavailable? Do the hearsay doctrine and its exceptions control or affect the meaning of the Clause? If so, in what way? Or does the Confrontation Clause drive hearsay doctrine in criminal cases?

Origins: Sir Walter Raleigh's case. Most accounts of the Confrontation Clause cite the trial of Sir Walter Raleigh for treason in 1603, though it is not clear that this case inspired the American framers. Raleigh was charged with conspiring against King James (raising money abroad to distribute among malcontents in England, to put Arabella Stuart on the throne).[15] He was convicted on what we would call "rank hearsay," despite his claim of right to confront his accusers "face to face." The most damning evidence was an out-of-court statement by alleged coconspirator Lord Cobham, given during an "examination" (questioning by officers of the Crown in the Tower, under pressure if not torture). There Cobham said Raleigh was fomenting insurrection. Raleigh offered

[15] The passages from the Raleigh trial are reported in 2 Howell's State Cases 15-20 (1803). See also Stephen, The Trial of Sir Walter Raleigh, 2 Trans. Royal Hist. Soc. 172 (4th Series 1919). Raleigh was sentenced to die, but King James found use for his talents and sent him to Guyana for gold. The expedition became an embarrassment because Raleigh attacked Spanish settlements, and executing him became convenient (gesture of good will toward Spain). He was beheaded 15 years after his trial, at the age of 66. Historians think he was not plotting against the crown.

explanations and showed that Cobham had recanted. He argued that the statute required two witnesses and urged the court to "call my Accuser" so they might stand "face to face." He conceded that a witness need not be called where he "is not to be had conveniently," but pointed out that Cobham was "alive, and in the house." The judges rejected Raleigh's position: One argued that the law permits conviction without witnesses (three may be convicted of conspiracy if "they all confess," so "here is never a Witness, yet they are condemned"!); another said "Many horse-stealers may escape, if they may not be condemned without witnesses"; yet another intoned that the law "presumes a man will not accuse himself to accuse another."

Early forays. In nineteenth-century decisions, the Court said the Clause preserved common law protections but was not an instrument of reform. We have opinions approving hearsay that fit standard exceptions in Mattox v. United States, 156 U.S. 237, 244-250 (1895) (testimony from first trial), and 146 U.S. 140 (1892) (dying declarations). The Court also intimated that the Clause accommodates evolving doctrine. See Snyder v. Massachusetts, 291 U.S. 97, 107 (1934) (dying declarations and documentary evidence are exceptions to the Clause, and these exceptions "may be enlarged from time to time").

Once, however, the Court came out the other way. See Kirby v. United States, 174 U.S. 47 (1899) (conviction of third party for theft was hearsay statement by jury in earlier proceeding that could not be used here to prove that property, which defendant was charged with possessing, had been stolen). *Kirby* inspired language in FRE 803(22) barring use of third-party felony convictions against the accused "to prove any fact essential" to the earlier judgment.

The 1960s. During the heyday of Warren Court reforms, the Confrontation Clause took on new importance. In Pointer v. Texas, 380 U.S. 400 (1965), defendant was convicted in state court of armed robbery, and the judge admitted testimony from a preliminary hearing where the accused was not represented. Justice Black wrote for the Court that the right of confrontation is "fundamental" and "obligatory on the States" under the Fourteenth Amendment. Admitting the preliminary hearing testimony under the former testimony exception violated defendant's rights, but the Court said it would be "different" if he had been "represented by counsel who had been given a complete and adequate opportunity to cross-examine."

Pointer brought interpretive difficulties. The quoted comment suggests that *prior* cross (or an opportunity) would be enough. It was not in *Pointer* because the accused did not have a lawyer. But later the Court said preliminary hearing testimony could not come in even if defense counsel "actually cross-examined" on the earlier occasion, because the witness was not shown to be unavailable. See Barber v. Page, 390 U.S. 719, 725 (1968).

In a companion case to *Pointer*, the Court condemned the practice of smuggling in, under the guise of cross-examination by the prosecutor, out-of-court statements by a witness who refuses to be cross-examined by the defense. The case was Douglas v. Alabama, 380 U.S. 415 (1965), where defendant was tried for assault with intent to commit murder. The prosecutor questioned co-offender Loyd (already convicted) on *his* confession, and read parts accusing Douglas of firing the gun. But Loyd refused to answer defense questions, and the Court concluded that the rights of Douglas were violated because he could not cross-examine ("effective" confrontation would be possible if Loyd "affirmed the statement as his," which he did not do). *Douglas* suggests that the Clause might be satisfied by deferred cross (questioning at trial on an earlier statement) *if* declarant affirms the statement as his. If that is right, the next question is whether acknowledging the statement suffices even if the witness is otherwise uncooperative.

After *Pointer* and *Douglas* came the holding in *Barber* that the state has a constitutional obligation to produce a declarant in preference to offering testimony from a preliminary hearing, and the holding in *Bruton* that admitting a confession by one defendant incriminating another by name violates the Clause despite limiting instructions, see Bruton v. United States, 391 U.S. 123 (1968). These narrow holdings led to distinct lines of authority that we explored earlier (see sections B1 and D1, supra).

Last decades of the Twentieth Century: The *Roberts* doctrine. Two decisions in the 1970s were harbingers of the *Roberts* doctrine. The first was California v. Green, 399 U.S. 149 (1970), which rejected challenges to the use of statements by a witness who was forgetful at trial but had incriminated defendant in a conversation with a police officer and in a preliminary hearing. Broadly read, *Green* suggested that statements would satisfy the Confrontation Clause if they were subject to *prior* cross-examination, as would be true if they were made in proceedings where defendant had a lawyer who tested them, or *deferred* cross-examination, as would be true if the declarant testified at trial and could *then* be cross-examined about what he said before.

The second harbinger was Dutton v. Evans, 400 U.S. 74 (1970), which rejected a challenge to a statement that was never tested by cross-examination because declarant never testified. The statement came in under a state coconspirator exception, which (unlike its federal counterpart) reached utterances by a conspirator who was already imprisoned. Broadly read, *Dutton* says the Confrontation Clause is satisfied if a statement possesses "indicia of reliability," similar to those underlying traditional exceptions. The Court stressed that the speaker had "no apparent reason to lie" and that his statement was "spontaneous" and "against his penal interest." Yet the message of *Dutton* is blurred because the Court stressed other factors: The speaker had participated in the crime and could not have had "faulty recollection," and he only obliquely incriminated the defendant ("If it hadn't been for that dirty son-of-a-bitch Alex Evans," said Williams, "we wouldn't be in this now"), so there was "no express assertion about past fact" and the statement "carried on its face a warning to the jury" against giving it "undue weight." Finally, defendant could have subpoenaed Williams, but decided not to do so.

In 1980 came the decision in Ohio v. Roberts, 448 U.S. 56 (1980), where the Court set out to systematize the Confrontation Clause as it relates to the use of hearsay against the accused. *Roberts* involved the trial of Herschel Roberts for possessing stolen credit cards and checks. At his preliminary hearing the *defense* called Anita Isaacs (unusual because defendants seldom call witnesses at this stage), and she testified that she knew Roberts and let him use her apartment for several days while she was away. The defense tried to get her to admit that she gave him the checks and credit cards, which belonged to Anita's parents, *without* telling him she lacked permission. Anita denied these points.

A year later the case came to trial, and the prosecutor tried five times to subpoena Anita Isaacs at her parents' home, but she was not found, and she did not telephone or appear at trial. Roberts testified that Anita gave him the checkbook and credit cards "with the understanding that he could use them." The court admitted her preliminary hearing testimony, and Roberts was convicted. He won a reversal in the Ohio Supreme Court, which ruled that the preliminary hearing testimony was inadmissible even though Isaacs was unavailable because the "mere opportunity" to cross-examine then did not satisfy the Confrontation Clause. The Supreme Court disagreed, and took the occasion to offer a systematic description of the Confrontation Clause as it relates to the use of hearsay:

> The Confrontation Clause operates in two separate ways to restrict the range of admissible hearsay. First, in conformance with the Framers' preference for face-to-face accusation, the Sixth Amendment establishes a rule of necessity. In the usual case (including cases where prior cross-examination has occurred), the prosecution must either produce, or demonstrate the unavailability of, the declarant whose statement it wishes to use against the defendant [citing *Barber*, *Green*, and other authority].[7]
>
> The second aspect operates once a witness is shown to be unavailable. Reflecting its underlying purpose to augment accuracy in the factfinding process by ensuring the defendant an effective means to test adverse evidence, the Clause countenances only hearsay marked with such trustworthiness that "there is no material departure from the reason of the general rule." [Court quotes passages from a decision that quotes *Dutton* and *Green*, including the idea that there must be "indicia of reliability" for hearsay offered against the accused.]
>
> The Court has applied this "indicia of reliability" requirement principally by concluding that certain hearsay exceptions rest upon such solid foundations that admission of virtually any evidence within them comports with the "substance of the constitutional protection" [citing *Mattox*]. This reflects the truism that "hearsay rules and the Confrontation Clause are generally designed to protect similar values" [quoting *Green*], and "stem from the same roots" [quoting *Dutton*]. It also responds to the need for certainty in the workaday world of conducting criminal trials.

---

[7] A demonstration of unavailability, however, is not always required. In Dutton v. Evans, 400 U.S. 74 (1970), for example, the Court found the utility of trial confrontation so remote that it did not require the prosecution to produce a seemingly available witness.

> In sum, when a hearsay declarant is not present for cross-examination at trial, the Confrontation Clause normally requires a showing that he is unavailable. Even then, his statement is admissible only if it bears adequate "indicia of reliability." Reliability can be inferred without more in a case where the evidence falls within a firmly rooted hearsay exception. In other cases, the evidence must be excluded, at least absent a showing of particularized guarantees of trustworthiness.

Ohio v. Roberts, 448 U.S. 56, 64-66 (1980).

■ NOTES ON THE *ROBERTS* DOCTRINE

1. *Roberts* adopted a two-pronged approach that required prosecutors to call declarants as witnesses or, if a declarant was unavailable, to show that her proffered statement was reliable. But *Roberts* watered down both these standards or requirements:

(a) From the beginning, the "unavailability" prong meant less than it seemed. Almost in the same breath, the Court said in a footnote that showing unavailability "is not always required," as in cases where utility of trial confrontation is "remote." The Court cited *Dutton*, which approved use of coconspirator statements without showing that the speaker was unavailable. In practice, courts applying *Roberts* required a showing of unavailability for statements, such as those offered in *Roberts* itself, that amounted to actual testimony from prior proceedings. Imposing a constitutional unavailability requirement dovetails with the former testimony exception which requires a showing of unavailability, see FRE 804(b)(1). For an analysis, see Kirkpatrick, Confrontation and Hearsay: Exemptions from the Constitutional Unavailability Requirement, 70 Minn. L. Rev. 665 (1986) (whether to require unavailability should turn on centrality of statement, reliability, likelihood that cross could test it, and adequacy of alternative means of challenge).

(b) From the beginning, the reliability prong also meant less than one might expect. In *Roberts*, the Court said hearsay fitting a "firmly rooted" exception satisfies the standard. In practice, courts applying *Roberts* approved use of hearsay fitting the most common exceptions, including those for coconspirator statements, agent's admissions, excited utterances, medical statements, business records, former testimony, dying declarations, and public records. The Court twice approved use of the conspirator exception while *Roberts* was in effect, see United States v. Inadi, 475 U.S. 387, 394 (1985), and Bourjaily v. United States, 483 U.S. 171 (1987), as well as exceptions for excited utterances and medical statements, see White v. Illinois, 502 U.S. 346 (1992). *Roberts* itself approved the former testimony exception, and mentioned with approval the exceptions for dying declarations and business records. See also United States v. De Water, 846 F.2d 528, 530 (9th Cir. 1988) (public records); United States v.

McLean-Davis, 785 F.2d 1534, 1536-1537 (11th Cir. 1986) (admissions by speaking agents).

(c) So common was resort to standard exceptions under *Roberts* that it is easier to list the ones that were *not* "firmly rooted." These included the catchall and the against-interest exception that came to be commonly used to admit statements by a co-offender implicating the accused, and the newly minted exceptions for child victim hearsay. Even though these exceptions were *not* viewed as firmly rooted, a statement could be offered under them if the prosecutor made a particularized showing of reliability—not just that the statement fit the exception, but that the particular statement was reliable.

2. Lest you conclude that *Roberts* was *completely* ineffective as an independent constitutional standard, you should know that in the *Wright* case the Court *disapproved* use of hearsay offered under a state catchall exception. There, the Court reversed a state conviction for child abuse on account of the use of statements by a child who was two and one-half years old: The examining physician asked "Does daddy touch you with his pee-pee?" and the child "did admit to that," adding "daddy does do this with me, but he does it a lot more with my sister," referring to a child then five years old. Writing for the Court, Justice O'Connor concluded that the catchall was *not* firmly rooted under *Roberts*, hence that hearsay admitted against the accused under it had to be analyzed for particularized guarantees of trustworthiness. Factors like "spontaneity and consistent repetition" count, as do the "mental state of the declarant" and "use of terminology unexpected of a child of similar age." But corroborative evidence does *not* count, and a statement "must possess indicia of reliability by virtue of its inherent trustworthiness." Idaho v. Wright, 497 U.S. 805, 820-821 (1990).

3. *Roberts* held sway for 24 years, until its rejection in *Crawford* and *Davis.* Even that rejection, which discarded *Roberts* as a standard in the case of "testimonial" statements, left room to argue that *Roberts* still applied to *other* hearsay, such as statements in purely private settings (not involving police). And oddly enough, the death of *Roberts* did not come in a decision that overruled it formally. Rather, *Roberts* was discarded somewhat indirectly in two decisions that came after *Crawford.* See Davis v. Washington, 547 U.S. 813 (2006) (section G3, infra); Whorton v. Bockting, 549 U.S. 406 (2007) (twice saying that *Crawford* "overruled" *Roberts*). It appears, then, that *Roberts* does not operate *at all* as a federal standard, even in cases of nontestimonial hearsay.

4. Although *Roberts* no longer announces a *federal* standard, some state courts follow the *Roberts* approach in applying *their own* constitutional standards (their counterparts to the Confrontation Clause). See State v. Comacho, 924 A.2d 99 (Conn. 2007) (applying *Roberts* to nontestimonial "dual inculpatory statement" incriminating defendant and declarant, and approving use of statement); State v. Birchfield, 157 P.3d 216 (Or. 2007) (in applying state confrontation clause, recognizing unavailability requirement based on *Roberts*). See generally Laird C. Kirkpatrick, Nontestimonial Hearsay After *Crawford, Davis* and *Bockting,* 19 Regent U. L. Rev. 367 (2007).

2. Modern Doctrine: *Crawford* and "Testimonial" Hearsay

You've already seen innumerable references to the case you're about to read, and it is fair to say that *Crawford* is one of those "paradigm shifting" cases that comes along rarely in constitutional jurisprudence. You will discover that *Crawford* is remarkable both for *how much* it changes things and for *how little* it changes things.

Justice Antonin Scalia

Tim Sloan / AFP / Getty Images

Appointed in 1986, Justice Antonin Scalia became an intellectual force on the Court. He describes himself as an "honest originalist" and holds that "a lot of stuff that's stupid is not unconstitutional." Thirteen years before *Crawford,* Scalia complained about the *Roberts* doctrine and signed on to the view that the Confrontation Clause applies to out-of-court statements only if "contained in formalized testimonial materials, such as affidavits, depositions, prior testimony, or confessions." See White v. Illinois, 502 U.S. 346, 365 (1992) (Justice Thomas, joined by Justice Scalia, dissenting). In *Crawford,* Scalia developed at length the historical basis for the testimonial approach, and you will read his opinion in *Crawford* and also his opinion in the *Davis* case, which develops the emergency doctrine. He also authored *Melendez-Diaz,* which holds that forensic lab reports are testimonial (section C6c, supra). More recent opinions on confrontation have led Scalia into sharp disagreement with colleagues. In 2011, Scalia sparred with Justice Sotomayor in the *Bullcoming* case (section C6c, supra) on the meaning of "testimonial," and in the *Bryant* case dealing with the emergency doctrine (described after *Davis,* infra), where he characterized her opinion for the majority as a "gross distortion" of the law and facts, and a "revisionist narrative" resuscitating the "reliability" criterion of *Roberts* and leaving confrontation jurisprudence "a shambles." Asked in 2013 why he writes such sharp dissents, Scalia replied that he writes them for law students: "They will read dissents that are breezy and have some thrust to them." The clarity and vigor of Scalia's opinions call to mind Nietzsche's comment that "it is not the least charm of a theory that it is refutable" (then it "attracts more subtle minds"): Scalia opinions definitely have charm, and they definitely draw attacks in the academy and in popular media (you can judge for yourself whether the attackers have "more subtle minds"). See generally Antonin Scalia, A Matter of Interpretation: Federal Courts and the Law (Princeton University Press 1998) (essays on originalism by Scalia, Gordon Wood, Mary Ann Glendon, and Ronald Dworkin).

CRAWFORD v. WASHINGTON

United States Supreme Court
541 U.S. 36 (2004)

Justice SCALIA delivered the opinion of the Court.

[Michael Crawford was convicted of assault after stabbing Kenneth Lee, a man who allegedly tried to rape Crawford's wife Sylvia.

Michael and Sylvia Crawford gave separate statements to police. In his statement, Michael said "I coulda swore I seen him goin' for somethin'" right before the stabbing, and he thought Lee "pulled somethin' out" and he "grabbed for it and that's how I got cut." In Sylvia's statement, she said that Lee "lifted his hand over his head maybe to strike Michael's hand down or something," and that "his hands were like . . . how do you explain this . . . open arms . . . with his hands open and he fell down . . . ." The court admitted both statements. The prosecutor used Sylvia's to refute Michael's claim that Lee was armed, which would support Michael's claim of self-defense. The Washington Supreme Court affirmed Michael's conviction, concluding that Sylvia's statement fit the against-interest exception because she had shown Michael where to find Lee and had gone with him and was present during the violent encounter, and thus faced issues of accomplice liability. Sylvia was unavailable as a witness because Michael had invoked the spousal testimonial privilege. Invoking the privilege did *not* waive Michael's confrontation rights, but Sylvia's statement satisfied the constitutional reliability criterion of the *Roberts* case.

The U.S. Supreme Court notes the findings of the Washington Supreme Court, including its finding that Michael did not waive his confrontation claims, and notes as well that the prosecutor conceded that admitting Sylvia's statement could not be harmless error. Justice Scalia comments that "We express no opinion" on these points.]

II

The Sixth Amendment's Confrontation Clause provides that, "in all criminal prosecutions, the accused shall enjoy the right . . . to be confronted with the witnesses against him." We have held that this bedrock procedural guarantee applies to both federal and state prosecutions . . . . *Roberts* says that an unavailable witness's out-of-court statement may be admitted so long as it has adequate indicia of reliability—*i.e.*, falls within a "firmly rooted hearsay exception" or bears "particularized guarantees of trustworthiness." Petitioner argues that this test strays from the original meaning of the Confrontation Clause and urges us to reconsider it.

A

The Constitution's text does not alone resolve this case. One could plausibly read "witnesses against" a defendant to mean those who actually testify at trial, those whose statements are offered at trial, or something in-between. We must therefore turn to the historical background of the Clause to understand its meaning.

The right to confront one's accusers is a concept that dates back to Roman times. The founding generation's immediate source of the concept, however, was the common law. English common law has long differed from continental civil law in regard to the manner in which witnesses give testimony in criminal trials. The common-law tradition is one of live testimony in court subject to adversarial testing, while the civil law condones examination in private by judicial officers. See 3 W. Blackstone, Commentaries on the Laws of England 373-374 (1768).

Nonetheless, England at times adopted elements of the civil-law practice. Justices of the peace or other officials examined suspects and witnesses before trial. These examinations were sometimes read in court in lieu of live testimony, a practice that "occasioned frequent demands by the prisoner to have his 'accusers,' *i.e.*, the witnesses against him, brought before him face to face." 1 J. Stephen, History of the Criminal Law of England 326 (1883). In some cases, these demands were refused.

Pretrial examinations became routine under two statutes passed during the reign of Queen Mary in the 16th century. These Marian bail and committal statutes required justices of the peace to examine suspects and witnesses in felony cases and to certify the results to the court. It is doubtful that the original purpose of the examinations was to produce evidence admissible at trial. See J. Langbein, Prosecuting Crime in the Renaissance 21-34 (1974). Whatever the original purpose, however, they came to be used as evidence in some cases, resulting in an adoption of continental procedure.

The most notorious instances of civil-law examination occurred in the great political trials of the 16th and 17th centuries. One such was the 1603 trial of Sir Walter Raleigh for treason. Lord Cobham, Raleigh's alleged accomplice, had implicated him in an examination before the Privy Council and in a letter. At Raleigh's trial, these were read to the jury. Raleigh argued that Cobham had lied to save himself: "Cobham is absolutely in the King's mercy; to excuse me cannot avail him; by accusing me he may hope for favour." 1 D. Jardine, Criminal Trials 435 (1832). Suspecting that Cobham would recant, Raleigh demanded that the judges call him to appear, arguing that "the Proof of the Common Law is by witness and jury: let Cobham be here, let him speak it. Call my accuser before my face . . . ." 2 How. St. Tr., at 15-16. The judges refused, and, despite

Raleigh's protestations that he was being tried "by the Spanish Inquisition," the jury convicted, and Raleigh was sentenced to death.

One of Raleigh's trial judges later lamented that "'the justice of England has never been so degraded and injured as by the condemnation of Sir Walter Raleigh.'" Through a series of statutory and judicial reforms, English law developed a right of confrontation that limited these abuses. For example, treason statutes required witnesses to confront the accused "face to face" at his arraignment. Courts, meanwhile, developed relatively strict rules of unavailability, admitting examinations only if the witness was demonstrably unable to testify in person. Several authorities also stated that a suspect's confession could be admitted only against himself, and not against others he implicated.

One recurring question was whether the admissibility of an unavailable witness's pretrial examination depended on whether the defendant had had an opportunity to cross-examine him. In 1696, the Court of King's Bench answered this question in the affirmative, in the widely reported misdemeanor libel case of King v. Paine, 5 Mod. 163, 87 Eng. Rep. 584. The court ruled that, even though a witness was dead, his examination was not admissible where "the defendant not being present when [it was] taken before the mayor . . . had lost the benefit of a cross-examination." . . . *Paine* had settled the rule requiring a prior opportunity for cross-examination as a matter of common law, but some doubts remained over whether the Marian statutes prescribed an exception to it in felony cases. The statutes did not identify the circumstances under which examinations were admissible, and some inferred that no prior opportunity for cross-examination was required. Many who expressed this view acknowledged that it meant the statutes were in derogation of the common law. Nevertheless, by 1791 (the year the Sixth Amendment was ratified), courts were applying the cross-examination rule even to examinations by justices of the peace in felony cases. When Parliament amended the statutes in 1848 to make the requirement explicit, the change merely "introduced in terms" what was already afforded the defendant "by the equitable construction of the law." Queen v. Beeston, 29 Eng. L. & Eq. R. 527, 529 (Ct. Crim. App. 1854) (Jervis, C. J.).

B

Controversial examination practices were also used in the Colonies. Early in the 18th century, for example, the Virginia Council protested against the Governor for having "privately issued several commissions to examine witnesses against particular men *ex parte*," complaining that "the person accused is not admitted to be confronted with, or defend himself against his defamers." A Memorial Concerning the Maladministrations of His Excellency Francis Nicholson, reprinted in 9 English Historical Documents 253, 257 (D. Douglas ed. 1955). A decade before the Revolution, England gave jurisdiction over Stamp Act offenses to the admiralty courts, which followed civil-law rather than common-law procedures and thus routinely took testimony by deposition or private judicial examination. Colonial representatives protested that the Act subverted their rights "by extending the jurisdiction of the courts of admiralty beyond its ancient limits." Resolutions of the Stamp Act Congress §8th (Oct. 19, 1765), reprinted in Sources of Our Liberties 270, 271 (R. Perry & J. Cooper eds. 1959). John Adams, defending a merchant in a high-profile admiralty case, argued: "Examinations of witnesses upon Interrogatories, are only by the Civil Law. Interrogatories are unknown at common Law, and Englishmen and common Lawyers have an aversion to them if not an Abhorrence of them." Draft of Argument in Sewall v. Hancock (1768-1769), in 2 Legal Papers of John Adams 194, 207 (K. Wroth & H. Zobel eds. 1965).

Many declarations of rights adopted around the time of the Revolution guaranteed a right of confrontation. [Court cites Declarations from Virginia, Pennsylvania, Delaware, Maryland, North Carolina, Vermont, Massachusetts, and New Hampshire.] The proposed Federal Constitution, however, did not. At the Massachusetts ratifying convention, Abraham Holmes objected to this omission precisely on the ground that it would lead to civil-law practices: "The mode of trial is altogether indetermined; . . . whether [the defendant] is to be allowed to confront the witnesses, and have the advantage of cross-examination, we are not yet told . . . . We shall find Congress possessed of powers enabling them to institute judicatories little less inauspicious than a certain tribunal in Spain, . . . the *Inquisition.*" 2 Debates on the Federal Constitution 110-111 (J. Elliot 2d ed. 1863). Similarly, a prominent Antifederalist writing under the pseudonym Federal Farmer criticized the use of "written evidence" while objecting to the omission of a vicinage right: "Nothing can be more essential than the cross examining [of] witnesses, and generally before the triers of the facts in question . . . . Written evidence . . . [is] almost useless; it must be frequently taken ex parte, and but very seldom leads to the proper discovery of truth." R. Lee, Letter IV by the Federal Farmer (Oct. 15, 1787). The First Congress responded by including the Confrontation Clause in the proposal that became the Sixth Amendment . . . .

III

This history supports two inferences about the meaning of the Sixth Amendment.

A

First, the principal evil at which the Confrontation Clause was directed was the civil-law mode of criminal procedure, and particularly its use of *ex parte* examinations as evidence against the accused. It was these practices that the Crown deployed in notorious treason cases like Raleigh's; that the Marian statutes invited; that English law's assertion of a right to confrontation was meant to prohibit; and that the founding-era rhetoric decried. The Sixth Amendment must be interpreted with this focus in mind.

Accordingly, we once again reject the view that the Confrontation Clause applies of its own force only to in-court testimony, and that its application to out-of-court statements introduced at trial depends upon "the law of Evidence for the time being." 3 Wigmore §1397, at 101; accord, Dutton v. Evans, 400 U.S. 74, 94 (1970) (Harlan, J., concurring in result). Leaving the regulation of out-of-court statements to the law of evidence would render the Confrontation Clause powerless to prevent even the most flagrant inquisitorial practices. Raleigh was, after all, perfectly free to confront those who read Cobham's confession in court.

This focus also suggests that not all hearsay implicates the Sixth Amendment's core concerns. An off-hand, overheard remark might be unreliable evidence and thus a good candidate for exclusion under hearsay rules, but it bears little resemblance to the civil-law abuses the Confrontation Clause targeted. On the other hand, *ex parte* examinations might sometimes be admissible under modern hearsay rules, but the Framers certainly would not have condoned them.

The text of the Confrontation Clause reflects this focus. It applies to "witnesses" against the accused—in other words, those who "bear testimony." 1 N. Webster, An American Dictionary of the English Language (1828). "Testimony," in turn, is typically "[a] solemn declaration or affirmation made for the purpose of establishing or proving some fact." An accuser who makes a formal statement to government officers bears testimony in a sense that a person who makes a casual remark to an acquaintance does not. The constitutional text, like the history underlying the common-law right of confrontation, thus reflects an especially acute concern with a specific type of out-of-court statement.

Various formulations of this core class of "testimonial" statements exist: "*ex parte* in-court testimony or its functional equivalent—that is, material such as affidavits, custodial examinations, prior testimony that the defendant was unable to cross-examine, or similar pretrial statements that declarants would reasonably expect to be used prosecutorially"; "extrajudicial statements . . . contained in formalized testimonial materials, such as affidavits, depositions, prior testimony, or confessions"; "statements that were made under circumstances which would lead an objective witness reasonably to believe that the statement would be available for use at a later trial." These formulations all share a common nucleus and then define the Clause's coverage at various levels of abstraction around it. Regardless of the precise articulation, some statements qualify under any definition—for example, *ex parte* testimony at a preliminary hearing.

Statements taken by police officers in the course of interrogations are also testimonial under even a narrow standard. Police interrogations bear a striking resemblance to examinations by justices of the peace in England. The statements are not *sworn* testimony, but the absence of oath was not dispositive. Cobham's examination was unsworn, yet Raleigh's trial has long been thought a paradigmatic confrontation violation. Under the Marian statutes, witnesses were typically put on oath, but suspects were not. Yet Hawkins [in Pleas of the Crown (T. Leach 6th ed. 1787)] and others went out of their way to caution that such unsworn confessions were not admissible against anyone but the confessor.

That interrogators are police officers rather than magistrates does not change the picture either. Justices of the peace conducting examinations under the Marian statutes were not magistrates as we understand that office today, but had an essentially investigative and prosecutorial function. England did not have a professional police force until the 19th century, so it is not surprising that other government officers performed the investigative functions now associated primarily with the police. The involvement of government officers in the production of testimonial evidence presents the same risk, whether the officers are police or justices of the peace.

In sum, even if the Sixth Amendment is not solely concerned with testimonial hearsay, that is its primary object, and interrogations by law enforcement officers fall squarely within that class.[4]

B

The historical record also supports a second proposition: that the Framers would not have allowed admission of testimonial statements of a witness who did not appear at trial unless he was unavailable to testify, and the defendant had had a prior opportunity for cross-examination. The text of the Sixth Amendment does not suggest any open-ended exceptions from the confrontation requirement to be developed by the courts. Rather, the "right . . . to be confronted with the witnesses against him," is most naturally read as a reference to the right of confrontation at common law, admitting only those exceptions established at the time of the founding. See Mattox v. United States, 156 U.S. 237, 243 (1895). As the English authorities above reveal, the common law in 1791 conditioned admissibility of an absent witness's examination on unavailability and a prior opportunity to cross-examine. The Sixth Amendment therefore incorporates those limitations. The numerous early state decisions applying the same test confirm that these principles were received as part of the common law in this country.

We do not read the historical sources to say that a prior opportunity to cross-examine was merely a sufficient, rather than a necessary, condition for admissibility of testimonial statements. They suggest that this requirement was dispositive, and not merely one of several ways to establish reliability. This is not to deny, as the Chief Justice notes, that "there were always exceptions to the general rule of exclusion" of hearsay evidence. Several had become well established by 1791. But there is scant evidence that exceptions were invoked to admit *testimonial* statements against the accused in a *criminal* case.[6] Most of

---

[4] We use the term "interrogation" in its colloquial, rather than any technical legal, sense. Just as various definitions of "testimonial" exist, one can imagine various definitions of "interrogation," and we need not select among them in this case. Sylvia's recorded statement, knowingly given in response to structured police questioning, qualifies under any conceivable definition.

[6] The one deviation we have found involves dying declarations. The existence of that exception as a general rule of criminal hearsay law cannot be disputed. See, e.g., Mattox v. United States, 156 U.S. 237, 243-244 (1895); [Court cites an English case and treatises from eighteenth and nineteenth centuries]; see also F. Heller, The Sixth Amendment 105 (1951) (asserting that this was the *only* recognized criminal hearsay exception at common law). Although many dying declarations may not be testimonial, there is authority for admitting even those that clearly are. We need not decide in this case whether the Sixth Amendment incorporates an exception for testimonial dying declarations. If this exception must be accepted on historical grounds, it is *sui generis*.

the hearsay exceptions covered statements that by their nature were not testimonial—for example, business records or statements in furtherance of a conspiracy. We do not infer from these that the Framers thought exceptions would apply even to prior testimony. Cf. Lilly v. Virginia, 527 U.S. 116, 134 (1999) (plurality opinion) ("Accomplices' confessions that inculpate a criminal defendant are not within a firmly rooted exception to the hearsay rule").[7]

IV

Our case law has been largely consistent with these two principles. Our leading early decision, for example, involved a deceased witness's prior trial testimony. Mattox v. United States, 156 U.S. 237 (1895). In allowing the statement to be admitted, we relied on the fact that the defendant had had, at the first trial, an adequate opportunity to confront the witness . . . .

Our later cases conform to *Mattox*'s holding that prior trial or preliminary hearing testimony is admissible only if the defendant had an adequate opportunity to cross-examine. Even where the defendant had such an opportunity, we excluded the testimony where the government had not established unavailability of the witness. See Barber v. Page, 390 U.S. 719 (1968). We similarly excluded accomplice confessions where the defendant had no opportunity to cross-examine. See Bruton v. United States, 391 U.S. 123 (1968). In contrast, we considered reliability factors beyond prior opportunity for cross-examination when the hearsay statement at issue was not testimonial. See Dutton v. Evans, 400 U.S., at 87-89 (plurality opinion).

Even our recent cases, in their outcomes, hew closely to the traditional line. *Roberts* admitted testimony from a preliminary hearing at which the defendant had examined the witness. *Lilly* excluded testimonial statements that the defendant had had no opportunity to test by cross-examination. And Bourjaily v. United States, 483 U.S. 171 (1987), admitted statements made unwittingly to an FBI informant after applying a more general test that did *not* make prior cross-examination an indispensable requirement.[8] . . .

Our cases have thus remained faithful to the Framers' understanding: Testimonial statements of witnesses absent from trial have been admitted only

General Rule

[7] We cannot agree with [the concurring and dissenting opinion of] the Chief Justice that the fact "that a statement might be testimonial does nothing to undermine the wisdom of one of these [hearsay] exceptions." Involvement of government officers in the production of testimony with an eye toward trial presents unique potential for prosecutorial abuse—a fact borne out time and again throughout a history with which the Framers were keenly familiar. This consideration does not evaporate when testimony happens to fall within some broad, modern hearsay exception, even if that exception might be justifiable in other circumstances.

[8] One case arguably in tension with the rule requiring a prior opportunity for cross-examination when the proffered statement is testimonial is White v. Illinois, 502 U.S. 346 (1992), which involved, *inter alia*, statements of a child victim to an investigating police officer admitted as spontaneous declarations . . . . [T]he only question presented in *White* was whether the Confrontation Clause imposed an unavailability requirement on the types of hearsay at issue. The holding did not address the question whether certain of the statements, because they were testimonial, had to be excluded even if the witness was unavailable. We "[took] as a given . . . that the testimony properly falls within the relevant hearsay exceptions."

where the declarant is unavailable, and only where the defendant has had a prior opportunity to cross-examine.[9]

V

Although the results of our decisions have generally been faithful to the original meaning of the Confrontation Clause, the same cannot be said of our rationales. *Roberts* conditions the admissibility of all hearsay evidence on whether it falls under a "firmly rooted hearsay exception" or bears "particularized guarantees of trustworthiness." This test departs from the historical principles identified above in two respects. First, it is too broad: It applies the same mode of analysis whether or not the hearsay consists of *ex parte* testimony. This often results in close constitutional scrutiny in cases that are far removed from the core concerns of the Clause. At the same time, however, the test is too narrow: It admits statements that *do* consist of *ex parte* testimony upon a mere finding of reliability. This malleable standard often fails to protect against paradigmatic confrontation violations.

Members of this Court and academics have suggested that we revise our doctrine to reflect more accurately the original understanding of the Clause. See, *e.g.*, *Lilly* (Breyer, J. concurring); *White* (Thomas, J., joined by Scalia, J., concurring in part and concurring in judgment); A. Amar, The Constitution and Criminal Procedure 125-131 (1997); Friedman, Confrontation: The Search for Basic Principles, 86 Geo. L. J. 1011 (1998). They offer two proposals: First, that we apply the Confrontation Clause only to testimonial statements, leaving the remainder to regulation by hearsay law—thus eliminating the overbreadth referred to above. Second, that we impose an absolute bar to statements that are testimonial, absent a prior opportunity to cross-examine—thus eliminating the excessive narrowness referred to above.

In *White*, we considered the first proposal and rejected it. Although our analysis in this case casts doubt on that holding, we need not definitively resolve whether it survives our decision today, because Sylvia Crawford's statement is testimonial under any definition. This case does, however, squarely implicate the second proposal.

A

Where testimonial statements are involved, we do not think the Framers meant to leave the Sixth Amendment's protection to the vagaries of the rules

[9] . . . Finally, we reiterate that, when the declarant appears for cross-examination at trial, the Confrontation Clause places no constraints at all on the use of his prior testimonial statements. See California v. Green, 399 U.S. 149 (1970). It is therefore irrelevant that the reliability of some out-of-court statements "'cannot be replicated, even if the declarant testifies to the same matters in court'" (quoting United States v. Inadi, 475 U.S. 387, 395 (1986)). The Clause does not bar admission of a statement so long as the declarant is present at trial to defend or explain it. (The Clause also does not bar the use of testimonial statements for purposes other than establishing the truth of the matter asserted. See Tennessee v. Street, 471 U.S. 409 (1985).)

of evidence, much less to amorphous notions of "reliability." Certainly none of the authorities discussed above acknowledges any general reliability exception to the common-law rule. Admitting statements deemed reliable by a judge is fundamentally at odds with the right of confrontation. To be sure, the Clause's ultimate goal is to ensure reliability of evidence, but it is a procedural rather than a substantive guarantee. It commands, not that evidence be reliable, but that reliability be assessed in a particular manner: by testing in the crucible of cross-examination. The Clause thus reflects a judgment, not only about the desirability of reliable evidence (a point on which there could be little dissent), but about how reliability can best be determined. Cf. 3 Blackstone, Commentaries, at 373 ("This open examination of witnesses . . . is much more conducive to the clearing up of truth"); M. Hale, History and Analysis of the Common Law of England 258 (1713) (adversarial testing "beats and bolts out the Truth much better").

The *Roberts* test allows a jury to hear evidence, untested by the adversary process, based on a mere judicial determination of reliability. It thus replaces the constitutionally prescribed method of assessing reliability with a wholly foreign one. In this respect, it is very different from exceptions to the Confrontation Clause that make no claim to be a surrogate means of assessing reliability. For example, the rule of forfeiture by wrongdoing (which we accept) extinguishes confrontation claims on essentially equitable grounds; it does not purport to be an alternative means of determining reliability. See Reynolds v. United States, 98 U.S. 145, 158-159 (1879).

The Raleigh trial itself involved the very sorts of reliability determinations that *Roberts* authorizes. In the face of Raleigh's repeated demands for confrontation, the prosecution responded with many of the arguments a court applying *Roberts* might invoke today: that Cobham's statements were self-inculpatory, that they were not made in the heat of passion, and that they were not "extracted from [him] upon any hopes or promise of Pardon." It is not plausible that the Framers' only objection to the trial was that Raleigh's judges did not properly weigh these factors before sentencing him to death. Rather, the problem was that the judges refused to allow Raleigh to confront Cobham in court, where he could cross-examine him and try to expose his accusation as a lie.

Dispensing with confrontation because testimony is obviously reliable is akin to dispensing with jury trial because a defendant is obviously guilty. This is not what the Sixth Amendment prescribes.

B

The legacy of *Roberts* in other courts vindicates the Framers' wisdom in rejecting a general reliability exception. The framework is so unpredictable that it fails to provide meaningful protection from even core confrontation violations.

Reliability is an amorphous, if not entirely subjective, concept. There are countless factors bearing on whether a statement is reliable; the nine-factor balancing test applied by the Court of Appeals below is representative. Whether a statement is deemed reliable depends heavily on which factors the judge considers and how much weight he accords each of them. Some courts wind up attaching the same significance to opposite facts. For example, the Colorado Supreme Court held a statement more reliable because its inculpation of the defendant was "detailed," while the Fourth Circuit found a statement more reliable because the portion implicating another was "fleeting," United States v. Photogrammetric Data Servs., Inc., 259 F.3d 229, 245 (2001). The Virginia Court of Appeals found a statement more reliable because the witness was in custody and charged with a crime (thus making the statement more obviously against her penal interest), see Nowlin v. Commonwealth, 579 S.E.2d 367, 371-372 (Va. App. 2003), while the Wisconsin Court of Appeals found a statement more reliable because the witness was *not* in custody and *not* a suspect, see State v. Bintz, 650 N.W.2d 913, 918 (Wis. App. 2002). Finally, the Colorado Supreme Court in one case found a statement more reliable because it was given "immediately after" the events at issue, while that same court, in another case, found a statement more reliable because two years had elapsed, Stevens v. People, 29 P.3d 305, 316 (2001).

The unpardonable vice of the *Roberts* test, however, is not its unpredictability, but its demonstrated capacity to admit core testimonial statements that the Confrontation Clause plainly meant to exclude. Despite the plurality's speculation in *Lilly* that it was "highly unlikely" that accomplice confessions implicating the accused could survive *Roberts*, courts continue routinely to admit them. [Court cites modern decisions from a federal Court of Appeals, and from the states of Colorado, Kentucky, Ohio, Wisconsin, Michigan, and Illinois.] One recent study found that, after *Lilly*, appellate courts admitted accomplice statements to the authorities in 25 out of 70 cases—more than one-third of the time. Kirst, Appellate Court Answers to the Confrontation Questions in Lilly v. Virginia, 53 Syracuse L. Rev. 87, 105 (2003). Courts have invoked *Roberts* to admit other sorts of plainly testimonial statements despite the absence of any opportunity to cross-examine. [Court cites federal and state decisions admitting plea allocutions, grand jury testimony, and prior trial testimony.]

To add insult to injury, some of the courts that admit untested testimonial statements find reliability in the very factors that *make* the statements testimonial. As noted earlier, one court relied on the fact that the witness's statement was made to police while in custody on pending charges—the theory being that this made the statement more clearly against penal interest and thus more reliable. Other courts routinely rely on the fact that a prior statement is given under oath in judicial proceedings. That inculpating statements are given in a testimonial setting is not an antidote to the confrontation problem, but rather the trigger that makes the Clause's demands most urgent. It is not enough to point out that most of the usual safeguards of the adversary process attend the statement, when the single safeguard missing is the one the Confrontation Clause demands.

C

Roberts' failings were on full display in the proceedings below. Sylvia Crawford made her statement while in police custody, herself a potential suspect in the case. Indeed, she had been told that whether she would be released "depended on how the investigation continues." In response to often leading questions from police detectives, she implicated her husband in Lee's stabbing and at least arguably undermined his self-defense claim. Despite all this, the trial court admitted her statement, listing several reasons why it was reliable. In its opinion reversing, the Court of Appeals listed several *other* reasons why the statement was *not* reliable. Finally, the State Supreme Court relied exclusively on the interlocking character of the statement and disregarded every other factor the lower courts had considered. The case is thus a self-contained demonstration of *Roberts'* unpredictable and inconsistent application . . . .

Where nontestimonial hearsay is at issue, it is wholly consistent with the Framers' design to afford the States flexibility in their development of hearsay law—as does *Roberts*, and as would an approach that exempted such statements from Confrontation Clause scrutiny altogether. Where testimonial evidence is at issue, however, the Sixth Amendment demands what the common law required: unavailability and a prior opportunity for cross-examination. We leave for another day any effort to spell out a comprehensive definition of "testimonial."[10] Whatever else the term covers, it applies at a minimum to prior testimony at a preliminary hearing, before a grand jury, or at a former trial; and to police interrogations. These are the modern practices with closest kinship to the abuses at which the Confrontation Clause was directed.

In this case, the State admitted Sylvia's testimonial statement against petitioner, despite the fact that he had no opportunity to cross-examine her. That alone is sufficient to make out a violation of the Sixth Amendment. *Roberts* notwithstanding, we decline to mine the record in search of indicia of reliability. Where testimonial statements are at issue, the only indicium of reliability sufficient to satisfy constitutional demands is the one the Constitution actually prescribes: confrontation.

The judgment of the Washington Supreme Court is reversed, and the case is remanded for further proceedings not inconsistent with this opinion.

It is so ordered.

[The opinion of Chief Justice Rehnquist, with whom Justice O'Connor joins, concurring in the judgment, is omitted.]

---

[10] We acknowledge the Chief Justice's objection that our refusal to articulate a comprehensive definition in this case will cause interim uncertainty. But it can hardly be any worse than the status quo. The difference is that the *Roberts* test is *inherently*, and therefore *permanently*, unpredictable.

■ NOTES ON *CRAWFORD*'S "TESTIMONIAL" APPROACH

1. Before you read *Crawford* you were familiar with its holding. You needed that introduction to make sense of important hearsay exceptions. Now that you've read the decision, what do you think? Justice Scalia goes very far in condemning efforts by courts to appraise the reliability of hearsay statements. If reliability is an unintelligible criterion for purposes of the Confrontation Clause, can it be intelligible for purposes of the hearsay doctrine and the exceptions?

2. The concept of "testimonial" hearsay lies at the heart of *Crawford*, and the Court quotes definitions but doesn't offer its own. We know "testimonial" includes *actual* testimony at a trial, before a grand jury, or in a preliminary hearing or pretrial motion or other proceeding (like plea hearings). We also know "testimonial" embraces eyewitness statements to police officers when they describe criminal acts (here everyone knows they will be used in investigation or prosecution). Should it be the same if someone talks to an undercover officer without knowing it? Or talks to a friend? In the latter case, if the statement is *not* testimonial, would it be testimonial if an officer overheard it? Consider these suggestions by Professor Friedman:

> A statement made knowingly to the authorities that describes criminal activity is almost always testimonial. A statement made by a person claiming to be the victim of a crime and describing the crime is usually testimonial, whether made to the authorities or not. In the case of a crime committed over a short period of time, if a statement is made before the crime is committed, it almost certainly is not testimonial. A statement made by one participant in a criminal enterprise to another, intended to further the enterprise, is not testimonial. And neither is a statement made in the course of going about one's ordinary business, made before the criminal act has occurred or with no recognition that it relates to criminal activity.

Richard D. Friedman, Confrontation: The Search for Basic Principles, 86 Geo. L.J. 1011, 1040-1043 (1998).

3. One question arising from *Crawford* relates to the role of intent:

(a) *Crawford* suggests that it is *the speaker* who counts, not the police, and it suffices that the speaker *expects* that his statement may be used in investigating or prosecuting crime. *Crawford* speaks of what an "objective witness" would "reasonably believe," apparently referring to "a reasonable person in the speaker's position." Later the decision in *Bryant* instructed courts to look at the state of mind of both the witness or victim *and* police. See Michigan v. Bryant, 131 S. Ct. 1143 (2011).

(b) To the extent the *speaker* counts, what state of mind is required? Is it enough that she *expects* (or a reasonable person in her position *should* expect) that what she says will play a role in investigating or prosecuting a crime? Or should it be necessary to prove that her *purpose* (or "primary" purpose) was to further the investigation or prosecution? An "expectation" standard seems more encompassing than a standard requiring "purpose" or "intent," and could

be met in cases of excited utterances by victims or eyewitnesses who see crimes being committed and call police or 911. See Richard Friedman, Grappling with the Meaning of "Testimonial," 71 Brooklyn L. Rev. 241, 251 (2005) ("anticipation" is better than "purpose" because it "better describes the testimonial function" and the inquiry is easier than asking about purpose or motivation).

4. Post-*Crawford* cases *reject* the notion that private statements are testimonial (witness or crime victim speaking to a friend or acquaintance, or to anyone other than law enforcement officers). Private statements are admitted as nontestimonial when they qualify as excited utterances, see Hartsfield v. Commonwealth, 277 S.W.3d 239, 245 (Ky. 2009) (sexual assault victim describes rape to bystander and daughter), or against-interest statements, see State v. Morales, 788 N.W.2d 737 (Minn. 2010) (admitting against *M* the statement by co-offender *VL* that he and *M* went to house to commit robbery; *M* was talking to friend; not testimonial). See also Robert P. Mosteller, Crawford v. Washington: Encouraging and Ensuring the Confrontation of Witnesses, 39 U. Rich. L. Rev. 511, 540 (2005) (courts treat private statements as nontestimonial). In a few cases, however, courts have found that private statements are testimonial after all. In the *Clark* case in 2013, for example, the Ohio Supreme Court held that a statement by a child to his preschool teacher describing abuse at home was testimonial, but the Supreme Court granted review of this case in 2014, and is expected to address the issue. The case is described in note 6(a), infra.

5. Let us think now about two places where *Crawford* has major impact:

(a) *Crawford* means that victims' statements to police describing violent crimes are testimonial, at least when they do not fit the emergency doctrine that you are about to look at. Hence they are often excludable even if they fit exceptions for excited utterances or present sense impressions. The same is true of 911 calls reporting crimes in progress or just completed. *Crawford* suggests that its approach leads to results consistent with prior law, but it did make a significant change. For a case illustrating the effect of *Crawford* on excited utterances, see Hayward v. State, 24 So. 3d 17, 32-33 (Fla. 2009) (in murder trial, error to admit victim's statement to police officer as first responder; victim spoke about "past events that could only be investigated or litigated") (harmless).

(b) *Crawford* also means statements by one of several alleged co-offenders to police, in which the speaker describes his role in a crime and incriminates another, who is later tried for his role, are also testimonial. In cases like *Williamson* (section E4, supra), statements by Reginald Harris are excludable as testimonial, and in that sense *Crawford* pre-empts *Williamson. Crawford* reinforces decisions like *Bruton*, which disapproved use of a confession by one naming another (section B1, supra). *Crawford* cites *Bruton* with approval, and *Crawford* reinforces this safeguard in the usual situation where one of several co-offenders speaks with law enforcement officers.

6. In child abuse trials, what should courts do with statements by young victims? Recall the various avenues for admitting such statements. Often they fit the excited utterance exception (section C1, supra), the medical statements exception (see the *Blake* case in section C3, supra), or the catchall and the rifle-shot child victim hearsay exceptions (section F3, supra). Less often, they fit the forfeiture provision (section E6, supra). In addition, special provisions let children give depositions or testify from remote locations, and these either modify the way of taking testimony from children or create what amount to new hearsay exceptions too. You will look at these later in this chapter.

(a) When children talk to family members and caregivers, usually these statements are not testimonial. See, e.g., State v. Ladner, 644 S.E.2d 684 (S.C. 2007) (statement to caretaker "aunt figure," made by child aged two and a half, saying "Bryan did it" in reference to defendant was nontestimonial) (excited utterance); State v. Hosty, 944 So. 2d 255 (Fla. 2006) (statement by mentally retarded woman to teacher was nontestimonial (under exception for disabled adult victims). In 2014, the Supreme Court granted certiorari in the *Clark* case, where an Ohio court held that statements describing abuse, made by a child (aged three and a half) to his preschool teacher, were testimonial. In granting review, the Supreme Court is expected to decide whether the obligation to report made the teacher a state agent, and whether the child's statement was testimonial. See State v. Clark, 999 N.E.2d 592 (Ohio 2013), *cert. granted*, 82 USLW 3688 (2014). See also Jerome C. Latimer, Confrontation After *Crawford*: The Decision's Impact on How Hearsay Is Analyzed Under the Confrontation Clause, 36 Seton Hall L. Rev. 327, 364-366 (2006) (children's statements in purely private settings are generally nontestimonial).

(b) When children speak to doctors in hospitals, usually again the statements are admitted, which seems surprising. Doctors have an obligation, imposed as a matter of professional ethics and often by statute, to alert social service people or law enforcement agencies when they suspect abuse. And often police or social service people are at hand in the examining room or nearby. See Hobgood v. State, 926 So. 2d 847, 851 (Miss. 2006) (admitting statements by five-year-old child describing abuse, including statements to psychotherapist and pediatrician, under tender years exception; purpose was to secure well-being of child, not further prosecution) (nontestimonial). But see Robert P. Mosteller, Testing the Testimonial Concept and Exceptions to Confrontation: "A Little Child Shall Lead Them," 82 Ind. L.J. 917, 957 (2007) (after medical status is assessed, later examinations should be "presumed prosecutorial in nature").

(c) When children speak to police or social service personnel, we find the opposite result: Here courts find their statements testimonial under *Crawford.* See Davison v. State, 282 P.3d 1262 (Ala. 2012) (error to admit statements by 14-year-old victim to doctor performing examination as part of Sexual Assault Response Team; victim had received treatment; police had arranged interview and were present, along with victim advocate; doctor emphasized "forensic purpose") (reversing conviction); Vega v. State, 236 P.3d 632, 636 (Nev. 2010) (statements by child victim to nurse at Child Advocacy Center were testimonial).

(d) Does the "testimonial" limitation apply to statements by very young children, say three to seven years old? Do they "expect" or "intend" their statements be used when investigating or prosecuting crimes? Compare Mosteller, supra note 6(b), at 975-976 (even young children "function as knowing witnesses who make pointed accusations," and "appear quite purposeful in communicating" accusations of wrong) with Richard Friedman, Grappling with the Meaning of "Testimonial," 71 Brook. L. Rev. 241, 271 (2005) (very young children cannot be witnesses for purposes of confrontation; their understanding is "so undeveloped that their words ought to be considered more like the bark of a bloodhound than like the testimony of an adult witness" and testimonial limit concept not apply to them).

7. Consider the situations in which *Crawford* indicates that out-of-court statements remain usable against defendants in criminal cases:

(a) "Statements in furtherance of a conspiracy" are nontestimonial, so decisions approving use of such statements remain good law, and FRE 801(d)(2)(E) operates as it did before (section B5, supra).

(b) The Confrontation Clause "does not bar the use of testimonial statements for purposes other than" proving the truth of the matter asserted. This comment in *Crawford* suggests that in cases like Problem 3-J ("My Husband Is in Denver") (Chapter 3D1, supra), where one lies to police to throw them off the scent, the statement is not testimonial. See, e.g., State v. Morris, 705 S.E.2d 583 (W. Va. 2010) (admitting statements by nurse to police; purpose was not to prove matter asserted, but to explain why defendant was arrested and as "background of the investigation") (no confrontation violation). What *else* falls under this rubric? For an argument that *Crawford* should generate a constitutional definition of hearsay that would treat as testimonial for confrontation purposes false statements to police and attempts to purchase drugs, see James L. Kainen, The Case For a Constitutional Definition of Hearsay: Requiring Confrontation of Testimonial, Nonassertive Conduct and Statements Admitted to Explain an Unchallenged Investigation, 93 Marq. L. Rev. 1415 (2010).

(c) Dying declarations can be admitted even if they are testimonial. For an argument that this exception is *not*, as the Court claims in *Crawford*, historically a "*sui generis*" exception, see Polelle, The Death of Dying Declarations in a Post-*Crawford* World, 71 Mo. L. Rev. 285 (2006) (dying declarations are *not* the only ones that were admitted historically; *res gestae* statements, normally what we would now call excited utterances, were also admitted against criminal defendants in earlier times).

(d) The forfeiture-by-misconduct provision in FRE 804(b)(6) remains valid. In situations like the one described in Problem 4-Q ("If You Want to Stay Healthy"), prosecutors can use testimonial hearsay. Forfeiture requires *intent* by the accused to silence the witness as a constitutional matter and for purposes of the forfeiture exception in FRE 804(b)(6) (section E6, supra).

(e) The Confrontation Clause does not require exclusion of statements by a declarant who can be cross-examined at trial or was cross-examinable previously (this matter is taken up in section G4, infra).

3. The Emergency Doctrine

DAVIS v. WASHINGTON

United States Supreme Court
547 U.S. 813 (2006)

Justice SCALIA delivered the opinion of the Court.

These cases require us to determine when statements made to law enforcement personnel during a 911 call or at a crime scene are "testimonial" and thus subject to the requirements of the Sixth Amendment's Confrontation Clause.

I

A

[In *Davis v. Washington,* a 911 operator received a call that ended before anyone spoke. She "reversed the call" and reached Michelle McCottry, who was in the middle of a domestic disturbance with her boyfriend Adrian Davis, defendant in this case:]

"911 Operator: Hello.
"Complainant: Hello.
"911 Operator: What's going on?
"Complainant: He's here jumpin' on me again.
"911 Operator: Okay. Listen to me carefully. Are you in a house or an apartment?
"Complainant: I'm in a house.
"911 Operator: Are there any weapons?
"Complainant: No. He's usin' his fists.
"911 Operator: Okay. Has he been drinking?
"Complainant: No.
"911 Operator: Okay, sweetie. I've got help started. Stay on the line with me, okay?
"Complainant: I'm on the line.
"911 Operator: Listen to me carefully. Do you know his last name?
"Complainant: It's Davis.
"911 Operator: Davis? Okay, what's his first name?
"Complainant: Adrian.
"911 Operator: What is it?
"Complainant: Adrian.
"911 Operator: Adrian?
"Complainant: Yeah.
"911 Operator: Okay. What's his middle initial?
"Complainant: Martell. He's runnin' now."

[McCottry said Davis had run out the door, that he had hit McCottry, and that he was leaving with someone else. The 911 Operator questioned McCottry ("Stop talking and answer my questions") and gathered information about Davis, learning that he had come to McCottry's house to "get his stuff" because McCottry was moving. The 911 Operator told McCottry that police were coming and would "check the area for him first" and would then talk with her. Minutes later they did arrive, and saw McCottry's "shaken state" and "fresh injuries on her forearm and her face" and her "frantic efforts to gather her belongings and her children" so they could leave.

Davis was charged with felony violation of a domestic no-contact order. The only state witnesses were the officers who responded to the call. They testified that McCottry had recent injuries, but neither knew the cause. Over an objection based on the Confrontation Clause, the court admitted the recorded 911 call. Davis was convicted, and the Washington Supreme Court affirmed, concluding that McCottry's identification of Davis was nontestimonial.]

B

[In *Hammon v. Indiana,* police responded to a reported domestic disturbance late at night, at the home of Herschel and Amy Hammon. Amy was on the front porch, "somewhat frightened," but she said nothing was the matter. She gave them permission to enter, and an officer saw a gas heater in the living room with flames coming out of the front and pieces of glass on the floor.

Herschel was in the kitchen, and he told police that he and Amy had been "in an argument" but that "everything was fine now," and the argument "never became physical." Amy had come back inside, and one officer stayed with her while the other talked with Herschel, who tried "to participate in Amy's conversation" but was "rebuffed." The officer testified that Herschel "became angry" when told to stay away from Amy. After hearing Amy's account, the officer asked her to fill out and sign a battery affidavit. She wrote "Broke our Furnace & shoved me down on the floor into the broken glass. Hit me in the chest and threw me down. Broke our lamps & phone. Tore up my van where I couldn't leave the house. Attacked my daughter."

Amy did not appear at Hammon's bench trial for domestic battery and violating probation (although she was subpoenaed). Over Hammon's objection, the officer testified to what Amy had said—that she and Herschel had argued, that he became irate over their daughter's going to a boyfriend's house, that the argument became "physical" and that Hammon was "breaking things in the living room," including the phone, a lamp, and the front of the heater, and that he "threw her down into the glass of the heater" and punched her twice in the chest.

The trial judge found Herschel Hammon guilty, and state courts affirmed.]

II

[*Crawford* held that the Confrontation Clause applies to testimonial statements.] Only statements of this sort cause the declarant to be a "witness" within the meaning of the Confrontation Clause. It is the testimonial character of the statement that separates it from other hearsay that, while subject to traditional limitations upon hearsay evidence, is not subject to the Confrontation Clause.

... [I]t suffices to decide the present cases to hold as follows: Statements are nontestimonial when made in the course of police interrogation under circumstances objectively indicating that the primary purpose of the interrogation is to enable police assistance to meet an ongoing emergency. They are testimonial when the circumstances objectively indicate that there is no such ongoing emergency, and that the primary purpose of the interrogation is to establish or prove past events potentially relevant to later criminal prosecution.[1]

III

A

[*Crawford* involved statements responding to police interrogation, which were testimonial by any definition. It was not necessary to define the scope of "interrogation," but here we must decide whether the Confrontation Clause applies "only to testimonial hearsay." Implicitly *Crawford* answered the question by emphasizing *testimony* as the focus of confrontation.] A limitation so clearly reflected in the text of the constitutional provision must fairly be said to mark out not merely it's "core," but its perimeter.

. . . .

The question before us in *Davis* . . . is whether, objectively considered, the interrogation that took place in the course of the 911 call produced testimonial statements.[2] When we said in *Crawford*, that "interrogations by law enforcement officers fall squarely within [the] class" of testimonial hearsay, we had immediately in mind (for that was the case before us) interrogations solely directed at establishing the facts of a past crime, in order to identify (or provide evidence to convict) the perpetrator. The product of such interrogation, whether reduced to a writing signed by the declarant or embedded in the memory (and perhaps notes) of the interrogating officer, is testimonial. It is, in the terms of the 1828 American dictionary quoted in *Crawford*, " '[a] solemn declaration or affirmation made for the purpose of establishing or proving some fact.' " (The solemnity of even an oral declaration of relevant past fact to an investigating officer is well enough established by the severe consequences that

[1] . . . [T]he statements . . . before us are the products of interrogations—which in some circumstances tend to generate testimonial responses. This is not to imply, however, that statements made in the absence of any interrogation are necessarily nontestimonial. The Framers were no more willing to exempt from cross-examination volunteered testimony or answers to open-ended questions than they were to exempt answers to detailed interrogation. (Part of the evidence against Sir Walter Raleigh was a letter from Lord Cobham that was plainly not the result of sustained questioning.) And of course even when interrogation exists, it is in the final analysis the declarant's statements, not the interrogator's questions, that the Confrontation Clause requires us to evaluate.

[2] [Relocated footnote 2 from earlier in the opinion. In that note the Court comments as follows: "If 911 operators are not themselves law enforcement officers, they may at least be agents of law enforcement when they conduct interrogations of 911 callers. For purposes of this opinion (and without deciding the point), we consider their acts to be acts of the police."]

can attend a deliberate falsehood.) A 911 call, on the other hand, and at least the initial interrogation conducted in connection with a 911 call, is ordinarily not designed primarily to "establis[h] or prov[e]" some past fact, but to describe current circumstances requiring police assistance.

The difference between the interrogation in *Davis* and the one in *Crawford* is apparent on the face of things. In *Davis*, McCottry was speaking about events *as they were actually happening*, rather than "describ[ing] past events," *Lilly v. Virginia*, 527 U.S. 116, 137 (1999) (plurality opinion). Sylvia Crawford's interrogation, on the other hand, took place hours after the events she described had occurred. Moreover, any reasonable listener would recognize that McCottry (unlike Sylvia Crawford) was facing an ongoing emergency. Although one *might* call 911 to provide a narrative report of a crime absent any imminent danger, McCottry's call was plainly a call for help against bona fide physical threat. Third, the nature of what was asked and answered in *Davis*, again viewed objectively, was such that the elicited statements were necessary to be able to *resolve* the present emergency, rather than simply to learn (as in *Crawford*) what had happened in the past. That is true even of the operator's effort to establish the identity of the assailant, so that the dispatched officers might know whether they would be encountering a violent felon. And finally, the difference in the level of formality between the two interviews is striking. Crawford was responding calmly, at the station house, to a series of questions, with the officer-interrogator taping and making notes of her answers; McCottry's frantic answers were provided over the phone, in an environment that was not tranquil, or even (as far as any reasonable 911 operator could make out) safe.

We conclude from all this that the circumstances of McCottry's interrogation objectively indicate its primary purpose was to enable police assistance to meet an ongoing emergency. She simply was not acting as a *witness;* she was not *testifying.* What she said was not "a weaker substitute for live testimony" at trial, *United States v. Inadi*, 475 U.S. 387, 394 (1986), like Lord Cobham's statements in *Raleigh's Case*, . . . or Sylvia Crawford's statement in *Crawford*. In each of those cases, the *ex parte* actors and the evidentiary products of the *ex parte* communication aligned perfectly with their courtroom analogues. McCottry's emergency statement does not. No "witness" goes into court to proclaim an emergency and seek help . . . .

This is not to say that a conversation which begins as an interrogation to determine the need for emergency assistance cannot, as the Indiana Supreme Court put it, "evolve into testimonial statements" once that purpose has been achieved. In this case, for example, after the operator gained the information needed to address the exigency of the moment, the emergency appears to have ended (when Davis drove away from the premises). The operator then told McCottry to be quiet, and proceeded to pose a battery of questions. It could readily be maintained that, from that point on, McCottry's statements were testimonial, not unlike the "structured police questioning" that occurred in *Crawford*. This presents no great problem . . . . Through *in limine* procedure, they should redact or exclude the portions of any statement that have become testimonial, as they do, for example, with unduly prejudicial portions of otherwise admissible evidence. Davis's jury did not hear the *complete* 911 call, although it may well have heard some testimonial portions. We were asked to classify only McCottry's early statements identifying Davis as her assailant, and we agree with the Washington Supreme Court that they were not testimonial. That court also concluded that, even if later parts of the call were testimonial, their admission was harmless beyond a reasonable doubt. Davis does not challenge that holding, and we therefore assume it to be correct.

B

Determining the testimonial or nontestimonial character of the statements that were the product of the interrogation in *Hammon* is a much easier task, since they were not much different from the statements we found to be testimonial in *Crawford.* It is entirely clear from the circumstances that the interrogation was part of an investigation into possibly criminal past conduct—as, indeed, the testifying officer expressly acknowledged. There was no emergency in progress; the interrogating officer testified that he had heard no arguments or crashing and saw no one throw or break anything. When the officers first arrived, Amy told them that things were fine, and there was no immediate threat to her person. When the officer questioned Amy for the second time, and elicited the challenged statements, he was not seeking to determine (as in *Davis*) "what is happening," but rather "what happened." Objectively viewed, the primary, if not indeed the sole, purpose of the interrogation was to investigate a possible crime—which is, of course, precisely what the officer *should* have done.

It is true that the *Crawford* interrogation was more formal. It followed a *Miranda* warning, was tape-recorded, and took place at the station house. While these features certainly strengthened the statements' testimonial aspect—made it more objectively apparent, that is, that the purpose of the exercise was to nail down the truth about past criminal events—none was essential to the point. It was formal enough that Amy's interrogation was conducted in a separate room, away from her husband (who tried to intervene), with the officer receiving her replies for use in his "investigat[ion]." What we called the "striking resemblance" of the *Crawford* statement to civil-law *ex parte* examinations is shared by Amy's statement here. Both declarants were actively separated from the defendant—officers forcibly prevented Hershel from participating in the interrogation. Both statements deliberately recounted, in response to police questioning, how potentially criminal past events began and progressed. And both took place some time after the events described were over. Such statements under official interrogation are an obvious substitute for live testimony, because they do precisely *what a witness does* on direct examination; they are inherently testimonial.

Both Indiana and the United States as *amicus curiae* argue that this case should be resolved much like *Davis.* For the reasons we find the comparison to *Crawford* compelling, we find the comparison to *Davis* unpersuasive. The statements in *Davis* were taken when McCottry was alone, not only unprotected by police (as Amy Hammon was protected), but apparently in immediate danger from Davis. She was seeking aid, not telling a story about the past. McCottry's present-tense statements showed immediacy; Amy's narrative of past events was delivered at some remove in time from the danger she described. And after Amy answered the officer's questions, he had her execute an affidavit, in order, he testified, "[t]o establish events that have occurred previously."

Although we necessarily reject the Indiana Supreme Court's implication that virtually any "initial inquiries" at the crime scene will not be testimonial, we do not hold the opposite—that *no* questions at the scene will yield nontestimonial answers. We have already observed of domestic disputes that "[o]fficers called to investigate . . . need to know whom they are dealing with in order to assess the situation, the threat to their own safety, and possible danger to the potential victim." *Hibel*, 542 U.S., at 186. Such exigencies may *often* mean that "initial inquiries" produce nontestimonial statements. But in cases like this one, where Amy's statements were neither a cry for help nor the provision of information enabling officers immediately to end a threatening situation, the fact that they were given at an alleged crime scene and were "initial inquiries" is immaterial. Cf. *Crawford*.[6]

IV

Respondents in both cases, joined by a number of their *amici*, contend that the nature of the offenses charged in these two cases—domestic violence—requires greater flexibility in the use of testimonial evidence. This particular type of crime is notoriously susceptible to intimidation or coercion of the victim to ensure that she does not testify at trial. When this occurs, the Confrontation Clause gives the criminal a windfall. We may not, however, vitiate constitutional guarantees when they have the effect of allowing the guilty to go free.

[When defendants "seek to undermine the judicial process by procuring or coercing silence" from witness or victim, the rule of forfeiture by wrongdoing extinguishes confrontation claims. Absent forfeiture, however, Amy Hammon's affidavit is excluded by the Sixth Amendment. The judgment affirms the conviction in the *Davis* case in Washington, and reverses the conviction of *Hammon* in the Indiana case.]

Justice THOMAS, concurring in the judgment in part and dissenting in part.

[The "emergency" standard is "disconnected from history and unnecessary to prevent abuse," and it "yields no predictable result." In many if not most cases where police respond to a report received by 911 call or otherwise, their purposes "are *both* to respond to the emergency *and* to gather evidence," so assigning one of these motives "requires constructing a hierarchy of purpose that

---

[6] Police investigations themselves are, of course, in no way impugned by our characterization of their fruits as testimonial. Investigations of past crimes prevent future harms and lead to necessary arrests. While prosecutors may hope that inculpatory "nontestimonial" evidence is gathered, this is essentially beyond police control. Their saying that an emergency exists cannot make it be so. The Confrontation Clause in no way governs police conduct, because it is the trial use of, not the investigatory collection of, ex parte testimonial statements which offends that provision. But neither can police conduct govern the Confrontation Clause; testimonial statements are what they are.

will rarely be present—and is not readily discernible," which entails "an exercise in fiction." An "objective" test is better than one that focuses on "subjective intentions" of officers, but it is "disconnected from the prosecutorial abuses" that were the target of the Confrontation Clause, and it shifts control to judges, whose decision will be "unpredictable and not necessarily tethered to the actual purpose" of police.]

Neither the 911 call at issue in *Davis* nor the police questioning at issue in *Hammon* is testimonial under the appropriate framework. Neither the call nor the questioning is itself a formalized dialogue.[5] Nor do any circumstances surrounding the taking of the statements render those statements sufficiently formal to resemble the Marian examinations; the statements were neither *Mirandized* nor custodial, nor accompanied by any similar indicia of formality. Finally, there is no suggestion that the prosecution attempted to offer the women's hearsay evidence at trial in order to evade confrontation. Accordingly, the statements at issue in both cases are nontestimonial and admissible under the Confrontation Clause.

The Court's determination that the evidence against Hammon must be excluded extends the Confrontation Clause far beyond the abuses it was intended to prevent . . . . The Court draws a line between the two cases based on its explanation that *Hammon* involves "no emergency in progress," but instead, mere questioning as "part of an investigation into possibly criminal past conduct," and its explanation that *Davis* involves questioning for the "primary purpose" of "enabl[ing] police assistance to meet an ongoing emergency." But the fact that the officer in *Hammon* was investigating Mr. Hammon's past conduct does not foreclose the possibility that the primary purpose of his inquiry was to assess whether Mr. Hammon constituted a continuing danger to his wife, requiring further police presence or action. It is hardly remarkable that Hammon did not act abusively towards his wife in the presence of the officers, and his good judgment to refrain from criminal behavior in the presence of police sheds little, if any, light on whether his violence would have resumed had the police left without further questioning, transforming what the Court dismisses as "past conduct" back into an "ongoing emergency." Nor does the mere fact that McCottry needed emergency aid shed light on whether the "primary purpose" of gathering, for example, the name of her assailant was to protect the police, to protect the victim, or to gather information for prosecution. In both of the cases before the Court, like many similar cases, pronouncement of the "primary" motive behind the interrogation calls for nothing more than a guess by courts.

---

[5] Although the police questioning in *Hammon* was ultimately reduced to an affidavit, all agree that the affidavit is inadmissible per se under our definition of the term "testimonial."

■ NOTES ON THE EMERGENCY DOCTRINE

1. *Davis* gave the Court its first chance after *Crawford* to explore the testimonial approach. The Court says a 911 call is "ordinarily not designed" to prove "some past fact," and the focus is "current circumstances requiring police assistance." Both Michelle McCottry and Amy Hammon described past events (as did Sylvia in *Crawford*). But the Court says the "primary purpose" in *Davis* case was to deal with an ongoing emergency, presumably because the assailant was at large, and the Court says the situation was different in *Hammon* because Herschel Hammon was in custody.

2. Five years after *Davis,* the Court addressed the emergency doctrine again in the *Bryant* Case. This time a bystander's 911 call at 3:25 A.M. brought police to a parking lot next to a gas station where Anthony Covington lay on the ground by his car dying of a gunshot wound. Asked "what happened, and who had shot him," Covington said Rick Bryant had shot him at Bryant's house about 20 minutes earlier, that he'd had a conversation with Bryant through the back door, and that he was shot through the door as he turned to leave. Taken to a hospital, Covington died several hours later. Police went to Bryant's house, about six blocks away. They found Covington's wallet, blood and a bullet on the back porch, and a bullet hole in the door. See Michigan v. Bryant, 131 S. Ct. 1143 (2011) (eight Justices participating; Justice Thomas concurs on narrow ground; Justices Scalia and Ginsburg dissent separately).

(a) In Justice Sotomayor's opinion for a five-Justice majority, the Court in *Bryant* found that the emergency doctrine applied, stressing that the suspect was armed, the victim was found in a public place and the whereabouts of his assailant was unknown. The domestic violence cases in *Davis* involved fewer potential victims than "cases involving threats to public safety," and the "duration and scope" of the emergency is affected by "the type of weapon employed." Whether there is an emergency turns on a "combined inquiry" that is "objective" in nature, focusing on motives of "both interrogators and declarants" at the time, "not with the benefit of hindsight." They usually have "mixed motives," and it is the "primary purpose" that counts.

(b) *Bryant* does two other important things. First, it stresses that an emergency is but one "primary purpose" that puts a statement outside the testimonial category. There may be "other circumstances" where out-of-court statements are nontestimonial because the primary purpose was not to create a substitute for testimony. The Court doesn't identify these: One might speculate that a purpose of obtaining medical care counts, or a purpose of guarding against risks to public health or safety. Second, *Bryant* says statements dealing with emergencies are less prone to "fabrication" than testimonial hearsay, and that many hearsay exceptions rest on similar logic. The Court cites FRE 803(2) covering excited utterances, where the declarant is unlikely to lie, and in a footnote cites FRE 803(4) (medical statements) and FRE 803(6) (business records) and 804(b)(3) (against interest statements). Implicitly, *Bryant* expanded

the "primary purpose" criterion in ways that make room for far more hearsay than *Crawford* or *Davis* seemed to envision.

(c) Justice Scalia (author of *Crawford, Davis,* and *Melendez*-Diaz) in dissent argued that the emergency rationale was "transparently false" and it was "absurdly easy" to see there was no emergency because the crime had occurred "six blocks away and 25 minutes earlier," and it was "beyond imagination" that Bryant would show up and begin shooting after police arrived. The Court's "distorted view" that is itself "dangerous," paving the way to obtain convictions through statements to police hours after the event.

3. Can a court determine the "primary purpose" of interactions between police and crime victims or witnesses, taking into account the perspective (and intent and purpose) of both sides? The majority says the primary purpose in *Bryant* was to resolve an ongoing emergency, but Justice Scalia is certain that resolving an emergency was *not* the primary purpose. It's two against five here.

4. *Bryant* aligns the "emergency" exception with the "public safety" exception to the *Miranda* doctrine. The latter derives from the decision in New York v. Quarles, 467 U.S. 649 (1984), referenced in a footnote in *Bryant.* In *Quarles*, a woman told police she had just been raped and her assailant was carrying a gun and had entered a nearby market. Officers found a man matching her description in the market, and frisked and arrested him after finding an empty shoulder holster. Without *Miranda* warnings, the officer asked where the gun was. He answered, the gun was found, and he was charged with possession. The Court put in place a "public safety" exception: "In a kaleidoscopic situation" in which "spontaneity rather than adherence to a police manual is necessarily the order of the day," failing to give warnings should not lead to excluding evidence. Like *Bryant*, *Quarles* adopted an "objective" standard (the "public safety" exception does *not* depend on "post hoc findings" on "the subjective motivation" of police; the officer "asked only the question necessary to locate the missing gun").

5. *Bryant* lays stress on "informality" as bearing on the "primary purpose" inquiry, and Justice Thomas reiterates in *Bryant* the views he expressed in *Davis* and elsewhere that *only* formalized statements (affidavits or other obvious testimonial equivalents) are testimonial. How much difference is there between the sit-down stationhouse talk that produced Sylvia Crawford's statement that was called "testimonial" in *Crawford* and Anthony Covington's parking lot statement that fit the emergency doctrine in *Bryant?*

6. *Bryant* has proved influential. See, e.g., People v. Chism, 324 P.3d 183 (Cal. 2014) (in trial for murder and robbery, applying excited utterance exception in admitting bystander's statement to police describing armed robbery of liquor store and gunshots resulting in death of clerk) (emergency doctrine applied).

4. The Cross-Examination Factor

Recall two statements from *Crawford.* In one place the Court says that for testimonial hearsay the Sixth Amendment demands "a prior opportunity to cross-examine," which satisfies the confrontation right if the witness is unavailable at trial. In another place the Court says that "when the declarant appears for cross-examination at trial, the Confrontation Clause places no constraints at all on the use of his prior testimonial statements." In short, *Crawford* emphatically affirms two related principles that the Court had endorsed before: Both a *prior* opportunity to cross-examine (in the case of an unavailable witness) and a *deferred* opportunity suffice. *Davis* has similar language.

a. *Cross-Examination at Trial (Deferred Cross)*

For two reasons, the fact that deferred cross-examination can suffice is important: First, some exceptions require the declarant to be cross-examinable about something he said earlier. Recall that FRE 801(d)(1) creates exceptions for prior statements of three different kinds by a declarant who is "subject to cross-examination" about them at trial (inconsistent statements under oath in a trial or proceeding or deposition; consistent statements; statements of identification). And FRE 803(5) on past recollection recorded assumes that the declarant testifies and is subject to cross. In short, important exceptions operate with a deferred opportunity to cross-examine. Many statements within these exceptions are testimonial, and the fact that deferred cross satisfies confrontation makes the difference between admitting and excluding.

Second, other exceptions *can* operate where the declarant testifies, including important ones in FRE 803 and the catchall in FRE 807. Many of these exceptions reach statements that might be excludable under *Crawford* as "testimonial," as is true of excited utterances to police reporting crimes. Hence once again the fact that deferred cross satisfies the Clause can make the difference between admitting and excluding.

The decision in *Green*. A pathbreaking 1970 decision in the *Green* case dealt with *both* deferred *and* prior cross. In *Green*, the state offered a statement by Melvin Porter, a 16-year-old who had been arrested for selling marijuana, to an undercover officer named Wade. Porter talked to Wade in the stationhouse, but at trial Porter retreated into evasions. The state called Wade, who testified that Porter had told him Green had called and asked Porter to sell marijuana ("stuff " or "grass"). Then Green personally delivered a sack containing 29 baggies of marijuana—the source of what Porter sold to Wade. Under a state statute allowing full use of prior inconsistent statements, the court admitted Porter's statement to Wade.[16] Ultimately the Supreme Court concluded that this procedure did not violate Green's confrontation rights:

---

[16] If *Green* arose under the Rules, the prosecutor probably could not use Porter's statement to Wade as substantive evidence. Unlike California law, the Rules do not permit substantive use of all inconsistent statements. You read the *Smith* case (section A1, supra), admitting a stationhouse affidavit (most decisions do not agree that such a statement was made in a "proceeding"). Porter did not sign an affidavit, so even *Smith* would not help on the facts of *Green*.

> [T]he inability to cross-examine the witness at the time he made his prior statement cannot easily be shown to be of crucial significance as long as the defendant is assured of full and effective cross-examination at the time of trial. The most successful cross-examination at the time the prior statement was made could hardly hope to accomplish more than has already been accomplished by the fact that the witness is now telling a different, inconsistent story, and—in this case—one that is favorable to the defendant . . . . The main danger in substituting subsequent for timely cross-examination seems to lie in the possibility that the witness' "[f]alse testimony is apt to harden and become unyielding to the blows of truth in proportion as the witness has opportunity for reconsideration and influence by the suggestions of others, whose interest may be, and often is, to maintain falsehood rather than truth." State v. Saporen, 285 N.W. 898, 901 (Minn. 1939). That danger, however, disappears when the witness has changed his testimony so that, far from "hardening," his prior statement has softened to the point where he now repudiates it.

California v. Green, 399 U.S. 149, 159 (1970). In this passage, the Court refers to elements that might be important conditions: The witness tells a "different" story that is "inconsistent" with what he said before; the present story is "favorable to" the defendant; the witness "repudiates" what he said before. The Court then says the question is *not* whether contemporaneous cross would put the jury "in a better position" to evaluate what the witness says, which acknowledges that optimal testing might require cross that occurs immediately after the statement being offered. Instead, the question is whether deferred cross can be "full and effective," which suggests that the opportunity to question the witness must be a real one.[17]

In *Green*, Porter claimed not to remember how he'd gotten the marijuana he sold to Officer Wade. The Court acknowledged "a narrow question lurking in this case," which was whether Porter's "apparent lapse of memory" had such negative impact on the right to cross-examine "as to make a critical difference," noting disagreement about the adequacy of cross if a witness "disclaims all present knowledge." On remand, the California Supreme Court concluded that Porter's performance could lead to "but one conclusion"—one must "disbelieve" his claimed lack of memory, and Porter "unmasked" his motive (he had "a conscience" and didn't want to incriminate his friend). The defense asked but one question, which was whether Porter thought he was telling the truth when he told Wade he'd gotten the marijuana from Green (Porter said yes). The defense "made no attempt" to explore the matter, so the opportunity to cross-examine was adequate.

Minimal opportunity suffices. Three other decisions address the question whether the opportunity to cross-examine is adequate.

[17] One of us has criticized *Green.* See Mueller, Cross-Examination Earlier or Later: When Is It Enough to Satisfy *Crawford?* 19 Regent U. L. Rev. 319 (2007) (*Green* "played *up* the extent" to which Porter was a friend to the defense and "played *down* the extent" to which cross was impeded; *Green* "ignored the practitioner's view of cross," requiring drama and appeal to emotions).

First is the *O'Neil* case, which held that cross can be effective even if the witness denies making a prior statement. There defendant *R*, whose confession to police implicated codefendant *O*, took the stand and denied having confessed. The Court said *O* would be *worse* off if *R* admitted making the confession. The fact that he denied it was "more favorable" for *O* than anything cross-examination could do if he "affirmed the statement as his." Nelson v. O'Neil, 402 U.S. 622, 628-630 (1971).

Second is the *Fensterer* case, which did not speak directly of hearsay. There the Court concluded that expert testimony could be admitted *even though* the expert could not recall, when cross-examined about his conclusion, what it rested on. In language that has become almost a mantra in decisions rejecting challenges to the adequacy of cross-examination about prior statements, the Court said: "Generally speaking, the Confrontation Clause guarantees an *opportunity* for effective cross-examination, not cross-examination that is effective in whatever way, and to whatever extent, the defense might wish." Delaware v. Fensterer, 474 U.S. 15, 19 (1985).

Third is the *Owens* case, which concluded that an unremembering witness is adequately cross-examinable. *Owens* did not address the constitutional issue (only a construction of the Rules). There an inmate was tried for beating correctional counselor John Foster with a metal pipe. Foster suffered a skull fracture and memory impairment. FBI Agent Mansfield interviewed Foster in the hospital, and he described the attack, naming Owens and picking his photo from an array. At trial, Foster again described the attack (feeling the blows, seeing his blood on the floor) and recalled talking to Mansfield and naming Owens, but admitted he couldn't remember "seeing his assailant" and couldn't remember other hospital visitors or whether they suggested Owens's name. The trial court let Mansfield testify to Foster's hospital statement under the exception for statements of identification in FRE 801(d)(1)(C), and the Supreme Court approved:

> [The] opportunity [to cross-examine] is not denied when a witness testifies as to his current belief but is unable to recollect the reason for that belief. It is sufficient that the defendant has the opportunity to bring out such matters as the witness's bias, his lack of care and attentiveness, his poor eyesight, and even (what is often a prime objective of cross-examination) the very fact that he has a bad memory. If the ability to inquire into these matters suffices to establish the constitutionally requisite opportunity for cross-examination when a witness testifies as to his current belief, the basis for which he cannot recall, we see no reason why it should not suffice when the witness's past belief is introduced and he is unable to recollect the reason for that past belief. In both cases the foundation for the belief (current or past) cannot effectively be elicited, but other means of impugning the belief are available. Indeed, if there is any difference in persuasive impact between the statement "I believe this to be the man who assaulted me, but can't remember why" and the statement "I don't know whether this is the man who assaulted me, but I told the police I believed so earlier," the former would seem, if anything, more damaging and hence gives

> rise to a greater need for memory-testing, if that is to be considered essential to an opportunity for effective cross-examination. We conclude . . . that it is not. The weapons available to impugn the witness's statement when memory loss is asserted will of course not always achieve success, but successful cross-examination is not the constitutional guarantee. They are . . . realistic weapons, as is demonstrated by defense counsel's summation in this very case, which emphasized Foster's memory loss and argued that his identification of respondent was the result of the suggestions of people who visited him in the hospital.

United States v. Owens, 484 U.S. 554, 559-560 (1988).

What emerges from these cases is that the opportunity for "full and effective" cross does not require much. If the opportunity is adequate when the witness has forgotten what happened, or denies making the statement being used, the situation is just about what Justice Scalia said in *Crawford*: The Clause "places no constraints at all" on using testimonial hearsay, provided only that declarant "appears for cross-examination" at trial.

Perhaps a glimmer of an argument survives. Suppose a witness stonewalls and answers *no* questions whatsoever: Can it *still* be said that he is adequately cross-examinable? In *Owens*, the Court left the door ajar. It said "limitations on the scope of examination by the trial court or assertions of privilege by the witness" might "undermine the process" so far that "meaningful" cross for purposes of FRE 801(d)(1)(C) "no longer exists." Arguably this point supports an argument under the Confrontation Clause, in light of the stress on cross in *Crawford*.

Waiver and sandbagging. In *Green*, the California Supreme Court said the defense failed to press Porter on cross. This idea looks like a move to shift responsibility to the defendant, bringing into play a notion of waiver—"you had a chance, and you blew it." Now that *Crawford* has appeared, restricting use of the excited utterance exception when witnesses or victims talk to police (unless the "emergency" doctrine applies) and barring use of some exceptions when children speak with authorities, a new question is arising: *If the defense* could have taken some initiative that it *did not pursue* at trial to cross-examine the declarant, or to summon him or her to testify, can we say that the defense *did have* the opportunity for cross that the Confrontation Clause requires?

■ PROBLEM 4-R. "Your Witness"

In 2015, Stan Vasko is tried for sexually abusing T.E., daughter of his girlfriend Natalia. The offense allegedly happened in September 2008, when T.E. was three years old (she was ten at the time of trial). The prosecutor calls T.E. to the witness stand:

Q: (*Mr. Prahl*): How old are you [T.E.]?
A: (*T.E.*): Ten.

Q: Can you tell us what year you were born in?
A: 2005.
Q: And are you in school now?
A: Yes I'm in fourth grade.
Q: And do you like school?
A: Yes.
Q: What's your teacher's name?
A: Mrs. Martin.
Q: Do you know what it means to tell the truth? If I said to you that it's snowing in this room right now, would that be true?
A: No, that's lying.
Q: Is it good to lie?
A: No, it's bad.
Q: I want you to think back to the time before you were in school, will you do that?
A: OK.
Q: Now do you remember being at home with your mommy before you started school?
A: No.
Q: What's your mommy's name?
A: Natalia.
Q: And your daddy, what's his name?
A: Frank.
Q: Well do you remember going to Mrs. Aston's kindergarten class?
A: No, I don't remember anything about that.
Q: Well what's the earliest thing you can remember?
A: I remember last year in third grade.
Q: Who was your teacher then?
A: Umm, hmmm.
Q: You don't remember?
A: No.
Q: Well do you remember anything from the time before you were in school?
A: No.
Q: Alright, I'm finished talking to [T.E.], your witness, Counsel.

Counsel for Vasko declines to cross-examine T.E., who is led out of the courtroom. For the state, Mr. Prahl makes an offer of proof, outside the hearing of the jury. For the defense, Ms. Dawson raises objection. Here is the relevant colloquy:

Mr. Prahl: Your Honor, we wish to call Dr. Booker and Anne Nelson. Dr. Booker examined T.E. at the hospital in October 2008, and Nelson is the Sexual Assault Nurse Examiner who was present. Natalia was there too. She had brought T.E. in because she was having mood swings, and said her "girl" hurt—that's the term used in the family for genital area. During the examination, T.E. repeated the statement, and said that "ga-ga" did it. Apparently "ga-ga" is a family term for monster. Dr. Booker asked T.E. to show him where it hurt, using an anatomically correct doll, and she put her finger into the doll's vagina. Dr. Booker conducted a pelvic exam and found an opening in T.E.'s hymen that was larger than any he had seen before in a child her age. T.E. then said "ga-ga" was Stan Vasko, whom T.E. referred to as "mommy's boyfriend." T.E. is still here, and the defense can call her, and we will stipulate that the defense can cross-examine by leading questions.

Ms. Dawson: Your Honor, what T.E. told Dr. Booker and Anne Nelson is hearsay, and I must object. It's also testimonial under *Crawford*. I'm sure Mr. Prahl will say that these statements are inconsistencies that fit our version of Rule 801(d)(1)(A), which embraces all such statements even if they were not under oath in proceedings, and he will say they fit our exception for child victim hearsay. But T.E. cannot be cross-examined about events she doesn't remember, and her lack of memory is not "inconsistent" with what she said years ago because there is no indication that she's lying in saying she doesn't remember. The child victim hearsay exception requires a finding of reliability, and these statements are anything but reliable, given her age and inability to remember. This child hasn't given evidence against my client, and I can't cross-examine a witness who hasn't even incriminated Mr. Vasko.

The judge concludes that the statements fit state Rule 801(d)(1)(A) because T.E.'s "claimed inability to remember what happened is inconsistent with her prior positive account to Dr. Booker and Nelson." The judge also says the statements fit the child victim hearsay provision "because they have the ring of truth." Dr. Booker and Anne Nelson testify in the manner indicated by the proffer.

Vasko is convicted, and he appeals. He argues that the court erred in admitting T.E.'s statements. He says the hearsay exceptions did not apply and that admitting the statements violated confrontation rights. The state's brief argues that the exceptions were satisfied. The appellate lawyer puts it this way to the reviewing court:

> Ms. Dawson on behalf of the defense could cross-examine T.E. to her heart's content: We tendered T.E. to the defense for cross-examination, but the defense did not ask a single question. That's not our fault, your honor, that was the strategic decision made by the defense. Even if T.E.'s statements were testimonial under *Crawford*, the defense had an opportunity to cross-examine, and that was enough.

How should the reviewing court dispose of this argument, and why?

■ NOTES ON DEFERRED CROSS-EXAMINATION

1. Did the defense have an adequate opportunity to cross-examine T.E.? That would entail reminding T.E. of what she told Dr. Booker and Anne Nelson. If the defense failed in this undertaking, it would be worse off than if it did nothing. It would be far less risky for the defense if the *prosecutor* had to broach T.E.'s prior statements while T.E. was on the stand. See generally Mueller, Cross-Examination Earlier or Later: When Is It Enough to Satisfy *Crawford*?, 19 Regent U. L. Rev. 319, 325, 336 (2007) (defendants can't cross-examine "if they must shoulder the risk of opening the subject" because "they cannot afford to make an effort that fails," but defendant "may be able to afford to cross-examine a witness called by the other side" even if the questioning does not prove much because "merely modifying or clarifying what the witness says can be viewed as contributing to the task at hand," and few witnesses "cannot at least be challenged" on their degree of certainty or their "interest or viewpoint or problems in perception or word choice").

2. In criminal cases, the prosecutor bears the burden of persuasion, which suggests that she must not only *call* their witnesses, *but also* obtain their testimony, or at the very least *ask them* about the points she seeks to establish. Under FRE 801(d)(1)(A), a declarant whose inconsistent statement is offered must be "subject to cross-examination" about the statement, which implies that the proponent must offer the statement. Alaska's version of this provision *requires* proponent to ask about the statement while declarant is on the stand. See Alaska Rule 801(d)(1)(A) (prior inconsistent statement is excludable unless declarant "was so examined while testifying" that she had "an opportunity to explain or deny"). See also Vaska v. State, 135 P.3d 1011 (Alaska 2006) (offering party "usually must meet" requirements of Rule 801(d)(1)(A) "by ensuring that the witness is so examined" that she has a chance to explain or deny the statement; otherwise defense "has no duty to cross-examine").

3. If T.E. persists in claiming not to remember the events, can the opportunity to cross-examine be sufficient? If she *also* claims not to remember even making the prior statements? On the basis of *Green*, *O'Neil*, *Owens*, and *Fensterer* (described above), courts have gotten the message that even nonresponsive witnesses are cross-examinable. See State v. Kennedy, 957 So. 2d 757 (La. 2007) (admitting videotaped statements by eight-year-old victim, made to persons in child advocacy center, describing rape; she was cross-examinable even if she could not "respond to questioning in a meaningful way").

4. On the question raised by the Problem, *Vaska* is not the only court to hold that the prosecutor must call the witness and broach the matter of her prior statement if it is to be used substantively. See also State v. Rohrich, 939 P.3d 697, 700-701 (Wash. 1997) (child victim was not asked about events or statement; she did not testify as required, and opportunity to cross-examine "means more than affording the defendant the opportunity to hail the witness to court"). But other courts conclude that making the witness available for cross is enough. See People v. Cookson, 830 N.E.2d 484, 490 (Ill. 2006); Peak v. Commonwealth, 197 S.W.3d 536, 543-544 (Ky. 2006).

5. Child victim hearsay exceptions pave the way for statements by children describing abuse if they are reliable and the child testifies or is unavailable and the statement is corroborated. On abuse prosecutions after *Crawford*, and the challenge of children who cannot be tested by cross, see Eileen Scallen, Coping With Crawford: Confrontation of Children and Other Challenging Witnesses, 35 Wm. Mitchell L. Rev. 1558 (2009).

b. Cross-Examination Before Trial (Prior Cross)

Recall the prior testimony exception in FRE 804(b)(1), covering testimony previously given by someone who is now unavailable, provided that the party against whom the testimony is offered (or in civil cases his "predecessor in interest") had motive and opportunity "to develop" the testimony in direct, cross, or redirect examination.

This situation arose in *Green.* Not only did Melvin Porter make statements to Officer Wade in the stationhouse, but he testified to the same point in the preliminary hearing. Counsel for Green cross-examined Porter then. Because Porter was evasive at trial, the prosecutor read excerpts from the preliminary hearing testimony. The California Supreme Court thought *prior* cross did not satisfy the Confrontation Clause (and later cross at trial did not make up the deficit), but again the Supreme Court disagreed:

> Porter's preliminary hearing testimony was admissible as far as the Constitution is concerned wholly apart from the question of whether [Green] had an effective opportunity for confrontation at the subsequent trial. For Porter's statement at the preliminary hearing had already been given under circumstances closely approximating those that surround the typical trial. Porter was under oath; [Green] was represented by counsel—the same counsel in fact who later represented him at the trial; [Green] had every opportunity to cross-examine Porter as to his statement; and the proceedings were conducted before a judicial tribunal, equipped to provide a judicial record of the hearings.

California v. Green, 399 U.S. 149, 165 (1970).

In a jurisdiction governed by the Rules, the prosecutor might invoke FRE 804(b)(1) to get in what Porter said at Green's preliminary hearing, raising two issues: First, is Porter "unavailable" under FRE 804(a) and the Confrontation Clause? Porter *would* be unavailable under FRE 804(a)(3) because he didn't remember "the subject matter" of his prior testimony (whether Green was his supplier), and probably this lack of memory would make him unavailable under the Confrontation Clause too. Second, did the opportunity to cross-examine Porter at the preliminary hearing satisfy FRE 804(b)(1) and the Confrontation Clause? Here we have to be careful. Since Green's lawyer *did* cross-examine Porter on substance, probably Green had the "opportunity and similar motive" required by FRE 804(b)(1). Arguably this cross means the Confrontation Clause is satisfied too. The Court thought so in *Roberts*, and *Crawford*'s statement about "adequate opportunity to cross-examine" points in the same direction.

If Green's lawyer had *not* cross-examined at the preliminary hearing, the question is whether *the opportunity he passed up* was enough to satisfy FRE 804(b)(1) and the Confrontation Clause. There are no easy answers: Defense lawyers usually think the best strategy is to *forego* cross at the preliminary hearing, because tipping their hand is worse than forging ahead on the slim chance that they can get the case thrown out. *Roberts* avoided answering this question, noting that it is hard to construe such conduct as waiver. Despite language in *Crawford* that a prior "opportunity" is enough, the question remains open. See generally Mueller & Kirkpatrick, Evidence §8.68 (5th ed. 2012).

5. Protected-Witness Testimony

The explosion in child abuse prosecutions led to new ways to get live testimony by child victims: States enacted statutes authorizing depositions and allowing their use at trial if the child is unavailable. The statutes define unavailability to include immaturity (too young to communicate or deal with the courtroom, or fear of testifying) and medical reasons (anticipated trauma from court appearance). Many states authorize child victims to give live testimony from outside the courtroom, with voice and image transmitted to the court by one-way video (people in court can see and hear child on monitor) or two-way (child can also see and hear courtroom on monitor).

In its decision in the *Coy* case, the Court threw cold water on such measures. *Coy* involved a trial for sexual assault in which a screen was put between the witness and the defense table so the complaining witnesses (13-year-old girls) could not see defendant while testifying, though he could see them. (The girls were assaulted while camping in the yard next door to defendant's house. The assailant wore a stocking over his head and shined a flashlight in their eyes, so they could not describe his face and did not identify defendant.) The Iowa statute authorizing the screen also provided for testimony by closed-circuit television, with parties in the same room. In an opinion by Justice Scalia, the Supreme Court disapproved: The Confrontation Clause guarantees defendant "a face-to-face meeting with witnesses." The interest of fairness is served because a witness may feel different when he repeats his story looking at the person he will harm by distortion or mistake, and it is harder to lie about someone "to his face" than "behind his back." While the witness need not look at defendant, the trier will "draw its own conclusions" if she "studiously look[s] elsewhere." The Clause has an "irreducible literal meaning" that guarantees a face-to-face encounter. Any exceptions must rest on "individualized findings" (not categories). See Coy v. Iowa, 487 U.S. 1012 (1988).

After *Coy*, several courts approved remote testimony, in which a child victim sat in another room and her image and words were transmitted through closed-circuit television (both lawyers being with the child, while defendant remained in the courtroom in voice contact with his lawyer). In *Craig* in 1990, the Court approved this technique, under certain circumstances. There the Maryland Court of Appeals thought *Coy* required a face-to-face courtroom encounter between victim and defendant before a judge could use this device. The Court disagreed: The state's interest in "physical and psychological well-being" of victims is important enough to outweigh the defense right to face accusers. The state must make a "case-specific" finding that this procedure is "necessary to protect the welfare of the particular child" and must find that "emotional distress" is "more than mere nervousness or excitement or some reluctance to testify," but can do so without bringing the child into defendant's presence. Maryland v. Craig, 497 U.S. 805 (1990).

■ NOTES ON PROTECTED-WITNESS TESTIMONY

1. Assume that a child is capable of entering the courtroom and describing abuse in the presence of the alleged perpetrator, but that doing so would be traumatic. Can a judge, or for that matter a psychologist or psychiatrist, distinguish between the fear and nervousness that would grip *anyone* in this setting and a reaction that would cause severe psychological damage? In *Coy*, the court thought the former was a good thing.

2. Do such procedures survive *Crawford*? Modern opinions apply *Craig* in other contexts, not in justifying a relaxation of the confrontation requirement, but in limiting the use of substitutes for live testimony in court. See United States v. Yates, 438 F.3d 1307 (11th Cir. 2006) (reversing convictions for offenses in operating internet pharmacy, on account of error in letting witnesses testify from Australia by two-way videoconference; court should have applied *Craig*; confrontation through video monitor "is not the same as physical face-to-face confrontation").

CHAPTER 5

Relevance Revisited

A CHARACTER EVIDENCE

1. Relevancy and Form

"Character" is a loaded term. In its broadest sense it suggests a unique combination of human qualities that defines the essence (and in a sense measures the worth) of a person. He is good or kind or caring, or awful, vicious or selfish. Even talking about character in this sense is awkward. It casts the speaker in a judgmental role and trenches on the privacy of the person in question.

"Character" also carries a narrower meaning, describing inclinations and suggesting their innateness. We speak of someone as being "by nature" cautious or careless, brave or fearful, combative or affable, meaning that these traits shape her natural tendencies.

Character as evidence of conduct. It is in the narrower sense that "character" has evidential significance because specific inclinations are predictive, suggesting patterns of behavior and telling us something about the likelihood that a person would or would not do certain acts. Emphasizing this predictive aspect, we may say that a person is "by disposition" tricky or deceitful, or "disposed" in the opposite direction, toward fairness and honesty. If the question is whether *X* knowingly made a false statement in selling his car, proof that he is honest is some indication he did not or (if he did) he thought it to be true, while proof he is tricky or deceitful is some indication that he made the statement *and* knew it was false. When proof of character is used in these ways, we speak of the "propensity argument," which describes using proof of character as "substantive evidence of conduct on a particular occasion."

Prohibition with exceptions. Now look at FRE 404, which states what seems to be a blanket prohibition: Character evidence cannot be used "to prove that on a particular occasion the person acted in accordance with the character or trait." But the devil here is in the details. Exceptions in FRE 404(a)(2) allow the defense in a criminal case to prove "a pertinent trait" of the defendant and, if such proof comes in, the prosecutor can "offer evidence to rebut it." The exceptions are huge, and we will take them up in detail. Notice two other major points: First, there are no "exceptions" in civil cases, which means that character cannot be used to prove conduct in that setting. Second, the same exclusionary principle is restated in FRE 404(b), *but* here we learn that "specific instances" of conduct can be used to show things like "motive" or "intent" or "plan."

Probative worth; prejudice. If character has a predictive aspect, why does Rule 404 begin with that broad prohibition? There are two reasons: First, the probative worth of character evidence is hard to assess. It turns in part on the inclination and the point to be proved: If, for example, we have in one case evidence of a fair and honest disposition and in another evidence of treachery and dishonesty, the former seems more persuasive as proof that the person did *not* utter the falsehood in issue than the latter in proving that he *did*. The reason is that fairness and honesty seem to lessen the likelihood that a person uttered any falsehood (hence necessarily the one at issue), while treachery and dishonesty seem only to increase the likelihood that the person utters falsehoods (but *not necessarily* the one in issue). More generally, it is hard to know how strong or deep run the currents of any trait, to be sure a person truly has the trait, or to grasp what it tells us about the person under the circumstances confronting her at the crucial moment. In the end, probative worth seems limited and hard to assess.

Second, we worry that "character evidence" can be prejudicial, and you have already seen that Rule 403 empowers trial judges to exclude evidence—even relevant evidence—on account of the risk of "unfair prejudice," which we defined to mean its tendency to make juries angry or to invite jury misuse. Recall the decisions in *Chapple* and *Old Chief II* (Chapter 2B), the first involving a photograph of the charred body and skull of a murder victim, where we were concerned about jury anger, the second involving proof of a prior violent crime, where we were concerned about jury misuse. It is in *Old Chief II* that we see most clearly the judgment reflected in the principle of exclusion stated in Rule 404—we think it would be misuse of a prior offense if it persuaded the jury to convict the defendant just because he did something wrong before.

The regulating scheme. FRE 404 and 405 restate principles that evolved at common law. Those principles are complicated and full of compromise. In *Michelson*, the Supreme Court took note of the common law scheme but declined to change it:

> [M]uch of this law is archaic, paradoxical and full of compromises and compensations by which an irrational advantage to one side is offset by a poorly reasoned counterprivilege to the other. But somehow it has proved a workable

> even if clumsy system when moderated by discretionary controls in the hands of a wise and strong trial court. To pull one misshapen stone out of the grotesque structure is more likely simply to upset its present balance between adverse interests than to establish a rational edifice.

Michelson v. United States, 335 U.S. 469, 486 (1948).

Now we focus on these issues: In what way (if at all) is character relevant? Is it provable under FRE 404 or 405? Why or why not? What form should the evidence take?

2. Character to Prove Conduct on a Particular Occasion

a. Character of Criminal Defendant

Consider evidence of the character of the accused, which has long presented the most common problem and acute difficulty.

■ PROBLEM 5-A. Fight in the Red Dog Saloon (Part 1)

Don and Vince come to blows in a local watering hole known as the Red Dog Saloon. Both suffer serious injuries, although Vince gets the worst of it: Wineglass in hand, Don takes a wild swing, and the glass shatters as it strikes Vince in the mouth, inflicting lacerations leading to permanent scars on his face. Don is charged with assault and battery. He pleads self-defense. Testimony conflicts as to who struck the first blow, though it appears that Don was seated at the bar enjoying his Chablis when Vince muttered something snide about what "real men" drink.

In the trial of Don, the prosecutor calls Coach Jones as a witness during the state's case-in-chief, offering his testimony that Don is "one mean aggressive physical man, quick tempered and prone to violence." Don objects that the proffered testimony is "irrelevant" and "barred by the character rule."

During the defense case-in-chief, Don calls Reverend Gram, offering his testimony that Don is "peaceably disposed toward all people, gentle and nonviolent, more likely to run from a fight than to defend himself, and certainly not likely to initiate violence." The prosecutor objects that the proffered testimony is "irrelevant" and "barred by the character rule."

What result on these objections and why? If the court lets Reverend Gram testify, can the prosecutor call Coach Jones during the state's case-in-rebuttal? See FRE 404(a).

■ NOTES ON EVIDENCE OF DEFENDANT'S CHARACTER

1. Under Rule 404, apparently it matters whether evidence of defendant's character is first offered by the defense or by the prosecution. Why?

2. What is a "pertinent" trait? That depends on the charges. In a battery trial, a court would likely exclude evidence that defendant is "honest" but admit proof that he is "peaceable" or "nonviolent." See United States v. Jackson, 588 F.2d 1046, 1055 (5th Cir.) (in drug trial, proof of defendant's reputation for truth and veracity was not admissible; truthfulness was "not pertinent to the criminal charges of conspiracy to distribute heroin or possession of heroin"), *cert. denied*, 442 U.S. 941 (1979).

3. What level of specificity is required? Rule 404(a)(1) and (2) speak of a pertinent "trait" of character, and the ACN speaks of limiting the evidence to such traits rather than proving "character generally." Compare State v. Blake, 249 A.2d 232, 234-235 (Conn. 1968) (alleged indecent assault; on retrial, defendant should be permitted to prove "specific traits" of "sexual morality and decency," but not "general good character") with United States v. John, 309 F.3d 298, 303 (5th Cir. 2002) (in trial for sexual assault against minor, admitting testimony by (a) wife of defendant indicating that the two "had a good marriage and a normal sexual relationship," (b) social service worker who placed eight foster children with defendant and his wife, indicating that she considered them "very good parents [who were] willing to do whatever needs to be done for the children," (c) defendant himself indicating that he was "fifty-one years old and had never been accused of sexual misconduct," and (d) defendant's 33-year-old daughter indicating that defendant had a "good" reputation in the community for "sexual morality and decency"). General proof that defendant is "law abiding" seems at least marginally relevant in all contexts, and courts seem disposed to admit it. See United States v. Diaz, 961 F.2d 1417 (9th Cir. 1992) (in drug trial, error to block defense from asking pastor about defendant's "character traits for being prone to criminal activity" since traits need not be specific and may be as general as being law abiding) (also "being prone to large-scale drug dealing" was not a character trait; court properly blocked defense cross raising this point).

4. If evidence of defendant's good character is admitted, what should the jury be told? Can it properly acquit on the proof of good character alone, or should it be told to consider character evidence in the context of all the proof? Compare Edgington v. United States, 164 U.S. 361, 366 (1896) and United States v. Pujana-Mena, 949 F.2d 24, 29-32 (2d Cir. 1991) (both implying that jury should be told to consider evidence of good character in the context of all evidence) with United States v. John, 309 F.3d 298, 304-305 (5th Cir. 2002) (reversible error to refuse to instruct jury that evidence of defendant's good character may itself create reasonable doubt).

5. Sometimes the best that defendant can offer is someone to testify that he "has heard nothing ill" of the defendant. Should such a lukewarm endorsement be permitted? See Michelson v. United States, 335 U.S. 469, 478 (1948) (Yes).

b. *Character of Crime Victim*

■ PROBLEM 5-B. Red Dog Saloon (Part 2)

In the trial of Don for the assault on Vince, Don calls Ernie, offering his testimony that Vince is "a belligerent, fight-picking, aggressive fellow with a real short fuse." The prosecutor objects that the proffered testimony is "irrelevant" and "barred by the rule against character evidence." Is this objection well taken on either ground? Spell out Don's argument that Ernie's testimony is relevant.

■ NOTES ON EVIDENCE OF THE VICTIM'S CHARACTER

1. The Rules let Don show that Vince is a violent person, and then the prosecutor can show that Don is violent too. Do these results make sense? Should the fact that Don attacks the character of Vince open the door for the prosecutor to attack Don's character?

2. If Vince sued Don for assault, could Don offer Ernie's testimony as described above? Could Don offer Reverend Gram's testimony, as described in Problem 5-A?

3. Assume that instead of calling Ernie to describe the character of Vince, Don calls an eyewitness to testify that Vince struck the first blow without provocation. Could the prosecutor then introduce evidence that Vince is by disposition peaceable? What if Don kills Vince and is charged with his murder?

4. In sexual assault trials, we follow different rules when it comes to defense attacks on the character of the complaining witness (the victim). Rule 412 addresses these cases, and we consider the differences and the reasons for them later (see section A5, infra).

5. Suppose the defense has proof that Vince had made threats to attack or kill Don. Should such evidence be admitted? What does it show? Do FRE 404 and 405 apply to such proof? See Torres v. State, 71 S.W.3d 758, 761 (Tex. Crim. App. 2002) (threats to harm defendant are not excludable as character evidence; they are admissible because they shed direct light on victim's intent, hence on the affray in issue).

c. *Methods of Proving Character*

If character (or a trait) is to be proved, how should it be done? There are three ways, all involving testimony by what we may call a "character witness." Such a witness might describe acts indicating the existence of the trait—that he falsified a document, for example, or rendered a correct account of moneys entrusted to him. Or she might give her opinion that the person has the trait in question—she thinks him "honest" or "deceitful." Or she might describe his reputation—"the shadow his daily life has cast in his neighborhood," as the Supreme Court called it in Michelson v. United States, 335 U.S. 469, 477 (1948). She might testify that he is "by reputation" honest or deceitful.

By longstanding common law tradition, only reputation testimony was allowed when the purpose was to prove character as circumstantial evidence of conduct on a particular occasion. Reputation evidence has been praised in eloquent terms as

> the slow growth of months and years, the resultant picture of forgotten incidents, passing events, habitual and daily conduct, presumably honest because disinterested, and safer to be trusted because prone to suspect . . . . It sums up a multitude of trivial details. It compacts into the brief phrase of a verdict the teaching of many incidents and the conduct of years. It is the average intelligence drawing its conclusion.

Finch, J., in Badger v. Badger, 88 N.Y. 546, 552 (1882), quoted in *Michelson*, supra. But many chafed at the common law restriction, arguing that opinion too should be allowed:

> Put any one of us on trial for a false charge, and ask him whether he would not rather invoke in his vindication, as Lord Kenyon said, "the warm, affectionate testimony" of those few whose long intimacy and trust has made them ready to demonstrate their faith to the jury, than any amount of colorful assertions about reputation. Take the place of a juryman, and speculate whether he is helped more by the witnesses whose personal intimacy gives to their belief a first and highest value, or by those who merely repeat a form of words in which the term "reputation" occurs . . . . The Anglo-American rules of evidence have . . . never done anything so curious in the way of shutting out evidential light as when they decided to exclude the person who knows as much as humanly can be known about the character of another, and have still admitted the secondhand, irresponsible product of multiplied guesses and gossip which we term "reputation."

7 J. Wigmore, Evidence §1986 (3d ed. 1940).

The common law restriction (allowing only reputation testimony) persevered, for reasons perhaps best summed up in these words:

> The answer to [Wigmore's] argument is found in overwhelming considerations of practical convenience. If a witness is to be permitted to testify to the character of an accused person, basing his testimony solely on his own knowledge and observation, he cannot logically be prohibited from stating the particular incidents affecting the defendant and the particular actions of the defendant which have led him to his favorable conclusion. In most instances it would

> be utterly impossible for the prosecution to ascertain whether occurrences narrated by the witness as constituting the foundation of his conclusion were or were not true. They might be utterly false, and yet incapable of disproof at the time of trial. Furthermore, even if evidence were accessible to controvert the specific statements of the witness in this respect, its admission would lead to the introduction into the case of innumerable collateral issues which could not be tried out without introducing the utmost complication and confusion into the trial, tending to distract the minds of the jurymen and befog the chief issue in litigation.

People v. Van Gaasbeck, 82 N.E. 718 (N.Y. 1907).

If you look now at Rule 405(a), you will see that this provision authorizes both reputation and opinion evidence, but sharply restricts evidence of specific instances.

■ PROBLEM 5-C. Red Dog Saloon (Part 3)

In Don's trial, if the judge lets Ernie testify about the Vince's character, should Ernie testify as described in Problem 5-B (Vince is "a belligerent, fight-picking fellow with a real short fuse")? What kind of testimony is that? If the judge lets Reverend Gram testify that Don is "peaceably disposed," and lets Coach Jones testify that Don is "quick tempered and prone to violence," is such testimony similar in nature? (See FRE 405.) What foundation should the proponent lay?

Suppose Ernie testified that Vince was "known in the community" as a belligerent person, or "has a reputation" for aggressiveness. What kind of testimony is that? (Again, see FRE 405.) What kind of foundation would be required? Could Reverend Gram and Coach Jones, in describing the character of Don, cast their testimony in similar form?

In support of his conclusion that Vince is "belligerent, fight-picking," and "aggressive," could Ernie describe past fights that he had seen Vince involved in? In support of his conclusion that Don is "quick-tempered and prone to violence," could Coach Jones describe specific acts by Don? What would be wrong with that?

■ NOTES ON OPINION AND REPUTATION

1. How well must a character witness know the defendant or victim if he is to testify to reputation? Is a college student qualified to give either positive or negative testimony on the character of the accused if the student has known defendant for two months around campus or in a dormitory, sorority, or fraternity? What about a business associate who has no social contact with defendant and knows nothing of his home life? See United States v. Parker, 447 F.2d 826, 831 (7th Cir. 1971) (error to exclude positive testimony on defendant's reputation among coworkers). How about an investigator hired to interview members of the community? See United States v. Perry, 643 F.2d 38, 52 (2d Cir.) (excluding testimony by private investigator hired by defendant's wife), *cert. denied*, 454 U.S. 835 (1981).

2. When Don claims Vince was the first aggressor, does that mean the character of Vince is an element in Don's defense?

(a) If Vince's character *were* an element in Don's defense, couldn't Don prove specific instances of aggressive behavior by Vince? See FRE 405(b). But the correct answer is that the character of Vince is *not* an element in Don's defense. Why? See State v. Hutchinson, 959 P.2d 1061, 1071 (Wash. 1998) (in murder trial, defendant claimed self-defense; he could only offer opinion or reputation evidence on victim's character).

(b) Suppose Don makes the different claim that *his* behavior was reasonable because *he knew* Vince had been violent in similar situations, so he needed to protect himself. *Now* can Don prove acts by Vince? See United States v. Burks, 470 F.2d 432, 434-435 (D.C. Cir. 1972) (victim's violent acts were admissible, if defendant knew of them, on question whether he "reasonably feared he was in danger of imminent great bodily injury"). Do FRE 404 and 405 even apply here?

3. Should the prosecutor be allowed to ask a character witness about the reputation of the defendant *after* the crime was committed? See United States v. Curtis, 644 F.2d 263, 268-269 (3d Cir. 1981) (No), *cert. denied*, 459 U.S. 1018 (1982). Why not?

4. Should FRE 405 be amended to bar reputation evidence, now that opinion is admissible? See Uviller, Evidence of Character to Prove Conduct: Illusion, Illogic, and Injustice in the Courtroom, 130 U. Pa. L. Rev. 845, 885 (1982) (reputation is the least trustworthy and least testable form of character evidence, and should be disallowed).

5. Can a defendant offer expert opinion that he is by disposition nonviolent? Compare United States v. MacDonald, 688 F.2d 224, 228 (4th Cir. 1982) (excluding psychiatric testimony that defendant's "personality configuration" is inconsistent with "outrageous and senseless murders") with United States v. Staggs, 553 F.2d 1073, 1075-1076 (7th Cir. 1977) (in trial for armed threats against official, error to exclude testimony by psychologist that defendant was "more likely to hurt himself than to direct his aggression toward others") (reversing). Later we view this matter from another perspective. See Chapter 9C2, infra (expert testimony on behavioral and psychological patterns).

COMMENT/PERSPECTIVE: Victim's Character in the Zimmerman Case

The 2013 trial of George Zimmerman for murder garnered national attention. The case arose out of the shooting death of 17-year-old Trayvon Martin in a gated community in Sanford, Florida, where defendant was a neighborhood watch coordinator. There were racial overtones (victim was African-American; defendant was mixed-race Hispanic) and some thought the stand-your-ground law was shielding defendant from responsibility. The two had a face-to-face encounter leading to a scuffle and shooting, but Zimmerman claimed self-defense. His lawyer called into question the victim's character, seeking to show that Martin had been suspended from school, that his mother had kicked him out and told him to go live with his father, that he had described himself as a "gangsta," had been in fights, used marijuana, and had a picture on his cellphone of a hand holding a pistol. Judge Nelson allowed discovery into these matters, but ruled at trial that the defense could not prove most of these points under Florida's counterpart to FRE 404. She did allow proof that Martin had traces of marijuana in his system, as bearing on his conduct on the occasion. Rule 404(a)(2)(B) says defendants can prove a "pertinent trait" of the victim, which includes aggressive disposition because it bears on self-defense, *but* the proof must be in the form of opinion or reputation, not specific acts. The prosecutor's objection stressed that Zimmerman didn't know of Martin's prior fights. If he *had* known of them, this fact might have been provable (bearing on the reasonableness of his behavior). The jury returned a verdict of "not guilty."

d. Cross-Examination and Rebuttal

PROBLEM 5-D. What Price Truth?

In Don's trial, the judge excludes the testimony of Coach Jones during the prosecutor's case-in-chief and admits the testimony of Reverend Gram during the defense's case-in-chief. After Gram has told the trier of fact that Don is a "peaceable nonviolent fellow," the prosecutor rises for cross-examination:

Q: Reverend Gram, you tell us that Don is not a violent man, is that right?
A: Yes, sir.
Q: And that he is not in the habit of striking his fellow man?

A: No, indeed.
Q: But that doesn't go for women, does it?
A: I beg your pardon—
Ms. Davenport: Your honor, I object to that last question and move that it be struck from the record. The question is whether the defendant starts fights, and the Reverend here has said he doesn't. The question is not proper cross-examination under Rule 405 and is beyond the scope of the direct besides.
Court: Overruled. It's a preliminary question, and I think maybe he's leading up to something. Go ahead, Mr. Irwin.
Mr. Irwin: Did you know, Reverend, that two weeks ago Don's wife was treated in the emergency room of Crosbie Clinic, suffering multiple bruises, lacerations, and two cracked ribs, all at the hands of the defendant, who you say wouldn't harm anyone?

Is the question proper, or did the court err in rejecting the defense objection? Can Mr. Irwin ask Reverend Gram whether he knows Don was fired for embezzling from his employer? Whether he knows Don was convicted of tax evasion? Whether he knows Don was arrested for brawling after a football game?

■ NOTES ON CROSS-EXAMINATION OF CHARACTER WITNESSES

1. When the accused calls a character witness to testify to his good character, the prosecutor may cross-examine about incidents from defendant's past that could not be proved otherwise. Recognizing that merely *asking* such questions may "waft an unwarranted innuendo into the jury box," the Supreme Court nevertheless concluded:

> A defendant . . . is powerless to prevent his cause from being irretrievably obscured and confused; but, in cases such as the one before us, the law foreclosed this whole confounding line of inquiry, unless defendant thought the net advantage from opening it up would be with him. Given this option, we think defendants . . . have no valid complaint at the latitude which existing law allows to the prosecution to meet by cross-examination an issue voluntarily tendered by the defense.

Michelson v. United States, 335 U.S. 469, 484-485 (1948).

2. What's going on with such cross-questions?

(a) Does this response to defense evidence let the prosecutor argue that the accused has bad character and probably did the deed? In *Michelson,*

the Court said the accused is entitled to limiting instructions even though the jury will likely find them "unintelligible." What sort of unintelligible instruction should the court give?

(b) Reverend Gram gave his opinion that Don was peaceable. Then the cross-examiner asked "Did you know" of specific instances of violence. In casting the question in that form, the prosecutor did the right thing. Why? How should the question be put if Reverend Gram testified to Don's *reputation* for peacefulness?

3. Mr. Irwin asked Reverend Gram about violent acts after he testified that Don is a "peaceable nonviolent fellow." Consider these variations in possible cross-examination:

(a) Irwin wants to ask Gram whether he knows Don "buys pornographic videos" or "cheats at cards" or "falsifies his charitable donations for tax purposes." Given Gram's direct testimony, are such questions proper on cross?

(b) Irwin wants to ask Gram whether he knows Don was "arrested for domestic assault." *Michelson* approved questions to a character witness about defendant being arrested before. The theory was that anyone who really *knew* him would know about such things, so asking about arrests tested knowledge. But even if most arrested people have done what they are arrested for, arrest is not a good proxy for the deed. And in today's more urbanized world, it seems questionable whether a knowledgeable character would know about arrests. See Mueller, "Of Misshapen Stones and Compromises: *Michelson* and the Modern Law of Character Evidence," in Evidence Stories 75 (Richard Lempert ed., 2006) (criticizing *Michelson* on this ground).

(c) Irwin dreams up the nastiest question he can think of: "Did you know, Reverend Gram, that Don beats up derelicts for kicks and throws rocks at little children?" Should we require a prosecutor to have a good faith basis for questions, so the jury, if it misuses them, will be misusing fact rather than fiction? How would the prosecutor do that?

4. Can *Don's* lawyer ask Coach Jones on cross whether Jones knows about times when Don "refused to fight back when attacked," and "intervened to prevent violence among his teammates"? Is the defense likely to follow this tactic?

e. Civil Cases

FRE 404(a) states a general rule excluding character when offered to prove conduct, and then sets out four exceptions, the first three of which apply only to criminal cases. Putting aside the fourth exception (covering character of witnesses, which we consider in Chapter 8), no provision touches civil cases.

It follows that character evidence, when offered to prove behavior in a particular instance, is *never* admissible in civil cases. Prior to an amendment in 2006 limiting the first three exceptions to criminal cases, courts sometimes admitted character evidence in civil cases where the conduct was criminal in nature. See Perrin v. Anderson, 784 F.2d 1040, 1043-1045 (10th Cir. 1986) (civil defendant may invoke exceptions when central issue "is in nature criminal"), and some state counterparts make limited provision to prove character in civil cases. See Oregon Evidence Rule 404(2)(d) (allowing character evidence in support of claim of self-defense in civil assault and battery cases). One commentator argues that we should more freely admit character evidence in civil cases. See Leonard, The Use of Character to Prove Conduct: Rationality and Catharsis in the Law of Evidence, 58 Colo. L. Rev. 1, 56-57 (1987) (admit character evidence unless it would waste time, confuse or mislead, or be unfairly prejudicial).

3. Character as an Element of a Charge, Claim, or Defense

a. *Criminal Cases*

We have seen that character evidence is usually inadmissible to prove conduct on a particular occasion. In criminal cases, the prosecutor may not offer such evidence in the case-in-chief to persuade the jury that defendant committed the crime. But exceptions in FRE 404(a) sometimes allow character evidence to prove conduct. For example, the accused may resort to such proof to show he did *not* commit the charged crime. We have also seen that *when* character evidence is admitted to prove conduct, the proof must take the form of opinion or reputation evidence (rather than specific instances). Finally, we have seen that specific instances may be raised on cross. Thus the cross-examiner may ask a character witness about acts by the person whose character he has described. Rule 405(a) makes that much clear.

Now look at something new. Rule 404 does *not* bar evidence of character when offered for *other reasons* than to prove conduct on a particular occasion. And note that Rule 405(b) provides that proof of "specific instances" of conduct is admissible whenever character is an "essential element" of a charge or defense.

So we have a new question: When is character an "element" of a charge or defense?

In criminal cases the answer is "almost never." In this country, we take some pride in the proposition that we punish people for what they *do,* and not for *who they are.* The Advisory Committee did cite an archaic example where the character of the victim is an element in a crime —"the chastity of the victim under a statute specifying her chastity as an element of the crime of seduction"! We don't put people on trial for such things today, but assume for a moment that such charges are brought and forget how appalling it would be to admit evidence of every "unchaste" act by the victim (offered to prove that she was not "chaste"). In such a trial, the accused could resort to Rule 405(b) if he wanted to prove such acts. Otherwise he would be limited by Rule 405(a) to opinion or reputation.

Now check your understanding, bearing in mind that the accused often does try to show innocence by proving his own good character. It is no exaggeration to say that the jury's opinion of his character may be his most important asset. But it does not follow that his character is "an essential element" of a charge or defense under FRE 405(b). In common parlance, character itself is not "in issue" regardless how vigorously it may be disputed or how important it may be in the jury's deliberations. Put yet another way, we do not (or should not) convict a person because he is "bad" (unless it also happens that he committed the offense) or acquit him because he is "good" (unless it also happens that he did not commit the offense).

Consider for a moment the character of the alleged victim. It would be possible to make the victim's character an element of a charge or defense. We could, for example, define battery as beating up a good person, which would mean that someone who beat up a bad person would not have committed this crime. But the criminal law has not gone in this direction, and constitutional principles such as equal protection and substantive due process would likely block any such move.

■ PROBLEM 5-E. "She's a Known Thief"

Gretta is charged with shoplifting from Bloomingdeal's. Helen, a plainclothes security guard in the women's clothing department, stopped her after she visited the changing room and was leaving the store. In searching Gretta's purse, Helen discovered a blouse and skirt that seemed new and matched items carried by the store. There were no store markings, however, and Gretta said she was carrying them "as a change of clothing because I'm meeting a friend for a drink after work."

Gretta pleaded innocent and advanced the same explanation at trial. During his case-in-chief, the prosecutor offered Helen's testimony that "I watched Gretta closely that day because I had learned by watching videotapes that Gretta stole other clothing items from the department in recent weeks, including a sweater, some gloves, and some lingerie." Helen would also testify (if allowed) that Gretta had a reputation among security guards as a shoplifter of small items from many departments, from electronics to homewares to cosmetics and jewelry. The prosecutor also offered evidence that Gretta had been convicted of shoplifting at other stores four times in the last five years.

Gretta objected that this evidence was "barred by the rule against character evidence." The prosecutor replied, "Your honor, she's a known thief, and being a thief is what she's charged with. She denies it. We're entitled to prove otherwise." What result, and why?

■ NOTES ON CHARACTER AS AN "ELEMENT" IN CRIMINAL CASES

1. The prosecutor has a point. Either Gretta is a thief or she isn't, and she says she isn't. She entered a plea of not guilty and offered an explanation. But the real question isn't whether she is a thief, but whether she was stealing the blouse and skirt. If FRE 404(a) doesn't apply, when would it ever apply? Compare State v. Demeritt, 813 A.2d 393 (N.H. 2002) (alleged vehicular manslaughter; defendant claimed victim caused accident by reckless driving; victim's "recklessness" was not an essential element of the defense; court properly excluded victim's specific acts).

2. Suppose the prosecutor offers Helen's testimony on the videotapes and Gretta's reputation among other guards in order to "explain why Helen followed Gretta and searched her purse." Should this argument overcome the "character" objection?

3. Consider defenses of "insanity" or "diminished capacity." Do FRE 404 and 405 apply, or do these defenses raise something apart from "character"? See United States v. Emery, 682 F.2d 493, 496-501 (5th Cir.) (admitting prior offense evidence as part of government's proof that defendant was sane), *cert. denied*, 459 U.S. 1044 (1982).

4. Consider repeat offender trials where a prior conviction is an element in the present charges (as in prosecutions for illegal possession of a firearm by a convicted felon). How about cases where prior offenses affect punishment? Do FRE 404 and 405 apply? Recall that the Court held in *Old Chief* that in this setting a defense offer to stipulate requires the court to exclude proof of prior crimes (see Chapter 2B1, supra).

5. When defendants claim entrapment, they are saying government action induced them to commit crimes they would not otherwise commit. Thus it becomes plausible to say character is an element in the defense. Typically, however, the response of the prosecution is not to introduce opinion or reputation evidence but to offer proof that defendant committed similar crimes before. Usually courts admit such evidence under FRE 404(b) rather than to refute an element of the defense under FRE 404(a)(2).

b. Civil Cases

In civil litigation (unlike criminal cases) there are several common situations in which character is an ultimate issue. Here the evidence is not offered as a predicate fact supporting an inference of behavior on a particular occasion, but as an end in itself.

Defamation. An obvious example is the defamation suit in which truth is raised as a defense: If a basketball player sues a newspaper for a story saying he "shaves points for cash," then evidence that in fact plaintiff did exactly that would be admissible. The proof would likely take the form of evidence of point-shaving in particular games. If the alleged libel is more general (accusing him of being a "thief"), a defense of truth would pave the way for evidence of particular thefts, or even opinion or reputation testimony that plaintiff is a thief. Sometimes reputation as such bears on damages. Defendant in a libel suit might allege that what was said did not damage plaintiff, simply because plaintiff already had a bad reputation, in which case evidence of that reputation is admissible. See Schafer v. Time, Inc., 142 F.3d 1361, 1370 (11th Cir. 1998) (in libel suit, admitting evidence of specific acts by plaintiff; character was at issue under FRE 405).

Negligent entrustment. Another example is the negligent entrustment claim, where plaintiff alleges that defendant negligently let another operate equipment (typically a car or truck) and that the other negligently injured plaintiff. Here plaintiff must prove that the latter was by disposition careless, in order to prevail on the point that defendant should not have entrusted the equipment to him. On this point it is clear that specific instances of negligence with such equipment may be proved. See Scroggins v. Yellow Freight Systems, Inc., 98 F. Supp. 928, 930 (E.D. Tenn. 2000) (truck driver); In re Aircrash in Bali, 684 F.2d 1301, 1315 (9th Cir. 1982) (airline pilot); Breeding v. Massey, 378 F.2d 171, 181 (8th Cir. 1967) (car driver). In these cases, plaintiff must also prove the person entrusted with the equipment was negligent at the time of the accident. Can you see why a plaintiff might seek recovery for negligent entrustment even though this theory requires proof of everything needed to recover in respondeat superior, plus one more thing?

Child custody. Yet another example is the custody dispute, where parental fitness of mother and father is assessed in order to serve the interests of the child. Here character, in the sense of being a good parent, is the ultimate issue. See Berryhill v. Berryhill, 410 So. 2d 416, 418-419 (Ala. 1982) (specific acts and reputation evidence admissible).

Wrongful death. A common instance of such use of character evidence is the wrongful death suit where the amount of damages may turn on the "worth" of the decedent to the plaintiff. Whatever tactical difficulties confront the defense in "speaking ill of the dead," the bereaved plaintiff should recover less if it can be shown that the deceased was an "alcoholic" or "compulsive gambler" than would be recoverable if the deceased was a hardworking, dedicated, loving spouse, parent, or child. See Perkins v. United Transport Co., 219 F.2d 422, 423 (2d Cir. 1955) (approving reputation evidence).

■ NOTES ON CHARACTER AS AN "ELEMENT" IN CIVIL CASES

1. In libel cases where the alleged defamatory statement was broad, can defendant advance a claim of truth by proving specific acts that support the broad statement? See Faigin v. Kelly, 184 F.3d 67, 83 (1st Cir. 1989) (where book suggested that athletic agent was untrustworthy, defendant could offer testimony by other athletes describing their dealings with plaintiff, to prove truth). If the statement charges specific acts of wrongdoing, can defendant support a defense of truth by evidence of *other* specific acts of a similar nature? See Roper v. Mabry, 551 P.2d 1381 (Wash. App. 1976) (No).

2. In a defamation case, could defendant use proof of different acts from those averred in the statement in question to show that the statement did not harm plaintiff's reputation? See Meiners v. Moriarity, 563 F.2d 343, 351 (7th Cir. 1977) (court should let party charged with libel cross-examine claimant on "relevant specific instances of conduct" that might have produced adverse publicity, including acts other than those mentioned in statement). What if plaintiff engaged in other misconduct that is not known in the community? See Shirley v. Freunscht, 735 P.2d 600 (Or. 1987) (in defamation suit, defendant tried to show that plaintiff had bad reputation beforehand; error to let witnesses relate specific instances of "business misconduct," which are irrelevant "unless they were generally known in the business community," which wasn't shown).

3. In a wrongful death action against the maker of a household spray purposefully inhaled by the 14-year-old decedent, can defendant prove that the boy also smoked marijuana? See Harless v. Boyld-Midway Division, American Home Products, 594 F.2d 1051, 1057-1058 (5th Cir. 1979) (No). Why not? How about evidence, in a suit for wrongful death of plaintiff's husband, that plaintiff and decedent had begun living together before decedent divorced his first wife? See St. Clair v. Eastern Air Lines, 279 F.2d 119, 121 (2d Cir.) (No), *cert. denied*, 364 U.S. 882 (1960). Why not? In a suit for wrongful death of a wage-earning spouse, should evidence be admitted that decedent was honest or dishonest? See Perkins v. United Transport Co., 219 F.2d 422, 423 (2d Cir. 1955) (Yes). How about evidence that he is or is not well regarded in his trade or calling? See *St. Clair*, supra (Yes).

4. Prior Acts as Proof of Motive, Intent, Plan, and Related Points

a. General Considerations

So elaborate and settled are the restrictions against using character evidence to prove conduct that it may come as a surprise that prosecutors often get in evidence of previous "bad acts" by the defendant. FRE 404(b) paves the way for such proof, and sets out a long (and nonexclusive) list of specific points on which it may be admitted, one of the most important being "intent." Nothing is more common in federal courts than drug cases in which the government proves that on some other occasion defendant sold drugs, to show that *on this* occasion he *intended* to sell similar drugs found in his possession. And specific acts are admitted on many other points, like knowledge, motive, and plan.

Yet in such cases the risk of prejudice to the defendant is manifest: Obviously the court must carefully analyze probative worth and risks of unfair prejudice and confusion of issues, and often the proof is excludable under FRE 403 even though it is marginally relevant on some point. Many courts endorse a four-part test or process under which the judge (a) decides whether the evidence is offered for a proper purpose, (b) decides whether it is relevant for that purpose, (c) decides whether its probative worth is outweighed by the risk of unfair prejudice, and (d) gives a limiting instruction on request. See Huddleston v. United States, 485 U.S. 681 (1988).

So common are such cases that a glance at the reporters yields hundreds of appellate decisions on point, usually rejecting defense arguments that the proof should have been excluded under FRE 403 or 404(a). Indeed, it sometimes seems that the basic rule against "character evidence" is a sham. It might better depict reality if reformulated as a narrow bar against the propensity inference: Prior offense evidence may be admitted in criminal cases on any issue to which it is relevant unless probative value is substantially outweighed by the risk of unfair prejudice, except that it is not admissible if its only relevance is to show a propensity on the part of the accused.

Viewing the cases this way can be misleading. Defendants take most appeals in criminal cases, and the times they successfully exclude such proof at trial are largely hidden from view. And prior acts seem especially relevant in drug cases, which are a staple in federal courts, and less often relevant in trials for offenses like theft and homicide, which are common in state courts. There is reason to think that trial judges are not quite as receptive to prior crimes evidence as appellate opinions seem to suggest, and to suppose such evidence is admitted somewhat less often in state than in federal court.

b. Proving Intent

■ PROBLEM 5-F. Drug Sale or Scam?

Rhoda Smith once lived with Ronald Moore, but after a quarrel she moves out and approaches the police, offering to act as a paid informant. After she tells them Moore "deals large quantities of cocaine," the police ask her to arrange for undercover officer Hardy to buy cocaine from Moore.

Smith tells Moore she has "a buyer from Virginia" who wants four ounces of cocaine. They arrange a sale to occur in Smith's motel room. Moore arrives, and Smith introduces Hardy as "the drug dealer from Virginia whose sources have run dry." Moore offers Hardy a small amount of hashish, which Hardy buys for $100. Then Moore agrees to sell Hardy four ounces of cocaine, but first asks to inspect the cash. Holding it up to the light, he complains that it is "dusty" and walks out, telling Smith "I won't do business with this turkey." (The cash had been dusted to pick up fingerprints.)

Police intercept Moore and recover a vial of cocaine from his pocket, but not enough to suggest that he came to deal. A search of Moore's home and car turns up nothing. Still Moore is charged with distribution of hashish and conspiracy to sell cocaine.

At trial Moore argues that the proposed cocaine transaction was "a scam to dupe the buyer," and that he planned to collect the money and depart without turning over any cocaine. The prosecutor offers testimony by Smith describing numerous hashish and cocaine sales by Moore during the 18 months the two lived together. Moore objects.

Should Smith be allowed to testify to the prior hashish sales? To the prior cocaine sales? What if Moore claims the government entrapped him by using Smith as its agent to induce him to commit the charged criminal acts?

■ NOTES ON PRIOR ACTS AS PROOF OF INTENT AND RELATED POINTS IN CRIMINAL CASES

1. On what point is Rhoda Smith's testimony describing Moore's prior hashish and cocaine sales relevant? Does this use of such testimony involve a propensity argument, or something else? Does the proper inference flow from prior sales of *both* drugs?

2. Would it be sensible (at least sometimes) to exclude prior crimes evidence offered during the prosecutor's case-in-chief but admit it (if necessary) during the prosecutor's case-in-rebuttal? Should it make a difference whether intent can be inferred from action (often true when the action is selling drugs) or requires extrinsic proof (often true in fraud cases)? Compare United States v. Colon, 880 F.2d 650, 660-662 (2d Cir. 1989) (in drug trial, reversible error to admit other transactions during government's case-in-chief since defendant's claim that he did not engage in the transaction removed issue of intent) with United States v. Parziale, 947 F.2d 123, 128-129 (5th Cir. 1991) (in drug conspiracy case, plea of not guilty raised issue of intent sufficiently to justify admitting other acts).

3. Should courts, if they admit prior acts, spell out reasons and findings in balancing the relevant factors? Reviewing courts would prefer such detail, but are reluctant to reverse simply because it does not appear in the record. Compare United States v. Osum, 943 F.2d 1394, 1403 (5th Cir. 1991) (when asked, court must make on-the-record findings, but objecting is not the same as requesting findings; if no request is made, reviewing court may still remand for findings if relevant factors are not apparent or there is doubt over ruling) with United States v. Smith, 292 F.3d 90, 98 (1st Cir. 2002) (absence of express findings in ruling under FRE 404(b) and 403 would not inhibit review; court assumes that trial judge undertook required balancing), *cert. denied*, 123 S. Ct. 332 (2003). How effective is it to remand to the trial judge a case that has already produced a conviction for a finding on the record of probative value versus prejudice?

4. If the defense offers to stipulate to such points, should that block the use of prior crimes? Recall *Old Chief* (Chapter 2B1, supra), which held that a defense stipulation requires exclusion of the names of prior convictions, in a felon-in-possession trial where convictions are elements of the charged offense. In *Old Chief*, the Court said its holding did not apply to prior crimes offered under FRE 404(b) to show intent and similar points. On this point, state courts may take a different course. See State v. Glodgett, 749 A.2d 283, 286 (N.H. 2000) (error to admit other crimes where defendant offered to stipulate that if jury found that he committed sexual assault, he had intent; to be relevant, "proffered evidence must be pertinent to an issue that is actually in dispute") (reversing), *appeal after new trial*, 813 A.2d 444 (N.H. 2002). Federal courts decline to require exclusion in this setting. See United States v. Cassell, 292 F.3d 788, 794 (D.C. Cir. 2002) (in felon-in-possession trial, fact that defense did not contest knowledge or intent did not prevent government from showing other instances to prove these points). See generally Mueller & Kirkpatrick, Evidence §4.16 (5th ed. 2012).

5. While intent is a central mental element in many crimes, it is not the only one that bears on guilt. Prior crimes often shed light on other mental conditions. See United States v. Loera, 933 F.2d 725, 729 (9th Cir. 1991) (to show malice, admitting misdemeanor convictions for drunk driving, which showed that defendant had reason to know the risk his drinking and driving posed to others); United States v. Ramirez, 894 F.2d 565, 568-569 (2d Cir. 1990) (defendant claimed lack of knowledge of drugs; court could admit later cocaine offense to rebut this claim); United States v. Dornhofer, 859 F.2d 1195, 1198-1199 (4th Cir. 1988) (in trial for possessing child pornography, admitting evidence that defendant had similar material as proof of "intent and lack of mistake or accident"), *cert. denied*, 490 U.S. 1005 (1990).

6. The entrapment defense raises the question of intent in its largest sense. The heart of this defense is that government action induced a crime the defendant would not otherwise commit, and the prosecutor's usual response is to prove that defendant committed similar crimes before. Courts admit such proof, typically citing FRE 404(b). See Sorrells v. United States, 287 U.S. 435, 451-452 (1932) (defendant who raises entrapment defense "cannot complain of an appropriate and searching inquiry into his own conduct and predisposition as bearing upon that issue"); United States v. Van Horn, 277 F.3d 48, 57-58 (1st Cir. 2002) (defense of entrapment meant prosecutor could cross-examine defendant about his involvement in prior similar crimes).

7. After some states added language requiring prosecutors to give pretrial notice of intent to prove prior acts, FRE 404(b) was amended in 1991 to require prosecutors to give notice before trial if the defense requests (which should be routine). For good cause, the notice requirement may be excused. Otherwise the notice must state "the general nature" of the evidence of prior acts or wrongs to be offered. Suppose the prosecutor *does* give notice, and defendant seeks a pretrial ruling that would exclude the evidence. Does the notification requirement imply that courts should resolve such issues before trial?

c. *Identity, Modus Operandi*

■ PROBLEM 5-G. "He Came Running in All Hunched Over"

Danzey and Gore are charged with bank robbery. The prosecutor calls eyewitnesses who describe the crime. One who was outside saw two men in ski masks and gloves emerge from a white car and enter the bank. Another in the bank said one of the men "came running in all hunched over" and vaulted the counter, taking the money trays from the teller and stuffing them into a bag. A third witness in an apartment two blocks away saw the perpetrators arrive at about 9:00 A.M. in separate cars, one white and the other brown. They returned a short time later, got into the brown car, and left the scene.

An eyewitness can identify Danzey as one of the robbers, but nobody can identify the other. As proof that the other was Gore, the government introduces his confession of involvement in eight similar robberies, all committed between 9:00 A.M. and 11:00 A.M., all using stolen cars of contrasting light and dark colors (one to drive to the bank, the other parked blocks away to be used after a "switch" in the getaway). In his confession Gore said he always wears a ski mask and gloves and always "runs hunched over and jumps over the counter."

Should the court admit Gore's confession of similar robberies? What if there is no confession, but Gore was convicted of the offenses? What if the government has neither a confession nor convictions but eyewitness testimony identifying Gore as the robber on the other occasions?

■ NOTES ON PRIOR ACTS TO PROVE MODUS OPERANDI

1. Does the proposed use of Gore's prior robberies involve a propensity argument or something else? Courts allow use of prior acts to prove identity or modus operandi only if prior acts and charged crime bear very close resemblance and are distinctive and unusual. Is this standard satisfied here? Compare United States v. Robinson, 161 F.3d 463, 467 (7th Cir. 1998) (in trial for April 8th bank robbery, admitting proof of defendant's involvement in April 18th robbery, to show modus operandi; prior act must bear singular strong resemblance to charged offense; similarities must be sufficiently idiosyncratic to permit inference of pattern; here both robbers entered bank "carrying a distinctive duffel bag in one hand and brandishing a handgun in the other," and "vaulted over the teller counter" and demanded money; in both cases the robber emptied drawers by himself after putting gun down; in both cases getaway car was blue Chevrolet Cavalier; robberies occurred within ten days and 25 miles of each other) with United States v. Lail, 846 F.2d 1299, 1300-1302 (11th Cir. 1988) (error to admit evidence that defendant committed prior robbery to show modus operandi; both involved lone gunman, handgun, lack of disguise, and proximity, but common elements did not amount to "signature" in light of striking differences; earlier crime involved dynamite, culprit posing as businessman, and hostage taking) (reversing).

2. FRE 404(b) speaks of a "prior crime, wrong, or other act," not of "convictions." In many cases, a prior crime has led to conviction, which makes the task of proof easy. (A hearsay exception in FRE 803(22) embraces many felony convictions, so they can be used as proof of underlying acts.) If we don't have a conviction, proof in the form of a confession can be used (the confession fits FRE 801(d)(2)(A) as an admission by the defendant). Absent a conviction or confession, the task of proof is harder, but eyewitness testimony is acceptable—in effect a "mini-trial" to determine previous events—and it brings procedural issues that we examine soon (section A4f, infra).

3. Suppose defendant wants to prove other crimes by a third person, called "reverse" 404(b) evidence. By its terms FRE 404(b) applies. Typically defendant argues that offenses by another so strikingly resemble the charged crime that the proof suggests that the other must have committed the charged offense too. Compare United States v. Alayeto, 628 F.3d 917, 921-922 (7th Cir. 2010) (in drug trial, excluding reverse 404(b) evidence of co-offender *G*'s postarrest conduct; such proof must be relevant and "survive the balancing of competing considerations" under FRE 403; standard is "less discriminating" than for evidence offered by prosecutor, but court properly excluded it; if *G* did do what defendant claims, it does not "demonstrate" that defendant was forced to take drugs from him and put it in her pants or body cavity, or show that *G* forced her to do such things) (no violation of due process) with United States v. Wright, 625 F.3d 583, 604 (9th Cir. 2010) (in trial for transporting and possessing child porn, error to exclude proof that defendant's roommate had "the kind of computer knowledge necessary to obtain" such material, that roommate knew defendant's computer had such images, and that roommate had intent to commit the offense; standard of admissibility of similar act evidence offered by defendants is not as restrictive as when prosecutor offers such proof).

d. Plan, Design

■ PROBLEM 5-H. The Undercover Cop Trick

Joe Gilmer is charged with robbing First Bristol Bank and carjacking resulting in death. Allegedly Ken Laver participated in the robbery, which the two had discussed while students in a vocational education program. Laver pled guilty to related charges and testifies for the government, telling this story:

Wanting a getaway car and some cash, they staked out a parking lot at Eastern State College and accosted freshman Stan Norton as he approached his Honda Civic. Gilmer told Norton he was an undercover cop, patted Norton down, pushed him into the back seat, accused him of being a drug dealer, and demanded "the cash that you got from dealing." Norton had none. When Norton asked to see a police ID, Gilmer threatened to kill him. Growing nervous, Laver left the car. Gilmer kept threatening Norton, and eventually choked him to death. Laver and Gilmer drove to a nearby field and buried the body. Taking Norton's keys, they went back to the college, sacked his room, and found money. After buying a gun the next day, Laver and Gilmer robbed First Bristol Bank, using the Honda Civic as getaway car.

Over Gilmer's objection outside the jury's presence, the prosecutor offers Laver's testimony in this vein: A month before the First Bristol robbery, Laver and Gilmer robbed Jimmy Waltz in a mall parking lot. They hadn't talked about it, but Gilmer represented himself as an undercover officer investigating drug dealing, showing Waltz a badge and his gun. Laver played along. Gilmer searched Waltz, found cash, and took it, telling Waltz he suspected it was drug money. Waltz protested that it was tips from his waiter's job, and went to get his supervisor to explain it. Laver and Gilmer left with the money, surprised at "how easy it was."

"Goes to plan and preparation under Rule 404(b)," says the prosecutor: "It shows these guys planned to test the undercover cop trick to see whether they could use it to steal seed money and a getaway car for the bank robbery.

"Not so fast," replies the defense. "The Waltz robbery wasn't planning for the First Bristol robbery, nor even planning for stealing the Honda. They hadn't discussed the cop thing, which was spur of the moment."

How should the court rule, and why?

■ NOTES ON PRIOR ACTS OFFERED TO PROVE PLAN OR DESIGN

1. Prosecutors are not required to prove planning or preparation for a crime, but proof along these lines makes more plausible the evidence offered to prove the crime itself. Does the Waltz robbery show the development of a plan culminating in the Bristol Bank robbery, or does it just paint Gilmer and Laver as thugs? The defense points out that the two hadn't discussed the undercover cop trick, and says the two just stumbled into it in the Waltz robbery. Does that matter? As always, proof of the prior act could be excluded under FRE 403 as unfairly prejudicial even if it is somehow relevant.

2. How can we distinguish the permissible use of other crimes to prove a plan from their impermissible use to prove conduct on the occasion? See Mendez & Imwinkelried, *People v. Ewoldt*: The California Supreme Court's About-Face on the Plan Theory for Admitting Evidence of an Accused's Uncharged Misconduct, 28 Loyola L.A. L. Rev. 473, 480-485 (1995) (true plan cases involve "a single, overall grand design that encompasses both the charged and uncharged offenses" where design is "overarching" and crimes are "integral components" of the plan so each amounts to a "step or stage" in executing it; in contrast are "spurious" or "unlinked" plans where prosecutor shows only that charged offense and prior acts are "similar and temporally proximate" without showing "common objective").

3. In abuse cases, proof that defendant also abused the victim's sibling is sometimes offered to show plan or design. Should it be admissible? Compare People v. Ewoldt, 867 P.2d 757 (Cal. 1994) (in trial of man for sexual assaults against wife's daughter *J* over three years, when she was 11-14 years old, admitting proof of other acts with *J* and her sister *N*; acts may prove common design or plan if "similar" to charged offense even if not part of "single, continuing conception or plot") with Government of Virgin Islands v. Pinney, 967 F.2d 912, 916-917 (3d Cir. 1992) (in trial for rape of seven-year-old girl in apartment, error to admit evidence that seven years earlier defendant raped victim's older sister in same apartment; insufficient temporal connection to show "common plan"). How about admitting proof of sexual misconduct toward others in the extended family? See State v. Wermerskirchen, 497 N.W.2d 235 (Minn. 1993) (in trial for sexual abuse of eight-year-old daughter, admitting proof that defendant abused 12-year-old stepdaughter *and* engaged in sexual touching and conversation with nieces years earlier, to show "design or intent" and "opportunistic fondling of young girls within the family context").

e. *Other Purposes*

■ PROBLEM 5-I. "It Was an Accident"

Late one night three-year-old Tim Valence was brought to the emergency room by his mother Donna. He was unconscious and suffering from head injuries and broken ribs. Despite best efforts of the hospital staff, he died the next day. Donna claimed Tim's injuries resulted from a fall down the stairs at home, but the treating doctor suspected abuse and notified police. After investigation, Donna was indicted for manslaughter.

At trial, to show that the injuries probably weren't accidental, the prosecutor offers evidence of two incidents in the last year: In both, Donna brought Tim to the hospital, once with broken bones and once with a concussion. Both times she said the injuries resulted from accidents. Admissible? What if such things had happened five times? Would it make a difference whether a doctor familiar with the injuries thought they were caused by abuse? Whether Donna or someone else was with Tim at the time?

■ NOTES ON OTHER USES OF PRIOR CRIMES EVIDENCE

1. Increasing concern to catch and punish child abuses has led courts to admit proof of previous abuse. One problem is that a doctor usually can't say who inflicted the injuries or when or how they happened. Often, however, circumstances indicate that one or another adult-in-charge must be the source or must at least know of the child's condition, and sometimes the nature or extent of injuries suggests that they must have been intentionally inflicted. See Estelle v. McGuire, 502 U.S. 62 (1991) (rejecting due process challenge to state conviction of father for murdering six-month-old daughter Tori; court admitted evidence that she had rectal tearing and fractured ribs; there was no proof that defendant caused the injuries, but evidence suggested that Tori died at hands of another, not by accident, and that the injuries must have been intentionally inflicted) (defendant and wife were her caretakers). The term "battered child syndrome" has come to mean a string of suspicious injuries, and it is also used to describe behavior patterns in children who suffer repeated sexual or physical abuse (see Chapter 9C2b, infra).

2. In cases like this one, where we have neither a confession nor a conviction, determining what happened before takes some doing. As we saw in Problem 5-G ("He Came Running in All Hunched Over"), proving the prior acts may require a "mini-trial" which raises procedural issues that we examine next (section A4f, infra).

3. Often proof of other acts is admitted to provide context of the charged crime, so it can be better understood. The problem is to draw a line between additional crimes that actually help broader understanding and other crimes that just paint defendant as a bad person. For a vivid example of a decision that approved proof of some additional crimes and disapproved proof of others, see United States v. Miller, 508 F.2d 444, 449 (7th Cir. 1974) (five defendants were charged with transporting a stolen Chevrolet; court could admit proof that they disarmed police and stole a police car trying to escape, but not proof that several defendants then kidnapped officer and towtruck driver).

4. Beyond the uses listed in FRE 404(b) are others that are not mentioned (the list is exemplary rather than exhaustive). Common but not on the list is the use of other acts to show motive and opportunity (which can mean skill or capacity). See United States v. Palmer, 809 F.2d 1504, 1505 (11th Cir. 1987) (in tax evasion case, admitting proof that defendant trafficked in drugs to show motive in using currency and not keeping records); United States v. Maravilla, 907 F.2d 216, 222 (1st Cir. 1990) (as proof that defendant "had the ability" to get victim through customs, admitting evidence that he did it before).

f. Proving Prior Acts

You have looked at examples of acts that can be proved under FRE 404(b)—acts suggesting things like intent, modus operandi, or plan. When the proponent (usually we mean the prosecutor) offers proof of such acts, the court must decide whether it is relevant in some permissible way and whether probative worth is outweighed by the risk of unfair prejudice. Relevant in some permissible way means relevant in some way *other than* proving character, hence action in conformity with character (forbidden propensity inference). Usually the prior acts are crimes, and inevitably proving crimes has prejudicial effect in suggesting that defendant is a bad actor generally, raising the possibility that the jury will draw the propensity inference, or will become angry and distracted, or conclude that defendant should go to jail for whatever else he has done, regardless whether he committed the charged crime. Thus evidence offered for a permissible purpose under FRE 404(b) is subject to possible exclusion under FRE 403.

Several questions remain: Who decides whether defendant committed the prior act, judge or jury? What standard of proof applies, preponderance or some higher standard, like clear and convincing or proof beyond reasonable doubt? If the prior act led to conviction, there is little room for dispute. If defendant confessed act, proof that he did so is likely to carry the day. If a police officer or other percipient witness testifies that he saw defendant commit the act, there may be a serious dispute, as defendant may deny having done it. Consider the following problem.

■ PROBLEM 5-J. "I Didn't Know They Were Stolen"

After his arrest for possession of 100 stolen iPad minis (market value of about $40,000), Huddleston is charged with knowingly receiving stolen property. At trial, the evidence shows that he was trying to sell them at less than cost, but he denies knowing that they were stolen. To refute this defense, the prosecutor offers testimony to the effect that Huddleston had been involved in selling stolen property before. The owner of a store is prepared to testify that he recently sold him 30 Apple Yosemite computers for $200 apiece (well below cost).

Huddleston objects under FRE 404 that this testimony is inadmissible character evidence that is only relevant if the jury interprets the act as proof that he is the kind of person who deals in stolen property, hence that he is guilty of the charged offense—the forbidden propensity inference. Huddleston also objects that the proof should be excluded as unfairly prejudicial under FRE 403.

Huddleston raises two additional points. First, he asserts that the court should exclude testimony by the shop owner unless the judge makes a preliminary finding under FRE 104(a) that the Yosemite computers were stolen and Huddleston knew it. Second, he argues that the prosecutor must prove these points by clear and convincing evidence. In response, the prosecutor argues that the question whether Huddleston sold them to the store owner is for the jury to decide and that the preponderance standard applies.

Who is right on these points, and why?

■ NOTES ON PROVING PRIOR ACTS

1. In Problem 5-J, everyone agrees that the court resolves "simple" relevancy issues: Is selling stolen computers relevant only because it supports the propensity inference, or is it also relevant in suggesting that Huddleston knew the iPad minis were stolen? (Most courts would say selling stolen computers does bear on knowledge that the iPad minis were stolen because dealers in stolen merchandise usually sell different kinds, and selling other stolen merchandise makes it more likely that Huddleston knew the iPad minis he sold this time were also stolen.) Everyone would also agree that the court resolves the question whether the proof is too prejudicial under FRE 403—whether the risk that the jury will make the forbidden propensity inference, or will become angry, or convict the defendant *not* because they he knowingly sold stolen iPad minis, but because they he should go to jail for selling Yosemite computers or because he's just "a bad apple." (Many courts would say these risks are *not* serious enough to exclude the evidence.)

2. In the *Huddleston* case, involving facts like those in Problem 5-J, the Supreme Court agreed with the prosecutor on the last two points raised by the defendant:

(a) The Rules do *not* require the court to make a "preliminary finding" that defendant committed the prior crime—that he knowingly sold stolen goods—before letting the store owner testify. These are questions for the jury under FRE 104(b) rather than for the court under FRE 104(a). In other words, whether Huddleston sold the stolen computers is *not* a matter of admissibility (which the judge decides), but a matter of conditional relevancy—whether a fact exists that is necessary for the relevance of the proffered evidence—and this point is for the jury under FRE 104(b). That is, the jury (not the court) decides whether defendant knowingly sold stolen Yosemite computers. The court still performs a "screening function," which entails insuring that prosecutor has evidence sufficient to support a jury finding that defendant sold the computers and knew they were stolen.

(b) The preponderance standard applies, so the prosecutor need not prove by "clear and convincing evidence" that defendant committed the prior acts, and certainly the prosecutor need not prove the point by proof beyond a reasonable doubt. See United States v. Huddleston, 485 U.S. 681 (1988).

3. *Huddleston* interprets the Federal Rules. It does not require states with similar rules to interpret them the same way. Some states follow the *Huddleston* approach while others reject it. Compare State v. Wheel, 587 A.2d 933, 943 (Vt. 1990) (adopting *Huddleston*) with People v. Garner, 806 P.2d 366, 370-374 (Colo. 1991) (rejecting *Huddleston;* court decides under FRE 104(a) whether prior crime occurred, applying preponderance standard). Some states take the most protective approach, making admissibility a question for the judge to decide by clear and convincing evidence. See, e.g., State v. Hernandez, 784 A.2d 1225, 1237-1238 (N.J. 2001); State v. Terrazas, 994 P.2d 1194 (Ariz. 1997).

4. *Huddleston* was a unanimous opinion, but many commentators and practitioners favor measures that would make it harder for prosecutors to prove other crimes. Consider these proposals: (1) amend FRE 404 to adopt the clear-and-convincing standard, see 120 F.R.D. 299, at 330 (1988) (American Bar Association); (2) amend FRE 404(b) to burden prosecutors with showing probative value outweighs prejudice, see Imwinkelried, The Need to Amend Federal Rule of Evidence 404(b): The Threat to the Future of the Federal Rules of Evidence, 30 Vill. L. Rev. 1465, 1497 (1985); (3) pay more attention to issues of fairness to the accused since the propensity argument cannot be effectively refuted even though it may not be right in any particular case, see Weissenberger, Making Sense of Extrinsic Act Evidence: Federal Rule of Evidence 404(b), 70 Iowa L. Rev. 607-611 (1985); (4) admit only acts that are distinguished by their "unusual nature" or "regular occurrence" so they really show "predisposition to behave in a similar fashion under similar circumstances," see Uviller, Evidence of Character to Prove Conduct: Illusion, Illogic, and Injustice in the Courtroom, 130 U. Pa. L. Rev. 845, 886-889 (1982).

5. What if defendant was charged but acquitted of a prior crime at trial? In the *Dowling* case, the Court approved testimony describing a crime leading to acquittal. *Dowling* was a trial for bank robbery in which the culprit wore a ski mask and carried a pistol. The court let Vena Henry testify that defendant and a man named Christian assaulted her at home two weeks later, when defendant was wearing a knit mask with cutout eyes and carrying a handgun (she could identify him because the man who assaulted her was unmasked in a struggle). Dowling had been acquitted of the assault, and in the bank robbery trial the government offered Henry's testimony to strengthen the identification of Dowling as the robber and link him with Christian (getaway driver). The Court held that acquittal of the assault did not block Henry's testimony under a concept of collateral estoppel, pointing out that the assault was not an ultimate issue in *both* the earlier case and the later one, and that *Huddleston* only requires the prosecutor to prove a prior crime by a preponderance. *Dowling* also rejected the argument that admitting Henry's testimony put defendant to the unfair burden of spending time and money relitigating points resolved before. See Dowling v. United States, 493 U.S. 342 (1990).

(a) *Dowling* is right in holding that acquittal on earlier charges is consistent with a later finding by a preponderance that defendant committed the earlier offense. Even if reformers throw out *Huddleston*, couldn't a later court find that Henry's testimony is clear and convincing evidence that Dowling committed the earlier offense?

(b) In a second prong, *Dowling* stressed that defendant failed to show that the acquittal proved that he was not one of the men involved in the assault (the jury might have agreed with his claim that the intruders were trying to retrieve money, not commit robbery), and declined to make the prosecutor prove this point. Even if the Court decided that collateral estoppel applies, the second prong of *Dowling* would still make things pretty hard on defendants because it is hard to know the basis for a jury verdict.

COMMENT/PERSPECTIVE: Ongoing Debate Over Character Evidence

As you will see when you look at the rape shield provision and Rules 413 and 414 on bad acts by defendants in sexual assault and child abuse trials, questions on the use of character evidence—particularly bad acts—are never put to rest. Broadly, there is the question whether character predicts human behavior (or how cogently it does), and some argue that situational considerations have more impact on behavioral choices, and that character has little if any predictive force. Some argue that persons with prior records are far more likely to be charged with new crimes, so in this skewed sample prior acts have no probative worth. Others argue that rules restricting proof of character are crucial in implementing the presumption of innocence, or that character evidence should be more readily admitted because the function of trials is not merely truth-finding, but catharsis. Still others stress that the main reason to exclude character evidence is that juries cannot appraise it and are prone to "attribution" error (to assume that traits or incidents tell more about behavior than they do in fact). Behind such arguments are debates over free will and the extent to which humans can shape their conduct, with philosophers like Aristotle and Kant stressing a greater role for free will in shaping character and conduct, and some like Freud arguing for a diminished role. Some European traditions embody a very different attitude from ours, as illustrated in the Camus novel The Stranger, where the prosecutor in a murder trial brings out that the defendant did not cry when his mother died, presumably indicating indifference toward others. For some of the better modern discussions, see Miguel A. Mendez, *Character Evidence Reconsidered: "People Do Not Seem to be Characters,"* 49 Hastings L.J. 871 (1998); David P. Leonard, *The Use of Character to Prove Conduct: Rationality and Catharsis in the Law of Evidence,* 38 U. Colo. L. Rev. 1 (1987); Roger Park, *Character at the Crossroads*, 49 Hastings. L.J. 717 (1998).

5. Character in Sex Offense Cases (Criminal and Civil)

a. Sexual History of Victim (Rape Shield Statutes)

Sex offense cases present a peculiarly difficult challenge for many reasons. The offense is serious, the punishment severe; the behavior is offensive and the psychological (and sometimes physical) injury to the victim may be serious; the charge is damaging to the defendant, and pressing the charge is stressful for the complainant; the subject of sex provokes strong emotions and gender-related reactions; often there are no "neutral" observers, and the complainant and defendant contradict each other, each having strong self-interested motivations.

Should past sexual conduct by the complaining witness be provable in such cases? Unfortunately, the common law tradition answered that question with an across-the-board yes, making women who brought rape charges fair game for cross-examination on their sexual behavior. This sorry sexist tradition had it that such cross-examination bore on both credibility and on the issue of consent. The underlying hypocrisy was exposed by the facts that such cross-examination was not thought to bear on credibility of women testifying elsewhere, and that in rape trials such questioning was permitted even where clinical evidence made any suggestion of consent ridiculous.

Against this backdrop, "rape shield" statutes were enacted everywhere. Congress did likewise by enacting FRE 412, which qualifies FRE 404(a)(2) by restricting the use of evidence relating to the sexual history of a sex crime victim.

That evidence of sexual behavior has no bearing on credibility standing by itself seems beyond dispute. That such evidence *often* has little or no bearing on the question whether a person consented to sex on a particular occasion seems also true. But it is not clear that such evidence is never relevant in sexual assault cases, and the operation of rape shield rules and statutes presents some difficulties. Rule 412 bars proof of the victim's "other sexual behavior" or "sexual predisposition" (meaning opinion or reputation testimony) in sexual assault prosecutions, with exceptions allowing (a) proof of specific instances to show that "someone other than the defendant" was responsible for "semen, injury, or other physical evidence," (b) proof of other "sexual behavior" with the accused to show consent (or "if offered by the prosecutor"), and (c) proof that that cannot constitutionally be excluded. Rule 412 also applies in civil cases, with important modifications. And Rule 412 requires a pretrial motion if proof of specific instances is to be offered, with the matter to be determined *in camera* and the record to be sealed.

Consider now the operation of Rule 412 in a "date rape" setting.

■ PROBLEM 5-K. Ordeal of Leslie or Fred

Leslie returns to her sorority sometime after midnight on Homecoming Saturday, earlier than most celebrants. She has been to a luau at the Beta Theta Sigma House, and a few of her more serious friends (who generally avoid such things) discover Leslie sometime later. She is in bed under the covers but not asleep, having taken off her coat and shoes but leaving the rest of her clothes on. She seems tense and sullen but flat in emotional affect and looks at her friends without expression.

Ultimately Leslie tells her roommate and a few others that she met a fellow named Fred at the luau. She says she met him several times in the previous summer while she worked at a pool as a lifeguard where he was a swimming instructor. She says she made the mistake of accepting Fred's offer of a ride home from the luau and that he took her to a lonely spot and made advances. At first she "didn't mind," but he "got completely out of hand" and finally raped her. Leslie is persuaded to go to the clinic, where she is clinically examined. Bruises are observed on her legs and forearms, and semen is found in her vagina.

As it turns out, Fred is an outsider (a casual acquaintance of Greg, one of the fraternity brothers) who had no business being at the luau. Fred is charged with rape. He pleads innocent. At his trial Fred claims that Leslie consented, and he testifies that he and Leslie had consensual sexual relations once during the previous summer. He also offers testimony by Greg that "Leslie is sexually very active" and "known as an easy mark." And he offers testimony by Thomas (another friend at Beta Theta Sigma) that *he* had sex with Leslie earlier that same night.

The prosecutor objects that the proffered testimony of Fred, Greg, and Thomas is "irrelevant" and "barred by the rape shield" law. Is the objection well taken on either ground? Spell out Fred's argument that the evidence is relevant and the prosecutor's response that it is not. *Should* such evidence be excluded?

■ NOTES ON EVIDENCE OF COMPLAINANT'S PRIOR SEXUAL CONDUCT IN CRIMINAL CASES

1. Does Rule 412 rest on relevancy or something else? What else? See Sandoval v. Acevedo, 996 F.2d 145, 149 (7th Cir. 1993) (Posner, J.) ("essential insight" of rape shield statute is that in post-Victorian age "in which most unmarried young women are sexually active," such activity on specific occasions "does not provide appreciable support for an inference that she *consented* to engage in this activity with the defendant").

2. Is defendant constitutionally entitled to prove the victim's sexual history when it suggests a motive for making a false charge? See Olden v. Kentucky, 488 U.S. 227 (1988) (error to refuse to let defendant ask complainant whether she claimed rape in order to preserve relationship with boyfriend with whom she was living) (reversing); Commonwealth v. Black, 487 A.2d 396 (Pa. Super. Ct. 1985) (unconstitutional to exclude proof of victim's incestuous relationship with brother, which might show complainant's "bias, interest or prejudice" against defendant father for stopping relationship). It is *Olden* and similar cases that the framers had in mind in including the exception in FRE 412(b)(1)(C) for "evidence whose exclusion would violate the defendant's constitutional rights." Suppose the prosecutor presents an alleged rape victim as being so naïve or inexperienced that she would not likely make a false accusation? See State v. Jacques, 558 A.2d 706, 708 (Me. 1989) (as a constitutional matter, defendant must be allowed "to rebut the inference that a jury might otherwise draw that the victim was so naïve sexually that she could not have fabricated the charge").

3. If defendant is charged with attempted rape, can he introduce evidence that he had been told beforehand that the woman would say no but mean yes? Is such proof the same thing as proof of "sexual behavior" or "predisposition" under FRE 412, or is it something else? See Doe v. United States, 666 F.2d 43, 46-48 (4th Cir. 1981) (court could *not* say that "extraordinary circumstances will never justify admission of [reputation and opinion] evidence to preserve a defendant's constitutional rights") (approving evidence of defendant's "state of mind as a result of what he knew of her reputation").

4. What if the defense wants to ask the complaining witness whether she previously charged someone with sexual assault, but the charge was false? As you will see in Chapter 8 (Impeachment of Witnesses), a party may ask a witness about making false statements of a serious sort, although the applicable rule (FRE 608(b)) does not let the attacking party prove such statements by calling other witnesses. (The theory in allowing the attack is that prior falsehoods suggest that the witness is by disposition untruthful.) So we are led to the following question: Does FRE 412 apply where the lawyer for the defendant asks the complaining witness whether she brought prior false charges of sexual assault? The ACN says FRE 412 does not apply to proof of "allegedly false claims" by complaining witnesses, but it seems that FRE 412 is implicated where false charges suggest sexual conduct, as happens if they describe what is usually called "date rape" (if such charges are false, they suggest sexual behavior). The matter is complicated because the defense is not trying to prove sexual acts, but *lies* that may relate to sexual acts.

(a) Courts have been cautious rather than rigid. The Rule leaves some leeway to conclude that questioning about false statements does *not* unduly compromise the protective policy because the focus is on the statement and its falsity, not on whatever underlying acts led to the statement. Compare State v. Guenther, 854 A.2d 308 (N.J. 2004) (setting out guidelines; remanding for court to determine whether charges were false) with State v. Dixon, 147 P.3d 991 (Wash. 2006) (excluding statement by child victim asking her aunt "what do I do if I'm lying?" because defense did not show she was speaking of the event that led to the present prosecution).

(b) Perhaps equally important, courts sometimes conclude that the Constitution entitles defendants to explore these matters. See United States v. Bartlett, 856 F.2d 1071, 1088 (8th Cir. 1988) (defendant has qualified constitutional right to offer evidence of prior false accusations by rape victim to show bias, prejudice, or ulterior motive, but not to attack general credibility of victim) (no violation to exclude here).

(c) Often the critical question is whether defendant has shown that prior charges were indeed false. Is it enough that prosecution was declined or the charges dismissed? See Hughes v. Raines, 641 F.2d 790, 792 (9th Cir. 1981) (failure to prosecute does not prove falsity of allegations). What if charges led to acquittal? See State v. Schwartzmiller, 685 P.2d 830, 833 (Idaho 1984) (acquittal "can never be taken to establish that the charges brought were based on false accusations"). What if complainant recanted earlier charges? See State v. Le Clair, 730 P.2d 609 (Or. 1986) (recantation is enough to establish falsity).

(d) These attacks on the credibility of the complaining witness raise the question whether it is the judge or the jury that decides whether the charges were false. In general, questioners who challenge witnesses by asking about false statements must have a good faith basis, but it is up to the jury to decide whether the witness spoke falsely as the question suggests. In sexual assault and abuse cases, this relaxed standard can be seen as compromising the protections of FRE 412. Most courts say judges decide under FRE 104(a) whether charges were false, and require the questioner to have more than a good faith basis, although some jurisdictions have no special rule. Compare State v. West,

24 P.3d 648, 652-655 (Haw. 2001) (judge decides whether prior charges were false) with State v. Smith, 743 So. 2d 199, 202 (La. 1999) (question is whether "reasonable jurors could find" prior charges were false).

5. If a male defendant is charged with sexual assault against another male, should rape-shield rules or statutes block proof that the complainant is homosexual, offered in support of the claim of consent? See generally Peter Nicholas, "They Say He's Gay": The Admissibility of Evidence of Sexual Orientation, 37 Ga. L. Rev. 793, 821 (2003) (reporting that most states hold that rape shield legislation blocks such proof).

6. FRE 412 requires written notice 14 days before trial, to be served on the other side (usually defendant is the moving party, and the other side is the prosecutor) and on the complaining witness, if proof covered by the Rule is to be offered. In any such hearing, the court must decide whether Rule 412 bars the proof or whether it fits one of the exceptions, and in the latter case the court may have to resolve further questions relating to probative worth, prejudice, and confusion of issues under FRE 403. Hearings of this kind are normally held *in camera* and out of public view. See State v. Bashaw, 672 P.2d 48, 49 n.3 (Or. 1983) (rape shield rule entails "a closed hearing"). If a court rules that evidence of prior sexual conduct by the complainant is admissible, at least some decisions allow her to appeal, even though she is not a party. See Doe v. United States, 666 F.2d 43, 46 (4th Cir. 1981) (allowing interlocutory appeal by complainant).

■ PROBLEM 5-L. Acting Out on the Assembly Line

Rita Haines works on the assembly line at Danmore Tractor Company. Most of the people she works with are men, although the number of women on the line is now approaching one-in-five.

In federal court, Haines sues Danmore and her supervisor Sam Torgenson, alleging sexual harassment. (Federal law affords relief against employers and others in the work force for sexual harassment, which can include hostile work environment. Whether employers are liable is affected by steps that they take—or don't take—in addressing problems through policies, enforcement, and response to complaints. To prevail, claimant must show that she personally found the conduct hostile, abusive, or offensive, and that a reasonable person in her position would react that way.) Haines alleges that she was regularly forced to endure unwanted sexual innuendo directed at her personally, that fellow-workers made comments about her appearance and figure, that Torgenson propositioned her in the presence of others, that she had to listen to stories about sexual encounters and adventures, and that pornography sometimes appeared in the lunchroom.

At trial, Danmore offers proof that (1) on weekends Rita works occasionally as an exotic dancer in a local club, (2) she sometimes reports to work in a mini-skirt and a tight blouse (although she changes to work clothes before starting her shift on the line), (3) she told at least one sexually explicit story in the lunchroom that apparently rested on some kind of personal experience, and (4) Rita made sexually suggestive remarks on several occasions to two of the men on the line.

Haines's lawyer objects to all of these items of proof, invoking FRE 412. How should the court rule, and why?

■ NOTES ON EVIDENCE OF COMPLAINANT'S PRIOR SEXUAL CONDUCT IN CIVIL CASES

1. Rule 412 applies in the context of Problem 5-L (the Court rejected an amendment extending the Rule to civil cases, but Congress amended the Rule in 1994). Note that in civil cases a court may admit proof of the victim's "sexual behavior" (specific acts) or "sexual predisposition" (opinion testimony) only if probative value "substantially outweighs" prejudice to parties or "the danger of harm to any victim"—a "reverse 403" standard weighted in favor of excluding rather than admitting evidence and extended to include consideration of harm to victims (whether or not they are parties). And reputation testimony is admissible "only if the victim has placed it in controversy."

2. Courts construe FRE 412 broadly. Obviously it reaches sexual acts and disposition ("consensual relations," being "sexually very active"), as illustrated by the testimony offered in Problem 5-K (Ordeal of Leslie or Fred). Less obviously, most courts extend the protective provisions much further. See generally Mueller & Kirkpatrick, Federal Evidence §4:78 (4th ed. 2013) (rule reaches "mode of dress, marital status or history, living arrangements where these imply something about sexual intimacy, sexual tastes or practices, sexual innuendo, flirting, propositions or offers, viewing or enjoyment of pornography (or collecting it or subscribing to internet services), participating in making pornography," and also such things as "employment as an exotic dancer or in some other aspect of the 'sex industry'").

3. Does proof that Rita made sexually suggestive remarks in the workplace bear on whether she was offended by "unwanted sexual innuendo directed at her personally"? See Wilson v. City of Des Moines, 442 F.3d 637, 643 (8th Cir. 2006) (admitting evidence that claimant used "sexually explicit language and behavior," that she "talked about vibrators and men's sex organs," amounting to "sexually charged comments" and "lewd, rude and unlady-like language" to show that she "might have welcomed the alleged harassment") (no violation of FRE 412).

b. Prior Offenses by Defendants in Sex Crime and Abuse Trials, and Civil Suits

In 1994, Congress enacted three provisions (FRE 413-415) inviting prosecutors to prove sexual assault or child molestation by proof that defendant assaulted or molested others, and paving the way to introduce such evidence in civil suits arising out of sexual assaults or child molestation. These sparked controversy and were delayed, but they took effect in 1995. Few sexual assault or molestation cases are tried in federal court, but they are if they arise in federal enclaves like national parks, military bases, and Indian Reservations. (Offenses committed on military bases by military personnel are tried in military courts under the Military Rules of Evidence.) In large measure, FRE 413-415 were enacted as examples for states to adopt as part of their own Rules.

FRE 413-415 was part of a politically charged crime bill, added at the last minute in a Conference Committee to win votes in the House. These provisions did not go through the rulemaking processes, and reaction was mixed. See Duane, The New Federal Rules of Evidence on Prior Acts of Accused Sex Offenders: A Poorly Drafted Version of a Very Bad Idea, 157 F.R.D. 95 (1994) (strongly criticizing these provisions). But see Cassell & Strassberg, Evidence of Repeated Acts of Rape and Child Molestation: Reforming Utah Law to Permit the Propensity Inference, 1998 Utah L. Rev. 145 (favoring generous rule of admissibility for prior rapes and child abuse); Park, The Crime Bill of 1994 and the Law of Character Evidence: Congress Was Right About Consent Cases, 22 Fordham Urban L.J. 271 (1995) (supporting FRE 413-415 where defense claims consent).

The Advisory Committees of the Judicial Conference opposed the new provisions, as did the Standing Committee. In its report, the Conference urged Congress to reconsider FRE 413-415. Even the ABA House of Delegates opposed them.

Consider these provisions. Briefly, FRE 413 provides that in sexual assault trials the court "may admit" evidence that defendant committed another "sexual assault." In parallel language, FRE 414 provides that in child abuse trials the court "may admit" evidence that defendant committed another "child molestation." Recall that FRE 404(b) bars the general propensity inference (can't use acts to show "character" in order to show acts "in accordance" with character). But FRE 404(b) allows use of other acts to prove particular points (intent, knowledge, and so forth). Note that FRE 413 and 414 contain no restriction against this general propensity inference, allowing such proof to be considered "on any matter to which it is relevant," thus discarding the bar against the general propensity inference in this setting.

FRE 415 extends FRE 413 and 414 to civil cases involving sexual assault or child molestation. Recall that in *criminal* cases defendants may seek acquittal by offering proof of good character under FRE 404(a)(2)(A), but this provision does not apply in civil cases. Since FRE 415 paves the way to proving defendant's bad character in these kinds of civil cases, shouldn't we *also* let defendant offer proof of his *good* character? Should we even do it when the claimant *does not* offer prove prior offenses? In criminal cases, we let would let defendants offer such proof.

As part of the compromise that produced these provisions, Congress invited the Judicial Conference to make alternative recommendations. The Conference did so, in the form of a suggested amendment to FRE 404(b) that would have allowed *some* use of prior assaults or child molestation, but with criteria directing courts to consider such factors as proximity in time between prior and charged offense, degree of resemblance, frequency of other acts, and so forth. Congress ignored this proposal.

■ PROBLEM 5-M. "I Told Him to Stop"

In his federal trial for the alleged rape of Karin on Fort Linden Air Force Base at 1:30 A.M. on Sunday, Craig claims consent. He is 32 years old, and works at Fort Linden as a civilian avionics technician and instructor. He resides in an apartment in town. Karin is a 27-year-old Air Force enlisted woman in the avionics training program. She is enrolled in a course that Craig teaches, and lives in women's barracks on Fort Linden.

Government proof shows that Craig and Karin met at the Aero Squad Bar, located in town. While there, Karin and Craig drank gin and tonics for several hours. Karin had come to the bar with other women from the base, but they left on the understanding that Craig would drive her back to Fort Linden.

Karin testified that on arriving at the base Craig suggested that they "go up the hill" to a secluded area of trees and grass that served as a picnic ground for base personnel. The two sat on a blanket that Craig produced from his trunk and continued to drink gin from a pint bottle he had bought at the package store before leaving the Aero Squad. Karin testified that Craig "put his arm around me and we kissed," but that she "physically resisted" when "he began touching me through my blouse and started to unbutton my blouse and skirt." She continued, "I told him to stop and that I didn't want to have sex with him tonight," but he "kept pressing himself against me and trying to reach up my blouse which had come untucked," until "I finally stood up and told him I was going to walk back to the barracks, and I proceeded to run as fast as I could." At that point, according to Karin, Craig dragged her back to the blanket, where he held her arms down with his knees, ripped off her clothes, and raped her.

On cross, Craig's lawyer tries to get Karin to admit she was "laughing and responding in kind" when Craig kissed her, and wasn't "resisting in any way" and in fact "co-operated in taking off" her clothes. Karin agrees that they were "laughing at first" and that she kissed him, and even helped unfasten her blouse and bra because she was "afraid he was going to rip the fabric," but she emphatically denies "helping him take my skirt off," and denies "cooperating when he raped me," saying she "told him to stop" and "tried to get him off me, but he was too heavy, and held my arms down."

Anticipating Craig's testimony, the government proposes two further proofs that what happened was rape rather than consensual sex:

First, the prosecutor calls Laura. In aid of an offer of proof, she testifies outside the jury's hearing that she "dated Craig for several weeks" a year earlier while they were living in another state, and that once when they returned to her apartment after a movie, Craig "tried to rape me." She "made the mistake" of letting him touch her, and he "kept coming on after I told him to stop," and "tried to rape me," except that she "screamed and kicked him in the privates" so hard that he "cried out in pain" and ran away.

Second, the prosecutor offers a certified copy of a judgment of conviction for sexual assault on a minor obtained against Craig in another state three years earlier. The victim was 13-year-old *N*, daughter of a woman named Rita, with whom Craig was living in a trailer at the time. The record indicates that Craig encouraged *N* to drink beer one afternoon while Rita was at work, that they then played strip poker, and that Craig fondled and sodomized *N*. He served a year in prison and was on probation at the time of the charged offense at Fort Linden.

Counsel for Craig objects to these proofs:

> Laura's testimony and the prior conviction amount to character assassination. Her story cannot be admitted to prove intent or modus operandi because it's too dissimilar from what supposedly happened at Fort Linden between Craig and Karin. And the conviction for abusing *N* shows acts of a totally different nature that cannot be relevant in any way to what the government claims here. If this evidence is admitted, the jury will be invited to convict the defendant just because it thinks Craig is "that sort of person." These proofs will inflame the jury, inviting it to convict Craig out of anger at what he may have done before, which is classic unfair prejudice.

How should the court rule on this objection under FRE 413 and FRE 403, and why?

■ NOTES ON PROVING DEFENDANT'S PRIOR SEXUAL CONDUCT IN TRIALS FOR SEXUAL ASSAULT AND CHILD ABUSE

1. If Craig did what Laura says, it was probably a crime of "abusive sexual contact" under 18 USC §2244 (in chapter 109A of title 18, to which FRE 413 refers). What Craig was convicted of doing to *N* was "sexual abuse of a minor" under 18 USC §2243 (another provision in chapter 109A of title 18). Does FRE 413 mean these instances of Craig's conduct may be considered as proof that he raped Karin?

2. Proof of other offenses fitting FRE 413 may be excluded under FRE 403 for unfair prejudice. Theoretically relevancy is one thing, prejudice another. But sometimes the two seem to meet. Compare Blind-Doan v. Sanders, 291 F.3d 1079 (9th Cir. 2002) (in suit by prisoner alleging that jailer sexually abused her, court should have admitted testimony by 17 others describing relevant acts; court may exclude under FRE 403, and may consider "similarity of the prior acts to the acts charged," but judge did not say how he "evaluated the factors," and some excluded testimony answered claim that defendant would not have abused plaintiff because presence of a witness deprived him of opportunity) (reversing judgment for defendant) with Johnson v. Elk Lake School District, 283 F.3d 138, 155 (3rd Cir. 2002) (in suit alleging sexual harassment of student by guidance counselor *S*, excluding testimony by former colleague *R* that *S* touched *R*'s crotch while lifting her onto his shoulders; *R* was "equivocal" on whether touching was intentional, and differences between "bizarre incident" with *R* and misconduct in issue was such that "dissimilarities reduced significantly the probative value") (FRE 403 applies).

3. Does the episode with Laura suggest that Craig raped Karin? If so, is that because it suggests that Craig is "that sort of person"? The general propensity inference allowed by FRE 413 is sometimes labeled the "lustful disposition" doctrine. See E. Imwinkelried, Uncharged Misconduct §§4.11-4.16 (1994); Reed, Reading Gaol Revisited: Admission of Uncharged Misconduct Evidence in Sex Offender Cases, 21 Am. J. Crim. L. 127 (1993) (describing this and other doctrines). States vary in their approach. See People v. Donoho, 788 N.E.2d 707, 716-717 (Ill. 2003) (four states added a propensity exception in sexual offense cases by statute or court rule, but 25 others recognize an exception to the bar against proving other offenses when they show lustful disposition or tendency toward sexual predation; some states limit doctrine to cases involving same victim, or where victim is a minor, or incest cases).

4. In sexual assault trials, is admitting proof of defendant's character or propensity to engage in sexual assaults a good thing? Should we admit it because otherwise it is so often "her word against his"? Because such a disposition is a reliable predictor of behavior? Is it true that lots of men who commit one or two rapes commit more rapes, but that only a few men who commit one or two robberies commit more robberies? See E. Imwinkelried, Uncharged Misconduct §4.16 (1994) (recidivism is *not* higher among those convicted of sexual assault than among those convicted of other crimes).

5. Suppose Craig calls others working at Fort Linden who frequent the Aero Squad, and five of them would testify that "Karin is a regular" who is often seen "arriving alone or with women friends and departing with a man she met there." Suppose each of two men would testify that he "picked up Karin at the Aero Squad," that he had "never met her before," and that he had "consensual sex with her." Under FRE 412, such testimony would not be admitted in support of Craig's claim of consent. Is it right to admit proof of sexual *misconduct* by the accused but not sexual *conduct* by the complaining witness? Consider Bryden & Park, "Other Crimes" Evidence in Sex Offense Cases, 78 Minn. L. Rev. 529, 568 (1994) (favoring admissibility of offenses by the accused in acquaintance rape cases; rape shield law excluding sexual history of the complainant "does not conflict with admission of evidence of the rape defendant's prior crimes").

6. Rule 413 does not require *convictions.* Should the judge in Problem 5-M determine that Laura's account proves sexual assault? This question is one of admissibility under FRE 104(a), and the jury would be excused during such an inquiry under FRE 104(c). Craig must have a chance to refute Laura's account. If he testifies, can the prosecutor cross-examine about what happened with Karin? See FRE 104(d) (testifying on a preliminary question does not open the accused to "cross-examination on other issues"). It seems that the judge must decide whether Laura's account shows a sexual assault by looking to the law of the state where they were. If Craig testifies that he didn't do what Laura says, should the judge decide the point under FRE 104(a), or must the question go to the jury under FRE 104(b)? See Johnson v. Elk Lake School District, 283 F.3d 138, 153 (3rd Cir. 2002) (jury decides) (court reluctantly follows *Huddleston*).

B HABIT AND ROUTINE PRACTICE

In contrast to "character" evidence, proof of personal habit is freely admitted. Indeed, Rule 406 stands out in Article IV in stating a rule of admissibility rather than limits. In fact Rule 406 *rejects* limits by providing that habit may be proved in order to show conduct whether "corroborated" or not and regardless whether there was any eyewitness. The same liberality extends to proof of the "routine practice" of an organization.

Why do we see such a difference—why do we give the cold shoulder to proof of character while being cordial toward habit evidence? Partly the answer lies in the moral overtones of the former and neutral quality of the latter. Partly it lies in the conviction that habit is simply more probative of conduct.

How should we distinguish between character and habit? Consider these attempts:

> "Character" is a generalized description of one's disposition in respect to a general trait such as honesty, temperance, or carefulness, while "habit" is more specific. The latter designates a regular practice of meeting a particular kind of situation with a certain type of conduct, or a reflex behavior in a specific set of circumstances. Evidence of habit or custom is relevant to an issue of behavior on a specific occasion because it tends to prove that the behavior on such occasion conformed to the habit or custom.

Frase v. Henry, 444 F.2d 1228, 1232 (10th Cir. 1971).

> [Habit] denotes one's regular response to a repeated situation. If we speak of a character for care, we think of the person's tendency to act prudently in all the varying situations of life—in business, at home, in handling automobiles and in walking across the street. A habit, on the other hand, is a person's regular practice of responding to a particular kind of situation with a specific type of conduct. Thus, a person may be in the habit of bounding down a certain stairway two or three steps at a time, of patronizing a particular pub after each day's work, or of driving his automobile without using a seatbelt. The doing of the habitual act may become semi-automatic, as with a driver who invariably signals before changing lanes.

McCormick, Evidence §195 (K. Broun ed., 7th ed. 2014).

> Why is such a sharp distinction drawn between habit and character evidence? The main reason is that habit describes particular behavior in a specific setting, and it is by nature at least regular if not invariable, so it has greater probative value in proving conduct on a particular occasion than does evidence of more general propensities. Also habit evidence is less likely to carry moral overtones or to present serious dangers of unfair prejudice or confusion.

2 Mueller & Kirkpatrick, Federal Evidence §4:46 (4th ed. 2013).

Usually habit evidence is offered in civil negligence cases, but occasionally it appears in criminal cases as well. See Derring v. State, 619 S.W.2d 644, 646-647 (Ark. 1981) (in murder trial, where body was never found, admitting proof that victim was "very dependable in his routine, kept a fairly rigid schedule, always had breakfast with the same person each day, attended school regularly, had no bad habits, and returned home to his apartment at the same time each evening," to prove he did not disappear on his own).

■ PROBLEM 5-N. Death on the Highway

Lance Teel and his wife Judy were driving westbound on Highway 46 when they collided with a car driven by Paul Finney, in which his wife Lena was a passenger. All four were killed, and no eyewitness saw the accident. The cars collided at the intersection of the highway and a county road, and the patrolman who examined the scene concluded that the Finney vehicle was entering the highway from the north and was in the process of turning left (eastward) when it was struck. The accident occurred at 8:00 A.M. on a cool cloudy gray September morning, when visibility was only about one-quarter of a mile.

The Teel estate sues the Finney estate for wrongful death. The patrolman testifies about the scene, and the court allows him to give his opinion as an expert in accident reconstruction on the probable speed and positions of the cars at the time of impact.

Because the accident looked like one that could happen only if one of the two drivers was at fault, and because there was no direct proof on this point, the Teel estate seeks to prove that Lance Teel was exercising due care. It calls witnesses Budge and Frese, who are prepared to testify that Lance Teel was "a good, careful driver." The Finney estate objects that the proffered evidence "is just proof of character, which cannot be admitted to show conduct on a particular occasion."

How should the court rule, and why?

■ PROBLEM 5-O. The Burning Sofa

Evan Girard co-owned and shared a house with Matt Rollins that caught fire and burned. The blaze took the life of Rollins, whose body was found in the laundry room near the back door. Rollins had been a successful developer of computer software, and had recently sold patent rights for more than $2 million. Girard sues the Rollins Estate to recover the value of Girard's interest in the house and the value of lost possessions.

An expert fire investigator testified that the blaze started in the den. The investigator was sure that the origin was not an electrical short, but he could not pinpoint the cause. Another expert testified on the basis of an autopsy that Rollins had a blood alcohol content of .15, which would have caused significant physical and mental impairment.

Girard thinks Rollins was a binge drinker who, when intoxicated, tended to smoke and fall asleep. The theory of the suit is that the fire started when Rollins drank too much, lit a cigarette, and passed out on the sofa in the den. The untended cigarette caught the sofa on fire, which led to the blaze that damaged the house. Rollins was trying to get out the back door when he succumbed to the smoke and later died from smoke inhalation.

Girard himself wants to testify to Rollins's drinking and smoking. If allowed, he would testify that Rollins was an episodic binge drinker who was usually functional, but would sometimes drink and smoke a lot—in the year before his death often "lapsing into unconsciousness" while drinking and smoking. These episodes led to four or five incidents in which his cigarette burned holes in the rug or scarred the furniture.

The defense objects that the proffered testimony is "barred by the rule against character evidence," but plaintiff's lawyer argues that Girard's account should be admitted as "evidence of habit under FRE 406." How should the court rule, and why?

■ NOTES ON HABIT EVIDENCE IN NEGLIGENCE CASES

1. The commentators quoted above describe habit as "reflex behavior" that is "semi-automatic" or "mechanistic." In Problem 5-N, can testimony that Teel was "a good, careful driver" be described that way? Or is it just character evidence, as the defense claims? Consider further description that Budge and Frese might provide about Lance Teel's driving habits. See Barton v. Plaisted, 256 A.2d 642, 647 (N.H. 1969) (admitting testimony on decedent's "customary driving speed over a period of years, along the 'flat' leading southerly into the curve where the accident occurred," as proof that his car crossed the center stripe there).

2. In Problem 5-O, should Girard be allowed to testify that Rollins habitually smoked while drinking? If he can say only that Rollins "occasionally" smoked a lot when drinking, that hardly seems to show habit, but testimony that Rollins "regularly" or "often" smoked while drinking would seem sufficient. See Henry v. Cline, 626 S.W.2d 958 (Ark. 1982) (excluding testimony that defendant drove this road "a dozen times" and "was speeding half of those times," which was "not sufficient to establish a mode of behavior that has become nearly or completely involuntary"). Does the judge decide such points under FRE 104(a), or let the jury decide under FRE 104(b)?

3. Litigants often invoke the rule allowing habit evidence in cases raising questions of negligence in driving. Probably wearing (or not wearing) a seatbelt counts as habit, see Sharpe v. Bestop, 730 A.2d 285 (N.J. 1999) (admitting proof of plaintiff's "habitual disregard" of warnings to wear seatbelts, but excluding proof of "occasional disregard of warnings not to drink and drive"), but getting lots of speeding tickets probably does not, see Hudelson v. Delta International Machinery Corp., 127 P.3d 147 (Idaho 2005) (excluding proof that defendant had stopsign and speeding violations in one year, two more the next year, and two more in the next two years) (these did not show habit of speeding).

4. Usually courts say violence toward others cannot be habit. Violence has to be consciously chosen behavior, doesn't it? Compare State v. Cotty, 899 A.2d 482 (R.I. 2006) (in murder trial, excluding 37 reports on encounters between victim and police, five involving drunken and aggressive behavior, which did not "rise to the level of semiautomatic conduct" or show habit of being violent when drunk) and State v. Brown, 543 S.E.2d 552 (S.C. 2001) (in trial of *B* for murdering nephew, proof that he became violent when angry was not habit) with State v. Huerta, 947 P.2d 483, 490 (Mont. 1997) (in trial of boyfriend of victim's mother, evidence that *she* regularly abused child, offered to show she caused his injuries, was habit) (can exclude under FRE 403). How about carrying a gun? See Ware v. State, 759 A.2d 764, 777 (Md. 2000) (Yes, can be habit).

5. If a pedestrian often crosses a certain street, evidence that she stays in a crosswalk can be habit. See Charmley v. Lewis, 729 P.2d 567, 570 (Or. 1986) (it tended to prove her "specific response to going to the grocery store"); Glatt v. Feist, 156 N.W.2d 819, 828 (N.D. 1968) (approving testimony that plaintiff "had been in the habit of crossing Main Street in returning from church at the point east of the crosswalk," to show that she was not in the crosswalk when struck by a car). If a young woman always tells friends or parents when leaving on a trip, does that qualify as habit? See State v. McKnight, 837 N.E.2d 315, 341 (Ohio 2005) (in murder trial, admitting testimony to this effect about victim, a 20-year-old woman who worked part time as waitress and was a college student; her repeated practice "became a semiautomatic form of behavior").

6. In Problem 5-O, we can be confident that Rollins was intoxicated when the fire started because we have blood alcohol content. If the blaze had consumed Rollins' body, could plaintiff prove Rollins had been drinking by describing his drinking "habits"? Unless the behavior resembles chronic alcoholism (basically drinking all the time), courts usually say No. Thus one court rejected an argument for habit based on four convictions for public intoxication in three and one-half years, see Reyes v. Missouri Pacific Ry., 589 F.2d 791, 794 (5th Cir. 1979). Suppose the question was whether Rollins had been drinking at work, and there was testimony that he routinely carries a cooler of beer in his car and drinks on the job, to the point of generating complaints from customers or colleagues. See Loughan v. Firestone Tire & Rubber Co., 749 F.2d 1519, 1523-1524 (11th Cir. 1985) (admit). But see generally Donald v. Triple S. Well Service, Inc., 708 So. 2d 1318 (Miss. 1998) (canvassing cases and counseling caution).

■ PROBLEM 5-P. Was He Served?

Manuel Gutierrez is charged with illegal entry after previous deportation. At trial, the government must prove that he was served a warrant of deportation and a letter in his native language warning him of the penalties of reentry.

As part of its proof, the government calls Agent Lesher, of the Immigration and Naturalization Service (INS). Lesher himself did not serve Gutierrez, nor did he ever serve deportation warrants. But he has worked for INS in a variety of positions for 12 years, serving on traffic check, line watch, and as warrant officer. If permitted, he would describe procedures followed by officers in carrying out deportations and the preparation and service of the forms. He would testify that normally an immigration officer picks up the "deportee," fills in blanks on the back of the warrant, signs it as witness, obtains the right thumb print of the deportee on the back, and hands him the letter and a copy of the warrant. In this case, no signature appears on the warrant, although it is otherwise filled out and has defendant's thumb print.

During defense voir dire, Agent Lesher testifies that he has never executed such a warrant and his knowledge of the procedures comes from "what I have been told by detention officers" and from knowing "normal rules and processes of deportation."

Defendant then objects that Agent Lesher's testimony cannot establish service in this case. Should Lesher be permitted to testify?

Allow testimony.
On cross – holes in his knowledge

NOTES ON ORGANIZATIONAL CUSTOM AND PRACTICE

1. Should proof of organizational routine (like serving warrants) be more readily admitted than proof of personal habit (like manner of driving or smoking while drinking)? There are workplace pressures that tend to insure regular compliance with "standard operating procedures," are there not? But there is something to be said for the regularity of personal habits too, isn't there, such as their being unconsciously repeated? Problem 5-P presents a new issue, which is that workplace routines may be learned by "what is said around the office" even more than they are learned by personal observation. Should "what is said around the office" be good enough as a basis for testimony?

2. If the question is whether a physician or dentist warned her patient of the hazards of a dental or medical procedure, should we admit evidence that she always gives such warnings? Does such proof show "habit," or is it "routine practice" of an organization? See Arthur v. Zearley, 292 S.W.2d 67 (Ark. 1999) (testimony by doctor about "what he told all of his patients" during informed consent conference qualified as "habit and routine") (but patients could testify that he did not warn them). See also Borley Storage and Transfer Co., Inc. v. Whitted, 710 N.W.2d 71, 83 (Neb. 2006) (in malpractice suit, lawyer could testify that he drafted documents and followed "a procedure or checklist" in seller-financed transactions, which he describes, and he "would have advised" client of need to continue financing statement after five years as "standard operating procedure").

3. Suppose the issue is whether a letter rescinding an agreement was posted. Suppose the author testifies that he dictated and signed the letter, that he saw the envelope in an "out" box in the office assistants' suite, and that a clerk periodically collects the contents of this box and posts letters or hand delivers interoffice material. Can such testimony prove mailing? Receipt in due course? See Wells Fargo Business v. Ben Kozloff, Inc., 695 F.2d 940, 944 (5th Cir.) (Yes), *cert. denied*, 464 U.S. 818 (1983).

4. Can organizational routine prove terms in an agreement? Compare Amoco Production Co. v. United States, 619 F.2d 1383, 1390 (10th Cir. 1980) (admitting evidence of "routine practice" of Federal Farm Mortgage Corporation "to reserve a one-half mineral interest in all property transferred," as proof of term in lost deed) with C.F.W. Construction Co. v. Travelers Insurance Co., 363 F.2d 557 (6th Cir. 1966) (when endorsement was required, practice was to submit contract to insurance company, but this evidence could not prove that contract was submitted to insurance company here).

5. Should proof of industry practice be admitted on standard of care? See Anderson v. Malloy, 700 F.2d 1208, 1211-1212 (8th Cir. 1983) (in suit against motel for failing to provide security, admitting evidence of measures taken by nearby motels). Does FRE 406 cover this use? Is the purpose to prove conduct, or something else?

C REMEDIAL MEASURES

Often someone involved in an accident takes later steps to avoid future mishaps. These may involve physical modifications of the machine or premises, changes in labels or instructions, or in procedures, or firing of employees thought responsible, or reorganization of departments or units. At common law, evidence of such "subsequent remedial measures" was long excludable, when offered to prove that the person in question was somehow at fault before, and FRE 407 continues tradition on this point.

The exclusionary doctrine rests on policy, relevance, and confusion of issues. As a matter of policy, it is thought wise to avoid discouraging efforts to make things better or safer (hence furthering an aim completely "extrinsic" to the conduct of litigation). Also it is considered unfair to introduce against a person, over his objection, evidence that he behaved responsibly after the fact. Concerns over relevancy arise because efforts to prevent future accidents may not show or even indicate that past practice or conditions amounted to negligence or fault. Concerns over confusion of issues arise partly because of the relevancy problem and partly because it may be impossible even to show that changes that follow an accident were made *because* of the accident.

Three major issues arise in the application of FRE 407. First, does the exclusionary doctrine apply in product liability cases? (An amendment to FRE 407 resolved this point in the affirmative, but many states did not make corresponding changes in their counterparts, and the original wording leaves the matter in doubt.) Second, does the *Erie* doctrine require federal courts to follow state practice on subsequent measures? (Most modern authority says no, but the matter is controversial.) Third, when may subsequent measures be shown to prove "feasibility"? (FRE 407 so permits if that point is disputed, but what constitutes a dispute?)

TUER v. MCDONALD

Court of Appeals of Maryland
701 A.2d 1101 (1997)

WILNER, Judge.

[Mary Tuer brought a malpractice suit against St. Joseph's Hospital in Baltimore, along with cardiac surgeons Garth McDonald and Robert Brawley, after her husband Eugene Tuer died of cardiac arrest on November 3, 1992, while awaiting coronary artery bypass graft surgery (CABG).

Eugene Tuer was 63, and had suffered angina for 16 years. Originally scheduled for surgery on Monday November 9th, he was admitted to St. Joseph's on Friday October 30th after suffering chest pains Thursday night. His surgery was rescheduled for 9 A.M. on Monday November 2nd, and he was put on Atenolol (beta blocker that reduces pressure on the heart) and Heparin (anticoagulant). His angina stabilized over the weekend, and he suffered no further pains or shortness of breath.

Following hospital protocol, an anesthesiologist stopped the Heparin at 5:30 A.M. on Monday morning, to allow the drug to be metabolized so Tuer would not have an anticoagulant in his blood during surgery. Drs. McDonald and Brawley prepared him, but an emergency involving another patient, more critically ill than Tuer, required postponement of his operation. Tuer was placed in the Coronary Surgery Unit and monitored. At 1:30 P.M., Dr. McDonald found Tuer short of breath and suffering arrhythmia and low blood pressure. He went into cardiac arrest. Resuscitation efforts and seven hours of surgery kept him alive, but he died the next day.

After Tuer's death, and apparently because of it, St. Joseph changed its protocol with respect to discontinuing Heparin for patients with stable angina. Under the new protocol, Heparin is continued until the patient is taken into the operating room.

Defendants made a motion in limine to exclude any reference to the change in protocol under Maryland Rule 5-407. Plaintiff countered that (a) the change was not a remedial measure because the defense claimed the prior protocol was correct, and (b) she was entitled to prove the change to show that continuing Heparin was "feasible." The trial court rejected the first argument (saying that defendants did not have to admit wrongdoing in order to claim that a change was remedial), but ruled that it would admit the proof if defendants denied feasibility.

Called by plaintiff as an adverse witness, Dr. McDonald testified that he approved discontinuing the Heparin to minimize the risk of excessive bleeding that would occur in the event of inadvertent puncture of the carotid artery. CABG requires puncturing the jugular vein with a needle, inserting a guide wire, then making an incision and inserting a catheter. The jugular is close to the carotid artery (high-pressure vessel bringing blood from the heart to the brain), and in 5 to 10 percent of the cases the anesthesiologist inadvertently punctures the artery when trying to insert the needle into the jugular, causing bleeding and sometimes death. Plaintiff got Dr. McDonald to say that under no circumstances would a patient in Tuer's condition (unstable angina stabilized by Heparin) continue on Heparin to the time of surgery. He considered restarting the Heparin when surgery was postponed, but decided against it. The court sustained a defense objection to the question whether it was "feasible to restart Heparin," but plaintiff got McDonald to say that restarting it would have been unsafe.

Plaintiff argued that she was entitled to prove the change in protocol, to impeach and to show it was not unsafe to restart Heparin, but the court disagreed. On cross, McDonald testified that he would have restarted Heparin if

Tuer had developed new chest pains indicating unstable angina, pointing out that Heparin is used later in CABG surgery to prevent clotting as blood circulates through a heart-lung machine.

Two doctors testified for plaintiff that Tuer had unstable angina, and that failing to restart Heparin departed from the customary standard. Three testified for defendant that it was right not to restart Heparin, since Tuer had stabilized.

The Court traces the law on subsequent measures in Maryland, describing the adoption of Maryland Rule 5-407, which is substantially identical to FRE 407 (before the 1997 amendment of the latter, which made changes not pertinent to this case).]

The Federal Advisory Committee on Rules of Evidence, which drafted FRE 407, offered two justifications for excluding evidence of subsequent remedial measures to prove culpability: first, that the subsequent conduct "is not in fact an admission, since the conduct is equally consistent with injury by mere accident or through contributory negligence," and second, the "social policy of encouraging people to take, or at least not discouraging them from taking, steps in furtherance of added safety." Although some commentators have since questioned the efficacy of the "social policy" argument, it was . . . sufficiently persuasive to cause the Federal rule to be proposed by the Supreme Court and adopted by Congress.[8]

These grounds and the commentary on them were considered by both the Rules Committee and this Court in deciding whether to adopt an analog to FRE 407 . . . . The discussion at the open hearing held by this Court [on proposed Maryland Rule 407 shows that the Court agreed] that evidence of subsequent remedial measures should no longer be admissible to show either what the applicable standard of care was at the time of the occurrence or a deviation from that standard of care. In that regard, the exclusionary aspect of the Rule is broader than the common law it replaced . . . .

[Plaintiff argues that proof of the change in protocol is admissible to show feasibility and impeach the testimony that restarting Heparin would be unsafe.]

[8]Criticism of the "social policy" argument centers on the notion that an exclusionary rule is not necessary to impel corrective action—that a defendant who is able to do so would likely take corrective action even in the absence of such a rule. [Court notes what it calls a "modified social policy argument" for the rule, which is that "people who take post-accident safety measures are doing exactly what good citizens should do" and that courts should not penalize behavior that seems "praiseworthy," at least so long as the probative worth of evidence of their behavior is small. Court notes as well the argument that the rule rests on relevancy, meaning that the "marginal relevance" of subsequent measures is "almost always substantially outweighed by the risk of jury confusion."]

FEASIBILITY

Rule 5-407(b) exempts subsequent remedial measure evidence from the exclusionary provision of Rule 5-407(a) when it is offered to prove feasibility, if feasibility has been controverted. That raises two questions: what is meant by "feasibility" and was feasibility, in fact, controverted? These two questions also tend to overlap and are often dealt with together; whether a defendant has controverted feasibility may well depend on how one defines the term.

The exception allowing subsequent conduct evidence to show feasibility has been a troublesome one, especially in negligence cases, for, as Judge Weinstein points out, "negligence and feasibility [are] often indistinct issues. The feasibility of a precaution may bear on whether the defendant was negligent not to have taken the precaution sooner." 2 Weinstein's Federal Evidence §407.04[3]. The Court of Special Appeals noted [in this case] that two seemingly divergent approaches have been taken in construing the feasibility exception. Some courts have construed the word narrowly, disallowing evidence of subsequent remedial measures under the feasibility exception unless the defendant has essentially contended that the measures were not physically, technologically, or economically possible under the circumstances then pertaining. Other courts have swept into the concept of feasibility a somewhat broader spectrum of motives and explanations for not having adopted the remedial measure earlier, the effect of which is to circumscribe the exclusionary provision.

Courts in the first camp have concluded that feasibility is not controverted—and thus subsequent remedial evidence is not admissible under the Rule—when a defendant contends that the design or practice complained of was chosen because of its perceived comparative advantage over the alternative design or practice [citing cases]; or when the defendant merely asserts that the instructions or warnings given with a product were acceptable or adequate and does not suggest that additional or different instructions or warnings could not have been given [citing cases]; or when the defendant urges that the alternative would not have been effective to prevent the kind of accident that occurred [citing cases].

Courts announcing a more expansive view have concluded that "feasible" means more than that which is merely possible, but includes that which is capable of being utilized successfully. In Anderson v. Malloy, 700 F.2d 1208 (8th Cir. 1983), for example, a motel guest who was raped in her room and who sued the motel for failure to provide safe lodging, offered evidence that, after the event, the motel installed peep holes in the doors to the rooms. The appellate court held that the evidence was admissible in light of the defendant's testimony that it had considered installing peepholes earlier but decided not to do so because (1) there were already windows next to the solid door allowing a guest to look out, and (2) based on the advice of the local police chief, peepholes would give a false sense of security. Although the motel, for obvious reasons, never suggested that the installation of peepholes was not possible, the court, over a strident dissent, concluded that, by inferring that the installation of peepholes would create a lesser level of security, the defendant had "controverted the feasibility of the installation of these devices." [Court describes other cases.]

The apparent divergence indicated by these cases may, at least to some extent, be less of a doctrinal division than a recognition that the concept of practicability is implicit in the notion of feasibility and allows some leeway in the application of the rule. [Court notes that dictionary definitions connote "practicability," but that some stress that which can be done "physically, technologically, or economically" and some stress "value, effectiveness, and overall utility."]

To some extent, the problem may be driven by special considerations arising from application of the rule to product liability cases, especially those grounded on strict liability. When the plaintiff is obliged to establish that there were feasible alternatives to the design, manufacturing method, or warnings used by the defendant, he or she necessarily injects the question of feasibility into the case, to which the defendant ordinarily responds by showing why those alternatives were not used. As [commentators] point out, if a remedial measure has, in fact, been taken that could have been taken earlier, the defendant is not likely to claim that the measure was not possible or practicable, and, indeed, defendants often are willing to stipulate to feasibility in order to avoid having the subsequent remedial evidence admitted. The issue arises when the defendant offers some other explanation for not putting the measure into effect sooner—often a judgment call as to comparative value or a tradeoff between cost and benefit or between competing benefits—and the plaintiff characterizes that explanation as putting feasibility into issue.[9] To the extent there can be said to be a doctrinal split among the courts, it seems to center on whether that kind of judgment call, which is modified later, suffices to allow the challenged evidence to be admitted.

That is essentially what occurred in this case. At no time did Dr. McDonald or any of his expert witnesses suggest that the Heparin could not have been restarted following the postponement of Mr. Tuer's surgery. Indeed, they indicated quite the opposite; Dr. McDonald, in fact, made clear that, had Mr. Tuer exhibited signs of renewed unstable angina, he would have restarted the Heparin. The only fair reading of his testimony and that of his supporting experts is that the protocol then in effect was the product of a professional judgment call that the risk to Mr. Tuer of having CABG surgery commence while there was a significant amount of Heparin in his blood outweighed the prospect of harm accruing from allowing him to remain Heparin-free for several hours.

Dr. McDonald's brief response to one question that, at the time, he regarded it as "unsafe" to restart the Heparin cannot be viewed in isolation but has to be read in the context of his whole testimony. Under any reasonable view of the meaning of feasibility, a flat assertion by a physician that the remedial

[9]Wright and Graham note that many of the cases in which the feasibility exception has been invoked are product liability cases, and that "it may be that courts had intuitive appreciation of the inappropriateness of the traditional rule in that context and were using the 'exception' as an alternative to holding the rule inapplicable in strict liability." 23 Wright and Graham, Federal Practice and Procedure §5288 (footnote omitted).

measure was inappropriate because it was medically "unsafe" would ordinarily be tantamount to asserting that the measure was not feasible and would thus suffice to controvert the feasibility of the measure. In a medical context at least, feasibility has to include more than mere physical possibility; as we have so sadly learned from history, virtually anything can physically be done to the human body. The practice of medicine is quintessentially therapeutic in nature. Its purpose is to comfort and to heal, and a determination of whether a practice or procedure is feasible has to be viewed in that light. The assertion that a given course would be unsafe, in the sense that it would likely cause paramount harm to the patient, necessarily constitutes an assertion that the course would not be feasible. Dr. McDonald was not asserting, however, in any absolute sense, that restarting the Heparin would have been unsafe but only that, given the complications that could have arisen, and that, in other cases had arisen, from an inadvertent puncture of the carotid artery, weighed against Mr. Tuer's apparently stable condition at the time and the intensive monitoring he would receive during the waiting period, there was a relative safety risk that, at the time, he and the hospital believed was not worth taking. That does not, in our view, constitute an assertion that a restarting of the Heparin was not feasible. It was feasible but, in their view, not advisable.

IMPEACHMENT

[The impeachment clause in the Rule creates similar interpretive problems. Most testimony by defense witnesses could be contradicted minimally by a subsequent measure. If a defendant says Yes when asked on cross whether he had taken all reasonable precautions, a subsequent measure can be seen as contradicting this testimony. But at common law plaintiff could not have called the defendant, asked whether he had been negligent, and impeached with proof of subsequent measures if he said No [presumably the thought here is that the rule against impeaching one's own witness would apply—EDS]. It might be different if the defendant said that the challenged product was perhaps the safest yet devised, but courts do not allow proof of a subsequent measure to impeach testimony that the measure was thought at the time to be less practical than the one actually used, or if the defendant simply says that due care was exercised. Hence the change in hospital protocol was not admissible to impeach McDonald's "brief statement that restarting the Heparin would have been unsafe." The judgment is affirmed.]

■ NOTES ON SUBSEQUENT REMEDIAL MEASURES

1. How does the court in *Tuer* read "feasibility" in FRE 407? How does it read "impeachment"? In effect, does the court in *Tuer* take a narrow view of both terms in order to achieve a broad protective purpose?

2. That protective purpose involves encouraging persons or companies (or institutions like hospitals) to implement remedial measures after injuries giving rise to claims. Isn't there an incentive to do so anyway, to avoid more injuries, deaths, and lawsuits? Or do we exclude such proof because we don't want to penalize socially responsible behavior? Would a hospital hesitate to change a protocol requiring cessation of anticoagulants before CABG surgery if proof of the change were admissible in cases like *Tuer*?

3. Like *Tuer* other courts apply the impeachment exception only when defendants appear to be making broad claims about the safety of prior practices or designs. See, e.g., MacDonald v. B.M.D. Golf Associates, Inc., 813 A.2d 488 (N.H. 2002) (in suit against golf course for injuries when cart tipped over, testimony that area was safe without warning sign did not pave way to prove that sign was later installed, but testimony that signs just create chaos *did* pave the way for such proof); Doe v. Walmart Stores, 558 S.E.2d 663 (W. Va. 2001) (in suit by kidnap victim claiming lack of lighting in parking lot was to blame, proof that Walmart used roving golf carts to cut parking lot crimes would be admissible if defendant claimed lot was as safe as it could be).

4. Nobody doubts that FRE 407 applies in negligence cases like *Tuer*. Since the 1997 amendment added language referring to defective "product" or "design," it has been clear that the exclusionary principle applies in product cases too. Before that, this matter remained in doubt: The language referred only to proving "negligence" or "culpable conduct," and arguably strict liability fit neither category. There was also considerable difference of opinion on the question whether the exclusionary principle *should* apply to product claims. Jurisdictions not governed by the Rules are divided on this point (the same is true of states retaining the original language of FRE 407).

(a) Consider the California Supreme Court's decision in the *Ault* case, which declined to apply a state provision (model for original FRE 407) in product claim. *Ault* involved a Scout vehicle that plunged 500 feet to the bottom of a canyon, allegedly caused by the failure of a gearbox from metal fatigue. The court held that plaintiff should have been permitted to prove that afterwards the manufacturer changed the metal in gearboxes from aluminum to malleable iron:

> Historically, the common law rule . . . was developed with reference to the usual negligence action, in which a pedestrian fell into a hole in a sidewalk or a plaintiff was injured on unstable stairs; in such circumstances, it may be realistic to assume that a landowner or potential defendant might be deterred from making repairs if such repairs could be used against him in determining liability for the initial accident.
>
> When the context is transformed from a typical negligence setting to the modern products liability field, however, the "public policy" assumptions justifying this evidentiary rule are no longer valid. The contemporary corporate mass producer of goods, the normal products liability defendant, manufactures tens of thousands of units of goods; it is manifestly unrealistic to suggest that such a producer will forego making improvements in its product, and risk innumerable additional lawsuits and the attendant adverse effect upon its public image,

> simply because evidence of adoption of such improvement may be admitted in an action founded on strict liability for recovery on an injury that preceded the improvement. In the products liability area, the exclusionary rule . . . does not affect the primary conduct of the mass producer of goods, but serves merely as a shield against potential liability. In short, the purpose . . . is not applicable to a strict liability case and hence its exclusionary rule should not be gratuitously extended to that field.

Ault v. International Harvester Co., 528 P.2d 1148 (Cal. 1974). In effect, *Ault* argues that the reason for the exclusionary principle is to affect out-of-court conduct by encouraging responsible behavior, but that it won't have that effect in product liability cases. For a contrary view, see Flaminio v. Honda Motor Co., Ltd., 733 F.2d 463 (7th Cir. 1984) (exposure to liability from *future* accidents if defect is *not* fixed is offset by exposure to liability from *past* accidents if defect *is* fixed and proof of the fix is admitted; hence "effects of scale are symmetrical" and *Ault* is wrong) (even pre-amendment FRE 407 applies in product cases).

(b) Tuer says feasibility is bound to come up in trying to figure out whether a product is defective, so it is impossible to avoid the subject. Doesn't excluding evidence of design changes lead to an inquiry that is incomplete and distorted? See generally Mueller & Kirkpatrick, Federal Evidence §4:53 (4th ed. 2013).

(c) On the matter of conflicting state rules, and the conflict between the federal rule and what some states do, consider these points: Counterparts to FRE 407 in Connecticut, Iowa, and Hawaii exempt product cases from the exclusionary principle. Decisions in at least ten other states do the same thing (Alaska, California, Colorado, Louisiana, Missouri, Nevada, New York, Ohio, Wisconsin, and Wyoming), but decisions in yet other states apply the exclusionary principle. Compare Minton v. Honda of America, 684 N.E.2d 648 (Ohio 1997) and Jeep Corp. v. Murray, 708 P.2d 297 (Nev. 1985) (declining to apply their counterparts to product liability claims) with Hyjek v. Anthony Industries, 944 P.2d 1036 (Wash. 1997) (state counterpart does apply in product suits). Some states resist the federal lead: The Colorado Supreme Court, knowing that the federal rule applies in product cases, declined to apply CRE 407 in this setting. See Forma Scientific, Inc. v. Biosera, Inc., 960 P.2d 108 (Colo. 1998). In 13 states, counterparts to FRE 407 were amended to apply in product cases (Delaware, Florida, Idaho, Kansas, Kentucky, Maine, Minnesota, North Dakota, Pennsylvania, Tennessee, Texas, Utah, and Vermont).

(d) Suppose an Ohio citizen sues an out-of-state carmaker alleging a defect in the ignition switch allowing the key to turn to the "accessory" position cutting power to the engine and turning off the airbags, leading to accident and injury. Suppose the automaker removes the suit to federal court. It is possible that plaintiff would win in state court in Ohio, which would admit proof of a design change repairing this problem, but would lose in federal court because this proof is excluded. If so, the *reason* she would lose is that federal and state law conflict on the question how best to affect out-of-court behavior by

automakers. This disagreement sounds more substantive than procedural, doesn't it? Doesn't the *Erie* doctrine seek *precisely* to avoid differences in outcome, as between state and federal court, when caused by conflicts in substantive law? Of course federal law *could* control all substantive issues relating to product liability. But FRE 407 is part of the *Federal Rules of Evidence*, not part of some "Federal Product Liability Law," which doesn't exist. Wouldn't it be better to apply *state* law on subsequent measures in product cases until and unless we adopt federal law governing the whole subject?

5. Plaintiff is hurt in 2015 in an accident caused by a steering defect in his 2012 car. The manufacturer, aware of similar accidents in 2012, corrects the defect by a design change in cars made in 2013 and after. Is evidence of the 2013 design change admissible? Does FRE 407 exclude only proof of measures taken after the accident generating the suit, or does it also reach measures taken after *earlier* accidents but *before* the accident in suit? See Trull v. Volkswagen of America, Inc., 187 F.3d 88, 96 (1999) ("measures that take place *before* the accident at issue do not fall within the prohibitions").

SETTLEMENT NEGOTIATIONS

1. Civil Settlements

FRE 408 bars proof of civil settlements, offers to settle, and conduct or statements made during settlement negotiations, when offered to prove or disprove the "validity or amount" of a disputed claim, to "impeach through a prior inconsistent statement or contradiction." Civil settlements (including offers, conduct, and statements during negotiations) are excludable in civil suits, and also in criminal cases (except that settlements in government enforcement civil suits are not excludable in criminal cases).

In part this exclusionary principle rests on relevancy: Payment of a small sum (or willingness to do so) does not tend strongly to prove liability; acceptance of a large sum (or willingness to do so) does not tend strongly to prove a claim is weak. But relevancy alone would not likely produce such rule because payment of larger sums *does* suggest liability, and acceptance of smaller sums *does* suggest that a claim lacks merit. In fact, the main reason for the rule is public policy: The system would grind to a halt if every filed case were tried, yet lawyers would not be able to risk negotiating if what they said or did in trying to settle were later provable if the attempt to settle failed.

Consider the principle in operation: While driving her car, Mason and her passenger Newell are struck by a car driven by Oscar. Mason and Newell bring civil claims against Oscar for personal injuries, but Newell settles his claim while Mason pursues hers. As an indication that Oscar was negligent, can Mason prove that Oscar paid money to Newell in settlement of his claim? No. That's exactly what FRE 408 prevents.

The situation becomes complicated if one of several defending parties settles. Suppose, for example, that Mason's accident involved a car driven by Oscar and a truck driven by Phil, and Mason sues both Oscar and Phil, seeking recovery of $1.5 million for personal injuries. Phil settles with Mason for $500,000 (usually such settlements are worked out and paid by the insurance carrier for the settling party), but Mason goes forward with her claim against Oscar. Can Oscar prove that Phil settled the parallel claim? Oscar might want to do so because the settlement makes Phil look responsible for Oscar's injuries, and it also suggests that Oscar has already recovered some compensation. Again the answer is No (Oscar cannot prove Phil's settlement with Mason). The claim against Phil would normally be dropped from the case after the settlement so he is no longer a party, but this fact doesn't matter. FRE 408 is not a "privilege" that protects only the paying party. Rather, it blocks "any party" from using a settlement, even if the person who paid the settlement is no longer in the case.

You might wonder whether, if proof of the Mason-Phil settlement is excluded, a jury could award Mason the full $1.5 million in a suit against Oscar alone, enabling her to collect $2 million altogether (in effect, collecting part of the total twice). The answer is No, at least in theory: In most states, damages are apportioned, so that even if the settlement were excluded, Oscar could try to prove that Phil is partially responsible for Mason's loss, which should reduce Oscar's liability.[1]

■ PROBLEM 5-Q. Two Potato, One Potato

Potato farmer Amos Perrin purchased from salesman Evan Sosbee an herbicide called Perquod made by Cheron Chemical Company, to apply to his crop. Sosbee was an agronomist, and his job was not only to sell Cheron products, but to deal with customers by offering suggestions on application and processing complaints. Appearing at the Perrin farm at the initial application of the Perquod, Sosbee advises Perrin that "Cheron will back up its recommendation of the product."

Midway through the growing season, Sosbee again appears on the farm, and Perrin comments that "the stuff we put on killed the weeds alright, but my potato plants don't look as healthy as they should." Sosbee replies, "Don't worry. We'll take care of you." At harvest time, Perrin again sees Sosbee, and Perrin, now clearly unhappy, advises Sosbee that "my yield isn't half what it was last year." Sosbee replies,

---

[1]Often states require defending parties to plead third-party liability or give pretrial notice of intent to offer proof along these lines. If an insurance carrier paid Mason's medical bills, it would be subrogated to her rights against Oscar and Phil, and could pursue the claims in her name. If it a jury awarded, in a suit that went forward against Oscar alone, recovery that was already part of the Mason-Phil settlement, the court could reduce the judgment accordingly. See Wright v. Moore, 931 A.2d 405 (Del. 2007).

"You just tell us the damages you're claiming, and we'll bill Cheron." Cheron doesn't pay.

Perrin sues Cheron. At trial, he offers to testify to the various statements by Sosbee. Assume that his comments fit FRE 801(d)(2)(D), but Cheron objects that his statements were "offers to settle Perrin's claim, and as such they are excludable under FRE 408."

How should the court rule and why?

■ NOTES ON CIVIL SETTLEMENT OFFERS IN CIVIL CASES

1. By nature a cautious bunch, lawyers conduct settlement talks by couching factual remarks in terms of "let us assume for sake of discussion that" or "just suppose" or "what if, hypothetically now." Is such caution still necessary under FRE 408?

2. In the example in the introduction, where Mason sues Oscar and Phil for an accident allegedly caused by them, suppose Oscar testifies that he was driving carefully. If he had admitted (or Oscar's lawyer speaking on his behalf), in negotiations with Phil (or Phil's lawyer), that Oscar had "dozed off momentarily," could Mason offer proof of this point, to impeach Oscar and contradict his testimony? If Phil testified on Mason's behalf, could Oscar bring out that Phil settled with Mason (thus avoiding further liability), the insinuation being that there is some kind of understanding under which Phil would shape his testimony to help Mason? Notice that FRE 408 bars the use of settlements (and statements made in settlement talks) to "impeach by a prior inconsistent statement or a contradiction," but FRE 408 does not bar use of settlements (and statements made in settlement talks) to prove bias. You will consider impeachment in Chapter 8, infra.

■ PROBLEM 5-R. "This Is Criminal; You Can't Exclude Civil Settlements Here"

Michael Prince founded First American Provident Company in Indianapolis, Indiana, with the purpose of overseeing and managing services used by insurance companies. Prince approached investors and persuaded 140 of them to provide more than $2 million in capital for First American. In fact, Prince did not use the money as promised, but spent it for his own personal pleasures, eventually looting First American of all its liquid assets and profiting to the tune of more than $1.5 million.

Alerted to the situation, the Securities Division of the State of Indiana investigated Prince for violations of the Indiana Blue Sky laws (statutes regulating sales of securities). The investigation led to negotiations involving Rachel Sanders, on behalf of the Attorney General, Quill, who acted as counsel for Prince, and Michael Prince himself. These discussions in turn led to a stipulated "cease and desist order," an agreement by Prince to pay a fine in the amount of $250,000, and his commitment not to solicit investments in the State of Indiana for ten years.

Later the Department of Justice indicted Prince in federal court in Indiana for mail fraud in connection with First American. At trial, the federal prosecutor offers a transcript of a conversation involving Prince, Quill, and Sanders, in which Prince admitted making personal use of more than $1.5 million raised from investors. The prosecutor also offers proof that Prince paid the civil fine in Indiana. Quill, once again representing Prince, objects: "Your Honor, that's settlement talk, he can't use that. Civil settlements are covered by the Rule, let's see, it's Rule 408." The prosecutor disagrees: "This is criminal, Your Honor, you can't exclude civil settlements here."

How should the court rule, and why?

■ NOTES ON CIVIL SETTLEMENT OFFERS IN CRIMINAL CASES

1. FRE 408 applies when statements in civil settlement negotiations are later offered in criminal cases. Some states do *not* exclude civil settlements from criminal prosecutions. See, e.g., State v. Mead, 27 P.3d 1115, 1127 (Utah 2001); Louisiana Code of Evidence, Art. 408 (this provision "does not require the exclusion in a criminal case" of civil settlements and negotiations). Prior to a 2006 amendment, one could not be sure whether FRE 408 made civil settlements excludable in criminal cases—there were cases both ways. Now there is no doubt. Excluding civil settlements from criminal trials means that an assailant who commits battery and settles the victim's civil claim can exclude, in a later criminal trial for battery, what he said in the civil settlement talks. This outcome is all to the good, isn't it? It encourages civil settlements. Under the contrary rule, those who commit acts that are both torts and crimes would be in a bind when it comes to negotiating an end to civil liability.

2. FRE 408 applies both to "furnishing" or "promising" to pay a civil settlement, and the language is broad enough to reach fines, so the fact that Prince paid a fine is excludable. The same principle reaches "conduct or statements" in civil negotiations, but does *not* apply to conduct or statements in proceedings relating to "a claim by a public office" exercising regulatory or enforcement authority. Hence the exclusionary principle does *not* apply to what Prince told

Rachel Sanders. Does it make sense to exclude proof that Prince paid a fine but not proof of what he said in negotiations? See ACN to amended Rule 408 (offering or accepting a compromise "is not very probative," and if it were provable in a civil suit, it might "deter a defendant from settling a civil regulatory action"). If you represented Prince in dealing with Sanders in the enforcement action, you'd tell Prince to "say nothing," wouldn't you? And you would say things like "let us assume for sake of discussion" or "just suppose," wouldn't you (just as lawyers used to do in *all* civil settlement talks)?

3. Betty Peed sought to buy a collection of dolls from Louise Stasko through the mail. Stasko sent the dolls in cartons to Peed, who opened the bottoms, removed the dolls, resealed the boxes, and then sought indemnity from the Postal Service, claiming the dolls had been stolen. Suspecting that Peed was the thief, inspectors arranged for Stasko to record a conversation in which Peed said she would return the dolls if Stasko would "drop the charges." In a trial of Peed for mail fraud, the government offers this incriminating remark. Peed objects that her statement was an attempt to compromise Stasko's civil claim, but the government claims it was "an effort to obstruct a criminal investigation or prosecution" under the last sentence of FRE 408. Which is it? See United States v. Peed, 714 F.2d 7, 9-10 (4th Cir. 1983) (admit statement as attempt to avoid prosecution). Shouldn't we encourage people to resolve their differences in this way without invoking the criminal process? Compare United States v. Davis, 596 F.3d 852 (D.C. Cir. 2010) (in prosecution of defendant for stealing funds from fraternity, reversible error under FRE 408 to admit evidence of defendant's offer to fraternity's treasurer to pay half of $29,000 worth of disputed checks to settle fraternity's claim).

2. Plea Bargaining in Criminal Cases

Plea bargaining statements are excludable for reasons similar to those that apply to civil settlement negotiations. Public policy favors plea bargaining as a way of disposing of criminal cases, and without protection such bargaining could not occur. And what is said during such bargaining sometimes does not really prove guilt or any weakness in the government's case, although it "looks bad" for one side or the other.

In the usual case, plea bargaining leads to a plea agreement, then to a plea, then to a judgment of conviction based on the plea. In the typical case, that's the end of it, and there's no occasion when plea bargaining statements would become important. Sometimes, however, things don't work out, and the plea bargain is broken, or the attempt to bargain does not lead to a plea, or the defendant withdraws from the bargain and persuades the court to allow the plea to be withdrawn. Then charges are pressed after all, and it is in these settings that FRE 410(4) excludes plea bargaining statements by the accused. (Other subdivisions exclude withdrawn pleas of guilty and courtroom statements by the accused explaining reasons for such pleas, which are called "allocutions.")

The effect of Rule 410 where a criminal trial goes forward was substantially limited in the *Mezzanatto* case. Let us assume that a conversation between the accused and the prosecutor amounts to plea bargaining, but no bargain was reached (or a plea was entered, then withdrawn) and the accused goes to trial. If the accused takes the stand and gives testimony contradicting his plea-bargaining statements, are such statements admissible to impeach? Legislative history made it clear that FRE 410 blocks this use of such statements, but what if—as part of the plea bargaining itself—defendant waives his right to exclude his statements in the event of trial? *Mezzanatto* held that such waivers are enforceable. United States v. Mezzanatto, 513 U.S. 196, 202 (1995) (prosecutor agreed to talk only if defendant was "completely truthful" and only if he agreed that "any statements he made during the meeting could be used to impeach any contradictory testimony" he might give at trial; can waive protections of FRE 410). Post-*Mezzanato* cases allow the substantive use of such statements. See United States v. Mitchell, 633 F.3d 997 (10th Cir. 2011) (admitting in government's case-in-chief defendant's withdrawn guilty plea, and statements in agreement and plea colloquy; *Mezzanatto* waiver covered these uses; refusing request to limit use of materials to impeachment). Given *Mezzanatto*, how often does plea bargaining go forward *without* a waiver?

Rule 410 does not exclude guilty pleas entered on the basis of plea bargains (it only excludes guilty pleas "later withdrawn"), nor does it exclude plea bargaining statements that lead to guilty pleas (it only excludes plea bargaining statements if no agreement was reached or a plea was entered but later withdrawn). See United States v. Gonzalez, 608 F.3d 1001, 1005 (7th Cir. 2010) (FRE 410 does not exclude statements in sentencing hearing; it covers statements in plea proceedings that do *not* result in a guilty plea or lead to a plea later withdrawn). Recall Problem 4-D (An Encounter Gone Bad), where the problem for the lawyer representing Kenneth Brixton was to deal with criminal charges when a civil suit by the victim was also in prospect (Chapter 4B1, supra). There you saw that the guilty plea is an admission that fits FRE 801(d)(2)(A) or (D) (either a personal admission or one by a speaking agent—the lawyer), and the same is true of plea bargaining statements. You saw then that the judgment itself might have preclusive effect in a later civil suit. One possible alternative is a nolo contendere plea, which *is* excludable under FRE 410(2). Why should such a plea be excluded? See Mueller & Kirkpatrick, Evidence (5th ed. 2012) §4.28 (this provision does not block consideration of such pleas in proceedings for deportation or license revocation).

■ PROBLEM 5-S. "I Used His Stuff"

Martin Rackly is charged with passing counterfeit bills. His lawyer Kent Slavin sets up an appointment with Assistant U.S. Attorney Amy Norton to discuss the situation. Slavin meets Norton and two Secret Service agents in the Federal Building, where Norton tells Slavin, "I'm not prepared to make a plea bargain because I haven't had a chance to study the case." Slavin replies that "Rackly's involvement in the counterfeiting operation is marginal, but he can help you get the guys you really want. So if you think you're interested in a deal, I think Rackly will cooperate with you."

Thereafter Slavin calls Norton's office and sets up another meeting in the Federal Building. He and Rackly attend, as do the Secret Service agents, but nobody from Norton's office is there. The agents deliver *Miranda* warnings, but Slavin protests that "We're here to talk about a plea, not a confession." On Slavin's advice, Rackly refuses to sign a Waiver of Rights Form (which would acknowledge receipt of *Miranda* warnings and say that "no promises have been made" and that Rackly "waives his right against self-incrimination"). He then makes a detailed statement, which includes the following crucial points: "Brody was my source. He had the bills, and I passed quite a few of them. I used his stuff at Wolf Brothers and Champion Electronics."

Ensuing telephone conversations between Slavin and Norton result in a draft plea agreement, but in the end Rackly does not sign. He is tried for passing bills at Wolf Brothers and Champion Electronics.

The prosecutor offers in evidence Rackly's statements admitting those transactions, but the defense objects: "Those are plea bargaining statements, and they should be excluded under Rule 410." What result, and why?

NOTES ON PLEA BARGAINING WITH AGENTS

1. In Problem 5-S, is it critical that the first meeting did not lead to real discussions? Can bargaining occur if no formal offer is made? What if agents announce in the second meeting that Norton "would go for a plea for passing the bill at Wolf Brothers"? See United States v. Grant, 622 F.2d 308, 313-315 (8th Cir. 1980) (FRE 410 applies).

2. Originally Rule 410 excluded any "offer to plead guilty" and statements "made in connection with, and relevant to" an offer. The language did not confine the exclusionary doctrine to discussions with prosecutors. The accused has a constitutional right to represent himself, see Faretta v. California, 422 U.S. 806 (1975), so it is plausible to argue that he does his own "plea bargaining" in talking to an arresting officer. What if he tells one he "wants to work something out" and the officer does nothing to discourage him? See United States v. Herman, 544 F.2d 791, 798 (5th Cir. 1977) (defendant made incriminating remarks in talks with postal inspectors during recess in hearing where he requested a lawyer for his defense; remarks were excludable; Congress did not want plea bargaining to be "formalized, ritualized or structured," and government, "as one of the dancing partners, should not be able to lead its partner to a trap door on the dance floor").

3. Concern that Rule 410 was too broad led to amendment. Now the Rule reaches plea bargaining statements only when made to "an attorney for the prosecuting authority." Under this language, can defendant's statements to an arresting agent *ever* be excluded as plea bargaining? Consider this comment:

> This change, it must be emphasized, does not compel the conclusion that statements made to law enforcement agents, especially when the agents purport to have authority to bargain, are inevitably admissible. Rather, the point is that such cases are not covered by the per se rule of [FRCrimP] 11(e)(6) [which was and is identical to FRE 410] and thus must be resolved by that body of law dealing with police interrogations.

Does this comment mean statements to an arresting officer are excludable if, for example, defendant says he wants to "work things out, like a lawyer would," and the officer promises "to help you out"? Decisions endorse a "two-tiered" approach, turning on whether (a) defendant "exhibited an actual subjective expectation to negotiate a plea," and (b) the expectation was reasonable under the circumstances. United States v. Robertson, 582 F.2d 1356, 1366 (5th Cir. 1978). Even courts following this approach often let statements in. See United States v. Sebetich, 776 F.2d 412, 421-422 (3d Cir. 1985) (cannot expect to bargain in "unplanned encounter" in parking lot); United States v. Karr, 742 F.2d 493, 496 (9th Cir. 1984) (any belief unreasonable).

■ PROBLEM 5-T. "Just Keep Them Out of It"

Executing a search warrant at the home of Bill Bragen in El Paso, DEA agents seize chemicals and laboratory equipment used to manufacture methamphetamine. They encounter and arrest Bragen and his wife Ann Bragen, as well as Al Roberts and his companion Judy Stall.

Thereafter Bragen and Roberts, each represented by counsel, meet with DEA Agents and U.S. Attorney George Kendall in the Federal Building. The lawyers for Bragen and Roberts tell Kendall that their clients "want to get the women out of this thing because they are not involved." Bragen and Roberts then make incriminating statements, saying in substance, "Just keep them out of it, they had nothing to do with it."

Kendall directs the two women to be released and obtains indictments against Bragen and Roberts. At trial, Kendall calls the DEA agents, who describe the results of their search. Kendall asks them to "describe what defendants said when we met in the Federal Building." Bragen and Roberts object. Outside the hearing of the jury, they argue that "what was said in that room was plea bargaining, and it is excludable under Rule 410."

■ NOTES ON PLEA BARGAINING, PLEAS, AND BARGAINING FOR OTHERS

1. In Problem 5-T, should the meeting with Bragen and Roberts be characterized as (a) an exchange in which the men confessed to get the women released or (b) an attempt to bargain a plea, leading to release of the women because they were innocent? If the first version is right, the government should be able to use the statements of Bragen and Roberts, shouldn't it? (The government did its part by releasing the women; if the confessions are excluded, it got nothing in return.) If the second version is right, the incriminating statements should be excluded under Rule 410, shouldn't they? Does Rule 410 address attempts by the accused to help others? See United States v. Robertson, 582 F.2d 1356 (5th Cir. 1978) (defendants were making "independent" confessions rather than engaging in plea negotiations; court applies earlier version of Rule 410); United States v. Brooks, 670 F.2d 625, 626-628 (5th Cir. 1982) (postarrest statements to agents in effort to "work something out" for defendant's girlfriend were not excludable).

2. Consider the last sentence in FRE 410, which makes some such statements admissible "in a criminal proceeding for perjury or false statement." What situation is that provision aimed at? See FRCrimP 11(c)(5) and (d) (the former contemplates that in considering a plea of guilty or nolo contendere the court may "question the defendant under oath, on the record, and in the presence of counsel"; the latter provides that the court shall not accept such a plea "without first, by addressing the defendant personally in open court, determining that the plea is voluntary and not the result of force or threats or of promises apart from a plea agreement").

3. FRE 410 prohibits only introduction of plea bargaining statements "against the defendant." What if the defense wants to suggest that the prosecutor lacks confidence in his case, so it must be weak, by introducing evidence that she offered to let defendant plead guilty to a lesser charge? See United States v. Verdoorn, 528 F.2d 103, 107 (8th Cir. 1976) (invoking FRE 408 rather than 410, court concludes that "government proposals concerning pleas should be excludable").

E PROOF OF PAYMENT OF MEDICAL EXPENSES

Where a person pays for injuries or other expenses incurred by another, in the belief that he is responsible or even simply as a Good Samaritan (believing himself blameless but wanting to help another in need), FRE 409 provides that proof of such behavior is excludable if offered to prove "liability." The bases for this exclusionary principle are similar to those underlying FRE 407 and 408: Responsible behavior after the fact does not necessarily prove legal fault, and the system should encourage such behavior.

The provision is useful in making it possible for an insurance carrier, which anticipates both liability and a possible dispute over amount, to advance sums necessary to compensate the claimant while still maintaining the position that it is not liable for the full amount claimed. A number of state statutes authorize advance payments of such sums, while providing for exclusion of evidence of payment.

By its terms, FRE 409 excludes only "furnishing" or "offering" or "promising to pay" medical and similar expenses, which seems narrower than the coverage of FRE 408. The latter excludes not only settlement offers, but conduct and statements in compromise negotiations. This difference in wording suggests that statements accompanying an offer to pay medical expenses might not be excludable, although such statements would be excludable if the context suggests that the parties were trying to settle the case.

F PROOF OF INSURANCE COVERAGE

Does having or not having liability coverage affect the exercise of care? Long ago litigants could argue either that a person with insurance (1) had bought a license to be careless, so proof of coverage tended to show he was negligent on the occasion, or that (2) they had exercised special caution, so proof of coverage tended to show that he was careful on the occasion. The speculative and contradictory nature of those arguments could not survive the growth of insurance to become commonplace. Thus concerns over relevance alone would justify Rule 411, which bars evidence of coverage offered in support of arguments such as these.

Rule 411 also helps keep juries from deciding cases or adjusting damage estimates in the belief that insurance will pay the judgment. In this respect, Rule 411 dovetails with the "collateral source" doctrine, which holds that one who carries casualty coverage, medical insurance, or life insurance can collect not only from the carrier but from the tortfeasor. In other words, the insured sometimes obtains "double recovery" because the party at fault cannot "take advantage of the thrift" of the insured party. Does this policy justify excluding evidence of the *absence* of insurance?

The exclusionary principle has not gone without criticism. Auto accident cases provide a common situation where insurance plays a role, and motorists are everywhere required to carry insurance. Jurors think everyone has coverage. Arguably there are more risks in keeping juries in the dark than in letting them know about coverage.

Rule 411 does not keep the involvement of insurance from the jury. For one thing, lawyers often insinuate the fact of insurance in other ways—during voir dire, for instance, where they put screening questions theoretically designed to prevent persons connected with the industry from sitting in cases where insurance is involved. And where a carrier retains counsel for plaintiff or defendant, lawyers on the other side have been known to refer to the carrier by a "slip of the tongue" heard by the jury. By way of caution, however, we should note that courts are attuned to lawyerly ploys, and some courts have *no patience* with lawyers who inject insurance into the case. Indeed, such behavior sometimes leads to mistrials. See, e.g., Neibauer v. Well, 319 N.W.2d 143 (N.D. 1982) (inadvertent reference to insurance is ground for mistrial on ground of prejudice).

Occasionally procedural or substantive principles inject insurance into the case. Consider these three: First, often any "second recovery" by the injured party (even where the collateral source doctrine applies) actually belongs to the carrier under rights of subrogation, created by the insurance contract or by law, as is often true with casualty insurance and medical coverage (not with life insurance). Second, in subrogation cases the insurance carrier is sometimes the "real party in interest." That is the case in some states and the federal system, where the carrier is the real party in interest to the extent of its subrogation rights. (Other states say the insured is the real party in interest, even though recovery goes to the carrier.) Third, a few states (Wisconsin and Arkansas) have "direct action" statutes that let injured claimants sue the insurance carrier as defendant.

Finally, Rule 411 is not "airtight," for it recognizes several situations where the fact of insurance is admissible. Consider the situations mentioned in the Notes below.

NOTES ON EVIDENCE OF INSURANCE COVERAGE

1. Insurance investigators sometimes gather pretrial statements from eyewitnesses, and these may be admissible for impeachment purposes. If a party uses such a statement in this way and the witness contests its accuracy, should the fact that an investigator prepared it be admissible? See Complete Auto Transit v. Wayne Broyles Engineering Corp., 351 F.2d 478, 481-482 (5th Cir. 1965) (Yes).

2. Plaintiff sues the alleged owner of a truck for personal injuries suffered when the truck ran into her car. Defendant denies ownership of (and responsibility for) the truck. Can plaintiff show that defendant carried insurance covering the truck? See Newell v. Harold Shaffer Leasing Co., 489 F.2d 103, 110 (5th Cir. 1974) (Yes). Why?

3. Recall Problem 2-G ("My Insurance Will Cover It") (Chapter 2B2, supra). If one admits fault by suggesting that his insurance will pay damages, should FRE 411 exclude his admission? Compare Reid v. Owens, 93 P.2d 680, 685 (Utah 1939) (reference to insurance admissible because "freighted with admission") with Cameron v. Columbia Builders, 320 P.2d 251, 254 (Or. 1958) (sever reference to insurance whenever possible).

CHAPTER 6

Competency of Witnesses

A HISTORICAL NOTE

FRE 601 provides that "[e]very person is competent to be a witness unless these rules provide otherwise." This rule provides a striking contrast with the common law, which imposed disabilities that made many potential witnesses incompetent to testify. Often, in fact, the most knowledgeable people could not testify.

Mental incapacity. Those who were insane or mentally impaired were incompetent as witnesses at common law. "It makes no difference from what cause this defect of understanding may have arisen; nor whether it be temporary and curable, or permanent; whether the party be hopelessly an idiot or maniac, or only occasionally insane, as a lunatic . . . . While the deficiency of understanding exists, be the cause of what nature soever, the person is not admissible to be sworn as a witness." S. Greenleaf, Evidence §365 (1883).

Religious belief. At common law, belief in a deity who would punish false swearing, either in this life or the hereafter, was an essential component of the oath. Christian beliefs were not required, and believers in most major religions were competent to take such an oath. But atheists, agnostics, and members of certain sects could not satisfy this religious test and were disqualified. This disqualification has been repudiated everywhere, and affirmations are now allowed as an alternative to the oath. This ground of incompetency is expressly prohibited in some state constitutions. See, e.g., Cal. Const. 1879, art. I, 14 (nobody is "incompetent to be a witness or juror" on account of "opinions on matters of religious belief").

Criminal conviction. A principle of law rooted in Greek and Roman traditions held that persons convicted of certain "infamous" crimes were "civilly dead." They could not vote, hold office, serve on a jury, or exercise other rights of citizenship. One effect of "civil death" that found voice in common law was that persons convicted of felonies or *crimen falsi* (crimes of falsehood) were disqualified as witnesses. They were viewed as having shown such disregard for morality and law that their testimony could not be trusted. This ground of incompetency was abolished by statute in England and most states. A few state statutes still make a person convicted of perjury incompetent to testify.

Infancy. The common law was much stricter than modern evidence law in disqualifying children as witnesses. The issue was generally approached as a disputable presumption of incompetency, in contrast to criminal law doctrines that conclusively presumed that children below a certain age were incapable of committing a crime. In evaluating the competency of child witnesses, courts tended to focus more on their ability to understand the oath than on their capacities of perception and recollection. Wigmore comments:

> In the earlier common-law precedents, . . . the paramount question has been the eligibility of children to take the oath; and the religious sense required for this has usually been the sole subject of argument, to the neglect of the question whether, independently of the oath, any particular degree of intelligence is necessary as a purely testimonial element.

2 J. Wigmore, Evidence §505 at 711 (J. Chadbourn ed., 1979).

Parties. The general rule of the common law was that a party could not be a witness for himself or a coparty in the case. According to an early treatise writer,

> This rule of the common law is founded, not solely in the consideration of interest, but partly also in the general expediency of avoiding the multiplication of temptations to perjury. In some cases at law, and generally by the course of proceedings in equity, one party may appeal to the conscience of the other, by calling him to answer interrogatories upon oath . . . . But where the party would volunteer his own oath, or a co-suitor, identified in interest with him, would offer it, this reason for the admission of the evidence totally fails: "and it is not to be presumed that a man, who complains without cause, or defends without justice, should have honesty enough to confess it."

S. Greenleaf, Evidence §329 (1892). Today this ground of incompetency has been abandoned everywhere.

Spouses of parties. At one time, one spouse was incompetent to testify for or against the other, although an exception allowed testimony about offenses against the family. Favorable testimony was barred because it was likely to be biased by interest and affection. Adverse testimony was barred in order to avoid marital discord and preserve family unity. Also a husband and wife were viewed as one by the common law. Today a spouse is no longer incompetent to give favorable testimony, and rules on adverse spousal testimony have been narrowed and reframed as a spousal testimonial privilege (see Chapter 12, infra). Usually the privilege applies only in criminal cases, and often the holder is the *witness* rather than the defendant (meaning that he cannot block testimony by a spouse who is willing to give it).

Accomplices. The common law barred testimony by accomplices, either for or against a criminal defendant, if they were parties of record to the same charge. This disability continued in some states until the mid-twentieth century. In Washington v. Texas, 388 U.S. 14 (1967), the Supreme Court declared the practice of barring accomplices from testifying for each other to be unconstitutional.

Other interested persons. As an extension of the disability of parties, spouses of parties, and accomplices, the common law also disqualified other persons having any direct interest in the litigation. Here is an early statement of the justification:

> It is founded on the known infirmities of human nature, which is too weak to be generally restrained by religious or moral obligations, when tempted and solicited in a contrary direction by temporal interests. There are, no doubt, many whom no interests could seduce from a sense of duty, and their exclusion by the operation of this rule may in particular cases shut out the truth. But the law must prescribe general rules; and experience proves that more mischief would result from the general reception of interested witnesses than is occasioned by their general exclusion.

T. Starkie, Evidence 83 (1824). This disqualification is now virtually obsolete in all jurisdictions, with the exception of the continuing existence of state Dead Man's Statutes (discussed in section F, infra).

■ NOTES ON HISTORICAL GROUNDS OF INCOMPETENCY

1. Do you agree with the modern view generally rejecting the grounds of incompetency described above? Isn't this repudiation likely to lead to greater perjury in the courtroom? What mechanisms, other than witness incompetence, can be employed to ensure trustworthy testimony?

2. Even though the grounds of incompetency have been generally repudiated, most remain available for another purpose—the impeachment of witnesses. Impeachment for bias is one of the most frequently used forms of impeachment. See also FRE 609 (criminal convictions allowed to impeach credibility). But see FRE 610 (religious beliefs may *not* be used to impeach credibility).

B COMPETENCY: THE MODERN VIEW

UNITED STATES v. LIGHTLY

United States Court of Appeals for the Fourth Circuit
677 F.2d 1027 (1982)

ERVIN, J.

On December 19, 1979, Terrance McKinley, an inmate at Lorton Reformatory in northern Virginia, sustained serious stab wounds from an assault in his cell. Two of McKinley's fellow inmates, Randy Lightly and Clifton McDuffie, were investigated, but only Lightly was formally charged. McDuffie was not indicted by the grand jury because a court appointed psychiatrist found him incompetent to stand trial and criminally insane at the time of the offense. He is presently confined in a mental hospital.

On May 22, 1980, Lightly was convicted of assault with intent to commit murder, and sentenced to ten years imprisonment to run consecutively with the sentence he already was serving. Lightly had also been charged with conspiracy to commit murder, but this charge was dropped.

At trial two different accounts of the stabbing developed. The government's case included testimony from the victim, Terrance McKinley, inmates Harvey Boyd and Robert Thomas, and McKinley's treating physician, Dr. Lance Weaver, which indicated that McDuffie and Lightly cornered McKinley in his cell and repeatedly stabbed him with half pairs of scissors. Lightly received a severe cut on his hand in the assault. Lightly's account of the stabbing was that he was walking along cell block three when he saw McDuffie and McKinley fighting in McKinley's cell. Lightly said he went into the cell to stop the fight and while he was pulling McDuffie off of McKinley, McDuffie turned around and cut him. His testimony was corroborated by three other inmates.

The defense also attempted to have McDuffie testify. McDuffie would have testified that only he and not Lightly had assaulted McKinley. The court ruled McDuffie incompetent to testify because he had been found to be criminally insane and incompetent to stand trial, and was subject to hallucinations.[1] We believe this was error and that Lightly is entitled to a new trial.

Every witness is presumed competent to testify, FRE 601, unless it can be shown that the witness does not have personal knowledge of the matters about which he is to testify, that he does not have the capacity to recall, or that he does not understand the duty to testify truthfully. This Rule applies to persons considered to be insane to the same extent that it applies to other persons. In this

[1]McDuffie believed that "Star Child" told him to kill McKinley because McKinley and Hodge, who apparently was a prison administrator, were going to kill him.

case, the testimony of McDuffie's treating physician indicated that McDuffie had a sufficient memory, that he understood the oath, and that he could communicate what he saw. The district judge chose not to conduct an in camera examination of McDuffie. On this record, it was clearly improper for the court to disqualify McDuffie from testifying....

McDuffie's potential testimony would have substantially corroborated Lightly's testimony. His disqualification from testifying, therefore, cannot be considered harmless error. In finding Lightly entitled to a new trial on this ground, we decline to rule on the other issues he raised in this appeal.

Reversed and remanded.

■ NOTES ON THE MODERN VIEW OF COMPETENCY

1. The ACN to FRE 601 says that a witness "wholly without [mental] capacity is difficult to imagine." Can you imagine such a witness? In extreme cases of insanity or mental incapacity, could not the testimony be excluded under other Rules, such as FRE 401, 403, 602, or 611(a)?

2. When mental capacity of a proposed witness is questioned, does the trial judge have authority to order a psychiatric examination? See United States v. Gutman, 725 F.2d 417, 420 (7th Cir.), *cert. denied*, 469 U.S. 860 (1984) (judge could condition admission of witness's testimony on his willingness to take a psychiatric examination). But see United States v. Raineri, 670 F.2d 702, 709 (7th Cir.), *cert. denied*, 459 U.S. 1035 (1982) (court "must consider the infringement on a witness's privacy, the opportunity for harassment, and the possibility that an examination will hamper law enforcement by deterring witnesses").

3. What if the witness is a drug addict or an alcoholic? See United States v. Jackson, 576 F.2d 46 (5th Cir. 1978) (fact that witness is a narcotics user goes not to competency but to credibility). What if the witness is under the influence of drugs or alcohol while testifying? See United States v. Van Meerbeke, 548 F.2d 415 (2d Cir.) (witness was competent even though, while on the stand, he consumed opium from a trial exhibit), *cert. denied*, 430 U.S. 974 (1976).

THE PERSONAL KNOWLEDGE REQUIREMENT

Before a witness is allowed to testify, FRE 602 requires that evidence must first be introduced "sufficient to support a finding that the witness has personal knowledge" of the matter about which the witness proposes to testify. Who decides whether the personal knowledge requirement is satisfied? Both the judge and the jury have a role to play. Under FRE 104(a) the judge must decide whether there is sufficient evidence to support a jury finding of personal knowledge.

But the ultimate determination of whether the witness has such knowledge is made by the jury under FRE 104(b). If the jury decides that personal knowledge is lacking, the jury is instructed to give the testimony no weight in its deliberations.

The personal knowledge requirement is usually addressed by preliminary questions that bring out how the witness happened to perceive the relevant acts, events, or conditions before she is asked to describe them. In an accident case, for example, a witness may be asked preliminary questions that show that she was walking along the street at the time and place of the accident and that she saw the accident, before she is asked about the accident itself.

How does the personal knowledge requirement apply to a hearsay statement? Even if the statement is admissible, the witness who relates it in court often does not know anything about the acts, events, or conditions described in the statement. Is the witness required to know anything more than that she heard the statement? See ACN to FRE 602 (rule "does not govern" a witness testifying about a hearsay statement "provided he has personal knowledge about the making of the statement"). Of course the hearsay declarant himself is required to have personal knowledge of the matter about which he makes an assertion, except in the case of statements by a party opponent.

D THE OATH REQUIREMENT

FRE 603 sets forth the requirement that every witness "must give an oath or affirmation to testify truthfully." However, the ACN makes clear that "no special verbal formula is required" and that flexibility is needed in dealing with a variety of religious beliefs and with "atheists, conscientious objectors, mental defectives, and children."

UNITED STATES v. FOWLER

United States Court of Appeals for the Fifth Circuit
605 F.2d 181 (1979)

GEE, J.

This cause provides eloquent testimony, albeit negative, to the value of counsel's assistance to criminal defendants. Appellant Fowler, a dealer in gravestones and an apparent tax protester among other things, ceased filing federal income tax returns in 1953. A wheel that did not squeak, Fowler's practices at last attracted Revenue's notice in time to result in his indictment for willful failure to file returns for the years 1971-75. During the investigation, he cooperated with investigating revenue agents no further than by providing them with partial records for the years in question. A trial at which the government employed the "bank-deposits" mode of proof resulted in his conviction on all counts, and he appeals.

Fowler, who conducted his own defense at trial but is represented by counsel here, advances seven points of error. Six present little of merit and may be dealt with rather briefly, but the seventh is of slight difficulty. Upon a careful consideration of all, however, we affirm his convictions. We treat his contentions in the order in which he presents them....

Fowler next complains that the court erred in refusing to allow him to testify after he refused either to swear or affirm that he would tell the truth or submit to cross-examination. At one point in their extended colloquy on the point, the judge offered to accept the simple statement, "I state that I will tell the truth in my testimony." Fowler was willing to do no more than laud himself in such remarks as, "I am a truthful man," and "I would not tell a lie to stay out of jail." Rule 603, Federal Rules of Evidence, is clear and simple: "Before testifying, every witness shall be required to declare that he will testify truthfully, by oath or affirmation ...." No witness has the right to testify but on penalty of perjury and subject to cross-examination. This contention is frivolous....

We cannot doubt that Fowler has derived substantial financial benefit from a long refusal to carry his share of the common burdens of citizenship. Sad to say, for he is a man no longer young, he must now respond not only in currency but in another coin: incarceration. Counsel's efforts on his behalf are commendable, but they came too late.

Affirmed.

■ NOTES ON THE OATH REQUIREMENT

1. What if a witness under subpoena refuses to be sworn? If refusing to testify can be punished as contempt, how about refusing to take an oath or make an affirmation? See Note, A Reconsideration of the Sworn Testimony Requirement: Securing Truth in the Twentieth Century, 75 Mich. L. Rev. 1681, 1698 n.89 (1977) (collecting state and foreign cases holding refusal to be sworn to be contempt of court).

2. An affirmation differs from an oath by eliminating reference to swearing or divine power. The words and ceremony to be used in administering an oath or affirmation are not specified in FRE 603 or similar state rules. It has been held that neither raising the hand nor using the word "solemn" is required. Flexibility in the wording of oaths or affirmations is often mandated by state constitutional provisions that prohibit religious tests for witnesses. With respect to the appropriate flexibility, see United States v. Looper, 419 F.2d 1405, 1407 n.4 (4th Cir. 1969) (English courts "have permitted Chinese to break a saucer, a Mohammedan to bow before the Koran and touch it to his head and a Parsee to tie a rope around his waist to qualify them to tell the truth").

3. One purpose of the oath is to impress on the mind of the witness a duty to speak only the truth. A less obvious purpose is to make him amenable to criminal prosecution if perjured testimony is given. Given possible criminal liability, should witnesses be warned of the penalties for perjury before testifying? See United States v. Mandujano, 425 U.S. 564 (1976) (no requirement to warn witness not to commit perjury or to tell the truth). Consider Oregon Rule of Evidence 603(2) (suggesting but not requiring this wording: "Under penalty of perjury, do you solemnly swear that the evidence you shall give in the issue (or matter) now pending between _________ and _________ shall be the truth, the whole truth and nothing but the truth, so help you God?").

4. Are there other factors, apart from the words in an oath or affirmation, that may have an effect in impressing on a witness the duty to tell the truth? What about the solemnity with which the oath is given and whether it is administered by the judge or a court clerk?

5. The typical oath or affirmation requires the witness to tell the "whole" truth. From what you have learned thus far, do you think witnesses are being asked to make a commitment that they may not be allowed to fulfill? Remember that witnesses can generally respond only to the questions asked.

The Reluctant Oath-Taker: The Bhagwan Shree Rajneesh

JP Laffont / Sygma / Corbis

Some witnesses have deep personal reservations to the oath requirement for a variety of reasons. The Bhagwan Shree Rajneesh was a spiritual leader from India who started a commune in a remote area of Oregon in the 1980s. He was involved in extensive litigation resulting from activities of his followers. In one lawsuit his deposition was taken, and he began with these words: "Your honor, before I take the oath, I have to say a few things, otherwise the oath will be a fraud. The first thing—I have always been against the ritual of oath-taking for the simple reason that if a man is capable of lying he can lie even while he is taking the oath. The oath can be a lie, and if a man is a man of truth, the oath creates a dilemma for that man. For the man of truth to take the oath means that he is capable of lying. Without the oath, he will lie and with the oath he will say the truth. You are putting me into a dilemma, but I am not a serious man. In life, I never take anything seriously, except the jokes. I will take this oath just to play the game of this deposition. I will follow the rule, but I would like you to remember that by taking the oath I am lying in the first place. It is against my philosophy of life and you are forcing me to take the oath; that means you are freeing me, giving me the freedom to lie later, although I am not going to lie. The oath allows me to lie, but in spite of that freedom I will only say the truth, because I am incapable of lying. This is impossible, that is against my being and my existence. Now, just to play the game, I will take the oath. . . ." Eugene (Oregon) Register Guard, p. 14A, August 30, 1984.

E THE CHILD WITNESS

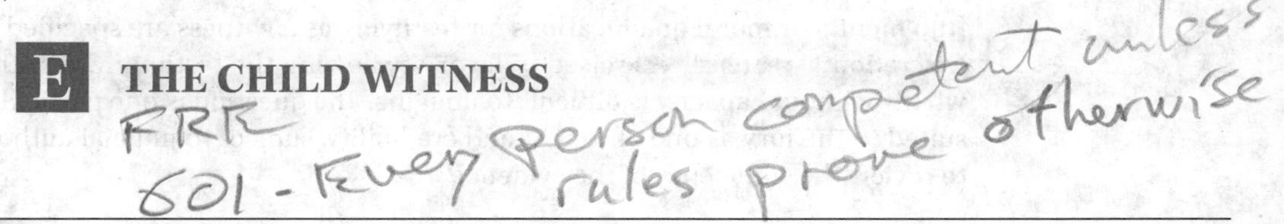

RICKETTS v. DELAWARE

Delaware Supreme Court
488 A.2d 856 (1985)

MOORE, J.

This is an appeal from a conviction of first degree rape of a five-year-old girl. The sole issue is whether the trial court committed reversible error in allowing the minor victim, then six years old, to testify without an adequate foundation to determine her competency as a witness. We find that under Rules 601 and 603 of the Delaware Rules of Evidence, the trial court did not err in permitting the child to testify. Accordingly, we affirm.

The defendant, Darrell Ricketts was indicted, tried and convicted on one count of first degree rape of a five year old girl. The child was the daughter of a woman the defendant was dating. At a bench trial, the victim, then six years old, testified with the use of anatomically correct dolls and drawings that Ricketts had anally raped her while her mother slept in an adjacent room.

Before testifying, a voir dire examination was conducted during which the child stated that she went to church, that a lie was a thing that is not true, and that it was a bad thing to tell a lie. She testified further that if you tell a lie you sometimes get a spanking. She also promised to tell the truth about everything that she was asked in court. However, in response to questions by the defense attorney and the court, the witness indicated that she was not sure what heaven was.

The court ruled that the child was competent to testify because, although she did not understand the concept of perjury, she knew the difference between truth and falsehood, which was the only test of competency.

The sole issue is whether the trial court erred in permitting the six-year-old to testify. A determination by the trial court that a witness is competent to testify pursuant to DRE 601 and 603 will be reversed only if the determination was an abuse of the trial judge's discretion. Thompson v. State, 399 A.2d 194, 198-99 (Del. Super. 1979).

Under DRE 601 "[e]very person is competent to be a witness except as otherwise provided in these rules."[1] The Advisory Committee's Note[2] to the Federal Rules of Evidence makes the following observations about Rule 601:

> [n]o mental or moral qualifications for testifying as a witness are specified .... Discretion is regularly exercised in favor of allowing the testimony. A witness wholly without capacity is difficult to imagine. The question is one particularly suited to the jury as one of weight and credibility, subject to judicial authority to review the sufficiency of the evidence.

ACN to FRE 601.

Thus, Rule 601 adopts the position that almost anyone is competent to testify, letting the concerns of mental or moral capacity go to the issues of credibility or weight given to the evidence.

Accordingly, under the Delaware Rules of Evidence the six-year-old rape victim is presumed competent to testify once the trial judge is satisfied by voir dire that the child understood her obligation to tell the truth, and the difference between truth and falsehood.

The defendant further argues that the child should not have been permitted to testify in this case because the voir dire examination demonstrated that she did not understand the oath. DRE 603 provides that "[b]efore testifying, every witness shall be required to declare that he will testify truthfully, by oath or affirmation administered in a form calculated to awaken his conscience and impress his mind with his duty to do so." DRE 603. We once again turn to the Federal Rules of Evidence Advisory Committee's Note, which states: "[t]he rule is designed to afford the flexibility required in dealing with . . . children."

Here, the child testified that she promised not to tell a lie and to tell the truth about everything that was asked of her in court. The trial court was correct in concluding that this was a sufficient affirmation that she would testify truthfully.

---

[1]The only rules specifically providing for the disqualification of a witness are those precluding the presiding judge or a member of the jury from testifying in the trial in which they are sitting. DRE 605, 606.

[2]As the comment to DRE 601 points out, this rule tracks URE 601 and the first sentence of FRE 601. The Delaware Study Committee, which drafted the DRE has stated that the historical materials surrounding the promulgation of the Federal Rules and the FRE official notes and comments, "should be considered as being part of the comments prepared by the Delaware Study Committee and a court should refer to these materials in construing these rules." DRE, Delaware Study Committee Prefatory Note.

Therefore, we conclude that this six-year-old was properly found to be competent to testify, and that her promise to "tell the truth" was an affirmation sufficient to impress on her mind her duty to be truthful as required by DRE 603.[3]

NOTES ON CHILDREN AS WITNESSES

1. Is a voir dire examination of a child witness always necessary? What questions should be asked of the child at such an examination? Usually the examination, when one occurs, focuses on the child's understanding of the duty to tell the truth as well as the child's ability to communicate.

2. Some states do not follow the approach of FRE 601 and presume incompetency of children below a certain age. See, e.g., N.Y. Crim. Proc. Law §60.20 (Consol. 2010) (one who is under nine years old cannot testify unless he or she "understands the nature of an oath").

3. What if a child satisfies the competency requirement, but because of age and the subject of her expected testimony the experience of testifying would be traumatic? In such circumstances, some states authorize presentation of the child's testimony by closed-circuit television or videotaped deposition. A "case specific" finding that such a procedure is necessary to protect the welfare of the child is constitutionally required in order to override the defendant's right to face his accuser. See Maryland v. Craig, 497 U.S. 836 (1990).

4. Could a child be found competent for purposes of direct examination but of insufficient maturity to withstand cross-examination? Perhaps, but cross-examination is what counts when analyzing a defendant's right of confrontation.

5. Courts often overlook competency issues or override objections on that ground when out-of-court statements by children are offered under hearsay exceptions. See, e.g., United States v. Nick, 604 F.2d 1199 (9th Cir. 1979) (excited utterance); People v. Wilkins, 349 N.W.2d 815 (Mich. App. 1984) (statement for medical diagnosis). Most, if not all, states recognize one or more hearsay exceptions for statements by children describing abuse or sexual assaults.

6. States have experimented with procedures in sex abuse prosecutions to facilitate testimony by child witnesses and reduce the trauma of testifying. Innovations include use of interdisciplinary teams from law enforcement and social service agencies, appointment of an advocate to support the child before and during trial, and assignment of one prosecutor to all stages of a case. Anatomical dolls are also used to help children overcome verbal inhibitions in describing sexual activity.

[3]Because all witnesses (except those specifically excluded by the rules) are competent to testify under DRE 601, we note it is no longer necessary to go through the guidelines for determining competency of a child witness set forth in Kelluem v. State, 396 A.2d 166, 168 (Del. Super. 1978).

PREVIOUSLY HYPNOTIZED WITNESSES

ROCK v. ARKANSAS

United States Supreme Court
483 U.S. 44 (1987)

Justice BLACKMUN delivered the opinion of the Court.

The issue presented in this case is whether Arkansas' evidentiary rule prohibiting the admission of hypnotically refreshed testimony violated petitioner's constitutional right to testify on her own behalf as a defendant in a criminal case.

Petitioner Vickie Lorene Rock was charged with manslaughter in the death of her husband, Frank Rock, on July 1, 1983. A dispute had been simmering about Frank's wish to move from the couple's small apartment adjacent to Vickie's beauty parlor to a trailer she owned outside town. That night a fight erupted when Frank refused to let petitioner eat some pizza and prevented her from leaving the apartment to get something else to eat. When police arrived on the scene they found Frank on the floor with a bullet wound in his chest. Petitioner urged the officers to help her husband, and cried to a sergeant who took her in charge, "please save him" and "don't let him die." The police removed her from the building because she was upset and because she interfered with their investigation by her repeated attempts to use the telephone to call her husband's parents. According to the testimony of one of the investigating officers, petitioner told him that "she stood up to leave the room and [her husband] grabbed her by the throat and choked her and threw her against the wall and . . . at that time she walked over and picked up the weapon and pointed it toward the floor and he hit her again and she shot him."

Because petitioner could not remember the precise details of the shooting, her attorney suggested that she submit to hypnosis in order to refresh her memory. Petitioner was hypnotized twice by Doctor Betty Back, a licensed neuropsychologist with training in the field of hypnosis. Doctor Back interviewed petitioner for an hour prior to the first hypnosis session, taking notes on petitioner's general history and her recollections of the shooting. Both hypnosis sessions were recorded on tape. Petitioner did not relate any new information during either of the sessions, but, after the hypnosis, she was able to remember that at the time of the incident she had her thumb on the hammer of the gun, but had not held her finger on the trigger. She also recalled that the gun had discharged when her husband grabbed her arm during the scuffle. As a result of the details that petitioner was able to remember about the shooting, her counsel arranged for a gun expert to examine the handgun, a single action Hawes .22 Deputy Marshal. That inspection revealed that the gun was defective and prone to fire, when hit or dropped, without the trigger's being pulled.

When the prosecutor learned of the hypnosis sessions, he filed a motion to exclude petitioner's testimony. The trial judge held a pretrial hearing on the motion and concluded that no hypnotically refreshed testimony would be admitted. The court issued an order limiting petitioner's testimony to "matters remembered and stated to the examiner prior to being placed under hypnosis." At trial, petitioner introduced testimony by the gun expert, but the court limited petitioner's own description of the events on the day of the shooting to a reiteration of the sketchy information in Doctor Back's notes. The jury convicted petitioner on the manslaughter charge and she was sentenced to 10 years imprisonment and a $10,000 fine.

On appeal, the Supreme Court of Arkansas rejected petitioner's claim that the limitations on her testimony violated her right to present her defense. The court concluded that "the dangers of admitting this kind of testimony outweigh whatever probative value it may have," and decided to follow the approach of States that have held hypnotically refreshed testimony of witnesses inadmissible per se. Although the court acknowledged that "a defendant's right to testify is fundamental," it ruled that the exclusion of petitioner's testimony did not violate her constitutional rights. Any "prejudice or deprivation" she suffered "was minimal and resulted from her own actions and not by any erroneous ruling of the court." We granted certiorari, to consider the constitutionality of Arkansas' per se rule excluding a criminal defendant's hypnotically refreshed testimony.

Petitioner's claim that her testimony was impermissibly excluded is bottomed on her constitutional right to testify in her own defense. At this point in the development of our adversary system, it cannot be doubted that a defendant in a criminal case has the right to take the witness stand and to testify in his or her own defense . . . .

The question now before the Court is whether a criminal defendant's right to testify may be restricted by a state rule that excludes her posthypnosis testimony. This is not the first time this Court has faced a constitutional challenge to a state rule, designed to ensure trustworthy evidence, that interfered with the ability of a defendant to offer testimony. In Washington v. Texas, 388 U.S. 14 (1967), the Court was confronted with a state statute that prevented persons charged as principals, accomplices, or accessories in the same crime from being introduced as witnesses for one another . . . . [T]he Court found that the mere presence of the witness in the courtroom was not enough to satisfy the Constitution's Compulsory Process Clause. By preventing the defendant from having the benefit of his accomplice's testimony, "the State *arbitrarily* denied him the right to put on the stand a witness who was physically and mentally capable of testifying to events that he had personally observed, and whose testimony would have been relevant and material to the defense." (Emphasis added.)

Just as a State may not apply an arbitrary rule of competence to exclude a material defense witness from taking the stand, it also may not apply a rule of evidence that permits a witness to take the stand, but arbitrarily excludes material portions of his testimony. In Chambers v. Mississippi, 410 U.S. 284 (1973), the Court invalidated a State's hearsay rule on the ground that it abridged the defendant's right to "present witnesses in his own defense." Chambers was tried for a murder to which another person repeatedly had confessed in the presence of acquaintances. The State's hearsay rule, coupled with a "voucher" rule that did not allow the defendant to cross-examine the confessed murderer directly, prevented Chambers from introducing testimony concerning these confessions, which were critical to his defense. This Court reversed the judgment of conviction, holding that when a state rule of evidence conflicts with the right to present witnesses, the rule may "not be applied mechanistically to defeat the ends of justice," but must meet the fundamental standards of due process. In the Court's view, the State in *Chambers* did not demonstrate that the hearsay testimony in that case, which bore "assurances of trustworthiness" including corroboration by other evidence, would be unreliable, and thus the defendant should have been able to introduce the exculpatory testimony.

Of course, the right to present relevant testimony is not without limitation. The right may, in appropriate cases, bow to accommodate other legitimate interests in the criminal trial process.[11] But restrictions of a defendant's right to testify may not be arbitrary or disproportionate to the purposes they are designed to serve. In applying its evidentiary rules a State must evaluate whether the interests served by a rule justify the limitation imposed on the defendant's constitutional right to testify.

The Arkansas rule enunciated by the state courts does not allow a trial court to consider whether posthypnosis testimony may be admissible in a particular case; it is a per se rule prohibiting the admission at trial of any defendant's hypnotically refreshed testimony on the ground that such testimony is always unreliable. Thus, in Arkansas, an accused's testimony is limited to matters that he or she can prove were remembered *before* hypnosis. This rule operates to the detriment of any defendant who undergoes hypnosis, without regard to the reasons for it, the circumstances under which it took place, or any independent verification of the information it produced.

[11]Numerous state procedural and evidentiary rules control the presentation of evidence and do not offend the defendant's right to testify. See, e.g., Chambers v. Mississippi, 410 U.S. 284, 302 (1973) ("In the exercise of this right, the accused, as is required of the State, must comply with established rules of procedure and evidence designed to assure both fairness and reliability in the ascertainment of guilt and innocence"); Washington v. Texas, 388 U.S. 14, 23 n.21 (1967) (opinion should not be construed as disapproving testimonial privileges or nonarbitrary rules that disqualify those incapable of observing events due to mental infirmity or infancy from being witnesses).

In this case, the application of that rule had a significant adverse effect on petitioner's ability to testify. It virtually prevented her from describing any of the events that occurred on the day of the shooting, despite corroboration of many of those events by other witnesses. Even more importantly, under the court's rule petitioner was not permitted to describe the actual shooting except in the words contained in Doctor Back's notes. The expert's description of the gun's tendency to misfire would have taken on greater significance if the jury had heard petitioner testify that she did not have her finger on the trigger and that the gun went off when her husband hit her arm.

In establishing its per se rule, the Arkansas Supreme Court simply followed the approach taken by a number of States that have decided that hypnotically enhanced testimony should be excluded at trial on the ground that it tends to be unreliable. Other States that have adopted an exclusionary rule, however, have done so for the testimony of *witnesses*, not for the testimony of a *defendant.* The Arkansas Supreme Court failed to perform the constitutional analysis that is necessary when a defendant's right to testify is at stake.

Although the Arkansas court concluded that any testimony that cannot be proved to be the product of prehypnosis memory is unreliable, many courts have eschewed a per se rule and permit the admission of hypnotically refreshed testimony. Hypnosis by trained physicians or psychologists has been recognized as a valid therapeutic technique since 1958, although there is no generally accepted theory to explain the phenomenon, or even a consensus on a single definition of hypnosis. See Council on Scientific Affairs, Scientific Status of Refreshing Recollection by the Use of Hypnosis, 253 J.A.M.A. 1918, 1918-1919 (1985) (Council Report).[17] The use of hypnosis in criminal investigations, however, is controversial, and the current medical and legal view of its appropriate role is unsettled.

Responses of individuals to hypnosis vary greatly. The popular belief that hypnosis guarantees the accuracy of recall is as yet without established foundation and, in fact, hypnosis often has no effect at all on memory. The most common response to hypnosis, however, appears to be an increase in both correct and incorrect recollections.[18] Three general characteristics of hypnosis may lead to the introduction of inaccurate memories: the subject becomes "suggestible" and may try to please the hypnotist with answers the subject

---

[17]Hypnosis has been described as "involving the focusing of attention; increased responsiveness to suggestions; suspension of disbelief with a lowering of critical judgment; potential for altering perception, motor control, or memory in response to suggestions; and the subjective experience of responding involuntarily." Council Report, 253 J.A.M.A. at 1919.

[18]"When hypnosis is used to refresh recollection, one of the following outcomes occurs: (1) hypnosis produces recollections that are not substantially different from nonhypnotic recollections; (2) it yields recollections that are more inaccurate than nonhypnotic memory; or, most frequently, (3) it results in more information being reported, but these recollections contain both accurate and inaccurate details.... There are no data to support a fourth alternative, namely, that hypnosis increases remembering of only accurate information." [Court cites Council Report, supra.]

thinks will be met with approval; the subject is likely to "confabulate," that is, to fill in details from the imagination in order to make an answer more coherent and complete; and, the subject experiences "memory hardening," which gives him great confidence in both true and false memories, making effective cross-examination more difficult. Despite the unreliability that hypnosis concededly may introduce, however, the procedure has been credited as instrumental in obtaining investigative leads or identifications that were later confirmed by independent evidence.

The inaccuracies the process introduces can be reduced, although perhaps not eliminated, by the use of procedural safeguards. One set of suggested guidelines calls for hypnosis to be performed only by a psychologist or psychiatrist with special training in its use and who is independent of the investigation. See Orne, The Use and Misuse of Hypnosis in Court, 27 Intl. J. Clinical & Experimental Hypnosis 311, 335-336 (1979). These procedures reduce the possibility that biases will be communicated to the hypersuggestive subject by the hypnotist. Suggestion will be less likely also if the hypnosis is conducted in a neutral setting with no one present but the hypnotist and the subject. Tape or video recording of all interrogations, before, during, and after hypnosis, can help reveal if leading questions were asked. Such guidelines do not guarantee the accuracy of the testimony, because they cannot control the subject's own motivations or any tendency to confabulate, but they do provide a means of controlling overt suggestions.

The more traditional means of assessing accuracy of testimony also remain applicable in the case of a previously hypnotized defendant. Certain information recalled as a result of hypnosis may be verified as highly accurate by corroborating evidence. Cross-examination, even in the face of a confident defendant, is an effective tool for revealing inconsistencies. Moreover, a jury can be educated to the risks of hypnosis through expert testimony and cautionary instructions. Indeed, it is probably to a defendant's advantage to establish carefully the extent of his memory prior to hypnosis, in order to minimize the decrease in credibility the procedure might introduce.

We are not now prepared to endorse without qualifications the use of hypnosis as an investigative tool; scientific understanding of the phenomenon and of the means to control the effects of hypnosis is still in its infancy. Arkansas, however, has not justified the exclusion of *all* of a defendant's testimony that the defendant is unable to prove to be the product of prehypnosis memory. A State's legitimate interest in barring unreliable evidence does not extend to per se exclusions that may be reliable in an individual case. Wholesale inadmissibility of a defendant's testimony is an arbitrary restriction on the right to testify in the absence of clear evidence by the State repudiating the validity of all posthypnosis recollections. The State would be well within its powers if it established guidelines to aid trial courts in the evaluation of posthypnosis testimony and it may be able to show that testimony in a particular case is so unreliable that exclusion is justified. But it has not shown that hypnotically enhanced testimony is always so untrustworthy and so immune to the traditional means of evaluating credibility that it should disable a defendant from presenting her version of the events for which she is on trial.

In this case, the defective condition of the gun corroborated the details petitioner remembered about the shooting. The tape recordings provided some means to evaluate the hypnosis and the trial judge concluded that Doctor Back did not suggest responses with leading questions. Those circumstances present an argument for admissibility of petitioner's testimony in this particular case, an argument that must be considered by the trial court. Arkansas' per se rule excluding all posthypnosis testimony infringes impermissibly on the right of a defendant to testify on his or her own behalf.

[The dissenting opinion of Chief Justice Rehnquist, joined by three other Justices, is omitted.]

NOTES ON HYPNOSIS IN THE COURTROOM

1. Is *Rock* limited to criminal defendants, or does it also prevent a per se ban of testimony by defense witnesses whose memory has been hypnotically refreshed? The Court doesn't say, but the case is based on a *criminal defendant's* right to produce evidence. Therefore, it would at least not prevent a per se ban on prosecution witnesses or witnesses in a civil case whose testimony has been hypnotically refreshed.

2. What are the dangers of hypnotically refreshed testimony that most concern courts and legislatures? The problem of "confabulation" has been described as follows:

> The hypnotic suggestion to relive a past event, particularly when accompanied by questions about specific details, puts pressure on the subject to provide information for which few, if any, actual memories are available. This situation may jog the subject's memory and produce some increased recall, but it will also cause him to fill in details that are plausible but consist of memories or fantasies from other times. It is extremely difficult to know which aspects of hypnotically aided recall are historically accurate and which aspects have been confabulated.

Orne, The Use and Misuse of Hypnosis in Court, 27 Intl. J. Clinical & Experimental Hypnosis 311, 317-318 (1979).

3. As the Court says in *Rock*, many states besides Arkansas also have a per se rule barring the admission of hypnotically refreshed testimony, although not necessarily that of criminal defendants. See, e.g., Contreras v. State, 718 P.2d 129 (Alaska 1986); State *ex rel.* Collins v. Superior Court, 644 P.2d 1266, 1293-1294 (Ariz. 1982); Bundy v. State, 471 So. 2d 9, 18-19 (Fla. 1985), *cert. denied*, 479

U.S. 894 (1986); Commonwealth v. Nazarovitch, 436 A.2d 170, 177 (Pa. 1981); State v. Martin, 684 P.2d 651 (Wash. 1984).

4. Some jurisdictions take the opposite view, and have adopted a per se rule of admissibility for hypnotically refreshed testimony, holding that the fact of hypnosis affects only credibility, not admissibility. See, e.g., Beck v. Norris, 801 F.2d 242, 244-245 (6th Cir. 1986); United States v. Awkard, 597 F.2d 667, 669 (9th Cir.), *cert. denied*, 444 U.S. 885 (1979); State v. Wren, 425 So. 2d 756 (La. 1983); State v. Brown, 337 N.W.2d 138, 151 (N.D. 1983); State v. Glebock, 616 S.W.2d 897, 903-904 (Tenn. Crim. App. 1981). In these jurisdictions, parties are often allowed to offer expert testimony on the reliability of hypnotically refreshed testimony and to request cautionary instructions to the jury that will enable the jury to assess the proper weight to be given to the evidence.

5. Some courts balance the probative value of the evidence against its prejudicial effect on a case-by-case basis. See, e.g., McQueen v. Garrison, 814 F.2d 951, 958 (4th Cir. 1987); Wicker v. McCotten, 783 F.2d 487, 492-493 (5th Cir.), *cert. denied*, 478 U.S. 1010 (1986); State v. Iwakiri, 682 P.2d 571, 578 (Idaho 1984) (weigh "totality of circumstances").

6. Finally, some courts will admit hypnotically refreshed testimony, provided proper procedural safeguards were followed. See Sprynczynatyk v. General Motors, 771 F.2d 1112 (8th Cir. 1985), *cert. denied*, 475 U.S. 1046 (1986):

> We adopt a rule which requires the district court, in cases where hypnosis has been used, to conduct pretrial hearings on the procedures used during the hypnotic session in question and assess the effect of hypnosis upon the reliability of the testimony before making a decision on admissibility. The proponent of the hypnotically enhanced testimony bears the burden of proof during this proceeding.

In making the determination whether the hypnotically refreshed testimony is sufficiently reliable, the *Sprynczynatyk* court instructed trial judges to consider the following safeguards:

> (1) The hypnotic session should be conducted by an impartial licensed psychiatrist or psychologist trained in the use of hypnosis and thus aware of its possible effects on memory so as to aid in the prevention of improper suggestions and confabulation. Appointment of the psychiatrist or psychologist should first be approved by the trial court . . . .
> (2) Information given to the hypnotist by either party concerning the case should be noted, preferably in written form, so that the extent of information the subject received from the hypnotist may be determined.
> (3) Before hypnosis, the hypnotist should obtain a detailed description of the facts from the subject, avoiding adding new elements to the subject's description.
> (4) The session should be recorded so a permanent record is available to ensure against suggestive procedures. Videotape is a preferable method of recordation.

(5) Preferably, only the hypnotist and subject should be present during any phase of the hypnotic session, but other persons should be allowed to attend if their attendance can be shown to be essential and steps are taken to prevent their influencing the results of the session.

771 F.2d at 1123 n.14.

G DEAD MAN'S STATUTES

In repealing statutes rendering a witness incompetent because of interest, legislatures encounter continuing concern about an interested witness testifying on a transaction with a person now deceased. Not only does the survivor have an incentive to testify falsely, but the death of the other may make it hard to expose or rebut false testimony. As a surviving remnant of incompetency by reason of interest, most states retain what are commonly referred to as Dead Man's Statutes, which limit testimony about transactions with deceased persons.

In a few states, such statutes apply to torts involving the deceased as well as contractual transactions. See, e.g., Zeigler v. Moore, 335 P.2d 425 (Nev. 1959) (survivor may not testify to manner in which automobile collision occurred when the other party is deceased). In their most extreme form, they bar testimony by the survivor on *any* fact occurring prior to the other's death, even facts that could not be personally disputed by the other if she had lived. See, e.g., Topkins v. DeLeon, 595 P.2d 242 (Colo. 1979) (plaintiffs who survived automobile accident barred from testifying regarding their pain and suffering that occurred prior to decedent's death).

A typical example of a dead person's statute is the following:

> Rule 601. General Rule of Competency; Disqualification of Witness West's North Carolina General Statutes Annotated
>
> (c) Disqualification of interested persons.—Upon the trial of an action .... party ... shall not be examined as a witness in his own behalf or interest ... against the executor, administrator or survivor of a deceased person ... concerning any oral communication between the witness and the deceased person or lunatic.

Scholars have long criticized the Dead Man's Statute as a crude legislative device that unfairly casts suspicion on all who pursue claims against estates of decedents. Consider this strong criticism by Dean Mason Ladd:

> Dead man statutes in different states continue to mystify able courts and good lawyers in their endless complexities of interpretation and application to the ever changing facts requiring proof to establish transactions and communications had with a person since deceased. Statutes vary greatly as do the interpretations of similar statutes. The basic objective of all statutes is the

> same. Survivors of a deceased person are looked upon with suspicion as persons ready on first opportunity to fabricate false claims against the decedent's estate because the deceased is unable to repudiate them. The right of living claimants to establish honest claims is sacrificed because of the danger that a substantially greater number of the survivors would take advantage of the situation and give perjured testimony for their gain. The existence of the dead man statutes represents the judgment of legislative bodies that the general honesty and truthfulness of people in modern society is at a pretty low ebb and that all it takes is the motive of interest plus a good chance created by death of one of the parties to cause the majority of people to concoct false claims to plunder the estates of deceased persons.

Ladd, The Dead Man Statute: Some Further Observations and a Legislative Proposal, 26 Iowa L. Rev. 207 (1941). See also Ray, The Dead Man's Statute—A Relic of the Past, 10 Sw. L.J. 390 (1956).

A few states have repealed their Dead Man's Statute entirely. See, e.g., Ariz. R. Evid. 601; Nev. Rev. Stat. §50.015. Many other states have narrowed the scope of testimony excluded by their statutes or have adopted approaches other than restricting the competency of witnesses. For example, New Jersey requires that in litigation against a decedent or a lunatic testimony about an alleged "promise, statement or act" of the decedent or lunatic must be established" by clear and convincing evidence." N.J. Stat. Ann. §2A:81-2 (West 2010).

California has adopted an interesting approach. In cases where a claim is made against the estate of a decedent, statements by the decedent may be admitted to rebut such claims. See California Evid. Code §1261 (West 2009). The California statute "opens the mouth" of both parties. It permits survivor to testify (simply because it does not restrict her testimony), and it does the next best thing for the decedent, which is to create a hearsay exception paving the way to admit much of what he said on the subject while alive. The California provision tries to help people with claims against estates, while accommodating the policy of protecting estates against fraudulent claims.

There is no federal Dead Man's Statute. However, the last sentence of FRE 601 was added by Congress in part to preserve recognition of state Dead Man's Statutes in diversity litigation. It provides that "state law governs the witness's competency regarding a claim or defense for which state law provides the rule of decision."

LAWYERS AS WITNESSES

The Federal Rules of Evidence do not prohibit lawyers from testifying. The problem is that testimony by an attorney who is acting as counsel violates applicable ethics rules, unless the testimony falls into one of several narrow exceptions. DR 5-101(B) of the Code of Professional Responsibility provides:

> A lawyer shall not accept employment in contemplated or pending litigation if he knows or it is obvious that he or a lawyer in his firm ought to be called as a witness, except that he may undertake the employment and he or a lawyer in his firm may testify: (1) If the testimony will relate solely to an uncontested matter. (2) If the testimony will relate solely to a matter of formality and there is no reason to believe that substantial evidence will be offered in opposition to the testimony. (3) If the testimony will relate solely to the nature and value of legal services rendered in the case by the lawyer or his firm to the client. (4) As to any matter, if refusal would work a substantial hardship on the client because of the distinctive value of the lawyer or his firm as counsel in the particular case.

See also DR 5-102(A) (requiring a lawyer to withdraw as counsel when "it is obvious that he or a lawyer in his firm ought to be called as a witness on behalf of his client").

The Code of Professional Responsibility explains the rationale for this ethical proscription as follows:

> Occasionally a lawyer is called upon to decide in a particular case whether he will be a witness or an advocate. If a lawyer is both counsel and witness, he becomes more easily impeachable for interest and thus may be a less effective witness. Conversely, the opposing counsel may be handicapped in challenging the credibility of the lawyer when the lawyer also appears as an advocate in the case. An advocate who becomes a witness is in the unseemly and ineffective position of arguing his own credibility. The roles of an advocate and of a witness are inconsistent; the function of an advocate is to advance or argue the cause of another, while that of a witness is to state facts objectively.

Model Code of Professional Responsibility, EC 5-9 (1980).

■ NOTES ON LAWYERS AS WITNESSES

1. The ABA Model Rules of Professional Conduct contain a similar proscription. See Rule 3.7, which provides:

> (a) A lawyer shall not act as advocate at a trial in which the lawyer is likely to be a necessary witness except where:
>
> (1) The testimony relates to an uncontested issue;
>
> (2) The testimony relates to the nature and value of legal services rendered in the case; or

(3) Disqualification of the lawyer would work substantial hardship on the client . . . .

(b) A lawyer may act as advocate in a trial in which another lawyer in the lawyer's firm is likely to be called as a witness unless precluded from doing so by Rule 1.7 or Rule 1.9. [Rules 1.7 and 1.9 deal with conflict of interest situations.]

2. It would be a simple matter to codify Disciplinary Rule 5-101(B) or Model Rule of Professional Conduct 3.7 as a ground of incompetency in an evidence code. What are the merits of such an approach?

3. Sometimes an attorney seeks to impeach a witness by inquiring about a prior inconsistent statement made to the attorney. If the witness denies making the statement, the attorney may be handicapped in proving the inconsistency because it would require the attorney to take the stand. What could an attorney do when interviewing witnesses to avoid this situation?

I JUDGES AS WITNESSES

Somewhat surprisingly, the common law did not consider a judge incompetent to testify in a trial over which the judge was presiding. FRE 605 is explicit in making this one of the few federal grounds of incompetency. Note that FRE 605 does not prohibit calling a judge as a witness in another trial or hearing, even a posttrial proceeding in the same case. Does it follow that any question may be asked of the judge at such a subsequent hearing? See Washington v. Strickland, 673 F.2d 879, 902-906 (5th Cir. 1982) (holding that trial judge could not be questioned regarding his reasons for giving the death sentence to defendant; rationale of FRE 606(b) barring testimony by jurors on mental processes "applies equally here"), *on reh'g*, 693 F.2d 1243 (5th Cir. 1982), *rev'd on other grounds*, 466 U.S. 668 (1984).

FRE 614 authorizes the court to question witnesses. Does this provision potentially conflict with FRE 605? In one pre-Rules criminal prosecution, the accused testified, and the judge asked him, about their prior conversation:

> [D]idn't I say to you at that time that if you wanted to do what was right you would tell the truth about it, no matter who it involved, and that I felt sure you had been selling liquor, and that you replied that you would not tell the truth, because you felt that it would involve so many people, and that you would rather take your punishment than tell the truth?

Doesn't such questioning improperly cast the judge as a witness in the case in which he presides? The reviewing court thought so, for it reversed the conviction:

> It is the right and duty of a federal judge to elicit by questions the relevant facts when they have not been brought out by counsel. But a judge cannot testify in

> the form of questions. If a judge has in his possession evidences of a defendant's guilt or innocence they can be adduced for or against him only by examination and cross-examination of the judge on the witness stand at a trial presided over by another judge.

Terrell v. United States, 6 F.2d 498, 499 (4th Cir. 1925).

J JURORS AS WITNESSES

1. Preverdict Testimony by Jurors

The common law did not disqualify a juror from testifying before a jury of which he was a member. There was concern that a juror whose testimony was excluded would simply relate the information to other jurors without cross-examination or impeachment and that it would be preferable to have such sharing of information in open court. Today the issue rarely arises because jurors who might be called as witnesses are usually identified in voir dire and excused from serving. Nonetheless, even where the potential of a juror to be called as a witness has been overlooked, FRE 606(a) prohibits testimony by that juror before the jury panel on which he serves.

PROBLEM 6-A. Outside Influence

In a highly publicized criminal prosecution of Volstad, a leading political figure, the jury is given strict instructions not to read newspaper accounts of the trial or discuss the case with anyone. During the trial, the judge receives information that one juror read newspaper accounts of the trial and discussed those accounts with others at lunch. The judge also hears that an associate of the defendant talked with the same juror outside of court and offered what may have been a bribe. During a recess in trial, after other jurors had been excused, the judge questions the juror about both matters. Does FRE 606(a) bar such inquiry?

2. Postverdict Testimony by Jurors

FRE 606(b) imposes severe limitations on a litigant's ability to seek a new trial by bringing evidence of jury misconduct to the attention of the court. It renders a juror incompetent to testify "about any statement made or incident that occurred during the jury's deliberations; the effect of anything on that juror's or another juror's vote; or any juror's mental processes concerning the verdict or indictment." The extent of this disqualification is well illustrated by the following case:

TANNER v. UNITED STATES

United States Supreme Court
483 U.S. 107 (1987)

Justice O'CONNOR delivered the opinion of the Court.

Petitioners William Conover and Anthony Tanner were convicted of conspiring to defraud the United States in violation of 18 U.S.C. §371, and of committing mail fraud in violation of 18 U.S.C. §1341. The United States Court of Appeals for the Eleventh Circuit affirmed the convictions. Petitioners argue that the District Court erred in refusing to admit juror testimony at a post-verdict hearing on juror intoxication during the trial....

The day before petitioners were scheduled to be sentenced, Tanner filed a motion, in which Conover subsequently joined, seeking continuance of the sentencing date, permission to interview jurors, an evidentiary hearing, and a new trial. According to an affidavit accompanying the motion, Tanner's attorney had received an unsolicited telephone call from one of the trial jurors, Vera Asbul. Juror Asbul informed Tanner's attorney that several of the jurors consumed alcohol during the lunch breaks at various times throughout the trial, causing them to sleep through the afternoons. The District Court continued the sentencing date, ordered the parties to file memoranda, and heard argument on the motion to interview jurors. The District Court concluded that juror testimony on intoxication was inadmissible under FRE 606(b) to impeach the jury's verdict. The District Court invited petitioners to call any nonjuror witnesses, such as courtroom personnel, in support of the motion for new trial. Tanner's counsel took the stand and testified that he had observed one of the jurors "in a sort of giggly mood" at one point during the trial but did not bring this to anyone's attention at the time....

Following the hearing the District Court filed an order stating that "[o]n the basis of the admissible evidence offered I specifically find that the motions for leave to interview jurors or for an evidentiary hearing at which jurors would be witnesses is not required or appropriate." The District Court also denied the motion for new trial.

While the appeal of this case was pending before the Eleventh Circuit, petitioners filed another new trial motion based on additional evidence of jury misconduct. In another affidavit, Tanner's attorney stated that he received an unsolicited visit at his residence from a second juror, Daniel Hardy. Despite the fact that the District Court had denied petitioners' motion for leave to interview jurors, two days after Hardy's visit Tanner's attorney arranged for Hardy to be interviewed by two private investigators. The interview was transcribed, sworn to by the juror, and attached to the new trial motion. In the interview Hardy stated that he "felt like... the jury was on one big party." Hardy indicated that seven of the jurors drank alcohol during the noon recess. Four jurors, including Hardy, consumed between them "a pitcher to three pitchers" of beer during various recesses. Of the three other jurors who were alleged to have consumed alcohol, Hardy stated that on several occasions he observed two jurors having one or two mixed drinks during the lunch recess, and one other juror, who was also the foreperson, having a liter of wine on each of three occasions. Juror Hardy also stated that he and three other jurors smoked marijuana quite regularly during the trial. Moreover, Hardy stated that during the trial he observed one juror ingest cocaine five times and another juror ingest cocaine two or three times. One juror sold a quarter pound of marijuana to another juror during the trial, and took marijuana, cocaine and drug paraphernalia into the courthouse. Hardy noted that some of the jurors were falling asleep during the trial, and that one of the jurors described himself to Hardy as "flying." Hardy stated that before he visited Tanner's attorney at his residence, no one had contacted him concerning the jury's conduct, and Hardy had not been offered anything in return for his statement. Hardy said that he came forward "to clear my conscience" and "[b]ecause I felt . . . that the people on the jury didn't have no business being on the jury. I felt . . . that Mr. Tanner should have a better opportunity to get somebody that would review the facts right."

The District Court, stating that the motions "contain supplemental allegations which differ quantitatively but not qualitatively from those in the April motions," denied petitioners' motion for a new trial . . . . Petitioners argue that the District Court erred in not ordering an additional evidentiary hearing at which jurors would testify concerning drug and alcohol use during the trial. Petitioners assert that, contrary to the holdings of the District Court and the Court of Appeals, juror testimony on ingestion of drugs or alcohol during the trial is not barred by FRE 606(b). Moreover, petitioners argue that whether or not authorized by Rule 606(b), an evidentiary hearing including juror testimony on drug and alcohol use is compelled by their Sixth Amendment right to trial by a competent jury.

By the beginning of this century, if not earlier, the near-universal and firmly established common-law rule in the United States flatly prohibited the admission of juror testimony to impeach a jury verdict.

Exceptions to the common-law rule were recognized only in situations in which an "extraneous influence" was alleged to have affected the jury . . . . The Court allowed juror testimony on influence by outsiders in Parker v. Gladden, 385 U.S. 363, 365 (1966) (bailiff's comments on defendant), and Remmer v. United States, 347 U.S. 227, 228-230 (1954) (bribe offered to juror). In situations that did not fall into this exception for external influence, however, the Court adhered to the common-law rule against admitting juror testimony to impeach a verdict . . . .

Lower courts used this external/internal distinction to identify those instances in which juror testimony impeaching a verdict would be admissible. The distinction was not based on whether the juror was literally inside or outside the jury room when the alleged irregularity took place; rather, the distinction was based on the nature of the allegation. Clearly a rigid distinction based only on whether the event took place inside or outside the jury room would have been quite unhelpful. For example, under a distinction based on location a juror could not testify concerning a newspaper read inside the jury room. Instead, of course, this has been considered an external influence about which juror testimony is admissible. Similarly, under a rigid locational distinction jurors could be regularly required to testify after the verdict as to whether they heard and comprehended the judge's instructions, since the charge to the jury takes place outside the jury room. Courts wisely have treated allegations of a juror's inability to hear or comprehend at trial as an internal matter.

Most significant for the present case, however, is the fact that lower federal courts treated allegations of the physical or mental incompetence of a juror as "internal" rather than "external" matters . . . .

Substantial policy considerations support the common-law rule against the admission of jury testimony to impeach a verdict. As early as 1915 this Court explained the necessity of shielding jury deliberations from public scrutiny:

> [L]et it once be established that verdicts solemnly made and publicly returned into court can be attacked and set aside on the testimony of those who took part in their publication and all verdicts could be, and many would be, followed by an inquiry in the hope of discovering something which might invalidate the finding. Jurors would be harassed and beset by the defeated party in an effort to secure from them evidence of facts which might establish misconduct sufficient to set aside a verdict. If evidence thus secured could be thus used, the result would be to make what was intended to be a private deliberation, the constant subject of public investigation—to the destruction of all frankness and freedom of discussion and conference.

McDonald v. Pless, 238 U.S. at 267-268 . . . .

There is little doubt that post-verdict investigation into juror misconduct would in some instances lead to the invalidation of verdicts reached after irresponsible or improper juror behavior. It is not at all clear, however, that the jury system could survive such efforts to perfect it. Allegations of juror misconduct, incompetency, or inattentiveness, raised for the first time days, weeks, or months after the verdict, seriously disrupt the finality of the process. Moreover, full and frank discussion in the jury room, jurors' willingness to return an unpopular verdict, and the community's trust in a system that relies on the decisions of laypeople would all be undermined by a barrage of post verdict scrutiny of juror conduct.

FRE 606(b) is grounded in the common-law rule against admission of jury testimony to impeach a verdict and the exception for juror testimony relating to extraneous influences . . . .

Petitioners have presented no argument that Rule 606(b) is inapplicable to the juror affidavits and the further inquiry they sought in this case, and, in fact, there appears to be virtually no support for such a proposition. See 3 D.

Louisell & C. Mueller, Federal Evidence §287, pp. 121-125 (1979) (under Rule 606(b), "proof to the following effects is excludable . . . that one or more jurors was inattentive during trial or deliberations, sleeping or thinking about other matters") . . . . [P]etitioners argue that substance abuse constitutes an improper "outside influence" about which jurors may testify under FRE 606(b). In our view the language of the Rule cannot easily be stretched to cover this circumstance. However severe their effect and improper their use, drugs or alcohol voluntarily ingested by a juror seems no more an "outside influence" than a virus, poorly prepared food, or a lack of sleep.

In any case, whatever ambiguity might linger in the language of Rule 606(b) as applied to juror intoxication is resolved by the legislative history of the Rule . . . .

[T]he legislative history demonstrates with uncommon clarity that Congress specifically understood, considered, and rejected a version of Rule 606(b) that would have allowed jurors to testify on juror conduct during deliberations, including juror intoxication. This legislative history provides strong support for the most reasonable reading of the language of Rule 606(b)—that juror intoxication is not an "outside influence" about which jurors may testify to impeach their verdict.

Finally, even if Rule 606(b) is interpreted to retain the common-law exception allowing post verdict inquiry of juror incompetence in cases of "substantial if not wholly conclusive evidence of incompetency," the showing made by the petitioners falls far short of this standard. The affidavits and testimony presented in support of the first new trial motion suggested, at worst, that several of the jurors fell asleep at times during the afternoons. The District Court judge appropriately considered the fact that he had "an unobstructed view" of the jury, and did not see any juror sleeping. The juror affidavit submitted in support of the second new trial motion was obtained in clear violation of the District Court's order and the court's local rule against juror interviews; on this basis alone the District Court would have been acting within its discretion in disregarding the affidavit. In any case, although the affidavit of juror Hardy describes more dramatic instances of misconduct, Hardy's allegations of *incompetence* are meager. Hardy stated that the alcohol consumption he engaged in with three other jurors did not leave any of them intoxicated. ("I told [the prosecutor] that we would just go out and get us a pitcher of beer and drink it, but as far as us being drunk, no we wasn't"). The only allegations concerning the jurors' ability to properly consider the evidence were Hardy's observation that some jurors were "falling asleep all the time during the trial," and that Hardy's own reasoning ability was affected on one day of the trial. These allegations would not suffice to bring this case under the common-law exception allowing post verdict inquiry when an extremely strong showing of incompetency has been made.

Petitioners also argue that the refusal to hold an additional evidentiary hearing at which jurors would testify as to their conduct "violates the sixth amendment's guarantee to a fair trial before an impartial and *competent* jury."

This Court has recognized that a defendant has a right to "a tribunal both impartial and mentally competent to afford a hearing." Jordan v. Massachusetts, 225 U.S. 167, 176 (1912). In this case the District Court held an evidentiary hearing in response to petitioners' first new trial motion at which the judge invited petitioners to introduce any admissible evidence in support of their allegations. At issue in this case is whether the Constitution compelled the District Court to hold an additional evidentiary hearing including one particular kind of evidence inadmissible under the Federal Rules.

As described above, long-recognized and very substantial concerns support the protection of jury deliberations from intrusive inquiry. Petitioners' Sixth Amendment interests in an unimpaired jury, on the other hand, are protected by several aspects of the trial process. The suitability of an individual for the responsibility of jury service, of course, is examined during voir dire. Moreover, during the trial the jury is observable by the court, by counsel, and by court personnel. Moreover, jurors are observable by each other, and may report inappropriate juror behavior to the court *before* they render a verdict. Finally, after the trial a party may seek to impeach the verdict by nonjuror evidence of misconduct. Indeed, in this case the District Court held an evidentiary hearing giving petitioners ample opportunity to produce nonjuror evidence supporting their allegations.

In light of these other sources of protection of the petitioners' right to a competent jury, we conclude that the District Court did not err in deciding, based on the inadmissibility of juror testimony and the clear insufficiency of the nonjuror evidence offered by petitioners, that an additional post-verdict evidentiary hearing was unnecessary.

[The dissenting opinion of Justice Marshall, joined by three other Justices, is omitted.]

■ NOTES ON THE *TANNER* CASE

1. Would evidence of juror intoxication be admissible if it could be proved without juror testimony? See United States v. Taliaferro, 558 F.2d 724, 725-726 (4th Cir. 1977) (admitting records of club where jurors dined, and testimony by marshal who was with them, to determine whether jurors were intoxicated during deliberations), *cert. denied*, 434 U.S. 106 (1978).

2. If the affidavit of Hardy had been admitted, would it justify a new trial? That issue is not addressed by FRE 606(b), but only the question of what evidence of jury misconduct or irregularity can be put before the judge.

3. What if the verdict were challenged on the ground that one juror was a neighbor of Tanner and told other jurors that "he has been in trouble with the law since he was a kid"? Does this statement fit the category of "outside influence" or "extraneous prejudicial information"?

4. What if, on voir dire, a juror had falsely denied knowing Tanner? Does FRE 606(b) block inquiry into perjury on voir dire? See Urseth v. City of Dayton, 680 F. Supp. 1084, 1089 (S.D. Ohio 1987) (No). Pending before the Supreme Court in 2014 was the *Warger* case, which presents the question whether a post-verdict challenge can use statements made during deliberations to prove falsehoods on voir dire. See Warger v. Shauers, 721 F.3d 606, 611-612 (8th Cir. 2013) (juror statements during deliberations cannot be used to for this purpose), *cert. granted,* 234 S. Ct. 1491 (2014). See generally Crump, Jury Misconduct, Jury Interviews, and the Federal Rules of Evidence: Is the Broad Exclusionary Doctrine of Rule 606(b) Justified?, 66 N.C. L. Rev. 509 (1988).

■ PROBLEM 6-B. Refusal to Take the Stand

Adkins is convicted of unlawful possession of narcotics at a trial in which he did not testify in his own defense. A week after trial, the judge receives a letter from a juror expressing concern that the jury violated the judge's instructions because it considered Adkins' refusal to take the stand as an admission of guilt. The judge informs both counsel of the letter, and the attorney for Adkins files a motion for a new trial based on juror misconduct. May the juror be called to testify on the matters in the letter? May the letter be considered?

■ PROBLEM 6-C. The Jury View

In a personal injury action arising out of an automobile accident, a verdict is returned for the plaintiff. After trial, counsel for defendant receives information that two jurors went to the accident scene one evening during the period of deliberations, apparently on a "factfinding" mission. At a hearing on a motion for a new trial, may the defense attorney make inquiry of the two jurors regarding the truth of this report?

■ PROBLEM 6-D. The Bomber

Jones is convicted of detonating an explosive device in a public building. Afterwards her lawyer is told that one juror is willing to testify that another informed the jury he was a demolitions expert in the Army and that the type of bomb Jones used was powerful enough to kill anyone within 20 feet, even though no injuries were inflicted by the explosion. If Jones moves for a new trial, may she offer such testimony in support of the motion? If so, may the prosecutor call other jurors to testify that this information had no influence on their votes?

■ PROBLEM 6-E. The $800,000 Jury Error

When Baker loses his farm to the bank in a foreclosure, he turns against his lawyer, Henderson, and brings a malpractice suit alleging that Henderson failed properly to advise him on the matter of redeeming the farm. In a bifurcated proceeding, the jury returns a verdict that Henderson was negligent, and the court then delivers the following instruction on the proper measure of damages:

"The Plaintiff's damages are the fair market value of the farm minus the redemption costs plus the mortgage balance on the property."

The evidence indicates that fair market value was about $500,000, that costs of redemption would have been about $10,000, and that the outstanding balance on the mortgage was about $400,000. During deliberations, the jury foreman sends a note to the judge asking whether the jury must follow this formula in calculating damages. With approval by both lawyers, the judge answers in the affirmative. After returning a verdict for Baker in the amount of $890,000, the jury is dismissed. The court enters judgment on the verdict.

Immediately Henderson's lawyer gets permission from the court to interview jurors. Within days, he obtains affidavits from all 12, saying that they understood that they were to add the mortgage balance to fair market value (rather than subtracting the former from the latter). Henderson seeks a new trial, arguing that the jury made an $800,000 mistake.

If the judge agrees that the jury erred, should she grant a new trial? Does FRE 606(b) allow such affidavits? Could Henderson have asked the trial judge, at the time the jury announced its verdict, to ask the jury how it understood the instruction?

CHAPTER 7

Direct and Cross-Examination Revisited

A DIRECT EXAMINATION

1. Nonleading Questions

Litigants usually present testimony of witnesses by means of direct examination. Remember the beginnings of the process: The lawyer develops background information about the witness, places him at the scene and establishes personal knowledge. With an expert witness, she develops the basis of expertise, then moves to substantive matters.

Especially on substantive matters, recall that direct examination usually means nonleading questions, as FRE 611(c) makes clear. The aim is to bring out what *the witness* has to say, and the attorney should not put words in his mouth or testify for him. But the system is not rigid, and the bar against leading the witness on direct is not absolute. Consider now the exceptions to the pattern.

2. Exceptions—Leading Questions Allowed

Under FRE 611(c), trial judges have discretion to permit leading questions, even during direct examination. By longstanding tradition, which changed little if any when the Rules were adopted, it is considered expedient to permit leading on direct in four situations:

(1) When necessary to develop testimony. FRE 611(c) contemplates direct examination of a witness by leading questions when these "may be necessary to develop his testimony." Thus the questioner can usually lead a witness who is (a) very young, hence apprehensive, uncomprehending, or confused, (b) timid, reticent, reluctant, or frightened, (c) ignorant, uncomprehending, or unresponsive, or (d) infirm. Of course the danger of leading may well be greater with people of such description, but if the choice is between running the risks associated with leading or doing without the knowledge of a witness, the risks seem acceptable. See United States v. Nabors, 762 F.2d 642, 650-651 (8th Cir. 1985) (rejecting objection that prosecutor improperly led 12-year-old boy, who hesitated in repeating "naughty" word allegedly used by defendant; trial judge could best "evaluate the emotional condition of the child witness and his hesitancy to testify").

(2) When witness is uncooperative. FRE 611(c) also contemplates leading questions on direct when the witness is "hostile" or "an adverse party" or "identified with an adverse party." Here the idea is that when a witness refuses to cooperate, the trial lawyer needs a little coercive power to get at what the witness knows. Leading questions enable the lawyer to press and may be the only way to get real answers. Adverse parties and their agents or associates are likely to be in this category, as are others described by the term "hostile." See United States v. Hicks, 748 F.2d 854, 859 (11th Cir. 1984) (prosecutor led defendant's girlfriend, who was "identified with an adverse party").

(3) When the Rule is more trouble than it is worth. Sometimes requiring nonleading questions on direct is simply not worth the trouble. On preliminary matters, for example, leading questions save time and are allowed:

Q (Phillips): You are Doctor Martin J. Young, are you not, and you reside at 1873 La Vista Drive in Atlanta?
A (Dr. Young): That is correct.
Q: And you are the chief surgeon at Brady Memorial Hospital in Atlanta, specializing in abdominal surgery?
A: Yes.

The same is true of matters that are not contested. Even without a formal stipulation, all parties may know that certain points are not seriously disputed, and on such matters leading questions can save time. Finally, most courts give short shrift to any objection to leading a witness who is qualified as an expert by formal professional training, on the theory that such witnesses simply "won't be led" in matters within their expertise while being examined by lawyers who are from their perspective laypersons. Physicians, for example, are unlikely to cave in to pressures from leading questions on subjects within their area of professional competence.

(4) When memory seems exhausted. Perhaps the most important and troublesome instance where leading questions are allowed on direct appears when the memory of the witness seems exhausted. Like all mortals, witnesses forget. When questioning is stymied by the inability of the witness to recollect, the lawyer can try to "refresh his recollection." Usually that means that the lawyer gently reminds the witness of something he said before, often in a written statement or affidavit or a deposition, and FRE 612 recognizes this technique: In time-honored tradition, the lawyer hands the statement to the witness, asks him to read it, then asks whether "his memory is now refreshed." If he says yes, the lawyer can proceed with questioning and elicit the desired information.

BAKER v. STATE

Maryland Court of Appeals

371 A.2d 699 (Md. App. 1977)

MOYLAN, J.

This appeal addresses the intriguing question of what latitude a judge should permit counsel when a witness takes the stand and says, "I don't remember." What are the available keys that may unlock the testimonial treasure vaults of the subconscious? What are the brush strokes that may be employed "to retouch the fading daguereotype of memory?" The subject is that of Present Recollection Revived.

The appellant, Teretha McNeil Baker, was convicted by a Baltimore City jury of both murder in the first degree and robbery. Although she raises two appellate contentions, the only one which we find it necessary to consider is her claim that the trial judge erroneously refused her the opportunity to refresh the present recollection of a police witness by showing him a report written by a fellow officer.

The ultimate source of most of the evidence implicating the appellant was the robbery and murder victim himself, Gaither Martin, a now-dead declarant who spoke to the jury through the hearsay conduit of Officer Bolton.[3] When Officer Bolton arrived at the crime scene, the victim told him that he had "picked these three ladies up . . . at the New Deal Bar"; that when he took them to their stated destination, a man walked up to the car and pulled him out; that "the other three got out and proceeded to kick him and beat him." It was the assertion made by the victim to the officer that established that his money, wallet and keys had been taken. The critical impasse, for present purposes, occurred when the officer was questioned, on cross-examination, about what happened en route to the hospital. The officer had received a call from Officer Hucke, of the Western District, apparently to the effect that a suspect had been picked up. Before proceeding to the hospital, Officer Bolton took the victim to the place where Officer Hucke was holding the appellant. The appellant, as part of this cross-examination, sought to elicit from the officer the fact that the crime victim confronted the appellant and stated that the appellant was not one of those persons who had attacked and robbed him. To stimulate the present memory of Officer Bolton, appellant's counsel attempted to show him the police report relating to that confrontation and prepared by Officer Hucke.

The record establishes loudly and clearly that appellant's counsel sought to use the report primarily to refresh the recollection of Officer Bolton and that he was consistently and effectively thwarted in that attempt:

---

[3]The exception to the Hearsay Rule urged by the State and utilized by the court to make the out-of-court assertion admissible was the "excited utterance" exception and not the "dying declaration" exception. We are not here considering the admissibility of this hearsay, but are rather assuming it to have been admissible.

By Mr. Harlan:

Q: Do you have the report filed by Officer Hucke and Officer Saclolo?

A: Right, I have copies.

Q: Okay.

Mr. Doory: I would object to that, Your Honor.

The Court: I will sustain the objection. This is not his report . . . .

By Mr. Harlan:

Q: All right. Would you consult your report and maybe it will refresh your recollection.

The Court: I think the response is he doesn't know who—

Mr. Harlan: He can refresh his recollection if he looks at the report.

The Court: He can't refresh his recollection from someone else's report, Mr. Harlan.

Mr. Harlan: I would object, Your Honor. Absolutely he can.

The Court: You might object, but—

Mr. Harlan: You are not going to permit the officer to refresh his recollection from the police report?

The Court: No. It is not his report . . . . He says he does not know who it was before. So, he can't refresh his recollection if he does not know simply because someone else put some name in there.

Mr. Harlan: He has to read it to see if it refreshes his recollection, Your Honor.

The Court: We are reading from a report made by two other officers which is not the personal knowledge of this officer.

Mr. Harlan: I don't want him to read from that report. I want him to read it and see if it refreshes his recollection.

On so critical an issue as possible exculpation from the very lips of the crime victim, appellant was entitled to try to refresh the memory of the key police witness. She was erroneously and prejudicially denied that opportunity. The reason for the error is transparent. Because they both arise from the common seedbed of failed memory and because of their hauntingly parallel verbal rhythms and grammatical structures, there is a beguiling temptation to overanalogize Present Recollection Revived and Past Recollection Recorded. It is a temptation, however, that must be resisted. The trial judge in this case erroneously measured the legitimacy of the effort to revive present recollection against the more rigorous standards for the admissibility of a recordation of past memory.

It is, of course, hornbook law that when a party seeks to introduce a record of past recollection, he must establish 1) that the record was made by or adopted by the witness at a time when the witness did have a recollection of the event and 2) that the witness can presently vouch for the fact that when the record was made or adopted by him, he knew that it was accurate . . . . Had the appellant herein sought to offer the police report as a record of past recollection on the part of Officer Bolton, it is elementary that she would have had to show, *inter alia*, that the report had either been prepared by Officer Bolton himself or had been read by him and that he can now say that at that time he knew it was correct. Absent such a showing, the trial judge would have been correct in declining to receive it in evidence.

When dealing with an instance of Past Recollection Recorded, the reason for the rigorous standards of admissibility is quite clear. Those standards exist to test the competence of the report or document in question. Since the piece of paper itself, in effect, speaks to the jury, the piece of paper must pass muster in terms of its evidentiary competence.[4]

Not so with Present Recollection Revived! By marked contrast to Past Recollection Recorded, no such testimonial competence is demanded of a mere stimulus to present recollection, for the stimulus itself is never evidence. Notwithstanding the surface similarity between the two phenomena, the difference between them could not be more basic.[5] *It is the difference between evidence and non-evidence.* Of such mere stimuli or memory-prods, McCormick says, "[T]he cardinal rule is that they are not evidence, but only aids in the giving of evidence." When we are dealing with an instance of Present Recollection Revived, the only source of evidence is the testimony of the witness himself. The stimulus may have jogged the witness's dormant memory, but the stimulus itself is not received in evidence. Dean McCormick makes it clear that even when the stimulus is a writing, when the witness "speaks from a memory thus revived, his testimony is what he says, not the writing." McCormick describes the psychological phenomenon in the following terms:

> It is abundantly clear from everyday observation that the latent memory of an experience may be revived by an image seen, or a statement read or heard. It is a part of the group of phenomena which the classical psychologists have called the law of association. The recall of any part of a past experience tends to bring with it the other parts that were in the same field of awareness, and a new experience tends to stimulate the recall of other like experiences.

The psychological community is in full agreement with the legal community in assessing the mental phenomenon. See Cairn, Law and the Social Sciences 200 (1935). . . .

The catalytic agent or memory stimulator is put aside, once it has worked its psychological magic, and the witness then testifies on the basis of the now-refreshed memory. The opposing party, of course, has the right to inspect the memory aid, be it a writing or otherwise, and even to show it to the jury. This examination, however, is not for the purpose of testing the competence of the

---

[4]. . . Maryland is in the minority position (preferred, however, by Wigmore) that where a proper foundation is laid, a past recollection recorded is admissible without regard to the state of declarant's recollection at the time of trial.

[5]"Under the guidance of Wigmore, we now recognize this as quite a different process. In the one instance, the witness stakes his oath on his present memory; in the other, upon his written recital of things remembered in the past." McCormick, Law of Evidence (1st Ed., 1954), p. 15.

memory aid (for competence is immaterial where the thing in question is not evidence) but only to test whether the witness's memory has in truth been refreshed. . . . And he cannot be allowed to read the writing in the guise of refreshment, as a cloak for getting in evidence an inadmissible document."[6] One of the most thorough reviews of this aspect of evidence law is found in United States v. Riccardi, 174 F.2d 883 (3d Cir. 1949), where the court said at 888:

> In the case of present recollection revived, the witness, by hypothesis, relates his present recollection, and under oath and subject to cross-examination asserts that it is true; his capacities for memory and perception may be attacked and tested; his determination to tell the truth investigated and revealed; protestations of lack of memory, which escape criticism and indeed constitute a refuge in the situation of past recollection recorded, merely undermine the probative worth of his testimony.

In solid accord with both the psychological sciences and the general common law of evidence, Maryland has long established it that even when a writing of some sort is the implement used to stir the embers of cooling memory, the writing need not be that of the forgetful witness himself, need not have been adopted by him, need not have been made contemporaneously with or shortly after the incident in question, and need not even be necessarily accurate. The competence of the writing is not in issue for the writing is not offered as evidence but is only used as a memory aid . . . .

When the writing in question is to be utilized simply "to awaken a slumbering recollection of an event" in the mind of the witness, the writing may be a memorandum made by the witness himself, 1) even if it was not made immediately after the event, 2) even if it was not made of firsthand knowledge and 3) even if the witness cannot now vouch for the fact that it was accurate when made. It may be a memorandum made by one other than the witness, even if never before read by the witness or vouched for by him. It may be an Associated Press account. It may be a highly selective version of the incident at the hands of a Hemingway or an Eliot. All that is required is that it ignite the flash of accurate recall—that it accomplish the revival which is sought . . . .

Not only may the writing to be used as a memory aid fall short of the rigorous standards of competence required of a record of past recollection, the memory aid itself need not even be a writing. What may it be? It may be anything.[10] It may be a line from Kipling or the dolorous refrain of "The Tennessee Waltz"; a whiff of hickory smoke; the running of the fingers across a swatch of corduroy; the sweet carbonation of a chocolate soda; the sight of a faded snapshot in a long-neglected album. All that is required is that it may trigger

[6]McCormick, Law of Evidence (2nd Ed., 1972), 19 n.66.

[10]Limited only, in the wise discretion of the trial judge, by such questions as time investment, logistics, and a sense of courtroom decorum or taste.

the Proustian moment.[11] It may be anything which produces the desired testimonial prelude, "It all comes back to me now."[12]

Of just such possibilities did Learned Hand speak in United States v. Rappy, 157 F.2d 964, 967 (2d Cir. 1946):

> Anything may in fact revive a memory: a song, a scent, a photograph, an allusion, even a past statement known to be false.

The United States Court of Appeals for the Ninth Circuit addressed the same issue in Jewett v. United States, 15 F.2d 955 (1926), and concluded, at 956:

> [I]t is quite immaterial by what means the memory is quickened; it may be a song, or a face, or a newspaper item, or a writing of some character. It is sufficient that by some material operation, however mysterious, the memory is stimulated to recall the event, for when so set in motion it functions quite independently of the actuating cause . . . .

Although the use of a memorandum of some sort will continue quantitatively to dominate the field of refreshing recollection, we are better able to grasp the process conceptually if we appreciate that the use of a memorandum as a memory aid is not a legal phenomenon unto itself but only an instance of a far broader phenomenon. In a more conventional mode, the process might proceed, "Your Honor, I am about to show the witness a written report, ask him to read it and then inquire if he can now testify from his own memory thus refreshed." In a far less conventional mode, the process could just as well proceed, "Your Honor, I am pleased to present to the court Miss Rosa Ponselle who will now sing 'Celeste Aida' for the witness, for that is what was playing on the night the burglar came through the window." Whether by conventional or unconventional means, precisely the same end is sought. One is looking for the effective elixir to revitalize dimming memory and make it live again in the service of the search for truth.

Even in the more conventional mode, it is quite clear that in this case the appropriate effort of the appellant to jog the arguably dormant memory of the key police witness on a vital issue was unduly and prejudicially restricted.

Judgments reversed; case remanded for a new trial; costs to be paid by Mayor and City Council of Baltimore.

---

[11]Marcel Proust, in his monumental epic In Remembrance of Things Past, sat, as a middle-aged man, sipping a cup of lime-flavored tea and eating a madeleine, a small French pastry. Through both media, two long-forgotten tastes from childhood were reawakened. By association, long-forgotten memories from the same period of childhood came welling and surging back. Once those floodgates of recall were opened, seven volumes followed.

[12]Generally speaking, the process of refurbishing a witness memory will take place as a part of astute counsel trial preparation. It is only when memory, through courtroom fear or otherwise unexpectedly bogs down on the witness' stand (or when the witness whose memory needs refreshing is one other than counsel own) that the courtroom becomes the arena for the refurbishing.

NOTES ON REFRESHING RECOLLECTION

1. In one sense *Baker* is an exceptional case. Usually the attempt to refresh memory involves a prior statement by the witness. *Baker* allows use of a report by a fellow officer.

2. Can a lawyer use anything at all to refresh recollection, or would a no-holds-barred approach invite inappropriate coaching? Under FRE 612 the opponent can cross-examine the witness about a writing used this way and offer it in evidence. Are these safeguards sufficient?

3. Consider how refreshing recollection relates to other devices—some of which you have seen already:

(a) *Past recollection recorded.* The attempt to refresh memory may fail, but the document may fit FRE 803(5) (past recollection recorded), allowing the document to itself to be used as evidence (but preventing it from going to the jury room during deliberations). Recall the *Scott* case (Chapter 4C4, supra).

(b) *Prior inconsistent statement as substantive evidence.* The attempt to refresh recollection may succeed only too well, reviving a memory of events very much at odds with a prior statement by the witness. If the prior statement was given under oath in a proceeding, and the witness is now cross-examinable about it, then the examining lawyer can use the prior statement as substantive evidence under FRE 801(d)(1)(A).

(c) *Prior inconsistent statement as impeaching proof.* Again the attempt to refresh memory may succeed only in bringing out a story conflicting with what the witness said before. Even if his prior statement fits no hearsay exception, it may be used to impeach.

B CROSS-EXAMINATION

1. Leading Questions

In the presentation of testimony, cross follows direct. Here the adverse party begins to test, to limit the impact, and to rebut the direct. Here the lawyer rather than the witness is the focus. Here substantive points are largely in the questions themselves, as the answers confirm or acknowledge what the questions in effect assert.

The mode of questioning on cross is (for the most part) leading under FRE 611(c). Only in rare instances must the cross-examiner avoid leading the witness: She cannot lead when the witness is her own client (or aligned with her client), as happens when, for example, defense counsel "cross-examines" the defendant after plaintiff called defendant as a witness.

One aim of cross is to develop the substance of the story as the adverse party hopes the jury will see it—to recast the story presented by the calling party. Another is to limit or confine the impact of the direct testimony. Yet another is to impeach the witness. The lines between these functions sometimes disappear, but in what follows we focus on tactics that aim to confine and limit the effect of adverse testimony.

2. Cross-Examining on Witness Preparation Material

In *Baker* you saw the process of refreshing memory on the stand, and the safeguards that FRE 612 provides for the cross-examining party. But witness preparation ("woodshedding") begins before trial, and almost invariably the cross-examiner tries to show that this process, and particularly the review of certain documents, affected the testimony.

Pre-Rules practice drew a sharp line between documents that a witness reviews before testifying and those he reviews on the stand to refresh memory. The cross-examiner was entitled to the latter but not the former. Under FRE 612(a), however, the court may order production not only of writings used to refresh memory "while testifying," but also of writings used "before testifying," if the court decides that justice so requires. The *James Julian* decision explores the tension between this discovery mechanism and the need to protect attorney work product.

JAMES JULIAN, INC. v. RAYTHEON CO.

United States District Court for the District of Delaware
93 F.R.D. 138 (1982)

[Plaintiff James Julian, Inc. (Julian) seeks injunctive relief and damages under the Sherman Act and National Labor Relations Act, naming as defendants several labor organizations and union officers, as well as Raytheon Co. (Raytheon) and Raytheon Service Co. (RSC). Here defendants Raytheon and RSC seek production of a binder of materials prepared by counsel for Julian for purposes of review by Julian's officers in preparation for their deposition testimony.]

MURRAY M. SCHWARTZ, J.

In the course of preparing witnesses for depositions plaintiff's counsel assembled a binder which was reviewed by current principals, officers and employees of Julian who were being deposed by the Raytheon defendants. The binder, which was not reviewed by the Court, contains: 1) selected documents obtained from RSC through discovery; 2) documents obtained by Julian from the public records of the Delaware Solid Waste Authority through a Freedom of Information Act request; and 3) documents prepared by Julian during the course of the project.

Julian does not object to defendants' obtaining the documents contained in the binder; indeed, Julian has represented that many of the documents were already turned over during the course of discovery. Rather, plaintiff objects to the production of the binder itself, arguing that the selection and ordering of documents constitute privileged work product reflecting counsel's opinions, mental impressions, conclusions or legal theories and is therefore entitled to special protection under Rule 26(b)(3) of the Federal Rules of Civil Procedure. The Raytheon defendants argue first, that production of the binder would not reveal the thought processes of plaintiff's counsel and second, that even if the binder was at one time entitled to special protection, plaintiff waived that entitlement by using the binder to prepare witnesses for deposition.

The threshold issue can be dispensed with quickly. The binder contains a small percentage of the extensive documents reviewed by plaintiff's counsel. In selecting and ordering a few documents out of thousands counsel could not help but reveal important aspects of his understanding of the case. Indeed, in a case such as this, involving extensive document discovery, the process of selection and distillation is often more critical than pure legal research. There can be no doubt that at least in the first instance the binders were entitled to protection as work product.

Even assuming the binder was once entitled to protection, the Raytheon defendants argue that plaintiff waived that protection. Relying on Rule 612 of the Federal Rules of Evidence, they argue that if a party uses protected documents to prepare a witness for deposition, those documents become discoverable . . . . [The provisions of FRE 612] are made applicable to depositions by virtue of Rule 30(c) of the Federal Rules of Civil Procedure. The legislative history and case law both discuss Rule 612 in terms of privilege without clearly distinguishing the attorney work product doctrine. As a result the following analysis will discuss the Rule's effect on protected documents generally before considering the effect, if any, of the fact that in this case plaintiff claims the protection of the work product doctrine.

There is no doubt that Rule 612(2) constituted a major departure from the settled rule that the use of a privileged document to refresh a witness' memory only constituted a waiver of the privilege if it occurred at the time of testimony. The precise issue presented by the Raytheon defendants' motion is whether in extending the rule to include documents used to refresh a witness' memory before testifying Congress intended to include all such documents or only those not subject to claims of privilege.

The legislative history of Rule 612 is ambiguous. It can be read to indicate a congressional intent to leave the decision as to privileged documents to the sound discretion of the district courts for resolution on a case by case basis. It is also possible to view the record as reflecting an intent to exempt privileged documents from the operation of the expanded rule.

As noted, prior case law required disclosure of privileged documents used to refresh memory at the time of testimony. Plaintiff argues, based largely on legislative history, that Congress intended to limit Rule 612's expansion of prior law to nonprivileged documents used to refresh witness' memory prior to testimony. As enacted, Rule 612 does limit the expansion of prior law, not, as plaintiff suggests, by exempting privileged documents, but by conditioning disclosure on the discretionary approval of the district court. It would thus appear that Congress left the task of striking a balance between the competing interests of full disclosure and the maintenance of confidentiality for case by case determination.

Those courts which have considered the issue have generally agreed that the use of protected documents to refresh a witness' memory prior to testifying constitutes a waiver of the protection. In what is perhaps the leading case, Berkey Photo, Inc. v. Eastman Kodak Co., 74 F.R.D. 613 (S.D.N.Y. 1977) (Frankel, J.), defendant's attorneys used four notebooks to prepare expert witnesses for deposition. The court noted that:

> [Given the] modern views favoring broad access to materials useful for effective cross-examination, embodied in rules like 612 [and the Jencks Act], it is disquieting to posit that a lawyer may "aid" a witness with items of work product and then prevent totally the access that might reveal and counteract the effects of such assistance. There is much to be said for a view that a party or its lawyer, meaning to invoke the privilege, ought to use other, and different materials, available later to a cross-examiner, in the preparation of witnesses. When this simple choice emerges the decision to give the work product to the witness could well be deemed a waiver of the privilege.

The court's actual holding that the notebook which had "the sound and quality of materials appropriate 'to promote the search of credibility and memory,'" need not be produced was based not on its reading of Rule 612 but on its perception that an order compelling discovery would work undue hardship on defendant, whose counsel were unaware of the scope of the then recently adopted rule. Indeed, the court was at pains to put the bar on notice that in the future a contrary result would obtain.

Judge Frankel's prediction has proved largely accurate. Thus, for example, the court in Wheeling-Pittsburgh Steel Corp. v. Underwriters Laboratories, Inc., 81 F.R.D. 8 (N.D. Ill. 1978), held that the use of privileged documents to refresh a witness' recollection prior to testimony served as an effective waiver of the privilege. Plaintiff attempts to distinguish *Wheeling* by arguing that because the witness had left the party's employ by the time of his deposition, his review of the documents destroyed their confidentiality. The *Wheeling* Court did hold that the use of the documents to refresh the witness' recollection constituted a waiver of the attorney-client privilege, but any notion that it was relying on concepts of publication to noncorporate personnel must be dispelled by its reliance on Bailey v. Meister Brau, Inc., 57 F.R.D. 11 (N.D. Ill. 1972), a pre-Rule 612 case. In *Bailey* privileged documents were used to refresh a witness's recollection at his deposition. In rejecting plaintiff's claim that privileged documents are excepted from the general rule that a party is entitled to inspect any document used to refresh recollection the court held that:

> To adopt such an exception would be to ignore the unfair disadvantage which could be placed upon the cross-examiner by the simple expedient of using only privileged writings to refresh recollection.

The *Bailey* court also considered the applicability of the attorney work product doctrine to the requested documents and concluded that the use of the documents to refresh recollection constituted a waiver of that doctrine for the same reasons that it constituted a waiver of the attorney-client privilege. [A]ccord, Marshall v. United States Postal Service, 88 F.R.D. 348 (D.D.C. 1980) (unsigned affidavit prepared by attorney from interview notes used to refresh recollection at deposition); Williamson v. Puritan Chemical Corp., 80 Civ. 1698 (S.D.N.Y. March 6, 1981) (statement made to counsel and reviewed prior to testifying); Peck & Peck, Inc. v. Jack La Lanne, 76 Civ. 4020 (S.D.N.Y. Jan. 12, 1978) (use of privileged investigative report to refresh recollection prior to testimony).

Aside from *Berkey* the only case Court or counsel have discovered in which the court denied production of privileged documents reviewed prior to testimony is Jos. Schlitz Brewing Co. v. Muller & Phipps (Hawaii) Ltd., 85 F.R.D. 118 (W.D. Mo. 1980). In *Schlitz* the witness, an attorney, testified that he had reviewed his correspondence file consisting of thirty-nine documents in preparation for his deposition. Although the Court did state that language and history of Rule 612 indicated that the Rule's adoption occasioned "little if any widening of disclosure obligations," the court's actual holding was simply that "there was insufficient establishment of actual use of any of the various documents [contained in the file], so as to authorize [the invocation of] Rule 612."

Plaintiff attempts to distinguish the above cited cases by asserting that, with the exception of *Bailey*, a pre-Rule 612 case, and *Berkey*, which is dismissed as containing mere dicta, none involved a claim of attorney opinion work product, the disclosure of which the court is obligated to protect against. FRCP 26(b)(3). Plaintiff's argument is not without merit. Each case must, of course, be evaluated on its own facts. In a given case the fact that the privileged documents contained attorneys' mental impressions might cause the Court to strike the balance in favor of nondisclosure. However, this is not that case. The binder at issue contains various documents selected and arranged by plaintiff's counsel and given to various witnesses prior to their depositions. Without reviewing those binders defendants' counsel cannot know or inquire into the extent to which the witnesses' testimony has been shaded by counsel's presentation of the factual background. The instant request constitutes neither a fishing expedition into plaintiff's files nor an invasion of counsel's "zone of privacy." Plaintiff's counsel made a decision to educate their witnesses by supplying them with the binders, and the Raytheon defendants are entitled to know the content of that education.

Based on the foregoing the Court concludes that the binders are properly within the scope of Rule 612(2) and in the interests of justice should be disclosed. An appropriate order will issue.

NOTES ON APPLYING RULE 612

1. Why did the defense want to discover what plaintiff's officers reviewed in preparing their testimony? If defense counsel already has the documents, what more can he reasonably request? Assuming the documents exchanged were voluminous, would it be helpful to the cross-examiner to know which specific documents had been reviewed by the officers prior to their deposition?

3. *James Julian* reads FRE 612 as authorizing judges to require production of material reviewed by a witness before testifying, even if covered by work product protection. It is not at all clear, however, that Congress intended to authorize judges to override protections otherwise afforded by privilege or the work product doctrine. See House Judiciary Committee's Report on FRE 612 (Committee intends that "nothing in the Rule be construed as barring the assertion of a privilege" for writings used by a witness to refresh memory).

4. Shouldn't a client whose communications with a lawyer fit the attorney-client privilege be able to review them before testifying without losing protection? Shouldn't a lawyer who develops work product be able to make reasonable use of that material in talking to witnesses, without losing protection? On the other hand, consider whether it is fair to deny the cross-examiner access to documents that play a role in shaping testimony. Courts split on these questions. See Donjon Marine Co., Inc. v Buchanan Marine, L.P., 2010 WL 2977044 (D. Conn. 2010) (some courts say a document reviewed by a witness before a deposition must always be produced; others say production is only required if privilege is waived, as by disclosure to outsiders, not when client reviews his own statements; third approach asks whether documents had impact on testimony). See also Sporck v. Peil, 759 F.2d 312, 317-319 (3d Cir. 1985) (prior to testimony there was "no basis for asking" defendant which documents he reviewed; afterwards, counsel may ask "which, if any, documents informed that testimony"), *cert. denied*, 474 U.S. 903 (1985).

5. Lawyers sometimes react to disclosure regimes by avoiding a "paper trail," coaching witnesses orally instead. Can the other side take the next logical step and require lawyers to record or transcribe all conversations with witnesses? See IBM Corp. v. Edelstein, 526 F.2d 37 (2d Cir. 1975) (no; court overrules order telling lawyer to transcribe witness interviews).

6. In civil cases, litigants turn over during discovery reports by experts that they will call at trial. As you can imagine, lawyers help prepare such reports, and the duty of disclosure once covered draft reports. As amended in 2010, however, FRCP 26(b)(4)(B) exempts "drafts" of expert reports from disclosure. Also the Rule also once required the lawyer to disclose "data or other information" considered by the expert in forming her opinions, but the amendment narrowed the obligation to "facts or data that the party's attorney provided and that the expert considered." This expansion of work product protection reflects complaints by lawyers that discovery into attorney-expert communications and draft reports has "undesirable effects," including higher costs and "two sets of experts—one for purposes of consultation and another to testify." And lawyers were being pushed into "a guarded attitude" in their interactions with testifying experts that impeded "effective communication," with the result that their efforts to protect against discovery tended to "interfere with their work." See ACN to 2010 Amendments to FRCP 26. This expanded protection if work product may lead courts to be more cautious about requiring disclosure of work product under FRE 612.

3. Cross-Examination as an Entitlement

In both civil and criminal cases, each party has the right to cross-examine witnesses called by the other side. Recall that absence of cross is the main reason why the hearsay doctrine so often requires exclusion of out-of-court statements. Hence it is no surprise that where cross-examination is cut short by the death or illness of the witness, this curtailment of the right is viewed as so serious that the direct testimony must often be stricken, and sometimes a mistrial is required. See United States v. Panza, 612 F.2d 432, 436-437 (9th Cir. 1979) (striking testimony by defendant when he refused to be cross-examined), *cert. denied*, 447 U.S. 925 (1980).

Consider this appraisal of what happened in a civil suit brought by a widow against an insurance carrier for an accident in which a car driven by her son, Lyle, collided head-on with another car, causing the death of Lyle's father (husband of plaintiff) who was a passenger. The widow sued the son's insurance carrier and alleged negligence by Lyle. It was likely the Lyle was torn in two directions—wanting his mother to recover from the insurance carrier but not wanting to be responsible for his father's death. The trial court ruled that plaintiff could not cross-examine Lyle (since she had called him as a witness), but the reviewing court disagreed:

> The process of truth-telling as is the process of truth-ascertainment is seldom the simple question whether there has been conscious, willful falsity. Nor is it even the simpler one of resolving the matter in terms of likely hostility *against* or friendliness *for* one party or the other. Thus, for every factor

> here tending Lyle toward the Plaintiff, there was one tugging in the opposite direction. Not the least of the latter was the suggestion hammered home by defense counsel that a finding of negligence was equivalent to a finding that Lyle had killed his father.
>
> Just what Lyle's real interests might be was not a matter for the District Judge, nor for us in the way of binding ex post facto parenthetical observations made from our remote position. That was for the jury to appraise in the light of a full and searching revelation. Our system of justice rests necessarily on the historic assumption that civilized moral people try their dead level best to tell the truth no matter how much it hurts or helps. But being a mechanism for the resolution of man's disputes, the instrument of cross examination is an integral part of that system in order to penetrate all of the conflicting impulses or obstacles to lay bare the whole truth. And yet from the nature of the strict procedural limitation imposed by the Judge, this could not be effectively done.
>
> Real cross examination was entirely missing. The Plaintiff's counsel was forbidden by the Court's ruling to engage either in it, or in the indigenous but powerful tool of leading questions. The Defendants, while having the nominal right to cross examine, did not for perfectly obvious reasons do so in fact. By this procedural ruling the defense was put in the fortunate position of being able to argue that the witness (Lyle)—for whose truthfulness and reliability the Plaintiffs generally vouched—by his court-testimony and a written statement given to an insurance adjuster, had made contradictory statements on his knowledge of the existence of the Stop Sign. This physical-mental fact was at the very heart of the reasonableness of his conduct in thinking (or in not thinking) that the oncoming car would or would not stop. And as to this issue, the jury may have taken the easy way out—the Plaintiff's failure to satisfy a preponderance of the evidence—simply because it could not ascertain for sure just when Lyle had stated the truth.
>
> This was not, therefore, the case of admission or exclusion of some bit of testimony asserted on appellate review to have been erroneous. This was the denial of the use of a tool of advocacy which our long judicial heritage marks as one of the most effective in the quest for truth. This was a substantial right. The experience of the bar is that it has substantial value. . . . It is sufficient if we can see, as we readily do here, that the development of this record and the development of the testimony of Lyle as a witness might well have been quite different had the Plaintiff been accorded the right to put Lyle through all of the rigors of a sharp, relentless, pressing, vigorous cross examination as he verbally retraced foot-by-foot, second-by-second the crucial moments during which the two vehicles pursued their tragic fatal collision course.

Degelos v. Fidelity & Casualty Co., 313 F.2d 809, 814 (5th Cir. 1963).

In criminal cases the Sixth Amendment entitles the accused to "confront the witnesses against him," and cross-examination is the most critical aspect of this constitutional right. This entitlement applies in state as well as federal prosecutions, see Pointer v. Texas, 380 U.S. 400 (1965), and the Supreme Court has found that a variety of court rulings that cut into this entitlement abridge defense confrontation rights. See Smith v. Illinois, 390 U.S. 129, 131-132 (1968) (requiring new trial where court let witness use alias instead of real name and refuse to state address); Davis v. Alaska, 415 U.S. 308, 316 (1974) (requiring new trial where court let witness refuse to answer questions on juvenile record).

Sometimes events beyond the control of the parties or the court cut short or deny completely the right to cross-examine a witness. He may fall ill or die or claim a privilege or refuse to cooperate despite the threat of contempt. In any such case, the problem arises in a different guise: What should be done about testimony that he has already given?

Generally the solutions have been either the draconian sanction of striking the direct testimony completely when no cross-examination could be had, or the more moderate sanction of striking portions of the direct if the interruption came after cross-examination had begun, thus keeping portions of the direct as to which cross-examination had occurred. Often the decisions are affected by an aroma of suspicion, particularly where the witness is a party or clearly allied with a party, or where the impediment to cross-examination arises from apparent illness or a claim of privilege, and in such cases completely striking the testimony is more likely.

EXCLUDING WITNESSES

1. The General Principle

Common sense calls out that similar independent accounts are more to be trusted than similar accounts by narrators who heard what others say about the same acts, events, or conditions. Of course suspicions would arise if witnesses give *identical* accounts, simply because no two persons are likely to use the same words, or to agree on every detail, in describing something. We expect descriptions to vary and even conflict on some points, and the very fact of variation leads us to trust even more accounts that agree on the essentials, and such accounts are even more persuasive if they are truly independent.

Police routinely interview suspects and witnesses separately, and in their questioning avoid disclosing what others said, except when it is useful to do otherwise. And courts routinely exclude ("sequester") witnesses, telling them to stay outside the courtroom before testifying, to minimize the risk that they will "shape" their testimony to agree with (or supplement or refute) what others have to say. Consider the modern embodiment of the "witness rule" in FRE 615, under which a court "must order witnesses excluded" so they cannot hear other testimony, if requested by a party. Then consider this illustration of the principle in the story of Susanna and the Elders, an apocryphal addition to the Old Testament book of Daniel.

SUSANNA AND THE ELDERS

from N. de Lange, Apocrypha:
Jewish Literature of the Hellenistic Age 130-132 (1978)

That year two elders of the people were appointed judges, and cases were brought before them even from other towns. These two both conceived a violent passion for the wife of one of their brother-Israelites, a certain Joakim. The woman's name was Susanna, the daughter of Helkiah. She was a beautiful woman, and she was in the habit of taking a walk in her husband's gardens toward evening. The elders' passion got the better of their good sense and made them forget all thought of Heaven or of justice....

"We must have her," one of them said. So they agreed on a plan and made advances to her and tried to force her to do what they wanted. But Susann.... said to them, "I know that if I give in to you I shall be killed, and I also know that if I refuse I won't escape unharmed. Still, it's better that I should reject you and face the consequences than sin before the Lord."

So the two lechers left her, bent on revenge and determined to bring about her death. They went to the assembly of the town, where all the Jews were gathered in session, and there they stood up and said, "Send for Susanna, the daughter of Helkiah, the wife of Joakim." ...

Susanna was a very attractive woman, and the two scoundrels ordered her to be unveiled so that they could feast their eyes on her beauty. At this her family and friends burst into tears. The two elder-judges came forward and put their hands on her head. Susanna, trusting in the Lord, looked up to heaven and said through her tears, "Lord, eternal God, who knows all things before they happen, you know that I have not done what these vicious men accuse me of."

The two elders said, "We were walking in her husband's garden, and as we were going past the stadium we saw this woman with a man. We stood and watched them making love, and they did not realize we were there. We decided we must find out who they were and moved closer. We recognized her, but the young man, who was masked, escaped. We seized the woman and asked her who the man was but she refused to tell us. This is our solemn testimony."

The whole assembly believed them because they were elders and judges of the people.

As Susanna was being led off to be executed, an angel of the Lord inspired a young man [Daniel], who parted the crowd and stood in their way.

"Are you such fools, you Israelites," he said, "as to condemn a Jewish woman to death without investigating the charge and discovering the truth? Separate these men and let me cross-examine them."

When they were separated, [Daniel] addressed the assembly. "Don't think," he said, "that these men can't be liars just because they are elders. I am going to confront them both now with a question that has been put in my mind."

He summoned one of the elders, and . . . said, "Listen to me, you hardened sinner. The sins you have committed in the past have finally found you out. You were empowered to try capital cases and you convicted the innocent and acquitted the guilty, even though the Lord says, 'You shall not put the innocent and the guiltless to death.'"

"Where were you in the garden, what kind of tree were you standing under, when you saw them together?"

"It was an ash tree," said the wretched man.

"Your perjury redounds on your own head," replied [Daniel]. "This very day the angel of the Lord will burn you to a fine ash!"

[Daniel] told them to take him away and fetch the other one. "You are more like a lewd Sidonian than a Jew. You were infatuated by beauty and dragged down by your lust. You had your way, no doubt, with Israelite women; they submitted to you out of fear. But this daughter of Judah was too proud to give in to your disgusting demands. Tell me, now, where exactly were you in the park, what tree were you standing under, when you saw them carrying on together?"

"It was a pear tree," said the elder.

"Sinner!" replied [Daniel]. "At this very moment the angel of the Lord is standing with his sword drawn, waiting for the people to finish with you so that he can pare you to the quick!"

The whole assembly began to shout and cheer the young man because he had convicted them of perjury out of their own mouths. They punished them, in accordance with the law, with the same penalty they had planned to inflict on their sister-Israelite. They gagged them and led them off and hurled them into a chasm, and there the angel of the Lord burned them with flames. And so an innocent life was saved that day.

■ NOTES ON EXCLUDING WITNESSES

1. If Susanna were tried under modern procedure with Daniel as her lawyer, he could invoke FRE 615. What could he ask the court to do?

2. The elders differ on what one might call a minor point of detail, but the author of the story tells us that the charges were made up, and the elders were guilty of what we would call rape or sexual assault, and their stories of Susanna's adultery were false. In a modern criminal trial, would such a discrepancy prove decisive? Suppose a man were tried for sexual assault against Susanna, and the state's main witnesses gave matching accounts except that one said the event occurred under an ash tree, and the other said under a pear tree. Is there truth to the idea that concocted stories are likely to match on "essential" points and differ only on "marginal" points? Should impeachment on "collateral points" be allowed when the situation suggests that two witnesses cooperated in preparing their testimony?

■ PROBLEM 7-A. Daily Transcripts

On the first day of the trial of Excel's claim against Mentor for patent infringement, counsel for plaintiff obtains a court order excluding all witnesses. Novick is the key expert witness for the defense, and he complies with the order. Just before Mentor calls Novick to testify, however, plaintiff learns that defense counsel has purchased daily transcripts of the trial, through private (and entirely proper) arrangement with the court reporter. Counsel for Excel suspects that defense counsel has at least gone over the pertinent portions of this transcript in preparing Novick for his time on the stand, and that in all likelihood Novick has actually read critical passages containing testimony given by witnesses for Excel.

Plaintiff's counsel seeks to bar Novick from testifying, arguing that any sharing of transcripts violates the order of exclusion. How should the court rule, and why?

■ NOTES ON BREADTH OF FRE 615

1. Pretty clearly courts must implement sequestration orders under FRE 615 by instructing excluded witnesses not to confer with others. Such instructions are routine. See Williams v. United States, 859 A.2d 130, 138 (D.C. 2004) (common to instruct witnesses not to discuss testimony with third parties until trial is over; such orders are "a corollary of the broader rule that witnesses may be sequestered"). Instructions to counsel are not usually considered necessary, as lawyers are expected to understand the reasons for orders of exclusion and act accordingly.

2. Where parties or witnesses violate a sequestration order, what remedies can a court put in play other than barring testimony by witnesses who hear testimony that they were not supposed to hear?

3. FRE 615 authorizes exclusion of witnesses "so that they cannot hear the testimony of other witnesses." Does the Rule authorize exclusion during opening statements? See United States v. Brown, 547 F.2d 36, 37 (3d Cir. 1976) (No), *cert. denied,* 431 U.S. 905 (1977).

4. What if the potential witness is a criminal defendant? He cannot be excluded from his own trial, and an order not to discuss the case with his attorney could violate his constitutional right to effective assistance of counsel. See

Geders v. United States 425 U.S. 80 (1976) (order prohibiting defendant from meeting with counsel during 17-hour overnight recess between direct and cross violated Sixth Amendment right to effective assistance of counsel).

Witness Sequestration in Terrorism Trial of Zacarias Moussaoui

Getty Images / Handout

Intentionally violating an order entered under FRE 615 can put a trial in jeopardy and an attorney at risk of discipline. In the trial of accused September 11th conspirator Zacarias Moussaoui, Reuters reported that Judge Brinkema said in court that she had "never seen such an egregious violation" of a sequestration order, after a lawyer from the Federal Aviation Administration apparently read the transcript of the first day of the trial and discussed the case with "several potential witnesses who were due to be called by both the prosecution and the defense." Reportedly the judge considered dismissing the case. Reuters News Service (Mar. 13, 2006). Ultimately Judge Brinkema barred testimony by several witnesses, but let others who had not violated the order testify to the same points. Moussaoui was convicted and sentenced to life in prison.

2. Traditional Exemptions from the Witness Rule

Under FRE 615, a person who is party to an action cannot be excluded. Nor can an "officer or employee" who is "designated as its representative." Sometimes the case agent who investigated the case is named as a government representative.

Parties are as likely as witnesses, aren't they, to shape their testimony to make it align better with what others say? How about requiring parties to testify first? Does the fact that parties or their designated representatives are exempt from sequestration mean judges should not try to accommodate concerns over "tailored testimony" by requiring a certain sequence in calling witnesses? See FRE 611(a) (courts may control "mode and order" of interrogating witnesses).

Also exempt from exclusion by FRE 615(c) is a person shown to be "essential to the presentation" of a cause. What kinds of witnesses likely qualify under this provision? Experts commonly fit this exemption, though not always. Compare United States v. Burgess, 691 F.2d 1146, 1157 (4th Cir. 1982) (psychiatrists for defense and prosecution both allowed to remain in court) with Miller v. Universal City Studios, 650 F.2d 1365, 1372-1374 (5th Cir. 1981) (doubting that expertise provides "automatic basis" for exemption, and suggesting that literary expert in copyright infringement suit might not qualify). See also United States v. Farnham, 791 F.2d 331, 335 (4th Cir. 1986) ("singular phrasing" in exemption (c) means that only one of two FBI agents remain in courtroom).

Suppose a witness excluded from the proceedings violates the order and *does* listen to other testimony (or talk to other witnesses). When the disadvantaged party learns of this violation of the court's order, what is the appropriate remedy? In an old case, the Supreme Court addressed the matter thus:

> If a witness disobeys the order of withdrawal, while he may be proceeded against for contempt and his testimony is open to comment to the jury by reason of his conduct, he is not thereby disqualified, and the weight of authority is that he cannot be excluded on that ground merely, although the right to exclude under particular circumstances may be supported as within the sound discretion of the trial court.

Holder v. United States, 150 U.S. 91, 92-93 (1893). See also Government of Virgin Islands v. Edinborough, 625 F.2d 472, 474 (3d Cir. 1980) (violating a sequestration order does not automatically call for excluding the testimony of the witness).

Should an aggrieved party have to show that violating the order prejudiced the outcome, or should prejudice be presumed? See United States v. Ell, 718 F.2d 291, 293-294 (9th Cir. 1983) (FRE 615 could be read as (a) requiring a showing of prejudice, (b) requiring automatic reversal, or (c) raising a presumption of prejudice; court decides that prejudice "is presumed and reversal is required unless it is manifestly clear" that the error was harmless or prosecutor proves harmless error by a preponderance).

3. The Special Case of Crime Victims

In our system, crime victims are not parties. The state or federal government as prosecuting authority acts on behalf of "the people" or "the State" or "the United States" on behalf of citizens and the larger body politic. Hence victims are not covered by FRE 615's exemption for "parties." Nor are victims normally categorized as persons "essential to the presentation of a case" (this exemption usually applies to agents and experts).

People who are personally and directly victimized by crime, such as those who suffer sexual or physical assault or robbery, are likely to be the first witnesses called by the prosecutor—or at least the first witnesses called to describe the crime itself. At least to this extent, concerns over "tailored" testimony can be accommodated without sequestering them. There are also victims who do not see what has happened, as is typically true in larceny and burglary cases, and people like these usually testify (if at all) about such things as the conditions of the premises or the items stolen, where once again concerns over tailored testimony are not great.

In the closing decade of the twentieth century, however, growing social and political concern led to enactment of statutes that create and protect certain rights for crime victims. Among these are the right to be treated with fairness and dignity, the right to be notified of important court proceedings, and to attend and be heard in such proceedings. See, e.g., Utah Constitution, Art. I §§12 and 28. The movement to guarantee such rights regained momentum when, in the Oklahoma City bombing trial of Timothy McVeigh in 1996, Judge Matsch excluded from the courtroom during the "guilt phase" all survivors of the bombing who were to give "victim impact" testimony during the punishment phase (in the event of conviction). Judge Matsch invoked FRE 615, which at the time had no exemption covering victims, and the reviewing court refused to disturb the ruling, even though the Victim Compensation and Assistance Act was already part of federal law, and it includes a provision entitling victims "to be present at all public court proceedings related to the offense" unless the court determines that their testimony "would be materially affected" by other testimony. See 42 USC §10606(a) and United States v. McVeigh, 106 F.3d 325 (10th Cir. 1997). Congress then enacted another statute, which provides that federal courts shall not exclude "any victim of an offense" from a trial merely because he may testify during sentencing. See 18 USC §3510. Judge Matsch acquiesced in the obvious legislative message and did *not* thenceforth exclude survivors of the Oklahoma City bombing, although he did conduct voir dire of these witnesses during the sentencing phase to satisfy himself that their testimony would not be affected by what they had heard.

In 1997, the fourth exemption was added to FRE 615, making it clear that people "authorized by statute" to be present at trial are not to be sequestered, and the intent was to accommodate the federal victim's right statutes. Many states have similar legislation, and similarly exempt crime victims from their sequestration provisions. Such statutes must be read carefully to determine who qualifies as a "victim."

CHAPTER 8

Impeachment of Witnesses

INTRODUCTION

Methods of impeachment. There are five ways to impeach a witness. Three focus on bringing out reasons to doubt his word in general, without pinpointing a particular error or lie in his testimony. The other two target particular misstatements or lies, but without suggesting reasons.

The first three methods are definite but nonspecific: They are definite in telling the trier why to doubt the witness, but nonspecific in not showing what testimony to doubt. They include (1) showing that the witness has some bias, animus, motivation, or corruption that might lead him to fabricate or shade his testimony to help or hurt one of the parties, (2) showing a defect in sensory or mental capacity (perception or memory) that undercuts his testimony, and (3) showing that he is by disposition untruthful. A party may mount this third attack in three different ways, including (a) cross-examining the target witness about nonconviction misconduct casting doubt on his honesty (Rule 608(b)), (b) cross-examining him about certain kinds of convictions (Rule 609), and (c) testimony by a character witness that the target witness is untruthful (Rule 608(a)).

The fourth and fifth methods are specific but indefinite: They are specific in calling into doubt particular points in the testimony of the witness (hence suggesting the possibility of error or falsehood on other points) but indefinite because they do not necessarily reveal the underlying cause. These include (4) showing that the witness has made a prior inconsistent statement (meaning one that conflicts with his current testimony), and (5) contradicting the witness—showing that he is just plain wrong on one or another point in his testimony.

Usually these attacks are mounted on cross-examination of the target witness. Most such attacks, however, may also be mounted by extrinsic evidence (testimony by another witness) after the target witness has left the stand. In one instance (attacking the character of the target by nonconviction misconduct), the Rules *limit* the attacking party to cross-examination of the target witness. In another (attacking the character of the target by means of convictions), the Rule now allows extrinsic evidence without restriction on timing. (Originally FRE 609 allowed use of a "public record," but only "during cross-examination.") In a third instance (inconsistent statements), the attack may be mounted on cross (and it usually is), but extrinsic evidence is also admissible, and Rule 613 regulates some aspects of the subject. Most importantly, it imposes a requirement that the witness be permitted to explain her prior statements.

Repairing credibility. Usually the calling party wants to repel the attack or otherwise repair the credibility of the witness. Subject to the discretion of the court under FRE 611 to limit excursions into side issues, a supporting party may examine the witness in an effort to refute points suggested during the attack or explain away any aspersions cast on his veracity. Sometimes the calling party mounts an offensive of his own. Under certain conditions, he may offer proof of the good character of the witness for truth and veracity or evidence of prior consistent statements (which harmonize with the direct testimony).

The regulating scheme. The drafters of the Federal Rules chose to regulate the subjects of impeaching and repairing witness credibility only in part. Thus the Rules make no mention of bias or mental or sensory capacity, no mention of contradiction, and only refer indirectly to the use of prior consistent statements to repair credibility.

A NONSPECIFIC IMPEACHMENT

1. Bias and Motivation

So active and motivated is the imagination of counsel, and so many and varied are the relationships that give rise to favor or animus, that the range of points the attacking party may raise in an attempt to impeach for bias or influence is wide indeed. There are few hard-edged rules, and the extent of permissible cross-examination for bias is very much a matter for the discretion of the trial judge. But it is clear that the court cannot properly cut off all apparently legitimate attempts to show that a witness is biased, and some subjects (like plea bargains affecting prosecution witnesses, or fees paid to experts) are so clearly proper that at least some questions are always allowed.

Of course much depends on the circumstance, so a question proper in one case might be improper in another. But bearing that warning in mind, consider the following questions, all of which have been upheld as means of indicating bias:[1]

Q (government to turncoat government witness): Defendants are paying your lawyer, aren't they?

Q (defense to government witness): Isn't it true, sir, that your livelihood depends entirely on government payment for your work as an informer and that you made up your testimony about my client in order to collect government bounty?

Q (plaintiff to defendant's expert in product liability case): Will you tell us, sir, what hourly rate you charge for testifying in cases such as this one?

Q (prosecutor to defense witness, an alleged co-offender): Isn't it true that defendant has been paying your wife's grocery and light bills since you were incarcerated?

Q (defense to government witness): Isn't it true, sir, that my client rebuffed your homosexual advance?

Q (defendant sheriff, charged with civil rights violations, to prosecution witness): Isn't it true that you were arrested on an earlier occasion by defendant's deputies?

So important is the defense right to develop bias in a prosecution witnesses that the Court has held that denying cross-examination on such a point can violate confrontation rights and due process. See Olden v. Kentucky, 488 U.S. 227 (1988) (blocking effort to show that complainant was living with boyfriend violated confrontation rights; theory was that rape charges were concocted to explain why she was driving with defendant and others after meeting them at bar, to protect relationship with boyfriend); Davis v. Alaska, 415 U.S. 308 (1974) (confrontation rights violated by preventing defense from cross-examining youthful witness under state statute blocking use of juvenile adjudications for impeachment purposes; probationer status might reveal "biases, prejudices, or ulterior motives"). Partly because of the importance of this impeaching mechanism, the Court has held that the trial judge must let the defense uncover identifying facts about government witnesses, such as name and address, and place of employment. See Smith v. Illinois, 390 U.S. 129 (1968) (where witness used pseudonym "James Jordan," sustaining objection to defense question seeking his true identity violated confrontation rights); Alford v. United States, 282 U.S. 687 (1931) (error to disallow defense question on "place of residence" of government witness).

Still, the court may impose reasonable limits on efforts to show bias and cut off questioning when the point has been made.

---

[1] The examples set out here rest on opinions in United States v. Coviello, 225 F.3d 54, 68 (1st Cir. 2000) (lawyer being paid), *cert. denied*, 531 U.S. 602 (2001); United States v. Leja, 568 F.2d 493, 495-499 (6th Cir. 1977) (work as informer); Collins v. Wayne Corp., 621 F.2d 777, 783-784 (5th Cir. 1980) (expert fees); United States v. Kerr, 464 F.2d 1367, 1372 (6th Cir. 1972) (grocery bills); United States v. Jones, 766 F.2d 412, 413-414 (9th Cir. 1985) (homosexual advance); and United States v. Garza, 754 F.2d 1202, 1206 (5th Cir. 1985) (arrests).

Deathrow Inmate John Clyde Abel

California Department of Corrections and Rehabilitation

You are about to read the *Abel* case, which establishes that bias is a legitimate method of impeachment under the Rules. The defendant John Clyde Abel has a long criminal record. In January 1991, he shot and killed a man in a parking lot in Orange, California during a robbery (his victim had withdrawn $20,000 from a bank to provide check-cashing services). Convicted of first degree murder, Abel was sentenced to death in September, 1997. During the penalty phase of his trial, evidence suggested that Abel participated in 15 robberies and was armed during 14 of them. The California Supreme Court upheld his conviction, and Abel is on death row in San Quentin. See People v. Abel, 271 P.3d 1040 (Cal. 2012). When Abel was arrested for the savings and loan robbery that gave rise to the appeal leading to Justice Rehnquist's opinion, he was probably incarcerated in the federal prison in Victorville, California, but he also spent time at the minimum security prison in Lompoc, and it was there that a witness in his later state trial testified that he had told Abel about the man whom Abel later murdered.

UNITED STATES v. ABEL

United States Supreme Court
469 U.S. 45 (1984)

Justice REHNQUIST delivered the opinion of the Court.

A divided panel of the Court of Appeals for the Ninth Circuit reversed respondent's conviction for bank robbery. The Court of Appeals held that the District Court improperly admitted testimony which impeached one of respondent's witnesses. We hold that the District Court did not err, and we reverse.

Respondent John Abel and two cohorts were indicted for robbing a savings and loan in Bellflower, Cal. . . . The cohorts elected to plead guilty, but respondent went to trial. One of the cohorts, Kurt Ehle, agreed to testify against respondent and identify him as a participant in the robbery.

Respondent informed the District Court at a pretrial conference that he would seek to counter Ehle's testimony with that of Robert Mills. Mills was not a participant in the robbery but was friendly with respondent and with Ehle, and had spent time with both in prison. Mills planned to testify that after the robbery Ehle had admitted to Mills that Ehle intended to implicate respondent falsely, in order to receive favorable treatment from the government. The prosecutor in turn disclosed that he intended to discredit Mills' testimony by calling Ehle back to the stand and eliciting from Ehle the fact that respondent, Mills, and Ehle were all members of the "Aryan Brotherhood," a secret prison gang that required its members always to deny the existence of the organization and to commit perjury, theft, and murder on each member's behalf.

Defense counsel objected to Ehle's proffered rebuttal testimony as too prejudicial to respondent. After a lengthy discussion in chambers the District Court decided to permit the prosecutor to cross-examine Mills about the gang, and if Mills denied knowledge of the gang, to introduce Ehle's rebuttal testimony concerning the tenets of the gang and Mills' and respondent's membership in it. The District Court held that the probative value of Ehle's rebuttal testimony outweighed its prejudicial effect, but that respondent might be entitled to a limiting instruction if his counsel would submit one to the court.

At trial Ehle implicated respondent as a participant in the robbery. Mills, called by respondent, testified that Ehle told him in prison that Ehle planned to implicate respondent falsely. When the prosecutor sought to cross-examine Mills concerning membership in the prison gang, the District Court conferred again with counsel outside of the jury's presence, and ordered the prosecutor not to use the term "Aryan Brotherhood" because it was unduly prejudicial. Accordingly, the prosecutor asked Mills if he and respondent were members of a "secret type of prison organization" which had a creed requiring members to deny its existence and lie for each other. When Mills denied knowledge of such an organization the prosecutor recalled Ehle.

Ehle testified that respondent, Mills, and he were indeed members of a secret prison organization whose tenets required its members to deny its existence and "lie, cheat, steal [and] kill" to protect each other. The District Court sustained a defense objection to a question concerning the punishment for violating the organization's rules. Ehle then further described the organization and testified that "in view of the fact of how close Abel and Mills were" it would have been "suicide" for Ehle to have told Mills what Mills attributed to him. Respondent's counsel did not request a limiting instruction and none was given.

The jury convicted respondent. On his appeal a divided panel of the Court of Appeals reversed. The Court of Appeals held that Ehle's rebuttal testimony was admitted not just to show that respondent's and Mills' membership in the same group might cause Mills to color his testimony; the court held that the contested evidence was also admitted to show that because Mills belonged to a perjurious organization, he must be lying on the stand. This suggestion of perjury, based upon a group tenet, was impermissible. The court reasoned:

> It is settled law that the government may not convict an individual merely for belonging to an organization that advocates illegal activity. Scales v. United

States, 367 U.S. 203, 219-24; Brandenburg v. Ohio, 395 U.S. 444. Rather, the government must show that the individual knows of and personally accepts the tenets of the organization. Neither should the government be allowed to impeach on the grounds of mere membership, since membership, without more, has no probative value. It establishes nothing about the individual's own actions, beliefs, or veracity. 707 F.2d 1013, 1016 (1983) (citations omitted).

The court concluded that Ehle's testimony implicated respondent as a member of the gang; but since respondent did not take the stand, the testimony could not have been offered to impeach him and it prejudiced him "by mere association."

We hold that the evidence showing Mills' and respondent's membership in the prison gang was sufficiently probative of Mills' possible bias towards respondent to warrant its admission into evidence. Thus it was within the District Court's discretion to admit Ehle's testimony, and the Court of Appeals was wrong in concluding otherwise.

Both parties correctly assume, as did the District Court and the Court of Appeals, that the question is governed by the Federal Rules of Evidence. But the Rules do not by their terms deal with impeachment for "bias," although they do expressly treat impeachment by character evidence and conduct, Rule 608, by evidence of conviction of a crime, Rule 609, and by showing of religious beliefs or opinion, Rule 610. Neither party has suggested what significance we should attribute to this fact. Although we are nominally the promulgators of the Rules, and should in theory need only to consult our collective memories to analyze the situation properly, we are in truth merely a conduit when we deal with an undertaking as substantial as the preparation of the Federal Rules of Evidence. In the case of these Rules, too, it must be remembered that Congress extensively reviewed our submission, and considerably revised it.

Before the present Rules were promulgated, the admissibility of evidence in the federal courts was governed in part by statutes or rules, and in part by case law. This Court had held in Alford v. United States, 282 U.S. 687 (1931), that a trial court must allow some cross-examination of a witness to show bias. This holding was in accord with the overwhelming weight of authority in the state courts as reflected in Wigmore's classic treatise on the law of evidence. Our decision in Davis v. Alaska, 415 U.S. 308 (1974), holds that the Confrontation Clause of the Sixth Amendment requires a defendant to have some opportunity to show bias on the part of a prosecution witness.

With this state of unanimity confronting the drafters of the Rules, we think it unlikely that they intended to scuttle entirely the evidentiary availability of cross-examination for bias. One commentator, recognizing the omission of any express treatment of impeachment for bias, prejudice, or corruption, observes that the Rules "clearly contemplate the use of the above-mentioned grounds of impeachment." E. Cleary, McCormick on Evidence, §40 p. 85 (3d ed. 1984). Other commentators, without mentioning the omission, treat bias as a permissible and established basis of impeachment under the Rules. 3 D. Louisell & C. Mueller, Federal Evidence §341 p. 470 (1979); 3 J. Weinstein & M. Berger, Weinstein's Evidence §607[03] (1981).

We think this conclusion is obviously correct. Rule 401 defines as "relevant evidence" evidence having any tendency to make the existence of any fact that is of consequence to the determination of the action more probable or less probable than it would be without the evidence. Rule 402 provides that all relevant evidence is admissible, except as otherwise provided by the United States Constitution, Act of Congress, or by applicable rule. A successful showing of bias on the part of a witness would have a tendency to make the facts to which he testified less probable in the eyes of the jury than it would be without such testimony.

The correctness of the conclusion that the Rules contemplate impeachment by showing of bias is confirmed by the references to bias in the Advisory Committee Notes to Rules 608 and 610, and by the provisions allowing any party to attack credibility in Rule 607, and allowing cross examination on "matters affecting the credibility of the witness" in Rule 611(b). The Courts of Appeals have upheld use of extrinsic evidence to show bias both before and after the adoption of the Federal Rules of Evidence.

We think the lesson to be drawn from all of this is that it is permissible to impeach a witness by showing his bias under the Federal Rules of Evidence just as it was permissible to do so before their adoption. In this connection, the comment of the Reporter for the Advisory Committee which drafted the Rules is apropos:

> In principle, under the Federal Rules no common law of evidence remains. "All relevant evidence is admissible, except as otherwise provided. . . ." In reality, of course, the body of common law knowledge continues to exist, though in the somewhat altered form of a source of guidance in the exercise of delegated powers.

Cleary, Preliminary Notes on Reading the Rules of Evidence, 57 Neb. L. Rev. 908, 915 (1978) (footnote omitted).

Ehle's testimony about the prison gang certainly made the existence of Mills' bias towards respondent more probable. Thus it was relevant to support that inference. Bias is a term used in the "common law of evidence" to describe the relationship between a party and a witness which might lead the witness to slant, unconsciously or otherwise, his testimony in favor of or against a party. Bias may be induced by a witness' like, dislike, or fear of a party, or by the witness' self-interest. Proof of bias is almost always relevant because the jury, as finder of fact and weigher of credibility, has historically been entitled to assess all evidence which might bear on the accuracy and truth of a witness' testimony. The "common law of evidence" allowed the showing of bias by extrinsic evidence, while requiring the cross-examiner to "take the answer of the witness" with respect to less favored forms of impeachment.

Mills' and respondent's membership in the Aryan Brotherhood supported the inference that Mills' testimony was slanted or perhaps fabricated in respondent's favor. A witness' and a party's common membership in an organization, even without proof that the witness or party has personally adopted its tenets, is certainly probative of bias. We do not read our holdings in *Scales* and *Brandenburg* to require a different conclusion. Those cases dealt with the constitutional requirements for convicting persons under the Smith Act and state syndicalism laws for belonging to organizations which espoused illegal aims and engaged in illegal conduct. Mills' and respondent's membership in the Aryan Brotherhood was not offered to convict either of a crime, but to impeach Mills' testimony. Mills was subject to no sanction other than that he might be disbelieved. Under these circumstances there is no requirement that the witness must be shown to have subscribed to all the tenets of the organization, either casually or in a manner sufficient to permit him to be convicted under laws such as those involved in *Scales* and *Brandenburg.* For purposes of the law of evidence the jury may be permitted to draw an inference of subscription to the tenets of the organization from membership alone, even though such an inference would not be sufficient to convict beyond a reasonable doubt in a criminal prosecution under the Smith Act.

Respondent argues that even if the evidence of membership in the prison gang were relevant to show bias, the District Court erred in permitting a full description of the gang and its odious tenets. Respondent contends that the District Court abused its discretion under Federal Rules of Evidence 403, because the prejudicial effect of the contested evidence outweighed its probative value. In other words, testimony about the gang inflamed the jury against respondent, and the chance that he would be convicted by his mere association with the organization outweighed any probative value the testimony may have had on Mills' bias.

Respondent specifically contends that the District Court should not have permitted Ehle's precise description of the gang as a lying and murderous group. Respondent suggests that the District Court should have cut off the testimony after the prosecutor had elicited that Mills knew respondent and both may have belonged to an organization together. This argument ignores the fact that the *type* of organization in which a witness and a party share membership may be relevant to show bias. If the organization is a loosely knit group having nothing to do with the subject matter of the litigation, the inference of bias arising from common membership may be small or nonexistent. If the prosecutor had elicited that both respondent and Mills belonged to the Book of the Month Club, the jury probably would not have inferred bias even if the District Court had admitted the testimony. The attributes of the Aryan Brotherhood—a secret prison sect sworn to perjury and self-protection—bore directly not only on the *fact* of bias but also on the *source* and *strength* of Mills' bias. The tenets of this group showed that Mills had a powerful motive to slant his testimony towards respondent, or even commit perjury outright.

A district court is accorded a wide discretion in determining the admissibility of evidence under the Federal Rules. Assessing the probative value of common membership in any particular group, and weighing any factors counseling against admissibility is a matter first for the district court's sound judgment under Rules 401 and 403 and ultimately, if the evidence is admitted, for the trier of fact.

Before admitting Ehle's rebuttal testimony, the District Court gave heed to the extensive arguments of counsel, both in chambers and at the bench. In an attempt to avoid undue prejudice to respondent the court ordered that the name "Aryan Brotherhood" not be used. The court also offered to give a limiting instruction concerning the testimony, and it sustained defense objections to the prosecutor's questions concerning the punishment meted out to unfaithful members. These precautions did not prevent *all* prejudice to respondent from Ehle's testimony, but they did in our opinion ensure that the admission of this highly probative evidence did not *unduly* prejudice respondent. We hold there was no abuse of discretion under Rule 403 in admitting Ehle's testimony as to membership and tenets.

Respondent makes an additional argument based on Rule 608(b). That Rule allows a cross-examiner to impeach a witness by asking him about specific instances of past conduct, other than crimes covered by Rule 609, which are probative of his veracity or "character for truthfulness or untruthfulness." The Rule limits the inquiry to cross-examination of the witness, however, and prohibits the cross-examiner from introducing extrinsic evidence of the witness' past conduct.

Respondent claims that the prosecutor cross-examined Mills about the gang not to show bias but to offer Mills' membership in the gang as past conduct bearing on his veracity. This was error under Rule 608(b), respondent contends, because the mere fact of Mills' membership, without more, was not sufficiently probative of Mills' character for truthfulness. Respondent cites a second error under the same Rule, contending that Ehle's rebuttal testimony concerning the gang was extrinsic evidence offered to impugn Mills' veracity, and extrinsic evidence is barred by Rule 608(b).

The Court of Appeals appears to have accepted respondent's argument to this effect, at least in part. It said:

> Ehle's testimony was not simply a matter of showing that Abel's and Mills' membership in the same organization might "cause [Mills], consciously or otherwise, to color his testimony." . . . Rather it was to show as well that because Mills and Abel were members of a gang whose members "will lie to protect the members," Mills must be lying on the stand.

It seems clear to us that the proffered testimony with respect to Mills' membership in the Aryan Brotherhood sufficed to show potential bias in favor of respondent; because of the tenets of the organization described, it might also impeach his veracity directly. But there is no rule of evidence which provides that testimony admissible for one purpose and inadmissible for another purpose is thereby rendered inadmissible; quite the contrary is the case. It would be a strange rule of law which held that relevant, competent evidence which tended to show bias on the part of a witness was nonetheless inadmissible because it also tended to show that the witness was a liar.

We intimate no view as to whether the evidence of Mills' membership in an organization having the tenets ascribed to the Aryan Brotherhood would be a specific instance of Mills' conduct which could not be proved against him by extrinsic evidence except as otherwise provided in Rule 608(b). It was enough that such evidence could properly be found admissible to show bias.

The judgment of the Court of Appeals is reversed.

■ NOTES ON SHOWING BIAS

1. In the Ninth Circuit's view, proof of Mills's membership in the "secret type of prison organization" had "no probative value" and prejudiced defendant "by mere association." Does "mere membership" in the Aryan Brotherhood tell nothing about Mills's inclinations as a witness? How does the Court deal with that point? Who is right, and why?

2. The Court (relying on Professor Cleary, principal draftsman of the Rules) reaches a sensible resolution of the problem of the Rules' failure to mention bias, doesn't it? How *does* it resolve this matter?

3. Often it happens that key prosecution witnesses are themselves involved in crimes giving rise to prosecution. The prosecutor must disclose information about deals and promises of leniency affecting such witnesses, see Giglio v. United States, 405 U.S. 150 (1972), and defendants follow up at trial by asking about these points. See United States v. Maloof, 205 F.3d 819, 829 (5th Cir. 2000) (defense questioned alleged co-offender extensively about plea agreement), *cert. denied*, 531 U.S. 873 (2000); United States v. Roberts, 618 F.2d 530, 535 (9th Cir. 1980) (court should allow defense questions on plea agreements between government and its witnesses), *cert. denied*, 452 U.S. 942 (1981). What if the witness lies about promises or deals? See Annunziato v. Manson, 566 F.2d 410 (2d Cir. 1977) (conviction set aside; witness falsely denied leniency agreement, and government failed to correct the falsehood).

4. Typically a deal takes the form of a written agreement that commits the witness to plead guilty to a lesser offense and testify against his cohorts in their trials, in exchange for the prosecutor's agreement to recommend that his plea be accepted and that a particular sentence be imposed. Given the inevitability of defense cross-examination on this subject, what should the prosecutor do on direct? See United States v. Gaev, 24 F.3d 473, 478-479 (3d Cir. 1994) (on direct, government could ask drug conspirator about plea agreement; otherwise jury would learn he was involved and might infer that he had not been punished). And see generally United States v. Smith, 232 F.3d 344 (D.C. 2000) (defense cross-examined government witness on plea agreement, and government showed previous truthful cooperation; court avoids deciding whether this tactic is proper because defense did not preserve claim).

5. Although the Supreme Court held (in *Alford* and *Smith*, described prior to the *Abel* case) that the defense should be able to uncover basic identifying facts about government witnesses, a concurring opinion by Justices White and Marshall in *Smith* sought to limit the reach of the principle:

> In *Alford* . . . the Court recognized that questions which tend merely to harass, annoy, or humiliate a witness may go beyond the bounds of proper cross-examination. I would place in the same category those inquiries which tend to endanger the personal safety of the witness. But in these situations, if the question asked is one that is normally permissible, the State or the witness should at the very least come forward with some showing of why the witness must be excused from answering the question.

Smith v. Illinois, 390 U.S. 129, 133-134 (1968). Where risks to the safety of the witness appear, trial judges frequently curtail defense cross on such basic facts.

6. Often bias is indicated by something the witness has said. When a party uses prior statements to impeach a witness on the theory that they are *inconsistent with* his present testimony, you will see that FRE 613(b) allows extrinsic evidence of such statements (testimony by another person) only if the witness under attack has a chance to explain (section B1, infra). Does this requirement apply when a statement is offered on the different theory that it shows bias? Courts sometimes say or imply that the answer is yes. See United States v. Betts, 16 F.3d 748, 764 (7th Cir. 1994) (although FRE 613 does not apply, still attacking party must show statement to witness first).

COMMENT/PERSPECTIVE: Using the Name "Aryan Brotherhood"

The Aryan Brotherhood (AB) took root in California prisons in the 1960s, and spread nationally from there. Its original purpose was to oppose and avenge acts by other prison organizations, particularly the Black Guerilla Family and Mexican Mafia. Now the AB is engaged in prison drug trafficking, murders, and intimidation of inmates and others. Prison violence linked to the AB and other gangs contributed to the increased use of solitary confinement, which has come under scrutiny because of its effects on prisoners who are denied most human contact. See generally Johnson v. California, 543 U.S. 499 (2005) (citing existence of racially based prison gangs, including Aryan Brotherhood, Black Guerrilla Family, Mexican Mafia, La Nuestra Familia, and Texas Syndicate, in sustaining policy of racial segregation of inmates for initial evaluation in prison). How to handle involvement in the AB has proved troublesome for courts. Compare Dawson v. Delaware, 503 U.S. 159 (1992) (vacating judgment imposing death penalty for error in admitting proof that defendant belonged to AB, to which defense stipulated in order to exclude expert testimony describing the group) with Fuller v. Johnson, 114 F.3d 491 (5th Cir. 1997) (admitting proof that defendant belonged to AB, "a gang that had committed unlawful acts, including homicides, multiple stabbings, drug dealing and aggravated assaults" because jury could conclude that membership in gang is relevant to future dangerousness). Crimes stemming from AB activities can lead to convictions, see U.S. v. Stinson, 647 F.3d 1196 (9th Cir. 2011) (upholding conviction for RICO conspiracy and related crimes for operating AB prison gang), and courts have admitted expert testimony on gang membership to explain such things as the unwillingness of an alleged co-offender to testify for the government, see United States v. Hankey, 203 F.3d 1160 (9th Cir. 2000) (admitting expert testimony that defendant and witness *W* were affiliated with Treetop Pyrus gang, and that if *W* testified against defendant he would "either be beaten or killed"). Alleged bias stemming from gang membership can bear on criminal trials in different ways. See, e.g., Cousins v. Commonwealth, 693 S.E.2d 283 (Va. App. 2010) (reversing murder conviction because judge refused to admit testimony that victim and state witnesses belonged to White Rock Crew); State v. Long, 647 N.W.2d 884 (Wis. App. 2002) (admitting proof that defendant and defense witnesses belonged to Sixth Ward gang, which bore on bias). In *Abel,* the trial court barred use of the name "Aryan Brotherhood" in order to reduce the risk of prejudice.

■ PROBLEM 8-A. The Hired Gun

In a product liability suit, defendant General Motors has called Dr. Norbert Riley as an expert witness. Riley is a professor of engineering design, holding a Ph.D. and an endowed chair at the University of Michigan. General Motors intends to elicit Riley's testimony that the accident could not have happened in the manner alleged because the design of the automatic shift mechanism made it impossible for the car to go into reverse unattended. On direct examination, counsel for the defendant broaches the subject of the fee arrangement between General Motors and Riley:

Q [defense counsel]: Now Professor Riley, of course you're here because General Motors has paid for your assistance in this case. Will you please advise the jury how you are paid?

A [Riley]: Our arrangement, I believe, is that I will receive $1600 per day for my appearances here in court.

Q: Thank you, sir. Now Professor Riley, you examined the vehicle involved in the accident, did you not?

Ensuing questioning go to substance, and no further mention was made of the fee arrangements. On cross-examination, plaintiff's counsel raises the subject anew:

Q [plaintiff's counsel]: Professor Riley, you mentioned that you are being paid here today. $1600 a day, is that right?
A [Riley]: That's correct.
Q: All right, sir, now could you tell us please how much you expect to be paid for your work on this case in total?
[Defense counsel]: Your Honor, we have nothing to hide here, but plaintiff's counsel is trying to browbeat this witness. The professor has said how much he gets paid, and it's a lot because he's a highly trained expert. There's no need to go into dollars and cents here. It wastes time and distracts everybody from what's really at stake here.
[Plaintiff's counsel]: Your Honor, the jury should know how much this man expects to get paid. I want them to know some other things too, including (1) how much he made testifying for GM last year, (2) whether he expects to testify for GM again, (3) how much he made, all told, last year testifying for automakers, and (4) approximately what proportion of his total income comes from such appearances.
Q [defense counsel]: Well, Your Honor, I have to object to that outburst. He's grandstanding here, and it's settled that inquiries of the sort he proposes are collateral. I'm asking you now to advise the jury not to consider the implications of those last remarks as evidence and to understand that GM is paying this man $1600 a day, just as we said in the beginning.

What should the judge do, and why?

NOTES ON CROSS-EXAMINING THE PAID WITNESS

1. Of course one party can cross-examine an expert on fees paid by the other side, which bears on bias. Invariably the calling party does pay for the services of any testifying expert, and brings out the fact of payment during initial phases of direct examination to avoid seeming to hide what will be laid bare by the other side. The harder questions are the ones posed above: How far can the cross-examiner go before we reach the point of diminishing returns? Compare Goldberg v. Boone, 912 A.2d 698 (Md. 2006) (can ask defense expert in malpractice case whether he was a "paid minimizer" who testified that medical problem was minor) and Collins v. Wayne Corp., 621 F.2d 777, 784 (5th Cir. 1980) (can ask about fees earned in other cases; pattern of compensation suggests possibility that witness "slanted his testimony" so he would be hired to testify in future cases) with United States v. 412.93 Acres of Land, 455 F.2d 1242, 1247 (3d Cir. 1972) (can bring out per diem fee for testifying) (but court blocked questions on compensation for whole project). See also Graham, Impeaching the Professional Expert Witness by a Showing of Financial Interest, 53 Ind. L.J. 35 (1977-1978).

2. Witnesses are sometimes paid special fees in criminal cases too—and the practice reaches not only experts but lay witnesses (informants) who would not cooperate otherwise. See United States v. Gray, 626 F.2d 494, 499 (5th Cir. 1980) (rejecting claim of misconduct where one government witness was paid $37,000, and another got $25,000; while high informant fees are suspicious, an informant's testimony is not excluded unless he was "promised payment contingent upon conviction"), *cert. denied*, 449 U.S. 1091 (1981). Should such witnesses be cross-examinable on fees they expect for their services in other cases? On yearly compensation for such services?

3. If a witness for the prosecution is in the Witness Protection Program (beholden to the government to protect his "new identity" and pay support), should defendant be able to bring out this fact? See United States v. Harris, 210 F.3d 165, 166 (3d Cir. 2000) (defense entitled to be informed, and cross-examine). Are there dangers in this strategy?

2. Sensory and Mental Capacity

The attacking party may seek to show that a witness had only a brief chance to see or hear what she has described in her testimony, or that she labors under defects in sensory capacity that affect her observation, or that human perceptive processes work in ways suggesting that her testimony is not so persuasive as it seems. Thus the cross-examining lawyer may bring out, for example, that the witness has poor eyesight or hearing, or may have been fooled by the angle of the sun or by noises that kept her from hearing what she thought she heard. Sometimes the attack proceeds on cross, but such points may also be proved by extrinsic evidence when the attacking party presents his case.

Such attacks sometimes go beyond commonplace matters, as the attacking party may show that the witness was under the influence of drugs or alcohol at the time of the events or even during trial. See Williams v. State, 749 N.E.2d 1139, 1142 (Ind. 2001).

An attack may broach the matter of mental afflictions or illness, including questions about treatment or stays in mental institutions. See United States v. Lindstrom, 698 F.2d 1154, 1159-1194 (11th Cir. 1983) (restricting cross on psychiatric history violated confrontation rights; defense sought to show that witness was motivated by "hatred" and "carrying out a vendetta" resulting from "continuing mental illness, for which she had been periodically treated and confined"). Courts may order production of medical records to assist in cross,

United States v. Honneus, 508 F.2d 566, 573 (1st Cir. 1974), *cert. denied*, 421 U.S. 948 (1975), and sometimes they admit psychiatric testimony when it bears on capacity to observe or report, United States v. Partin, 493 F.2d 750 (5th Cir.) (error to exclude expert testimony that government witness suffered from undifferentiated schizophrenic reaction, which bore on his "ability to see and hear accurately"), *cert. denied*, 434 U.S. 903 (1974).

■ NOTES ON PROVING LACK OF CAPACITY

1. The Rules do not mention impeachment for limits or impairment of sensory or mental capacity. Arguably it deserved coverage, and courts allow impeaching attacks that focus on such matters, usually invoking FRE 611 (which speaks of cross-examination on "credibility" and authorizes courts to control the proceedings to determine "truth" while protecting witnesses from "harassment or undue embarrassment").

2. Impeaching efforts that focus on psychiatric history raise concerns over privacy, sometimes putting courts to difficult choices between allowing important questions that might affect credibility and protecting witnesses from embarrassment or abuse. In one case, defendant sought to cross-examine a government witness over a psychiatric report that had found him competent, but the judge didn't allow it. In an instructive opinion by Judge Russell, the reviewing court affirmed:

> One's psychiatric history is an area of great personal privacy which can only be invaded in cross-examination when required in the interests of justice. This is so because cross-examination of an adverse witness on matters of such personal privacy, if of minimal probative value, is manifestly unfair and unnecessarily demeaning of the witness. Moreover, such cross-examination will generally introduce into the case a collateral issue, leading to a large amount of testimony substantially extraneous to the essential facts and issues of the controversy being tried . . . . [M]any psychiatric problems or fixations which a witness may have had are without any relevancy to the witness' credibility, concerned as it is with whether the witness' mental impairment is related to "his capacity to observe the event at the time of its occurrence, to communicate his observations accurately and truthfully at trial, or to maintain a clear recollection in the meantime." It follows that the witness' mental impairment, to constitute a proper subject for cross-examination, must have been "at a time probatively related to the time period about which he was attempting to testify," must go to the witness' qualification to testify and ability to recall, and must not "introduce into the case a collateral issue which would confuse the jury and which would necessitate allowing the Government to introduce testimony explaining the matter."
>
> Whether the cross-examination is to be permitted under the above principles is an issue committed to the discretion of the trial court, which, in its determination, is "entitled to weigh the potential unfairness of a freewheeling inquiry intended to stigmatize the witness against whatever materiality the

> evidence might have." To enable the trial court to make that determination, the party seeking to engage in the determination should make an offer of proof of the evidence it seeks to develop on the witness' mental impairment. The decision of the trial court, finally, on the allowability of such cross-examination may be reversed only for abuse of discretion.

United States v. Lopez, 611 F.2d 44, 45-46 (4th Cir. 1979) (court relies on FRE 403). See also Bennett v. United States, 876 A.2d 623, 632-633 (D.C. 2005) (psychiatric history involves personal privacy; can control cross accordingly; court allowed questions to prosecution witness about mental illness, but disallowed term "schizophrenia").

3. No witness is incompetent because of mental illness, but courts claim authority to order psychiatric examinations in rare cases raising acute concerns. See United States v. Gutman, 725 F.2d 417, 420 (7th Cir.) (judge has power and sometimes duty to hold hearing to determine whether witness should be permitted to testify only if he agrees to psychiatric examination), *cert. denied*, 105 U.S. 244 (1984). Such orders are very rare. For an example, see Hamill v. Powers, 164 P.3d 1086 (Okla. 2007) (in rape trial, state planned to use expert to prove that adult victim lacked capacity to consent; defense was entitled to order requiring psychological or psychiatric examination) ("admittedly rare").

4. Should experts testify on reliability of eyewitness identification? Courts sometimes let experimental psychologists testify that (a) memory diminishes exponentially (quickly losing its edge, then gradually fading), (b) stress causes inaccuracies in perception and recall, (c) observers assimilate or incorporate new and potentially inaccurate information they learn afterward and confuse or conflate this data with their original memory, (d) later conversations reinforce opinions about identification (feedback factor), (e) accuracy bears little or no relationship with certainty, and (f) cross-racial identifications contain more mistakes. Some appellate opinions criticize courts for excluding such evidence, see United States v. Downing, 753 F.2d 1224 (3d Cir. 1985) (error to apply per se rule of exclusion; court should assess scientific basis and utility), and there are occasional reversals because such evidence was excluded, see State v. Chapple, 660 P.2d 1208 (Ariz. 1983) (Chapter 2B1, supra). Most opinions, however, find such testimony inadmissible or defer to the discretion of the judge. See State v. Butterfield, 27 P.3d 1133, 1146 (Utah 2001) (must give cautionary instruction; whether to admit expert testimony is discretionary); Johnson v. State, 526 S.E.2d 549 (Ga. 2000) (court has discretion).

3. Character for "Truth and Veracity"

Proving "bad character for truth and veracity" (in the catchphrase of the profession) is a standard impeaching strategy, long part of our law. The Rules continue this tradition, recognizing three ways to show untruthfulness: Cross-examination on nonconviction misconduct, cross-examination on convictions, and use of character witnesses.

Recall that FRE 404 generally bars character evidence to prove conduct out of court. Showing that a person is untruthful involves character evidence to show a particular kind of conduct *in* court—lying on the stand—and FRE 404(a)(3) makes an exception to allow this strategy. FRE 608 and 609 authorize this attack, with certain restrictions that protect witnesses and parties alike. It is embarrassing, even humiliating, to have one's veracity questioned, and FRE 611 lets judges protect witnesses from "harassment or undue embarrassment." When the witness is a party, such impeachment raises a risk of prejudice similar to that which FRE 404 guards against.

The fact is that a party loses much of the protection of FRE 404 if he testifies, because doing so opens him up to questions exposing misconduct bearing on truthfulness. In practice, it is the accused in a criminal case who suffers most from this fact. Still, testifying does not sacrifice all the protection in FRE 404. For one thing, an impeaching attack must focus on veracity. If defendant in a murder trial testifies, for example, FRE 608 and 609 entitle the prosecutor to try to suggest that he is "dishonest," but FRE 404 continues to bar evidence that he is violent. Cf. United States v. Fountain, 768 F.2d 790, 795 (7th Cir.) (can't ask defendant whether he was "peaceable," as violent men "are not necessarily liars"), *reh'g denied*, 777 F.2d 345 (1985). Also prosecutors cannot use the misdeeds exposed in these impeaching attacks as proof of the charged crime.

a. Cross-Examination on Nonconviction Misconduct

One way to suggest that a witness is disposed to be untruthful is to bring out on cross instances of nonconviction misconduct that seem to bear on veracity. You may decide for yourself whether such instances indicate untruthfulness, but it is a long-cherished belief that they do, and for most people this belief makes intuitive sense. FRE 608(b) endorses questions on such points if the court in its discretion decides that the acts point toward this conclusion. Consider the inquiries, all approved in appellate opinions:[2]

Q (prosecutor to defendant): Isn't it a fact that you lied on two employment applications nine years ago, when you replied no to the question whether you had ever been convicted, fined, imprisoned, or placed on probation?

Q (prosecutor to defendant): Weren't you involved in persuading ineligible voters to fill out false registration forms? Didn't you even steal the forms? Didn't you misrepresent to the registrar that persons you found in the park

[2] The examples set out here rest, respectively, on opinions in United States v. Howard, 774 F.2d 838, 844-845 (7th Cir. 1985) (lying on employment applications, defendant said he thought applications covered only convictions in last ten years); United States v. Girdner, 773 F.2d 257, 260 (10th Cir. 1985) (persuading ineligible voters to falsify registrations), *cert. denied*, 475 U.S. 1066 (1986); United States v. Zandi, 769 F.2d 229, 236 (4th Cir. 1985) (false information on loan applications and tax returns); United States v. Mansaw, 714 F.2d 785, 789 (8th Cir.) (aliases; defendant not entitled to bring out that witness worked as prostitute), *cert. denied*, 464 U.S. 964 (1983); State v. Fields, 730 N.W.2d 777, 782 (Minn. 2007) (stealing from employer); United States v. Irwin, 354 F.2d 192, 198 (2d Cir. 1965) (bribery), *cert. denied*, 383 U.S. 967 (1966).

were the persons named in the forms? Didn't you tell falsely registered voters to lie if questioned?

Q (prosecutor to defendant): Didn't you give false information on a bank loan application and your tax returns?

Q (defense counsel to government witness): Isn't it a fact, ma'am, that you used false names or aliases?

Q (prosecutor to defendant): Sir, are there times in your past when you haven't been necessarily honest? Specifically, was there a time when you got in trouble basically from stealing from an employer?

Q (defense counsel to government IRS agent): Isn't it a fact, ma'am, that you have accepted bribes in the performance of your official duties?

Just putting such questions can impeach, no matter how the witness replies, for the odor raised by a question lingers after a denial. If there were no regulating mechanism, the cross-examining lawyer could inflict damage just by coming up with the nastiest question he can think of (taking care to link it to some actual condition or event so it doesn't sound like a shot in the dark): "You lied to your spouse about what you were doing on that trip to Orlando, didn't you?" or "You inflated your credentials when you applied for that job at Northern Bell, didn't you?" You don't need much imagination to see the mischief such questions can cause, and the Court suggested long ago that lawyers cannot ask them without adequate basis. See Michelson v. United States, 335 U.S. 469, 481 (1948) (judge properly ascertained that defendant, testifying as witness, had actually been arrested before cross-examiner was permitted to ask about underlying deeds, so "groundless question" would not "waft an unwarranted innuendo into the jury box").

The modern attitude is even more cautious: The thinking is that *even if* the cross-examiner has a factual basis, such questions can be damaging beyond their power to shed light on veracity. Hence trial judges have discretion to block even well-founded questions. FRE 608(b) says the court "may" allow questions about "specific instances" of conduct by the witness relating to "character for truthfulness." Here is the way one court described the appropriate caution:

> "[A] witness may be cross-examined on a prior bad act that has not resulted in a criminal conviction only where (1) the examiner has a factual predicate for the question, and (2) the bad act bears directly upon the veracity of the witness in respect to the issues involved [i]n the trial." Portillo v. United States, 609 A.2d 687, 690-691 (D.C. 1992) (citations and internal quotation marks omitted). The second prong of this test [asks whether the prior bad acts are probative of truthfulness or untruthfulness] . . . . [T]his court has looked to decisions of the federal courts applying FRE 608(b) in determining whether a bad act "bears directly upon the veracity of the witness in respect to the issues involved in the trial." Woodward & Lothrop v. Hillary, 598 A.2d 1142, 1150 (D.C. 1991).
>
> In ruling on proposed inquiry into specific prior acts, the trial court "is vested with broad discretion" in two ways. "First, notwithstanding the fact that a party proposing cross-examination claims to have a 'factual predicate' for inquiry into

> prior bad acts, the trial court may assess the questioner's offer of proof to determine whether such a factual predicate exists." Second, the court (a) may "impose reasonable limits" on cross-examination to prevent, among other things, "harassment, prejudice, confusion of the issues," physical harm to the witness, "or interrogation that is repetitive or only marginally relevant," *Roundtree* [*v. United States*, 581 A.2d 315, 320 (D.C. App. 1990)] (quoting Delaware v. Van Arsdall, 475 U.S. 673, 679 (1986)); or (b), "[w]ith regard to prejudice, . . . may preclude a proposed line of cross-examination 'if it appears that the danger of unfair prejudice will outweigh its probative value.'" *Roundtree* (quoting Lee v. United States, 454 A.2d 770, 775 (D.C. 1982), *cert. denied*, 464 U.S. 972 (1983)).

Murphy v. Bonanno, 663 A.2d 505, 508 (D.C. App. 1995). See also State v. Gomez, 63 P.3d 72, 79 (Utah 2002) (in rape trial, not allowing defense to ask victim whether she used false identification card to gain entry into bars; probative value was "fairly low" when compared with potential to "inflame the jury").

Rule 608 does not require pretrial notice. A responsible lawyer, if there is any doubt whether a question is proper (as there often is), advises the court so the matter can be aired in advance. Some judges insist that lawyers warn them, and one state court grafted a notice requirement onto the Rule, at least for prosecutors. See State v. Fallin, 540 N.W.2d 518 (Minn. 1995). The decision in *Fallin* led to formal amendment (the Minnesota rule now expressly requires prosecutors to give notice).

Most modern cases disapprove cross-examination about behavior that does not directly involve lies or deception. Thus questioning about drug use, violence, or sexual relationships is generally disapproved,[3] although occasionally such points come out in attacks that show bias or motivation on the part of the witness.

UNITED STATES v. MANSKE

United States Court of Appeals for the Seventh Circuit
186 F.3d 770 (1999)

Before FLAUM, RIPPLE, and ROVNER, Circuit Judges.

FLAUM, Circuit Judge.

[In his trial for conspiracy to distribute cocaine, Thomas Manske sought to cross-examine alleged co-offenders Stephen Pszeniczka and Daniel Knutowski, who had "fingered Manske as their drug source." Pszeniczka and Knutowski testified that Manske was their primary supplier of cocaine between 1993 and 1996, and that he delivered one to two ounces to them every Wednesday. Over

---

[3] See United States v. Fountain, 768 F.2d 790, 795 (7th Cir. 1985) (violent men "are not necessarily liars"); United States v. Rubin, 733 F.2d 837, 841-842 (11th Cir. 1984) (drug overdose "unrelated to truthfulness"); United States v. Cox, 536 F.2d 65, 71 (5th Cir. 1976) (illicit sex "totally immaterial to credibility").

the three-year period, Manske sold them 5.78 kilograms of cocaine. This testimony made up "the bulk" of the government's case.

Manske testified that he knew Pszeniczka and Knutowski, and admitted engaging in illegal sports betting and bookmaking with them. He also testified that the weekly Wednesday meetings and phonecalls involved gambling.

Manske attacked the credibility of Pszeniczka and Knutowski and two other government witnesses (Mary Colburn and Jacky Campbell), bringing out that they were receiving leniency in exchange for testifying, and that they had histories of drug use and drug dealing.

The government made a motion in limine to block defense cross-examination of Pszeniczka about threats he had made to witnesses testifying in a related case, and from cross-examining Colburn and Campbell on this subject. Jeffrey Matter had told police that Pszeniczka was involved in drug dealing, and Matter gave a sworn statement that Pszeniczka threatened him by phone, telling him "if you don't change your statement you might as well be dead" because "[e]ither I'll kill you or my friends will." Matter changed his story, and Pszeniczka (on learning of the switch) told Matter that "if you go back to what you first said, I'll put a cap in your head." A witness told a Wisconsin police officer that Pszeniczka had come looking for Mary Colburn and said, on learning that Colburn had left town, that it was "good" because "if [Colburn] hadn't [she'd] be dead."

Manske also wanted to question Jackie Campbell about things that Pszeniczka had said to her about "mob connections" and his willingness to use violence against people who "crossed him." Colburn and her boyfriend were prepared to describe an incident in which they found "dolls with ropes around their necks hanging from a tree" on Colburn's front yard and a sign saying "Narcs Live Here" and "You're dead."

In its motion in limine, the government argued that the threats amounted to "conduct not probative of truthfulness or untruthfulness" because they tended only to show "propensity for violence." Manske argued that "threats calculated to encourage people to break the law" are probative of truthfulness or untruthfulness, and that the threats supported the defense theory that the government's case rested on an "elaborate set-up" depending on testimony by Pszeniczka and others who were afraid to contradict him. The trial court granted the government's motion. Manske was convicted, and he appeals.]

FRE 608(b) is a rule of limited admissibility. Other than certain criminal convictions allowed into evidence by FRE 609, a witness's specific instances of conduct may only be raised on cross-examination if they are probative of truthfulness or untruthfulness.... The defendant argues that these threats deal with more than mere violence—Pszeniczka's willingness to threaten violence was a means to achieve an end of dissuading people from testifying truthfully in legal proceedings—and thus clearly implicates Pszeniczka's truthfulness.

As a leading treatise notes, there are three ways of looking at 608(b): a broad one, a narrow one, and a middle one. See Mueller & Kirkpatrick, Federal Evidence, 154-155 (2d ed. 1994). The broad view holds that "virtually any conduct indicating bad character indicates untruthfulness, including robbery and assault." *Id.* This view is untenable, as it would open the door to a potentially mind-numbing array of questions on every cross-examination. It would also "pave the way to an exception [to 608(b)'s limitations] that swallows the rule . . . [because it] adopts the hypothesis that all bad people are liars, which is an unverifiable conclusion." McLaughlin, Weinstein's Federal Evidence, §608.12[4][c] 608-639 (2d ed. 1999). The narrow reading of the rule, which the government essentially urges on us, considers a crime as bearing on veracity only if it involves falsehood or deception, such as forgery or perjury. Mueller & Kirkpatrick at 154. The middle view "is that behavior seeking personal advantage by taking from others in violation of their rights reflects on veracity." *Id.* While this generally does not cover "personal crimes" involving violence, it does not necessarily exclude all such acts. The threat evidence would clearly be allowed in under the broad view, and probably excluded under the narrow one. Whether it would fit under the middle view is a more vexing question.

Mueller and Kirkpatrick note that "[u]nder some circumstances, it seems wise to allow questions that would not be embraced by the more focused view but would pass muster under the middle view, and there appears to be a trend in this direction [among courts]." *Id.* at 159-160. Their treatise discusses a circumstance nearly identical to this one, where although the specific instance of conduct may not facially appear relevant to truthfulness, closer inspection reveals that it bears on that issue. "[W]hen [a party's question is] specific and well-founded, the cross-examiner should be allowed to ask . . . questions on acts better described as dishonest than false . . . [including questions related to] *concealing or frightening off witnesses* or suborning perjury (even in unrelated cases.)" *Id.* at 160-161 (emphasis added).

We have not had many occasions to address the scope of 608(b); however, when we have, our approach has been closest to the middle view. For example, in Varhol v. National RR Pass. Corp., 909 F.2d 1557, 1566 (7th Cir. 1990) (en banc) (per curiam), we rejected the plaintiff's contention that 608(b) only allowed questioning about acts involving fraud or deceit, such as perjury, subornation of perjury, false statements, embezzlement and false pretenses. We held that although "receiving stolen goods [fell] into a gray area," the plaintiff could be questioned about buying stolen railroad tickets because "people generally regard stealing (and receiving and using stolen property) as acts that 'reflect adversely on a [person's] honesty and integrity.'" *Id.* (*quoting* Gordon v. United States, 383 F.2d 936, 940 (D.C. Cir. 1967)) [Court describes other cases approving questions on theft, receiving stolen tires, failing to file tax returns, bribery, and loss of professional license on account of deceptive practices.] In *Varhol*, the full court observed that "if the witness has no compunctions against stealing another's property . . . it is hard to see why he would hesitate to obtain an advantage for himself or a friend in trial by giving false testimony . . . . As a practical matter, it is difficult to distinguish between untruthfulness and dishonesty."

Although the factual context of *Varhol* differs, the relationship between the specific acts of misconduct and truthfulness is, if anything, more compelling in this case. Threatening to cause physical harm to a person who proposes to testify against you is at least as probative of truthfulness as receiving stolen tires or a stolen railroad ticket. Also, because Stephen Pszeniczka had no compunction about intimidating potential witnesses in previous legal proceedings, "it is hard to see" why he would hesitate to obtain an advantage for himself in Manske's trial by giving false testimony against Manske. The advantage he hoped to obtain, it appears, was leniency from the government in return for his testimony. Pszeniczka had already been given ten years off of his sentence for cooperation in a prior prosecution, and acknowledged that if the remaining thirty years of his sentence was not reduced, he would likely die in prison. Because of the sum of these facts, we conclude it was legally erroneous for the district court to conclude that the threat evidence was irrelevant under 608(b).

The government urges us to reject the defendant's argument that this was error because the district court is entitled to great deference. See FRE 608(b) (specific instances of conduct may be inquired into "in the discretion of the court"). Recognizing that a district court's decision as to 608(b) is ordinarily reviewed for an abuse of discretion does not change our view of this matter. The usual deference does not apply when a district court incorrectly categorizes the nature of the evidence. Here, the trial court construed the threat evidence too narrowly: its error was in perceiving the threats as probative only of violence (which—if correct—would have been a proper reason to grant the government's motion in limine). However, because the threat evidence also implicated Pszeniczka's truthfulness, the government's motion should have been denied. Thus, this is not the prototypical case where we give deference to a district court's decision to exclude evidence because it was repetitive, unfairly prejudicial, or might cause confusion.[8]

The government maintains that even if the district court's decision was erroneous, the error was harmless. While we might have accepted this argument if 608(b) was the only issue the defendant raised on appeal, because of the inter-relatedness of Manske's two claims, we cannot assess the level of harm this error caused in a vacuum. Instead, we can only determine whether it was harmless in conjunction with our discussion of the district court's ruling prohibiting the defendant from using the threat evidence to probe the biases of other witnesses.

[The defense also sought to adduce testimony from Mary Colburn and Jackie Campbell that corroborated Pszeniczka's false story because "they feared what Pszeniczka or his associates would do to them." The trial court

[8] We also note that the questions Manske sought to ask were not part of a broad fishing expedition. The district court, government, and defense were all familiar with the threat subject matter. This is salient, in light of Mueller & Kirkpatrick's point referenced above—which we endorse—that questions such as those asked by Manske should be allowed when they are "specific and well founded."

blocked this testimony, but it was admissible to show bias arising out of fear.] Bias is always relevant, and parties should be granted reasonable latitude in cross-examining target witnesses. United States v. Frankenthal, 582 F.2d 1102, 1106 (7th Cir. 1978). This latitude is wide enough, we believe, to encompass the case before us, where the defendant's theory was that the witnesses were biased against him because they feared for their personal safety, even though the incidents upon which they based that fear arose outside the context of this case . . . . See Mueller and Kirkpatrick, Federal Evidence, 401-402 (2d ed. 1994) ("[P]arties should be given considerable leeway, by wide-ranging inquiry on cross . . . . Proof of bias may properly show the following . . . fear by the witness for his [or her] personal safety or the safety of friends or family, relating to the parties or issues in suit"). See also *Abel*, 469 U.S. at 52 ("Bias may be induced by a witness's likes, dislikes, [or] fear . . . or by the witness's self-interest.") . . . In reaching our conclusion, we emphasize how closely this point and the FRE 608(b) issue are entwined. If the bias question arose alone and was not, in combination, so central to the case, we might not consider it relevant.

[Trial courts have "wide latitude" of discretion to set reasonable limits on scope and extent of cross for bias, and may prevent harassment, confusion of issues, and prejudice. But deferential review is appropriate for areas on the periphery of the right of cross-examination, and de novo review is appropriate for rulings affecting the core value of the right to confront witnesses, which includes aspects of exploring bias. Here the court kept defendant from asking Colburn and Campbell about their fear of Pzeniczka and how it might affect their testimony against Manske, which was a "complete ban" that cut off an important topic. Nor was the ruling proper because the government didn't lay a foundation, for questions about bias do not carry special foundational requirements.] Thus, the only "necessary" questions the defendant need ask are the "who, what, why, where, and when" of the specific incidents he claims give rise to bias.[9] If accepted, the government's argument in its brief that the defendant needed to explicitly ask questions like: "are you presently afraid of Steve Pszeniczka?" or "do you feel pressured to testify a certain way because of Steve Pszeniczka?" would dramatically limit the effectiveness of many cross-examinations. (Most experienced counsel avoid attempts to obtain a direct concession from a witness that he is biased, because the witness rarely makes the concession, and "in the attempt to force the concession, the counsel might become argumentative. Experienced counsel prefer to invite the jury to draw the inference of bias during closing arguments."); see also Thomas A. Mauet, Fundamentals of Trial Techniques 254-259 (2d ed. 1988) (cross-examiner should not ask directly about bias, but instead should make point through suggestion that a witness has a motive or bias to lie). Thus, since such a "foundation" was

[9] Of course, a district court may require some showing that the answers the cross-examination hopes to elicit are relevant, but the "who, what, why" questions are designed to achieve this result. Moreover, in this case, the relevance of Pszeniczka's prior threats seems readily apparent.

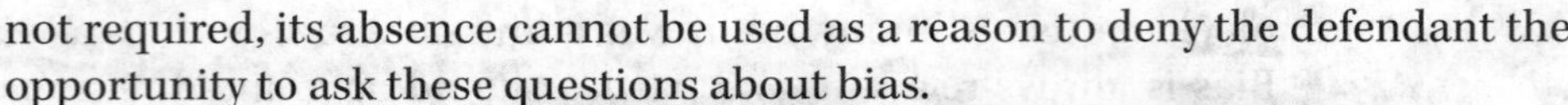

not required, its absence cannot be used as a reason to deny the defendant the opportunity to ask these questions about bias.

[The errors were not harmless. Court reverses and remands for a new trial.]

■ NOTES ON CROSS-EXAMINATION ON NONCONVICTION MISCONDUCT

1. *Manske* describes a broad, narrow, and middle view of the breadth of questioning under FRE 608(b). The broad view allows questioning on almost any misconduct. The narrow view confines the cross-examiner to acts that are themselves false or misleading. The middle view reaches conduct "seeking personal advantage by taking from others in violation of their rights." Courts applying FRE 608(b) have rejected the broad view, and generally allow questions that satisfy the narrow view by asking directly about deceptive statements or behavior. Compare United States v. Geston, 299 F.3d 1130, 1137 (9th Cir. 2002) (cannot ask about violence while intoxicated) with United States v. Simonelli, 237 F.3d 19, 23 (1st Cir. 2001) (can ask about altering time cards and inflating bills). It is in settings like *Manske*, where the conduct has a wrongful and exploitive aspect but is not false or deceptive in itself, that courts split. Compare United States v. Alaniz, 148 F.3d 929, 935 (8th Cir. 1998) (can't ask jailer whether he "turned his head" to allow inmates to beat another inmate) with United States v. Zidell, 323 F.3d 412, 426 (6th Cir. 2003) (can ask defendant whether he attempted to secure perjured testimony). *Manske* approves impeachment by questioning on such matters, doesn't it? Does the outcome seem right?

2. In asking Pszeniczka (pronounced "Zen eek a") about his threatening behavior, Manske was trying to impeach him in two different ways: One involved suggesting that Pszeniczka was untruthful, and the other involved suggesting that he was "framing" Manske, indicating bias. (Pszeniczka was under investigation for money laundering, and there was logic behind Manske's strategy in suggesting that he couldn't be trusted because he too was in trouble.) If the latter theory dropped out of the case—if the *only* argument for questioning Pszeniczka about threatening witnesses was that it showed an untruthful disposition, the decision indicates that the questions would still be proper under FRE 608(b). Do you agree?

3. When *Manske* was decided, FRE 608(b) covered cross on specific instances of conduct to attack or support "credibility." Since 2003, FRE 608(b) has covered cross on specific instances to attack or support "character for truthfulness." The change made express what was always intended—FRE 608(b) covers attacks on truthfulness and nothing else. *Manske* gets this point right in concluding that FRE 608(b) does *not* apply to questioning that aims to show bias. Courts sometimes misunderstood this point, but *Abel* recognized that FRE 608 does not block extrinsic evidence of statements or acts that show bias. See United States v. Abel, 469 U.S. 45 (1984) (section A1, supra). Sometimes courts also mistakenly invoked FRE 608 in dealing with impeachment by contradiction. The amended language makes it clear that FRE 608 also does not apply to impeachment by contradiction. See United States v. Magallanez, 408 F.3d 672 (10th Cir. 2005) (FRE 608 does not keep government from calling rebuttal witness to contradict).You will read about impeachment by contradiction in section B2, infra.

4. When FRE 608 *does* apply (questioner seeks to show the witness is by character or disposition untruthful), cross-examination is allowed, but not "extrinsic evidence." Thus in *Manske*, if efforts to scare witnesses into lying were only relevant in showing that Pzenickzka was untruthful, defendant would have to take his answer, and could not call Colburn or Campbell or Matter to testify to the threats. Why does FRE 608(b) block resort to "extrinsic evidence"? *Manske* doesn't tell us, but the reason is that impeachment can be largely accomplished by questions (even if the witness denies the implied charge of misconduct), and separately proving or disproving the conduct is not worth the time.

5. There are fewer cases applying FRE 608 than you might think, probably because litigants often do not uncover acts of deception by witnesses. In contrast, many cases apply FRE 609 (proving convictions) because the information is available in public records. When opposing litigants know each other, however, as in lawsuits arising in the aftermath of relationships that have gone sour, clients give their lawyers ammunition that becomes the basis for impeachment. See Murphy v. Bonanno, 663 A.2d 505 (D.C. App. 1995) (in suit by defendant *B*'s estranged wife *E* and a woman friend *D*, with whom *E* was staying, plaintiffs alleged that *B* forced his way into *E*'s home and assaulted them; *B* sought to cross-examine *E* about false statements in loan application, about "false and fraudulent" claims after an accident, and about *E*'s tactics in extorting settlement from doctor who loaned her money, whom *E* accused of sexual harassment). In *Murphy* and similar cases, the parties use FRE 608(b) to enlarge the fight and vent frustrations.

6. How about asking a witness about engaging in adultery? See State v. Moses, 726 A.2d 250, 252-253 (N.H. 1999) (cannot ask about adulterous relationship; does not relate directly to truthfulness) (marital infidelities are not proper basis for impeachment).

7. Sometimes it is unclear whether statements, which an adverse party wants to raise on cross to impeach, were false. They may be subject to doubt that is hard to resolve, or may have led to an investigation or to criminal charges, but the matter was dropped or led to dismissal or acquittal. Should questioning proceed such settings? See State v. Miller, 921 A.2d 942 (N.H. 2007) (in trial for sexual assault, defendant sought to cross-examine minor victim about false allegations that her father abused her; defense need not prove falsity by clear and convincing evidence; court sets out guidelines for exercise of discretion); United States v. Crowley, 318 F.3d 401, 417 (2d Cir. 2003) (in trial for sexual abuse, blocking effort to cross-examine complainant *V* about prior false charges of abuse; claimant would deny that charges were false, producing "little of probative value"), *cert. denied*, 124 S. Ct. 239 (2003). Recall the Notes on Evidence of Complainant's Prior Sexual Conduct in Criminal Cases (Chapter 5A5a), on the effect of the rape shield rule (FRE 412) when complainants in sex offense cases are asked about bringing allegedly false charges.

8. Can a cross-examiner ask whether the witness has ever stolen anything (even if he was not charged)? How many people can truthfully say No to this question? Doesn't it put almost any witness on the spot? Professor Lilly says the question whether thefts shed light on truthfulness is close: "Theft, if unaccompanied by falsehood or stealth, falls somewhere between" filing false statements on a license application and engaging in "drunken or disorderly conduct," and courts are divided on such matters. See Lilly, Principles of Evidence 297 (2006). Some courts say theft *does* suggest untruthfulness. See People v. Segovia, 196 P.3d 1126, 1132 (Colo. 2008) ("theft is probative of truthfulness or dishonesty") (dishonest is synonym for untruthful). Others say theft is *not* probative of truthfulness, or is probative only if it involves deception. See Riddick v. United States, 806 A.2d 631, 637 (D.C. App. 2002) (cannot ask about being expelled from neighborhood stores for theft, absent showing that stealing "involved an element of deceit or falsification"); State v. Bashaw, 785 A.2d 897, 900 (N.H. 2001) (cannot ask about stealing police badge; petty theft does not suggest untruthfulness). Still others allow inquiry only when the theft leads to conviction, or when the questioner has a specific basis and focuses on particular instances. Compare Brent v. State, 632 So. 2d 936, 942-945 (Miss. 1994) (counsel engaged in "fishing expedition" and may not ask "open-ended questions," like whether witness has "ever stolen or lied"); Robinson v. State, 468 A.2d 328, 332 (Md. 1983) (can ask about conviction for theft, but not whether witness ever stole property; value of "groundless inquiry" outweighed by prejudice).

b. Proving Prior Convictions

A second way to suggest that a witness is untruthful involves his prior convictions. This form of impeachment happens far more often in criminal than in civil cases (can you imagine why?), but it is permissible in both settings. Usually this attack is accomplished on cross. FRE 609(a) states the principle in two parts. First, the cross-examiner can ask about convictions for crimes "punishable by death or imprisonment in excess of one year" (in the federal system and most states, these are felonies), but such convictions can be used to impeach defendant in a criminal trial only if probative value "outweighs" their "prejudicial effect" (a "reverse 403" standard that favors exclusion). For witnesses other than a criminal defendant, admissibility is subject to FRE 403. Second, the cross-examiner can ask about any convictions (felonies or misdemeanors) that entail dishonesty or "false statement," and there is no discretion to disallow questions on such convictions.

Consider these points: First, convictions are matters of public record, so counsel is likely to know about them. In any criminal case, prosecutor and defense counsel know about defendant's convictions—the former because defendant's "rap sheet" affects the decision whether to charge, and what charges to bring; the latter because defense counsel always looks at his client's record, if only because that affects the decision whether to testify. Second, a conviction is compelling evidence not only that the person committed the deed, but that it was a crime for which he is culpable, magnifying and dramatizing it.

Dual approach: First and second prongs of FRE 609(a). Rule 609 takes a dual approach. FRE 609(a)(1)—the "first prong"—covers convictions for crimes "punishable by death or by imprisonment for more than one year" (basically felonies). In other words, what counts for first prong convictions is the seriousness of the offense. FRE 609(a)(2) is the "second prong," and it covers crimes involving "a dishonest act or false statement," so it is the nature of the offense (more than its seriousness) that counts. Thus the second prong covers misdemeanors as well as felonies. More precisely, the second prong covers crimes in which "establishing the elements" of the offense "required proving" a dishonest act or false statement (or "the witness's admitting" to such things).

Reasonable people differ on the question whether felonies like murder or drug-dealing tell anything about veracity. Would you be surprised to learn that most courts think theft crimes do not involve dishonesty? See United States v. Givens, 767 F.2d 574, 579 n.1 (9th Cir.) (theft conviction does not involve dishonesty or false statement), *cert. denied*, 474 U.S. 953 (1985). Reacting to rulings similar to *Givens*, the principal architect of the Rules commented that the author of *Alice in Wonderland* "would have been pleased"! Cleary, Preliminary Notes on Reading the Rules of Evidence, 57 Neb. L. Rev. 908, 919 (1978). Recall that courts are similarly reluctant to allow questions to a witness about thefts under FRE 608(b) when there has been no conviction. See item 8 in Notes on Cross-Examination on Nonconviction Misconduct (immediately prior to this section, supra).

For these reasons, using prior convictions to impeach engenders much variety in approach,[4] brings problems of interpretation, raises many trial issues, and generates many appeals. Able observers continue to ask whether this game is worth the candle, and whether this form of impeachment is fair or just. A salient fact, and one often advanced by those favoring abolition of such impeachment, is that defendants often decide not to take the stand if they have a

[4] States adopting codes based on the Federal Rules differ sharply. Consider these examples: Hawaii Rule 609 permits impeaching use of convictions only for crimes involving "dishonesty." Alaska Rule 609 permits use of convictions only if the underlying crimes involve "dishonesty or false statement." Maryland Rule 609 permits use of convictions for any crime that is "infamous" or "relevant" to credibility. A Colorado statute allows use of felony convictions only, with no discretion. Colo. Rev. Stat. §13-90-101. Montana Rule 609 *disallows* use of all convictions for impeachment, while counterparts to FRE 609 in Louisiana and Rhode Island *allow* use of all convictions for this purpose.

prior record. See generally the criticism of this form of impeachment in Spector, Impeaching the Defendant by His Prior Convictions and the Proposed Federal Rules of Evidence: A Half Step Forward and Three Steps Backward, 1 Loy. U. Chi. L.J. 247 (1970); Nichol, Prior Crime Impeachment of Criminal Defendants: A Constitutional Analysis of Rule 609, 82 W. Va. L. Rev. 391 (1980).

Beyond the question what kinds of convictions bear on veracity, the framers of FRE 609 focused on five main questions:

(1) Discretion. Should courts have discretion to block this kind of impeachment by applying the principles in FRE 403? Before the Rules were drafted, a federal court had interpreted a District of Columbia statute as allowing discretion to exclude for unfair prejudice to the accused, even though the statute was silent on this point. See Luck v. United States, 348 F.2d 763 (D.C. Cir. 1965). FRE 609 authorizes discretion to exclude felonies (the "reverse 403 standard" described in the introduction), but not to exclude convictions for crimes that entail dishonesty or false statement, and it is settled that there is no discretion to bar questioning about (or proof of) such convictions.[5]

(2) Time limit. Should there be a time limit, or can the cross-examiner ask even about convictions from the distant past? FRE 609(b) contains a ten-year limit (with room for flexibility), in effect creating a presumption that convictions older than that are excludable. Sometimes older convictions are admitted, pursuant to the notice provision, but ordinarily they are excluded. If the person convicted flees when released on parole, should the ten-year period be extended? See United States v. McClintock, 748 F.2d 1278, 1288 (9th Cir. 1984) (Yes), *cert. denied*, 474 U.S. 822 (1985). The beginning point of the ten-year period is the later moment of the date of conviction or the date of release from confinement (normally release comes later, but not if a defendant is sentenced to time served), and the end point is either the date of trial or testimony or the date of indictment (courts differ). See Mueller & Kirkpatrick, Federal Evidence §6:53 (4th ed. 2013).

(3) Effect of pardon or annulment. Should convictions be usable if we can be sure the witness has been rehabilitated or was innocent? FRE 609(c) disallows use of convictions if the witness has been formally pardoned or the conviction has been annulled and there are no later felony convictions, but this provision has not been expansively interpreted. See Wilson v. Attaway, 757 F.2d 1227, 1244-1246 (11th Cir. 1985) (first offender statute authorizes judge to put defendant on probation without entering judgment, if he pleads guilty; on fulfilling terms of probation, he is discharged; completing probation exonerates him, signifying rehabilitation; still it is a conviction under FRE 609).

---

[5] As enacted, FRE 609 spoke of "prejudice to the defendant," which made sense if it referred to the accused. But the clause didn't *say* that, and *seemed* to refer to civil and criminal defendants alike. When the question arose whether the clause allowed exclusion of felony convictions offered against *a civil plaintiff,* the Court said no, see Green v. Bock Laundry Machine Co., 490 U.S. 504 (1989), leading to the 1990 amendment with language close to what we now find—discretion clauses covering all witnesses.

(4) Juvenile adjudications. Should youthful offenses be usable? FRE 609(d) imposes major limits. They are admissible only in criminal cases, and only for witnesses "other than the accused." This provision reflects the view that transgressions by young people are not as serious as adult crimes, nor as probative of credibility. What counts is not the age of the offender but the nature of the proceedings: Convictions under statutes allowing prosecution of youthful offenders as adults but providing alternate penalties fall outside FRE 609(d), which embraces only special juvenile offense schemes. See United States v. Ashley, 569 F.2d 975, 978 (5th Cir.) (sentence under Youth Corrections Act was not within FRE 609(d), which reaches only delinquency findings under Juvenile Delinquency Act and similar state schemes), *cert. denied*, 439 U.S. 853 (1978).

This part of Rule 609 responded to the decision in Davis v. Alaska, 415 U.S. 308 (1974), where defendant was convicted of burglary on testimony by one Green, who was on probation after a juvenile adjudication for burglary. On cross, the defense asked Green whether he might have been under suspicion for the charged offense and whether he had "ever been questioned" on such subjects (Green said no, apparently untruthfully). The trial court disallowed efforts to bring out that Green had been found delinquent for a similar offense and was on probation. The Court reversed, noting that Green may have been biased because of his "vulnerable status as a probationer" and his "possible concern that he might be a suspect." The Court distinguished between the use of prior crimes to suggest untruthful disposition, and a "more particular attack" aimed at "revealing possible biases, prejudices, or ulterior motives" directly related to the case. Thus *Davis* does not necessarily mean defendant has a constitutional right to cross-examine on prior juvenile adjudications in all cases. Rule 609 does not always entitle the defense to cross-examine on such matters either, for juvenile adjudications are the proper subject of defense cross-examination only if necessary "to fairly determine guilt or innocence."

(5) Pendency of appeal. Should convictions be usable even if they are on appeal? FRE 609(e) answers in the affirmative, the thought being that convictions are usually affirmed. The principle suggests that an actual judgment may not be necessary and that the cross-examiner may ask about pleas and guilty verdicts (even though these have not yet led to judgment or sentence). See United States v. Klein, 560 F.2d 1236, 1241 (5th Cir. 1977) (approving questions on guilty verdict, but warning that pleas might be different as a less reliable indication of guilt), *cert. denied*, 434 U.S. 1073 (1978); United States v. Smith, 623 F.2d 627, 630-631 (9th Cir. 1980) (permitting questions on plea). Allowing in a later case the impeaching use of an earlier conviction that is on appeal can hardly be error, given FRE 609(e), but a later reversal of the earlier conviction creates argument for a new trial in the second case, on the basis of new evidence. See United States v. Soles, 482 F.2d 105, 107-108 (2d Cir.), *cert. denied*, 414 U.S. 1027 (1973).

■ PROBLEM 8-B. "Hit the Deck"

A man wearing a Halloween mask and carrying a sawed-off shotgun entered Franklin First Bank in Little Rock, ordered customers to "hit the deck," and forced tellers at gunpoint to put cash from their drawers into a canvas sports bag that he was carrying. He then fled the scene. Two weeks later Dan Dennet is arrested and charged with robbery.

Ray Elmo is the state's main witness: He is expected to testify that Dennet confessed the robbery to him and sought his help in hiding the money and escaping to Mexico. Dennet is asserting the defense of alibi. He expects to testify that he and his old friend George Farr were on a fishing trip in the Ozarks at the time of the robbery, and he plans to call Farr to corroborate his story.

Dennet and Farr have prior bank robbery convictions, arising out of separate incidents. Anticipating that the prosecutor will ask about his prior conviction, which led to a term of three years and ended eight years ago, Dennet makes a pretrial motion to exclude the conviction and bar questions about it. Also anticipating that the prosecutor will question George Farr on *his* bank robbery conviction, which led to an eight-year sentence from which Farr was released one year ago, Dennet moves to exclude it and bar questions about it.

The prosecutor opposes these motions, arguing that "prior felonies are per se relevant" on veracity, and there is no need to inquire into the underlying facts or the trial records. Dennet argues that "felony convictions for robbery have nothing to do with veracity," and the court "should look at the record for insight into what really happened."

It turns out that Ray Elmo also has a bank robbery conviction that led to his release from confinement three years earlier. The prosecutor, having argued that robbery convictions are "per se relevant," cannot very well claim the robbery conviction of Ray Elmo is "irrelevant." Suppose, however, the court rules in favor of the defense and blocks questions to Dennet and Farr about their robbery convictions as unfairly prejudicial. Can the prosecutor also object that defense questions to Ray Elmo about his bank robbery conviction should be precluded on account of unfair prejudice?

■ NOTES ON APPLYING THE FIRST PRONG—FRE 609(a)(1)

1. Rule 609(a)(1) covers convictions for crimes punishable by "death or imprisonment for more than one year." These first prong convictions are felonies, and the robbery convictions of Dennet, Farr, and Elmo fit this provision. They do not fit FRE 609(a)(2) (the second prong) because they do not require proof of a false statement and, although it may seem surprising, most courts have concluded that robbery does not involve a dishonest act either (see item 4 in the Notes on Applying the Second Prong, infra). Thus Rule 609(a)(1) applies on the facts of the Problem, and guides the exercise of discretion by slightly favoring exclusion of a prior conviction of the accused (it is usable only if probative value "outweighs its prejudicial effect to the defendant"), and slightly favoring admission of a prior conviction of any other witness (it is "subject to Rule 403," meaning admit unless probative value is outweighed by the danger of unfair prejudice).

2. In the Problem, if the court allows use of the robbery convictions to impeach these witnesses, how much detail can come out? Most courts let the cross-examiner bring out only limited information—typically the fact of conviction, name of the crime, date and place of conviction, and sentence. See State v. Robb, 723 N.E.2d 1019, 1036 (Ohio 2000) (imposing these limits). Almost all courts agree that the cross-examiner may not go into details. See Banks v. State, 761 N.E.2d 403, 405 (Ind. 2002) (can show that witness was convicted of robbery, but cannot ask about "details"); Acevedo v. State, 467 So. 2d 220, 225-226 (Miss. 1985) (questioning should not "go into the details of the former crime nor the punishment given").

3. In the Problem, how should the court exercise its discretion? A prominent pre-Rules decision in the *Gordon* case stressed five factors as important: (1) the nature of the conviction, (2) its recency or remoteness, (3) whether it is similar to the charged offense, (4) whether defendant's record is otherwise clean (convictions are more probative if they show a continuing pattern rather than isolated instances), (5) the importance of credibility issues, and (6) the importance of getting the defendant's own testimony. See Gordon v. United States, 383 F.2d 936 (D.C. Cir.), *cert. denied*, 390 U.S. 1029 (1967). In the *Lipscomb* case that was decided after the Rules took effect, the same court applied the *Gordon* factors, and commented about the probative worth of a bank robbery conviction:

> Robbery is generally less probative than crimes that involve deception or stealth. But it does involve theft and is a serious crime that shows conscious disregard for the rights of others. Such conduct reflects more strongly on credibility than, say, crimes of impulse, or simple narcotics or weapons possession. The age of the conviction (eight years ago) and [defendant's] age when it was committed (16) reduce the probativeness of the conviction. On the other hand, credibility was central to the trial, and prejudice was not especially great because the prior conviction was not similar to the present one. Cf. *Gordon* ("convictions which are for the same crime should be admitted sparingly") . . . . Any possible doubt on the propriety of admitting [defendant's] prior robbery conviction is eliminated by the underlying facts that were submitted to the district court at the close of trial. This additional information shows that [defendant], although convicted eight years ago, had been released from prison only a year-and-a-half ago, and was a repeat offender with a more recent burglary conviction which the government had not proffered to impeach his credibility. This subsequent conviction enhances the probativeness of [defendant's] earlier robbery conviction because

> it shows that the robbery was not merely an isolated criminal episode from which Lipscomb has since been rehabilitated. Cf. *Gordon* (subsequent "legally blameless life" affects probativeness of prior conviction).

United States v. Lipscomb, 702 F.2d 1049, 1070 (D.C. Cir. 1983). Reviewing courts urge judges to spell out their reasoning in applying the *Gordon* factors, and sometimes reverse or remand because they have not done so. See State v. Flowers, 734 N.W.2d 239 (Minn. 2007) (remanding with instructions to address factors bearing on unfair prejudice and probative value); State v. Bryant, 633 S.E.2d 152, 155 (S.C. 2006) (court must articulate reasons on the record).

4. Among the *Gordon* factors, most important are the nature of the conviction, and (when it comes to a prior conviction of the defendant) its resemblance to the crime charged and the overall record. Most felonies that seem highly probative (perjury, embezzlement, and fraud) can be left out for the moment because they fit the second prong of FRE 609(a). Among *other* felonies, crimes like smuggling and some forms of theft (like burglary and larceny) are more probative than others because they involve stealth and sometimes deception. Crimes of violence (particularly assault or homicide) and drug crimes rank low. The more closely a prior crime resembles the charged offense, the greater the risk of unfair prejudice in the form of jury misuse (to prove guilt rather than untrustworthiness), pointing toward a decision to exclude. And defendant's record counts too: If he has other convictions, we can be more confident that any particular conviction is an accurate indicator.

5. At issue in *Lipscomb* (note 3, supra) was the question whether the court should examine the "facts and circumstances" of a prior conviction. The prosecutor argued that doing so was improper, but the defense argued that additional information was important in deciding to admit or exclude. The reviewing court held that *all* felony convictions are relevant on credibility "in some degree" and that the structure of Rule 609 "strongly suggests" that such inquiry is not *always* required. Mostly, however, the court agreed with the defense position: Policy considerations suggest that such inquiry can be helpful, and sometimes useful information is easily available (the prosecutor's "case jacket" listing docket entries affecting the defendant may help). The defense won the battle in *Lipscomb,* but lost the war: The court looked at other factors, but concluded that Lipscomb's own conviction was rightly admitted—his later burglary conviction made the earlier robbery conviction more probative by showing that it was not an isolated episode. *Lipscomb* states the majority rule, but some decisions agree with the prosecutor's view that the judge should not look into the facts. See Hopkins v. State, 768 A.2d 89, 91 (Md. Spec. App. 2001) (in deciding whether conviction is for "infamous crime" or is otherwise relevant to credibility, court must consider only name of crime) (no mini-trial).

6. Consider the three witnesses in the Problem:

(a) What are Dennet's strongest arguments for barring mention of his prior robbery conviction? If he testified in the prior case but was convicted anyway, would that bear on probative worth? His three-year sentence was light

(bank robbery can lead to 20 years in prison), and he completed it eight years ago. How do these facts bear on the matter?

(b) Will Dennet suffer prejudice if the prosecutor asks Farr about *his* bank robbery conviction? Convictions of nonparty witnesses can be excluded on this ground under Rule 609 (although they are subject to the Rule 403 standard that favors admissibility). How do Farr's recent release date and relatively long sentence bear on the matter?

(c) Can the prosecution suffer prejudice if the defense asks Ray Elmo about *his* bank robbery conviction?

COMMENT/PERSPECTIVE: Prior Convictions and Untruthfulness

For years, commentators have called for abolishing use of convictions to impeach, particularly in the common circumstance in which they are used against criminal defendants. The tradition allowing this use of convictions grew out of the change in doctrine that permitted convicted felons to testify (the common law rule disqualified them as witnesses), and the thought was to accept their testimony but reveal the convictions to aid in assessing credibility. In the European tradition, convictions are *not* generally usable to impeach, but this difference appears to reflect other differences between continental and American practice: It was once the case that criminal defendants were tried to a judge rather than a jury, although modern reforms have incorporated lay jurors into the process, and criminal defendants have no right to testify under oath, their credibility being "automatically discounted." See Mirjan R. Damaska, Propensity Evidence In Continental Legal Systems, 70 Chi.-Kent L. Rev. 55, 59 (1994-1995). In this country, the debate focuses on the question whether prior criminal behavior, even when it involves lying, sheds light on truthfulness. Those who hold that the answer is No argue that truthfulness is contextualized, and that willingness to lie on an employment application, for example, tells nothing about willingness to lie in a criminal trial, and this argument seems even stronger with crimes like burglary that do not even involve lying. With respect to criminal defendants, those arguing against the use of convictions stress that factfinders are *already* skeptical because the accused is trying to preserve life or liberty, and the marginal effect of a conviction on credibility is low. Those who take the other side argue that when *any* witness testifies, the factfinder should know something about the person in order to assess credibility, and that a criminal past is one of the most important things that one might want to know.

7. When a witness is asked about a conviction under FRE 609, should he be allowed to offer an explanation on redirect? See United States v. Jackson, 627 F.2d 1198, 1208-1210 (D.C. Cir. 1980) (on redirect, defendant "could have brought out" facts that might "mitigate somewhat the 'bad man' image" that the conviction might suggest). *Jackson* was a drug trial. Defendant had been convicted of manslaughter for "shooting and killing his wife" and "had also shot the man who was with his wife." If these additional facts lessened the impact of his prior conviction, would it make more sense to bar all mention of it? If the evidence in the earlier trial indicated that defendant and his wife had a stormy marriage, that he knew about her involvement with the other man, and had beaten her in quarrels, should the prosecutor be able to bring out *these* facts? Where does it end?

8. Other than barring questions, is there any way to minimize prejudice from questions about a conviction for a crime similar to the one charged? In the Problem, for example, if the court admits Dennet's prior robbery conviction in his present trial for a similar offense, can the court do anything to lessen risk of prejudice? Sometimes courts limit the attacking party to showing the fact of conviction but not its *nature*. Would that help? See State v. Montano, 65 P.3d 61, 74 (Ariz. 2003) (in murder trial, "sanitizing" conviction by allowing defense to bring out only fact of conviction, not that it was for child pornography, to minimize prejudice); State v. Demeritt, 813 A.2d 393, 399 (N.H. 2002) (in vehicular homicide trial, letting state bring out defendant's convictions for "felony assaults" but not that they were "sexual" assaults); United States v. Beahm, 664 F.2d 414, 418-419 (4th Cir. 1981) (where defendant was accused of indecent liberties with children, error to impeach him with conviction for similar offenses; court should have excluded the evidence "or at the very least limited disclosure to the fact of conviction without revealing its nature"). Can a jury appraise truthfulness if it does not know what the conviction was for? See Bells v. State, 759 A.2d 1149, (Md. Spec. App. 2000) (in drug trial, reversible error to impeach defendant with sanitized prior conviction, which was "totally undefined" and left jury "completely unable to assess what, if any, impact" the conviction has on credibility; should have excluded altogether).

■ PROBLEM 8-C. "A History of Lying"

Ryan Dewald is charged with embezzling union funds in violation of 28 USC §501, a crime that carries a potential fine of $10,000 and imprisonment up to five years. The charges stem from his actions as Treasurer of the Transportation Workers Local 681 in Tampa, Florida, where he allegedly wrote checks adding up to more than $650,000 payable to various law firms for performing legal business for the union. Allegedly these firms submitted inflated bills on Dewald's request and paid him cash kickbacks exceeding $125,000. Wendy Pickett is the principal government witness, and she testifies that she saw couriers from the law firms deliver envelopes apparently containing cash to Dewald. Dewald testifies that the envelopes described by Pickett contained legal documents, not cash kickbacks, and that Pickett is motivated to testify against him in anger over a personal relationship with Dewald that he ended.

After Pickett's testimony during the prosecutor's case, defense counsel tells the court and the prosecutor, in a colloquy that the jury does not hear, "this woman has a history of lying," and proposes to ask her about the following on cross:

1. Her misdemeanor conviction nine years ago for displaying a false handicapped symbol in her car in violation of city ordinance, leading to a fine of $500;
2. Her misdemeanor conviction six years ago for petit theft (she shoplifted, leaving a store with expensive women's scarves hidden in the bag with items she had bought, after telling a suspicious clerk she "put the scarves back");

After Dewald testifies during the defense case, the prosecutor tells the court and defense counsel, again in a colloquy that the jury does not hear, "you talk about a history of lying, consider this guy," and he proposes to ask Dewald about the following on cross:

3. His felony conviction eight years earlier for forgery (Dewald signed the name of another official on travel authorizations, and served a year in prison);
4. His misdemeanor conviction a year earlier for petit theft (he altered the electrical meter attached to his house, reducing his monthly bills by more than half, and paid a fine of $500).

Which if any of these questions should be allowed?

■ NOTES ON APPLYING THE SECOND PRONG—FRE 609(a)(2)

1. Rule 609(a)(2) covers convictions for crimes whose "elements" require proof of "a dishonest act or false statement" (or an admission of such points). These second prong convictions can be felonies or misdemeanors (including violations of local ordinances). The present wording came by amendment in 2006 that aimed to reduce the number of convictions that fit the second prong and simplify the task of applying it. Before the amendment, FRE 609(a)(2) covered convictions for crimes that "involved" dishonesty or false statement, leading some courts to look at the facts underlying a conviction, not just the elements of the crime. See United States v. Payton, 159 F.3d 49, 56-57 (2d Cir. 1998) (larceny conviction based on false statements in food stamp application fit second prong; court would "look beyond the elements of the offense"). Under this approach, *any* crime (murder, kidnapping, theft), if *accomplished* by lying or dishonesty, fit the second prong, and courts could become involved in time-consuming and contentious inquiries. According to the ACN, the amendment was designed to "tighten up" the second prong, so fewer convictions fit and the inquiry could be less complicated.

2. Rule 609(a)(2) expresses the view that convictions within a core area are especially relevant on veracity because the acts constituting the crime include false statements or dishonest acts. The core area includes perjury, fraud, forgery, embezzlement, counterfeiting, and false statement or false pretenses. The core does *not* include many crimes, such as those involving violence (murder, forcible rape, assault), prostitution, drunkenness, and drug trafficking.[5] Some crimes are hard to classify, like smuggling (not within the core) and failure to file a tax return (again probably not within the core). See generally Mueller & Kirkpatrick, Federal Evidence §6:46 (4th ed. 2013).

3. Consider again the 2006 amendment. The ACN says the purpose was "to give effect to the legislative intent to limit" convictions fitting the second prong. By implication, the framers reject decisions like *Payton* (note 1) finding that convictions fit the second prong if underlying facts show dishonesty or false statements.

(a) Under the amendment, the ACN says, a conviction for "a crime of violence, such as murder," does not fit the second prong "even if the witness acted *deceitfully*" in committing the crime. But the ACN also says convictions for "crimes in the nature of *crimen falsi* [crimes of falsehood] must be admitted" regardless how they are "specifically charged." Thus a conviction for "making a false claim" fits the second prong "regardless" whether the charges rest on a statute "that expressly references deceit" (like one covering "material misrepresentations" to the government) or on one "that does not" (like a statute covering obstruction of justice). See, e.g., 28 USC §1215 (which covers killing someone to keep him from testifying, and which also covers altering documents to affect their use in official proceedings.)

(b) Does the ACN's language suggest that Pickett's shoplifting conviction does not fit the second prong, but Dewald's conviction for stealing electricity does? Both were convicted of petit larceny, but the prosecutor did *not* have to prove false or misleading conduct in Pickett's case (only that she left

---

[5] Cases approving resort to FRE 609(a)(2) include United States v. Bay, 762 F.2d 1314, 1317-1318 (9th Cir. 1984) (forgery); United States v. Williams, 642 F.2d 136, 140 (5th Cir. 1981) (bribery); United States v. Lester, 749 F.2d 1288, 1300 (9th Cir. 1984) (filing false police report); United States v. McClintock, 748 F.2d 1278, 1288 (9th Cir. 1984) (mail fraud). Cases disapproving resort to FRE 609(a)(2) include United States v. Mansaw, 714 F.2d 785, 789 (8th Cir.) (prostitution), *cert. denied*, 464 U.S. 986 (1983); Czajka v. Hickman, 703 F.2d 317, 319 (8th Cir. 1983) (rape); United States v. Mehrmanesh, 689 F.2d 822, 833-834 (9th Cir. 1982) (narcotics); Reyes v. Missouri P. R.R., 589 F.2d 791, 795 (5th Cir. 1979) (public intoxication); United States v. Harvey, 588 F.2d 1201, 1203 (8th Cir. 1978) (assault).

the store with merchandise that she didn't pay for), and *did* have to prove false or misleading conduct in Dewald's (altering the meter). See Altobello v. Borden Confectionery Products, Inc., 872 F.2d 215, 216-217 (7th Cir. 1989) (misdemeanor theft fit second prong where facts showed that defendant tampered with electric meter, which was "*necessarily* a crime of deception"). And see Mueller & Kirkpatrick, Federal Evidence §6:47 (4th ed. 2013) (discussing this matter).

4. As noted in the introduction, convictions for theft in its various forms have proved problematic. Courts usually conclude that theft does not fit the second prong core category. One can see why the question is difficult: On the one hand, theft seems quintessentially "dishonest," and theft *often* involves deceit or even false statement: In cases of larceny or burglary, for example, the perpetrator takes advantage of the owner's absence or inattention, or distracts the owner, or at the very least conceals the crime. On the other hand, one can be guilty of theft by taking something belonging to another without falsehood or deception, using threats or violence instead, as is usually true with the crime of robbery. Before the 2006 amendment, most courts decided that theft crimes did not fit the core category, and the amendment *narrowed* or *tightened* the language, so theft is even *less* likely to qualify. See, e.g., State v. Pacheco, 26 P.3d 572, 587 (Haw. 2001) (petty theft did not qualify under rule allowing only questions on convictions for crimes of dishonesty); United States v. Owens, 145 F.3d 923, 927 (7th Cir. 1998) (excluding misdemeanor theft conviction for stealing car stereo). A few courts come out the other way. See, e.g., McHenry v. Chadwick, 896 F.2d 184, 188-189 (6th Cir. 1990) (shoplifting and concealing stolen property involved dishonesty or false statement).

■ PROBLEM 8-D. Faker, Thug?

Allen is charged with burglary, arising out of an incident in which a masked intruder allegedly gained entrance at night through the ground floor window of a condominium owned by Beatrice and stole jewelry and silverware. State witnesses place Allen in the neighborhood at the time of the offense. Beatrice testifies that she returned home on the occasion in question and surprised the intruder, and in court she identifies Allen as the culprit. But defense cross-examination shakes her testimony, bringing out that in pretrial statements she said the perpetrator wore a "class ring" on his right hand and a "silver banded watch" on his left. (Allen has testified that he wears neither a ring nor a watch, and acquaintances from his place of employment support him on these points.)

During cross-examination of Allen, the prosecutor proposes to ask him about an incident four years earlier in which he allegedly falsified his federal income tax return. That event led to a tax fraud prosecution, a conviction on a felony count after a trial, and incarceration for one and one-half years. In the present burglary proceedings, the trial judge holds an in camera hearing in aid of the defense objection. There the prosecutor asks permission to bring out on cross-examination of Allen that

1. He claimed an exemption on his tax return for a child, though he has no children;
2. He claimed a deduction in the amount of $4,000 for mortgage interest, though he lived in a rented house and was entitled to no such deduction; and
3. He claimed a deduction in the amount of $800 for "charitable contributions," for which he "possessed receipts," when in fact he had no proof of any charitable contributions.

Allen objects, arguing that cross-examination under FRE 609 "is restricted to bringing out the fact of conviction, the date and place, and the sentence imposed." The prosecutor replies in this vein:

> I have no intention of mentioning any conviction. I want to ask about the acts under FRE 608(b). There is no doubt that Allen did precisely what the questions imply, for the record of the proceedings against him establishes these points. There is nothing in Rule 609 that says I must proceed under that provision, and FRE 608(b) authorizes the court to permit cross-examination about "[s]pecific instances of the conduct of a witness" that bear upon "his credibility," as these "instances" certainly do. This man is asking the jury to believe him when he says he did not commit the burglary, and I think the jury is entitled to know that he lied repeatedly on his tax return.

How should the judge rule and why? *Should* the specific limits developed in cases applying FRE 609 apply when the misbehavior of the witness has resulted in conviction, even if the prosecutor proposes to make no mention of the conviction?

■ NOTES ON COORDINATING FRE 608 WITH 609

1. One can read FRE 608 and 609 as the prosecutor suggests in the Problem. But FRE 609 seems designed to cover the whole subject of impeachment by convictions, and FRE 608 seems designed to cover only use of nonconviction misconduct. Hence it seems more plausible to read FRE 609 as governing whenever the conduct in question has led to conviction, so FRE 609's limits on cross apply.

2. Federal circuits split on this matter. In 2009, the Ninth Circuit agreed that FRE 608 should not be available when conduct has resulted in a conviction, and the First Circuit is on the same page. See United States v. Osazuwa, 564

F.3d 1169, 1175 (9th Cir. 2009) (government should not have cross-examined defendant about acts underlying bank fraud conviction; FRE 608(b) "permits impeachment only by specific acts that have not resulted in a criminal conviction," and impeaching use of criminal convictions "is treated exclusively under Rule 609") (reversing); United States v. Rogers, 41 F.3d 25 (1st Cir. 1994) (prosecutor asked about acts underlying convictions, but should have proceeded under FRE 609). But see United States v. Barnhart, 599 F.3d 737, 747 (7th Cir. 2010) (rejecting claim of error where prosecutor "paraded" facts underlying defendant's convictions; cases applying limits in FRE 609 are "inapplicable" because FRE 608 permits cross on "facts underlying his theft and deceptive practices convictions").

3. States are split as well. Compare Childers v. Commonwealth, 332 S.W.3d 64 (Ky. 2010) (impeachment by specific instances of conduct that led to conviction is "governed exclusively by Rule 609," while impeachment by conduct not resulting in conviction is governed by Rule 608) with State v. Hoverson, 710 N.W.2d 890, 898 (N.D. 2006) (court erred in thinking it had no discretion to allow defense to ask about facts underlying informant's conviction for theft; court can allow inquiry into acts under Rule 608).

4. Isn't the *Osazuwa* approach far preferable as a matter of sound policy? Consider the following argument:

> [Q]uestioning about criminal acts without mentioning a conviction would generate a distorted and incomplete picture, inviting the factfinder to believe, for instance, that the witness not only misbehaved but "got away with it." This strategy would also allow the impeaching party to avoid the ten-year rule in FRE 609(b), the bar in FRE 609(c) against questions on convictions that have generated pardon or annulment or a certificate of rehabilitation, and the restriction against questions on juvenile adjudications contained in FRE 609(d). Arguably the purpose of these various restrictions in FRE 609 is not only to bar questions on convictions but to limit all reference to the whole subject and put certain aspects of it out of bounds.

Mueller & Kirkpatrick, Evidence §6.34 (5th ed. 2012).

LUCE v. UNITED STATES

United States Supreme Court
469 U.S. 38 (1984)

CHIEF JUSTICE BURGER delivered the opinion of the Court.

We granted certiorari to resolve a conflict among the Circuits as to whether the defendant, who did not testify at trial, is entitled to review of the District Court's ruling denying his motion to forbid the use of a prior conviction to impeach his credibility.

I

Petitioner was indicted on charges of conspiracy, and possession of cocaine with intent to distribute, in violation of 21 U.S.C. §§846 and 841(a)(1). During his trial in the United States District Court for the Western District of Tennessee, petitioner moved for a ruling to preclude the Government from using a 1974 state conviction to impeach him if he testified. There was no commitment by petitioner that he would testify if the motion were granted, nor did he make a proffer to the court as to what his testimony would be. In opposing the motion, the Government represented that the conviction was for a serious crime—possession of a controlled substance.

The District Court ruled that the prior conviction fell within the category of permissible impeachment evidence under Federal Rule of Evidence 609(a). The District Court noted, however, that the nature and scope of petitioner's trial testimony could affect the court's specific evidentiary rulings; for example, the court was prepared to hold that the prior conviction would be excluded if petitioner limited his testimony to explaining his attempt to flee from the arresting officers. However, if petitioner took the stand and denied any prior involvement with drugs, he could then be impeached by the 1974 conviction. Petitioner did not testify, and the jury returned guilty verdicts.

II

The United States Court of Appeals for the Sixth Circuit affirmed. The Court of Appeals refused to consider petitioner's contention that the District Court abused its discretion in denying the motion in limine without making an explicit finding that the probative value of the prior conviction outweighed its prejudicial effect. The Court of Appeals held that when the defendant does not testify, the court will not review the District Court's in limine ruling.

Some other Circuits have permitted review in similar situations;[3] we granted certiorari to resolve the conflict. We affirm.

III

It is clear, of course, that had petitioner testified and been impeached by evidence of a prior conviction, the District Court's decision to admit the impeachment evidence would have been reviewable on appeal along with any other claims of error. The Court of Appeals would then have had a complete record detailing the nature of petitioner's testimony, the scope of the cross-examination, and the possible impact of the impeachment on the jury's verdict.

[3] . . . The Ninth Circuit allows review if the defendant makes a record unequivocally announcing his intention to testify if his motion to exclude prior convictions is granted, and if he proffers the substance of his contemplated testimony. See United States v. Cook, 608 F.2d 1175, 1186 (1979) (en banc), *cert. denied,* 444 U.S. 1034 (1980).

A reviewing court is handicapped in any effort to rule on subtle evidentiary questions outside a factual context.[4] This is particularly true under Rule 609(a)(1), which directs the court to weigh the probative value of a prior conviction against the prejudicial effect to the defendant. To perform this balancing, the court must know the precise nature of the defendant's testimony, which is unknowable when, as here, the defendant does not testify.[5]

Any possible harm flowing from a district court's in limine ruling permitting impeachment by a prior conviction is wholly speculative. The ruling is subject to change when the case unfolds, particularly if the actual testimony differs from what was contained in the defendant's proffer. Indeed even if nothing unexpected happens at trial, the district judge is free, in the exercise of sound judicial discretion, to alter a previous in limine ruling. On a record such as here, it would be a matter of conjecture whether the District Court would have allowed the Government to attack petitioner's credibility at trial by means of the prior conviction.

When the defendant does not testify, the reviewing court also has no way of knowing whether the Government would have sought to impeach with the prior conviction. If, for example, the Government's case is strong, and the defendant is subject to impeachment by other means, a prosecutor might elect not to use an arguably inadmissible prior conviction.

Because an accused's decision whether to testify "seldom turns on the resolution of one factor," New Jersey v. Portash, 440 U.S. 450, 467 (1979) (Blackmun, J., dissenting), a reviewing court cannot assume that the adverse ruling motivated a defendant's decision not to testify. In support of his motion a defendant might make a commitment to testify if his motion is granted; but such a commitment is virtually risk free because of the difficulty of enforcing it.

Even if these difficulties could be surmounted, the reviewing court would still face the question of harmless error. Were in limine rulings under Rule 609(a) reviewable on appeal, almost any error would result in the windfall of automatic reversal; the appellate court could not logically term "harmless" an error that presumptively kept the defendant from testifying. Requiring that a defendant testify in order to preserve Rule 609(a) claims, will enable the reviewing court to determine the impact any erroneous impeachment may have had in light of the record as a whole; it will also tend to discourage making such motions solely to "plant" reversible error in the event of conviction.

Petitioner's reliance on Brooks v. Tennessee, 406 U.S. 605 (1972), and *New Jersey v. Portash*, supra, is misplaced. In those cases we reviewed Fifth Amendment challenges to state-court rulings that operated to dissuade

---

[4] Although the Federal Rules of Evidence do not explicitly authorize in limine rulings, the practice has developed pursuant to the district court's inherent authority to manage the course of trials. See generally FRE 103(c); cf. Fed. Rule Crim. Proc. 12(e).

[5] Requiring a defendant to make a proffer of testimony is no answer; his trial testimony could, for any number of reasons, differ from the proffer.

defendants from testifying. We did not hold that a federal court's preliminary ruling on a question not reaching constitutional dimensions—such as a decision under Rule 609(a)—is reviewable on appeal.

However, Justice Powell, in his concurring opinion in *Portash*, stated essentially the rule we adopt today:

> The preferred method for raising claims such as [petitioner's] would be for the defendant to take the stand and appeal a subsequent conviction . . . . Only in this way may the claim be presented to a reviewing court in a concrete factual context.

440 U.S., at 462.

We hold that to raise and preserve for review the claim of improper impeachment with a prior conviction, a defendant must testify. Accordingly, the judgment of the Court of Appeals is affirmed.

[Justice Stevens did not participate. Justices Brennan and Marshall joined in a separate concurring opinion, which is omitted.]

■ NOTES ON PRESERVING ERROR FOR REVIEW

1. Why do defendants like Edward Luce make pretrial motions to bar impeachment under FRE 609? Would the Court have reached the merits of the Luce claim of error if defense counsel had indicated that Luce would testify (if his conviction could not be used against him) and described in detail the tenor of the expected testimony?

2. In New Jersey v. Portash, 440 U.S. 450, 454-455 (1979), defendant was prosecuted for misconduct and extortion in office. He twice sought a ruling that his prior grand jury testimony, given under a grant of use immunity, would not be admissible if he testified. The judge ruled that the testimony would be admissible to impeach if he contradicted what he said before, and he did not testify. Still the Court reached the merits of his claim, holding that immunized testimony was involuntary, hence inadmissible under the Fifth Amendment. The state had objected that the question was "abstract and hypothetical" because defendant did not testify, but the Court said the trial judge "did rule on the merits" and the "case or controversy" requirement was satisfied. Should the Court resolve a constitutional issue in cases like *Portash* but not evidence issues in cases like *Luce*?

3. In *Cook* (cited in *Luce*), the Ninth Circuit held that a defendant who does not testify may still challenge an adverse ruling in limine under FRE 609 if he "establishes on the record that he will in fact take the stand and testify if his challenged prior convictions are excluded" and he "sufficiently outlines the nature of his testimony" so the trial court and the reviewing court can do the necessary balancing. The court argued:

> [I]t is unrealistic to continue to refuse to review these rulings unless the defendant takes the stand. The effect of the preliminary ruling can substantially change the course of the trial, and any ruling which so changes the course of a trial ought to be subject to judicial review.
>
> Defendants and their counsel make many tactical choices during a trial. Ordinarily, these choices are binding upon the defendant. However, assuming only for the purpose of argument that the trial court erred in announcing its application of Rule 609, the error may cause a defendant to make a choice that he might otherwise not have made. The government must admit that the tactical choice to remain silent is more likely a product of the court's ruling than of the defendant's free selection among strategic options.
>
> It pushes the doctrine of waiver beyond its usual criminal-law application to say that a defendant responding to an erroneous ruling by the trial court by remaining silent has waived his right to testify. And waiver becomes even less convincing if we say that by remaining silent under the constraints of an erroneous ruling on a point of law the defendant has waived his right to challenge that ruling on appeal.

United States v. Cook, 608 F.2d 1175, 1183-1184, 1186 (9th Cir. 1979), *cert. denied*, 444 U.S. 1304 (1980). Decisions from eight circuits similarly allowed review, despite defendant's failure to testify, although not all required a commitment and proffer. Did the court in *Luce* adequately answer the points made in *Cook*?

4. *Luce* establishes the procedure to be followed in federal criminal prosecutions, but states can follow *Cook* if they choose. A number of states do just that, rejecting *Luce*. See People v. Moore, 156 A.2d 394, 346 (N.Y. 1989); Commonwealth v. Jackson, 561 A.2d 335 (Pa. Super. 1988); State v. McClure, 692 P.2d 579, 583-584 & n.4 (Or. 1984). In one state, the Rule expressly provides that defendant need not take the stand to preserve the claim of error. See Tennessee Rule 609(e) ("reasonable written notice" of intent to impeach by prior convictions must be given in advance of trial, and court "may rule" on admissibility prior to trial "but in any event shall rule prior to the testimony of the accused," who "need not actually testify at the trial to later challenge the propriety" of admitting the conviction). But see Walker v. State, 790 A.2d 1214 (Del. 2002); State v. Wickham, 796 P.2d 1354, 1356 (Alaska, 1990); People v. Finley, 431 N.W.2d 19, 24 (Mich. 1988) (all following *Luce*).

5. Under *Luce*, a defendant who decides against testifying because the court refuses to exclude his prior conviction loses the right to claim error. If he *does* testify, his lawyer would prefer to "make a clean breast of it" by bringing out the conviction on direct, rather than waiting until the prosecutor raises the matter on cross (it will appear that the defense is hiding something). So the question arises whether this strategy also forecloses a right of appeal on the point (on the theory that defendant waived error by broaching the subject himself). In the *Ohler* case, the Court answered in the affirmative. See Ohler v. United States, 529 U.S. 753 (2000) (bringing out convictions on direct waives claim of error in a ruling that they can be used). Between them, *Luce* and *Ohler* put the accused in a difficult position, don't they? Some states have fallen in line behind *Ohler*, but some have not. Compare Brown v. State, 817 A.2d 241 (Md. 2003) (following *Ohler*) with State v. Daly, 623 N.W.2d 799 (Iowa 1999) (declining to follow *Ohler*).

c. Character Witnesses

The third way of suggesting lack of veracity is to introduce testimony by a character witness that the witness in question (we may call him the "principal witness") is untruthful. FRE 608(a) authorizes testimony of this sort. Here too the Rules expand common law tradition by permitting "opinion" as well as "reputation" testimony (FRE 405 does likewise in the case of character evidence used to prove out-of-court conduct), meaning that the character witness may say what he personally thinks of the veracity of the principal witness.

In either case a foundation is necessary, and some elaboration is typically allowed:

Q (to character witness): Coach Jones, are you acquainted with the reputation of [principal witness] Grace Gardner in the community of Riverdale for truth and veracity?
A (Coach Jones): Yes sir, I am.
Q: And what is that reputation?
A: It is very bad.
Q: And knowing what you know of that reputation, would you believe Grace Gardner in a serious matter?
A: Well, not exactly.
Q: Would you believe her under oath?
A: No, I honestly would not.

The foundation for opinion testimony is substantially the same, except that what is needed is a period of personal acquaintance.

Usually the character witness has resided in the same community with the principal witness and knows him personally or knows his reputation. But the character witness need not satisfy a formal residency requirement. One decision put it this way:

> We also think there should be no restriction necessarily limited to the community in which the witness sought to be impeached lives, and that the realities of our modern, mobile, impersonal society should also recognize that a witness may have a reputation for truth and veracity in the community in which he works and may have impressed on others in that community his character for truthfulness or untruthfulness. Therefore, we believe the community in which the witness worked, the law office of [character witness] Cory in this instance, was a proper locality in which to prove [principal witness] O'Toole's reputation or character for truthfulness or untruthfulness. We do not imply that such character in the community in which she lived might not have been proved.

United States v. Mandel, 591 F.2d 1347, 1350 (4th Cir. 1979), *cert. denied*, 445 U.S. 961 (1980).

Admitting opinion testimony suggests the possibility that experts might testify—perhaps psychiatrists or psychologists. But such testimony is seldom admitted, and modern cases repeatedly uphold rulings excluding proffered psychiatric testimony. See Nichols v. American National Insurance Co., 154 F.3d 875, 882-884 (8th Cir. 1998) (in suit alleging sexual harassment and constructive discharge, error to let psychiatrist testify to plaintiff's "poor psychiatric credibility," and describe her supposed "recall bias, secondary gain, and malingering"; record does not show testimony satisfied *Daubert*, and witness "sought to answer the very question at the heart of the jury's task," which is whether plaintiff could be believed; this testimony created "a serious danger of confusing or misleading the jury" and might cause jury to "substitute the expert's credibility assessment for its own common sense"); United States v. Cecil, 836 F.2d 1431, 1440-1441 (4th Cir.) (in drug trial, excluding psychiatrist's out-of-court statement that government witness was incapable of telling the truth, partly because credibility is strictly for jury), *cert. denied*, 487 U.S. 1205 (1988). But there are exceptions to this pattern. One outstanding exception is an old and famous case—the prosecution of Alger Hiss for perjury. See United States v. Hiss, 88 F. Supp. 559 (S.D.N.Y. 1950) (admitting defense psychiatric testimony on mental condition of main prosecution witness Whittaker Chambers; his credibility was "one of the major issues upon which the jury must pass," and insanity bears importantly on question of credibility).

NOTES ON EXPERT OPINION RELATING TO CREDIBILITY

1. Are you surprised that courts disallow expert testimony on witness credibility? Why shouldn't such testimony get in?

2. Do cases that let experts testify on accuracy of eyewitness identification (Notes on Proving Lack of Capacity in section A2, supra) suggest that experts should testify on lack of veracity too? Some courts admit expert testimony concerning the trauma suffered by victims of rape or child abuse, which sometimes has the effect of bolstering credibility. See Notes on Proving Truthfulness: Character and Behavioral Syndrome Evidence (section C2, infra).

3. Suppose the party who calls Grace Gardner wants to cross-examine Coach Jones about instances of good conduct in Gardner's life, reflecting truthfulness. "Coach Jones," counsel might say, "have you heard that Grace Gardner has for years acted as faculty treasurer in the school where you both teach and that she has rendered scrupulously correct accounts year after year?" Is such a question proper under FRE 608? Why do you suppose that such questions are seldom asked?

B SPECIFIC IMPEACHMENT

1. Prior Inconsistent Statements

Almost always a witness has made previous statements on the subject of her testimony. If that testimony differs from her prior statements, the attacking party may cross-examine on those statements and (subject to some conditions) prove them by "extrinsic evidence" (testimony by other witnesses).

Depending on the situation and his forensic skills, the attacking lawyer may be able to make devastating use of this "self-contradiction." He can argue that the prior statement has the specific effect of refuting testimony by the witness on the point in question. And while the mere fact of the prior inconsistent statement is indefinite in that it does not explain *why* the witness has changed her view, the cross-examiner may be able to draw from the larger setting all sorts of theories: The witness changed her story out of bias for the calling party, or because she has been "bought" or "frightened" off, or because her memory is poor, and so forth. And with theories of this sort the cross-examiner may take a small blot on the credibility of the witness and make it spread, arguing thus: "If she has contradicted herself on this one point, how can we rely on anything else she says?"

A moment's reflection explains why prior statements are so commonly known to the attacking party: In civil cases many witnesses give depositions that produce a permanent record of what they have said; in criminal cases key witnesses for the prosecution testify before grand juries or in preliminary hearings; insurance investigators regularly (often promptly) seek out witnesses and obtain formal written or recorded statements, and lawyers send investigators out for the same purpose; the prosecuting attorney does the same thing, and statements gotten this way are turned over to the defense.[6] Moreover, in life it often happens that witnesses have written letters or made business records or notes, or have spoken to others on the transactions in issue, and all these matters may be unearthed during discovery or pretrial investigation.

a. *Procedural issues*

By longstanding common law tradition, the attacking lawyer observed certain delicate conventions when raising the issue of prior inconsistencies. First, on

[6] Under Brady v. Maryland, 373 U.S. 83 (1963), the prosecutor has a constitutional obligation, if asked by the defense, to turn over evidence tending to exculpate the defendant. But FRCrimP 16(a)(2) delays defense discovery of prior statements by "government witnesses or prospective government witnesses." The Jencks Act (18 USC §3500) provides that such statements are discoverable only after "said witness has testified on direct examination." The purpose of this delay is to protect prosecution witnesses from threats or reprisals by defendants or their friends. In practice, pretrial statements by prosecution witnesses are commonly turned over to the defense at the start of trial, to avoid delays that would result if proceedings had to be halted to let defense counsel read the statement as he rises to commence cross-examination.

cross-examination he was expected to lead the witness gently to her inconsistency. The lawyer was to show the statement to the witness, if written, and in other cases to remind her of its substance; the lawyer was to draw her attention to the time of the statement and the surrounding circumstances; only after these preliminaries was he to ask whether the witness in fact wrote the statement or spoke the words and to suggest that they undercut her credibility.

Second, the attacking lawyer was not allowed to prove the statement by extrinsic evidence (offering the writing into evidence, or adducing testimony by another witness as to what the first had said) unless he had first raised the matter on cross-examination.

These conventions, which were known as The Rule in Queen Caroline's Case, 2 Brod. & Bing. 284, 129 Eng. Rep. 976, 977 (1820), came to be seen as a nuisance. However "fair" they may be in civil discourse, they seemed out of place in an adversary trial. They blunted the impeaching attack by providing the witness an opportunity to explain away the inconsistency even before the attacker could "spring" it on her, and they blocked extrinsic evidence if the cross-examiner forgot to lay the foundation properly.

FRE 613 changes common law practice. The message of FRE 613(a) is simple. No longer need the cross-examiner worry about approaching the subject gently. Instead, he may go straight to the point: "You just testified that the light was red for the blue car, but didn't you tell Charles that the blue car had the green light?" The only restriction is that "opposing counsel" (usually the lawyer who called the witness) is entitled on request to see the statement or learn its contents, so he can repair, if possible, the damage done by the attacker if he distorted the statement or wrenched it out of context.

The message of FRE 613(b) is more complicated. If a prior inconsistency is proved by "extrinsic evidence," generally the witness must have an opportunity "to explain or deny" it (unless "the interests of justice otherwise require"), and the adverse party (usually the one who called the witness) must have a chance to interrogate her. Sequence is not specified: The Rule does not say the chance to explain must *come before* extrinsic evidence is admitted, as *Queen Caroline's Case* would require, and it is clear that if a witness *later* has a chance to explain, the Rule is satisfied. See Wilmington Trust Co. v. Manufacturers Life Insurance, 749 F.2d 694, 699 (11th Cir. 1985) (FRE 613(b) contains "no specification of any particular time or sequence"; defendant could have requested that the witness be permitted to take the stand in surrebuttal but made no such request).

■ PROBLEM 8-E. "He's Trying to Sandbag Us!"

In his civil suit seeking recovery for injuries sustained during an assault, Plimpton claims that Dirk struck him in the chest with a shovel, causing severe injuries. During plaintiff's case-in-chief, Welch testifies for Plimpton that Dirk struck the blow without provocation. Counsel for Dirk then cross-examines Welch, but does not ask whether Welch made any prior statement about the event.

During the defense case, Dirk calls Murphy, the police officer who investigated the incident. Murphy testifies that Welch told him that he did not actually see the blow being struck, and thinks Plimpton may have thrown a rock at Dirk.

Plaintiff's counsel is immediately on her feet:

> Your Honor, he's trying to sandbag us. Mr. Welch is gone, and he has had no opportunity to respond to the suggestion that he's changed his story. Defendant had a chance to put the same question to Welch, and deliberately did not. He should have laid a foundation back then. Rule 613(b) requires that Welch have a chance to explain.

How should the court rule, and why? Does it matter whether Welch has left the courtroom? What if he was told that he may go home and not told that he remains subject to recall? What if it is learned that he joined the French Foreign Legion and is beyond reach of subpoena?

■ NOTES ON APPLYING FRE 613(b)

1. Under FRE 611, courts have discretion to set the "mode and order" of examining witnesses, which includes deciding whether to allow parties to recall them. If an adverse party elects to cross-examine without mentioning a prior inconsistent statement, and wants later to call another witness to prove the statement (which is what Dirk's lawyer did in calling Murphy), either the court winds up recalling the witness being attacked (Welch), or the extrinsic evidence must be excluded, at least on objection by the calling party (Plimpton's counsel raised the point). The reason for excluding extrinsic evidence on objection is that the protection afforded by FRE 613(b) has not been provided (the witness must have "an opportunity to explain or deny").

2. Rule 613 is silent on sequence. It does not say who bears the risk if the witness is no longer available and did not have a chance to "explain or deny" his prior statement. But the fact that FRE 613(b) puts a condition on admitting extrinsic evidence suggests that the attacking party bears the risk. Even if the witness could be recalled, a court can (and probably should) exclude extrinsic evidence, unless the attacking party secures the court's assent in advance to recall the witness. The cases have been pragmatic. Compare Jones v. Collier, 762 F.2d 71, 72 (8th Cir. 1985) (excluding proof of prior statement by witness who had testified the day before and returned to his place of incarceration 300 miles away; plaintiff "did not lay any foundation for his rebuttal," apparently as "part of trial strategy") with United States v. McLaughlin, 663 F.2d 949, 953-954 (9th Cir. 1981) (defense could offer extrinsic evidence of statement, after reminding declarant of meeting in question on cross; government could offer witness to provide opportunity to explain).

3. Rule 613 does have an escape clause, allowing extrinsic evidence of a prior statement even if the witness had no chance to explain "if justice so requires." Arguably justice would so require if the attacking party only learned of the statement after the witness had testified and had been released, particularly if he could no longer be subpoenaed to return, or if (for example) the attacking party had some other good reason to defer proving the prior statement and, when he decided to do so, the witness had left the jurisdiction. Imagine, for example, Dirk's lawyer wanting to hear Plimpton's testimony before deciding whether to use Welch's prior statement, which seems a plausible reason to defer decision on this point. If Welch left the jurisdiction after his initial testimony, the question whether to allow extrinsic evidence might turn on whether Dirk's lawyer knew or should have anticipated this eventuality. Rule 613 also exempts prior statements by the opposing party from the requirement of a chance to explain, presumably because that party is usually present and courts are likely to allow such a party to take the stand again to explain or deny.

b. Inconsistent Statements and Misuse of the Impeachment Process

Recall from Problem 3-C ("The Blue Car Ran a Red Light") that the impeaching use of prior inconsistent statements is considered a nonhearsay use. Traditionally such statements were almost always admitted for the impeaching (nonhearsay) purpose of proving vacillation, even where the hearsay doctrine prohibited their substantive (hearsay) use to prove what they asserted. This tradition persisted despite doubts that juries would consider such statements only as impeachment. Recall too that the Advisory Committee wanted to define all prior inconsistent statements as nonhearsay, but that Congress refused to go along. So we live still in a world in which many prior inconsistencies may be admitted to impeach, but not as substantive evidence.

Concern that a prior inconsistent statement will be taken as proof of what it asserts is the most obvious reason that might persuade a court to exclude it (this "substantive" use of a statement admitted only to impeach is a form of misuse that could lead to exclusion for prejudice under FRE 403). Concern over jury misuse of inconsistent statements was exacerbated by a development that finds expression in FRE 607, which is that *any* party may impeach a witness, "including the party that called the witness." The "voucher rule" used to prevent this kind of thing from happening (it barred the calling party from impeaching its own witnesses), but FRE 607 did away with the voucher rule. As you will see when you read the *Webster* case, this development makes it possible for a party to call a witness *not* with the expectation of getting useful testimony, but for the purpose of proving whatever he said before, under the *guise* of impeachment, but with the real purpose of getting the jury to consider prior statements as substantive evidence.

Before we look at *Webster,* recall that sometimes there are other reasons to exclude prior statements by testifying witnesses. For example, statements in civil settlement talks are usually excludable under FRE 408, and plea bargaining statements are excludable under FRE 410 under some circumstances. If a litigant has made statements covered by such exclusionary provisions and he then testifies at trial, may the statements be used to impeach credibility? Usually the answer is No in the case of statements during settlement negotiations (FRE 408 bars their use as inconsistent statements or to contradict), and FRE 410 points toward the same conclusion for plea bargaining statements, but this conclusion is misleading because defendants are usually forced to waive the right to exclude as a condition of bargaining (see Chapter 5D, supra).

UNITED STATES v. WEBSTER

United States Court of Appeals for the Seventh Circuit
734 F.2d 1191 (1984)

POSNER, J.

The defendant, Webster, was convicted of aiding and abetting the robbery of a federally insured bank and receiving stolen bank funds, was sentenced to nine years in prison, and appeals. Only one issue need be discussed. The government called the bank robber, King (who had pleaded guilty and been given a long prison term), as a witness against Webster. King gave testimony that if believed would have exculpated the defendant, whereupon the government introduced prior inconsistent statements that King had given the FBI inculpating Webster. Although the court instructed the jury that it could consider the statements only for purposes of impeachment, Webster argues that this was not good enough, that the government should not be allowed to get inadmissible evidence before the jury by calling a hostile witness and then using his out-of-court statements, which would otherwise be inadmissible hearsay, to impeach him.

... [I]t would be an abuse of [FRE 607], in a criminal case, for the prosecution to call a witness that it knew would not give it useful evidence, just so it could introduce hearsay evidence against the defendant in the hope that the jury would miss the subtle distinction between impeachment and substantive evidence—or, if it didn't miss it, would ignore it. The purpose would not be to impeach the witness but to put in hearsay as substantive evidence against the defendant, which Rule 607 does not contemplate or authorize. We thus agree that "impeachment by prior inconsistent statement may not be permitted where employed as a mere subterfuge to get before the jury evidence not otherwise admissible." United States v. Morlang, 531 F.2d 183, 190 (4th Cir. 1975). Although *Morlang* was decided before the Federal Rules of Evidence became effective, the limitation that we have quoted on the prosecutor's rights under Rule 607 has been accepted in all circuits that have considered the issue. We agree with these decisions.

But it is quite plain that there was no bad faith here. Before the prosecutor called King to the stand she asked the judge to allow her to examine him outside the presence of the jury, because she didn't know what he would say. The defendant's counsel objected and the voir dire was not held. We do not see how in these circumstances it can be thought that the prosecutor put King on the stand knowing he would give no useful evidence. If she had known that, she would not have offered to voir dire him, as the voir dire would have provided a foundation for defense counsel to object, under *Morlang*, to the admission of King's prior inconsistent statements.

Webster urges us, on the authority of Graham, Handbook of Federal Evidence §607.3 (1981 and Supp. 1983), to go beyond the good-faith standard and hold that the government may not impeach a witness with his prior inconsistent statements unless it is surprised and harmed by the witness's testimony. But we think it would be a mistake to graft such a requirement to Rule 607, even if such a graft would be within the power of judicial interpretation of the rule. Suppose the government called an adverse witness that it thought would give evidence both helpful and harmful to it, but it also thought that the harmful aspect could be nullified by introducing the witness's prior inconsistent statement. As there would be no element of surprise, Professor Graham would forbid the introduction of the prior statements; yet we are at a loss to understand why the government should be put to the choice between the Scylla of forgoing impeachment and the Charybdis of not calling at all a witness from whom it expects to elicit genuinely helpful evidence. The good-faith standard strikes a better balance; and it is always open to the defendant to argue that the probative value of the evidence offered to impeach the witness is clearly outweighed by the prejudicial impact it might have on the jury, because the jury would have difficulty confining use of the evidence to impeachment. See FRE 403.

The judgment of conviction is affirmed.

■ NOTES ON "ABUSE" OF FRE 607

1. *Webster* suggests a "good faith" standard to distinguish between abuse of FRE 607 and legitimate impeachment by the calling party. Let's look at this standard. Assume that King told investigators that he and Webster planned and did the robbery. Assume he changes his story at trial: Testifying on voir dire outside the jury's hearing, he says the two planned the robbery, but Webster begged off and did not go to the bank. With the jury back, the prosecutor adduces from King that he and Webster planned the robbery. Under the good faith standard, if the prosecutor asked King whether Webster actually participated, it appears that the prosecutor could not then impeach the expected response ("no, Webster backed out") by proving the earlier statement (Webster did participate). But if the prosecutor only asked King about the planning, wouldn't she be misleading the jury? If she stopped there and *defendant* got King to say Webster did not go to the bank, would it then be an abuse for the prosecutor to ask about the prior statement?

2. The court in *Webster* refers to the opinion in *Morlang.* There the prosecutor called Wilmoth, ostensibly to adduce his testimony that Morlang admitted participating in a scheme to divert federal funds. But Wilmoth had told the prosecutor before trial that he would not testify this way, and (true to his latest word) he denied the conversation on the stand. Then the prosecutor called Crist (Wilmoth's cellmate), who testified that Wilmoth said that Morlang admitted his involvement. The reviewing court decided that refuting Wilmoth's denial of Morlang's confession by getting Crist to testify was improper:

> While it is the rule in this circuit that a party calling a witness does not vouch for his credibility, it has never been the rule that a party may call a witness where his testimony is known to be adverse for the purpose of impeaching him. To so hold would permit the government, in the name of impeachment, to present testimony to the jury by indirection which would not otherwise be admissible. The courts have consistently refused to sanction such a practice....
>
> We ... recognize that the strict rule against impeaching one's own witness has long been discredited .... The overwhelming weight of authority is, however, that impeachment by prior inconsistent statement may not be permitted where employed as a mere subterfuge to get before the jury evidence not otherwise admissible.
>
> Witnesses may, of course, sometimes fail to come up to the expectations of counsel and in such situations there is an understandable temptation to get before the jury any prior statement made by the witness. And it may be that in certain instances impeachment might somehow enhance the truth-finding process. Yet, whatever validity this latter assertion may have, it must be balanced against the notions of fairness upon which our system is based. Foremost among these concepts is the principle that men should not be allowed to be convicted on the basis of unsworn testimony.

United States v. Morlang, 531 F.2d 183, 189-190 (4th Cir. 1975). Accord United States v. Gomez-Gallardo, 915 F.2d 553, 555 (9th Cir. 1990) (impeachment improper when used as guise to put before jury otherwise inadmissible substantive evidence; question is whether government examined witness for "primary purpose" of doing that). Pretty clearly *Webster* kept the *Morlang* doctrine intact.

3. When Congress balked at the suggestion of the drafters of the Rules to let all prior inconsistencies be used as substantive evidence, arguably Congress should have kept the voucher principle in some form. In any event, *Morlang* means that sometimes the calling party will be restricted in much the same way that the voucher principle would restrict him. See generally Graham, Employing Inconsistent Statements for Impeachment and as Substantive Evidence: A Critical Review and Proposed Amendments of Federal Rules of Evidence

801(d)(1)(A), 613, and 607, 75 Mich. L. Rev. 1565 (1977); Ordover, Surprise! That Damaging Turncoat Witness Is Still with Us: An Analysis of Federal Rules of Evidence 607, 801(d)(1)(A) and 403, 5 Hofstra L. Rev. 65 (1976).

4. Recall that *some* inconsistencies *are* admissible as substantive evidence—namely, those that fit FRE 801(d)(1)(A) because they were given in proceedings under oath and the declarant is now cross-examinable. As we saw in Problem 4-A ("I Got Amnesia") (Chapter 4A1), grand jury testimony can fit FRE 801(d)(1)(A), and so can preliminary hearing testimony, and for that matter testimony in suppression motions, depositions, or other trials. If the calling party offers an inconsistent statement that fits this (or some other) exception, the *Morlang* issue disappears. No longer can it be said that the calling party is offering inconsistent statements in hope that the jury will misuse them as substantive evidence: Making substantive use of such statements *simply isn't* misuse anymore.

5. The *DeLillo* case seems to restrict the *Morlang* doctrine. *DeLillo* holds that *Morlang* does not apply to witnesses crucial to the calling party's case. There, the government sought to prove that Vincent DeLillo installed substandard concrete pipes and conspired with others to hide leaks. A participant in the scheme named Gorman testified that Vincent told a subordinate to hide the leaks, but another participant named Monahan testified that Vincent said no such thing. Then the government introduced a taped statement in which Monahan said that Vincent *had* told them to hide the leaks, after all. The reviewing court decided it was alright to adduce Gorman's testimony, then to offer Monahan's testimony contradicting Gorman, and *then* prove Monahan's prior inconsistent statement supporting Gorman's description of events:

> Beyond doubt, Monahan was not called . . . as a subterfuge with the primary aim of getting to the jury a statement impeaching him. Monahan's corroborating testimony was essential in many areas of the government's case. Once there, the government had the right to question him, and to attempt to impeach him, about those aspects of his testimony which conflicted with Gorman's account of the same events. *Morlang* itself explicitly recognizes the propriety of impeachment where it is "necessary to alleviate the harshness of subjecting a party to the mercy of a witness who is recalcitrant or may have been unscrupulously tampered with." To the extent that defendants rely on *Morlang* for the principle that a witness cannot be put on the stand if the side calling him knows that he will give testimony that it will have to impeach, it seems clear to us that the effect of [FRE] 607 . . . is to nullify the plausibility of such a reading.

United States v. DeLillo, 620 F.2d 939, 946-947 (2d Cir.), *cert. denied*, 449 U.S. 835 (1980). The argument in *DeLillo* turns not on the government's good faith, but on the government's need for Gorman's testimony: As a participant in the scheme, Gorman was an essential witness, which justified allowing the impeachment.

6. Should *Morlang* apply to defense impeachment of defense witnesses? See United States v. MacDonald, 688 F.2d 224, 233-234 (4th Cir. 1982) (Yes).

c. Constitutional issues

The Fourth, Fifth, and Sixth Amendments are the sources of critical exclusionary doctrines. Under the decision in *Mapp,* evidence collected in a search that violates the Fourth Amendment (requiring a warrant based on probable cause) is excludable from a later trial; under *Miranda,* a statement by the accused taken after arrest during police questioning is excludable under the Fifth Amendment (source of privilege against self-incrimination) unless the police gave the warnings required by that famous decision and obtained his consent to talk; under *Massiah,* statements by the accused taken by police after he has a lawyer are similarly excludable from trial as violating the Sixth Amendment (which entitles the accused to counsel). See Mapp v. Ohio, 367 U.S. 643 (1961); Miranda v. Arizona, 384 U.S. 436 (1966); Massiah v. United States, 377 U.S. 201 (1964). Bear in mind these decisions as you read *Harris.*

Recall Doyle v. Ohio, 426 U.S. 610 (1976) (Chapter 4B2, supra), where the Court said that using postwarning silence by the accused (while in official custody) to impeach his trial testimony violates *Miranda.* Now we consider the use of postwarning *statements* and prewarning *silence* to impeach trial testimony.

HARRIS v. NEW YORK

United States Supreme Court
401 U.S. 222 (1971)

[Harris was charged with selling heroin in transactions on January 4 and 6. On both occasions the buyer was an undercover police officer who became the state's principal witness. Taking the stand in his own defense, Harris testified that he knew the police officer, but he denied engaging in any transaction with him on January 4. He further testified that on January 6 he had sold the officer two glassine bags containing what appeared to be heroin, but he contended that in reality they contained only baking powder and that his motive in making the sale was to gain the sum of $12.

On cross-examination, the prosecutor asked defendant about certain statements he had apparently made after his arrest on January 7. (At that time, Harris had not gotten *Miranda* warnings, and the state conceded that his statements were inadmissible under the rule in that case. The prosecutor had made no reference to those statements during the state's case-in-chief. The Supreme Court opinion comments that Harris "makes no claim that the statements made to the police were coerced or involuntary.")

Defendant replied that he could not remember much about what he said in the stationhouse, and the prosecutor essentially read the statements to the defendant and (at defense request, for purposes of appeal) included the transcript of the statements in the record. Those statements "partially contradicted" Harris's direct testimony. (In his dissenting opinion, Justice Brennan says that in those statements Harris said that on January 4 "the officer had used [Harris] as a middleman to buy some heroin from a third person with money furnished by the officer" and that on January 6 Harris "had again acted for the officer in buying two bags of heroin from a third person for which [Harris] received $12 and a part of the heroin.") The trial judge told the jury that the statements "could be considered only in passing on [Harris's] credibility and not as evidence of guilt," and both the prosecutor and the defense commented on the statements in closing argument.]

MR. CHIEF JUSTICE BURGER delivered the opinion of the Court.

Some comments in the *Miranda* opinion can indeed be read as indicating a bar to use of an uncounseled statement for any purpose, but discussion of that issue was not at all necessary to the Court's holding and cannot be regarded as controlling. *Miranda* barred the prosecution from making its case with statements of an accused made while in custody prior to having or effectively waiving counsel. It does not follow from *Miranda* that evidence inadmissible against an accused in the prosecution's case in chief is barred for all purposes, provided of course that the trustworthiness of the evidence satisfies legal standards.

In Walder v. United States, 347 U.S. 62 (1954), the Court permitted physical evidence, inadmissible in the case in chief, to be used for impeachment purposes.

> It is one thing to say that the Government cannot make an affirmative use of evidence unlawfully obtained. It is quite another to say that the defendant can turn the illegal method by which evidence in the Government's possession was obtained to his own advantage, and provide himself with a shield against contradiction of his untruths. Such an extension of the *Weeks* doctrine would be a perversion of the Fourth Amendment.
>
> [T]here is hardly justification for letting the defendant affirmatively resort to perjurious testimony in reliance on the Government's disability to challenge his credibility.

It is true that Walder was impeached as to collateral matters included in his direct examination, whereas petitioner here was impeached as to testimony bearing more directly on the crimes charged. We are not persuaded that there is a difference in principle that warrants a result different from that reached by the Court in *Walder.* Petitioner's testimony in his own behalf concerning the events of January 7 contrasted sharply with what he told the police shortly after his arrest. The impeachment process here undoubtedly provided valuable aid to the jury in assessing petitioner's credibility, and the benefits of this process should not be lost, in our view, because of the speculative possibility that impermissible police conduct will be encouraged thereby. Assuming that the exclusionary rule has a deterrent effect on proscribed police conduct, sufficient deterrence flows when the evidence in question is made unavailable to the prosecution in its case in chief. Every criminal defendant is privileged to testify in his own defense, or to refuse to do so. But that privilege cannot be construed to include the right to commit perjury. Having voluntarily taken the stand, petitioner was under an obligation to speak truthfully and accurately, and the prosecution here did no more than utilize the traditional truth-testing devices of the adversary process.[2] Had inconsistent statements been made by the accused to some third person, it could hardly be contended that the conflict could not be laid before the jury by way of cross-examination and impeachment.

The shield provided by *Miranda* cannot be perverted into a license to use perjury by way of a defense, free from the risk of confrontation with prior inconsistent utterances. We hold, therefore, that petitioner's credibility was appropriately impeached by use of his earlier conflicting statements.

Affirmed.

Mr. Justice BLACK dissents.

Mr. Justice BRENNAN, with whom Mr. Justice DOUGLAS and Mr. Justice MARSHALL join, dissenting.

It is conceded that the question-and-answer statement used to impeach petitioner's direct testimony was, under Miranda v. Arizona, 384 U.S. 436 (1966), constitutionally inadmissible as part of the State's direct case against petitioner. I think that the Constitution also denied the State the use of the statement on cross-examination to impeach the credibility of petitioner's testimony given in his own defense. The decision in Walder v. United States, 347 U.S. 62 (1954), is not, as the Court today holds, dispositive to the contrary. Rather, that case supports my conclusion.

[Justice Brennan summarizes the facts.]

Walder v. United States was not a case where tainted evidence was used to impeach an accused's direct testimony on matters directly related to the case against him. In *Walder* the evidence was used to impeach the accused's testimony on matters *collateral* to the crime charged. Walder had been indicted in 1950 for purchasing and possessing heroin. When his motion to suppress use of the narcotics as illegally seized was granted, the Government dismissed the prosecution. Two years later Walder was indicted for another narcotics violation completely unrelated to the 1950 one. Testifying in his own defense, he said on direct examination that he had never in his life possessed narcotics. On cross-examination he denied that law enforcement officers had seized narcotics from his home two years earlier. The Government was then permitted to

[2] If, for example, an accused confessed fully to a homicide and led the police to the body of the victim under circumstances making his confession inadmissible, the petitioner would have us allow that accused to take the stand and blandly deny every fact disclosed to the police or discovered as a "fruit" of his confession, free from confrontation with his prior statements and acts. The voluntariness of the confession would, on this thesis, be totally irrelevant. We reject such an extravagant extension of the Constitution.

introduce the testimony of one of the officers involved in the 1950 seizure, that when he had raided Walder's home at that time he had seized narcotics there. The Court held that on facts where "the defendant went beyond a mere denial of complicity in the crimes of which he was charged and made the sweeping claim that he had never dealt in or possessed any narcotics," the exclusionary rule of Weeks v. United States, 232 U.S. 383 (1914), would not extend to bar the Government from rebutting this testimony with evidence, although tainted, that petitioner had in fact possessed narcotics two years before. The Court was careful, however, to distinguish the situation of an accused whose testimony, as in the instant case, was a "denial of complicity in the crimes of which he was charged," that is, where illegally obtained evidence was used to impeach the accused's direct testimony on matters directly related to the case against him. As to that situation, the Court said:

> Of course, the Constitution guarantees a defendant the fullest opportunity to meet the accusation against him. He must be free to deny all the elements of the case against him without thereby giving leave to the Government to introduce by way of rebuttal evidence illegally secured by it, and therefore not available for its case in chief.

From this recital of facts it is clear that the evidence used for impeachment in *Walder* was related to the earlier 1950 prosecution and had no direct bearing on "the elements of the case" being tried in 1952. The evidence tended solely to impeach the credibility of the defendant's direct testimony that he had never in his life possessed heroin. But that evidence was completely unrelated to the indictment on trial and did not in any way interfere with his freedom to deny all elements of that case against him. In contrast, here, the evidence used for impeachment, a statement concerning the details of the very sales alleged in the indictment, was directly related to the case against petitioner.

While *Walder* did not identify the constitutional specifics that guarantee "a defendant the fullest opportunity to meet the accusation against him . . . [and permit him to] be free to deny all the elements of the case against him," in my view *Miranda* identified the Fifth Amendment's privilege against self-incrimination as one of those specifics. That privilege has been extended against the States. Malloy v. Hogan, 378 U.S. 1 (1964). It is fulfilled only when an accused is guaranteed the right "to remain silent unless he chooses to speak in the *unfettered* exercise of his own will" (emphasis added). The choice of whether to testify in one's own defense must therefore be "unfettered," since that choice is an exercise of the constitutional privilege, Griffin v. California, 380 U.S. 609 (1965). *Griffin* held that comment by the prosecution upon the accused's failure to take the stand or a court instruction that such silence is evidence of guilt is impermissible because it "fetters" that choice—"[i]t cuts down on the privilege by making its assertion costly." For precisely the same reason the constitutional guarantee forbids the prosecution to use a tainted statement to impeach the accused who takes the stand: The prosecution's use of the tainted statement "cuts down on the privilege by making its assertion costly." Thus, the accused is denied an "unfettered" choice when the decision whether to take the stand is burdened by the risk that an illegally obtained prior statement may be introduced to impeach his direct testimony denying complicity in the crime charged against him. We settled this proposition in *Miranda* where we said:

> The privilege against self-incrimination protects the individual from being compelled to incriminate himself in *any* manner . . . . [S]tatements merely intended to be exculpatory by the defendant are often *used to impeach his testimony at trial . . . . These statements are incriminating in any meaningful sense of the word and may not be used without the full warnings and effective waiver required for any other statement.*

This language completely disposes of any distinction between statements used on direct as opposed to cross-examination. "An incriminating statement is as incriminating when used to impeach credibility as it is when used as direct proof of guilt and no constitutional distinction can legitimately be drawn." People v. Kulis, 221 N.E.2d 541, 543 (N.Y. 1966) (dissenting opinion).

The objective of deterring improper police conduct is only part of the larger objective of safeguarding the integrity of our adversary system. The "essential mainstay" of that system is the privilege against self-incrimination, which for that reason has occupied a central place in our jurisprudence since before the Nation's birth. Moreover, "we may view the historical development of the privilege as one which groped for the proper scope of governmental power over the citizen . . . . All these policies point to one overriding thought: the constitutional foundation underlying the privilege is the respect a government . . . must accord to the dignity and integrity of its citizens." *Miranda.* These values are plainly jeopardized if an exception against admission of tainted statements is made for those used for impeachment purposes. Moreover, it is monstrous that courts should aid or abet the law-breaking police officer. It is abiding truth that "[n]othing can destroy a government more quickly than its failure to observe its own laws, or worse, its disregard of the charter of its own existence." Mapp v. Ohio, 367 U.S. 643, 659 (1961). Thus, even to the extent that *Miranda* was aimed at deterring police practices in disregard of the Constitution, I fear that today's holding will seriously undermine the achievement of that objective. The Court today tells the police that they may freely interrogate an accused incommunicado and without counsel and know that although any statement they obtain in violation of *Miranda* cannot be used on the State's direct case, it may be introduced if the defendant has the temerity to testify in his own defense. This goes far toward undoing much of the progress made in conforming police methods to the Constitution. I dissent.

■ NOTES ON IMPEACHMENT BY *MIRANDA*-BARRED STATEMENTS

1. If *Harris* had gone the other way, would the prosecutor lose a critical way to keep defendants honest? Does *Harris* significantly increase police incentive to violate *Miranda* rights? Does *Miranda* also establish a moral principle? If it offends a moral standard for the state to offer *Miranda*-barred statements, what weight (if any) should we assign to the fact that the accused takes the stand and apparently commits perjury?

2. In *Miranda,* the Court was concerned with the "interrogation atmosphere and the evils it can bring," emphasizing that the Fifth Amendment protects personal "dignity and integrity," requiring the state "to respect the inviolability of the human personality." 384 U.S. 436, at 456 & 460 (1967). The Court noted that abuses in interrogation procedures "may even give rise to a false confession" and that the presence of counsel during interrogation "can mitigate the dangers of untrustworthiness," 384 U.S. 436, at 455 n.24 & 470 (1967). Still, reliability of stationhouse confessions seems not to have been the main concern, and the Court said that confessions "remain a proper element in law enforcement" and that police need not "stop a person" from making voluntary statements, 384 U.S. 436, at 478 (1967). Does an assumption of reliability of stationhouse confessions underlie the decision in *Harris*?

3. In *Harris,* does it matter that the statement was offered to impeach direct testimony by the accused, as opposed to testimony adduced on cross? Long before *Harris,* the Court touched on this point in a related context. In a drug conspiracy trial, the accused testified on direct that he received packages but did not know they contained cocaine. On cross, the prosecutor asked whether he had ever seen cocaine before, and he replied "never." The government then offered a can of cocaine, seized in violation of the Fourth Amendment on an unrelated occasion. The Supreme Court disapproved. It quoted the principle that the "essence of a provision forbidding the acquisition of evidence in a certain way is not merely that evidence so acquired shall not be used before the court but that it shall not be used at all," and commented that defendant "did not testify [on direct] concerning the can of cocaine," hence that he "did nothing to waive his constitutional protection." Agnello v. United States, 269 U.S. 20 (1925).

4. *Miranda* requires police not only to warn the arrested suspect but to stop asking questions if he claims his right to counsel. If he does so but police keep questioning him, does *Harris* permit the use for impeachment purposes of what he says thereafter? See Oregon v. Hass, 420 U.S. 714 (1975) (Yes). Is *Hass* different enough from *Harris* that it should have been decided the other way even if *Harris* is right?

5. Rufus Mincey was hospitalized after an exchange of gunfire with an arresting officer. While in the emergency room with an intravenous feeding tube, a catheter in his bladder, and tubes in his throat and nose, he was questioned by a detective. He could not speak, so he wrote his answers. Questioning continued despite his requests for a lawyer, and his replies were admitted to impeach him at his murder trial. The Court distinguished *Harris* and reversed the conviction, holding that this use of an "*involuntary* statement" by a "seriously wounded" defendant in his "debilitated and helpless condition . . . on the edge of consciousness" violated due process. Mincey v. Arizona, 437 U.S. 385, 398-401 (1978). Why the different outcome?

6. Local official Joseph Portash was subpoenaed to testify before a grand jury, and he invoked his privilege against self-incrimination. Through counsel, he negotiated an immunity agreement, under which his testimony and evidence derived from it could not be used in later proceedings against him (apart from a perjury prosecution). Portash was later indicted for misconduct in office and extortion. He sought a pretrial ruling barring the use for impeachment purposes of his immunized grand jury testimony, but the motion was denied. Portash did not testify and was convicted. The Supreme Court reversed, distinguishing *Harris* and *Hass* on the ground that no contention was made there that the statements were "involuntary," while in this case—

> Testimony given in response to a grant of legislative immunity is the essence of coerced testimony. In such cases there is no question whether physical or psychological pressures overrode the defendant's will; the witness is told to talk or face the government's coercive sanctions, notably, a conviction for contempt. The information given in response to a grant of immunity may well be more reliable than information beaten from a helpless defendant, but it is no less compelled. The Fifth and Fourteenth Amendments provide a privilege against *compelled* self-incrimination, not merely against unreliable self-incrimination.

New Jersey v. Portash, 440 U.S. 450, 459 (1979). Can *Portash* be reconciled with *Harris*?

7. Daryl James is tried for murder, arising out of a confrontation between eight boys returning from a party and three others demanding money. The defense suppressed statements James made on arrest to the effect that his hair was reddish brown, long, and combed straight back on the day of the crime, and that he went to his mother's salon to get his hair dyed black and curled to change his appearance. At trial, state witnesses described the assailant as having reddish hair worn shoulder length in a "butter" style, and remembered seeing James weeks earlier wearing his hair that way. The defense called a family friend named Henderson, who testified that on the day of the crime she took James to register for school and that his hair was black. Can the state now introduce James' suppressed statements on the theory that *Harris* allows use of these statements to contradict Henderson's testimony? See James v. Illinois, 493 U.S. 307 (1990) (No; threat of perjury deters witnesses from lying, but not defendants faced with other charges; expanding impeachment exception would "chill some defendants from presenting their best defense" and "significantly weaken" deterrent effect of exclusionary rule).

JENKINS v. ANDERSON

United States Supreme Court
447 U.S. 231 (1980)

Mr. Justice Powell delivered the opinion of the Court.

The question in this case is whether the use of prearrest silence to impeach a defendant's credibility violates either the Fifth or Fourteenth Amendment to the Constitution.

I

On August 13, 1974, the petitioner stabbed and killed Doyle Redding. The petitioner was not apprehended until he turned himself in to governmental authorities about two weeks later. At his state trial for first-degree murder, the petitioner contended that the killing was in self-defense.

The petitioner testified that his sister and her boyfriend were robbed by Redding and another man during the evening of August 12, 1974. The petitioner, who was nearby when the robbery occurred, followed the thieves a short distance and reported their whereabouts to the police. According to the petitioner's testimony, the next day he encountered Redding, who accused him of informing the police of the robbery. The petitioner stated that Redding attacked him with a knife, that the two men struggled briefly, and that the petitioner broke away. On cross-examination, the petitioner admitted that during the struggle he had tried "[t]o push that knife in [Redding] as far as [I] could," but maintained that he had acted solely in self-defense.

During the cross-examination, the prosecutor questioned the petitioner about his actions after the stabbing:

Q. And I suppose you waited for the Police to tell them what happened?
A. No, I didn't.
Q. You didn't?
A. No.
Q. I see. And how long was it after this day that you were arrested, or that you were taken into custody?

After some discussion of the date on which petitioner surrendered, the prosecutor continued:

Q. When was the first time that you reported the things that you have told us in Court today to anybody?
A. Two days after it happened.
Q. And who did you report it to?
A. To my probation officer.
Q. Well, apart from him?

A. No one.
Q. Who?
A. No one but my—
Q. (Interposing) Did you ever go to a Police Officer or to anyone else?
A. No, I didn't.
Q. As a matter of fact, it was two weeks later, wasn't it?
A. Yes.

In closing argument to the jury, the prosecutor again referred to the petitioner's prearrest silence. The prosecutor noted that petitioner had "waited two weeks, according to the testimony—at least two weeks before he did anything about surrendering himself or reporting [the stabbing] to anybody." The prosecutor contended that the petitioner had committed murder in retaliation for the robbery the night before.

The petitioner was convicted of manslaughter and sentenced to 10 to 15 years' imprisonment in state prison.... [Federal habeas corpus relief is denied, and the Supreme Court here affirms.]

II

At trial the prosecutor attempted to impeach the petitioner's credibility by suggesting that the petitioner would have spoken out if he had killed in self-defense. The petitioner contends that the prosecutor's actions violated the Fifth Amendment as applied to the States through the Fourteenth Amendment. The Fifth Amendment guarantees an accused the right to remain silent during his criminal trial and prevents the prosecution from commenting on the silence of a defendant who asserts the right.... In this case, of course, the petitioner did not remain silent throughout the criminal proceedings. Instead, he voluntarily took the witness stand in his own defense.

This Court's decision in Raffel v. United States, 271 U.S. 494 (1926), recognized that the Fifth Amendment is not violated when a defendant who testifies in his own defense is impeached with his prior silence. The defendant in *Raffel* was tried twice. At the first trial, a Government agent testified that Raffel earlier had made an inculpatory statement. The defendant did not testify. After the first trial ended in deadlock the agent repeated his testimony at the second trial, and Raffel took the stand to deny making such a statement. Cross-examination revealed that Raffel had not testified at the first trial.... The Court held that inquiry into prior silence was proper because "[t]he immunity from giving testimony is one which the defendant may waive by offering himself as a witness.... When he takes the stand in his own behalf, he does so as any other witness, and within the limits of the appropriate rules he may be cross-examined...." Thus, the *Raffel* Court concluded that the defendant was "subject to cross-examination impeaching his credibility just like any other witness." Grunewald v. United States, 353 U.S. 391 (1957).[2]

It can be argued that a person facing arrest will not remain silent if his failure to speak later can be used to impeach him. But the Constitution does not forbid "every government-imposed choice in the criminal process that has the effect of discouraging the exercise of constitutional rights." Chaffin v. Stynchcombe, 412 U.S. 17, 30 (1973) .... The "'threshold question is whether compelling the election impairs to an appreciable extent any of the policies behind the rights involved.'" *Chaffin v. Stynchcombe*, supra [quoting another authority]. The *Raffel* Court explicitly rejected the contention that the possibility of impeachment by prior silence is an impermissible burden upon the exercise of Fifth Amendment rights. "We are unable to see that the rule that [an accused who] testified ... must testify fully, adds in any substantial manner to the inescapable embarrassment which the accused must experience in determining whether he shall testify or not."

[Court describes and quotes *Harris* and stresses the obligation of the defendant, if he takes the stand, to testify truthfully, and the importance of cross-examination in enhancing the reliability of the criminal process.]

Thus, impeachment follows the defendant's own decision to cast aside his cloak of silence and advances the truth-finding function of the criminal trial. We conclude that the Fifth Amendment is not violated by the use of prearrest silence to impeach a criminal defendant's credibility.

III

The petitioner also contends that use of prearrest silence to impeach his credibility denied him the fundamental fairness guaranteed by the Fourteenth Amendment. We do not agree. Common law traditionally has allowed witnesses to be impeached by their previous failure to state a fact in circumstances in which that fact naturally would have been asserted .... Each jurisdiction may formulate its own rules of evidence to determine when prior silence is so inconsistent with present statements that impeachment by reference to such silence is probative. For example, this Court has exercised its supervisory powers over federal courts to hold that prior silence cannot be used for impeachment where silence is not probative of a defendant's credibility and where prejudice to the defendant might result. See United States v. Hale, 422 U.S. 171, 180-181 (1975).[5]

---

[2] In *Raffel*, the defendant's decision not to testify at his first trial was an invocation of his right to remain silent protected by the Fifth Amendment. In this case, the petitioner remained silent before arrest, but chose to testify at his trial. Our decision today does not consider whether or under what circumstances prearrest silence may be protected by the Fifth Amendment. We simply do not reach that issue because the rule of *Raffel* clearly permits impeachment even if the prearrest silence were held to be an invocation of the Fifth Amendment right to remain silent.

[5] Mr. Justice Marshall contends that the petitioner's prearrest silence is not probative of his credibility. In this case, that is a question of state evidentiary law. In federal criminal proceedings the relevance of such silence, of course, would be a matter of federal law .... Mr. Justice Marshall's further conclusion that introduction of the evidence in this trial violated due process relies upon the Court's reasoning in *Doyle* and *Hale*. But the Court's decision in *Hale* rested upon nonconstitutional grounds, and *Doyle* is otherwise distinguishable.

Only in Doyle v. Ohio, 426 U.S. 610 (1976), did we find that impeachment by silence violated the Constitution. In that case, a defendant received the warnings required by *Miranda* when he was arrested for selling marihuana . . . .

In this case, no governmental action induced petitioner to remain silent before arrest. The failure to speak occurred before the petitioner was taken into custody and given *Miranda* warnings. Consequently, the fundamental unfairness present in *Doyle* is not present in this case. We hold that impeachment by use of prearrest silence does not violate the Fourteenth Amendment.

IV

Our decision today does not force any state court to allow impeachment through the use of prearrest silence. Each jurisdiction remains free to formulate evidentiary rules defining the situations in which silence is viewed as more probative than prejudicial. We merely conclude that the use of prearrest silence to impeach a defendant's credibility does not violate the Constitution. The judgment of the Court of Appeals is affirmed.

[The concurring opinion of Justice Stewart and the dissenting opinion of Justices Marshall and Brennan are omitted.]

■ NOTES ON THE USE OF SILENCE TO IMPEACH

1. If Jenkins had fled after the killing, taking the earliest flight to Florida, would proof of this fact at trial violate his right to travel? Would it impose a duty not to travel? Can it be seriously argued that the use against him of his silence violates his privilege against compelled self-incrimination or imposes on him a duty to confess?

2. Jenkins was a black resident of Detroit, apparently on parole, when he killed Redding. Did the fact that he did not look for police to tell them what happened refute his testimony that he acted in self-defense? Wasn't his reticence as "insolubly ambiguous" as defendant's silence in *Doyle* (Chapter 4B2, supra)?

3. Eric Weir stabbed Ronnie Buchanan to death in a parking lot near a poolhall. Weir left in his truck, and the next afternoon (17 hours later) police came to his trailer with a warrant to arrest him for murder. They advised him of the warrant, and for five to ten minutes nothing more was said, as Weir put on his socks and boots. After putting him in the police cruiser, officers gave him *Miranda* warnings. At trial, the evidence suggested that Buchanan pinned Weir to the ground. Weir testified that Buchanan attacked him, that Weir drew a knife from a scabbard at his waist, and that Buchanan "fell on it." Weir said he put the knife in a toolbox in his truck, but it was not found. On cross, the prosecutor suggested that Weir had fled and asked why he didn't tell friends what happened. The prosecutor also asked these questions:

> The next day when the State Police came to your house and searched it, why didn't you just tell them, "I lost it"?
> Why didn't you tell the State Police where the knife was?
> Why didn't you go to the police department?

Weir v. Fletcher, 658 F.2d 1126, 1127-1128 nn.3 & 4 (6th Cir. 1980). Weir challenged his conviction, but the Court concluded that questioning about post-arrest prewarning silence did not violate the Fifth Amendment:

> [W]e have consistently explained *Doyle* as a case where the government had induced silence by implicitly insuring the defendant that his silence would not be used against him.... In *Jenkins*, we noted that the failure to speak involved in that case occurred before the defendant was taken into custody and was given his *Miranda* warnings, commenting that no governmental action induced the defendant to remain silent before his arrest....
>
> In the absence of the sort of affirmative assurances embodied in the *Miranda* warnings, we do not believe that it violates due process of law for a State to permit cross-examination as to post-arrest silence when a defendant chooses to take the stand. A State is entitled, in such situations, to leave to the judge and jury under its own rules of evidence the resolution of the extent to which post-arrest silence may be deemed to impeach a criminal defendant's own testimony.

Fletcher v. Weir, 455 U.S. 603, 606-607 (1982). Does *Weir* mean police may arrest a suspect, sit with him in an interview room for 30 minutes, then Mirandize him, thus providing the prosecutor the benefit of the impeaching use of both prewarning silence (if he refuses to cooperate) and postwarning statements (if he talks after being warned)?

4. Suppose a suspect asks a police officer, after arrest but before *Miranda* warnings, "Do I have to talk to you?" or "Can I discuss the situation with a lawyer before talking about it?" If he gives the right answers, the officer will say no to the first question and yes to the second. In this situation, can the prosecutor ask defendant on cross why he didn't tell the officer the story he tells at trial? If the arresting officer doesn't reply to these queries, could the prosecutor ask such questions?

5. Glenn Charles was charged with murder after being found with the victim's car and other personal effects. He received *Miranda* warnings, then Charles told the arresting officer that he stole the car after finding it near Washtenaw and Hill Streets, two miles from the bus station. At trial, Charles testified that he stole the car from the parking lot of Kelly's Tire Co. in Ann Arbor (next to the bus station). On cross, the prosecutor brought out that the bus station and Kelly's Tire were next to the jail and asked whether that was where he "got the idea to come up with the story that you took a car from that location." Defendant claimed he was telling the truth, and the prosecutor then asked:

> Don't you think it's rather odd that if it were the truth that you didn't come forward and tell anybody at the time you were arrested, where you got the car? . . . Well, you told Detective LeVanseler back when you were first arrested, you stole the car back on Washtenaw and Hill Street?

Does the former question violate *Doyle*, or is the attack saved by the latter? See Anderson v. Charles, 447 U.S. 404, 406-407 (1980) (*Doyle* "does not apply to cross-examination that merely inquires into prior inconsistent statements" because it "makes no unfair use of silence" and cross cannot be "bifurcated" neatly; ambiguity in initial question was "quickly resolved" by later reference to what defendant told the arresting officer).

2. Contradiction

Impeaching a witness by contradiction entails a showing that something he said in his testimony is not so. Sometimes the impeachment is done by cross-examination, as questions force the witness to admit that he erred (even lied) on some point, but often it is accomplished by extrinsic evidence (testimony or something else, like a writing or recording), which for convenience we may call counterproof.

Assume that George is a witness for defendant Florence in Ernie's suit against her for property damage and personal injuries, arising out of a collision in which Florence drove her car into the rear of Ernie's at an intersection stop. On direct, George testifies that (1) Ernie caused the accident by suddenly backing up into the car driven by Florence after she had come to a full stop, (2) he (George) saw the accident from the curb and first met Florence when he spoke to her afterward about what he had seen, and (3) he was returning from making a purchase at Jason's Drugs when he saw the accident. During his case-in-rebuttal Ernie offers testimony (a) by Hal that Ernie's car was standing still when Florence ran into him, (b) by Ike (who is acquainted with George) that Florence and George had been seeing each other socially for at least a year prior to the accident, and (c) by Jason that his drugstore was closed for remodeling on the day of the accident.

If any one of Ernie's rebuttal witnesses is believed, his testimony is counterproof that contradicts George. Like inconsistent statements, the counterproof refutes him on specific points, though standing alone it is indefinite because it doesn't explain why George erred or lied. But the forensic skill of counsel and the psychology of the moment, taken in the larger factual setting of the case, may allow for lots of theories that explain why George should not be believed, and once these theories are expounded the stain on credibility may spread to other points in his testimony.

Setting a limit. Few witnesses testify so perfectly that nothing they say can be challenged. While no lawyer worth her salt would chase a witness at every opportunity, sometimes a lawyer pushes too far and courts react by setting limits, barring contradiction on trivial points. In doing so, courts recognize that *all* contradicting counterproof has some impeaching effect but let it in only if it has *additional* relevance—some relevance *independent* of its contradicting effect. Three kinds of counterproof appear in the cases:

The first is counterproof that not only contradicts but also tends to prove a substantive point, as is true of Hal's testimony that Ernie's car was standing still at the time of the accident. Here the counterproof ordinarily gets in, as it would even if it did not have contradicting effect, for it goes to the merits. Its impeaching (contradicting) effect is often forgotten, being overshadowed by the struggle of each party to establish one version of the facts and destroy the competing version. (In the example, Ernie is more intent on having Hal's version of events accepted as the truth than in persuading the jury through Hal's testimony that George is not a believable witness.)

The second is counterproof that not only contradicts but tends to prove some other impeaching point, as is true of Ike's testimony that Florence and George have been seeing each other. Here too the counterproof usually gets in, as would be true once again even if it did not have contradicting effect, for it tends to show bias. (Recall that bias may be proved by extrinsic evidence, so the attacking party is not limited to cross-examination.) The fact that it also catches George in a lie (if he has been seeing Florence socially, he is unlikely to be *merely mistaken* in saying he first met her at the time of the accident) adds a second impeaching dimension to the counterproof.

The third is counterproof that *only* contradicts, as is true of Jason's testimony that the drugstore was closed on the day of the accident. Here the evidence is usually excluded, for it has no relevancy *apart* from contradicting the witness. The fact that it catches George in an error or lie (who knows whether he has forgotten about the errand he was on that day or lied about it?) would not be viewed as reason enough to admit the evidence. It contradicts on what courts usually call a "collateral" point and would usually be excluded. Sometimes, however, courts admit counterproof on such a point where it seems that a witness could not be innocently mistaken. After all, even a point that seems collateral from the perspective of a trial may be a telltale point, perhaps the linchpin in the story, from the perspective of the witness. In other words, what is collateral in the suit may not be collateral in the life of the witness, so counterproof contradicting him on the point may convincingly suggest that he must be lying.

To sum up: Courts generally exclude counterproof that contradicts only on a collateral point. In effect, they require a dual relevancy of evidence offered to contradict a witness, for such proof must tend not only to prove that he lied or erred, but also to prove some other point that could make a difference in the case.

Why contradiction? Reconsider what you've just read. It seems to suggest that counterproof gets in to contradict only if it could get in anyway. Then why recognize "contradiction" as a fifth method of impeachment, rather than just an opportunity for making arguments to the jury?

There are two reasons.

One is that the contradicting effect of counterproof justifies departing from normal trial sequence. Thus Hal testified during the case-in-rebuttal of plaintiff Ernie, rather than during his case-in-chief, simply because the *occasion* to prove that Ernie did not suddenly drive backwards arose most strongly after defendant Florence presented her case. Though Hal's testimony went to substantive issues, Ernie could delay offering that testimony until after George had testified for Florence.

The other is that the contradicting effect of counterproof persuades courts to admit some evidence that would otherwise be excluded. If, for example, Florence had taken the witness stand and testified that she never had an accident before, Ernie would be allowed to prove (if he had the evidence) that in fact Florence had been in several prior accidents, particularly if she were at fault in them. Normally such proof would not get in: Such evidence would not be admissible to show she was a bad driver, hence careless on the occasion in question, for proving this point in that way would be disallowed by FRE 404 and 405. But if Florence "opens the door" by testifying to her accident-free past (which suggests that she is a careful driver, hence careful on the occasion in question), counterproof of prior accidents would be admitted to impeach her by contradiction, particularly if she were at fault.

Otherwise-excludable counterproof. Ponder for a moment the destination we have reached. It is paradoxical.

To avoid wasting time on trivia, we bar impeachment on collateral matters, admitting only counterproof that has dual relevancy. But then counterproof gets in that would not otherwise come in at all, just *because* it contradicts. When Florence testifies to her accident-free past, counterproof of prior accidents involving fault on her part comes in: It is admissible because it contradicts Florence (thus impeaches her) and bears on the question whether she is a careful driver, hence careful or negligent at the time of the accident. But the evidence comes in only to contradict her, not to prove she was negligent, because we can't use character evidence to prove negligence. So we insist that counterproof be relevant on some point other than contradiction, then let in counterproof that is incompetent on that other point, just because it contradicts!

Consider this point: When otherwise-excludable counterproof come in to contradict a witness, usually the testimony being contradicted *could itself* have been excluded. If counsel for Florence had asked her on direct whether she considered herself a careful driver, for example, counsel for Ernie might plausibly have objected in this vein:

> Your honor, whether Florence is or is not generally careful is beside the point. The issue is whether she was negligent in colliding with Ernie. She cannot prove she exercised due care then by testifying that she is normally careful. In the first place, her own testimony on that point is so hopelessly self-serving that it is unworthy of belief. In the second place, even if another witness was willing to testify to that point, that testimony would not be admissible. It would be barred by the rule against character evidence—Rules 404 and 405. And it could not get in as habit either, because it's too general to qualify under Rule 406.

Isn't that objection sound? Yet counsel for Ernie would not likely make the objection for a simple reason: There is glee in Ernie's camp when Florence is foolish enough to suggest that she has never been negligent in an accident before (counsel would know she had other accidents; he would have taken her deposition or gotten the record of her motor vehicle infractions), and being able to impeach her unwise claim is better for Ernie than keeping her from making the claim.

The unmentioned mechanism. If you look through the Rules, you will find that impeachment by contradiction is hardly mentioned. No provision addresses this kind of impeachment, and yet it goes on every day, and the scheme of limitation sketched above is more or less instinctively understood by courts and litigators. It is probable that if a party challenges this impeaching technique one day, a court will resolve the matter the way the Supreme Court resolved the question of impeachment by showing bias in *Abel.*

The concerns that lead to exclusion of counterproof that contradicts on collateral points are very much the concerns that find expression in FRE 403 and 611, and these can be and are read to limit this form of impeachment.

Procedural issues. You can see that the question whether the attacking lawyer can contradict by otherwise-excludable evidence raises questions of procedural fairness. If Florence testifies *on direct* that she has never been in an accident before, it seems fair to permit cross-examination and extrinsic evidence to prove the contrary. See Atkinson v. Atchison, Topeka & Santa Fe Ry., 197 F.2d 244 (10th Cir. 1952) (approving cross-examination of plaintiff like that set out above after she testified *on direct* to her cautious driving habits). But imagine a case in which Florence makes no reference to her driving history on direct, and *Ernie* first raises the matter on cross-examination:

Q (Ernie's counsel): Now can you tell me, ma'am, whether you consider yourself to be a careful driver.

A (Florence): Yes, sir, I do.

Q: Well isn't it a fact, ma'am, that last year you were involved in a collision with another car while you were in the wrong lane of the highway?

Should Ernie be allowed to "open his own door" for otherwise-excludable counterproof, contradicting a denial that he himself elicits? The answer is No, as courts recognize. See Nesbit v. Cumberland Contracting Co., 75 A.2d 339 (Md. 1950) (disapproving cross-examination of plaintiff on convictions for reckless driving and similar infractions, after defendant elicited on cross that plaintiff considered himself a good driver; this questioning "was not directed at any testimony of general competence developed in direct examination"). Reconsider this question after reading *Havens*, infra.

FRE 608 doesn't apply. Now ask yourself this question: Why doesn't FRE 608(b) prevent Ernie's lawyer from offering extrinsic evidence that Florence has had previous accidents, after she has testified that she never had an accident before?

The answer is that FRE 608(b) doesn't apply to impeachment by contradiction, except in one narrow situation. FRE 608(b) regulates *only* attacks on "character for truthfulness," so it does not block Ernie's lawyer from proving by extrinsic evidence that Florence was negligent in prior accidents. See United States v. Magallanez, 408 F.3d 672 (10th Cir. 2005) (FRE 608 does not block government from calling witness to contradict defendant's testimony). The one narrow situation, where FRE 608(b) does affect impeachment by contradiction, is this one: After a party cross-examines a witness on nonconviction misconduct in order to suggest untruthfulness, FRE 608(b) blocks use of "extrinsic evidence" to prove the misconduct. If the witness has denied the misconduct when asked about it, the attacking party is stuck with the answer.

■ PROBLEM 8-F. "That's Just Collateral, Your Honor"

Oswald is charged with a robbery in Seattle at 7:00 P.M. on July 14. Defendant claims alibi. As principal witness for the defense, Ardiss testifies that he operates the Jolly Roger Restaurant in Portland, that Oswald is a regular customer, and that he was there for the entire evening on July 14. The prosecutor cross-examines:

Q [prosecutor]: To the best of your knowledge, Mr. Ardiss, would you say that Oswald was in the Jolly Roger in Portland every day during the weeks prior to July 14, or was he gone for occasional periods of three or four days, or what?

A [Ardiss]: No, it would be my testimony that Mr. Oswald was in there every day during that time.

During the state's case-in-rebuttal, the prosecutor calls Detective Kinney of Seattle. Kinney testifies that he saw Oswald in Seattle on June 27 and that "Mr. Oswald told me that he had been there, in Seattle I mean, for the last couple of days before I ran into him." The prosecutor also calls Samuels, a waiter at the Jolly Roger in Portland, and elicits his testimony that "I never laid eyes on Mr. Oswald in the Jolly Roger."

Oswald has raised timely objection to the testimony of both Kinney and Samuels: "We have to object to this whole approach. He's just trying to distract the jury here. That's just collateral, Your Honor, what he's going into now. We strenuously object to these delaying and distracting tactics. It's just not proper impeachment."

How should the court rule, and why?

■ NOTES ON "COLLATERAL MATTERS" AND THE RELEVANCY OF COUNTERPROOF OFFERED TO CONTRADICT

1. In the Problem, Kinney contradicted what Ardiss said. Kinney's testimony put Oswald in Seattle on June 27th and for a couple of days before that, challenging Ardiss' testimony that Oswald was at the Jolly Roger in Portland every day in the weeks before July 14th. Would giving full credit to Kinney's testimony contradict Ardiss on a point that was relevant? Suppose the prosecutor called Detective Kinney during the state's case-in-chief to show that Oswald was in Seattle on June 27th and for a couple of days before. That wouldn't be very helpful to the prosecutor's case, would it?

2. Samuels also contradicted what Ardiss said. According to Samuels, Oswald was "never" at the Jolly Roger in Portland, which contradicts Ardiss' testimony that Oswald was there on July 14th. Doesn't this testimony contradict Ardiss on a point that counts?

3. Consider a case that raises both the question whether counterproof contradicts and the question whether it is collateral. Ivy Kelly is charged with the shooting murder of her husband Jack. She claims self-defense. She calls an expert who describes the battered woman syndrome and suggests that she fits the profile. The characteristics include frustration, stress disorders, depression, economic and emotional dependence, hope that the relationship will improve, poor self-image, and (most important) "isolation" and "learned helplessness." Should the prosecutor be allowed to rebut this testimony by proof that Ivy threatened injury to a trespasser, beat on the back door of her house with a shovel while Jack was inside, and became "verbally abusive" with a neighbor trying to clean an easement between their properties? See State v. Kelly, 685 P.2d 564, 569-571 (Wash. 1984) (No; this proof has no bearing on defendant's "inability to extricate herself from the marital relationship" and does not refute "evidence explaining her gradual loss of contact with her family and friends"). Is the court right? Or does the counterproof contradict testimony that she suffered from "learned helplessness"? If so, does it escape the "collateral matters" bar because "learned helplessness" is relevant to self-defense?

UNITED STATES v. HAVENS

United States Supreme Court
446 U.S. 620 (1980)

Mr. Justice WHITE delivered the opinion of the Court.

The petition for certiorari filed by the United States in this criminal case presented a single question: whether evidence suppressed as the fruit of an unlawful search and seizure may nevertheless be used to impeach a defendant's

Can evid obtained unlawfully be used to impeach Δ?

false trial testimony, given in response to proper cross-examination, where the evidence does not squarely contradict the defendant's testimony on direct examination.

I

Respondent was convicted of importing, conspiring to import, and intentionally possessing a controlled substance, cocaine. According to the evidence at his trial, Havens and John McLeroth, both attorneys from Ft. Wayne, Ind., boarded a flight from Lima, Peru, to Miami, Fla. In Miami, a customs officer searched McLeroth and found cocaine sewed into makeshift pockets in a T-shirt he was wearing under his outer clothing. McLeroth implicated respondent, who had previously cleared customs and who was then arrested. His luggage was seized and searched without a warrant. The officers found no drugs but seized a T-shirt from which pieces had been cut that matched the pieces that had been sewn to McLeroth's T-shirt. The T-shirt and other evidence seized in the course of the search were suppressed on motion prior to trial.

Both men were charged in a three-count indictment, but McLeroth pleaded guilty to one count and testified against Havens. Among other things, he asserted that Havens had supplied him with the altered T-shirt and had sewed the makeshift pockets shut. Havens took the stand in his own defense and denied involvement in smuggling cocaine. His direct testimony included the following:

Q. And you heard Mr. McLeroth testify earlier as to something to the effect that this material was taped or draped around his body and so on, you heard that testimony?
A. Yes, I did.
Q. Did you ever engage in that kind of activity with Mr. McLeroth and Augusto or Mr. McLeroth and anyone else on that fourth visit to Lima, Peru?
A. I did not.

On cross-examination, Havens testified as follows:

Q. Now, on direct examination, sir, you testified that on the fourth trip you had absolutely nothing to do with the wrapping of any bandages or tee shirts or anything involving Mr. McLeroth; is that correct?
A. I don't—I said I had nothing to do with any wrapping or bandages or anything, yes. I had nothing to do with anything with McLeroth in connection with this cocaine matter . . . .
Q. And your testimony is that you had nothing to do with the sewing of the cotton swatches to make pockets on that tee shirt?
A. Absolutely not.
Q. Sir, when you came through Customs, the Miami International Airport, on October 2, 1977, did you have in your suitcase Size 38-40 medium tee shirts?

An objection to the latter question was overruled and questioning continued:

Q. On that day, sir, did you have in your luggage a Size 38-40 medium man's tee shirt with swatches of clothing missing from the tail of that tee shirt?
A. Not to my knowledge. . . .
Q. Mr. Havens, I'm going to hand you what is Government's Exhibit 9 for identification and ask you if this tee shirt was in your luggage on October 2nd, 1975 [*sic*]?
A. Not to my knowledge. No.

Respondent Havens also denied having told a Government agent that the T-shirts found in his luggage belonged to McLeroth.

On rebuttal, a Government agent testified that Exhibit 9 had been found in respondent's suitcase and that Havens claimed the T-shirts found in his bag, including Exhibit 9, belonged to McLeroth. Over objection, the T-shirt was then admitted into evidence, the jury being instructed that the rebuttal evidence should be considered only for impeaching Havens' credibility.

The Court of Appeals reversed relying on Agnello v. United States, 269 U.S. 20 (1925), and Walder v. United States, 347 U.S. 62 (1954). The court held that illegally seized evidence may be used for impeachment only if the evidence contradicts a particular statement made by a defendant in the course of his direct examination. We reverse.

II . . .

These cases were understood by the Court of Appeals to hold that tainted evidence, inadmissible when offered as part of the Government's main case, may not be used as rebuttal evidence to impeach a defendant's credibility unless the evidence is offered to contradict a particular statement made by a defendant during his direct examination; a statement made for the first time on cross-examination may not be so impeached. This approach required the exclusion of the T-shirt taken from Havens' luggage because, as the Court of Appeals read the record, Havens was asked nothing on his direct testimony about the incriminating T-shirt or about the contents of his luggage; the testimony about the T-shirt, which the Government desired to impeach, first appeared on cross-examination, not on direct.

It is true that *Agnello* involved the impeachment of testimony first brought out on cross-examination and that in *Walder*, *Harris*, and *Hass*, the testimony impeached was given by the defendant while testifying on direct examination. In our view, however, a flat rule permitting only statements on direct examination to be impeached misapprehends the underlying rationale of *Walder*, *Harris*, and *Hass.* These cases repudiated the statement in *Agnello* that no use at all may be made of illegally obtained evidence. Furthermore, in *Walder*, the Court said that in *Agnello*, the Government had "smuggled in" the impeaching opportunity in the course of cross-examination. The Court also relied on the statement in *Agnello* that Agnello had done nothing "to justify cross-examination in respect of the evidence claimed to have been obtained by the search." The implication of *Walder* is that *Agnello* was a case of cross-examination having too tenuous a connection with any subject opened upon direct examination to permit impeachment by tainted evidence.

In reversing the District Court in the case before us, the Court of Appeals did not stop to consider how closely the cross-examination about the T-shirt and the luggage was connected with matters gone into in direct examination. If these questions would have been suggested to a reasonably competent cross-examiner by Havens' direct testimony, they were not "smuggled in"; and forbidding the Government to impeach the answers to these questions by using contrary and reliable evidence in its possession fails to take account of our cases, particularly *Harris* and *Hass.* In both cases, the Court stressed the importance of arriving at the truth in criminal trials, as well as the defendant's obligation to speak the truth in response to proper questions. We rejected the notion that the defendant's constitutional shield against having illegally seized evidence used against him could be "perverted into a license to use perjury by way of a defense, free from the risk of confrontation with prior inconsistent utterances." Both cases also held that the deterrent function of the rules excluding unconstitutionally obtained evidence is sufficiently served by denying its use to the government on its direct case. It was only a "speculative possibility" that also making it unavailable to the government for otherwise proper impeachment would contribute substantially in this respect.

Neither *Harris* nor *Hass* involved the impeachment of assertedly false testimony first given on cross-examination, but the reasoning of those cases controls this one. There is no gainsaying that arriving at the truth is a fundamental goal of our legal system. We have repeatedly insisted that when defendants testify, they must testify truthfully or suffer the consequences. This is true even though a defendant is compelled to testify against his will. It is essential, therefore, to the proper functioning of the adversary system that when a defendant takes the stand, the government be permitted proper and effective cross-examination in an attempt to elicit the truth. The defendant's obligation to testify truthfully is fully binding on him when he is cross-examined. His privilege against self-incrimination does not shield him from proper questioning. He would unquestionably be subject to a perjury prosecution if he knowingly lies on cross-examination. In terms of impeaching a defendant's seemingly false statements with his prior inconsistent utterances or with other reliable evidence available to the government, we see no difference of constitutional magnitude between the defendant's statements on direct examination and his answers to questions put to him on cross-examination that are plainly within the scope of the defendant's direct examination. Without this opportunity, the normal function of cross-examination would be severely impeded.

We also think that the policies of the exclusionary rule no more bar impeachment here than they did in *Walder*, *Harris*, and *Hass.* In those cases, the ends of the exclusionary rules were thought adequately implemented by denying the government the use of the challenged evidence to make out its case in chief. The incremental furthering of those ends by forbidding impeachment of the defendant who testifies was deemed insufficient to permit or require that false testimony go unchallenged, with the resulting impairment of the integrity of the factfinding goals of the criminal trial. We reaffirm this assessment of the competing interests, and hold that a defendant's statements made in response to proper cross-examination reasonably suggested by the defendant's direct examination are subject to otherwise proper impeachment by the government, albeit by evidence that has been illegally obtained that is inadmissible on the government's direct case, or otherwise, as substantive evidence of guilt.

In arriving at its judgment, the Court of Appeals noted that in response to defense counsel's objection to the impeaching evidence on the ground that the matter had not been "covered on direct" the trial court had remarked that "[i]t does not have to be covered on direct." . . . [W]e cannot accept respondent's suggestions that because of the illegal search and seizure, the Government's questions about the T-shirt were improper cross-examination. McLeroth testified that Havens had assisted him in preparing the T-shirt for smuggling. Havens, in his direct testimony, acknowledged McLeroth's prior testimony that the cocaine "was taped or draped around his body and so on" but denied that he had "ever engage[d] in that kind of activity with Mr. McLeroth . . . ." This testimony could easily be understood as a denial of any connection with McLeroth's T-shirt and as a contradiction of McLeroth's testimony. Quite reasonably, it seems to us, the Government on cross-examination called attention to his answers on direct and then asked whether he had anything to do with sewing the cotton swatches on McLeroth's T-shirt. This was cross-examination growing out of Havens' direct testimony; and, as we hold above, the ensuing impeachment did not violate Havens' constitutional rights.

We reverse the judgment of the Court of Appeals and remand the case to that court for further proceedings consistent with this opinion.

So ordered.

Mr. Justice BRENNAN, joined by Mr. Justice MARSHALL and joined in Part I by Mr. Justice STEWART and Mr. Justice STEVENS, dissenting.

The Court upholds the admission at trial of illegally seized evidence to impeach a defendant's testimony deliberately elicited *by the Government* under the cover of impeaching an accused who takes the stand in his own behalf. I dissent. Criminal defendants now told that prosecutors are licensed to insinuate otherwise inadmissible evidence under the guise of cross-examination no longer have the unfettered right to elect whether or not to testify in their own behalf. Not only is today's decision an unwarranted departure from prior controlling cases, but, regrettably, it is yet another element in the trend to depreciate the constitutional protections guaranteed the criminally accused . . . .

The Court's opinion attempts to discredit *Agnello* by casting a strawman as its holding, and then demolishing the pitiful scarecrow of its own creation. . . .

[T]he actual principle of *Agnello*, as discerned by *Walder*, is that the Government may not employ its power of cross-examination to predicate the admission of illegal evidence. In other words, impeachment by cross-examination about—or introduction of—suppressible evidence must be warranted by defendant's statements upon direct questioning. That principle is not at all inconsistent with later cases holding that the defendant may not take advantage of evidentiary suppression to advance specific perjurious claims as part of his direct case.

Nor is it correct to read *Agnello* as turning upon the tenuity of the link between the cross-examination involved there and the subject matter of the direct examination. The cross-examination about Agnello's previous connection with cocaine was reasonably related to his direct testimony that he lacked knowledge that the commodity he was transporting was cocaine. For "[t]he possession by Frank Agnello of the can of cocaine which was seized tended to show guilty knowledge and criminal intent on his part . . . ." Thus, the constitutional flaw found in *Agnello* was that the introduction of the tainted evidence had been prompted by statements of the accused first elicited upon cross-examination. And the case was so read in *Walder v. United States*. That decision specifically stated that a defendant "must be free to deny all the elements of the case against him without thereby giving leave to the Government to introduce by way of rebuttal evidence illegally secured by it, and therefore not available for its case in chief." Since as a matter of the law of evidence it would be perfectly permissible to cross-examine a defendant as to his denial of complicity in the crime, the quoted passage in *Walder* must be understood to impose a further condition before the prosecutor may refer to tainted evidence—that is, some particular direct testimony by the accused that relies upon "the Government's disability to challenge his credibility."

In fact, the Court's current interpretation of *Agnello* and *Walder* simply trivializes those decisions by transforming their Fourth Amendment holdings into nothing more than a constitutional reflection of the common-law evidentiary rule of relevance.

Finally, the rationale of *Harris v. New York* and *Oregon v. Hass* does not impel the decision at hand. The exclusionary rule exception established by *Harris* and *Hass* may be fairly easily cabined by defense counsel's willingness to forgo certain areas of questioning. But the rule prescribed by the Court in this case passes control of the exception to the Government, since the prosecutor can lay the predicate for admitting otherwise suppressible evidence with his own questioning. To be sure, the Court requires that cross-examination be "proper"; however, traditional evidentiary principles accord parties fairly considerable latitude in cross-examining opposing witnesses. In practical terms, therefore, today's holding allows even the moderately talented prosecutor to "work in . . . evidence on cross-examination [as it would] in its case in chief . . . ." Walder v. United States, 347 U.S., at 66. To avoid this consequence, a defendant will be compelled to forgo testifying on his own behalf . . . .

. . . .

Accordingly, I dissent.

■ NOTES ON CONTRADICTING A WITNESS BY CONSTITUTIONALLY EXCLUDABLE COUNTERPROOF

1. Given the decision in *Harris*, the outcome in *Havens* is hardly a surprise. Is *Havens* likely to have an impact on how police gather evidence?

2. The T-shirt not only contradicted what Havens said on cross; it also contradicted his direct. The Court takes pains to say the prosecutor may offer constitutionally excludable evidence to contradict testimony elicited on cross, but it is not clear why it does so. Isn't Justice Brennan right that letting the government impeach testimony elicited *on cross* by illegally seized evidence "passes control"? Doesn't it let the government evade the exclusionary principle?

3. *Havens* says that in *Agnello* the government "'smuggled in" the impeaching opportunity. There, defendant testified that he did not know what certain packages contained (it was cocaine), and was asked on cross whether he had ever seen cocaine before (he replied, essentially, "never"). If *Agnello* arose today, would such cross be "reasonably suggested" by the direct, so a denial paves the way to admit illegally seized evidence? In a case similar to *Agnello*, one court said yes (cross is related; illegally seized evidence comes in). It was another drug prosecution, and defendant testified on direct that he didn't know the packages he delivered contained Quaaludes (he thought they were "Greek statues"). On cross, the government asked whether he was "familiar with Quaaludes." Defendant said no, and the government contradicted the denial by showing that agents seized Quaaludes from his car at the time of the offense (the search was illegal). See United States v. Hernandez, 646 F.3d 970 (5th Cir. 1981) (although never overruled, *Agnello* has been "practically eviscerated," and *Havens* controls), *cert. denied*, 454 U.S. 1082 (1981). Cases like *Havens* and *Hernandez* suggest, don't they, that if *Havens* arose today, defendant could not avoid paving the way to admit the T-shirt by confining his direct to saying he "knew nothing about what McLeroth was carrying"? Doesn't this outcome make Justice Brennan's point (control has passed to the government)?

4. One small consolation for defendants. As decisions from Illinois illustrate, courts sometimes *do* find that the prosecutor went too far by expanding cross into new areas. See People v. Lawson, 762 N.E.2d 633 (Ill. App. 2001) (defendant testified on direct that he was going from a pool hall to a store at time of robbery; prosecutor asked on cross whether he told detective, in suppressed statement, that he "had witnesses" who saw him at the pool hall but "couldn't name them," since this question was "not related to any specific statements that defendant made on direct") (reversing), *app. denied*, 770 N.E.2d 222 (2002); People v. Williams, 564 N.E.2d 168 (Ill. App. 1990) (defendant described his military service on direct; on cross, prosecutor asked whether he had "ever" seen a .38 caliber weapon or bullet, and defendant said no; prosecutor should not then have introduced .38 caliber bullet illegally seized on arrest) (reversing), *app. denied*, 567 N.E.2d 341 (1991).

5. State courts remain free to fashion rules giving more protection to defendants. See, e.g., State v. Brunelle, 534 A.2d 198 (Vt. 1987) (refusing to follow *Havens,* and rejecting even *Harris* in holding that suppressed evidence may not be introduced to impeach defendants; even if defendant had stayed off the stand because the court ruled that the evidence could be used to impeach, defendant could still raise the point on appeal).

COMMENT/PERSPECTIVE: *Harris, Harvey, Havens* (3 Hs Limiting 3 Ms)

Broadly speaking, the subjects of *Havens* and *Harris* (which you have read) and the *Harvey* case (which you have not seen) are exclusionary doctrines that discourage law enforcement from violating citizen rights. These are attempts to control police by excluding from criminal trials evidence obtained in violation of rights secured by the Fourth, Fifth, and Sixth amendments (covering, respectively, searches and seizures, self-incrimination, and right of counsel). Courts did not always exclude evidence seized in violation of constitutional rights, although the practice began in the federal system more than a century ago. See Weeks v. United States, 232 U.S. 383 (1914) (requiring exclusion, in federal criminal trials, of evidence seized in violation of the Fourth Amendment). In the days of *Weeks,* it was thought that most provisions in the Bill of Rights applied only to the federal government, not to the states. Gradually most of these were "incorporated" into the Due Process Clause of the Fourteenth Amendment (which does apply to the states), and now these three exclusionary doctrines apply to the states too. *Harris* and *Havens* address the question whether these doctrines block use of illegally seized evidence *to impeach by contradiction* testimony by the accused (both say no, and allow the impeaching use of such evidence). All three doctrines are developed in detail by many cases over many years, so the memory aid suggested here does not tell the whole story. Still, it may help if you bear in mind that three salient opinions on the exclusionary doctrines have defendant names beginning with M and three opinions on the impeachment question have defendant names beginning with H: *Mapp* and *Havens* (Fourth Amendment); *Miranda* and *Harris* (Fifth Amendment); *Massiah* and *Harvey* (Sixth Amendment). Here are the full cites: Mapp v. Ohio, 367 U.S. 643 (1961) (Fourth Amendment exclusionary doctrine applies to states); United States v. Havens, 446 U.S. 620 (1980) (evidence seized in violation of Fourth Amendment can be used to impeach); Miranda v. Arizona, 384 U.S. 436 (1966) (Fifth Amendment requires warnings before custodial interrogation); Harris v. New York, 401 U.S. 222 (1971) (statements taken in violation of right to warning may be used to impeach); Massiah v. United States, 377 U.S. 201 (1964) (Sixth Amendment right to counsel requires exclusion of statements taken from defendants in custody who have lawyers); Michigan v. Harvey, 494 U.S. 344 (1989) (statements taken in violation of Sixth Amendment right of counsel can be used to impeach).

■ PROBLEM 8-G. "Have You Ever Sold Narcotics Before?"

Young is charged with selling narcotics. He testifies on direct that he did not commit the charged offense and he was elsewhere at the time. On cross-examination, the prosecutor asks, "Have you ever sold narcotics before?"

The defense timely objects. Is the question improper? On what ground?

What if defendant answers before counsel interposes an objection: "No, sir, I never have sold narcotics, not this time and not before either." During the state's case-in-rebuttal, the prosecutor offers testimony by undercover agents that they saw defendant sell narcotics on three previous unrelated occasions. The defense raises timely objection. Should this testimony be excluded? Why or why not?

■ NOTES ON CONTRADICTING A WITNESS BY COUNTERPROOF EXCLUDABLE UNDER THE RULES

1. Does *Havens* suggest that the tactic pursued by the prosecutor in Problem 8-G is proper? In theory, the answer is no because both the rule in *Havens* and the rationale behind it differ from the rule involved in Problem 8-G and the rationale behind it.

(a) *Havens* involves a constitutional principle (a limit on an exclusionary doctrine, under which illegally seized evidence can be used to contradict defendant's testimony). In contrast, the rule involved in Problem 8-G is a principle of evidence law (a limit on the protective policy in FRE 404).

(b) The constitutional principle seeks to balance incentives—encouraging police to respect individual rights while discouraging defendants from lying on the witness stand. The evidence rule seeks to achieve fairness (it is unfair to ask defendants to defend their whole lives, as opposed to specific charges) and sound verdicts (we don't want juries thinking about other crimes when the question is guilt of the *charged* crime).

(c) Still, the bad news is that decisions on constitutional points sometimes affect other areas, and *Havens* is sometimes cited as authority for the point that cross-examination and contradiction are proper because testimony

elicited on cross is reasonably related to the direct, even if no constitutional issue is involved. See, e.g., United States v. Sotomayor-Vazquez, 249 F.3d 1, 11 (1st Cir. 2001) (sweeping denial of involvement in schemes like the one charged paved the way for proof that defendant engaged in such a scheme before; court invokes *Havens* although no constitutional issue was raised).

(d) More bad news: Often the facts raise *both* a constitutional issue and an evidence issue, but the bright glare of the constitutional issue distracts courts from seeing or paying attention to related issues of evidence law. See, e.g., United States v. Martinez, 967 F.2d 1343, 1346 (9th Cir. 1992) (defendant denied knowing about cocaine in house; on cross, government asked whether he "ever used or sold cocaine," then contradicted his denial by proving that earlier he engaged in illegally intercepted conversation about cocaine transaction; cross reasonably suggested by direct); Ware v. United States, 579 A.2d 701 (D.C. App. 1990) (defendant testified on direct that he did not sell dilaudid to *B* or "to anyone else" that day; government properly showed 17 dilaudid tablets recovered from his car in illegal search).

2. In Problem 8-G, assume that Young testified *on direct* that he had "never been involved with drugs before." Then it should be all right for the prosecutor to raise on cross (or show by extrinsic evidence) defendant's prior drug convictions. United States v. Gaertner, 705 F.2d 210, 214-216 (7th Cir. 1983) (defendant "raised the issue of his lack of prior involvement in drug trafficking," thus "opened the door on the question of his prior or present drug involvement"), *cert. denied*, 464 U.S. 1071 (1984); United States v. Paulsen, 645 F.2d 13, 14-15 (8th Cir.) (admitting "collateral evidence" of drug run after defendant testified on direct that he "had never been involved with drugs or drug dealing"), *cert. denied*, 454 U.S. 848 (1981).

3. Some good news for defendants is that not all modern courts apply the logic of *Havens* to evidence excludable under the Rules. Consider the trial of Gerald Simpson for possession of cocaine with intent to distribute, and possession of dilaudid and marijuana. Simpson testified, sticking to the facts underlying the charges. On cross, the government tried to broaden the inquiry, asking whether he had "ever seen these yellow pills before" (referring to dilaudid) and he admitted that he had and said he was familiar with the pills, but denied knowing how the drug is commonly packaged. To undermine the claim of unfamiliarity with packaging, the prosecutor asked whether he had been carrying dilaudid when he was arrested six years before (he denied it). The reviewing court disapproved. Prior possession was not "relevant to any permissible purpose," and the initial question served only "to demonstrate Simpson's criminal propensities," which is forbidden by FRE 404. The claim that the government could contradict his denial by proving the prior conviction was "circular." It might have been proper to ask whether Simpson had dilaudid when arrested *this* time, but the government "may not use impermissible means" to get at this point by asking about general knowledge of dilaudid packaging. See United States v. Simpson, 992 F.2d 1224, 1225-1226 (D.C. Cir. 1993) (reversing conviction for plain error), *cert. denied*, 510 U.S. 906 (1993).

REPAIRING CREDIBILITY

When a witness has been impeached, ordinarily some party (generally the one who called the witness) has an interest in repairing the damage. The Rules allow for this strategy, but two conditions are paramount: First, generally courts disallow any attempt to repair credibility before the attack has come. In the specific context of character witnesses, FRE 608(a) states this "no bolstering" principle directly (allowing proof of truthfulness "only after" an attack suggesting untruthfulness). Second, the repair should be made at the point of attack. Both these limits bring some difficulties in application, as you will see.

Generally courts take the view that a party who anticipates an attack—her witness has some obvious vulnerability—may bring out the impeaching facts first. This strategy is not viewed as violating the first condition mentioned above. Thus it is permissible on direct (1) for a party to adduce testimony by his expert that she is being paid for her services (recall Problem 8-A, The Hired Gun), (2) for the calling party (prosecutor or defense or civil litigant) to bring out that its witness has been convicted of crimes, (3) for the prosecutor to bring out that its witness entered into a plea bargain, and (4) for the calling party to bring out any connection or affinity that she has with the witness, such as personal or business relationships, which are obvious grounds of bias that the other side would likely raise. *Failing* to raise such points would make the calling party appear to be "hiding something," which would to some extent inflate artificially the impeaching impact if the adversary first raised these points on cross.

1. What Constitutes an Attack on Credibility That Paves the Way for Repair?

Obviously credibility is attacked if the other side engages in any of the three recognized attacks on character—cross-examining the target witness on nonconviction misconduct under FRE 608(b), adducing testimony by a character witness that the target witness has bad character for truth and veracity, which is provable by opinion or reputation testimony under FRE 608(a), or proving that the target witness has prior convictions, which FRE 609 allows. *Sometimes* proving bias or prior inconsistent statements is viewed as inviting repair, but not usually, and we revisit these matters in the next sections.

Generally, however, evidence that simply *contradicts or refutes* testimony given by a witness does not invite rehabilitation or repair. The question whether evidence should be admitted when it contradicts or refutes other evidence is dealt with under the principles we examined in Problems 8-F ("That's Just Collateral, Your Honor") and 8-G ("Have You Ever Sold Narcotics Before?") and the *Havens* case.

In an Oregon case, the question arose whether a prosecutor could repair the credibility of an alleged sexual assault victim (14-16 years old at the time) in the trial of her stepfather for the crimes. On cross, the prosecutor asked the stepfather whether he was "trying to tell the jury" that the victim and her sister were "lying because they don't like the way you discipline them?" He answered yes, and the prosecutor then adduced testimony from the girls' aunt to the effect that she had known the victim since she was born and she was "honest and truthful." The Oregon Supreme Court held that "merely contradicting" the testimony of an adverse witness is not an attack on truthfulness that opens the door to character evidence. The court added that the prosecutor cannot create a foundation for character evidence by asking whether a witness has lied: "An affirmative response to such an inquiry does not put the character for truthfulness of the prosecution witness at issue, nor does it open the door to rehabilitation evidence of truthful character." State v. Carr, 725 P.2d 1287 (Or. 1986) (reversing conviction).

■ NOTES ON REBUTTING IMPEACHING ATTACKS

1. If the calling party tries to disarm an expected attack, the other side faces the dilemma of regaining the rhetorical initiative. If, for example, a party who calls an expert forthrightly puts on the table the financial arrangements that are in place, the other side more-or-less *has* to raise the matter again in order to convey that these arrangements really have *impeaching* effect. On this point, recall Problem 8-A (The Hired Gun).

2. Similar situations recur in other settings where the calling party tries to disarm an expected attack. If defendant testifies on direct, for example, that he has been twice before convicted (the defense knows the prosecutor will ask about the convictions if they are not already "out there"), what can the prosecutor do? See Acevedo v. State, 467 So. 2d 220, 225 (Miss. 1985) (where defendant doesn't mention all his prior convictions, prosecutor can "ask the defendant of what crimes or misdemeanors he has been convicted," and whether he "denies being convicted of a particular crime on a particular date in a particular court"). What if defendant has listed every past conviction?

3. Do you agree with *Carr,* described above, that the father's testimony did not suggest untruthfulness on the part of the daughter? Whether or not to believe the mother and stepfather (who testified that they act "as one" in disciplining their children), the defense was certainly proper—perhaps their program of discipline really does explain the accusations. Once that defense is tendered, what can a prosecutor do, other than trying to prove that the girls are truthful? In the end, however, *Carr* seems correct under FRE 608.

4. In the trial of Andre Maltais for murder, the state calls his girlfriend Robin Murphy, who saw the crime. On cross, the defense brings out that Murphy was "totally drunk" at the time, that she was a longtime drug user, that she "lied to police" about the murder, and that she is "a prostitute, a lesbian, and an alcoholic." On redirect examination of Murphy, can the prosecutor bring out that defendant introduced her to drugs when "she was eleven years old and he picked her up hitchhiking"? Commonwealth v. Maltais, 438 N.E.2d 847, 854 (Mass. 1982) (Yes). Do these questions rehabilitate Murphy, or only prejudice the defense? Are they justified because defendant "opened the door"?

2. Evidence of Good Character

Recall the example of witness Grace Gardner, whose credibility was attacked through testimony by Coach Jones that she has a bad reputation in Riverdale for truth and veracity (section A3c, supra). After such attack, the calling party might seek to repair the damage by offering testimony that in fact she is truthful:

Q (to character witness): Reverend Gram, are you acquainted with Grace Gardner?
A (Reverend Gram): Yes, sir, I am.
Q: She is a member of your Riverdale congregation, is she not?
A: Yes, she is.
Q: And you have had occasion to work with her on church projects?
A: Yes, sir, I did. She served as chair of our building committee several years ago and did a superb job, I might add.
Q: Yes, and you got to know her quite well during that period, did you not?
A: Yes, sir.
Q: How would you estimate her character for truth and veracity?
A: Oh, it is of the very highest order, sir, the very highest order. She is a scrupulously honest woman.
Q: And you would believe her under oath?
A: Oh, yes, absolutely. I would believe her whether she is under oath or not.
Q: Thank you, Reverend. Your witness, counsel.

Such supporting testimony is allowed under FRE 608(a), which paves the way for "opinion or reputation" testimony supporting credibility after "character for truthfulness has been attacked." See United States v. Bonner, 302 F.3d 776, 780 (7th Cir. 2002) (after defense suggested that *A* gained by cooperating with government, prosecutor could ask *G* "what kind of woman" *A* was; he said *A* was "an honest mother" and "a good wife" and "a friend of mine") (defense objected, and court required a "more precise question").

Note that the supporting party laid a foundation for Reverend Gram's good opinion, and of course the supporting party hopes very much that any stature and esteem that the character witness might bring with him to the stand will "rub off" a little on the witness being supported, and generally on the cause of the supporting party.

Cross-examination. There are risks in this strategy. If Coach Jones harbors a bad opinion of Gardner, presumably he has reasons, perhaps arising out of specific instances of her behavior. The attacking party (who called Coach Jones) may learn of these reasons and is entitled (if he can) to turn these to good use in cross-examining Reverend Gram:

Q (attacking party): Now Reverend Gram, you say Grace Gardner is an honest woman, is that right?
A (Reverend Gram): Yes, sir.
Q: And you would believe her, regardless whether she is sworn to tell the truth or not?
A: Yes, sir.
Q: Well, sir, did you know that she embezzled money from her employer the Seacoast Bank? Did you know that?
A: No sir, and I don't know it now. Whatever people may have said—
Q: And that she pleaded guilty to embezzlement charges, did you know that?
A: No.

Here as in the case of cross-examination of character witnesses under FRE 405, the ostensible purpose is to test the knowledge and judgment of the good character witness. With questions as damning as those suggested here, the attacking party comes out ahead regardless how the character witness replies. If Gram did not know of the incidents, then he lacked important information about Gardner; if he did know of them, then his good opinion of her honesty is hard to understand. Here as before, the cross-examiner must have a reasonable basis for the questions, or they amount to gross misconduct.

Sometimes it is hard to figure out whether an impeaching attack really calls truthfulness into question. Consider now a case raising a real challenge on this point.

UNITED STATES v. MEDICAL THERAPY SCIENCES

United States Court of Appeals for the Second Circuit
583 F.2d 36 (1978)

[Stanley Berman and his Connecticut company, Medical Therapy Sciences, were convicted of filing false claims for Medicare payments, and related charges. Government proof suggested that Berman devised a scheme to obtain payment from insurance carriers in Connecticut and New York, using Medical Therapy and its New York branch, Respiratory Specialties, to double bill for the same patients, and to charge for more expensive equipment than was provided and for supplies neither delivered nor needed. Barbara Russell, a trusted employee and personal intimate of Berman, was an unindicted coconspirator who testified for the government. She supervised much of the billing and testified that she and Berman often discussed the applicable rules and practices of the companies, suggesting that both knew they were obtaining funds to which they were not entitled. On appeal, Berman contended that the trial judge erred in permitting the prosecutor to call character witnesses to bolster Russell's credibility, and that this error was crucial in light of Berman's claim that Russell alone perpetrated the frauds.]

MOORE, J.

Rule 608(a) . . . provides that character evidence may be used to support a witness, but limits its use so that "evidence of truthful character is admissible only after the character of the witness for truthfulness has been attacked by opinion or reputation evidence or otherwise." Berman's claim is that the foundation for character evidence was not present in this case because Russell's character for truthfulness had not been attacked within the meaning of the Rule. He argues that cross examination elicited only matters of Russell's bias in favor of the Government and against Berman and that, in any event, the Government itself initially brought to the jury's attention, on its direct examination of Russell, the facts that she had had two prior convictions and that she had been accused by Berman of having embezzled money from Medical Therapy. Berman contends that the Government should not thereafter have been allowed to bolster her credibility when the defense cross examined only as to matters brought out on direct.

The Government's argument is that, in questioning Russell on direct as to her prior convictions, the prosecutor was only anticipating defense impeachment, as it had the right to do, so that the jury would not gain the impression that the Government was attempting to hide information from them. Because Russell's truthfulness was "attacked" on cross examination, the Government argues that Rule 608(a) by its terms permits it the use of character evidence, notwithstanding its own elicitation of Russell's background.[2] Although the issue is a close one, we believe that the decision to permit the evidence in question was one within the trial judge's discretion.

As to the point that the Government first elicited the impeaching facts, we agree that the Government had the right to proceed as it did. Rule 608 itself contains no limitation that precludes a party from offering character evidence under circumstances where it anticipates impeachment; rather, the event that triggers the applicability of the Rule is an "attack" on the witness' veracity. While under the Federal Rules, a party *may* impeach his own witness, FRE 607, there is a vast difference between putting that witness' veracity in issue by eliciting the impeaching facts and merely revealing the witness' background. Indeed, even in

[2] The Government also argues that Berman waived any objection on the ground that the Government had been the first to elicit the "impeachment facts" from its own witness. While it is true that this precise point was not raised below, defense counsel did interpose an objection to the character witnesses pursuant to Rule 608(a), and we think that the issue is properly before us.

jurisdictions where a party may not discredit his own witness, it has been held that the fact of prior convictions may be brought out on direct examination for non-impeachment purposes. As stated by the New York Court of Appeals,

> The law does not limit a party to witnesses of good character, nor does it compel a party to conceal the bad record of his witnesses from the jury, to have it afterwards revealed by the opposing party with telling effect. Such a rule would be unfair alike to the party calling the witness and the jury .... [W]hen a disreputable witness is called and frankly presented to the jury as such, the party calling him represents him for the occasion and the purposes of the trial as worthy of belief.

People v. Minsky, 124 N.E. 126, 127 (N.Y. 1919).

While we do not think that Rule 608(a) should make supporting character evidence available to a party who elicits impeachment material on direct examination for impeaching purposes, we do believe that, when the tenor of the direct examination does not suggest an "attack" on veracity, and when cross examination *can* be characterized as such an attack, the trial judge should retain the discretion to permit the use of character witnesses. His proximity to the situation allows him to make the determination of when, and by whom, an attack is made. Were the rule to be otherwise, a party would have to choose between revealing, on direct, the background of a witness and its right to use character evidence if the witness' veracity is subsequently impugned.

In the instant case, the Government's direct questioning of Russell was brief and to the point. She was simply asked whether, when she left Medical Therapy to establish a business which was in competition with Berman's, she had taken patients from Berman's operation; she answered in the negative. This questioning covered about one page. The prosecutor also elicited the fact that, near the end of Russell's employment with Berman, at a time when relations between the two were strained, Berman had accused Russell of taking $70 from him, and that she had denied the charge (claiming, in fact, that Berman had owed her and her husband for past loans), but had repaid the money to avoid any further problem. Finally, she admitted her two prior convictions for obtaining amphetamines by fraudulent practices, but explained that she had committed the acts at a time when she had been addicted to the drug for weight control purposes and that she had sought help after her second conviction. Even this interchange covered only five pages of transcript. At least on the basis of the cold record before us, it appears that, in a very real sense, the Government did not put Russell's veracity in issue. Thus, though we believe that the trial judge should retain discretion to disallow the use of character evidence under circumstances such as this, we think he must also be permitted to allow it when, subsequent to the revelation of a witness' problems on direct, the opponent paints the witness with more accusatory strokes—especially where, as here, wrongdoing which implicates veracity is alleged and denied.

In this case, however, Berman argues that his counsel did not open the door to character evidence because his cross examination of Russell did not constitute an "attack on veracity." We conclude, however, that Judge Carter could have properly characterized the defense's treatment of Russell as an attack within the meaning of Rule 608(a).

In this case, cross examination of Russell included sharp questioning about her prior convictions, which were predicated on activities characterized as fraudulent. When such convictions are used for impeachment purposes, as they were on cross examination here, we think that the door is opened to evidence in support of truthfulness.[3]

Russell's character was also attacked by "specific act" evidence, to wit, allegations that she had embezzled money and stolen patients from Berman's company. While Berman argues that such evidence, because it involved her efforts to set up a competing business, bore solely on her bias against him, and, as such, did not constitute an attack on character, we do not think that the implications were so limited. As noted by the commentators, evidence of bias can take many forms. Some types of bias, for example bias stemming from a relationship with a party, do not necessarily involve any issue relating to the moral character of the witness, but suggest only that the witness' testimony may perhaps unwittingly be slanted for reasons unrelated to general propensity for untruthfulness. As such, character evidence is not relevant to meet such an attack. On the other hand, alleged partiality based on hostility or self-interest may assume greater significance if it is sought to be proven by conduct rising to the level of corruption.[4] Certainly, the embezzlement and theft of which Russell was accused can be said to fall within the category of corrupt conduct, within the contemplation of Rule 608(a).[5] Furthermore, Russell consistently denied the larceny that was ascribed to her by the defense attack.[6] Under such

---

[3] Indeed, under Rule 609(a)(2), a witness may always be impeached by proof of a prior conviction if the crime involved "dishonesty or false statement." . . . Since the attack on Russell was predicated in part on convictions for fraud, which are deemed to have a bearing on a witness' truthfulness, supporting character evidence would be relevant under Rule 608(a) to meet the impeachment.

[4] Here, Berman did attempt to prove Russell's embezzlement by extrinsic evidence—i.e., the testimony of defense witness Spyek. Further, defense witness Menti testified that Russell had suggested that he "steal" from Medical Therapy to supply her competing business with equipment, contrary to Russell's denials; he also testified that he had seen Medical Therapy equipment at Russell's company. While this evidence may have suggested bias, and while it was admissible pursuant to the defense theory that Russell had falsified claims in order to obtain money for her own purposes, it also served to attack Russell's veracity in a severe manner by suggesting that she had lied when she denied the embezzlement and theft.

[5] Embezzlement convictions are treated by the Conference Report as relevant to truthfulness. See n.3 supra. If embezzlement is alleged, but it never was the subject of a conviction, logically the accusation does not lose its character as an attack on truthfulness.

[6] See n.4 supra, to the effect that the defense attack here went far beyond mere accusation by cross-examination and denial. Other witnesses were called to contradict Russell's denials in order to support the defense's theory that Russell had the motive to commit the frauds, on her own, and for her own purposes—that she could have submitted false claims to cover up for her embezzlement. Though contradiction cannot usually be characterized as an "attack" on character, here the contradiction specifically implicated Russell's veracity.

We think that trial judges should be permitted, under Rule 608, to exercise sound discretion to permit or deny a party the use of character evidence to support veracity. As is always the case, the balancing test under Rule 403 must be considered before any such evidence is permitted over objection. Furthermore, it is always open to the trial judge to deny a party the opportunity to present only cumulative evidence bearing solely on credibility.

a circumstance, the commentators again agree that "rehabilitating evidence should be allowed in the judge's discretion if he finds the witness' denial has not erased the jury's doubts." [3 J. Weinstein & M. Berger, Weinstein's Evidence ¶608[05], at 608-41-42 (1977).]

We think, in sum, that the decision to permit the character evidence must be affirmed on the facts. We emphasize, however, that discretion in this area must be exercised with circumspection so that the jury's attention is not diverted from the main issues to be tried. It is not every cross examination that should trigger the authority of Rule 608(a)'s provision for supporting character evidence. However, since the attack in this case went even beyond cross examination, and since Berman's guilt was established not only by Russell's testimony, but also by ample supporting evidence, both documentary and in the form of testimony from the Blue Cross specialist and from other employees of Medical Therapy, we affirm.

Judgment affirmed.

■ NOTES ON PROVING TRUTHFULNESS: CHARACTER AND BEHAVIORAL SYNDROME EVIDENCE

1. Did the prosecutor succeed in "suckering" the defense into an attack that paved the way for supporting evidence? Does the strategy of the prosecution amount to advance (and hidden) support that should be disallowed?

2. Should courts admit expert testimony that a person is telling the truth? Generally they exclude such testimony and express suspicion when an expert even gets close to endorsing the truthfulness of a litigant or major player. See State v. Leahy, 78 P.3d 136 (Or. App. 2006) (error to let police officer testify, "I believe that it most definitely happened exactly the way the victim described it to me") (cannot allow witness, expert or lay, to comment on credibility of another witness); United States v. Muckala, 303 F.3d 1207, 1217 (10th Cir. 2002) (in suit by nurse alleging sexual harassment at hospital, allowing treating psychiatrist to describe her psychological condition but not to give his opinion on her truthfulness in bringing the complaint or to say whether he believes she was harassed). Often courts raise two objections: One is that experts do not know how to distinguish truthful from untruthful tendencies or dispositions in people; the other is that juries can resolve credibility issues, and expert testimony might even infringe on the prerogatives of the jury. The latter ground is obsolete, see FRE 704 (abolishing "ultimate issue" objection), but courts continue to express apprehension that expert testimony on credibility issues will discourage juries from making their own independent judgment.

3. The deluge of prosecutions for child sexual abuse that began in the 1980s put pressure on courts to relax this attitude and make room for such proof. Often experts now give social framework testimony describing familial or other settings in which abuse occurs, or syndrome testimony focusing on behavioral patterns of the actors. Parallel developments appear in sexual assault cases, where experts sometimes testify to Rape Trauma Syndrome, and in homicide prosecutions in which women being tried for killing men raise the defense that they were battered, hence justifiably acting in self-defense (Battered Woman Syndrome). See generally C. Mueller & L. Kirkpatrick, Evidence §7.22 (5th ed. 2012) (describing child sexual abuse accommodation syndrome, rape trauma syndrome, and battered woman syndrome). And see Chapter 9C2b, infra. Such testimony occasionally draws close to commenting directly on veracity or "believability" of particular witnesses, and some modern opinions approve. See State v. Bachman, 446 N.W.2d 271, 276 (S.D. 1989) (expert testified that allegations were truthful); State v. Kim, 645 P.2d 1330, 1338-1339 (Haw. 1982) (expert found 13-year-old daughter of defendant believable). But most modern opinions insist that experts should not testify that the child is truthful or her story is believable. See State v. Keller, 844 P.2d 195, 201 (Or. 1993) (reversible error to let expert testify that five-year-old child was telling truth); People v. Fasy, 829 P.2d 1314, 1318 (Colo. 1992) (expert did not comment on truthfulness); State v. Sims, 608 A.2d 1149, 1153-1154 (Vt. 1991) (error to let expert convey impression that she believed victim).

4. Testimony describing child abuse and rape trauma syndromes differs from standard testimony supporting veracity, doesn't it? An expert who describes syndromes and ventures the opinion that the story of the complaining witness fits a pattern is actually saying the story is plausible, isn't she? Is she also saying that people who give such accounts fit a pattern in which truthfulness is a common element? Doesn't that mean such testimony is covered by FRE 608? See State v. Grecinger, 569 N.W.2d 189 (Minn. 1997); State v. Rimmasch, 775 P.2d 388 (Utah 1989); People v. Snook, 745 P.2d 647 (Colo. 1987) (all applying FRE 608 to such testimony). If so, it would seem at the very least that an expert should not give such testimony about the complaining witness unless she testifies and her character for veracity is attacked. And arguably the effect of FRE 608 is to bar direct comment on the truthfulness or believability of a particular story, since the Rule contemplates generalized testimony about the disposition of the witness toward truthfulness.

5. Whatever reservations a court might have about admitting expert testimony based on someone's apparent mental or emotional condition, a court should let experts testify on the basis of physical symptoms, shouldn't it? See United States v. Bowers, 660 F.2d 527, 528-529 (5th Cir. 1981) (approving testimony by pediatrician describing "battered child syndrome," which "may show that the parent's explanation of the child's injuries is a fabrication" and let jury infer not only that child's injuries were not accidental but that parent deliberately caused them), and State v. Taylor, 663 S.W.2d 235, 239-240 (Mo. 1984) (disapproving testimony by psychologist that seemed to vouch for credibility of complaining witness in rape case, but indicating that physician may opine that victim's wounds "were caused by forcible sexual intercourse").

6. If expert testimony on child abuse and rape trauma syndromes indicates that a story is plausible, does it have a bearing on the case that goes beyond credibility issues? Does it shed light on all the proof, typically tending to support the contention that abuse or rape occurred by suggesting that what happened fits a broader pattern? Putting aside for a moment those cases where experts base conclusions on physical injuries, do you think they know enough about human nature to know whether abuse or rape has occurred? Do they know enough to know when a particular person is being truthful? These questions bring into play the legal doctrines governing expert testimony, and the subject is revisited in Chapter 9 (Opinion and Expert Testimony; Scientific Evidence).

7. Much has been written on child abuse and rape trauma syndromes. Among the best articles in the legal literature are Mosteller, Legal Doctrines Governing the Admissibility of Expert Testimony Concerning Social Framework Evidence, 52 Law & Contemp. Probs. 85 (1989); McCord, Expert Psychological Testimony About Child Complainants in Sexual Abuse Prosecutions: A Foray into the Admissibility of Novel Psychological Evidence, 77 J. Crim. L. & Criminology 1 (1986); Massaro, Experts, Psychology, Credibility, and Rape: The Rape Trauma Syndrome Issue and Its Implications for Expert Psychological Testimony, 69 Minn. L. Rev. 395 (1985); McCord, The Admissibility of Expert Testimony Regarding Rape Trauma Syndrome in Rape Prosecutions, 26 B.C. L. Rev. 1143 (1985).

3. Prior Consistent Statements

Prior consistent statements are often admissible to rehabilitate a witness, primarily in cases where the attacking party suggests that her testimony is tainted by recent fabrication or undue influence or motive. Here a prior statement by the witness, consistent with her direct testimony, might tend to refute the attack. This rehabilitating effect is clearest if the witness spoke before the motive or influence came into play: Evidence that she previously said the same thing she says at trial suggests that her testimony should *not* be rejected as a fabrication or discounted for improper motive.

Sometimes the attacking party clearly suggests that the witness is fabricating or allowing improper motives to affect her testimony. (Examples are suggested in the discussion of FRE 801(d)(1)(B) in Chapter 4A2, supra.) But an attack for bias may convey this message subtly (improper influence being a kind of bias): *Something* is fishy here, we don't know what, but this witness has been frightened or cajoled or "bought off," so she now favors one side. See United States v. Sutton, 732 F.2d 1483, 1493-1494 (10th Cir. 1984) (government witness testified that he phoned defendant and got instructions; defense asked him on cross to identify the first person he told about the call; prosecutor properly called wife of witness to say he told her the same thing; defense was trying to suggest that no conversation took place, hence that testimony was "recently fabricated"), *cert. denied*, 469 U.S. 1157 (1985).

Attack by prior inconsistent statement. One might think an attack by prior inconsistent statements *must* invite repair by consistent ones. But inconsistent statements don't *necessarily* suggest that the witness fabricated her testimony or colored her story on account of improper influence or motive. Such vacillation might reflect confusion arising from problems in perception or memory, so the "hornbook rule" is that impeachment by inconsistent statement does *not* pave the way to prove consistent statements. Professor Lilly put it this way:

> Producing evidence that [a witness] also made a statement consistent with his testimony [after he was attacked by a prior inconsistent statement] adds very little: the trier already has before it two conflicting accounts.

See G. Lilly, Principles of Evidence 318 (2006).

If, however, the attacking lawyer uses inconsistent statements to suggest fabrication or improper influence or motive, then consistent statements become useful after all. Recall the example in Chapter 4A2, supra, where Marian testified on direct that David was driving within the speed limit. Change the facts slightly. Assume this time that Paul's lawyer cross-examines Marian on a prior inconsistent statement, in this vein:

Q (Paul's lawyer to Marian): Didn't you say, some ten days after the accident, that the Ford was speeding?
A (Marian): Yes, sir, I did.
Q: Isn't it true, ma'am, that your testimony today is just a fabrication—you're just hiding what you've known from the beginning to be the truth?
A: No, not at all—
Q: Did David tell you what to say here in court?
A: No, he didn't—
Q: Thank you, ma'am. No further questions.

Marian's inconsistent statement on Day 10 *could* reflect vacillation born of inattentiveness or problems of perception (what we call lack of capacity), but Paul's lawyer has suggested something different: He implies that Marian was (as they say) "reached" or "gotten to" *after* Day 10 when she said David was speeding—maybe at some later date (perhaps Day 20) when she met with David and he insisted he was driving within the speed limit. It is for that reason that she changed her story. Thus, depending on the way in which the cross-examiner plays his hand, argues his point, and perhaps on the degree to which other circumstances come to light, an attack predicated on a prior inconsistent statement *may be interpreted* as raising charges of fabrication or improper motive.

There are other situations where consistencies are relevant to repair credibility. In the example set out above, if Paul's lawyer had contented himself with suggesting lack of memory, prior consistent statements can be used to rebut the suggestion that the witness has simply forgotten what happened. If she said the same thing close to the time of the events that she says in her testimony, then conflicting statements at other times don't show that her testimony reflects failed memory. And prior consistent statements can even show that a supposed prior inconsistent statement was never made, or that it was not really inconsistent with trial testimony. See, e.g., United States v. Coleman, 631 F.2d 908, 913-914 (D.C. Cir. 1980) (consistent statements are admissible where impeachment suggests lack of memory); United States v. Castillo, 14 F.3d 802, 805-806 (2d Cir. 1994) (after impeachment by inconsistent statements, admitting consistent statement to "aid the jury in determining whether the two statements meant the same thing"); United States v. Payne, 944 F.2d 1458, 1471 (9th Cir.) (admitting consistent statements to put prior statements in context and show that inconsistencies were minor part of consistent account), *cert. denied*, 503 U.S. 975 (1991).

The premotive requirement. Assuming that a prior inconsistency, or an attack stressing some form of bias or collusion, suggests that she's fabricating her testimony or was affected by improper influence or motive, do *all* consistent statements tend to refute the charge? Referring again to Marian, recall that she said on Days 1 and 30 that David "was driving within the speed limit," but we learn that on Day 10 she said that David "was speeding."

By tradition, the statement on Day 1 could rehabilitate Marian. *That* one indicates that she believed from the beginning that David was not at fault. See G. Lilly, Introduction to the Law of Evidence 432 (3d ed. 1996) ("a prior consistent statement *that predates* the alleged recent fabrication or the motive to falsify has sufficient probative value to be admitted because it tends to rebut the cross-examiner's charge of recent contrivance") (original emphasis). In contrast, Marian's statement on Day 30 would not rehabilitate her: On Day 10 she said that David "was speeding," and Paul argues that she later changed her tune (perhaps when she met with David on Day 20?), so what she said on Day 30 actually reinforces the attack (she was "reached").

In short, it is *premotive* statements, consistent with trial testimony, that tend most clearly to refute an attack suggesting fabrication or improper influence or motive. You saw the premotive requirement at work in Problem 4-B ("He Thinks I'm His Wife"), in Chapter 4A2, supra. That problem tracks the facts of the *Tome* case, where the Court found that the premotive requirement is built into FRE 801(d)(1)(B), which in effect creates a hearsay exception for certain prior consistent statements. See Tome v. United States, 513 U.S. 150 (1995). As amended in 2014, this provision paves the way for the *substantive use* of consistent statements when offered "to rebut an express or implied charge" of recent fabrication or improper influence or motive, or to repair credibility "when attacked on another ground." Before the amendment, this provision did not expressly cover all situations where consistent statements are considered relevant to repair credibility. Now it does. Importantly, the ACN says the 2014 amendment retains *Tome's* premotive requirement.

Substantive and rehabilitative uses compared. Using a consistent statement for a rehabilitative purpose is not itself a hearsay use. The rehabilitative use turns on the point that "staying with the same story" by speaking consistently shows an unchanging view of the matter at hand. We are not taking the consistent statement as proof of what it asserts, but as proof of consistency.[7] In the example above, the rehabilitating party (David) argues in this vein: "When Marian said before that I was within the speed limit, her statement shows that she has long held the view to which she testified here, and this showing does not involve a hearsay use."

What is important here is to recognize that proper rehabilitative use of a consistent statement turns on considerations of relevancy, which is what the premotive requirement is all about. A consistent statement is only *relevant* to refute a claim of improper motive if made *before* the motive arose—or at least it is *most clearly* relevant under this condition. Similar considerations affect the relevancy of a consistent statement offered to refute a claim that the trial testimony reflects lack of memory. If the cross-examiner finishes an attack by saying to the witness "you just don't remember the true facts, do you?" and the calling party then offers a consistent statement made one day earlier, it has little or no relevancy to refute the suggestion of lost memory, but it would be very relevant if made two years earlier and only days or minutes after the event.

Rule 801(d)(1)(B) *rests on* the use of consistent statements to repair credibility, but doesn't *regulate this repairing use*. Yet this provision is the only one that mentions consistent statements, and one scholar argues that it should be reworded to avoid any implication that consistent statements are admissible whenever a witness is impeached. The rewording would say the exception applies only when a consistent statement is "independently admissible for the nonhearsay purpose of repairing a specific impeaching attack." See Liesa Richter, Seeking Consistency for Prior Consistent Statements: Amending Federal Rule of Evidence 801(d)(1)(B), 46 Conn. L. Rev. 937, 986 (2014) (also saying that *Tome* "appeared to shift some of the authority for rehabilitation standards to the hearsay rules," and the rewording would keep judges and litigants from being "lulled into thinking that any prior consistent statement 'offered' to rehabilitate becomes automatically admissible for its truth").

Because FRE 801(d)(1)(B) could be misread as regulating rehabilitation, we need to look now at the relevancy concerns that apply to the rehabilitative use of consistent statements. We also need to do so because the premotive requirement bears on the relevancy of consistent statements, and *Tome*'s endorsement of this requirement as embedded in FRE 801(d)(1)(B) might indicate that the same requirement should apply to the purely rehabilitative use of such statements—not because FRE 801(d)(1)(B) regulates the subject, but because

[7] Recall the similar-but-opposite reasons for treating an *inconsistent* statement as nonhearsay when offered to impeach, which we saw in Problem 3-C ("The Blue Car Ran the Red Light"). The impeaching use of an inconsistent statement turns on the fact that "blowing hot and cold" by speaking in contradictory ways shows vacillation, which does not involve taking an inconsistent statement as proof of what it asserts.

Tome's effort to limit the substantive use of consistent statements would be undercut if the premotive requirement didn't also apply to the rehabilitative use. Recall that post-*Tome* decisions split on the question whether the requirement applies in this setting. Compare State v. Bujan, 190 P.3d 1255 (Utah 2008) (prior consistent statements may be admitted to rehabilitate even if made after motive arose) with United States v. Brooks, 736 F.3d 921, 935 (10th Cir. 2013) (premotive requirement applies even when consistent statement is offered to rehabilitate and not for its truth).

The next Problem provides an opportunity to consider relevancy factors and the premotive requirement too.

■ PROBLEM 8-H. "She Handed Me the Heroin"

Clair and Arla are suspected of conspiring to distribute heroin. An informant introduces undercover FBI Agent Turner to the two women, and during lunch at a restaurant Clair agrees to sell Turner 100 grams of heroin. Turner suggests that Clair go to the women's restroom to put a sample of the heroin in a paper towel so Turner can test it. Both women go to the restroom and later return with the heroin, and the sale is made.

Clair and Arla are arrested and charged with selling heroin. Matrons do a search and discover that Clair (not Arla) is carrying a large quantity of heroin. Thereafter Clair pleads guilty to a drug offense.

Eighteen months later Arla goes to trial on the charge of selling heroin. Turner testifies for the government that when the two women returned from the restroom, it was Arla who produced the heroin from her purse, wrapped in a paper towel. Counsel for Arla vigorously cross-examines:

Q: Isn't it a fact, Mr. Turner, that you really remember which woman was carrying the heroin because you were focused more on the women than on the drugs?

A: No, sir, I remember very well. It was the woman in the black and white dress.

Q: Aren't you really just trying to put *two* women in jail, and you think my client is guilty because she was with Clair—in effect, mere guilt by association?

A: No, sir.

During the defense case-in-chief, both Clair and defendant Arla testify that it was *Clair* who carried the heroin back and handed it to Turner.

During the government's case-in-rebuttal, the prosecutor offers a recorded statement by Turner, made outside the restaurant moments after Clair and Arla were arrested, in which Turner said: "The woman in the black and white dress had the stuff in her purse. She took the heroin out of her purse after she came out of the restroom and handed it to me." It is undisputed that Arla was wearing the black-and-white dress, while Clair wore slacks and a blouse.

Arla raises a hearsay objection, and argues in addition that the prosecutor is engaging in "improper rehabilitation." How should the court rule, and why?

NOTES ON PRIOR CONSISTENCIES

1. Arla's lawyer implies that Turner forgot who produced the heroin sample. Does this attack suggest that his recorded statement outside the restaurant should be admitted to repair his credibility? Should it also be admissible under FRE 801(d)(1)(B) as substantive evidence?

2. Arla's lawyer also implies that Turner was trying at trial to railroad Arla into jail. Does this attack suggest that his recorded statement outside the restaurant should be admitted to repair his credibility? Should it too be admissible under FRE 801(d)(1)(B) as substantive evidence?

3. If we apply a premotive requirement, which *Tome* demands in federal courts if the statement is to be used substantively—and maybe to the rehabilitative use of the statement too, because otherwise we undermine *Tome*—then we have to figure out whether the alleged improper motivation was already operating at the moment of arrest. A moment's reflection suggests that almost any law enforcement officer might be charged with harboring a motive to build a case the moment he arrests the defendant, which would mean that any statement he made thereafter could never satisfy a premotive requirement, so imposing such a requirement would block use of prior consistencies by police (if we applied the requirement to both uses) or limit their use (if we applied the requirement only to the substantive use).

4. On facts like those in Problem 8-H, a federal trial court admitted the agent's recorded statement. The decision came before *Tome,* and the court wasn't convinced that a premotive requirement should apply. It commented that agent's motive arose when it was discovered that the other woman (Clair, in the Problem) was carrying the heroin, and it was "at that point that the moment to fabricate arose in order to convict [Arla] of possessing the sample." See United States v. Obayagbona, 627 F. Supp. 329, 337-338 (E.D.N.Y. 1985). Are you convinced? Notice that the cross-examiner in the Problem framed the question in the present tense: "Aren't you really just trying to put *two* women in jail, and you think my client is guilty because she was with Clair—in effect, mere guilt by association?" Does that framing make it easier to admit the recorded statement? Would it be harder to do so, if the premotive requirement applies, if the questioner had asked "Haven't you been trying all along to railroad Arla and Clair into jail, from the moment you met them in the restaurant?"

5. In criminal cases, often an important prosecution witness has participated in the alleged offense. When defendant cross-examines such a witness in an effort to show that he is trying to help himself by helping the prosecutor, this attack often amounts to a charge of improper motive or fabrication. Once again it makes a difference whether the premotive requirement applies. Does the involvement of witnesses in the alleged offense mean that everything they say afterwards is already tainted by improper motive? Or does the motive arise only after arrest, or maybe not until plea bargaining begins? These questions have posed real difficulties for courts. Compare United States v. Awon, 135 F.3d 96, 99-100 (1st Cir. 1998) (error to admit consistent statements by brothers hired to set fires, made in conversations in which police promised not to prosecute if they cooperated; they had same "desire for leniency" that they had at trial, so premotive requirement was not satisfied) with United States v. Prieto, 232 F.3d 816, 819-822 (11th Cir. 2000) (admitting alleged co-offender's postarrest statements as prior consistencies; such statements "are not automatically and necessarily contaminated by a motive to fabricate in order to curry favor"), *cert. denied*, 534 U.S. 950 (2001).

D FORBIDDEN ATTACKS

FRE 610 disallows impeaching attempts that attack credibility on the basis of "beliefs or opinions" on matters of religion. The idea is that religious belief is intensely personal, that religious attitudes may evoke strong feelings in jurors, that our society tolerates diversity of religious conviction, and that in the end the subject brings great risk of prejudice and little prospect of developing anything that helps.

Note that FRE 603 requires a witness to declare "by oath or affirmation" that he will speak the truth. Here too some sensitivity to religious diversity is appropriate, and a person who objects to an "oath" must be allowed to commit himself to the truth by some other means. See Chapter 6D, supra.

■ NOTES ON RELIGIOUS BELIEF AND IMPEACHMENT

1. Does FRE 610 bar cross-examination aiming to uncover bias on account of the affiliation of a witness with a religious organization having an interest in the case?

2. Recall that the decision in *Abel* (section A1, supra) upheld cross-examination by the prosecutor that uncovered the common membership of the defendant and a defense witness in the Aryan Brotherhood. Would the result have been different if the Aryan Brotherhood were a "religious" organization? Cf. Government of Virgin Islands v. Petersen, 553 F.2d 324, 328 (3d Cir. 1977) (in murder trial, disallowing defense effort to establish that defendant and alibi witness were Rastafarians who "reject violence," for FRE 610 "prohibits such testimony when it is used to enhance the witness' credibility").

3. In State v. Zobel, 222 N.W.2d 570, 572 (Neb. 1974), defendant asked an undercover officer testifying for the prosecutor whether he had "ever made an oath rejecting the power of God and Christ and accepting Satan as omnipotent." Defendant claimed that the witness was a priest of Satan. Would FRE 610 block this attack? See United States v. Sampol, 636 F.2d 621, 666 (D.C. Cir. 1980) (cutting off inquiry aiming to show that government witness adhered to "Luceme religion," where witness testified on voir dire that "he faithfully adhered to the teaching of that sect and consulted with spirits of his religion" before acting, but his religious belief would not cause him to violate his oath to testify truthfully).

CHAPTER 9

Opinion and Expert Testimony; Scientific Evidence

A LAY OPINION TESTIMONY

By longstanding tradition, lay witnesses testify to facts, not opinions based on facts. They did so before the Rules came, and they do so now. Yet lay witnesses *do* give opinion testimony, and always have. The Rules did not bring a day-and-night change, but they altered the approach, and are more generous than common law in allowing lay opinions.

Common law approach. Many pre-Rules cases tried to draw a bright line between fact and opinion, welcoming fact testimony by lay witnesses and rejecting opinions. You know already how hard it is (even futile) to maintain this distinction. Ask any of us to estimate a person's height. Is our answer fact or opinion? Consider the redness of a barn, speed of a car, intoxication of a driver. Is lay testimony on such points fact or opinion?

Still, courts tried to separate "fact" from "opinion," for three reasons:

First was a misreading of English precedents, which sometimes expressed the (entirely sound) requirement of firsthand knowledge by rejecting opinion testimony. American courts seemed to overlook the purpose of the distinction and rejected opinions even where the witness had firsthand knowledge.

Second was the emergence of the idea that an expert (one trained in science) should be allowed to state his "opinion," in the sense of analyzing and interpreting data so as to paint a picture understandable by a lay trier of fact. It came to be understood that lay opinions were improper because, by definition, lay witnesses lacked special training.

Third was the notion that the trier of fact should draw its own conclusions, and lay opinion testimony would "invade the province of the jury."

The Rules approach. The modern view recognizes that "facts" and "opinions" are regions in a continuum, differing in degree rather than kind: Facts are more specific or concrete, opinions more general or conclusory. Courts agree that testimony by lay witnesses should be specific rather than general, concrete rather than conclusory. But Rule 701 does not preserve a fact-opinion dichotomy. Instead it speaks functionally. It sets two conditions and a limit (or proviso): Lay opinion testimony is admissible if (1) "rationally based" on "perception" and (2) "helpful" to the trier of fact in understanding his testimony or determining a fact in issue, provided that it does not reflect "scientific, technical, or other specialized knowledge" covered by FRE 702. Thus FRE 701 is more generous than the common law, allowing more latitude to admit lay opinion testimony.

The Rules address the underlying concerns in other ways. Thus, Rule 602 requires lay witnesses to have "personal knowledge," treating this matter as an aspect of witness competency rather than testimonial form. On the issue of invading the province of the jury, FRE 704 says lay opinion testimony is not objectionable "because it embraces an ultimate issue." *Any* relevant testimony speaks to issues that a jury must resolve, so the old objection was overbroad, even simplistic. More refined concerns remain: Opinion testimony that is conclusory is *still* excludable if (as is likely) it is not "helpful," and FRE 704(b) restricts expert testimony on the "mental state or condition" of the accused. And the fear remains that some testimony may confuse or overwhelm a lay jury, so it can be rejected for that reason.

The Rules cover expert testimony separately in FRE 702 and 703. As you will see, the modern approach is to require that scientific and technical testimony satisfy a reliability standard. This standard covers people like doctors and geologists, where nobody is likely to imagine that FRE 701 applies. The boundary line between lay and expert opinions is not always clear, however, because people like police officers and auto mechanics often testify on points lying beyond everyday experience, and can sometimes qualify as experts themselves. It is partly because the line is blurred that we find the proviso in Rule 701 (barring lay testimony resting on scientific and other technical or specialized knowledge), which means that police officers and auto mechanics must qualify as experts (a process that takes some doing) before testifying as such.

Modern practice. Even common law tradition recognized that lay opinions should be welcomed on many points, and courts applying Rule 701 continue to admit such testimony. The so-called collective facts doctrine makes the point that certain ideas well within common experience can best be expressed, and reliably so, by means of a shorthand word or phrase. One court put it this way:

> If it is impossible or difficult to reproduce the data observed by the witnesses, or the facts are difficult of explanation, or complex, or are of a combination of circumstances and appearances which cannot be adequately described and presented with the force and clearness as they appeared to the witness, the witness may state his impressions and opinions based upon what he observed. It is a means of conveying to the jury what the witness has seen or heard. If the jury can be put into a position of equal vantage with the witness for drawing the opinion, then the witness may not give an opinion. Because it is sometimes

> difficult to describe [various matters,] witnesses may relate their opinions or conclusions of what they observed.

United States v. Skeet, 665 F.2d 983, 985 (9th Cir. 1982) ("mental or physical condition of a person, his character or reputation, the emotions manifest by his acts," and "speed of a moving object," as well as matters like "size, heights, odors, flavors, color, heat").

An early opinion provides an even longer list, with which courts applying FRE 701 would likely be equally comfortable. Lay opinions should be admissible

> upon a great variety of unscientific questions arising every day, and in every judicial inquiry. These are questions of identity, handwriting, quantity, value, weight, measure, time, distance, velocity, form, size, age, strength, heat, cold, sickness, and health; questions also concerning various mental and moral aspects of humanity, such as disposition and temper, anger, fear, excitement, intoxication, veracity, general character, and particular phases of character, and other conditions and things, both moral and physical, too numerous to mention.

Hardy v. Merrill, 56 N.H. 227, 22 Am. Rep. 441 (1878).

Another insight that has proved durable animates Rule 701: A witness should not be so closely confined by rules of legal diction that he is effectively muzzled. As Judge Learned Hand put it:

> Every judge of experience in the trial of causes has again and again seen the whole story garbled, because of insistence upon a form with which the witness cannot comply, since, like most men, he is unaware of the extent to which inference enters into his perceptions. He is telling the "facts" in the only way that he knows how, and the result of nagging and checking him is often to choke him altogether, which is, indeed, usually its purpose.

Central Ry. v. Monahan, 11 F.2d 212, 214 (2d Cir. 1926). Consider this elaboration of that thought, in an opinion approving testimony describing the understanding of another:

> The question ought always to be whether it is more convenient to insist that the witness disentangle in his own mind—which, much more often than not, he is quite unable to do—those constituent factors on which his opinion is based; or to let him state his opinion and leave to cross examination a searching inquisition to uncover its foundations . . . . To require him to unravel that nexus will, unless he is much practiced in self scrutiny, generally make him substitute an utterly unreal—though honest—set of constituents, or will altogether paralyze his powers of expression.

United States v. Petrone, 185 F.2d 334, 336 (2d Cir. 1950) (per curiam, before Judges Hand, Swan, and Frank), *cert. denied*, 340 U.S. 931 (1951).

In the spirit of these comments, modern reviewing courts have approved opinion testimony of the following sorts:[1]

1. In deciding not to promote *T*, *M* did not base his decision on her national origin;
2. After accidental fall in stairwell, 10-year-old boy underwent "personality change" and his physical, behavioral, and educational performance in school declined;
3. The railroad crossing was in poor condition and difficult to get across;
4. Claimant was an alcoholic unable to work;
5. It seemed that plaintiff had time to get out of the way.

Still, courts are not always generous or flexible in their approach to these matters. Despite its accommodating attitude, for example, the reviewing court in *Skeet* saw fit to approve a ruling by the trial court excluding, in an assault trial, testimony by defense witnesses opining that "the shooting was accidental"!

■ PROBLEM 9-A. "It Was My Impression"

In the trial of Cox for unlawful detonation of explosives, arising from the firebombing of cars, the prosecutor calls defendant's former girlfriend Carter. She testifies that Cox told her twice that he knew someone who would blow up cars for $50 and that he showed her a newspaper account of one of the bombings giving rise to the charges. During the state's case-in-chief, the following exchange occurs:

Q [prosecutor]: Did Mr. Cox admit being involved in this bombing?

A [Carter]: He never actually said that, you know, he had blown it up, but it was my understanding by his mentioning that he had a friend and showing me the article that it was my impression when we were done talking that he was involved in having blown it up.

Ms. Dreeves: The defense objects to that, your Honor. It calls for opinion and speculation, and nothing she says can be helpful in understanding her testimony or determining the facts in issue in this case.

How should the court rule, and why?

---

[1] The ensuing passages are not direct quotations, but they fairly describe testimony approved, respectively, by the decisions in Torres v. County of Oakland, 758 F.2d 147, 149-150 (6th Cir. 1985); Kurczy v. St. Joseph Veterans Ass'n, 820 A.2d 929, 940 (R.I. 2003); Young v. Illinois C.G. Ry., 618 F.2d 332, 337 (5th Cir. 1980); Singletary v. Secretary of Health, Educ. & Welfare, 623 F.2d 217, 219 (2d Cir. 1980); Virginia Ry. & Power Co. v. Burr, 133 S.E. 776 (Va. 1926).

NOTES ON LAY TESTIMONY ON ANOTHER'S MEANING OR STATE OF MIND

1. When it comes to understanding the meaning, intention, or comprehension of another on the basis of what he says, it would be a hard rule indeed that either barred all testimony or required a witness to sort out the particulars underlying his conclusion. In *Petrone* (quoted prior to the Problem), the Second Circuit recognized this difficulty:

> Nothing is less within the powers of the ordinary witness than to analyze the agglomerate of sensations which combine in his mind to give him an "impression" of the contents of another's mind.

United States v. Petrone, 185 F.2d 334, 336 (2d Cir. 1950) (per curiam) (admitting federal agent's testimony that defendant "had not given 'the impression . . . that he did not know those bills were in that room' "), *cert. denied*, 340 U.S. 931 (1951). See also United States v. Davis, 787 F.2d 1501, 1505 (11th Cir. 1986) (*V* testified that in asking *V* whether he "wanted to make a trip," *L* was referring to "an illegal act" and that in telling *V* not to worry about *M*, *L* meant that *M* "must have known about the 'dope business' "), *cert. denied*, 479 U.S. 852 (1986). Do *Petrone* and *Davis* suggest that Carter can testify that Cox was admitting involvement in a bombing? Or did she go too far beyond the ordinary meaning of the words that Cox spoke?

2. What about interpreting what another thinks or feels on the basis of nonverbal behavior? In a suit on an accidental death policy, arising out of the death of a husband killed in a fight he started with his wife, liability turned on whether the husband thought he would be killed in the fight. The trial court let the daughter testify that he "did not believe his wife would ever kill him," and the reviewing court approved:

> When . . . the witness observes firsthand the altercation in question, her opinions on the feelings of the parties are based on her personal knowledge and rational perceptions and are helpful to the jury. The Rules require nothing more for admission of the testimony.

John Hancock Mutual Life Insurance Co. v. Dutton, 585 F.2d 1289, 1294 (7th Cir. 1978). See also Bohannon v. Pegelow, 652 F.2d 729, 731-732 (7th Cir. 1981) (in suit alleging that police officer violated civil rights in arresting plaintiff for pandering, admitting testimony by plaintiff's girlfriend, whose favors plaintiff allegedly offered to sell to defendant, that the arrest was "motivated by racial prejudice," for she "observed" it).

3. Should a lay witness testify that a person is sane or insane? At common law, laypersons could describe conduct bearing on sanity but could venture an opinion on sanity itself only on the basis of longer observation. United States v. Alden, 476 F.2d 378, 385 (7th Cir. 1973) (should admit lay testimony describing "acts, conduct, declarations, spoken words, appearance, and manner of speech," but opinion "can only be expressed where the witness has been qualified by sufficient association with an opportunity to observe the subject"). There is reason to think FRE 701 opens the door even further. Compare United States v. Goodman, 2011 WL 258282 (10th Cir. 2011) (error to bar lay opinion that defendant was insane, which is admissible if witness is acquainted with subject and has observed his conduct) (reversing conviction) with United States v. Lawson, 653 F.2d 299, 303 (7th Cir. 1981) (admitting testimony by FBI agents that defendant was sane, based on investigation of extortion scheme and dealing with him at a rendezvous; Rules admit "substantially more evidence" than common law, relying on cross "as a means of verification"), *cert. denied*, 454 U.S. 1150 (1982).

■ PROBLEM 9-B. The Watchful Neighbor

A pickup truck driven by defendant Al Davis collides with a car driven by Sandy Pinkston, seriously injuring her child Amy, who is in the right front seat. In the ensuing lawsuit by Sandy Pinkston against Al Davis, plaintiff calls Luke Hanson as a witness.

Peruse the following transcript of Hanson's testimony on direct and cross-examination. Consider whether either side has proper objections under FRE 701. Consider too how you would avoid or cure any problems in Hanson's testimony.

Direct Examination

Q [plaintiff's counsel]: Please state your name and address for the court reporter.

A: Luke Hanson, 1623 Elm Street, in Fayetteville.

Q: Mr. Hanson, directing your attention now to the afternoon of June 12 of last year, did you see an automobile accident in the 1600 block of Elm Street, near your home?

A [Mr. Hanson]: Yes, sir. I was sitting outside on my front porch swing. It happened practically in front of me.

Q: Please tell the jury what you saw.

A: Well, the lady across the street, Mrs. Pinkston, was backing her car out of the driveway to take her daughter to ballet lessons when a pickup truck plowed right into the side of her.

Q: Did you see the driver of the pickup?

A: I did.

Q: Do you see him here today?

A: I'm really not sure. It's been almost a year. The driver had a beard and that fellow is clean-shaven. But I would guess that's him over there [pointing to the defendant].

Q: Let the record show that the witness pointed to the defendant. Now Mr. Hanson, how fast was the pickup going at the time of the collision?
A: I would say he was going at least 35 miles per hour.
Q: And what is the speed limit on that street?
A: Well, generally it's 35 miles per hour, but the law says you can go only 20 if you're within 500 feet of a school, and we are. So he was breaking the speed limit, no question about it.
Q: Did you go over to the pickup after the accident?
A: Yes, sir.
Q: Did you notice any unusual odor coming from the truck?
A: Yes, sir. There was a strong smell of pot. I'm sure the driver was smoking a joint—had been, anyway.
Q: Would you say he was stoned?
A: I really can't say.
Q: Well, how did he seem?
A: It's hard to say, but he had a real guilty look, like he was afraid he was going to lose his license or get sued.
Q: What was Mrs. Pinkston doing after the accident?
A: She was crying, real hard.
Q: What about?
A: I think she was upset about her little girl Amy, who got hurt the worst of anyone.
Q: What injuries did Amy and her mother suffer?
A: Well, Amy looked like she had a broken back, but Mrs. Pinkston only had a dislocated shoulder.
Q: How extensive was the damage to the station wagon?
A: The whole right side was caved in. The car was totaled.
Q: And do you know the approximate value of the car?
A: I'd say about $5,000.
Q: No further questions. Thank you, Mr. Hanson.

Cross-Examination

Q: Mr. Hanson, isn't it true that Mrs. Pinkston barreled out of her driveway without stopping or looking to see whether anyone was coming?
A: Well, she looked like she was in a hurry, and she didn't turn around to look at the street as she came out.
Q: And Mr. Davis, in the pickup, did everything he could to avoid a collision, isn't that so?
A: Yes, he couldn't have stopped in that short a space. Mrs. Pinkston just backed out right in front of him. It was sad to see.
Q: Now Mr. Hanson, let's assume that we can identify the most careful driver in the world. If he or she had been driving along Elm Street on that fateful afternoon, could that hypothetical perfect driver have avoided Mrs. Pinkston's car, backing out the way she did?
A: No, I don't believe so.

FURTHER NOTES ON LAY OPINION TESTIMONY

1. As the Problem illustrates, it is almost impossible to talk about ordinary events without giving opinions and conclusions. How could Hanson know Mrs. Pinkston was taking Amy to a ballet lesson? Behind such inferences are things like conversations about Amy, observations of comings and goings, and maybe what the child was wearing. We "know" these things for such reasons, but might have a hard time explaining how we know them. Lawyers would not object to such testimony unless it touches an important issue. If it does, and if the reason for the conclusion is a conversation, the court would sustain an objection based on hearsay or lack of knowledge required by FRE 602.

2. Hanson is not sure whether defendant was the other driver. Does uncertainty require exclusion for lack of personal knowledge? Most courts say No. See, e.g., Huckin v. Connor, 928 S.W.2d 180, 184 (Tex. App. 1996) (if witness testifies to facts from his observation but he is uncertain, "he may qualify his testimony by the use of such phrases as 'I believe,' 'I think,' 'It is my impression,' without detracting from its admissibility").

3. Hanson is asked whether the truck driver seemed stoned. Not everyone knows enough to answer such questions, and people who do may not want to admit it. Testimony of this sort is sometimes given, and obviously being stoned (or intoxicated) can bear on negligence. See, e.g., State v. Robertson, 831 So. 2d 389, 391 (La. App. 2002) (witness says defendant looked "a little stoned," explaining that he knew she was using "because of her motions, actions, and the way her eyes looked, basing his opinion on his past experience as a drug user"). Can someone who "went to Berkeley in the sixties" testify on such points if he didn't use drugs but "knew people who did"?

4. Hanson can certainly testify that he thinks the truck was going 35 mph. See, e.g., United States v. Conn, 297 F.3d 548, 554 (7th Cir. 2002) ("quintessential Rule 701 testimony" includes "speed of a vehicle").

5. Consider the question to Hanson on the "hypothetical perfect driver." Does it smack too much of speculation and guesswork? In a personal injury case arising out of a collision between a pickup truck and a semi-tanker, the defense offered lay testimony by one Highlan (driver of another car) that Welsch (driver of the tanker) "did everything he could to avoid this accident" and that plaintiff Gorby "could have avoided" it. The trial court excluded this testimony, and the reviewing court affirmed:

> Highlan . . . was not present in the truck's cab with Welsch. Highlan could only observe the semi-tanker truck from a car in the opposite lane of traffic and thus could not know the exact measures Welsch took to avoid the accident. More significantly, Highlan could not know when Welsch perceived Gorby's truck. Furthermore, even if Highlan had been present in the cab with Welsch, we would still find that the opinion was not based upon firsthand knowledge or observation. Appellant never established that Highlan was familiar with

> the Schneider semi-tanker truck. In particular, appellant never established that Highlan was familiar with the safety equipment semi-tanker trucks carry, the distances over which trucks may safely stop, the load the Schneider truck carried, or the brake and steering equipment of such trucks. The mere fact that Highlan was a motorist with twenty-nine years of experience did not give him the personal knowledge necessary to formulate an admissible lay opinion....

Gorby v. Schneider Tank Lines, 741 F.2d 1015, 1021-1022 (7th Cir. 1984).

EXPERT WITNESSES

Expert testimony is the subject of Rules 702-706 (part of Rule 704 also applies to lay witnesses). Rule 702 is the basic provision, and the ensuing four provisions deal with important aspects of expert testimony. The ensuing discussion takes up the subject in the following order:

(1) Qualified expert. A witness must qualify as an expert to be able to testify as such. Rule 702 refers to a witness "qualified as an expert" through "knowledge, skill, experience, training, or education." It is only such persons who can give "opinion" testimony on "scientific" or "technical" matters or offer "specialized knowledge."

(2) Helpfulness standard. An expert may provide opinion testimony under FRE 702 only if it would "help the trier of fact" understand the evidence or determine a fact.

(3) Reasonable reliance standard. Often experts testify on the basis of personal knowledge. Unlike lay witnesses (who must have such knowledge), however, Rule 703 allows experts also to rely on hearsay and other material, provided that other experts in the field "would reasonably rely" on such information.

(4) Mental state restriction. Under FRE 704(b), experts may not give opinion testimony that the accused "did nor did not have a mental state or condition that constitutes an element of the crime charged or a defense."

(5) Stating Opinion Directly. Under FRE 705, an expert may provide opinion testimony "without first testifying to the underlying facts," which represents a purposeful departure from the conventions that generally attend the presentation of testimony. The departure is designed to lessen the emphasis on labored foundations provided by elaborate hypothetical questions.

(6) Court appointment. Under Rule 706, a court may appoint an expert witness, on its own motion or on request by a party. In fact this power is rarely used. (Under FRE 614, courts can call ordinary witnesses as well, but this power is used even less frequently.)

(7) Reliability standard. Section C of this chapter explores the reliability standard. Once thought to apply only to "scientific" evidence, the standard now applies across the board to expert testimony.

1. Qualifying the Witness: Who Is an Expert?

Expertise in astonishing variety finds its way into courts. Physicians and psychiatrists are familiar figures, as are real estate appraisers and engineers. And these represent only the tip of the iceberg.

Under Rule 702, an expert is someone with specialized knowledge. Clearly FRE 702 embraces persons with formal education or training, like physicians, engineers, and geologists. The standard is lenient, and many others qualify. A person with suitable training or education can be an expert even if he is not a specialist or not renowned, and even if he lacks a certification or experience. See Garrett v. Desa Industries, 705 F.2d 721, 724-725 (4th Cir. 1983) (though lacking "prior experience," one with master's in engineering qualified as expert); Payton v. Abbott Laboratories, 780 F.2d 147, 155-156 (1st Cir. 1985) (physicians could testify about injuries resulting from use of DES during pregnancy, even though neither was a research scientist or specialist).

Rule 702 reaches further still, embracing people with practical experience but no formal training. See United States v. Thomas, 676 F.2d 239, 245 (7th Cir. 1980) (admitting testimony by one who worked in car repair shop and rebuilt cars as hobby, that defendant was not operating such a shop, because he only had tools for "taking apart" cars, none for "assembling, repairing or painting"), *cert. denied*, 450 U.S. 931 (1981).

The ACN to FRE 702 also refers to "skilled" witnesses, listing "bankers or landowners testifying to land values." Thus an owner can testify to the value of his real property, and a business person can describe its financial picture (estimating profits or losses), and farmers and ranchers may estimate values of crops or livestock. See United States v. 79.20 Acres of Land, 710 F.2d 1352, 1357 (8th Cir. 1983) (landowner testifies to value of property); Rossi v. Mobil Oil Corp., 710 F.2d 821, 830 (Temp. Emer. App. 1983) (bookkeeper employed by gasoline retailer testifies to gallonage and profitability figures); Greenwood Ranches v. Skie Construction Co., 629 F.2d 518, 522-523 (8th Cir. 1980) (rancher testifies to probable value at maturity that failed crop would have had).

2. Helpfulness Standard: When Can Experts Testify?

Under Rule 702, an expert can testify only if what he says will help the trier of fact understand the evidence or determine a fact in issue. This standard—it is too vague to be a test—is also generous, and under it courts have admitted a wide range of testimony.

Consider the following modern examples, all approved as proper:[2]

[2] Ensuing passages are not quotations, but they describe testimony approved, respectively, by United States v. McCollum, 802 F.2d 344, 345-346 (9th Cir. 1986); American Home Assur. Co. v. Sunshine Supermarket, 753 F.2d 321, 325 (3d Cir. 1985); Davis v. Combustion Eng., 742 F.2d 916, 919 (6th Cir. 1984); United States v. Pugliese, 712 F.2d 1574, 1582 (2d Cir. 1983); Bauman v. Volkswagenwerk Aktiengesellschaft, 621 F.2d 230, 233-234 (6th Cir. 1980); United States v. Cyphers, 553 F.2d 1064, 1071-1072 (7th Cir.), *cert. denied*, 434 U.S. 843 (1977).

1. Testimony in a mail fraud trial on "the typical structure of mail fraud schemes";
2. Testimony by fire marshals, in a suit for fire loss, that arson started the blaze;
3. Testimony by a professor of management and marketing, in employment discrimination suit, that plaintiff "was terminated because of his age";
4. Testimony by a DEA agent in drug trial describing purity of heroin commonly sold on the street;
5. Testimony, in a product liability suit against an automaker, describing hammer tests in which one person struck the outer handle of a car door while another pushed from the inside with his feet, to support plaintiff's theory that door popped open during sideswipe accident; and
6. Testimony that hairs recovered from articles used by robbers were microscopically like hair samples taken from defendants.

The question arises whether the helpfulness requirement means experts should testify only on subjects beyond the ken of lay juries (as common law courts often held). Modern decisions conflict. Compare In re Japanese Electric Products Antitrust Litigation, 723 F.2d 238, 278-279 (3d Cir. 1983) (FRE 702 does not limit expert testimony to matters "beyond the jury's sphere of knowledge") with K-Mart Corporation v. Honeycutt, 24 S.W.3d 357 (Tex. 2000) (in suit by customer injured while sitting on lower rail of shopping-cart corral when employee pushed other carts into corral, error to let "human factors and safety expert" testify that missing top rail presented unreasonable risk; where subject is within common knowledge of jurors, expert testimony should be excluded).

Japanese Products reaches the preferable result. Experts can help a jury understand even familiar matters, in virtue of experience or training that provides a more thorough understanding than ordinary experience provides. See Garbincius v. Boston Edison Co., 621 F.2d 1171, 1174-1175 (1st Cir. 1980) (approving testimony by civil engineer on adequacy in number and placement of devices warning motorists of excavation). Where expertise is only marginally helpful because the subject is simple or familiar, special education or experience may not add to common understanding. If so, a decision excluding such testimony better rests on FRE 403. Where the subject *is* beyond lay understanding, testimony by someone with special knowledge will likely help.

3. Reasonable Reliance Standard: The Bases of Expert Testimony

Rule 703 lets an expert testify on the basis of facts or data of three sorts, including (1) facts or data that he learns by firsthand observation beforehand, (2) facts or data that he learns at the trial or hearing itself, or (3) outside facts or data, meaning information he gleans before trial by consulting other sources, provided that they are the kinds of data on which experts in the field would "reasonably" rely.

Firsthand knowledge. The first category embraces personal knowledge (firsthand experience), which is very much the same thing that Rule 602 requires of lay witnesses. Often an expert personally observes, examines, or tests the place, object, or person that he describes in his testimony. Routinely, for example, a doctor examines an injured claimant and testifies to the diagnosis of ailment or injury and the prognosis for future difficulties or recovery. In these cases, the question is whether he has sufficient data to support an opinion, and on this point the expert himself is likely to have a view worth hearing.

Facts learned at trial. The second category is unique to experts. It embraces information that the expert learns at trial. For all practical purposes, this category means (1) testimony heard by the expert while sitting in the courtroom listening to other witnesses before taking the stand himself and (2) information conveyed in hypothetical questions summing up evidence previously admitted. (Note that Rule 602 contains a clause making the personal knowledge requirement inapplicable to expert testimony offered under Rule 703, which accommodates these techniques.)

Outside data. The third category, again unique to experts, is very broad. Rule 703 lets experts rely on facts or data on which other experts in the field would reasonably rely. This category amounts to formal recognition (not openly acknowledged prior to adoption of the Rules in 1975) of what was long the reality: *Necessarily* experts rely on facts and data that are not mentioned at trial.[3] Here too the intent of Rule 703 is to be generous in admitting expert testimony, as illustrated in the following examples approved by modern reviewing courts:[4]

1. Testimony by an expert from the Bureau of Alcohol, Tobacco, and Firearms on the origin of a firearm, based on markings on the gun, on trade publications, and on company catalogues;
2. Testimony by psychologist that injuries suffered by a railroad employee, while working in control tower on account of nearby lightning strike, could have caused hearing and psychological damage and impaired ability to work;

---

[3] Prior 1975, courts indulged a kind of Puritan fiction that acknowledged only the first two categories (personal knowledge or information provided at trial). But it was understood that experts—especially those with formal training, like physicians, and engineers—rely on background data from books and articles, conversations and conferences, courses, and experiments, and it is impossible to introduce such material into evidence. Most such information amounts to "hearsay" that would be inadmissible. For early recognition of this truth, see Jenkins v. United States, 307 F.2d 637, 641-642 & n.21 (D.C. Cir. 1962) (better decisions allow opinion "based, in part, upon reports of others which are not in evidence but which the expert customarily relies upon") (yet expert cannot "rest solely" on unintroduced reports, which "would amount to offering an opinion of another" in violation of hearsay rule).

[4] United States v. Harper, 802 F.2d 115, 121 (5th Cir. 1986); Cashman v. Allied Prod. Corp., 761 F.2d 1250, 1254-1255 (8th Cir. 1985); Walker v. Soo Line R. Co., 208 F.3d 581, 586 (7th Cir. 2000), *cert. denied*, 591 U.S. 930; American Universal Ins. Co. v. Falzone, 644 F.2d 65, 66-67 (1st Cir. 1981); United States v. Sims, 514 F.2d 147, 149 (9th Cir.), *cert. denied*, 423 U.S. 845 (1975).

3. Testimony of a biomechanical engineer, based on a seminar sponsored by an automaker, papers on accidents prepared by the Society of Automotive Engineers, and literature in biomechanics, that an infant car seat was improperly designed;
4. Testimony by a fire marshal, based in part on information from other marshals on fire inspection team, to the effect that the fire was caused by a person; and
5. Psychiatric testimony on the sanity of the accused, based in part on conversations of the psychiatrist with IRS agents recounting their dealings with the accused.

But courts have not always accepted expert opinions as reasonably based. Consider these opinions, rejected by reviewing courts:[5]

1. Testimony by an investigative agent, based on a psychological stress evaluation (voice stress analysis), that plaintiff knew about and authorized setting the fire;
2. Testimony by an expert, based on accident information compiled by a safety director for a truck company summarizing 3,000 accident reports, that a fuel system fire probably did not cause the crash.

Use at trial of outside information. The relationship between expert testimony and outside data is a matter of exquisite subtlety. On one important point we can be clear. The intent of Rule 703, in authorizing expert testimony based on outside information, is *not* to make underlying data admissible for all purposes or to create a new hearsay exception. The framers of Rule 703 had nearly the opposite purpose in mind—simply recognizing that experts do rely on outside data and that one cannot ignore this reality.

On a second point we can also be clear. The framers thought (and said as much in Rule 705) that sometimes the outside data comes before the factfinder, if only because the adverse party cross-examines the expert on the basis of his opinion in hopes of showing it to be ill-founded. (On this point, more below.) The framers also may have thought the *calling party* would ask about the underlying data on direct: The justification is to make the opinion-to-come more convincing by explaining its basis. But the risk of abuse seemed too great, and FRE 703 now blocks the proponent from disclosing to the jury facts or data underlying expert testimony that are "otherwise" inadmissible (the court *can* admit such material if "probative value" in assessing the testimony "substantially outweighs" prejudicial effect).

Here is the rub. These impeaching and supporting uses do not mean the data are admissible for all purposes. Hence we face a paradox: Rule 703

[5] Barrel of Fun, Inc. v. State Farm Fire & Cas. Co., 739 F.2d 1028, 1033 (5th Cir. 1984); Soden v. Freightliner Corp., 714 F.2d 498, 503-504 (5th Cir. 1983).

envisions outside data that experts may reasonably rely on, but not the trier of fact. We also face the difficulty of admitting evidence susceptible of misuse, and of tempting the parties to exploit the opening thus provided. In other words, Rule 403 has a role to play.

Consider the paradox. Experts often rely on out-of-court statements that would be hearsay if introduced to prove what they assert, and Rule 703 does not obviate the hearsay objection to this use of such statements, even where a testifying witness relies on them. Here is a description of what we are doing:

> [T]he expert is fully capable of judging for himself what is, or is not, a reliable basis for his opinion. This relates directly to one of the functions of the expert witness, namely to lend his special expertise to the issue before him . . . . In a sense, the expert synthesizes the primary source material—be it hearsay or not—into properly admissible evidence in opinion form. The trier of fact is then capable of judging the credibility of the witness as it would that of anyone else giving expert testimony. This rule respects the functions and abilities of both the expert witness and the trier of fact, while assuring that the requirement of witness confrontation is fulfilled.

United States v. Sims, 514 F.2d 147, 149 (9th Cir.), *cert. denied*, 423 U.S. 845 (1975). Are you convinced? How true is it that experts like physicians and engineers acquire the ability "to separate the wheat from the chaff," as the court in *Sims* later remarked?

Consider the problem of jury misuse and party exploitation of data. In one case, a reviewing court approved, in the trial of Wright and Moss, testimony by Wright's psychiatrist, who referred (on cross) to something Wright said. Moss was bothered by the risk that the jury might use Wright's statement as proof of what Moss did. The reviewing court gave more weight to Rule 703 than to dangers of exploitation and misuse. See United States v. Wright, 783 F.2d 1091, 1100 (D.C. Cir. 1986) (psychiatrists can "rely on conversations with their patients" in diagnosing them; under FRE 705, expert may be required on cross "to disclose the facts or data" underlying an opinion; FRE 703 and 705 mean these data are not "substantive evidence," and they come in for the limited purpose of helping the jury "scrutinize the expert's reasoning").

In another case, however, the reviewing court was more troubled by the risk of abuse. Charged with attempted bank robbery, defendant McCollum called Dr. Jorgensen (a "forensic hypnotist") in support of his claim that he had been drugged, threatened, and hypnotized before entering the bank. Jorgensen described his interview with McCollum, and repeated some of what he said, but experts disagreed on the question whether McCollum was under hypnosis in the interview. The defense offered a videotape, which the trial court excluded, and the reviewing court agreed. See United States v. McCollum, 732 F.2d 1419, 1423 (9th Cir.) (offering tape "amounted to an effort to put the defendant's testimony directly before the jury without subjecting him to the cross-examination and impeachment"), *cert. denied*, 469 U.S. 920 (1984).

■ PROBLEM 9-C. "They Saw It the Same Way I Did"

Shana Lynn sues Dr. Mark Filer and Florida West Hospital for malpractice in Tampa. She claims that he negligently failed to diagnose injuries she suffered in a diagnostic laparoscopy performed earlier by Dr. Donald Lewis, when Shana went to Tampa Family Hospital complaining of abdominal pain and nausea. In Florida West, Filer ordered a renal ultrasound and scan, which indicated the possibility of urine leaking into the abdomen ("excessive fluid above the bladder"). Filer performed a bilateral retrograde pyelogram, but results were "negative for a urine leak," and he did nothing further.

Lynn alleges permanent injuries resulting from Filer's failure to use stents to drain excess fluids. By the time Filer correctly diagnosed Lynn's condition, she suffered internal injuries, infection, and pain. At trial, Lynn's experts (Drs. Debra Miller of Atlanta and Nancy Nielson of Cleveland) testify that Filer breached the standard of professional care observed in the Tampa area.

As its expert the defense called urologist Donna Weaver, who described the problems in diagnosing Lynn's condition. Here is the critical part of her direct testimony:

Q: How did you determine the appropriate standard of medical care in this case?

A: Well I'm a urologist and I practice medicine here, and I'm familiar with Ms. Lynn's condition. I also spoke with eleven colleagues in urology here in Tampa.

Q: And at some point were you able to meet with your colleagues?

Plaintiff's Counsel: Objection, your honor. We're happy to hear what Dr. Weaver thinks, but she's about to say what her colleagues think, which is hearsay.

Defense counsel: The issue is standard of care, and that's what she's describing.

Court: Overruled. You may answer the question.

A: Well I presented Shana Lynn's case in two different forums. One involved five urologists with whom I spoke at our regular meeting. We did what you might call a "curbside consult" and I described the case and asked what my colleagues thought. I also made a formal presentation of her case to six urologists on staff at Tampa State Medical School. These urologists have been in practice here for many years.

Q: Based on those consultations, can you say to a reasonable medical certainty whether Dr. Filer met the prevailing standard of care in this area?

Plaintiff's counsel: Well your Honor, please, she can give her opinion, but not the opinion of others.

Court: Overruled, counsel, Dr. Weaver, you may answer.

A: Yes, he met the standard.

Q: Do you think you have a solid basis for that conclusion?
A: Yes, all eleven urologists share my view. They all see it the same way I do.
Plaintiff's counsel: Your Honor, please! She can't testify to what her colleagues think. That's blatant hearsay.
Court: Overruled, counsel. She's testifying to the standard in Tampa.

The jury returns a verdict for the defendant, and the court enters judgment dismissing the claim. Plaintiff appeals. Did the court commit error?

■ NOTES ON BASES FOR EXPERT TESTIMONY AND THE CONDUIT PROBLEM

1. Dr. Weaver can testify that Dr. Filer "met the standard" if that is her opinion. An objection that testifying to this point "invades the province of the jury" or "embraces an ultimate issue" would fail under FRE 704 (no such objection was raised). The hearsay objection is more challenging: Dr. Weaver testified that her eleven colleagues "share" her view and "see it the same way," which rests on—and conveys the substance of—her conversations with them. Is that going too far? FRE 703 seems to block *defendant* from exploring this point, but *plaintiff* could do so under FRE 705. Of course cross-examining Dr. Weaver on *her* opinion about Dr. Filer's performance may be helpful, but plaintiff can't cross-examine the other urologists.

2. The question before the factfinder in Problem 9-C involves standard of care. It wouldn't be realistic to allow only testimony by doctors relying on first-hand observations of treatments given to scores (maybe hundreds) of patients. Plaintiff called doctors from Atlanta and Cleveland, who must have gotten their information about Tampa standards by talking to Florida doctors. Medical experts *must* testify to local standards because there is no national standard. Often plaintiffs cannot find *local* doctors to testify, and must resort to out-of-town doctors. Whether Dr. Weaver (local doctor) testifies to the standard of care, or Dr. Miller (Atlanta) and Dr. Neilson (Cleveland), they *all* describe a standard that exists in "common professional knowledge and understanding," which can itself be found only in things like manuals and articles and "what professional people say." One modern opinion commented perceptively on professional knowledge, approving testimony by business executives on the quality of a paper copier:

> Business executives do not make assessments of a product's quality and marketability by inspecting the product at first hand. Their assessments are inferential, and as long as they are the sorts of inference that businessmen customarily draw they count as personal knowledge, not hearsay. All perception is inferential, and most knowledge social; since Kant we have known that there is no unmediated contact between nature and thought. Knowledge acquired

> through others may still be personal knowledge within the meaning of FRE 602, rather than hearsay, which is the repetition of a statement made by someone else—a statement offered on the authority of the out-of-court declarant and not vouched for as to truth by the actual witness. Such a statement is different from a statement of personal knowledge merely based, as most knowledge is based, on information obtained from other people.

Agfa-Gevaert, A.G. v. A.B. Dick Co., 879 F.2d 1518, 1523 (7th Cir. 1989). Similarly Dr. Weaver should be allowed to testify to the standard of care in Tampa by relying at least in part on what her 11 colleagues said.

3. Is there a problem because Dr. Weaver says her 11 colleagues "see it the same way," which suggests that they agree that Dr. Filer's conduct conformed to the standard? Suppose she testified this way: "I know the standard of care in Tampa, on the basis of my own practice, and from talking to others. I used my 'curbside consult' and 'formal presentation' to check my knowledge. I also know what Dr. Filer did, and I think he satisfied the standard." This testimony should be acceptable. Is it different enough from her actual testimony to matter? See State v. Towne, 453 A.2d 1133 (Vt. 1982) (error to let forensic expert testify that he consulted physician who wrote book with "the best description" of psychosexual disorders and that he concurred with expert's opinion) (reversing); Linn v. Fossum, 946 So. 2d 1032, 1039 (Fla. 2006) (error to admit testimony like that in Problem 9-C; opinion "by consensus" is "immune to challenge," as other side cannot cross-examine nontestifying experts; court cannot determine whether consulting expert, on whom witness relied, was qualified or had proper foundation) (reversing).

4. An expert must give *her* opinion, even if she relies on others. How can Dr. Miller of Atlanta and Dr. Neilson of Cleveland testify? Could they say they relied on their "experiences in practice, knowledge of the field, and conversations with local experts," and that Dr. Filer's treatment of Shana Lynn "did not meet the prevailing standard in Tampa"? The more heavily an expert relies on hearsay instead of experience, the more likely a court will exclude. See United States v. Tomasian, 784 F.2d 782, 785-786 (7th Cir. 1986) (expert could not testify to value of ivory tusks; he "consulted outside sources to ascertain the price per pound of ivory and then multiplied" that by weight; it would be different if he had given "an opinion based on hearsay," but he "could only relay another's opinion of the price per pound of ivory" and "had no opinion of his own" and did not know whether price per pound measures real value).

5. Can experts reasonably rely on statements by interested witnesses? See Dallas & Mavis Forwarding Co. v. Stegall, 659 F.2d 721, 722 (6th Cir. 1981) (excluding testimony by state trooper that car moved into left lane before accident; opinion did not rest on physical evidence, and came primarily from "story of a biased eyewitness"). But recall Baker v. Elcona Homes, 588 F.2d 551 (6th Cir. 1978) (officer Hendrickson relied on truckdriver in deciding who had the green light) (Chapter 4C6b, supra).

6. Should the judge alone decide, pursuant to FRE 104(a), whether an expert like Dr. Weaver has an adequate basis for her opinion, or should the judge act as screening agent and pass the decision to the jury under FRE 104(b)? What about a third possibility—that the expert herself might be the judge of the reasonableness of reliance? Compare In re Japanese Electric Products Antitrust Litigation, 723 F.2d 238, 276-277 (3d Cir. 1983) (experts testified that underlying data were of a type reasonably relied upon by similar experts, and court erred in "substituting its own opinion") with Soden v. Freightliner Corp., 714F.2d 498, 505 (5th Cir. 1983) (experts have "wide latitude in picking and choosing," but FRE 703 requires courts to examine "reliability of those sources"). Most courts agree more with *Soden* than with *Japanese Electric Products*, but judges pay close attention to what experts *say* that they need for a useful opinion.

7. In the *Crawford* era, courts generally *reject* defense attacks on expert testimony relying on hearsay. Recall the discussion of forensic lab reports and the suggestion in the *Bullcoming* case (described in Chapter 4C6c, supra) that an expert can offer an "independent opinion" based on tests performed by others without violating defense confrontation rights.

8. Some states have balked at the use of experts to present conclusions resting on unseen and untestable data. See Michigan Rule 703 (facts or data on which expert bases opinion "shall be in evidence"); Ohio Rule 703 (facts or data upon which expert bases an opinion "may be those perceived by the expert or admitted in evidence at the hearing").

4. Formal Problems—The Mental State Restriction

Tradition restricted expert testimony in ways that seem more formal than substantive. Rule 704 abolished one restriction—the one barring testimony on an "ultimate issue." But Congress amended Rule 704 to reinstate this restriction when it comes to expert testimony on the mental conditions amounting to elements of charges or defenses in criminal cases. And some of the traditional concerns persist in modern cases.

Ultimate issue restriction. At common law, witnesses (experts and laypeople) could not testify to ultimate issues, lest they "invade the province of the jury." This quaint phrase expressed a fear that certain testimony might push the jury into abandoning its responsibility to weigh evidence and determine facts, adopting uncritically whatever a witness might say. Still, relevant testimony can hardly help but address ultimate facts, and there is no particular reason to think that it is just such testimony that overwhelms juries. Rule 704 abolishes this old saw, and nobody has missed it.

One aspect of the old thought remains. Modern courts reject expert testimony on proper application of legal standards. The ACN to Rule 704 says courts ought to disallow questions phrased "in terms of inadequately explored legal criteria," but permit more specific questions, apparently phrased in readily understood terms. Thus an expert could not testify that decedent had "capacity to make a will" but could testify that he knew "the nature and extent of his property and the natural objects of his bounty."

Mental condition as element of claim or defense. As amended by Congress, Rule 704(b) bars experts in criminal trials from stating opinions that defendant had or lacked a mental state or condition "constituting an element of the crime charged or of a defense."[6] The purpose, as reflected in the Senate Report was to limit psychiatrists to "presenting and explaining their diagnoses," and prevent them from speaking in terms of "legal or moral constructs." Long before this change, an opinion in the District of Columbia Circuit argued for much the same result:

> [T]here is no justification for permitting psychiatrists to testify on the ultimate issue. Psychiatrists should explain how defendant's disease or defect relates to his alleged offense, that is, how the development, adaptation and functioning of defendant's behavioral processes may have influenced his conduct.

Washington v. United States, 390 F.2d 444, 456 (D.C. Cir. 1967) (applying older test in which insanity turned on whether crime was a "product" of mental illness).

■ NOTES ON FORMAL RESTRICTIONS

1. Courts have been challenged in trying to distinguish between adequately and inadequately explained criteria in a legal standard. Compare United States v. Burton, 737 F.2d 439, 443 (5th Cir. 1984) (excluding tax professor's opinion that taxpayer's theory was not implausible; evidence as to "uncertainty of the controlling law" is excludable under FRE 403) and Owen v. Kerr-McGee Corp., 698 F.2d 236, 239-240 (5th Cir. 1983) (excluding expert opinion on "legal" as opposed to "factual" cause of accident) with United States v. Gold, 743 F.2d 800, 817 (11th Cir. 1984) (approving expert testimony that claims were reimbursable under Medicare), *cert. denied,* 469 U.S. 1217 (1985).

2. Consider whether FRE 704(b) should apply in the following cases:

(a) In the trial of Bennett on charges arising out of a Ponzi scheme, in which he encouraged charities and donors to deposit money with New Era by promising that after a holding period such deposits would be matched by other donors, defendant offers psychiatric testimony that he suffers mental disorders that kept him from forming an intent to defraud, or made it unlikely that he would have had such purpose. Admit or exclude? See United States v. Bennett, 161 F.3d 171, 183 (3d Cir. 1998) (exclude; expert was to "go beyond" assisting jury by explaining the nature of the mental disease or describing its "typical effect," and was to "state expressly" whether he had the requisite intent).

---

[6] Congress also codified the insanity defense, in dissatisfaction over the acquittal of John Hinckley in the shooting of President Reagan. Hinckley was acquitted as insane. The statute defines insanity to mean that defendant, "as a result of a severe mental disease or defect, was unable to appreciate the nature and quality or the wrongfulness of his acts." It puts on defendant the burden of proving insanity "by clear and convincing evidence," and provides that mental disease or defect is not "otherwise" a defense. 18 USC §17.

(b) Lawyers sometimes use "mirroring hypotheticals" in cases like *Bennett*, asking "whether a person who suffers from the disorder attributed to the defendant would intend to defraud people if he set up the scheme that the defendant set up?" In *Bennett*, the court mentioned such techniques, citing United States v. Levine, 80 F.3d 129, 134 (5th Cir. 1996) ("hypothetical questions mirroring" facts in evidence violate FRE 704(b) when the answers reflect "a necessary inference as to whether the defendant did or did not have the mental state or condition" that is an element of a crime or defense).

(c) In his trial for attempted bank fraud involving phony instruments resembling checks submitted in payment of a mortgage along with a demand to refund the difference between the amount of the phony check and the amount of the debt, Joseph Finley offers a psychologist's testimony that he suffers from an "atypical belief system" that is "fixed and rigid," in support of his claim that he lacked intent. Admit or exclude? See United States v. Finley, 301 F.3d 1000, 1007-1013 (9th Cir. 2002) (admit; expert can testify on mental state as long as he doesn't "draw the ultimate inference or conclusion").

3. Rule 704(b) doesn't limit *lay* testimony on the mental condition of the accused, but FRE 701 blocks lay testimony based on "scientific, technical or other specialized knowledge within the scope of Rule 702," thus preventing an "end run" around the restrictions on experts, and the testimony described above *would* rest on "scientific, technical, or other specialized knowledge."

4. Should the judge admit expert testimony only if the witness states her conclusions to a "reasonable certainty"? Or can experts testify that the data suggest something that "could be" or "might be" so? See State v. Hebert, 480 A.2d 742, 749 (Me. 1984) (no "special degree of certainty" required). But see In re Air Disaster at Lockerbie, Scotland, on December 21, 1988, 37 F.3d 804, 824-825 (2d Cir. 1994) (excluding evidence suggesting alternative explanations to claim that bombing was work of terrorists, as "speculative and conjectural" since alternative theories lacked foundation). Traditionally expert testimony on medical prognoses had to satisfy a standard of "reasonable medical certainty," see Kimball v. Bahl, 727 N.W.2d 256, 261 (N.D. 2007) (expert medical opinion must be "expressed in terms of reasonable medical certainty, not mere possibilities"); State v. Kuehn, 728 N.W.2d 589, 597 (Neb. 2007) (expert need not use term "reasonable medical certainty," but opinion must be "sufficiently definite and relevant to provide a basis" for factfinder to determine issue). Some modern courts have backed away from this tradition. See People v. Ramirez, 155 P.3d 371 (Colo. 2007) (abandoning medical certainty standard; Colorado Rule 702 governs, and turns on reliability; even opinion stated with something "less than certainty" is admissible).

5. Presenting Expert Testimony: Stating Opinion Directly

When a party calls an expert, usually the first questions establish that the matter at hand could benefit from expertise. Then comes the foundation. In the case of a professional person (like a physician or engineer), usually the calling party brings out (1) educational background, including degree and certificate or license to practice, (2) experience, such as employment or practice, and (3) familiarity with the subject. The pattern is similar (but less elaborate) with skilled people having informal expertise resting on experience.

Qualifying the witness. Before the witness testifies on substance, the calling party asks the court to "qualify the witness as an expert." Sometimes initial questioning thoroughly establishes qualifications, and the court grants the request. (The adverse party may be all too willing to stipulate, hoping the preliminaries can be dispensed with, before the jury gets *too* impressed. But if credentials are impressive, the calling party usually declines this invitation and goes through the motions of qualifying the witness.)

Sometimes quite the opposite happens. The adverse party thinks he has a shot at undercutting the credentials, maybe even blocking qualification. He asks for "voir dire"—meaning essentially questioning him on his credentials and familiarity with the subject. After voir dire, the court rules. The question is governed by FRE 104(a): The court alone resolves this point (question is whether the witness is "qualified") and does not ask the jury to decide. If the expert qualifies, the calling party proceeds to substance. The most important point achieved by qualifying the witness as an expert is that he then can state his opinion on technical matters.[7]

Bringing out expert opinion. Recall the three bases for expert testimony—firsthand knowledge, facts learned at trial, and outside information (facts on which others in the field reasonably rely). How does one offer an opinion resting on such sources?

In somewhat elliptical fashion, Rule 705 provides the answer. The calling party may ask directly for the expert's "opinion," and the expert may offer her opinion "without first testifying" to the underlying basis. Of course establishing the basis first is not *prohibited*, and a party may prefer to do so. The point here is that he need not. Before looking closer at these two approaches, be advised that in the mild language of Rule 705, which speaks only to order of proof, lies an extraordinary change. (The Rule does contain qualifiers: The court may require "otherwise"—may force the proponent to bring out the underlying facts or data first. And the expert may have to yield up the basis for his opinion "on cross-examination.")

---

[7] Lesser advantages flow from qualifying the witness as an expert. Courts allow the calling party more latitude in phrasing questions. (The objection against "leading the witness" gets short shrift, at least in the case of professional people, who are unlikely to be led by a lawyer.) Qualifying the witness as an expert paves the way to compute witness "costs" at the statutory rate for experts. (In civil suits, the prevailing party normally recovers costs.) But most jurisdictions do not permit out-of-pocket costs of hiring an expert to be taxed to the losing party, and the statutory rate is set at a much lower level than experts actually charge, so this point is less important than it might seem. In the federal system, the statutory fee for both lay and expert witnesses is $40 per day. 28 USC §1821(b). See also Crawford Fitting Co. v. J.T. Gibbons, Inc., 482 U.S. 437 (1987) (expert fees taxed to losing party may not exceed amount authorized by §1821).

(1) Asking directly. Consider it a minute. Essentially Rule 705 permits a party to call a witness, qualify him as an expert, then go straight to the heart of the matter:

Q: Doctor Kirsten, do you have an opinion as to what caused Linda McMartin's nervous condition?
A (Kirsten): I do.
Q: What caused it?
A: The accident in May, in which her stationary car was struck from behind and rammed into the stopped car in front of her. The effect of the first impact was to ram her body sharply forward, which in turn snapped her neck and head sharply backward. The effect of the second impact, when her car struck the one in front, was just the reverse: Her body struck the steering wheel while her head and neck snapped forward. Essentially she suffered what we call severe whiplash, and that led to physical pain and dislocation of vertebra, then to nervous shock, and finally to what we call traumatic neurosis or anxiety, which was aggravated by her pregnancy and her natural fear over the health and life of her baby.

Testimony by a lay witness would never come out so directly. The proponent would be expected first to lay a foundation—to show that the witness has personal knowledge. The proponent would place her at the scene, show that she saw what happened, then bring out what she saw. Of course laying the foundation for a doctor to testify in the manner of Dr. Kirsten would differ. She would not have seen the impact, and would have acquired his knowledge after the fact. But analogy to the lay witness suggests that the proponent should establish that Dr. Kirsten examined and diagnosed Linda McMartin and bring out whatever facts might be essential to support her opinion that McMartin suffered a whiplash injury. Yet FRE 705 permits a qualified physician to testify *without* first establishing such points. Why?

There are two somewhat related reasons:

First is the frustration felt by lawyers, courts, and experts alike with the clumsiness of eliciting opinions by hypothetical questions. Experts traditionally based their testimony on information laid out in the form of questions summarizing that portion of the evidence that supported the answer sought by the questioning lawyer. But hypothetical questions became long and complex, taking up pages of trial record and requiring as much as 15 minutes to recite. Rule 705 takes the position that there must be a better way.

Second is the stride made by Rule 703 in letting the expert base opinion testimony on outside information (facts on which experts "reasonably" rely). To the extent that one can anticipate that an expert will be wise and responsible in sifting outside data, drawing on what is trustworthy and ignoring what is not, the risk in letting her state her opinion at the outset is not great—there is not much risk of a mistrial or need to strike testimony.

(2) Hypothetical questions. Rule 705 leaves open the more traditional approach, which proceeded by hypothetical questions. Imagine for a moment how the examination of Dr. Kirsten might have gone if plaintiff's counsel had embodied the necessary factual basis in a hypothetical question:

Q: Doctor Kirsten, I want to ask you what you think caused Linda McMartin's present nervous condition. Please assume the following facts to be true:

First, Linda was sitting in the driver's seat of her car at a full stop;
Second, her car was struck from behind by another car traveling at a speed on impact of ten to fifteen miles per hour;
Third, the force of that impact impelled Linda's car forward so that it struck another stopped car approximately eight feet in front of it;
Fourth, Linda was in good general health at the time, experiencing no particular anxiety, nervousness, or other disability;
Fifth, she was seven months pregnant at the time of the accident;
Sixth, Linda immediately experienced great pain in her neck and head;
Seventh, it was later discovered that she had suffered two dislocated vertebra; and finally
Eighth, from that time forward she became extremely nervous and anxious, suffering fears and constant worries, nightmares, and emotional distress leading to frequent crying and depression.

Now Doctor Kirsten, based on these facts, which I ask you to assume to be true, can you tell us what caused Linda's present physical and emotional condition?

A: Yes, sir. I would say that the accident caused Linda McMartin to suffer what we call severe whiplash injury. That in turn led to physical pain, dislocation of vertebra, to nervous shock, and finally to what we call traumatic neurosis or anxiety, aggravated by her pregnancy and natural fear for the health and life of her baby.

Eliciting expert opinion this way is cumbersome. The question is long and clumsy, and the supposing takes on a surreal quality—why should one have to suppose anything, when actual evidence has been presented? Besides, the focus is all wrong: When the point is to get at what the expert knows, the lawyer does most of the talking, and the answer, when finally given, seems almost an anticlimax.

There is more. The hypothetical question generated objection and argument: Opposing counsel would contend (if for no other reason than to be disruptive) that the question did not accurately sum up the evidence, or omitted crucial facts, or that the recited facts could not support the opinion sought, and so forth. So customary are such objections that typically the court instructs the witness please to wait and not to answer until the other party has a chance to object. While FRE 705 reduces the need to resort to the hypothetical question, lawyers still sometimes use it. Better reasoned decisions are more flexible, holding that the hypothetical question need not embody all pertinent facts, as long as it is reasonably complete and not misleading.

Implications of the new approach. Letting the calling party ask the expert directly for his opinion has greatly increased the importance of cross-examination as a means of testing that opinion. The framers anticipated this result, commenting in the ACN to Rule 705 that the cross-examiner may bring out data "unfavorable to the opinion," while acknowledging that the effectiveness of this approach depends upon "advance knowledge" acquired (in civil cases at least) through discovery under FRCP 26.

Recall the breadth of modern discovery. In criminal cases, the relevant provision is FRCrimP 16(g), which requires the government, on defense request, to turn over written summaries of expected expert testimony. In civil cases, the parties automatically turn over the names of experts they expect to call as witnesses, and provide written reports of such experts setting out their opinions and the underlying "facts or data." See FRCP 26(a)(2). Adverse parties may depose such experts, paying for their time. See FRCP 26(b)(4). If there are court-ordered physical examinations (as often happens in personal injury cases), a party who requests any resultant report must provide similar reports prepared by others who examined the person. See FRCP 35.

In a scheme that readily admits expert opinion by direct questioning, the lawyer's ability at trial to cross-examine effectively may depend on effective use of discovery.

■ NOTES ON PRESENTING EXPERT TESTIMONY

1. Assume that you are counsel for Linda McMartin, and you know Dr. Kirsten is qualified and prepared. Probably you would rather elicit Kirsten's testimony in the direct manner, and not by hypothetical questions. You might even hope the lawyer for the other side will bring out, on cross, the solid basis of Kirsten's opinion. But what if your adversary, knowing she is qualified and prepared, asks only a few questions probing at weak spots, or none at all? It might be wise for the proponent, even if she elicits an expert opinion directly, to bring out the underlying basis by further questions.

2. Are there circumstances in which eliciting opinion by hypothetical questions might still be useful? The answer is Yes—if your expert has *not* made a thorough investigation, or if you want to make use of an expert called by the other side (but in such cases lawyers often can't take the risk of getting unwelcome answers to hypothetical questions).

3. Traditionally the adverse party could demand and conduct a voir dire before the expert gave his opinion. Voir dire provided a chance at the outset to challenge credentials or show that the expert lacked sufficient foundation. A moment's reflection suggests that voir dire could expand into a full-fledged impeaching attack, and in this sense the approach authorized by Rule 705 came into tension with the voir dire process. Maine's counterpart to FRE 705 includes an additional subdivision that addresses this point:

> (b) *Objection.* An adverse party may object to the testimony of an expert on the ground that the expert does not have a sufficient basis for expressing an opinion. Counsel may before the witness gives an opinion be allowed to conduct in the absence of the jury a voir dire examination directed to the underlying facts or data on which the opinion is based. If a prima facie case is made that the expert does not have sufficient basis for the expert's opinion, the opinion is inadmissible unless the party offering the testimony first establishes the underlying facts or data.

See also Alaska Rule 705(b) and Delaware Rule 705(b), containing similar provisions. Is such language a good idea? See also Hawaii Rule 705 (expert may give opinion without first disclosing basis if underlying facts or data were "disclosed in discovery").

4. Is a lawyer, cross-examining a professional person on a technical subject, really up to the task of discrediting testimony already given? Some lawyers and judges entertain doubts. One experienced federal trial judge (since retired) used to require experts to testify by prepared scripts, exchanged with opposing counsel in advance:

> [A]dvance knowledge is so important that in civil cases I require an expert's direct testimony to be written out, in full, and provided to the other side well in advance of trial. Whether the testimony is presented in narrative or in question and answer form is optional with the attorney. In the courtroom, when the expert appears, I read or summarize her qualifications to the jury, clarify how an expert's testimony differs from that of an ordinary witness, and explain why her testimony will be different in form. I further caution the jury not to draw an inference from the fact that the expert will read the testimony. After the expert reads her direct testimony to the jury, the opposing attorney cross-examines her, and any loose ends are then picked up on redirect examination.

Pratt, A Judicial Perspective on Opinion Evidence Under the Federal Rules, 39 Wash. & Lee L. Rev. 313, 322 (1982). What benefits do you see from this approach? What drawbacks? It is at least open to doubt that judges have authority to require the calling party to "stick to a script" or to order exchanges of scripts among parties.

5. Most states following the federal model go along with Rule 705, but Ohio balked. Its corresponding provision says that the expert may give opinion testimony and reasons for it "after disclosure of the underlying facts or data." Would you prefer this approach?

6. The burden put on the cross-examiner by Rule 705 justifies strict enforcement, against a party offering expert testimony, of discovery obligations. Consider the *Smith* case, where the Tenth Circuit reversed an $800,000 judgment in a suit against an automaker for injuries in an accident allegedly caused by badly designed seatbelts. Plaintiff had given notice of his intent to call Dr. Freston to testify about "medical treatment" and "prognosis," but at trial Freston also said "the seat belt was involved" in the injury. The reviewing court noted that (a) two other experts, called by plaintiff and deposed by defendant, said they had no opinion about cause, (b) plaintiff did not disclose Freston's expected testimony in interrogatory responses, (c) plaintiff never said Freston would testify about cause, and (d) Ford did not get until trial a copy of an article that Freston relied on in his direct, and had "only eleven minutes" to prepare for cross:

> [T]he Federal Rules of Evidence contemplate that the "full burden of exploration of the facts and assumptions underlying the testimony of an expert witness [falls] squarely on the shoulders of opposing counsel's cross-examination." [Court cites Graham, Discovery of Experts Under Rule 26(b)(4) of the Federal Rules of Civil Procedure: Part One, An Analytical Study, 1976 U. Ill. L.F. 895, 897.] "Before an attorney can even hope to deal on cross-examination with unfavorable expert opinion he must have some idea of the basis of that opinion and the data relied upon. If the attorney is required to await examination at trial to get this information, he often will have too little time to recognize and expose vulnerable spots in the testimony." [Court cites Friedenthal, Discovery and Use of an Adverse Party's Expert Information, 14 Stan. L. Rev. 455, 486 (1962).] Finally, proper impeachment or rebuttal may have required advance knowledge so that Ford's own experts could have been consulted.

Smith v. Ford Motor Co., 626 F.2d 784, 799 (10th Cir. 1980), *cert. denied*, 450 U.S. 918 (1981).

6. Court-Appointed Experts

Regularly trial lawyers and commentators complain that expert testimony has become a cottage industry, that experts can be hired to advance any cause, and that trials become "battles of experts" that bewilder lay juries. Some believe the way out of this dilemma is for the court to appoint "independent" experts. Rule 706 authorizes this procedure.

Not surprisingly, segments of the trial bar vigorously oppose court appointment of experts, and Rule 706 seeks to solve or ameliorate some of their objections. Worries over surprise are answered by a provision that the expert will "advise the parties" of his findings and submit to a deposition taken "by any party." The fear that a court-appointed expert will be viewed as the responsibility of one party or another is answered in part by language allowing any party actually to call the expert and entitling all to cross-examine. Finally, the converse fear that the court-appointed expert will bask in a special aura of respectability is answered (at least in part) by language in Rule 706(c) implying that the source of the appointment need not be disclosed (the court may "authorize disclosure to the jury" that the court appointed the expert).

Yet court appointment of experts continues to be a rarity in American practice, perhaps for two reasons:

First is the adversary tradition. For the most part, judges are reluctant to interfere in presenting evidence. Trial lawyers deeply resent judicial participation, worrying that the judge does not understand the issues, strengths or weaknesses of the evidence, or the dynamics of the unfolding trial, so the judge will only "mess up the case" by meddling. They worry too over erosion of party control.

Second is the awkward problem of compensation. Rule 706(b) does address the point: It enables the court to fix compensation from funds "provided by law" in criminal cases and condemnation actions, and in civil cases to tax the parties for court-appointed experts "as other costs" are taxed. But courts are reluctant to draw on public funds for such purposes, and in civil cases the power to tax costs at the end may not satisfy an expert who is paid as he works. (Taxing costs earlier is awkward, as the loser usually pays.)

RELIABILITY STANDARD FOR SCIENTIFIC AND OTHER TECHNICAL EVIDENCE

1. Defining a Standard

For years American courts required evidence offered as science to satisfy a special standard: Such evidence must be "generally accepted" in the pertinent scientific community. There were many fears, but the central concern was that false and unreliable evidence would be offered and juries would be unable to appraise it wisely. Universally the standard was known as the *Frye* standard, after the two-page decision in Frye v. United States, 293 F. 1013, 1014 (D.C. Cir. 1923) (rejecting lie detector evidence).

In the last decade of the twentieth century, things changed. First, the Supreme Court decided the *Daubert* case in 1993, discarding *Frye* for federal courts in favor of a more flexible approach that was still designed to insure the reliability of scientific evidence. Second, the Court decided *Kumho Tire* in 1999, extending the *Daubert* standard to *all* expert testimony presenting technical or specialized material. Third, FRE 702 was amended in 2002 "in response to" *Daubert* (as the ACN says), so it formally requires expert testimony to rest on sufficient facts or data, reflect reliable principles and methods, and reliably apply these principles and methods.

Almost half the states follow *Daubert*, but 17 states (including California and New York) do not, and most of these follow their own versions of the *Frye* rule.[8] Perhaps equally significant, only about half the states followed the lead

[8] On a count taken in 2014, we find opinions in these 35 states that follow *Daubert* or adopt similar standards: Alabama, Alaska, Arizona, Arkansas, Colorado, Connecticut, Delaware, Florida, Georgia, Hawaii, Indiana, Iowa, Kentucky, Louisiana, Massachusetts, Michigan (by statute covering suits for injury or death), Mississippi, Montana, Nebraska, New Jersey, Maine, New Hampshire, New Mexico, North Carolina, Ohio, Oklahoma, Oregon, Rhode Island, South Dakota, Tennessee, Texas, Vermont, West Virginia, Wisconsin, and Wyoming. Opinions in 14 other states refrain from following *Daubert*, and most prefer something close to a *Frye* standard, including these: California, Idaho, Illinois, Kansas, Maryland, Minnesota, Missouri, Nevada, New York, North Dakota, Pennsylvania, South Carolina, Utah, and Washington. One state (Virginia) continues to defer any decision about *Daubert*.

of the federal Advisory Committee by revising their own counterparts to FRE 702, and the rest retain the original version, requiring only that the expert be qualified and that his testimony be helpful.[9]

As you read *Daubert*, consider its reasons for rejecting *Frye*. Bear in mind that *Frye* was the almost-universal the rule for 70 years. Consider why you might find the *Frye* approach attractive if you were a judge. Suppose you were presiding in a toxic tort case where claimants offered proof of causation in the form of expert testimony describing epidemiological studies indicating a statistical correlation between exposure (or taking medication) and outcome (ailments or birth defects). Suppose further that the defendants offered expert testimony that these studies were flawed because the reported correlations were not "statistically significant" and because variables ignored by the claimant's experts might account for the observed outcomes.

As trial judge, you might find yourself drawn to one or another of the following three approaches: First, admit the evidence because the experts are qualified and let the jury resolve the dispute. Second, decide for yourself whether plaintiff's proof is valid science and admit or exclude accordingly. Third, defer to the scientific community for its judgment on the validity of the proof, asking the proponent to show not only what the proof is and what it means, but that scientists generally agree with it. The *Frye* standard most clearly resembles the third approach. *Frye* would let you say to yourself, "I'm not going to let everything in and I'm not going to resolve scientific disputes myself; if I exclude anything I'll do it because other scientists don't accept the proof and I can tell the expert it's not my opinion that counts, but the verdict of other scientists."

Even before *Daubert*, courts were beginning to reject *Frye* as vague, manipulable, and too restrictive in excluding cutting-edge scientific learning. In 1985, Judge Becker wrote an influential opinion for the Third Circuit rejecting *Frye*. See United States v. Downing, 753 F.2d 1224 (3d Cir. 1985). As you will see, *Daubert* drew so heavily on *Downing* that the new standard might well be called the *Daubert-Downing* standard.

---

[9] These 19 states amended their counterparts, adding the three criteria described in the text above, but with some local variation: Arizona, Arkansas, Connecticut, Delaware, Florida, Georgia, Kansas, Kentucky, Michigan, Missouri, North Carolina, North Dakota, Ohio, Oklahoma, South Dakota, Utah, Vermont, West Virginia, and Wisconsin,. A few states have provisions with reliability criteria phrased differently. See counterparts in Indiana, Maryland, Minnesota, and Pennsylvania (referring to general acceptance criterion). The Colorado Supreme Court considered and rejected a proposal to amend its counterpart, and retained the original language. Again with local variation, most other state counterparts remain similar to the original federal language, as is true in these 20 states: Alaska, Hawaii, Idaho, Iowa, Louisiana, Maine, Montana, Nebraska, Nevada, New Hampshire, New Jersey, New Mexico, Oregon, Rhode Island, South Carolina, Tennessee, Texas, Virginia, Washington, and Wyoming.

Thomas Kuhn and Karl Popper: The Nature of Science

You are about to read *Daubert,* which came during an ongoing conversation in the academy about the nature of science. Thomas Kuhn had written *The Structure of Scientific Revolutions* in 1962, advancing a thesis that had become well-accepted—that science mostly advances in a normal way as experiments are conducted within a paradigm of theories and beliefs that are universally accepted. The scientist works out these theories and resolves anomalies where they appear. If too many anomalies appear; the paradigm comes into question and must be replaced (consider the shift from an earth-centered to a sun-centered view of the what we now call the solar system). Kuhn pushed further, and became controversial: Paradigm shifts are not, he argued, purely the product of reason and objective science, but are affected by social factors and historical situations—what we might term subjectivity. On a different side of this conversation stood Karl Popper, whose earlier work, *The Logic of Scientific Discovery* (1934), stressed that science means propositions that can be "falsified," meaning that replicable experiments can be devised that will show they are wrong, if they are. His point was not that science is purely objective, but that the conjectures that lead to discovery become accepted only if examined by exacting tests that detect weakness or error. When enough tests fail to falsify a proposition, it becomes accepted as true. Consider whether *Daubert's* view of science more closely resembles that of Kuhn or Popper.

Thomas Kuhn
(b. 1922; d. 1996)
Bill Pierce / The LIFE Images Collection / Getty Images

Karl Popper
(b. 1902; d. 1994)
The Estate of Sir Karl Popper

DAUBERT v. MERRELL DOW PHARMACEUTICALS

United States Supreme Court
509 U.S. 579 (1993)

Justice BLACKMUN delivered the opinion of the Court.

In this case we are called upon to determine the standard for admitting expert scientific testimony in a federal trial.

Petitioners Jason Daubert and Eric Schuller are minor children born with serious birth defects. They and their parents sued respondent in California state court, alleging that the birth defects had been caused by the mothers' ingestion of Bendectin, a prescription anti-nausea drug marketed by respondent. Respondent removed the suits to federal court on diversity grounds.

After extensive discovery, respondent moved for summary judgment, contending that Bendectin does not cause birth defects in humans and that petitioners would be unable to come forward with any admissible evidence that it does. In support of its motion, respondent submitted an affidavit of Steven H. Lamm, physician and epidemiologist, who is a well-credentialed expert on the risks from exposure to various chemical substances. Doctor Lamm stated that he had reviewed all the literature on Bendectin and human birth defects—more than 30 published studies involving over 130,000 patients. No study had found Bendectin to be a human teratogen (i.e., a substance capable of causing malformations in fetuses). On the basis of this review, Doctor Lamm concluded that maternal use of Bendectin during the first trimester of pregnancy has not been shown to be a risk factor for human birth defects.

Petitioners did not (and do not) contest this characterization of the published record regarding Bendectin. Instead, they responded to respondent's motion with the testimony of eight experts of their own, each of whom also possessed impressive credentials. These experts had concluded that Bendectin can cause birth defects. Their conclusions were based upon "in vitro" (test tube) and "in vivo" (live) animal studies that found a link between Bendectin and malformations; pharmacological studies of the chemical structure of Bendectin that purported to show similarities between the structure of the drug and that of other substances known to cause birth defects; and the "reanalysis" of previously published epidemiological (human statistical) studies.

The District Court granted respondent's motion for summary judgment. The court stated that scientific evidence is admissible only if the principle upon which it is based is "sufficiently established to have general acceptance in the field to which it belongs." The court concluded that petitioners' evidence did not meet this standard. Given the vast body of epidemiological data concerning Bendectin, the court held, expert opinion which is not based on epidemiological evidence is not admissible to establish causation. Thus, the animal-cell studies, live-animal studies, and chemical-structure analyses on which petitioners had relied could not raise by themselves a reasonably disputable jury issue regarding causation. Petitioners' epidemiological analyses, based as they were on recalculations of data in previously published studies that had found no causal link between the drug and birth defects, were ruled to be inadmissible because they had not been published or subjected to peer review.

The United States Court of Appeals for the Ninth Circuit affirmed. Citing Frye v. United States, 293 F. 1013, 1014 (D.C. Cir. 1923), the court stated that expert opinion based on a scientific technique is inadmissible unless the technique is "generally accepted" as reliable in the relevant scientific community. The court declared that expert opinion based on a methodology that diverges "significantly from the procedures accepted by recognized authorities in the field . . . cannot be shown to be 'generally accepted as a reliable technique.'"

The court emphasized that other Courts of Appeals considering the risks of Bendectin had refused to admit reanalyses of epidemiological studies that had been neither published nor subjected to peer review. Those courts had found unpublished reanalyses "particularly problematic in light of the massive weight of the original published studies supporting [respondent's] position, all of which had undergone full scrutiny from the scientific community." Contending that reanalysis is generally accepted by the scientific community only when it is subjected to verification and scrutiny by others in the field, the Court of Appeals rejected petitioners' reanalyses as "unpublished, not subjected to the normal peer review process and generated solely for use in litigation." The court concluded that petitioners' evidence provided an insufficient foundation to allow admission of expert testimony that Bendectin caused their injuries and, accordingly, that petitioners could not satisfy their burden of proving causation at trial.

We granted certiorari, in light of sharp divisions among the courts regarding the proper standard for the admission of expert testimony.

II

A

In the 70 years since its formulation in the *Frye* case, the "general acceptance" test has been the dominant standard for determining the admissibility of novel scientific evidence at trial. Although under increasing attack of late, the rule continues to be followed by a majority of courts, including the Ninth Circuit. The *Frye* test has its origin in a short and citation-free 1923 decision concerning the admissibility of evidence derived from a systolic blood pressure deception test, a crude precursor to the polygraph machine. In what has become a famous (perhaps infamous) passage, the then Court of Appeals for the District of Columbia described the device and its operation and declared:

> Just when a scientific principle or discovery crosses the line between the experimental and demonstrable stages is difficult to define. Somewhere in this twilight zone the evidential force of the principle must be recognized, and while courts will go a long way in admitting expert testimony deduced from a well-recognized scientific principle or discovery, the thing from which the deduction is made must be sufficiently established to have gained general acceptance in the particular field in which it belongs.

Because the deception test had "not yet gained such standing and scientific recognition among physiological and psychological authorities as would justify the courts in admitting expert testimony deduced from the discovery, development, and experiments thus far made," evidence of its results was ruled inadmissible.

The merits of the *Frye* test have been much debated, and scholarship on its proper scope and application is legion [Court cites articles in footnote].

Petitioners' primary attack, however, is not on the content but on the continuing authority of the rule. They contend that the *Frye* test was superseded by the adoption of the Federal Rules of Evidence. We agree.

We interpret the legislatively-enacted Federal Rules of Evidence as we would any statute. Beech Aircraft Corp. v. Rainey, 488 U.S. 153 (1988). Rule 402 provides the baseline [Court quotes Rule]. "Relevant evidence" is defined as that which has "any tendency to make the existence of any fact that is of consequence to the determination of the action more probable or less probable than it would be without the evidence." FRE 401. The Rule's basic standard of relevance thus is a liberal one.

Frye, of course, predated the Rules by half a century. In United States v. Abel, 469 U.S. 45 (1984), we considered the pertinence of background common law in interpreting the Rules of Evidence. We noted that the Rules occupy the field, but, quoting Professor Cleary, the Reporter, explained that the common law nevertheless could serve as an aid to their application:

> In principle, under the Federal Rules no common law of evidence remains. "All relevant evidence is admissible, except as otherwise provided . . . ." In reality, of course, the body of common law knowledge continues to exist, though in the somewhat altered form of a source of guidance in the exercise of delegated powers.

We found the common-law precept at issue in the *Abel* case entirely consistent with Rule 402's general requirement of admissibility, and considered it unlikely that the drafters had intended to change the rule. In Bourjaily v. United States, 483 U.S. 171 (1987), on the other hand, the Court was unable to find a particular common-law doctrine in the Rules, and so held it superseded.

Here there is a specific Rule that speaks to the contested issue. Rule 702, governing expert testimony, provides: "If scientific, technical, or other specialized knowledge will assist the trier of fact to understand the evidence or to determine a fact in issue, a witness qualified as an expert by knowledge, skill, experience, training, or education, may testify thereto in the form of an opinion or otherwise." Nothing in the text of this Rule establishes "general acceptance" as an absolute prerequisite to admissibility. Nor does respondent present any clear indication that FRE 702 or the Rules as a whole were intended to incorporate a "general acceptance" standard. The drafting history makes no mention of *Frye*, and a rigid "general acceptance" requirement would be at odds with the "liberal thrust" of the Federal Rules and their "general approach of relaxing the traditional barriers to 'opinion' testimony." Beech Aircraft Corp. v. Rainey (citing Rules 701 to 705). See also Weinstein, Rule 702 of the Federal Rules of Evidence is Sound; It Should Not Be Amended, 138 F.R.D. 631, 631 (1991) ("The Rules were designed to depend primarily upon lawyer-adversaries and sensible triers of fact to evaluate conflicts"). Given the Rules' permissive backdrop and their inclusion of a specific rule on expert testimony that does not mention "general acceptance," the assertion that the Rules somehow assimilated *Frye* is unconvincing. *Frye* made "general acceptance" the exclusive test for admitting expert scientific testimony. That austere standard, absent from and incompatible with the Federal Rules of Evidence, should not be applied in federal trials.

B

That the *Frye* test was displaced by the Rules of Evidence does not mean, however, that the Rules themselves place no limits on the admissibility of purportedly scientific evidence.[7] Nor is the trial judge disabled from screening such evidence. To the contrary, under the Rules the trial judge must ensure that any and all scientific testimony or evidence admitted is not only relevant, but reliable.

The primary locus of this obligation is FRE 702, which clearly contemplates some degree of regulation of the subjects and theories about which an expert may testify. "*If scientific*, technical, or other specialized *knowledge will assist the trier of fact* to understand the evidence or to determine a fact in issue" an expert "may testify *thereto*." The subject of an expert's testimony must be "scientific . . . knowledge."[8] The adjective "scientific" implies a grounding in the methods and procedures of science. Similarly, the word "knowledge" connotes more than subjective belief or unsupported speculation. The term "applies to any body of known facts or to any body of ideas inferred from such facts or accepted as truths on good grounds." Webster's Third New International Dictionary 1252 (1986). Of course, it would be unreasonable to conclude that the subject of scientific testimony must be "known" to a certainty; arguably, there are no certainties in science. See, e.g., Brief for Nicolaas Bloembergen

[7] The Chief Justice "does not doubt that FRE 702 confides to the judge some gatekeeping responsibility," but would neither say how it does so, nor explain what that role entails. We believe the better course is to note the nature and source of the duty.

[8] FRE 702 also applies to "technical, or other specialized knowledge." Our discussion is limited to the scientific context because that is the nature of the expertise offered here.

et al. as Amici Curiae 9 ("Indeed, scientists do not assert that they know what is immutably 'true'—they are committed to searching for new, temporary theories to explain, as best they can, phenomena"); Brief for American Association for the Advancement of Science and the National Academy of Sciences as Amici Curiae 7-8 ("Science is not an encyclopedic body of knowledge about the universe. Instead, it represents a *process* for proposing and refining theoretical explanations about the world that are subject to further testing and refinement") (emphasis in original). But, in order to qualify as "scientific knowledge," an inference or assertion must be derived by the scientific method. Proposed testimony must be supported by appropriate validation—i.e., "good grounds," based on what is known. In short, the requirement that an expert's testimony pertain to "scientific knowledge" establishes a standard of evidentiary reliability.[9] FRE 702 further requires that the evidence or testimony "assist the trier of fact to understand the evidence or to determine a fact in issue." This condition goes primarily to relevance. "Expert testimony which does not relate to any issue in the case is not relevant and, ergo, non-helpful." 3 Weinstein & Berger Par. 702[02], pp.702-18. See also United States v. Downing, 753 F.2d 1224, 1242 (CA3 1985) ("An additional consideration under FRE 702—and another aspect of relevancy—is whether expert testimony proffered in the case is sufficiently tied to the facts of the case that it will aid the jury in resolving a factual dispute"). The consideration has been aptly described by Judge Becker as one of "fit." "Fit" is not always obvious, and scientific validity for one purpose is not necessarily scientific validity for other, unrelated purposes. See Starrs, Frye v. United States Restructured and Revitalized: A Proposal to Amend Federal Evidence Rule 702, and 26 Jurimetrics J. 249, 258 (1986). The study of the phases of the moon, for example, may provide valid scientific "knowledge" about whether a certain night was dark, and if darkness is a fact in issue, the knowledge will assist the trier of fact. However (absent creditable grounds supporting such a link), evidence that the moon was full on a certain night will not assist the trier of fact in determining whether an individual was unusually likely to have behaved irrationally on that night. FRE 702's "helpfulness" standard requires a valid scientific connection to the pertinent inquiry as a precondition to admissibility.

---

[9] We note that scientists typically distinguish between "validity" (does the principle support what it purports to show?) and "reliability" (does application of the principle produce consistent results?). See Black, A Unified Theory of Scientific Evidence, 56 Ford. L. Rev. 595, 599 (1988). Although "the difference between accuracy, validity, and reliability may be such that each is distinct from the other by no more than a hen's kick," Starrs, *Frye v. United States* Restructured and Revitalized: A Proposal to Amend Federal Evidence Rule 702, 26 Jurimetrics J. 249, 256 (1986), our reference here is to evidentiary reliability—that is, trustworthiness. Cf., e.g., ACN on FRE 602 ("'The rule requiring that a witness who testifies to a fact which can be perceived by the senses must have had an opportunity to observe, and must have actually observed the fact' is a 'most pervasive manifestation' of the common law insistence upon 'the most reliable sources of information.'"); ACN on Art. VIII of the Rules of Evidence (hearsay exceptions will be recognized only "under circumstances supposed to furnish guarantees of trustworthiness"). In a case involving scientific evidence, evidentiary reliability will be based upon scientific validity.

That these requirements are embodied in FRE 702 is not surprising. Unlike an ordinary witness, see FRE 701, an expert is permitted wide latitude to offer opinions, including those that are not based on firsthand knowledge or observation. See FRE 702 and 703. Presumably, this relaxation of the usual requirement of firsthand knowledge—a rule which represents "a 'most pervasive manifestation' of the common law insistence upon 'the most reliable sources of information,'" ACN on FRE 602 (citation omitted)—is premised on an assumption that the expert's opinion will have a reliable basis in the knowledge and experience of his discipline.

C

Faced with a proffer of expert scientific testimony, then, the trial judge must determine at the outset, pursuant to FRE 104(a),[13] whether the expert is proposing to testify to (1) scientific knowledge that (2) will assist the trier of fact to understand or determine a fact in issue.[14] This entails a preliminary assessment of whether the reasoning or methodology underlying the testimony is scientifically valid and of whether that reasoning or methodology properly can be applied to the facts in issue. We are confident that federal judges possess the capacity to undertake this review. Many factors will bear on the inquiry, and we do not presume to set out a definitive checklist or test. But some general observations are appropriate.

Ordinarily, a key question to be answered in determining whether a theory or technique is scientific knowledge that will assist the trier of fact will be whether it can be (and has been) tested. "Scientific methodology today is based on generating hypotheses and testing them to see if they can be falsified; indeed, this methodology is what distinguishes science from other fields of human inquiry." Green, Expert Witnesses and Sufficiency of Evidence in Toxic Substances Litigation: The Legacy of Agent Orange and Bendectin Litigation, 86 Nw. U. L. Rev. 643, at 645 (1992). See also C. Hempel, Philosophy of Natural Science 49 (1966) ("The statements constituting a scientific explanation must be capable of empirical test"); K. Popper, Conjectures and Refutations: The Growth of Scientific Knowledge 37 (5th ed. 1989) ("The criterion of the scientific status of a theory is its falsifiability, or refutability, or testability").

Another pertinent consideration is whether the theory or technique has been subjected to peer review and publication. Publication (which is but one element of peer review) is not a sine qua non of admissibility; it does not

[13] [Court quotes FRE 104(a).] These matters should be established by a preponderance of proof. See Bourjaily v. United States, 483 U.S. 171, 175-176 (1987).

[14] Although the *Frye* decision itself focused exclusively on "novel" scientific techniques, we do not read the requirements of FRE 702 to apply specially or exclusively to unconventional evidence. Of course, well-established propositions are less likely to be challenged than those that are novel, and they are more handily defended. Indeed, theories that are so firmly established as to have attained the status of scientific law, such as the laws of thermodynamics, properly are subject to judicial notice under FRE 201.

necessarily correlate with reliability, see S. Jasanoff, The Fifth Branch: Science Advisors as Policymakers 61-76 (1990), and in some instances well-grounded but innovative theories will not have been published, see Horrobin, The Philosophical Basis of Peer Review and the Suppression of Innovation, 263 J. Am. Med. Assn. 1438 (1990). Some propositions, moreover, are too particular, too new, or of too limited interest to be published. But submission to the scrutiny of the scientific community is a component of "good science," in part because it increases the likelihood that substantive flaws in methodology will be detected. The fact of publication (or lack thereof) in a peer-reviewed journal thus will be a relevant, though not dispositive, consideration in assessing the scientific validity of a particular technique or methodology on which an opinion is premised.

Additionally, in the case of a particular scientific technique, the court ordinarily should consider the known or potential rate of error, see, e.g., United States v. Smith, 869 F.2d 348, 353-354 (7th Cir. 1989) (surveying studies of the error rate of spectrographic voice identification technique), and the existence and maintenance of standards controlling the technique's operation. See United States v. Williams, 583 F.2d 1194, 1198 (CA2 1978) (noting professional organization's standard governing spectrographic analysis), *cert. denied*, 439 U.S. 1117 (1979).

Finally, "general acceptance" can yet have a bearing on the inquiry. A "reliability assessment does not require, although it does permit, explicit identification of a relevant scientific community and an express determination of a particular degree of acceptance within that community." *Downing*. Widespread acceptance can be an important factor in ruling particular evidence admissible, and "a known technique that has been able to attract only minimal support within the community," *Downing*, may properly be viewed with skepticism.

The inquiry envisioned by FRE 702 is, we emphasize, a flexible one.[15] Its overarching subject is the scientific validity—and thus the evidentiary relevance and reliability—of the principles that underlie a proposed submission. The focus, of course, must be solely on principles and methodology, not on the conclusions that they generate.

Throughout, a judge assessing a proffer of expert scientific testimony under FRE 702 should also be mindful of other applicable rules. FRE 703 provides that expert opinions based on otherwise inadmissible hearsay are to be admitted only if the facts or data are "of a type reasonably relied upon by experts in

[15] A number of authorities have presented variations on the reliability approach, each with its own slightly different set of factors. See, e.g., *Downing*, 753 F.2d 1238-1239 (on which our discussion draws in part); 3 Weinstein & Berger, Weinstein's Evidence Par. 702[03] (on which the *Downing* court in turn partially relied); McCormick, Scientific Evidence: Defining a New Approach to Admissibility, 67 Iowa L. Rev. 879, 911-912 (1982); and Symposium on Science and the Rules of Evidence, 99 F.R.D. 187, 231 (1983) (statement by Margaret Berger). To the extent that they focus on the reliability of evidence as ensured by the scientific validity of its underlying principles, all these versions may well have merit, although we express no opinion regarding any of their particular details.

the particular field in forming opinions or inferences upon the subject." FRE 706 allows the court at its discretion to procure the assistance of an expert of its own choosing. Finally, FRE 403 permits the exclusion of relevant evidence "if its probative value is substantially outweighed by the danger of unfair prejudice, confusion of the issues, or misleading the jury . . . ." Judge Weinstein has explained: "Expert evidence can be both powerful and quite misleading because of the difficulty in evaluating it. Because of this risk, the judge in weighing possible prejudice against probative force under FRE 403 of the present rules exercises more control over experts than over lay witnesses." Weinstein, 138 F.R.D., at 632.

III

We conclude by briefly addressing what appear to be two underlying concerns of the parties and amici in this case. Respondent expresses apprehension that abandonment of "general acceptance" as the exclusive requirement for admission will result in a "free-for-all" in which befuddled juries are confounded by absurd and irrational pseudoscientific assertions. In this regard respondent seems to us to be overly pessimistic about the capabilities of the jury, and of the adversary system generally. Vigorous cross-examination, presentation of contrary evidence, and careful instruction on the burden of proof are the traditional and appropriate means of attacking shaky but admissible evidence. See Rock v. Arkansas, 483 U.S. 44, 61 (1987). Additionally, in the event the trial court concludes that the scintilla of evidence presented supporting a position is insufficient to allow a reasonable juror to conclude that the position more likely than not is true, the court remains free to direct a judgment, FRCP 50(a), and likewise to grant summary judgment, FRCP 56. Cf., e.g., Turpin v. Merrell Dow Pharmaceuticals, Inc., 959 F.2d 1349 (CA6) (holding that scientific evidence that provided foundation for expert testimony, viewed in the light most favorable to plaintiffs, was not sufficient to allow a jury to find it more probable than not that defendant caused plaintiff's injury), *cert. denied*, 506 U.S. 826 (1992); Brock v. Merrell Dow Pharmaceuticals, Inc., 874 F.2d 307 (CA5 1989) (reversing judgment entered on jury verdict for plaintiffs because evidence regarding causation was insufficient), *modified*, 884 F.2d 166 (CA5 1989), *cert. denied*, 494 U.S. 1046 (1990); Green 680-681. These conventional devices, rather than wholesale exclusion under an uncompromising "general acceptance" test, are the appropriate safeguards where the basis of scientific testimony meets the standards of FRE 702.

Petitioners and, to a greater extent, their amici exhibit a different concern. They suggest that recognition of a screening role for the judge that allows for the exclusion of "invalid" evidence will sanction a stifling and repressive scientific orthodoxy and will be inimical to the search for truth. It is true that open debate is an essential part of both legal and scientific analyses. Yet there are important differences between the quest for truth in the courtroom and the quest for truth in the laboratory. Scientific conclusions are subject to perpetual revision. Law, on the other hand, must resolve disputes finally and quickly. The scientific project is advanced by broad and wide-ranging consideration of a multitude of hypotheses, for those that are incorrect will eventually be shown to be so, and that in itself is an advance. Conjectures that are probably wrong are of little use, however, in the project of reaching a quick, final, and binding legal judgment—often of great consequence—about a particular set of events in the past. We recognize that in practice, a gatekeeping role for the judge, no matter how flexible, inevitably on occasion will prevent the jury from learning of authentic insights and innovations. That, nevertheless, is the balance that is struck by Rules of Evidence designed not for the exhaustive search for cosmic understanding but for the particularized resolution of legal disputes.[16]

IV

To summarize: "general acceptance" is not a necessary precondition to the admissibility of scientific evidence under the Federal Rules of Evidence, but the Rules of Evidence—especially FRE 702—do assign to the trial judge the task of ensuring that an expert's testimony both rests on a reliable foundation and is relevant to the task at hand. Pertinent evidence based on scientifically valid principles will satisfy those demands.

The inquiries of the District Court and the Court of Appeals focused almost exclusively on "general acceptance," as gauged by publication and the decisions of other courts. Accordingly, the judgment of the Court of Appeals is vacated and the case is remanded for further proceedings consistent with this opinion.

It is so ordered.

Chief Justice Rehnquist, with whom Justice Stevens joins, concurring in part and dissenting in part.

The petition for certiorari in this case presents two questions: first, whether the rule of *Frye* remains good law after the enactment of the Federal Rules of Evidence; and second, if *Frye* remains valid, whether it requires expert scientific testimony to have been subjected to a peer-review process in order to be admissible. The Court concludes, correctly in my view, that the *Frye* rule did not survive the enactment of the Federal Rules of Evidence, and I therefore join Parts I and II-A of its opinion. The second question presented in the petition for certiorari necessarily is mooted by this holding, but the Court nonetheless proceeds to construe FRE 702 and 703 very much in the abstract, and then offers some "general observations."

"General observations" by this Court customarily carry great weight with lower federal courts, but the ones offered here suffer from the flaw common to

[16] This is not to say that judicial interpretation, as opposed to adjudicative factfinding, does not share basic characteristics of the scientific endeavor: "The work of a judge is in one sense enduring and in another ephemeral . . . . In the endless process of testing and retesting, there is a constant rejection of the dross and a constant retention of whatever is pure and sound and fine." B. Cardozo, The Nature of the Judicial Process 178, 179 (1921).

most such observations—they are not applied to deciding whether or not particular testimony was or was not admissible, and therefore they tend to be not only general, but vague and abstract. This is particularly unfortunate in a case such as this, where the ultimate legal question depends on an appreciation of one or more bodies of knowledge not judicially noticeable, and subject to different interpretations in the briefs of the parties and their *amici.* Twenty-two *amicus* briefs have been filed in the case, and indeed the Court's opinion contains no less than 37 citations to *amicus* briefs and other secondary sources.

The various briefs filed in this case are markedly different from typical briefs, in that large parts of them do not deal with decided cases or statutory language—the sort of material we customarily interpret. Instead, they deal with definitions of scientific knowledge, scientific method, scientific validity, and peer review—in short, matters far afield from the expertise of judges. This is not to say that such materials are not useful or even necessary in deciding how FRE 703 should be applied; but it is to say that the unusual subject matter should cause us to proceed with great caution in deciding more than we have to, because our reach can so easily exceed our grasp.

But even if it were desirable to make "general observations" not necessary to decide the questions presented, I cannot subscribe to some of the observations made by the Court. In Part II-B, the Court concludes that reliability and relevancy are the touchstones of the admissibility of expert testimony. FRE 402 provides, as the Court points out, that "evidence which is not relevant is not admissible." But there is no similar reference in the Rule to "reliability." The Court constructs its argument by parsing the language "if scientific, technical, or other specialized knowledge will assist the trier of fact to understand the evidence or to determine a fact in issue . . . an expert . . . may testify thereto." FRE 702. It stresses that the subject of the expert's testimony must be "scientific . . . knowledge," and points out that "scientific" "implies a grounding in the methods and procedures of science," and that the word "knowledge" "connotes more than subjective belief or unsupported speculation." From this it concludes that "scientific knowledge" must be "derived by the scientific method." Proposed testimony, we are told, must be supported by "appropriate validation." Indeed, in footnote 9, the Court decides that "in a case involving scientific evidence, evidentiary reliability will be based upon scientific validity."

Questions arise simply from reading this part of the Court's opinion, and countless more questions will surely arise when hundreds of district judges try to apply its teaching to particular offers of expert testimony. Does all of this dicta apply to an expert seeking to testify on the basis of "technical or other specialized knowledge"—the other types of expert knowledge to which FRE 702 applies—or are the "general observations" limited only to "scientific knowledge"? What is the difference between scientific knowledge and technical knowledge; does FRE 702 actually contemplate that the phrase "scientific, technical, or other specialized knowledge" be broken down into numerous subspecies of expertise, or did its authors simply pick general descriptive language covering the sort of expert testimony which courts have customarily received? The Court speaks of its confidence that federal judges can make a "preliminary assessment of whether the reasoning or methodology underlying the testimony is scientifically valid and of whether that reasoning or methodology properly can be applied to the facts in issue." The Court then states that a "key question" to be answered in deciding whether something is "scientific knowledge" "will be whether it can be (and has been) tested." Following this sentence are three quotations from treatises, which speak not only of empirical testing, but one of which states that "the criterion of the scientific status of a theory is its falsifiability, or refutability, or testability."

I defer to no one in my confidence in federal judges; but I am at a loss to know what is meant when it is said that the scientific status of a theory depends on its "falsifiability," and I suspect some of them will be, too.

I do not doubt that FRE 702 confides to the judge some gatekeeping responsibility in deciding questions of the admissibility of proffered expert testimony. But I do not think it imposes on them either the obligation or the authority to become amateur scientists in order to perform that role. I think the Court would be far better advised in this case to decide only the questions presented, and to leave the further development of this important area of the law to future cases.

■ NOTES ON *DAUBERT* AND THE RELIABILITY STANDARD

1. The question whether *Frye*'s "general scientific acceptance" standard survived enactment of the Rules led to a long debate. Are you convinced by *Daubert*'s analysis? Recall United States v. Abel, 469 U.S. 45 (1984) (Chapter 8A1, supra), where the Court said the failure of the Rules to mention bias did not end this kind of impeachment: Citing the "state of unanimity" on this point, the Court in *Abel* said it was "unlikely" that the drafters of the Rules "intended to scuttle entirely" this kind of attack. Wasn't the *Frye* doctrine universal too?

2. Does *Daubert* discard *Frye*? If not, what is left of it? Clearly *Daubert* does not say the only question is whether the expert is qualified by training or experience, holding as well that the expert (in addition to being qualified) must present valid science. Where in the Rules does the Court find a requirement for valid science?

3. *Daubert* refines the method of scrutinizing scientific evidence. What factors does *Daubert* emphasize? In addition to factors enumerated in *Daubert*, a court could also take into account types of error, existence of a professional literature appraising the process or technique, nonjudicial uses and experience with it, its newness and relationship to established processes or techniques, and qualifications or stature of the witnesses. See United States v. Downing, 753 F.2d 1224 (3d Cir. 1985) (mentioning these factors).

4. One criticism was that *Frye* excluded too much evidence, but a new concern had arisen by the time *Daubert* was decided, which was that courts were being flooded with "junk science," and were taking more responsibility for risk management than they could handle. The term "junk science" was popularized in Peter Huber's *Galileo's Revenge: Junk Science in the Courtroom* (1991), which the Ninth Circuit cited in *Daubert.*[10] Huber's argument is that technology has made our environment safer, but that popular fears over toxicity and risk combine with lax evidentiary and legal standards to produce counterproductive court judgments that burden and stifle technology while undervaluing its contributions. Does *Daubert* respond more to the view that *Frye* kept too much expert testimony out, or to the view that lax standards let too much in? On remand, the Ninth Circuit again found that plaintiff's proof was not valid science. See Daubert v. Merrell Dow Pharmaceuticals, 43 F.3d 1311 (9th Cir. 1995) (without peer reviews, proponent must show validity another way, including testimony by experts explaining "how they went about reaching their conclusions" and showing that they "followed the scientific method" as practiced by at least a recognized minority; proof that Bendectin caused limb reduction defects must also satisfy criterion of "fit," which means it must show that "children whose mothers took Bendectin are more than twice as likely" to suffer defects as children of mothers who did not) (neither showing was made).

COMMENT/PERSPECTIVE: What Did *Daubert* Do?

In the Supreme Court, *Daubert* attracted attention as a potential watershed, and interest groups filed 22 amicus briefs, including trade associations, prosecutors, defense lawyers, scientists, physicians, and legal scholars. Some urged the Court to adopt a stricter standard; others urged a more flexible one. When the decision came down it was hard to figure out who won. All parties expressed satisfaction, perhaps because "no one is exactly sure what the new standard is." See Stewart, A New Test: Decision Creates Uncertain Future for Admissibility of Expert Testimony, 79 A.B.A. J. 48 (Nov. 1993). In the early years, it remained hard to assess. Some thought most cases would come out the same way, which happened in *Daubert* itself on remand. Some courts thought *Daubert* opened the door to evidence that would be excludable under *Frye.* See, e.g., United States v. Cordoba, 104 F.3d 225 (9th Cir. 1997) (remanding to reconsider admissibility of polygraph evidence under *Daubert*). Empirical work has yielded conflicting results, but two scholars doing extensive research (measuring removals by defendants to federal court to take advantage of *Daubert*) have concluded that it imposes a more stringent standard. See Jurs & DeVito,

[10] For scholarly developments of these themes, see Huber, Safety and the Second Best: The Hazards of Public Risk Management in the Courts, 85 Colum. L. Rev. 277 (1985); Epstein, The Legal and Insurance Dynamics of Mass Tort Litigation, 13 J. Legal Stud. 475 (1984).

The Stricter Standard: An Empirical Assessment of *Daubert*'s Effect on Civil Defendants, 62 Cath. U. L. Rev. 675 (2013) (civil defendants think the *Daubert* standard is "more restrictive"). See also Dixon & Gill, Rand Institute For Civil Justice, Changes in the Standards for Admitting Expert Evidence in Civil Cases Since the Daubert Decision xv (2001) ("after *Daubert*, judges scrutinized reliability more carefully and applied stricter standards in deciding whether to admit expert evidence"). In criminal cases, however, most studies have not found significant change. See Grosscup, et al., The Effects of Daubert on the Admissibility of Expert Testimony in State and Federal Criminal Cases, 8 Psychol. Pub. Pol'y & L. 339, 363 (2002) (appellate decisions in criminal cases show no change in "overall rate" of admitting of expert evidence). See also Michael Risinger, Navigating Expert Reliability: Are Criminal Standards of Certainty Being Left on the Dock, 64 Albany L. Rev. 99 (2000) (civil defendants win *Daubert* challenges "most of the time"; criminal defendants "virtually always lose").

5. For cutting-edge science, *Daubert* means the trial judge should determine issues of validity in a pretrial hearing, doesn't it? Such hearings can be major undertakings. In United States v. Bonds, 12 F.3d 540, 558-560 (6th Cir. 1993), the judge assigned to a magistrate the task of appraising DNA testing of blood in an FBI laboratory. The hearing took six weeks. The magistrate issued a 120-page report approving the evidence, and the reviewing court affirmed a conspiracy conviction and upheld the evidence ruling. Such an inquiry cannot be undertaken every time the government offers such proof. Must the next court undertake a similar inquiry?

6. Integrating the insights of science into the factfinding process of an adversary system is challenging. Some argue that the problem is the bias of experts who are paid by one side or the other. In *Melendez-Diaz* (described in Chapter 4C6c) the Court stressed the bias factor in requiring prosecutors to call lab technicians in criminal cases. For an argument that *Daubert*'s reliability standard does not adequately address adversarial bias in civil cases either, see David E. Bernstein, Expert Witnesses, Adversarial Bias, and The (Partial) Failure of the *Daubert* Revolution, 93 Iowa L. Rev. 451 (2008).

KUMHO TIRE COMPANY, LTD. v. CARMICHAEL

United States Supreme Court
526 U.S. 137 (1998)

Justice Breyer delivered the opinion of the Court.

[The right rear steel-belted radial tire of a minivan driven by Patrick Carmichael blew out, causing an accident that killed one passenger and severely injured others. The Carmichaels sued Kumho Tire (maker and distributor) in federal court. Plaintiffs relied on deposition testimony by Dennis Carlson, an expert in tire failure analysis.

Carlson in turn relied on certain features of tire technology: A steel-belted radial has a "carcass" containing layers of flexible cords ("plies"), and steel strips ("belts") that are laid between the plies and outer tread. Steel wire loops ("beads") hold the plies together along the inner circumference. The outer layer ("tread") encases the carcass, and the whole is bound together in rubber by the use of heat and chemicals. The tire rests on the "bead seat" of the wheel assembly, which contains a "rim flange" extending over the bead and holding the side of the tire.

Carlson assumed that the tire had traveled far. It had been made in 1988 and installed before the Carmichaels bought the minivan in March 1993. They had driven it about 7,000 miles before the tire blew out in July 1993. The tread depth (11/32 of an inch when new) was worn to depths ranging from 3/32 of an inch to nothing. The tire tread had punctures that had been inadequately repaired.

Nevertheless, Carlson concluded that a manufacturing or design defect caused the blowout. He relied in part on three premises, not disputed: First, the carcass should stay bound to the inner side of the tread, even after the tread is worn. Second, in this case the tread separated from its carcass prior to the accident. Third, this separation caused the blowout.

Carlson's conclusions rested on other propositions that are in dispute. First, if misuse in the form of "overdeflection" does *not* cause tire failure, then usually the cause is a tire defect. (Overdeflection means underinflating the tire or putting too much weight on it, generating heat that can undo the bond between the tread and the carcass.) Second, a tire misused in this way will reveal (a) greater tread wear on the shoulder than the center, (b) a "bead groove" where the bead pushes too hard against the bead seat inside the rim, (c) signs of deterioration on the sidewalls, such as discoloration, and (d) marks on the rim flange. The *absence* of two or more of these signs means that a defect caused the separation.

On inspecting the tire, Carlson found greater tread wear on the shoulder than the center, signs of a bead groove, discoloration, marks on the rim flange, and inadequately filled puncture holes (which cause heat leading to separation). Carlson thought these symptoms were not significant and did not show overdeflection. The extra shoulder wear, for example, appeared mostly on one shoulder (an overdeflected tire shows wear on both shoulders). Hence the tire did not reveal two of the four symptoms, so a defect caused the blowout.

The trial court ruled Carlson's testimony inadmissible because his methodology failed the reliability requirement of FRE 702 and *Daubert*, and granted summary judgment for the defense. Plaintiffs appealed, and the Eleventh Circuit reversed, concluding that *Daubert* applies only to scientific evidence, not to expert testimony more generally. The Supreme Court granted certiorari.]

II

A

In *Daubert,* this Court held that FRE 702 imposes a special obligation upon a trial judge to "ensure that any and all scientific testimony . . . is not only relevant, but reliable." The initial question before us is whether this basic gatekeeping obligation applies only to "scientific" testimony or to all expert testimony. We, like the parties, believe that it applies to all expert testimony.

[Court quotes FRE 702, which then consisted of the first sentence of present FRE 702.]

This language makes no relevant distinction between "scientific" knowledge and "technical" or "other specialized" knowledge. It makes clear that any such knowledge might become the subject of expert testimony. In *Daubert,* the Court specified that it is the Rule's word "knowledge," not the words (like "scientific") that modify that word, that "establishes a standard of evidentiary reliability." Hence, as a matter of language, the Rule applies its reliability standard to all "scientific," "technical," or "other specialized" matters within its scope. We concede that the Court in *Daubert* referred only to "scientific" knowledge. But as the Court there said, it referred to "scientific" testimony "because that [wa]s the nature of the expertise" at issue.

Neither is the evidentiary rationale that underlay the Court's basic *Daubert* "gatekeeping" determination limited to "scientific" knowledge. *Daubert* pointed out that FRE 702 and 703 grant expert witnesses testimonial latitude unavailable to other witnesses on the "assumption that the expert's opinion will have a reliable basis in the knowledge and experience of his discipline" (pointing out that experts may testify to opinions, including those that are not based on firsthand knowledge or observation). The Rules grant that latitude to all experts, not just to "scientific" ones.

Finally, it would prove difficult, if not impossible, for judges to administer evidentiary rules under which a gatekeeping obligation depended upon a distinction between "scientific" knowledge and "technical" or "other specialized" knowledge. There is no clear line that divides the one from the others. Disciplines such as engineering rest upon scientific knowledge. Pure scientific theory itself may depend for its development upon observation and properly engineered machinery. And conceptual efforts to distinguish the two are unlikely to produce clear legal lines capable of application in particular cases. Cf. Brief for National Academy of Engineering as *Amicus Curiae* (scientist seeks to understand nature while the engineer seeks nature's modification); Brief for Rubber Manufacturers Association as *Amicus Curiae* (engineering, as an "'applied science,'" relies on "scientific reasoning and methodology"); Brief for John Allen et al. as *Amici Curiae* (engineering relies upon "scientific knowledge and methods").

Neither is there a convincing need to make such distinctions. Experts of all kinds tie observations to conclusions through the use of what Judge Learned Hand called "general truths derived from . . . specialized experience." Hand,

Historical and Practical Considerations Regarding Expert Testimony, 15 Harv. L. Rev. 40, 54 (1901). And whether the specific expert testimony focuses upon specialized observations, the specialized translation of those observations into theory, a specialized theory itself, or the application of such a theory in a particular case, the expert's testimony often will rest "upon an experience confessedly foreign in kind to [the jury's] own." The trial judge's effort to assure that the specialized testimony is reliable and relevant can help the jury evaluate that foreign experience, whether the testimony reflects scientific, technical, or other specialized knowledge.

We conclude that *Daubert*'s general principles apply to the expert matters described in Rule 702. The Rule, in respect to all such matters, "establishes a standard of evidentiary reliability." It "requires a valid . . . connection to the pertinent inquiry as a precondition to admissibility." And where such testimony's factual basis, data, principles, methods, or their application are called sufficiently into question, the trial judge must determine whether the testimony has "a reliable basis in the knowledge and experience of [the relevant] discipline."

B

Petitioners ask more specifically whether a trial judge determining the "admissibility of an engineering expert's testimony" *may* consider several more specific factors that *Daubert* said might "bear on" a judge's gatekeeping determination. These factors include:

1. Whether a "theory or technique . . . can be (and has been) tested";
2. Whether it "has been subjected to peer review and publication";
3. Whether, in respect to a particular technique, there is a high "known or potential rate of error" and whether there are "standards controlling the technique's operation"; and
4. Whether the theory or technique enjoys "general acceptance" within a "relevant scientific community."

Emphasizing the word "may" in the question, we answer that question yes.

Engineering testimony rests upon scientific foundations, the reliability of which will be at issue in some cases. In other cases, the relevant reliability concerns may focus upon personal knowledge or experience. As the Solicitor General points out, there are many different kinds of experts, and many different kinds of expertise. See Brief for United States as *Amicus Curiae* (citing cases involving experts in drug terms, handwriting analysis, criminal *modus operandi*, land valuation, agricultural practices, railroad procedures, attorney's fee valuation, and others). Our emphasis on the word "may" thus reflects *Daubert's* description of the Rule 702 inquiry as "a flexible one." *Daubert* makes clear that the factors it mentions do *not* constitute a "definitive checklist or test." And *Daubert* adds that the gatekeeping inquiry must be "tied to the facts" of a particular "case" (quoting United States v. Downing, 753 F.2d 1224, 1242

(C.A.3 1985)). We agree with the Solicitor General that "[t]he factors identified in *Daubert* may or may not be pertinent in assessing reliability, depending on the nature of the issue, the expert's particular expertise, and the subject of his testimony." Brief for United States as *Amicus Curiae*. The conclusion, in our view, is that we can neither rule out, nor rule in, for all cases and for all time the applicability of the factors mentioned in *Daubert*, nor can we now do so for subsets of cases categorized by category of expert or by kind of evidence. Too much depends upon the particular circumstances of the particular case at issue.

Daubert itself is not to the contrary. It made clear that its list of factors was meant to be helpful, not definitive. Indeed, those factors do not all necessarily apply even in every instance in which the reliability of scientific testimony is challenged. It might not be surprising in a particular case, for example, that a claim made by a scientific witness has never been the subject of peer review, for the particular application at issue may never previously have interested any scientist. Nor, on the other hand, does the presence of *Daubert*'s general acceptance factor help show that an expert's testimony is reliable where the discipline itself lacks reliability, as, for example, do theories grounded in any so-called generally accepted principles of astrology or necromancy.

At the same time, and contrary to the Court of Appeals' view, some of *Daubert*'s questions can help to evaluate the reliability even of experience-based testimony. In certain cases, it will be appropriate for the trial judge to ask, for example, how often an engineering expert's experience-based methodology has produced erroneous results, or whether such a method is generally accepted in the relevant engineering community. Likewise, it will at times be useful to ask even of a witness whose expertise is based purely on experience, say, a perfume tester able to distinguish among 140 odors at a sniff, whether his preparation is of a kind that others in the field would recognize as acceptable.

We must therefore disagree with the Eleventh Circuit's holding that a trial judge may ask questions of the sort *Daubert* mentioned only where an expert "relies on the application of scientific principles," but not where an expert relies "on skill- or experience-based observation." We do not believe that Rule 702 creates a schematism that segregates expertise by type while mapping certain kinds of questions to certain kinds of experts. Life and the legal cases that it generates are too complex to warrant so definitive a match.

To say this is not to deny the importance of *Daubert*'s gatekeeping requirement. The objective of that requirement is to ensure the reliability and relevancy of expert testimony. It is to make certain that an expert, whether basing testimony upon professional studies or personal experience, employs in the courtroom the same level of intellectual rigor that characterizes the practice of an expert in the relevant field. Nor do we deny that, as stated in *Daubert*, the particular questions that it mentioned will often be appropriate for use in determining the reliability of challenged expert testimony. Rather, we conclude that the trial judge must have considerable leeway in deciding in a particular case how to go about determining whether particular expert testimony is reliable. That is to say, a trial court should consider the specific factors identified in *Daubert* where they are reasonable measures of the reliability of expert testimony.

C

The trial court must have the same kind of latitude in deciding *how* to test an expert's reliability, and to decide whether or when special briefing or other proceedings are needed to investigate reliability, as it enjoys when it decides *whether or not* that expert's relevant testimony is reliable. Our opinion in General Electric Co. v. Joiner, 522 U.S. 166 (1997), makes clear that a court of appeals is to apply an abuse-of-discretion standard when it "review[s] a trial court's decision to admit or exclude expert testimony." That standard applies as much to the trial court's decisions about how to determine reliability as to its ultimate conclusion. Otherwise, the trial judge would lack the discretionary authority needed both to avoid unnecessary "reliability" proceedings in ordinary cases where the reliability of an expert's methods is properly taken for granted, and to require appropriate proceedings in the less usual or more complex cases where cause for questioning the expert's reliability arises. Indeed, the Rules seek to avoid "unjustifiable expense and delay" as part of their search for "truth" and the "jus[t] determin[ation]" of proceedings. FRE 102. Thus, whether *Daubert*'s specific factors are, or are not, reasonable measures of reliability in a particular case is a matter that the law grants the trial judge broad latitude to determine. And the Eleventh Circuit erred insofar as it held to the contrary.

III

We further explain the way in which a trial judge "may" consider *Daubert*'s factors by applying these considerations to the case at hand, a matter that has been briefed exhaustively by the parties and their 19 *amici.* The District Court did not doubt Carlson's qualifications, which included a masters degree in mechanical engineering, 10 years' work at Michelin America, Inc., and testimony as a tire failure consultant in other tort cases. Rather, it excluded the testimony because, despite those qualifications, it initially doubted, and then found unreliable, "the methodology employed by the expert in analyzing the data obtained in the visual inspection, and the scientific basis, if any, for such an analysis." After examining the transcript in "some detail," and after considering respondents' defense of Carlson's methodology, the District Court determined that Carlson's testimony was not reliable. It fell outside the range where experts might reasonably differ, and where the jury must decide among the conflicting views of different experts, even though the evidence is "shaky." In our view, the doubts that triggered the District Court's initial inquiry here were reasonable, as was the court's ultimate conclusion.

For one thing, and contrary to respondents' suggestion, the specific issue before the court was not the reasonableness *in general* of a tire expert's use of a visual and tactile inspection to determine whether overdeflection had caused the tire's tread to separate from its steel-belted carcass. Rather, it was the reasonableness of using such an approach, along with Carlson's particular method of analyzing the data thereby obtained, to draw a conclusion regarding *the particular matter to which the expert testimony was directly relevant.* That matter concerned the likelihood that a defect in the tire at issue caused its tread to separate from its carcass. The tire in question, the expert conceded, had traveled far enough so that some of the tread had been worn bald; it should have been taken out of service; it had been repaired (inadequately) for punctures; and it bore some of the very marks that the expert said indicated, not a defect, but abuse through overdeflection. The relevant issue was whether the expert could reliably determine the cause of *this* tire's separation.

Nor was the basis for Carlson's conclusion simply the general theory that, in the absence of evidence of abuse, a defect will normally have caused a tire's separation. Rather, the expert employed a more specific theory to establish the existence (or absence) of such abuse. Carlson testified precisely that in the absence of *at least two* of four signs of abuse (proportionately greater tread wear on the shoulder; signs of grooves caused by the beads; discolored sidewalls; marks on the rim flange), he concludes that a defect caused the separation. And his analysis depended upon acceptance of a further implicit proposition, namely, that his visual and tactile inspection could determine that the tire before him had not been abused despite some evidence of the presence of the very signs for which he looked (and two punctures).

For another thing, the transcripts of Carlson's depositions support both the trial court's initial uncertainty and its final conclusion. Those transcripts cast considerable doubt upon the reliability of both the explicit theory (about the need for two signs of abuse) and the implicit proposition (about the significance of visual inspection in this case). Among other things, the expert could not say whether the tire had traveled more than 10, or 20, or 30, or 40, or 50 thousand miles, adding that 6,000 miles was "about how far" he could "say with any certainty." The court could reasonably have wondered about the reliability of a method of visual and tactile inspection sufficiently precise to ascertain with some certainty the abuse-related significance of minute shoulder/center relative tread wear differences, but insufficiently precise to tell "with any certainty" from the tread wear whether a tire had traveled less than 10,000 or more than 50,000 miles. And these concerns might have been augmented by Carlson's repeated reliance on the "subjective[ness]" of his mode of analysis in response to questions seeking specific information regarding how he could differentiate between a tire that actually had been overdeflected and a tire that merely looked as though it had been. They would have been further augmented by the fact that Carlson said he had inspected the tire itself for the first time the morning of his first deposition, and then only for a few hours. (His initial conclusions were based on photographs.)

Moreover, prior to his first deposition, Carlson had issued a signed report in which he concluded that the tire had "not been . . . overloaded or underinflated," not because of the absence of "two of four" signs of abuse, but simply because "the rim flange impressions . . . were normal." That report also said that the "tread depth remaining was 3/32 inch," though the opposing expert's (apparently undisputed) measurements indicate that the tread depth taken at various positions around the tire actually ranged from 5/32 of an inch to 4/32 of an inch, with the tire apparently showing greater wear along *both* shoulders than along the center.

Further, in respect to one sign of abuse, bead grooving, the expert seemed to deny the sufficiency of his own simple visual-inspection methodology. He testified that most tires have some bead groove pattern, that where there is reason to suspect an abnormal bead groove he would ideally "look at a lot of [similar] tires" to know the grooving's significance, and that he had not looked at many tires similar to the one at issue.

Finally, the court, after looking for a defense of Carlson's methodology as applied in these circumstances, found no convincing defense. Rather, it found (1) that "none" of the *Daubert* factors, including that of "general acceptance" in the relevant expert community, indicated that Carlson's testimony was reliable; (2) that its own analysis "revealed no countervailing factors operating in favor of admissibility which could outweigh those identified in *Daubert*"; and (3) that the "parties identified no such factors in their briefs." For these three reasons *taken together*, it concluded that Carlson's testimony was unreliable.

Respondents now argue to us, as they did to the District Court, that a method of tire failure analysis that employs a visual/tactile inspection is a reliable method, and they point both to its use by other experts and to Carlson's long experience working for Michelin as sufficient indication that that is so. But no one denies that an expert might draw a conclusion from a set of observations based on extensive and specialized experience. Nor does anyone deny that, as a general matter, tire abuse may often be identified by qualified experts through visual or tactile inspection of the tire. As we said before, the question before the trial court was specific, not general. The trial court had to decide whether this particular expert had sufficient specialized knowledge to assist the jurors "in deciding the particular issues in the case." 4 J. McLaughlin, Weinstein's Federal Evidence ¶702.05[1], p. 702-733 (2d ed. 1998); see also ACN on Proposed FRE 702, Preliminary Draft of Proposed Amendments to the Federal Rules of Civil Procedure and Evidence: Request for Comment 126 (1998) (stressing that district courts must "scrutinize" whether the "principles and methods" employed by an expert "have been properly applied to the facts of the case").

The particular issue in this case concerned the use of Carlson's two-factor test and his related use of visual/tactile inspection to draw conclusions on the basis of what seemed small observational differences. We have found no indication in the record that other experts in the industry use Carlson's two-factor test or that tire experts such as Carlson normally make the very fine distinctions about, say, the symmetry of comparatively greater shoulder tread wear that were necessary, on Carlson's own theory, to support his conclusions. Nor, despite the prevalence of tire testing, does anyone refer to any articles or papers that validate Carlson's approach. Indeed, no one has argued that Carlson himself, were he still working for Michelin, would have concluded in a report to his employer that a similar tire was similarly defective on grounds identical to those upon which he rested his conclusion here. Of course, Carlson himself claimed that his method was accurate, but, as we pointed out in *Joiner*, "nothing in either *Daubert* or the Federal Rules of Evidence requires a district court to admit opinion evidence that is connected to existing data only by the *ipse dixit* of the expert."

Respondents additionally argue that the District Court too rigidly applied *Daubert's* criteria. They read its opinion to hold that a failure to satisfy any one of those criteria automatically renders expert testimony inadmissible. The District Court's initial opinion might have been vulnerable to a form of this argument. There, the court, after rejecting respondents' claim that Carlson's testimony was "exempted from *Daubert*-style scrutiny" because it was "technical analysis" rather than "scientific evidence," simply added that "none of the four admissibility criteria outlined by the *Daubert* court are satisfied." Subsequently, however, the court granted respondents' motion for reconsideration. It then explicitly recognized that the relevant reliability inquiry "should be 'flexible,'" that its "'overarching subject [should be] . . . validity' and reliability," and that "*Daubert* was intended neither to be exhaustive nor to apply in every case." And the court ultimately based its decision upon Carlson's failure to satisfy either *Daubert's* factors *or any other* set of reasonable reliability criteria. In light of the record as developed by the parties, that conclusion was within the District Court's lawful discretion.

In sum, Rule 702 grants the district judge the discretionary authority, reviewable for its abuse, to determine reliability in light of the particular facts and circumstances of the particular case. The District Court did not abuse its discretionary authority in this case. Hence, the judgment of the Court of Appeals is

Reversed.

Justice SCALIA, with whom Justice O'CONNOR and Justice THOMAS join, concurring.

[Trial judges have discretion to "choose among *reasonable* means" of appraising science; they do not have discretion to perform the gatekeeping responsibility "inadequately."]

Justice STEVENS, concurring in part and dissenting in part.

[The question whether Dennis Carlson should have been allowed to testify should be decided by the trial court under the correct standard, as set forth in this opinion.]

■ NOTES ON *KUMHO TIRE* AND THE BROADENING OF THE *DAUBERT* STANDARD

1. *Daubert* emphasized the term "scientific" in FRE 702, so applying *Daubert* to all expert testimony was not a foregone conclusion. Yet prior to

Kumho Tire courts were not sure whether *Daubert* applied to experts in technical fields like engineering, medicine, psychiatry, and economics. *Kumho Tire* put an end to those doubts, and got rid of the problem of distinguishing science from other expertise: Are you convinced that *Daubert* extends as far as *Kumho Tire* said, or that it was wise to extend *Daubert* that far?

2. *Daubert* says the judge should look not only at "reasoning or methodology," but at *application* of reasoning and methodology. The focus is the "task at hand," not the contours of theory or method. *Kumho Tire* makes the same point: The question was not "the reasonableness in general of a tire expert's use of visual and tactile inspection," but the reasonableness of the method and approach "regarding the *particular matter*" to which he testifies. That means the judge is supposed to take a close look, doesn't it?

3. Consider FRE 702, as amended in 2000 after *Daubert* and *Kumho Tire*. Paraphrasing, expert testimony must be based on "sufficient facts or data," and must be "the product of reliable principles and methods" that are "reliably applied" to the facts. This amendment encapsulates the standard emerging from *Daubert* and *Kumho Tire*.

(a) The idea of sufficient basis is implicit in *Daubert*, and one can reasonably insist on such a basis in assessing reliability. Under *Daubert*, judges play a "gatekeeping" function. The criteria in amended Rule 702 look like specifications of admissibility, which are for judges to apply under FRE 104(a), not for juries under 104(b).

(b) The question whether technicians followed lab protocol determines whether principles and methods were "reliably applied to the facts," doesn't it? That means judges determine the point (it affects admissibility under 104(a)), rather than juries determining it as a matter of "weight." Giving the matter to the judge seems the right thing to do because it is part of the reliability standard, but pre-amendment decisions split on this point. The same issues affect weight as well, however, so the jury can take another look at this element if the evidence is admitted. See Edward J. Imwinkelried, The Debate in the DNA Cases Over the Foundation for the Admission of Scientific Evidence: The Importance of Human Error as a Cause of Forensic Misanalysis, 69 Wash. U. L.Q. 19 (1991) (matters of protocol should affect admissibility, not just weight).

4. *Kumho Tire* says an expert can testify on the basis of experience, citing the perfume tester. The ACN picks up this thought: "Nothing in this amendment is intended to suggest that experience alone . . . may not provide a sufficient foundation for expert testimony." An expert who relies "solely or primarily" on experience, however, must explain how experience "leads to [her] conclusion," why it is "a sufficient basis," and "how that experience [can be] reliably applied to the facts." How does an expert relying on experience provide an explanation? Consider this hypothetical exchange suggested by Professor David Crump:

Question: Mr Perfume Sniffer, the Supreme Court says that I must first ask you whether your testimony identifying perfumes by the nasal method is based upon "sufficient facts or data."

Answer: Well, I sniffed the perfume. Is that "sufficient facts or data?"
Q: And I have to ask you whether your testimony is the product of "reliable principles and methods."
A: Look, I smelled Chanel No. 5. I know I smelled Chanel No. 5.
Q: And did you "apply the principles and methods reliably to the facts of the case?"
A: I used my nose. That's all I can do.

See David Crump, The Trouble with *Daubert-Kumho*: Reconsidering the Supreme Court's Philosophy of Science, 68 Mo. L. Rev. 1, 15 (2003). Does such an examination satisfy the FRE 702 standard?

5. *Kumho Tire* stresses that the judge has discretion in deciding whether any particular criterion is satisfied *and* in deciding what criteria to apply in the first place.

(a) The discretionary element came less from *Daubert*, which alludes to discretion only in calling for flexibility, than from the later decision in the *Joiner* case. *Joiner* reviewed a decision by the Eleventh Circuit interpreting *Daubert* to mean that any ruling *excluding* scientific evidence was subject to a "particularly stringent" standard of review—suggesting, in other words, that *Daubert* loosened the standard for admitting scientific evidence. The Court rejected this holding, taking the position that rulings either way—admitting or excluding scientific evidence—involve discretion and should be reviewed for abuse. See General Electric Co. v. Joiner, 522 U.S. 136 (1997). In *Kumho Tire*, discretion gets even more emphasis, becoming central to the *Daubert* standard.

(b) Discretion is important in applying general principles, such as those in FRE 403 (weighing probative value against unfair prejudice) and 611 (controlling mode and order of presenting evidence). Discretion is also a key concept where rules and appellate scrutiny cannot do much better in handling problems than trial courts can do on their own, with only general guidance. Is *Daubert* a good setting in which to confer broad discretion on trial courts? Don't *Daubert* and *Kumho Tire*, taken together, tell trial judges, "You must be careful, but we won't look hard at what you do"? Not surprisingly, opinions reviewing *Daubert* issues reverse only for abuse of discretion. But this hands-off attitude is not universal. Decisions in at least nine states and the District of Columbia endorse far more searching appellate review. See, e.g., Schultz v. State, 664 A.2d 60, 64 (Md. App. 1994) (question of reliability of scientific technique "does not vary according to the circumstances of each case," so it is inappropriate to apply abuse of discretion standard on review). There is no reason, is there, to think trial judges can better appraise the validity of science than appellate judges? For an argument that trial judges need more guidance and appellate courts should exercise closer scrutiny, see Christopher Mueller, *Daubert* Asks the Right Questions: Now Appellate Courts Should Help Find the Right Answers, 33 Seton Hall L. Rev. 987 (2003).

(c) Did the decision to extend *Daubert* to expertise in general lead the Court in *Kumho Tire* to stress discretion? Could *Daubert* work in the broader setting otherwise?

6. The question often arises, when scientific evidence is statistical, whether the results would be viewed as significant in the scientific community. The convention is to insist on results that are so strong that there is only a 5 percent probability that the observed correlation, which itself might be large (like a 50 percent increase in ailment from exposure) or small (like an 8 percent increase), is the result of chance or accident.

(a) Should we make do with less persuasive evidence because courts, unlike scientists and scholars, must answer today's questions today and cannot wait for better results? One scholar argues that a scientist should be allowed to testify that, although the correlation would not satisfy the usual required level of statistical significance (p = .05), still the scientist herself finds the correlation persuasive, and might base a personal decision on it. See Neil Cohen, The Gatekeeping Role in Civil Litigation and the Abdication of Legal Values in Favor of Scientific Values, 33 Seton Hall L. Rev. 943 (2003).

(b) In thinking about this question, don't equate the conventional level of statistical significance with the certainty of the conclusion:

> [T]he conventional standard does *not* mean that science usually accepts only results that are 95% certain. Statistical significance at the level of p = .05 means that there is but one chance in 20 that the observed results could happen by chance. *Satisfying* the standard means that there is one chance in 20 (or less) that mere accidental variation would produce such a result, not that we can be 95% certain that the outcome (22 out of 42 observed ailments were caused by exposure . . .) is correct. We do not and cannot know that. All we know is that the observed outcome would rarely be produced by chance alone, which gives us *some reason* to believe that the indicated correlation is correct. Any suggestion, however, that the conventional standard produces results of which we are 95% certain is false.

Christopher Mueller, *Daubert* Asks the Right Questions: Now Appellate Courts Should Help Find the Right Answers, 33 Seton Hall L. Rev. 987, 1013 (2003) (acknowledging that "we should consider carefully the possibility of accepting results in lawsuits that scientists are not yet prepared to accept," but stating reservations).

(c) Some modern courts stress that the conventional p-value standard is but one indicator of the probative value of statistical studies. See, e.g., King v. Burlington Northern Santa Fe Ry. Co., 762 N.W.2d 24 (Neb. 2009) (declining to impose statistical significance requirement "if an expert shows that others in the field would nevertheless rely on the study to support a causation opinion and that the probability of chance causing the study's results is low"); DeLuca v. Merrell Dow Pharmaceuticals, Inc., 911 F.2d 941, 955 (3d Cir. 1990) (when p-value exceeds .05, it is common to reject results as statistically insignificant,

but confidence levels and statistical significance are "but a part of a meaningful evaluation").

(d) In the *Milward* case, the First Circuit reversed a judgment dismissing a toxic tort case for error in excluding expert testimony for the plaintiff, who alleged that his rare form of leukemia known as APL was caused by benzene compounds to which he was exposed as a refrigeration technician. A toxicologist was prepared to testify, on the basis of a "weight of the evidence" approach to general causation pioneered by Bradford Hill, that exposure to benzene "can cause" APL. The trial court challenged the conclusion as flawed for technical reasons (insufficient evidence of common etiology for APL, insufficient knowledge on relationship between "chromosomal translocations" and APL, insufficient evidence that benzene can cause these translocations), and because the indicated conclusion was not generally accepted. The reviewing court faulted the judge for analyzing each component of the analysis on its own, and for not recognizing that the toxicologist looked at each body of evidence when "combined with other evidence" in drawing an inference of cause. The reviewing court approved an approach counting many viewpoints, stressing that different scientists reach different conclusions but that this fact does not mean the approach is "any less scientific." See Milward v. Acuity Specialty Products Group, Inc., 639 F.3d 11 (1st Cir. 2011).

7. More generally, does *Daubert* exclude too much scientific evidence out of a concern to conform legal standards to scientific standards? See David E. Bernstein, Expert Witnesses, Adversarial Bias, and The (Partial) Failure of the Daubert Revolution, 93 Iowa L. Rev. 451, 488 (2008) (*Daubert* weeds out junk science in exposure cases, but at the price of excluding "speculative" evidence that "most experts" would credit); Charles R. Nesson, Agent Orange Meets the Blue Bus: Factfinding at the Frontier of Knowledge, 66 B.U. L. Rev. 521, 529-530 (1986) (scientist exploring hypothesis that exposure causes cancer is "likely to suspend scientific judgment" until testing or study can eliminate alternatives; doctor, lawyer, or judge "does not have the luxury of postponing a decision," and juries must reach conclusions without "waiting for scientific demonstration"). But see Ronald Allen, Rationality, Mythology, and the "Acceptability of Verdicts" Thesis, 66 B.U. L. Rev. 541, 561-562 (1986) (courts should not depart from reality as best we can reconstruct it; system should "strive for rationality").

COMMENT/PERSPECTIVE: *Daubert* in Civil Cases

Some think *Daubert* is too stringently applied to exclude proof of causation in toxic exposure cases, praising the *Milward* case (note 6(d), supra) as the better approach. Professor Michael Green argues that scientists "do not think in probabilistic terms about causation," but consider "comparative costs of false positives and false negatives," which points toward resorting even to treatment with low probability of success if the ailment would otherwise bring death. Scientists, Green argues, consider the "weight of the evidence" in resolving such dilemmas, often using the Hill criteria (strength of observed correlations, consistency, specificity, coherence, etc.). Green's point is that experts exercise "judgment" and there is "no algorithm" that yields a definite answer. See Michael D. Green, Pessimism About Milward, 3 Wake Forest J.L. & Policy 41, 46-47 (2013) (but conscious bias, affiliation bias, and selection bias make it unlikely that *Milward* approach will prevail in court). Professor Joseph Sanders argues that *Milward* exposed a "rhetorical conflict" emerging from *Daubert*, and that Justice Rehnquist in *Joiner* (note 5(a), supra) took an "atomistic" approach in a "deconstructive exercise" in which he concluded that elements in plaintiff's proof did not support the conclusion. *Milward,* in contrast, recognizes that the weakness in elements of proof may not matter, as "the sum of the parts *may* be greater than each study by itself." See Joseph Sanders, Milward v. Acuity Special Products Group: Constructing and Deconstructing Science and Law In Judicial Opinions, 3 Wake Forest J.L. & Pol'y 141, 158-170 (2013).

Others are not sure that *Milward* improved the situation. Professor David Bernstein faults *Milward* for having "misapplied basic scientific concepts" in suggesting that its "weight of the evidence" approach reflects "a reasoning process that is both scientific and reliable," in the process inviting any expert to testify "in light of the weight he chooses to give each item," which ignores the directive in *Joiner* to examine each item of evidence and decide whether it is valid science. See David E. Bernstein, The Misbegotten Judicial resistance to the *Daubert* Revolution, 89 Notre Dame L. Rev. 27, 60-63 (2013).

2. Modern Science in the Courtroom

Even to survey the field of scientific evidence with a sample of cases from each area would make this book much too long. Standard treatises address these areas, offering both scientific and legal insights. See D. Faigman, D. Kaye, M. Saks & J. Sanders, Modern Scientific Evidence (2013); P. Giannelli & E. Imwinkelried, Scientific Evidence (4th ed. 2012). Suffice it to say that technical evidence relating to ballistics, epidemiology, fingerprints, intoxication, footprints, analysis of hair and human tissue, and innumerable other subjects are staples in the trial process.

Scientific evidence sometimes presents great challenge. Questions of causation in toxic tort cases like *Daubert* have proved difficult. The same is true of "syndrome" evidence developed by psychologists working with techniques of social science, which is commonplace in trials on charges of child abuse, sexual assault, and domestic violence. A third area of challenge involves DNA evidence in criminal and paternity cases. With DNA evidence comes statistics (these play a role in toxic tort cases too), which in turn lead to Bayesian estimates of the likelihood that important propositions are true, as is visible in paternity cases. To these areas we now turn.

a. Toxic Tort Cases

In toxic tort cases like *Daubert*, science often has no answer to the crucial question. Proof of causation takes the form of cluster studies (people in exposed area experience higher rates of illness), short-term screening assays (testing effects of chemicals on bacteria or cells in culture dishes), "differential diagnosis" (by process of elimination, doctor concludes that only exposure to the agent in question could account for the ailment), animal studies, and epidemiology (statistical analyses of disease incidence). The first three kinds of proof can be obtained relatively quickly and cheaply, but the latter two are expensive and take a long time to develop.

The strength of epidemiological evidence, which is in some respects the most persuasive kind, varies widely in ways requiring the skills of a statistician to explain. One great difficulty in all such proof is that it typically leaves the question of causation in any particular case unanswered. The problem for the factfinder is compounded when issues of multiple or synergistic causation appear (did asbestos cause lung cancer, or was smoking the cause, or both?). Another difficulty is that such proof often shows only an increase in ailments from exposure (20 out of 1,000 unexposed people suffer the ailment; 35 out of 1,000 exposed people suffer the ailment), which suggests "general" or "possible" cause, but cannot support an inference of cause in any particular case. To support an inference that a particular person caught the ailment from the exposure, it is sometimes thought that the proof must show at least a "doubling" of risk (20 out of 1,000 unexposed people suffer the ailment; 50 out of 1,000 exposed people suffer the ailment).

The increased scrutiny of such proof that *Daubert* invites has led to increased use of summary judgment throwing out cases that depend on unproven science. Some criticize this development. See Margaret A. Berger, Upsetting the Balance Between Adverse Interests: The Impact of the Supreme Court's Trilogy on Expert Testimony in Toxic Tort Litigation, 64 Law & Contemp. Probs. 289 (2001) (courts mistakenly require epidemiological evidence to prove doubling of risk; federal courts should look to state requirements for proving causation); Lucinda Finley, Guarding the Gate to the Courthouse: How Trial Judges are Using their Evidentiary Screening Role to Remake Tort Causation Rules, 49 DePaul L. Rev. 335 (1999) (courts should not place burden of scientific uncertainty on plaintiffs). For defenses of *Daubert*, see Joseph Sanders, The Paternalistic Justification for Restrictions on the Admissibility of Expert Evidence, 33 Seton Hall L. Rev. 881 (2003) (judges can better appraise science than juries); Christopher Mueller, *Daubert* Asks the Right Questions: Now Appellate Courts Should Help Find the Right Answers, 33 Seton Hall L. Rev. 987, 993 (2003) (reaching similar conclusion).

Proposals to address these matters vary, from resort to procedural mechanisms like class actions, allowing use of statistics to prove causation, allowing recovery proportional to the likelihood of cause, and creating funds to compensate victims. But the road has been rocky, and innovative reforms have not succeeded. The Court has warned that class suits may not be able to reach global solutions. See Ortiz v. Fibreboard Corp., 527 U.S. 815 (1999) (disapproving proposed settlement of asbestos cases because, among other things, interests of claimants were too disparate); Amchem Products, Inc. v. Windsor, 521 U.S. 591 (1997) (disapproving relaxation of procedural requirements in connection with "settlement class"). Congress has not stepped into the picture, although legislative proposals to resolve massive cases routinely appear.

b. Syndrome and Social Framework Evidence

In the 1990s, expert testimony describing syndromes and social frameworks came of age. In three settings such proof has become commonplace, although controversy and disagreement continue on points of detail.

Child abuse trials. In child abuse cases, courts admit testimony on battered child syndrome (BCS) and child sexual abuse accommodation syndrome (CSAAS). In abuse cases, experts describe delay in reporting, initial reporting of only part of what happened, behavioral problems at school, vomiting, sexualized play, regression in toilet training (younger children), disclosure to a friend, withdrawal and daydreaming, and low self-esteem (older children). See People v. Spicola, 947 N.E.2d 620 (N.Y. 2011) (admitting expert testimony on CSAAS, which can explain behavior that might be puzzling to a jury). Less often, similar testimony is offered in prosecutions of children for killing parents. See, e.g., Nemeth, 694 N.E.2d 1332, 1335 (Ohio 1998) (in trial of 16-year-old boy for killing mother with bow and arrow, testimony on BCS shed light on question whether he acted with requisite state of mind). Courts comment that such experts should not say that the child was abused, nor that her account is truthful or right. See State v. Huntington, 575 N.W.2d 268, 278 (Wis. 1998) (can't testify that child is telling truth).

Sexual assault trials. In sexual assault trials, courts admit evidence of "rape trauma syndrome" (RTS) to help assess conduct by the victim afterwards and evaluate claims of consent. See People v. Hampton, 746 P.2d 947, 951-954 (Colo. 1987) (psychologist describes pattern of emotional adjustment, to help jury assess delay in reporting) (should not argue that reaction "paralleled" typical victims). Courts have tended not to allow use of RTS to prove that an attack occurred (or criminal penetration). See People v. Taylor, 552 N.E.2d 131 (N.Y. 1990); People v. Bledsoe, 681 P.2d 291 (Cal. 1984).

Spousal battering or murder trials. In trials of men for beating women in intimate relationships and in trials of women for killing men in such relationships (on issue of self-defense), courts often admit evidence of battered woman syndrome (BWS) to shed light on the woman's behavior. See State v.

Stewart, 719 S.E.2d 876 (W. Va. 2011) (in trial of woman for murdering husband, reversible error to exclude testimony on BWS); State v. Vega, 788 A.2d 1221, 1234 (Conn. 2001) (in trial of man for kidnapping and assaulting girlfriend, admitting testimony on BWS), *cert. denied*, 537 U.S. 836 (2002).

Framework versus character evidence. When such testimony describes generalized behavioral patterns based on observing many people, the term "social framework" seems an apt description. In terms of FRE 702, important questions are whether the expert has an adequate basis in observation and theory and whether the jury needs the kind of help an expert can provide.

When such testimony describes the behavior of a crime victim or criminal defendant, the term "social framework" is no longer accurate, and syndrome evidence draws close to being character evidence of the sort regulated by FRE 404 and 405. Recall that the latter restrict the use of character to prove conduct, although they are generous in allowing defendants to try to show innocence by proving good character. Unlike typical character witnesses, however, where the testifying witness learned what she knows before the events in suit, witnesses giving syndrome testimony glean what they know afterward and are looking for (even expecting to find) confirmation of alleged events.

When expert testimony comments on the credibility of victims or defendants, it draws close to character evidence regulated by FRE 608. See State v. Grecinger, 569 N.W.2d 189, 193-194 (Minn. 1997) (in trial of man for attempted murder and battery against intimate companion, admitting expert testimony on BWS under MRE 608 as bearing on her veracity). The latter allows opinion evidence but blocks proof of *good* character until the other side brings credibility into question. Here too, witnesses testify with specific reference to a defendant or victim, having gleaned what they know after the fact.

■ PROBLEM 9-D. "They Become Anxious and Guilt-Ridden"

Art Milton is charged with sexual assault on his 14-year-old daughter Sandra, which allegedly took place in the family home. Jean Milton (Art's wife and Sandra's mother) was out, as was Sandra's sister Terri (age 16). Art Milton has pleaded innocent.

At trial Sandra testifies that Art Milton ordered her to hold still while he removed her clothes and touched her between her legs and "did what I know he does to mom." Under questioning by the district attorney, Sandra states that Milton had touched her similarly on other occasions and describes what seems to have been rape or attempted rape, although she is not entirely sure whether penetration was accomplished.

During defense cross-examination, Sandra concedes that three months later she wrote out a statement indicating that she had lied about the incident. She explained her accusations had been motivated by her desire "to be able to stay out at night like other girls my age," adding that "after I reported it to the social worker and the prosecutor, everybody has been pushing me really hard to stick to the story, which isn't true."

Art Milton testifies that Sandra had gotten in trouble in school for truancy and for stealing money and shoplifting, and had run away from home several times. He also testifies to facts suggesting that Terri too resents "the 10:00 curfew we insist on during the week, and 11:30 on weekends," and that Terri pressed Sandra "to get me in trouble."

During its case-in-rebuttal, the prosecutor calls Dr. Clara Burton, a clinical psychologist:

Q [prosecutor]: Dr. Burton, how long have you worked with domestic sex abuse?
A [Burton]: A little over 12 years.
Q: And how many sexually abused children have you seen in that time?
A: Between three and four hundred.
Q: So you are familiar with the behavior patterns of such children?
A: Oh yes, very much so.
Q: Could you describe it, please?
Q [defense]: Objection, Your Honor. May we approach the bench?

The jury is excused, and the following discussion takes place:

Defense counsel: Your Honor, we object to Dr. Burton's testimony for many reasons:

First, there is no model of behavior for sexually abused children that is accepted by psychologists or reliable enough for use in a criminal prosecution. In short, this testimony cannot satisfy the *Daubert* standard.

Second, if Dr. Burton is allowed to testify, she will be taking the case away from the jury, invading the jury's province and testifying on the very question which the jury has to decide—who is telling the truth here.

Third, the jury doesn't need help appraising Sandra's behavior, and what Dr. Burton has to say cannot help. Either she's going to talk in generalities about how *most* abused children behave or she's going to speculate about what did or did not happen to Sandra.

Fourth, it is axiomatic that credibility issues are for the jury to decide. Juries don't need help deciding who to believe.

Fifth, if we let Dr. Burton testify, the jury won't know how to evaluate what she has to say. She'll snow them with her expertise, and they, the common people on the jury, will just throw in the sponge.

Prosecutor: Your Honor, the question is whether Dr. Burton is a qualified expert, and whether the underlying theories and technique are reliable under *Daubert*. Dr. Burton is qualified, and she can help. The defense has suggested in lots of ways that Sandra is just lying, and the jury doesn't know how to evaluate that. Could we just put Dr. Burton on the stand now, and make a proffer of what she would testify to?

Court: Go ahead.

Dr. Burton: Well, I would say that what Sandra did in this case is characteristic of sexually abused children. What happens is that they become anxious and guilt-ridden. They actually carry a heavy burden of guilt, thinking that it was somehow their fault. They often retract what they say at first because they realize that the guilty party is their parent, and they still care for them. Sandra fits the profile exactly. Another thing is that children in Sandra's position worry that they might be blamed or punished, and that they might break up the family. Often children like Sandra don't trust their mother. I can also say that it's extremely rare for children to make up stories of this sort. Thus I find her story entirely credible. We have many studies that confirm all these points, and they are reliable and generally accepted in the professional community.

How should the judge rule in this case, and why?

■ NOTES ON SYNDROME AND FRAMEWORK EVIDENCE

1. Do jurors need help understanding battered or abused children? See People v. McAlpin, 812 P.2d 563, 570-571 (Cal. 1991) (describing myths surrounding child abuse). Is the same true of battered women? See Commonwealth v. Anestal, 978 N.E.2d 37, 41 n.5 (Mass. 2012) (effects of BWS are not within common experience). Rape victims? See People v. Taylor, 552 N.E.2d 131, 136 (N.Y. 1990) (describing cultural myths on rape). If jurors need help, is it because they lack experience in human relationships? In abuse, battering, or rape? In arson or murder trials, should jurors be brought up to speed on effects of these crimes on victims or on social factors leading to such crimes? On pressures of inner city life when gang members are charged with crimes?

2. If experts give syndrome evidence in child abuse cases, should they use terms like "battered child syndrome"? Should they say the victim suffers from (or exhibits) this syndrome? Should experts refer to "battered woman syndrome" and "rape trauma syndrome"? Should they say the woman suffers from (or exhibits) the syndrome? Courts tend to say no to all these questions. Why? See State v. Favoccia, 51 A.3d 1002 (Conn. 2012) (should not say minor exhibited characteristics of sexual assault victims); State v. Haines, 860 N.E.2d 91, 102 (Ohio 2006) (should not say woman suffers syndrome, that defendant is batterer or that woman is telling truth); State v. Gettier, 438 N.W.2d 1, 5-6 (Iowa 1989) (should not use RTS label).

3. Absent clinical symptoms, do experts understand children well enough to know whether they were likely beaten or sexually abused? Compare United States v. St. Pierre, 812 F.2d 417, 419-420 (8th Cir. 1987) (scientific community recognizes "certain emotional and psychological characteristics" in sexually abused children) with Miller v. Commonwealth, 77 S.W.2d 566 (Ky. 2002) (CSAAS not generally accepted in scientific community, and may invade province of jury; one may not introduce "evidence of the habit of a class of individuals either to prove that another member of the class acted the same way under similar circumstances or to prove that the person was a member of that class because he/she acted the same way"). Do experts understand women well enough to know whether they were likely raped? See People v. Bledsoe, 681 P.2d 291 (Cal. 1984) (RTS is a "therapeutic tool" to find and treat emotional problems; counselors try to help victims deal with trauma, and accuracy of descriptions is not "vital" to task; rape counselors avoid credibility judgments, do not probe inconsistencies) (RTS inadmissible to show rape). If *Bledsoe* is right that RTS is a therapeutic rather than an investigative technique, does it follow that such evidence should be excluded altogether?

4. In trials of women for killing intimate companions, syndrome evidence often describes the defendant and supports the claim of self-defense. See State v. Koss, 551 N.E.2d 970, 974-975 (Ohio 1990). Should similar evidence be admitted when it relates to behavioral patterns of the defendant and supports the claim that he did the deed? See, e.g., United States v. Long, 328 F.3d 655, 667-669 (D.C. Cir. 2003) (in trial for transporting a minor for purposes of sexual activity, admitting expert testimony on modus operandi of "preferential sex offenders," describing "typology, identification, characteristics, and strategies," as well as "characteristics and behavior of child victims").

5. In the 1995 trial of O.J. Simpson for the double homicide of Nicole Brown and Ronald Goldman, the prosecutor thought of offering expert testimony on patterns of domestic abuse. Should such proof be allowed? The California Evidence Code makes expert testimony on "battered women's syndrome" admissible for the state or the defense "except when offered against a criminal defendant to prove the occurrence of the act or acts of abuse which form the basis of the criminal charge." See Cal. Evid. Code §1107. This provision appears to mean that such expert testimony would be inadmissible in the Simpson trial. The statute describes BWS as including "physical, emotional or mental effects upon the beliefs, perceptions, or behavior of victims of domestic violence."

6. After *Kumho Tire,* syndrome evidence must satisfy the scientific validity standard of *Daubert.* See United States v. Young, 316 F.3d 649, 656-657 (7th Cir. 2002) (in domestic abuse trial, admitting testimony by Professor of Nursing that domestic abuse victims often recant accusations, and victim in this case "exhibited this not uncommon behavior pattern," which satisfied *Daubert*); State v. Weaver, 648 N.W.2d 355, 364-365 (S.D. 2002) (in domestic abuse trial, admitting BWS testimony as satisfying *Daubert*).

7. How about other kinds of psychological profiles that support defendants? See State v. Davis, 645 N.W.2d 913 (Wis. 2002) (in trial for sexual contact with minor, defendant may offer expert testimony that he lacks psychological characteristics typical of such offenders, but must give pretrial notice; prosecutor may ask for an examination of the accused by its own expert; privilege against self-incrimination may be waived as necessary to enable prosecutor to meet defense evidence); United States v. Rahm, 993 F.2d 1405, 1409-1410 (9th

Cir. 1993) (in trial for possessing counterfeit currency, error to exclude defense expert testimony based on Wechsler Adult Intelligence Scale and Minnesota Multiphasic Personality Inventory that defendant's intelligence was average but scores on subtests were below average and indicated tendency to overlook visual details). How about admitting such proof to help the state? See United States v. Gillespie, 852 F.2d 475, 479-481 (9th Cir. 1988) (error to admit testimony offered by state describing "characteristics common to child molesters").

c. DNA Evidence

Courts everywhere admit scientific evidence based on analysis of deoxyribonucleic acid (DNA). Sometimes described as genetic profiling (or "gene mapping" or "genetic fingerprinting"), DNA evidence offers the possibility of a "match" or "nonmatch" between tissue or fluid samples of unknown origin and known exemplars. In forms that are variable and individualized, DNA is found in human tissue and fluids, from saliva to blood to semen, and in fingernails, skin, and hair. In any person, DNA from *any* and *all* such samples shows a pattern that differs from patterns in most other people.

In criminal trials, especially involving rape and homicide, DNA evidence can be powerfully incriminating or exculpatory. In the clinical setting of a paternity suit, analyzing DNA in blood samples taken from the child and the mother can yield precise information on the nature of the DNA that the child's father must have.

The technical challenges to proof in this form are daunting. In 1992, the National Research Council published a report by a committee of scientists and jurists, see DNA Technology in Forensic Science (1992) (*NRC Report*). It made recommendations for handling DNA evidence, and it had considerable impact on modern decisions. In 1996, the NRC published a followup study revisiting areas of difficulty, see The Evaluation of Forensic DNA Evidence (1996) (*NRC Update*). This study too had considerable impact.

The following excerpt from the Montana decision in *Moore* presents a lucid description of technical concepts. Read it to get your sea legs. Then use Problem 9-E ("We Found a Match") and the following Notes to consider the evidentiary issues.

STATE v. MOORE

Supreme Court of Montana
885 P.2d 457 (1994)

[Larry Moore was charged with murdering Brad Brisbin, who disappeared without trace on the morning of November 9, 1990. No body was recovered, but Brisbin's wife Rene testified that Brad said Moore had called and asked to meet him at a truckstop. There was proof that Brisbin headed up Gallatin

Canyon toward West Yellowstone, and Moore returned from that direction in his truck sometime later. Moore made inconsistent statements about Brisbin, commenting that he had seen Brisbin climb into a car with a woman on the morning he disappeared, that Brisbin and Moore had been together, and that Brisbin had an accident with a gun in Moore's truck

The defense moved to exclude DNA evidence, but the court denied the motion. The defense then moved to exclude testimony describing statistical calculations "which would have presented a probability that any alleged match between the tissue samples and the Brisbin children is not coincidental." The trial court granted this motion.

The court admitted DNA analyses of human blood and pieces of human muscle and brain tissue found in the cab of defendant's truck. Cellmark Diagnostics conducted RFLP analysis ("restriction fragment length polymorphism") on a muscle fragment and the Analytic Genetic Testing Center (AGTC) performed PCR analysis ("polymerase chain reaction") on another muscle fragment and the cerebellum tissue. An expert from AGTC testified that the samples "could not be excluded as having come from the biological father" of Brisbin's children. A Cellmark expert testified that DNA in the muscle was "consistent with" that of Brisbin's mother.

The Montana Supreme Court provides the following account:]

DNA is a fundamental material, which determines the genetic properties of all living things. All nucleated cells of every human being contain DNA, and every cell of a particular individual contains the same configuration of DNA. The significance of DNA for forensic purposes is that, with the exception of identical twins, no two individuals have identical DNA. Another important fundamental aspect of human genetics is that, except for unusual but recognized occurrences of mutation, offspring inherit genes from their parents, receiving one-half from the mother and one-half from the father.

The DNA molecule is composed of a long double helix, which looks like a twisted ladder. The sides of the ladder are made up of alternating units of phosphate and sugar. Attached to the sides of the ladder are the rungs, which are made up of four types of organic bases: adenine, guanine, cytosine, and thymine. Due to their chemical compositions, adenine will only bond with thymine, and cytosine will only bond with guanine. Thus, the bases on one side of the rung will determine the order on the other side. For the purpose of DNA profiling, these base pairs are the critical components of the ladder. It is the order or sequence of the base pairs (the rungs) that determines the genetic traits of an individual life form and each human being. A specific sequence of base pairs that is responsible for a particular trait is called a gene.

Genetically, humans are more alike than dissimilar. Approximately 99 percent of human DNA molecules, i.e., base pair sequences, are the same, creating such shared features as arms and legs. Other sections of the DNA ladder, however, vary distinctly from one person to another. It is these variable regions, called "polymorphisms," which make it possible to establish identity and differences between individuals.

The length of each polymorphism is determined by the number of repeat core sequences of base pairs. The core sequence is called a Variable Number Tandem Repeat (VNTR) while the total fragment length is called a Restriction Fragment Length Polymorphism (RFLP). Alternative forms of RFLP's are called alleles.

A particular region on the DNA molecule where a specific VNTR occurs is called a "locus." A locus is considered polymorphic when the number of VNTR's varies from one person to another. Of the approximately three billion base pairs contained in one DNA molecule, roughly three million are thought to be polymorphic. DNA profiling focuses on several highly polymorphic or hypervariable segments of the DNA. Different people will have the same VNTRs in a particular hypervariable locus, but the loci will differ in length because varying numbers of the VNTRs are linked together. Although a person may not have a unique polymorphic area at any one locus, the frequency with which two people will exhibit eight or ten of these alleles at four or five different locations is extremely low. Thus DNA analysis attempts to detect these highly variable regions and distinguish among the alleles that exist there.

At the time the testing was conducted in this case, there were two technologies generally used in forensic DNA analysis to detect the polymorphic regions: restriction fragment length polymorphism (RFLP), and polymerase chain reaction (PCR). Both methods were employed in this case.

RFLP ANALYSIS

As is explained in [several cases], RFLP analysis involves several steps.

1. Extraction of DNA. The DNA must be extracted from the evidentiary sample by using chemical enzymes. An enzyme is then added to digest cellular material that is not DNA, thereby providing a purer sample.

2. Restriction or Digestion. The DNA is then mixed with restriction enzymes which cut the DNA molecules into fragments at specific base sequences. The restriction enzymes recognize particular sequences of base pairs. The enzymes sever the DNA molecule at targeted locations within the sequence. The process severs the DNA molecule at all sites targeted at locations along the three billion base pair length of the molecule. Therefore, some of the resulting "restriction fragments" will contain polymorphic DNA segments, although most will not. Because the alleles differ markedly in length from one person to the next, the restriction fragments containing the alleles will also differ in length.

3. Gel Electrophoresis. This technique entails placing the DNA fragments into an agarose gel which has a negative and positive electrode at either end. An electrical current is then run through the gel. The restriction fragments, which are negatively charged in their natural state, travel toward the positive charge. The process is able to sort the restriction enzymes by length, as the shorter fragments—which are lighter and less bulky—will travel further in the gel. Several samples are run on the gel but in different tracks or lanes which run parallel to each other. In addition to the samples, fragments of known base-pair lengths are placed in separate lanes to facilitate measurement.

4. Southern Transfer. This procedure transfers the fragments to a more functional surface. A nylon membrane is placed over the gel and, through capillary action, the DNA fragments attach themselves to the membrane while occupying the same position relative to one another as they had on the gel. The restriction fragments are then treated with a chemical which cuts the fragments of DNA lengthwise along each base pair, by sawing through the middle of each rung. The result is a collection of single stranded restriction fragments.

5. Hybridization. The nylon membrane is dipped into a solution containing various "genetic probes," which are single stranded DNA fragments of known length and sequence designed to link with identified polymorphic alleles. The probes will link only to those DNA fragments which contain base pair sequences that are complementary to the base sequences of the probe. The genetic probes are tagged with a radioactive marker so that after the probe links with a particular allele, its position relative to the other restriction fragments can be observed.

6. Autoradiography. The nylon membrane is placed on an x-ray film and exposed by the radioactively charge probes. The result is a pattern of bands called an "autoradiograph," or "autorad." Each band represents a different polymorphic allele, and its position indicates the length of the restriction fragment in which that allele occurs. Because individuals differ in length of their polymorphic alleles, the position of the bands on the DNA prints will tend to differ from person to person.

7. Interpretation of the DNA Print. The DNA print of the crime sample and the DNA print of the defendant are then compared both visually and with a machine to determine if both samples of DNA came from the same person. A match will be declared if the samples fall within a certain distance of one another. Cellmark Diagnostics, the laboratory conducting the RFLP analysis in this case, will declare a match if the bands from two DNA prints fall within one millimeter of each other.

8. Statistical Analysis. Statistical analysis is used in both RFLP and PCR analysis. If the two DNA samples match, then population geneticists determine the likelihood that the match is unique. The scientists determine the frequency with which a particular allele is found in the population, then by using a multiplication or product rule, compute an aggregate estimate of the statistical probability that the suspect's combination of alleles would be found in the relevant racial population.

[The trial court properly admitted the DNA testimony. By requesting exclusion of statistics, the defense waived the claim that DNA evidence should not be admitted without statistical correlations. The question whether such proof should be presented without statistics in other cases is reserved. DNA evidence satisfies the *Daubert* standard. Problems with missing bands in the autorads for the wife and children did not require exclusion, nor did inconsistencies in test results for defendant's mother, nor did problems with the "thermal cycler."]

■ PROBLEM 9-E. "We Found a Match"

Donald Vanbart is charged with first degree murder in the slaying of Kim Gosberg, whose body was found three days after she disappeared, partially buried under leaves and forest debris in a wooded area about 200 yards from the home where she lived with her husband and children. The autopsy indicates that Gosberg died of strangulation and had been raped. (An athletic sock was tied around her neck; her hands were tied behind her with shoelaces and pantyhose; semen stains were found on her body and clothing.) The prosecutor proposes to offer evidence of a match between DNA isolated from semen found on the clothing and body of the victim and DNA isolated from a blood sample obtained from the defendant.

In a pretrial hearing on evidence issues, the prosecutor shows that the case against Vanbart is strong. Shortly after the murder of Karen Gosberg was generally reported, he told his sister in reference to her, "this time I went too far." A neighbor of Gosberg was prepared to testify that he heard a woman scream in the woods where the body was later discovered (the time being close to that later determined to be the probable time of death); another neighbor would testify that he saw the defendant driving away from the neighborhood in a blue sedan; another neighbor noted the license number, and the car was shown to be a blue sedan registered to Vanbart. Two other women were prepared to testify that on separate occasions within the last six months Vanbart had assaulted them in separate incidents, by dragging them into wooded areas, tying them up with shoelaces and undergarments, choking them with an athletic sock, and raping them. (The court ruled in favor of admitting this evidence under FRE 404(b) as proof of "modus operandi and identity.")

In the evidence hearing, the prosecutor calls Dr. Lawrence Mullens, who holds advanced degrees in biochemistry and human genetics. Mullens is employed by Lifemark Laboratories, a private firm specializing in DNA analysis, and he describes the underlying theory and technique of RFLP analysis in substantially the terms outlined in the quoted passage from the Montana decision in *Moore*. Mullens is prepared to say "we found a match" in the DNA taken from the semen sample found at the crime scene and the DNA extracted from the blood of the defendant (also that DNA from the semen sample did *not* match DNA from the blood of Karen Gosberg's husband). If allowed, Mullens would say "only one Hispanic person in 187,000 would produce such a match" (Vanbart being Hispanic).

After cross-examining Dr. Mullens, counsel for Vanbart makes the following objections:

(1) Your Honor, I pass over the question whether the underlying theory is valid, realizing that courts accept DNA profiling, but *Daubert* also requires valid lab technique. How do we know Lifemark's technique

is reliable? *Daubert* speaks of industry standards and peer review literature. Has the Lifemark technique been peer reviewed? Is it subject to industry standards?

(2) Your Honor, *Daubert* also requires the offering party to follow lab protocol in this particular case, which is why confrontation decisions under *Crawford,* like *Melendez-Diaz* and *Bullcoming,* require a percipient witness to testify. The proponent has to show that the chemists who did the work didn't slip up by contaminating the sample or misreading or misinterpreting the autorads.

(3) Your Honor, *Daubert* requires valid statistics. Dr. Mullens talks about one in 187,000, but they need to show what they're multiplying by what because the variables have to be independent. Also his figure relates to the Hispanic population, and my client is Hispanic, but the NSC Study recognizes that there may be population substructures in which the combination of alleles seen here is more common, so the figure may be exaggerated.

(4) Your honor, why compare semen samples with data from "Hispanics" specifically? Again, my client is Hispanic, but we can't assume his guilt in making such comparisons. We should compare the "matching alleles" here with *all* population subgroups, taking as the basis of comparison the subgroup where the allele is most common, to minimize the risk of error.

(5) Finally, your honor, I object that this proof is prejudicial and misleading. Presenting astronomical numbers, with all the fancy labels and apparatus of science will distract the jury from what it should be doing, which is considering the real evidence in the case. *Without* the numbers, the proof of "match" will be assumed to be conclusive, which is not correct at all. *With* the numbers, the jury will forget about the other proof, including *our* defense evidence that others were seen leaving the neighborhood at the time of the crime, and the culprit may well be among those.

How should the judge handle these various objections, and why?

■ NOTES ON DNA EVIDENCE

1. In his first objection, Vanbart's lawyer omitted any direct challenge to genetic profiling because the theory is universally accepted. A court would find appellate authority establishing this point in the jurisdiction, or could take judicial notice of the validity of the theory, either as a matter of general understanding or in virtue of a decision from elsewhere. Vanbart's lawyer was right that *Daubert* covers the analytic process. In the early years, RFLP and PCR were the most common techniques, as *Moore* reflects. They remain common, but others have appeared more recently.

2. Doesn't the judge also have to decide whether lab protocols are reliable? Vanbart's second objection raises this point. The lab protocols are prescribed steps involving entries of data and recording of observed results, and these implement the RFLP process described in *Moore*. In effect *Moore* approved the Cellmark protocol, and the question for the judge in the Vanbart case is whether *Moore* bears on the Lifemark protocol. Perhaps the judge could use the Cellmark protocol approved in *Moore* as a baseline, asking the offering party to explain any differences.

3. Under *Daubert* and FRE 702, judges *also* resolve objections that the lab did not run the tests right or got unreliable results because something went wrong (Vanbart's third objection). Many mishaps are possible: Technicians can put DNA from a single sample in two lanes of gel, obtaining a perfect (but false) band match; restriction enzymes can cut DNA in the wrong places (producing "star activity"); the gel can vary in consistency, producing band-shifting, hence false matches or nonmatches (band-shifting is more likely to prevent matches than cause false matches; corrective measures are sometimes applied, including test lanes with material from a single sample); occasionally tagged probes do not bond properly to unzipped fragments (those that have been "restricted" or "digested" in the second phase of the process), producing autorads that are hard to interpret. Even if it is better to ask judges to resolve these issues than to expect juries to do so, we are putting a pretty heavy burden on judges, aren't we?

4. The *Daubert* validity standard applies to the statistical method used to determine a match and describe the probability of finding it (Vanbart's fourth objection). In a 1991 article, two scholars suggested that information in data banks supporting frequency estimates might produce misleading results. Essentially these estimates depend on the product rule we saw in *Collins* (Chapter 2C, supra): If one match were found in 1/10 of the relevant populace and another in 1/20 of the populace, and *if these matches are independent* (Hardy-Weinberg equilibrium), the product rule suggests that both matches would be found in 1/100 of the populace.[12] The 1991 article advanced the population substructure thesis, which holds that subgroups within larger populations contain band matches that are *not* independent because mating patterns are not random, and some combinations of matches might not be independent. So powerful was this thesis that courts began to exclude DNA evidence or bar frequency estimates.

(a) The 1992 NRC Report took the substructure thesis seriously and suggested that estimates should employ an interim "ceiling principle" (using the higher of 10 percent or the highest frequency for any observed match in

[12] The computation is $2(1/10 \times 1/20) = 1/100$. "The factor of 2 arises in the heterozygous case [subject carries different alleles and autorad shows two bands at any one locus], because one must consider the case in which allele a1 was contributed by the father and allele a2 by the mother and vice versa: each of the two cases has a probability pa1pa2." NRC Report, at 78.

any population group). The intended result is a conservative estimate giving defendant the benefit of a doubt.

(b) Later research, including findings published in the 1996 NRC Update, led experts to conclude that variations due to population substructuring did not significantly affect the calculations. Some modern decisions now say the precautions are not required. See Commonwealth v. Blasioli, 713 A.2d 1117, 1125 (Pa. 1998) (substructuring does not significantly affect frequency estimates) (collecting cases); Lempert, DNA, Science and the Law: Two Cheers for the Ceiling Principle, 34 Jurimetrics J. 41 (1993).

5. What about Vanbart's fifth objection that the relevant comparison is not defendant's subgroup, but a group containing all possible suspects? For each observed match, should the prosecutor choose the highest observed frequency in *all* population groups, which would (like the ceiling principle) produce an estimate benefiting defendants? See State v. Carter, 524 N.W.2d 763 (Neb. 1994) (in trial of black defendant for murder, state introduced probabilities based on comparison with black and white databases, ignoring possibility that perpetrator was from another group) (reversing).

6. What about Vanbart's last objection that the proof is prejudicial and misleading? *Collins* complained that astronomical numbers might distract and hypnotize a jury. In *Collins*, there were other problems (no *proof* of probabilities; independence requirement not satisfied). But the Court was also concerned at the magnitude of the numbers. The same potentially hypnotic effect comes in DNA cases, doesn't it? See State v. Pierce, 597 N.E.2d 107 (Ohio 1992) ("only one in forty billion blacks would have the same DNA composition"). *Moore* rejected the claim that admitting proof of a match was misleading without probability estimates (the defense waived this objection, instead challenging the estimates themselves). But Vanbart has a point when he says proof of "a match" *without* numbers may lead the jury to accept the proof as conclusive and that admitting proof *with* the numbers may overwhelm. How about a compromise in which the testimony is limited to saying that DNA tests "place the defendant in a group of people who might have left" the semen or blood? See State v. Bloom, 516 N.W.2d 159 (Minn. 1994) (expert can say that "given a reliable multi-locus match, the probability that the match is random or coincidental is extremely low," and that "to a reasonable scientific certainty," defendant is the source, and may "give an opinion as to random match probability").

d. Serologic and DNA Testing and Paternity

In paternity suits, scientific evidence plays a critical role. Here modern serologic and DNA testing combines with probabilistic analysis, despite doubts expressed in *Collins* about distraction and distortion that can come with the numbers, to produce something called a "Paternity Index" that usually suggests a very high probability that the defendant in the case is the biological father.

Until the 1970s, standard "blood tests" were useful but inconclusive. They could be categorical in proving nonpaternity, but could weed out only about 15 percent of nonfathers falsely accused (they could not eliminate most men mistakenly named as father). The tests were even less effective in the other direction (identifying defendant as father) because they could only place a man in a group of about one-fifth to one-third of the population with the blood type of the biological father. In the 1970s, immunologic systems became testable by blood or tissue sample, and these more powerful serologic tests could exclude about 98 percent of nonfathers falsely accused. HLA tests (the letters stand for human leucocite antigen) attained a power exceeding 95 percent, often reducing the pool of potential fathers to as little as 2 percent of the male population. It came to be recognized that these tests could support a positive (but less than certain) inference that a particular man was the father.

In the 1990s, DNA evidence brought the promise of even greater power to identify the father. DNA profiling ("gene mapping") may some day become conclusive, producing a unique profile for each person, but we are not quite there yet. Still, DNA profiling leads to a Paternity Index that expresses the scarcity of indicators common to the biological father and the defendant.

The Paternity Index involves an application of something called Bayesian analysis, which employs a standard equation developed in the nineteenth century. Bayes' Theorem describes the degree to which a new item of evidence, when it can be expressed as a datum of known frequency, affects our assessment of an issue. Suppose X stands for the proposition to be proved (like biological fatherhood), E stands for the evidence (like lab tests placing defendant in a small group of possible fathers), and the notation | stands for "given" or "assuming." Then Odds ($X|E$) stands for the odds of X given evidence E. Bayes' Theorem says *these* odds (the odds of X, given E) are equal to the *prior* odds of X (without evidence E) multiplied by something called the Likelihood Ratio (LR). In other words, Odds ($X|E$) = P(X) × LR. The Likelihood Ratio is a fraction in which the numerator is the probability that evidence E would exist if X were so, and the denominator is the probability that Evidence E would exist if X were *not* so. Hence:

$$\textbf{(1)}\ \text{Odds}\ (X \mid E) = \frac{\text{P}(E \mid X)}{\text{P}(E \mid \text{not-}\ X)} \times \text{Odds}\ (X)$$

Bayes' Theorem may also be cast in numeric form to yield likelihood expressed as a fraction or decimal number (probability), which is easier to use, although the equation in this form is more complicated.[13] In what follows, the expression $P(X|E)$ stands for the probability of X, given evidence E:

[13] The probability of getting heads on a coin flip is one half, usually written 1/2 or .5. The odds of getting heads are one to one, usually written 1:1. Probability converts to odds by this equation: Odds = P/(1–P). Thus the probability of one-half converts this way to odds: Odds = .5/(1–.5) = 1:1. Odds convert to probability by treating the number to the left of the colon as the numerator in a fraction whose denominator is the *sum* of the numbers on each side of the colon. Thus, odds of 1:1 convert in this way to probability: Probability = 1/(1+1) = 1/2 or .5.

$$(\mathbf{2})\ P(X \mid E) = \frac{\mathrm{P}(X \mid X)\ \mathrm{P}(X)}{\mathrm{P}(E \mid X) \times \mathrm{P}(\ X) + \mathrm{P}(E \mid \text{not- } X)\ \mathrm{P}(\text{not- } X)}$$

Equation (1), expressing the Theorem in odds form, makes the idea close to intuitively obvious because the Likelihood Ratio expresses an easy-to-grasp idea. Remember that this equation says our new assessment of *X* (Odds (*X*|*E*)) equals the likelihood that evidence *E* would exist if we knew the matter to be proved *were so* (*P*(*E*|*X*)) divided by the likelihood that such evidence would exist if we knew it was *not* so (*P*(*E*|not-*X*)) multiplied by our *prior assessment* of *X* (Odds (*X*)). Try using the Theorem with a simple card problem. Suppose we want to know whether a card drawn from a hat containing a full mixed deck is the Queen of Hearts. If asked for an initial estimate of the likelihood of drawing that card, we would say the odds are 1:51 (one chance of drawing that card against 51 chances of drawing some other), and that the probability is 1/52 (or .019). If we were told a red card was drawn and asked how this datum affects the likelihood that this card is a Queen of Hearts, we would say the new odds are 1:25 (one chance of getting the Queen of Hearts against 25 chances of getting other red cards), and the probability is 1/26 (or .03846).

Bayes' Theorem expresses this reasoning mathematically. For *X*, substitute *QH* to mean drawing the Queen of Hearts; for *E*, substitute *R* to mean drawing a red card. The equation shows how to modify our original estimate of the odds of drawing the Queen of Hearts, given that the card drawn is red. Using the theorem in odds form, we have:

$$\text{Odds}\ (QH \mid R) = \frac{P(R \mid QH)}{P(R \mid \text{not- } QH)} \times \text{Odds}\ (QH) = \frac{1}{(25/51)} \times 1{:}51$$

$$= 2.04 : 51\ (\text{probability of } .03846)$$

Dividing the number on each side of the colon by 2.04 yields odds of 1:25 (as we expect). The calculations are harder, but we reach the probability of .03846 by applying Equation (2)—the Theorem in numeric form.

■ PROBLEM 9-F. Paternity Index 624

In her paternity suit, Lisa claims Richard is the father of her child Jason. Lisa testifies that she had an ongoing relationship with Richard during the probable time of conception and that they had frequent intercourse. Richard testifies that he saw Lisa only occasionally during the time, and they had intercourse twice. He also testifies that thereafter Lisa turned down his overtures, telling him she wanted to see other men, and that she was seeing four other men that Richard knew about.

Important to Lisa's case is a report prepared by Lifemark Diagnostics, a private laboratory specializing in DNA and HLA testing. The report analyzes blood samples taken from Lisa, Jason, and Richard. It contains the following statements:

> On the attached protocol are results obtained in our laboratory on blood specimens from the mother Lisa, the child Jason, and Richard. The samples were tested for both serologic and genetic factors to determine whether Richard might be or is not the biological father. Shown on the protocol are certain serologic and genetic characteristics of these persons and the combined probability, based on estimates of the frequency of these characteristics in the Caucasian population, that Richard, as compared to a random Caucasian man, could be the source of the paternal genes and antigens observed in Jason.
>
> From the testing performed here, falsely accused males would be excluded in 95% of the cases. The results do not provide evidence of nonpaternity for Richard. Since parentage cannot be excluded for him, the test results have been used to calculate a Paternity Index (PI), which reflects the number of unrelated random Caucasian men who would have to be tested to find another with the appropriate genes and antigens to be the father of Jason. Here the index is 624, which converts to a probability of paternity of 99.84%. These figures indicate the plausibility of Richard being the father of Jason. The significance of this evidence must be weighed with other factors, such as access to the mother by Richard or other men at the time of conception.
>
> Signed,
> Hilston K. Pool, Ph.D.
> Certified Pathologist
> Lifemark Laboratories

The protocol shows that Lifemark performed HLA and DNA tests on the blood samples and describes the findings in detail. Dr. Pool testifies and is prepared to explain the report and, in substance, to testify from present memory on what it says and means.

Richard objects. He concedes the relevance and admissibility of evidence of (1) the genotypes and serologic factors found in the blood of Lisa, Jason, and himself, (2) the fact that Jason's father must have certain serologic and genetic characteristics, and (3) the fact that Richard has them too, and could pass them to his child. But he argues that the numeric data, including the Paternity Index and probability of paternity, should be excluded. How should the court rule, and why?

■ NOTES ON SEROLOGIC AND GENETIC TESTS IN PATERNITY CASES

1. Testing labs routinely produce reports like in the Problem, with a Paternity Index expressed as a number (624) and a "probability of paternity" expressed as a percentage (99.84%). The Paternity Index states the number of men who would probably have to be tested to find another who could be the father. The probability of paternity involves doing the division in a fraction (the numerator is the Paternity Index; the denominator is that number plus one) and converting the result to a percentage. In the Problem, 624/625 = .9984 or 99.84%. Both the Paternity Index and the probability of paternity are admitted in paternity cases. Both are always high, and they go to the jury. See Child Support Enforcement Agency v. Doe, 51 P.3d 366, 367 (Haw. 2002) (2542 to 1 or 99.96%). See generally Peterson, A Few Things You Should Know about Paternity Tests (But Were Afraid to Ask), 22 Santa Clara L. Rev. 667 (1982).

2. Suppose Hilston Pool testifies that the Lifemark test has the power to exclude 95 percent of all men falsely accused. The test did not exclude Richard. Does it follow that the probability is 95 percent that he is the father? That only 5 percent of the men in the general populace could be the father? The answer to both questions is No. Using playing cards in an example makes it easier to see why. Suppose the question is whether a card drawn at random from a mixed deck is the Queen of Hearts. Suppose a test that recognizes all red face cards yields a positive result (a red face card). Among the possible "wrong" cards (all cards that are not the Queen of Hearts), this test has the power to exclude 46/51, or 90.2% (it will exclude 26 black cards and 20 red cards that are not face cards). The positive result means the drawn card is one out of six red face cards, so the odds are 1:5 that the card is the Queen of Hearts (a probability of 1/6, or 16.7 percent, not 88.2%). The percentage of cards that is a Queen of Hearts is 1.96% (not 9.8%, which is the difference between 90.2% and 100%). It is easy for a layperson to misinterpret the power of a test, and courts caution against this risk. See Commonwealth v. Beausoleil, 490 N.E.2d 788, 792 n.5, and 795 (Mass. 1986) (cannot equate probability of exclusion with probability that nonexcluded man is father).

3. Consider the Paternity Index, which comes from the Likelihood Ratio in Bayes' Theorem. The number (624 in the Problem) is derived by carrying out the division in the fraction that makes up the Ratio. The numerator is the probability that Richard, if he were the father, would pass to a child the genetic characteristics that Jason got from his father. The denominator is the probability that a random man in the populace would pass these characteristics to Jason. For nonexcluded males, the numerator might be .4486—a probability that is realistically substantial but less than half.[14] The denominator might be .000719—a probability that is realistically tiny since any particular combination of observed markers is likely to be rare in the general population. These figures produce the Paternity Index (.4486/.000719 = 624). The higher the Index, the stronger the indication of paternity, and the number is likely to *be* high for *any* nonexcluded male. See Koehler, DNA Matches and Statistics, 76 Judicature

[14] Half the genetic information from each parent, but the genetic markers a father passes to his offspring combine in innumerable ways, so any *particular* combination of paternal genes will not likely appear in as many as half his children. The same comment applies on the mother's side.

222, 224 (1993) (Paternity Index measures "the strength of the genetic evidence, where higher numbers are more probative"). Consider this explanation of the Paternity Index, offered by one modern court:

> [T]he denominator of the paternity index will be the same for every putative father. This is because the denominator is the gene frequency in the population. The numerator, however, will vary from putative father to putative father because their phenotypes will vary. . . . Because the numerator varies from putative father to putative father, the paternity index will also vary. Thus, even though all men not excluded by a paternity test are capable of fathering the child, they will have different paternity indexes and thus different relative likelihoods of having fathered the child.

Plemel v. Walker, 735 P.2d 1209, 1214 (Or. 1987) (expert must explain this point to jury). Do you think a jury can understand such explanations?

4. Suppose Lisa is a 32-year-old woman in a metropolitan area containing 100,000 unmarried men within 12 years of her age (20-44 years). Richard can reasonably argue that the evidence suggests there are likely to be 72 men who could be Jason's father, but the argument is weakened by the fact that he cannot identify them or link them to Lisa.

5. Consider the probability of paternity (99.84 percent in Problem 9-F). If we take this figure as describing the probability that Richard is the father, given the test results, it reflects an application of Bayes' Theorem *with a hidden assumption.*

(a) From note 1, recall that the percentage is computed by dividing the Paternity Index by that number plus one (624/625 = .9984, or 99.84 percent). The same idea can be expressed as Odds 624:1, meaning the odds that Richard is the father are 624 to 1.

(b) From note 3, recall that the Index comes from dividing the probability that Richard (if he were the father) would pass along the observed paternal genetic markers by the probability that a random man would do so. In note 3, the larger figure (.4476) is the numerator in the Likelihood Ratio in Equation (1), which is $P(E|X)$—the probability that Jason would have the observed paternal markers (*E*) if we knew Richard was his father (*X*). The smaller figure (.000719) is the denominator, which is $P(E|\text{ non-}X)$—the probability that Jason would have the paternal genetic markers (*E*) if we knew Richard was *not* his father (non-*X*) because someone else is. Doing the arithmetic gives us the Index as well as the probability (99.84 percent) and Odds (624:625).

(c) Equation (1) says estimating the odds that Richard is the father *given* the test data (Odds $(X|E)$) requires a *prior* estimate of the odds (Odds (*X*)). *The hidden assumption in presenting the probability of paternity is that the prior odds are 1:1.* See Plemel v. Walker, 735 P.2d 1209, 1217 n.9 (Or. 1987) ("standard assumption" in calculating probability of paternity is that "prior probability of paternity is 50 percent"). In effect, converting an estimate of the scarcity of Jason's paternal genes into an estimate of probability that Richard is the father involves *a prior assumption of a substantial probability* that he is the father—the odds are already 1:1 (probability .5). You can see that this estimate means an assumption

that the other evidence in the case is evenly balanced, which might or might not be the case. Are there special problems with using such an assumption in *criminal* cases? See State v. Skipper, 637 A.2d 1101 (Conn. 1994) (in trial for sexual assault resulting in pregnancy, proving probability of paternity infringed right to be presumed innocent because it assumed prior probability of .5).

6. Suppose the jury thinks Lisa was intimate with four other men during the probable period of conception. Would it make sense to take the prior odds of Richard's paternity to be 1:4 (probability 20 percent)? If we did, applying Bayesian logic and using the same figures set out above would lead us to new odds 156:1 (probability 99.36 percent) favoring the conclusion that Richard is the father. A reduction from 99.84 percent to 99.36 percent leaves the probability overwhelmingly high in favor of Richard's paternity. If you experiment, you will discover that the paternity index would have to be in the neighborhood of 36 (Richard's was 624) before proof of relations with four other men would reduce the new calculation to odds of 9:1 (probability 90 percent). At least in the common situation where the paternity index for the defendant is very high, then, even multiple relationships have little effect on the final probability.

7. Should we describe inclusionary impact without numbers? How about translating a number like 99.84 percent into a statement that tests "put defendant in a small group of men who might be the father" or that he is "very likely" to be the father or "much more likely to be the father" than a man selected at random? How about telling the jury there is a likelihood of "more than 40 percent" that Richard would pass to his child the paternal genetic markers found in Jason, and fewer than "one man in a thousand" would do so? See Joint AMA-ABA Guidelines: Present Status of Serologic Testing in Problems of Disputed Parentage, 10 Fam. L.Q. 247, 262 (1976) (suggesting "practically proved" for PI 99.8-99.9, "extremely likely" for PI 99.1-99.75, "very likely" for PI 95-99, "likely" for PI 90-95, "undecided" for PI 80-90, and "not useful" for PI less than 80). But see County of El Dorado v. Misura, 38 Cal. Rptr. 2d 908, 911 n.1 (Cal. App. 1995); Plemel v. Walker, 735 P.2d 1209, 1219 (Or. 1987) (both disapproving use of these verbal predicates).

8. How about having the expert apply the Paternity Index to a range of prior estimates, perhaps using a chart like this one:

	1	*2*
Select from column 1 a prior estimate of the likelihood that defendant is the father, without considering the blood typing evidence. The appropriate new estimate, given the blood typing evidence, is set out directly across in column 2.	0	0
	.1	.48
	.2	.67
	.3	.78
	.4	.85
	.5	.89
	.6	.93
	.7	.95
	.8	.97
	.9	.99
	1.0	1.0

See Plemel v. Walker, 735 P.2d 1209, 1219 (Or. 1987) (on request, expert must "calculate the probability that the defendant is the father by using more than a single assumption about the strength of the other evidence" so results are shown "without overstating the information that can be derived from them").

9. Some statutes create a "presumption of paternity" when genetic evidence is convincing. See California Family Code §7555 (presumption arises when paternity index is "100 or greater" and may be rebutted by a preponderance of the evidence); New York Family Court Act §532 (DNA test indicating at least 95 percent probability raises rebuttable presumption of paternity). Is there any proof that can dislodge the presumption? See County of El Dorado v. Misura, 38 Cal. Rptr. 2d 908, 913-914 (Cal. App. 1995) (showing untested other men had access does not dislodge presumption) (but if test was improperly conducted or wrong tables were used, index might be too low to trigger presumption; defendant might show nonaccess or infertility, which would establish prior probability of zero, proving nonpaternity; defendant might show another man with high paternity index had access).

10. Regardless whether a presumption is deployed, a test showing a high paternity index should suffice to take the issue of paternity to a jury if there is proof of intimacy *despite* defense denials or counterproof. See Brooks v. Rogers, 445 S.E.2d 725 (Va. App. 1994) (despite claim that defendant had vasectomy and that his son had relations with plaintiff, affirming judgment of paternity) (absent medical record, judge did not believe vasectomy; no evidence of sexual relations between plaintiff and son of defendant). What if tests foreclose paternity? See Pondexter v. Washington, 1995 WL 57224 (Ohio App. 1995) (dismissing where HLA test indicated exclusion *despite* affidavit that plaintiff had relations with no other man before or after conception). If powerful test evidence is presented and is met only by denials of intimacy or proof that other men had access, can a court or jury reasonably find *against* paternity? Compare Matter of Debra L. v. William J., 594 N.Y.S.2d 810 (App. Div. 1993) (reversing dismissal of petition based on proof of intimacy and test showing 99 percent probability of paternity, and directing court to enter judgment of paternity despite testimony denying intercourse) with Zearfoss v. Frattaroli, 646 A.2d 1238 (Pa. Super. 1994) (where plaintiff and defendant offered conflicting evidence on crucial question of timing, error to award summary judgment to plaintiff based on test results indicating 99.99 percent probability of paternity) (test evidence is not conclusive).

CHAPTER 10

Burdens of Proof and Presumptions

A BURDENS AND PRESUMPTIONS IN CIVIL CASES

Courts normally act only when parties ask them to do so and "prove their case," so it comes naturally to say that litigants must carry "burdens" or lose if they fail. Unfortunately the subject of burdens is among the most slippery in the areas of procedure and evidence, and attempts to refine what we know lead to difficulty. No thoughtful person emerges from considering the subject without feeling apprehension that the devices that define and impose burdens can be misunderstood and misapplied, that they may disguise what is happening, and that they gloss over real problems.

Bear in mind these points. First, burdens are functionally related, as are the concerns and policies that underlie them. Second, every burden raises questions of allocation (who bears it?) and weight or degree (how much must a party do in order to carry it?). Third, the various burdens, despite their similarities, have different consequences in a lawsuit.

With respect to trial burdens, bear in mind these questions: Is it appropriate, when the evidence leaves a matter in doubt, to act *as if* we know the answer? If doubt is unresolvable, would it be wise to redefine what is in issue? Should a burden-imposing device always impose *the same* burden, or should weight or consequences be adjustable to the particular case or category of cases?

1. Pretrial Burdens (Pleading, Pretrial Statement)

In some ways, the burden of pleading is least important. Despite a move toward tightening pleading burdens led by the *Twombly* and *Iqbal* cases,[1] a century-long

[1] Bell Atlantic Corp. v. Twombly, 550 U.S. 544 (2007) ("plausibility" standard) (antitrust complaint inadequate); Ashcroft v. Iqbal, 556 U.S. 662 (2009) (plausibility does not mean probability, but requires more than possibility) (civil rights complaint inadequate).

trend reduced the impact of pleadings. Parties set out claims and defenses in a short and plain manner; amendments are allowed as of course; motions to dismiss for failure to state a claim or judgment on the pleadings seldom succeed. Discovery and pretrial proceedings have more impact than pleadings. And many pleading conventions are clear and settled, some by rule or statute, others by decisions. In a suit for breach of contract, plaintiff normally pleads agreement, consideration, performance, breach, and damages (with particular allegations if she seeks "consequential" damages). These are not all the points that might affect right to recover (others include capacity to contract, legality, and accord and satisfaction), but they suffice in a complaint.

Yet figuring out what to plead is not easy in suits that rest on remedial statutes or assert new rights. Resolving uncertainties by "overpleading" is not satisfactory, as it tempts everyone to assume the pleader bears the burden of persuasion on points pleaded.

It is a challenging task (and largely thankless) to develop a coherent rationale explaining pleading burdens—a system for assigning burdens when no rule, statute, or case provides the answer. Courts sometimes grasp at straws. They look to the grammar of statutes for clues (even where phrasing seems accidental), and resort to shibboleths as if they provide guidance (plaintiff pleads everything in the "affirmative" case; defendant pleads "denials"). See generally Cleary, Presuming and Pleading: An Essay on Juristic Immaturity, 12 Stan. L. Rev. 5 (1959).

Sometimes pleading burdens are allocated out of concerns peculiar to pleading. The purpose may be to help the pleadings make sense: In a suit on a promissory note, plaintiff pleads nonpayment; in a defamation action, plaintiff pleads untruth (think how odd such complaints would seem if these allegations were missing). Here the burden of pleading does not match later trial burdens. That is, usually at trial a defendant sued on a promissory note must prove payment, and a defendant sued for defamation must prove truth. Another purpose peculiar to pleading is to provide certainty, so litigators know what to do at the beginning of the lawsuit. Cf. Palmer v. Hoffman, 318 U.S. 109 (1943) (FRCP 8 requires defendant to plead contributory negligence in diversity case, even though state law puts burden of persuasion on this point on plaintiff).

2. Trial Burdens (Production and Persuasion)

The term "burden of proof" embraces two related but different concepts that come into play in the trial of an action. One is the burden of production (burden of producing evidence); the other is the burden of persuasion.

Burden of production. To say a party bears the burden of producing evidence is to say she runs the risk of losing automatically (on motion for judgment as a matter of law, before or after the verdict) if she does not offer sufficient evidence to enable a reasonable person to find in her favor. At the outset, usually the party who bears the burden of persuasion also bears the burden of production. If Agnes sues Burt for personal injuries arising from an automobile accident, for example, she ordinarily bears the burden of producing evidence of Burt's negligence. If she carries that burden, she is assured that the trier will consider and weigh her evidence, a benefit most visible in a jury-tried case.

Success in carrying the burden of production does not necessarily shift it to the adversary. If Agnes offers sufficient evidence to support a finding that Burt was negligent, the trier of fact ordinarily remains free to reject her proof. Hence the burden of production does not pass to Burt, and he can win even if he produces no counterproof, although the risk that the trier will find against him may be higher if he stands silent rather than offering credible counterproof.

If the party bearing the burden of production carries it very well, however, it does shift to her opponent. That means the opponent loses automatically if he does not offer rebuttal evidence. Jurisdictions vary in defining proof that shifts the burden of production to the opponent. As a convenient shorthand, we use the term "cogent and compelling," but the concept is not uniform. (Most jurisdictions agree that testimonial proof cannot have burden-shifting effect if a reasonable person could disbelieve the witnesses. Jurisdictions vary as to whether all the evidence may be considered, or only that offered by the opponent.) Agnes might shift the burden to Burt if she offers unequivocal testimony by neutral observers that he rear-ended her car while she was stopped at the intersection for a red light, and if Burt fails to make headway in discrediting the witnesses by cross-examination. At this juncture, Burt must offer *some* counterproof—such as evidence that he did not run into Agnes from behind, or did so only because *he* was struck by a car from his rear. Failing to produce such counterproof puts him at risk of a partial judgment as a matter of law on negligence, leaving only damages to be determined by the jury.

Burden of persuasion. To say a party bears the burden of persuasion (or risk of nonpersuasion) is to say that she can win only if the evidence persuades the trier of the existence of the facts that she needs in order to prevail. (Ordinarily that means that she wins only if, on the basis of the evidence, the facts seem more likely true than not.) Perhaps because this burden operates at the end of trial, courts often say it never "shifts." Usually it is actually mentioned only in jury trials, in argument and instructions.

Elements in these burdens. Parties need not produce evidence on every point that might bear on liability, any more than they must plead them. The best reason to ignore many such points is that ordinarily they do not affect outcome. As Professor Cleary put it, requiring plaintiff in a contract suit "to establish the existence or nonexistence . . . of every concept treated in Corbin and Williston" would indeed be burdensome, and would force the lawsuit to cover "unnecessary territory." Cleary, supra at 7.

Thus evidence sufficient to enable the trier to find agreement, consideration, performance, breach, and damages normally satisfies the burden of production in a contract suit. In the absence of defense evidence, plaintiff prevails if the trier is persuaded on these points. Yet the right to recover might turn on matters like fulfillment of conditions, legality of agreement or performance, modification of terms, waiver, estoppel, or accord and satisfaction. If such issues are raised (normally defendant must do so), the outcome might turn on how they are resolved.

Allocating the burdens. On any particular element, usually burdens of pleading, producing evidence, and persuading the trier of fact are all put on the same party. Unfortunately textwriters give confusing signals on the relationship between the pretrial burden of pleading and the trial burdens, implying one burden impels the others, but disagreeing on which is in the driver's seat.[2] And (as is true of the burden of pleading) it is easy enough to discern the custom on such matters, but hard to explain *why* the trial burdens are allocated as they are, or to come up with rules of general application.

In the typical contract suit, plaintiff bears the burdens of production and persuasion on agreement, consideration, performance, breach, and damages. If nonfulfillment of a condition (including nonperformance by plaintiff) is an issue, plaintiff bears the burdens on this point too. (Normally it becomes an issue only if defendant pleads it with specificity under FRCP 8(c), so here is a place where pleading and trial burdens diverge.) If failure of consideration becomes an issue, the burdens of production and persuasion usually fall on defendant. (Here too the point usually becomes an issue only if he pleads it; it is an "affirmative defense," which is but another way of saying that defendant bears all the burdens—pleading, production, persuasion.)

Reasons for allocating burdens. Precedent aside, reasons behind assignment of burdens are usually framed in four broad concerns:

First and perhaps most important, burdens are allocated to serve substantive policy, making it easier or harder for plaintiffs to recover or defendants to avoid liability. In negligence cases, plaintiffs will more likely recover if defendants bear the burdens on the issue of contributory negligence. In a suit against an insurance carrier on a double indemnity life insurance policy, seeking recovery for accidental death, the beneficiary will more likely recover the full sum if the carrier bears the burdens on the question whether suicide was the cause of death.[3]

Second, we allocate burdens so as to recognize what is probably true. In a contract suit, for example, it is unlikely that *none* of the conditions precedent to defendant's obligations have occurred, for few plaintiffs would waste time and

---

[2] Compare McCormick on Evidence §337, at 509 (K. Broun ed., 7th ed. 2014) (usually "the party who has the burden of pleading a fact will have the burdens of producing evidence and of persuading the jury of its existence") with J. Friedenthal, A. Miller, J. Sexton, H. Hershkoff, Civil Procedure Cases and Materials 527 (10th ed. 2009) (burden of pleading "usually is assigned to the party who has the burden of producing evidence on that issue at trial"). The evidence people want the procedure people to bear the laboring oar, and vice versa. For the most part, we think the burden of pleading should follow the burden of persuasion.

[3] On a life insurance policy with double indemnity, the carrier pays the face amount of the policy if the insured died of natural causes, and twice that sum if accident was the cause of death. But if death resulted from suicide, the carrier generally owes nothing if the policy is new, or owes the face amount if the policy has existed for a minimum statutory period (such as two years). If the carrier takes the position that suicide was the cause of death, usually it bears the burden of persuasion on this issue. See 10 Couch on Insurance 2d §41:49 (1982); 19 id. §79:386; 21A J. Appleman, Insurance Law and Practice §12571 (rev. ed. 1981).

money bringing suit in such cases. It is more likely that most conditions have occurred. In light of this reality, the Rules put on defendant the burden of specifically alleging that certain conditions have not occurred. (Recall, however, that when a defendant does allege that conditions have not occurred, plaintiff bears the burden of persuading the trier of fact that the conditions have occurred.) In similar vein, we all know that a properly posted letter is almost always delivered to the addressee in due course, so we have a presumption to this effect.

Third, we allocate burdens so as to place them on the party most likely to have access to the necessary proof. In a suit against a bailee for damage to goods, for example, defendant is more likely than plaintiff to be able to show (if such be the case) that something other than its own negligence was the cause, and typically such defendant bears the burdens on this issue. Similarly, it is easier for a debtor to prove payment of an obligation than for the creditor to prove nonpayment, and for this reason usually the burden of proving payment is allocated to the defendant.

Fourth, we allocate burdens to help resolve cases where definitive proof is unavailable. Thus, absence for seven years without tidings raises a presumption of death, which can be important when surviving spouses seek to recover benefits or to remarry.

Weight of the burdens. In civil cases, the burden of pleading a point requires the party to include allegations in the appropriate complaint, answer, or reply. You likely spent time studying this subject in the basic procedure course.

The burdens of production and persuasion are related: The first requires a party to produce sufficient evidence to permit reasonable persons on the jury to find the point with the requisite measure of certainty, as defined by the burden of persuasion. The second means, in most civil actions,[4] proof by a preponderance—that is, evidence that persuades the jury (acting as reasonable persons) that the points to be proved are more likely so than not.

3. A Special Device for Shifting and Allocating Burdens: The Presumption

a. Sources and Nature of Presumptions

Burdens in civil cases may be allocated by presumptions: In a suit against a bailee for damage to goods placed in his care and custody, for example, it is

[4] In some civil actions (like suits for fraud or to reform a contract), the party bearing those burdens can prevail only on the basis of "clear and convincing evidence." This standard seems to enhance both burdens. That is, a particular body of evidence might suffice to carry the burden of coming forward in an ordinary case, but would not do so under the "clear and convincing" standard. And such a body of evidence might persuade the jury in an ordinary case, but fail to persuade if the instruction calls for "clear and convincing" proof. In some other special cases, there are similar heavy burdens. See, e.g., Addington v. Texas, 441 U.S. 418 (1979) (commitment proceedings; due process requires burden of persuasion "equal to or greater than" clear and convincing standard).

usually "presumed" that *if* the goods were in good shape when turned over to the bailee, but damaged on retrieval, *then* the bailee caused the damage by his negligence. Normally the bailor bears the burdens (pleading, production, persuasion) on the "basic facts" (delivery of undamaged goods; retrieval of damaged goods), but if the bailor succeeds on the basic facts, he gets the benefit of a presumption that the bailee was negligent and that his negligence caused the damage.

The term "presumption" describes a device that *requires* the trier to draw a particular conclusion when the basic facts are established, in the absence of evidence tending to disprove the presumed fact ("counterproof"). Thus in the bailor's suit (if the basic facts are proved) the trier *must* conclude that the bailee's negligence caused the damage unless he offers counterproof of some other cause—like earthquake, crime, or fire spreading from nearby property. Here is the essence of it: A presumption unopposed controls decision on the point in question.

There are many presumptions. Some (like the bailed goods presumption) apply again and again in a particular setting; they are context specific. Others are unattached. They roam the terrain of procedural conventions like Don Quixote—out to do good and operating in random and independent fashion. Consider the mailed letter presumption: If it is shown that a letter was properly posted (addressed, stamped, put in the mailbox), a presumption directs the trier to conclude that it was delivered to the addressee in due course (three days or so for domestic mail) unless there is counterproof that the addressee never got it. Here is a presumption of obvious utility (mailers are seldom in a position to show that what they sent was delivered at the distant end), and it is unattached: It can arise in a suit against an insurance carrier, where it might help the claimant prove renewal of the policy or the carrier prove cancellation; it can arise in an infringement action to prove the date or fact of registration of a patent. In short, this presumption comes into play whenever a party must prove delivery of a mailed letter.

Some presumptions grew out of common law. They appear as courts wrestle with recurrent problems. See, e.g., Owens v. Publix Supermarkets, Inc., 802 So. 2d 315, 330 (Fla. 2001) (creating presumption, arising on proof of slip-and-fall on business premises where a "transitory foreign substance" is found on the floor, that the condition was "not safe" and the owner "did not maintain the premises in a reasonably safe condition") (burden of persuasion shifts to owner). A full list of such presumptions would be long indeed. Other presumptions are statutory: The one for bailed goods is embodied in the UCC, which contains many provisions on matters of burden. Presumptions also grow out of efforts to implement remedial statutes, as you will see later. Here is a sampling:

1. In a suit against the owner of an automobile involved in an accident, upon proof of ownership, a presumption that the driver had the owner's permission (the "loaned auto" presumption); also a presumption, arising upon proof that defendant owned the car and employed the driver, that

the driver was acting within the scope of his duties (the "scope-of-employment" presumption);

2. In a suit on an accidental death policy or a life insurance policy with a double indemnity feature, upon proof that decedent came to a sudden violent end, a presumption that accident (as opposed to suicide or crime) caused the death;[5]
3. In a suit for death benefits, upon proof that the insured has been absent without tidings for a period of seven years, a presumption that he is dead; and
4. In a suit for death benefits, upon proof that plaintiff and decedent entered into a ceremonial marriage, a presumption that the marriage is valid and ongoing.

Presumptions such as these resolve recurring problems of proof without the need for extended debate: If a party seeking to prove delivery of a document shows that it was properly posted and the adversary offers no counterproof, the matter is settled, without need for extended argument or additional evidence.

Unfortunately, talking about presumptions bogs down in verbiage using differing terms and meanings. Here are the common ones:

(1) Conclusive or irrebuttable presumption. Rules of substantive law sometimes borrow the language of presumptions.

Under the Coal Mine Health and Safety Act of 1969, for example, a miner shown by X-ray or other clinical evidence to have pneumoconiosis (black lung disease) is "irrebuttably presumed" to be totally disabled, which "operates conclusively to establish entitlement to benefits." Usery v. Turner Elkhorn Mining Co., 428 U.S. 1, 11 (1976). And it was once true in California that a husband was irrebuttably presumed to be the father of a child born to his wife during marriage (absent proof that they did not cohabit or that he was impotent). The presumption still cannot be rebutted by ordinary evidence (testimony denying intercourse or evidence that the wife had intercourse with another), but the statute now requires a finding of nonpaternity if blood tests so indicate. Cal. Evid. Code §621. These legal rules are not presumptions at all, as the term is ordinarily used. They are principles of substantive law, expressed in the language of presumptions.

---

[5] In poignant cases, cause of sudden death is hard to determine because circumstances suggest accident or suicide (other alternatives may appear—death while committing a crime, or a natural cause like heart attack): When the beneficiary sues, generally she bears the burden of persuasion on the question of accident. The presumption comes to her aid, and it determines either (1) *the way* her case is conveyed to the jury in the court's instructions or (2) *whether* her case gets to the jury, if the facts suggest suicide. The presumption dislodges any assumption that death came from natural causes (which is unlikely if the insured died in a collision or is found with a bullet in his head), and sometimes it is phrased as a presumption *against* suicide. The insurance carrier normally bears the burden of persuasion when it claims that the insured committed suicide (see footnote 2, supra), and the presumption of accidental death is sometimes viewed as the *source* of this burden or as playing some role in it. Generally the carrier also bears the burden of proving that some other exclusion in the policy applies (such as death while committing a crime), and the presumption of accidental death sometimes plays a role in this matter too.

(2) Mandatory presumption or presumption of law. Generally these terms refer to the true presumption—the device that is the principal focus of this section. It controls decision if unopposed, so in jury-tried cases an instruction is in order and in bench trials the judge has no option but to find the presumed fact. "Mandatory" is redundant, for "presumption" by itself conveys this meaning.

(3) Permissive presumption, inference, presumption of fact. These terms usually refer to conclusions that are permitted but not required. The term "inference" adequately captures the meaning, and using the word "presumption" in this context clouds the message (an inference never controls decision, so the term "presumption" is inapposite). Jurors draw inferences from the evidence in the case, viewed in the light of their own lifetime experiences, and we expect them to do so. In this sense, inferences are simply conclusions drawn by reasonable persons on the basis of factual information.

But there is another kind of inference. We mean the kind that the judge mentions in formal instructions—a conclusion permissible on the basis of the evidence, to which the judge expressly draws the jury's attention. Inference instructions amount to judicial comment on the evidence, and they almost "nudge" or invite the jury to draw a conclusion.[5] They are discouraged in many states, used sparingly in others, and sometimes particular instructions are disallowed altogether. Even federal judges may be reluctant to give inference instructions, though traditionally they have more latitude than their state counterparts to comment on the evidence.

Probably the best known inference is the "*res ipsa loquitur*" device from tort law. Under certain conditions, it permits a finding of negligence to rest on circumstantial evidence, even though the defense might otherwise hope for a directed verdict. This particular inference is special in expressing an important policy that certain plaintiffs should be allowed to recover, if the jury chooses to find in their favor. It is special too in that it is conveyed to the jury in careful and explicit instructions, which (in most jurisdictions) are given even in the face of counterproof offered by the defense.

(4) Prima facie case. This supremely ambiguous term is used in two very different ways. It means either that the evidence *requires* a particular conclusion (like a presumption unanswered) or that the evidence *permits* that conclusion (like an inference).

b. Easy Cases: Presumption Controls, Disappears, or Is Contingent

In civil cases, we can identify three situations in which the operation of a civil presumption is easy and straightforward. The first two can be called "one-sided

[5] The question whether to instruct a civil jury that it may draw an inference gets mixed up in the analysis of presumptions. It is sometimes hard to figure out whether anything remains when a presumption is met by counterproof indicating the nonexistence of the presumed fact. One possibility is that an inference remains. If so, the next question is whether to mention the inference to the jury.

situations" because the presumption either controls the matter to which it is addressed (such as delivery of a properly posted letter), or falls out of the case altogether.

The third situation can be called "contingent" because the basic facts giving rise to the presumption are not clearly established at the end of trial (like proper posting of a letter). Hence a jury receives a contingent instruction to the effect that the presumption applies if the basic facts are found to exist, but not otherwise.

Let us now look more closely at these situations.

The two one-sided situations. In trials where a presumption is called into operation because the basic facts are established (such as proper posting of a letter), it can happen that there is no evidence tending to disprove the presumed fact (delivery of the letter in due course), or it can happen that there is cogent and compelling evidence disproving the presumed fact. In these one-sided situations, at the opposite end of the spectrum of possibilities, everyone agrees on how a presumption works.

At one end of the spectrum, the presumption controls. If the basic facts are established and there is no counterproof indicating that the presumed fact is not so, then the trier must find the presumed fact. In the mailed letter example, the trier of fact must find that the letter was delivered to the addressee in due course. In short, the unopposed presumption requires a finding of the presumed fact.

At the other end of the spectrum, the presumption disappears. If the basic facts are established but there is cogent and compelling proof that the presumed fact is not so, the presumption drops from the case. In the mailed letter example, the trier of fact must find that the addressee did not receive the letter. In short, the presumption, if met with cogent and compelling counterproof against the presumed fact, drops from the case.

The contingent case. Sometimes there is enough proof of the basic facts to support a finding that they exist, but not enough to require such a finding. Or evidence relating to the basic fact conflicts (some proof supports the basic facts; other proof points toward the contrary conclusion). In short, there is room to reach either conclusion. In the case of the mailed letter presumption, one could reasonably decide either that the letter was properly posted, or that it was not. Here the presumption can operate only if the trier finds the basic facts to be so. In a jury-tried case the judge must give a contingent (or conditional) instruction that *if* the jury finds the basic facts, *then* it must find the presumed fact.

■ PROBLEM 10-A. The Unhappy Harpsichordist

Atlas Moving Company advertises as follows: "We are the ones who care. Trust our people to move your most cherished possessions as carefully as you would."

Glen, a professional pianist and harpsichordist, is famed for his modern interpretation of Bach's Goldberg Variations. On moving from New Haven to Los Angeles to become pianist in residence at the University of Southern California, Glen hired Atlas to move his valued antique harpsichord, along with other household furniture. The month was April, and one Larson (an experienced mover for Atlas) picked up and loaded Glen's possessions on the 12th and drove straight to Los Angeles, arriving there on the 16th. When the shipment arrived, Glen discovered a deep crack in the inner casing of the harpsichord, which severely impaired its tonal quality.

Glen sues Atlas for $20,000, supporting his damage claim with expert testimony. Glen himself testifies that he plays the instrument nearly every day and that it was in perfect condition when Atlas picked it up in New Haven.

Atlas introduces the deposition of Keenan, another accomplished keyboard artist in New Haven. The transcript contains Keenan's testimony that he played Glen's harpsichord in New Haven and noticed the crack in the casing at the time, along with impaired tonality.

At the close of the evidence, Glen requests the court to instruct the jury that if it finds that the harpsichord was undamaged when Larson picked it up, it must find Atlas responsible for damage to the instrument. Should the instruction be given?

■ NOTES ON PRESUMPTIONS IN THE CONTINGENT SITUATION

1. The jury should be free to believe or reject Glen's testimony, and the same is true for Keenan's deposition testimony. If the jury *does* believe Glen's testimony, doesn't that mean the basic facts of the presumption are established? Absent counterproof against the presumed fact (there is no such proof), the jury should be told that if it *does* credit Glen's testimony, then Atlas is responsible. See St. Mary's Honor Center v. Hicks, 509 U.S. 502, 506 and n.3 (1993) (with statutory presumption of discrimination, basic facts make out prima facie case; if "reasonable minds could *differ* as to whether a preponderance of the evidence establishes the facts of a prima facie case" *and* if factfinder "finds that the prima facie case *is*" made out, *then* factfinder "*must* find the existence of the presumed fact" of discrimination) (original emphasis).

2. Language originally proposed by the Advisory Committee would have told courts and lawyers how to handle the contingent situation. Proposed Rule 3-02(2)(C) would have provided that if "reasonable minds would not necessarily agree" on the evidence whether or not the basic facts exist, the judge should tell the jury to "find in favor of the presumed fact" if they found the basic facts, "but otherwise to find against the existence of the presumed fact." Preliminary

Draft, Rule 3-03(2), 46 F.R.D. 161, 212-213 (1969). This language was deleted before the Rules were adopted, perhaps because the last phrase could be incorrect if there is independent evidence—meaning evidence apart from the basic facts of the presumption—that could support a finding of the presumed fact.

c. Hard Cases—Presumption Operates a Little, or Maybe Disappears

In the situations just examined, the presumption either controls or disappears or turns on a contingency. The presumption controls if the basic facts are established and there is no counterproof against the presumed fact. It disappears if cogent and compelling counterproof refutes the presumed fact. It operates contingently if the basic facts are up in the air—there is enough evidence to find that they exist, but not so much that a reasonable mind *must* conclude that they exist, or there is evidence both for and against the basic facts. The latter situation calls for a contingent instruction.

Now we take up the civil presumption in a truly challenging setting. We assume the basic facts are established, so we don't have to worry about the contingent case. Here is what we do have to worry about: The party against whom the presumption operates has offered evidence refuting the presumed fact—what we have called "counterproof"—but this evidence does not by nature fit either of the book-end categories we have already examined. That is to say, this evidence is not so cogent and compelling that it would require any reasonable person to find against the presumed fact. Nor is it so weak and unpersuasive that a reasonable person could not find against the presumed fact on the basis of the evidence. In short, the counterproof is neither cogent and compelling nor insufficient. Hence we are not in the situation in which the counterproof has vanquished the presumption (it has disappeared), nor in the opposite situation in which the presumption is effectively unopposed (the presumption controls). Instead, we are in what we might call the "in-between" situation, in which there is enough evidence to find against the presumed fact, but not so much that the presumed fact must be rejected.

In our in-between case, everyone can agree that the presumption no longer controls. The remaining question—and it is a hard one—is whether the presumption disappears, as it would if the counterproof were cogent and compelling. In this setting, a debate has long raged between what has come to be called the "bursting bubble" approach (associated with the name of Thayer) and the reformist approach (associated with Morgan). The tension between these two views greatly affected Rule 301.

The bursting bubble. Common law had it that the presumption vanished in this in-between situation. Courts and commentators waxed poetic in mixed metaphors: Presumptions "smoke out" the opponent, making him produce sufficient counterproof that the presumed fact is not so; when he does produce, the presumption is "put to flight"; hence presumptions are like "bursting bubbles"; also "like bats of the law, flitting in the twilight, but disappearing in the sunshine of actual facts"; and like "Maeterlinck's male bee" ("having functioned they disappear").[6] Thayer endorsed this view, and it is associated with his name.

Less poetically, common law tradition meant that the presumption shifted, to the party against whom it operated, the burden of coming forward with evidence (burden of production) and *not* the burden of persuasion. In its pure form, the traditional approach meant the bailor could lose automatically if the bailee offered evidence that fire damaged the goods. Even though the bailor had a presumption working for him, the bailee's counterproof caused it to burst and the jury never got the case.

The language of FRE 301 is consistent with the bursting bubble approach, and most federal courts that pronounce on this matter say that indeed FRE 301 adopts the bursting bubble approach. See, e.g., McCann v. Newman Irrevocable Trust, 458 F.3d 281, 287-288 (3d Cir. 2006) (FRE 301 embodies "bursting bubble theory"); A.C. Auckerman Co. v. R.L. Chaides Constr. Co., 960 F.2d 1020, 1037-1038 (Fed. Cir. 1999) (similar).

The reformist approach. The bursting bubble effect seemed absurd to commentators. Most astute was Professor Edmund Morgan, who argued that a presumption should shift the burden of persuasion. How, he asked, can a presumption be strong enough to *require* a finding in the absence of counterproof, yet so weak that it vanishes in the face of counterproof which the jury could reject? He had in mind the poignant circumstance in which only a presumption can take the case to the jury, which means that if counterproof "bursts" the presumption, then indeed the case fails, even though a jury would remain free (if only it got the chance) to disbelieve the counterproof. Here is his argument:

> MR. MORGAN . . . In McIver v. Schwartz, [145 A. 101 (R.I. 1929),] the basic fact was the general employment of a servant by the defendant to drive the defendant's automobile. The presumed fact was that the servant . . . was in the scope of his employment at the time of the collision with the plaintiff . . . . The only evidence in the case on this point was testimony by the defendant himself who got on the stand and said that the boy was not authorized to drive the car at this particular hour. He had been driving the car in the morning. He had the keys to the car, and the employer explained [that] this was because he had neglected to turn the keys back. The boy was not called as a witness. The Supreme Court of Rhode Island assumed that both the trial judge and the jury positively disbelieved the testimony of the defendant. The plaintiff had a verdict; the defendant appealed on the ground that there was no question for the jury . . . because the only testimony on scope of employment was the testimony as to the general employment

[6] E.L. Cheeney Co. v. Gates, 346 F.2d 197, 202 (5th Cir. 1965) ("smoke out" the opponent); Cleary, Presuming and Pleading: An Essay in Juristic Immaturity, 12 Stan. L. Rev. 5, 16-17 (1959) ("bursting bubble"); Mackowik v. Kansas City, St. J. & C.B.R.R., 94 S.W. 256, 262 (Mo. 1906) ("bats of the law"); Bohlen, The Effect of Rebuttable Presumptions of Law Upon the Burden of Proof, 68 U. Pa. L. Rev. 307, 314 (1920) ("Maeterlinck's male bee").

> of the servant by the defendant to drive the defendant's automobile. The plaintiff as respondent said: "That is true under previous Rhode Island decisions, but I had a presumption to help me." The Supreme Court of Rhode Island answered, "Yes, you had a presumption to help you, until the defendant introduced that testimony; it was testimony which a jury might have believed, and if the jury had believed the testimony, it would have justified them in finding no scope of employment. So your presumption was destroyed by the mere introduction of the evidence, and the fact that neither the jury nor the trial judge believed the testimony is entirely immaterial. The mere introduction of the evidence wipes out the total effect of the presumption." That is straight Thayer . . . . Mr. Thayer says in so many words that the sole effect of the presumption is to put on the opposing party the burden of producing evidence which would justify a trier in finding [against] the presumed fact.
>
> . . . What I object to in the Thayerian rule is this: the creation of a presumption for a reason that the court deems sufficient, a rule of law [that] if this basic fact stands by itself [unrebutted] there must be a finding of a presumed fact, whether the jury would ordinarily find it from the basic fact or not; but some testimony is put in which anybody can disbelieve, which comes from interested witnesses, and which is of a sort that is usually disbelieved. It seems to me it is futile to create a presumption if it is to be so easily destroyed . . . . I say that the slightest definite weight you can give [to presumptions] . . . is to [let them] fix the burden of persuasion because the burden of persuasion is important . . . where the mind of the jury or the trier of fact is in equilibrium.

18 American Law Institute Proceedings 201-221 (1940-1941). Morgan lost the battle, but his view prevailed in other times and other places, and the war is not over yet.

FRE 301 and modern practice. The Morgan argument convinced the drafters of the Rules. In all three preenactment versions, the Committee included the following:

> [A] presumption imposes on the party against whom it is directed the burden of proving that the nonexistence of the presumed fact is more probable than its existence.

See 46 F.R.D. 161, 212 (1969) (Preliminary Draft); 51 F.R.D. 315, 336 (1971) (Revised Draft); 56 F.R.D. 183, 208 (1972) (draft sent to Congress).

Congress was not persuaded. The House sought a compromise between the bursting bubble and Morgan approaches, and proposed treating civil presumptions as evidence. By this view, a presumption would not shift the burden of persuasion, but would not burst like a bubble either. Here is the critical language in the House proposal: "[E]ven though met with contradicting evidence, a presumption is sufficient evidence of the fact presumed, to be considered by the trier of the facts." See House Judiciary Print of H.R. 6453, November 15, 1973. But this approach had been discredited and had been tested in only a few jurisdictions. The problem is that a presumption is *not* evidence, but a way of looking at evidence—so telling a jury that a presumption is evidence can only confuse.

The Senate rejected both the Committee's proposal and the House version, and settled on the language ultimately adopted. That language could be read as a straight adoption of the bursting bubble approach. The crucial passage is as follows:

> [A] presumption imposes on the party against whom it is directed the burden of going forward with evidence to rebut or meet the presumption, but does not shift to such party the burden of proof in the sense of the risk of nonpersuasion, which remains throughout the trial upon the party on whom it was originally cast.

Here is an instance in which the Rules did not carry their usual influence. The framers of the new Uniform Rules of Evidence (URE) preferred the Morgan approach, so Uniform Rule 301 follows the Committee's initial proposal rather than the congressional revision. And states adopting codes based on the federal model are split on this point.[7]

■ PROBLEM 10-B. The Death of Mason Parnell

Mason Parnell was a wheat farmer. At age 49, he died of a head wound inflicted by discharge of a 30.06 rifle while alone in the spare sleeping room in the basement of his house.

His widow Vera Parnell sues Midcontinent Casualty Company on an accidental death policy covering her husband, seeking recovery in the amount of $100,000. Midcontinent claims that suicide was the cause of death and denies all liability. In such cases claimant bears the burden of pleading that death came by accident, and also the burdens of production and persuasion on that point.

Physical evidence shows that Mason Parnell was flat on his back on the bed when the gun discharged and that the muzzle was close to his chin at the time.

There is other circumstantial evidence. Vera Parnell introduces testimony that (1) Mason Parnell did not shoot himself intentionally because no soot pattern or flash burn was found on his face (indicating that the muzzle

[7] Out of 44 states adopting codes based on the Rules, 12 provide that civil presumptions shift the burden of persuasion (Arkansas, Delaware, Maine, Mississippi, Montana, Nebraska, Nevada, North Dakota, Oregon, Utah, Wisconsin, and Wyoming). Another 19 states follow FRE 301 to the extent of providing that civil presumptions affect the burden of production and not the burden of persuasion (Alaska, Colorado, Idaho, Illinois, Indiana, Kentucky, Maryland, Michigan, Minnesota, New Hampshire, New Jersey, New Mexico, North Carolina, Ohio, South Carolina, South Dakota, Vermont, Virginia, and West Virginia). Eight other states either omit any provision for civil presumptions or omit any directive on their effect (Arizona, Connecticut, Iowa, Louisiana, Pennsylvania, Tennessee, Texas, and Washington). The other five states provide that *some* presumptions shift the burden of persuasion, while others shift only the burden of production (Alabama, Florida, Hawaii, Oklahoma, and Rhode Island).

was more than 12 inches away), (2) a rifle owned by Parnell accidentally discharged during an earlier hunting trip, (3) Parnell died clutching a cigarette lighter (hence he may have had only one hand free to hold the rifle and pull the trigger), and (4) Parnell was in good financial condition, healthy, happily married, and not moody or morose.

But Midcontinent also introduces evidence that (a) the rifle that caused Parnell's death was in perfect order and was not the one that had accidentally discharged earlier, (b) some nasal hairs were found on the front gunsight, and (c) Parnell had experienced marital difficulties and may have been suffering from Alzheimer's disease.

At the close of the evidence, Vera requests that the jury be instructed on the presumption, arising from proof of sudden violent death, that death resulted from accident rather than suicide. Midcontinent argues that no such instruction is proper under the circumstances and moves for a directed verdict. The jurisdiction has adopted Rule 301, in the form enacted by Congress. What should the court do, and why?

NOTES ON PRESUMPTIONS IN THE "IN-BETWEEN" CASES

1. Almost all American jurisdictions recognize the presumption that Vera Parnell invoked. Why? If the presumption were not recognized, do you think a reasonable person could think, on the facts of the Problem, that the evidence establishes by a preponderance that Mason Parnell died an accidental death?

2. Courts in the in-between situation, where there is some counterproof against the presumed fact, have found ways to avoid the bursting bubble effect. Consider the following alternative approaches, discussed in C. Mueller & L. Kirkpatrick, Evidence §3.8 (5th ed. 2012), and ask whether any of them has more promise than the bursting bubble approach:

(a) "Substantial" or "uncontradicted" evidence. A presumption survives the introduction of counterproof, and is rebutted only by counterproof of high quality—"substantial" or "uncontradicted" evidence, or counterproof that is "undisputed" or "clear and positive" or "unimpeached." Under this approach, counterproof sufficient to support a finding for the adverse party does not vanquish the presumption altogether. The presumption, now reduced in force, protects an inference from extinction—in other words, it takes the case to the jury and lets it find the presumed fact. See Bieszck v. Avis Rent-A-Car System, Inc., 583 N.W.2d 691, 696 (Mich. 1998) (loaned auto presumption does not shift burden of persuasion, but can only be overcome by "positive, unequivocal, strong and credible" evidence; this high threshold serves the underlying legislative purpose underlying and "helps promote public safety") (standard was met here); Gaither v. Myers, 404 F.2d 216 (D.C. Cir. 1968) (owner denied driving car, but his testimony "was not so consistent and conclusive" as to overcome the

presumption); E.L. Cheeney Co. v. Gates, 346 F.2d 197, 201-204 (5th Cir. 1965) (employee testified that he was supposed to drive truck only to and from home and he had been visiting a friend; his credibility was attacked by inconsistent statement that he had been "working in an oilfield," which "would not carry the day on agency," and presumption "alone suffices until it is rebutted by clear, positive, uncontradicted testimony") (counterproof did not "conclusively overcome" presumption).

(b) "Believe the evidence." A presumption survives the introduction of counterproof challenging the presumed fact, and the jury should be told to find the presumed fact unless it "believes" the counterproof. See Sutphen v. Hagelin, 344 A.2d 270 (Conn. 1975) ("family car" presumption that driver had owner's permission does not disappear in the face of counterproof; jury should be told that presumption applies if it disbelieves the counterproof).

(c) "Equipoise." A presumption survives the introduction of counterproof, and the trier must find the presumed fact unless the counterproof makes its nonexistence as likely as its existence. This "equipoise" approach is best expounded in an opinion by the Maine Supreme Court in Hinds v. John Hancock Mutual Life Insurance Co., 155 A.2d 721 (Me. 1959). There the court decided that presumptions should have "maximum coercive force short of shifting the burden of persuasion," and endorsed a rule that the presumption controls "until the contrary evidence persuades the factfinder that the balance of probabilities is in equilibrium, or, stated otherwise, until the evidence satisfies the jury or factfinder that it is as probable that the presumed fact does not exist as that it does exist." (*Hinds* involved a presumption against suicide similar to the Problem. Later Maine adopted Uniform Rule 301, under which presumptions shift burden of persuasion.)

3. Sometimes courts avoid deciding how much counterproof is required before the presumption disappears, and instead focus on instructing the jury. Like Morgan's favorite example of *McIver*, the Maryland decision in *Grier* involved the presumption, arising on proof of car ownership, that the driver was the owner's agent. In *Grier*, defendant driver testified that he did not remember a near-miss incident in which he allegedly cut in front of a bus, and had checked with others who drove his car, who didn't recall it either. The Maryland Supreme Court said the judge should "mention the presumption, so that the jury may appreciate the legal recognition of a slant of policy or probability." See Grier v. Rosenberg, 131 A.2d 737 (Md. 1957). See also Murphy v. 24th Street Cadillac Corp., 727 A.2d 915, 920 (Md. 1999) (if party against whom presumption operates produces "some evidence" against the presumed fact, the matter goes to the jury, who should be "informed of the presumption"). Should a court say "presumption" in instructions? Does the term oversell the underlying policy, or undersell it? Or just confuse things?

4. Alaska Rule 301(a) includes the following:

> When the burden of producing evidence to meet a presumption is satisfied, the court must instruct the jury that it may, but is not required to, infer the

existence of the presumed fact from the proved fact, but no mention of the word "presumption" may be made to the jury.

Similar language appears in other provisions. See, e.g., Maryland Rule 5-301(a) (when counterproof is offered, "the presumption will retain the effect of creating a question to be decided by the trier of fact" unless presumption has been rebutted "as a matter of law"); North Carolina Rule 301 (similar to Alaska provision, but with no admonition about the word "presumption"). Is this position an improvement over the bursting bubble approach? It's not clear, is it, that the "proved fact[s]" in Problem 10-B suffice to show that Mason Parnell died accidentally? How about providing that these cases should get to the jury without *any* instruction? Vermont takes this approach. Its rule says that where the party opposed to the presumption has carried its burden of production, "the court shall submit the question of the existence of the presumed fact to the jury on the evidence as a whole without reference to the presumption," unless a reasonable juror could not find the presumed fact on all the evidence. Vermont Rules of Evidence, Rule 301(c)(2) (1983).

5. Some commentators endorse the bursting bubble approach, as do some decisions. See Lansing, Enough Is Enough: A Critique of the Morgan View of Rebuttable Presumptions in Civil Cases, 62 Or. L. Rev. 485 (1983); O'Brien v. Equitable Life Assurance Society, 212 F.2d 383, 388-389 (8th Cir.) (while in bed with a woman, decedent was shot by her husband; decedent's widow sued insurer, invoking presumption of accidental death, which could apply if decedent died as *victim* of criminal assault; but woman testified that decedent forced her onto bed and that she could not remember anything further; presumption was "destroyed" because her testimony suggested that decedent died while *perpetrating* an assault), *cert. denied*, 348 U.S. 835 (1954). Was the purpose of the presumption of accidental death adequately served in *O'Brien*?

6. Some state rules and decisions take the view that presumptions affect the burden of persuasion. In a variety of contexts, often interpreting statutory presumptions, court decisions also take this approach. See, e.g., Frederick v. Shankle, 785 A.2d 749, 751 (Md. 2001) (with statutory presumption that police officer with heart condition or hypertension contracted the disease at work, applying rule that policy-based presumptions shift burden of persuasion); Smith v. Atkinson, 771 So. 2d 429, 435 (Ala. 2000) (in context of presumption that plaintiff would have prevailed but for destruction of evidence by spoliation, applying similar rule); Knowles v. Gilchrist Co., 289 N.E.2d 879 (Mass. 1972) (bailed goods presumption shifts to bailee burden of persuasion on issue of due care).

d. Operation of Rule 301

Consider the language in Rule 301, which (we said above) "could be read as a straight adoption of the bursting bubble approach." Recall, however, how common law courts struggled to avoid this outcome, and consider following decisions where the Court could have adopted the bursting bubble approach but chose not to.

In the *Burdine* case in 1981, the Court wrestled with proof of discrimination in suits under the Civil Rights Act of 1964. Plaintiff had alleged gender discrimination. The Court said that in disparate treatment cases plaintiff makes out a "prima facie case" by proving "that she applied for an available position for which she was qualified, but was rejected under circumstances which give rise to an inference of unlawful discrimination." Citing McDonnell Douglas Corp. v. Green, 411 U.S. 792 (1973), the Court sketched a model of the prima facie case. *McDonnell Douglas* involved race discrimination, but the model serves in gender cases too. Plaintiff makes a prima facie case by showing he "belongs to a racial minority," that he "applied and was qualified for a job for which the employer was seeking applicants," that he was rejected despite being qualified, and that "the position remained open and the employer continued to seek" applicants. Then the Court in *Burdine* came to the place where the rubber hits the road:

> [T]he prima facie case "raises an inference of discrimination only because we presume these acts, if otherwise unexplained, are more likely than not based on the consideration of impermissible factors." Establishment of the prima facie case in effect creates a presumption that the employer unlawfully discriminated against the employee. If the trier of fact believes the plaintiff's evidence, and if the employer is silent in the face of the presumption, the court must enter judgment for the plaintiff because no issue of fact remains in the case.

This presumption, the Court went on to say, "shifts to the defendant" the burden of introducing evidence that plaintiff was rejected "for a legitimate, nondiscriminatory reason," but the presumption does not shift to defendant the burden of persuasion. In fact the burden of persuasion "never shifts," and the presumption operates to allocate the burden of production. In a footnote the Court included a "See" citation referencing FRE 301, implying that this arrangement of burdens of production and persuasion is consistent with the latter. (One might read this reference to mean that FRE 301 actually *applies* here, but that conclusion is "iffy" for reasons explored further below.)

When *Burdine* was decided, Title VII suits were tried to courts without juries, but in 1991 Congress amended the statute. Now suits like *Burdine* claiming intentional discrimination carry the right to a jury trial when plaintiff seeks damages, and pave the way to recover compensatory damages (only backpay and injunctive relief were available before). See 42 USC §1981a. In effect, the statute "ups the ante" so *Burdine*'s holding on presumptions now applies in jury trials for much larger sums.

■ NOTES ON *BURDINE* AND FRE 301 IN "IN-BETWEEN" CASES

1. *Burdine* says plaintiff makes out a prima facie case by showing she was a member of a protected class, that she applied for a job, that she was qualified, that the job remained open, and that the job went to someone else. Proving those points would not suffice, as a matter of logic, to take a case to a jury or let a judge find for the claimant. Thousands of job applicants experience rejection in identical circumstances simply because there are usually many qualified applicants for any opening. Yet if the facts of the prima facie case are proved and defendant offers no counterproof, *Burdine* says plaintiff prevails. Need more proof that presumptions serve policy goals?

2. Suppose a new case like *Burdine* is tried to a jury and plaintiff seeks compensatory damages. This time defendant offers proof sufficient to support a finding that a man who was promoted in preference to plaintiff was better qualified. But plaintiff attacks this proof by cross-examining defense witnesses, and in the end the factfinder *could conclude* that the man was *not* better qualified, or that his qualifications were *not* the reason he was preferred. Could defendant still win judgment as a matter of law? Could plaintiff hope for a conditional instruction telling the jury to find in her favor if the jury rejects the defense explanation? In St. Mary's Honor Center v. Hicks, 509 U.S. 502 (1993), a five-Justice majority answered the first question no (defendant does not win automatically) and the second question yes (she could hope for an instruction). *St. Mary's* was a judge-tried race discrimination case, and the Court said that once defendant carried its burden of production, the *McDonnell Douglas* framework (with "presumptions and burdens") is "no longer relevant" and "resurrect[ing] it later . . . flies in the face of *Burdine*." So defendant does not *win* automatically, but plaintiff doesn't necessarily lose either:

> The presumption, having fulfilled its role of forcing the defendant to come forward with some response, simply drops out of the picture. The defendant's "production" (whatever its persuasive effect) having been made, the trier of fact proceeds to decide the ultimate question: whether plaintiff has proven "that the defendant intentionally discriminated against [him]" because of his race. The factfinder's disbelief of the reasons put forward by the defendant (particularly if disbelief is accompanied by a suspicion of mendacity) may, together with the elements of the prima facie case, suffice to show intentional discrimination. Thus, rejection of the defendant's proffered reasons, will *permit* the trier of fact to infer the ultimate fact of intentional discrimination, and the Court of Appeals was correct when it noted that, upon such rejection, "no additional proof of discrimination is *required*." But the Court of Appeals' holding that the rejection of the defendant's proffered reasons *compels* judgment for the plaintiff disregards the fundamental principle of Rule 301 that a presumption does not shift the burden of proof, and ignores our repeated admonition that the Title VII plaintiff at all times bears the "ultimate burden of persuasion."

St. Mary's Honor Center v. Hicks, 509 U.S. 502, 511 (1993).

3. *Burdine* cites FRE 301 but stops short of saying it applies in Title VII suits. *St. Mary's* goes a step further, referring to "the fundamental principle of Rule 301" and implying that FRE 301 does apply. Both cases suggest that counterproof against the presumed fact does not cause the presumption to vanish, since plaintiff's case lives on. Since the native probative force of the basic facts do not justify this conclusion, it seems that the presumption has not "burst like a bubble," but survives to insure that the factfinder can still draw an inference of discrimination. *Burdine* and *St. Mary's* reject the bursting bubble approach implicitly, and they cite FRE 301 in doing so. The Court also cites FRE 301 in an important "black lung" case involving statutory presumptions designed to help coal miners recover compensation for black lung disease, but without discussing what happens when defendants introduce counterproof against the presumed facts. See Usery v. Turner Elkhorn Mining Co., 428 U.S. 1, 27 (1976).

4. Not surprisingly in light of *Burdine* and *St. Mary's*, some courts applying FRE 301 reject the bursting bubble approach. See, e.g., Rice v. Office of Servicemembers' Group Life Insurance, 260 F.3d 1240 (10th Cir. 2001) (rejecting bursting bubble interpretation of FRE 301; approving instruction conveying a presumption of competency despite proof of incompetency) and United States v. Jessup, 757 F.2d 378, 380-384 (1st Cir. 1985) (citing FRE 301 and rejecting bursting bubble approach for statutory bail presumption applied by magistrate; seeking "middle ground" where magistrate should "still keep in mind" that Congress found that major drug offenders "pose special risks").

■ NOTES ON FRE 301 AND FEDERAL STATUTORY REMEDIES

1. Long ago the Court held that a "legislative presumption" could pass muster under the Due Process and Equal Protection Clauses if there were "some rational connection between the fact proved and the ultimate fact presumed," such that finding the latter on the basis of the former is not "so unreasonable as to be a purely arbitrary mandate." Mobile, J. & K.C. Ry. v. Turnipseed, 219 U.S. 35, 43 (1910). In *Turner Elkhorn*, the Court quotes another opinion to the effect that courts judging rationality should give "significant weight" to the capacity of Congress "to amass the stuff of actual experience and cull conclusions from it," and concludes that the black lung presumptions are valid. Usery v. Turner Elkhorn Mining Co., 428 U.S. 1, 28 (1976). Given *Turner Elkhorn*, it seems that *Burdine*'s prima facie case satisfies the "rational basis" standard, and Congress may enact statutory presumptions serving substantive policy even where the basic facts would not, as a matter of mere logic, suffice to prove the presumed fact.

2. *Turner Elkhorn*'s "black lung" presumptions express a policy favoring recovery for coal miners and their families. They also help resolve cases where positive and particularized proof cannot be had. Can the same things be said of the prima facie case in *Burdine*? Don't these points suggest that bursting bubble treatment is inappropriate for the presumptions in both cases? What do these points suggest about FRE 301?

3. Federal law (Carmack Amendment to Interstate Commerce Act) makes common carriers liable to shippers for "loss, damage or injury" to property they receive for transportation. The Court has held that under this statute the shipper makes out a "prima facie case" by showing "delivery in good condition, arrival in damaged condition, and the amount of damages," and thereafter "the burden of proof is upon the carrier" to show that it was free from negligence and that the damage was due to "one of the excepted causes relieving the carrier of liability." Missouri Pacific R.R. v. Elmore & Stahl, 377 U.S. 134, 137 (1964). In a judge-tried post-Rules suit by the shipper of 198,568 aerosol cans of Solarcaine spray, seeking recovery because the caps in the top two layers of cartons were "discolored" (apparently road dirt came through a hole in the truck), the trial court gave judgment for defendant. The Sixth Circuit reversed, concluding that the Carmack Amendment as interpreted in *Missouri Pacific* shifts the burden of persuasion. The reviewing court rejected defendant's contention that the judge did right under FRE 301:

> It is immediately apparent that Rule 301 does not affect the burden of proof in Carmack Amendment cases. For well-articulated reasons Congress chose to place the burden of proof on a carrier in whose hands goods are damaged rather than on the shipper. This is more than a burden of going forward with the evidence. It is a true burden of proof in the sense of the risk of nonpersuasion and it remains on the carrier once the prima facie showing has been made.

Plough, Inc. v. Mason & Dixon Lines, 630 F.2d 468, 472 (6th Cir. 1980). See also Tenneco Chemical v. William T. Burnett & Co., 691 F.2d 658, 663-664 (4th Cir. 1982) (statutory presumption of validity of patent shifts burden of persuasion, and FRE 301 does not apply). *Plough* and *Tenneco* illustrate the use of policies found in federal statutes in justifying strong presumptions, and in rejecting application of FRE 301 if it weakens presumptions.

e. *Bifurcated Approaches*

Some states take a bifurcated approach to presumptions. In California, Florida, and Hawaii, for example, a presumption designed to further a "public policy" shifts the burden of persuasion, but a presumption designed "to facilitate the determination of the particular action" shifts only the burden of production. See Cal. Evid. Code §§603-606 (West 1995); Fla. Stat. Ann. §§90.301-90.303 (1999); Haw. R. Evid. 301-303 (1983). California and Florida have statutory lists of presumptions in each category. In both states, the presumption of validity of a ceremonial marriage and the presumption of death of a person not heard from for seven years belong in the public policy category (affecting the burden of persuasion), and the mailed letter presumption only facilitates determination of the action (affecting only burden of production).

Surely these jurisdictions are on to something. Not all presumptions are created equal, and some should have greater effect than others. Unfortunately it is hard to decide which presumption belongs in which category and even to define the scope of the categories. In a dual scheme, how should we treat the bailed goods presumption? The presumption that accident rather than suicide caused the death? The black lung presumption? The problem may be that we have no rank ordering of presumptions and might never agree on one. The common law failed to develop a comprehensive approach; the jurisdictions that tackle the problem by code disagree on the categories and offer incomplete lists. If we must live in a one-rule world, which one should we choose, URE 301 or FRE 301?

f. State Presumptions in Diversity Cases

Rule 302 provides that in federal courts state law controls the "effect" of presumptions relating to "a fact which is an element of a claim or defense as to which State law supplies the rule of decision." This provision expresses the view that presumptions are "substantive" for *Erie* purposes, in expectation that *Erie* requires federal courts to apply state presumptions. Many state counterparts to Rule 302 require state courts to recognize federal presumptions in the unusual case in which state courts apply federal law in civil litigation.

B BURDENS, PRESUMPTIONS, AND INFERENCES IN CRIMINAL CASES

1. Burden of Persuasion

When it comes to burdens in criminal cases, two points are most important. First, the Due Process Clauses of the Fifth and Fourteenth Amendments require the prosecutor to prove beyond a reasonable doubt every element in the charged crime, in state and federal court alike. Second, a court cannot instruct the jury to find a fact against the accused, no matter how powerful the evidence may be, and this notion grew out of the jury trial entitlement, which is also protected as a matter of due process in state and federal court alike.

The reasonable doubt standard is central to American criminal law, universally known even among lay people, and included in jury instructions everywhere. In 1970, the Court took note that it had long been "assumed" that this standard was guaranteed as a matter of due process, deciding in the *Winship* case that indeed due process does protect against conviction "except upon proof beyond a reasonable doubt of every fact necessary to constitute the crime." See In re Winship, 397 U.S. 358, 364 (1970) (standard also applies to delinquency proceedings against juvenile offenders).

The rule that the jury cannot be instructed to find a fact against the accused has an even longer provenance, although its source is harder to pinpoint.

See, e.g., Sparf v. United States, 156 U.S. 51, 105 (1895) (cannot instruct jury to find the accused guilty of the charged offense or any offense less than that charged); United States v. Martin Linen Supply Co., 430 U.S. 564, 572 (1977) (jurors are "primary finders of fact," so judge cannot enter judgment of conviction or direct jury to come forward with such a verdict, regardless "how overwhelmingly the evidence may point"); Sandstrom v. Montana, 442 U.S. 510, 516 n.5 (1979) ("verdicts may not be directed against defendants in criminal cases").

The proposition that proof beyond reasonable doubt is required leads to another question: How far does the obligation extend? Are prosecutors constitutionally required to prove beyond reasonable doubt every fact that bears on culpability? Must they prove that defendant, if he pleads insanity, is sane? Or, if he pleads self-defense, that he was in fact *not* entitled for that reason to do what he did? These are ordinarily viewed as affirmative defenses, meaning that the accused must both plead and prove them. The question is whether—and to what extent—the burdens on these elements can be allocated to defendants.

In two cases in the 1970s, the Court took up these questions. First came the *Mullaney* case from Maine, and then *Patterson* from New York. Both involved murder convictions, and in both the defendant claimed temporary incapacity—in Maine, where criminal law was set forth in traditional terms, the defense was "heat of passion," and in New York, where the law was set out in the spare clinical wording of modern statutes, the defense was "extreme emotional disturbance."

In *Mullaney*, the law of Maine defined both murder and manslaughter as unlawful intentional killing. The difference was that murder required "malice aforethought." At the end of trial, the court instructed the jury that if the prosecutor proved "intentional and unlawful" killing, then malice aforethought was to be "conclusively implied" unless defendant proved he acted in "heat of passion on sudden provocation." The court also told the jury that malice aforethought and heat of passion were "inconsistent things." This approach violated due process, the Court concluded. It stressed that Maine treats murder different from manslaughter in punishment, and said the obligation to prove guilt beyond reasonable doubt cannot be "limited to those facts that constitute a crime as defined by state law" because that would allow the state to "undermine" (without changing substantive law) what *Winship* sought to achieve: A legislature could "redefine the elements that constitute different crimes, characterizing them as factors that bear solely on the extent of punishment." See Mullaney v. Wilbur, 421 U.S. 684, 698 (1975).

In *Patterson*, the New York statute defined murder as intentionally causing the death of another person. The defense was not "heat of passion" (as in Maine), but acting "under the influence of extreme emotional disturbance for which there was a reasonable explanation or excuse." In New York, as in Maine, the defense reduced murder to manslaughter—in New York, intentional killing was manslaughter if defendant killed the victim under circumstances that do not constitute murder because defendant acted "under the influence of extreme emotional disturbance." Like Maine, New York put the burden on defendant to prove the defense. In *Patterson*, however, the Court found that New York's approach comported with due process. The Court recognized similarities with *Mullaney,* but thought there were differences: First, New York criminalized killing as murder if the state approved intent and causation, and no "further facts" had to be "proved" or "presumed." Second, the defense of extreme emotional disturbance "[did] not serve to negative any facts" that the prosecutor had to prove, but constituted a "separate" matter. In other words, "extreme emotional disturbance" could coexist with intent to kill, and burdening defendant with proving the defense could not be construed as burdening him with *disproving* an element in the prosecutor's case. See Patterson v. New York, 432 U.S. 197, 205-206 (1977).

■ NOTES ON BURDEN OF PERSUASION IN CRIMINAL CASES

1. *Mullaney* sent shockwaves through prosecutors' offices. The opinion could be read—perhaps *should be read*—to mean that prosecutors must bear the burden of proving beyond reasonable doubt every fact bearing on culpability. That would mean, for example, that prosecutors would have to prove that self-defense did not apply if defendant pled self-defense. For an argument based on this "purely procedural" interpretation of due process, see Barbara Underwood, The Thumb on the Scales of Justice: Burdens of Persuasion in Criminal Cases, 86 Yale L.J. 1299, 1317-1325 (1977) (the Constitution regulates criminal procedure extensively, and has little to say about the substance of criminal law, leaving that to legislatures, but the latter cannot alter procedural burdens, and must leave them on prosecutors for every element bearing on culpability). Is this "purely procedural" interpretation of due process what the Court had in mind in *Mullaney* when it said courts should not "undermine" *Winship* by redefining the elements so as to characterize them as bearing only on "extent of punishment"?

2. Are *Mullaney* and *Patterson* really different cases? The instruction in *Mullaney* said "heat of passion" was "inconsistent" with intent to kill, but the instruction in *Patterson* did not imply that "extreme emotional disturbance" would negate intent. The Court in *Patterson* seized on this point (defense did not "negative any facts of the [charged] crime"). Is this distinction a matter of definition (Maine taking one view, New York another)? Should the Court determine, as a constitutional matter, whether one can entertain a culpable intent to kill while acting in heat of passion (or extreme emotional disturbance), or is it just a matter of what the jury is told? In *Patterson,* Justice Powell wrote in dissent that the Court managed "to run a constitutional boundary line through the barely visible space that separates Maine's law from New York's." See Patterson v. New York, 432 U.S. 197, 221 (1977). He had a point, didn't he?

3. *Mullaney* saw a threat to due process in the possibility that states might manipulate their criminal codes, but *Patterson* raised a different concern. If prosecutors must prove beyond reasonable doubt "any fact affecting" criminality, legislatures would be deprived of "any discretion whatsoever" in allocating burdens, which would "discourage" efforts at reforming criminal law. Consider the so-called "accommodation" drug sale recognized in some jurisdictions. If defendant sells drugs to a friend for purposes of "accommodation" (not to make a profit or encourage addiction), arguably the offense should carry a lesser penalty than "arm's length" drug transactions. If recognizing this point means prosecutors must prove beyond a reasonable doubt that a sale did *not* fit this category, a legislature might say the price is too high—better to penalize all sellers the same way. The legislature in Iowa adopted this accommodation notion, which was interpreted as putting on defendants the burden of proving accommodation (an affirmative defense). After *Mullaney*, the Iowa Supreme Court held that the statute could not constitutionally put the burden on the defense, and the prosecutor had to prove beyond reasonable doubt that a sale was *not* an accommodation. See State v. Monroe, 236 N.W.2d 24, 34 (Iowa 1975). Inhibiting such reform efforts is not a good thing, is it?

4. Decisions prior to *Mullaney* and *Patterson* had sustained affirmative defenses in criminal cases as constitutional. See Martin v. Ohio, 480 U.S. 228 (1987) (defendant may be burdened with proving self-defense) (reporting, however, that all but two states place the burden on prosecutors to disprove self-defense); Rivera v. Delaware, 429 U.S. 877 (1976) (defendant may be burdened with proving insanity by a preponderance). Ways of treating these defenses vary widely. In some states, for example, a defendant need only plead insanity (then the prosecutor bears the burdens of producing evidence and persuading the jury); in others, he must plead and produce evidence of insanity (though the burden of persuasion rests with the state); in still others, he must plead, offer evidence, and persuade. See also 18 USC §17 (defendant must establish insanity by clear and convincing evidence). Doesn't *Patterson* in effect approve these practices?

5. Does *Patterson* go too far in the other direction? Under *Patterson*, could a legislature define murder as "unlawful killing," and recognize an affirmative defense of "lack of intent to kill"? The majority in *Patterson* recognized that leaving the door ajar might tempt some to go too far, and offered this comment: "There are obviously constitutional limits beyond which the States may not go." See Patterson v. New York, 432 U.S. 197, 210 (1977) (legislature cannot declare that someone is "presumptively guilty" or that proving "identity of the accused" should create a presumption of "facts essential to guilt"). Justice Powell in dissent addressed this matter: Due process, he wrote, requires the prosecutor to shoulder the burden of proof beyond reasonable doubt "only if the factor at issue makes a substantial difference in punishment and stigma" *and* has "historically" operated this way in our tradition. See *Patterson*, 432 U.S. at 226-227.

6. Justice Powell was looking for a middle ground between a "purely procedural" interpretation of due process in which the prosecutor must bear the burden on all points bearing on culpability, and a "no-holds-barred" interpretation that would give total freedom to legislatures. Professors Jeffries and

Stephan suggested what we might call a "final check" approach. They argued that the Eighth Amendment (barring "cruel and unusual punishments") limits legislative capacity to define criminality in three different ways, by requiring an act ("actus reus"), a blameworthy mental attitude ("mens rea"), and proportionality in punishment.[8] The "accommodation" factor in drug cases (note 3, supra) can illustrate the approach. Assume the legislature wants to amend the drug crime statute by exempting anyone who transfers narcotics to accommodate a friend, without seeking profit or trying to encourage addiction. The Constitution does not require an exemption for accommodation suppliers, so an exemption is "gratuitous" (a matter of choice). For this reason, the legislature can put on defendant the burden of proving he is an accommodation supplier. Suppose the legislature wanted to decriminalize sexual assault, or lessen the penalty, in a case not involving physical force in which a defendant made a reasonable mistake on the age of the victim? If such an exemption is also gratuitous, the legislature could put on defendant the burden of proving that he was reasonably mistaken in thinking the victim had attained the age of consent. See Jeffries & Stephan, Defenses, Presumptions, and Burden of Proof in the Criminal Law, 88 Yale L.J. 1325 (1979).

7. Can a legislature sidestep due process by directing courts to impose higher sentences if certain factors appear, authorizing judges to apply them under the preponderance standard? See McMillan v. Pennsylvania, 477 U.S. 79 (1986) (approving scheme requiring five years' imprisonment if judge determines in sentencing that perpetrator visibly possessed firearm); Almendez-Torres v. United States, 523 U.S. 224 (1998) (approving scheme letting judge impose 20-year sentence because defendant, convicted of illegal entry carrying penalty of two years, was previously convicted of aggravated felonies). But see Apprendi v. New Jersey, 530 U.S. 466 (2000) (finding due process violation where defendant was convicted of illegal possession of firearm, carrying penalty of 5-10 years, but judge imposed 12 years under statute increasing penalties for hate crimes; "any fact that increases the penalty for a crime beyond the prescribed statutory maximum," apart from prior convictions, "must be submitted to a jury, and proved beyond a reasonable doubt").

---

[8] See, e.g., Enmund v. Florida, 458 U.S. 782 (1982) (defendant drove getaway car used in robbery and killing; death penalty was cruel and unusual); Robinson v. California, 370 U.S. 660 (1962) (punishment for status of drug addiction is cruel and unusual); Morissette v. United States, 342 U.S. 246 (1952) (mens rea is essential in defining criminality); United States v. Weems, 217 U.S. 349 (1910) (15 years' hard labor, imposed on Coast Guard disbursing officer for minor falsifications that harmed no one, was cruel and unusual). But see Tison v. Arizona, 481 U.S. 137 (1987) (upholding death sentence for participant in prison escape leading to murder; defendant acted with reckless indifference); Rummel v. Estelle, 445 U.S. 263 (1980) (upholding life sentence under habitual offender statute; defendant had been convicted three times for fraudulently obtaining money and goods worth $229.11).

■ PROBLEM 10-C. Killing by "Calculation and Design"?

Esther Marlin is prosecuted for alleged aggravated murder of her husband Wilbur. The offense is defined as "purposefully killing another with prior calculation and design." The evidence indicates that Esther and Wilbur quarreled over grocery money in the kitchen of their home, that Wilbur struck Esther in the head, that she went upstairs, donned a robe, and then returned with Wilbur's pistol. Wilbur saw that Esther was carrying something, asked her about it, and then came at her. She fired six shots, three of which struck and killed Wilbur.

At trial, Esther claims that she acted in self-defense.

Applying state law, the trial judge advises the jury that Esther bears the burden of proving self-defense. He instructs that self-defense requires that defendant (1) be not at fault in creating the situation giving rise to the argument and (2) have an honest belief that she was in imminent danger of death or great bodily harm and that only such force could provide a means of escape.

The jury finds Esther guilty. In the U.S. Supreme Court, she argues that the instruction putting on her the burden of persuasion on self-defense violates *Winship-Mullaney-Patterson.* Specifically, she argues that requiring her to prove that she believed that she was in "imminent danger of death or great bodily harm" unconstitutionally relieved the state of its burden to prove that she acted with "prior calculation and design."

What result, and why?

2. Presumptions and Inferences

Presumptions and inferences present greater difficulty in criminal than in civil cases.[9]

Both the constitutional entitlement to a jury trial and considerations of due process restrict use of these devices in criminal cases. Probably *no* presumption operating against the accused on an element in the offense can *control* decision, even if he offers no counterproof. The reason is that directed verdicts against the accused are not allowed, and a presumption instruction binding

[9] The presumptions that concern us have nothing to do with the "presumption of innocence," which is a hallmark of Anglo-American criminal jurisprudence, giving positive expression to the truth that the prosecutor bears the burden of persuasion on each element of the offense. See Taylor v. Kentucky, 436 U.S. 478 (1978) (failure to instruct on presumption of innocence violates due process). Instead, we focus on presumptions that operate in favor of the prosecutor, and there are more of these than you might think. See United States v. Gainey, 380 U.S. 63 (1965) (approving a statutory presumption, arising from proof that defendant was present at a still, that he was "carrying on" the business of a distillery); Leary v. United States, 395 U.S. 6 (1969) (former Harvard professor was tried for importing marijuana, after being stopped entering country from Mexico; Court upholds statutory presumption, arising on proof of possession of marijuana, that it was imported, but strikes down presumption that he *knew* the marijuana was imported).

the jury amounts to a partial directed verdict. A binding directive is improper even where the evidence is so cogent and compelling that any reasonable person would conclude beyond reasonable doubt that defendant is guilty.

The Supreme Court has addressed criminal presumptions in three different ways:

(1) Instructions. Sometimes the Court asks whether instructions misled the jury on its prerogative to determine the facts, or on allocation of the burden of persuasion. The Court has found that instructions are ambiguous where they suggest, on the one hand, that defendant may be convicted only on proof beyond a reasonable doubt, but on the other hand that he may be convicted on the strength of a presumption. The Court has reversed convictions following such "double track" instructions where the jury may have relied on a presumption that could not satisfy the beyond-reasonable-doubt standard. See United States v. Romano, 382 U.S. 136 (1965) (in trial for being in possession, custody, or control of illegal still, jury was told that presence at still was "sufficient" to authorize conviction) (reversing even though there was enough other evidence to convict; jury "may have disbelieved or disregarded" the evidence and convicted for "presence alone").

(2) Relationship between basic and presumed fact. Often the Court appraises the logical relationship between the predicate fact of a presumption and the conclusion. Does the one support an inference of the other beyond reasonable doubt? By this approach, some presumptions fail because they cannot satisfy even the preponderance standard. See Leary v. United States, 395 U.S. 6 (1969) (striking down presumption, arising on proof of possession of marijuana, that defendant knew it was imported; much is grown domestically, so possession does not make it more probable than not that defendant knew it was imported). Others survive because they satisfy the beyond-reasonable-doubt standard. See Turner v. United States, 396 U.S. 398 (1970) (upholding presumption, arising on proof of possession of heroin, that defendant knew it was imported: "To possess heroin *is* to possess imported heroin," for "little if any" is made domestically, and defendant "doubtless knew" it came from abroad; presumption satisfies reasonable doubt standard). The decision in *Allen*, infra, addresses the intermediate situation, where the presumption satisfies the lower but fails the higher standard.

(3) Effect on other safeguards. Occasionally the Court considers arguments that criminal presumptions violate other constitutional safeguards, including the rights (a) to a *trial* of guilt or innocence, (b) to be *tried by a jury*, both of which are arguably infringed by a *statute* prescribing that one fact supports a finding of another, see Leary v. United States, 395 U.S. 6 (1969) (Black, concurring), (c) against self-incrimination, since a presumption instruction arguably amounts to a comment about defendant's failure to refute an inference by testifying, see United States v. Gainey, 380 U.S. 63 (1965) (Black, dissenting), and (d) to be presumed innocent, which seems to be undermined by "presumed" facts. See Ashford & Risinger, Presumptions, Assumptions, and Due Process in Criminal Cases: A Theoretical Overview, 79 Yale L.J. 165, 176 (1969). So far these arguments have not commanded a majority on the Court.

Now look at *Sandstrom* and *Allen*, which reflect the Court's current thinking.

SANDSTROM v. MONTANA

United States Supreme Court
442 U.S. 510 (1979)

Mr. Justice BRENNAN delivered the opinion of the Court.

The question presented is whether, in a case in which intent is an element of the crime charged, the jury instruction, "the law presumes that a person intends the ordinary consequences of his voluntary acts," violates the Fourteenth Amendment's requirement that the State prove every element of a criminal offense beyond a reasonable doubt.

I

On November 22, 1976, 18-year-old David Sandstrom confessed to the slaying of Annie Jessen. Based upon the confession and corroborating evidence, petitioner was charged on December 2 with "deliberate homicide," in that he "purposely or knowingly caused the death of Annie Jessen." At trial, Sandstrom's attorney informed the jury that, although his client admitted killing Jessen, he did not do so "purposely or knowingly," and was therefore not guilty of "deliberate homicide" but of a lesser crime. The basic support for this contention was the testimony of two court-appointed mental health experts, each of whom described for the jury petitioner's mental state at the time of the incident. Sandstrom's attorney argued that this testimony demonstrated that petitioner, due to a personality disorder aggravated by alcohol consumption, did not kill Annie Jessen "purposely or knowingly."

The prosecution requested the trial judge to instruct the jury that "[t]he law presumes that a person intends the ordinary consequences of his voluntary acts." Petitioner's counsel objected, arguing that "the instruction has the effect of shifting the burden of proof on the issue of" purpose or knowledge to the defense, and that "that is impermissible under the Federal Constitution, due process of law." He offered to provide a number of federal decisions in support of the objection, including this Court's holding in Mullaney v. Wilbur, 421 U.S. 684 (1975), but was told by the judge: "You can give those to the Supreme Court. The objection is overruled." The instruction was delivered, the jury found petitioner guilty of deliberate homicide, and petitioner was sentenced to 100 years in prison.

Sandstrom appealed to the Supreme Court of Montana, again contending that the instruction shifted to the defendant the burden of disproving an element of the crime charged, in violation of *Mullaney v. Wilbur*, supra, In re Winship, 397 U.S. 358 (1970), and Patterson v. New York, 432 U.S. 197 (1977). The Montana court conceded that these cases did prohibit shifting the burden of proof to the defendant by means of a presumption, but held that the cases "do not prohibit allocation of *some* burden of proof to a defendant under certain circumstances." Since in the court's view, "[d]efendant's sole burden under instruction No. 5 was to produce *some* evidence that he did not intend the ordinary consequences of his voluntary acts, not to disprove that he acted 'purposely' or 'knowingly,' . . . the instruction does not violate due process standards as defined by the United States or Montana Constitution . . ." (emphasis added).

Both federal and state courts have held, under a variety of rationales, that the giving of an instruction similar to that challenged here is fatal to the validity of a criminal conviction. We granted certiorari to decide the important question of the instruction's constitutionality. We reverse.

II

The threshold inquiry in ascertaining the constitutional analysis applicable to this kind of jury instruction is to determine the nature of the presumption it describes. That determination requires careful attention to the words actually spoken to the jury, for whether a defendant has been accorded his constitutional rights depends upon the way in which a reasonable juror could have interpreted the instruction.

Respondent argues, first, that the instruction merely described a permissive inference—that is, it allowed but did not require the jury to draw conclusions about defendant's intent from his actions—and that such inferences are constitutional. These arguments need not detain us long, for even respondent admits that "it's possible" that the jury believed they were required to apply the presumption. Sandstrom's jurors were told that "[t]he law presumes that a person intends the ordinary consequences of his voluntary acts." They were not told that they had a choice, or that they might infer that conclusion; they were told only that the law presumed it. It is clear that a reasonable juror could easily have viewed such an instruction as mandatory.

In the alternative, respondent urges that, even if viewed as a mandatory presumption rather than as a permissive inference, the presumption did not conclusively establish intent but rather could be rebutted. On this view, the instruction required the jury, if satisfied as to the facts which trigger the presumption, to find intent *unless* the defendant offered evidence to the contrary. Moreover, according to the State, all the defendant had to do to rebut the presumption was produce "some" contrary evidence; he did not have to "prove" that he lacked the required mental state. Thus, "[a]t most, it placed a *burden of production* on the petitioner," but "did not shift to petitioner the *burden of persuasion* with respect to any element of the offense . . ." (emphasis added). Again, respondent contends that presumptions with this limited effect pass constitutional muster.

We need not review respondent's constitutional argument on this point either, however, for we reject this characterization of the presumption as well. Respondent concedes there is a "risk" that the jury, once having found petitioner's act voluntary, would interpret the instruction as automatically directing a finding of intent. Moreover, the State also concedes that numerous courts "have differed as to the effect of the presumption when given as a jury instruction without further explanation as to its use by the jury," and that some have found it to shift more than the burden of production, and even to have conclusive effect. Nonetheless, the State contends that the only authoritative reading of the effect of the presumption resides in the Supreme Court of Montana. And the State argues that by holding that "[d]efendant's sole burden under instruction No. 5 was to produce *some* evidence that he did not intend the ordinary consequences of his voluntary acts, not to disprove that he acted 'purposely' or 'knowingly,'" the Montana Supreme Court decisively established that the presumption at most affected only the burden of going forward with evidence of intent—that is, the burden of production.[5]

The Supreme Court of Montana is, of course, the final authority on the legal weight to be given a presumption under Montana law, but it is not the final authority on the interpretation which a jury could have given the instruction. If Montana intended its presumption to have only the effect described by its Supreme Court, then we are convinced that a reasonable juror could well have been misled by the instruction given, and could have believed that the presumption was not limited to requiring the defendant to satisfy only a burden of production. Petitioner's jury was told that "*[t]he law presumes* that a person intends the ordinary consequences of his voluntary acts." They were not told that the presumption could be rebutted, as the Montana Supreme Court held, by the defendant's simple presentation of "some" evidence; nor even that it could be rebutted at all. Given the common definition of "presume" as "to suppose to be true without proof," Webster's New Collegiate Dictionary 911 (1974), and given the lack of qualifying instructions as to the legal effect of the presumption, we cannot discount the possibility that the jury may have interpreted the instruction in either of two more stringent ways.

First, a reasonable jury could well have interpreted the presumption as "conclusive," that is, not technically as a presumption at all, but rather as an irrebuttable direction by the court to find intent once convinced of the facts triggering the presumption. Alternatively, the jury may have interpreted the instruction as a direction to find intent upon proof of the defendant's voluntary actions (and their "ordinary" consequences), unless *the defendant* proved the contrary by some quantum of proof which may well have been considerably greater than "some" evidence—thus effectively shifting the burden of persuasion on the element of intent. Numerous federal and state courts have warned that instructions of the type given here can be interpreted in just these ways. And although the Montana Supreme Court held to the contrary in this case, Montana's own Rules of Evidence expressly state that the presumption at issue

---

[5] For purposes of argument, we accept respondent's definition of the production burden when applied to a defendant in a criminal case. We note, however, that the burden is often described quite differently when it rests upon the prosecution. We also note that the effect of a failure to meet the production burden is significantly different for the defendant and prosecution. When the prosecution fails to meet it, a directed verdict in favor of the defense results. Such a consequence is not possible upon a defendant's failure, however, as verdicts may not be directed against defendants in criminal cases.

here may be overcome only "by a preponderance of evidence contrary to the presumption." Montana Rule of Evidence 301(b)(2). Such a requirement shifts not only the burden of production, but also the ultimate burden of persuasion on the issue of intent.[7]

We do not reject the possibility that some jurors may have interpreted the challenged instruction as permissive, or, if mandatory, as requiring only that the defendant come forward with "some" evidence in rebuttal. However, the fact that a reasonable juror could have given the presumption conclusive or persuasion-shifting effect means that we cannot discount the possibility that Sandstrom's jurors actually did proceed upon one or the other of these latter interpretations. And that means that unless these kinds of presumptions are constitutional, the instruction cannot be adjudged valid. It is the line of cases urged by petitioner, and exemplified by *Winship*, that provides the appropriate mode of constitutional analysis for these kinds of presumptions.

III

In *Winship*, this Court stated:

> Lest there remain any doubt about the constitutional stature of the reasonable-doubt standard, we explicitly hold that the Due Process Clause protects the accused against conviction except upon proof beyond a reasonable doubt *of every fact* necessary to constitute the crime with which he is charged.

Id., at 364 (emphasis added). Accord, *Patterson*. The petitioner here was charged with and convicted of deliberate homicide, committed purposely or knowingly. It is clear that under Montana law, whether the crime was committed purposely or knowingly is a fact necessary to constitute the crime of deliberate homicide. Indeed, it was the lone element of the offense at issue in Sandstrom's trial, as he confessed to causing the death of the victim, told the jury that knowledge and purpose were the only questions he was controverting, and introduced evidence solely on those points. Moreover, it is conceded that proof of defendant's "intent" would be sufficient to establish this element. Thus, the question before this Court is whether the challenged jury instruction had the effect of relieving the State of the burden of proof enunciated in *Winship* on the critical question

---

[7] The potential for these interpretations of the presumption was not removed by the other instructions given at the trial. It is true that the jury was instructed generally that the accused was presumed innocent until proved guilty, and that the State had the burden of proving beyond a reasonable doubt that the defendant caused the death of the deceased purposely or knowingly. But this is not rhetorically inconsistent with a conclusive or burden-shifting presumption. The jury could have interpreted the two sets of instructions as indicating that the presumption was a means by which proof beyond a reasonable doubt as to intent could be satisfied. For example, if the presumption were viewed as conclusive, the jury could have believed that, although intent must be proved beyond a reasonable doubt, proof of the voluntary slaying and its ordinary consequences constituted proof of intent beyond a reasonable doubt. Cf. *Mullaney* ("These procedural devices require (in the case of a presumption) . . . the trier of fact to conclude that the prosecution has met its burden of proof with respect to the presumed . . . fact by having satisfactorily established other facts").

of petitioner's state of mind. We conclude that under either of the two possible interpretations of the instruction set out above, precisely that effect would result, and that the instruction therefore represents constitutional error.

We consider first the validity of a conclusive presumption. This Court has considered such a presumption on at least two prior occasions. In Morissette v. United States, 342 U.S. 246 (1952), the defendant was charged with willful and knowing theft of Government property. Although his attorney argued that for his client to be found guilty, "the taking must have been with felonious intent," the trial judge ruled that "[t]hat is presumed by his own act." After first concluding that intent was in fact an element of the crime charged, and after declaring that "[w]here intent of the accused is an ingredient of the crime charged, its existence is . . . a jury issue," *Morissette* held:

> It follows that the trial court may not withdraw or prejudge the issue by instruction that the law raises a presumption of intent from an act. It often is tempting to cast in terms of a "presumption" a conclusion which a court thinks probable from given facts . . . . [B]ut [w]e think presumptive intent has no place in this case. A conclusive presumption which testimony could not overthrow would effectively eliminate intent as an ingredient of the offense. A presumption which would permit but not require the jury to assume intent from an isolated fact would prejudge a conclusion which the jury should reach of its own volition. A presumption which would permit the jury to make an assumption which all the evidence considered together does not logically establish would give to a proven fact an artificial and fictional effect. In either case, this presumption would conflict with the overriding presumption of innocence with which the law endows the accused and which extends to every element of the crime. (Emphasis added.)

Just last Term, . . . we reaffirmed the holding of *Morissette* . . . .

As in *Morissette* . . . , a conclusive presumption in this case would "conflict with the overriding presumption of innocence with which the law endows the accused and which extends to every element of the crime," and would "invade [the] factfinding function" which in a criminal case the law assigns solely to the jury. The instruction announced to David Sandstrom's jury may well have had exactly these consequences. Upon finding proof of one element of the crime (causing death), and of facts insufficient to establish the second (the voluntariness and "ordinary consequences" of defendant's action), Sandstrom's jurors could reasonably have concluded that they were directed to find against defendant on the element of intent. The State was thus not forced to prove "beyond a reasonable doubt . . . every fact necessary to constitute the crime . . . charged," and defendant was deprived of his constitutional rights as explicated in *Winship.* A presumption which, although not conclusive, had the effect of shifting the burden of persuasion to the defendant, would have suffered from similar infirmities. If Sandstrom's jury interpreted the presumption in that manner, it could have concluded that upon proof by the State of the slaying, and of additional facts not themselves establishing the element of intent, the burden was shifted to the defendant to prove that he lacked the requisite mental state. Such a presumption was found constitutionally deficient in *Mullaney.* In *Mullaney,* the charge was murder, which under Maine law required proof not only of intent but of malice. The trial court charged the jury that "malice aforethought is an essential and indispensable element of the crime of murder." However, it also instructed that if the prosecution established that the homicide was both intentional and unlawful, malice aforethought was to be implied unless the defendant proved by a fair preponderance of the evidence that he acted in the heat of passion on sudden provocation. As we recounted just two Terms ago in *Patterson,* "[t]his Court . . . unanimously agreed with the Court of Appeals that Wilbur's due process rights had been invaded by the presumption casting upon him the burden of proving by a preponderance of the evidence that he had acted in the heat of passion upon sudden provocation." And *Patterson* reaffirmed that "a State must prove every ingredient of an offense beyond a reasonable doubt, and . . . may not shift the burden of proof to the defendant" by means of such a presumption.

Because David Sandstrom's jury may have interpreted the judge's instruction as constituting either a burden-shifting presumption like that in *Mullaney,* or a conclusive presumption like those in *Morissette* . . . and because either interpretation would have deprived defendant of his right to the due process of law, we hold the instruction given in this case unconstitutional . . . .

Accordingly, the judgment of the Supreme Court of Montana is reversed, and the case is remanded for further proceedings not inconsistent with this opinion. It is so ordered.

[A concurring opinion by Justice Rehnquist, joined by Chief Justice Burger, is omitted.]

■ NOTES ON THE SIGNIFICANCE OF *SANDSTROM*

1. The *Sandstrom* majority considers four possible instructions, or four *interpretations* of the instruction actually given. Going from strongest to mildest, the four possibilities are these: First, the instruction could say the jury *must* find that defendant acted purposefully if he acted voluntarily. Second, it could say the jury should find that he acted purposefully if he acted voluntarily unless he proves otherwise. Third, it could say the jury can find that he acted purposefully unless he offers evidence to the contrary. Fourth, it could say that the jury can decide whether he acted purposefully and can decide whether proof that his act was voluntary also shows that it was purposeful.

2. *Sandstrom* disapproves the first of these instructions or interpretations, doesn't it? The reason is that such instruction amounts to a partial directed verdict, telling the jury that it must interpret certain proof in a certain way. And *if* the instruction given in the case *could be interpreted* this way, it presents the "double track" problem identified in the *Romano* case (described in the text above) and is improper for this reason.

3. *Sandstrom* seems to approve the fourth kind of instruction (or interpretation), doesn't it? Let us look at this instruction more closely. The judge says:

> You may find that defendant acted purposefully or knowingly only if you conclude that the evidence proves that point beyond a reasonable doubt. Depending on the circumstances, it is sometimes possible to reach that conclusion on the basis of proof that a person acted voluntarily.

Does this instruction seem proper? Does it avoid the "double track" problem?

4. *Sandstrom* leaves open the second and third instructions (or interpretations), which it describes as types of "mandatory presumption." The second instruction (or interpretation) would put the burden of persuasion on defendant, and the third would put a milder burden of production on him. Montana urged this third interpretation in *Sandstrom.* Consider an *even milder* form of instruction, in which the trial judge says:

> If you find that defendant acted voluntarily, you should find that he acted purposefully or knowingly unless there is other evidence in the case that indicates that he did not.

Would this instruction be proper under *Sandstrom*? Note the Court's suggestion that "some jurors may have interpreted the challenged instruction . . . as requiring only that the defendant come forward with 'some' evidence."

5. Would the problems in *Sandstrom* be cured if the trial judge had emphasized that the prosecutor bears the burden of persuasion beyond a reasonable doubt on intent? See Francis v. Franklin, 471 U.S. 307 (1985) (No). But see United States v. Nelson, 277 F.3d 164, 197 (2d Cir. 2002) (instruction that jury "may infer and find that defendants intended all consequences that a person, standing in circumstances and posing like knowledge, should have expected to result from acts he knowingly committed" does not violate *Sandstrom*; it merely let jury infer that accused intends consequences of actions), *cert. denied*, 537 U.S. 835 (2002).

5. David Sandstrom was charged with "deliberate homicide," punishable by death or imprisonment for life or a term of two to 100 years. Montana law defined the crime as "purposely or knowingly" causing another's death. The state also recognized a crime of "mitigated deliberate homicide," defined as deliberate homicide "committed under the influence of extreme mental or emotional stress for which there is reasonable explanation or excuse," punishable by imprisonment for not less than two nor more than 40 years. See Mont. Code §§94-5-102 and 94-5-103 (1973). Assume that Sandstrom claimed he was under "extreme mental or emotional stress," but the state offered sufficient evidence that he acted "purposely or knowingly." Suppose that Montana (like New York in *Patterson*) took the view that one can "purposely or knowingly" kill while being under "extreme mental or emotional stress," but had a presumption that one acting on such purpose or knowledge is *not* under extreme mental or emotional stress. The trial judge tells the jury:

> The law presumes that a person acting purposefully or knowingly is not under the influence of extreme mental or emotional stress. If you find beyond a reasonable doubt that defendant acted purposefully or knowingly, you should conclude, if you believe it to be the case, that he was not acting under the influence of extreme mental or emotional stress, unless other evidence persuades you to the contrary.

Under *Patterson,* couldn't Montana allocate to defendant the burden of proving extreme mental or emotional stress? Under *Sandstrom,* could Montana do the same thing through a presumption? See Harris, Constitutional Limits on Criminal Presumptions as an Expression of Changing Concepts of Fundamental Fairness, 77 J. Crim. L. & Criminology 308, 335 (1986) (*Sandstrom* "tends to encourage the legislature to express in more straightforward ways what the state must prove to justify punishing a person").

COUNTY OF ULSTER v. ALLEN

United States Supreme Court
442 U.S. 140 (1979)

Mr. Justice STEVENS delivered the opinion of the Court.

A New York statute provides that, with certain exceptions, the presence of a firearm in an automobile is presumptive evidence of its illegal possession by all persons then occupying the vehicle.[1] The United States Court of Appeals for

---

[1] New York Penal Law §265.15(3) (McKinney 1967):

> The presence in an automobile, other than a stolen one or a public omnibus, of any firearm, defaced firearm, firearm silencer, bomb, bombshell, gravity knife, switchblade knife, dagger, dirk, stiletto, billy, blackjack, metal knuckles, sandbag, sandclub or slingshot is presumptive evidence of its possession by all persons occupying such automobile at the time such weapon, instrument or appliance is found, except under the following circumstances:
>
> > (a) if such weapon, instrument or appliance is found upon the person of one of the occupants therein; (b) if such weapon, instrument or appliance is found in an automobile which is being operated for hire by a duly licensed driver in the due, lawful and proper pursuit of his trade, then such presumption shall not apply to the driver; or (c) if the weapon so found is a pistol or revolver and one of the occupants, not present under duress, has in his possession a valid license to have and carry concealed the same.

In addition to the three exceptions delineated in §§265.15(3)(a)-(c) above as well as the stolen-vehicle and public-omnibus exception in §265.15(3) itself, §265.20 contains various exceptions that apply when weapons are present in an automobile pursuant to certain military, law enforcement, recreational, and commercial endeavors.

the Second Circuit held that respondents may challenge the constitutionality of this statute in a federal habeas corpus proceeding and that the statute is "unconstitutional on its face." We granted certiorari to review these holdings and also to consider whether the statute is constitutional in its application to respondents.

Four persons, three adult males (respondents) and a 16-year-old girl (Jane Doe, who is not a respondent here), were jointly tried on charges that they possessed two loaded handguns, a loaded machinegun, and over a pound of heroin found in a Chevrolet in which they were riding when it was stopped for speeding on the New York Thruway shortly after noon on March 28, 1973. The two large-caliber handguns, which together with their ammunition weighed approximately six pounds, were seen through the window of the car by the investigating police officer. They were positioned crosswise in an open handbag on either the front floor or the front seat of the car on the passenger side where Jane Doe was sitting. Jane Doe admitted that the handbag was hers.[2] The machinegun and the heroin were discovered in the trunk after the police pried it open. The car had been borrowed from the driver's brother earlier that day; the key to the trunk could not be found in the car or on the person of any of its occupants, although there was testimony that two of the occupants had placed something in the trunk before embarking in the borrowed car.[3] The jury convicted all four of possession of the handguns and acquitted them of possession of the contents of the trunk.

Counsel for all four defendants objected to the introduction into evidence of the two handguns, the machinegun, and the drugs, arguing that the State had not adequately demonstrated a connection between their clients and the contraband. The trial court overruled the objection, relying on the presumption of possession created by the New York statute. Because that presumption does not apply if a weapon is found "upon the person" of one of the occupants of the car, the three male defendants also moved to dismiss the charges relating

[2] The arrest was made by two state troopers. One officer approached the driver, advised him that he was going to issue a ticket for speeding, requested identification, and returned to the patrol car. After a radio check indicated that the driver was wanted in Michigan on a weapons charge, the second officer returned to the vehicle and placed the driver under arrest. Thereafter, he went around to the right side of the car and, in "open view," saw a portion of a .45-caliber automatic pistol protruding from the open purse on the floor or the seat. He opened the car door, removed that gun, and saw a .38-caliber revolver in the same handbag. He testified that the crosswise position of one or both of the guns kept the handbag from closing. After the weapons were secured, the two remaining male passengers, who had been sitting in the rear seat, and Jane Doe were arrested and frisked. A subsequent search at the police station disclosed a pocketknife and marihuana concealed on Jane Doe's person.

[3] Early that morning, the four defendants had arrived at the Rochester, N.Y., home of the driver's sister in a Cadillac. Using her telephone, the driver called their brother, advised him that "his car ran hot" on the way there from Detroit and asked to borrow the Chevrolet so that the four could continue on to New York City. The brother brought the Chevrolet to the sister's home. He testified that he had recently cleaned out the trunk and had seen no weapons or drugs. The sister also testified, stating that she saw two of the defendants transfer some unidentified item or items from the trunk of one vehicle to the trunk of the other while both cars were parked in her driveway.

to the handguns on the ground that the guns were found on the person of Jane Doe. Respondents made this motion both at the close of the prosecution's case and at the close of all evidence. The trial judge twice denied it, concluding that the applicability of the "upon the person" exception was a question of fact for the jury.

At the close of the trial, the judge instructed the jurors that they were entitled to infer possession from the defendants' presence in the car. He did not make any reference to the "upon the person" exception in his explanation of the statutory presumption, nor did any of the defendants object to this omission or request alternative or additional instructions on the subject.

[Defendants sought relief by post-trial motion and appeal in the state courts in New York, arguing that apart from the presumption there was not enough evidence to convict. They lost. Then they sought and obtained a writ of habeas corpus in the United States District Court, which concluded that the presence of two guns in a woman's handbag in a car could not reasonably support an inference that the guns were in the possession of three other persons in the car. The Second Circuit Court of Appeals affirmed, but on a different ground, finding that the statute creating the presumption was unconstitutional on its face because it "sweeps within its compass (1) many occupants who may not know they are riding with a gun (which may be out of their sight), and (2) many who may be aware of the presence of the gun but not permitted access to it." The Supreme Court granted certiorari. Before reaching the presumption itself, the Court concluded that the District Court had jurisdiction to entertain the constitutional challenge, since the New York state courts had themselves reached the constitutional question, and had not ruled against defendants on the basis of any "independent and adequate state procedural ground" that would foreclose adjudication of the constitutional challenge.]

In this case, the Court of Appeals undertook the task of deciding the constitutionality of the New York statute "on its face." Its conclusion that the statutory presumption was arbitrary rested entirely on its view of the fairness of applying the presumption in hypothetical situations—situations, indeed, in which it is improbable that a jury would return a conviction,[14] or that a prosecution would ever be instituted. We must accordingly inquire whether these respondents had standing to advance the arguments that the Court of Appeals considered decisive. An analysis of our prior cases indicates that the answer to this inquiry depends on the type of presumption that is involved in the case.

Inferences and presumptions are a staple of our adversary system of factfinding. It is often necessary for the trier of fact to determine the existence of an element of the crime—that is, an "ultimate" or "elemental" fact—from the

---

[14] Indeed, in this very case the permissive presumptions in §265.15(3) and its companion drug statute, N.Y. Penal Law §220.25(1), were insufficient to persuade the jury to convict the defendants of possession of the loaded machinegun and heroin in the trunk of the car notwithstanding the supporting testimony that at least two of them had been seen transferring something into the trunk that morning. . . .

existence of one or more "evidentiary" or "basic" facts. The value of these evidentiary devices, and their validity under the Due Process Clause, vary from case to case, however, depending on the strength of the connection between the particular basic and elemental facts involved and on the degree to which the device curtails the factfinder's freedom to assess the evidence independently. Nonetheless, in criminal cases, the ultimate test of any device's constitutional validity in a given case remains constant: the device must not undermine the factfinder's responsibility at trial, based on evidence adduced by the State, to find the ultimate facts beyond a reasonable doubt.

The most common evidentiary device is the entirely permissive inference or presumption, which allows—but does not require—the trier of fact to infer the elemental fact from proof by the prosecutor of the basic one and which places no burden of any kind on the defendant. In that situation the basic fact may constitute prima facie evidence of the elemental fact. When reviewing this type of device, the Court has required the party challenging it to demonstrate its invalidity as applied to him. Because this permissive presumption leaves the trier of fact free to credit or reject the inference and does not shift the burden of proof, it affects the application of the "beyond a reasonable doubt" standard only if, under the facts of the case, there is no rational way the trier could make the connection permitted by the inference. For only in that situation is there any risk that an explanation of the permissible inference to a jury, or its use by a jury, has caused the presumptively rational factfinder to make an erroneous factual determination.

A mandatory presumption is a far more troublesome evidentiary device. For it may affect not only the strength of the "no reasonable doubt" burden but also the placement of that burden; it tells the trier that he or they *must* find the elemental fact upon proof of the basic fact, at least unless the defendant has come forward with some evidence to rebut the presumed connection between the two facts.[16] In this situation, the Court has generally examined the presumption on its face to determine the extent to which the basic and

---

[16] This class of more or less mandatory presumptions can be subdivided into two parts: presumptions that merely shift the burden of production to the defendant, following the satisfaction of which the ultimate burden of persuasion returns to the prosecution; and presumptions that entirely shift the burden of proof to the defendant. The mandatory presumptions examined by our cases have almost uniformly fit into the former subclass, in that they never totally removed the ultimate burden of proof beyond a reasonable doubt from the prosecution.

To the extent that a presumption imposes an extremely low burden of production—e.g., being satisfied by "any" evidence—it may well be that its impact is no greater than that of a permissive inference, and it may be proper to analyze it as such. See generally Mullaney v. Wilbur, 421 U.S. 684, 703 n.31 (1975).

In deciding what type of inference or presumption is involved in a case, the jury instructions will generally be controlling, although their interpretation may require recourse to the statute involved and the cases decided under it. Turner v. United States [319 U.S. 463 (1970)] provides a useful illustration of the different types of presumptions. It analyzes the constitutionality of two different presumption statutes (one mandatory and one permissive) as they apply to the basic fact of possession of both heroin and cocaine, and the presumed facts of importation and distribution of narcotic drugs. The jury was charged essentially in the terms of the two statutes.

The importance of focusing attention on the precise presentation of the presumption to the jury and the scope of that presumption is illustrated by a comparison of United States v. Gainey, 380 U.S. 63 (1965),

elemental facts coincide. To the extent that the trier of fact is forced to abide by the presumption, and may not reject it based on an independent evaluation of the particular facts presented by the State, the analysis of the presumption's constitutional validity is logically divorced from those facts and based on the presumption's accuracy in the run of cases.[17] It is for this reason that the Court has held it irrelevant in analyzing a mandatory presumption, but not in analyzing a purely permissive one, that there is ample evidence in the record other than the presumption to support a conviction.

---

with United States v. Romano [382 U.S. 136 (1965)]. Both cases involved statutory presumptions based on proof that the defendant was present at the site of an illegal still. In *Gainey* the Court sustained a conviction "for carrying on" the business of the distillery in violation of 26 U.S.C. §5601(a)(4), whereas in *Romano*, the Court set aside a conviction for being in "possession, or custody, or . . . control" of such a distillery in violation of §5601(a)(1). The difference in outcome was attributable to two important differences between the cases. Because the statute involved in *Gainey* was a sweeping prohibition of almost any activity associated with the still, whereas the *Romano* statute involved only one narrow aspect of the total undertaking, there was a much higher probability that mere presence could support an inference of guilt in the former case than in the latter.

Of perhaps greater importance, however, was the difference between the trial judge's instructions to the jury in the two cases. In *Gainey*, the judge had explained that the presumption was permissive; it did not require the jury to convict the defendant even if it was convinced that he was present at the site. On the contrary, the instructions made it clear that presence was only "a circumstance to be considered along with all the other circumstances in the case." As we emphasized, the "jury was thus specifically told that the statutory inference was not conclusive." In *Romano*, the trial judge told the jury that the defendant's presence at the still "shall be deemed sufficient evidence to authorize conviction." Although there was other evidence of guilt, that instruction authorized conviction even if the jury disbelieved all of the testimony except the proof of presence at the site. This Court's holding that the statutory presumption could not support the *Romano* conviction was thus dependent, in part, on the specific instructions given by the trial judge. Under those instructions it was necessary to decide whether, regardless of the specific circumstances of the particular case, the statutory presumption adequately supported the guilty verdict.

[17] In addition to the discussion of *Romano* in n.16, supra, this point is illustrated by Leary v. United States [395 U.S. 6 (1969)]. In that case, Dr. Timothy Leary, a professor at Harvard University, was stopped by customs inspectors in Laredo, Tex., as he was returning from the Mexican side of the international border. Marihuana seeds and a silver snuffbox filled with semirefined marihuana and three partially smoked marihuana cigarettes were discovered in his car. He was convicted of having knowingly transported marihuana which he knew had been illegally imported into this country in violation of 21 U.S.C. §176a. That statute included a mandatory presumption: "possession shall be deemed sufficient evidence to authorize conviction [for importation] unless the defendant explains his possession to the satisfaction of the jury." Leary admitted possession of the marihuana and claimed that he had carried it from New York to Mexico and then back.

Mr. Justice Harlan for the Court noted that under one theory of the case, the jury could have found direct proof of all of the necessary elements of the offense without recourse to the presumption. But he deemed that insufficient reason to affirm the conviction because under another theory the jury might have found knowledge of importation on the basis of either direct evidence or the presumption, and there was accordingly no certainty that the jury had not relied on the presumption. The Court therefore found it necessary to test the presumption against the Due Process Clause. Its analysis was facial. Despite the fact that the defendant was well educated and had recently traveled to a country that is a major exporter of marihuana to this country, the Court found the presumption of knowledge of importation from possession irrational. It did so, not because Dr. Leary was unlikely to know the source of the marihuana, but instead because "a majority of possessors" were unlikely to have such knowledge. Because the jury had been instructed to rely on the presumption even if it did not believe the Government's direct evidence of knowledge of importation (unless, of course, the defendant met his burden of "satisfying" the jury to the contrary), the Court reversed the conviction.

Without determining whether the presumption in this case was mandatory,[18] the Court of Appeals analyzed it on its face as if it were. In fact, it was not, as the New York Court of Appeals had earlier pointed out.

The trial judge's instructions make it clear that the presumption was merely a part of the prosecution's case,[19] that it gave rise to a permissive inference available only in certain circumstances, rather than a mandatory conclusion of possession, and that it could be ignored by the jury even if there was no affirmative proof offered by defendants in rebuttal. The judge explained that possession could be actual or constructive, but that constructive possession could not exist without the intent and ability to exercise control or dominion over the weapons. He also carefully instructed the jury that there is a mandatory presumption of innocence in favor of the defendants that controls unless it, as the exclusive trier of fact, is satisfied beyond a reasonable doubt that the defendants possessed the handguns in the manner described by the judge. In short, the instructions plainly directed the jury to consider all the circumstances tending to support or contradict the inference that all four occupants of the car had possession of the two loaded handguns and to decide the matter for itself without regard to how much evidence the defendants introduced.

Our cases considering the validity of permissive statutory presumptions such as the one involved here have rested on an evaluation of the presumption as applied to the record before the Court. None suggests that a court should pass on the constitutionality of this kind of statute "on its face." It was error for the Court of Appeals to make such a determination in this case.

As applied to the facts of this case, the presumption of possession is entirely rational. Notwithstanding the Court of Appeals' analysis, respondents were not "hitchhikers or other casual passengers," and the guns were neither "a few inches in length" nor "out of [respondents'] sight." The argument against possession by any of the respondents was predicated solely on the fact that the guns were in Jane Doe's pocketbook. But several circumstances—which, not surprisingly, her counsel repeatedly emphasized in his questions and his argument—made it highly improbable that she was the sole custodian of those weapons.

Even if it was reasonable to conclude that she had placed the guns in her purse before the car was stopped by police, the facts strongly suggest that Jane

---

[18] Indeed, the court never even discussed the jury instructions.

[19] "It is your duty to consider all the testimony in this case, to weigh it carefully and to test the credit to be given to a witness by his apparent intention to speak the truth and by the accuracy of his memory to reconcile, if possible, conflicting statements as to material facts and in such ways to try and get at the truth and to reach a verdict upon the evidence."

"To establish the unlawful possession of the weapons, again the People relied upon the presumption and, in addition thereto, the testimony of Anderson and Lemmons who testified in their case in chief."

"Accordingly, you would be warranted in returning a verdict of guilt against the defendants or defendant if you find the defendants or defendant was in possession of a machine gun and the other weapons and that the fact of possession was proven to you by the People beyond a reasonable doubt, and an element of such proof is the reasonable presumption of illegal possession of a machine gun or the presumption of illegal possession of firearms, as I have just before explained to you."

Doe was not the only person able to exercise dominion over them. The two guns were too large to be concealed in her handbag. The bag was consequently open, and part of one of the guns was in plain view, within easy access of the driver of the car and even, perhaps, of the other two respondents who were riding in the rear seat.

Moreover, it is highly improbable that the loaded guns belonged to Jane Doe or that she was solely responsible for their being in her purse. As a 16-year-old girl in the company of three adult men she was the least likely of the four to be carrying one, let alone two, heavy handguns. It is far more probable that she relied on the pocketknife found in her brassiere for any necessary self-protection. Under these circumstances, it was not unreasonable for her counsel to argue and for the jury to infer that when the car was halted for speeding, the other passengers in the car anticipated the risk of a search and attempted to conceal their weapons in a pocketbook in the front seat. The inference is surely more likely than the notion that these weapons were the sole property of the 16-year-old girl.

Under these circumstances, the jury would have been entirely reasonable in rejecting the suggestion—which, incidentally, defense counsel did not even advance in their closing arguments to the jury—that the handguns were in the sole possession of Jane Doe. Assuming that the jury did reject it, the case is tantamount to one in which the guns were lying on the floor or the seat of the car in the plain view of the three other occupants of the automobile. In such a case, it is surely rational to infer that each of the respondents was fully aware of the presence of the guns and had both the ability and the intent to exercise dominion and control over the weapons. The application of the statutory presumption in this case therefore comports with the standard laid down in *Tot* and restated in *Leary*. For there is a "rational connection" between the basic facts that the prosecution proved and the ultimate fact presumed, and the latter is "more likely than not to flow from" the former.

Respondents argue, however, that the validity of the New York presumption must be judged by a "reasonable doubt" test rather than the "more likely than not" standard employed in *Leary*. Under the more stringent test, it is argued that a statutory presumption must be rejected unless the evidence necessary to invoke the inference is sufficient for a rational jury to find the inferred fact beyond a reasonable doubt. Respondents' argument again overlooks the distinction between a permissive presumption on which the prosecution is entitled to rely as one not necessarily sufficient part of its proof and a mandatory presumption which the jury must accept even if it is the sole evidence of an element of the offense.[29]

---

[29] The dissenting argument rests on the assumption that "the jury [may have] rejected all of the prosecution's evidence concerning the location and origin of the guns." Even if that assumption were plausible, the jury was plainly told that it was free to disregard the presumption. But the dissent's assumption is not plausible; for if the jury rejected the testimony describing where the guns were found, it would necessarily also have rejected the only evidence in the record proving that the guns were found in the car. The conclusion that the jury attached significance to the particular location of the handguns follows inexorably from the acquittal on the charge of possession of the machinegun and heroin in the trunk.

In the latter situation, since the prosecution bears the burden of establishing guilt, it may not rest its case entirely on a presumption unless the fact proved is sufficient to support the inference of guilt beyond a reasonable doubt. But in the former situation, the prosecution may rely on all of the evidence in the record to meet the reasonable-doubt standard. There is no more reason to require a permissive statutory presumption to meet a reasonable-doubt standard before it may be permitted to play any part in a trial than there is to require that degree of probative force for other relevant evidence before it may be admitted. As long as it is clear that the presumption is not the sole and sufficient basis for a finding of guilt, it need only satisfy the test described in *Leary*.

The permissive presumption, as used in this case, satisfied the *Leary* test. And, as already noted, the New York Court of Appeals has concluded that the record as a whole was sufficient to establish guilt beyond a reasonable doubt.

The judgment is reversed.

So ordered.

[The concurring opinion of Chief Justice Burger is omitted.]

Mr. Justice POWELL, with whom Mr. Justice BRENNAN, Mr. Justice STEWART and Mr. Justice MARSHALL join, dissenting . . . .

In the criminal law, presumptions are used to encourage the jury to find certain facts, with respect to which no direct evidence is presented, solely because other facts have been proved.[1] The purpose of such presumptions is plain: Like certain other jury instructions, they provide guidance for jurors' thinking in considering the evidence laid before them. Once in the juryroom, jurors necessarily draw inferences from the evidence—both direct and circumstantial. Through the use of presumptions, certain inferences are commended to the attention of jurors by legislatures or courts.

Legitimate guidance of a jury's deliberations is an indispensable part of our criminal justice system. Nonetheless, the use of presumptions in criminal cases poses at least two distinct perils for defendants' constitutional rights. The Court accurately identifies the first of these as being the danger of interference with "the factfinder's responsibility at trial, based on evidence adduced by the State, to find the ultimate facts beyond a reasonable doubt." If the jury is instructed that it must infer some ultimate fact (that is, some element of the offense) from proof of other facts unless the defendant disproves the ultimate fact by a preponderance of the evidence, then the presumption

[1] Such encouragement can be provided either by statutory presumptions, or by presumptions created in the common law. Unless otherwise specified, "presumption" will be used herein to refer to "permissible inferences," as well as to "true" presumptions.

shifts the burden of proof to the defendant concerning the element thus inferred.[2]

But I do not agree with the Court's conclusion that the only constitutional difficulty with presumptions lies in the danger of lessening the burden of proof the prosecution must bear. As the Court notes, the presumptions thus far reviewed by the Court have not shifted the burden of persuasion; instead, they either have required only that the defendant produce some evidence to rebut the inference suggested by the prosecution's evidence, or merely have been suggestions to the jury that it would be sensible to draw certain conclusions on the basis of the evidence presented.[3] Evolving from our decisions, therefore, is a second standard for judging the constitutionality of criminal presumptions which is based—not on the constitutional requirement that the State be put to its proof—but rather on the due process rule that when the jury is encouraged to make factual inferences, those inferences must reflect some valid general observation about the natural connection between events as they occur in our society . . . . In sum, our decisions uniformly have recognized that due process requires more than merely that the prosecution be put to its proof.[6] In addition, the Constitution restricts the court in its charge to the jury by requiring that, when particular factual inferences are recommended to the jury, those factual inferences be accurate reflections of what history, common sense, and experience tell us about the relations between events in our society. Generally, this due process rule has been articulated as requiring that the truth of the inferred fact be more likely than not whenever the premise for the inference is true. Thus, to be constitutional a presumption must be at least more likely than not true.

In the present case, the jury was told:

> Our Penal Law also provides that the presence in an automobile of any machine gun or of any handgun or firearm which is loaded is presumptive evidence of their unlawful possession. In other words, [under] these presumptions or this

---

[2] The Court suggests that presumptions that shift the burden of persuasion to the defendant in this way can be upheld provided that "the fact proved is sufficient to support the inference of guilt beyond a reasonable doubt." As the present case involves no shifting of the burden of persuasion, the constitutional restrictions on such presumptions are not before us, and I express no views on them.

It may well be that even those presumptions that do not shift the burden of persuasion cannot be used to prove an element of the offense, if the facts proved would not permit a reasonable mind to find the presumed fact beyond a reasonable doubt. My conclusion makes it unnecessary for me to address this concern here.

[3] The Court suggests as the touchstone for its analysis a distinction between "mandatory" and "permissive" presumptions. I have found no recognition in the Court's prior decisions that this distinction is important in analyzing presumptions used in criminal cases.

[6] The Court apparently disagrees, contending that "the factfinder's responsibility . . . to find the ultimate facts beyond a reasonable doubt" is the only constitutional restraint upon the use of criminal presumptions at trial.

> latter presumption upon proof of the presence of the machine gun and the hand weapons, you may infer and draw a conclusion that such prohibited weapon was possessed by each of the defendants who occupied the automobile at the time when such instruments were found. The presumption or presumptions is effective only so long as there is no substantial evidence contradicting the conclusion flowing from the presumption, and the presumption is said to disappear when such contradictory evidence is adduced.

Undeniably, the presumption charged in this case encouraged the jury to draw a particular factual inference regardless of any other evidence presented: to infer that respondents possessed the weapons found in the automobile "upon proof of the presence of the machine gun and the hand weapon" and proof that respondents "occupied the automobile at the time such instruments were found." I believe that the presumption thus charged was unconstitutional because it did not fairly reflect what common sense and experience tell us about passengers in automobiles and the possession of handguns. People present in automobiles where there are weapons simply are not "more likely than not" the possessors of those weapons . . . .

In another context, this Court has been particularly hesitant to infer possession from mere presence in a location, noting that "[p]resence is relevant and admissible evidence in a trial on a possession charge; but absent some showing of the defendant's function at the [illegal] still, its connection with possession is too tenuous to permit a reasonable inference of guilt—'the inference of the one from proof of the other is arbitrary . . . .'" *United States v. Romano.* We should be even more hesitant to uphold the inference of possession of a handgun from mere presence in an automobile, in light of common experience concerning automobiles and handguns. Because the specific factual inference recommended to the jury in this case is not one that is supported by the general experience of our society, I cannot say that the presumption charged is "more likely than not" to be true. Accordingly, respondents' due process rights were violated by the presumption's use.

As I understand it, the Court today does not contend that in general those who are present in automobiles are more likely than not to possess any gun contained within their vehicles. It argues, however, that the nature of the presumption here involved requires that we look, not only to the immediate facts upon which the jury was encouraged to base its inference, but to the other facts "proved" by the prosecution as well. The Court suggests that this is the proper approach when reviewing what it calls "permissive" presumptions because the jury was urged "to consider all the circumstances tending to support or contradict the inference."

It seems to me that the Court mischaracterizes the function of the presumption charged in this case. As it acknowledges was the case in *Romano,* the "instruction authorized conviction even if the jury disbelieved all of the testimony except the proof of presence" in the automobile.[7] The Court nevertheless relies on all of the evidence introduced by the prosecution and argues that the "permissive" presumption could not have prejudiced defendants. The possibility that the jury disbelieved all of this evidence, and relied on the presumption, is simply ignored . . . .

■ NOTES ON THE SIGNIFICANCE OF *ALLEN*

1. In *Allen*, the Court concludes that the "presumption" was "permissive." (You know this term is confusing and misleading and it would better be described as an "inference.") What made the Court say it was "permissive"? Do you agree that it was?

2. *Allen* also refers to a "mandatory presumption" that "tells the trier that he or they *must* find the elemental fact" unless defendant comes forward with counterproof. (You know that here "presumption" is the proper term.) Could a presumption operate that way against the accused on elements in the offense? Doesn't *Sandstrom*, which was decided only two weeks after *Allen*, make it clear that the answer is No?

3. Referring now to the "permissive" presumption (inference), what standard must it satisfy? How strongly must the basic fact (presence of guns in car) support the presumed (or inferred) fact? Beyond reasonable doubt, preponderance, or more likely than without the presumed fact—these are the choices. The Court answers the question, doesn't it? If the presumption is delivered to the jury *in isolation* (relying solely on the presence of the guns in the car, you may infer that defendant possessed them), then the basic fact must tend to prove the presumed (or inferred) fact beyond reasonable doubt. But if the presumption is delivered to the jury *in context* (looking at the presence of the guns in the car and all the other evidence, you may conclude, if you think the point is proved beyond a reasonable doubt, that defendant possessed the guns), then all that is required is a "rational connection" between the basic and the presumed (or inferred) fact, and the "more likely than not" standard from *Leary* applies.

---

[7] In commending the presumption to the jury, the court gave no instruction that would have required a finding of possession to be based on anything more than mere presence in the automobile. Thus, the jury was not instructed that it should infer that respondents possessed the handguns only if it found that the guns were too large to be concealed in Jane Doe's handbag; that the guns accordingly were in the plain view of respondents; that the weapons were within "easy access of the driver of the car and even, perhaps, of the other two respondents who were riding in the rear seat"; that it was unlikely that Jane Doe was solely responsible for the placement of the weapons in her purse; or that the case was "tantamount to one in which the guns were lying on the floor or the seat of the car in the plain view of the three other occupants of the automobile."

■ PROBLEM 10-D. Presence of a Firearm

College student Sam Alden returns to home in Rochester, New York, for a Christmas visit with his family. During his visit he encounters his former high school classmate Burnell, and late one evening the two drive around town in Burnell's car. Police stop them, and it turns out that the car matches the description of a getaway car used in a nearby liquor store holdup in which the salesperson was killed 20 minutes earlier. The arresting officers direct Burnell to open the trunk, where they discover a sawed-off shotgun and three Uzi automatic rifles. Alden and Burnell are charged with unlawful possession of firearms.

At trial, the prosecutor offers evidence of the facts outlined above. He also calls Clayton as a witness, and he testifies that he and Burnell belong to a gun club and that Burnell once bragged that "I have a bunch of Uzis, and a modified shotgun."

At the close of the evidence, the prosecutor requests that the court instruct the jury as follows:

> The presence in a car of a loaded firearm is presumptive evidence of unlawful possession. On proof of the presence of guns in the car, you may infer that each defendant in the car possessed them. The presumption is effective only so long as there is no substantial evidence contradicting that conclusion, and it disappears when contradictory evidence is adduced. To establish unlawful possession of the weapon, the prosecutor relied on the presumption as well as testimony. Accordingly, you would be warranted in returning a verdict of guilty if you find beyond a reasonable doubt that possession is proved, and an element of such proof is the presumption of illegal possession.

Alden and Burnell both object, claiming the instruction violates due process. The prosecutor replies that the Supreme Court in *Allen* has approved such an instruction. On these facts, is the instruction proper as against Alden? As against Burnell?

■ NOTES ON INFERENCES IN CRIMINAL CASES

1. Doesn't the requested instruction in Problem 10-D fairly paraphrase the instruction approved in *Allen*? Can the court and the parties know before all the evidence is in whether such an instruction is proper in any given case?

2. The legislative device in *Allen* might be described as a "nudging inference" because it encourages the jury to infer one fact on the basis of another, where the inference is plausible but less than certain. Why do we have (and permit) use of such a nudging instruction relating to the elements of an offense in criminal cases?

3. Consider what courts tell jurors about the prosecutor's burden: Invariably they learn that the state must prove its case beyond a reasonable doubt. But courts often advise juries as well that the prosecutor need not prove guilt "beyond all possible doubt," see Kevin F. O'Malley, Jay E. Grenig & Hon. William C. Lee, Federal Jury Practice and Instructions §12.10 (6th ed. 2014). Sometimes they add that "reasonable doubt" does not mean "a mere possible doubt or a speculative, imaginary, or forced doubt, because everything relating to human affairs is open to some possible or imaginary doubt." See United States v. Muckenstrum, 515 F.2d 568, 571 (5th Cir.) (criticizing instruction that reasonable doubt means "substantial rather than speculative doubt"), *cert. denied*, 423 U.S. 1032 (1975). Does the "nudging" inference sabotage the reasonable doubt standard? Or serve as a constructive reminder to a lay factfinder that it need not abandon common sense?

4. Is there reason, *apart* from the "nudging" effect, to be uncomfortable with a conviction that follows such an instruction? Wouldn't Burnell likely be convicted even without the instruction? Usually a trial is decided on the basis of conflicting testimony, circumstantial evidence, questions of credibility, or combinations of these. Is there a reason to prefer convictions resting on such proof over convictions resting on the weight that the jury gives to a presumption? See Nesson, Reasonable Doubt and Permissive Inferences: The Value of Complexity, 92 Harv. L. Rev. 1187 (1979).

5. Look at the presumption instruction in *Allen,* which is paraphrased in the Problem. Do you like the language? Professor Nesson suggests telling the jury that "it is often possible to infer" a conclusion from the basic fact. In *Allen,* the judge could say:

> It is often possible to infer from the presence of loaded firearms in a car that the occupants possessed them. You must decide whether, in the context of this case, such a conclusion is justified as to each defendant. You should consider all the facts. For example, consider where the guns were found, whether they were in plain sight, how easy they were to reach. Based on your consideration of all the evidence, you must decide whether the prosecution has proved beyond reasonable doubt that each defendant is guilty as charged.

Nesson, Rationality, Presumptions, and Judicial Comment: A Response to Professor Allen, 94 Harv. L. Rev. 1574, 1589 (1981). What do you think of this suggestion?

6. In federal court Timothy Leary was charged with possession and concealment of imported marijuana. See Leary v. United States, 395 U.S. 6 (1969). Does the element of importation relate to culpability or to federalism—the division of responsibility between federal government and states? Sometimes Congress can decide for itself that certain kinds of acts affect "interstate commerce," and if the finding is reasonable Congress can criminalize the acts. The statute is a proper exercise of power to regulate interstate commerce. See Perez v. United States, 402 U.S. 146 (1970) (upholding statute criminalizing extortionate credit transactions; Congress could conclude that extortion is a problem affecting interstate commerce). Suppose Congress finds that traffic in cocaine affects interstate commerce, so it enacts penalties, but only if it is imported or taken across state lines. Can Congress determine that these points "affect only federal jurisdiction," thus avoid constitutional restraints that ordinarily apply in criminal prosecutions? Consider (1) allocating to the court (rather than the jury) the responsibility to decide them, (2) authorizing decision on such points by a preponderance, (3) giving such questions to the jury to decide under the lesser standard, and (4) burdening *the defense* with proving by a preponderance that the cocaine did *not* come from abroad or cross state lines. Should Congress be allowed to choose any or all of these procedures?

CHAPTER 11

Judicial Notice

A INTRODUCTION

Judicial notice describes the process by which a court determines certain matters without formal proof. It saves attorneys the time and expense of proving matters that are beyond reasonable dispute. Judicial notice covers four areas: adjudicative facts, which is the *only* type governed by FRE 201, evaluative facts, legislative facts, and law. Notice of legislative and evaluative facts is unregulated; judicial notice of law is regulated by a different set of rules and conventions.

Adjudicative facts are not defined in FRE 201, but the ACN quotes the suggestion by Professor Davis that they are "the facts that normally go to the jury in a jury case." It is also said that adjudicative facts are those that would have to be proved by evidence if notice were not taken. Judicial notice of indisputable adjudicative facts thus serves as a substitute for evidence, furthering trial efficiency. In a nonjury trial, the judge takes judicial notice merely by making an announcement or ruling, and she might or might not use the term "judicial notice." In a jury trial, judicial notice requires an instruction telling the jury that notice has been taken and explaining what that means. See FRE 201(f).

Evaluative facts include matters of common knowledge that judges and jurors bring to their deliberations. These facts amount to background information, appearing "inconspicuously and interstitially in [the] elementary processes of understanding and reasoning." McNaughton, Judicial Notice—Excerpts Relating to the Morgan-Wigmore Controversy, 14 Vand. L. Rev. 779, 789 (1961). Because evidence is not usually offered to prove evaluative facts, they are also known as "nonevidence" facts. When jurors consider such matters, we sometimes refer to the process as "jury notice."

The most basic evaluative facts are those that help judge and jury understand testimony and other evidence, such as the usual meaning of words, idioms, and slang expressions and what is meant by various forms of assertive conduct. When a witness says "fire engine," we assume a jury understands what is meant without resort to a dictionary or evidence. When a witness testifies that defendant nodded on being asked whether he was the person driving the car, we assume a jury understands the usual meaning of a nod.

Other evaluative facts help the trier assess formal evidence. Such facts are likely to be comprised of arrays of factual data that underlie ordinary judgments about the world, which are captured in terms like "human nature" and "physical laws." When a witness is impeached, for example, by a showing that he has a close romantic or economic relationship with one of the parties, we assume a jury understands how and why such relationships might affect credibility. And when evidence is offered that an airplane crashed to the ground after its engine failed in flight, we assume a jury understands the connection between these events, without testimony describing principles of physics.

Because an evaluative fact is normally a matter of general knowledge, there is usually no need to instruct the jury to take notice of such a fact. If a party asks for an instruction, it is an indication that she views the matter as an adjudicative fact. But a general instruction on evaluative facts is sometimes given, telling jurors they may use their experience in the affairs of life in evaluating evidence, and also their general knowledge of the natural tendencies and inclinations of human beings and their common sense.

Legislative facts are those that are considered by a trial or appellate court in ruling on questions of law. Such questions may involve interpreting a statute or constitutional provision or creating, modifying, or rejecting a common law rule. As Professor Davis put it: "When a court . . . develops law or policy, it is acting legislatively; the courts have created the common law through judicial legislation, and the facts which inform the tribunal's legislative judgment are called legislative facts." Davis, Judicial Notice, 55 Colum. L. Rev. 945, 952 (1955). Legislative facts include legislative history of a statute or rule, but the category is much broader. Legislative facts include nonlegal matters, like scientific propositions, sociological or historical facts, and any other propositions about the world that a court considers in making legal rulings. Jury instructions are not given on such matters because legal rulings are beyond the province of juries.

Judicial notice of law refers to the process by which the court determines controlling law. To the extent judicial notice is taken, parties are relieved of the burden of proving law, although they generally help the court in this task. If judicial notice of law is not taken, responsibility for proving the applicable law rests with the parties. Federal courts traditionally take judicial notice not only of federal law, but also of the law of the forum state and sister states. State courts traditionally take judicial notice of federal law and the law of the forum state, and more recently, many have been willing to notice the law of sister states. There is a strong trend toward expanding the scope of judicial notice of law. Although the Federal Rules of Evidence do not address the issue, most states specify the scope of judicial notice of law by statute or rule.

The four categories of judicial notice are easy to describe, but there is sometimes confusion on the question how a particular matter should be classified. Sometimes a fact overlaps two or more categories (meaning essentially that it is used for more than one purpose in the case). Classification is important because the restrictions and procedures of FRE 201 apply only if the matter noticed is an adjudicative fact.

B JUDICIAL NOTICE OF ADJUDICATIVE FACTS

■ PROBLEM 11-A. Dry Pavement

Paulsen sues Davis for injuries sustained in an automobile accident at an intersection in Indianapolis on September 8, 2010. Paulsen asks the court to take judicial notice that it did not rain in Indianapolis on that date and that the pavement at the intersection was dry. In support of this request, Paulsen furnishes the court with a copy of the official weather bureau record for Indianapolis on September 8, 2010, which clearly indicates that no precipitation was recorded. Davis objects on grounds that the record is hearsay and has not been properly authenticated. Should the request for judicial notice be granted, in whole or in part? Is FRE 104(a) applicable?

■ PROBLEM 11-B. The Subpoena

West is cited to show cause why he should not be held in contempt for failure to appear as a witness at a trial after being served a subpoena. West denies getting the subpoena. The petitioning party asks the court to take judicial notice that West was served, directing court's attention to a properly executed return of service filed by the sheriff and included as part of the record of the case. The petitioning party also asks the court to take judicial notice that West had been held in contempt for failure to appear at an earlier trial of the same case, and had also been held in contempt for refusing to testify in related cases in two other states. What ruling?

■ PROBLEM 11-C. Interstate Call

Lauro is charged with knowingly using the telephone in interstate commerce for purposes of transacting bets or wagers. Telephone records show the call was placed interstate from Baborian in New Haven, Connecticut, to Lauro in Rhode Island, but Lauro denies knowing that it was an interstate call. At trial the only evidence of knowledge was testimony that Lauro, who admittedly was in Rhode Island, spoke to Baborian's father in New Haven, Connecticut, at 6:36 P.M., and the father said Baborian was with him in New Haven at that time, but was driving to Rhode Island and would be calling Lauro shortly. At 6:51 P.M., Lauro got Baborian's call. The prosecutor asks the court to take judicial notice (1) that the driving time from New Haven, Connecticut, to Rhode Island is more than 15 minutes and (2) that therefore Lauro must have known Baborian's call was from out of state. What ruling?

■ PROBLEM 11-D. The Football Fan

Rogers is charged with armed robbery. He asserts an alibi defense, claiming that he was watching a professional football game on television with friends at the time of the robbery. To rebut this defense, the prosecutor supplies the court with a copy of TV Guide and asks the court to take judicial notice that there was no football game of any type being televised at the time of the robbery. What ruling?

■ PROBLEM 11-E. Delayed Shipment

Pellum Construction Company of Los Angeles was interested in bidding on a project to construct a new hospital in Long Beach. Pellum hired a New York architectural firm to draft a design proposal. All bids, accompanied by the proposed architectural design, were required to be submitted to the Long Beach hospital board by September 15, 2001. Pellum hired Air Courier Services to fly the design proposal from New York to Los Angles on September 11. The design proposal failed to arrive in time, and Pellum lost the contract to another construction company. Pellum sues Air Courier Services Inc. for failing to deliver the architectural design proposal. Air Courier defends on grounds of impossibility of performance. At trial, Air Courier asks the judge to take judicial notice that there was a terrorist attack on New York City that occurred on September 11, 2001, and that conditions following that attack made it impossible to get shipment to Los Angeles by September 15th. Should the court take judicial notice of these points?

■ PROBLEM 11-F. Asbestos and Cancer

Plaintiffs who contracted cancer after exposure to asbestos file a product liability action against a leading asbestos manufacturer. Plaintiffs request that the court take judicial notice that asbestos causes cancer. What ruling? Assume the request is granted. Is defendant then barred from trying to prove the contrary? Is defendant barred from arguing to the jury that asbestos does not cause cancer?

GOVERNMENT OF THE VIRGIN ISLANDS v. GEREAU

United States Court of Appeals for the Third Circuit
523 F.2d 140 (1975)

Defendants-appellants contend that the District Court of the Virgin Islands, Division of St. Croix, erred in denying their motion for a new trial. Rejecting this contention, we affirm the district court.

On August 13, 1973, defendants were found guilty of first degree murder, first degree assault, and robbery. The jury which returned the verdicts had deliberated for nine days. The jurors were polled individually and each acknowledged the verdict as his own. Two days later, defendants filed a motion requesting a new trial on the ground that the verdict had not been freely assented to by all the jurors....

Juror Agneta Cappin testified that one of the jury attendants, Matron Foye, spoke to her about the case.

> She just asked me how everything is going and I tell her not so good. And I say two of them that don't understand, they don't come in yet. And she say to me she want them to hurry up so she can get to go home, that is all.

Matron Foye denied the conversation. The trial judge, finding both women to be credible witnesses, chose to believe Foye rather than Cappin because he knew that Foye "was grateful for the opportunity to earn extra income as a jury matron." We do not consider these credibility findings to lack adequate support in the record. However, we do hold that the trial judge's reliance on his personal, subjective belief about the needs and motive of Matron Foye was an improper ground for rejecting Cappin's concededly credible testimony.

In basing his fact-finding on personal knowledge, the trial judge was, in effect, taking judicial notice of extra-record, adjudicative facts. "With respect to judicial notice of adjudicative facts, the tradition has been one of caution in requiring that the matter be beyond reasonable controversy." Advisory Committee's Notes to FRE 201(b); cf. FRE 201(a) and (b). A second hallmark of facts properly the subject of judicial notice is that they be either matters of common knowledge or "capable of immediate and accurate determination by resort to easily accessible sources of indisputable accuracy...." Weaver v. United States, 298 F.2d 496, 498 (5th Cir. 1962). Facts possessing these characteristics are entitled to be considered by a judge without first being proved through the routine processes of introducing evidence. The necessary cachet is not, however, bestowed merely by a judge's knowledge of a particular fact.

> There is a real but elusive line between the judge's *personal knowledge* as a private man and these matters of which he takes judicial notice as a judge. The latter does not necessarily include the former; as a judge, indeed, he may have to ignore what he knows as a man, and contrariwise....

> It is therefore plainly accepted that the judge is not to use from the bench, under the guise of judicial knowledge, that which he knows *only as an individual* observer outside of court. The former [judicial knowledge] is in truth "known" to him merely in the fictional sense that it is known and notorious to all men, and the dilemma is only the result of using the term "knowledge" in two senses. Where to draw the line between knowledge by notoriety and knowledge by personal observation may sometimes be difficult, but the principle is plain.

J. Wigmore, Evidence, §2569, at 539-40 (3d ed. 1940). It is apparent that the trial judge's knowledge about Matron Foye falls into this latter category of personal knowledge and, therefore, does not qualify for judicial notice. It follows that the trial judge erred in rejecting Cappin's testimony on the ground stated . . . .

As an antidote to these errors in the fact-finding process, our inquiry into the validity of the verdict will assume . . . that Cappin's testimony was accurate . . . .

In the present case, Cappin did not indicate whether she considered herself influenced by the matron's statement. However, the trial judge found that she had voted guilty from the first ballot to the last. Since Cappin did not mention the incident to any of the other jurors, no juror could have been moved by the remarks to change his vote.

It thus appearing that no prejudice accrued to the defendants from the only occurrence which was both legally cognizable and sufficient to impeach the jury verdict, we find no abuse of discretion in the trial judge's refusal to order a new trial. The judgment of the district court will be affirmed.

■ NOTES ON JUDICIAL NOTICE OF ADJUDICATIVE FACTS

1. The *Gereau* rule that judges may not base judicial notice on personal knowledge is well established but occasionally violated. See SEC v. Musella, 578 F. Supp. 425, 439 (S.D.N.Y. 1984), where the court took judicial notice of the following:

> [A]ll law firms, especially those such as Sullivan & Cromwell that routinely handle sensitive matters, impress upon their incoming employees the firm's expectation that they will not publicly discuss matters pertaining to their clients . . . . I have not been so long removed from the world inhabited by firms like Sullivan to have forgotten what life is like there.

See also In re National Airlines, 434 F. Supp. 269 (D. Fla. 1977) (taking judicial notice of attractiveness of flight attendants based on judge's own observations).

2. Does FRE 201 require a party to notify an opposing party that judicial notice is requested of a particular matter at trial? See FRE 201(c) (No). Does the Rule require a court to notify parties prior to taking judicial notice on its own motion? See FRE 201(e) (No, but court must allow party an opportunity to be heard). Compare Model Code, Rule 804(1) (1942): "The judge shall inform the parties of the tenor of any matter to be judicially noticed," and allow "reasonable opportunity" to present information "relevant to the propriety of taking such judicial notice or to the tenor of the matter to be noticed."

3. Does the Constitution guarantee parties a right to be heard on the propriety of taking judicial notice? See Ohio Bell Telephone v. Public Utilities Commission, 301 U.S. 292, 302-303 (1937) (judicial notice without providing opportunity for parties to be heard violates due process) (review of administrative determination).

4. Judicial notice is mandatory under FRE 201(c) on request by a party if the court is "supplied with the necessary information." A purpose of mandatory judicial notice is to assure attorneys that it will be possible to establish certain facts by judicial notice, relieving them of the obligation to produce evidence. Does the Rule accomplish this purpose? Isn't there still uncertainty about what is the "necessary information?"

5. For additional examples of judicial notice of adjudicative facts, see Barnes v. Bosley, 568 F. Supp. 1406, 1410 n.4 (E.D. Mo. 1983) (judicial notice "that currently the Democratic Party is firmly in control of political offices within the city of St. Louis"), *modified in part, rev'd in part on other grounds*, 745 F.2d 501 (8th Cir. 1984), *cert. denied*, 471 U.S. 1017 (1985); Sinatra v. Heckler, 566 F. Supp. 1354 (E.D.N.Y. 1983) (substantial number of federal employees take vacations during year-end holiday period when the mails are heavily burdened, resulting in slowdown of office operations and retarded delivery); Allen v. Allen, 518 F. Supp. 1234, 1235 n.2 (E.D. Pa. 1981) (Father's Day occurred on June 17 in 1979); Caufield v. Board of Education, 486 F. Supp. 862, 885 (E.D.N.Y. 1979) (judicial notice that "historically in New York City, a large percentage of the teaching force, particularly at the lower school levels, has been composed of women"), *aff'd*, 632 F.2d 999 (2d Cir. 1980), *cert. denied*, 450 U.S. 1020 (1981); United Klans of America v. McGovern, 453 F. Supp. 836 (N.D. Ala. 1978) (judicial notice that United Klans "has been and continues to be a 'white supremacy' organization whose purposes and policies are implemented by acts of terror and intimidation"), *aff'd*, 621 F.2d 152 (5th Cir. 1980); State *ex rel.* Chalka v. Johnson, 292 N.W.2d 835, 840 (Wis. 1980) (judicial notice that Southern Comfort is "an intoxicating liquor and that excessive consumption of an intoxicating liquor can cause death").

6. In light of these examples, do you agree with Professor Davis that adjudicative facts are "facts concerning the immediate parties—who did what, where, when, how, and with what motive or intent"? 2 K. Davis, Administrative Law Treatise §15.03, at 353 (1984). Aren't many adjudicative facts general in nature and unrelated to the parties?

COMMENT/PERSPECTIVE:
How Broad Should Judicial Notice Be?

The scope of judicial notice of adjudicative facts under FRE 201(b) is narrow. See Hardy v. Johns-Manville Sales Corp., 681 F.2d 334, 347 (5th Cir. 1982) (judicial notice "applies to self-evident truths that no reasonable person could question, truisms that approach platitudes or banalities"). Is the standard of FRE 201(b) ("not subject to reasonable dispute") too stringent? Professors Thayer and Wigmore thought so, and Professor Davis agreed. They urged that judicial notice should have a broader focus and should encompass not only indisputable facts but also facts that are unlikely to be challenged. Under the Thayer-Wigmore-Davis view, judicial notice would be like a presumption. The fact judicially noticed would *not* be binding upon the jury, and the opposing party could introduce evidence to the contrary. See J. Thayer, A Preliminary Treatise on Evidence at the Common Law 308 (1898); 9 J. Wigmore, Evidence §2567 (J. Chadbourn rev. 1981); Davis, Judicial Notice, 1969 Law & Social Order 513. Professors Morgan and McNaughton took the opposing position, ultimately adopted by FRE 201(b), that judicial notice should be limited to matters that are not subject to reasonable dispute. Under their view, because the matter must be indisputable, controverting proof is inappropriate. Hence taking notice is conclusive and conflicting evidence should not be admitted. E. Morgan, Basic Problems of Evidence 9 (1962); McNaughton, Judicial Notice—Excerpts Relating to the Morgan-Wigmore Controversy, 14 Vand. L. Rev. 779 (1961).

C JUDICIAL NOTICE IN CRIMINAL CASES

FRE 201 is one of the few rules that distinguishes between civil and criminal cases. FRE 201(f) says that in criminal cases a judicial notice instruction does not bind the jury. Could this provision limit a prosecutor's ability to obtain judicial notice on appeal to repair a gap in the government's proof? Consider the following case:

UNITED STATES v. JONES

United States Court of Appeals for the Sixth Circuit
580 F.2d 219 (1978)

[Defendant was convicted of illegally intercepting telephone conversations of his estranged wife. After the jury convicted defendant on three of five counts, the district judge granted defendant's motion for a judgment of acquittal on the ground that the government failed to prove that South Central Bell Telephone

Company was "a common carrier . . . providing or operating . . . facilities for the transmission of interstate or foreign communications," a requirement of the federal eavesdropping statute under which defendant was prosecuted. The government appealed the ruling of the trial court and urged that judicial notice be taken by the appellate court of South Central Bell's status as a common carrier.]

The government did not at any time during the jury trial specifically request the district court to take judicial notice of the status of South Central Bell. Nevertheless, it relies upon the provisions of Rule 201(d) which state that "[j]udicial notice may be taken at any stage of the proceeding." It is true that the Advisory Committee Note to 201(f) indicates that judicial notice is appropriate "in the trial court *or on appeal.* "It is also true that the language of 201(d) does not distinguish between judicial notice in civil or criminal cases. There is, however, a critical difference in the manner in which the judicially noticed fact is to be submitted to the jury in civil and criminal proceedings:

> *Instructing jury.* In a civil action or proceeding, the court shall instruct the jury to accept as conclusive any fact judicially noticed. In a criminal case, the court shall instruct the jury that it may, but is not required to, accept as conclusive any fact judicially noticed.

FRE 201(f). Thus under subsection (f) judicial notice of a fact in a civil case is conclusive while in a criminal trial the jury is not bound to accept the judicially noticed fact and may disregard it if it so chooses.

It is apparent from the legislative history that the congressional choice of language in Rule 201 was deliberate. In adopting the present language, Congress rejected a draft of subsection (f) proposed by the Supreme Court, which read:

The judge shall instruct the jury to accept as established any facts judicially noticed.

The House Report explained its reason for the change:

> Rule 201(f) as received from the Supreme Court provided that when judicial notice of a fact is taken, the court shall instruct the jury to accept that fact as established. Being of the view that mandatory instruction to a jury in a criminal case to accept as conclusive any fact judicially noticed is inappropriate because contrary to the spirit of the Sixth Amendment right to a jury trial, the Committee adopted the 1969 Advisory Committee draft of this subsection, allowing a mandatory instruction in civil actions and proceedings and a discretionary instruction in criminal cases.

H. Rep. No. 93-650, 93d Cong., 1st Sess. 6-7 (1973), U.S. Code Cong. & Admin. News 7075, 7080 (1974). Congress intended to preserve the jury's traditional prerogative to ignore even uncontroverted facts in reaching a verdict. The legislature was concerned that the Supreme Court's rule violated the spirit, if not the letter, of the constitutional right to a jury trial by effectively permitting a partial directed verdict as to facts in a criminal case.[8]

As enacted by Congress, Rule 201(f) plainly contemplates that the jury in a criminal case shall pass upon facts which are judicially noticed. This it could not do if this notice were taken for the first time after it had been discharged and the case was on appeal. We, therefore, hold that Rule 201(d), authorizing judicial notice at the appellate level, must yield in the face of the express congressional intent manifested in 201(f) for criminal jury trials. To the extent that the earlier practice may have been otherwise, we conceive that it has been altered by the enactment of Rule 201.

Accordingly, the judgment of the district court is affirmed.

■ NOTES ON JUDICIAL NOTICE IN CRIMINAL CASES

1. Was *Jones* correctly decided? Does the decision succeed in protecting the doctrine of jury nullification? Consider the following criticism:

> It is extremely difficult to see the working of the process of jury nullification under such circumstances. If they wished to exercise their power of nullification, they certainly did not need to do so by finding that South Central Bell was not engaged in interstate commerce. Moreover the jury already convicted the defendant. Whenever the fact judicially noticeable against the defendant is needed to support a conviction actually rendered by a jury, it makes no practical sense to discuss the possibility of jury nullification.

M. Graham, Handbook of Federal Evidence 84 n.15 (3d ed. 1991).

2. The Advisory Committee had trouble making up its mind on judicial notice in criminal cases. Originally it favored the nonbinding notice that FRE 201(f) now endorses, on the ground that "a verdict cannot be directed against the accused in a criminal case." 46 F.R.D. 161, 205 (1969). Later it concluded that mandatory notice was proper because "the right of jury trial does not extend to matters which are beyond reasonable dispute." 51 F.R.D. 315, 335 (1971). But Congress agreed with the Committee's first thought, and adopted the original proposal. The House Committee Report cites "the spirit of the Sixth Amendment right to a jury trial." Who is right here? Consider the following critique of FRE 201(f) as enacted:

[8] The Supreme Court of Utah expressed a similar concern in State v. Lawrence, 234 P.2d 600 (Utah 1951): "If a court can take one important element of an offense from the jury and determine the facts for them because such fact seems plain enough to him, then which element cannot be similarly taken away, and where would the process stop?"

> With deference, [FRE 201(f) as it emerged from Congress] is irrational. Actual application of the Congressional version makes fools of the judge, the law and the jury. If for example, the facts warrant a finding that a woman was taken by the defendant for immoral purposes from Newark, New Jersey, to New York City, New York, the judge under the Court's [proposed] Rule would by a proper instruction leave that issue to the jury, while further instructing them that such a journey would constitute a crossing of state lines. The Congressional rule, intended to preserve the power of the jury, requires him to instruct the jury that it "may, but is not required to accept" the proposition that to go from Newark to New York is to cross state lines. Under the Court's [proposed] rule the jury would still have the power to acquit the defendant though the evidence warranted a judgment of conviction—but on the ground of mercy and not under an instruction permitting it to find that Newark is not really in New Jersey but is a New York suburb of "fun city," and that, after all, state lines were not crossed.
>
> Under the Congressional rule, in the morning when the judge tries a civil case the world is round. That afternoon when he tries a criminal case the world is flat.

10 Moore's Federal Practice §201.70 (2d ed. 1985).

3. Consider the *Lawrence* case, which *Jones* cites in footnote 8. *Lawrence* involved a prosecution for grand larceny, arising out of the alleged theft in 1950 of a 1947 Ford two-door sedan. The trial judge instructed the jury to "take the value of this property as being in excess of $50.00," and the jury convicted. Not coincidentally, that sum represented the dividing line between grand and petty larceny. The Utah Supreme Court reversed, on the ground that judicial notice improperly took away the jury's power to "make findings which are not based on logic, nor even common sense." State v. Lawrence, 234 P.2d 600, 603 (Utah 1951). Do you agree with *Lawrence* that a mandatory instruction is out of line? A court applying FRE 201(f) could not give such an instruction. If the jury wanted to convict for petty larceny, would that be equivalent to finding that "the world is flat"?

4. On the facts in *Lawrence*, what exactly should a trial judge applying FRE 201(f) tell the jury? Consider the following proposal, advanced by the Federal Judicial Center Committee:

> Even though no evidence has been introduced about it, I have decided to accept as proved that [e.g., the city of San Francisco is north of the city of Los Angeles]. I believe that this fact is of such common knowledge [or alternative justification per rule 201(b)(2) of the Federal Rules of Evidence] that it would be a waste of our time to hear evidence about it. Thus, you may treat it as proved, even though no evidence was brought out on the point. Of course, with this fact, as with any fact, you will have to make the final decision and you are not required to agree with me.

Federal Judicial Center, Committee to Study Jury Instructions 12 (1982). Would similar language work on the facts of *Lawrence*?

5. Does the Moore argument (note 2, supra) overstate the degree to which FRE 201(f) protects the freedom of the jury? The ABA Section on Litigation thinks so: "Federal courts recognize a sound distinction between adjudicative facts and the legal significance of those facts. Thus, an instruction to a jury that, if it finds that a defendant traveled from Newark to New York, then the defendant traveled in interstate commerce is consistent with Rule 201." ABA Section of Litigation, Emerging Problems Under the Federal Rules of Evidence 36-37 (1983).

6. *Jones* fits into the modern trend of decisions. See United States v. Dior, 671 F.2d 351 (9th Cir. 1982) (refusing to take judicial notice after trial that $13,690 in Canadian currency had a value of $5,000 or more in United States currency); United States v. Bliss, 642 F.2d 390 (10th Cir. 1981); United States v. Thomas, 610 F.2d 1166 (3d Cir. 1979). But see Government of the Canal Zone v. Burjan, 596 F.2d 690 (5th Cir. 1979), and United States v. Lavender, 602 F.2d 639 (4th Cir. 1979) (judicial notice taken on appeal that place of crime was within federal jurisdiction).

7. Is there a drafting error in the second sentence of FRE 201(f)? It bars binding notice "in a criminal case." What is wrong with binding judicial notice when taken *in favor* of a criminal defendant?

■ PROBLEM 11-G. Deadly Weapon

Stimson, a karate expert, is charged with "assault with a deadly weapon, to wit, his hands," arising out of an attack on Boyer. Under the law of the jurisdiction, whether a weapon is deadly under the statute is an adjudicative fact for the jury. But on request by the prosecutor, the court instructs the jury under FRE 201(f) that "you may, but are not required to find, that the hands of karate expert qualify as a deadly weapon under the statute." In his case-in-chief, Stimson calls Osaga, a fellow karate expert, who will testify that karate is not a dangerous sport and that the hands of a karate expert are not a deadly weapon. The prosecutor objects, arguing that rebutting evidence cannot be presented with respect to a fact that has already been judicially noticed. What ruling?

D EVALUATIVE FACTS

Evaluative facts are those facts known to the jury which are used to consider and evaluate the evidence introduced at trial. Thayer described evaluative facts as a part of judicial reasoning:

> In conducting a process of judicial reasoning, as of other reasoning, not a step can be taken without assuming something which has not been proved; and

> the capacity to do this, with competent judgment and efficiency, is imputed to judges and juries as part of their necessary mental outfit.

J. Thayer, Preliminary Treatise on Evidence at the Common Law 279-280 (1898).

PROBLEM 11-H. "Okay, Maurie"

Defendant is prosecuted for extortion in violation of federal law. At trial, the prosecution offers into evidence a note from the defendant to the alleged victim containing the following statements: "Okay, Maurie, this is it, get it and get it straight because you only have one chance . . . . Please Maurie, make it easy on yourself by cooperating fully." The prosecutor requests an instruction under FRE 201 telling the jury that it may, but is not required to, find that in the language of the criminal underworld such statements constitute an implicit death threat. What ruling?

NOTES ON JUDICIAL NOTICE OF EVALUATIVE FACTS

1. Do jurors really need to be told that the note to Maurie might convey a veiled death threat? If underworld code or jargon carries sinister meaning not common in ordinary discourse, shouldn't the prosecutor call an expert to testify on such points?

2. Courts have long understood that jurors bring certain "mental baggage" to the cases they decide. Indeed, this baggage seems part and parcel of the common sense that we seek from juries. Consider the following description of what jurors bring to their task:

> But any juror must consider the testimony in light of that knowledge and experience which is common to all men. For instance, it is a matter of common knowledge that a bullet piercing the brain of a human being will in all likelihood prove fatal. It is common knowledge also that a forest tree cut nearly in two at the butt will fall, if a high wind blows against it. If a witness should testify to the contrary of these ordinary phenomena the common knowledge of the juror derived from his experience in such matters would naturally compel him to discredit that witness. Many illustrations might be given where men are normally and legitimately influenced in considering testimony by their general knowledge and experience.

Rostad v. Portland Ry., Light & Power Co., 201 P. 184, 187 (Or. 1921). See also Head v. Hargrave, 105 U.S. 45, 49-50 (1882).

3. Is the doctrine described in *Rostad*, supra, subject to abuse? How can attorneys regulate the amount of relevant, extrarecord information possessed by jurors sitting on a case? Presumably the voir dire of prospective jurors should provide such an opportunity.

4. A jury's knowledge of evaluative facts is one of the factors that affect choice of venue. See Pereza v. Mark, 423 F.2d 149, 151 (2d Cir. 1970) (Vermont jurors "are very likely better acquainted with rifles than we are"); Chance v. Du Pont De Nemours & Co., 371 F. Supp. 439, 449 (E.D.N.Y. 1974) (federal court in West Virginia "is best equipped to decide whether blasting caps are familiar articles around coal mines," and community standards comprise "a vital element in assessing the actions of the parties").

5. Isn't an attorney's most direct involvement with evaluative facts likely to be in closing argument? To what extent can an attorney refer to matters outside the record, such as historical facts, scientific facts, and current events? See Levin & Levy, Persuading the Jury with Facts Not in Evidence: The Fiction-Science Spectrum, 105 U. Pa. L. Rev. 139 (1956) (references to current and historical events should be permitted).

6. What limits are imposed on a jury's use of information outside the record in deciding a case? Consider the following incident in a civil case, which the reviewing court considered jury misconduct calling for reversal:

> After the jury was discharged on the afternoon of November 13, juror Noll borrowed a book on electricity from a friend, took it home with him, and thereafter read from it extensively until the early hours of the next morning, paying particular attention to the arcing and jumping characteristics of electricity while being transmitted through electric transmission lines. The next morning, after the jury returned to the jury room to resume its deliberations, he proceeded, in the presence of all the jurors, to discuss with most, if not all, of them matters and things he had learned from the book about the subject in question.

Thomas v. Kansas Power & Light Co., 340 P.2d 379 (Kan. 1959).

7. Scholars who conducted extensive surveys on the jury system concluded:

> [J]urors bring to their deliberations much extra knowledge—some of which certainly would not be known to the judge. The jury's extra information tends to be some item of personal experience not part of the trial, or some generalization about human nature. . . . Bringing knowledge such as this to bear on its deliberations is, of course, one of the jury's most engaging and flavorsome characteristics. It raises the interesting problem of how the legal system expects the jurors to confine their deliberations to the trial record on the one hand, and yet on the other to bring into their deliberations their common experience with life. In any case, to the extent that the jury utilizes in its deliberations things it knows about life in general or about human nature, it is using a kind of knowledge which the judge, as a human being, must also have, although twelve jurors coming from many strata of the society may well produce more knowledge than one judge.

H. Kalven & H. Zeisel, The American Jury 131-132 (1966).

 JUDICIAL NOTICE OF LEGISLATIVE FACTS

Recall that legislative facts are those facts used by a court to make a legal ruling. Recall also that notice of legislative facts is not regulated by FRE 201. What limits are there on such notice? Consider the following cases:

MULLER v. OREGON

United States Supreme Court
208 U.S. 412 (1907)

[In this case, the Court finds a rational basis for an Oregon statute limiting the hours women can work in laundries and factories to a maximum of ten hours per day, and therefore upholds its constitutionality.]

It may not be amiss, in the present case, before examining the constitutional question, to notice the course of legislation as well as expressions of opinion from other than judicial sources. In the brief filed by Mr. Louis D. Brandeis, for the defendant in error, is a very copious collection of all these matters, an epitome of which is found in the margin.[1]

The legislation and opinions referred to in the margin may not be, technically speaking, authorities, and in them is little or no discussion of the constitutional question presented to us for determination, yet they are significant of a widespread belief that woman's physical structure, and the functions she performs in consequence thereof, justify special legislation restricting or qualifying the conditions under which she should be permitted to toil. Constitutional questions, it is true, are not settled by even a consensus of present public opinion, for it is the peculiar value of a written constitution that it places in unchanging form limitations upon legislative action, and thus gives a permanence

---

[1] The following legislation of the States impose restrictions in some form or another upon the hours of labor that may be required of women. In foreign legislation Mr. Brandeis calls attention to these statutes: Great Britain: Factories Act of 1844, chap. 15, pp. 161, 171; Factory and Workshop Act of 1901, chap. 22, pp. 60, 71; and see 1 Edw. VII, chap. 22. France, 1848; Act Nov. 2, 1892, and March 30, 1900. Switzerland, Canton of Glarus, 1848; Federal Law 1877, art. 2, §1. Austria, 1855; Acts 1897, art. 96a, §§1-3. Holland, 1889; art. 5, §1. Italy, June 19, 1902, art. 7. Germany, Laws 1891.

Then follow extracts from over ninety reports of committees, bureaus of statistics, commissioners of hygiene, inspectors of factories, both in this country and in Europe, to the effect that long hours of labor are dangerous for women, primarily because of their special physical organization. The matter is discussed in these reports in different aspects, but all agree as to the danger. It would of course take too much space to give these reports in detail. Following them are extracts from similar reports discussing the general benefits of short hours from an economic aspect of the question. In many of these reports individual instances are given tending to support the general conclusion. Perhaps the general scope and character of all these reports may be summed up in what an inspector for Hanover says: "The reasons for the reduction of the working day to ten hours—(a) the physical organization of women, (b) her maternal functions, (c) the rearing and education of the children, (d) the maintenance of the home—are all so important and so far reaching that the need for such reduction need hardly be discussed."

and stability to popular government which otherwise would be lacking. At the same time, when a question of fact is debated and debatable, and the extent to which a special constitutional limitation goes is affected by the truth in respect to that fact, a widespread and long continued belief concerning it is worthy of consideration. We take judicial cognizance of all matters of general knowledge.

HOUSER v. STATE

Washington Supreme Court
540 P.2d 412 (Wash. 1975)

UTTER, J.

Charles Houser, III, brought this action on his own behalf and that of the class of all 18- to 20-year-olds in this state, challenging the constitutionality of the legislation that established a minimum age of 21 for the consumption of alcoholic beverages. The trial court rendered summary judgment in favor of the defendant state agencies, and Houser appeals. We affirm the ruling of the trial court.

Appellant sought from the court below a declaratory judgment that the 21-year-old drinking age deprived persons between the ages of 18 and 20 of the equal protection of the laws in violation of the Fourteenth Amendment and Const. art. 1, §12. He contended that no rational basis exists for the present statutory scheme under which Washington citizens are considered to be adults at the age of 18 for all purposes except the possession and consumption of alcohol. He supported this contention with evidence in the form of an expert's affidavit that indicated that several traditional arguments for maintaining the drinking age at 21 were without scientific support. The State countered this claim by submitting to the court's notice two technical studies which contained data supporting the statutory age discrimination, and by citing the single federal case in point, Republican College Council v. Winner, 357 F. Supp. 739 (E.D. Pa. 1973), which upheld Pennsylvania's drinking age limitation against equal protection attack. The trial court found the State's studies and the reasoning of the *Republican College* case adequate to uphold the drinking-age statutes, regardless of the truth of the statements in appellant's expert's affidavit. It therefore granted the State's motion for summary judgment. Appellant's appeal challenges both the trial court's judicial notice of the State's studies and its refusal to grant him a trial on the merits of the contradictory factual claims . . . .

To ascertain whether a rational relationship existed between the 21-year-old drinking age and a legitimate state purpose, the trial court took judicial notice of the studies submitted to it by the State. Appellant contends these studies were not judicially noticeable because the facts they contain were not "well established and authoritatively settled." This argument misconceives the function the court was performing in ruling on the constitutional issue before it. The State's summary judgment motion required the court to inquire not into the facts of the particular case at bar but into the general relationship between the attainment of the age of 21 and the effect of alcohol consumption. The question it presented was essentially one of law, not fact: whether there was a "rational relationship" between the statutory distinction and the state purposes it was alleged to serve. The finding that it was rational to believe that the discrimination did correspond to a permissible state objective was a step in the court's legal reasoning, not a conclusion regarding the factual background of the particular dispute before it.

A court "may ascertain as it sees fit any fact that is merely a ground for laying down a rule of law. . . ." Chastleton Corp. v. Sinclair, 264 U.S. 543, 548 (1924). The restrictive rules governing judicial notice are not applicable to factual findings that simply supply premises in the process of legal reasoning. In interpreting and developing the constitution and laws, courts cannot operate in a vacuum. In order to determine whether there is a "rational relationship" between a statutory classification and an objective said to justify it, a court must look beyond the case reports and statute books into a world that is rich with probability and conjecture and almost devoid of settled certainty. It must make the best assessment it can from the best information it can obtain. Reputable scientific studies are one source of such information, increasingly utilized by courts in constitutional decision making. The trial court thus did not err in noticing the studies submitted to it in this case.

NOTES ON JUDICIAL NOTICE OF LEGISLATIVE FACTS

1. Why don't the Rules regulate judicial notice of legislative facts? Could it be that the requirement of indisputability sets too high a bar? If Congress tried to limit what legislative facts could be noticed, wouldn't that interfere with the judicial function to such a degree that it would be unconstitutional?

2. Why is judicial notice of legislative facts usually an invisible process? Do judges invite criticism when they reveal their extrarecord sources? Consider the following passage in a dissenting opinion by Judge Frank in an appeal from an injunction prohibiting defendants, who made and sold girdles, from using the trade name Miss Seventeen Foundations Co. because of the likelihood of confusion with *Seventeen* magazine, which was published by the plaintiff:

> Like the trial judge's, our surmise [as to confusion between the names] must here rest on "judicial notice." As neither the trial judge nor any member of this court is (or resembles) a teen-age girl or the mother or sister of such a girl, our judicial notice apparatus will not work well unless we feed it with information directly obtained from "teen-agers" or from their female relatives accustomed to shop for them. Competently to inform ourselves, we should have a staff of investigators like those supplied to administrative agencies. As we have no such

> staff, I have questioned some adolescent girls and their mothers and sisters, persons I have chosen at random. I have been told uniformly by my questionees that no one could reasonably believe that any relation existed between plaintiff's magazine and defendant's girdles.

Triangle Publications v. Rohrlich, 167 F.2d 969, 976 (2d Cir. 1948).

3. For other examples of judicial notice of legislative facts, see Population Services International v. Wilson, 398 F. Supp. 321, 332-333 (S.D.N.Y. 1975) (challenging New York statute prohibiting distribution of contraceptives to anyone under 16; "it is not beyond the power of this Court to note that some young persons under the age of sixteen do engage in sexual intercourse and the consequence of such activity is often venereal disease, unwanted pregnancy, or both"), *aff'd*, Carey v. Population Services International, 431 U.S. 678 (1977). See also Record Museum v. Lawrence Township, 481 F. Supp. 768, 771 (D.N.J. 1979) (challenge to drug paraphernalia ordinance; court takes judicial notice of "the phenomenon known as the Counterculture of the Seventies wherein untraditional attire such as spoons and hand-crafted pipes adorn both home and person").

F JUDICIAL NOTICE OF LAW

As noted earlier, the term "judicial notice of law" is sometimes used to describe the process by which the court determines applicable law, relieving the parties of proving the point. Long ago, if judicial notice of law was not taken, the law had to be pleaded and, at least in the case of foreign law, proved to the jury as though it were a question of fact. Often an expert would testify to the nature of the law or its proper interpretation. With respect to issues of foreign law, this testimony would be weighed by the jury along with the other evidence. Under the modern view, if judicial notice of the law is not taken, the proof is presented to the court, and the determination of controlling law is made by the judge, not the jury. Once this determination is made, whether by judicial notice or proof to the court, the jury is instructed at the end of trial to apply the law in deciding the case.

Judicial notice of law is not addressed in FRE 201. The ACN to Rule 201 says that "the manner in which law is fed into the judicial process is never a proper concern of the rules of evidence, but rather of the rules of procedure." Federal procedural rules, however, regulate this process only when it comes to proving the law of foreign nations. See FRCP 44.1 and FRCrimP 26.1.

Common law tradition requires federal judges to take judicial notice of all domestic statutory and case law, state as well as federal:

> The states of the Union are not foreign to the United States or to its courts. Such courts are required to take judicial notice of the statute and case law of each of the states. "The law of any State of the Union, whether depending upon statutes

> or *upon judicial opinions*, is a matter of which the courts of the United States are bound to take judicial notice, *without plea or proof*."

Schultz v. Tecumseh Products, 310 F.2d 426, 433 (6th Cir. 1962) (emphasis in original). A few federal statutes regulate judicial notice of law. See 44 USC §§1507, 1510 (authorizing notice of Code of Federal Regulations and content of Federal Register).

NOTES ON JUDICIAL NOTICE OF LAW

1. Many states have provisions in their evidence codes regulating judicial notice of law. See, e.g., Hawaii Rule of Evidence 202:

> (a) *Scope of rule.* This rule governs only judicial notice of law.
>
> (b) *Mandatory judicial notice of law.* The court shall take judicial notice of (1) the common law, (2) the constitutions and statutes of the United States and of every state, territory, and other jurisdiction of the United States, (3) all rules adopted by the U.S. Supreme Court or by the Hawaii Supreme Court, and (4) all duly enacted ordinances of cities or counties of this State.
>
> (c) *Optional judicial notice of law.* Upon reasonable notice to adverse parties, a party may request that the court take, and the court may take, judicial notice of (1) all duly adopted federal and state rules of court, (2) all duly published regulations of federal and state agencies, (3) all duly enacted ordinances of municipalities or other governmental subdivisions of other states, (4) any matter of law which would fall within the scope of this subsection . . . but for the fact that it has been replaced, superseded, or otherwise rendered no longer in force, and (5) the laws of foreign countries, international law, and maritime law.
>
> (d) *Determination by court.* All determinations of law made pursuant to this rule shall be made by the court and not by the jury, and the court may consider any relevant material or source, including testimony, whether or not submitted by a party or admissible under these rules.

2. Other states regulate judicial notice of law by statute outside their evidence code. Many of these statutes are based on the Uniform Interstate and International Procedure Act, which extends judicial notice to the law of any foreign jurisdiction. It provides:

> *§4.01 [Notice]* A party who intends to raise an issue concerning the law of any jurisdiction or governmental unit thereof outside this state shall give notice in his pleadings or other reasonable written notice.
>
> *§4.02 [Materials to Be Considered]* In determining the law of any jurisdiction, or governmental unit thereof outside this state, the court may consider any relevant material or source, including testimony whether or not submitted by a party or admissible under the rules of evidence.

> *§4.03 [Court Decision and Review]* The court, not jury, shall determine the law of any governmental unit outside this state. Its determination is subject to review on appeal as a ruling on a question of law.
>
> *§4.04 [Other Provisions of Law Unaffected]* This Article does not repeal or modify any other law of this state permitting another procedure for the determination of foreign law.

13 U.L.A. 459 (1980).

3. Courts seem more reluctant to extend judicial notice of law to municipal ordinances, probably because they are not always well catalogued or readily accessible. See Howard v. United States, 306 F.2d 392, 394 (10th Cir. 1962) (refusing to take judicial notice of Albuquerque vagrancy ordinance); Bryant v. Liberty Mutual Insurance Co., 407 F.2d 576, 579 n.2 (4th Cir. 1969) (collecting cases).

4. The limitations on the scope of judicial notice of law resulted from the historical unavailability or scarcity of legal materials and uncertainties regarding their accuracy. In this era of electronic publishing and computerized legal research, are these concerns any longer valid? Consider the following observation:

> As all law has become increasingly accessible and judges have tended to assume the duty to rule on the tenor of all law, the notion that this process is part of judicial notice has become increasingly an anachronism. Evidence, after all, involves the proof of facts. How the law is fed into the judicial machine is more appropriately an aspect of the law pertaining to procedure.

McCormick on Evidence §335, at 507 (J. Strong ed., 5th ed. 1999).

G THE PROBLEM OF CLASSIFICATION

Because so many different doctrines use the term "judicial notice," it is important to distinguish them. Proper classification is necessary to determine whether FRE 201 applies and what precedential value an appellate case taking judicial notice may have.

UNITED STATES v. GOULD

United States Court of Appeals for the Eighth Circuit
536 F.2d 216 (1976)

Defendants, Charles Gould and Joseph Carey, were convicted of conspiring to import (Count I) and actually importing (Count II) cocaine from Colombia, South America, into the United States in violation of the Controlled Substances Import and Export Act.

The evidence persuasively showed that defendants and David Miller enlisted the cooperation of Miller's sister, Barbara Kenworthy, who agreed to travel to Colombia with defendants and smuggle the cocaine into the United States by placing it inside two pairs of hollowed-out platform shoes. In May of 1975, defendants and Ms. Kenworthy traveled to Colombia where the cocaine was purchased and packed in Ms. Kenworthy's shoes. The success of the importation scheme was foiled when, upon Ms. Kenworthy's arrival to the Miami airport from Colombia, a customs agent insisted upon x-raying the cocaine-laden shoes. Approximately two pounds of cocaine were discovered and seized by customs officials . . . .

At trial, two expert witnesses for the Government testified as to the composition of the powdered substance removed from Ms. Kenworthy's platform shoes at the Miami airport. One expert testified that the substance was comprised of approximately 60 percent cocaine hydrochloride. The other witness stated that the white powder consisted of 53 percent cocaine. There was no direct evidence to indicate that cocaine hydrochloride is a derivative of coca leaves. In its instructions to the jury, the District Court stated:

> If you find the substance was cocaine hydrochloride, you are instructed that cocaine hydrochloride is a schedule II controlled substance under the laws of the United States.

[Defendants claim the prosecutor should have been required to prove that the substance seized was on the schedule of controlled substances. The schedule listed "coca leaves" and any "derivative thereof" but did not specifically mention cocaine hydrochloride.]

Our inquiry on this first assignment of error is twofold. We must first determine whether it was error for the District Court to take judicial notice of the fact that cocaine hydrochloride is a schedule II controlled substance. Secondly, if we conclude that it was permissible to judicially notice this fact, we must then determine whether the District Court erred in instructing the jury that it must accept this fact as conclusive.

The first aspect of this inquiry merits little discussion . . . . The fact that cocaine hydrochloride is derived from coca leaves is, if not common knowledge, at least a matter which is capable of certain, easily accessible and indisputably accurate verification. See Webster's Third New International Dictionary 434 (1961). Therefore, it was proper for the District Court to judicially notice this fact. Our conclusion on this matter is amply supported by the weight of judicial authority . . . .

Our second inquiry involves the propriety of the District Court's instruction to the jurors that this judicially noticed fact must be accepted as conclusive by them. Defendants, relying upon FRE 201(f), urge that the jury should have been instructed that it could discretionarily accept or reject this fact. Rule 201(f) provides:

> In a civil action or proceeding, the court shall instruct the jury to accept as conclusive any fact judicially noticed. In a criminal case, the court shall instruct the jury that it may, but is not required to, accept as conclusive any fact judicially noticed.

It is clear that the reach of rule 201 extends only to adjudicative, not legislative, facts. FRE 201(a). Consequently, the viability of defendants' argument is dependent upon our characterization of the fact judicially noticed by the District Court as adjudicative, thus invoking the provisions of rule 201(f). In undertaking this analysis, we note at the outset that rule 201 is not all-encompassing. "Rule 201 . . . was deliberately drafted to cover only a small fraction of material usually subsumed under the concept of 'judicial notice.'" 1 J. Weinstein, Evidence ¶201[01] (1975).

The precise line of demarcation between adjudicative facts and legislative facts is not always easily identified. Adjudicative facts have been described as follows:

> When a court . . . finds facts concerning the immediate parties—who did what, where, when, how, and with what motive or intent—the court . . . is performing an adjudicative function, and the facts are conveniently called adjudicative facts . . . .
>
> Stated in other terms, the adjudicative facts are those to which the law is applied in the process of adjudication. They are the facts that normally go to the jury in a jury case. They relate to the parties, their activities, their properties, their businesses.

2 K. Davis, Administrative Law Treatise §15.03, at 353 (1958).

Legislative facts, on the other hand, do not relate specifically to the activities or characteristics of the litigants. A court generally relies upon legislative facts when it purports to develop a particular law or policy and thus considers material wholly unrelated to the activities of the parties.

> Legislative facts are ordinarily general and do not concern the immediate parties. In the great mass of cases decided by courts . . . the legislative element is either absent or unimportant or interstitial, because in most cases the applicable law and policy have been previously established. But whenever a tribunal engages in the creation of law or of policy, it may need to resort to legislative facts, whether or not those facts have been developed on the record.

2 K. Davis, Administrative Law Treatise, supra, at §15.03. Legislative facts are established truths, facts or pronouncements that do not change from case to case but apply universally, while adjudicative facts are those developed in a particular case.

Applying these general definitions, we think it is clear that the District Court in the present case was judicially noticing a legislative fact rather than an adjudicative fact. Whether cocaine hydrochloride is or is not a derivative of the coca leaf is a question of scientific fact applicable to the administration of the Comprehensive Drug Abuse Prevention and Control Act of 1970. The District Court reviewed the schedule II classifications contained in 21 U.S.C. §812, construed the language in a manner which comports with common knowledge and understanding, and instructed the jury as to the proper law so interpreted. It is undisputed that the trial judge is required to fully and accurately instruct the jury as to the law to be applied in a case. When a court attempts to ascertain the governing law in a case for the purpose of instructing the jury, it must necessarily rely upon facts which are unrelated to the activities of the immediate parties. These extraneous, yet necessary, facts fit within the definition of legislative facts and are an indispensable tool used by judges when discerning the applicable law through interpretation....

It is clear to us that the District Court took judicial notice of a legislative, rather than an adjudicative, fact in the present case and rule 201(f) is inapplicable. The District Court was not obligated to inform the jury that it could disregard the judicially noted fact. In fact, to do so would be preposterous, thus permitting juries to make conflicting findings on what constitutes controlled substances under federal law.

■ PROBLEM 11-I. Obscene Books

Roost, an adult bookstore owner, is charged with possession of obscene material. At trial, the books in question are admitted. The court concludes as a matter of law that they are obscene within the meaning of the statute and so instructs the jury. The jury is left with only the question of whether the defendant possessed the books. Has the court erred? Is this case distinguishable from *Gould*?

■ NOTES ON THE PROBLEM OF CLASSIFICATION

1. Courts have some leeway to find a matter to be a legal issue for the court rather than a factual issue for the jury. If it is a legal matter for the court, then any fact noticed in making the ruling is legislative rather than adjudicative and is outside the scope of FRE 201. Isn't that the approach taken by the court in *Gould*? But the Sixth Amendment right to a jury trial limits what issues can be taken from the jury and shifted to the court. In Problem 11-I, deciding whether books were obscene is likely to be an issue for the jury.

2. Professor Davis said that it is important to recognize that many facts are not "readily classifiable as either adjudicative or legislative," likening the difficulties in this area to those of distinguishing between questions of "law" and "fact," concluding that some facts may be both "adjudicative" and "legislative" just as there are "mixed" questions of "law" and "fact." 2 K. Davis, Administrative Law Treatise §15.03, at 528 (2010 Supp.). Still, FRE 201 requires us to make the classification, in order to decide whether the requirements of FRE 201 apply or not.

3. Does FRE 201 regulate judicial notice usefully? One commentator points out that "there have been thousands of cases in which courts have taken judicial notice of some fact" since the Rules were adopted, but only "a few dozen" indicate that the fact is legislative or adjudicative. He concludes that FRE 201 "has not been well-received by the judges who actually have to work with it." Turner, Judicial Notice and Federal Rule of Evidence 201—A Rule Ready for Change, 45 U. Pitt. L. Rev. 181, 185 (1983).

4. The problem of classification is of practical importance to attorneys trying to deal with precedents. The reports are laden with decisions taking "judicial notice" of multifarious facts, but a decision taking judicial notice of a matter as a legislative fact is not authority for noticing the same matter as an adjudicative fact. Consider this comment by the Oregon Supreme Court:

> In determining the appropriateness of a court's action in taking judicial notice, it must constantly be borne in mind that judicial notice may be employed for a wide variety of purposes. A failure to distinguish between the purposes for which courts take judicial notice of fact creates the danger that someone will assume that once an appellate court has at one time or another taken judicial notice of a fact for one purpose it is a proper subject for notice for a completely different purpose.

Chartrand v. Coos Bay Tavern, 696 P.2d 513, 517 (Or. 1985).

■ PROBLEM 11-J. "Drunk as a Skunk"

Prizi, a pedestrian, is seriously injured after being struck by a pickup truck driven by Davenport. The accident occurred one block from the Red Dog Saloon, where Davenport had spent the afternoon drinking. Davenport is described by one patron as "drunk as a skunk" at the time of his departure. Prizi sues the Red Dog Saloon for negligence in serving liquor to an intoxicated person whom the saloon should have foreseen was likely to drive off in a car. Prizi's action rests on a recent decision of the state supreme court recognizing a tort cause of action against tavern owners on behalf of third parties injured by patrons driving away in cars while intoxicated ("dramshop liability"). In deciding to create the new cause of action, the supreme court took "judicial notice that traveling by motor vehicle to and from a tavern is commonplace." Relying on this language, Prizi asks the trial judge to remove the issue of foreseeability from the jury. Prizi requests judicial notice that the employees of the Red Dog Saloon should have foreseen that Davenport would drive a motor vehicle upon leaving the tavern. What ruling?

■ PROBLEM 11-K. Lighter Fluid Explosion

Goodman sues Inland Chemical (Inland) for injuries suffered when a can of charcoal lighter fluid manufactured by defendant exploded. Goodman had attempted to light the charcoal in his outdoor grill, but when he checked 15 minutes later he did not see any flames or feel much heat. He did notice that some of the briquettes were grayish-white at the corners. He poured more fluid on the charcoal. Immediately, a flame shot up the stream of fluid and the can blew up in his hand. Inland asserts the defense of contributory negligence, which under the applicable law constitutes a complete defense if proven. Inland moves for a summary judgment, on the ground that Goodman was contributorily negligent as a matter of law. Inland asks the court to take judicial notice that once combustion occurs in a bed of charcoal, the addition of flammable fluid is certain to result in instantaneous flare-up of the volatile liquid coming into contact with the charcoal. Should judicial notice be taken? Is this matter adjudicative, evaluative, or legislative?

■ PROBLEM 11-L. Speed Trap

Danielson is clocked by police radar driving 53 mph in a 35 mph speed zone. The jurisdiction requires that before scientific evidence may be received the court must find that there is general acceptance of the technique within the relevant scientific community. The prosecutor asks the court to take judicial notice that radar has achieved general scientific acceptance as a reliable speed-measuring technique. What ruling?

CHAPTER 12

Privileges

A INTRODUCTION

Almost all the evidence rules, apart from those relating to privilege, seek to enhance accurate and efficient factfinding. Privileges are different. Their purpose is to protect certain relationships and values, even if protection imposes significant costs on litigation. Their effect in any given trial may be to impede the search for truth.

A primary goal of most privileges is to encourage communication in favored relationships, such as marriages. To this end, privileges block government interference with those relationships. Some privileges encourage communication within government, limiting access to state secrets or confidential advice given by officials. The scope of privilege law concerns everyone, because it fixes a balance between the interest of society in maintaining privacy or protecting government functions and the right of litigants to obtain evidence needed to advance claims or defenses in court.

There is often confusion between evidentiary privileges and related but distinct ethical or professional obligations of confidentiality. Various professions, including law and medicine, have codes of ethics that impose duties on members to protect the confidentiality of disclosures by clients or patients, regardless whether privilege law covers similar material. Violating ethical duties may lead to professional censure and possible suspension or loss of license. Of course one may also adopt ethical standards of confidentiality as matters of conscience, without professional standards or licensing laws.

As a practical matter, ethical obligations of confidentiality may provide more protection than privileges, which are usually available only in judicial, legislative, or administrative proceedings. Ethical duties impose general proscriptions against disclosure, and extend to matters beyond reach of evidentiary privileges, like communications by client or patient that do not satisfy confidentiality requirements of privilege law. Thus a client's communication to a lawyer in the presence of an outsider may not be privileged, but the lawyer is still ethically obliged not to discuss the matter.

Nonetheless, privilege law is fundamentally important. Without a privilege, a professional person called as a witness may have to disclose confidential communications from a client or patient, regardless of ethical standards and regardless what assurance may have been given to client or patient. Hence practitioners are careful not to commit to confidentiality in court proceedings beyond what privilege law covers, and ethical codes usually allow disclosure if required by law or court order. See, e.g., ABA Model Code of Professional Responsibility, DR 4-101(C)(2); AMA Principles of Medical Ethics IV (2001). A practitioner who wants to maintain confidentiality in areas broader than those protected by privileges puts herself at risk of being held in contempt of court.

Privileges remain the most significant area of evidence law not codified in the Rules. The Advisory Committee drafted (and the Court promulgated) 13 privilege rules. But these proved controversial in Congress, in part because privileges seem substantive in nature, and some thought they exceeded the Court's authority under the Rules Enabling Act. Also concerns arose because the proposed Rules omitted the physician-patient and marital confidences privileges, and included what some saw as an overbroad state secret privilege. There was also concern that the Rules would have displaced state privilege law in diversity cases.

Congress reacted by deleting the privilege rules, and instead adopted FRE 501, under which privileges are matters of federal common law developed and interpreted in light of "reason and experience." And Congress went further, barring the Court from adopting privilege rules on its own. The revised Enabling Act provides that rules "creating, abolishing, or modifying an evidentiary privilege" shall have "no force or effect" unless enacted by Congress. See 28 USC §2074(b). Most states with codes modeled on the Rules have codified their privilege law, and state provisions vary considerably.

■ NOTES ON FRE 501

1. Is deference to state privilege law in diversity cases required by the *Erie* doctrine? See Erie Railroad v. Tompkins, 304 U.S. 64 (1938). Most rules of evidence are considered "procedural," and can be applied in federal court even when state law supplies the rule of decision. But privileges are generally viewed as "substantive." Why?

2. Does FRE 501 undermine state policy choices, given that it does not defer to state privilege law in federal question cases and federal criminal prosecutions? Clearly state privilege law is less effective in protecting communications if it is not also recognized in these settings. See, e.g., United States v. Schenheinz, 548 F.2d 1389 (9th Cir. 1977) (under IRS summons, stenographer must testify and produce records on employer's tax matters even though information was covered by state employer-stenographer privilege).

3. In light of congressional insistence that any amendment to the Rules respecting privileges be approved by statute, should federal courts hesitate to change privilege law by decision? Does it matter how sweeping the change is? Keep this question in mind as you read the decisions in *Trammel* and *Upjohn*, infra.

B ATTORNEY-CLIENT PRIVILEGE

1. Reasons for the Privilege

5 J. BENTHAM, RATIONALE OF JUDICIAL EVIDENCE 301

(John Stuart Mill ed. 1827)

When in consulting with a law adviser, attorney or advocate, a man has confessed his delinquency, or disclosed some fact which, if stated in court, might tend to operate in proof of it, such law adviser is not to be suffered to be examined as to any such point. The law adviser is neither to be compelled, nor so much as suffered, to betray the trust thus reposed in him. Not suffered? Why not? Oh, because to betray a trust is treachery; and an act of treachery is an immoral act....

But if such confidence, when reposed, is permitted to be violated, and if this be known (which, if such be the law, it will be), the consequence will be, that no such confidence will be reposed. Not reposed?—Well: and if it be not, wherein will consist the mischief? The man by the supposition is guilty; if not, by the supposition there is nothing to betray: let the law adviser say every thing he has heard, every thing he can have heard from his client, the client cannot have any thing to fear from it. That it will often happen that in the case supposed no such confidence will be reposed, is natural enough: the first thing the advocate or attorney will say to his client, will be—Remember that, whatever you say to me, I shall be obliged to tell, if asked about it. What, then, will be the consequence? That a guilty person will not in general be able to derive quite so much assistance from his law adviser, in the way of concerting a false defence, as he may do at present.

Except the prevention of such pernicious confidence, of what other possible effect can the rule for the requisition of such evidence be productive? Either of none at all, or of the conviction of delinquents, in some instances in which, but for the lights thus obtained, they would not have been convicted. But in this effect, what imaginable circumstances is there that can render it in any degree pernicious and undesirable? None whatever. The conviction of delinquents is the very end of penal justice.

■ NOTES ON JUSTIFICATIONS FOR THE PRIVILEGE

1. Is Bentham right that the privilege protects only the guilty? Justifications for the privilege can stress instrumental or humanistic values, depending on whether they relate to the effective performance of the attorney's functions or to preserving privacy. Do instrumental justifications answer Bentham's arguments? Humanistic justifications?

2. Although Bentham takes the most extreme position, he does not stand alone as critic of the privilege. See McCormick on Evidence §87 (K. Broun ed., 1996) (privilege may make "marginal alteration" in client behavior, which falls short of adequate justification; privilege may be "integrally related to an entire code of professional conduct" that would have to be modified if privilege were eliminated). Wigmore, who generally supported the privilege, was even more critical. He argued that its benefits are "indirect and speculative," while "its obstruction is plain and concrete," and that the privilege was "an obstacle to the investigation of the truth" that "ought to be strictly confined within the narrowest possible limits consistent with the logic of its principle." See 8 Wigmore on Evidence §2291 (McNaughton rev. 1961). If we could shed the habits of history, would we be better off without the privilege? Should it be narrowly construed?

3. Other commentators have defended the privilege, notably the late David Louisell, who began with a point stressed by Wigmore. The latter had commented that "any honorable man" would be repelled if the confidences that the attorney-client relationship "naturally invite" were open to inspection by adverse parties in litigation, and that such a "double-minded attitude would create an unhealthy moral state" in the lawyer. See 8 Wigmore on Evidence §2291 (McNaughton rev. 1961). Here is Louisell's argument:

> Why would compellability to reveal his clients' secrets "create an unhealthy moral state in the practitioner?" Because, it is submitted, he would know that he was perverting the function of counseling. Perhaps the notion is as well put by Francis Bacon as anyone: "The great Truste, between Man and Man, is the Truste of *Giving Counsell.* For in other Confidences, Men commit the parts of their life; Their lands, their Goods, their Children, their Credit, some particular affaire; But to such, as they make their *Counsellors*, they commit the whole: By how much the more, they are obliged to all Faith and integrity."

Louisell, Confidentiality, Conformity and Confusion: Privileges in Federal Court Today, 31 Tulane L. Rev. 101, 112-113 (1956) (quoting Bacon's Essays, XX, Of Counsel).

4. How much does the privilege obstruct truth? Recall that civil litigants enjoy the benefits of many discovery devices, including depositions (FRCP 30) and interrogatories (FRCP 31). Recall too that discovery under FRCP 26 may probe "any matter, not privileged," that is relevant to any "claim or defense." Suppose a civil plaintiff asks defendant in his deposition, "Isn't it a fact that you ran the red light?" If defendant had told her lawyer the light was red for him, could the lawyer tell her not to answer because of the privilege? If plaintiff asked the question in an interrogatory, could the defendant or her lawyer refuse to answer? (Interrogatories are typically served on counsel, not the client, and counsel normally prepares the answers, even though her responses speak for the client.) The answer in both cases is "no," because the privilege covers *communications,* not *facts reported* in communications. It is different if plaintiff calls the lawyer to testify to what defendant said, or asks defendant "what she told her lawyer."

5. Consider the picture in criminal cases, where the prosecutor cannot require the defendant to testify. Does it appear that the attorney-client privilege is more costly in this setting, in terms of blocking access to proof?

6. In the wake of the September 11th attacks in 2001, the Bureau of Prisons (part of the Justice Department) amended regulations governing federal inmates, to allow the Attorney General to order monitoring of attorney-client communications on "reasonable suspicion" that an inmate may use them "to further or facilitate acts of terrorism." 28 C.F.R. §501.3(d) (2010). Safeguards apply. Unless the feared acts are "imminent," a federal judge must approve. Also the inmate and attorneys receive written notice. And monitoring is conducted by persons uninvolved in the case against the inmate. Are such measures sensible? For critical views, see Lance Cole, Revoking Our Privileges: Federal Law Enforcement's Multi-Front Assault on the Attorney-Client Privilege (and Why It Is Misguided), 48 Vill. L. Rev 469 (2003); Paul R. Rice & Benjamin Parlin Saul, Is the War on Terrorism a War on Attorney-Client Privilege?, 17 Crim. Just. 22 (2002).

Jeremy Bentham, Skeptical Curmudgeon

Jeremy Bentham
(b. 1748; d. 1832)
Library of Congress

Jeremy Bentham was a British philosopher, social reformer, and jurist, who is viewed as the founder of modern utilitarianism. Two of Bentham's most famous works are: (1) *Fragment on Government* (1776), which challenged William Blackstone's *Commentaries on the Laws of England* and criticized its defense of judge-made law; and (2) *Introduction to Principles of Morals and Legislation* (1789), which set forth the "greatest happiness principle" underlying utilitarian philosophy that "it is the greatest happiness of the greatest number that is the measure of right and wrong." However, Bentham also wrote the first multi-volume treatise on the law of evidence entitled *Rationale of Judicial Evidence* (1827). This treatise sharply criticized the common law grounds of witness incompetency discussed at the beginning of Chapter 6 and was highly influential in persuading English courts eventually to modify or abandon them. Bentham also challenged the underlying rationale for an attorney-client privilege, as can be seen in the excerpt quoted above. He also had caustic criticism for the spousal testimonial privilege, saying that it permits a person to convert his house into a "den of thieves" and "secures to every man, one safe and unquestionable and ever ready accomplice for every imaginable crime." 5 Rationale of Judicial Evidence 340 (1827).

■ PROBLEM 12-A. "A Bum Rap"

After a long publicized trial, Dr. McNary is convicted of slaying his wife and two children, who were stabbed in the family home on October 20th. Dr. McNary claims innocence, and the case against him is circumstantial. His attorney Ashbrooke makes an eloquent argument for clemency, but McNary receives the death sentence. The night after the sentence is announced, Ashbrooke receives a call from Barton, an acquaintance who is also a criminal defense lawyer. On the phone, Barton tells Ashbrooke:

> I hesitate to call you, but I'm doing it because your client's facing a bum rap. You should know I'm the court-appointed lawyer for a man named Frank Gallo, who is charged with robbing a liquor store on October 20. Just between us, Gallo may be a little crazy. He's been in trouble before, but we don't need to talk about that. He tells me he didn't rob the liquor store, and I believe him because his alibi is too amazing to be false. He told me that at the very moment when the liquor store was being robbed, he—Gallo—was in fact in the McNary house committing what amounts to burglary and murder. Apparently the husband wasn't home, but the wife and kids were, and Gallo told me he killed them with a knife. Now he could have read the story in the paper and made up the part about him doing it, but I've listened to him and frankly I believe him. He even told me where he buried the knife, but I haven't looked for it. I'm not quite sure what to do with this information myself, but I felt I had to tell you about it.

The next day Ashbrooke seeks a new trial on ground of newly discovered evidence. At the hearing, he calls Gallo and Barton to the stand. Gallo refuses to testify, claiming the privilege against self-incrimination. When Barton is called, Gallo claims the attorney-client privilege. Should the claim be sustained? What constitutional arguments can be made on McNary's behalf for overriding the privilege? What constitutional arguments can be made on Gallo's behalf?

■ NOTES ON THE CONSTITUTIONAL RIGHT TO PRESENT A DEFENSE

1. The Compulsory Process clause of the Sixth Amendment provides that defendant in a criminal case has the right to "compulsory process for obtaining witnesses in his favor." In 2006, the Court acknowledged that there is a constitutional right to present a defense that is rooted in the Compulsory Process and Due Process Clauses. See Holmes v. South Carolina, 547 U.S. 319 (2006) (whether "rooted directly" in the Due Process or Compulsory Process clauses, the Constitution "guarantees criminal defendants 'a meaningful opportunity to present a complete defense'"). This right lends support to the argument that Dr. McNary has the right to call Gallo and Barton and get their testimony about the crime McNary has been charged with. The problem is that this claim of right would force Barton to do something he is ethically obliged *not* to do, which is to testify to what his client told him in professional confidence, and it would threaten the attorney-client privilege that belongs to Gallo, as well as Gallo's own right not to incriminate himself and his right to effective representation in his own trial by Barton.

2. The constitutional right to present a defense does not override all evidence rules that restrict what defendants can do. See United States v. Scheffer, 523 U.S. 303, 308 (1998) (rejecting challenge to rule excluding polygraph evidence; constitutional entitlement to present a defense is abridged only by evidence rules that infringe "a weighty interest of the accused" and are "'arbitrary' or 'disproportionate' to the purposes they are designed to serve"). The attorney-client privilege isn't in the category of "arbitrary" or "disproportionate" rules, is it? Can privilege rules ever be overridden by the right to present a defense? See United States v. Lindstrom, 698 F.2d 1154, 1167 (11th Cir. 1983) (Yes; sometimes privileges must "yield to the paramount right of the defendant to cross-examine effectively the witness in a criminal case"); In re John Doe, 964 F.2d 1325, 1329 (2d Cir. 1992) (confrontation right overrides psychotherapist-patient privilege). See generally Mueller & Kirkpatrick, Evidence §5.5 (5th ed. 2012) (discussing circumstances where constitutional right to present evidence may override privileges).

3. Would the case for overriding the privilege be stronger if Gallo were deceased? In one case, the Court refused to recognize an exception merely because the client had died. There the government sought testimony by the lawyer describing his client's statements, and the Court concluded that the privilege applies. See Swidler & Berlin v. United States, 524 U.S. 399 (1998) (blocking government from obtaining conversation between Vince Foster, who had committed suicide, and his lawyer; privilege must continue after death to encourage client to talk "fully and frankly" with lawyer; even limited exception allowing disclosure for use in criminal trials of others would damage the privilege, as clients "may be concerned about reputation, civil liability, or possible harm to friends or family"). But see Restatement Third, The Law Governing

Lawyers, §77, Comment d (court may withhold privilege of deceased client if communication "bears on a litigated issue of pivotal significance") (balance "interest in confidentiality" against "exceptional need").

4. We have seen other settings where the right to present a defense arises. Recall FRE 412(b)(1)(C), making exception to the rape shield statute for evidence that the accused has a constitutional right to offer (Chapter 5A5, supra). Recall too Rock v. Arkansas, 483 U.S. 44 (1987) (striking down rule barring hypnotically refreshed testimony as applied to defendant on ground that he has constitutional right to testify) (Chapter 6E, supra). See also the decision in *Holmes*, supra note 1 (constitutional error to bar defendant from introducing proof that third party committed charged crime); Chambers v. Mississippi, 410 U.S. 284 (1973) (error to bar defendant from proving that witness confessed to murder for which defendant was charged and from cross-examining about his earlier statements); Washington v. Texas, 388 U.S. 14 (1967) (striking down state statute barring defendant from calling accomplice as witness); Crane v. Kentucky, 476 U.S. 683 (1986) (error to prevent defendant from showing at trial that his confession was unreliable).

2. Professional Services

The privilege applies only to confidential communications made for the purpose of rendering professional legal services to the client. Yet often attorneys are consulted for more than legal advice. They may also be asked questions soliciting business, financial, or personal advice. And often they are asked or expected to perform services on behalf of their clients that do not require formal legal training. How much of what attorneys do on behalf of their clients is protected by the attorney-client privilege?

■ PROBLEM 12-B. The Bail Jumper

Woodburn is out on bail pending trial on an indictment charging him with bank robbery. One of the conditions is that he stay in touch with his attorney Nash and appear at the time set for trial. Woodburn fails to appear, and the government seeks an indictment against Woodburn for bail jumping. The government subpoenas Nash before the grand jury and asks him whether he advised his client of the time and place of trial. Nash declines to answer, asserting the privilege on behalf of Woodburn. The government obtains a court order requiring Nash to answer, but he continues in his refusal and is held in contempt. What ruling in an appeal by Nash from his contempt citation?

NOTES ON PROVIDING PROFESSIONAL SERVICES

1. Does the Nash statement telling Woodburn the time and place of trial constitute legal advice? Isn't he serving as a conduit for information from the court? Is such a communication properly viewed as confidential? Most federal courts hold that no privilege applies. See, e.g., United States v. Posin, 996 F.2d 1229, 1229 (9th Cir. 1993); United States v. Woodruff, 383 F. Supp. 696, 698 (E.D. Pa. 1974) (communications between counsel and defendant about trial date "do not involve the subject matter of defendant's legal problem"; they are "nonlegal in nature" and counsel "is simply performing a notice function"). In states adopting proposed FRE 503 (applying privilege to provision of legal services, not just legal advice), courts sometimes find the issue harder. See State v. Ogle, 682 P.2d 267 (Or. 1984) (denying privilege on ground of policy and precedent over dissent arguing that notification fits language extending privilege to communications made in "rendition of professional legal services") (court splits 4-3).

2. For examples of activities by lawyers that courts have held not to be legal services, see United States v. Lawless, 709 F.2d 485 (7th Cir. 1983) (accounting); United States v. Palmer, 536 F.2d 1278 (9th Cir. 1976) (shipping agent); Canaday v. United States, 354 F.2d 849, 857 (8th Cir. 1966) (scrivener); Diamond v. City of Mobile, 86 F.R.D. 324 (S.D. Ala. 1978) (investigator); J.P. Foley & Co. v. Vanderbilt, 65 F.R.D. 523 (S.D.N.Y. 1974) (business agent, negotiator); Federal Savings & Loan Insurance Corp. v. Fielding, 343 F. Supp. 537, 546 (D. Nev. 1972) (business partner); Jones v. Smith, 56 S.E.2d 462, 465 (Ga. 1949) (attesting witness).

3. Is preparation of tax returns "professional legal services"? Compare United States v. Davis, 636 F.2d 1028, 1043 (5th Cir.) (accountants are not covered by privilege in preparing returns; it makes "little sense" to let taxpayer invoke privilege "merely because he hired an attorney"), *cert. denied*, 454 U.S. 862 (1981) with Colton v. United States, 306 F.2d 633, 637 (2d Cir. 1962) (giving tax advice and preparing returns "are basically matters sufficiently within the professional competence of an attorney" to make them "prima facie" privileged), *cert. denied*, 371 U.S. 951 (1963). Most courts hold that the privilege does not apply to matters intended for inclusion in a return, on the theory that such information was not intended to be kept confidential. Most courts also hold that tax planning advice is privileged, but not preparation of returns. See, e.g., In re Grand Jury Investigation, 842 F.2d 1223, 1225 (11th Cir. 1987) (admittedly preparation of a return "requires some knowledge of the law," and the manner of preparation "can be viewed as an implicit interpretation" of law, but a taxpayer "should not be able to invoke a privilege simply because he hires an attorney to prepare his tax returns").

4. How should we distinguish between business and legal advice? Should the privilege apply if the client seeks a mixture of business and legal advice? Most courts say that the privilege attaches only if the lawyer's work is "primarily legal." See Sedco International, S.A. v. Cory, 683 F.2d 1201 (8th Cir.), *cert. denied*, 459 U.S. 1017 (1982).

3. Communications

The attorney-client privilege is described as a doctrine protecting "communications" from the client. Assume that a person charged with murder tells his lawyer he was "really angry" at the victim. If the two are speaking in private, there is no doubt that the statement is privileged, and the result would be the same if the client wrote such a message in a note or letter to the lawyer.

It is hard to say how much further the privilege reaches. Assume, for example, that the client rolls up his sleeve and displays a scab-covered wound on his forearm that "came from the fight" with the victim. Or suppose he pulls out a knife and says "that's what I used." Both gestures have a communicative aspect, but neither is *solely* communicative. Does the privilege apply to viewing the wound or the knife? And consider whether the privilege applies to a page in the client's diary, written hours after the event, which the client shows to the lawyer later. And think about whether the privilege applies if the lawyer tells the client, "Yes, you better take care of that wound, it looks like someone slashed you with a knife." Is the *lawyer's* statement covered?

■ PROBLEM 12-C. The Tipsy Client

Murphy arrives 35 minutes late for his afternoon appointment with Finch, his attorney, about a probate matter. Finch sees that Murphy has been drinking heavily, for he staggers as he is ushered into Finch's office and his breath smells of alcohol. In a slurred voice, he apologizes for being late, and explains that he had a "few drinks" with some friends and "lost track" of time. During the interview, Murphy is rambling and incoherent, and Finch finally suggests that the appointment be rescheduled.

As Murphy leaves the office, Finch offers to call a taxicab, but Murphy insists on driving. Finch watches with trepidation as Murphy drives away. Two blocks down the street Murphy collides with a parked car. He is not injured and flees the scene on foot. In his later trial for hit-and-run and drunk driving, Murphy is represented by another lawyer. The state calls Finch as a witness. To what may Finch be required to testify, if Murphy claims the privilege?

■ NOTES ON OBSERVATIONS AND ADVICE BY COUNSEL

1. If Finch may be compelled to testify to what he saw when his client came in, does it follow that defense counsel may be compelled to testify about his client's mental capacity? Compare Clanton v. United States, 488 F.2d 1069, 1071 (5th Cir.) (lawyer could testify that client was competent to stand trial; testimony "did not relate to private, confidential, communications"), *cert. denied*,

419 U.S. 877 (1974) with Gunther v. United States, 230 F.2d 222, 223-224 (D.C. Cir. 1956) (lawyer should not testify that client was competent to stand trial; necessarily the lawyer then opens himself to questions on "factual data" underlying opinion, opening up "the entire relationship," violating privilege and right to counsel). See generally Pizzi, Competency to Stand Trial in Federal Courts: Conceptual and Constitutional Problems, 45 U. Chi. L. Rev. 21, 57-64 (1977).

2. May a lawyer be compelled to testify to his client's physical appearance? See United States v. Kendrick, 331 F.2d 110, 113-114 (4th Cir. 1964) ("physical characteristics of the client, such as his complexion, his demeanor, his bearing, his sobriety and his address," are not privileged; such matters "are observable by anyone who talked with the client; there is nothing, in the usual case, to suggest that the client intends his attorney's observations of such matters to be confidential"). What about testifying to a client's lifestyle? See In re Grand Jury Proceedings (Chesnoff), 13 F.3d 1293, 1296 (9th Cir. 1994) (no privilege for observations about client's "expenditures" on European cruise, "income-producing activities," and "lifestyle").

3. How about statements by the lawyer to the client? If they are within the privilege, does the protection cover only legal advice or all statements? Compare Wells v. Rushing, 755 F.2d 376, 379 n.2 (5th Cir. 1985) (what lawyer tells client is privileged only to extent necessary to avoid revealing "confidential information provided by the client" or "advice or opinions of the attorney") with United States v. Ramirez, 608 F.2d 1261, 1268 n.12 (9th Cir. 1979) (lawyer-client communications "in both directions" are covered). See also Upjohn Co. v. United States, 449 U.S. 383, 389 (1981) (purpose is "to encourage full and frank communication" between attorney and client). And consider this description:

> [A]dvice does not spring from lawyers' heads as Athena did from the brow of Zeus. Inevitably, attorneys' opinions reflect an accumulation of education and experience in the law and the larger society law serves. In a given case, advice prompted by the client's disclosures may be further and inseparably informed by other knowledge and encounters. We have therefore stated that the privilege cloaks a communication from attorney to client " 'based, *in part at least*, upon a confidential communication [to the lawyer] from [the client].' "

In re Sealed Case, 737 F.2d 94, 99 (D.C. Cir. 1984).

PEOPLE v. MEREDITH

Supreme Court of California
631 P.2d 46 (Cal. 1981)

TOBRINER, J.

Defendants Frank Earl Scott and Michael Meredith appeal from convictions for the first degree murder and first degree robbery of David Wade. Meredith's conviction rests on eyewitness testimony that he shot and killed Wade. Scott's conviction, however, depends on the theory that Scott conspired with Meredith and a third defendant, Jacqueline Otis, to bring about the killing and robbery. To support the theory of conspiracy the prosecution sought to show the place where the victim's wallet was found, and, in the course of the case this piece of evidence became crucial. The admissibility of that evidence comprises the principal issue on this appeal....

On the night of April 3, 1976, Wade (the victim) and Jacqueline Otis, a friend of the defendants, entered a club known as Rich Jimmy's. Defendant Scott remained outside by a shoeshine stand. A few minutes later codefendant Meredith arrived outside the club. He told Scott he planned to rob Wade, and asked Scott to go into the club, find Jacqueline Otis, and ask her to get Wade to go out to Wade's car parked outside the club.

In the meantime, Wade and Otis had left the club and walked to a liquor store to get some beer. Returning from the store, they left the beer in a bag by Wade's car and reentered the club. Scott then entered the club also and, according to the testimony of Laurie Ann Sam (a friend of Scott's who was already in the club), Scott asked Otis to get Wade to go back out to his car so Meredith could "knock him in the head."

When Wade and Otis did go out to the car, Meredith attacked Wade from behind. After a brief struggle, two shots were fired; Wade fell, and Meredith, witnessed by Scott and Sam, ran from the scene.

Scott went over to the body and, assuming Wade was dead, picked up the bag containing the beer and hid it behind a fence. Scott later returned, retrieved the bag, and took it home where Otis and Meredith joined him.

We now recount the evidence relating to Wade's wallet, basing our account primarily on the testimony of James Schenk, Scott's first appointed attorney. Schenk visited Scott in jail more than a month after the crime occurred and solicited information about the murder, stressing that he had to be fully acquainted with the facts to avoid being "sandbagged" by the prosecution during the trial. In response, Scott gave Schenk the same information that he had related earlier to the police. In addition, however, Scott told Schenk something Scott had not revealed to the police: that he had seen a wallet, as well as the paper bag, on the ground near Wade. Scott said that he picked up the wallet, put it in the paper bag, and placed both behind a parking lot fence. He also said that he later retrieved the bag, took it home, found $100 in the wallet and divided it with Meredith, and then tried to burn the wallet in his kitchen sink. He took the partially burned wallet, Scott told Schenk, placed it in a plastic bag, and threw it in a burn barrel behind his house.

Schenk, without further consulting Scott, retained Investigator Stephen Frick and sent Frick to find the wallet. Frick found it in the location described by Scott and brought it to Schenk. After examining the wallet and determining that it contained credit cards with Wade's name, Schenk turned the wallet and its contents over to Detective Payne, investigating officer in the case. Schenk told Payne only that, to the best of his knowledge, the wallet had belonged to Wade.

The prosecution subpoenaed Attorney Schenk and Investigator Frick to testify at the preliminary hearing. When questioned at that hearing, Schenk said that he received the wallet from Frick but refused to answer further questions on the ground that he learned about the wallet through a privileged communication. Eventually, however, the magistrate threatened Schenk with contempt if he did not respond "yes" or "no" when asked whether his contact with his client led to disclosure of the wallet's location. Schenk then replied "yes," and revealed on further questioning that this contact was the sole source of his information as to the wallet's location.

At the preliminary hearing Frick, the investigator who found the wallet, was then questioned by the district attorney. Over objections by counsel, Frick testified that he found the wallet in a garbage can behind Scott's residence.

Prior to trial, a third attorney, Hamilton Hintz, was appointed for Scott. Hintz unsuccessfully sought an in limine ruling that the wallet of the murder victim was inadmissible and that the attorney-client privilege precluded the admission of testimony concerning the wallet by Schenk or Frick.

At trial Frick, called by the prosecution, identified the wallet and testified that he found it in a garbage can behind Scott's residence . . . .

The jury found both Scott and Meredith guilty of first degree murder and first degree robbery . . . .

Defendant Scott concedes, and we agree, that the wallet itself was admissible in evidence. Scott maintains, however, that Evidence Code section 954 bars the testimony of the investigator concerning the location of the wallet . . . .

Section 954 provides, "[T]he client . . . has a privilege to refuse to disclose, and to prevent another from disclosing, a confidential communication between client and lawyer . . . ."

Scott's statements to Schenk regarding the location of the wallet clearly fulfilled the statutory requirements. Moreover, the privilege did not dissolve when Schenk disclosed the substance of that communication to his investigator, Frick. Under Evidence Code section 912, subdivision (d), a disclosure which is "reasonably necessary" to accomplish the purpose for which the attorney has been consulted does not constitute a waiver of the privilege. If Frick was to perform the investigative services for which Schenk had retained him, it was "reasonably necessary," that Schenk transmit to Frick the information regarding the wallet. Thus, Schenk's disclosure to Frick did not waive the statutory privilege.

The statutes codifying the attorney-client privilege do not, however, indicate whether that privilege protects facts viewed and observed as a direct result of confidential communication . . . .

Judicial decisions have recognized that the implementation of . . . [the policies underlying the attorney-client privilege] may require that the privilege extend not only to the initial communication between client and attorney but also to any information which the attorney or his investigator may subsequently acquire as a direct result of that communication. In a venerable decision involving facts analogous to those in the instant case, the Supreme Court of West Virginia held that the trial court erred in admitting an attorney's testimony as to the location of a pistol which he had discovered as the result of a privileged communication from his client. That the attorney had observed the pistol, the court pointed out, did not nullify the privilege: "All that the said attorney knew about this pistol, or where it was to be found, he knew only from the communications which had been made to him by his client confidentially and professionally, as counsel in this case. And it ought therefore, to have been entirely excluded from the jury. . . . " State of West Virginia v. Douglass (1882) 20 W. Va. 770, 783.

More recent decisions reach similar conclusions. In State v. Olwell, 394 P.2d 681 (Wash. 1964), the court reviewed contempt charges against an attorney who refused to produce a knife he obtained from his client. The court first observed that "[t]o be protected as a privileged communication . . . the securing of the knife . . . must have been *the direct result of information* given to Mr. Olwell by his client." (Emphasis added.) The court concluded that defense counsel, after examining the physical evidence, should deliver it to the prosecution, but should not reveal the source of the evidence; "[b]y thus allowing the prosecution to recover such evidence, the public interest is served, and by refusing the prosecution an opportunity to disclose the source of the evidence, the client's privilege is preserved and a balance reached between these conflicting interests."

Finally, we note the decisions of the New York courts in People v. Belge, 372 N.Y.S.2d 798 (Sup. Ct. 1975), affirmed, 376 N.Y.S.2d 771 (App. Div. 1975). Defendant, charged with one murder, revealed to counsel that he had committed three others. Counsel, following defendant's directions, located one of the bodies. Counsel did not reveal the location of the body until trial, 10 months later, when he exposed the other murders to support an insanity defense.

Counsel was then indicted for violating two sections of the New York Public Health Law for failing to report the existence of the body to proper authorities in order that they could give it a decent burial. The trial court dismissed the indictment; the appellate division affirmed, holding that the attorney-client privilege shielded counsel from prosecution for actions which would otherwise violate the Public Health Law.

The foregoing decisions demonstrate that the attorney-client privilege is not strictly limited to communications, but extends to protect observations made as a consequence of protected communications. We turn therefore to the question whether that privilege encompasses a case in which the defense, by removing or altering evidence, interferes with the prosecution's opportunity to discover that evidence.[7] . . .

---

[7] We agree with the parties' suggestion that an attorney in Schenk's position often may best fulfill conflicting obligations to preserve the confidentiality of client confidences, investigate his case, and act as an officer of the court if he does not remove evidence located as the result of a privileged communication. We must recognize, however, that in some cases an examination of evidence may reveal information critical to the defense of a client accused of crime. If the usefulness of the evidence cannot be gauged without taking possession of it, as, for example, when a ballistics or fingerprint test is required, the attorney may properly take it for a reasonable time before turning it over to the prosecution. Similarly, in the present case the defense counsel could not be certain the burnt wallet belonged in fact to the victim: in taking the wallet to examine it for identification, he violated no ethical duty to his client or to the prosecution.

When defense counsel alters or removes physical evidence, he necessarily deprives the prosecution of the opportunity to observe that evidence in its original condition or location. As the Amicus Appellate Committee of the California District Attorneys Association points out, to bar admission of testimony concerning the original condition and location of the evidence in such a case permits the defense in effect to "destroy" critical information; it is as if, he explains, the wallet in this case bore a tag bearing the words "located in the trash can by Scott's residence," and the defense, by taking the wallet, destroyed this tag. To extend the attorney-client privilege to a case in which the defense removed evidence might encourage defense counsel to race the police to seize critical evidence.

We therefore conclude that courts must craft an exception to the protection extended by the attorney-client privilege in cases in which counsel has removed or altered evidence. Indeed, at oral argument defense counsel acknowledged that such an exception might be necessary in a case in which the police would have inevitably discovered the evidence in its original location if counsel had not removed it. Counsel argued, however, that the attorney-client privilege should protect observations of evidence, despite subsequent defense removal, unless the prosecution could prove that the police probably would have eventually discovered the evidence in the original site.

We have seriously considered counsel's proposal, but have concluded that a test based upon the probability of eventual discovery is unworkably speculative. Evidence turns up not only because the police deliberately search for it, but also because it comes to the attention of policemen or bystanders engaged in other business. In the present case, for example, the wallet might have been found by the trash collector. Moreover, one [sic] physical evidence (the wallet) is turned over to the police, they will obviously stop looking for it; to ask where, how long, and how carefully they would have looked is obviously to compel speculation as to theoretical future conduct of the police.

We therefore conclude that whenever defense counsel removes or alters evidence, the statutory privilege does not bar revelation of the original location or condition of the evidence in question.[8] We thus view the defense decision to remove evidence as a tactical choice. If defense counsel leaves the evidence where he discovers it, his observations derived from privileged communications are insulated from revelation. If, however, counsel chooses to remove

---

[8] In offering the evidence, the prosecution should present the information in a manner which avoids revealing the content of attorney-client communications or the original source of the information. In the present case, for example, the prosecutor simply asked Frick where he found the wallet; he did not identify Frick as a defense investigator or trace the discovery of the wallet to an attorney-client communication. In other circumstances, when it is not possible to elicit such testimony without identifying the witness as the defendant's attorney or investigator, the defendant may be willing to enter a stipulation which will simply inform the jury as to the relevant location or condition of the evidence in question. When such a stipulation is proffered, the prosecution should not be permitted to reject the stipulation in the hope that by requiring defense counsel personally to testify to such facts, the jury might infer that counsel learned those facts from defendant.

evidence to examine or test it, the original location and condition of that evidence loses the protection of the privilege. Applying this analysis to the present case, we hold that the trial court did not err in admitting the investigator's testimony concerning the location of the wallet....

NOTES ON APPLYING THE PRIVILEGE TO OBJECTS

1. Didn't Scott reveal the information about the wallet to his lawyer Schenk only because he reasonably thought that what he was saying was within the privilege? Yet his disclosure led his attorney to retrieve the wallet from his yard and deliver it to the police, and the prosecutor can tell the jury that it came from Scott's yard. Is the decision fair to Scott? What *should* a criminal defense lawyer do when his client tells him about the existence and location of physical evidence?

2. *Meredith* holds that an attorney who removes or alters physical evidence may be required to disclose its original location or condition. Is this rule consistent with the *Olwell* case (discussed in *Meredith*), which held that a defense lawyer who receives physical evidence from a client must deliver it to the prosecutor, but need not reveal the source? Does the *Olwell* doctrine mean that if Scott had brought the wallet to Schenk, instead of Schenk sending an investigator to retrieve it, the jury would never learn of Scott's connection to the wallet? Does *Olwell* give too much protection by enabling the client to sever his connection by turning incriminating evidence over to his lawyer?

3. Consider the compromise suggested by the defense in *Meredith*—that where counsel receives evidence and turns it over, the connecting information given by the accused should remain privileged unless the prosecutor shows that police would "inevitably" have discovered it. A similar doctrine appears in the context of the Sixth Amendment. If police obtain a confession that cannot itself be admitted because of the *Massiah* doctrine (barring *ex parte* questioning by police after proceedings have commenced, unless the accused clearly initiates discussions), evidence discovered as a result is nevertheless admissible if the prosecutor shows that police would "inevitably" have discovered it or found it by means of an "independent source." See Nix v. Williams, 467 U.S. 431 (1984). Should courts take this approach in cases like *Meredith*?

4. What if a lawyer destroys or conceals evidence? See United States v. Kellington, 139 F.3d 909 (9th Cir. 1998) (affirming felony conviction of lawyer for burning envelope at request of client facing extradition hearing; an "honest and unwitting" lawyer would want to know "what he was causing to be destroyed for his fugitive client before putting the torch to it," and burning envelopes with unknown contents "is not taught in American law schools."); In re Ryder, 263 F. Supp. 360 (E.D. Va. 1967) (attorney suspended from practice for 18 months for receiving stolen money and sawed-off shotgun from client and keeping it in his own safe deposit box, knowing that money had been stolen and gun was used in armed robbery). See also ABA Model Rules of Professional Conduct, Rule 3.4

(providing that a lawyer shall not "unlawfully obstruct" access to evidence or "unlawfully alter, destroy or conceal a document or other material having potential evidential value," nor help another person do any such act).

4. Required Confidentiality

It has long been understood that the privilege protects only communications intended by the client to be confidential. This limit confines the privilege within reasonable bounds and expresses the point that a privilege for public statements to others would serve no purpose. It is also clear, however, that disclosure may be made to other selected persons, such as agents of the attorney, without losing the cloak of confidentiality.

What obligation should be imposed on client and attorney to ensure the confidentiality of communications? Certainly the privilege should be denied for a conversation between lawyer and client in a room full of outsiders, conducted so as to be heard by all. But what if an eavesdropper or wiretapper hears what lawyer and client say behind closed doors, or if their correspondence is stolen by outsiders?

a. Involving or Disclosing to Communicative Intermediaries

The privilege covers confidential communications between clients and their lawyers. But lawyers often have the assistance of other persons, like secretaries, receptionists, paralegals, law clerks, legal assistants, interns, investigators, and other office personnel. If such persons are present when a client consults his lawyer, or are used to convey a message between client and lawyer, the communication is still confidential *if* their role was to help the lawyer represent the client. See proposed-but-rejected FRE 503 (extending privilege to "representative of the lawyer," defined as one employed "to assist the lawyer in the rendition of professional legal services").

The attorney privilege can extend to experts retained by the lawyer. A leading case is United States v. Kovel, 296 F.2d 918 (2d Cir. 1961), which held that an accountant hired by a lawyer to assist in representing a client in a complicated tax matter was within the privilege. The court stated:

> [T]he complexities of modern existence prevent attorneys from effectively handling clients' affairs without the help of others; few lawyers could now practice without the assistance of secretaries, file clerks, telephone operators, messengers, clerks not yet admitted to the bar, and aides of other sorts . . . .
>
> We cannot regard the privilege as confined to "menial or ministerial" employees . . . .
>
> Accounting concepts are a foreign language to some lawyers in almost all cases, and to almost all lawyers in some cases. Hence the presence of an accountant, whether hired by the lawyer or by the client, while the client is relating a complicated tax story to the lawyer, ought not destroy the privilege,

> any more than would that of the linguist [who assists in interpreting a foreign language] . . . . [I]f the lawyer has directed the client, either in the specific case or generally, to tell his story in the first instance to an accountant engaged by the lawyer, who is then to interpret it so that the lawyer may better give legal advice, communications by the client reasonably related to that purpose ought fall within the privilege . . . .

296 F.2d at 921-922.

■ NOTES ON COMMUNICATIVE INTERMEDIARIES AND OTHER AIDES

1. If the privilege is to survive in the modern world, the *Kovel* doctrine is necessary, isn't it? Does the doctrine reach a physician retained by a personal injury lawyer to diagnose the client in preparation for litigation? See City & County of San Francisco v. Superior Court, 231 P.2d 26 (Cal. 1951) (attorney-client privilege applies).

2. It is the lawyer, not the client, who determines what intermediaries are needed to help in representation. See United States v. Brown, 478 F.2d 1038, 1040 (7th Cir. 1973) (privilege inapplicable where accountant was present by invitation of client, not lawyer's request).

3. *Kovel* recognized that there is no federal accountant-client privilege, a point that the Supreme Court confirmed much later in United States v. Arthur Young & Co., 465 U.S. 805 (1984). The Internal Revenue Service Restructuring and Reform Act of 1998 (26 USC §7525) creates a privilege for communications to federal tax practitioners (many of whom are accountants), but it applies only in noncriminal federal proceedings.

4. The concern in *Kovel* was to apply the privilege where an expert acts as interpreter or intermediary between client and lawyer. Should it apply where the expert does not transmit or even rely on communications from the client? Consider the report of an appraiser in a condemnation case or an engineer in a product case. Would such reports be privileged under proposed-but-rejected Rule 503? They would likely qualify as work product under FRCP 26(b)(3) (work product includes "documents and tangible things prepared in anticipation of litigation or for trial by or for another party or by or for that other party's representative," which includes "attorney, consultant, surety, indemnitor, insurer, or agent"). Is work product protection enough?

b. Joint Clients and Pooled Defenses

If two or more clients consult the same attorney on matters of common interest, communications between joint clients and attorney are privileged as against outsiders. Thus one of two joint clients can communicate with an attorney in the presence of another without destroying confidentiality.

What if the clients retain separate attorneys but have a common interest in the matter being litigated, as happens when both are charged for their roles in a single crime? Can they pool information or otherwise collaborate (even mount a joint defense) without destroying confidentiality? Most courts say yes. Allowing pooling of information among clients with overlapping interests is thought to encourage better preparation and conserve time and expense. Presumably little is lost by recognizing the privilege because collaborative communications are unlikely to be made in absence of the privilege.

■ PROBLEM 12-D. A Failed Venture

Samuel and Thomas consult with lawyer Ullman on forming a partnership to import computer chips from Asia. The three discuss the venture, to be called Accu-Chip, Limited. Samuel indicates that he has "lots of contacts in Tokyo and Taipei who will supply quality chips," but he acknowledges that "many cheap chips available in those markets don't meet American specifications." Thomas provides most of the start-up money and some expertise on customs law and import fees.

The two sign a partnership and go into business. But Accu-Chip falls on hard times. It has difficulty with the chip quality; the market for chips declines because of technological changes and falling prices. The government brings criminal charges against Samuel and Thomas for alleged conspiracy to violate customs and import tariffs.

1. In a suit against Accu-Chip and the partners (Samuel and Thomas), dissatisfied customer Vanden alleges breach of implied warranty and misrepresentation of the quality of Accu-Chip products. Vanden takes the deposition of Ullman (who represents the defendants) and asks, "What did your clients tell you about the quality of the chips they intended to import?" On behalf of defendants, Ullman invokes the attorney-client privilege and refuses to answer. Vanden moves to compel answers. What result and why?

2. Samuel retains Wilson as counsel and files suit against Thomas for alleged breach of the partnership contract and an accounting for partnership profits. At trial, Samuel takes the witness stand and proposes to testify to what Thomas said in Ullman's office when the partnership was formed. For Thomas, Ullman invokes the attorney-client privilege. What result, and why?

3. In the criminal trial of Samuel and Thomas for alleged conspiracy to evade customs inspections and import fees, Wilson represents Samuel and Ullman represents Thomas. The four meet together to coordinate

strategy. During the meeting, Samuel angrily reminds Thomas that "you were supposed to be the expert on customs and taxes." Thomas replies, "I carried out that end and handled it as well as anybody could." At trial, Samuel proposes to testify to what Thomas said, but Ullman objects, raising the attorney-client privilege. What result, and why?

■ NOTES ON INTENTIONAL DISCLOSURE

1. Courts considering the first situation described in Problem 12-D speak in terms of "joint clients." The assumption is that the clients have the same interest. Here the privilege claim is usually sustained against outsiders. Why does that outcome seem right? Courts considering the third situation speak of "pooled strategy" or "defense," where the assumption is that the clients have overlapping but disparate interests. Here proposed Rule 503(b)(3) would uphold the privilege, and most courts agree. Why does that outcome seem right? The second situation stands between the first and the third. Once the clients had the same interest, but now they have conflicting interests. Here proposed Rule 503(d)(5) would deny the privilege, and most courts agree. Why?

2. If joint clients have no privilege for earlier attorney-client communications after they have a falling out, does the lawyer have an ethical obligation to warn them before providing joint representation? See ABA Model Rules of Professional Conduct, Rule 1.7(b)(2) (in representing multiple clients on a matter, lawyer shall provide "explanations of the implications of the common representation and the advantages and risks").

3. Usually the privilege does not apply to communications uttered in the known presence of an outsider. See United States v. Landof, 591 F.2d 36, 39 (9th Cir. 1978) (no privilege for statements in presence of third person, a lawyer who was not acting as counsel). The same result obtains if the lawyer later discloses the communication to a third party at her client's direction. See United States v. El Paso Co., 682 F.2d 530, 538-541 (5th Cir. 1982) (tax pool analysis disclosed to outside auditors), *cert. denied*, 466 U.S. 944 (1984).

4. Suppose a client communicates facts to his lawyer with the expectation that they will be disclosed to a third party. Should the privilege apply? What if no disclosure is actually made? See United States v. (Under Seal), 748 F.2d 871, 875-876 (4th Cir. 1984) (where client communicates information to attorney with understanding that it will be revealed to others, privilege does not apply, even if "a fortuity" prevents actual publication, but information intended for disclosure may regain protection if client later "decides not to publish his communications and tells his attorney before the release").

c. *Scavengers and Eavesdroppers*

SUBURBAN SEW 'N SWEEP v. SWISS-BERNINA

United States District Court, Northern District of Illinois
91 F.R.D. 254 (N.D. Ill. 1981)

[Sewing machine retailers sue manufacturer Swiss-Bernina and others alleging antitrust violations (price discrimination and conspiracy). In building their case, plaintiffs search a dumpster in the parking lot of an office building occupied by Swiss-Bernina. Over a two-year period, they find hundreds of relevant documents, including handwritten drafts of confidential letters from the President of Swiss-Bernina to a lawyer for the corporation. These had been put in wastebaskets, which were emptied by a company employee into a large trash container, which was in turn emptied into the dumpster. Only Swiss-Bernina used the dumpster. Ultimately it was emptied by a scavenging company hired by Swiss-Bernina.

All agree that the drafts of letters were intended to remain confidential and would be privileged but for the fact that they were retrieved from the dumpster. The privilege issue arose in the setting of a motion to compel answers during discovery, when plaintiffs filed interrogatories seeking transcriptions and other information relating to the letters. The Magistrate refused to compel, apparently because he considered the tactics pursued by the plaintiffs to be improper.

In reviewing what the Magistrate did, the District Court notes that property put in the garbage is "no longer protected by the Fourth Amendment." Even if it was, what plaintiffs did would not be a violation because the Fourth Amendment covers only government agents, and the exclusionary doctrine does not apply in civil cases anyway. The Court also notes a "diversity" in approaches to the question whether failure to maintain secrecy should be viewed in terms of waiver or voluntary disclosure, both of which result in loss of the attorney-client privilege.]

LEIGHTON, J. . . .

The traditional rule . . . placed near absolute responsibility for maintaining confidentiality on the parties to the communication. The underlying principle is well summarized by Wigmore:

> The law provides subjective freedom for the client by assuring him of exemption from its processes of disclosure against himself or the attorney or their agents of communication. This much, but no more, is necessary for the maintenance of the privilege. Since the means of preserving secrecy of communication are largely in the client's hands and since the privilege is a derogation

> from the general testimonial duty and should be strictly construed, it would be improper to extend its prohibition to third persons who obtain knowledge of the communications.

8 Wigmore on Evidence §2326 (McNaughton Rev. 1961); see Id. §2325.

Under this rule, the privilege does not extend to prevent third parties who are not agents of the parties to the communication from testifying, with the result that a purloined letter, a stolen document, or a surreptitiously overheard conversation are not privileged. McCormick, Evidence §75 (2nd Ed. 1972). However, as McCormick points out:

> Perhaps these incidental hazards may have been thought so remote as not to be likely to discourage disclosure; simple eavesdropping could be guarded against by taking simple precautions. With the advent of more sophisticated techniques for invading privacy in general and intercepting confidential communications in particular, the picture changed and a very different concept of the eavesdropper emerged. As a consequence . . . statutes and rules defining privileges began to include provisions entitling the holder to prevent anyone from disclosing a privileged confidential communication.

Id. One such provision is Rule 503 of the Proposed Federal Rules of Evidence which were prescribed and approved by the Supreme Court . . . .

The advisory committee notes specifically reject the former rule, adhered to by Wigmore. Commentators, noting that "(w)hile it may perhaps have been tolerable in Wigmore's day to penalize a client for failing to achieve secrecy, such a position is outmoded in an era of sophisticated eavesdropping devices against which no easily available protection exists," have endorsed the Supreme Court view, and rejected the older rule. 2 Weinstein's Evidence ¶503(b)[2] (1980) . . . .

Nevertheless, "allowing the client to invoke the privilege to prevent testimony by eavesdroppers does not . . . in any way reduce the client's need to take all possible precautions to insure confidentiality." 2 Weinstein's Evidence ¶503(b)[2]. Nor does the new rule alter the well established principle that the privilege is to be strictly confined. The case before the court must be distinguished from the involuntary disclosure cases because the documents were not taken from some place where defendants had put them for safekeeping, diligently trying to safeguard their confidentiality, but rather were taken from defendants' garbage. This case lies between the inadvertent disclosure cases, where the information is transmitted in public or otherwise clearly not adequately safeguarded, and the involuntary disclosure cases, where the information is acquired by third parties in spite of all possible precautions.

Thus . . . the relevant consideration is the intent of the defendants to maintain the confidentiality of the documents as manifested in the precautions they took. In determining whether the precautions taken were adequate, two considerations are paramount: (1) the effect on uninhibited consultation between attorney and client of not allowing the privilege in these circumstances;

and (2) the ability of the parties to the communication to protect against the disclosures.

Though this case presents a very close question, the court concludes that consideration of these factors requires that the privilege not be applied to these documents. The likelihood that third parties will have the interest, ingenuity, perseverance and stamina, as well as risk possible criminal and civil sanctions, to search through mounds of garbage in hopes of finding privileged communications, and that they will then be successful, is not sufficiently great to deter open attorney-client communication. Furthermore, if the client or attorney fear such disclosure, it may be prevented by destroying the documents or rendering them unintelligible before placing them in a trash dumpster.[6] While requiring this degree of precaution may seem extreme, if the parties feel that the likelihood of disclosure is sufficiently great, the precautions may be justified, and it is within their power to decide what precautions to take, and so to protect against disclosure. Accordingly, that part of the Magistrate's order pertaining to the documents allegedly protected by the attorney-client privilege must also be reversed.

NOTES ON SCAVENGERS AND EAVESDROPPERS

1. Do you agree that the client in *Sew 'N Sweep* didn't take adequate precautions? If police can search trashcans for evidence without a warrant, does it follow that the privilege should be lost if private parties recover discarded documents? Had you better buy a shredder when you enter practice? What about people listening at the door, or picking up a phone extension? See proposed-but-rejected Rule 503(b) (client can refuse to disclose and "prevent any other person from disclosing" confidential communications).

2. The confidentiality requirement imposes an obligation on parties who want to claim the privilege to ensure privacy both when the communication occurs and thereafter. Is it the client's obligation, or does the attorney have a similar duty? Should the nature of the duty be more precisely defined, or should we let courts gauge intention by looking at the precautions taken? See proposed-but-rejected FRE 503(a)(4) ("confidential" means "not *intended* to be disclosed to third persons.") (emphasis added). As you will see in section B7b, infra, intentional disclosure to outsiders normally waives the privilege.

3. In each of the following situations, consider the question whether confidentiality, hence protection of the privilege, should be lost:

(a) A letter from a client is stolen from her lawyer's office. Should it matter whether the door is locked? What if the thief is the night janitor?

(b) A letter from a client is left on her lawyer's desk, where it is seen and read by another client during an interview.

[6] It was revealed at oral argument that defendants now have a paper shredder.

(c) A letter from the attorney is mistakenly addressed to and read by the wrong client, or is sent to the client at the wrong address, and read by the occupant.

(d) A fax from attorney to client is mistakenly sent to opposing counsel. The fax cover sheet contains instructions for recipients that material is privileged and should not be read by unintended recipients.

Compare Sampson Fire Sales, Inc. v. Oaks, 201 F.R.D. 351, 361-362 (M.D. Pa. 2001) (privilege not waived for inadvertently sent fax; recipient lawyer ordered to return fax) with In re Sealed Case, 877 F.2d 976, 980 (D.C. Cir. 1989) (refusing to "grant greater protection to those who assert the privilege than their own precautions warrant") (parties must "treat the confidentiality of attorney-client communications like jewels—if not crown jewels"). And see generally Mitchel L. Winick et al., Playing "I Spy" with Client Confidences: Confidentiality, Privilege and Electronic Communications, 31 Tex. Tech L. Rev. 1225 (2000).

4. What about conversations that are overheard? See United States v. Lentz, 419 F. Supp. 2d 820 (E.D. Va. 2005) (no privilege for phone call to attorney from jail because client was warned that jailhouse phone calls are monitored); United States v. Gann, 732 F.2d 714, 723 (9th Cir. 1984) (no privilege where defendant made statements to attorney on phone within earshot of law enforcement agents; defendant was "surrounded by officers searching his residence").

5. The Corporate Client

Before enactment of the Rules, it could be said that the privilege extended to corporations, but it was not clear how many people in the organization were within the charmed circle—how many could communicate with counsel in ways that would be protected by a corporate claim of privilege.

In the drafting process, the framers of the Rules seized on the control group test, which limited the privilege to corporate employees who were in a position to control action that the corporation might take on advice of the attorney. They proposed a rule covering communications to lawyers by a "representative of the client," to include only "one having authority to obtain legal services" and to act "on behalf of the client" on the basis of "advice rendered" by the lawyer. See Revised Draft of March, 1971, Rule 503, 51 F.R.D. 315, 361 (1971).

Before the Rules were enacted, however, another approach appeared. This one came to be known as the "subject matter" test:

> [A]n employee of a corporation, though not a member of its control group, is sufficiently identified with the corporation so that his communication to the corporation's attorney is privileged where the employee makes the communication at the direction of his superiors in the corporation and where the subject matter upon which the attorney's advice is sought by the corporation and dealt with in the communication is the performance by the employee of the duties of his employment.

Harper & Row Publishers v. Decker, 423 F.2d 487 (7th Cir.), *aff'd*, 400 U.S. 348 (1970). The Supreme Court affirmed the decision in *Harper & Row*, but was divided 4-4.

In this environment, the Advisory Committee thought the matter was "too hot to handle." See Hearings on Proposed Rules of Evidence Before the Special Subcommittee on Reform of Federal Criminal Laws of the House Committee on the Judiciary, 93d Cong., 1st Sess., Ser. 2, at 524 (1973) (testimony by Professor Cleary). The Committee withdrew its endorsement of the control group test, and Congress rejected all the privilege rules and left this question (and all privilege issues) to courts to resolve. The matter came again to the Supreme Court in *Upjohn.*

UPJOHN CO. v. UNITED STATES

United States Supreme Court
449 U.S. 383 (1981)

Justice REHNQUIST delivered the opinion of the Court.

We granted certiorari in this case to address important questions concerning the scope of the attorney-client privilege in the corporate context and the applicability of the work-product doctrine in proceedings to enforce tax summonses. With respect to the privilege question the parties and various *amici* have described our task as one of choosing between two "tests" which have gained adherents in the courts of appeals. We are acutely aware, however, that we sit to decide concrete cases and not abstract propositions of law. We decline to lay down a broad rule or series of rules to govern all conceivable future questions in this area, even were we able to do so. We can and do, however, conclude that the attorney-client privilege protects the communications involved in this case from compelled disclosure and that the work-product doctrine does apply in tax summons enforcement proceedings.

I

Petitioner Upjohn Co. manufactures and sells pharmaceuticals here and abroad. In January 1976 independent accountants conducting an audit of one of Upjohn's foreign subsidiaries discovered that the subsidiary made payments to or for the benefit of foreign government officials in order to secure government business. The accountants so informed Mr. Gerard Thomas, Upjohn's Vice-President, Secretary, and General Counsel. Thomas is a member of the Michigan and New York bars, and has been petitioner's General Counsel for 20 years. He consulted with outside counsel and R.T. Parfet, Jr., Upjohn's Chairman of the Board. It was decided that the company would conduct an internal investigation of what were termed "questionable payments." As part of this investigation the attorneys prepared a letter containing a questionnaire which was sent to "All Foreign General and Area Managers" over the Chairman's signature. The letter began by noting recent disclosures that several American companies made "possibly illegal" payments to foreign government officials and emphasized that the management needed full information concerning any such payments made by Upjohn. The letter indicated that the Chairman had asked Thomas, identified as "the company's General Counsel," "to conduct an investigation for the purpose of determining the nature and magnitude of any payments made by the Upjohn Company or any of its subsidiaries to any employee or official of a foreign government." The questionnaire sought detailed information concerning such payments. Managers were instructed to treat the investigation as "highly confidential" and not to discuss it with anyone other than Upjohn employees who might be helpful in providing the requested information. Responses were to be sent directly to Thomas. Thomas and outside counsel also interviewed the recipients of the questionnaire and some 33 other Upjohn officers or employees as part of the investigation.

On March 26, 1976, the company voluntarily submitted a preliminary report to the Securities and Exchange Commission on Form 8-K disclosing certain questionable payments. A copy of the report was simultaneously submitted to the Internal Revenue Service, which immediately began an investigation to determine the tax consequences of the payments. Special agents conducting the investigation were given lists by Upjohn of all those interviewed and all who had responded to the questionnaire. On November 23, 1976, the Service issued a summons pursuant to 26 U.S.C. §7602 demanding production of:

> All files relative to the investigation conducted under the supervision of Gerard Thomas to identify payments to employees of foreign governments and any political contributions made by the Upjohn Company or any of its affiliates since January 1, 1971 and to determine whether any funds of the Upjohn Company had been improperly accounted for on the corporate books during the same period.
>
> The records should include but not be limited to written questionnaires sent to managers of the Upjohn Company's foreign affiliates, and memoranda or notes of the interviews conducted in the United States and abroad with officers and employees of the Upjohn Company and its subsidiaries.

The company declined to produce the documents specified in the second paragraph on the grounds that they were protected from disclosure by the attorney-client privilege and constituted the work product of attorneys prepared in anticipation of litigation. On August 31, 1977, the United States filed a petition seeking enforcement of the summons . . . . That court adopted the recommendation of a Magistrate who concluded that the summons should be enforced. Petitioner appealed to the Court of Appeals for the Sixth Circuit which rejected the Magistrate's finding of a waiver of the attorney-client privilege, but agreed that the privilege did not apply "[t]o the extent that the communications were made by officers and agents not responsible for directing Upjohn's actions in response to legal advice . . . for the simple reason that the communications were not the 'client's.'" The court reasoned that accepting petitioner's claim for a broader application of the privilege would encourage upper-echelon management to ignore unpleasant facts and create too broad a "zone of silence." Noting that Upjohn's counsel had interviewed officials such as the Chairman and President, the Court of Appeals remanded to the District Court so that a determination of who was within the "control group" could be made. In a concluding footnote the court stated that the work-product doctrine "is not applicable to administrative summonses issued under 26 U.S.C. §7602."

II

FRE 501 provides that "the privilege of a witness . . . shall be governed by the principles of the common law as they may be interpreted by the courts of the United States in light of reason and experience." The attorney-client privilege is the oldest of the privileges for confidential communications known to the common law. Its purpose is to encourage full and frank communication between attorneys and their clients and thereby promote broader public interests in the observance of law and administration of justice. The privilege recognizes that sound legal advice or advocacy serves public ends and that such advice or advocacy depends upon the lawyer being fully informed by the client. . . . This rationale for the privilege has long been recognized by the Court. . . . Admittedly complications in the application of the privilege arise when the client is a corporation, which in theory is an artificial creature of the law, and not an individual; but this Court has assumed that the privilege applies when the client is a corporation, and the Government does not contest the general proposition.

The Court of Appeals, however, considered the application of the privilege in the corporate context to present a "different problem," since the client was an inanimate entity and "only the senior management, guiding and integrating the several operations, . . . can be said to possess an identity analogous to the corporation as a whole." The first case to articulate the so-called "control group test" adopted by the court below, Philadelphia v. Westinghouse Electric Corp., 210 F. Supp. 483, 485 (E.D. Pa.), reflected a similar conceptual approach:

> Keeping in mind that the question is, Is it the corporation which is seeking the lawyer's advice when the asserted privilege communication is made?, the most satisfactory solution, I think, is that if the employee making the communication, of whatever the rank he may be, is in a position to control or even to take a substantial part in a decision about any action which the corporation may take upon the advice of the attorney, . . . then, in effect, *he is (or personifies) the corporation* when he makes his disclosure to the lawyer and the privilege would apply. (Emphasis supplied.)

Such a view, we think, overlooks the fact that the privilege exists to protect not only the giving of professional advice to those who can act on it but also the giving of information to the lawyer to enable him to give sound and informed advice. The first step in the resolution of any legal problem is ascertaining the factual background and sifting through the facts with an eye to the legally relevant. [The Court quotes the Code of Professional Responsibility to the effect that a lawyer should be "fully informed of all the facts."]

In the case of the individual client the provider of information and the person who acts on the lawyer's advice are one and the same. In the corporate context, however, it will frequently be employees beyond the control group as defined by the court below—"officers and agents . . . responsible for directing [the company's] actions in response to legal advice"—who will possess the information needed by the corporation's lawyers. Middle-level—and indeed lower-level—employees can, by actions within the scope of their employment, embroil the corporation in serious legal difficulties, and it is only natural that these employees would have the relevant information needed by corporate counsel if he is adequately to advise the client with respect to such actual or potential difficulties. . . .

The control group test adopted by the court below thus frustrates the very purpose of the privilege by discouraging the communication of relevant information by employees of the client to attorneys seeking to render legal advice to the client corporation. The attorney's advice will also frequently be more significant to noncontrol group members than to those who officially sanction the advice, and the control group test makes it more difficult to convey full and frank legal advice to the employees who will put into effect the client corporation's policy.

The narrow scope given the attorney-client privilege by the court below not only makes it difficult for corporate attorneys to formulate sound advice when their client is faced with a specific legal problem but also threatens to limit the valuable efforts of corporate counsel to ensure their client's compliance with the law. In light of the vast and complicated array of regulatory legislation confronting the modern corporation, corporations, unlike most individuals, "constantly go to lawyers to find out how to obey the law," Burnham, The Attorney-Client Privilege in the Corporate Arena, 24 Bus. Law 901, 913 (1969), particularly since compliance with the law in this area is hardly an instinctive matter.[2] The test adopted by the court below is difficult to apply in practice, though no abstractly formulated and unvarying "test" will necessarily enable courts to decide questions such as this with mathematical precision. But if the purpose of the attorney-client privilege is to be served, the attorney and client must be able to predict with some degree of certainty whether particular

[2] The Government argues that the risk of civil or criminal liability suffices to ensure that corporations will seek legal advice in the absence of the protection of the privilege. This response ignores the fact that the depth and quality of any investigations to ensure compliance with the law would suffer, even were they undertaken. The response also proves too much, since it applies to all communications covered by the privilege: an individual trying to comply with the law or faced with a legal problem also has strong incentive to disclose information to his lawyer, yet the common law has recognized the value of the privilege in further facilitating communications.

discussions will be protected. An uncertain privilege, or one which purports to be certain but results in widely varying applications by the courts, is little better than no privilege at all. The very terms of the test adopted by the court below suggest the unpredictability of its application. The test restricts the availability of the privilege to those officers who play a "substantial role" in deciding and directing a corporation's legal response. Disparate decisions in cases applying this test illustrate its unpredictability. Compare, e.g., Hogan v. Zletz, 43 F.R.D. 308, 315-316 (N.D. Okla. 1967), aff'd in part sub nom. Natta v. Hogan, 392 F.2d 686 (CA10 1968) (control group includes managers and assistant managers of patent division and research and development department) with Congoleum Industries, Inc. v. GAF Corp., 49 F.R.D. 82, 83-85 (E.D. Pa. 1969), aff'd, 478 F.2d 1398 (CA3 1973) (control group includes only division and corporate vice presidents, and not two directors of research and vice president for production and research).

The communications at issue were made by Upjohn employees to counsel for Upjohn acting as such, at the direction of corporate superiors in order to secure legal advice from counsel . . . . Information, not available from upper-echelon management, was needed to supply a basis for legal advice concerning compliance with securities and tax laws, foreign laws, currency regulations, duties to shareholders, and potential litigation in each of these areas. The communications concerned matters within the scope of the employees' corporate duties, and the employees themselves were sufficiently aware that they were being questioned in order that the corporation could obtain legal advice. The questionnaire identified Thomas as "the company's General Counsel" and referred in its opening sentence to the possible illegality of payments such as the ones on which information was sought. A statement of policy accompanying the questionnaire clearly indicated the legal implications of the investigation. . . . This statement was issued to Upjohn employees worldwide, so that even those interviewees not receiving a questionnaire were aware of the legal implications of the interviews. Pursuant to explicit instructions from the Chairman of the Board, the communications were considered "highly confidential" when made, and have been kept confidential by the company. Consistent with the underlying purposes of the attorney-client privilege, these communications must be protected against compelled disclosure.

The Court of Appeals declined to extend the attorney-client privilege beyond the limits of the control group test for fear that doing so would entail severe burdens on discovery and create a broad "zone of silence" over corporate affairs. Application of the attorney-client privilege to communications such as those involved here, however, puts the adversary in no worse position than if the communications had never taken place. The privilege only protects disclosure of communications; it does not protect disclosure of the underlying facts by those who communicated with the attorney . . . . Here the Government was free to question the employees who communicated with Thomas and outside counsel. Upjohn has provided the IRS with a list of such employees, and the IRS has already interviewed some 25 of them. While it would probably be more convenient for the Government to secure the results of petitioner's internal investigation by simply subpoenaing the questionnaires and notes taken by petitioner's attorneys, such considerations of convenience do not overcome the policies served by the attorney-client privilege. As Justice Jackson noted in his concurring opinion in Hickman v. Taylor, 329 U.S. at 516: "Discovery was hardly intended to enable a learned profession to perform its functions . . . on wits borrowed from the adversary."

Needless to say, we decide only the case before us, and do not undertake to draft a set of rules which should govern challenges to investigatory subpoenas. Any such approach would violate the spirit of FRE 501 . . . . While such a "case-by-case" basis may to some slight extent undermine desirable certainty in the boundaries of the attorney-client privilege, it obeys the spirit of the Rules. At the same time we conclude that the narrow "control group test" sanctioned by the Court of Appeals in this case cannot, consistent with "the principles of the common law as . . . interpreted . . . in light of reason and experience," FRE 501, govern the development of the law in this area.

III

Our decision that the communications by Upjohn employees to counsel are covered by the attorney-client privilege disposes of the case so far as the responses to the questionnaires and any notes reflecting responses to interview questions are concerned. The summons reaches further, however, and Thomas has testified that his notes and memoranda of interviews go beyond recording responses to his questions. To the extent that the material subject to the summons is not protected by the attorney-client privilege as disclosing communications between an employee and counsel, we must reach the ruling by the Court of Appeals that the work-product doctrine does not apply to summonses issued under 26 U.S.C. §7602.

The Government concedes, wisely, that the Court of Appeals erred and that the work-product doctrine does apply to IRS summonses. This doctrine was announced by the Court over 30 years ago in Hickman v. Taylor, 329 U.S. 495 (1947). In the case the Court rejected "an attempt, without purported necessity or justification, to secure written statements, private memoranda and personal recollections prepared or formed by an adverse party's counsel in the course of his legal duties." The Court noted that "it is essential that a lawyer work with a certain degree of privacy" and reasoned that if discovery of the material sought were permitted

> much of what is now put down in writing would remain unwritten. An attorney's thoughts, heretofore inviolate, would not be his own. Inefficiency, unfairness and sharp practices would inevitably develop in the giving of legal advice and in the preparation of cases for trial. The effect on the legal profession would be demoralizing. And the interests of the clients and the cause of justice would be poorly served.

The "strong public policy" underlying the work-product doctrine was reaffirmed recently in United States v. Nobles, 422 U.S. 225, 236-240 (1975), and has been substantially incorporated in Federal Rule of Civil Procedure 26(b)(3).

... Rule 26(b)(3) codifies the work product doctrine, and the Federal Rules of Civil Procedure are made applicable to summons enforcement proceedings by Rule 81(a)(3). While conceding the applicability of the work-product doctrine, the Government asserts that it has made a sufficient showing of necessity to overcome its protections. The Magistrate apparently so found. The Government relies on the following language in *Hickman:*

> We do not mean to say that all written materials obtained or prepared by an adversary's counsel with an eye toward litigation are necessarily free from discovery in all cases. Where relevant and nonprivileged facts remain hidden in an attorney's file and where production of those facts is essential to the preparation of one's case, discovery may properly be had . . . . And production might be justified where the witnesses are no longer available or can be reached only with difficulty.

The Government stresses that interviewees are scattered across the globe and that Upjohn has forbidden its employees to answer questions it considers irrelevant. The above-quoted language from *Hickman*, however, did not apply to "oral statements made by witnesses . . . whether presently in the form of [the attorney's] mental impressions or memoranda." As to such material the Court did "not believe that any showing of necessity can be made under the circumstances of this case so as to justify production . . . . If there should be a rare situation justifying production of these matters, petitioner's case is not of that type." Forcing an attorney to disclose notes and memoranda of witnesses' oral statements is particularly disfavored because it tends to reveal the attorney's mental processes ("what he saw fit to write down regarding witnesses' remarks") ("the statement would be his [the attorney's] language, permeated with his inferences") (Jackson, J., concurring) . . . .

... [S]ome courts have concluded that *no* showing of necessity can overcome protection of work product which is based on oral statements from witnesses. See, e.g., In re Grand Jury Proceedings, 473 F.2d 840, 848 (8th Cir. 1973) (personal recollections, notes, and memoranda pertaining to conversation with witnesses); In re Grand Jury Investigation, 412 F. Supp. 943, 949 (E.D. Pa. 1976) (notes of conversation with witness "are so much a product of the lawyer's thinking and so little probative of the witness's actual words that they are absolutely protected from disclosure"). Those courts declining to adopt an absolute rule have nonetheless recognized that such material is entitled to special protection. See, e.g., In re Grand Jury Investigation, 599 F.2d 1224, 1231 (CA3 1979) ("special considerations . . . must shape any ruling on the discoverability of interview memoranda . . . ; such documents will be discoverable only in a 'rare situation' "); cf. In re Grand Jury Subpoena, 599 F.2d 504, 511-512 (CA2 1979).

We do not decide the issue at this time. It is clear that the Magistrate applied the wrong standard when he concluded that the Government had made a sufficient showing of necessity to overcome the protections of the work-product doctrine. The Magistrate applied the "substantial need" and "without undue hardship" standard articulated in the first part of Rule 26(b)(3). The notes and memoranda sought by the Government here, however, are work product based on oral statements. If they reveal communications, they are, in this case, protected by the attorney-client privilege. To the extent they do not reveal communications, they reveal the attorney's mental process in evaluating the communications. As rule 26 and *Hickman* make clear, such work product cannot be disclosed simply on a showing of substantial need and inability to obtain the equivalent without undue hardship.

While we are not prepared at this juncture to say that such material is always protected by the work-product rule, we think a far stronger showing of necessity and unavailability by other means than was made by the Government or applied by the Magistrate in this case would be necessary to compel disclosure. Since the Court of Appeals thought that the work-product protection was never applicable in an enforcement proceeding such as this, and since the Magistrate whose recommendations the District Court adopted applied too lenient a standard of protection, we think the best procedure with respect to this aspect of the case would be to reverse the judgment of the Court of Appeals for the Sixth Circuit and remand the case to it for such further proceedings in connection with the work-product claim as are consistent with this opinion.

Accordingly, the judgment of the Court of Appeals is reversed, and the case remanded for further proceedings.

■ NOTES ON CORPORATE ATTORNEY-CLIENT PRIVILEGE

1. *Upjohn* adopts something close to the "subject matter" test that had produced a stalemate when the Court reviewed *Harper & Row*. The *Upjohn* opinion lists several factors supporting its conclusion that the privilege applies. It notes that (1) the communications were made by employees to corporate counsel for the purpose of enabling counsel to provide legal advice to the corporation; (2) they were made at the direction of corporate superiors; (3) the communications concerned matters within the scope of the employee's corporate duties; and (4) the communications were treated as confidential when made and were kept confidential. Is the second factor essential? Aren't the first and fourth simply restatements of general requirements of the privilege?

2. If there is a need for a corporate privilege, why limit it? Why not apply the privilege to a confidential statement to the corporation's lawyer by *any* employee?

3. Do lower-echelon employees need the privilege that *Upjohn* endorses, or are they likely to be motivated to disclose for other reasons? Can't employees be ordered to talk with the lawyer? See generally Saltzburg, Corporate and Related Attorney-Client Privilege Claims: A Suggested Approach, 12 Hofstra L. Rev. 279 (1984) (employees do not own and cannot invoke corporate privilege, so extending it to them is unnecessary).

4. Without extending the privilege to employees as *Upjohn* does, would counsel and corporate management be willing to investigate the facts? Isn't the motivation of management and the legal team important too? See Richard A. Bierschbach & Alex Stein, Overenforcement, 93 Geo. L.J. 1743 (2005) (*Upjohn* lets corporations police themselves without risking criminal liability).

5. If the interests of the corporation are potentially adverse to those of the employee, the corporate attorney has an ethical obligation to warn the employee that she does not represent the employee, that he may obtain separate counsel, and that the corporation holds the privilege with respect to any communications. See ABA Model Rules of Professional Conduct, Rule 4.3. Would such warnings undermine the attorney's ability to obtain information from employees? But see Diversified Industries v. Meredith, 572 F.2d 596, 611 n.5 (8th Cir. 1977) (communications to corporate counsel "may reveal potential liability of the employee," so employee himself may have privilege where he seeks legal advice from corporate counsel "for himself " or where counsel acts as "joint attorney").

6. When corporate management changes, who then has the power to decide whether to claim the corporate attorney-client privilege with respect to statements made by displaced officers? New management, says the Supreme Court:

> [W]hen control of a corporation passes to new management, the authority to assert and waive the corporation's attorney-client privilege passes as well. New managers installed as a result of a takeover, merger, loss of confidence by shareholders, or simply normal succession, may waive the attorney-client privilege with respect to communications made by former officers and directors. Displaced managers may not assert the privilege over the wishes of current managers, even as to statements that the former might have made to counsel concerning matters within the scope of their corporate duties.

Commodity Futures Trading Commission v. Weintraub, 470 U.S. 1026 (1985). This language does not mean that new management has the power to waive whatever claim the prior manager might have to a personal attorney-client privilege, does it?

7. Consider a claim of privilege in the context of a stockholders' derivative suit, where minority stockholders sue managers to recover damages *for the corporation.* Can managers claim the corporate privilege to block discovery by plaintiff stockholders of corporate communications? See Garner v. Wolfinbarger, 430 F.2d 1093 (5th Cir. 1970), *cert. denied*, 401 U.S. 974 (1971) (recognizing qualified privilege that may be overcome for good cause); Saltzburg, Corporate-Attorney-Client Privilege in Shareholder Litigation and Similar Cases: *Garner* Revisited, 12 Hofstra L. Rev. 817 (1984).

8. Should the scope of the privilege for governmental entities be similar to that for corporations? See Deuterium Corp. v. United States, 19 Cl. Ct. 697, 699 (1990) (applying reasoning of *Upjohn* to government employees "at all levels"). But in this setting the privilege is sometimes qualified. See In re Lindsey, 148 F.3d 1100 (D.C. Cir. 1998) (governmental attorney-client privilege may not shield information about possible criminal misconduct by public officials from disclosure to grand jury).

COMMENT/PERSPECTIVE: Attorney-Client Privilege and Work Product Protection

As *Upjohn* shows, attorney-client privilege and work product protection overlap. Basic points may help untangle things: First, the privilege belongs to the client, but work product protection belongs to the lawyer. Second, the privilege covers communications between client and lawyer, but work product covers efforts by the lawyer in preparation for litigation, including the lawyer's theories and thoughts, and also the statements that the lawyer gets from witnesses. Third, the purpose of the privilege is to encourage the client to be candid, but the purpose of work product protection is to encourage the lawyer to work hard in representing his client. Fourth, there are exceptions to the privilege, but it is more-or-less absolute when it applies, while work product protection (even when it applies) can be overcome by a showing of substantial need. Both privilege and work product protection apply in *Upjohn.* The managers' responses to the questionnaire were statements by the corporate client to its lawyer Thomas, according to *Upjohn,* so the privilege applies. Thomas sought the statements about the time the company told the SEC and IRS about "questionable payments," so litigation was anticipated and work product protection applies. And the subpoena sought "all files," including "memoranda and notes," thus going after what Thomas was thinking. The procedure course usually includes the decision in Hickman v. Taylor, 329 U.S. 495 (1947), cited in *Upjohn. Hickman* made it clear that work product covers statements by witnesses to lawyers, but not facts, so work product does not excuse the party (usually acting through the lawyer) to reply to "searching interrogatories." Hence the lawyer need not turn over statements, but the information they contain must be reflected in discovery responses by the client, at least to the extent such information is accepted as correct.

6. Exceptions to Coverage

The attorney-client privilege gives way in several circumstances. Suits between client and lawyer present an obvious example: If the client sues for malpractice, she cannot invoke the privilege to keep her lawyer from proving whatever was said on either side that might be relevant in defending the suit; similarly, if the lawyer sues for his fee, the client cannot invoke the privilege to block relevant proof of what was said on each side during the period of service.

A second example involves the lawyer who acts as attesting witness on a document executed by his client. The privilege survives the death of the client, but a lawyer who attests his client's will is usually permitted to testify to the execution of the document in probate proceedings, the theory being that the client would want such disclosure.

Two other exceptions are much harder in practice. One holds that certain basic facts about the attorney-client relationship are not privileged, even though the attorney may know such facts only through his confidential association with the client: Thus, it is usually said that the identity of the client and the fee arrangement with the lawyer are not privileged, and sometimes the same is said of the address or whereabouts of the client. Finally, all courts seem to agree that the privilege does not apply to communications in furtherance of a crime or fraud. But as you are about to see, sometimes identity *is* privileged (courts speak of "an exception," which means that the exception excluding identity from protection has its own exception in which identity is protected after all). And the crime or fraud exception is sometimes particularly difficult to apply.

a. Client Identity

IN RE OSTERHOUDT

United States Court of Appeals for the Ninth Circuit
722 F.2d 591 (1983)

PER CURIAM:

[Seeking information about legal fees that Luxana Phaksuan paid his attorney William Osterhoudt, the government issued a subpoena to him. Phaksuan moved the district court to quash the subpoena. The motion was denied and Phaksuan appealed.]

The government stipulated that only the amount, form, and date of payment of legal fees need be disclosed. Appellant recognizes that generally "[t]he identity of an attorney's clients and the nature of his fee arrangements with his clients are not confidential communications protected by the attorney-client privilege." He argues, however, that the subpoena fell within an exception to this general rule barring disclosure where "a strong probability exists that disclosure of such information would implicate that client in the very criminal activity for which legal advice was sought."

Appellant contends the exception applies in this case because he hired the attorney to represent him in a grand jury investigation of possible income tax and controlled substance violations, and the government represented in an affidavit filed with the court below that (1) the grand jury inquiry was based upon information that appellant was a "major distributor of several multi-ton loads of marijuana" in 1976, 1980 and 1981 from which he had made "substantial sums of money"; (2) that "a complete financial investigation" of appellant was relevant to the grand jury's inquiry; and (3) that the information regarding the date and amount of legal fees paid by appellant was necessary to complete that investigation.

Appellant's argument rests on the premise that the requisites of the privilege are met whenever evidence regarding the fees paid the attorney would implicate the client in a criminal offense regarding which the client sought the attorney's legal advice. That is not the law.

The purpose of the attorney-client privilege is to protect every person's right to confide in counsel free from apprehension of disclosure of confidential communications. Fee arrangements usually fall outside the scope of the privilege simply because such information ordinarily reveals no confidential professional communication between attorney and client, and not because such information may not be incriminating.

In Chirac v. Reinicker, 24 U.S. (11 Wheat.) 280 (1826), an attorney objected to the question whether he was employed as counsel to conduct an ejectment suit for the benefit of Reinicker, as landlord of the premises. The Court held:

> The fact [of representation] is preliminary, in its own nature, and establishes only the existence of the relation of client and counsel, and therefore, might not necessarily involve the disclosure of any *communication* arising from that relation, after it was created.

Id. at 295 (emphasis added). The same rationale applies to the fee arrangement. Information regarding the fee arrangement ordinarily is not part of the subject matter of the professional consultation and therefore is not privileged communication even though it may evidence wrongdoing by the client.

Cases recognizing the exception to the general rule that the client's identity and the amount of the fee paid the attorney are not within the privilege rely upon Baird v. Koerner, 279 F.2d 623 (9th Cir. 1960). Appellant's confusion as to the meaning of the exception is based upon a misstatement of the *Baird* rule in subsequent opinions. See, e.g., United States v. Hodge & Zweig, 548 F.2d at 1353.

In *Baird* the client had engaged the lawyer for advice in tax matters and, on the attorney's recommendation, had anonymously tendered to the United States Treasury through the attorney sums due for unpaid taxes. The government sought disclosure of the client's name. This court held the general rule that the identity of the client was not protected by the attorney-client privilege was inapplicable. The exception to the general rule stated in *Baird* was that the identification of the client was not within the privilege when the identification "conveys information which ordinarily would be conceded to be part of the usual *privileged communication* between attorney and client." *Id.* at 632 (emphasis added). As an illustration of this principle (and one on all fours with the facts of *Baird*), the court quoted the following passage from 97 C.J.S. Witnesses, §283e, at 803:

> The name of the client will be considered privileged matter where the circumstances of the case are such that the name of the client is material only for the purpose of showing an *acknowledgment* of guilt on the part of such client of the very offense on account of which the attorney was employed....

279 F.2d at 633 (emphasis added).

Hodge & Zweig and other subsequent cases have mistakenly formulated the exception not in terms of the principle itself, but rather in terms of this example of circumstances in which the principle is likely to apply. The principle of *Baird* was not that the privilege applied because the identity of the client was incriminating, but because in the circumstances of the case disclosure of the identity of the client was in substance a disclosure of the confidential communication in the professional relationship between the client and the attorney.

Another source of the confusion may be that applying the label "general rule" to the doctrine that client identity and fee arrangement must be disclosed has distracted attention from the fact that the governing principle is that only professional communications are privileged. The case upon which *Baird* relied, Ex parte McDonough, 170 Cal. 230, 149 P. 566 (1915), did not speak in terms of the "general rule" and its "exception" but rather whether the facts disclosed the presence of the requisites of the privilege: a confidential communication:

> [T]he identity of the attorney's client . . . will seldom be a matter that can be held, under the law, to have been *communicated in confidence.* The mere fact of retaining an attorney to act as such is not ordinarily a matter occurring in the course of the confidential relation of attorney and client, but is something that precedes the establishment of that relation.

Id. at 235 (emphasis added).

Colton v. United States, 306 F.2d 633, 637 (2d Cir. 1962), properly cites *Baird* for its true principle:

> [T]he authorities are clear that the privilege extends essentially only to the substance of matters communicated to an attorney in professional confidence. Thus the identity of a client, or the fact that a given individual has become a client are matters which an attorney normally may not refuse to disclose, even though the fact of having retained counsel may be used as evidence against the client.... To be sure, there may be circumstances under which the identification

of a client may amount to the prejudicial disclosure of a confidential communication, as where the substance of a disclosure has already been revealed but not its source.

Nothing in the circumstances of this case suggests that disclosure of the amounts and dates of payments of fees by appellant to his attorney would in any way convey the substance of confidential professional communications between appellant and his attorney. Accordingly, in this case this information is not protected by the attorney-client privilege.

Appellant also argues that enforcement of the subpoena "would violate fundamental rights guaranteed by the Fifth and Sixth Amendments to the Constitution." He contends that compelling an attorney to provide evidence against his client is destructive of the trust and confidence essential to the relationship and may create a conflict of interest requiring the attorney to sever the relationship, thus denying the client counsel of his choice.

We need not consider whether in some circumstances a suspect's right to counsel may be impaired by requiring the attorney to produce evidence or a hearing may be required to protect against such impairment. We are satisfied that appellant's relationship with his counsel was not threatened and no hearing was required on the record made in this case.

The government stipulated that counsel need produce only the date, amount, and form of payment. . . . The information required was so distinct from any confidential communication between appellant and his counsel and so clearly unprotected by the attorney-client privilege that no reasonably informed client could have supposed that it would be protected from disclosure. . . .

Affirmed.

■ NOTES ON PRIVILEGE FOR CLIENT'S IDENTITY

1. The government knows Luxana Phaksuan was the client of William Osterhoudt. The government wants details on the fees Osterhoudt collected from his client, which apparently bore on tax matters or drug crimes. *Osterhoudt* recognizes that ordinarily the client's identity and fee arrangements (and fact of representation) are not privileged. Why should such matters be excepted from coverage? If the answer is that normally the client does not expect to keep the fact of consultation confidential (or fee arrangements or identity), what should we do when he *does* want to keep such facts under wraps?

2. *Osterhoudt* cites the earlier pathbreaking decision in *Baird*, which recognized an exception allowing such matters to be privileged after all. As *Osterhoudt* says, the pivotal point in *Baird* was the client's identity. The government had received an anonymous payment of taxes, and wanted to know where it came from. It could trace the money to Baird's lawyer, and the question was whether the lawyer had to reveal his client's name. The Ninth Circuit concluded on these facts that identity *was* privileged. *Baird* was understood variously as meaning that the privilege applied to the identity of the client if disclosing it would (a) reveal the legal advice that the lawyer had given, or (b) constitute the last link in a chain of incriminating evidence, or (c) reveal confidential statements or communications by the client himself. See In re Grand Jury Investigation 83-2-35 (Durant), 723 F.2d 447 (9th Cir. 1983) (suggesting these interpretations).

3. *Osterhoudt* says *Baird* has been misinterpreted and should only apply if disclosure would reveal things the client told his lawyer in confidence—things at the heart of the privilege. In *Baird*, presumably forcing the lawyer to name his client would reveal that he told his lawyer he thought he had unpaid taxes. In *Osterhoudt*, won't forcing the lawyer to name Luxana Phaksuan as his client necessarily reveal the fact that he sought advice about tax or drug matters, which is what piqued the interest of the government? Or is it sufficient, as a basis to distinguish *Baird*, that in *Osterhoudt* disclosing the fee arrangement will not reveal what Phaksuan told Osterhoudt? Other decisions give similar construction to the *Baird* doctrine. See Tornay v. United States, 840 F.2d 1424, 1428 (9th Cir. 1988) ("careful reading" of later decisions shows that *Baird* applies only where, in exceptional circumstances, disclosing client's identity "would reveal information that is tantamount to a confidential professional communication").

4. Consider three situations where an attorney claims the privilege when asked to identify her client:

(a) Lawyer returns stolen property for an unnamed client. See Hughes v. Meade, 453 S.W.2d 538, 542 (Ky. App. 1970) (privilege inapplicable to identity of client who hired attorney to return stolen typewriter; not professional legal service).

(b) Lawyer reports illegal misdeeds or misconduct by third person on behalf of anonymous client. See In re Kozlov, 398 A.2d 882 (N.J. 1979) (privilege applies); In re Kaplan, 168 N.E.2d 660 (N.Y. 1960) (privilege applies).

(c) Lawyer represents a person charged with a crime but is hired and paid by an anonymous third party. Compare In re Grand Jury Subpoena for Attorney Representing Criminal Defendant Reyes-Requena, 913 F.2d 1118, 1123 (5th Cir. 1990) (privilege denied; no contention that fee payer was current or former client) with Ralls v. United States, 52 F.3d 223, 226 (9th Cir. 1995) (fee payer was previous client in matter; identity and fee arrangements were "intertwined" with confidential communications made to obtain legal advice for fee payer himself).

Are there good reasons to permit nondisclosure in these cases? Is the lawyer providing "legal services" in these situations?

5. While driving his car home late at night, Dale runs over and kills a pedestrian named Baltes. Dale panics and speeds away from the scene. Media reports indicate that police are looking for the driver. They have a description of Dale's car but not the license number or enough detail to identify him. Dale feels remorse and retains Arnold as his attorney. He asks Arnold to negotiate a plea bargain but not to reveal his identity if negotiations fail. The prosecutor refuses to negotiate without knowing who Arnold represents. The Baltes family learns from the district attorney that Arnold represents the hit-and-run driver. The family files a wrongful death suit against "John Doe" and seeks a court order compelling Arnold to reveal his client's identity. Arnold claims the identity is privileged. How should the court rule? See Note, Public Assault on the Attorney-Client Privilege: Ramifications of Baltes v. Does, 3 Geo. J. Legal Ethics 351 (1989) (approving Florida trial court ruling that privilege applies in situation described here); D'Alessio v. Gilbert, 617 N.Y.S.2d 484 (1994) (upholding privilege on similar facts).

6. Some courts have declined to apply the privilege to other basic facts about the relationship. See Matter of Walsh, 623 F.2d 489 (7th Cir.), *cert. denied*, 449 U.S. 994 (1980) (times and places when attorney met with client, and bills sent and fees paid); In re Grand Jury Witness (Waxman), 695 F.2d 359, 361-362 (9th Cir. 1982) (amounts and form of attorney fees received); Condon v. Petacque, 90 F.R.D. 53 (N.D. Ill. 1981) (dates when attorney consulted); United States v. Blackman, 72 F.3d 1418, 1424-1426 (9th Cir. 1995) (requiring disclosure of identity of client who paid in cash fees exceeding $10,000, under government reporting requirement).

7. Should the address or location of the client be disclosable where it relates directly to the legal advice he sought? Consider Matter of Grand Jury Subpoenas Served upon Field, 408 F. Supp. 1169 (S.D.N.Y. 1976) (address privileged, where client sought advice on relocating); In re Stolar, 397 F. Supp. 520 (S.D.N.Y. 1975) (address and phone number privileged; client sought advice on right to refuse to be interviewed by FBI).

b. Future Crime or Fraud

The exception to the privilege for future crimes or frauds is challenging. It is hard to prove that a communication furthered a crime or fraud when the opposing party does not have access to what was said. The *Zolin* case takes up this matter.

UNITED STATES v. ZOLIN

United States Supreme Court
491 U.S. 554 (1989)

Justice Blackmun delivered the opinion of the Court.

[The IRS investigated L. Ron Hubbard, founder of the Church of Scientology, on tax matters. Seeking documents and tapes that were filed under seal in state court in Los Angeles in unrelated litigation involving the Church, the IRS brought the present suit against Frank Zolin, as clerk of the California court, to obtain the material. Meanwhile Hubbard died, and his widow Mary Sue Hubbard and the Church intervened, claiming the documents were privileged.

The IRS claimed the crime-fraud exception applied, and submitted declarations by Agent Petersell, who described the content of the tapes based on information received during interviews, and submitted partial transcripts obtained from a confidential source. The court rejected the IRS request to listen to the tapes, and held that the material was privileged. It concluded that the crime-fraud exception did not apply because there was "no clear indication" that any future crime or fraud was planned. The Ninth Circuit affirmed.]

A variety of questions may arise when a party raises the crime-fraud exception. The parties to this case have not been in complete agreement as to which of these questions are presented here. In an effort to clarify the matter, we observe, first, that we need not decide the quantum of proof necessary ultimately to establish the applicability of the crime-fraud exception.[7] Rather, we are concerned here with the type of evidence that may be used to make that ultimate showing. Within that general area of inquiry, the initial question in this case is whether a district court, at the request of the party opposing the privilege, may review the allegedly privileged communications *in camera* to determine whether the crime-fraud exception applies. If such *in camera* review is permitted, the second question we must consider is whether some threshold evidentiary showing is needed before the district court may undertake the requested review....

(1)

At first blush, two provisions of the Rules of Evidence would appear to be relevant. Rule 104(a) provides: "Preliminary questions concerning the qualification of a person to be a witness, the existence of a privilege, or the admissibility of evidence shall be determined by the court.... In making its determination it is not bound by the rules of evidence except those with respect to privileges." Rule 1101(c) provides: "The rule with respect to privileges applies at all stages of all actions, cases, and proceedings." Taken together, these Rules might be read to establish that in a summons-enforcement proceeding, attorney-client communications cannot be considered by the district court in making its crime-fraud ruling: to do otherwise, under this view, would be to make the crime-fraud determination without due regard to the existence of the privilege.

---

[7] We note, however, that this Court's use in Clark v. United States, 289 U.S. 1, 14 (1933), of the phrase "prima facie case" to describe the showing needed to defeat the privilege has caused some confusion. See Gardner, The Crime or Fraud Exception to the Attorney-Client Privilege, 47 A.B.A. J. 708, 710-711 (1961); Note, 51 Brooklyn L. Rev. 913, 918-919 (1985) ("The *prima facie* standard is commonly used by courts in civil litigation to *shift* the burden of proof from one party to the other. In the context of the fraud exception, however, the standard is used to dispel the privilege altogether *without* affording the client an opportunity to rebut the *prima facie* showing" (emphasis in original)). In using the phrase in *Clark*, the Court was aware of scholarly controversy concerning the role of the judge in the decision of such preliminary questions of fact. The quantum of proof needed to establish admissibility was then, and remains, subject to question.

Even those scholars who support this reading of Rule 104(a) acknowledge that it leads to an absurd result.

> Because the judge must honor claims of privilege made during his preliminary fact determinations, many exceptions to the rules of privilege will become "dead letters," since the preliminary facts that give rise to these exceptions can never be proved. For example, an exception to the attorney-client privilege provides that there is no privilege if the communication was made to enable anyone to commit a crime or fraud. There is virtually no way in which the exception can ever be proved, save by compelling disclosure of the contents of the communication; Rule 104(a) provides that this cannot be done.

21 C. Wright & K. Graham, Federal Practice & Procedure: Evidence §5055, p. 276 (1977).

We find this Draconian interpretation of Rule 104(a) inconsistent with the Rule's plain language. The Rule does not provide by its terms that all materials as to which a "clai[m] of privilege" is made must be excluded from consideration. In that critical respect, the language of Rule 104(a) is markedly different from the comparable California evidence rule, which provides that "the presiding officer may not require disclosure of information claimed to be privileged under this division in order to rule on the claim of privilege." Cal. Evid. Code §915(a) (1989). There is no reason to read Rule 104(a) as if its text were identical to that of the California rule.

Nor does it make sense to us to assume, as respondents have throughout this litigation, that once the attorney-client nature of the contested communications is established, those communications must be treated as presumptively privileged for evidentiary purposes until the privilege is "defeated" or "stripped away" by proof that the communications took place in the course of planning future crime or fraud. We see no basis for holding that the tapes in this case must be deemed privileged under Rule 104(a) while the question of crime or fraud remains open . . . . We thus shall not adopt a reading of Rule 104(a) that would treat the contested communications as "privileged" for purposes of the Rule, and we shall not interpret Rule 104(a) as categorically prohibiting the party opposing the privilege on crime-fraud grounds from relying on the results of an in camera review of the communications.

(2)

Having determined that Rule 104(a) does not prohibit the *in camera* review sought by the IRS, we must address the question as a matter of the federal common law of privileges. See FRE 501. We conclude that a complete prohibition against opponents' use of *in camera* review to establish the applicability of the crime-fraud exception is inconsistent with the policies underlying the privilege.

We begin our analysis by recognizing that disclosure of allegedly privileged materials to the district court for purposes of determining the merits of a claim of privilege does not have the legal effect of terminating the privilege. Indeed, this Court has approved the practice of requiring parties who seek to avoid disclosure of documents to make the documents available for *in camera* inspection, and the practice is well established in the federal courts. Respondents do not dispute this point: they acknowledge that they would have been free to request *in camera* review to establish the fact that the tapes involved attorney-client communications, had they been unable to muster independent evidence to serve that purpose.

Once it is clear that *in camera* review does not destroy the privileged nature of the contested communications, the question of the propriety of that review turns on whether the policies underlying the privilege and its exceptions are better fostered by permitting such review or by prohibiting it. In our view, the costs of imposing an absolute bar to consideration of the communications *in camera* for purpose of establishing the crime-fraud exception are intolerably high.

> No matter how light the burden of proof which confronts the party claiming the exception, there are many blatant abuses of privilege which cannot be substantiated by extrinsic evidence. This is particularly true . . . of . . . situations in which an alleged illegal proposal is made in the context of a relationship which has an apparent legitimate end.

Note, The Future Crime or Tort Exception to Communications Privileges, 77 Harv. L. Rev. 730, 737 (1964). A per se rule that the communications in question may never be considered creates, we feel, too great an impediment to the proper functioning of the adversary process. This view is consistent with current trends in the law.

B

We turn to the question whether *in camera* review at the behest of the party asserting the crime-fraud exception is always permissible, or, in contrast, whether the party seeking *in camera* review must make some threshold showing that such review is appropriate.

Our endorsement of the practice of testing proponents' privilege claims through *in camera* review of the allegedly privileged documents has not been without reservation. This Court noted in United States v. Reynolds, 345 U.S. 1 (1953), a case which presented a delicate question concerning the disclosure of military secrets, that "examination of the evidence, even by the judge alone, in chambers" might in some cases "jeopardize the security which the privilege is meant to protect." Analogizing to claims of Fifth Amendment privilege, it observed more generally: "Too much judicial inquiry into the claim of privilege would force disclosure of the thing the privilege was meant to protect, while a complete abandonment of judicial control would lead to intolerable abuses." . . .

A blanket rule allowing *in camera* review as a tool for determining the applicability of the crime-fraud exception, as *Reynolds* suggests, would place the policy of protecting open and legitimate disclosure between attorneys and clients at undue risk. There is also reason to be concerned about the possible due process implications of routine use of *in camera* proceedings. Finally, we cannot ignore the burdens *in camera* review places upon the district courts, which may well be required to evaluate large evidentiary records without open adversarial guidance by the parties.

There is no reason to permit opponents of the privilege to engage in groundless fishing expeditions, with the district courts as their unwitting (and perhaps unwilling) agents. Indeed, the Government conceded at oral argument (albeit reluctantly) that a district court would be mistaken if it reviewed documents *in camera* solely because "the government beg[ged it]" to do so, "with no reason to suspect crime or fraud." We agree.

In fashioning a standard for determining when in camera review is appropriate, we begin with the observation that "*in camera* inspection . . . is a smaller intrusion upon the confidentiality of the attorney-client relationship than is public disclosure." We therefore conclude that a lesser evidentiary showing is needed to trigger *in camera* review than is required ultimately to overcome the privilege. The threshold we set, in other words, need not be a stringent one.

We think that the following standard strikes the correct balance. Before engaging in *in camera* review to determine the applicability of the crime-fraud exception, "the judge should require a showing of a factual basis adequate to support a good faith belief by a reasonable person," Caldwell v. District Court, 644 P.2d 26, 33 (Colo. 1982), that *in camera* review of the materials may reveal evidence to establish the claim that the crime-fraud exception applies.

Once that showing is made, the decision whether to engage in *in camera* review rests in the sound discretion of the district court. The court should make that decision in light of the facts and circumstances of the particular case, including, among other things, the volume of materials the district court has been asked to review, the relative importance to the case of the alleged privileged information, and the likelihood that the evidence produced through *in camera* review, together with other available evidence then before the court, will establish that the crime-fraud exception does apply. The district court is also free to defer its *in camera* review if it concludes that additional evidence in support of the crime-fraud exception may be available that is not allegedly privileged, and that production of the additional evidence will not unduly disrupt or delay the proceedings.

D

In sum, we conclude that a rigid independent evidence requirement does not comport with "reason and experience," FRE 501, and we decline to adopt it as part of the developing federal common law of evidentiary privileges. We hold that *in camera* review may be used to determine whether allegedly privileged attorney-client communications fall within the crime-fraud exception. We further hold, however, that before a district court may engage in *in camera* review at the request of the party opposing the privilege, that party must present evidence sufficient to support a reasonable belief that *in camera* review may yield evidence that establishes the exception's applicability....

[Court vacates judgment of Ninth Circuit, and remands the case.]

■ NOTES ON THE CRIME-FRAUD EXCEPTION

1. Why do we need a crime-fraud exception? Does the exception amount to a concession that Bentham was right about the privilege—that its function is to protect the guilty, and the crime-fraud exception reduces that tendency? Should the exception extend to all future torts? This broader formulation of the exception was adopted by the Model Code of Evidence, Rule 212 (1942) and Uniform Rule 26(2)(a) (1974).

2. Suppose the client does not know that what she proposes is criminal or fraudulent? See In re Grand Jury Subpoena, 745 F.3.d 681 (3d Cir. 2014) (for crime-fraud exception to apply, client must be committing or intending to commit crime or fraud when consulting lawyer). See also proposed-but-rejected Rule 503(d)(1) (privilege denied only if client obtained lawyer's services to commit "what the client knew or reasonably should have known to be a crime or fraud").

3. *Zolin* addresses the question whether a judge can require production of the underlying material in order to rule on a privilege claim when the adversary claims the crime-fraud exception applies. *Zolin* also describes the standard that the adversary must satisfy. Production may be required, but is not "automatic," and the adversary must show a "factual basis adequate to support a good faith belief" that inspection will reveal that the exception applies. Isn't it obvious that a judge must see the material in order to rule? What is the concern? Could we solve the problem by a rule that privileged material stays privileged, even if disclosed to court and counsel for the other side, while the court rules on the privilege claim?

4. *Zolin* describes the standard required for *in camera* inspection, but doesn't answer the next question, which is what standard to use in deciding whether the crime-fraud exception applies. The traditional view, based on the pre-*Zolin* notion that the judge had to decide without seeing the material, is that the adversary had to make a prima facie showing that the purpose of the communication was to commit a crime or fraud. But as *Zolin* says in footnote 7, that standard has been criticized because it doesn't make room for the privilege claimant to be heard in rebuttal. If a court takes advantage of the procedure approved in *Zolin*, there is no excuse for ruling on the matter without hearing the privilege claimant, is there? Indeed, a court that has the information that inspection provides should be able to resolve the issue one way or another, and *Zolin* makes obsolete the notion that a prima facie showing of a criminal or fraudulent purpose suffices. Modern opinions recognize this point, allowing both parties to be heard and resolving the issue under the preponderance standard. In short, the privilege claimant must show by a preponderance that the requirements of the privilege are met, but the adverse party can then overcome the privilege claim if he can show by a preponderance that the crime-fraud exception applies. See In re Napster, Inc. Copyright Litigation, 479 F.3d 1078 (9th Cir. 2007) (in civil case, rejecting traditional "prima facie" standard for proving crime-fraud exception; adverse party must prove by a preponderance under FRE 104(a) that exception applies; privilege claimant can then offer evidence rebutting adverse party's proof).

5. Does a lawyer have an ethical duty to report crimes or frauds that a client appears to be planning? Compare ABA Model Code of Professional Responsibility, DR 4-101(C) (lawyer may reveal "intention of his client to commit a crime and the information necessary to prevent the crime") with ABA Model Rules of Professional Conduct, Rule 1.6(b), which was amended in 2003 in the wake of the Enron scandal (lawyer may disclose confidences as necessary "to prevent reasonably certain death or substantial bodily harm" or to keep client "from committing crime or fraud that is reasonably certain to result in substantial injury to the financial interests or property of another," if the client "has used or is using the lawyer's services" and "to prevent, mitigate or rectify substantial injury to the financial interests or property of another" resulting from such fraud). See also Restatement (Third) of Law Governing Lawyers §117A. Could an attorney face civil liability for *not* reporting contemplated future crimes by a client?

7. Assertion and Waiver

As holder, the client must claim the privilege at the right moment or risk losing its protection. The attorney cannot claim the privilege if her client wants to disclose (she has no separate stake in the protection), but she is presumptively authorized to assert the privilege for her client. You know that disclosure to necessary intermediaries (and some disclosure to others, as in the pooled defense and joint client cases) does not cause loss of protection, but disclosing to other parties during the discovery process often does. Problems of claim and waiver can become complicated.

a. *Asserting the Privilege*

As holder of the privilege, the client decides whether to assert or waive it. She may claim the privilege independently or through her lawyer, who is ethically required to assert the privilege on the client's behalf unless she waives it or authorizes waiver. Third parties may call the privilege to the attention of the court, which may seek assurance that the privilege is inapplicable or has been waived before permitting disclosure.

The privilege claimant bears the burden of establishing his entitlement. The question whether a privilege claim should be sustained is for the court to resolve under FRE 104(a). As you saw in *Zolin*, typically the court needs basic information in order to rule, like a description of the communication and the services rendered. As *Zolin* indicates, generally courts resolve privilege claims without requiring disclosure of communications, and the information seeker then bears the burden of proving an exception, if there is one.

Review of privilege rulings. As noted in Chapter 1, ordinarily rulings on evidence issues are interlocutory and cannot be reviewed until final judgment, but sometimes immediate review is possible where a court overrules a claim of attorney-client privilege.

On this point, the cases are in disarray, even within the federal system. Under one approach, the threshold question is whether the person from whom information was sought has been held in contempt. If not, no review may be had. If so, some authority permits the reviewing court to consider the privilege ruling on the merits if the person has been held in criminal contempt. If he has been held in civil contempt, all that can be reviewed is the authority of the trial judge to impose the contempt sanction.

Under another approach, the threshold question is whether the nondisclosing person is a party to the suit. If so, he may obtain review of the privilege ruling only by suffering an adverse judgment on the merits of the case, then raising the privilege issue (and other points of error) on appeal from the judgment. See IBM Corp. v. United States, 493 F.2d 112, 117 (2d Cir. 1973) (IBM held in civil contempt and fined $150,000 per day for refusing to produce documents under claims of attorney-client privilege and work product; interlocutory review denied), *cert. denied*, 416 U.S. 995 (1974). If he is not a party, he may obtain review of the privilege issue without suffering a judgment of contempt, simply because the final judgment in the proceedings will never afford him a chance to obtain such review.

Many modern cases present the issue of review in the context of orders of production directed to criminal defense lawyers during grand jury proceedings. Of course the lawyer is not herself a party, and technically the potential defendant is not a party either (he has not yet been indicted). In this circumstance, some modern federal authority applies the doctrine of Perlman v. United States, 247 U.S. 7 (1918) (party may appeal, on ground of Fourth Amendment violation, from disclosure order directed to court clerk), which lets the client intervene to appeal immediately from an order overruling her claim of privilege. One court explained the outcome thus:

> We suspect that the willingness of a lawyer to protect a client's privilege in the face of a contempt citation will vary greatly, and have a direct relationship to the value of the client's business and the power of the client in relation to the attorney. We are reluctant to pin the appealability of a district court order upon such precarious considerations. Moreover, there is a paradoxical element in even looking for indications of the lawyer's intent. If the attorney will submit to a contempt citation rather than testify, the efficient administration of justice is best served by hearing the client-intervenor's appeal immediately, rather than waiting for an appeal of the contempt judgment against the attorney. If the

attorney will testify rather than risk contempt, the client-intervenor's appeal is most certainly proper because there will be no later opportunity to appeal and the order is definitely "final" as to the client.

In re Grand Jury Proceedings (Fine), 641 F.2d 199, 201-203 (5th Cir. 1981).

■ PROBLEM 12-E. The Reluctant Lawyer

A federal grand jury is deciding whether to indict Kastin for fraud based on his alleged use of the mail to send false and misleading brochures soliciting investments in a real estate partnership. Walters, a real estate attorney who had represented Kastin, is called before the grand jury to describe discussions with Kastin relating to the brochure prior to mailing. The government is trying to show that Kastin knew there were false statements in the brochure, but Walters claims the attorney-client privilege on behalf of Kastin and refuses to testify. The court orders Walters to answer, finding that the discussions fit the future crime or fraud exception to the privilege.

Assume that Walters has a reasonable basis for believing that the court has erred. Does he have an ethical obligation to protect Kastin by defying the order, at the cost of being held in contempt, so the merits of the privilege claim can be reviewed? What if Walters is unwilling to be held in contempt? Should Kastin be allowed to intervene and to appeal the order requiring Walters to disclose?

■ NOTES ON APPELLATE REVIEW OF PRIVILEGE ISSUES

1. If the court *sustains* the privilege claim and bars testimony by Walters, can the government obtain immediate review? See 18 USC §3731 (allowing interlocutory appeals when evidence is suppressed before trial). Why should the government be allowed such an appeal? Consider the fact that double jeopardy blocks a government appeal if Kastin is acquitted after trial on the merits.

2. If a civil litigant refuses to testify after a privilege claim is overruled, she can be cited for contempt. If it is civil contempt (which she can discharge by testifying), normally she cannot obtain immediate review on the merits. Why? Should such an appeal be allowed if she is cited for criminal contempt? See Powers v. Chicago Transit Authority, 846 F.2d 1139, 1140 (7th Cir. 1988) (upholding $150 per day fine for failure to turn over material for which petitioner claimed privilege; refusing review because civil contempt is not a final judgment; criminal contempt is appealable "on the theory that it is the terminating order of a separate proceeding, the criminal prosecution").

3. If the privilege holder ultimately discloses privileged matter at trial pursuant to a court order after a privilege claim is denied, can the ruling be challenged on appeal from a final judgment, or is the claim waived? See proposed-but-rejected Rule 512 (disclosure of privileged matter is not a waiver if disclosure was "compelled erroneously").

b. Waiver

The protection of the attorney-client privilege can be lost by waiver, which usually happens in one of three ways:

(1) Voluntary Disclosure. The privilege is waived by *voluntary* disclosure of any significant part of the covered matter, but not if the disclosure is itself privileged. Thus the privilege is waived if the client discloses to his barber a communication he had with his attorney, but not if he discloses it to his wife in a confidential conversation, which is itself protected by the spousal confidences privilege. If the disclosure is compelled by an erroneous court order, however, it is involuntary and the privilege is *not* waived. The protection is restored if the order is set aside or reversed.

The attorney can also waive the client's privilege if she has authority from the client to do so. If the client authorizes the lawyer to conduct negotiations or perform other legal tasks, and in doing so the lawyer discloses a privileged communication, the disclosure waives the client's privilege. In the unlikely event that a lawyer discloses a privileged communication *without the client's express or implied consent,* however, there is no waiver, and the privilege can still prevent use of the privileged communication at trial.

Suppose the lawyer discloses privileged matter to a government agency in order to settle a dispute or resolve an investigation. Does such "selective" disclosure waive the privilege with respect to third parties seeking disclosure of the information? Most courts say yes. See In re Qwest Communications Int'l, 450 F.3d 1179, 1187-1197 (10th Cir. 2006) (most courts reject rule allowing selective disclosure to government agencies); Permian Corp. v. United States, 665 F.2d 1214, 1216-1221 (D.C. Cir. 1981) (voluntary cooperation with investigations may be "laudable," but client "cannot be permitted to pick and choose among his opponents, waiving the privilege for some and resurrecting the claim of confidentiality to obstruct others"). But see Diversified Industries v. Meredith, 572 F.2d 596, 611 (8th Cir. 1977) (surrender of privileged documents to SEC under agency subpoena did not result in waiver of privilege with respect to third parties).

(2) Waiver by asserting claims or defenses. The privilege can be waived, even without disclosure, if the client puts the content of the communications at issue by making certain claims or raising certain defenses. Thus the privilege is waived if the client asserts a defense that he relied on "advice of counsel." See Nguyen v. Excel Corp., 197 F.3d 200 (5th Cir. 1999) (reliance on an advice of counsel defense waives privilege with respect to communications pertinent to the defense). The privilege is also sometimes waived by the assertion of a claim where it is necessary for the opposing party to use privileged communications to mount a defense. See, e.g., Ryers v. Burleson, 100 F.R.D. 436 (D.D.C. 1983) (allegations of lawyer malpractice constituted a waiver of confidential communications under the circumstances).

(3) Waiver by inadvertent disclosure. Sometimes even accidental or inadvertent disclosure by the lawyer waives the privilege, which often happens during discovery in complex cases that involves thousands (sometimes millions) of documents or files. This kind of waiver is both controversial and challenging. There were three views at common law about waiver of this sort. Under the strict view, any disclosure of protected communications waived the privilege. Under the lenient view, waiver resulted only if disclosure was intentional. Most courts, however, sought a middle position in which waiver occurred only where the lawyer failed to take adequate care. The middle position is now codified in federal proceedings by FRE 502(b), which Congress enacted in 2008.

Ironically, while intentional-but-unauthorized disclosure by an attorney does not waive the privilege, *negligent* disclosure by the attorney sometimes does. Such waiver-by-inadvertence rests on the idea that the attorney has the client's authority to respond to discovery requests and undertake other actions, so the attorney's negligence is in effect the client's negligence, and the client is responsible for the attorney's shortcomings.

The danger of inadvertent disclosure during discovery has increased exponentially because of the explosion in the quantity of electronically stored information (ESI). See Schaefer, The Future of Inadvertent Disclosure: The Lingering Need to Revise Professional Conduct Rules, 69 Md. L. Rev. 195, 196 (2010) (in 2006, volume of ESI was estimated to be more than 3 million times the information in all the books ever written, and amount was expected to increase tenfold by 2011); Paul & Baron, Information Inflation: Can the Legal System Adapt?, 13 Rich. J.L. & Tech. 1, 5-6 (2007) (typical small business today has equivalent of 2,000 four-drawer file cabinets of records, in form of ESI). As one commentator noted:

> In only the past twenty years, inadvertent disclosure has evolved from the slim possibility of misaddressing an envelope, which seemed preventable, to a substantial risk faced by every practicing attorney regardless of the care taken to prevent it. The prospect of inadvertent disclosure strikes fear and sometimes pain in the hearts of attorneys.

Schaefer, supra, at 196.

The concern of lawyers about inadvertent waiver in discovery is amplified by another common law doctrine–subject matter waiver. Under this doctrine, waiving the privilege on part of what it covers also waives the privilege on everything related to the part disclosed. In other words, negligent disclosure of a privileged document could result in loss of privilege for the disclosed document and also lead to a successful demand by the other side for all related documents on the same subject matter.

Lawyers have responded to these concerns in two ways:

First, they have devoted more resources to pre-production review during discovery, escalating costs. Law firms often allocate many hours of the time of associates, paralegals, and outside consultants to review documents and computer files to be sure that privileged matter is not inadvertently disclosed. In a recent antitrust investigation, Verizon Corp. reportedly spent $13.5 million on privilege review.[1] Computer programs now help cull out privileged material from ESI. But even costly review processes are imperfect, and mistaken production of privileged material is commonplace.

Second, lawyers have resorted to private "nonwaiver" agreements before beginning discovery. Typically such an agreement contains a "clawback" provision stating that if privileged documents or files are inadvertently released, the receiving party will return them on request and will not copy or use them or claim waiver. Sometimes parties even negotiate a "quick peek" agreement under which they disclose documents without pre-production privilege review for brief examination without waiving the privilege. Such agreements are enforceable between the parties, but generally cannot bind outsiders who may later seek production of the disclosed material. A 2006 amendment to FRCP 26(b)(5)(B) includes a clawback feature allowing the producing party to assert a late privilege claim and obligating the receiving party to challenge this claim by making a motion in court, thus accomplishing part of what typical nonwaiver agreements achieve.

To address these problems further, Congress enacted FRE 502 in 2008.[2] The rule applies to disclosures in a federal proceeding or to a federal office or agency, and it sometimes preempts state privilege law (a point we will examine). The three most significant provisions are as follows: First, FRE 502(a) speaks to the scope of waiver by disclosure. Thus disclosure of privileged matter, whether intentional or inadvertent, does not waive the privilege for related matter, except in one narrow circumstance—where the disclosure was intentional and the undisclosed communications "ought in fairness to be considered together" with already disclosed material. If, for example, a party introduces an email from her attorney that supports her position, her adversary may be entitled to see other communications from the attorney that place the email in context. The ACN says subject-matter waiver "is limited to situations in which a party intentionally puts protected information into the litigation in a selective, misleading and unfair manner" and that inadvertent disclosure "can never result in subject matter waiver."

Second, FRE 502(b) codifies the majority view that inadvertent disclosure waives the privilege only when adequate precautions were not taken. FRE

[1] Alvin F. Lindsay, New Rule 502 to Protect Against Privilege Waiver, Nat'l L.J. (Aug. 25, 2008).

[2] Congressional enactment was necessary because the Court lacks authority to promulgate rules modifying evidentiary privileges without approval by Act of Congress. See 28 USC §2074(b). And FRE 502 probably exceeds the Court's rulemaking power because it displaces state law in some circumstances.

502(b) says inadvertent disclosure is not a waiver if the privilege holder "took reasonable steps to prevent disclosure" and "promptly took reasonable steps to rectify the error." The ACN says the following factors may be helpful: "the reasonableness of the precautions taken, the time taken to rectify the error, the scope of discovery, the extent of disclosure, and the overriding issue of fairness" as well as "the number of documents to be reviewed, and the time constraints for production." Thus FRE 502(b) does not provide a definitive test but requires inquiry and balancing on a case-by-case basis.

Third, FRE 502(d) addresses the question whether a nonwaiver agreement is binding on outsiders. It says that a federal court "may order that the privilege or protection is not waived by disclosure connected with the litigation pending before the court—in which event the disclosure is also not a waiver in any other federal or state proceeding." This provision is controversial because it says a federal court order binds third parties not only in later federal proceedings but in state proceedings, even if the privilege would be waived under state law. As the ACN explains, "if a federal court's confidentiality order is not enforceable in a state court then the burdensome costs of privilege review and retention are unlikely to be reduced." It should be noted that a court can enter a FRE 502(d) order on its own motion, even without party agreement about nonwaiver.

■ PROBLEM 12-F: "The Disclosure Was Inadvertent"

Milton & Associates, a general contractor, sued Beacon Building Supply (BBS) in federal court alleging breach of contract in connection with the construction of a large office complex. BBS was represented in the litigation by Carol Brock, a partner in the Frank/Carlton law firm, and associate Kevin Marlow. Milton filed a discovery request for all the BBS internal emails relating to the construction project. To assist in identifying such emails, and screening out any that might be privileged, Brock hired a technology consulting company, Discovery Manager Inc.

Anticipating massive discovery requests, the two sides negotiate a nonwaiver agreement that provides as follows: "If either Milton or BBS discloses information in this litigation that the disclosing party thereafter claims to be privileged or subject to work product protection, the disclosure will not constitute or be deemed a waiver or forfeiture—in this or any other action—of any claim of privilege or work product protection that the disclosing party would otherwise be entitled to assert with respect to the disclosed information. The provisions of FRE 502(b) are inapplicable to this agreement."[1]

[1]See Model Draft of a Rule 502(d) Order, 81 Fordham L. Rev. 1587 (2012).

Using its own specially designed software, Discovery Manager was able to identify 63,200 internal BBS emails relating to the project. Then in consultation with Brock and Marlow, Discovery Manager sought to screen out and remove any of those emails that might be protected from disclosure by the attorney-client privilege or work product doctrine. It did so by isolating all emails addressed to or received from attorneys at Frank/Carlton. The software identified 840 such emails, and they were removed. Marlow then did a manual review of the remaining 62,360 emails, largely by sampling, and identified 38 additional emails that he removed as privileged or work product. Once the protected emails were removed and entered on a privilege log, the remaining 62,322 emails were turned over to Milton on May 14.

On June 20, counsel for Milton notified Brock that 62 emails were found in the disclosed emails that appeared to be subject to the attorney-client privilege. Brock responded the same day stating that the disclosure was inadvertent and she would be back in touch shortly. Over the next three weeks, Brock and Marlow were involved in eight depositions in the case, as well as a summary judgment motion brought by another defendant. On July 18, Brock called Milton's counsel and learned that the 62 privileged emails involved correspondence with Frank/Carlton attorneys that were attachments to other emails so the connection to Frank/Carlton did not appear in the headers of the emails. On July 22, Brock sent a letter to Milton's counsel asserting the privilege claim and demanding return of the emails. Milton refused, contending that any claim of privilege had been waived by the failure of BBS to conduct a proper privilege review prior to disclosing the emails and by its delay in demanding their return.

On August 1, Brock filed a motion seeking a court ruling that the 62 emails are privileged and compelling their return. How should the court rule? If there were no nonwaiver agreement, what would happen?

NOTES ON FRE 502

1. Under the nonwaiver agreement, the answer is easy, isn't it? The privilege claim applies to the 62 emails, which cannot be used against BBS if they were privileged communications. The parties signed an enforceable agreement that the privilege would not be waived regardless what care was taken when the emails were produced. FRE 502(e) provides that an agreement "on the effect of disclosure in a federal proceeding is binding . . . on the parties." See Chubb Integrated Systems, Ltd. v. National Bank of Washington, 103 F.R.D. 52, 67 (D.D.C. 1984) (such agreement is a contract between parties to refrain from "raising the issue of waiver" or "otherwise utilizing" information). Although Milton could not claim the privilege was *waived*, it could ask the court to rule that they were not privileged for some other reason, as would be true if the emails related to business advice rather than legal advice. But until the court rules, Milton is bound by FRCP 26(b)(5), which provides that an attorney who receives material claimed to be privileged during discovery must "promptly return, sequester, or destroy" it and "may not use or disclose the information until the claim is resolved."

2. If the parties had no agreement, the issue is more challenging because FRE 502(b) protects against waiver by inadvertent disclosure only on a showing that the holder of the privilege or protection "took reasonable steps to prevent disclosure" and "promptly took reasonable steps to rectify the error." Thus the court would have to examine the efforts BBS made to screen out privileged material from the disclosed emails and the promptness and reasonableness of its later conduct after the disclosure was discovered.

3. Is it reasonable to rely on computer software to screen for privileged material? In cases involving massive document exchanges, computer screening is likely to be the only feasible way. See ACN to FRE 502(b) (party that uses analytical software applications and linguistic tools in screening for privilege and work product "may be found to have taken 'reasonable steps' to prevent inadvertent disclosure"). Still, a court might be troubled by the limited search terms used by BBS and Discovery Manager and Marlow's minimal hands-on review. See Rhoads Industries v. Building Materials Corp., 254 F.R.D. 216 (E.D. Pa. 2008) (criticizing limitation of email search to address lines and not bodies of emails, and reliance on keyword searches without other quality assurance measures). Could the parties agree what search terms suffice? See Race Tires America v. Hoosier Racing Tire Corp., 674 F.3d 158, 162 (3d Cir. 2012) (in antitrust suit involving discovery of more than 500,000 documents, the parties agreed that certain search terms raised "presumption" that each conducted a reasonable search).

4. How could BBS claim it took reasonable steps to rectify the error when it did not even learn of the disclosure until notified by the receiving party? It seems that the disclosing party has no obligation to review material that it has already produced. See ACN to FRE 502(b) (producing party need not "engage in a post-production review" to locate protected material produced by mistake, but the producing party must "follow up on any obvious indications" that the material was produced inadvertently).

5. After receiving notice of the disclosures on June 20th, Brock took more than a month to demand their return (acting on July 22nd). Is that prompt enough? Compare Sheet Metal Workers' Nat. Pension Fund v. Palladium Equity Partners, LLC, 722 F. Supp. 2d 845, 851 (E.D. Mich. 2010) (inadvertent production discovered late Friday led to notification of opposing counsel the following Monday, which satisfied promptness requirement) with Ceeglia v. Zuckerberg, 2012 WL 1392965 (W.D.N.Y. 2012) (two month delay in requesting return of inadvertently disclosed email was not reasonable).

6. When privileged material is inadvertently disclosed, what is the obligation of the *receiving party*? See ABA Model Rule of Professional Conduct 4.4(b):

"A lawyer who receives a document [including emails] relating to the representation of the lawyer's client and knows or reasonably should know that the document was inadvertently sent shall promptly notify the sender." Milton's attorney complied with this ethical obligation by notifying BBS of the receipt of apparently privileged documents. But the Model Rule does not address the waiver question, leaving the matter to a judge to resolve by applying the law of evidence. The Comment in the Model Code says that lawyers may return inadvertently sent documents "unread" as a matter of their own "professional judgment."

7. A nonwaiver agreement can provide more protection than FRE 502(b) itself, but FRE 502(e) says such agreements do not bind outsiders unless "incorporated in a court order." Thus outsiders may seek discovery of documents or files in related or subsequent litigation, claiming that privilege or work product protection was waived by disclosure. Hence litigants like Milton and BBS normally present nonwaiver agreements to the court to be incorporated in an order, if the court is willing to do so. As noted above, such an order would mean that disclosure did not amount to waiver in any other federal or state proceeding.

8. Should a court enter a FRE 502(d) order if the parties agree to a regime in which neither side has to make any effort to cull out material subject to privilege or work product protection? Compare Radian Asset Assurance, Inc. v. College of the Christian Brothers of New Mexico, 2010 WL 4928866 (D.N.M. 2010) (entering order without predisclosure privilege review) with Spieker v. Quest Cherokee, LLC, 2009 WL 2168892 (D. Kan. 2009) (refusing to enter order without predisclosure privilege review). Allowing such orders without privilege review was contemplated by the drafters of FRE 502 in order to reduce litigation costs. See ACN to FRE 502 (court order "may provide for return of documents without waiver irrespective of the care taken by the disclosing party," and the parties may agree to "quick-peek" arrangements in order to control "excessive costs of pre-production review"). Under a "quick peek" agreement, the requesting party examines documents produced by the other side without any privilege review, and designates the material that it seeks. Then the producing party does a privilege review and asserts any privilege claims. But see Wang, Nonwaiver Agreements After Federal Rule of Evidence 502: A Glance at Quick-Peek and Clawback Agreements, 56 UCLA L. Rev. 1835 (2009) (expressing concern about loss of confidentiality even where privilege is preserved and arguing that courts should not grant protective orders where there is no privilege review). See generally Symposium on Rule 502, 81 Fordham L. Rev. 1533 (2012).

9. It was once the case that the producing party could simply withhold documents or files on ground of privilege or work product. Under this regime, the information seeker might never learn about the existence of such material. In 1993, however, an amendment to FRCP 26(b)(5) added language requiring any party claiming privilege or work product protection to "make the claim expressly" and "describe the nature" of material not being produced. This provision put in effect the convention of the "privilege log," which the producing party must make in order to claim privilege or work product protection. In the *Rhoads Industries* case (note 3, supra), a young associate withheld many documents and files from production on ground of privilege without making a privilege log, and the court later held that this failure resulted in waiver of the privilege for all that material.

THE PSYCHOTHERAPIST-PATIENT PRIVILEGE

JAFFEE v. REDMOND

Supreme Court of the United States
518 U.S. 1 (1996)

Justice STEVENS delivered the opinion of the Court.

After a traumatic incident in which she shot and killed a man, a police officer received extensive counseling from a licensed clinical social worker. The question we address is whether statements the officer made to her therapist during the counseling sessions are protected from compelled disclosure in a federal civil action brought by the family of the deceased. Stated otherwise, the question is whether it is appropriate for federal courts to recognize a "psychotherapist privilege" under FRE 501.

I

On June 27, 1991, Redmond was the first officer to respond to a "fight in progress" call at an apartment complex. As she arrived at the scene, two of Allen's sisters ran toward her squad car, waving their arms and shouting that there had been a stabbing in one of the apartments. Redmond testified at trial that she relayed this information to her dispatcher and requested an ambulance. She then exited her car and walked toward the apartment building. Before Redmond reached the building, several men ran out, one waving a pipe. When the men ignored her order to get on the ground, Redmond drew her service revolver. Two other men then burst out of the building, one, Ricky Allen, chasing the other. According to Redmond, Allen was brandishing a butcher knife and disregarded her repeated commands to drop the weapon. Redmond shot Allen when she believed he was about to stab the man he was chasing. Allen died at the scene. Redmond testified that before other officers arrived to provide support, "people came pouring out of the buildings," and a threatening confrontation between her and the crowd ensued.

Petitioner filed suit in Federal District Court alleging that Redmond had violated Allen's constitutional rights by using excessive force during the encounter at the apartment complex. The complaint sought damages under 42 U.S.C. §1983 and the Illinois wrongful death statute. At trial, petitioner presented testimony from members of Allen's family that conflicted with Redmond's version of the incident in several important respects. They testified, for example, that Redmond drew her gun before exiting her squad car and that Allen was unarmed when he emerged from the apartment building.

During pretrial discovery petitioner learned that after the shooting Redmond had participated in about 50 counseling sessions with Karen Beyer, a clinical social worker licensed by the State of Illinois and employed at that time by the Village of Hoffman Estates. Petitioner sought access to Beyer's notes concerning the sessions for use in cross-examining Redmond. Respondents vigorously resisted the discovery. They asserted that the contents of the conversations between Beyer and Redmond were protected against involuntary disclosure by a psychotherapist-patient privilege. The district judge rejected this argument. Neither Beyer nor Redmond, however, complied with his order to disclose the contents of Beyer's notes. At depositions and on the witness stand both either refused to answer certain questions or professed an inability to recall details of their conversations.

In his instructions at the end of the trial, the judge advised the jury that the refusal to turn over Beyer's notes had no "legal justification" and that the jury could therefore presume that the contents of the notes would have been unfavorable to respondents. The jury awarded petitioner $45,000 on the federal claim and $500,000 on her state law claim.

II

FRE 501 authorizes federal courts to define new privileges by interpreting "common law principles . . . in the light of reason and experience." The authors of the Rule borrowed this phrase from our opinion in Wolfle v. United States, 291 U.S. 7, 12 (1934), which in turn referred to the oft-repeated observation that "the common law is not immutable but flexible, and by its own principles adapts itself to varying conditions." Funk v. United States, 290 U.S. 371, 383 (1933). See also Hawkins v. United States, 358 U.S. 74, 79 (1958) (changes in privileges may be "dictated by 'reason and experience'"). The Senate Report accompanying the 1975 adoption of the Rules indicates that FRE 501 "should be understood as reflecting the view that the recognition of a privilege based on a confidential relationship . . . should be determined on a case-by-case basis." The Rule thus did not freeze the law governing the privileges of witnesses in federal trials at a particular point in our history, but rather directed federal courts to "continue the evolutionary development of testimonial privileges." Trammel v. United States, 445 U.S. 40, 47 (1980).

The common-law principles underlying the recognition of testimonial privileges can be stated simply. "'For more than three centuries it has now been recognized as a fundamental maxim that the public . . . has a right to every man's evidence. When we come to examine the various claims of exemption, we start with the primary assumption that there is a general duty to give what testimony one is capable of giving, and that any exemptions which may exist are distinctly exceptional, being so many derogations from a positive general rule.'" United States v. Bryan, 339 U.S. 323, 331 (1950) (quoting 8 J. Wigmore, Evidence §2192, p. 64 (3d ed. 1940)). Exceptions from the general rule disfavoring testimonial privileges may be justified, however, by a "'public good transcending the normally predominant principle of utilizing all rational means for ascertaining the truth.'" *Trammel*, quoting Alkanes v. United States, 364 U.S. 206, 234 (1960) (Frankfurter, J., dissenting).

Guided by these principles, the question we address today is whether a privilege protecting confidential communications between a psychotherapist and her patient "promotes sufficiently important interests to outweigh the need for probative evidence . . ." [quoting *Trammel* case]. Both "reason and experience" persuade us that it does.

III

Like the spousal and attorney-client privileges, the psychotherapist-patient privilege is "rooted in the imperative need for confidence and trust." *Trammel.* Treatment by a physician for physical ailments can often proceed successfully on the basis of a physical examination, objective information supplied by the patient, and the results of diagnostic tests. Effective psychotherapy, by contrast, depends upon an atmosphere of confidence and trust in which the patient is willing to make a frank and complete disclosure of facts, emotions, memories, and fears. Because of the sensitive nature of the problems for which individuals consult psychotherapists, disclosure of confidential communications made during counseling sessions may cause embarrassment or disgrace. For this reason, the mere possibility of disclosure may impede development of the confidential relationship necessary for successful treatment. As the Judicial Conference Advisory Committee observed in 1972 when it recommended that Congress recognize a psychotherapist privilege as part of the Proposed Federal Rules of Evidence, a psychiatrist's ability to help her patients

> is completely dependent upon [the patients'] willingness and ability to talk freely. This makes it difficult if not impossible for [a psychiatrist] to function without being able to assure patients of confidentiality and, indeed, privileged communication. Where there may be exceptions to this general rule . . . , there is wide agreement that confidentiality is a sine qua non for successful psychiatric treatment.

CAN to Proposed Rules, 56 F.R.D. 183, 242 (1972).

By protecting confidential communications between a psychotherapist and her patient from involuntary disclosure, the proposed privilege thus serves important private interests.

Our cases make clear that an asserted privilege must also "serv[e] public ends." Upjohn Co. v. United States, 449 U.S. 383, 389 (1981) . . . . The psychotherapist privilege serves the public interest by facilitating the provision of appropriate treatment for individuals suffering the effects of a mental or emotional problem. The mental health of our citizenry, no less than its physical health, is a public good of transcendent importance.[10]

In contrast to the significant public and private interests supporting recognition of the privilege, the likely evidentiary benefit that would result from the denial of the privilege is modest. If the privilege were rejected, confidential conversations between psychotherapists and their patients would surely be chilled, particularly when it is obvious that the circumstances that give rise to the need for treatment will probably result in litigation. Without a privilege, much of the desirable evidence to which litigants such as petitioner seek access—for example, admissions against interest by a party—is unlikely to come into being. This unspoken "evidence" will therefore serve no greater truth-seeking function than if it had been spoken and privileged.

That it is appropriate for the federal courts to recognize a psychotherapist privilege under FRE 501 is confirmed by the fact that all 50 States and the District of Columbia have enacted into law some form of psychotherapist privilege. [Court's footnote catalogues the state provisions.] We have previously observed that the policy decisions of the States bear on the question whether federal courts should recognize a new privilege or amend the coverage of an existing one. Because state legislatures are fully aware of the need to protect the integrity of the factfinding functions of their courts, the existence of a consensus among the States indicates that "reason and experience" support recognition of the privilege. In addition, given the importance of the patient's understanding that her communications with her therapist will not be publicly disclosed, any State's promise of confidentiality would have little value if the patient were aware that the privilege would not be honored in a federal court.[12] Denial of the federal privilege therefore would frustrate the purposes of the state legislation that was enacted to foster these confidential communications.

The uniform judgment of the States is reinforced by the fact that a psychotherapist privilege was among the nine specific privileges recommended by the Advisory Committee in its proposed privilege rules. In United States v. Gillock, 445 U.S. 360, 367-368 (1980), our holding that FRE 501 did not include a state legislative privilege relied, in part, on the fact that no such privilege was included in the Advisory Committee's draft. The reasoning in *Gillock* thus supports the opposite conclusion in this case. In rejecting the proposed draft that

---

[10] This case amply demonstrates the importance of allowing individuals to receive confidential counseling. Police officers engaged in the dangerous and difficult tasks associated with protecting the safety of our communities not only confront the risk of physical harm but also face stressful circumstances that may give rise to anxiety, depression, fear, or anger. The entire community may suffer if police officers are not able to receive effective counseling and treatment after traumatic incidents, either because trained officers leave the profession prematurely or because those in need of treatment remain on the job.

[12] At the outset of their relationship, the ethical therapist must disclose to the patient "the relevant limits on confidentiality." See American Psychological Association, Ethical Principles of Psychologists and Code of Conduct, Standard 5.01 (Dec. 1992). See also National Federation of Societies for Clinical Social Work, Code of Ethics V(a) (May 1988); American Counseling Association, Code of Ethics and Standards of Practice A.3.a (effective July 1995).

had specifically identified each privilege rule and substituting the present more open-ended FRE 501, the Senate Judiciary Committee explicitly stated that its action "should not be understood as disapproving any recognition of a psychiatrist-patient . . . privilege contained in the [proposed] rules."

Because we agree with the judgment of the state legislatures and the Advisory Committee that a psychotherapist-patient privilege will serve a "public good transcending the normally predominant principle of utilizing all rational means for ascertaining truth," *Trammel*, we hold that confidential communications between a licensed psychotherapist and her patients in the course of diagnosis or treatment are protected from compelled disclosure under FRE 501.

IV

All agree that a psychotherapist privilege covers confidential communications made to licensed psychiatrists and psychologists. We have no hesitation in concluding in this case that the federal privilege should also extend to confidential communications made to licensed social workers in the course of psychotherapy. The reasons for recognizing a privilege for treatment by psychiatrists and psychologists apply with equal force to treatment by a clinical social worker such as Karen Beyer.[15] Today, social workers provide a significant amount of mental health treatment. Their clients often include the poor and those of modest means who could not afford the assistance of a psychiatrist or psychologist, but whose counseling sessions serve the same public goals.[16] Perhaps in recognition of these circumstances, the vast majority of States explicitly extend a testimonial privilege to licensed social workers.[17] We therefore agree with the

---

[15] If petitioner had filed her complaint in an Illinois state court, respondents' claim of privilege would surely have been upheld, at least with respect to the state wrongful death action. An Illinois statute provides that conversations between a therapist and her patients are privileged from compelled disclosure in any civil or criminal proceeding. Ill. Comp. Stat., ch. 740, §110/10 (1994). The term "therapist" is broadly defined to encompass a number of licensed professionals including social workers. Karen Beyer, having satisfied the strict standards for licensure, qualifies as a clinical social worker in Illinois.

Indeed, if only a state law claim had been asserted in federal court, the second sentence in FRE 501 would have extended the privilege to that proceeding. We note that there is disagreement concerning the proper rule in cases such as this in which both federal and state claims are asserted in federal court and relevant evidence would be privileged under state law but not under federal law. Because the parties do not raise this question and our resolution of the case does not depend on it, we express no opinion on the matter.

[16] The Judicial Conference Advisory Committee's proposed psychotherapist privilege defined psychotherapists as psychologists and medical doctors who provide mental health services. This limitation in the 1972 recommendation does not counsel against recognition of a privilege for social workers practicing psychotherapy. In the quarter-century since the Committee adopted its recommendations, much has changed in the domains of social work and psychotherapy. While only 12 States regulated social workers in 1972, all 50 do today. Over the same period, the relative portion of therapeutic services provided by social workers has increased substantially.

[17] [Court cites statutes of Arizona, Arkansas, California, Colorado, Connecticut, Delaware, Florida, Georgia, Idaho, Illinois, Indiana, Iowa, Kansas, Kentucky, Louisiana, Maine, Massachusetts, Minnesota, Mississippi, Missouri, Montana, Nebraska, Nevada, New Hampshire, New Jersey, New Mexico, New York, North Carolina, Ohio, Oklahoma, Oregon, Rhode Island, South Carolina, South Dakota, Tennessee, Texas, Utah, Vermont, Virginia, Washington, Wisconsin, and Wyoming.]

Court of Appeals that "[d]rawing a distinction between the counseling provided by costly psychotherapists and the counseling provided by more readily accessible social workers serves no discernible public purpose."

We part company with the Court of Appeals on a separate point. We reject the balancing component of the privilege implemented by that court and a small number of States.[18] Making the promise of confidentiality contingent upon a trial judge's later evaluation of the relative importance of the patient's interest in privacy and the evidentiary need for disclosure would eviscerate the effectiveness of the privilege. As we explained in *Upjohn*, if the purpose of the privilege is to be served, the participants in the confidential conversation "must be able to predict with some degree of certainty whether particular discussions will be protected. An uncertain privilege, or one which purports to be certain but results in widely varying applications by the courts, is little better than no privilege at all."

These considerations are all that is necessary for decision of this case. A rule that authorizes the recognition of new privileges on a case-by-case basis makes it appropriate to define the details of new privileges in a like manner. Because this is the first case in which we have recognized a psychotherapist privilege, it is neither necessary nor feasible to delineate its full contours in a way that would "govern all conceivable future questions in this area." [19]

V

The conversations between Officer Redmond and Karen Beyer and the notes taken during their counseling sessions are protected from compelled disclosure under FRE 501. The judgment of the Court of Appeals is affirmed.

It is so ordered.

Justice SCALIA, with whom THE CHIEF JUSTICE joins as to Part III, dissenting.

I

The case before us involves confidential communications made by a police officer to a state-licensed clinical social worker in the course of psychotherapeutic counseling. Before proceeding to a legal analysis of the case, I must observe that the Court makes its task deceptively simple by the manner in which it proceeds. It begins by characterizing the issue as "whether it is appropriate for federal courts to recognize a 'psychotherapist privilege,'" and devotes almost all of its opinion to that question. Having answered that question (to its satisfaction) in the affirmative, it then devotes less than a page of text to answering

---

[18] [Court cites statutes in Maine, New Hampshire, North Carolina, and Virginia.]

[19] Although it would be premature to speculate about most future developments in the federal psychotherapist privilege, we do not doubt that there are situations in which the privilege must give way, for example, if a serious threat of harm to the patient or to others can be averted only by means of a disclosure by the therapist.

in the affirmative the small remaining question whether "the federal privilege should also extend to confidential communications made to licensed social workers in the course of psychotherapy."

Relegating the question actually posed by this case to an afterthought makes the impossible possible in a number of wonderful ways. For example, it enables the Court to treat the Proposed Federal Rules of Evidence developed in 1972 by the Judicial Conference Advisory Committee as strong support for its holding, whereas they in fact counsel clearly and directly against it. The Committee did indeed recommend a "psychotherapist privilege" of sorts; but more precisely, and more relevantly, it recommended a privilege for psychotherapy conducted by "a person authorized to practice medicine" or "a person licensed or certified as a psychologist," Proposed Rule of Evidence 504, 56 F.R.D. 183, 240 (1972), which is to say that it recommended against the privilege at issue here. That condemnation is obscured, and even converted into an endorsement, by pushing a "psychotherapist privilege" into the center ring. The Proposed Rule figures prominently in the Court's explanation of why that privilege deserves recognition, and is ignored in the single page devoted to the sideshow which happens to be the issue presented for decision.

II

To say that the Court devotes the bulk of its opinion to the much easier question of psychotherapist-patient privilege is not to say that its answer to that question is convincing. At bottom, the Court's decision to recognize such a privilege is based on its view that "successful [psychotherapeutic] treatment" serves "important private interests" (namely those of patients undergoing psychotherapy) as well as the "public good" of "[t]he mental health of our citizenry." I have no quarrel with these premises. Effective psychotherapy undoubtedly is beneficial to individuals with mental problems, and surely serves some larger social interest in maintaining a mentally stable society. But merely mentioning these values does not answer the critical question: are they of such importance, and is the contribution of psychotherapy to them so distinctive, and is the application of normal evidentiary rules so destructive to psychotherapy, as to justify making our federal courts occasional instruments of injustice? On that central question I find the Court's analysis insufficiently convincing to satisfy the high standard we have set for rules that "are in derogation of the search for truth."

When is it, one must wonder, that the psychotherapist came to play such an indispensable role in the maintenance of the citizenry's mental health? For most of history, men and women have worked out their difficulties by talking to, inter alios, parents, siblings, best friends and bartenders—none of whom was awarded a privilege against testifying in court. Ask the average citizen: Would your mental health be more significantly impaired by preventing you from seeing a psychotherapist, or by preventing you from getting advice from your mom? I have little doubt what the answer would be. Yet there is no mother-child privilege.

How likely is it that a person will be deterred from seeking psychological counseling, or from being completely truthful in the course of such counseling, because of fear of later disclosure in litigation? And even more pertinent to today's decision, to what extent will the evidentiary privilege reduce that deterrent? The Court does not try to answer the first of these questions; and it cannot possibly have any notion of what the answer is to the second, since that depends entirely upon the scope of the privilege, which the Court amazingly finds it "neither necessary nor feasible to delineate."

The Court confidently asserts that not much truth-finding capacity would be destroyed by the privilege anyway, since "[w]ithout a privilege, much of the desirable evidence to which litigants such as petitioner seek access . . . is unlikely to come into being." If that is so, how come psychotherapy got to be a thriving practice before the "psychotherapist privilege" was invented? Were the patients paying money to lie to their analysts all those years? Of course the evidence-generating effect of the privilege (if any) depends entirely upon its scope, which the Court steadfastly declines to consider. And even if one assumes that scope to be the broadest possible, is it really true that most, or even many, of those who seek psychological counseling have the worry of litigation in the back of their minds? I doubt that, and the Court provides no evidence to support it.

III

Turning from the general question that was not involved in this case to the specific one that is: The Court's conclusion that a social-worker psychotherapeutic privilege deserves recognition is even less persuasive . . . .

[The Court's] brief analysis like the earlier, more extensive, discussion of the general psychotherapist privilege contains no explanation of why the psychotherapy provided by social workers is a public good of such transcendent importance as to be purchased at the price of occasional injustice. Moreover, it considers only the respects in which social workers providing therapeutic services are similar to licensed psychiatrists and psychologists; not a word about the respects in which they are different. A licensed psychiatrist or psychologist is an expert in psychotherapy—and that may suffice (though I think it not so clear that this Court should make the judgment) to justify the use of extraordinary means to encourage counseling with him, as opposed to counseling with one's rabbi, minister, family or friends. One must presume that a social worker does not bring this greatly heightened degree of skill to bear, which is alone a reason for not encouraging that consultation as generously. Does a social worker bring to bear at least a significantly heightened degree of skill—more than a minister or rabbi, for example? I have no idea, and neither does the Court. The social worker in the present case, Karen Beyer, was a "licensed clinical social worker," a job title whose training requirements consist of "master's degree in social work from an approved program," and "3,000 hours of satisfactory, supervised clinical professional experience." It is not clear that the degree in social work requires any training in psychotherapy . . . .

Another critical distinction between psychiatrists and psychologists, on the one hand, and social workers, on the other, is that the former professionals, in their consultations with patients, do nothing but psychotherapy. Social workers, on the other hand, interview people for a multitude of reasons. The Illinois definition of "[l]icensed social worker," for example, is as follows:

> "Licensed social worker" means a person who holds a license authorizing the practice of social work, which includes social services to individuals, groups or communities in any one or more of the fields of social casework, social group work, community organization for social welfare, social work research, social welfare administration or social work education.

Thus, in applying the "social worker" variant of the "psychotherapist" privilege, it will be necessary to determine whether the information provided to the social worker was provided to him in his capacity as a psychotherapist, or in his capacity as an administrator of social welfare, a community organizer, etc. Worse still, if the privilege is to have its desired effect (and is not to mislead the client), it will presumably be necessary for the social caseworker to advise, as the conversation with his welfare client proceeds, which portions are privileged and which are not.

[A]lthough the Court is technically correct that "the vast majority of States explicitly extend a testimonial privilege to licensed social workers," that uniformity exists only at the most superficial level. No State has adopted the privilege without restriction; the nature of the restrictions varies enormously from jurisdiction to jurisdiction; and 10 States, I reiterate, effectively reject the privilege entirely. It is fair to say that there is scant national consensus even as to the propriety of a social-worker psychotherapist privilege, and none whatever as to its appropriate scope. In other words, the state laws to which the Court appeals for support demonstrate most convincingly that adoption of a social-worker psychotherapist privilege is a job for Congress....

In its consideration of this case, the Court was the beneficiary of no fewer than 14 amicus briefs supporting respondents, most of which came from such organizations as the American Psychiatric Association, the American Psychoanalytic Association, the American Association of State Social Work Boards, the Employee Assistance Professionals Association, Inc., the American Counseling Association, and the National Association of Social Workers. Not a single amicus brief was filed in support of petitioner. That is no surprise. There is no self-interested organization out there devoted to pursuit of the truth in the federal courts. The expectation is, however, that this Court will have that interest prominently indeed, primarily in mind. Today we have failed that expectation, and that responsibility. It is no small matter to say that, in some cases, our federal courts will be the tools of injustice rather than unearth the truth where it is available to be found. The common law has identified a few instances where that is tolerable. Perhaps Congress may conclude that it is also tolerable for the purpose of encouraging psychotherapy by social workers. But that conclusion assuredly does not burst upon the mind with such clarity that a judgment in favor of suppressing the truth ought to be pronounced by this honorable Court. I respectfully dissent.

■ NOTES ON *JAFFEE* AND THE FEDERAL PSYCHOTHERAPIST-PATIENT PRIVILEGE

1. On remand, a second jury in *Jaffee* awarded plaintiff $100,000 on her federal claim (more than twice what the first jury awarded), but nothing on her state law claim (the first jury had awarded $2 million). The case again went up on appeal, this time focusing on the question whether plaintiffs' attorneys could recover fees for advancing the ultimately unsuccessful argument claiming entitlement to the therapist's records. The trial judge had awarded just over $446,000 in fees and $19,000 in costs, about half the amount sought, disallowing the fee petition for the second trial because it was "necessitated by plaintiffs having incorrectly argued against a privilege in the first trial." See Jaffee v. Redmond, 142 F.3d 409 (7th Cir. 1998) (reversing to reconsider awarding fees connected with the unsuccessful challenge to the privilege claim and to reconsider awarding fees for the second trial).

2. In ringing terms, *Jaffee* confirms the federal psychotherapist-patient privilege, derived from common law under FRE 501.

(a) The first decision by the Court of Appeals stressed that the privilege rests on both instrumental and humanistic bases. See Jaffee v. Redmond, 51 F.3d 1346, 1355 (7th Cir. 1994) (confidentiality encourages people to get help and right of privacy is "fundamental tenet" in American legal system). In contrast, the Supreme Court stressed the instrumental rationale. To be sure, the majority nods toward privacy in recognizing "the sensitive nature" of problems leading to therapy, so disclosure may lead to "embarrassment or disgrace," and the next paragraph concludes that the privilege "serves important private interests." Does *Jaffee* adequately support privacy?

(b) Has the instrumental justification been adequately made? The dissent argues that psychotherapy was a "thriving practice" before the privilege was "invented," and that we have no idea whether one is deterred from seeking therapy by the absence of a privilege (hence the risk that confidences will come out later). Others have argued in a similar vein. See Daniel W. Shuman, Myron F. Weiner & Gilbert Pinard, The Privilege Study (Part III): Psychotherapist-Patient Communications in Canada, 9 Int'l J.L. & Psychiatry 393, at 416-417 (1986) (treatment occurs without regard to privilege); Myron F. Weiner & Daniel W. Shuman, The Privilege Study: An Empirical Examination of the Psychotherapist-Patient Privilege, 60 N.C. L. Rev. 893 (1982) (survey of lay persons, patients, therapists, and judges shows privilege may affect therapy for only a "small percentage" of people). And see Edward Imwinkelried, The Rivalry Between Truth and Privilege: The Weakness of the Supreme Court's Instrumental Reasoning in

Jaffee v. Redmond, 49 Hastings L.J. 969 (1998) (instrumentalist justification has not been made; Court should have rested its decision on privacy).

(c) Consider these facts: Everyone thinks trusting the therapist is essential, and therapy depends on frank disclosure of acts, fears, and thoughts that are likely to be personal and embarrassing, and therapists are ethically required to warn patients of limits of confidentiality. Should we hesitate to ground the privilege in an instrumentalist rationale because we cannot find empirical verification that the privilege is needed?

3. Sometimes critics argue that neither privacy nor the instrumental rationale justifies the privilege because so much of what we say is unprotected. Thus the dissent in *Jaffee* argues that there is no privilege for conversations with "parents, siblings, best friends and bartenders." And the dissent asks "the average citizen" whether "your mental health" would be more impaired by discouraging psychiatric treatment or "preventing you from getting advice from your mom?" On the law of privilege for communication between parents and children, see Catherine J. Ross, Implementing Constitutional Rights for Children: The Parent-Child Privilege in Context, 14 Stan. L. & Pol'y Rev. 85 (2003) (proposing privilege covering communications from minor child to parent, based on liberty interest of parent in freedom from government intrusion into parent-child relationship). Some might think Justice Scalia shot himself in the foot by putting the last question, but his serious point is that many conversations that are doubtless crucial to psychological wellbeing are not privileged. So why a privilege here? One of us tried to answer this argument in these terms:

> [O]ther aspects of privacy are protected. The privilege for spousal confidences covers the most critical realm of private communications (the area that seems most important to the greatest number) and a privilege covers religious consultations (including the confessional). A broader familial privilege reaching conversations between parent and child and among siblings is not out of the question and may be warranted. It is true that other private conversations are not privileged, even if private, intimate and "therapeutic." People sometimes have such talks in the belief that what they say "cannot come back to haunt" them, like conversations with trusted friends, bartenders or running partners. And people sometimes "bear their souls" or "unload" on passing acquaintances in the belief that the conversation is "safe" because neither expects to see the other again, or to have overlapping contacts. But lack of privilege here does not mean the psychotherapist-patient privilege is fatally narrow, nor undercut the theory that it provides important protection for privacy as a value in itself. The area covered by the privileges mentioned above is, after all, very substantial. And what is not covered is often undiscoverable and unusable anyhow, meaning privacy is preserved even without a privilege: Familial communications are hard to get at if the witness is reluctant to cooperate, and conversations with bartenders and passing acquaintances are beyond reach in all but high-profile criminal prosecutions or civil litigation (O.J. Simpson, JonBenet Ramsey, the cigarette litigation).

Mueller, The Federal Psychotherapist-Patient Privilege After *Jaffee*: Truth and Other Values in a Therapeutic Age, 49 Hastings L.J. 947, 955-957 (1998) (also arguing that one can be "too embarrassed about crafting an imperfect rule," as we must choose between "a failsafe rule that is too general and uncertain for ready application and a clear rule that is too broad or narrow," and suggesting that *Jaffee* merits respect as "a compromise between functionality and precision").

Karen Beyer and the Psychotherapist-Patient Privilege

Karen Beyer

After the *Jaffee* decision, therapist Karen Beyer wrote about what happened. She said Mary Lu Redmond was "traumatized" by the shooting, having called an ambulance while the victim's relatives "stared in horror and anger," and that she sought counseling from the Human Services Department of the Village for which she worked. Beyer, as Director of the Department, took her case, and worked with Redmond for almost two years. When the subpoena came, Redmond did not want the records disclosed, and Beyer agreed. The subpoena was "the beginning of the end" of their therapeutic relationship because of the "extreme pressure" both felt. Lawyers advised Beyer to turn over the records, but she refused "because of the devastating effect I believed this would have had on Redmond," who was a "proud and very private person" whose records reflected "nothing more than her private struggle to heal." The refusal to hand over the records led to a referral to the office of the US Attorney. No charges were brought, but Beyer reports believing that she "might go to jail." See Karen Beyer, First Person: *Jaffee v. Redmond* Therapist Speaks, 34 American Psychoanalyst 1 (2000). Medical and psychiatric records are often in the hands of doctors and hospitals or other institutions, so the privilege holder and the possessor of the information are different persons. The same is often true of records covered by attorney-client privilege, but lawyers are in a good position to assert their clients' rights. Doctors and psychotherapists—and hospitals and similar institutions—are often reluctant to expend efforts resisting court orders, which may require hiring a lawyer and becoming "involved" in matters they'd rather steer away from. Some states have special rules requiring the information seeker, if she seeks medical or other records that are likely covered by a privilege, to obtain a court order first (not just a subpoena), with notice to the privilege holder and an opportunity for a hearing, or a waiver signed by the privilege holder. See, e.g., Colorado Civil Rule 45(c)(2)(B).

4. Without hesitation, *Jaffee* extends privilege protection to sessions with licensed clinical social workers. But in 1975, when the Court promulgated the Rules, the relevant provision extended only to psychiatrists and psychologists, not social workers. See Proposed Rule 504(a)(2). Should it extend to social workers? What about arguments that social workers have less training and often engage in activity other than psychotherapy?

5. Should the privilege extend to receptionists, secretaries, and other aides? See State v. Miller, 709 P.2d 225 (Or. 1985) (defendant called state mental hospital and asked to speak to psychiatrist; receptionist asked his problem and he confessed to murder; communications to aides "reasonably necessary" for transmitting communication are privileged; even though no psychotherapist-patient relationship was yet established, privilege protects communications that defendant believed necessary to obtain diagnosis or treatment).

6. Although refusing to delineate the scope of the privilege, the Court in a footnote expresses "no doubt" that there are situations where the privilege must "give way," mentioning the case where "a serious threat of harm to the patient or to others can be averted only by means of a disclosure." Should there be a "future crimes" exception? Proposed-but-rejected Rule 504 did not have such an exception, perhaps in the belief that "less harm" will occur if patients "feel free to ventilate their intentions." 2 J. Weinstein & M. Berger, Weinstein's Evidence 504-524 (1981). Is a policy of letting patients "ventilate their intentions" undermined by developments in tort law allowing claims against psychotherapists who fail to warn potential victims of threats by patients? A famous California decision held that a therapist must disclose threats by the patient if he suspects that the patient may act on the threats, and the decision has wide following. See Tarasoff v. Regents of University of California, 551 P.2d 334 (Cal. 1976). See United States v. Hayes, 227 F.3d 578 (6th Cir. 2000) (discussing tension between privilege and *Tarasoff*; recognizing doctor's duty to warn potential victims and perhaps testify in proceedings to hospitalize patient, but refusing to find broad waiver that would allow psychotherapist to testify against patient in criminal case). The Ninth Circuit declined to recognize a "dangerous patient" exception under federal law, because it would "significantly injure" the underlying interests and offers "little practical advantage" while encroaching on "policy prerogatives of the states." United States v. Chase, 340 F.3d 978, 992 (9th Cir. 2003). But see United States v. Auster, 517 F.3d 312 (5th Cir. 2008) (patient had no reasonable expectation of confidentiality where psychotherapist had informed him repeatedly that any violent threats would be communicated to potential victims).

7. *Jaffee* stresses state law, and state statutory law at that, as important to the federal privilege that the Court crafts in the civil rights suit brought on behalf of Ricky Allen against Officer Redmond. From one perspective, this reference is fitting, since state law constitutes legitimate expressions of social concerns and normative principles. From other perspectives, however, the stress on state law is troublesome. For one thing, how is a federal court to fashion federal law in a manner that is consistent both with the methods of common law development mandated by FRE 501 and directive of *Jaffee* to look to state statutes? In some states, the statutory privilege covers counseling obtained by a person charged with child abuse, but other states carve out an exception in this situation, on the theory that getting at whatever the defendant told his psychotherapist is more important than encouraging therapy or protecting privacy. How should a federal court faced with the issue (as might happen if a Native American or a person working on a military base were prosecuted for child abuse) fashion the appropriate federal rule? Deciding which statute embodies the better policy is surely difficult, and the process of choice here does not look much like common law evolution. See generally Mueller, supra note 3, at 959-961 (1998) (it would be better to recognize that this privilege is substantive, and for federal courts to apply the law of the state where they sit).

8. The psychotherapist-patient privilege is an outgrowth of the physician-patient privilege, which federal courts do not recognize, although it exists by statute in most states. The drafters of the Federal Rules concluded that "exceptions [to the physician-patient privilege] which have been found necessary in order to obtain information required by the public interest or to avoid fraud are so numerous as to leave little if any basis for the privilege." ACN to Proposed FRE 504. Commonly recognized exceptions make the physician-patient privilege inapplicable in criminal cases, in civil cases where the patient puts his medical condition in issue, or when reporting of a wide variety of illnesses or injuries as required by statute.

SPOUSAL PRIVILEGES

1. Introduction

Early in the common law tradition, one spouse was incompetent to testify for or against the other. This incompetency grew out of the rule making parties themselves incompetent as witnesses, combined with the legal fiction that husband and wife were but one person. When this ground of incompetency disappeared, the spouse of a party was still prevented from testifying adversely, but the issue came to be viewed in terms of privilege, based on considerations of marital harmony and privacy.

Common law and most modern statutes recognize two related but distinct spousal privileges. One bars adverse spousal testimony; the other protects spousal confidences. The two doctrines often overlap, but there are significant differences as well.

In one sense, the testimonial privilege is the broader of the two. It goes beyond protecting communications and blocks all testimony by one spouse against another, including accounts of premarital acts or events. The spousal confidences privilege excludes only testimony about private communications between spouses (and perhaps some behavior in private settings) while they were married. In another sense, the testimonial privilege is the narrower of the two. It applies only if the spouses are married when the testimony is sought. But the spousal confidences privilege is usually said to protect the interval of the marriage forever, hence blocking post-dissolution testimony describing private communications occurring during marriage.

These privileges generally apply to same-sex couples in states that recognize same-sex marriages, civil unions, or domestic partnerships. A variety of statutes, either expressly or by implication, extend these privileges to same-sex couples. See, e.g., 15 Vt. Stat. Ann. §8 (2009) (terms relating to "marital" or "familial" relationships shall be construed consistently with statutes authorizing same-sex marriage and "for all purposes throughout the law"); N.J. Stat. Ann. 2A:84A-17(2) (2006) (extending spousal testimonial privilege to partners in civil unions); Or. Rev. Stat. §106.340(1) (2007) (conferring to domestic partners "any privilege" or "immunity" enjoyed by married persons); Rev. Code. Wash. 26.60.015 (2009) (same).

2. Testimonial Privilege

The testimonial privilege serves two purposes. The first is to preserve ongoing marriages:

> The basic reason the law has refused to pit wife against husband or husband against wife in a trial where life or liberty is at stake was a belief that such a policy was necessary to foster family peace, not only for the benefit of the husband, wife and children, but for the benefit of the public as well.

Hawkins v. United States, 358 U.S. 74, 77 (1958) (opinion by Justice Black). The other is somewhat harder to state, but it relates to the unseemliness of casting one spouse as the accuser of the other. Pitting spouse against spouse seems to invade and deny human dignity—an enterprise in which the government should not engage. Testifying against a spouse would likely amount to what Justice Black called an "unforgivable act" sealing the fate of any marriage.

The underlying logic suggests that the privilege should apply in civil and criminal cases alike. But it is only rarely claimed in civil litigation, and in federal courts it is doubtful that the privilege applies in civil suits. See Ryan v. Commissioner of Internal Revenue, 568 F.2d 531, 542-544 (7th Cir. 1977) (in civil suit, court leaves the question open but denies the privilege), *cert. denied*, 439 U.S. 820 (1978).

Jurisdictions disagree on the question whether both spouses hold the testimonial privilege, or only one—whether only the witness holds the privilege (so he or she can refuse to testify) or only the defendant (so he or she can block the spouse from testifying), or both. If both hold the privilege, then one spouse can testify against the other only in the unlikely event that both agree.

TRAMMEL v. UNITED STATES

United States Supreme Court
445 U.S. 40 (1980)

MR. CHIEF JUSTICE BURGER delivered the opinion of the Court.

We granted certiorari to consider whether an accused may invoke the privilege against adverse spousal testimony so as to exclude the voluntary testimony of his wife. This calls for a re-examination of Hawkins v. United States, 358 U.S. 74 (1958).

I

On March 10, 1976, petitioner Otis Trammel was indicted with two others, Edwin Lee Roberts and Joseph Freeman, for importing heroin into the United States from Thailand and the Philippine Islands and for conspiracy to import heroin . . . . The indictment also named six unindicted co-conspirators, including petitioner's wife Elizabeth Ann Trammel.

According to the indictment, petitioner and his wife flew from the Philippines to California in August 1975, carrying with them a quantity of heroin. Freeman and Roberts assisted them in its distribution. Elizabeth Trammel then traveled to Thailand where she purchased another supply of the drug. On November 3, 1975, with four ounces of heroin on her person, she boarded a plane for the United States. During a routine customs search in Hawaii, she was searched, the heroin was discovered, and she was arrested. After discussions with Drug Enforcement Administration agents, she agreed to cooperate with the Government.

Prior to trial on this indictment, petitioner moved to sever his case from that of Roberts and Freeman. He advised the court that the Government intended to call his wife as an adverse witness and asserted his claim to a privilege to prevent her from testifying against him. At a hearing on the motion, Mrs. Trammel was called as a Government witness under a grant of use immunity. She testified that she and petitioner were married in May 1975 and that they remained married.[1] She explained that her cooperation with the Government was based on assurances that she would be given lenient treatment.[2] She then described, in considerable detail, her role and that of her husband in the heroin distribution conspiracy.

After hearing this testimony, the District Court ruled that Mrs. Trammel could testify in support of the Government's case to any act she observed during the marriage and to any communication "made in the presence of a third

---

[1] In response to the question whether divorce was contemplated, Mrs. Trammel testified that her husband had said that "I would go my way and he would go his."

[2] The Government represents to the Court that Elizabeth Trammel has not been prosecuted for her role in the conspiracy.

person"; however, confidential communications between petitioner and his wife were held to be privileged and inadmissible. The motion to sever was denied.

At trial, Elizabeth Trammel testified within the limits of the court's pretrial ruling; her testimony, as the Government concedes, constituted virtually its entire case against petitioner. He was found guilty on both the substantive and conspiracy charges and sentenced to an indeterminate term of years pursuant to the Federal Youth Corrections Act.

In the Court of Appeals petitioner's only claim of error was that the admission of the adverse testimony of his wife, over his objection, contravened this Court's teaching in Hawkins v. United States, supra, and therefore constituted reversible error. The Court of Appeals rejected this contention. It concluded that *Hawkins* did not prohibit "the voluntary testimony of a spouse who appears as an unindicted co-conspirator under grant of immunity from the Government in return for her testimony."

II

The privilege claimed by petitioner has ancient roots. Writing in 1628, Lord Coke observed that "it hath beene resolved by the Justices that a wife cannot be produced either against or for her husband." 1 E. Coke, A Commentarie upon Littleton 6b (1628). This spousal disqualification sprang from two canons of medieval jurisprudence: first, the rule that an accused was not permitted to testify in his own behalf because of his interest in the proceeding; second, the concept that husband and wife were one, and that since the woman had no recognized separate legal existence, the husband was that one. From those two now long-abandoned doctrines, it followed that what was inadmissible from the lips of the defendant-husband was also inadmissible from his wife.

Despite its medieval origins, this rule of spousal disqualification remained intact in most common-law jurisdictions well into the 19th century. It was applied by this Court in Stein v. Bowman, 13 Pet. 209, 220-223, 10 L. Ed. 129 (1839) . . . and again in Jin Fuey Moy v. United States, 254 U.S. 189 (1920), where it was deemed so well established a proposition as to "hardly requir[e] mention." Indeed, it was not until 1933, in Funk v. United States, 290 U.S. 371, that this Court abolished the testimonial disqualification in the federal courts, so as to permit the spouse of a defendant to testify in the defendant's behalf. *Funk*, however, left undisturbed the rule that either spouse could prevent the other from giving adverse testimony. The rule thus evolved into one of privilege rather than one of absolute disqualification.

The modern justification for this privilege against adverse spousal testimony is its perceived role in fostering the harmony and sanctity of the marriage relationship. Notwithstanding this benign purpose, the rule was sharply criticized. Professor Wigmore termed it "the merest anachronism in legal theory and an indefensible obstruction to truth in practice." 8 Wigmore, §2228, at 221 . . . . In its place, Wigmore and others suggested a privilege protecting only private marital communications, modeled on the privilege between priest and penitent, attorney and client, and physician and patient.[5]

These criticisms influenced the American Law Institute, which, in its 1942 Model Code of Evidence, advocated a privilege for marital confidences, but expressly rejected a rule vesting in the defendant the right to exclude all adverse testimony of his spouse. [See Rule 215 (1942).] In 1953 the Uniform Rules of Evidence, drafted by the National Conference of Commissioners on Uniform State Laws, followed a similar course; it limited the privilege to confidential communications and "abolishe[d] the rule, still existing in some states, and largely a sentimental relic, of not requiring one spouse to testify against the other in a criminal action." See Rule 23(2) and comments. Several state legislatures enacted similarly patterned provisions into law.

In Hawkins v. United States, 358 U.S. 74 (1958), this Court considered the continued vitality of the privilege against adverse spousal testimony in the federal courts. There the District Court had permitted petitioner's wife, over his objection, to testify against him. With one questioning concurring opinion, the Court held the wife's testimony inadmissible; it took note of the critical comments that the common-law rule had engendered, but chose not to abandon it. Also rejected was the Government's suggestion that the Court modify the privilege by vesting it in the witness-spouse, with freedom to testify or not independent of the defendant's control. The Court viewed this proposed modification as antithetical to the widespread belief, evidenced in the rules then in effect in a majority of the States and in England, "that the law should not force or encourage testimony which might alienate husband and wife, or further inflame existing domestic differences."

Hawkins, then, left the federal privilege for adverse spousal testimony where it found it, continuing "a rule which bars the testimony of one spouse against the other unless both consent." Accord, Wyatt v. United States, 362 U.S. 525 (1960).[7] However, in so doing, the Court made clear that its decision was not meant to "foreclose whatever changes in the rule may eventually be dictated by 'reason and experience.'"

III

A

The Federal Rules acknowledge the authority of the federal courts to continue the evolutionary development of testimonial privileges in federal criminal trials

---

[5] This Court recognized just such a confidential marital communications privilege in Wolfle v. United States, 291 U.S. 7 (1934), and in Blau v. United States, 340 U.S. 332 (1951). In neither case, however, did the Court adopt the Wigmore view that the communications privilege be substituted *in place* of the privilege against adverse spousal testimony. The privilege as to confidential marital communications is not at issue in the instant case; accordingly, our holding today does not disturb *Wolfle* and *Blau*.

[7] The decision in *Wyatt* recognized an exception to *Hawkins* for cases in which one spouse commits a crime against the other. This exception, placed on the ground of necessity, was a longstanding one at common law. It has been expanded since then to include crimes against the spouse's property, and in recent years crimes against children of either spouse. Similar exceptions have been found to the confidential marital communications privilege.

"governed by the principles of the common law as they may be interpreted . . . in the light of reason and experience." FRE 501. The general mandate of Rule 501 was substituted by the Congress for a set of privilege rules drafted by the Judicial Conference Advisory Committee on Rules of Evidence and approved by the Judicial Conference of the United States and by this Court. That proposal defined nine specific privileges, including a husband-wife privilege which would have codified the *Hawkins* rule and eliminated the privilege for confidential marital communications. See proposed FRE 505. In rejecting the proposed Rules and enacting Rule 501, Congress manifested an affirmative intention not to freeze the law of privilege. Its purpose rather was to "provide the courts with the flexibility to develop rules of privilege on a case-by-case basis," 120 Cong. Rec. 40891 (1974) (statement of Rep. Hungate), and to leave the door open to change.[8]

Although Rule 501 confirms the authority of the federal courts to reconsider the continued validity of the *Hawkins* rule, the long history of the privilege suggests that it ought not to be casually cast aside. That the privilege is one affecting marriage, home, and family relationships—already subject to much erosion in our day—also counsels caution. At the same time, we cannot escape the reality that the law on occasion adheres to doctrinal concepts long after the reasons which gave them birth have disappeared and after experience suggests the need for change . . . . Mr. Justice Black admonished in another setting, "[w]hen precedent and precedent alone is all the argument that can be made to support a court-fashioned rule, it is time for the rule's creator to destroy it." Francis v. Southern Pacific Co., 333 U.S. 445, 471 (1948) (dissenting opinion).

B

Since 1958, when *Hawkins* was decided, support for the privilege against adverse spousal testimony has been eroded further. Thirty-one jurisdictions, including Alaska and Hawaii, then allowed an accused a privilege to prevent adverse spousal testimony. The number has now declined to 24.[9] In 1974, the National Conference on Uniform State Laws revised its Uniform Rules of Evidence, but again rejected the *Hawkins* rule in favor of a limited privilege for confidential

---

[8] Petitioner's reliance on 28 U.S.C. §2076 for the proposition that this Court is without power to reconsider *Hawkins* is ill-founded. That provision limits this Court's *statutory* rulemaking authority by providing that rules "creating, abolishing, or modifying a privilege shall have no force or effect unless . . . approved by act of Congress." It was enacted principally to insure that state rules of privilege would apply in diversity jurisdiction cases unless Congress authorized otherwise. In Rule 501 Congress makes clear that §2076 was not intended to prevent the federal courts from developing testimonial privilege law in federal criminal cases on a case-by-case basis "in light of reason and experience"; indeed, Congress encouraged such development.

[9] [Court collects state statutes and suggests that they show that (a) eight states "provide that one spouse is incompetent to testify against the other in a criminal proceeding," (b) 16 states "provide a privilege against adverse spousal testimony and vest the privilege in both spouses or in the defendant-spouse alone," (c) nine states "entitle the witness-spouse alone to assert a privilege against adverse spousal testimony," and (d) 17 states "have abolished the privilege in criminal cases." The District of Columbia has a statute "which vests the privilege against adverse spousal testimony in the witness spouse."]

communications. See Uniform Rules of Evidence, Rule 504. That proposed rule has been enacted in Arkansas, North Dakota, and Oklahoma— each of which in 1958 permitted an accused to exclude adverse spousal testimony.[10] The trend in state law toward divesting the accused of the privilege to bar adverse spousal testimony has special relevance because the laws of marriage and domestic relations are concerns traditionally reserved to the states. Scholarly criticism of the *Hawkins* rule has also continued unabated.

C

Testimonial exclusionary rules and privileges contravene the fundamental principle that "'the public . . . has a right to every man's evidence.'" United States v. Bryan, 339 U.S. 323, 331 (1950). As such, they must be strictly construed and accepted "only to the very limited extent that permitting a refusal to testify or excluding relevant evidence has a public good transcending the normally predominant principle of utilizing all rational means for ascertaining truth." Elkins v. United States, 364 U.S. 206, 234 (1960) (Frankfurter, J., dissenting). Here we must decide whether the privilege against adverse spousal testimony promotes sufficiently important interests to outweigh the need for probative evidence in the administration of criminal justice.

It is essential to remember that the *Hawkins* privilege is not needed to protect information privately disclosed between husband and wife in the confidence of the marital relationship—once described by this Court as "the best solace of human existence." Stein v. Bowman, 13 Pet., at 223, 10 L. Ed. 129 [1839]. Those confidences are privileged under the independent rule protecting confidential marital communications. The *Hawkins* privilege is invoked, not to exclude private marital communications, but rather to exclude evidence of criminal acts and of communications made in the presence of third persons.

No other testimonial privilege sweeps so broadly. The privileges between priest and penitent, attorney and client, and physician and patient limit protection to private communications. These privileges are rooted in the imperative need for confidence and trust. The priest-penitent privilege recognizes the human need to disclose to a spiritual counselor, in total and absolute confidence, what are believed to be flawed acts or thoughts and to receive priestly consolation and guidance in return. The lawyer-client privilege rests on the

---

[10] In 1965, California took the privilege from the defendant-spouse and vested it in the witness-spouse, accepting a study commission recommendation that the "latter [was] more likely than the former to determine whether or not to claim the privilege on the basis of the probable effect on the marital relationship." See Cal. Evid. Code Ann. §§970-973 (West 1966 and Supp. 1979) and 1 California Law Revision Commission, Recommendation and Study Relating to the Marital "For and Against" Testimonial Privilege, at F-5 (1956). See also 6 California Law Revision Commission, Tentative Privileges Recommendation—Rule 27.5, pp. 243-244 (1964). Support for the common-law rule has also diminished in England. In 1972, a study group there proposed giving the privilege to the witness-spouse, on the ground that "if [the wife] is willing to give evidence . . . the law would be showing excessive concern for the preservation of marital harmony if it were to say that she must not do so." Criminal Law Revision Committee, Eleventh Report, Evidence (General) 93.

need for the advocate and counselor to know all that relates to the client's reasons for seeking representation if the professional mission is to be carried out. Similarly, the physician must know all that a patient can articulate in order to identify and to treat disease; barriers to full disclosure would impair diagnosis and treatment.

The *Hawkins* rule stands in marked contrast to these three privileges. Its protection is not limited to confidential communications; rather it permits an accused to exclude all adverse spousal testimony. As Jeremy Bentham observed more than a century and a half ago, such a privilege goes far beyond making "every man's house his castle," and permits a person to convert his house into "a den of thieves." 5 Rationale of Judicial Evidence 340 (1827). It "secures, to every man, one safe and unquestionable and ever ready accomplice for every imaginable crime."

The ancient foundations for so sweeping a privilege have long since disappeared. Nowhere in the common-law world—indeed in any modern society—is a woman regarded as chattel or demeaned by denial of a separate legal identity and the dignity associated with recognition as a whole human being. Chip by chip, over the years those archaic notions have been cast aside so that "[n]o longer is the female destined solely for the home and the rearing of the family, and only the male for the marketplace and the world of ideas."

The contemporary justification for affording an accused such a privilege is also unpersuasive. When one spouse is willing to testify against the other in a criminal proceeding—whatever the motivation—their relationship is almost certainly in disrepair; there is probably little in the way of marital harmony for the privilege to preserve. In these circumstances, a rule of evidence that permits an accused to prevent adverse spousal testimony seems far more likely to frustrate justice than to foster family peace. Indeed, there is reason to believe that vesting the privilege in the accused could actually undermine the marital relationship. For example, in a case such as this, the Government is unlikely to offer a wife immunity and lenient treatment if it knows that her husband can prevent her from giving adverse testimony. If the Government is dissuaded from making such an offer, the privilege can have the untoward effect of permitting one spouse to escape justice at the expense of the other. It hardly seems conducive to the preservation of the marital relation to place a wife in jeopardy solely by virtue of her husband's control over her testimony.

IV

Our consideration of the foundations for the privilege and its history satisfy us that "reason and experience" no longer justify so sweeping a rule as that found acceptable by the Court in *Hawkins.* Accordingly, we conclude that the existing rule should be modified so that the witness-spouse alone has a privilege to refuse to testify adversely; the witness may be neither compelled to testify nor foreclosed from testifying. This modification—vesting the privilege in the witness-spouse—furthers the important public interest in marital harmony without unduly burdening legitimate law enforcement needs.

Here, petitioner's spouse chose to testify against him. That she did so after a grant of immunity and assurances of lenient treatment does not render her testimony involuntary. Accordingly, the District Court and the Court of Appeals were correct in rejecting petitioner's claim of privilege, and the judgment of the Court of Appeals is Affirmed.

■ NOTES ON SPOUSAL TESTIMONIAL PRIVILEGE

1. *Trammel* endorses a testimonial privilege held only by the witness-spouse. Are you convinced by the argument that when one spouse is willing to testify against the other, "their relationship is almost certainly in disrepair," and that enabling the defendant to bar testimony could "undermine the marital relationship"? What new tool does *Trammel* provide to prosecutors when both spouses are implicated in criminal activity?

2. The Tenth Circuit in *Trammel* invoked a "joint participants" exception. See United States v. Trammel, 583 F.2d 1166, 1168-1169 (10th Cir. 1980). Under it, the testimonial privilege does not apply, regardless who holds it, if spouses were joint participants in crime. Nowhere does the Court mention this point. Does that mean that there is, or that there is not, a joint participants exception after *Trammel*? Consider the case in which an unindicted wife is unwilling to testify against her husband. If they are coparticipants in the venture, a joint participants exception would enable the government to force her to testify, even if it could not otherwise do so under *Trammel.* Should her testimony be compellable? Most courts hold that the privilege continues even if both spouses were involved in criminal activity. See In re Grand Jury Subpoena (Koecher), 755 F.2d 1022, 1026-1027 (2d Cir. 1985) (*Trammel* does not announce a joint participants exception, and reviewing court is "unable to accept the proposition that a marriage cannot be a devoted one simply because at some time the partners have decided to engage in a criminal activity"), *vacated and dismissed as moot*, 475 U.S. 133 (1986). But see United States v. Clark, 712 F.2d 299, 300-301 (7th Cir. 1983) (joint participants exception applies; "rehabilitative effect of a marriage, which in part justifies the privilege, is diminished when both spouses are participants in the crime").

3. Of course a marriage must be valid when the privilege is invoked, see People v. Catlin, 26 P.3d 357, 389 (2001) (denying privilege because murder defendant's second marriage was bigamous). Given *Trammel*'s comments about a relationship "in disrepair," should courts inquire broadly into the health of the marriage when the privilege is invoked, denying protection where the marriage seems "on the rocks"? Compare United States v. Brown, 605 F.2d 389, 396 (8th Cir.) (in overruling privilege claim, court notes that wife had been with defendant husband for only two weeks and had not seen him for eight months after he left her; "difficult to visualize" how underlying values could be served by applying privilege), *cert. denied*, 444 U.S. 972 (1979) with United States v. Lilley, 581 F.2d 182, 189 (8th Cir. 1978) (declining invitation to condition claim of testimonial privilege on "judicial determination that the marriage is a happy or successful one"). See Note, "Honey, the Judge Says We're History": Abrogating the Marital Privileges via Modern Doctrines of Marital Worthiness, 77 Cornell L. Rev. 843 (1992).

4. What if the spouses are recently married, and the primary purpose of the marriage seems to be blocking testimony by one against the other? See Lutwak v. United States, 344 U.S. 604, 614-615 (1953) (war brides case in which defendants and aliens married abroad without intending to live together as spouses; "sham, phony, empty ceremony" rendered testimonial privilege unavailable); United States v. Saniti, 604 F.2d 603, 604 (9th Cir.) (where marriage was a sham, wife of defendant could testify against him), *cert. denied*, 444 U.S. 969 (1979). Is a marriage entered into after the crime and prior to trial *necessarily* a sham? See San Fratello v. United States, 340 F.2d 560, 566 (5th Cir. 1965) (fact that defendant marries witness after crime and shortly before trial did not entitle prosecutor to call spouse to testify).

5. Consider the exceptions recognized by *Trammel* in footnote 7, which include prosecutions of one spouse for a crime against the other or the children of either. Should that exception embrace situations in which a spouse is an apparently willing victim in a consensual criminal act? See Wyatt v. United States, 362 U.S. 525 (1960) (spousal testimonial privilege inapplicable in Mann Act prosecution where defendant was charged with prostituting his own wife, even though both defendant-husband and witness-wife sought to invoke the privilege, for the statute assumes that husbands induce their wives against their will to engage in such acts).

6. Five years before *Trammel* the Court had accepted the Advisory Committee's proposal of a privilege held only by the party spouse (see proposed-but-rejected Rule 505). And 20 years before that the Court in *Hawkins* had endorsed a privilege that either witness-spouse or party-spouse could invoke. Does *Trammel* represent the kind of common law evolution that Congress had in mind in adopting FRE 501 in preference to specific provisions? Is *Trammel* consistent with the spirit of the Enabling Act that bars rulemaking by the Court in the privilege area?

■ PROBLEM 12-G. Hit-and-Run

Charley and his wife Edith were returning home late one night from a party where they both had too much to drink. Charley, who was driving, failed to see Max, an elderly pedestrian who was crossing the street at a properly marked crosswalk. He struck and killed him. Charley panicked and, over Edith's screams, fled the scene without stopping and returned to their home.

After they entered their house, Pam, the babysitter, asked Edith why she was so upset. She tearfully replied, "Because Charley ran over someone on the way home." After a police investigation, criminal charges are brought against Charley for vehicular manslaughter.

At trial, Edith refuses to testify for the prosecution, claiming the testimonial privilege. The prosecutor then calls Pam as a witness at trial to relate what Edith had said to her. The court finds that Edith's statement to Pam qualifies under the excited utterance exception to the hearsay rule, but both Charley and Edith object to Pam's testimony, again asserting the testimonial privilege. What ruling?

3. Spousal Confidences Privilege

The privilege for spousal confidences has long been recognized as a necessary protection for the marital relationship. Long ago the Court praised the privilege as one based on "the deepest and soundest principles of our nature," suggesting that any inroad on the privilege would "destroy the best solace of human existence." Stein v. Bowman, 38 U.S. 209, 222-223 (1839). And recall that the modern Court, even as it sliced the testimonial privilege in half in *Trammel*, was at pains to say that the spousal confidences privilege was "not at issue" there, and that it did not "disturb" prior holdings on that privilege.

A doctrine under attack. Despite such statements of support, the privilege has come under siege. Modern courts, scholars, and reformers have attacked the doctrine.

Consider these arguments: Spousal confidences, covered at the time of their utterance, should be stripped of protection if the couple later obtains a divorce. McCormick on Evidence §85 (K. Broun ed., 6th ed. 2006). The privilege should be abolished altogether (position taken by the drafters of the Rules) for these reasons:

> The traditional justifications for privileges not to testify against a spouse and not to be testified against by one's spouse have been the prevention of marital dissension and the repugnancy of requiring a person to condemn or be condemned by his spouse. These considerations bear no relevancy to marital communications. Nor can it be assumed that marital conduct will be affected by a privilege for confidential communications of whose existence the parties in all likelihood are unaware.

ACN to Proposed Rule 505, 56 F.R.D. 245-246 (1972).

The privilege defended. The Advisory Committee may have been surprised at the vigor of modern defenders of the privilege, whose reaction helped scuttle *all* the privilege proposals in Congress. Consider this defense, advanced by the late David Louisell in response to what he considered to be the overemphasis on the instrumentalist approach:

> A marriage without the right of complete privacy of communication would necessarily be an imperfect union. Utter freedom of marital communication from all government supervision, constraint, control or observation, save only when the communications are for an illegal purpose, is a psychological necessity for the perfect fulfillment of marriage. Recognition by the state that spouses possess such right of confidential communication by reason of the nature of their relationship, promotes the public policy of furthering and safeguarding the objectives of marriage just as other institutions in the area of domestic relations or family law promote it.

Louisell, Confidentiality, Conformity and Confusion: Privileges in Federal Court Today, 31 Tul. L. Rev. 101, 111-113 (1956). Recall too the constitutional right of privacy recognized in Griswold v. Connecticut, 381 U.S. 479 (1965) (state cannot bar contraceptive use by married couples).

Consider this response by Professor Krattenmaker to the instrumentalist argument advanced by the Advisory Committee. Assuming that spousal conversations "take place without conscious, simultaneous awareness of the privilege," he replied:

> This proves little without the further assumption that subconscious, unarticulated knowledge never can influence human conduct. Surely, there is little reason to doubt that where they exist, interpersonal privileges such as that for confidential marital communications as well as confessions to clergymen provide at the very least a subconscious backdrop to the exercise of the right of privacy.

Krattenmaker, Testimonial Privileges in Federal Courts: An Alternative to the Proposed Federal Rules of Evidence, 62 Geo. L.J. 60, 92 (1973).

Finally, consider Professor Black's protest against the Advisory Committee's position:

> It ought to be enough to say of such a rule that it could easily—even often—force any decent person—anybody any of us would want to associate with—either to lie or to go to jail. No rule can be good that has that consequence—that compels the decent and honorable to evade or to disobey it.

Black, The Marital and Physician Privileges—A Reprint of a Letter to a Congressman, 1975 Duke L.J. 45, 48.

Notwithstanding the views of the Advisory Committee, the marital confidences privilege remains alive and well. Courts must address such issues as (a) what level of confidentiality suffices, (b) which spouse holds the privilege and can waive it, and (c) whether there is a joint participant exception. Consider the following case:

UNITED STATES v. MONTGOMERY

United States Court of Appeals for the Ninth Circuit
384 F.3d 1050 (2004)

GOODWIN, Circuit Judge.

[James Montgomery and Mary Lou O'Connor formed Sun Village Realty for the purpose of managing property in a resort community in Sunriver, Oregon. Sun Village contracted with owners to rent their vacation homes in return for commissions of 25-30 percent. Louise Montgomery oversaw the operation from 1989 until October 1992, when Mary O'Connor (sister of James, sister-in-law of Louise) moved to Sunriver to help James on legal issues "unrelated to this case."

Unwilling to work with O'Connor, Louise Montgomery left the office, and O'Connor took over the operations, and specifically the preparation of monthly statements of account that were sent to homeowners. O'Connor bought a duplex in Sunriver called "Goldfinch," which she sometimes rented to customers.

In January 1994, Louise Montgomery returned, and noticed "unusual situations." Suspecting that O'Connor was diverting money by assigning reservations that were not managed by Sun Village and deleting reservations from the monthly accounting, Louise "discussed the irregularities" with James, and once commented that O'Connor was "hiding reservations." When James did nothing, Louise expressed her concerns in a letter she left for him on the kitchen counter of their home. There she said that she would not "be part of a dishonest operation" and would not prepare monthly statements unless O'Connor "stops stealing" and would not solicit new owners because they "will probably be cheated."

In a later change of heart, Louise Montgomery joined her husband and sister-in-law in cheating customers, and began omitting one-night rentals from the monthly statements and creating inaccurate accounts.

Eventually owners became suspicious: Some focused on declines in rental income; others learned from neighbors that people were in their homes when the statements did not reflect occupancy; some discovered that renters signed guestbooks during periods when statements did not reflect occupancy. Sun Village allowed certain people, including Montgomery, O'Connor herself, and various members of the office staff, to stay in vacant units without cost, and these arrangements too were not reported to owners or even reflected in computer entries, being described in the office as "freebies" or "complimentary uses." When complaints were tendered to O'Connor, she referred them to Louise Montgomery, who replied simply that rent was down, sometimes on account of bad weather.

In October 1998, the IRS Criminal Division searched the records of Sun Village. In the bedroom of the Montgomery residence, they seized the note from Louise Montgomery to her husband. In October 1999, a grand jury indicted James and Louise Montgomery and Mary O'Connor on count of conspiracy and mail fraud.

Louise Montgomery agreed to testify against her husband and sister-in-law. James Montgomery and Mary O'Connor were convicted of conspiracy and mail fraud. Montgomery was sentenced to 24 months (including perjury enhancement) and O'Connor was sentenced to 18 months. The sentences were augmented because of the amount of loss. Defendants were ordered to pay $184,814.70 in restitution.]

II

Montgomery contends that the district court erred by not permitting him to claim the marital communications privilege to exclude from trial his wife's correspondence and his wife's testimony about conversations with him. The government counters that Mrs. Montgomery did not intend the information in the letter to remain confidential, that Mrs. Montgomery controls the privilege, and that the privilege does not apply because Mrs. Montgomery became an accessory after the fact. We review de novo the district court's construction of a federal rule of evidence.

A. Marital Privileges

FRE 501 provides that "the privilege of a witness [or] person . . . shall be governed by the principles of the common law as they may be interpreted by the courts of the United States in the light of reason and experience." The Supreme Court has recognized two privileges that arise from the marital relationship. The first permits a witness to refuse to testify against his or her spouse. See Trammel v. United States, 445 U.S. 40, 53 (1980). The witness spouse alone holds the privilege and may choose to waive it. Because Mrs. Montgomery decided to testify, the first privilege is not at issue.

The second privilege, called the "marital communications" privilege, provides that "[c]ommunications between the spouses, privately made, are generally assumed to have been intended to be confidential, and hence they are privileged . . . ." Wolfle v. United States, 291 U.S. 7, 14 (1934). The privilege (1) extends to words and acts intended to be a communication; (2) requires a valid marriage; and (3) applies only to confidential communications, i.e., those not made in the presence of, or likely to be overheard by, third parties. Recognizing that the privilege "obstructs the truth-seeking process," we have construed it narrowly, particularly in criminal proceedings, "because of society's strong interest in the administration of justice." United States v. Marashi, 913 F.2d 724, at 730 (9th Cir. 1990). The government bears the burden of showing that the communication was not intended to be confidential. Blau v. United States, 340 U.S. 332, 333 (1951).

There is no dispute that the letter Mrs. Montgomery wrote to her husband was a communication or that the communication was made during a valid marriage, so we must decide whether the information in the letter was intended to remain confidential. In *Wolfle*, the Court stated that "wherever a communication, because of its nature or the circumstances under which it was made, was obviously not intended to be confidential, it is not a privileged communication." Similarly, in Pereira v. United States, 347 U.S. 1 (1954), the Court stated:

> Although marital communications are presumed to be confidential, that presumption may be overcome by proof of facts showing that they were not intended to be private. The presence of a third party negatives the presumption of privacy. So too, the intention that the information conveyed be transmitted to a third person.

347 U.S. at 6 (citations omitted).

In United States v. McCown, 711 F.2d 1441 (9th Cir. 1983), we concluded that a defendant's instruction to his wife to write a check was not privileged. The defendant had directed two codefendants, who lived with the defendant and his wife, to purchase a gun, and he gave them a check written by his wife. We found the "obvious inference" to be that the defendant had not intended to keep his instruction to his wife hidden or secret from his co-defendants.

Here, the letter begins, "Dear Jimmy," and ends, "Love, Louise." Mrs. Montgomery left the letter on the kitchen counter of the couple's home, and it was recovered from the couple's bedroom during the execution of a search warrant. The letter states, "If you can't stop [O'Connor] or if we can't stop her together I am going to write to her or talk to her." When asked at trial whether she intended for Montgomery to keep "that information" to himself, Mrs. Montgomery answered: "No, I was hoping he would communicate it to his sister, Mary O'Connor."

As in *Blau*, the nature of the communication—a handwritten letter from a wife to a husband that was left on the kitchen counter of the couple's home—is "of the kind likely to be confidential." Unlike in *McCown*, we cannot draw the "obvious inference" that Mrs. Montgomery understood her request of Montgomery would be transmitted to O'Connor or that O'Connor would infer that Montgomery was acting at Mrs. Montgomery's direction. That the letter implored Montgomery to communicate the substance of her concerns to O'Connor does not render the letter itself nonconfidential.

The government has also failed to show that letter's location on the kitchen counter was an indication that it was not intended to be confidential. The fact that the couple's children resided in the house is not sufficient to establish this intention. There is no evidence that the children would likely have seen or read the letter, or that Mrs. Montgomery acted without regard to whether the children would have seen it. We will not cast aside the presumption of confidentiality by speculating that the communication was made in the presence of, or was likely to be seen by, the couple's children.

B. Holder of the Privilege

We must next decide whether Montgomery could invoke the marital communications privilege to exclude Mrs. Montgomery's communications. In admitting the evidence, the district court relied on United States v. Figueroa-Paz, 468 F.2d 1055 (9th Cir. 1972), where we stated: "Another privilege protects marital communications. It belongs to the communicating spouse, and likewise may be waived." The waiver we referred to, however, was the appellant's failure "to object to his wife's testimony as to his communications when it was offered." *Figueroa-Paz* stands for the rule that the marital communications privilege will be waived if an objection is not timely made. Our statement that the communicating spouse alone holds the privilege was nonbinding dictum. The identity of the holder of the privilege was not germane to the resolution of the case.

Neither the Supreme Court, nor this court, has interpreted the privilege as belonging exclusively to the communicating spouse. In *Blau*, the Court had "no doubt" that the recipient of a marital communication could claim "his privilege" to refuse to reveal the information to authorities. Since *Figueroa-Paz*, and without once endorsing its narrow interpretation of the privilege, we have construed the privilege to bar testimony "concerning communications between the spouses." See In re Grand Jury Investigation (Hipes), 603 F.2d 786, 788 (9th Cir. 1979) (privilege "permits either spouse . . . to assert the privilege to bar testimony concerning confidential communications between the spouses during their marriage"); see also United States v. White, 974 F.2d 1135, at 1137-38 (9th Cir. 1992); *Marashi*, 913 F.2d at 729; United States v. Bolzer, 556 F.2d 948, 951 (9th Cir. 1977).

Our sister circuits have also ruled that communications between the spouses are privileged, without vesting the privilege exclusively in the communicating spouse. [Court quotes cases from the First, Third, Fourth, Seventh, and Tenth Circuits.]

Although "federal courts follow the federal common law regarding privileges in federal criminal proceedings," United States v. Espino, 317 F.3d 788, 795 (8th Cir. 2003), in *Trammel* the Supreme Court found "special relevance" in state law trends "because the laws of marriage and domestic relations are concerns traditionally reserved to the states." Following the Court's lead by looking to the states, we count thirty-three states plus the District of Columbia that permit the non-communicating spouse to invoke the privilege outright or on behalf of the communicating spouse.[1]

Considering the language in *Blau*, our decisions since *Figueroa-Paz*, and the decisions of our sister circuits—as well as the practice of the majority of the states—we hold that either spouse may assert the privilege to prevent testimony regarding communications between spouses. Vesting the privilege in both spouses recognizes that allowing the communicating spouse to disclose

[1] [As jurisdictions that permit both spouses to invoke the privilege, court lists Alabama, Alaska, Arizona, Arkansas, California, Delaware, District of Columbia, Florida, Hawaii, Idaho, Illinois, Iowa, Kansas, Louisiana, Maryland, Minnesota, Mississippi, Missouri, Montana, Nebraska, Nevada, New Hampshire, New York, North Dakota, Ohio, Oklahoma, Oregon, Pennsylvania, South Dakota, Utah, Washington, West Virginia, Wisconsin, and Wyoming, adding that the other states either vest the privilege "in the communicating spouse" or do not have "a clear rule."]

one side of a conversation would eviscerate the privilege. As one treatise has observed, permitting each spouse to testify as to his or her own statements "invites attempts to prove circumstantially the statements of one spouse by proof of what the other had said." 2 Christopher B. Mueller & Laird C. Kirkpatrick, Federal Evidence §207 (2d ed. 1994).

Here, Mrs. Montgomery's letter was received as proof that she had conveyed her suspicions to Montgomery and that he therefore had notice of O'Connor's culpable activities. The government makes its purpose clear in its opening brief: "James Montgomery's criminal intent was proved by his inaction when confronted by his wife about his sister's theft from the clients." The government was able to prove circumstantially that he and Mrs. Montgomery had discussed O'Connor's theft. Accordingly, we conclude that the district court erred in admitting the letter and in allowing the government to inquire at trial about their communications.

C. Exceptions

The government's alternative argument, that the letter was not privileged because Mrs. Montgomery was an accessory after the fact, is a nonstarter. The government contends that Mrs. Montgomery became an accessory when she returned to the business in January 1994 and participated in the conspiracy until its completion. However, the government does not explain the crime to which Mrs. Montgomery served as an accessory after the fact, or how Mrs. Montgomery could be both a co-conspirator and an accessory after the fact during the conspiracy.

According to 18 USC §3, an accessory after the fact is one who, "knowing that an offense against the United States has been committed, receives, relieves, comforts or assists the offender to hinder or prevent his apprehension." Mrs. Montgomery was indicted on the conspiracy count, which was alleged to have continued until 1996, and each of the substantive counts of mail fraud, all of which occurred after January 1, 1995. Because we can find no completed crime to which Mrs. Montgomery served as an accessory after the fact, and the government suggests none, we need not decide whether the exception would permit admission of her testimony.

The government concedes that the "partnership in crime" exception does not apply because Mrs. Montgomery's statements were not in furtherance of any criminal activity. Although we are inclined to agree with this rationale, a more fundamental element is wanting. Here, Mrs. Montgomery's communications encouraged Montgomery to take action to end O'Connor's stealing. According to the government, Mrs. Montgomery joined the conspiracy only after those efforts proved fruitless.

In *Marashi*, we held that "the marital communications privilege does not apply to statements made in furtherance of joint criminal activity." Because Mrs. Montgomery had not become a participant at the time of her communications, no joint criminal activity had been undertaken. Accordingly, the exception does not apply. The majority of our sister circuits agree that communications made before a spouse begins to participate in the criminal activity are privileged.[2] In sum, the district court erred in admitting Mrs. Montgomery's letter and her testimony recounting her conversations with Montgomery. Because the government conceded at oral argument that any error was prejudicial, we reverse Montgomery's convictions.

[Court rejects additional challenges raised by Mary O'Connor, but agrees that the trial court mistakenly applied the Mandatory Victim's Restitution Act of 1996 because it was enacted after the crimes were committed.]

NOTES ON SPOUSAL CONFIDENCES

1. Federal courts generally limit the privilege to confidential communications, but recognize private acts as privileged when they are communicative in nature. See United States v. Estes, 793 F.2d 465 (2d Cir. 1986) (privilege applies to husband's act of pouring bag of stolen cash onto marital bed while discussing his crime; it was a communicative act). Compare Garcia-Jaramillo v. Immigration and Naturalization Service, 604 F.2d 1236, 1238 (9th Cir. 1979) (no privilege applies to spouse's post-divorce testimony on "sexual relations"). Some states take a broader view, and extend the spousal confidences privilege to private acts by one spouse in the other's presence. See People v. Daghita, 86 N.E.2d 172 (N.Y. 1949) (privilege reaches "knowledge derived from the observance of disclosive acts done in the presence or view of one spouse by the other because of the confidence existing between them by reason of the marital relation and which would not have been performed except for the confidence so existing").

2. Consider the following exceptions to the privilege:

(a) Most courts recognize a joint participants exception on the ground that "greater public good will result from permitting the spouse of an accused to testify willingly concerning their joint criminal activities than would come from permitting the accused to erect a roadblock against the search for truth." United States v. Estes, 793 F.2d 465, 466 (2d Cir. 1986) (privilege protects husband's statements to wife before she became a participant but not those made afterwards). See also United States v. Marashi, 913 F.2d 724, 730 (9th Cir. 1990) (marital communications privilege does not apply to "present or future crimes in which both spouses are participants").

(b) The privilege does not apply if one spouse is charged with a crime against the other or a child of either. See United States v. White, 974 F.2d 1135,

[2] Even were we to conclude that Mrs. Montgomery could be classified as an accessory after the fact, we would not find that exception applicable for the same reason—Mrs. Montgomery's statements were made prior to her participation.

1138 (9th Cir. 1992) (privilege does not apply to statements about crimes against "a spouse or a spouse's children"). There is a similar exception to the testimonial privilege. Hence a spouse charged with child abuse usually cannot block any kind of testimony by the other spouse, and the latter cannot refuse to testify. Usually these exceptions do not reach abuse against an outsider (someone who is not a child of either spouse), and it is unclear whether these exceptions apply if the abuse targets *both* a child of the spouses (or of one of them) and an outsider. See proposed-but-rejected FRE 505(c) (no testimonial privilege if spouse is charged with crime against "the person or property of the other, or of a child of either," or a crime against a third person "committed in the course of" a crime against the other).

(c) The privilege does not apply in spousal suits, like divorce or child custody litigation. See Chamberlain v. Chamberlain, 230 S.W.2d 184 (Mo. App. 1950) (husband's "unnatural sexual demands" were not privileged—not made verbally!).

(d) The privilege does not apply to communications in the presence of outsiders. What about children living with the spouses? See Wolfle v. United States, 291 U.S. 7, 17 (1934) (privilege does not reach spousal communications voluntarily made in presence of their children "old enough to comprehend").

THE PRIVILEGE AGAINST SELF-INCRIMINATION

1. Overview

The only privilege expressly recognized by the U.S. Constitution is the privilege against self-incrimination, guaranteed by the Fifth Amendment. Such a privilege is also recognized, in varying language, by most state constitutions. In Malloy v. Hogan, 378 U.S. 1 (1964), the Court held that the federal privilege applies to the states as a component of due process under the Fourteenth Amendment. State provisions are important if they provide more protection than the federal privilege, but the Fifth Amendment establishes a constitutional minimum in both state and federal proceedings.

The Fifth Amendment provides that "No person shall be . . . compelled in any criminal case to be a witness against himself." This language could be interpreted as guaranteeing the privilege only in criminal trials, and then only when asserted by the defendant. The Court rejected this narrow reading, however, and it is settled that the privilege applies in civil cases too, in pretrial proceedings as well as trial, and it may be asserted by any party or witness (not just defendants). The privilege applies not only in judicial proceedings, but in administrative and legislative proceedings as well. It applies whenever government power can be used to compel testimony (usually we're speaking of contempt). This broader reading seems necessary if the privilege is to have any real meaning.

The Court has summed up the reasons for the privilege in these terms:

> It reflects many of our fundamental values and most noble aspirations; our unwillingness to subject those suspected of crime to the cruel trilemma of self-accusation, perjury or contempt; our preference for an accusatorial rather than an inquisitorial system of criminal justice; our fear that self-incriminating statements will be elicited by inhumane treatment and abuses; our sense of fair play which dictates "a fair state-individual balance by requiring the government to leave the individual alone until good cause is shown for disturbing him and by requiring the government in its contest with the individual to shoulder the entire load," . . . ; our respect for the inviolability of the human personality and of the right of each individual "to a private enclave where he may lead a private life," . . . ; our distrust of self-deprecatory statements; and our realization that the privilege, while sometimes "a shelter to the guilty," is often "a protection to the innocent."

Murphy v. Waterfront Commission, 378 U.S. 52, 55 (1964). Modern commentators have suggested another rationale:

> By exercising the right to silence, a criminal abandons the lying alternative that would have involved perjurious pooling with innocents. Any such pooling might impair the credibility of the stories told by innocent suspects not possessing evidence that could corroborate their stories. Factfinders would rationally consider such stories as suspicious as all self-exonerating accounts, including those coming from guilty suspects and defendants. The probability of stories told by the innocents would consequently go down. By not pooling with innocents, a criminal defendant therefore minimizes the exposure of an innocent suspect to the risk of wrongful conviction.

Alex Stein & Daniel J. Seidmann, The Right to Silence Helps the Innocent: A Game-Theoretic Analysis of the Fifth Amendment Privilege, 114 Harv. L. Rev. 430 (2000). For opposing views, see Gordon Van Kessel, Quieting the Guilty and Acquitting the Innocent: A Close Look at a New Twist on the Right to Silence, 35 Ind. L. Rev. 925 (2002), and Staphanos Bibas, The Right to Remain Silent Helps Only the Guilty, 88 Iowa L. Rev. 421 (2003).

2. Persons Protected

The privilege against self-incrimination belongs only to natural persons. It cannot be asserted by legal entities like corporations or labor unions. Nor, for the most part, can the privilege be claimed by unincorporated associations or partnerships. According to the Court, the test is

> whether one can fairly say under all the circumstances that a particular type of organization has a character so impersonal in the scope of its membership and activities that it cannot be said to embody or represent the purely private

> or personal interest of its constituents, but rather to embody their common or group interests only. If so, the privilege cannot be invoked on behalf of the organization or its representatives in their official capacity.

United States v. White, 322 U.S. 694, 701 (1944).

Because the privilege is personal, one of several codefendants cannot claim a privilege belonging to another. Nor can an attorney or agent rely on the Fifth Amendment in refusing to testify or produce evidence that would incriminate a client or principal. A corporate employee must produce records held in an official capacity even if they would incriminate him personally.

3. Scope of Privilege

The Fifth Amendment could be interpreted so broadly that it would block any action against a defendant that might produce incriminating evidence, like compelling him to come to court if that would facilitate identification. But the Court has adopted a narrower reading: The privilege applies only to "testimonial" proof, meaning evidence that is communicative. In a leading case, the Court held that forcing defendant to give a blood sample does not violate the privilege. See Schmerber v. California, 384 U.S. 757 (1966). Other cases hold that the privilege is not offended by requiring defendant to be fingerprinted or photographed, participate in a lineup, submit a handwriting sample, wear or remove clothing or a toupee for identification purposes, speak for purposes of voice identification, or submit a hair sample.

■ PROBLEM 12-H. The Uncooperative Driver

While driving home from a tavern late one night, Darrell sideswipes a parked car. He does not stop, but a passerby notes his license number and phones the police. Darrell is stopped by a police officer ten minutes later. After failing a field sobriety test, he is placed under arrest for driving under the influence of intoxicants and failing to leave his name at the scene of an accident. At the police station, he is asked whether he would be willing to take a breathalyzer test. He is informed that under the state's implied consent law, refusal to take the test will result in automatic suspension of his driver's license for 90 days. Darrell nonetheless declines.

At trial, the prosecutor offers evidence of Darrell's refusal to take the breathalyzer test as evidence against him. Darrell objects, claiming the privilege against self-incrimination. In addition, he challenges the constitutionality of the statute requiring him to leave his name at the scene of an accident, claiming that this requirement also violates his privilege against self-incrimination. What result?

4. Incrimination

The privilege protects only against compelled disclosure that could lead to criminal liability, not disclosure that provides the basis for a civil damage claim or results in social embarrassment or public condemnation. In one case, the Supreme Court held that a claim of privilege should be upheld whenever it is "evident from the implications of the question, in the setting in which it was asked, that a responsive answer or an explanation of why it cannot be answered might be dangerous because injurious disclosure could result." But the Court added that a privilege claim may be overruled only when it is "perfectly clear, from a careful consideration of all the circumstances in the case, that the witness is mistaken, and the answer[s] cannot possibly have such tendency to incriminate." Hoffman v. United States, 341 U.S. 479, 486-488 (1951).

The privilege applies only where a danger of criminal liability still exists. If the statute of limitations has run, or the witness has received a pardon, or the Double Jeopardy Clause would bar prosecution, the privilege does not apply. The fact that one has already been convicted does not necessarily end protection, however, at least where an appeal is available, as there is a possibility of reversal and new trial. Where a conviction can only be challenged by collateral attack, courts overrule privilege claims.

An important mechanism for eliminating the danger of incrimination is a grant of immunity, which makes it possible to compel a witness to testify. There are two types: One is "transactional immunity," which protects the witness against any future prosecution relating to the matter to which he is to testify; the other is "use immunity," which precludes use of his testimony in a future prosecution, but does not block prosecution based on independent evidence. Use immunity provides less protection, and for years it was assumed that only transactional immunity could overcome a privilege claim. In Kastigar v. United States, 406 U.S. 441 (1972), however, the Court held that use immunity is sufficient. To be sure, in a later prosecution the government bears the burden of proving that its evidence derived from sources independent of any testimony that the defendant gave when his privilege claim was overruled.

The privilege applies even where the threat of criminal liability comes from another sovereign—one *other than* the jurisdiction seeking to compel the testimony. However, the fact that the testimony would be incriminating under the law of another jurisdiction does not necessarily provide a basis for refusal to testify, but is a ground under the Constitution for preventing use of that testimony in the other jurisdiction.

In Murphy v. Waterfront Commission, 378 U.S. 52 (1964), the Court held that the privilege protects a witness whose testimony was compelled in a state proceeding from suffering the use of that testimony against him in a federal trial. The Court said it would exercise its supervisory powers to require exclusion of such testimony. In dictum, the Court said testimony must also be excluded in the reverse situation, where it is compelled from a witness in a federal proceeding and later offered in a state proceeding. It also seems clear that testimony compelled from a witness in one state cannot be used against that witness in a prosecution in another state.

The most problematic case, where courts are divided, arises where potential criminal liability exists under the laws of a foreign sovereign. Because courts in this country cannot prevent future use of that testimony in a foreign court, recognizing such potential incrimination as a basis for the privilege could result in loss of the testimony. Such a result is more extreme than the outcome in domestic cases, where the testimony can be obtained if future use is restricted. Compare Mishima v. United States, 507 F. Supp. 131 (D. Alaska 1981) (privilege applies) with In re Campbell, 628 F.2d 1260 (9th Cir. 1980) (possibility of use of grand jury testimony abroad does not violate privilege).

5. Drawing Adverse Inferences

The most common form of governmental compulsion against which the privilege is directed is a contempt citation for refusal to answer questions. However, compulsion can come in other forms, including physical force and psychological coercion. In the *Miranda* case, the Court held that even custodial police interrogation is coercive enough to justify applying the privilege. See Miranda v. Arizona, 384 U.S. 436 (1966). Sometimes a later penalty or adverse consequence is imposed because a witness has asserted the privilege. If he knows such a consequence will be imposed, does this threat amount to compulsion under the Fifth Amendment? Consider the following case.

GRIFFIN v. CALIFORNIA

United States Supreme Court
380 U.S. 609 (1965)

Mr. Justice DOUGLAS delivered the opinion of the Court.

Petitioner was convicted of murder in the first degree after a jury trial in a California court. He did not testify at the trial on the issue of guilt, though he did testify at the separate trial on the issue of penalty. The trial court instructed the jury on the issue of guilt, stating that a defendant has a constitutional right not to testify. But it told the jury:

> As to any evidence or facts against him which the defendant can reasonably be expected to deny or explain because of facts within his knowledge, if he does not testify or if, though he does testify, he fails to deny or explain such evidence, the jury may take that failure into consideration as tending to indicate the truth of such evidence and as indicating that among the inferences that may be reasonably drawn therefrom those unfavorable to the defendant are the more probable . . . .

Petitioner had been seen with the deceased the evening of her death, the evidence placing him with her in the alley where her body was found. The prosecutor made much of the failure of petitioner to testify:

> . . . He would know how she got down the alley. He would know how the blood got on the bottom of the concrete steps. He would know how long he was with her in that box. He would know how her wig got off. He would know whether he beat her or mistreated her . . . .
>
> These things he has not seen fit to take the stand and deny or explain.
>
> And in the whole world, if anybody would know, this defendant would know.
>
> Essie Mae is dead, she can't tell you her side of the story. The defendant won't.

The death penalty was imposed and the California Supreme Court affirmed. The case is here on a writ of certiorari . . . .

If this were a federal trial, reversible error would have been committed. Wilson v. United States, 149 U.S. 60, so holds. It is said, however, that the *Wilson* decision rested not on the Fifth Amendment, but on an Act of Congress, now 18 U.S.C. §3481. That indeed is the fact, as the opinion of the Court in the *Wilson* case states. But that is the beginning, not the end, of our inquiry. The question remains whether, statute or not, the comment rule, approved by California, violates the Fifth Amendment.

We think it does. It is in substance a rule of evidence that allows the State the privilege of tendering to the jury for its consideration the failure of the accused to testify. No formal offer of proof is made as in other situations; but the prosecutor's comment and the court's acquiescence are the equivalent of an offer of evidence and its acceptance. The Court in the *Wilson* case stated:

> . . . It is not every one who can safely venture on the witness stand though entirely innocent of the charge against him. Excessive timidity, nervousness when facing others and attempting to explain transactions of a suspicious character, and offences charged against him, will often confuse and embarrass him to such a degree as to increase rather than remove prejudices against him. It is not every one, however honest, who would, therefore, willingly be placed on the witness stand. The statute, in tenderness to the weakness of those who from the causes mentioned might refuse to ask to be a witness, particularly when they may have been in some degree compromised by their association with others, declares that the failure of the defendant in a criminal action to request to be a witness shall not create any presumption against him.

If the words "Fifth Amendment" are substituted for . . . "statute," the spirit of the Self-Incrimination Clause is reflected. For comment on the refusal to testify is a remnant of the "inquisitorial system of criminal justice," which the Fifth Amendment outlaws. It is a penalty imposed by courts for exercising a constitutional privilege. It cuts down on the privilege by making its assertion costly.

It is said, however, that the inference of guilt for failure to testify as to facts peculiarly within the accused's knowledge is in any event natural and irresistible, and that comment on the failure does not magnify that inference into a penalty for asserting a constitutional privilege. People v. Modesto, 62 Cal. 2d 436, 452-453, 398 P.2d 753, 762-763. What the jury may infer, given no help from the court is one thing. What it may infer when the court solemnizes the silence of the accused into evidence against him is quite another. That the inference of guilt is not always so natural or irresistible is brought out in the *Modesto* opinion itself:

> Defendant contends that the reason a defendant refuses to testify is that his prior convictions will be introduced in evidence to impeach him and not that he is unable to deny the accusations. It is true that the defendant might fear that his prior convictions will prejudice the jury, and therefore another possible inference can be drawn from his refusal to take the stand.

We said in *Malloy v. Hogan* that "the same standards must determine whether an accused's silence in either a federal or state proceeding is justified." We take that in its literal sense and hold that the Fifth Amendment, in its direct application to the Federal Government, and in its bearing on the States by reason of the Fourteenth Amendment, forbids either comment by the prosecution on the accused's silence or instructions by the court that such silence is evidence of guilt.

Reversed.

Mr. Justice STEWART, with whom Mr. Justice WHITE joins, dissenting. . . .

We must determine whether the petitioner has been "compelled . . . to be a witness against himself." Compulsion is the focus of the inquiry. Certainly, if any compulsion be detected in the California procedure, it is of a dramatically different and less palpable nature than that involved in the procedures which historically gave rise to the Fifth Amendment guarantee. When a suspect was brought before the Court of High Commission or the Star Chamber, he was commanded to answer whatever was asked of him, and subjected to a far-reaching and deeply probing inquiry in an effort to ferret out some unknown and frequently unsuspected crime. He declined to answer on pain of incarceration, banishment, or mutilation. And if he spoke falsely, he was subject to further punishment. Faced with this formidable array of alternatives, his decision to speak was unquestionably coerced.

Those were the lurid realities which lay behind enactment of the Fifth Amendment, a far cry from the subject matter of the case before us. I think that the Court in this case stretches the concept of compulsion beyond all reasonable bounds, and that whatever compulsion may exist derives from the defendant's choice not to testify, not from any comment by court or counsel. In support of its conclusion that the California procedure does compel the accused to testify, the Court has only this to say: "It is a penalty imposed by courts for exercising a constitutional privilege. It cuts down on the privilege by making its assertion costly." Exactly what the penalty imposed consists of is not clear . . . .

It is not at all apparent to me, on any realistic view of the trial process, that a defendant will be at more of a disadvantage under the California practice than he would be in a court which permitted no comment at all on his failure to take the witness stand. How can it be said that the inferences drawn by a jury will be more detrimental to a defendant under the limiting and carefully controlling language of the instruction here involved than would result if the jury were left to roam at large with only its untutored instincts to guide it, to draw from the defendant's silence broad inferences of guilt? . . .

Moreover, no one can say where the balance of advantage might lie as a result of the attorneys' discussion of the matter. No doubt the prosecution's argument will seek to encourage the drawing of inferences unfavorable to the defendant. However, the defendant's counsel equally has an opportunity to explain the various other reasons why a defendant may not wish to take the stand, and thus rebut the natural if uneducated assumption that it is because the defendant cannot truthfully deny the accusations made.

I think the California comment rule is not a coercive device which impairs the right against self-incrimination but rather a means of articulating and bringing into the light of rational discussion a fact inescapably impressed on the jury's consciousness . . . .

. . . No constitution can prevent the operation of the human mind. Without limiting instructions, the danger exists that the inferences drawn by the jury may be unfairly broad. Some States have permitted this danger to go unchecked, by forbidding any comment at all upon the defendant's failure to take the witness stand. Other States have dealt with this danger in a variety of ways, as the Court's opinion indicates. Some might differ, as a matter of policy, with the way California has chosen to deal with the problem, or even disapprove of the judge's specific instructions in this case. But, so long as the constitutional command is obeyed, such matters of state policy are not for this Court to decide.

I would affirm the judgment.

■ NOTES ON *GRIFFIN* CASE

1. Consider how *Griffin* might apply in other situations. Which of the following examples of prosecutorial questions and comments are proper under the *Griffin* standard?

(a) Who else could have testified in this case? Eberhardt v. Bordenkircher, 605 F.2d 275, 278 (6th Cir. 1979) (improper).

(b) How many witnesses did the defense put on for your consideration? Adams v. State, 566 S.W.2d 387 (Ark. 1978) (improper).

(c) The question where defendant was on the night of the crime—that question he never answered. State v. Cannon, 576 P.2d 132 (Ariz. 1978) (improper).

(d) The defense has failed to produce any evidence in this case. United States v. Bright, 630 F.2d 804, 825 (5th Cir. 1980) (proper, so long as prosecutor says *defense*, not *defendant*, failed to produce evidence).

(e) "The government's evidence is uncontradicted," People v. Garcia, 420 N.E.2d 482 (Ill. App. 1981) (proper). But see Todd v. State, 598 S.W.2d 286 (Tex. App. 1980) (improper if defendant would have to testify in person to supply the contradiction).

(f) "Get [defendant] to explain 14 blows to you." State v. Barden, 572 S.E.2d 108 (N.C. 2002) (proper; statement responded to argument that defendant lacked intent to kill and asked why 14 blows did not amount to premeditated murder).

2. Does defendant have a constitutional right to an instruction that no inference may be drawn from the fact that he did not testify? See Carter v. Kentucky, 450 U.S. 288 (1981) (Yes). What if he does not want an instruction, concerned that it calls the jury's attention to the fact that he did not testify? See Lakeside v. Oregon, 435 U.S. 333 (1978) (giving "no inference" instruction over objection does not violate Fifth Amendment).

■ PROBLEM 12-I. "He Claimed the Fifth"

The City of St. Louis entered a contract with Bink's Armored Cars to collect and transport coins from city parking meters. The City sues Bink's for alleged negligence in supervising its employees, claiming that substantial sums were lost because of pilferage by Carlton, supervisor of Bink's employees assigned to collect money from the meters. Carlton is also named as a defendant.

As proof that Carlton unlawfully took the money, the City offers proof that Carlton had asserted the privilege against self-incrimination when called before a grand jury investigating the incident. Both defendants object. Again over their objections, the City calls Carlton as a witness, where he again asserts the privilege against self-incrimination.

In her summation, the attorney for the City argues that Carlton's Fifth Amendment claims should be considered as circumstantial evidence supporting its claim against Bink's and Carlton. The judge tells the jury that "a witness has a constitutional right to decline to answer on the ground that it may incriminate him, and you may (but need not) infer from such refusal that the answers would be adverse to the witness' interest."

The jury returns a large verdict against both defendants. On appeal, Bink's and Carlton argue that the court erred in (a) admitting proof of Carlton's claim of privilege before the grand jury, (b) letting the City call Carlton as a witness when it knew he would claim the privilege, (c) letting the City's attorney comment on Carlton's claim of the privilege, and (d) inviting the jury to draw an adverse inference. What result?

6. Writings

The Fifth Amendment protects against compelled writing as much as compelled testimony. Forcing a person to give an incriminating statement in writing is not different from compelling him to give it orally. But what if the government seeks a pre-existing statement or writing, forcing its production but not its making? Or what if such a writing is seized from defendant in a lawful search and used against him at trial? Is the writer being compelled to "be a witness against himself "under the Fifth Amendment?

■ PROBLEM 12-J. The Inculpatory Diary

Acting on information from a reliable informant, the Secret Service obtains a federal warrant to search a warehouse in Midville for "counterfeit currency and records pertaining to the printing and distribution of counterfeit currency." In the search, agents locate and seize $500,000 in counterfeit $20 bills along with personal papers, including a diary, kept by George Belknap, owner of the warehouse. The diary contains incriminating statements painting Belknap as the ringleader of a counterfeit currency operation.

Agents learn that he is the sole proprietor of a printing company, "Andrew Jackson Offset Printing." They also discover that he is secretary-treasurer of an unincorporated association known as the "Society for a Return to the Gold Standard," which may be the distribution network for counterfeit currency. The evidence is presented to a grand jury, which indicts Belknap for possession of counterfeit currency.

In investigating possible further charges against Belknap and others for making and distributing counterfeit currency, the grand jury issues a subpoena to Belknap for production of the records of "Andrew Jackson Offset Printing" and the "Society for a Return to the Gold Standard." Belknap resists, asserting the privilege against self-incrimination. He also moves to suppress the personal diary seized in the initial search of the warehouse, asserting that its use against him would violate his privilege.

What rulings? In formulating your answer, consider the following case and notes:

UNITED STATES v. DOE

United States Supreme Court
465 U.S. 605 (1984)

Justice Powell delivered the opinion of the Court.

This case presents the issue whether, and to what extent, the Fifth Amendment privilege against compelled self-incrimination applies to the business records of a sole proprietorship.

Respondent is the owner of several sole proprietorships. In late 1980, a grand jury, during the course of an investigation of corruption in the awarding of county and municipal contracts, served five subpoenas on respondent. The first two demanded the production of the telephone records of several of respondent's companies and all records pertaining to four bank accounts of respondent and his companies . . . . The third subpoena demanded the production of a list of virtually all the business records of one of respondent's companies for the period between January 1, 1976, and the date of the subpoena. The fourth subpoena sought production of a similar list of business records belonging to another company. The final subpoena demanded production of all bank statements and cancelled checks of two of respondent's companies that had accounts at a bank in the Grand Cayman Islands.

Respondent filed a motion in federal district court seeking to quash the subpoenas. The District Court for the District of New Jersey granted his motion except with respect to those documents and records required by law to be kept or disclosed to a public agency. In reaching its decision, the District Court noted that the Government had conceded that the materials sought in the subpoena were or might be incriminating. The court stated that, therefore, "the relevant inquiry is . . . whether the *act* of producing the documents has communicative aspects which warrant Fifth Amendment protection." The court found that the act of production would compel respondent to "admit that the records exist, that they are in his possession, and that they are authentic." While not ruling out the possibility that the Government could devise a way to ensure that the act of turning over the documents would not incriminate respondent, the court held that the Government had not made such a showing.

The Court of Appeals for the Third Circuit affirmed . . . .

The Court of Appeals next considered whether the documents at issue in this case are privileged. The court noted that this Court held in Fisher v. United States, 425 U.S. 391 (1976), that the contents of business records ordinarily are not privileged because they are created voluntarily and without compulsion. The Court of Appeals nevertheless found that respondent's business records were privileged under either of two analyses. First, the court reasoned that, notwithstanding the holdings in *Bellis* and *Fisher*, the business records of a sole proprietorship are no different from the individual owner's personal records. Noting that Third Circuit cases had held that private papers, although created voluntarily, are protected by the Fifth Amendment, the court accorded the same protection to respondent's business papers. Second, it held that respondent's act of producing the subpoenaed records would have "communicative aspects of its own." 680 F.2d at 335. The turning over of the subpoenaed documents to the grand jury would admit their existence and authenticity. Accordingly, respondent was entitled to assert his Fifth Amendment privilege rather than produce the subpoenaed documents.

The Government contended that the court should enforce the subpoenas because of the Government's offer not to use respondent's act of production against respondent in any way. The Court of Appeals noted that no formal request for use immunity under 18 U.S.C. §§6002 and 6003 had been made. In light of this failure, the court held that the District Court did not err in rejecting the Government's attempt to compel delivery of the subpoenaed records.

We granted certiorari to resolve the apparent conflict between the Court of Appeals holding and the reasoning underlying this Court's holding in *Fisher*. We now affirm in part, reverse in part, and remand for further proceedings.

The Court in *Fisher* expressly declined to reach the question whether the Fifth Amendment privilege protects the contents of an individual's tax records in his possession.[7] The rationale underlying our holding in that case is, however, persuasive here. As we noted in *Fisher*, the Fifth Amendment protects the person asserting the privilege only from *compelled* self-incrimination. Where the preparation of business records is voluntary, no compulsion is present.[8] A subpoena that demands production of documents "does not compel oral testimony; nor would it ordinarily compel the taxpayer to restate, repeat, or affirm the truth of the contents of the documents sought." Applying this reasoning in *Fisher*, we stated:

> [T]he Fifth Amendment would not be violated by the fact alone that the papers on their face might incriminate the taxpayer, for the privilege protects a person only against being incriminated by his own compelled testimonial communications. Schmerber v. California [384 U.S. 757 (1966)]; United States v. Wade [388 U.S. 218 (1967)]; and Gilbert v. California [388 U.S. 263 (1967)]. The accountant's workpapers are not the taxpayer's. They were not prepared by the taxpayer, and they contain no testimonial declarations by him. Furthermore, as far as this record demonstrates, the preparation of all of the papers sought in these cases was wholly voluntary, and they cannot be said to contain compelled testimonial evidence, either of the taxpayers or of anyone else. The taxpayer cannot

---

[7] In *Fisher*, the Court stated: "Whether the Fifth Amendment would shield the taxpayer from producing his own tax records in his possession is a question not involved here; for the papers demanded here are not his 'private papers.' . . ." We note that in some respects the documents sought in *Fisher* were more "personal" than those at issue here. The *Fisher* documents were accountant's workpapers in the possession of the taxpayers' lawyers. The workpapers related to the taxpayers' individual personal returns. To that extent, the documents were personal, even though in the possession of a third party. In contrast, each of the documents sought here pertained to respondent's businesses.

[8] Respondent's principal argument is that the Fifth Amendment should be read as creating a "zone of privacy which protects an individual and his personal records from compelled production." This argument derives from language in Boyd v. United States, 116 U.S. 616 (1886). This Court addressed substantially the same argument in *Fisher*:

> Within the limits imposed by the language of the Fifth Amendment, which we necessarily observe, the privilege truly serves privacy interests; but the Court has never on any ground, personal privacy included, applied the Fifth Amendment to prevent the otherwise proper acquisition or use of evidence which, in the Court's view, did not involve compelled testimonial self-incrimination of some sort.

425 U.S. at 399. In Andresen v. Maryland, 427 U.S. 463 (1976), the petitioner also relied on *Boyd*. In rejecting his argument, we observed that "the continued validity of the broad statements contained in some of the Court's earlier cases [has] been discredited by later opinions." See also United States v. Nobles, 422 U.S. 225, 233, n.7 (1975).

> avoid compliance with the subpoena merely by asserting that the item of evidence which he is required to produce contains incriminating writing, whether his own or that of someone else.

Id., at 409-410.

This reasoning applies with equal force here. Respondent does not contend that he prepared the documents involuntarily or that the subpoena would force him to restate, repeat, or affirm the truth of their contents. The fact that the records are in respondent's possession is irrelevant to the determination of whether the creation of the records was compelled. We therefore hold that the contents of those records are not privileged.[10]

Although the contents of a document may not be privileged, the act of producing the document may be. A government subpoena compels the holder of the document to perform an act that may have testimonial aspects and an incriminating effect. As we noted in *Fisher*:

> Compliance with the subpoena tacitly concedes the existence of the papers demanded and their possession or control by the taxpayer. It also would indicate the taxpayer's belief that the papers are those described in the subpoena. Curcio v. United States, 354 U.S. 118, 125 (1957). The elements of compulsion are clearly present, but the more difficult issues are whether the tacit averments of the taxpayer are both "testimonial" and "incriminating" for purposes of applying the Fifth Amendment. These questions perhaps do not lend themselves to categorical answers; their resolution may instead depend on the facts and circumstances of particular cases or classes thereof.

In *Fisher*, the Court explored the effect that the act of production would have on the taxpayer and determined that the act of production would have only minimal testimonial value and would not operate to incriminate the taxpayer. Unlike the Court in *Fisher*, we have the explicit finding of the District Court that the act of producing the documents would involve testimonial

---

[10] *Accord* In re Grand Jury Proceedings, 626 F.2d 1051, 1055 (C.A.1 1980) ("The line of cases culminating in *Fisher* have stripped the content of business records of any Fifth Amendment protection"). While not directly on point, Andresen v. Maryland, 427 U.S. 463 (1976), is consistent with our holding. In *Andresen*, investigators from a bicounty fraud unit obtained warrants to search the petitioner's office. During the search, the investigators seized several incriminating business records relating to the petitioner's practice as a sole practitioner of real estate law. The petitioner sought suppression of the documents on Fourth and Fifth Amendment grounds. The petitioner based his Fifth Amendment argument on "dicta in a number of cases which imply, or state, that the search for and seizure of a person's private papers violate the privilege against self-incrimination." The Court dismissed this argument and found the documents not to be privileged because the petitioner "had voluntarily committed to writing" any incriminating statements contained therein. Although *Andresen* involved a search warrant rather than a subpoena, the underlying principle is the same in this context. If the party asserting the Fifth Amendment privilege has voluntarily compiled the document, no compulsion is present and the contents of the document are not privileged.

self-incrimination.[11] The Court of Appeals agreed.[12] The District Court's finding essentially rests on its determination of factual issues. Therefore, we will not overturn that finding unless it has no support in the record. Traditionally, we also have been reluctant to disturb findings of fact in which two courts below have concurred. We therefore decline to overturn the finding of the District Court in this regard, where, as here, it has been affirmed by the Court of Appeals.[13]

The Government, as it concedes, could have compelled respondent to produce the documents listed in the subpoena. [Sections 6002 and 6003 of Title 18] provide for the granting of use immunity with respect to the potentially incriminating evidence. The Court upheld the constitutionality of the use immunity statute in Kastigar v. United States, 406 U.S. 441 (1972).

The Government did state several times before the District Court that it would not use respondent's act of production against him in any way. But counsel for the Government never made a statutory request to the District Court to grant respondent use immunity.[15] We are urged to adopt a doctrine of constructive use immunity. Under this doctrine, the courts would impose a requirement on the Government not to use the incriminatory aspects of the act of production against the person claiming the privilege even though the statutory procedures have not been followed.

---

[11] The District Court stated: With few exceptions, enforcement of the subpoenas would compel [respondent] to admit that the records exist, that they are in his possession, and that they are authentic. These communications, if made under compulsion of a court decree, would violate [respondent's] Fifth Amendment rights . . . . The government argues that the existence, possession and authenticity of the documents can be proved without [respondent's] testimonial communication, but it cannot satisfy this court as to how that representation can be implemented to protect the witness in subsequent proceedings. 541 F. Supp., at 3.

[12] The Court of Appeals stated: In the matter *sub judice*, however, we find nothing in the record that would indicate that the United States knows, as a certainty, that each of the myriad documents demanded by the five subpoenas in fact is in the appellee's possession or subject to his control. The most plausible inference to be drawn from the broadsweeping subpoenas is that the Government, unable to prove that the subpoenaed documents exist—or that the appellee even is somehow connected to the business entities under investigation—is attempting to compensate for its lack of knowledge by requiring the appellee to become, in effect, the primary informant against himself. 680 F.2d at 335.

[13] The Government concedes that the act of producing the subpoenaed documents might have had some testimonial aspects, but, it argues that any incrimination would be so trivial that the Fifth Amendment is not implicated . . . . On the basis of the findings made in this case we think it clear that the risk of incrimination was "substantial and real" and not "trifling or imaginary." Respondent did not concede in the District Court that the records listed in the subpoena actually existed or were in his possession. Respondent argued that by producing the records, he would tacitly admit their existence and his possession. Respondent also pointed out that if the Government obtained the documents from another source, it would have to authenticate them before they would be admissible at trial. See FRE 901. By producing the documents, respondent would relieve the Government of the need for authentication. These allegations were sufficient to establish a valid claim of the privilege against self-incrimination. This is not to say that the Government was foreclosed from rebutting respondent's claim by producing evidence that possession, existence, and authentication were a "foregone conclusion." *Fisher*. In this case, however, the Government failed to make such a showing.

[15] Despite repeated questioning at oral argument, counsel for the Government gave no plausible explanation for the failure to request official use immunity rather than promising that the act of producing the documents would not be used against respondent.

We decline to extend the jurisdiction of courts to include prospective grants of use immunity in the absence of the formal request that the statute requires. As we stated in Pillsbury Co. v. Conboy, 459 U.S. 248 (1983), in passing the use immunity statute, "Congress gave certain officials in the Department of Justice exclusive authority to grant immunities." "Congress foresaw the courts as playing only a minor role in the immunizing process . . . ." The decision to seek use immunity necessarily involves a balancing of the Government's interest in obtaining information against the risk that immunity will frustrate the Government's attempts to prosecute the subject of the investigation. Congress expressly left this decision exclusively to the Justice Department. If, on remand, the appropriate official concludes that it is desirable to compel respondent to produce his business records, the statutory procedure for requesting use immunity will be available.[17]

We conclude that the Court of Appeals erred in holding that the contents of the subpoenaed documents were privileged under the Fifth Amendment. The act of producing the documents at issue in this case is privileged and cannot be compelled without a statutory grant of use immunity pursuant to 18 U.S.C. §§6002 and 6003. The judgment of the Court of Appeals is, therefore, affirmed in part, reversed in part, and the case is remanded to the District Court for further proceedings in accordance with this decision.

Justice O'CONNOR, concurring.

I concur in both the result and reasoning of Justice Powell's opinion for the Court. I write separately, however, just to make explicit what is implicit in the analysis of that opinion: that the Fifth Amendment provides absolutely no protection for the contents of private papers of any kind. The notion that the Fifth Amendment protects the privacy of papers originated in Boyd v. United States, 116 U.S. 616, 630 (1886), but our decision in Fisher v. United States, 425 U.S. 391 (1976), sounded the death-knell for *Boyd.* "Several of *Boyd*'s express or implicit declarations [had] not stood the test of time[,]" and its privacy of papers concept "had long been a rule searching for a rationale . . . ." Today's decision puts a long-overdue end to that fruitless search.

Justice MARSHALL, with whom Justice BRENNAN joins, concurring in part and dissenting in part.

I concur in the Court's affirmance of the Court of Appeals' ruling that the act of producing the documents could not be compelled without an explicit grant

[17] Respondent argues that any grant of use immunity must cover the contents of the documents as well as the act of production. We find this contention unfounded. To satisfy the requirements of the Fifth Amendment, a grant of immunity need be only as broad as the privilege against self-incrimination. Murphy v. Waterfront Commission, 378 U.S. 52, 107 (1964) (White, J., concurring); see *Pillsbury Co.*; United States v. Calandra, 414 U.S. 338 at 346 (1974). As discussed above, the privilege in this case extends only to the act of production. Therefore, any grant of use immunity need only protect respondent from the self-incrimination that might accompany the act of producing his business records.

of use immunity pursuant to 18 U.S.C. §§6002 and 6003. I dissent, however, with respect to that part of the Court's opinion reversing the Court of Appeals. The basis for the reversal is the majority's disagreement with the Court of Appeals' discussion of whether the Fifth Amendment protected the contents of the documents respondent sought to withhold from disclosure. Inasmuch as the Court of Appeals' judgment did not rest upon the disposition of this issue, this Court errs by reaching out to decide it. As Justice Stevens rightly insists, "[t]his Court . . . reviews judgments, not statements in opinions."

Contrary to what Justice O'Connor contends, I do not view the Court's opinion in this case as having reconsidered whether the Fifth Amendment provides protection for the contents of "private papers of any kind." This case presented nothing remotely close to the question that Justice O'Connor eagerly poses and answers. First, as noted above, the issue whether the Fifth Amendment protects the contents of the documents was obviated by the Court of Appeals' rulings relating to the act of production and statutory use immunity. Second, the documents at stake here are business records which implicate a lesser degree of concern for privacy interests than, for example, personal diaries.

Were it true that the Court's opinion stands for the proposition that "the Fifth Amendment provides absolutely no protection for the contents of private papers of any kind," I would assuredly dissent. I continue to believe that under the Fifth Amendment "there are certain documents no person ought to be compelled to produce at the Government's request." Fisher v. United States, 425 U.S. 391 (Justice Marshall, concurring).

Justice STEVENS, concurring in part and dissenting in part.

"This Court . . . reviews judgments, not statements in opinions." Black v. Cutter Laboratories, 351 U.S. 292 (1956). When both the District Court and the Court of Appeals correctly apply the law, and correctly dispose of the issue before them, I think it is poor appellate practice for this Court to reverse.

The question in this case is whether, without tendering statutory immunity, the Government can compel the sole proprietor of a business to produce incriminating records pursuant to a grand jury subpoena. Except for the records that are required by law to be kept or to be disclosed to public agencies, the District Court held that production could not be required. The basis for that decision turned, not on any suggestion that the contents of the documents were privileged, but rather on the significance of the act of producing them . . . .

This Court's opinion is entirely consistent with both the reasoning of the Court of Appeals and its disposition of the case. This Court agrees that the subpoena directed to respondent should have been quashed—which is all that the judgment we review today contains. Accordingly, the Court of Appeals' judgment should be affirmed.

To the extent that the Court purports to reverse the judgment of the Court of Appeals, I respectfully dissent.

■ NOTES ON REQUIRED DISCLOSURE AND THE FIFTH AMENDMENT

1. In *Doe,* the Court draws a distinction between the contents of a previously-created private or business record and the *act of producing* such a record. Even if the contents of the record are not protected, the act of producing the record in response to a government demand may indeed be incriminating, because it would authenticate the record for use in a criminal prosecution of the defendant. Production of the record may nonetheless be compelled where the government grants immunity, but as the Court observed in note 17 "any grant of use immunity need only protect respondent from the self-incrimination that might accompany the act of producing his business records."

2. In 2002, the Court considered a claim of the Fifth Amendment privilege in connection with private documents of Webster Hubbell, an Associate Attorney General. The question was whether producing documents is a "testimonial communication" covered by the Fifth Amendment. Hubbell invoked his privilege, declining to produce tax papers and other documents relating to the Whitewater investigation, in response to a subpoena issued by Independent Counsel Kenneth Starr.

(a) Already under indictment for one set of offenses, Hubbell did produce the material after the court granted him immunity with Starr's consent, but the information led to a new indictment for tax-related crimes. The Court held that the immunity Hubbell got in the first case precluded the later prosecution to the extent that the "testimonial aspect" of producing the subpoenaed documents was a necessary precursor to the second prosecution. See United States v. Hubbell, 530 U.S. 27 (2002). As in *Doe,* so in *Hubbell* defendant could not "avoid compliance with the subpoena served on him merely because the demanded documents contained incriminating evidence." Yet the subpoena demanded communications (a testimonial matter). Absent immunity, Hubbell would have incriminated himself by identifying documents relevant to the subpoena.

(b) Consider whether *Hubbell,* fairly read, stands for the following: If a witness has a private document, and the government either doesn't know the document exists or doesn't know whether the witness has it, the document may be protected by the Fifth Amendment. If the witness produces the document under a grant of immunity, he performs a "testimonial act." The contents of the document, and its connection with the witness, may not be used as evidence against him. *Hubbell,* then, provides an important corrective to Justice O'Connor's statement in *Doe* that "the Fifth Amendment provides absolutely no protection for the contents of private papers of any kind."

(c) Consider the following attempt to predict the consequences of *Hubbell*:

> [T]he Supreme Court appeared to conclude that unless the government knows—really knows—of a particular document's existence, a subpoena's

> target is free to refuse to turn the document over, because the act of producing the document would testify to the fact that it does indeed exist. Of course, if the government really does know that the document exists, and hence knows what is in it . . . the government can probably get a warrant to search for and seize the document. Thus, after *Hubbell*, the working rule will be something like the following: When faced with subpoenas for documents, suspects can comply or not as they wish. For its part, the government can search for the evidence as it wants, so long as it satisfies the probable cause and warrant requirements.

William J. Stuntz, Commentary: O.J. Simpson, Bill Clinton, and the Transsubstantive Fourth Amendment, 114 Harv. L. Rev. 842, 865 (2001).

7. Required Records and Reports

If compelling the making or production of a writing can raise Fifth Amendment concerns, what is the status of records or reports required by law? Many governmental regulatory schemes mandate the keeping of various records or the submission of certain reports, often enforcing compliance by criminal sanctions.

The *Shapiro* case is the leading authority upholding the government's right to require such records. Shapiro was convicted under the Emergency Price Control Act of 1942, based on records he was required to keep, which he produced in response to a government subpoena. The Court rejected his argument that he should have immunity from prosecution because he produced the records under compulsion. The Court said there are limits on the extent to which the government can require a person to keep and produce records for use in later criminal prosecutions, but held that records could be required "when there is a sufficient relationship between the activity sought to be regulated and the public concern." See Shapiro v. United States, 335 U.S. 1 (1948).

Later cases have been more sympathetic to the privilege. In the *Albertson* case, the Court declared unconstitutional a provision of the Subversive Activities Control Act of 1950 requiring that officers of the Communist Party file a registration statement. See Albertson v. Subversive Activities Control Board, 382 U.S. 70 (1965). In a trilogy of decisions in 1968, the Court held that persons engaged in wagering activities could not be required to register or pay an occupational tax, see Marchetti v. United States, 390 U.S. 39 (1968); Grosso v. United States, 390 U.S. 62 (1968), nor to register a regulated firearm as required by a federal statute, see Haynes v. United States, 390 U.S. 85 (1968). The Court delineated the limits of the doctrine allowing required records as follows:

> The premises of the doctrine, as it is described in *Shapiro*, are evidently three: first, the purposes of the United States' inquiry must be essentially regulatory; second, information is to be obtained by requiring the preservation of records of a kind which the regulating party has customarily kept; and third, the records themselves must have assumed "public aspects" which render them at least analogous to public documents.

Grosso v. United States, 390 U.S. 62, 67-68 (1968). With respect to federal wagering tax and firearm registration statutes, *Grosso* held that these criteria were not satisfied. The registration requirements were not "essentially regulatory," but were directed at "a highly selective group inherently suspect of criminal activities." Moreover, they were not related to the types of records customarily kept and lacked sufficient "public aspects."

Later decisions have upheld amended versions of both the federal wagering tax and the firearm registration statutes, and these cases help illuminate further the boundaries of the required records doctrine. The federal wagering tax provisions were amended to allow information obtained from the required records to be used only in prosecutions under the tax statute, not in prosecutions for other gambling offenses. The act has been upheld in this more narrow form, apparently because the amended act is perceived as more "regulatory" in nature. See United States v. Haydel, 649 F.2d 1152 (5th Cir. 1981), *cert. denied*, 455 U.S. 1022 (1982).

The National Firearms Act was amended to apply to all possessors of regulated firearms, not just those suspected of unlawful activity. In addition, the registration filing is required only of the manufacturer or importer, not the transferee. The registration must include the transferee's photograph and fingerprints, and the Act prohibits receipt or possession of a firearm by anyone other than the person to whom the firearm is registered. In the *Freed* case, defendant challenged the amended Act, arguing that requiring cooperation by the transferee in providing a photograph and fingerprints for the registration form was compelled self-incrimination. The Court upheld the amended Act, partly because it specifically prohibits use, in a prosecution for a violation occurring prior to or concurrently with submission of the information or with compiling the records, of any evidence provided in complying with the statute. Justice Douglas commented:

> Appellee's argument assumes the existence of a periphery of the Self-Incrimination Clause which protects a person against incrimination not only against past or present transgressions but which supplies insulation for a career of crime about to be launched. We cannot give the Self-Incrimination Clause such an expansive interpretation.

United States v. Freed, 401 U.S. 601, 606-607 (1971).

■ NOTES ON THE REQUIRED RECORDS DOCTRINE

1. Are you satisfied that the rationale and boundaries of the required records doctrine have been adequately articulated? See Saltzburg, The Required Records Doctrine: Its Lessons for the Privilege Against Self-Incrimination, 53 U. Chi. L. Rev. 6 (1986). McCormick took the view that the only justification for the required records doctrine is "essentially a conclusion that the need for disclosure outweighs relatively minimal intrusion upon protected interests," and now that the privilege "applies only to the act of production," the limits on the protection of self-incrimination interests "may not justify" a balancing approach. See McCormick on Evidence §139 (K. Broun ed., 6th ed. 2006).

2. If one furnishes incriminating information to the government in compliance with a reporting requirement, does he lose the right to assert privilege if the information is used against him in a later prosecution? See Garner v. United States, 424 U.S. 648 (1976) (in trial for gambling, admitting return reporting gambling income; taxpayer complied with reporting requirement without claiming privilege) (disclosure not "compelled").

3. If a court-appointed guardian is suspected of abusing a child, can the guardian assert the Fifth Amendment privilege and refuse to comply with a court order to produce the child on the ground that production would be self-incriminating? See Baltimore City Department of Social Services v. Bouknight, 493 U.S. 549 (1990) (upholding order requiring parent as court-appointed custodian to produce child despite claim that production would be incriminatory, relying on cases approving compelled production in "regulatory scheme constructed to effect the State's public purposes unrelated to enforcement of its criminal laws") (leaving open question of state's "ability to use the testimonial aspects" of the act of production in later criminal proceeding).

CHAPTER 13

Foundational Evidence, Authentication

A INTRODUCTION

Before tangible evidence is admitted, such as a contract or a gun used in a crime, the proponent must show that what he offers is what he says it is—the very contract that is in issue in the case, the very gun used in the crime. The term that describes this aspect of proof is "authentication," and we say that the proponent must authenticate the exhibits that he offers. Technically, the authentication requirement reaches beyond tangible evidence, as is indicated by provisions such as FRE 901(b)(6), which addresses the matter of authenticating "telephone conversations."

Broadly speaking, authenticating an item of evidence under FRE 901(a) means offering "evidence sufficient to support a finding" that the matter is what the proponent claims that it is. In fact, a kind of "authentication" occurs when live witnesses give firsthand accounts of what they know or have seen, because the calling party asks the witness to identify himself or herself and "lays a foundation" by having her testify that she was at the crucial place at the critical time, and that she has firsthand knowledge about the matters to which she is to testify. For example, a lawyer might begin his questioning of a witness to an accident by having her testify that she was at Fourth and Green (where the accident occurred) at the relevant time on June 16th (the date of the accident). Failing to satisfy the authentication requirement, and failing to show that a percipient witness actually has relevant knowledge, can result in excluding evidence.

Common law courts were strict in applying the authentication requirement, and a notorious example involves the exclusion of a can bearing the label Green Giant in a suit alleging that plaintiff was injured by a piece of metal in a can of peas. Keegan v. Green Giant Co., 110 A.2d 599 (Me. 1954) (rejecting proffered can for failing to prove defendant's connection; defendant wins directed verdict). See also Mancari v. Frank P. Smith, Inc., 114 F.2d 834 (D.C. Cir.

won directed verdict

Lays foundation witness testifies at crucial place at critical time

1940) (ad with defendant's name advertising its product could not be taken as originating with defendant). Under the Rules, *Keegan* and *Mancari* would come out differently. FRE 902 allows "self-authentication" for trade inscriptions that would include the label on a can of peas, and probably logos in newspaper advertising. More generally, FRE 901 liberalizes authentication, relaxing the requirement by letting courts consider such things as "appearance" and "contents" and "internal patterns," and by the list of things that are self-authenticating. See FRE 901(b)(4) and 902. Still, the authentication requirement remains a significant evidentiary hurdle that must be surmounted.

Authentication gives rise to issues of conditional relevancy under FRE 104(b). Here is a place where literal language has meaning: Something offered in evidence becomes relevant only if the proponent proves that the thing is what he claims it to be. And here is a place where the division of functions contemplated by FRE 104 makes good sense. Authenticity speaks to common understanding, and it is right to trust a jury to decide whether an object is the real thing and ignore an item the jury thinks is not authentic.

FRE 104(b) contemplates that judges play a screening function, passing the ultimate decision on authenticity to the jury. The proponent must offer enough proof to enable a jury to find an exhibit authentic. If he offers no proof (or not enough to support the finding), the exhibit must be excluded. If he does offer enough, the exhibit is admitted and the jury makes the ultimate decision on authenticity. Of course the opponent remains free to challenge authenticity by offering evidence in rebuttal, hoping to persuade the jury to reject the exhibit as not authentic. The jury's usual function may be preempted if evidence for or against authenticity is so compelling that it permits only one conclusion by a reasonable jury. Here the court resolves the issue, by excluding the exhibit or instructing the jury to accept it as authentic.

In connection with witnesses we speak of "laying the foundation" for their testimony, and this phrase also describes the process of proving that an object is what its proponent claims, and the phrase is almost a synonym for "authentication." Rule 901(b) sets out an illustrative list of ten methods of authentication that satisfy the standard of Rule 901(a).

Here are the traditional steps to authenticate an exhibit: (1) Getting the court reporter to mark the exhibit for identification; (2) offering testimony identifying or describing the exhibit (heart of the process); (3) offering the exhibit in evidence; (4) letting counsel for other parties examine it; (5) giving other lawyers a chance to object; (6) submitting the exhibit to the court to examine if it wishes; (7) getting a ruling; (8) asking permission to present the exhibit, if admitted, to the jury by reading or showing it to them (or letting them pass it around). The sequence of steps may vary, depending on the jurisdiction. Until a exhibit is ruled admissible, counsel should not display it or read its contents or ask the authenticating witness to do so, or even describe the exhibit in ways that reveal its substance when handing it to the authenticating witness.

NOTES ON THE AUTHENTICATION REQUIREMENT

1. FRE 901 assumes an authentication requirement and sets out a list of ways to satisfy it. Interestingly, however, no provision expressly imposes such a requirement. Presumably it is implicit in the notion that only relevant evidence is admissible (FRE 401-402). The ACN to FRE 901 says the authentication requirement represents an "attitude of agnosticism" toward documents and other exhibits that "departs sharply from men's customs in ordinary affairs." Why should the judge screen exhibits before they are seen by the jury? If the jury can be trusted to determine authenticity, why can't it be trusted to ignore exhibits lacking authenticating evidence? See Broun, Authentication and Contents of Writings, 1969 Law & Soc. Ord. 611.

2. Look at FRE 901(b): You can see that it reaches beyond tangible objects. Among other things, it also covers voice identification and phone calls, because the identity of a person in a conversation or phone call is usually critical to its relevancy.

3. FRE 901(b)(4) allows exhibits to be authenticated by "appearance, contents, substance, internal patterns, or other distinctive characteristics of the item, taken together with all the circumstances." To what extent does FRE 901(b)(4) let the trier of fact take exhibits at "face value"? Consider United States v. Blackwell, 694 F.2d 1325, 1329-1333 (D.C. Cir. 1982) (approving photograph apparently showing defendant in hotel room holding gun like the one he was charged with possessing, despite failure to show origin of photograph or what gun he was holding).

4. In civil cases, discovery lets parties resolve authentication questions before trial. FRCP 26(a)(1)(A) requires each, even without a request from the other side, to provide copies or descriptions of "all documents, electronically stored information, and tangible things" in its possession or control that it "may use to support its claims or defenses." Production under this Rule authenticates such. In addition, at least 30 days before trial each party must provide the others with an appropriate "identification of each document or other exhibit." FRCP 26(a)(3)(A). With some qualifications, objections not made within 14 days are waived, except for objections under FRE 402 or 403. These provisions go far toward removing issues of authentication from civil trials.

5. Authentication is also accomplished by stipulations or, in civil cases, by use of FRCP 36, which lets a party file a request for admission of facts, including genuineness of documents. Under FRCP 37(c), if the other side refuses to admit genuineness without good reason (and the requesting party proves genuineness), the latter may seek from the other side reasonable expenses incurred in making that proof, including attorney's fees.

6. Authentication continues to be a bigger hurdle in criminal trials than in civil litigation, and fewer authentication issues are resolved by stipulation. Why?

B TANGIBLE OBJECTS

Tangible objects offered as exhibits must be authenticated by showing "the item is what the proponent claims it is." How much detail must be described by the authenticating witness to meet this standard? Consider the following case:

UNITED STATES v. JOHNSON

United States Court of Appeals for the Ninth Circuit
637 F.2d 1224 (1980)

[Johnson was convicted of assault resulting in serious bodily injury for an attack with an ax on a victim named Papse.]

Spencer WILLIAMS, J.

At Johnson's trial, the United States called Papse as a witness. A long-handled ax was offered into evidence during his testimony. Pursuant to a search warrant, this ax had been seized at Johnson's residence five days after the assault. Papse identified the ax, apparently with some hesitancy, as the weapon used to commit the assault on him. Over Johnson's objection that there had been insufficient foundation or authentication, the ax was admitted into evidence . . . .

Johnson argues the ax allegedly used in the assault was admitted into evidence without first being authenticated properly. He contends Papse's testimony was inadequate as authentication because the witness failed to state specifically that he could distinguish this ax from any other, because he did not identify specific characteristics of this ax which could tie it to the incident, and because he appeared to base his identification largely on an assumption, derived from his belief that this ax was the only ax on the premises, that this ax *must* have been the weapon in question. In addition, Johnson contends the ax introduced into evidence was in a changed condition from the ax noted at the scene of the incident, and for this reason the court should have been especially cautious about its admission.[34]

FRE 901(a) provides that "[t]he requirement of authentication or identification as a condition precedent to admissibility is satisfied by evidence sufficient to support a finding that the matter in question is what its proponent claims." The terms of the Rule are thus satisfied, and the proffered evidence should ordinarily be admitted, once a prima facie case has been made on the issue. At that point the matter is committed to the trier of fact to determine the evidence's credibility and probative force.

Here, although the trial record reveals the identification of the ax made by Papse may not have been entirely free from doubt, the witness did state that he

[34] Johnson inaccurately states in his brief that testimony revealed the ax observed at the crime scene had "blood and hair upon the blade end of it." In fact, the testimony was that Rose Edmo, a witness, had been told by Barney Dixie, another witness, only that "there was hair on the axe." The ax admitted as an exhibit did not have hair on it. Assuming the testimony about the hair is believed, the absence of hair represents the only change in the ax's condition which was noted between the time of the alleged assault and its seizure five days later.

was "pretty sure" this was the weapon Johnson had used against him, that he saw the ax in Johnson's hand, and that he was personally familiar with this particular ax because he had used it in the past. Based on Papse's testimony, a reasonable juror could have found that this ax was the weapon allegedly used in the assault. Papse's ability or inability to specify particular identifying features of the ax, as well as the evidence of the ax's alleged changed condition, should then go to the question of the weight to be accorded this evidence, which is precisely what the trial court ruled. In other words, although the jury remained free to reject the government's assertion that this ax had been used in the assault, the requirements for admissibility specified in Rule 901(a) had been met.

Finally, the trial court did not abuse its discretion in failing to exclude the ax for being more prejudicial than probative under Evidence Rule 403. "District judges have wide latitude in passing on the admissibility of evidence, and admission will not be overturned on appeal absent an abuse of discretion." United States v. Kearney, 560 F.2d 1358, 1369 (9th Cir.), cert. denied, 434 U.S. 971 (1977). The ax, as the suspected assault weapon, was very relevant to the government's case and the jury was entitled to see it....

■ NOTES ON AUTHENTICATING TANGIBLE OBJECTS

1. The nature of the necessary authenticating proof depends on the purpose for which the exhibit is offered. The foundation required to prove the ax was the one used in the assault differs from the foundation required merely to show that defendant owned an ax.

2. Could the prosecutor offer an ax for the limited purpose of *illustrating* the type of weapon used in the assault? Such use is sometime allowed, in which case any ax similar to the one used in the assault could be offered, even if it has no connection to defendant.

3. When police seize a tangible object like a weapon, what should they do to ease the task of authenticating the object? Wouldn't it be desirable to mark the object in some way so it is distinguishable from other weapons of a similar nature?

■ PROBLEM 13-A. A White Granular Substance

Swenson is arrested and three baggies containing a white granular substance are seized from his person. Arresting officer Taylor delivers the baggies to Ursula at the state crime lab for analysis. Ursula turns them over to a chemist named Vic, who runs tests and determines that they contain cocaine. Taylor picks them up from Vic on the day of trial and brings them to court. You are the prosecutor. What foundation is necessary to introduce the baggies? Must you call Taylor, Ursula, and Vic? What routine steps could these people take to make the process easier?

UNITED STATES v. HOWARD-ARIAS

United States Court of Appeals for the Fourth Circuit
679 F.2d 363 (1982)

[Appellant was a crew member on the fishing trawler "Don Frank" who was rescued when the vessel became disabled 60 miles off the Virginia coast on December 29, 1980. The crew was taken aboard an Italian ship, and Coast Guard cutters arrived. An officer boarded the Don Frank and discovered a large quantity of marijuana. The Coast Guard cutter "Cherokee" tried to tow the Don Frank to shore, but it foundered and sank. Approximately 240 bales of marijuana were salvaged. On return to port, the marijuana was turned over to Coast Guard and Drug Enforcement Administration (DEA) investigators. Appellant was charged with possessing marijuana with intent to distribute while on a vessel within U.S. jurisdiction, and related offenses.]

The appellant's claims regarding the admission of certain evidence need not long detain us. His first argument is that the government failed to establish a continuous "chain of custody" for the marijuana from the time of its seizure on the seas off the Virginia coast until introduction at trial. It is conceded that one of the DEA agents involved in the transfer and testing of the bales and samples drawn from them did not testify at trial. The Coast Guard officer who seized and tested the marijuana, the officer to whom he surrendered it, the DEA custodian at Norfolk, and the DEA chemist all appeared as witnesses. The special agent who received the marijuana from the Coast Guard for transit to the DEA in Norfolk did not.

The "chain of custody" rule is but a variation of the principle that real evidence must be authenticated prior to its admission into evidence. The purpose of this threshold requirement is to establish that the item to be introduced, i.e., marijuana, is what it purports to be, i.e., marijuana seized from the "Don Frank." Therefore, the ultimate question is whether the authentication testimony was sufficiently complete so as to convince the court that it is improbable that the original item had been exchanged with another or otherwise tampered with. Contrary to the appellant's assertion, precision in developing the "chain of custody" is not an iron-clad requirement, and the fact of a "missing link does not prevent the admission of real evidence, so long as there is sufficient proof that the evidence is what it purports to be and has not been altered in any material aspect." United States v. Jackson, 649 F.2d 967 (3d Cir.), *cert. denied*, 454 U.S. 871, 1034 (1981). Resolution of this question rests with the sound discretion of the trial judge, and we cannot say that he abused that discretion in this case . . . .

■ NOTES ON CHAIN OF CUSTODY

1. What types of exhibits require a foundation showing chain of custody? See United States v. Yeley-Davis, 632 F.3d 673, 683 (10th Cir. 2011) (when evidence is fungible, not readily identifiable, or susceptible to tampering or alteration, court may require proof of chain of custody).

2. How is chain of custody established? See C. Mueller & L. Kirkpatrick, Evidence §9.5 (5th ed. 2012) ("[A] chain of custody normally requires calling each of the persons who had custody of the item from the time of the relevant event until trial and offering testimony showing (1) when they took custody and from whom, (2) the precautions they took to preserve the item, (3) the item was not changed, substituted, or tampered with while they had it, and (4) when they relinquished custody and to whom. Each witness should also testify that the item offered appears to be in the same condition as when they had custody of it.").

3. How big a break in the chain of custody can be tolerated? See United States v. Clark, 664 F.2d 1174, 1176 (11th Cir. 1981) ("minor break in the chain of possession" would affect weight but should not keep evidence out). But what about a major break? For example, what if the Coast Guard officer who originally seized and tested the marijuana in this case were the missing link? Presumably the court would be reluctant to admit without a clear connection between the drugs and the defendant.

4. Some courts say there must be a "reasonable probability" that no tampering occurred. See United States v. Briley, 319 F.3d 360, 363 (8th Cir. 2003). Sometimes prosecutors are aided by a presumption that public officers discharged their responsibilities with due care. See United States v. Turner, 591 F.3d 928, 934 (7th Cir. 2010) (citing presumption of regularity in police practices).

5. What procedures can law enforcement officers follow to maintain a complete chain of custody? See generally Giannelli, Chain of Custody and the Handling of Real Evidence, 20 Am. Crim. L. Rev. 527 (1983). Should law enforcement agencies be required to maintain a round-the-clock watch? See United States v. Santiago, 534 F.2d 768, 770 (7th Cir. 1976) (rejecting claim that narcotics should have been excluded because "many people had access" to safes where envelopes storing the material were sealed) (no evidence of tampering).

C WRITINGS

There are several ways to authenticate writings under FRE 901(b). Consider the following case and the problem that follows:

UNITED STATES v. BAGARIC

United States Court of Appeals for the Second Circuit
706 F.2d 42 (1983)

[Defendants Milan Bagaric, Mile Markich, Ante Ljubas, Vinko Logarusic, Ranko Primorac, and Drago Sudar were convicted of violations of the Racketeer Influenced and Corrupt Organizations Act (RICO). Miro Baresic was an unindicted co-racketeer, who participated in the enterprise's affairs during 1977 and 1978.]

KAUFMAN, J.

Logarusic challenges the admission of additional evidence linking him to Baresic. We refer to a letter discovered during a consent search of Logarusic's home on April 3, 1981, after his arrest. Appellant claims the letter was not properly authenticated. Fed. R. Evid. 901(a). We disagree. The requirement of authentication "is satisfied by evidence sufficient to support a finding that the matter is what its proponent claims." This finding may be based entirely on circumstantial evidence, including "[a]ppearance, contents, substance . . . and other distinctive characteristics" of the writing. 901(b)(4). Here, the letter was addressed to Logarusic and postmarked Asuncion, Paraguay, where Baresic resided. It began with the salutation "Dear Vinko" and ended "your Miro Baresic . . . your Miro Toni." "Toni Saric" was the alias Baresic had used in gaining entry into the United States. The letter referred to "our people in Chicago," where four of the defendants lived, and it asked Logarusic to contact "Crni," which the proof showed was Ljubas's sobriquet among his confederates. It also contained references to "Mercedes," a friend of Logarusic who testified on his behalf and admitted knowing Baresic, and to "the Razov family," Logarusic's landlord. Finally, the letter stated that "[t]he Swedes, Americans, and Yugoslavs are requesting expulsion because I am a terrorist and dangerous," a fact confirmed by testimony that Baresic was a fugitive from Sweden where he was sought for the murder of the Yugoslavian ambassador. In sum, as Chief Judge Motley found, there was ample demonstration "that the letter was in fact what the Government claimed, i.e., a letter from Miro Baresic to Vinko Logarusic."

NOTES ON AUTHENTICATING WRITINGS

1. Can stylistic patterns, such as spelling errors, authenticate writings? See United States v. Larson, 596 F.2d 759, 765 n.5 (8th Cir. 1979) (admitting evidence that defendant "misspelled approach as 'approuch' three times in one ransom note" and "previously did the same in a letter to the Pardon Board"); United States v. Clifford, 704 F.2d 86 (3d Cir. 1983) (letters authenticated in part by unusual misspellings).

2. Is a letter authenticated by the fact that it is written on letterhead and appears to be signed by the defendant? Is letterhead accessible to outsiders, or so easily made on private order, that admitting on such grounds is dangerous? Traditionally courts have been unwilling to authenticate a writing based on letterhead, but modern decisions are more accepting of letterhead as at least a partial basis for authentication. See United States v. Gordon, 634 F.2d 639, 643-644 (1st Cir. 1980) (admitting documents because they appeared "on their face" to come from J. John Gordon, President and Senior Counsel of International Bank of Commerce, with residential address at 8 Creswell Road, Worcester, and phone number 617-754-5000, which matched those of the defendant).

■ PROBLEM 13-B. The Land-Sale Contract

In a suit filed in 2007 to quiet title to Ridgeview Estates, plaintiff seeks to offer as an exhibit a land-sale contract between Greta Higgins, a previous owner, and plaintiff for the sale of the property to the plaintiff. The land-sale contract was executed in 1985, and the original was obtained from the property records office of the county courthouse. Identify the ways this exhibit could be authenticated under FRE 901(b).

R. KEETON, BASIC EXPRESSIONS FOR TRIAL LAWYERS (1979)

§2.25 Offering Documentary Evidence

Q: Have you ever before seen Plaintiff's Exhibit 7 for Identification?
A: Yes, I have.
Q: When did you first see it?
A: In the early part of February of this year.
Q: Where were you when you first saw it?
A: In my office.
Q: How did it come to your attention?
A: It came to me in the regular mail at my office.
Q: Please answer my next question just *yes* or *no*: Do you know who sent it to you?
A: Yes.
Q: How do you know?
A: I recognize the signature.
Q: Without saying whose signature you recognized it to be, please tell us how you were able to recognize that signature.
A: Well, I've been doing business with this person for more than ten years.
Q: Have you ever seen him sign his name during that period?
A: Yes, many times.
Q: Have you received letters from him during those ten years you have been doing business with him?
A: Yes, dozens of them.
Q: Have you completed transactions based on those letters?
A: Yes, often.
Q: Whose signature is it that appears on Plaintiff's Exhibit 7 for Identification?
A: John J. Jones.
Q: Is that the John J. Jones against whom you have brought this lawsuit?
A: Yes, it is.
Plaintiff's Counsel: Your Honor, . . . I offer in evidence what has been marked as Plaintiff's Exhibit 7 for Identification.

Defense Counsel: Objection, Your Honor.
Court: Objection overruled. The document is in evidence as Plaintiff's Exhibit 7.
Plaintiff's Counsel: Your honor, may I hand Plaintiff's Exhibit 7 to the jury for their examination?
Court: You may.

[Wait until all jurors have read the document before proceeding.]

D ELECTRONIC EVIDENCE AND SOCIAL MEDIA

■ PROBLEM 13-C. "The Wizard" and the Incriminating Email

On Friday July 19, 2007, 14-year-old Tiffany is reported missing from her home in Phoenix, Arizona. Her anguished parents invite police to examine her computer files, where they discover email messages from someone using the moniker "The Wizard." Apparently the two "met" in an online chatroom. Police recover the following messages from Tiffany's computer:

W: Think of it as the first of many road trips. Let's take a camera, so the pictures will show everyone just how grown up you are. Tickets are in my hand. Everyone knows the first visit to Vegas is the luckiest. Don't empty out your mom's purse until just before you leave. The more you play, the more they pay!

T: You promised it is only for the concert, and then we have to come back that night. I don't want to wind up on a milk carton. Anyway, after the concert I know my mom will lock me up for awhile, so don't be surprised if I can't take any more trips anytime soon. This concert better be worth it!

W: Not to worry. You can trust me. You'll love the band. Can't wait to see you on Friday.

On Sunday July 20, 2007, police find Tiffany at the Lucky Lady Hotel in Las Vegas, in a room with 28-year-old Morris Tate. He is arrested, and Tiffany is returned to her home.

Federal investigators learn that Tate is the internet account holder who calls himself "The Wizard." He is charged with inducing a minor to cross state lines for immoral purposes and sexual assault against a minor. As proof that Tate induced Tiffany to go with him from Arizona to Nevada, and to show how Tate persuaded Tiffany to meet him, the prosecutor offers the emails found on Tiffany's computer. She is willing to testify about the email exchange.

What foundation is needed to authenticate these emails? Is a different foundation required for The Wizard's emails than for those sent by Tiffany?

NOTES ON AUTHENTICATION OF SOCIAL MEDIA

1. Can one authenticate emails by relying on the header and footer of a message, which includes the IP address, date, and email addresses of the parties? Assuming that Tate is shown to have an Internet account in the name of "The Wizard," is it sufficient that the email purports to have been sent by an account holder with that name? See Tienda v. State, 358 S.W.3d 633 (Tex. Crim. App. 2012) (that an email "on its face purports to come from a certain person's email address, that the respondent in an internet chat room dialogue purports to identify himself, or that a text message emanates from a cell phone number assigned to the purported author—none of these circumstances, without more, has typically been regarded as sufficient").

2. Which illustrations in FRE 901(b) are helpful in authenticating emails or other social media? Consider 901(b)(4) (writings may be authenticated on basis of "appearance, contents, substance, internal patterns, or other distinctive characteristics, taken together with all the circumstances"). What about using the "reply doctrine (mentioned in the ACN to FRE 901(b)(4)), under which a letter may be authenticated as coming from a person by showing that it replies to an earlier communication to that person, provided that the earlier communication has itself been authenticated. Could the "reply doctrine" help here?

3. Can emails or other social media entries such as Facebook profiles or messages be fabricated or disguised as coming from someone else? What about claims that an email account was compromised or available to more than one person, so an email or Facebook entry did not come from the account holder? See State v. Eleck, 130 Conn. App. 632, 23 A.3d 818, 820 (2011) (witness claimed Facebook account was hacked; court rejects Facebook entries, noting "general lack of security of the medium"); Munshani v. Signal Lake Venture Fund II, 2001 WL 1526954 (Mass. Super. 2001) (forged emails submitted; case dismissed and monetary sanctions imposed).

4. What is sufficient to authenticate an email or social media posting? See Smith v. Mississippi, 136 So. 3d 424 (2014) (citing as examples where "the purported sender admits authorship" or "is seen composing the communication," and approving use of the business records of an internet service provider or cellphone company showing that a communication "originated from the purported sender's personal computer or cell phone under circumstances in which it is reasonable to believe" that only he would have access to the computer or cell phone, and citing the circumstance in which a communication "contains information that only the purported sender could be expected to know," or in which he "responds to an exchange in such a way as to indicate circumstantially that he was in fact the author").

5. What about Web postings? Consider the following:

> To authenticate a printout of a web page, the proponent must offer evidence that: (1) the printout accurately reflects the computer image of the web page as of a specified date; (2) the website where the posting appears is owned or

> controlled by a particular person or entity; and (3) the authorship of the website posting is reasonably attributable to that person or entity . . . . If a web posting is offered for the truth of what it asserts, it is necessary to lay an additional foundation to admit it under an exception to the hearsay rule . . . . If the web posting is adequately authenticated as being from a party opponent, it normally will be admissible as an admission. If the web posting is by a third party and is offered for its truth, an additional foundation is necessary [to fit a hearsay exception].

5 C. Mueller & L. Kirkpatrick, Federal Evidence §9:9 at 396 (4th ed. 2013).

E RECORDINGS

■ PROBLEM 13-D. The Hidden Microphone

Jenkins is charged with selling heroin to Kirsch, an undercover agent. The transaction took place in a motel room where narcotics officers had planted a hidden microphone. The microphone picked up and transmitted to a nearby recording device the entire conversation between Jenkins and Kirsch. Officer Enyart was in a nearby room, where he operated the device, which made and stored a digitized version of the conversation. Enyart did not listen as the conversation went forward, but can describe the set up, operation, and reliability of the recording device. On what is commonly called a flashdrive (or external memory chip), he made a backup copy of the conversation. He had custody of the recording device and the flashdrive backup for the entire period prior to trial. What foundation is necessary to authenticate this recording? Can both Kirsch and Enyart authenticate the recording? Are both needed?

UNITED STATES v. OSLUND

United States Court of Appeals for the Eighth Circuit
453 F.3d 1048 (2006)

HANSEN, Circuit Judge.

[Defendant Richard Oslund was convicted by a jury for the robbery and murder of a Brinks security guard who was making a delivery at a Target store in Minnesota and was sentenced to two consecutive life terms. The perpetrator hid near the entrance, shot the guard three times, grabbed the bag of cash, and ran. The police and FBI conducted a joint investigation of the murder and set up a tip hotline. Over 500 tips were received, and one of them identified Oslund as a suspect. The tip came from an attorney representing Zachary Koehler. Koehler first met Oslund in 1992, and they later served time together in several

Minnesota prisons and became good friends. Koehler was in Stillwater State Prison when the Target robbery occurred, and shortly thereafter Oslund was also incarcerated at Stillwater for a parole violation. Koehler sought out Oslund and spoke to him briefly, noticing a new, large tattoo on Oslund's neck. He asked Oslund about it, and Oslund replied that he "had to do it after the Target." Koehler knew about the Brinks robbery and to what Oslund was referring. He then asked Oslund what happened, and Oslund replied that "things got out of control and I had to blast him." Koehler had recently received $1,000 from Oslund, and asked him if the money came from the Brinks robbery, to which Oslund replied that it had. After this conversation, Koehler called his attorney to pass the information along to the FBI.]

FBI Agent James Walden approached one of Oslund's close friends and former roommates, Thomas Russell, who agreed to cooperate in the investigation and tape conversations between Oslund and him. Taping did not begin until August 28, 2000, though, due to difficulty in finding a time when neither Russell nor Oslund was in custody. Hundreds of hours of conversations between Russell and Oslund were recorded by the FBI between August 28, 2000, and March 17, 2001.

Oslund was reluctant at first to discuss the robbery but eventually began discussing the Target robbery after Russell told him he wanted to rob an armored car and was looking for some advice about how to do it. There were both inculpatory statements, some confessional in nature, and exculpatory statements on the tapes. Both the defense and the prosecution used excerpts from the tapes at trial.

On the two-year anniversary of the crime, the FBI installed video and audio recording equipment in a car and had Russell drive Oslund to the Bloomington Target store. Oslund and Russell again discussed the robbery and how Oslund had carried it out . . . .

Oslund first challenges the admission of the taped conversations, alleging that no proper foundation for their admission had been made. Specifically, he challenges the authenticity of the tapes and claims that the tapes were the result of unlawful inducement. "The admission of tape recordings is 'within the sound discretion of the trial court and will not be reversed unless there has been an abuse of that discretion.'" *United States v. Webster,* 84 F.3d 1056, 1064 (8th Cir. 1996).

Several nonexclusive factors should be considered when determining the admissibility of tape-recorded conversations. *United States v. McMillan,* 508 F.2d 101, 104 (8th Cir. 1974). They include

> (1) That the recording device was capable of taking the conversation now offered in evidence. (2) That the operator of the device was competent to operate the device. (3) That the recording is authentic and correct. (4) That changes, additions or deletions have not been made in the recording. (5) That the recording has been preserved in a manner that is shown to the court. (6) That the speakers are identified. (7) That the conversation elicited was made voluntarily and in good faith, without any kind of inducement.

Id.

These factors are useful to determine if a "tape's 'substance and the circumstances under which it was obtained [provide] sufficient proof of its reliability.'" *Webster,* 84 F.3d at 1064 (quoting *United States v. Roach,* 28 F.3d 729, 733 n.4 (8th Cir. 1994)). "These requirements do not, however, exist *in vacuo;* they become meaningful only when viewed in light of the facts of a specific case." *Durns v. United States,* 562 F.2d 542, 547 (8th Cir. 1977). Not only do we look to the specific facts of a case, but it is worth noting that the technology related to recording devices has greatly advanced since *McMillan* was decided, a fact that supports the premise that the *McMillan* factors are guidelines to be viewed in light of specific circumstances, not a rigid set of tests to be satisfied. *See Webster,* 84 F.3d at 1064 (the *McMillan* factors are general guidelines for a district court to use in evaluating if the Government has met its burden); *see also United States v. Clark,* 986 F.2d 65, 68 (4th Cir. 1993) (government not required to meet every *McMillan* factor; the "factors, while helpful, merely 'provide guidance to the district court when called upon to make rulings on authentication issues.'") (quoting *United States v. Branch,* 970 F.2d 1368, 1372 (4th Cir. 1992)). In this light, we turn to the district court's admission of the tapes.

[Oslund moved to suppress the tapes, but the court denied the motion after a hearing at which Russell, Agent Walden, and a police officer testified. At trial, Oslund objected that the government did not properly authenticate the tapes. At this time, Russell was in custody in Wisconsin, and the government did not call him, relying instead on testimony by Agent Walden.]

Oslund contends that because Russell did not testify at trial, the government failed to properly authenticate the tapes and that Agent Walden's testimony was not sufficient to do so. While it may have been better for Russell to have testified about the recordings at trial, the district court did not abuse its discretion in holding that the government met its burden under *McMillan. See United States v. Buchanan,* 985 F.2d 1372, 1378-79 (8th Cir. 1993) (finding tapes admissible between defendant and informant even though informant did not testify at trial; *McMillan* factors were satisfied through testimony of officer). Agent Walden testified that Russell would contact him prior to meeting with Oslund, that he would then provide Russell with a digital recorder, that Agent Walden would turn the recorder on and then turn it off after receiving it back, and that it was not possible for Russell to turn the recorder off. In addition, Agent Walden was able to identify each speaker in the recordings and thus authenticate the identity of the participants. *See United States v. Frazier,* 280 F.3d 835, 849 (8th Cir.) (testimony of federal drug agent that he was familiar with voices through work on wiretap provided sufficient foundation to identify participants in recorded conversation). *United States v. Cerone,* 830 F.2d 938, 949 (8th Cir. 1987) ("Any person may identify a speaker's voice if he has heard the voice at any time.").

Oslund also contends that Russell's testimony is required to explain the existence of various "gaps" in the recordings. The "gaps" are periods of the

Russell did not testify.

recordings when no voices or conversation can be heard, as when the recording occurred in a bar and ambient or background noise is all that is discernable at times. Oslund argues that these "gaps" could show alterations or modifications or reflect times when Russell had moved the recorder to a location to avoid memorializing exculpatory statements by Oslund that could cause an inaccurate perception of the recorded conversation. However, this court has held that gaps in an audiotape affect "the weight of the evidence, not its admissibility." *United States v. Byrne,* 83 F.3d 984, 990 (8th Cir. 1996). *See also United States v. Ray,* 250 F.3d 596, 602 (8th Cir. 2001) (gaps in tape recording were not so substantial as to render entire recording untrustworthy and defendant could argue to jury that he was entrapped by informant into making incriminating statements); *cf. Webster,* 84 F.3d at 1065 (finding court did not abuse its discretion in admitting videotape where lens was partially obscured and did not cover all of the actions of those being recorded and the audio was partially unclear because the "infirmities are not so pervasive as to render the tape as a whole untrustworthy"). The "gaps" themselves, whether or not Russell testified at the trial, are not enough to render the recordings inadmissible and instead go to the weight a jury should assign the recordings.

Oslund also argues that the seventh element of *McMillan* was not met for two reasons: (1) that he was induced to speak to Russell and (2) that Russell was induced to cooperate with the government and to orchestrate the conversations because he wanted to collect part of the $115,000 reward money offered in this case. According to Oslund, this potential for a financial reward induced Russell to manipulate the conversations in order to get certain statements from Oslund. Oslund argues that because Agent Walden was not simultaneously monitoring the conversations as they occurred, and because Agent Walden cannot speak as to Russell's state of mind, that only Russell's testimony would satisfy this *McMillan* factor. We respectfully disagree.

In *United States v. Brown* we held that the seventh factor in *McMillan* referred to the statements of the defendant in a recorded conversation, and as such, the defendant's statement must be made in good faith, without inducement, and voluntarily. 604 F.2d 557, 560 (8th Cir. 1979). We are presented with no evidence that Oslund did not voluntarily enter into these conversations with Russell or that he was somehow induced to do so, and as such, this argument fails. *Id.; see also United States v. Risken,* 788 F.2d 1361, 1370 (8th Cir.) (no inducement when defendant voluntarily enters into conversation with informant). . . .

The *McMillan* factors are a guide for the court to use, and if the totality of the circumstances surrounding the recordings satisfies the court as to their reliability, even if not every factor is explicitly and completely met, admission is proper. Looking at the totality of the circumstances here, we conclude that the district court did not abuse its discretion in allowing the admission of the taped conversations between Oslund and Russell . . . .

Accordingly, we affirm the judgment of the district court.

NOTES ON AUTHENTICATING RECORDED CONVERSATIONS

1. If the government had brought Russell from his place of incarceration in Wisconsin to the trial court in Minnesota, Russell could have testified that the recordings accurately captured his conversations with Oslund. In Problem 13-D (The Hidden Microphone), Kirsch probably could have done the same thing. Would this alternative satisfy the authentication requirement? See FRE 901(b)(1) (authorizing authentication by testimony that the thing being offered is "what it is claimed to be").

2. In cases where a participant to the recorded conversation is *not* available or is unwilling to provide such testimony, the proponent generally must rely on FRE 901(b)(9) and produce "evidence describing a process or system and showing that it produces an accurate result." Typically this evidence is supplied by the person who operated the recording device. The *Oslund* court cites the *McMillan* factors, which provide guidance for laying such a foundation, but notes that they are outdated (*McMillan* was decided before the adoption of the FRE and before the coming of modern digital recording technology). For a more modern formulation of the foundation for authenticating audio recordings, consider the following:

> It is sufficient to authenticate a tape recording if the proponent offers testimony establishing: (1) the device was capable of making a true recording and was in good working order; (2) the operator was qualified to operate it and did so properly; (3) no changes were made in the recording (no additions or deletions); (4) the identities of the speakers; and (5) that the tape was properly preserved.

5 C. Mueller & L. Kirkpatrick, Federal Evidence §9:14 at 435 (4th ed. 2013).

3. *Oslund* is an unusual case because Agent Walden did not actually make the recording—the informant Russell did. However, the court found the authentication requirement to be satisfied because only Walden could turn the recording device on or off, and he took the device from Russell immediately after each conversation with Oslund. For a similar case, see United States v. Emerson, 501 F.3d 804 (7th Cir. 2007) (admitting recording of conversation with defendant made by informant who was unable to turn off recording device).

4. In *Oslund* the court considers whether statements on the recording were made "voluntarily" and "without inducement." Do these issues bear on authentication? Most courts say no, and do not consider them as part of the foundation for introducing a recording. See United States v. Anderton, 679 F.2d 1199, 1202 (5th Cir. 1982) ("we have declined to require proof that the conversation was made 'voluntarily and in good faith without any kind of inducement' ").

5. Note that FRE 901(b)(5) contemplates testimony based on "hearing the voice." What if the conversation were not in English, and the testifying witness did not know the language being spoken? See United States v. Zepeda-Lopez, 478 F.3d 1213 (10th Cir. 2007) (agent could identify voices in conversation spoken in Spanish even though he could not speak it; he heard six recordings, including a call in which defendant "identified himself by his nickname 'Cacho,'" which amounted to a "baseline call" to which agent could compare later recordings). Can a proponent of a recorded conversation rely on "voiceprint" analysis to identify the speaker? See generally State v. Coon, 974 P.2d 386 (Alaska 1999) (approving voiceprint evidence in authenticating recorded conversation, under *Daubert* standard; expert testified that more than 30 states accept such evidence) (court notes that cases conflict).

6. Describing the background of a recording and identifying participants in a conversation may be just the beginning of the proponent's task in getting a jury to understand what it hears. In drug cases, expert testimony interpreting coded drug jargon in recordings has become commonplace. See United States v. Griffith, 118 F.3d 318 (5th Cir. 1997) (approving expert testimony that "days of work" meant "pounds of marijuana," that "30" meant "a $30,000 shipment of marijuana," and that "5 price" and "8 price" meant $500 and $800 per pound); United States v. Villarman-Oviedo, 325 F.3d 12 (1st Cir. 2003) (DEA Agent testifies to "use of coded terms to denote drugs and about the meaning of those terms").

COMMENT/PERSPECTIVE: Transcripts of Recordings as Jury Aids

Transcripts are sometimes provided to assist juries, particularly when parts of a recording are hard to hear. The proponent must of course show that the transcript is accurate, which ordinarily entails testimony by the person who prepared the transcript. But it is possible to authenticate a transcript by means of testimony by anyone who hears the conversation and reads the transcript for accuracy. See United States v. Anderson, 452 F.3d 66, 76 (1st Cir. 2006) (prosecutor prepared transcript, and was not allowed to testify; agent who recorded conversation and listened to it could authenticate transcript). If opposing parties take issue with the accuracy of transcripts, they can prepare alternate transcripts. See United States v. Onori, 535 F.2d 938, 948-949 (5th Cir. 1976) (endorsing use of divergent transcripts offered by government and defense). The judge can play the role of at least insuring that any transcript submitted to the jury could be viewed as correct, on the basis of listening to the recording. See United States v. Chiarizio, 525 F.2d 289, 293 (2d Cir. 1975) (judge should hold *in camera* hearing, personally listening to recordings, reading transcripts, and hearing objections). Transcripts, however, are not themselves the evidence on which juries are to decide the case:

> The best evidence of the conversation is the tape itself; the transcript should normally be used only after the defendant has had an opportunity to verify its accuracy and then only to assist the jury as it listens to the

> tape . . . . Transcripts should not ordinarily be read to the jury or given independent weight. The trial judge should carefully instruct the jury that differences in meaning may be caused by such factors as the inflection in a speaker's voice or inaccuracies in the transcript and that they should, therefore, rely on what they hear rather than on what they read when there is a difference. Transcripts should not ordinarily be admitted into evidence unless both sides stipulate to their accuracy . . . .
>
> United States v. McMillan, 508 F.2d 101, 105-106 (8th Cir. 1974), *cert. denied*, 421 U.S. 916 (1975).

F OTHER EXHIBITS

■ PROBLEM 13-E. The Photograph

In an automobile accident case, plaintiff Harris offers a photograph of the intersection where the accident occurred, taken one month afterwards. State the foundation necessary to authenticate the photograph. Must the photographer testify in order to establish authenticity? What if the photograph shows a new traffic sign or physical feature that was not there at the time of the accident? Is the photograph still admissible?

■ PROBLEM 13-F. X-Ray

Mason is struck by a car while crossing a street as a pedestrian. He sues for personal injuries, including a fractured leg. If Mason offers an X-ray of his leg, what foundation is necessary? What part of FRE 901(b) applies? How does the foundation for X-rays differ from that for photographs?

■ PROBLEM 13-G. Computer Printout

Georgia Pacific sues Allied Construction Company to recover on an unpaid account for the sale of lumber and other construction materials. To prove the amount of the account, Georgia Pacific offers a computer printout. What foundation is necessary to authenticate this exhibit?

 TELEPHONE CONVERSATIONS

UNITED STATES v. POOL

United States Court of Appeals for the Fifth Circuit
660 F.2d 547 (1981)

[Eight defendants were convicted of several charges arising from participation in a scheme to import approximately 225,000 pounds of marijuana worth $60 million into the United States. Defendant Loye appealed his conviction under Count 9 of the indictment (for violation of 21 U.S.C. §843(b) for using a telephone to facilitate the illegal importation) on the ground that the phone call alleged to be from him was insufficiently authenticated.]

HILL, J.

. . . On August 5, 1978, at 10:40 A.M. DEA Agent Starratt received a call from a person who identified himself as "Chip," a nickname used by appellant Loye throughout the investigation. The caller told the agent that Petrulla wanted DEA Agent Story to obtain another boat. Based on this conversation Agent Starratt identified Loye as the telephone participant charged with the §843(b) violation in Count 9. The conversation was not recorded. Starratt never met Chip and he never made any voice comparison with Loye. The only way Starratt could identify the caller was through the caller's self-identification. Under these circumstances, Loye argues that Starratt's testimony identifying him is inadmissible because it was not authenticated, Fed. R. Evid. 901. Loye also argues that the identification was hearsay. Loye's contention that the identity of the caller was not properly authenticated finds support in our case law . . . .

We have previously remarked that "a telephone call out of the blue from one who identifies himself as X may not be, in itself, sufficient authentication of the call as in fact coming from X." United States v. Register, 496 F.2d 1072, 1077 (5th Cir. 1974). We agree with the government that the standard of admissibility of voice identification testimony is prima facie. We also agree that circumstantial evidence may be used in meeting this standard. However, there is not sufficient evidence to support the conclusion that Agent Starratt actually heard Loye's voice. As noted, Starratt had never met Loye and no voice comparisons were made. Under these circumstances, Loye's use of the nickname "Chip" does not make out a prima facie case that he was the caller. The possibility that someone else was using his nickname in this clandestine operation is too great to properly admit Agent Starratt's identification. This identification was essential to Loye's §843(b) conviction. Accordingly, we reverse Loye's conviction for Count 9 . . . .

NOTES ON AUTHENTICATING PHONE CALLS

1. The decision would be different, would it not, if Starratt had been able to recognize Loye's voice? How familiar does a witness have to be with a caller's voice before being allowed to testify to the identity of the caller? See United States v. Axselle, 604 F.2d 1330, 1338 (10th Cir. 1979) (hearing voice one other time sufficient familiarity); United States v. Vitale, 549 F.2d 71 (8th Cir.) (two other occasions sufficient), *cert. denied,* 431 U.S. 907 (1977).

2. By what other methods might the telephone call be authenticated as being from Loye? See FRE 901(b)(4) and (b)(5).

3. In *Pool* the witness *received* an incoming call. How can a witness authenticate a call that he places himself? See FRE 901(b)(6).

PROBLEM 13-H. "This Is O'Rourke"

In his third year of law school, Paul Michaud was a finalist for an associate position with O'Rourke & Kelly, the largest law firm in the state. He had returned from what he considered to be a successful interview with the firm and had been promised a decision within ten days. Although he did not have a chance to meet the senior partner, Jeremy O'Rourke, he learned that O'Rourke would make the final hiring decision. The firm was aware that he had two offers with deadlines, one from a prestigious firm in another city and the other from a federal judge.

On returning to his apartment on the fourth day after his interview, he found a phone message on his answering machine. The caller identified herself as the secretary to Jeremy O'Rourke of O'Rourke & Kelly. She stated that Mr. O'Rourke would like to speak with Paul and that "he will be leaving soon, but can be reached by phone at the Metropolitan Country Club, at 407-8965 after 5 P.M. this evening." Because it was after 5 P.M., Paul dialed the number indicated on the phone message. He asked to speak to Mr. O'Rourke. A voice came on the line and said "This is O'Rourke." Paul asked whether a decision had been made on the associate position. To his delight, the response was unhesitating, cordial, and positive—"When can you start?" After the negotiation of a starting date, the conversation was concluded.

The next day Paul wrote letters declining his other two offers. Paul heard nothing more for two months. Then he received the following letter:

> Dear Mr. Michaud:
>
> We are writing to inform you and our other job applicants that, because of recent internal restructuring within our law firm, we have decided not to hire any new associates for next year. We appreciate your interest in our firm.

Sincerely,
Jeremy O'Rourke
O'Rourke & Kelly

Paul was devastated. Against the recommendation of friends and ignoring possible legal impediments, he hired an attorney and filed suit against O'Rourke & Kelly for breach of contract. At trial, Paul takes the stand as the first witness. When Paul is asked to recount his telephone conversation with O'Rourke, the attorney for O'Rourke & Kelly objects on grounds of lack of authentication. What ruling?

 SELF-AUTHENTICATING EXHIBITS

FRE 902 provides for the admissibility of "self-authenticating" exhibits, i.e., exhibits that do not require "extrinsic evidence" of authenticity. The exhibit on its face provides its own foundation, and there is no need to call a witness to prove what it is. Being self-authenticating means only that the thing can be admitted and considered by a jury. It does not mean the opponent is barred from offering counterproof challenging authenticity or arguing that it should have little or no weight.

1. Acknowledged Documents

■ PROBLEM 13-I. The Rejected Easement

Byron sues Casey, alleging trespass on Greenacre. Casey claims to be entitled to drive on a dirt road over the parcel. At trial, Casey offers a document that purports to be an acknowledged grant of easement covering the road in question given to her by Arthur, who had later given a quitclaim deed for Greenacre to Byron. There is evidence that Arthur mentioned "some easement on the property" to Byron, and all agree that Casey has a good defense if indeed she holds the easement.

Casey offers the document without foundation testimony, and Byron offers no proof at all on the subject. At the end of trial, Casey seeks a directed verdict, arguing that the jury "cannot reject this easement because the document is acknowledged and self-authenticating under FRE 902(8)." She seeks an instruction "telling the jury that they must accept this document for what it is, proof of the easement."

The court rejects Casey's motion and refuses the instruction. In his close, Byron argues that the purported easement is "obviously faked" and asks the jury to "pay no attention to that trumped up document." The jury returns a verdict for Byron. Should Casey have gotten her directed verdict or the requested instruction?

NOTES ON ACKNOWLEDGED DOCUMENTS

1. The recording acts that are important in protecting land titles require deeds, easements, mortgages and similar documents to be acknowledged before they can be recorded in records of land titles. FRE 902(8) provides that an acknowledged document is self-authenticating, and the process of acknowledgement entails going to a notary, producing identification (like a driver's license) and swearing to having actually signed the document, or actually signing it in the notary's presence. The notary adds his certificate and seal to attest this matter.

2. In the Problem, Byron won without having challenged in any way the certified easement that Casey introduced. The easement fits FRE 902(8), and the question is whether self-authentication merely permits the factfinder to draw an inference of authenticity, or does it mean the opponent, if he means to suggest that the easement is "faked," must offer some kind of evidence or suffer an adverse instruction on the point. What do you think?

2. Certified Copies of Public Records

The most common example of self-authentication is the certified copy of a public record. Rule 902(4) addresses this matter, and serves an important purpose because such records are so often important in litigation, and public officials seldom release original documents for use in litigation. What is required to authenticate a copy of a public record under this rule? Consider the following problem.

PROBLEM 13-J. The Death Certificate

Walter Bellamy Jr. died in a single-car accident when his car went off the road while he was driving home. His life insurance company refused to pay death benefits to his widow, the designated beneficiary, claiming that his death was a suicide, hence outside the coverage of the policy. His widow files an action against the life insurance company. To prove the cause of his death at trial, she offers the certified copy of his death certificate shown below. Is it admissible as a self-authenticating document under FRE 902(4)? Why or why not?

To satisfy the requirement of a seal, what if a second certificate were stapled to the death certificate, apparently signed by "Charles Burkett" above the title "Clerk of Cook County," bearing the apparent seal of the Office of County Clerk and containing the following statement:

> I certify that I am the Clerk of Cook County, and that Emily F. Bundy is personally known to me as the Deputy Clerk of Cook County, having legal

custody of the records of the county pertaining to births, deaths, and motor vehicle registration.

Would *this* certificate authenticate the death certificate in a jurisdiction that requires a seal?

Certified Copy of a Death Record

STATE OF ILLINOIS

MEDICAL CERTIFICATE OF DEATH

REGISTRATION DISTRICT NO. 2.28

REGISTERED NUMBER 48736

STATE FILE NUMBER

DECEASED – NAME (First, Middle, Last) 1. Walter Herbert Bellamy — SEX 2. M — DATE OF DEATH 3. Jan. 11, 2006

RACE 4a. White — ORIGIN OR DESCENT 4b. -- — AGE 5a. 47 — UNDER 1 YEAR 5b. — UNDER 1 DAY 5c. — DATE OF BIRTH 6. Oct. 27, 1960 — COUNTY OF DEATH 7a. Cook

CITY, TOWN, TWP OR ROAD DISTRICT NUMBER 7b. Chicago — HOSPITAL OR OTHER INSTITUTION 7c. Metro General — 7d. DOA

STATE OF BIRTH 8. Mass. — CITIZEN OF WHAT COUNTRY 9. USA — MARRIED, NEVER MARRIED, WIDOWED, DIVORCED 10. Married — NAME OF SURVIVING SPOUSE 11. Elaine Schwartz

SOCIAL SECURITY NUMBER 12. 317-42-6307 — USUAL OCCUPATION 13a. Salesman — KIND OF BUSINESS OR INDUSTRY 13b. Electronics — U.S. WAR VETERAN 13c. No — WAR OR DATES OF SERVICE 13d. N/A

RESIDENCE STREET AND NUMBER 14a. 1022 N. 141st — CITY, TOWN, TWP OR ROAD DISTRICT NO. 14b. Chicago — INSIDE CITY LIMITS 14c. Yes — COUNTY 14d. Cook — STATE 14e. Ill.

FATHER – NAME 15. George Walter Bellamy — MOTHER – MAIDEN NAME 16. Karen Kay Dietz

INFORMANT'S SIGNATURE 17a. ▶ Elaine Bellamy — RELATIONSHIP 17b. Wife — MAILING ADDRESS 17c. 1022 N. 141st. Chicago, IL 60627

18. DEATH WAS CAUSED BY (ENTER ONLY ONE CAUSE PER LINE FOR (a), (b), AND (c))

PART I. IMMEDIATE CAUSE

(a) Head injury — APPROXIMATE INTERVAL BETWEEN ONSET AND DEATH: Instantaneous

CONDITIONS, IF ANY, WHICH GAVE RISE TO IMMEDIATE CAUSE (a), STATING THE UNDERLYING CAUSE LAST

DUE TO, OR AS A CONSEQUENCE OF

(b) Automobile accident - Lake St. & Route 43

DUE TO, OR AS A CONSEQUENCE OF

(c)

PART II. OTHER SIGNIFICANT CONDITIONS — AUTOPSY 19a. No — 19b.

DATE OF OPERATION, IF ANY 20a. — MAJOR FINDINGS OF OPERATION 20b.

ATTENDED THE DECEASED FROM 21a. Jan. 11, 2006 TO 21b. Jan. 11, 2006 — 21c. DOA — HOUR OF DEATH 21d. approximately 3:00 PM

22a. SIGNATURE ▶ Randall Lewis — DATE SIGNED 22b. Jan. 11, 2006

NAME AND ADDRESS OF CERTIFIER 22c. Randall Lewis, Metro General Hosp., Chicago, IL — ILLINOIS LICENSE NUMBER 22d. 2837

NAME OF ATTENDING PHYSICIAN IF OTHER THAN CERTIFIER 23.

NOTE: IF AN INJURY WAS INVOLVED IN THIS DEATH THE CORONER MUST BE NOTIFIED

BURIAL, CREMATION, REMOVAL 24a. Burial — CEMETERY OR CREMATORY – NAME 24b. Forrest Park — LOCATION 24c. Glenview — STATE IL — DATE 24d. Jan. 14, 2006

FUNERAL HOME 25a. Resthaven Mortuary 819 Main St. Chicago IL 60627

FUNERAL DIRECTOR'S SIGNATURE 25b. ▶ Robert Babcox — FUNERAL DIRECTOR'S ILLINOIS LICENSE NUMBER 25c. 4222

LOCAL REGISTRAR'S SIGNATURE 26a. ▶ William Hutchinson — DATE REC'D BY LOCAL REGISTRAR 26b. Jan. 22, 2006

I HEREBY CERTIFY THAT the foregoing is a true and correct copy of the death record for the decedent named at item 1, and that this record was established and filed in my office in accordance with the provisions of the Illinois Vital Records Act.

DATE March 21, 2006 *SIGNED* Emily F. Bundy

AT Chicago *Illinois OFFICIAL TITLE* Deputy Clerk

The original record of this death is permanently filed with the ILLINOIS DEPARTMENT OF PUBLIC HEALTH at Springfield. County clerks and local registrars are authorized to make certifications from copies of the original record. The Illinois statutes provide that the certification of a death record by the Department of Public Health, local registrar or county clerk shall be prima facie evidence in all courts and places of the facts therein stated.

VR-201C (1978) OFFICE OF VITAL RECORDS · ILLINOIS DEPARTMENT OF PUBLIC HEALTH · SPRINGFIELD 62761

■ NOTES ON CERTIFIED COPIES OF PUBLIC RECORDS

1. Under FRE 902(1)(A), an original signed-and-sealed public record is self-authenticating. Under FRE 902(1)(B), an original public record *without* a seal is self-authenticating if a public official with "duties within the same entity" certifies the authenticity of the document by signing a certificate "under seal—or its equivalent." Either way, signature and seal are required.

2. Far more common, because public officials don't release original documents, is the method employed in the Problem, which is to offer a certified *copy* of the public record. As you can see on the form, the copy mechanism is built into the system: The original Death Certificate for Walter Herbert Bellamy includes, at the bottom, a certificate, so that the original can be copied and the public official can sign and seal the copy in the appropriate place at the bottom of the document, so the whole becomes a copy of the death certificate and an original certification of authenticity. Unfortunately for the plaintiff in the Problem, Emily Bundy apparently did not seal her certification.

3. There is something else that is unfortunate. The 2011 restyling project introduced an error into FRE 902(4). Before restyling, this provision required certification "by" a certificate that complies with FRE 902(1), (2), or (3), meaning a signed certificate with a seal. After restyling, FRE 902(4) speaks of certification by an official "or" a certificate complying with FRE 902(1), (2), or (3), implying that a certificate with signature and seal is optional. States with rules following the federal model mostly retain the original language, making it clear that a signed-and-sealed certificate is needed, and it is clear that the restylers did not mean to change the meaning of the federal language.

4. The poor widow didn't get a seal with Emily Bundy's signature, but she got Charles Burkett to seal *his* certificate. Surely *that's* good enough. Well, not so fast. Burkett doesn't say Emily Bundy's signature is genuine, and FRE 902(1), (2) and (3) contemplate a certificate saying "the signature is genuine." But wait, maybe the widow has another arrow in her quiver: Provisions in the Criminal and Civil Rules address this matter, and both say an official record may be evidenced by a copy "attested by the officer with legal custody," or by his deputy, if "accompanied by a certificate that the officer has custody," and requiring that the certificate be made under seal. See FRCrimP 27 and FRCP 44(a)(1). Are these requirements consistent with FRE 902(2)? In case of conflict, which controls? Do these provisions get the widow home free?

3. Newspapers, Periodicals, and Other Self-Authenticating Material

FRE 902(6) says that "[p]rinted material purporting to be a newspaper or periodical" is self-authenticating. Note, however, that this provision does not make newspapers or periodicals admissible to prove the truth of statements they contain except where such statements fit an exception to the hearsay rule. But an exhibit purporting to be a newspaper or periodical may be taken as an actual or true impression of the publication whose identification it carries. The name of the publisher or printer, date and place of publication, all as indicated by appropriate legends on the face of the document, may be taken at face value as showing that the contents were published at the time and place and in the source indicated. What else may be proven under this rule? Consider the following problem.

■ PROBLEM 13-K. The House of the Rising Sun

Under the headline "Mayor Linked to Prostitution," the *Daily Post* ran a story stating that Mayor Cook was found to have a one-half ownership in the House of the Rising Sun, a local prostitution establishment. The story appeared under the by-line of Ron Bellamy, who was identified as "staff reporter." A week later, a letter to the editor was published in the *Post*, signed by George Ramsey, congratulating the *Post* on its exposé of the mayor and stating that "Cook has been the prostitution kingpin in this town for years, and it is time the public knew about it." Mayor Cook files a libel action against the *Post*, Bellamy, and Ramsey. Bellamy defends on the ground that the published version of the story was not the same as the version he submitted to the city editor. Ramsey defends on the ground that he never wrote the letter in question. The *Post* settles prior to trial. At trial Mayor Cook offers as exhibits the two issues of the *Post* where the story and letter appeared. Bellamy and Ramsey object on grounds of lack of authentication. What ruling?

■ NOTES ON NEWSPAPERS, PERIODICALS, AND OTHER SELF-AUTHENTICATING EXHIBITS

1. The ACN to FRE 902(6) states "[e]stablishing the authenticity of the [newspaper or periodical] may, of course, leave still open questions of authority and responsibility for items therein contained." What does this mean?

2. For examples of exhibits found self-authenticating, see Stahl v. Novartis Pharm. Corp., 283 F.3d 254 (5th Cir. 2002) (photocopies of medical journal articles); United States v. Hitsman, 604 F.2d 443 (5th Cir. 1979) (college transcript bearing seal of registrar); United States v. Alvarez, 972 F.2d 1000 (9th Cir. 1992) (firearm with inscribed words "Garnika, Spain" to prove origin under FRE 902(7)); Crossley v. Lieberman, 868 F.2d 566 (3d Cir. 1989) (certified record of Philadelphia Court of Common Pleas).

3. Under FRE 902(9), commercial paper and related documents are self-authenticating to the extent "allowed by general commercial law." This body of law is now found largely in the Uniform Commercial Code (UCC), and FRE 902(9) in effect incorporates provisions of the UCC as rules of evidence. UCC §1-201(3) defines presumption to mean that the trier "must find the existence of the fact presumed unless and until evidence is introduced which would support a finding of its non-existence," and other provisions appear to use the term "prima facie" to mean essentially enough evidence to support (but not to require) a particular finding. There are at least five other pertinent sections: UCC §1-202 provides that bills of lading and certain other documents are "prima facie" authentic; UCC §3-114(3) provides that a date on an instrument is "presumed to be correct"; UCC §3-307(1)(b) provides that a signature on an instrument is "presumed to be genuine or authorized," except in certain cases; UCC §3-510 provides for the admissibility of certain documents that "create a presumption of dishonor and of any notice of dishonor therein shown"; and UCC §8-105(3)(b) provides that the signature on a security "is presumed to be genuine or authorized." Thus in cases where the UCC applies, a check or a security is generally admissible as proof that it was signed by the person whose apparent signature appears on it, and there is no need to call an authenticating witness.

4. FRE 902(10) incorporates by reference the multiplicity of federal statutes making certain documents "presumptively or prima facie genuine or authentic." Among the more important of such statutes is 28 USC §753(b), which provides that a "transcript" of court proceedings is "deemed prima facie" correct as a statement of "testimony taken and proceedings had," but that no transcript is "considered as official" except those made from records "certified by the reporter" or other authorized person.

5. Recall the matchbook from Problem 3-H (Eagle's Rest Bar and Grill), which dealt with the hearsay problem of using the legend on the matchbook to prove its origin. Recall as well the example of the can of Green Giant peas that figured in a mid-century case in Maine, which led to a loss for a plaintiff who claimed injury from a piece of metal in such a can, but lost because he didn't prove where the can came from. Both these issues are easily resolved by FRE 902(7), which cuts through hearsay and authentication problems by providing that a commercially affixed "inscription, sign, tag, or label" can establish "origin, ownership, or control."

I DEMONSTRATIVE EVIDENCE GENERALLY

BELLI, DEMONSTRATIVE EVIDENCE: SEEING IS BELIEVING

16 Trial 70 (July 1980)

Everyone is familiar with the saying that a picture is worth a thousand words. To the trial lawyer, a picture can be worth much, much more. It could spell the difference between victory and defeat, or between a nominal award and an "adequate" one. Yet photographs comprise merely one fact of that vast expanse referred to as "demonstrative evidence." This article will examine the purposes and uses of demonstrative evidence, as well as some of its forms and variations.

WHAT IS DEMONSTRATIVE EVIDENCE?

Broadly speaking, demonstrative evidence is anything which appeals to the jurors' senses. It can be something for them to look at, to touch, to smell, to taste, or listen to. Demonstrative evidence is premised upon the theory that it is easier and much more effective simply to show the jurors what is being described, rather than to waste time and to risk possible confusion by relying solely upon oral testimony.

Demonstrative evidence clearly and concisely communicates to the jury that precise image which no amount of verbal description by itself could convey. In addition, by giving jurors something they can see, feel, smell, taste, or hear, their attention spans and interests in the case are revived and renewed. More importantly, they now have something they can take back into the jury room with them as they begin their deliberations.

From this, one sees that another advantage to using demonstrative evidence is the *continual communication* with the jury that it provides. Unlike a witness' spoken testimony which disappears as soon as it is stated, tangible demonstrative evidence remains in the jury's presence throughout the trial, a constant reminder of the point it is intended to make. To illustrate this concept of continuous communications, I would like briefly to relate a burn case I recently tried with Vincent Igoe of East St. Louis, Illinois.

The case involved a plaintiff who had suffered thermal burns over 80 percent of his body. Among a myriad of other demonstrative evidence, we introduced and had accepted into evidence a six-foot high, full-color photograph of the plaintiff, who was clad only in a diaper-like cloth. The picture had been taken shortly after the incident occurred, and graphically illustrated the severity of the plaintiff's condition. Having the picture in the sight of the jury throughout the trial played a large factor in the defendant's decision to settle the case for $1 million.

One note on the continuous use of a single piece of demonstrative evidence throughout a trial such as this: Every once in a while, cases come about involving such "shocking" evidence. Sometimes it is more useful to bring in this evidence during the latter stage of the trial, so that the jurors do not become immune or indifferent to it, thereby losing some of its initial potency. This is a factor which must be taken into consideration and weighed on its own merits in every case involving such evidence, the trial lawyer then proceeding the way he deems best.

THE USES OF DEMONSTRATIVE EVIDENCE

Demonstrative evidence is utilized for three major purposes: (1) to establish the liability of the defendant; (2) to illustrate the full extent and severity of the plaintiff's injuries; and (3) to complement the written transcript for use on appeal.

(1) As every trial lawyer is fully aware, without liability there is no case; there can be no recompense to an injured party. . . .

The use of models, tests, and experiments for reconstructing the accident in front of the jury to establish liability can prove invaluable. Simply telling a jury how one came to be injured involves not only general questions of the witness' credibility, but also the query of whether such an accident could have occurred even assuming all facts to be true as stated. To re-create the incident in the courtroom instantly removes this latter inquiry. Now the jury knows that such an accident can in fact occur, and is not quite so incredible as it may at one time have thought.

(2) Demonstrative evidence, especially in the form of photographs and motion pictures—and particularly "day-in-the-life" films, which show the plaintiff's condition immediately after the accident and during the recovery period—is instrumental in communicating the plaintiff's injuries, pain, and suffering to the jury . . . .

. . . What often occurs is that, in the three to four years that it takes before the case goes to trial (and even considerably longer if one takes into consideration the possibility of various appeals followed by a second, or even third, trial), the plaintiff will have substantially recovered from the once horrendous scars, bruises, lacerations and other telltale markings of the distressful event. The jury, without such photos and movies, sees only the plaintiff as he now stands before them, in a fairly healthy, rehabilitated state. Once-hideous scars will have since faded away, leaving only faint traces of their one-time gruesome existence . . . .

(3) Demonstrative evidence is also important as it aids in the creation of the record for review in the event the case is appealed. Many verdicts in favor of the plaintiff are appealed on the basis that there were insufficient facts upon which the jury or court could have found that the defendant was negligent, or frequently that the damages awarded the plaintiff were "excessive." By placing before the appellate justices a comprehensive record, replete with demonstrative evidence which clearly shows the defendant's liability and accurately reflects the *full* extent of the plaintiff's injuries, pain, and suffering, the plaintiff's lawyer stands a much better chance of not having the verdict overturned, or the damages awarded reduced.

TYPES OF DEMONSTRATIVE EVIDENCE

Of all types of demonstrative evidence, photographs have historically been the most frequently employed, and even today the trend continues. Although many restrictions were originally placed on the use of photographs, most of these have since disappeared. Color photographs and enlargements are routinely permitted. The fact that the scene captured on film is gory or gruesome does not make it any less admissible, unless it is being offered for the sole purpose of inflaming the jury . . . .

Motion pictures likewise may be utilized, but judges tend to exercise their discretion more frequently in refusing to admit this type of evidence, due to their susceptibility to editing and staging. One of the more common uses of motion pictures that has blossomed in the past few years is the use of a "day-in-the-life" film. The object of such a film is to record the injured plaintiff's daily routine since the injury was incurred. The camera begins rolling the moment the plaintiff wakes, and continues until he falls asleep.

The impact of these films is very powerful. The jury must watch as the plaintiff lives through one full day. These films are especially potent when the plaintiff has lost a limb, suffered severe internal injuries, has become a paraplegic, has sustained considerable brain damage, or someone, especially in the case of children, who for the rest of their lives will be confined to an iron lung.

Each juror sees how the plaintiff can no longer care for even his simplest needs. They learn how his condition demands constant care and attention. The jurors watch as the plaintiff's face writhes with pain as he tries to walk or make even the most elementary of movements. In short, the jurors watch as the plaintiff suffers through a typical day, which will be repeated over and over again until death.

Often, rather than show a picture of the injury, it is more effective to show the wound itself. Courts commonly allow scars, bruises, burnt tissue, and even the stump of an amputated limb to be bared and shown. In some cases, the court will allow the jurors to *touch* the injury. This is particularly true where the injury is hidden, such as a dent in the scalp. Often, jurors are given the chance to touch burned skin, so they may feel how hardened it has become.

Where the plaintiff has lost a limb due to the malfeasance of the defendant, the prosthesis he must wear for the remainder of his days may be admitted into evidence. The artificial limb may be put on and its workings demonstrated for the jury. Once in a while, in an amputation case, the courts are presented with the question of whether the amputated limb itself may be entered into evidence.

In one celebrated case, the plaintiff's hand was severed as he was operating a stamping press. One issue in the case involved exactly where the hand had been when it was caught. The Supreme Court of California held that the trial court had properly admitted into evidence a jar containing the plaintiff's amputated hand, which had been preserved in fluid. A streak of ink along the hand supported the plaintiff's contentions as to the whereabouts of the hand at the time of the injury. Other courts have admitted a severed kneecap, a bottle containing four ounces of brain matter and eight pieces of splintered bone, and a few toes.

Models, charts and diagrams are most effective tools for communicating with the jury. A skeleton, an electric train set, or a magnetized map upon which magnetic cars, trains, pedestrians and the like may be mounted play important roles in the successful handling of many cases. More often than not, the costs in having a model or chart prepared are not nearly as exorbitant as the trial lawyer may think . . . .

CONCLUSION

Many other forms of demonstrative evidence are widely employed. Tests, experiments, sound recordings, "real" evidence and untold others help the trial lawyer every day in making known to the jurors *exactly* what it is they should know. The varieties of demonstrative evidence available to the trial attorney are enormous. They are limited only by the creativity and originality of the trial lawyer's mind and the trial court's discretion. New forms of demonstrative evidence are being invented daily by innovative lawyers seeking to show the jurors precisely what they should consider.

The last 25 years have seen great advances in the field of demonstrative evidence and its uses. The next 25 years shall be at the very least equally exciting. Right now some trial lawyer may be formulating a new concept which will once again revolutionize this area. It is with eager anticipation that all trial lawyers await such new discoveries in further strengthening their skills and competence in the greatest of all professions.

■ NOTES ON DEMONSTRATIVE EVIDENCE

1. Belli refers to demonstrative evidence as anything that "appeals to the jurors' senses." This definition is overbroad because it could even encompass testimony. Most commentators and cases distinguish between *real* evidence and *demonstrative* evidence. The former refers to tangible objects or matters that had a direct part in the events giving rise to the suit. The latter usually refers to evidence having no independent probative value that serves as a *visual or perceptual aid* in understanding testimony or other evidence. Sometimes demonstrative evidence is referred to as *illustrative* evidence.

2. If evidence is admitted merely for illustrative purposes, should it be treated differently from other evidence? Certainly the jury should be told it is not substantive evidence. Should it be allowed to go the jury room? Usually not, but courts are not uniform on this point.

3. Is demonstrative evidence ever hearsay? See Grimes v. Employers Mutual Liability Insurance Co., 73 F.R.D. 607 (D. Alaska 1977) ("day in life" film of plaintiff is hearsay but admissible under catchall exception).

4. The generally accepted standards for the admissibility of experiments or tests were stated as follows in Ramseyer v. General Motors Corp., 417 F.2d 859, 864 (8th Cir. 1969):

> Admissibility of evidence depends upon a foundational showing of substantial similarity between the tests conducted and actual conditions. Perfect identity between experimental and actual conditions is neither attainable nor required. Dissimilarities effect [sic] the weight of the evidence, not admissibility . . . .

> Finally, the decision whether to admit or exclude evidence of experiments in a particular case rests largely in the discretion of the trial judge and his decision will not be overturned on appeal absent a clear showing of an abuse of discretion.

When a litigant seeks to conduct an experiment in court, it is a form of demonstrative evidence. Trial courts have great discretion in deciding whether to allow in-court experiments, and are strongly influenced by considerations such as the amount of time the experiment will consume and the danger of unfair prejudice or of confusing or misleading the jury. If what the litigant seeks to offer is testimony regarding an experiment conducted out-of-court, prior to trial, the rules governing expert witnesses and scientific evidence must also be considered.

J COMPUTER ANIMATIONS AND SIMULATIONS

Computer technology has made possible a powerful new type of demonstrative evidence—animations or simulations. Animations are visual depictions that illustrate or clarify an eyewitness account, an expert's opinion on what happened, or that demonstrate a process, principle, mechanism or other phenomenon relevant to the suit. Animations are illustrative evidence. Simulations, on the other hand, are attempted recreations of an event. They are developed by entering known data into a computer program which analyses the data according to certain rules (e.g., the laws of physics or mathematics) to produce a conclusion about what happened and usually a visual recreation of the event. Because simulations are focused on the event and support a particular version of what happened, they are usually classified as substantive evidence. How should the foundation required for a simulation differ from those required for an animation? What role should FRE 403 play in regulating the use of such exhibits? Consider the following problem:

■ PROBLEM 13-L. "The Animation Will Help the Jury"

Brandon Sayles is charged with involuntary manslaughter in connection with the death of Melissa, the seven-month-old daughter of his live-in girlfriend Naomi Lyell. Sayles and Lyell rushed Melissa to the emergency room, but Melissa died from severe neck injuries within an hour. As Melissa's treating physician, Dr. Gerdes concluded that her injuries resulted from "Shaken Baby Syndrome" and contacted police.

Interviewed by a detective, Sayles says Melissa fell down the stairs and was unconscious when he found her. Sayles tells the detective he "panicked" and then shook Melissa "in the hope of reviving her." But he says her injuries were the result of the fall.

The prosecutor offers a computer animation prepared by the National Center on Shaken Baby Syndrome. "The animation will help the jury understand the testimony by Dr. Gerdes," the prosecutor announces, "so it can comprehend how Melissa suffered her fatal injuries." The animation depicts a representational figure of a typical infant about six months in age being shaken so the head is whipped back and forth with such force that the chin touches the chest in the forward motion and the head almost touches the child's back at the other extreme. Later the animation depicts physical damage that to blood vessels and nerves located in the brain and eyes of a child shaken in this manner.

As foundation, on the basis of medical training and experience, Dr. Gerdes testifies that (1) the computer animation accurately represents Shaken Baby Syndrome and the injuries it causes, and (2) his examination of Melissa persuades him that she suffered brain and eye damage similar to the injuries demonstrated on the animation. Sayles objects to the animation, claiming lack of adequate authentication and unfair prejudice.

How should the judge rule? Would it make a difference if the judge were willing to give the following instruction:

> Ladies and Gentlemen, we are going to watch a computer animation, and I want you to understand that it is not meant to be a recreation of events in this case. What happened in this case is for you to decide on the basis of the evidence presented, and not on the basis of the animation. The purpose of the animation is merely to help you understand the testimony by Dr. Gerdes and the concepts he is presenting here.

■ NOTES ON COMPUTER-CREATED ANIMATIONS

1. Does the proponent need an expert to authenticate such computer animations? Who would be sufficient? Should the court also require testimony by the person who prepared the animation to explain the data or parameters on which it rests?

2. What if a criminal defendant like Sayles, or a civil litigant for that matter, cannot afford an expert to prepare computer-generated video imagery to present his version of the facts? What if he cannot even afford an expert to challenge the preparation or accuracy of the opponent's images? Should an imbalance in available resources bear on the decision whether to admit such evidence?

3. What role does FRE 403 play in this context? Consider the following suggestion:

> Computer-generated video imagery can have a powerful impact on the jury, perhaps overwhelming its fair consideration of other conflicting evidence.

> Moreover, unlike experimental evidence, computer-generated imagery is not restricted by the laws of gravity or other scientific principles. For these reasons, courts retain broad discretion under FRE 403 to exclude computer animations, particularly where they are based on questionable assumptions or project such a slanted or distorted view of the evidence as to be unfairly prejudicial or misleading.

C. Mueller & L. Kirkpatrick, Evidence §9.34 (5th ed. 2012). And see generally Fred Galves, Where the Not-So-Wild Things Are: Computers in the Courtroom, The Federal Rules of Evidence, and the Need for Institutional Reform and More Judicial Acceptance, 13 Harv. J.L. & Tech. 161 (2000).

CHAPTER 14

The "Best Evidence" Doctrine

A INTRODUCTION

Litigants have a natural incentive to offer the most direct, reliable, and persuasive evidence they can find, if only because they want to win. That means that they must satisfy whatever burdens are allocated to them in proving charges, claims, or defenses, and it means ultimately that they must persuade the factfinder (judge or jury). Of course the most effective or persuasive evidence is not always the most reliable evidence, and litigants sometimes try to win by means of unfair tactics, but still it is often the case that the most persuasive evidence is also the best proof that one can find. Hence it is often unnecessary to *require* parties to produce the best evidence, and in fact the law does not generally impose any such requirement. Litigants are mostly free to choose among admissible forms of proof, and they may offer "lesser" forms for reasons of practicality, economy, or tactics. Testimony describing the scene of an accident may be given instead of taking the jury for a view. A photograph or testimonial description of a wrecked car is almost always offered in lieu of the car itself. And hearsay is often admissible even though the declarant could be called as a witness.

The main exception to this pattern—the place where we do impose a rule of preference—arises in proving the contents of writings. Common law tradition long included a requirement to offer the original writing whenever the purpose was to prove its contents, or at least to explain in a satisfactory way why the original was not being offered. This rule precludes proof of the terms of a writing not only by testimony, but also by a copy (even if reliable), unless the original is unavailable through no fault of the party seeking to prove its content. The rule is commonly called the "Best Evidence" doctrine, although the name is misleading in suggesting that it applies across the board. Less commonly but more accurately, the rule is also known as the original writing or original document rule.

The Best Evidence doctrine (we will stick with the most common name) rests on five considerations. First, the written word traditionally has special sanctity in legal affairs, justifying more stringent proof requirements. Second, any method of proving the content of a writing *other* than the writing itself, is distinctly inferior. Language is complex, and the slightest variation in wording or punctuation can make a big difference. Unless a writing is very short, human memory cannot summarize it with the precision that is often needed. The burden that comes with requiring an original writing is minor when compared to the increased accuracy that an original makes possible. Third, modern photocopy methods have not always been available, and copies of writings have been viewed with suspicion. Requiring the proponent to produce the original is a safeguard against forgeries and inadvertent errors that may come with the copying process. This safeguard is less important now that the technology of document production is more advanced. Fourth, production of the original writing assures completeness and prevents segments from being removed from their context. Fifth, examining the writing may help resolve disputes over authenticity.

■ NOTES ON THE "BEST EVIDENCE" DOCTRINE

1. FRE 1002 not only codifies the common law Best Evidence rule but extends it to recordings and photographs. What is the justification for this extension? On the other hand, note that FRE 1003 significantly qualifies the Best Evidence doctrine by making "duplicates" generally admissible in lieu of originals. For the definition of "duplicate" see FRE 1001(e).

2. In view of the general admissibility of duplicates under FRE 1003, what kind of secondary evidence proving contents of a "writing, recording, or photograph" is now most likely to be excluded by FRE 1002?

3. Examine FRE 1005 carefully. It prevents disruption of public record-keeping systems by allowing litigants to submit a copy rather than an original of a public record. But there must be either testimony or a certification that the copy is accurate. This requirement effectively qualifies, at least for public records, the broad statement in FRE 1003 that duplicates are generally admissible without a certification.

4. To what extent is an "escape clause" to FRE 1002 provided by FRE 1004(d), which dispenses with the requirement of producing the original when the writing, recording, or photograph is "not closely related to a controlling issue"? For examples of "collateral" writings, see the ACN to FRE 1004(d). See also United States v. Johnson, 413 F.2d 1396, 1400 (5th Cir. 1969), *on reh'g*, 431 F.2d 441 (5th Cir. 1970) (in trial for receiving and concealing a stolen car, letting FBI agent testify that registration papers at courthouse did not match car with that tag seen in front of defendant's house, leading to discovery that it was stolen; this testimony was not offered to prove "identity," but rather "to explain the reason for the agent's subsequent inspection," which led to conclusive proof of identity); McCormick on Evidence §234, at 364 (J. Strong ed., 5th ed. 1999) (witness can refer to newspaper in explaining why he knows date of event because next day he saw newspaper account of event and made mental note of date); 5 Mueller & Kirkpatrick, Federal Evidence §10:30 (4th ed. 2013):

> It seems impossible to define "collateralness" or matters "not closely related to a controlling issue" with any precision. Perhaps for this reason the exception is often invoked with little or no discussion of its intended meaning. The exception is useful in preserving flexibility in administering the Best Evidence doctrine, enabling the trial judge to protect continuity and flow in presenting testimony and avoiding unnecessary distraction and delay—the exception is "a necessary concession to expedition of trials and clearness of narration."

5. Are you persuaded that the Best Evidence rule is needed? To the extent that the parties want to present the most complete and accurate evidence of the content of a writing, recording, or photograph, they will certainly offer the thing itself, won't they? Does the rule serve to block parties from presenting inferior proof in the circumstances in which they might be most tempted to do so? See Cleary & Strong, The Best Evidence Rule: An Evaluation in Context, 51 Iowa L. Rev. 825 (1966) (Best Evidence rule does offer minimal protection against inaccurate or fraudulent presentations and against attempts to present evidence out of context).

■ PROBLEM 14-A. The Defamatory Letter

Paula brings a defamation action against Daniel based on statements made by Daniel in a letter to Paula's employer. At trial, the letter is neither produced nor shown to be unavailable. Over a Best Evidence objection, the employer is allowed to testify regarding the contents of the letter. Paula is awarded a substantial verdict. On appeal, Daniel contends that it was a clear violation of the Best Evidence rule to allow the employer to testify to the contents of the letter without being required to produce it. Assuming the appellate court agrees with this contention, is the error likely to be found to be harmful? Should the judgment be reversed and the case retried? To resolve this question, what question is Daniel likely to be asked at oral argument?

B DEFINING A "WRITING, RECORDING, OR PHOTOGRAPH"

UNITED STATES v. DUFFY

United States Court of Appeals for the Fifth Circuit
454 F.2d 809 (1972)

WISDOM, J.

The defendant-appellant James H. Duffy was convicted by a jury of transporting a motor vehicle in interstate commerce from Florida to California knowing it to have been stolen in violation of 18 U.S.C.A. §2312. He was sentenced to imprisonment for a term of two years and six months. On this appeal, Duffy complains of error in the admission of certain evidence and of prejudice resulting from members of the jury having been present during a sentencing in an unrelated case. We affirm.

At the trial, the Government established that Duffy was employed in the body shop of an automobile dealership in Homestead, Florida; that the stolen vehicle was taken by the dealership as a trade-in on the purchase of a new car; that the vehicle was sent to the body shop for repair; and that the vehicle and the defendant disappeared over the same weekend. The Government also presented testimony as to the discovery of the car in California including the testimony of (1) a witness who was found in possession of the vehicle and arrested and who testified he had received the vehicle from the defendant, (2) a San Fernando, California police officer who made the arrest and recovered the automobile, and (3) an F.B.I. agent who examined the vehicle, its contents, and the vehicle identification number. The defense stipulated to the authenticity of fingerprints, identified as Duffy's found on the rear-view mirror of the vehicle. The defense sought, through the testimony of three witnesses including the defendant, to establish that Duffy had hitchhiked to California and that, although he had worked on the stolen vehicle in the automobile dealership in Florida, he had not stolen it and had not transported it to California.

Both the local police officer and the F.B.I. agent testified that the trunk of the stolen car contained two suitcases. Found inside one of the suitcases, according to the witnesses, was a white shirt imprinted with a laundry mark reading "D-U-F." The defendant objected to the admission of testimony about the shirt and asked that the government be required to produce the shirt.[1] The trial judge overruled the objection and admitted the testimony. This ruling is assigned as error.

The appellant argues that the admission of the testimony violated the "Best Evidence Rule." According to his conception of the "Rule," the Government should have been required to produce the shirt itself rather than testimony about the shirt. This contention misses the import of the "Best Evidence Rule." The "Rule," as it exists today, may be stated as follows:

> [I]n proving the terms of *a writing*, where such terms are material, the original writing must be produced, unless it is shown to be unavailable for some reason other than the serious fault of the proponent. (Emphasis supplied)

McCormick, Evidence 409 (1954). Although the phrase "Best Evidence Rule" is frequently used in general terms, the "Rule" itself is applicable only to the proof of the contents of a writing. McCormick summarizes the policy-justifications for the rule preferring the original writing:

---

[1] It is undisputed that the shirt was available to be produced and that there was no reason for failure to produce the shirt.

> (1) . . . precision in presenting to the court the exact words of the writing is of more than average importance, particularly as respects operative or dispositive instruments, such as deeds, wills and contracts, since a slight variation in words may mean a great difference in rights, (2) . . . there is a substantial hazard of inaccuracy in the human process of making a copy by handwriting or typewriting, and (3) as respects oral testimony purporting to give from memory the terms of a writing, there is a special risk of error, greater than in the case of attempts at describing other situations generally. In the light of these dangers of mistransmission, accompanying the use of written copies or of recollection, largely avoided through proving the terms by presenting the writing itself, the preference for the original writing is justified.

McCormick, Evidence 410 (1954).

The "Rule" is not, by its terms or because of the policies underlying it, applicable to the instant case. The shirt with a laundry mark would not, under ordinary understanding, be considered a writing and would not, therefore, be covered by the "Best Evidence Rule." When the disputed evidence, such as the shirt in this case, is an object bearing a mark or inscription, and is, therefore, a chattel *and* a writing, the trial judge has discretion to treat the evidence as a chattel or as a writing. In reaching his decision, the trial judge should consider the policy-consideration behind the "Rule." In the instant case, the trial judge was correct in allowing testimony about the shirt without requiring the production of the shirt. Because the writing involved in this case was simple, the inscription "D-U-F," there was little danger that the witness would inaccurately remember the terms of the "writing." Also, the terms of the "writing" were by no means central or critical to the case against Duffy. The crime charged was not possession of a certain article, where the failure to produce the article might prejudice the defense. The shirt was collateral evidence of the crime. Furthermore, it was only one piece of evidence in a substantial case against Duffy.

The appellant relies on Watson v. United States, 5 Cir. 1955, 224 F.2d 910 for his contention that the testimony was inadmissible without production of the shirt. *Watson* involved a prosecution for possession of liquor without internal revenue stamps affixed to the containers in violation of what was then 26 U.S.C. §2803(a). This Court held that admission of testimony that there were no revenue stamps on seized containers without requiring production of the containers was erroneous. This case, however, does not provide support for appellant's assertion. First, the only case cited in *Watson* in support of application of the "Best Evidence Rule" to an object was a 1917 Ninth Circuit case involving a writing and not an object. See Simpson v. United States, 9 Cir. 1917, 245 F. 278. Second, the containers in *Watson* were critical to the proof of the crime. Possession of the containers was an element of the crime. As mentioned above, the shirt in the instant case, was not critical and possession of the shirt was not an element of the crime. Finally, *Watson*, although it has never been specifically overruled, has been distinguished into oblivion by this and other courts. Where *Watson* has been followed, a writing has been involved. In *Burney*, [5 Cir.

1965, 339 F.2d 91,] we held that oral testimony describing the contents of two containers as distilled spirits was admissible without producing the containers or their contents.

> The *Watson* decision is a minority decision on this point. As far as we are able to ascertain, the *Watson* case is the only case in all of the Circuits which does not confine the scope of the best evidence rule to the production of original documents or writings whenever feasible.

339 F.2d at 93.

In sum, the admission of the testimony in the instant case did not violate the "Best Evidence Rule." . . .

Affirmed.

■ NOTES ON DEFINING A "WRITING, RECORDING, OR PHOTOGRAPH"

1. *Duffy* asks whether the Best Evidence doctrine applies to inscribed chattels. The question whether an inscription is a "writing" can also arise if a witness testifies to the number on a car's license, or the number on a police officer's badge, or for that matter the words on a traffic sign. Doesn't the definition of "writing" in FRE 1001(a) ("letters, words, or numbers" that are "set down in any form") embrace these as well as the laundry mark in *Duffy*?

2. Even if the Best Evidence doctrine applies, courts can excuse nonproduction under the collateral writing exception of FRE 1004(d) if the inscription is tangential to the dispute. So the court could still take such an "end run" in *Duffy* if it arose today.

3. Is a painting subject to the Best Evidence rule? See Seiler v. Lucasfilm, 808 F.2d 1316 (9th Cir. 1986) (Best Evidence rule applies to drawings). A musical score? (yes) A live performance of a musical score? (no) A recorded performance? (yes)

4. Trial judges have wide discretion to determine on the facts whether the Best Evidence doctrine should apply to inscribed chattels. Consider the following suggested guidelines:

> The term "collateral" and the defining phrase used in FRE 1004(4) imply that it is the unimportance of the matter in question to the issues in the case which counts. No doubt this factor is significant, but the examples described above suggest that other factors are equally important, if not more so. These include:
>
> a. the simplicity or complexity of content and consequent risk of error in admitting a testimonial account;
>
> b. the strength of the proffered evidence of content, taking into account corroborative witnesses or evidence and the presence or absence of bias or self-interest on the part of the witnesses;

c. the breadth of the margin for error within which mistake in a testimonial description would not undermine the point to be proved;
d. the presence or absence of an actual dispute as to content,
e. the ease or difficulty of producing the original, and
f. the reasons why the proponent of other proof of content does not have or offer the original itself.

5 Mueller & Kirkpatrick, Federal Evidence §10:30 (4th ed. 2013).

DEFINING AN "ORIGINAL"

It can sometimes be challenging to define an "original." Note that FRE 1001(d) defines it as "the writing or recording itself." What does that mean? Consider the following problem:

■ PROBLEM 14-B. The Unprivate Physician

Denise retains Dr. Murphy to arrange a private adoption of her newborn daughter with an express understanding that her identity as mother will never be disclosed to the adoptive parents or the child. Eighteen years later the daughter seeks her biological parents and is put in touch with Dr. Murphy. At her request, he gives her a photocopy of his adoption records, which identify Denise as the mother. The daughter contacts Denise, which results in psychological anguish for Denise. She sues Dr. Murphy for outrageous conduct and breach of promise. At trial, Denise offers the photocopy of the adoption records that Dr. Murphy gave her daughter. His lawyer objects, saying the Best Evidence rule requires production of the original records, not the photocopy. What ruling? Would it matter whether the jurisdiction had adopted Rule 1003?

■ NOTES ON DEFINING AN "ORIGINAL"

1. The definition of an "original" writing, recording, or photograph is set forth in FRE 1001(d). Can a photocopy or carbon copy ever qualify as an original? To decide which of several writings is "the original," one must consider the elements of the charge, claim, or defense, the intention of the parties, surrounding circumstances, the use to which the writing in question was put, and the purposes of the offering party. Consider United States v. Rangel, 585 F.2d 344, 346 (8th Cir. 1978) (photocopies of customer's carbon copies of Master Charge receipts were "originals" when they were submitted in support of false claim for travel expenses); Cartier v. Jackson, 59 F.3d 1046, 1048 (10th Cir. 1995) (in infringement suit alleging that Michael Jackson appropriated a song from a demo tape sent by plaintiff; the demo tape and not a prior "master" tape was the "original" because it was all that defendant heard).

2. Why is it usually easy to satisfy the Best Evidence doctrine when it comes to photographs? See FRE 1001(d) an original of a photograph "includes a negative or print from it."

USE OF DUPLICATES

In the days of Bob Cratchit, making copies involved great labor and risk of inaccuracy or illegibility.[1] Little wonder, then, that common law tradition frowned as much on "copies" as on testimony describing the original. Even the advent of more advanced copies (produced by carbon paper and the Thermofax machine) did not immediately open the door to copies.

This traditional skepticism, however, could not long survive the coming of the modern office copier. The genius of these machines is that they make full and accurate copies as readable as the original. (The technology involves an electrostatic process, but reproduction of black-and-white printed pages is so good that the product is sometimes called a "photocopy.") In recognition of this technology, Rule 1003 permits the use in evidence of any "duplicate" *without* need to make excuses for nonproduction of the original under FRE 1004. Note that "duplicate" is defined in FRE 1001(e) to mean essentially a machine-made copy, and not handmade copies from the Bob Cratchit era.

Rule 1003 does not quite open the door all the way to duplicates. A duplicate is *nearly* as usable in evidence as an original, but not quite. Rule 1003 contains two escape clauses, permitting exclusion of duplicates when concerns arise over "authenticity of the original" or under the circumstances it would be "unfair to admit the duplicate." In the following problems, consider whether duplicates should be admissible or required. Consider too FRE 1008, which allocates to the jury the responsibility of determining whether "(a) an asserted writing ever existed; (b) another one produced at the trial or hearing is the original; or (c) other evidence of content accurately reflects the original."

■ PROBLEM 14-C. "There Never Was Such an Original"

Dan sues Eva in contract and offers in evidence what he claims to be a "photocopy of the original agreement." On inspecting the proffered photo-

[1] The scrivener copied the original by hand, or used "letterpress" or "blotterpress" method. These involved pressing the inked original on porous paper to produce a reverse (mirror image), then pressing this reverse copy on a second porous sheet to make a second reversal (producing a faint forward-reading document) or, when times were slow in bookkeeping, simply using the first reversal in producing a new forward-reading handmade copy.

copy and consulting with his client, counsel for Eva raises a Best Evidence objection. In proceedings in aid of the objection, Eva takes the stand, and testifies thus:

Q (defense counsel): Have you examined this so-called photocopy?
A (Eva): Yes, I have.
Q: Is that a copy of a written agreement between you and Dan?
A: I have no idea what that's a copy of. I never saw such a document in my life. We did have an agreement, and we did type it out, in a way that looks sort of like this, but *this* says that I promised not to go to work for any of Dan's competitors, and what we signed never contained anything like that. Our agreement, the original that we signed, never said that.

Counsel for Eva then states, "Your honor, there never was such an original as this. Therefore this purported copy—whatever it is—cannot be admitted. We've raised a genuine question about authenticity, and you cannot properly admit this purported copy—this forgery, if you want to call it what it really is."

You are counsel for Dan. How can you reply to Eva's objection? If Dan can testify that "I made this photocopy from the very agreement Eva and I signed, and it accurately reproduces our contract," should the judge resolve the issue produced by the conflict between Dan and Eva, or should the jury decide it? If the jury should decide it, does that mean that the copy should be admitted? Hasn't Eva raised a "genuine issue" about the authenticity of the original?

■ PROBLEM 14-D. Nine Hours or One?

Gretchen sues St. Anne's Hospital and Dr. Mazo for negligence in an operation that caused her permanent brain damage. At the time, Gretchen was pregnant and had been admitted for emergency surgery. While under a general anesthetic, she vomited in her oxygen mask, which blocked the flow of oxygen to her brain. After the operation she was permanently comatose, living on life support, and her baby died unborn.

In his testimony, Dr. Mazo admits that it would be negligent to place Gretchen under anesthesia if she had eaten only one hour earlier. But St. Anne's introduces her admitting record, which shows that nine hours had passed since she last ate.

In a dramatic development during rebuttal, Gretchen's attorney calls Sally Abrams, the nurse who admitted Gretchen to St. Anne's. Abrams testifies that Gretchen told her she had eaten a meal just one hour prior to coming to the hospital. Abrams wrote the number "1" on the admitting form, and she testifies that after the failed surgery Dr. Mazo forced her (on threat of dismissal) to change the "1" to a "9." Before altering the form, however, she made a photocopy showing her prior entry.

Gretchen offers the photocopy. The defense raises a Best Evidence objection, both to the copy and to Abrams' testimony, arguing that the copy is a forgery that does not accurately reflect the contents of the original. How should the court rule, and why? What if the judge is personally persuaded that the photocopy is a forgery?

E BEST EVIDENCE DOCTRINE IN OPERATION

By its terms, the Best Evidence Doctrine applies only when a party seeks to prove "the content" of a writing. On this point Rule 1002 made no change, though to be sure it did broaden the coverage of the doctrine to embrace recordings and photographs.

When the doctrine applies. Obviously it is critical to understand just when "the content" is what a party seeks to prove. Speaking broadly and focusing mostly on writings, there are two situations in which content is indeed the point to be proved. First is the circumstance in which the substantive law forces the content of a writing into prominence, and in effect simply requires one party or another to prove that content. Second is the circumstance in which a party chooses to prove content, even though she might theoretically present an adequate claim or defense without such proof—the situation, in other words, in which party strategy forces the writing into prominence.

Recall, as one instance in which substantive law forces the content of a writing into prominence, what you learned in the contracts course about the parol evidence doctrine and the statute of frauds. Here is not the place to exhaust those subjects, but we can agree that the former holds essentially that when the parties have integrated their agreement into a writing, they may not later alter or vary the terms of that agreement by "parol evidence" (meaning, for the most part, evidence of oral statements uttered during negotiation or signing). We can agree that the latter holds essentially that when a contract is "within the statute of frauds" (such as an agreement for the sale of goods at a price exceeding $500), there must be an adequate writing.

Imagine now that a party sues on a contract covered by either of these substantive doctrines. What is the effect of the doctrine? Its effect is to force any party who would rely on the agreement to prove "the content" of the writing. And what is the effect of the Best Evidence doctrine? Its effect (oversimplifying for a moment) is to force the party to offer the writing itself. Note well that the substantive law, standing alone, does not require production of the document, for its focus is on the rights of the parties, not the mechanics of proof. Nevertheless the effect of these substantive principles is to force the parties to prove content, and then the Best Evidence doctrine steps in to require production of the document, as the proper means of proving content.

Now consider a case in which party strategy forces a writing into prominence. Recall Baker v. Elcona Homes, 588 F.2d 551 (6th Cir. 1978), *cert. denied*, 441 U.S. 933 (1979) (Chapter 4C6, supra), where defendant sought to prove that the Valiant ran a red light and offered as proof the accident report prepared by Officer Hendrickson. As long as defendant chose to rely on the report as proof that the light was red for the Valiant, the Best Evidence doctrine required defendant to offer the report itself. No principle of substantive law required proof in that form. Testimony by an eyewitness who saw the accident would serve as well—and possibly better. But the Best Evidence doctrine says, in effect, that if defendant *wants to use* the police report to prove that the Valiant ran a red light, then defendant must offer the report itself.

Perhaps there was no bystander, or none known to the defendant in *Elcona Homes.* He may have had no other option when he decided to prove the point by using the report. Necessity may have been the mother of this strategy, but it was strategy plus the Best Evidence doctrine that led him to proceed this way, not substantive law or the Best Evidence doctrine alone.

When the doctrine does not apply. As you are soon to discover, there are many cases in which it might appear at first glance that the Best Evidence doctrine applies, but in fact it does not. Speaking broadly once again, most of these cases are commonly described as situations in which the matter to be proved has been "incidentally recorded," but in which neither substantive law nor party strategy actually forces the writing into prominence.

Think again about *Elcona Homes.* If Officer Hendrickson had remained on the stand (in fact he had left), and if defendant had succeeded in qualifying him as an expert in accident investigation and had asked him which vehicle probably had the light, could plaintiffs raise a Best Evidence objection? Clearly not, at least if Officer Hendrickson can testify from present memory about the conclusions he reached (the ones he also put in his report). Can you see why?

Consider now some problems and cases that illustrate the Best Evidence doctrine.

■ PROBLEM 14-E. The XXX-Rated Movies

In a trial for alleged interstate transportation of obscene films, the prosecutor tries to establish the obscene content of the films seized from the defendant by the testimony of a police officer who viewed them. The films themselves are not offered into evidence or shown to the jury. The attorney for the defendant makes a Best Evidence objection to the police officer's testimony. What ruling?

■ PROBLEM 14-F. The Surveillance Photograph

During a bank robbery, a hidden surveillance camera takes digitized pictures of the robber. At trial the bank security officer, who was not present at the robbery, testifies that he downloaded the digitized files that were created automatically at the time of the robbery, and he examined the image of the robber. He offers to testify that the person shown in the image is the defendant. The image is not offered in evidence. Defendant makes a Best Evidence objection. What ruling?

MEYERS v. UNITED STATES

United States Court of Appeals, District of Columbia Circuit
171 F.2d 800 (1948)

[In the trial of Bleriot Lamarre for perjury, and of Bennett Meyers for suborning perjury, the government sought to prove that Lamarre lied in his testimony before a Senate Committee. To prove what Lamarre had said, the government called William P. Rogers, then Chief Counsel to the Committee. Rogers had examined Lamarre before the Committee and consequently heard all his testimony. Later in the trial the government also introduced in evidence a stenographic transcript of Lamarre's testimony.

According to the indictment, Lamarre falsely testified to the Committee that (a) he was "not financially interested" in Aviation Electric Corporation in the years 1940-1947, (b) a Cadillac purchased by Meyers was for company use; and (c) the payment of $10,000 to decorate and furnish Meyers's Washington apartment was made by Lamarre when actually the money was paid by means of an Aviation Electric check.

On appeal, Meyers claimed that using Rogers to prove what Lamarre had said represented a "bizarre procedure."]

WILBUR K. MILLER, J.

The dissenting opinion . . . asserts it was reversible error to allow Rogers to testify at all as to what Lamarre had said to the subcommittee, on the theory that the transcript itself was the best evidence of Lamarre's testimony before the subcommittee.

That theory is, in our view, based upon a misconception of the best evidence rule. As applied generally in federal courts, the rule is limited to cases where the contents of a writing are to be proved. Here there was no attempt to prove the contents of a writing; the issue was what Lamarre had said, not what the transcript contained. The transcript made from shorthand notes of his testimony was, to be sure, evidence of what he had said, but it was not the only admissible evidence concerning it. Rogers' testimony was equally competent, and was admissible whether given before or after the transcript was received in evidence. Statements alleged to be perjurious may be proved by any person who heard them, as well as by a reporter who recorded them in shorthand . . . .

As we have pointed out, there was no issue as to the contents of the transcript, and the government was not attempting to prove what it contained; the issue was what Lamarre actually had said. Rogers was not asked what the transcript contained but what Lamarre's testimony had been.

After remarking, ". . . there is a line of cases which holds that a stenographic transcript is not the best evidence of what was said. There is also a legal cliche that the best evidence rule applies only to documentary evidence," the dissenting opinion asserts that the rule is outmoded and that "the courts ought to establish a new and correct rule." We regard the principle set forth in the cases which we have cited as being, not a legal cliche, but an established and sound doctrine which we are not prepared to renounce.

With the best evidence rule shown to be inapplicable, it is clearly seen that it was neither "preposterously unfair," as the appellant asserts, nor unfair at all, to permit the transcript of Lamarre's evidence to be introduced after Rogers had testified. Since both methods of proving the perjury were permissible, the prosecution could present its proof in any order it chose.

There is no substance in the criticism, voiced by the appellant and in the dissent, of the fact that Rogers testified early in the unduly protracted trial and the transcript was introduced near its close. Appellant's counsel had a copy of the transcript from the second day of the trial, and had full opportunity to study it and to cross-examine Rogers in the light of that study. The mistaken notion that, had the transcript been first put in evidence, Rogers' testimony would have been incompetent is, of course, based on the erroneous idea that the best evidence rule had application.

It is quite clear that Meyers was in no way prejudiced by the order in which the evidence against him was introduced, nor does it appear that his position before the jury would have been more favorable had the transcript been offered on an earlier day of the trial . . . .

Since we perceive no prejudicial error in appellant's trial, the judgment entered pursuant to the jury's verdict will not be disturbed.

Affirmed.

PRETTYMAN, J. (dissenting).

I am of strong opinion that the judgment in this case should be reversed.

The testimony given by Lamarre before the Senate Committee was presented to the jury upon the trial in so unfair and prejudicial a fashion as to constitute reversible error.

Lamarre testified before the Committee in executive session, only Senators, Mr. William P. Rogers, who was counsel to the Committee, the clerk, the reporter, and the witness being present. An official stenographic record was made of the proceedings. The testimony continued for two days, and the transcript is 315 typewritten pages. When Meyers was indicted, he moved for a copy of the transcript. The United States Attorney opposed, on the ground that the executive proceedings of a Senate Committee are confidential. The court denied Meyers' motion.

When the trial began, the principal witness called by the Government was Mr. Rogers. He was asked by the United States Attorney, "Now, will you tell the Court and the jury in substance what the testimony was that the defendant Lamarre gave before the Committee concerning the Cadillac automobile?" Two counts of the indictment related to this automobile.

The court at once called counsel to the bench and said to the prosecutor:

> Of course, technically, you have the right to proceed the way you are doing . . . . I do not think that is hearsay under the hearsay rule, but it seems to me . . . that, after all, when you have a prosecution based on perjury, and you have a transcript of particular testimony on which the indictment is based, that you ought to lay a foundation for it or ought to put the transcript in evidence, instead of proving what the testimony was by someone who happens to be present, who has to depend on his memory as to what was said.

Counsel for the defense, objecting, insisted that the procedure was "preposterously unfair." The trial judge said that it seemed to him that the transcript ought to be made available to defense counsel. That was then done, but the prosecutor insisted upon proceeding as he had planned with the witness.

Mr. Rogers then testified: "I will try to give the substance of the testimony . . . . I am sure your Honor appreciates that I do not remember exactly the substance of the testimony. The substance of testimony was this . . . ." And then he gave "in substance" the testimony in respect to the Cadillac car. The same process was followed in respect to the matters covered by the other counts of the indictment, i.e., the redecoration of Meyers' apartment and Meyers' interest in the Aviation Electric Corporation. Defense counsel reserved part of his cross-examination until he could read the transcript.

The notable characteristics of this testimony of Rogers are important. In each instance, the "substance" was a short summation, about half a printed page in length. The witness did not purport to be absolute in his reproduction but merely recited his unrefreshed recollection, and his recollection on each of the three matters bears a striking resemblance to the succinct summations of the indictment . . . .

From the theoretical viewpoint, I realize that there is a line of authority that (absent or incompetent the original witness) a bystander who hears testimony or other conversation may testify as to what was said, even though there be a stenographic report. And there is a line of cases which holds that a stenographic transcript is not the best evidence of what was said. There is also a legal cliché that the best evidence rule applies only to documentary evidence. The trial judge in this case was confronted with that authority, and a trial court is probably not the place to inaugurate a new line of authority. But I do not know why an appellate court should perpetuate a rule clearly outmoded by scientific development. I know that courts are reluctant to do so. I recognize the view that such matters should be left to Congress. But rules of evidence were originally judge-made and are an essential part of the judicial function. I know of no reason why the judicial branch of Government should abdicate to the legislative branch so important a part of its responsibility.

I am of opinion, and quite ready to hold, that the rules of evidence . . . are outmoded and at variance with known fact, and that the courts ought to establish a new and correct rule. The rationale of the so-called "best evidence rule" requires that a party having available evidence which is relatively certain may not submit evidence which is far less certain. The law is concerned with the true fact, and with that alone; its procedures are directed to that objective, and to that alone. It should permit no procedure the sole use of which is to obscure and confuse that which is otherwise plain and certain . . . .

The doctrine that stenographic notes are not the best evidence of testimony was established when stenography was not an accurate science. The basis for the decisions is succinctly stated in the 1892 case quoted as leading by Professor Wigmore:

> Stenographers are no more infallible than any other human beings, and while as a rule they may be accurate, intelligent, and honest, they are not always so; and therefore it will not do to lay down as a rule that the stenographer's notes when translated by him are the best evidence of what a witness has said, in such a sense as to exclude the testimony of an intelligent bystander who has heard and paid particular attention to the testimony of the witness.

[4 Wigmore, Evidence, §1330 (3d ed. 1940), quoting McIver, C.J., in Brice v. Miller, 1892, 35 S.C. 537, 549, 15 S.E. 272.]

But we have before us no such situation. Stenographic reporting has become highly developed, and official stenographic reports are relied upon in many of the most important affairs of life . . . . In the present instance, at least, no one has disputed the correctness of the transcript.

From the theoretical point of view, the case poses this question: Given both (1) an accurate stenographic transcription of a witness' testimony during a two-day hearing and (2) the recollection of one of the complainants as to the substance of that testimony, is the latter admissible as evidence in a trial of the witness for perjury? I think not. To say that it is, is to apply a meaningless formula and ignore crystal-clear actualities. The transcript is, as a matter of simple, indisputable fact, the best evidence. The principle and not the rote of the law ought to be applied . . . .

■ NOTES ON *MEYERS* AND THE LIMITS OF THE BEST EVIDENCE DOCTRINE

1. If the case arose today, it would likely be decided the same way under the Federal Rules. The case would also be decided the same way if the prosecutor had never offered the transcript and had relied solely on Rogers' testimony.

2. Would this case be decided differently if Rogers had not been present at the hearing and had learned of Lamarre's testimony only by reading the transcript? When a witness testifies on a matter that has been recorded, application of the Best Evidence doctrine turns on whether the witness has independent knowledge of the matter, apart from the recording.

3. Judge Prettyman's dissent rests on the view that a transcript is the best evidence of former testimony. What if the only available transcript had been prepared by an unofficial court reporter? By a secretary to the defendant's attorney? Can a court always judge what is the "best evidence"? Shouldn't the government be allowed to try its own case and choose its own form of proof?

4. Suppose the transcript of Lamarre's testimony was introduced first, and Rogers was asked to summarize or interpret it. Could Meyers object? Perhaps on grounds that "the writing speaks for itself," but not for violating the Best Evidence rule.

■ PROBLEM 14-G. The Recorded Conversation

In a drug surveillance operation, DEA agent Nolan monitors a conversation between Peter and Quinn that takes place in a room in the Quality Court Motel. Using a planted bug and recording equipment in an adjacent room, Nolan both hears and records what Peter and Quinn are saying. The conversations relate to drug transactions, past and ongoing.

After arresting Peter and Quinn, Nolan interrogates them separately at DEA headquarters. First Nolan questions Peter, who admits his involvement in a drug scheme and implicates Quinn. After getting Peter's story, Nolan summons a stenographer and has Peter repeat his statement. The stenographer prints out a hardcopy, and Peter signs it. Then Nolan questions Quinn and tape records the interview.

Consider the following evidence issues:

1. At the trial of Peter and Quinn, should Nolan be allowed to testify to the conversation he overheard at the Quality Court Motel or does the Best Evidence Doctrine require the government to produce the recording?
2. Can Nolan testify to Peter's admissions about his own conduct, or does a Best Evidence objection by Peter force the government to offer the signed written statement instead? What if Nolan thinks the signed statement omits important points that Peter uttered in his original recitation, before the retelling that the stenographer used in making the written version?
3. Can Nolan testify to what Quinn said at DEA headquarters, or does a Best Evidence objection force the government to offer the recording?

■ PROBLEM 14-H. The Sick Chickens

Best Chix, a company that specializes in breeding chickens and selling them to poultry farmers, sues one such farmer, Curt Duval, to recover the balance owed on the purchase price for a flock of chickens. Duval, who claims he is entitled to a price adjustment because many of the chickens were infected with leukosis, seeks to prove this point by testifying to the substance of a veterinarian's report he received, but does not offer the report itself. Best Chix makes a Best Evidence objection. What ruling, and why?

■ PROBLEM 14-I. Cash Payment

Teresa Feiler, who rents apartments to students in College Station, seeks to evict Ashley Gibson for nonpayment of rent for the month of October. Gibson testifies that she paid the October rent in cash. Under questioning in aid of an objection, counsel for Feiler gets Gibson to admit that Feiler always gave her a written receipt for her rent payments. Then Feiler's lawyer objects to Gibson's testimony, arguing that "the receipt constitutes the Best Evidence of payment, your Honor, and she cannot testify that she made the October payment unless she has a good reason for not producing the receipt." What result, and why?

■ PROBLEM 14-J. The Unreported Burglary

In a suit by homeowner Eric Hoskins against Frontier Casualty Company to recover losses suffered when a burglar allegedly stole a valuable Jackson Pollock painting from his home in St. Louis on December 14th, Frontier denies liability and asserts that any coverage that might have existed was lost when Hoskins failed to report the theft to the police. As proof, Frontier offers testimony by its claims examiner Jensen, who would testify that she "looked through the records of reported burglaries in every police station in greater St. Louis for the time period December 14th through December 20th, and found no record of a report by Hoskins and no record of any complaint regarding stolen artwork." Hoskins makes a Best Evidence objection, arguing that "Frontier must produce the logs and records themselves, not just testimony by someone who looked through the written materials." What result, and why? Notice, if helpful, the comments in the ACN to FRE 1002.

■ PROBLEM 14-K. The Unproduced X-Ray

In a personal injury suit brought by Sid Landon against Leigh Mills after a two-car collision, Dr. Sherry Nash (Landon's treating physician) testifies for Landon that X-ray of his leg showed a fractured femur. Landon does not offer the X-ray. Mills objects, citing the Best Evidence rule. What ruling? Does it make any difference whether the doctor is relying on the X-ray as part of the basis of a medical opinion rather than merely describing what the X-ray depicts? See FRE 703 and the ACN to FRE 1002.

F PRODUCTION OF ORIGINAL EXCUSED

SYLVANIA ELECTRIC PRODUCTS v. FLANAGAN

United States Court of Appeals for the First Circuit
352 F.2d 1005 (1965)

McEntee, J.

Plaintiff, Paul L. Flanagan, d/b/a Paul L. Flanagan and Sons, is a trucker and hauler of sand, gravel, stone and other similar materials. In the spring of 1963, defendant, Sylvania Electric Products, Inc., engaged a general contractor to construct a parking lot for it at its plant in Needham, Massachusetts. There was a hill or ledge on this site which had to be removed at the beginning of the job. Although the general contractor was obliged to level off the hill, he was not required under his contract to truck the ledge material away. Plaintiff alleges that on May 27, 1963, which is the date the parking lot job was commenced, the defendant made an oral agreement with him whereby he agreed to supply the trucks and haul this ledge material away and the defendant agreed to pay him for this work at the rate of $13 per hour per truck. Plaintiff proceeded immediately with the hauling operation which extended over two periods: May 27 to June 10, 1963 and June 17 to July 1, 1963. In the performance of this work he used his own trucks and trucks rented from others, as was his practice on jobs of this size. Plaintiff claimed that the entire job took a total of 1932 1/2 truck hours work for which he billed defendant at the rate of $13 an hour. This amount, plus an item of $145 for bulldozer hire, which was not disputed, came to $25,267.50. Defendant refused to pay this bill. Whereupon plaintiff brought suit in the Massachusetts Superior Court for breach of contract. The case was removed to the United States District Court for the District of Massachusetts on the ground of diversity. The jury found for the plaintiff in the full amount of his claim. This is an appeal by the defendant from the judgment entered by the district court based on the jury verdict. Defendant's principal ground of appeal is that the district court erred in admitting certain evidence in violation of the best evidence rule; that this evidence should have been excluded and a verdict should have been directed for the defendant.

Plaintiff offered the following evidence in support of his claim, all of which he alleged is based on daily truck hour slips on tally sheets made at the site of the job which recorded the number of trucks on the job and the number of hours worked by each truck: (1) Exhibit A in the declaration filed in this case, which he says is a summary of the data contained in the invoices and the tally sheets. (2) A number of photostatic copies of bills and invoices sent to plaintiff by other truckers for the rental of their trucks on this job. (3) Copies of two bills sent by plaintiff to defendant, one in the amount of $12,521 for work done during the first period and the other reflecting the total amount of $25,267.50 due for both periods. The contents of these two bills is identical with the claim set forth in Schedule A of the plaintiff's declaration (supra).

Plaintiff testified that the data contained in the above exhibits is the same as that contained in the tally sheets. In the course of the trial when plaintiff was asked whether the information contained in these exhibits was the same as that contained in the tally sheets, defendant objected on the ground that this was secondary evidence and thus was barred by the best evidence rule. At this point, the trial court inquired as to whether the plaintiff had those tally sheets, to which he replied that he knew he had some at home but was not sure whether he had them all. The court then suggested that he bring in those that he had. Later in the course of the trial this line of inquiry was resumed by plaintiff's counsel and again defendant objected. The court allowed plaintiff's testimony that the information contained in the invoices "checked out" with that contained in the tally sheets. The defendant adequately objected. None of the tally sheets were ever produced at the trial.

It is well settled that the best evidence that is obtainable in the circumstances of the case must be adduced to prove any disputed fact. Here, the plaintiff's claim is based on performance of the work. The best evidence of his performance is the truck hour records (tally sheets). Those records were made for the very purpose of recording this performance. Instead of producing these records plaintiff offered the secondary evidence of their content enumerated above. In proving the terms of a writing, which terms are material to the issues in the case, the original writing must be produced unless it is shown to be unavailable for some reason other than the serious fault of the proponent. McCormick, Evidence §196 (1954). Upon a proper showing of the unavailability of the original writing, secondary evidence of its contents may be received. However, secondary evidence of the content of the original is not admissible unless the proponent of the testimony shows that a reasonable and diligent search has been made for the original without success.

From a careful examination of the evidence in this case we feel there is not sufficient proof that the original tally sheets in question were in fact unavailable or that a reasonable search had been made to find them. Although plaintiff stated that it was not his practice to keep these tally sheets after checking them with the truckers' invoices, he did testify on several occasions that he knew he had some of them at home and that he would bring into court what he had. This he did not do. It is also apparent from the evidence that plaintiff had tally sheets in his possession when he conferred with officials of the defendant in June 1963, at which time he knew there was a dispute concerning the work and payment for it. Although plaintiff stated in open court that he would make a search for the tally sheets there is little if any evidence that he in fact made such a search and there is no evidence at all as to the extent of any such search. There is no universal or fixed rule that determines the sufficiency of the proof required to show that a reasonable or diligent search has been made. Each case is governed in large measure by its own particular facts and circumstances. He who seeks to introduce secondary evidence must show that he has used all reasonable means to obtain the original, i.e., such search as the nature of the case would suggest. The best evidence rule should not be applied as a mere technicality. But where the missing original writings in dispute are the very foundation of the claim, which is the situation in this case, more strictness in proof is required than where the writings are only involved collaterally. Plaintiff failed to satisfy this requirement.

Moreover, under the best evidence rule, in order to permit proof by secondary evidence of the allegedly lost or otherwise unavailable original writing, the trial judge must make preliminary findings that the original had become unavailable, otherwise than through the fault of the proponent of the testimony and that reasonable search had been made for it. The record in this case does not reveal that the trial court made these necessary preliminary findings. . . .

Ordinarily prejudicial error with respect to damages should require that the new trial be on damages only. However, in this case the whole case depended largely upon plaintiff's credibility. The record was left in such condition that he was never called upon to explain the absence of his records, his search, if any, therefor, or why, when he knew from the beginning that there was a dispute, he had not preserved them, if, in fact, he had not. Actually, plaintiff has never denied that the records no longer exist. In view of the fact that examination of the records might well corroborate the defendant's account, rather than plaintiff's, as to other issues between the parties, we believe that justice would be best served by ordering an entirely new trial.

The judgment of the district court will be vacated, the verdict set aside and the case remanded for a new trial consistent with this opinion.

■ NOTES ON ADMISSIBILITY OF "OTHER EVIDENCE OF CONTENTS"

1. If Paul Flanagan testified, in a hearing before the judge, that he had asked his bookkeeper where the tally sheets were and that the bookkeeper had replied, "Paul, I'm afraid those were lost when we moved the office from the first floor to the second, and the only records we still have are the copies of the bills and invoices," would Paul's testimony restating what his bookkeeper had told him be admissible to prove loss of the records? Note that FRE 1004(a) would permit resort to secondary evidence of what the tally sheets contained if their loss without bad faith were satisfactorily explained. And note further that in deciding this matter under FRE 104(a) the court is not bound by evidence rules.

2. As the principal case suggests, the extent of search required for the original is a matter to be determined by the trial judge. The appellate cases provide relatively few guidelines. A cursory search should not suffice:

> Ordinarily it is not sufficient that the paper is not found in its usual place of deposit, but all papers in the office or place should be examined . . . . It is true the party need not search every possible place where it might be found, for then the search might be interminable, but he must search every place where there is a reasonable possibility that it might be found.

Stipe v. First National Bank, 301 P.2d 175, 181 (Or. 1956).

3. Whether a writing, recording, or photograph is beyond the reach of judicial process under FRE 1004(b) depends on the applicable process statutes or rules. Process provisions usually extend farther in criminal cases than civil. If the writing, recording, or photograph is in the hands of a third party, the process typically used to compel production is a subpoena duces tecum. The party seeking discovery is usually able to obtain only a duplicate, not the original. Does inability to obtain the original through discovery mean that at trial the party will be allowed to offer any form of secondary evidence? Or if a duplicate was available through discovery, is the party required to offer that duplicate? The literal language of FRE 1004(b) appears to excuse a party from compliance with the Best Evidence doctrine on a showing that the *original* is unobtainable. But see 5 Mueller & Kirkpatrick, Federal Evidence §10:28 (4th ed. 2013) (suggesting that FRE 1004(b) should be read as requiring a party who can get a duplicate through discovery to prove contents by offering the duplicate).

4. FRE 1004 recognizes two categories of unavailability that justify proof by secondary evidence. Would showing extreme difficulty or impracticality of producing a writing, like a billboard or tombstone, be sufficient justification for not producing the original? See People v. Mastin, 171 Cal. Rptr. 780, 783 (Cal. App. 1981) (court could "visualize situations" where Best Evidence doctrine should not apply, like proving "an inscription on a 30 ton piece of heavy equipment or an item of personal property which should be promptly returned" to its owner).

5. FRE 1004(c) sets up a procedure that permits use of secondary evidence of contents when the writing, recording, or photograph is under the control of the opponent and the opponent is on notice, by pleadings or otherwise, of the party's intent to prove contents at the hearing. This procedure is not the same as a request for production, and the rule does not require showing of an inability to obtain the original through discovery or other means.

■ PROBLEM 14-L. Testimony versus Photocopy

In a breach of contract action, Corrigan, the plaintiff, establishes that the original written contract was destroyed in a fire through no fault of his own. Even though Corrigan has an accurate and legible photocopy of the original contract, he chooses at trial to prove the terms of the contract by his testimony rather than by offering the photocopy. Defendant Gregor makes a Best Evidence objection to the testimony, arguing that the photocopy must be introduced. What ruling? See FRE 1004 and the ACN to FRE 1004.

■ PROBLEM 14-M. The Tax Evader

Brad Trimble is prosecuted for alleged tax evasion, and the government calls Charles Urban, an IRS accountant, to testify. Urban has examined Trimble's bank records, which reflect more than 90 deposits and 300 withdrawals over the year, and the prosecutor offers (1) Urban's testimonial summary of deposits and disbursements from the account and (2) a chart prepared by Urban from bank records summarizing entries that the prosecutor considered significant. Trimble raises a Best Evidence objection. The prosecutor invokes FRE 1006. What result?

■ PROBLEM 14-N. "No Pets"

Owner Ann Brindon seeks to evict tenant Clay Dobbs from the apartment he rents from her because he has broken his lease by keeping a dog. At the hearing, Brindon seeks to testify that the lease contains a "no pets" provision, but Dobbs' Best Evidence objection is sustained.

Counsel for Brindon does not have the lease at hand, but she discovers in the file a signed letter from Dobbs acknowledging that "the lease says I cannot have any pets" and requesting special permission to keep the dog. She offers the letter, but Dobbs renews his Best Evidence objection. Brindon invokes FRE 1007. How should the court rule, and why? If Dobbs had written no letter but had orally sought exemption from the "no pets" provision from Brindon, could she prove the clause by testifying to what he said?

NOTES ON OTHER ESCAPES FROM PRODUCING THE ORIGINAL

1. When someone offers a summary under FRE 1006, should the jury be told that it is not "evidence" because only the documents themselves have that status? Does it matter whether the documents themselves were admitted? See United States v. Bray, 139 F.3d 1104, 1111 (6th Cir. 1998) (summary, whether or not underlying documents are introduced, is "evidence to be considered by the factfinder").

2. Sometimes a summary of exhibits or other trial evidence is introduced for "pedagogical" purposes to help the jury understand the evidence rather than to prove its content. Such use of summaries is governed by FRE 611(a) rather than FRE 1006. See Gomez v. Great Lakes Steel Division National Steel Corp., 803 F.2d 250, 257-258 (6th Cir. 1986) (charts used only as visual aid or "pedagogical device" should be accompanied by limiting instruction telling jury the purpose of the summary and that "it does not itself constitute evidence").

3. When a summary is offered, does it matter whether the underlying documents are *admissible*? See Hackett v. Housing Authority of San Antonio, 750 F.2d 1308, 1312 (5th Cir.) (summary inadmissible when based on inadmissible hearsay), *cert. denied*, 474 U.S. 50 (1985). Thus in Problem 14-M isn't it clear that before offering Urban's testimony the government must lay a foundation establishing the admissibility of the underlying records?

4. Does the proponent of summary evidence have to offer the underlying documents? (No, although the court may require production under FRE 1006). Must he give advance notice of intent to offer a summary? See FRCP 26(a)(3)(A)(iii) (requiring pretrial disclosure "of each document or other exhibit, including summaries of other evidence").

TABLE OF CASES

Italic type indicates principal cases.

TABLE OF RULES

Federal Rules of Evidence

Proposed Federal Rules of Evidence

Federal Rules of Criminal Procedure

Federal Rules of Civil Procedure

Uniform Rules of Evidence

Uniform Rules of Evidence (1974)

Model Code of Evidence

American Bar Association Model Rules of Professional Conduct

American Bar Association Model Code of Professional Responsibility

TABLE OF AUTHORITIES

Books and Treatises

AMA Principles of Medical Ethics IV (2001), 790

Appleman, J., Insurance Law and Practice (rev. ed. 1981), 716 n.3

Barker, S., The Elements of Logic (3d ed. 1980), 65

Bentham, J., Fragment of Government (1776), 793

________, Introduction to Principles of Morals and Legislation (1789), 793

________, Rationale of Judicial Evidence (J.S. Mill ed., 1827), 791, 793, 794

Blackstone, W., Commentaries on the Laws of England, 793

Brammer, D., Edges of Truth: The Mary Weaver Story (2013), 378

Cohen, L., The Probable and the Provable (1977), 109

Couch on Insurance (1982), 716 n.3

Davis, K., Administrative Law Treatise (1984 & Supp. 2010), 769, 786

Dombroff, M., Direct and Cross-Examination (1985), 22

Faigman, D., D. Kaye, M. Saks, & J. Sanders, Modern Scientific Evidence (2013), 691

Friedenthal, J., A. Miller, J. Sexton, & H. Hershkoff, Civil Procedure Cases and Materials (10th ed. 2009), 716 n.2

Giannelli, P. & E. Imwinkelried, Scientific Evidence (4th ed. 2012), 691

Graham, M., Handbook of Federal Evidence (3d ed. 1991), 772

Greenleaf, S., Evidence (1892), 488

________, Evidence (1883), 487

Huber, P., Galileo's Revenge: Junk Science in the Courtroom (1991), 677

Imwinkelried, E., Uncharged Misconduct (1994), 460

Kalven, H. & H. Zeisel, The American Jury (1966), 776

Kamisar, Police Interrogation and Confessions: Essays in Law and Policy (1980), 211

Keeton, R., Basic Expressions for Trial Lawyers (1979), 903

Kuhn, T., The Structure of Scientific Revolutions (1962), 665

Lilly, G., Introduction to the Law of Evidence (3d ed. 1996), 630

________, Principles of Evidence (2006), 564, 629

Longfellow, H.W., Tales of a Wayside Inn (1864-1873), 116 n.3

McCormick, Evidence (K. Broun ed., 7th ed. 2014), 23, 62, 462, 716 n.2

________, Evidence (K. Broun ed., 6th ed. 2006), 867, 894

________, Evidence (J. Strong ed., 5th ed. 1999), 782, 930

________, Evidence (K. Broun ed., 1996), 792

Morgan, E., Basic Problems of Evidence (1962), 770

Moore's Federal Practice (2d ed. 1985), 773

Mueller, C., "Of Misshapen Stones and Compromises: *Michelson* and the Modern Law of Character Evidence," in Evidence Stories 75 (Richard Lempert ed., 2006), 433

Mueller, C. & L. Kirkpatrick, Evidence (5th ed. 2012), 61, 71, 171, 207, 216, 248, 258, 289, 380, 421, 441, 480, 577, 627, 727, 795, 901, 927

________, Federal Evidence (4th ed. 2013), 21, 89, 182, 231, 290, 361, 456, 462, 474, 566, 574, 575, 906, 910, 930, 935, 949

O'Malley, K., J. Grenig, & W. Lee, Federal Jury Practice and Instructions (6th ed. 2014), 71, 107-108, 760

Park, R., D. Leonard, & S. Goldberg, Evidence Law: A Student's Guide to the Law of Evidence as Applied in American Trials (3d ed. 2011), 33

Popper, K., The Logic of Scientific Discovery (1934), 665

Sandburg, C., The People, Yes (1936), 55

Scalia, A., A Matter of Interpretation: Federal Courts and the Law (Princeton Univ. Press 1998), 389

Starkie, T., Evidence (1824), 489

Thayer, J., A Preliminary Treatise on Evidence at the Common Law (1898), 53, 54, 770, 775

Traynor, R., The Riddle of Harmless Error (1970), 45 n.7

Articles

INDEX

10/27

451-66; Rules 412-15 & 406

467-85 (skip prob 5 - T, Note 1 p 483)

Rules 407-11

539-564

607, 611, 608(b)